Beginning XML
3rd Edition

David Hunter
Andrew Watt
Jeff Rafter
Jon Duckett
Danny Ayers
Nicholas Chase
Joe Fawcett
Tom Gaven
Bill Patterson

PARK LEARNING CENTRE
UNIVERSITY OF GLOUCESTERSHIRE
P.O. Box 220, The Park
Cheltenham GL50 2RH
Tel: 01242 532721

WILEY

Wiley Publishing, Inc.

Beginning XML, 3rd Edition

Copyright © 2004 by Wiley Publishing, Inc., Indianapolis, Indiana. All rights reserved.

Published simultaneously in Canada

No part of this publication may be reproduced, stored in a retrieval system, or transmitted in any form or by any means, electronic, mechanical, photocopying, recording, scanning, or otherwise, except as permitted under Section 107 or 108 of the 1976 United States Copyright Act, without either the prior written permission of the Publisher, or authorization through payment of the appropriate per-copy fee to the Copyright Clearance Center, Inc., 222 Rosewood Drive, Danvers, MA 01923, (978) 750-8400, fax (978) 646-8700. Requests to the Publisher for permission should be addressed to the Legal Department, Wiley Publishing, Inc., 10475 Crosspoint Blvd., Indianapolis, IN 46256, (317) 572-3447, fax (317) 572-4355, E-mail: `brandreview@wiley.com`.

LIMIT OF LIABILITY/DISCLAIMER OF WARRANTY: THE PUBLISHER AND THE AUTHOR MAKE NO REPRESENTATIONS OR WARRANTIES WITH RESPECT TO THE ACCURACY OR COMPLETENESS OF THE CONTENTS OF THIS WORK AND SPECIFICALLY DISCLAIM ALL WARRANTIES, INCLUDING WITHOUT LIMITATION WARRANTIES OF FITNESS FOR A PARTICULAR PURPOSE. NO WARRANTY MAY BE CREATED OR EXTENDED BY SALES OR PROMOTIONAL MATERIALS. THE ADVICE AND STRATEGIES CONTAINED HEREIN MAY NOT BE SUITABLE FOR EVERY SITUATION. THIS WORK IS SOLD WITH THE UNDERSTANDING THAT THE PUBLISHER IS NOT ENGAGED IN RENDERING LEGAL, ACCOUNTING, OR OTHER PROFESSIONAL SERVICES. IF PROFESSIONAL ASSISTANCE IS REQUIRED, THE SERVICES OF A COMPETENT PROFESSIONAL PERSON SHOULD BE SOUGHT. NEITHER THE PUBLISHER NOR THE AUTHOR SHALL BE LIABLE FOR DAMAGES ARISING HEREFROM. THE FACT THAT AN ORGANIZATION OR WEBSITE IS REFERRED TO IN THIS WORK AS A CITATION AND/OR A POTENTIAL SOURCE OF FURTHER INFORMATION DOES NOT MEAN THAT THE AUTHOR OR THE PUBLISHER ENDORSES THE INFORMATION THE ORGANIZATION OR WEBSITE MAY PROVIDE OR RECOMMENDATIONS IT MAY MAKE. FURTHER, READERS SHOULD BE AWARE THAT INTERNET WEBSITES LISTED IN THIS WORK MAY HAVE CHANGED OR DISAPPEARED BETWEEN WHEN THIS WORK WAS WRITTEN AND WHEN IT IS READ.

For general information on our other products and services please contact our Customer Care Department within the United States at (800) 762-2974, outside the United States at (317) 572-3993 or fax (317) 572-4002.

Trademarks: Wiley, the Wiley logo, Wrox, the Wrox logo, Programmer to Programmer, and related trade dress are trademarks or registered trademarks of John Wiley & Sons, Inc. and/or its affiliates, in the United States and other countries, and may not be used without written permission. All other trademarks are the property of their respective owners. Wiley Publishing, Inc., is not associated with any product or vendor mentioned in this book.

Wiley also publishes its books in a variety of electronic formats. Some content that appears in print may not be available in electronic books.

Library of Congress Cataloging-in-Publication Data:

ISBN: 0-7645-7077-3

Printed in the United States of America

10 9 8 7 6 5 4 3 2 1

About the Authors

David Hunter

David is a Senior Technical Consultant for CGI, the largest Canadian independent information technology (IT) services firm and the fifth largest in North America. With a career that has spanned design, development, support, training, writing, and other roles, he has had extensive experience building scalable, enterprise-class applications using various Internet technologies.

"For the first two editions of this book, I thanked God and I thanked Andrea. They're both still helping and supporting me, and should continue to be thanked for my contributions to this edition."

David Hunter contributed Chapters 1–3 and Appendix B to this book.

Andrew Watt

Andrew Watt is an independent consultant and computer book author with an interest and expertise in various XML technologies. Currently, he is focusing on the use of XML in Microsoft technologies. He is a Microsoft Most Valuable Professional for Microsoft InfoPath 2003.

"I would like to thank Jim Minatel, Acquisitions Editor, and Mark Enochs, Development Editor, for their help, patience, and encouragement during the writing of the chapters I contributed to this book."

Andrew Watt contributed Chapters 7–11 and 19, and Appendixes C–D to this book.

Jeff Rafter

Jeff Rafter's involvement in the computer industry began with his work on *Future Lock*, a Commodore 64 classic published by *Compute's Gazette*. For the past eight years his focus has shifted to web development and markup languages, and he is always eager to explore emerging technologies. Jeff currently resides in Redlands, California, where he enjoys restoring his turn-of-the-century house, playing frisbee with his Border Collie and writing sonnets.

"I thank God for his love and grace, and would also like to thank my wife Ali who is the embodiment of that love in countless ways. She has graciously encouraged me to pursue my dreams at any cost. I would also like to express my gratitude for my fellow authors and our editors, who worked tirelessly through the process of completing this book."

Jeff Rafter contributed Chapters 4–5 and 12, and Appendixes E–G to this book.

Jon Duckett

Jon published his first website in 1996 while studying for a BSc (Hons) in Psychology at Brunel University, London. Since then he has helped create a wide variety of websites and has co-authored more than 10 programming-related books on topics from ASP to XML (via many other letters of the alphabet) that have covered diverse aspects of web programming including design, architecture, and coding. After graduating, Jon worked for Wrox Press first in their Birmingham (UK) offices for three years and then in Sydney (Australia) for another year. He is now a freelance developer and consultant based in a leafy suburb of London, working for a range of clients spread across three continents. When not stuck in front of a computer screen, Jon enjoys writing and listening to music.

Jon Duckett contributed Chapters 16–17 to this book.

Danny Ayers

Danny Ayers is a freelance developer and writer specializing in cutting-edge web technologies. His personal focus is on using Semantic Web technologies to make the Internet a whole lot more useful. He lives in rural Tuscany with his wife, Caroline, a dog, Basil, and numerous cats. The animals regularly appear alongside XML-oriented material on his weblog at `http://dannyayers.com`.

"Thanks to Andrew Watt and the Wrox team for giving a very busy person something useful to do."

Danny Ayers contributed Chapters 13 and 18 to this book.

Nicholas Chase

Nicholas Chase has been involved in website development for companies such as Lucent Technologies, Sun Microsystems, Oracle, and the Tampa Bay Buccaneers. Nick has been a high school physics teacher, a low-level radioactive waste facility manager, an online science fiction magazine editor, a multimedia engineer, and an Oracle instructor. More recently, he was the Chief Technology Officer of an interactive communications firm. He is the host of the XML Reference Guide on InformIT.com, a frequent contributor to IBM's developerWorks, and the author of several books on XML and web development. He's currently trying to buy a farm so he and his wife can raise alpacas and mutant chickens. He loves to hear from readers and can be reached through his website, `http://www.nicholaschase.com`.

"I would like to thank my wife Sarah and my family for their understanding, and Andrew Watt, Laura Lewin, Jim Minatel, and Michelle (you know who you are) for their assistance in helping me to get this done."

Nick Chase contributed Chapters 14–15 to this book.

Joe Fawcett

Joe Fawcett began programming 30 years ago and started working in development after leaving college. A career change saw him become a professional bridge player until 10 years ago when he returned to programming, becoming especially interested in XML as it was emerging in 1997. He was awarded the status of Microsoft Most Valuable Professional in XML in 2003. Joe works as head of software development for Chesterton Ltd., a large property company based in the U.K. He lives with Gillian and their two young children, Persephone and Xavier.

Joe Fawcett contributed Chapter 20 to this book.

Tom Gaven

Tom Gaven has been in the IT industry for over 25 years and has developed and delivered technical training on programming languages, operating systems, user interfaces, and architecture. Recently, Tom has focused on XML and all related technologies. Currently, Tom works for Exostar, the B2B exchange for the aerospace and defense industry, maintaining the XML interfaces and schemas for the exchange. He also co-authored a freely available XML editor, XMLDE. The editor supports RELAX NG and is available at `http://www.xmldistilled.com`.

"I would like to acknowledge the support of my adorable wife, Maria, and three fantastic kids, Julie, Marissa, and Gregory. I would also like to thank Joe Hughes, for all his hard effort creating the XMLDE editor."

Tom Gaven contributed Chapter 6 to this book.

Bill Patterson

Bill Patterson has worked in the computer field for longer than he would care to admit. He holds a masters' degree in both business and computer science. He first began working with PHP and XML in 2000, and works as an independent consultant in New Jersey.

"I want to thank my mother, Doris Patterson, who has never stopped teaching me, and my wife Judy and daughters Meg and Karen, who give me reasons to keep learning."

Bill Patterson contributed Chapter 21 to this book.

The authors would also like to thank Kurt Cagle for his contribution to this edition, which provided a lot of groundwork for a few chapters, in particular, Chapter 13 on RSS and content syndication.

Credits

Vice President & Executive Group Publisher
Richard Swadley

Vice President and Publisher
Joseph B. Wikert

Senior Acquisitions Editor
Jim Minatel

Development Editor
Mark Enochs

Editorial Manager
Mary Beth Wakefield

Production Editor
Angela Smith

Technical Editing
Wiley-Dreamtech India Pvt Ltd

Text Design & Composition
TechBooks

Contents

Introduction

Welcome to *Beginning XML*, Third Edition, the book I wish I'd had when I was first learning the language!

When we wrote the first edition of this book, XML was a relatively new language but already gaining ground fast and becoming more and more widely used in a vast range of applications. By the time we started the second edition, XML had already proven itself to be more than a passing fad, and was in fact being used throughout the industry for an incredibly wide range of uses. As we began the third edition it was clear that XML was a mature technology, but, more importantly, it became evident that the XML landscape was dividing into several areas of expertise. We needed to categorize the increasing number of specifications surrounding XML, which either use XML or provide functionality in addition to the XML core specification.

So what is XML? It's a markup language, used to describe the structure of data in meaningful ways. Anywhere that data is input/output, stored, or transmitted from one place to another, is a potential fit for XML's capabilities. Perhaps the most well-known applications are web-related (especially with the latest developments in handheld web access—for which some of the technology is XML-based). However, there are many other nonweb-based applications where XML is useful—for example, as a replacement for (or to complement) traditional databases, or for the transfer of financial information between businesses. News organizations, along with individuals, have also started using XML to distribute syndicated news stories.

This book aims to teach you all you need to know about XML—what it is, how it works, what technologies surround it, and how it can best be used in a variety of situations, from simple data transfer to using XML in your web pages. It will answer the fundamental questions:

- What is XML?
- How do I use XML?
- How does it work?
- What can I use it *for*, anyway?

Who Is This Book For?

This book is for people who know that it would be a pretty good idea to learn XML but aren't 100 percent sure why. You've heard the hype but haven't seen enough substance to figure out what XML is and what it can do. You may already be somehow involved in web development and probably even know the basics of HTML, although neither of these qualifications is absolutely necessary for this book.

What you don't need is knowledge of SGML (XML's predecessor) or even markup languages in general. This book assumes that you're new to the concept of markup languages, and we have tried to structure it in a way that will make sense to the beginner and yet quickly bring you to XML expert status.

The word "Beginning" in the title refers to the style of the book, rather than the reader's experience level. There are two types of beginner for whom this book will be ideal:

- Programmers who are already familiar with some web programming or data exchange techniques. You will already be used to some of the concepts discussed here, but you will learn how you can incorporate XML technologies to enhance those solutions you currently develop.
- Those working in a programming environment but with no substantial knowledge or experience of web development or data exchange applications. As well as learning how XML technologies can be applied to such applications, you will be introduced to some new concepts to help you understand how such systems work.

How This Book Is Organized

We've tried to arrange the subjects covered in this book to take you from no knowledge to expert, in as logical a manner as we could. In the third edition, we have structured the book in sections that are based on various areas of XML expertise. Unless you are already using XML, you should start by reading the introduction to XML in Part I. From there, you can quickly jump into specific areas of expertise, or if you prefer, you can read through the book in order. It is important to remember that there is quite a lot of overlap in XML, and that some of the sections make use of techniques learned earlier in the book.

- First, we'll be looking at what exactly XML is and why the industry felt that a language like this was needed.
- After covering the *why*, the next logical step is the *how*, so we'll be seeing how to create well-formed XML.
- Once we understand the whys and hows of XML, we'll go on to some more advanced things you can do when creating your XML documents, to make them not only well formed, but valid. (And we'll talk about what "valid" really means.)
- Now that you're comfortable with XML and have seen it in action, we'll unleash the programmer within you and look at an XML-based programming language that we can use to transform XML documents from one format to another.
- At some point we will need to store and retrieve XML information from databases. We'll not only learn the state of the art for XML and databases, we will also learn how to query XML information using an SQL-like syntax called XQuery.
- XML wouldn't really be useful unless we could write programs to read the data in XML documents and create new XML documents, so we'll get back to programming and look at a couple of ways that we can do that.
- Understanding how to program and use XML within our own business is one thing, but sending that information to a business partner or publishing it to the Internet is another. We'll look at technologies that use XML that allow us to send messages across the Internet, publish information, and discover services that provide information.
- Since we have all of this data in XML format, it would be great if we could easily display it to people, and it turns out we can. We'll look at an XML version of HTML called XHTML, and we'll also look at a technology you may already have been using in conjunction with HTML documents that also works great with XML called CSS. In addition, we'll learn how to design stunning graphics and make interactive forms using XML.
- Finally, we'll finish off with some case studies, which should help to give you ideas on how XML can be used in real-life situations, and which could be used in your own applications.

What's Covered in This Book?

This book builds on the strengths of the first and second editions, and provides new material to reflect the changes in the XML landscape—notably RELAX NG, XQuery, RSS, and SVG. Updates have been made to reflect the most recent versions of specifications and best practices throughout the book. In addition to the many changes in the chapters, each chapter now has a set of exercise questions to test your understanding of the material. The answers to these questions appear in Appendix A.

Part I: Introduction

The introduction is where most readers should begin. In the first three chapters we will introduce some of the goals of XML as well as the specific rules for constructing XML. Once you have read this part you should be able to read and create your own XML documents.

Chapter 1: What Is XML?

Here we'll cover some basic concepts, introducing the fact that XML is a markup language (a bit like HTML) where you can define your own elements, tags, and attributes (known as a vocabulary). We'll see that tags have no presentation meaning—they're just a way of describing the structure of data.

Chapter 2: Well-Formed XML

As well as explaining what well-formed XML is, we'll take a look at the rules that exist (the XML 1.0 Recommendation) for naming and structuring elements—you need to comply with these rules if your XML is to be well formed.

Chapter 3: XML Namespaces

Because tags can be made up, we need to avoid name conflicts when sharing documents. Namespaces provide a way to uniquely identify a group of tags, using a URI. This chapter explains how to use namespaces.

Part II: Validation

In addition to the well-formedness rules you learn in Part I, you will most likely want to learn how to create and use different XML vocabularies. In this Part, we will introduce you to DTDs, XML Schemas, and RELAXNG, three languages that define custom XML vocabularies. We will also show you how to utilize these definitions to validate your XML documents.

Chapter 4: Document Type Definitions

We can specify how an XML document should be structured, and even give default values, using Document Type Definitions (DTDs). If XML conforms to the associated DTD, it is known as valid XML. This chapter covers the basics of using DTDs.

Chapter 5: XML Schemas

XML Schemas, like DTDs, allow you to define how a document should be structured. In addition to defining document structure, they also allow you to specify the individual data types of attribute values and element content. They are a more powerful alternative to DTDs and are explained here.

Chapter 6: RELAX NG

RELAX NG is a third technology used to define the structure of documents. In addition to a new syntax and new features, it takes the best from XML Schemas and DTDs, and is therefore very simple and very powerful. Both the full syntax and compact syntax are discussed.

Part III: Processing

In addition to defining and creating XML documents, you are going to need to know how to work with documents to extract information and convert it to other formats. In fact, easily extracting information and converting to other formats is what makes XML so powerful.

Chapter 7: XPath

The XPath language is used to locate sections in the XML document, and it's important in many other XML technologies. In this edition we dedicated an entire chapter to this technology in order to expand our existing information and introduce the new version of XPath.

Chapter 8: XSLT

XML can be transformed into other XML, HTML, and other formats using XSLT stylesheets, which are introduced here. This chapter has been completely overhauled from the second edition.

Part IV: Databases

Creating and processing XML documents is good, but eventually you will want to store those documents. In this section we discuss strategies for storing and retrieving XML documents and document fragments from different databases.

Chapter 9: XQuery, the XML Query Language

Very often you will need to retrieve information from within a database. XQuery, which is built on XPath and XPath2, allows you to do this in an elegant way.

Chapter 10: XML and Databases

XML is perfect for structuring data, and some traditional databases are beginning to offer support for XML. These are discussed along with a more general overview of how XML can be used in an n-tier architecture. In addition, new databases based on XML are introduced.

Part V: Programming

At some point in your XML career, you will need to work with an XML document from within a custom application. The two most popular methodologies, the Document Object Model (DOM) and the Simple API for XML (SAX) are explained in this Part.

Chapter 11: The Document Object Model

Programmers can use a variety of programming languages to manipulate XML, using the Document Object Model's objects, interfaces, methods, and properties, which are described here.

Chapter 12: Simple API for XML

An alternative to the DOM for programmatically manipulating XML data is to use the Simple API for XML (SAX) as an interface. This chapter shows how to use SAX and has been updated from the second edition to focus on SAX 2.0.2.

Part VI: Communication

Sending and receiving data from one computer to another is often difficult. However, several technologies have been created to make communication with XML much easier. In this section we will discuss RSS and content syndication, as well as Web services and SOAP.

Chapter 13: RSS and Content Syndication

RSS is an actively changing technology that is used to publish syndicated news stories and website summaries on the Internet. In this chapter we not only discuss how to use the different versions of RSS and Atom, we also cover the history and future direction of the technology. In addition, we demonstrate how to create a simple newsreader application that works with any of the currently published versions.

Chapter 14: Web Services

Web services enable you to perform cross-computer communications. This chapter describes Web services and introduces you to using remote procedure calls in XML (using XML-RPC and REST), as well as giving you a brief look at major topics such as SOAP. Finally, it breaks down the assortment of specifications designed to work in conjunction with Web services.

Chapter 15: SOAP and WSDL

Fundamental to XML Web services, the Simple Object Access Protocol (SOAP) is one of the most popular specifications for allowing cross-computer communications. Using SOAP, you can package up XML documents and send them across the Internet to be processed. This chapter explains SOAP and the Web services Description Language (WSDL) that is used to publish your service.

Part VII: Display

There are several XML technologies devoted to displaying the data that is stored inside of an XML document. Some of these technologies are web-based, and some are designed for applications and mobile devices. Here we will discuss the primary display strategies and formats used today.

Chapter 16: XHTML

XHTML is a new version of HTML that follows the rules of XML. In this chapter we discuss the differences between HTML and XHTML, and show you how XHTML can help make your sites available to a wider variety of browsers, from legacy browsers to the latest browsers on mobile phones.

Chapter 17: Cascading Style Sheets

Website designers have long been using Cascading Style Sheets (CSS) with their HTML to easily make changes to a website's presentation without having to touch the underlying HTML documents. This power is also available for XML, allowing you to display XML documents right in the browser. Or, if you need a bit more flexibility with your presentation, you can use XSLT to transform your XML to HTML or XHTML and then use CSS to style these documents.

Chapter 18: Scalable Vector Graphics

Do you want to produce a custom graphics from XML? SVG allows you to describe a graphic using XML-based vector commands. In this chapter we will teach you the basics of SVG and then dive into a more complex SVG-based application that can be published to the Internet.

Chapter 19: XForms

XForms are XML-based forms that can be used to design desktop applications, paper-based forms, and of course XHTML-based forms. In this chapter we will demonstrate the basics as well as some of the more interesting uses of XForms.

Part VIII: Case Studies

Throughout the book you'll gain an understanding of how XML is used in web, business-to-business (B2B), data storage, and many other applications. These case studies cover some example applications and show how the theory can be put into practice in real-life situations. Both are new to this edition.

Case Study 1: .NET XML Web Services

In this case study we explore some of the possibilities and strategies for using XML in .NET. This includes an example that demonstrates creating and consuming a Web service.

Case Study 2: XML and PHP

There are XML tools available for most programming languages. In this case study we explore PHP (including an introduction to PHP) and how to work with XML documents using the language.

Part IX: Appendixes

The first appendix provides answers to the exercise questions that appear throughout the book. Additionally, these provide reference material that you may find useful as you begin to apply the knowledge gained throughout the book in your own applications.

Programming Languages

We have also tried to demonstrate the ubiquity of XML throughout the book. Some of the examples are specific to Windows; however, most of the examples include information on working with other platforms, such as Linux.

Additionally, we have attempted to show the use of XML in a variety of programming languages. Some of these include Java, JavaScript, PHP, Python, Visual Basic, ASP, and C#. So, while there is a good chance that you will see an example written in your favorite programming language, there is also a good chance you will encounter an example in a language you have never used. Whenever a new language is introduced, we include information on downloading and installing the necessary tools to use it. It is important to remember that our focus is XML, so whichever programming language is used in an example, the core XML concept will be explained in detail.

What You Need to Use This Book

Because XML is a text-based technology, all you really need to create in XML documents is Notepad or your equivalent text editor. However, to really see some of these samples in action, you might want to have a current Internet browser that can natively read XML documents, and even provide error messages if something is wrong. In any case, there will be some screenshots throughout the book, so that you can see what things should look like. Also, note the following:

- If you do have Internet Explorer, you should also have an implementation of the DOM, which you may find useful in the chapters on that subject.
- Some of the examples and the case studies require access to a web server, such as Microsoft's IIS (or PWS).
- Throughout the book, other (freely available) XML tools will be used, and we'll give instructions for obtaining these at the appropriate place.

Conventions

To help you get the most from the text and keep track of what's happening, we've used a number of conventions throughout the book.

Boxes like this one hold important, not-to-be forgotten information that is directly relevant to the surrounding text.

Tips, hints, tricks, and asides to the current discussion are offset and placed in italics like this.

The following describes the styles used in the text:

- We *highlight* important words in italics when we introduce them.
- We show keyboard strokes like this: Ctrl+A.
- We show file names, URLs, and code within the text like so: `persistence.properties`.
- We present code in two different ways:

```
In code examples we highlight new and important code with a gray background.
```

```
For code that's less important in the present context or that has been shown
before, no gray background is used.
```

Source Code

As you work through the examples in this book, you may choose either to type in all the code manually or to use the source code files that accompany the book. All of the source code used in this book is available for downloading at `http://www.wrox.com`. Once you're at the site, simply locate the book's title (either by using the Search box or by using one of the title lists) and click the Download Code link on the book's detail page to obtain all the source code for the book.

Because many books have similar titles, you may find it easiest to search by ISBN; for this book the ISBN is 0-7645-7077-3.

Once you download the code, just decompress it with your favorite compression tool. Alternately, you can go to the main Wrox code download page at `http://www.wrox.com/dynamic/books/download.aspx` to see the code available for this book and all other Wrox books.

Errata

We make every effort to ensure that there are no errors in the text or in the code. However, no one is perfect, and mistakes do occur. If you find an error in one of our books, like a spelling mistake or faulty piece of code, we would be very grateful for your feedback. By sending in errata you may save another reader hours of frustration, and at the same time you will be helping us provide even higher quality information.

To find the errata page for this book, go to `http://www.wrox.com` and locate the title using the Search box or one of the title lists. Then, on the book details page, click the Book Errata link. On this page you can view all errata that has been submitted for this book and posted by Wrox editors. A complete book list including links to each book's errata is also available at www.wrox.com/misc-pages/booklist.shtml.

If you don't spot "your" error on the Book Errata page, go to www.wrox.com/contact/techsupport.shtml and complete the form there to send us the error you have found. We'll check the information and, if appropriate, post a message to the book's errata page and fix the problem in subsequent editions of the book.

p2p.wrox.com

For author and peer discussion, join the P2P forums at p2p.wrox.com. The forums are a web-based system for you to post messages relating to Wrox books and related technologies as well as interact with other readers and technology users. The forums offer a subscription feature to e-mail you topics of interest of your choosing when new posts are made to the forums. Wrox authors, editors, other industry experts, and your fellow readers are present on these forums.

At http://p2p.wrox.com you will find a number of different forums that will help you not only as you read this book, but also as you develop your own applications. To join the forums, just follow these steps:

1. Go to p2p.wrox.com and click the Register link.
2. Read the terms of use and click Agree.
3. Complete the required information to join as well as any optional information you wish to provide and click Submit.
4. You will receive an e-mail with information describing how to verify your account and complete the joining process.

You can read messages in the forums without joining P2P but in order to post your own messages, you must join.

Once you join, you can post new messages and respond to messages other users post. You can read messages at any time on the web. If you would like to have new messages from a particular forum e-mailed to you, click the Subscribe to this Forum icon by the forum name in the forum listing.

For more information about how to use the Wrox P2P, be sure to read the P2P FAQs for answers to questions about how the forum software works as well as many common questions specific to P2P and Wrox books. To read the FAQs, click the FAQ link on any P2P page.

Part I: Introduction

What Is XML?

Extensible Markup Language (XML) is a buzzword you will see everywhere on the Internet, but it's also a rapidly maturing technology with powerful real-world applications, particularly for the management, display, and organization of data. Together with its many related technologies, which are covered in later chapters, XML is an essential technology for anyone working with data, whether on the web or internally. This chapter introduces you to some XML basics and begins to show you why learning about it is so important.

We will cover the following:

- The two major categories of computer file types—binary files and text files—and the advantages and disadvantages of each
- The history behind XML, including other markup languages such as SGML and HTML
- How XML documents are structured as hierarchies of information
- A brief introduction to some of the other technologies surrounding XML, which you will work with throughout the book
- A quick look at some areas where XML is useful

While there are some short examples of XML in this chapter, you aren't expected to understand what's going on just yet. The idea is simply to introduce the important concepts behind the language, so that throughout the book you can see not only how to use XML, but also why it works the way it does.

Of Data, Files, and Text

XML is a technology concerned with the description and structuring of *data*, so before we can really delve into the concepts behind XML, we need to understand how computers store and access data. For our purposes, computers understand two kinds of data files: binary and text files.

Binary Files

A *binary file*, at its simplest, is just a stream of *bits* (1s and 0s). It's up to the application that created a binary file to understand what all of the bits mean. That's why binary files can only be read and produced by certain computer programs, which have been specifically written to understand them.

For example, when a document is created with Microsoft Word, the program creates a binary file with an extension of "doc," in its own proprietary format. The programmers who wrote Word decided to insert certain binary codes into the document to denote bold text, codes to denote page breaks, and other codes for all of the information that needs to go into a "doc" file. When you open a document in Word, it interprets those codes and displays the properly formatted text on-screen or prints it to the printer.

The codes inserted into the document are *meta data*, or information about information. Examples could be "this word should be in bold," "that sentence should be centered," and so on. This meta data is really what differentiates one file type from another; the different types of files use different kinds of meta data.

For example, a word processing document has different meta data than a spreadsheet document, because they are describing different things. Not so obviously, documents from different word processing applications also have different metadata, because the applications were written differently (see Figure 1-1).

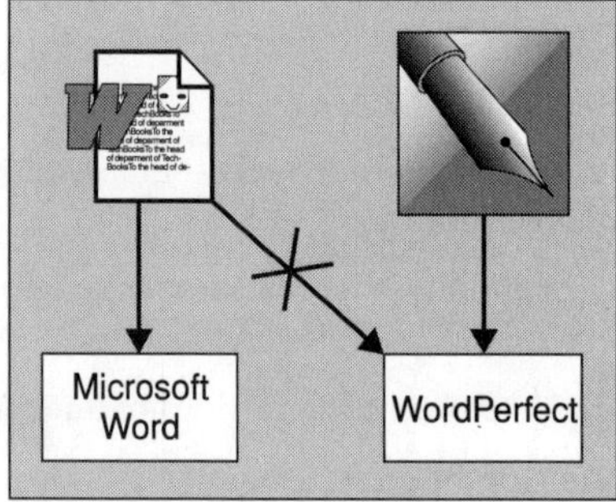

Figure 1-1

We can't assume that a document created with one word processor will be readable by another, because the companies who write word processors all have their own proprietary formats for their data files. So, Word documents open in Microsoft Word, and WordPerfect documents open in WordPerfect.

Luckily for us, most word processors come with translators or import utilities, which can translate documents from other word processors into formats that can be understood natively. If I have Microsoft Word installed on my computer and someone gives me a WordPerfect document, I might be able to import it into Word, so that I can read the document. Of course, many of us have seen the garbage that sometimes occurs as a result of this translation; sometimes applications are not as good as we'd like them to be at converting the information.

Binary file formats are advantageous because it is easy for computers to understand these binary codes, meaning that they can be processed much faster, and they are very efficient for storing this meta data. There is also a disadvantage, as we've seen, in that binary files are proprietary. You might not be able to open binary files created by one application in another application, or even in the same application running on another platform.

Text Files

Like binary files, *text files* are also streams of bits. However, in a text file these bits are grouped together in standardized ways, so that they always form numbers. These numbers are then further mapped to characters. For example, a text file might contain the following bits:

```
1100001
```

This group of bits would be translated as the number `97`, which could then be further translated into the letter `a`.

This example makes a number of assumptions. A better description of how numbers are represented in text files is given in the "Encoding" section in Chapter 2.

Because of these standards, text files can be read by many applications, and can even be read by humans, using a simple text editor. If I create a text document, anyone in the world can read it (as long as they understand English, of course) in any text editor they wish. Some issues still exist, such as the fact that different operating systems treat line-ending characters differently, but it is much easier to share information when it's contained in a text file than when the information is in a binary format.

Figure 1-2 shows some of the applications on my machine that are capable of opening text files. Some of these programs only allow me to *view* the text, while others will let me *edit* it, as well.

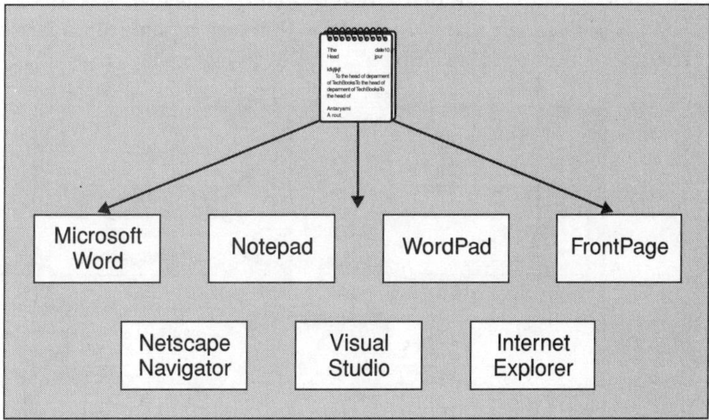

Figure 1-2

In its beginning, the Internet was almost completely text-based, which allowed people to communicate with relative ease. This contributed to the explosive rate at which the Internet was adopted, and to the ubiquity of applications like e-mail, the World Wide Web, newsgroups, and so on.

The disadvantage of text files is that adding other information—our meta data, in other words—is more difficult and bulky. For example, most word processors allow you to save documents in text form, but if you do, you can't mark a section of text as bold or insert a binary picture file. You will simply get the words with none of the formatting.

A Brief History of Markup

We can see that there are advantages to binary file formats (easy to understand by a computer, compact, the ability to add meta data), as well as advantages to text files (universally interchangeable). Wouldn't it be ideal if there were a format that combined the universality of text files with the efficiency and rich information storage capabilities of binary files?

This idea of a universal data format is not new. In fact, for as long as computers have been around, programmers have been trying to find ways to exchange information between different computer programs. An early attempt to combine a universally interchangeable data format with rich information storage capabilities was *Standard Generalized Markup Language* (SGML). This is a text-based language that can be used to mark up data—that is, add meta data—in a way that is *self-describing*. We'll see in a moment what self-describing means.

SGML was designed to be a standard way of marking up data for any purpose, and took off mostly in large document management systems. When it comes to huge amounts of complex data there are a lot of considerations to take into account and, as a result, SGML is a very complicated language. However, with that complexity comes power.

A very well-known language, based on the SGML work, is the *HyperText Markup Language* (HTML). HTML uses many of SGML's concepts to provide a universal markup language for the display of information, and the linking of different pieces of information. The idea was that any HTML document (or web page) would be presentable in any application that was capable of understanding HTML (termed a web browser). A number of examples are given in Figure 1-3.

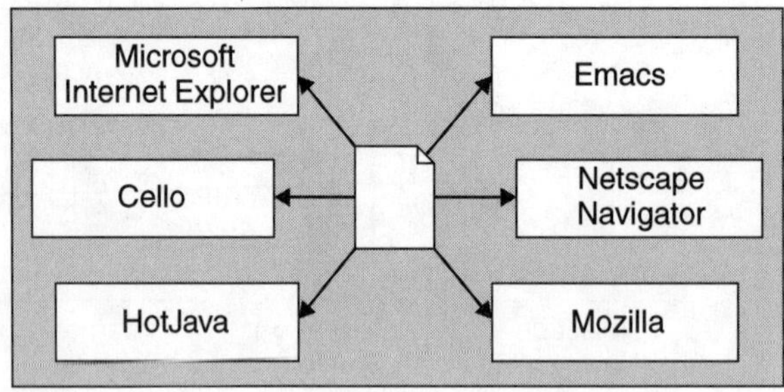

Figure 1-3

Not only would that browser be able to display the document, but if the page contained links (termed *hyperlinks*) to other documents, the browser would also be able to seamlessly retrieve them as well.

Furthermore, because HTML is text-based, anyone can create an HTML page using a simple text editor, or any number of web page editors, some of which are shown in Figure 1-4.

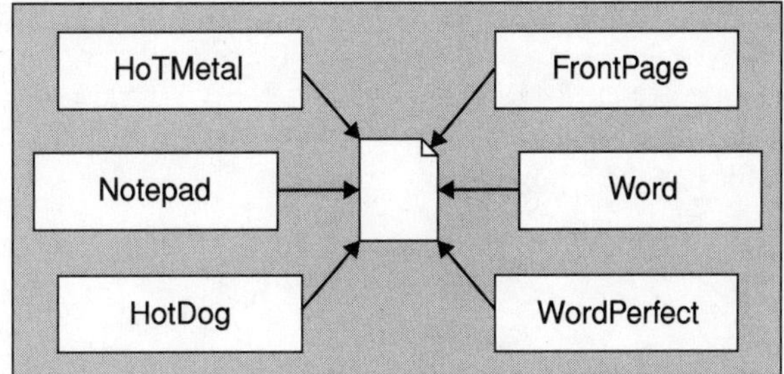

Figure 1-4

Even many word processors, such as WordPerfect and Word, allow you to save documents as HTML. Think about the ramifications of Figures 1-3 and 1-4: any HTML editor, including a simple text editor, can create an HTML file, and that HTML file can then be viewed in any web browser on the Internet!

So What Is XML?

Unfortunately, SGML is such a complicated language that it's not well suited for data interchange over the web. And, although HTML has been incredibly successful, it's limited in scope: it is only intended for displaying documents in a browser. The tags it makes available do not provide any information about the content they encompass, only instructions on how to display that content. This means that I could create an HTML document that displays information about a person, but that's about all I could do with the document. I couldn't write a program to figure out from that document which piece of information relates to the person's first name, for example, because HTML doesn't have any facilities to describe this kind of specialized information. In fact, HTML wouldn't even know that the document was about a person at all. *Extensible Markup Language* (XML) was created to address these issues.

Note that it's spelled "Extensible," not "eXtensible." Mixing these up is a common mistake.

XML is a subset of SGML, with the same goals (markup of any type of data), but with as much of the complexity eliminated as possible. XML was designed to be fully compatible with SGML, meaning any document that follows XML's syntax rules is by definition also following SGML's syntax rules, and can therefore be read by existing SGML tools. It doesn't go both ways though, so an SGML document is not necessarily an XML document.

It is important to realize, however, that XML is not really a "language" at all, but a standard for creating languages that meet the XML criteria (we'll go into these rules for creating XML documents in Chapter 2). In other words, XML describes a syntax that you use to create your own languages. For example, suppose I have data about a name, and I want to be able to share that information with others as well as use that information in a computer program. Instead of just creating a text file like this:

```
John Doe
```

or an HTML file like this:

```
<html>
<head><title>Name</title></head>
<body>
```

```
<p>John Doe</p>
</body>
</html>
```

I might create an XML file like the following:

```
<name>
  <first>John</first>
  <last>Doe</last>
</name>
```

Even from this simple example, you can see why markup languages such as SGML and XML are called "self-describing." Looking at the data, you can easily tell that this is information about a `<name>`, and you can see that there is data called `<first>` and more data called `<last>`. I could have given the tags any names I liked, however, if you're going to use XML, you might as well use it right and give things *meaningful* names.

You can also see that the XML version of this information is much larger than the plain-text version. Using XML to mark up data adds to its size, sometimes enormously, but achieving small file sizes isn't one of the goals of XML; it's only about making it easier to write software that accesses the information, by giving structure to the data.

> **This larger file size should not deter you from using XML. The advantages of easier-to-write code far outweigh the disadvantages of larger bandwidth issues.**

If bandwidth is a critical issue for your applications, you can always compress your XML documents before sending them across the network—compressing text files yields very good results.

Try It Out — Opening an XML File in Internet Explorer

If you're running Internet Explorer 5 or later, you can view the preceding XML in your browser.

1. Open up Notepad and type in the following XML:

```
<name>
  <first>John</first>
  <last>Doe</last>
</name>
```

2. Save the document to your hard drive as `name.xml`. If you're using Windows XP, be sure to change the Save as type drop down to "All Files." (Otherwise, Notepad will save the document with a `.txt` extension, causing your file to be named `name.xml.txt`.) You might also want to change the Encoding drop down to Unicode, as shown in Figure 1-5. (Find more information on encodings in Chapter 2.)
3. You can then open it up in Internet Explorer (for example, by double-clicking on the file in Windows Explorer), where it will look something like Figure 1-6.

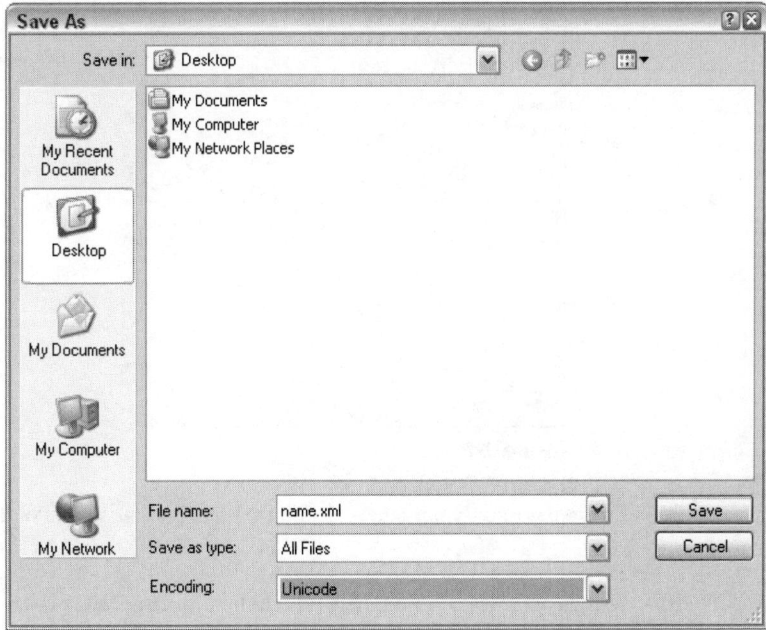

Figure 1-5

Figure 1-6

How It Works

Although our XML file has no information concerning display, the browser formats it nicely for us, with our information in bold and our markup displayed in different colors. Also, `<name>` is collapsible, like your file folders in Windows Explorer; try clicking on the minus sign (–) next to `<name>` in the browser window. It should then look like Figure 1-7.

Figure 1-7

For large XML documents, where you only need to concentrate on a smaller subset of the data, this can be quite handy.

This is one reason why Internet Explorer can be so helpful when authoring XML: it has a default *stylesheet* built in, which applies this default formatting to any XML document.

> *XML styling is accomplished through another document dedicated to the task, called a stylesheet. In a stylesheet the designer specifies rules that determine the presentation of the data. The same stylesheet can then be used with multiple documents to create a similar appearance among them. A variety of languages can be used to create stylesheets. Chapter 8 explains a transformation stylesheet language called Extensible Stylesheet Language Transformations (XSLT), and Chapter 17 looks at a stylesheet language called Cascading Style Sheets (CSS).*

As you'll see in later chapters, you can also create your own stylesheets for displaying XML documents. This way, the same data that your applications use can also be viewed in a browser. In effect, by combining XML data with stylesheets, you can separate your data from your presentation. That makes it easier to use the data for multiple purposes (as opposed to HTML, which doesn't provide any separation of data from presentation—in HTML, *everything* is presentation).

What Does XML Buy Us?

But why go to the trouble of creating an XML document? Wouldn't it be easier to just make up some rules for a file about names, such as "The first name starts at the beginning of the file, and the last name comes after the first space?" That way, our application could still read the data, but the file size would be much smaller.

How Else Would We Describe Our Data?

As a partial answer, suppose that we want to add a middle name to our example:

```
John Fitzgerald Doe
```

Okay, no problem. We'll just modify our rules to say that everything after the first space and up to the second space is the middle name, and everything after the second space is the last name. However, if there is no second space, we have to assume that there is no middle name, and the first rule still applies. So we're still fine, unless a person happens to have a name like the following:

```
John Fitzgerald Johansen Doe
```

Whoops! There are two middle names in there. The rules get more complex. While a human might be able to tell immediately that the two middle words compose the middle name, it is more difficult to program this logic into a computer program. We won't even discuss "John Fitzgerald Johansen Doe the 3rd"!

Unfortunately, when it comes to problems like this, many software developers simply define more restrictive rules, instead of dealing with the complexities of the data. In this example, the software developers might decide that a person can only have *one* middle name, and the application won't accept anything more than that.

This is pretty realistic, I might add. My full name is David John Bartlett Hunter, but because of the way many computer systems are set up, a lot of the bills I receive are simply addressed to David John Hunter or David J. Hunter. Maybe I can find some legal ground to stop paying my bills, but in the meantime, my vanity takes a blow every time I open my mail.

This example is probably not all that hard to solve, but it points out one of the major focuses behind XML. Programmers have been structuring their data in an infinite variety of ways, and every new way of structuring data brings a new methodology for pulling out the information we need. With those new methodologies comes much experimentation and testing to get it just right. If the data changes, the methodologies also have to change, and testing and tweaking has to begin again. With XML there is a standardized way to get the information we need, no matter how we structure it.

In addition, remember how trivial this example is. The more complex the data you have to work with, the more complex the logic you'll need to do that work. You'll appreciate XML the most in larger applications.

XML Parsers

If we just follow the rules specified by XML, we can be sure that getting at our information will be easy. This is because there are programs written, called *parsers*, which can read XML syntax and get the information out for us. We can use these parsers within our own programs, meaning our applications will never have to look at the XML directly; a large part of the workload will be done for us.

Parsers are also available for parsing SGML documents, but they are much more complex than XML parsers. Because XML is a subset of SGML, it's easier to write an XML parser than an SGML parser.

In the past, before these parsers were around, a lot of work would have gone into the many rules we were looking at (such as the rule that the middle name starts after the first space, and so on). But with our data in XML format, we can just give an XML parser a file like this:

```
<name>
  <first>John</first>
  <middle>Fitzgerald Johansen</middle>
  <last>Doe</last>
</name>
```

The parser can tell us that there is a piece of data called `<middle>`, and that the information stored there is `Fitzgerald Johansen`. The parser writer didn't have to know any rules about where the first name ends and where the middle name begins. The parser didn't have to know anything about my application at all, nor about the types of XML documents the application works with. The same parser could be used in my application, or in a completely different application. The language my XML is written in doesn't matter to the parser either; XML written in English, Chinese, Hebrew, or any other language could all be read by the same parser, even if the person who wrote it didn't understand any of these languages.

> **Just as any HTML document can be displayed by any web browser, any XML document can be read by any XML parser, regardless of what application was used to create it, or even what platform it was created on. This goes a long way to making your data universally accessible.**

There's another added benefit here: if I had previously written a program to deal with the first XML format, which had only a first and last name, that application could also accept the new XML format, without me having to change the code. So, because the parser takes care of the work of getting data out of the document for us, we can add to our XML format without breaking existing code, and new applications can take advantage of the new information if they wish.

If we subtracted elements from our `<name>` example, or changed the names of elements, we would still have to modify our applications to deal with the changes.

On the other hand, if we were just using our previous text-only format, any time we changed the data at all, every application using that data would have to be modified, retested, and redeployed.

Because it's so flexible, XML is targeted to be the basis for defining data exchange languages, especially for communication over the Internet. The language facilitates working with data within applications, such as an application that needs to access the previously listed `<name>` information, but it also facilitates sharing information with others. We can pass our `<name>` information around the Internet and, even without our particular program, the data can still be read. People can even pull the file up in a regular text editor and look at the raw XML, if they like, or open it in a viewer such as Internet Explorer.

Why "Extensible?"

Since we have full control over the creation of our XML document, we can shape the data in any way we wish, so that it makes sense for our particular application. If we don't need the flexibility of our `<name>` example, we could decide to describe a person's name in XML like this:

```
<designation>John Fitzgerald Johansen Doe</designation>
```

If we want to create data in a way that only one particular computer program will ever use, we can do so. And if we feel that we want to share our data with other programs, or even other companies across the Internet, XML gives us the flexibility to do that as well. We are free to structure the same data in different ways that suit the requirements of an application or category of applications.

This is where the extensible *in Extensible Markup Language comes from: anyone is free to mark up data in any way using the language, even if others are doing it in completely different ways.*

HTML, on the other hand, is not extensible, because you can't add to the language; you have to use the tags that are part of the HTML specification. For example, web browsers can understand the following:

```
<p>This is a paragraph.</p>
```

The `<p>` tag is a predefined HTML tag. However, web browsers can't understand the following:

```
<paragraph>This is a paragraph.</paragraph>
```

The `<paragraph>` tag is not a predefined HTML tag.

The benefits of XML become even more apparent when people use the same format to do common things, because this allows us to interchange information much more easily. There have already been numerous projects to produce industry-standard vocabularies to describe various types of data. For example, *Scalable Vector Graphics* (SVG) is an XML vocabulary for describing two-dimensional graphics (we'll look at SVG in Chapter 18); *MathML* is an XML vocabulary for describing mathematics as a basis for machine-to-machine communication; *Chemical Markup Language* (CML) is an XML vocabulary for the management of chemical information. The list goes on and on. Of course, you could write your own XML vocabularies to describe this type of information if you so wished, but if you use other, more common, formats, there is a better chance that you will be able to produce software that is immediately compatible with other software. Better yet, you can reuse code already written to work with these formats.

Since XML is so easy to read and write in your programs, it is also easy to convert between different vocabularies when required. For example, if you want to represent mathematical equations in your particular application in a certain way, but MathML doesn't quite suit your needs, you can create your own vocabulary. If you wanted to export your data for use by other applications, you might convert the data in your vocabulary to MathML for the other applications to read. In fact, Chapter 8 covers a technology called *XSLT*, which was created for transforming XML documents from one format to another, and that could potentially make these kinds of transformations very simple.

HTML and XML: Apples and Red Delicious Apples

What HTML does for display, XML is designed to do for data exchange. Sometimes XML isn't up to a certain task, just as HTML is sometimes not up to the task of displaying certain information. How many of us have Adobe Acrobat readers installed on our machines for those documents on the web that HTML just can't display properly? When it comes to display, HTML does a good job most of the time, and those who work with XML believe that, most of the time, XML will do a good job of communicating information. Just as HTML authors sometimes give up precise layout and presentation for the sake of making their information accessible to all web browsers, XML developers give up the small file sizes of proprietary formats for the flexibility of universal data access.

Of course, a fundamental difference exists between HTML and XML: HTML is designed for a *specific* application, to convey information to humans (usually visually, through a web browser), whereas XML has no specific application; it is designed for whatever use you need it for.

This is an important concept. Because HTML has its specific application, it also has a finite set of specific markup constructs (`<P>`, `<UL>`, `<H2>`, and so on), which are used to create a correct HTML document. In theory, we can be confident that any web browser will understand an HTML document because all it has to do is understand this finite set of tags. In practice, of course, I'm sure you've come across web pages that displayed properly in one web browser and not another, but this is usually a result of nonstandard HTML tags, which were created by browser vendors instead of being part of the HTML specification itself.

On the other hand, if we create an XML document, we can be sure that any XML parser will be able to retrieve information from that document, even though we can't guarantee that any application will be able to understand *what that information means*. That is, just because a parser can tell us that there is a piece of data called `<middle>` and that the information contained therein is `Fitzgerald Johansen`, it doesn't mean that there is any software in the world that knows what a `<middle>` is, what it is used for, or what it means.

So we can create XML documents to describe any information we want, but before XML can be considered useful, applications must be written that understand it. Furthermore, in addition to the capabilities provided by the base XML specification, there are a number of related technologies, some of which are covered in later chapters. These technologies provide more capabilities for us, making XML even more powerful than we've seen so far.

Unfortunately, some of these technologies exist only in draft form. Exactly how powerful these tools will be, or in what ways they'll be powerful, is yet to be seen.

Hierarchies of Information

The syntactical constructs that make up XML are discussed in the next chapter, but first it might be useful to examine how data is structured in an XML document.

When it comes to large, or even moderate, amounts of information, it's usually better to group it into related subtopics, rather than to have all of the information presented in one large blob. For example, this chapter is broken down into subtopics, and further broken down into paragraphs; a tax form is broken down into subsections, across multiple pages. This makes the information easier to comprehend, as well as making it more accessible.

Software developers have been using this paradigm for years, using a structure called an *object model*. In an object model, all of the information being modeled is broken up into various objects, and the objects themselves are then grouped into a hierarchy.

Hierarchies in HTML

For example, when working with Dynamic HTML (DHTML) there is an object model available for working with HTML documents, called the *Document Object Model* (DOM). This allows us to write code in an HTML document, such as the following JavaScript:

```
alert(document.title);
```

Here we are using the `alert()` function to pop up a message box telling us the title of an HTML document. That's done by accessing an object called `document`, which contains all of the information needed about the HTML document. The `document` object includes a property called `title`, which returns the title of the current HTML document.

The information that the object provides comes to us in the form of properties, and the functionality available comes to us in the form of methods.

Hierarchies in XML

XML also groups information in hierarchies. The items in our documents relate to each other in parent/child and sibling/sibling relationships.

> **These "items" are called elements. Chapter 2 provides a more precise definition of what exactly an element is. For now, just think of them as the individual pieces of information in the data.**

Consider our `<name>` example, shown hierarchically in Figure 1-8.

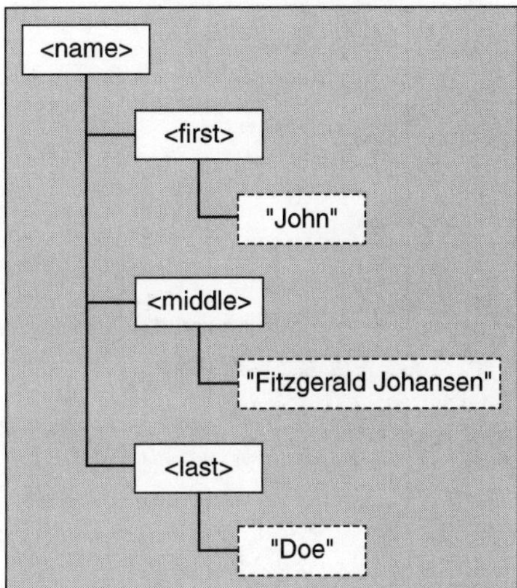

Figure 1-8

`<name>` is a parent of `<first>`. `<first>`, `<middle>`, and `<last>` are all siblings to each other (they are all children of `<name>`). Note, also, that the text is a child of the element. For example the text `John` is a child of `<first>`.

This structure is also called a *tree*; any parts of the tree that contain children are called *branches*, while parts that have no children are called *leaves*.

These are fairly loose terms, rather than formal definitions, which simply facilitate discussing the tree-like structure of XML documents. I have also seen the term "twig" in use, although it is much less common than "branch" or "leaf."

Because the `<name>` element has only other elements for children, and not text, it is said to have *element content*. Conversely, because `<first>`, `<middle>`, and `<last>` have only text as children, they are said to have *simple content*.

Elements can contain both text and other elements. They are then said to have *mixed content*.

For example:

```
<doc>
  <parent>this is some <em>text</em> in my element</parent>
</doc>
```

Here, `<parent>` has three children:

- A text child containing the text `this is some`
- An `<em>` child
- Another text child containing the text `in my element`

The structure is shown in Figure 1-9.

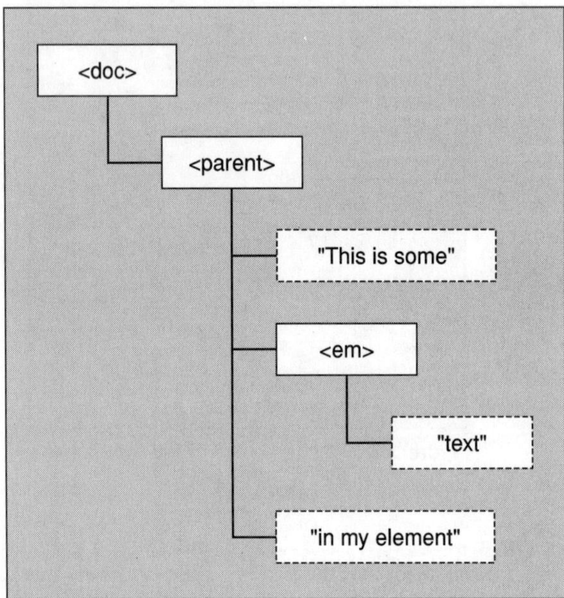

Figure 1-9

Relationships can also be defined by making the family tree analogy work a little bit harder: `<doc>` is an *ancestor* of `<em>`; `<em>` is a *descendant* of `<doc>`.

Once you understand the hierarchical relationships between your items (and the text they contain), you'll have a better understanding of the nature of XML. You'll also be better prepared to work with some of the other technologies surrounding XML, which make extensive use of this paradigm.

Chapter 11 gives you an opportunity to work with the Document Object Model mentioned earlier, which allows you to programmatically access the information in an XML document using this tree structure.

What's a Document Type?

XML's beauty comes from its ability to create a document to describe any information we want. It's completely flexible as to how we structure our data, but eventually we're going to want to settle on a particular design for our information, and say "to adhere to our XML format, structure the data like this."

For example, when we created our <name> XML above, we created *structured data*. We not only included all of the information about a name, but our hierarchy also contains implicit information about how some pieces of data relate to other pieces (our <name> contains a `<first>`, for example).

But it's more than that; we also created a specific set of elements, which is called a *vocabulary*. That is, we defined a number of XML elements that all work together to form a name: `<name>`, `<first>`, `<middle>`, and `<last>`.

But, it's even more than that! The most important thing we created was a *document type*. We created a specific type of document, which must be structured in a specific way, to describe a specific type of information. Although we haven't explicitly defined them yet, there are certain rules to which the elements in our vocabulary must adhere in order for our <name> document to conform to our document type. For example:

- ❑ The top-most element must be the <name> element.
- ❑ The `<first>`, `<middle>`, and `<last>` elements must be children of that element.
- ❑ The `<first>`, `<middle>`, and `<last>` elements must be in that order.
- ❑ There must be information in the `<first>` element and in the `<last>` element, but there doesn't have to be any information in the `<middle>` element.

In later chapters, you'll see different syntaxes that you can use to formally define an XML document type. Some XML parsers know how to read these syntaxes, and can use them to determine if your XML document really adheres to the rules in the document type or not.

However, all of the syntaxes used to define document types so far are lacking; they can provide some type checking, but not enough for many applications. Furthermore, they can't express the human meaning of terms in a vocabulary. For this reason, when creating XML document types, human-readable documentation should also be provided. For our <name> example, if we want others to be able to use the same format to describe names in their XML, we should provide them with documentation to describe how it works.

In real life, this human-readable documentation is often used in conjunction with one or more of the syntaxes available. Ironically, the self-describing nature of XML can sometimes make this human-readable documentation even more important. Often, because the data is already labeled within the document structure, it is assumed that people working with the data will be able to infer its meaning, which can be dangerous if the inferences made are incorrect, or even just different from the original author's intent.

No, Really—What's a Document Type?

Well, okay, maybe I was a little bit hasty in labeling our <name> example a document type. The truth is that others who work with XML may call it something different.

One of the problems people encounter when they communicate is that they sometimes use different terms to describe the same thing or, even worse, use the same term to describe different things. For example, I might call the thing that I drive a car, whereas someone else might call it an auto, and someone else again might call it a G-Class Vehicle. Furthermore, when I say car I *usually* mean a vehicle that has four wheels, is made for transporting passengers, and is smaller than a truck. (Notice how fuzzy this definition is, and that it depends further on the definition of a truck.) When someone else uses the word car, or if I use the word car in certain circumstances, it may instead just mean a land-based motorized vehicle, as opposed to a boat or a plane.

The same thing happens in XML. When you're using XML to create document types, you don't really have to think (or care) about the fact that you're creating document types; you just design your XML in a way that makes sense for your application, and then use it. If you ever did think about exactly what you were creating, you might have called it something other than a document type.

We picked the terms "document type" and "vocabulary" for this book because they do a good job of describing what we need to describe, but they are not universal terms used throughout the XML community. Regardless of the terms you use, the concepts are very important.

What Is the World Wide Web Consortium?

One of the reasons that HTML and XML are so successful is that they're *standards*. That means that anyone can follow these standards, and the solutions they develop will be able to interoperate. So who creates these standards?

The *World Wide Web Consortium* (W3C) was started in 1994, according to their web site (`http://www.w3.org/`), "to lead the World Wide Web to its full potential by developing common protocols that promote its evolution and ensure its interoperability." Recognizing this need for standards, the W3C produces *recommendations* that describe the basic building blocks of the web. They call them recommendations instead of standards because it is up to others to follow the recommendations to provide the interoperability.

Their most famous contribution to the web is the HTML Recommendation; when web browser producers claims that their product follows version 3.2 or 4.01 of the HTML Recommendation, they're talking about the Recommendation developed under the authority of the W3C.

The reason specifications from the W3C are so widely implemented is that the creation of these standards is a somewhat open process: any company or individual can join the W3C's membership, and membership allows these companies or individuals to take part in the standards process. This means that web browsers such as Netscape Navigator and Microsoft Internet Explorer are more likely to implement the same version of the HTML Recommendation, because both Microsoft and Netscape were involved in the evolution of that Recommendation.

Because of the interoperability goals of XML, the W3C is a good place to develop standards around the technology. Most of the technologies covered in this book are based on standards from the W3C; the XML 1.0 Specification, the XSLT Specification, the XPath Specification, and so on.

What Are the Pieces That Make Up XML?

"Structuring information" is a pretty broad topic, and it would be futile to try and define a specification to cover it fully. For this reason, a number of interrelated specifications all work together to form the XML family of technologies, with each specification covering different aspects of communicating information. Here are some of the more important ones:

- *XML 1.0* is the base specification upon which the XML family is built. It describes the syntax that XML documents have to follow, the rules that XML parsers have to follow, and anything else you need to know to read or write an XML document. It also defines DTDs, although they sometimes get treated as a separate technology.
- Because we can make up our own structures and element names for our documents, *DTDs* and *Schemas* provide ways to define our document types. We can check to make sure other documents adhere to these templates, and other developers can produce compatible documents. DTDs and Schemas are discussed in Chapters 4 and 5.
- *Namespaces* provide a means to distinguish one XML vocabulary from another, which allows us to create richer documents by combining multiple vocabularies into one document type. Namespaces are discussed in detail in Chapter 3.
- *XPath* describes a querying language for addressing parts of an XML document. This allows applications to ask for a specific piece of an XML document, instead of having to always deal with one large chunk of information. For example, XPath could be used to get "all the last names" from a document. We discuss XPath in Chapter 7.
- As we discussed earlier, in some cases, we may want to display our XML documents. For simpler cases, we can use *Cascading Style Sheets* (CSS) to define the presentation of our documents. For more complex cases, we can use *Extensible Stylesheet Language* (XSL); this consists of *XSLT*, which can transform our documents from one type to another, and *Formatting Objects*, which deal with display. These technologies are covered in Chapters 8 and 17.
- Although the syntax for HTML and the syntax for XML look very similar, they are actually not the same—XML's syntax is much more rigid than that of HTML. This means that an XML parser cannot necessarily read an HTML document. This is one of the reasons that *XHTML* was created—an XML version of HTML. XHTML is very similar to HTML, so HTML developers will have no problem working with XHTML, but the syntax used is more rigid and readable by XML parsers (since XHTML *is* XML). XHTML is discussed in Chapter 16.
- The *XQuery* recommendation is designed to provide a means of querying data directly from XML documents on the web and is discussed in Chapter 9.
- To provide a means for more traditional applications to interface with XML documents, there is a document object model (DOM), which we discuss in Chapter 11. An alternative way for programmers to interface with XML documents from their code is to use the Simple API for XML (SAX), which is the subject of Chapter 12.
- In addition to the specifications for the various XML technologies, some specifications also exist for specific XML document types:
    - The *RDF Site Summary* (RSS) specification is used by web sites that want to syndicate news stories (or similar content that can be treated similarly to news stories), for use by other web sites or applications. RSS is discussed in Chapter 13.
    - The *Scalable Vector Graphics* (SVG) specification is used to describe two-dimensional graphics, and is discussed in Chapter 18.

Where Is XML Used, and Where Can It Be Used?

Well, that's quite a question. XML can be used anywhere. It is platform- and language-independent, which means it doesn't matter that one computer may be using, for example, a Visual Basic application on a Microsoft operating system, and another computer might be a UNIX machine running Java code. Any time one computer program needs to communicate with another program, XML is a potential fit for the exchange format. The following are just a few examples, and such applications are discussed in more detail throughout the book.

Reducing Server Load

Web-based applications can use XML to reduce the load on the web servers by keeping all information on the client for as long as possible, and then sending the information to those servers in one big XML document.

Web Site Content

The W3C uses XML to write its specifications. These XML documents can then be transformed into HTML for display (by XSLT), or transformed into a number of other presentation formats.

Some web sites also use XML entirely for their content, where, traditionally, HTML would have been used. This XML can then be transformed into HTML via XSLT, or displayed directly in browsers via CSS. In fact, the web servers can even determine dynamically what kind of browser is retrieving the information, and then decide what to do. For example, transform the XML into HTML for older browsers, and just send the XML straight to the client for newer browsers, reducing the load on the server.

In fact, this could be generalized to *any* content. If your data is in XML, you can use it for any purpose. Presentation on the web is just one possibility.

Remote Procedure Calls

XML can also be used as a means of sending data for *Remote Procedure Calls* (RPC). RPC is a protocol that allows objects on one computer to call objects on another computer to do work, allowing distributed computing. As Chapters 14 and 15 show, using XML and HTTP for these RPC calls, with web services and/or SOAP, allows this to occur even through a firewall, which would normally block such calls, providing greater opportunities for distributed computing.

e-Commerce

e-commerce is one of those buzzwords that you hear all over the place. Companies are discovering that by communicating via the Internet, instead of by more traditional methods (such as faxing, human-to-human communication, and so on), they can streamline their processes, decreasing costs and increasing response times. Whenever one company needs to send data to another, XML is the perfect format for the exchange.

When the companies involved have some kind of ongoing relationship, this is known as *business-to-business* (B2B) e-commerce. *Business-to-consumer* (B2C) transactions also take place—a system you may have used if you bought this book on the Internet. Both types of e-commerce have their potential uses for XML.

And XML is a good fit for many other applications. After reading this book, you should be able to decide when XML will work in your applications and when it won't.

Summary

This chapter provided an overview of what XML is and why it's so useful. We've seen the advantages of text and binary files, and the way that XML combines the advantages of both, while eliminating most of the disadvantages. We have also seen the flexibility we have in creating data in any format we wish.

Because XML is a subset of a proven technology, SGML, there are many years of experience behind the standard. Also, because other technologies are built around XML, we can create applications that are as complex or simple as our situation warrants.

Much of the power that we get from XML comes from the rigid way in which documents must be written. Chapter 2 takes a closer look at the rules for creating well-formed XML.

Exercise Questions

Suggested solutions to these questions can be found in Appendix A.

Question 1

Modify the "`name`" XML document you've been working with to include the person's title (Mr., Ms., Dr., and so on).

Question 2

The "`name`" example we've been using so far has been in English. However, XML is language-agnostic, so we can create XML documents in any language we wish. Therefore, create a new French document type to represent a name. You can use the following table for the names of the XML elements.

English	French
name	identité
first	prénom
last	nom
middle	deuxième-prénom

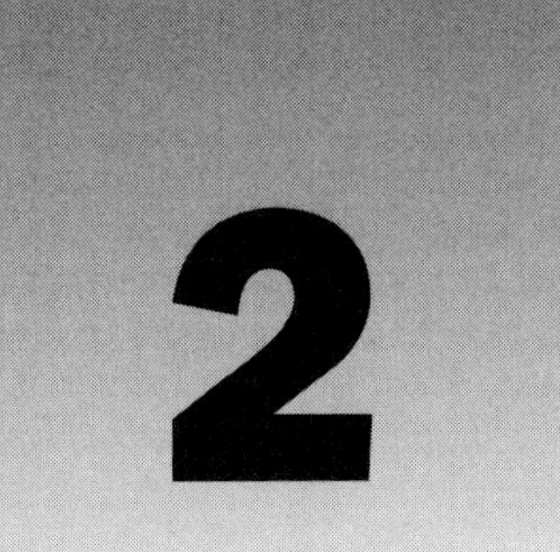

Well-Formed XML

We've discussed some of the reasons why XML makes sense for communicating data, so now let's get our hands dirty and learn how to create our own XML documents. This chapter covers all you need to know to create *well-formed* XML. Well-formed XML is XML that meets certain syntactical rules outlined in the XML 1.0 specification.

You will learn the following:

- ❑ How to create XML elements using start-tags and end-tags
- ❑ How to further describe elements with attributes
- ❑ How to declare your document as being XML
- ❑ How to send instructions to applications that are processing the XML document
- ❑ Which characters aren't allowed in XML—and how to use them in your documents anyway!

Because the syntax rules for XML and HTML are so similar, and because you may already be familiar with HTML, we'll be making comparisons between the two languages in this chapter. However, if you don't have any knowledge of HTML, you shouldn't find it too hard to follow along.

If you have Microsoft Internet Explorer 5 or later, you may find it useful to save some of the examples in this chapter on your hard drive and view the results in the browser. If you don't have IE5 or later, some of the examples will have screenshots to show what the end results look like. One nice result of doing this is that the browser will tell you if you make a syntax mistake. I do this quite often, just to sanity-check myself and make sure I haven't mistyped anything.

Parsing XML

The main reason for creating all these rules about writing well-formed XML documents is so that we can create a computer program to read in the data, and easily tell markup from information.

> *According to the XML specification (`http://www.w3.org/TR/REC-xml#sec-intro`): "A software module called an XML processor is used to read XML documents and provide access to their content and structure. It is assumed that an XML processor is doing its work on behalf of another module, called the application."*

An XML processor is more commonly called a *parser*, since it simply parses XML and provides the application with any information it needs. That is, it reads through the characters in the document, determines which characters are part of the document's markup and which are part of the document's data, and does all of the other processing of an XML document that happens before an application can make use of it. There are quite a number of XML parsers available, many of which are free. Some of the better-known ones include:

- **Microsoft Internet Explorer Parser**—Microsoft's XML parser, MSXML, first shipped with Internet Explorer 4, and implemented an early draft of the XML specification. With the release of IE5, the XML implementation was upgraded to reflect the XML version 1 specification. The latest version of the parser is available for download from Microsoft's MSDN site, at `http://msdn.microsoft.com`, and also comes built-in with the Internet Explorer browser.
- **Apache Xerces**—The Apache Software Foundation's Xerces subproject of the Apache XML Project (`http://xml.apache.org/`) has resulted in XML parsers in Java and C++, plus a Perl wrapper for the C++ parser. These tools are free, and the distribution of the code is controlled by the GNU Public License (GPL).
- **James Clark's Expat**—Expat is an XML 1.0 parser toolkit written in C. You can find more information at `http://www.jclark.com/xml/expat.html`, and Expat can be downloaded from `ftp://ftp.jclark.com/pub/xml/expat.zip`. It is free for both private and commercial use.
- **Xml4j**—IBMs AlphaWorks site (`http://www.alphaworks.ibm.com`) offers a number of XML tools and applications, including the xml4j parser. This is another parser written in Java, available for free, though there are some licensing restrictions regarding its use.

Tags and Text and Elements, Oh My!

It's time to stop calling things just "items" and "text;" we need some names for the pieces that make up an XML document. To get cracking, let's break down the simple `name.xml` document we created in Chapter 1:

```
<name>
  <first>John</first>
  <middle>Fitzgerald Johansen</middle>
  <last>Doe</last>
</name>
```

The text starting with a < character and ending with a > character is an XML *tag*. The information in our document (our data) is contained within the various tags that constitute the markup of the document. This makes it easy to distinguish the *information* in the document from the *markup*.

As you can see, the tags are paired, so that any opening tag (for example, `<name>`) must have a closing tag (`</name>`). In XML parlance, these are called *start-tags* and *end-tags*. The end-tags are the same as the start-tags, except that they have a `/` right after the opening < character.

In this regard, XML tags work the same as start-tags and end-tags in HTML. For example, you would mark a section of HTML bold like this:

```
<B>This is bold.</B>
```

As you can see, there is a `<B>` start-tag, and a `</B>` end-tag, just like we use for XML.

All of the information from the start of a start-tag to the end of an end-tag, and including everything in between, is called an *element*. So:

- `<first>` is a start-tag
- `</first>` is an end-tag
- `<first>John</first>` is an element

The text between the start-tag and end-tag of an element is called the *element content*. The content between our tags will often just be data (as opposed to other elements). In this case, the element content is referred to as *Parsed Character DATA*, which is almost always referred to using its acronym, *PCDATA*, or with a more general term such as "text content" or even "text node."

Whenever you come across a strange-looking term like PCDATA, it's usually a good bet the term is inherited from SGML. Because XML is a subset of SGML, there are a lot of these inherited terms.

The whole document, starting at `<name>` and ending at `</name>`, is also an element, which happens to include other elements. (And, in this case, since it contains the entire XML document, the element is called the *root element*, which we'll talk about later.)

If you wish, you can include a space before the closing > of a tag. For example, you could create markup like the following, with a space between the first `<first` and the closing tag:

```
<first >John</first>
```

or the following with a space between both `<first` and `</first` and their closing tags:

```
<first >John</first >
```

or even

```
<first
>John</first>
```

Later on, we'll see where this might come in handy.

To put this newfound knowledge into action, let's create an example that contains more information than just a name.

Try It Out Distribution

For the examples in this chapter, we'll create a fictional company, Serna Inc., which has developed a new portable music device. Serna Inc. provides a subscription service called sernaDirect that works with the devices so that the subscribers can regularly update the musical selection on their devices by downloading songs from Serna Inc. Since Serna Inc. wishes to focus on developing its product line and building the subscription service, it has contracted another company, Ferna Distribution, to handle distribution of the products to customers. The distribution process works like this:

1. The customer calls a Ferna Distribution Customer Service Representative (CSR) or visits the Ferna website to place an order. The customer can also change or cancel an order.
2. The order is captured into Ferna Distribution's back-end systems, and once a day a file is sent to Serna Inc. with all of the day's orders (including canceled and updated orders).
3. Once Serna Inc. has received a file, its systems are updated with the new, cancelled, and updated orders. Based on this, the music for the sernaDirect subscription service can be sent to the appropriate subscribers (based on the ID of their device).

This process is illustrated in Figure 2-1.

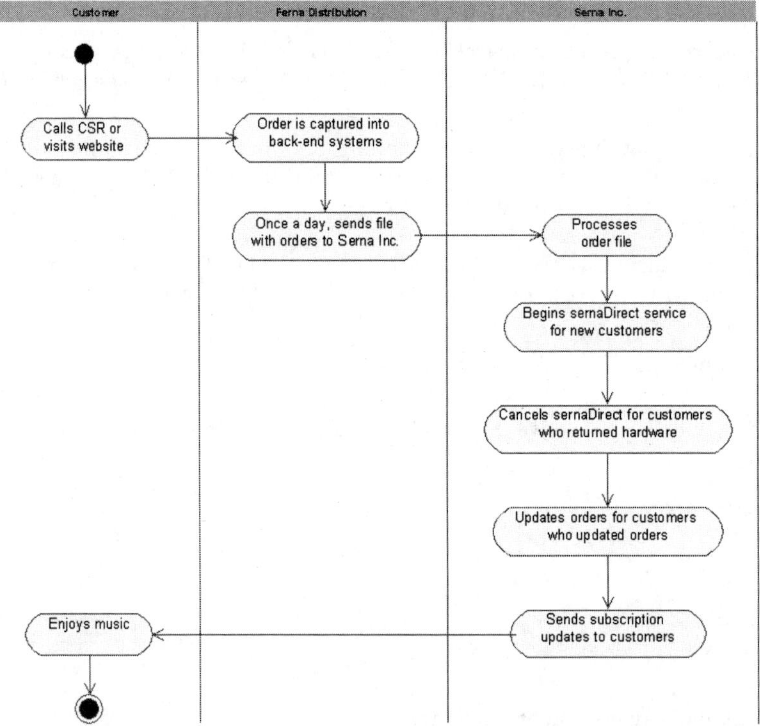

Figure 2-1

For this *Try It Out*, we're concerned with the file that Ferna Distribution sends to Serna Inc. each day, with the new, cancelled, and updated orders. This is exactly the place where XML shines, and we'll use XML to create the daily file to Serna Inc. But before we break out Notepad and start typing, we need to know what information we're capturing.

In Chapter 1, we learned that XML is hierarchical in nature; information is structured like a tree, with parent/child relationships. This means that we have to arrange our order information in a tree structure as well.

1. Since this XML layout will contain information about orders, we need to capture information like the customer's name and address, the type of hardware which has been purchased, information about the subscription to sernaDirect, and so on.

   Figure 2-2 shows the hierarchy we'll be creating:

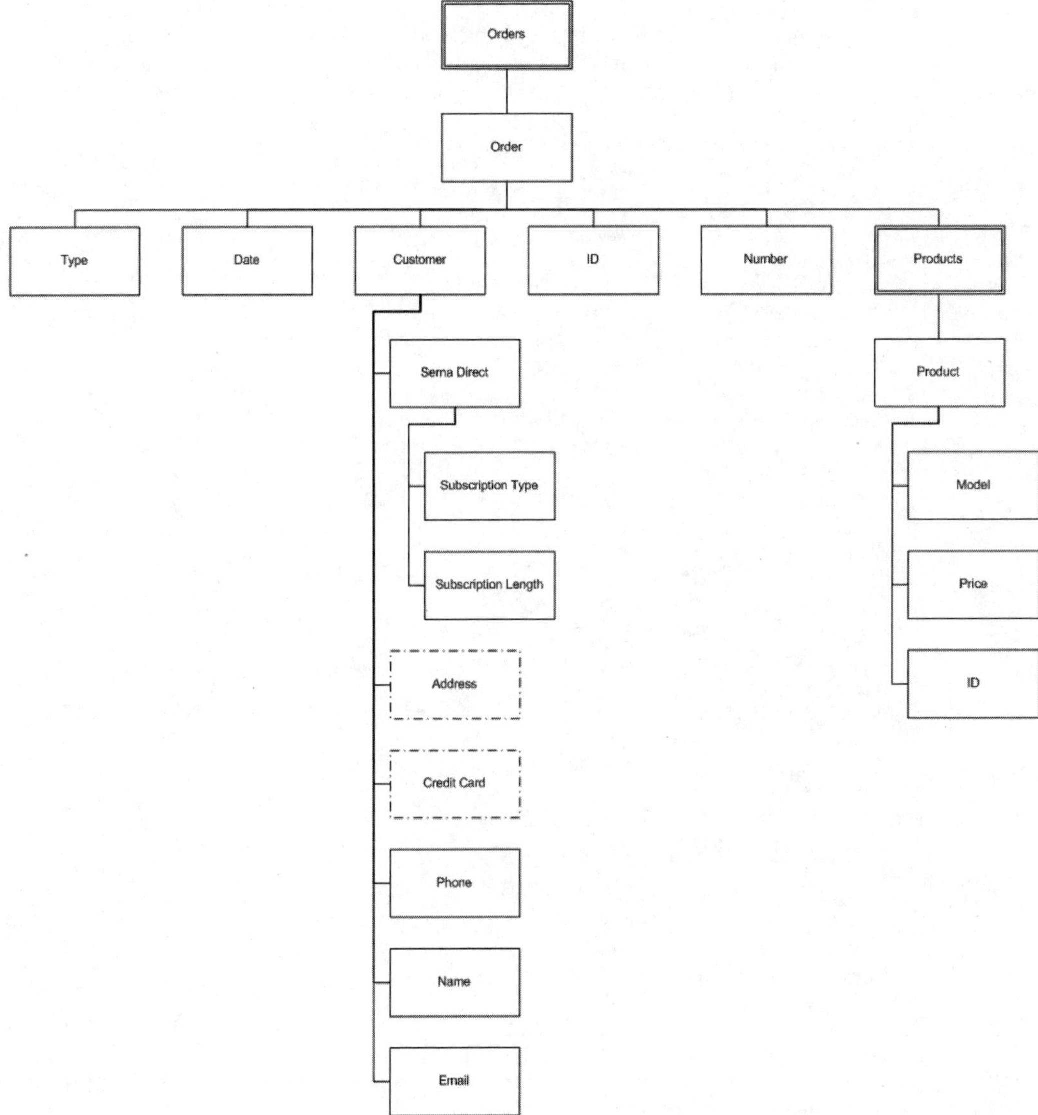

Figure 2-2

Notice that for the sake of brevity, I haven't included all of the layers of information. For example, the Address will be further broken down for the address information, and the Credit Card will contain child elements for the credit card information.

Some of these elements, like <Date>, will only appear once; others, like <Product> or <Order>, might appear multiple times in the document. Also, some will have PCDATA only, while some will include their information as child elements instead. For example, the <Date> element will contain PCDATA (no child elements) only: the date the order was placed. On the other hand, the <Address> element won't contain any PCDATA of its own, but will contain child elements that further break down the information, such as <State> and <City>.

2. With this in mind, we're ready to start entering XML. If you have Internet Explorer 5 or later, installed on your machine, type the following into Notepad and save it to your hard drive as order.xml:

```
<Orders>
  <Order>
    <Type>N</Type>
    <Date>Jan 1, 2004, 14:29</Date>
    <Customer>
      <SernaDirect>
        <SubscriptionType>B</SubscriptionType>
        <SubscriptionLength>12</SubscriptionLength>
      </SernaDirect>
      <Address>
        <Address1>123 Somewhere Ave.</Address1>
        <Address2></Address2>
        <City>Some Town</City>
        <State>TA</State>
        <Zip>000000000</Zip>
      </Address>
      <CreditCard>
        <Number>4111111111111111</Number>
        <CardHolderName>John Q Public</CardHolderName>
        <Expiry>11/09</Expiry>
      </CreditCard>
      <Phone>5555555555</Phone>
      <Name>John Public</Name>
      <Email>jpublic@someprovider.com</Email>
    </Customer>
    <ID>0000000001</ID>
    <Number>x582n9</Number>
    <Products>
      <Product>
        <Model>X9</Model>
        <Price>129.95</Price>
        <ID>x9000059</ID>
      </Product>
    </Products>
  </Order>
  <Order>
    <Type>N</Type>
    <Date>Jan 1, 2004, 16:00</Date>
    <Customer>
      <SernaDirect>
        <SubscriptionType>D</SubscriptionType>
        <SubscriptionLength>12</SubscriptionLength>
      </SernaDirect>
```

```
      <Address>
        <Address1>89 Subscriber's Street</Address1>
        <Address2>Box 882</Address2>
        <City>Smallville</City>
        <State>XQ</State>
        <Zip>000000000</Zip>
      </Address>
      <CreditCard>
        <Number>4512451245124512</Number>
        <CardHolderName>Helen P Someperson</CardHolderName>
        <Expiry>01/08</Expiry>
      </CreditCard>
      <Phone>5554443333</Phone>
      <Name>Helen Someperson</Name>
      <Email>helens@isp.net</Email>
    </Customer>
    <ID>0000000002</ID>
    <Number>a98f78d</Number>
    <Products>
      <Product>
        <Model>Y9</Model>
        <Price>229.95</Price>
        <ID>y9000065</ID>
      </Product>
    </Products>
  </Order>
</Orders>
```

For the sake of brevity, we'll only enter two orders.

3. Now open the file in IE. (Navigate to the file in Explorer and double-click on it, or open up the browser and type in the path in the URL bar.) If you have typed in the tags exactly as shown, the `order.xml` file will look something like Figure 2-3.

I've made use of IE's handy collapse feature to collapse some of the elements, so that more of the document would fit on the screen.

How It Works

Here we've created a hierarchy of information about a series of orders that have been placed through Ferna Distribution, so we've named the root element accordingly: `<Orders>`.

Each `<Order>` element has children for the type of order, the date the order was placed, and the ID and number of the order (these types of systems often have multiple IDs attached to an order, since there are multiple systems dealing with it, so I added two separate numbers for realism—the `<ID>` and `<Number>` elements). There are also child elements for handling information about the customer, and the products purchased by that customer.

You may have noticed that the browser changed `<Address2></Address2>` in our first order to `<Address2/>` when it displayed the information. We'll talk about this shorthand syntax a little later, but don't worry: this is called a *self-closing tag* and it's perfectly legal.

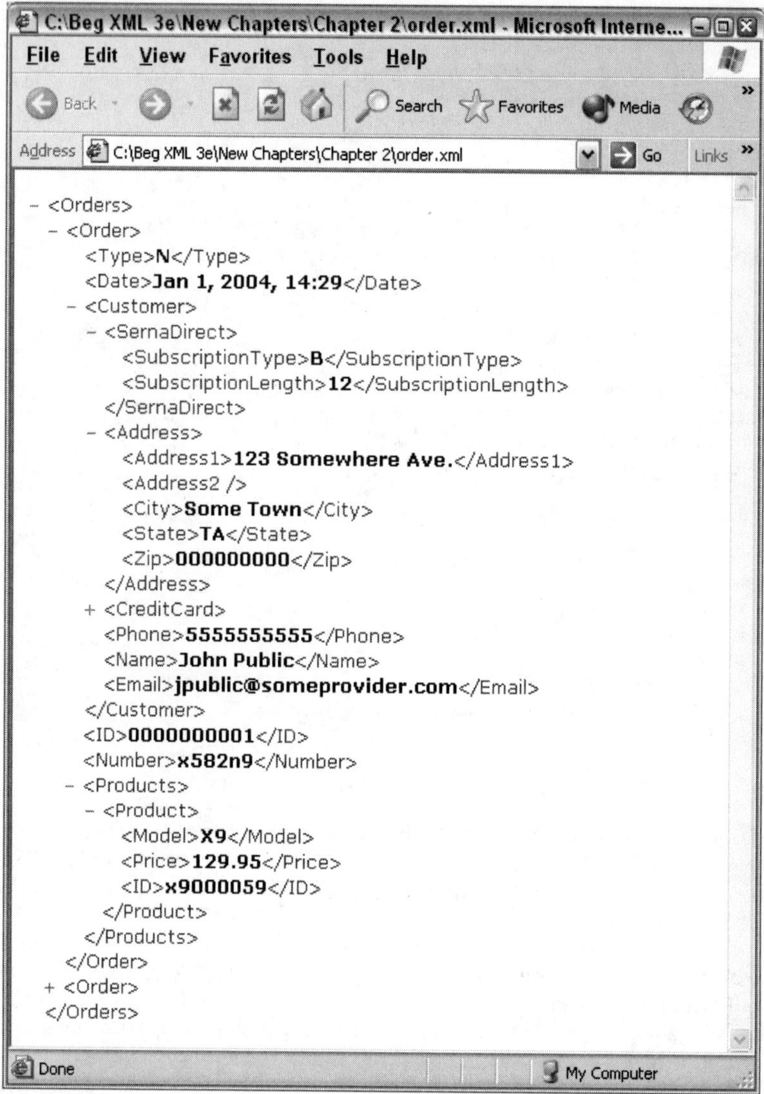

Figure 2-3

Rules for Elements

Obviously, if we could just create elements in any old way we wanted, we wouldn't be any further along than our text file examples from the previous chapter. There must be some rules for elements, which are fundamental to the understanding of XML.

> **XML documents must adhere to certain rules to be well formed.**

We'll list them, briefly, before getting down to details:

- Every start-tag must have a matching end-tag, or be a self-closing tag.
- Tags can't overlap; elements must be properly nested.
- XML documents can have only one root element.
- Element names must obey XML naming conventions.
- XML is case sensitive.
- XML will keep whitespace in your PCDATA.

It is these rules that make XML such a universal format for interchanging data. As long as your XML documents follow all of the rules in the XML Recommendation, any available XML parser will be able to read the information it contains.

Every Start-Tag Must Have an End-Tag

One of the problems with parsing HTML documents is that not every element requires a start-tag and an end-tag. Take the following example:

```
<HTML>
<BODY>
<P>Here is some text in an HTML paragraph.
<BR>
Here is some more text in the same paragraph.
<P>And here is some text in another HTML paragraph.</p>
</BODY>
</HTML>
```

Notice that the first `<P>` tag has no closing `</P>` tag. This is allowed—and sometimes even encouraged—in HTML, because most web browsers can figure out where the end of the paragraph should be. In this case, when the browser comes across the second `<P>` tag, it knows to end the first paragraph and begin a new paragraph. Then there's the `<BR>` tag (line break), which by definition has no closing tag.

Also, notice that the second `<P>` start-tag is matched by a `</p>` end-tag, in lowercase. This is not a problem for HTML browsers, because HTML is not case sensitive, but as we'll soon see, this would cause a problem for an XML parser.

The problem is that this makes HTML parsers harder to write. Developers must add code to take into account all of these factors, which often makes the parsers larger and much harder to debug. What's more, the way files are parsed is not standardized—different browsers do it differently, leading to incompatibilities. (Perhaps not in this simple example, but when it comes to HTML tables, browser inconsistencies are a nightmare, and badly created HTML markup makes things much worse!)

For now, just remember that in XML the end-tag is required, and its name has to exactly match the start-tag's name.

Elements Must Be Properly Nested

Because XML is strictly hierarchical, you have to be careful to close the child elements before you close their parents. (This is called *properly nesting* your tags.) Let's look at another HTML example to demonstrate this:

```
<P>Some <STRONG>formatted <EM>text</STRONG>, but</EM> no grammar no good!</P>
```

This would produce the output shown in Figure 2-4 on a web browser.

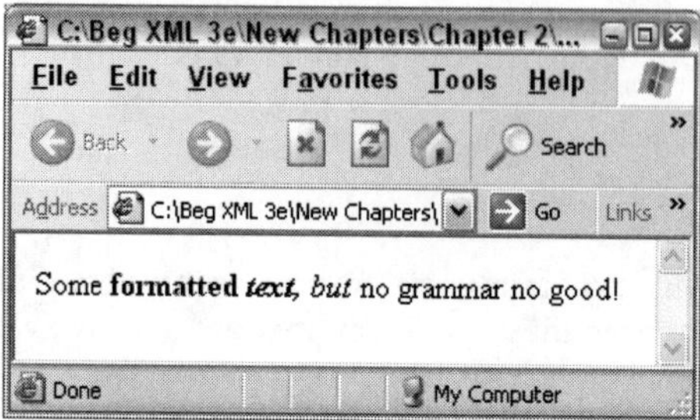

Figure 2-4

As you can see, the <STRONG> tags cover the text "`formatted text`", while the <EM> tags cover the text "`text, but`".

But is <EM> a child of <STRONG>, or is <STRONG> a child of <EM>? Or are they both siblings, and children of <P>? According to our stricter XML rules, the answer is none of the above. The HTML code, as written, can't be arranged as a proper hierarchy, and therefore could not be well-formed XML.

Actually, in later versions of the HTML Recommendation, the HTML example here isn't really proper HTML either; according to the HTML 4 Recommendation, tags should not overlap like this, but web browsers will do their best to render the content anyway.

If ever you're in doubt as to whether your XML tags are overlapping, try to rearrange them visually to be hierarchical. If the tree makes sense, then you're okay. Otherwise, you'll have to rework your markup.

For example, we could get the same effect as above by doing the following:

```
<P>Some <STRONG>formatted <EM>text</EM></STRONG><EM>, but</EM>
no grammar no good!</P>
```

Which can be properly formatted in a tree, like this:

```
<P>
  Some
  <STRONG>
    formatted
    <EM>
      text
    </EM>
  </STRONG>
  <EM>
    , but
  </EM>
  no grammar no good!
</P>
```

Our example now makes it clear which elements are parents of which other elements, and what element each piece of text belongs to, which makes it properly nested. Not only is this a better way to write HTML, but it also makes the example well-formed to an XML parser.

An XML Document Can Have Only One Root Element

In our `<name>` document from Chapter 1, the `<name>` element is called the *root element*. This is the top-level element in the document, and all the other elements are its children or descendants. An XML document must have one and only one root element: in fact, it must have a root element even if it has no content.

For example, the following XML is not well-formed, because it has two root elements:

```
<name>John</name>
<name>Jane</name>
```

To make this well-formed, we'd need to add a top-level element, like this:

```
<names>
  <name>John</name>
  <name>Jane</name>
</names>
```

So while it may seem a bit of an inconvenience, it turns out that it's incredibly easy to follow this rule. If you have a document structure with multiple root-like elements, simply create a higher-level element to contain them.

Elements Must Obey XML Naming Conventions

If we're going to be creating elements we're going to have to give them names, and XML is very generous in the names we're allowed to use. For example, there aren't any reserved words to avoid in XML, as there are in most programming languages, so we have a lot of flexibility in this regard.

However, there are some rules that we must follow:

- Names can start with letters (including non-Latin characters) or the - character, but not numbers or other punctuation characters.
- After the first character, numbers, hyphens, and periods are allowed.
- Names can't contain spaces.
- Names can't contain the `:` character. Strictly speaking, this character *is* allowed, but the XML specification says that it's "reserved." You should avoid using it in your documents, unless you are working with namespaces (which we'll be looking at in the next chapter).
- Names can't start with the letters `xml`, in uppercase, lowercase, or mixed—you can't start a name with `xml`, `XML`, `XmL`, or any other combination.

Unfortunately, the XML parser shipped with Internet Explorer doesn't enforce this rule. However, even if you are using IE's XML parser, you should never name elements starting with the characters `xml`, because your documents would not be considered well-formed by other parsers.

- There can't be a space after the opening < character; the name of the element must come immediately after it. However, there can be space before the closing > character, if you desire.

Here are some examples of valid names:

```
<first.name>
<résumé>
```

And here are some examples of invalid names:

```
<xml-tag>
```

which starts with `xml`,

```
<123>
```

which starts with a number,

```
<fun=xml>
```

because the "=" sign is illegal, and

```
<my tag>
```

which contains a space.

> **Remember these rules for element names—they also apply to naming other things in XML.**

Case Sensitivity

Another important point to keep in mind is that the tags in XML are *case sensitive*. (This is a big difference from HTML, which is case insensitive.) This means that `<first>` is different from `<FIRST>`, which is different from `<First>`.

> *This sometimes seems odd to English-speaking users of XML, since English words can easily be converted to upper or lowercase with no loss of meaning. But in many languages, the concept of case is either not applicable (in other words, what's the uppercase of "β"? Or the lowercase, for that matter?), or is extremely important (what's the uppercase of "é"? The answer may be different, depending on the context—sometimes it will be "É", but other times it will just be "é".). To put intelligent rules into the XML specification for converting between uppercase and lowercase (sometimes called case folding) would probably have doubled or trebled its size, and still only benefited certain sections of the population. Luckily, it doesn't take long to get used to having case-sensitive names.*

Our previous `<P></p>` HTML example would not work in XML; because XML is case sensitive, an XML parser would not be able to match the `</p>` end-tag with any start-tags, and neither would it be able to match the `<P>` start-tag with any end-tags.

> **Warning! Because XML is case sensitive, you could legally create an XML document that has both `<first>` and `<First>` elements, which have different meanings. This is a bad idea, and will cause nothing but confusion! You should always try to give your elements distinct names, for your sanity, and for the sanity of those to come after you.**

To help combat these kinds of problem, it's a good idea to pick a naming style and stick to it. Some examples of common styles are:

- `<first_name>`
- `<firstName>`
- `<first-name>`
- `<FirstName>`

Which style you choose isn't important; what is important is that you stick to it. A naming convention only helps when it's used consistently. For this book, we'll usually use the `<FirstName>` convention.

Whitespace in PCDATA

There is a special category of characters called `whitespace` that includes things like the space character, new lines (what you get when you hit the Enter key), and tabs. Whitespace is used to separate words, as well as to make text more readable.

Those familiar with HTML are probably quite aware of the practice of *whitespace stripping*. In HTML, any whitespace considered insignificant is stripped out of the document when it is processed. For example, take the following HTML:

```
<P>This is a paragraph.     It has a whole bunch
   of space.</P>
```

As far as HTML is concerned, anything more than a single space between the words in a `<P>` is insignificant. So all of the spaces between the first period and the word `It` would be stripped, except for one. Also, the line feed after the word `bunch` and the spaces before `of` would be stripped down to one space. As a result, the previous HTML would be rendered in a browser as shown in Figure 2-5.

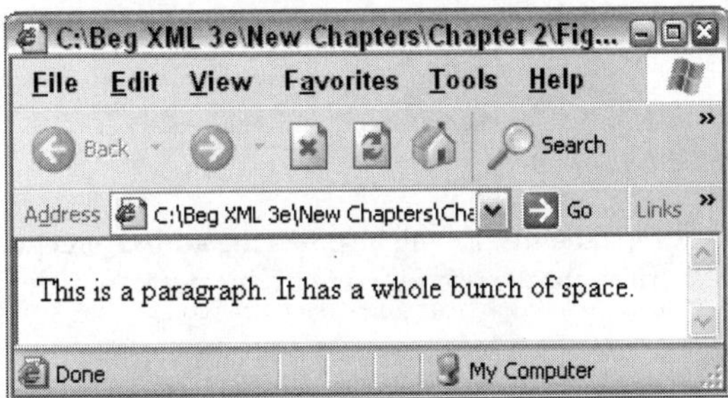

Figure 2-5

In order to get the results as they appear in the HTML example, we'd have to add special HTML markup to the source, like the following:

```
<P>This is a paragraph.     It has a whole
bunch<BR>  of space.</P>
```

Here, ` ` signifies that we should insert a space (`nbsp` stands for *Non-Breaking SPace*), and the `<BR>` tag specifies that there should be a line feed. This would format the output as it appears in Figure 2-6.

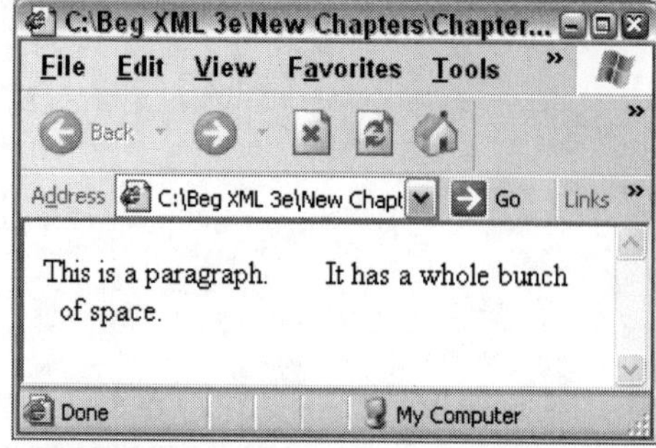

Figure 2-6

Alternatively, if we wanted to have the text displayed *exactly* as it is in the source file, we could use the <PRE> tag. This specifically tells the HTML parser not to strip the whitespace, but to display the text exactly as it appears in the HTML document, so we could write the following and also get the desired results:

```
<PRE>This is a paragraph.    It has a whole bunch
  of space.</PRE>
```

This would produce output like that in Figure 2-7.

Figure 2-7

However, in most web browsers, the <PRE> tag also has the added effect that the text is rendered in a fixed width font, like the courier font we use for code in this book (which is why Figure 2-7 looks slightly different than Figure 2-6).

Whitespace stripping is very advantageous for a language like HTML, which is primarily a means for displaying information. It allows the source for an HTML document to be formatted in a readable way for the person writing the HTML, while displaying it formatted in a readable, and possibly quite different, way for the user who views the document in a browser.

In XML, however, no whitespace stripping takes place for PCDATA. This means that for the following XML tag:

```
<tag>This is a paragraph.    It has a whole bunch
  of space.</tag>
```

the PCDATA is:

```
This is a paragraph.    It has a whole bunch
  of space.
```

Just like our second HTML example, none of the whitespace has been stripped out. As far as whitespace stripping goes, all XML elements are treated just as for the HTML <PRE> tag. This makes the rules much easier to understand for XML than they are for HTML.

In XML, the whitespace stays.

Unfortunately, if you view the preceding XML example in Internet Explorer, the whitespace will be stripped out—or will seem to be. This is because IE is not actually showing you the XML directly; it uses a technology called XSL to transform the XML to HTML, and it displays the HTML. Then, because IE is an HTML browser, it strips out the whitespace.

End-of-Line Whitespace

There is one form of whitespace stripping that XML does perform on PCDATA, which is the handling of *new line* characters. The problem is that there are two characters that are used for new lines—the *line feed* character and the *carriage return* character—and computers running Windows, UNIX, and Macintosh computers all use these characters differently.

For example, to get a new line in Windows, an application would use both the line feed and the carriage return character together, whereas on UNIX only the line feed would be used. This could prove to be very troublesome when creating XML documents, because UNIX machines would treat the new lines in a document differently from the Windows boxes, which would treat them differently from the Macintosh boxes, and our XML interoperability would be lost.

For this reason, it was decided that XML parsers would change all new lines to a single line feed character before processing. This means that any XML application will know, no matter which operating system it's running under, that a new line will be represented by a single line feed character. This makes data exchange among multiple computers running different operating systems that much easier, since programmers don't have to deal with the (sometimes annoying) end-of-line logic.

Whitespace in Markup

As well as the whitespace in our data, there could also be whitespace within an XML document that's not actually part of the data. For example:

```
<Tag>
  <AnotherTag>This is some XML</AnotherTag>
</Tag>
```

While any whitespace contained within <AnotherTag>'s PCDATA is part of the data, there is also a new line after <tag>, and some spaces before <anotherTag>. These spaces could be there just to make the document easier to read, while not actually being part of its data. This "readability" whitespace is called *extraneous whitespace*.

While an XML parser must pass all whitespace through to the application, it can also inform the application which whitespace is not actually part of an element's PCDATA, but is just extraneous whitespace.

So how does the parser decide whether this is extraneous whitespace or not? That depends on what kind of data we specify `<tag>` should contain. If `<tag>` can only contain other elements (and no PCDATA) then the whitespace will be considered extraneous. However, if `<tag>` is allowed to contain PCDATA, then the whitespace will be considered to be part of that PCDATA, so it will be retained.

Unfortunately, from this document alone an XML parser would have no way to tell whether `<tag>` is supposed to contain PCDATA or not, which means that it has to assume none of the whitespace is extraneous. We'll see how we can get the parser to recognize this as extraneous whitespace in Chapter 5, when we discuss content models.

Attributes

In addition to tags and elements, XML documents can also include *attributes*. Attributes are simple name/value pairs associated with an element. They are attached to the start-tag, but not to the end-tag, as shown in the following code:

```
<name nickname="Shiny John">
  <first>John</first>
  <middle>Fitzgerald Johansen</middle>
  <last>Doe</last>
</name>
```

Attributes must have values—even if that value is just an empty string (like `""`)—and those values must be in quotes. So the following, which is part of a common HTML tag, is not legal in XML:

```
<INPUT checked>
```

and neither is this:

```
<INPUT checked=true>
```

Either single quotes or double quotes are fine, but they have to match. For example, to make this into well-formed XML, you can use either of these:

```
<INPUT checked='true'>
```

or

```
<INPUT checked="true">
```

but you can't use:

```
<INPUT checked="true'>
```

Because either single or double quotes are allowed, it's easy to include quote characters in your attribute values, like "John's nickname" or 'I said "hi" to him'. You just have to be careful not to accidentally close your attribute, like 'John's nickname'; if an XML parser sees an attribute value like this, it will think you're closing the value at the second single quote, and will raise an error when it sees the "s" which comes right after it.

The same rules apply to naming attributes as apply to naming elements: names are case sensitive, can't start with `xml`, and so on. Also, you can't have more than one attribute with the same name on an element. So if we create an XML document like the following line of code, we will get the IE5 error shown in Figure 2-8.

```
<bad att="1" att="2"></bad>
```

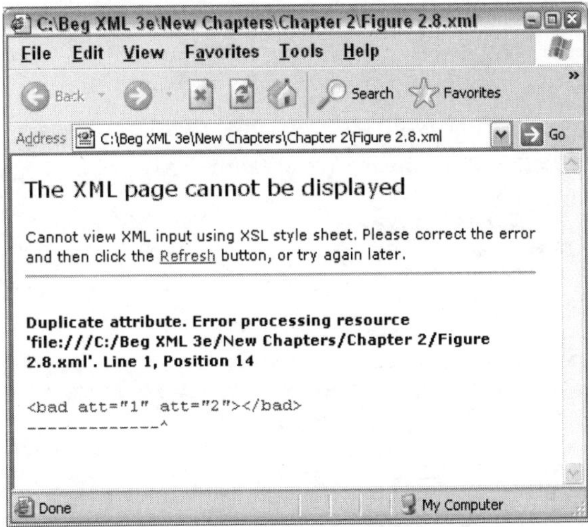

Figure 2-8

Finally, the order in which attributes are included on an element is not considered relevant. In other words, if an XML parser encounters an element like this:

```
<name first="John" middle="Fitzgerald Johansen" last="Doe"></name>
```

it doesn't necessarily have to give us the attributes in that order, but can do so in any order it wishes. Therefore, if there is information in an XML document that must come in a certain order, you should put that information into elements, rather than attributes.

Try It Out — Adding Attributes to Our Orders

In our previous *Try It Out*, we entered a lot of information about the various orders captured throughout the day. However, notice that the `<Orders>` element can contain multiple `<Order>` elements, and the `<Products>` element can contain multiple `<Product>` elements. Often programmers find it handy to include an attribute on these types of "container" elements to indicate how many items are in the list. We could get the same value by counting the child elements, but it's sometimes useful to have this as a separate piece of information, for a sanity check. Also, both `<Order>` and `<Product>` have child elements for ID—this is often the type of information that's captured in an attribute, instead of a child element.

1. Open your `order.xml` file created earlier, and resave it to your hard drive as `order2.xml`.
2. With your new-found attributes knowledge, add count attributes to <Orders> and <Products>, and change any `<ID>` elements to an ID attribute on the parent, instead. The result should look like this:

```
<Orders Count="2">
  <Order ID="0000000001">
    <Type>N</Type>
    <Date>Jan 1, 2004, 14:29</Date>
    <Customer>
      <SernaDirect>
        <SubscriptionType>B</SubscriptionType>
        <SubscriptionLength>12</SubscriptionLength>
      </SernaDirect>
      <Address>
        <Address1>123 Somewhere Ave.</Address1>
        <Address2></Address2>
        <City>Some Town</City>
        <State>TA</State>
        <Zip>000000000</Zip>
      </Address>
      <CreditCard>
        <Number>4111111111111111</Number>
        <CardHolderName>John Q Public</CardHolderName>
        <Expiry>11/09</Expiry>
      </CreditCard>
      <Phone>5555555555</Phone>
      <Name>John Public</Name>
      <Email>jpublic@someprovider.com</Email>
    </Customer>
    <Number>x582n9</Number>
    <Products Count="1">
      <Product>
        <Model>X9</Model>
        <Price>129.95</Price>
        <ID>x9000059</ID>
      </Product>
    </Products>
  </Order>
  <Order ID="0000000002">
    <Type>N</Type>
    <Date>Jan 1, 2004, 16:00</Date>
    <Customer>
      <SernaDirect>
        <SubscriptionType>D</SubscriptionType>
        <SubscriptionLength>12</SubscriptionLength>
      </SernaDirect>
      <Address>
        <Address1>89 Subscriber's Street</Address1>
        <Address2>Box 882</Address2>
```

```
        <City>Smallville</City>
        <State>XQ</State>
        <Zip>000000000</Zip>
      </Address>
      <CreditCard>
        <Number>4512451245124512</Number>
        <CardHolderName>Helen P Someperson</CardHolderName>
        <Expiry>01/08</Expiry>
      </CreditCard>
      <Phone>5554443333</Phone>
      <Name>Helen Someperson</Name>
      <Email>helens@isp.net</Email>
    </Customer>
    <Number>a98f78d</Number>
    <Products Count="1">
      <Product>
        <Model>Y9</Model>
        <Price>229.95</Price>
        <ID>y9000065</ID>
      </Product>
    </Products>
  </Order>
</Orders>
```

3. Save the file and view it in IE. It will look something like Figure 2-9.

How It Works

Using attributes, we added some extra information about the number of items contained in any "lists." Again, this is information that could easily be inferred from the content of the document, but if a list showed that it was supposed to have two elements and only one was in the document, we'd know that we had a problem.

Why Use Attributes?

There have been many debates in the XML community about whether attributes are really necessary, and if so, where they should be used. The following subsections address some of the main points in that debate.

Attributes Can Separate Different Types of Information

In the previous example, the number of `<Order>` elements under `<Orders>` isn't really part of the data we're sending, so it may make sense to make that information an attribute. This logically separates the data most applications will need from the data that most applications won't need.

In reality, there is no such thing as *pure* meta data—all information is data to *some* application. Think about HTML; you could break the information in HTML into two types of data: the data to be shown to a human, and the data to be used by the web browser to format the human-readable data. From one standpoint, the data used to format the data would be meta data, but to the browser or the person writing the HTML, the meta data *is* the data. Therefore, attributes can make sense when we're separating one type of information from another.

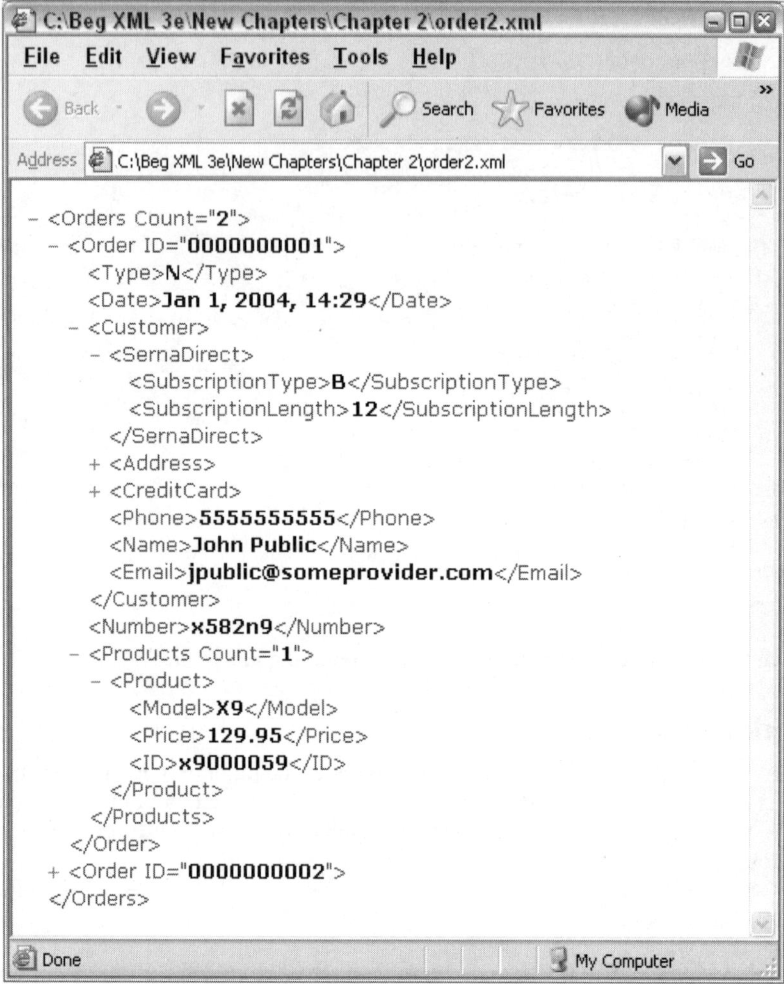

Figure 2-9

What Do Attributes Buy Me That Elements Don't?

Can't elements do anything attributes can do? In other words, on the face of it there's really no difference between:

```
<name nickname='Shiny John'></name>
```

and

```
<name>
  <nickname>Shiny John</nickname>
</name>
```

So why bother to pollute the language with two ways of doing the same thing?

The main reason that XML was invented was that SGML could do some great things, but it was too massively difficult to use without a full-fledged SGML expert on hand. So one concept behind XML is a kinder, gentler, simpler SGML. For this reason, many people don't like attributes, because they add a complexity to the language that they feel isn't needed.

On the other hand, some people find attributes easier to use—for example, they don't require nesting and you don't have to worry about crossed tags.

Why Use Elements If Attributes Take Up So Much Less Space?

Wouldn't it save bandwidth to use attributes instead? For example, if we were to rewrite our <name> document to use only attributes, it might look like the following, which takes up much less space than our earlier code using elements:

```
<name nickname='Shiny John' first='John'
middle='Fitzgerald Johansen' last='Doe'></name>
```

However, in systems where size is really an issue, it turns out that simple compression techniques would work much better than trying to optimize the XML. And because of the way compression works, you end up with almost the same file sizes regardless of whether attributes or elements are used.

Besides, when you try to optimize XML this way, you lose many of the benefits XML offers, such as readability and descriptive tag names.

Elements Can Be More Complex Than Attributes

When you use attributes, you are limited to simple text as a value. However, when you use elements, your content can be as simple or as complex as you need. That is, when your data is in an element, you have room for expansion, by adding other child elements to further break down the information.

Sometimes Elements Can Get in the Way

Imagine a case where you have a <note> element, which contains annotations about the text in your XML document. Sometimes the note will be informational, and sometimes a warning. You could include the type of note using an element, such as:

```
<note>
  <type>Information</type>
  This is a note.
</note>
```

or:

```
<note><Information>This is a note.</Information></note>
```

However, it would probably be much less intrusive to include the information in an attribute, such as

```
<note type="Information">This is a note.</note>
```

Attributes Are Un-Ordered

The order of attributes is considered irrelevant. Hence, sometimes you may need to use elements, rather than attributes, for information that must come in the document in a certain order.

Visual Preferences

Many people have different opinions as to whether attributes or child elements "look better." The answer comes down to a matter of personal preference and style.

In fact, much of the attributes versus elements debate comes from personal preference. Many, but not all, of the arguments boil down to "I like the one better than the other." But since XML has both elements and attributes, and neither one is going to go away, you're free to use both. Choose whichever works best for your application, whichever looks better to you, or whichever you're most comfortable with.

Comments

Comments provide a way to insert text into an XML document that isn't really part of the document, but rather is intended for people who are reading the XML markup itself.

Anyone who has used a programming language will be familiar with the idea of comments: You want to be able to annotate your code (or your XML), so that those coming after you will be able to figure out what you were doing. (And remember: the one who comes after you may be you! Code you wrote 6 months ago might be as foreign to you as code someone else wrote.)

Of course, comments may not be as relevant to XML as they are to programming languages; after all, this is just data, and it's self-describing to boot. But you never know when they're going to come in handy, and there are cases where comments can be very useful, even in data.

Comments start with the string `<!--` and end with the string `-->`, as shown here:

```
<name nickname='Shiny John'>
  <first>John</first>
  <!--John lost his middle name in a fire-->
  <middle></middle>
  <last>Doe</last>
</name>
```

There are a couple of points that we need to note about comments. First, you can't have a comment inside a tag, so the following is illegal:

```
<middle></middle <!--John lost his middle name in a fire--> >
```

Second, you can't use the string `--` inside a comment, so the following is also illegal:

```
<!--John lost his middle name -- in a fire-->
```

The XML specification states that an XML parser doesn't need to pass these comments on to the application, meaning that you should never count on being able to use the information inside a comment from your application. Comments are only there for the benefit of someone reading your XML markup.

> **HTML programmers have often used the trick of inserting scripting code in comments, to protect users with older browsers that didn't support the `<script>` tag. That kind of trick can't be done in XML, since comments won't necessarily be available to the application. Therefore, if you have data that you need to get at later from your applications, put it in an element or an attribute!**

Try It Out — Some Comments On Our Orders

The type of distribution system we're working with can be very complicated. Let's add some comments to our order XML to clarify how and why we've structured some of the data the way we have.

1. Open up your `order2.xml` file, make the following changes, and save the modified XML file as `order3.xml`:

```
<Orders Count="2">
  <Order ID="0000000001">
    <Type>N</Type>
    <!--Indicates the type of order: N(ew), C(ancel), or U(pdate)-->
    <Date>Jan 1, 2004, 14:29</Date>
    <!--we're only capturing order date, but often systems will capture
    a separate shipment date as well-->
    <Customer>
      <SernaDirect>
        <SubscriptionType>B</SubscriptionType>
        <!--Type of subscription: B(asic) or D(eluxe)-->
        <SubscriptionLength>12</SubscriptionLength>
        <!--length of subscription in months-->
      </SernaDirect>
      <Address>
      <!--systems often require separate Home, Billing, and Delivery
      addresses, but for the sake of simplicity we're only capturing one-->
        <Address1>123 Somewhere Ave.</Address1>
        <Address2></Address2>
        <City>Some Town</City>
        <State>TA</State>
        <Zip>000000000</Zip>
      </Address>
      <CreditCard>
        <Number>4111111111111111</Number>
        <CardHolderName>John Q Public</CardHolderName>
        <Expiry>11/09</Expiry>
      </CreditCard>
      <Phone>5555555555</Phone>
      <!--systems often require separate home and business #'s, but we're
      only capturing the one-->
      <Name>John Public</Name>
      <Email>jpublic@someprovider.com</Email>
    </Customer>
    <Number>x582n9</Number>
    <!--in this type of distributed system, there are often multiple
    ID's/numbers associated with an order, because of the multiple
    back-end systems involved-->
```

```
      <Products Count="1">
       <Product>
          <Model>X9</Model>
          <Price>129.95</Price>
          <ID>x9000059</ID>
      </Product>
      </Products>
    </Order>
    <Order ID="0000000002">
      <Type>N</Type>
      <Date>Jan 1, 2004, 16:00</Date>
      <Customer>
        <SernaDirect>
          <SubscriptionType>D</SubscriptionType>
          <SubscriptionLength>12</SubscriptionLength>
        </SernaDirect>
        <Address>
          <Address1>89 Subscriber's Street</Address1>
          <Address2>Box 882</Address2>
          <City>Smallville</City>
          <State>XQ</State>
          <Zip>000000000</Zip>
        </Address>
        <CreditCard>
          <Number>4512451245124512</Number>
          <CardHolderName>Helen P Someperson</CardHolderName>
          <Expiry>01/08</Expiry>
        </CreditCard>
        <Phone>5554443333</Phone>
        <Name>Helen Someperson</Name>
        <Email>helens@isp.net</Email>
      </Customer>
      <Number>a98f78d</Number>
      <Products Count="1">
        <Product>
          <Model>Y9</Model>
          <Price>229.95</Price>
          <ID>y9000065</ID>
        </Product>
      </Products>
    </Order>
  </Orders>
```

2. Figure 2-10 shows the new document in IE.

How It Works

With the new comments, anyone who reads the source for our XML document will be able to learn a bit more about how to create their own order file. This particular XML document might be used as a sample document that can be sent to new distributors as they begin working with Serna Inc.

In this example, the XML parser included with IE *does* pass comments up to the application, so the browser has displayed our comments. But remember that, for all intents and purposes, this information is only available to people reading the source file. The information in comments *may or may not* be passed

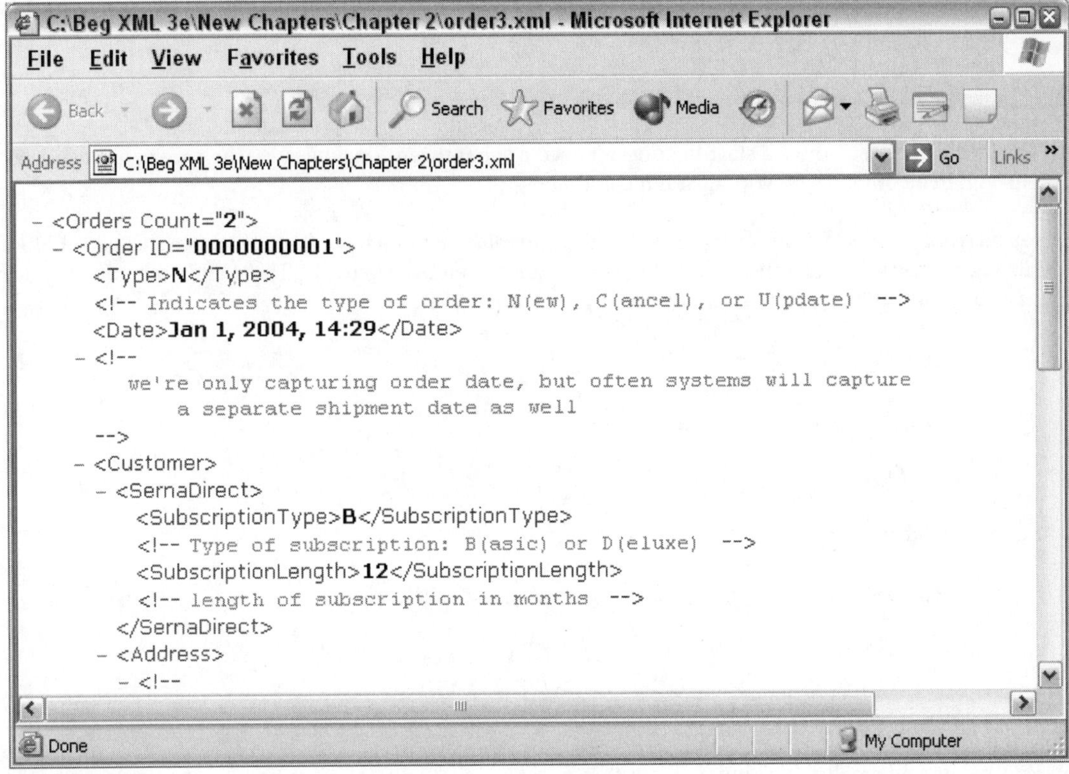
C:\Beg XML 3e\New Chapters\Chapter 2\order3.xml - Microsoft Internet Explorer
File Edit View Favorites Tools Help
Back Search Favorites Media
Address C:\Beg XML 3e\New Chapters\Chapter 2\order3.xml
Go Links
- <Orders Count="2">
- <Order ID="0000000001">
<Type>N</Type>
<!-- Indicates the type of order: N(ew), C(ancel), or U(pdate) -->
<Date>Jan 1, 2004, 14:29</Date>
- <!--
we're only capturing order date, but often systems will capture
a separate shipment date as well
-->
- <Customer>
- <SernaDirect>
<SubscriptionType>B</SubscriptionType>
<!-- Type of subscription: B(asic) or D(eluxe) -->
<SubscriptionLength>12</SubscriptionLength>
<!-- length of subscription in months -->
</SernaDirect>
- <Address>
- <!--
Done
My Computer

Figure 2-10

up to our application, depending on which parser we're using. We can't count on it, unless we specifically choose a parser that does pass them through.

If a developer uses this XML document as a sample and forgets to delete the comments before sending it to Serna Inc., it won't matter. They'll be in the document, but they won't actually be part of the document's data, and so they won't do any harm.

Empty Elements

Sometimes an element has no PCDATA. Recall our earlier example, where the `<middle>` element contained no name:

```
<name nickname='Shiny John'>
  <first>John</first>
  <!--John lost his middle name in a fire-->
  <middle></middle>
  <last>Doe</last>
</name>
```

In this case, you also have the option of writing this element using the special *empty element* syntax (this syntax is also called a *self-closing tag*):

```
<middle/>
```

This is the one case where a start-tag doesn't need a separate end-tag, because they are combined into this one tag. In all other cases, you must have both tags.

Recall from our discussion of elements that the only place we can have a space within the tag is before the closing >. This rule is slightly different when it comes to empty elements. The / and > characters always have to be together, so you can create an empty element like this:

```
<middle />
```

or this:

```
<middle/>
```

but not like these:

```
<middle/ >
```

or

```
<middle / >
```

Empty elements really don't buy you anything—except that they take less typing—so you can use them, or not, at your discretion. Keep in mind, however, that as far as XML is concerned `<middle></middle>` is *exactly* the same as `<middle/>`; for this reason, XML parsers will sometimes change your XML from one form to the other. You should never count on your empty elements being in one form or the other, but since they're syntactically exactly the same, it doesn't matter. (This is the reason that Internet Explorer felt free to change our earlier `<Address2></Address2>` syntax to just `<Address2/>`.)

> *Interestingly, the XML community doesn't seem to mind the empty element syntax, even though it doesn't add anything to the language. This is especially interesting considering the passionate debates that have taken place on whether attributes are really necessary.*

One place where empty elements are very often used is for elements that have no (or optional) PCDATA, but instead have all of their data contained in attributes. So if we rewrote our `<name>` example without child elements, instead of a start-tag and end-tag we would probably use an empty element, like this:

```
<name first="John" middle="Fitzgerald Johansen" last="Doe"/>
```

Or, for readability, XML authors will often write the XML like this:

```
<name first="John"
      middle="Fitzgerald Johansen"
      last="Doe"
      />
```

Another common example is the case where just the element name is enough; for example, the HTML `<BR>` tag would be converted to an XML empty element, such as the XHTML `<br/>` tag. (XHTML is the latest "XML-compliant" version of HTML, and is discussed in Chapter 16.)

XML Declaration

It is often very handy to be able to identify a document as being of a certain type. On computers running Windows, giving the file an extension of `.xml` identifies the file as an XML file to Windows, but on other operating systems this will not work. Also, we might want the flexibility of creating XML files with other extensions.

XML provides the *XML declaration* to label documents as being XML, along with giving the parsers afew other pieces of information. You don't need to have an XML declaration—a parser can usually tell a document is XML without it—but it's considered good practice to include it. A typical XML declaration looks like this:

```
<?xml version='1.0' encoding='UTF-16' standalone='yes'?>
<name nickname='Shiny John'>
  <first>John</first>
  <!--John lost his middle name in a fire-->
  <middle/>
  <last>Doe</last>
</name>
```

Some things to note about the XML declaration:

- The XML declaration starts with the characters `<?xml`, and ends with the characters `?>`.
- If you include a declaration, you must include the `version`, but the `encoding` and `standalone` attributes are optional.
- The `version`, `encoding`, and `standalone` attributes must be in that order.
- Currently, the version should be `1.0`. If you use a number other than `1.0`, XML parsers that were written for the version 1.0 specification can reject the document. (If a new version of XML is ever created, the version number in the XML declaration will be used to signal which version of the specification your document claims to support.)
- The XML declaration must be right at the beginning of the file. That is, the first character in the file should be that <; no line breaks or spaces. Some parsers are more forgiving about this than others.

So an XML declaration can be as full as the previous one, or as simple as:

```
<?xml version='1.0'?>
```

The next two sections describe more fully the `encoding` and `standalone` attributes of the XML declaration.

Encoding

It should come as no surprise that text is stored in computers using numbers, since 1s and 0s are all that computers really understand. A *character code* is a one-to-one mapping between a set of characters and the corresponding numbers to represent those characters. A character encoding is the method used to represent the numbers in a character code digitally (in other words how many bytes should be used for each number, and so on).

One character code that you might have come across is the *American Standard Code for Information Interchange* (ASCII). In ASCII, for example, the lowercase character "a" is represented by the number 97, and the uppercase character "A" is represented by the number 65.

There are 7-bit and 8-bit ASCII encoding schemes. 7-bit ASCII uses 7 bits for each character, which limits it to 128 different values, while 8-bit ASCII uses one byte (8 bits) for each character, which limits it to 256 different values. 7-bit ASCII is a much more universal standard for text, while there are a number of 8-bit ASCII character codes, which were created to add additional characters not covered by ASCII, such as ISO-8859-1. Each 8-bit ASCII encoding scheme might have slightly different sets of characters represented, and those characters might map to different numbers. However, the first 128 characters are always the same as the 7-bit ASCII character code.

ASCII can easily handle all of the characters needed for English, which is why it was the predominant character encoding used on personal computers in the English-speaking world for many years. But there are way more than 256 characters in all of the world's languages, so obviously ASCII (or any other 8-bit encoding limited to 256 characters) can only handle a small subset of these. This is why Unicode was invented.

Unicode

Unicode is a character code designed from the ground up with internationalization in mind, aiming to have enough possible characters to cover all of the characters in any human language. There are two major character encodings for Unicode: *UTF-16* and *UTF-8*. UTF-16 takes the easy way, and simply uses 2 bytes for every character (2 bytes = 16 bits = 65,356 possible values).

UTF-8 is more clever: it uses 1 byte for the characters covered by 7-bit ASCII, and then uses some tricks so that any other characters may be represented by two or more bytes. This means that 7-bit ASCII text can actually be considered a subset of UTF-8, and processed as such. For text written in English, where most or all of the characters would fit into the ASCII 7-bit character encoding, UTF-8 will result in smaller file sizes (because each character requires only 1 byte), but for text in other languages, UTF-16 can be smaller (since UTF-8 can require three or more bytes for some characters, while UTF-16 always requires two).

Because of the work done with Unicode to make it international, the XML specification states that all XML processors must use Unicode internally. Unfortunately, very few of the documents in the world are encoded in Unicode. Most are encoded in ISO-8859-1, or windows-1252, or EBCDIC (used very commonly in mainframe computers), or one of a large number of other character codes. (Many of these character codes, such as ISO-8859-1 and windows-1252, are actually 8-bit ASCII character codes. They are not, however, subsets of UTF-8 in the same way that "pure" 7-bit ASCII is.)

Specifying a Character Encoding for XML

This is where the `encoding` attribute in our XML declaration comes in. It allows us to specify to the XML parser what character encoding our text is in. The XML parser can then read the document in the proper encoding and translate it into Unicode internally. If no encoding is specified, UTF-8 or UTF-16 is assumed (parsers must support at least UTF-8 and UTF-16). If no encoding is specified, and the document is not UTF-8 or UTF-16, the parser raises an error.

That being said, sometimes an XML processor is allowed to ignore the encoding specified in the XML declaration. If the document is being sent via a network protocol such as HTTP, there may be protocol-specific headers that specify a different encoding than the one specified in the document. In such a case, the HTTP header would take precedence over the encoding specified in the XML declaration. However, if there are no external sources for the encoding, and the encoding specified is different from the actual encoding of the document, it results in an error.

If you're creating XML documents in Notepad on a machine running an earlier version of the Microsoft Windows operating system, in the English speaking world, the character encoding you are probably using by default is *windows-1252*. So the XML declarations in your documents should look like this:

```
<?xml version="1.0" encoding="windows-1252"?>
```

However, not all XML parsers understand the windows-1252 character set, meaning that a document that claims to use it may cause the parser to raise an error, indicating that it can't be processed. If that's the case, try substituting ISO-8859-1, which happens to be very similar to windows-1252. Or, if your document doesn't contain any special characters (like accented characters, for example), you could use ASCII instead, or leave the `encoding` attribute out, and let the XML parser treat the document as UTF-8.

If you're running Windows NT or later, Notepad also gives you the option of saving your text files in Unicode, in which case you can leave out the `encoding` attribute in your XML declarations (see Figure 2-11).

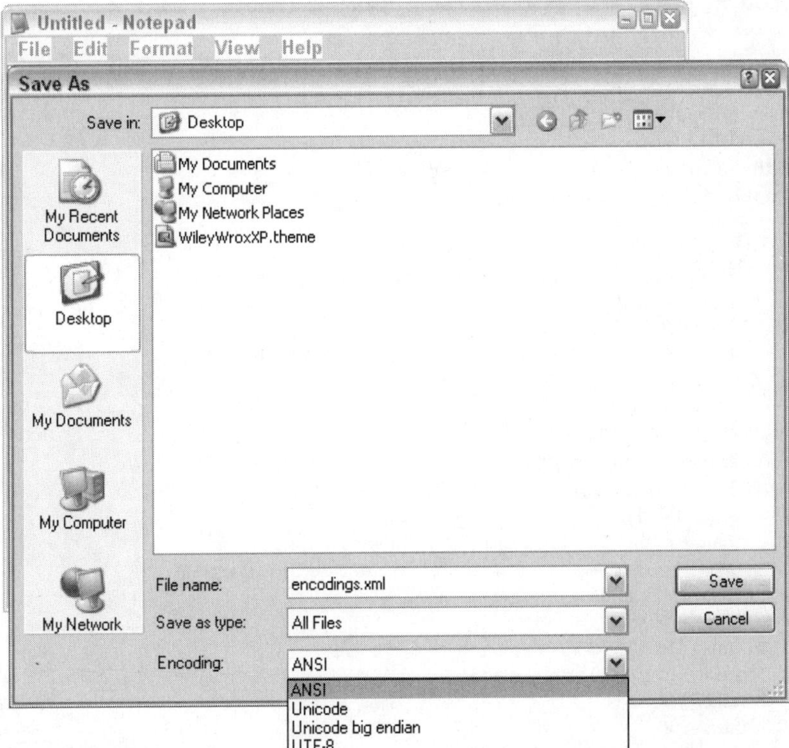

Figure 2-11

Standalone

If the `standalone` attribute is included in the XML declaration, it must be set to either `yes` or `no`.

- `yes` specifies that this document exists entirely on its own, without depending on any other files.
- `no` indicates that the document may depend on an external DTD (DTDs are covered in Chapter 4).

This little attribute actually has its own name: the *Standalone Document Declaration*, or SDD. The XML specification doesn't actually require a parser to do anything with the SDD. It is considered more of a hint to the parser than anything else.

It's time to take a look at how the XML declaration works in practice.

Try It Out — Declaring Our Orders to the World

Let's declare our XML document, so that any parsers will be able to tell right away what it is. And, while we're at it, let's take care of any elements that don't have any content, and change them to use the empty element syntax, just to get familiar with it.

1. Open up the file `order2.xml` (we'll ignore the version with all of our comments, to reduce clutter), and make the following changes. If you have an earlier version of Windows, and can't save the file in Unicode from Notepad (which is UTF-16), you may have to change the `encoding` to a more appropriate value (usually `windows-1252`).

```
<?xml version="1.0" encoding="UTF-16" standalone="yes"?>
<Orders Count="2">
  <Order ID="0000000001">
    <Type>N</Type>
    <Date>Jan 1, 2004, 14:29</Date>
    <Customer>
      <SernaDirect>
        <SubscriptionType>B</SubscriptionType>
        <SubscriptionLength>12</SubscriptionLength>
      </SernaDirect>
      <Address>
        <Address1>123 Somewhere Ave.</Address1>
        <Address2/>
        <City>Some Town</City>
        <State>TA</State>
        <Zip>000000000</Zip>
      </Address>
      <CreditCard>
        <Number>4111111111111111</Number>
        <CardHolderName>John Q Public</CardHolderName>
        <Expiry>11/09</Expiry>
      </CreditCard>
      <Phone>5555555555</Phone>
      <Name>John Public</Name>
      <Email>jpublic@someprovider.com</Email>
    </Customer>
    <Number>x582n9</Number>
    <Products Count="1">
```

```
        <Product>
          <Model>X9</Model>
          <Price>129.95</Price>
          <ID>x9000059</ID>
        </Product>
      </Products>
    </Order>
    <Order ID="0000000002">
      <Type>N</Type>
      <Date>Jan 1, 2004, 16:00</Date>
      <Customer>
        <SernaDirect>
          <SubscriptionType>D</SubscriptionType>
          <SubscriptionLength>12</SubscriptionLength>
        </SernaDirect>
        <Address>
          <Address1>89 Subscriber's Street</Address1>
          <Address2>Box 882</Address2>
          <City>Smallville</City>
          <State>XQ</State>
          <Zip>000000000</Zip>
        </Address>
        <CreditCard>
          <Number>4512451245124512</Number>
          <CardHolderName>Helen P Someperson</CardHolderName>
          <Expiry>01/08</Expiry>
        </CreditCard>
        <Phone>5554443333</Phone>
        <Name>Helen Someperson</Name>
        <Email>helens@isp.net</Email>
      </Customer>
      <Number>a98f78d</Number>
      <Products Count="1">
        <Product>
          <Model>Y9</Model>
          <Price>229.95</Price>
          <ID>y9000065</ID>
        </Product>
      </Products>
    </Order>
  </Orders>
```

2. Save the file as `order4.xml`, and view it in IE, as shown in Figure 2-12.

How It Works

With our new XML declaration, any XML parser can tell right away that it is indeed dealing with an XML document, and that the document is claiming to conform to version 1.0 of the XML specification.

Furthermore, the document indicates that it is encoded using the UTF-16 character encoding. In addition, because the Standalone Document Declaration declares that this is a standalone document, the parser knows that this one file is all that it needs to fully process the information.

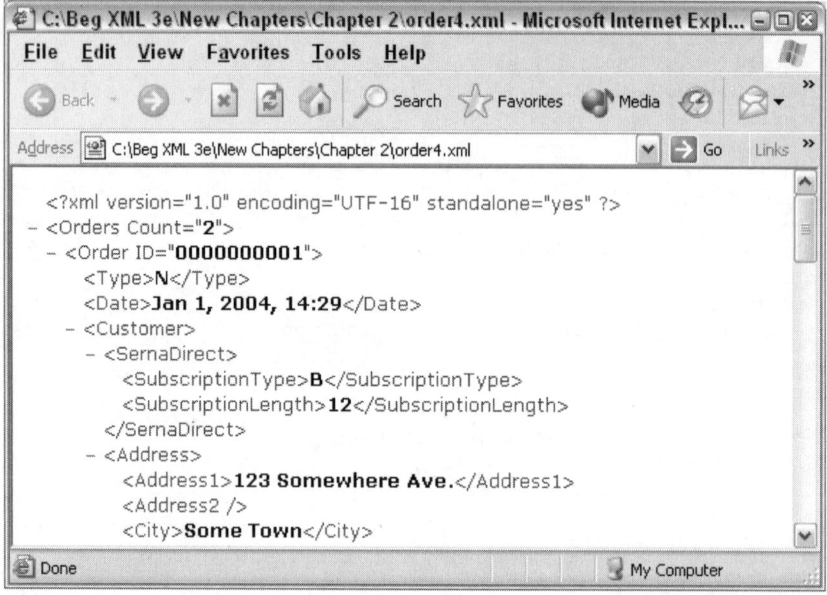

Figure 2-12

And finally, because the address for the first order has no information in the <Address2> element, the syntax has been changed to the empty element syntax. Remember though, that to the parser <Address2/> is exactly the same as <Address2></Address2>, which is why this part of our document looks the same in the browser as it did in our earlier screenshots.

Processing Instructions

Although it isn't all that common, sometimes you need to embed application-specific instructions into your information to affect how it will be processed. XML provides a mechanism to allow this, called *processing instructions* or *PIs*. These allow you to enter instructions into your XML which are not part of the data of the document, but which are passed up to the application, as shown in the following code:

```
<?xml version='1.0'?>
<name nickname='Shiny John'>
  <first>John</first>
  <!--John lost his middle name in a fire-->
  <middle/>
  <?nameprocessor SELECT * FROM blah?>
  <last>Doe</last>
</name>
```

There aren't really a lot of rules on PIs. They're basically just a <? followed by the name of the application that is supposed to receive the PI (the *PITarget*). The rest, up until the ending ?> is whatever you want the instruction to be. The PITarget is bound by the same naming rules as elements and attributes. So, in this example, the PITarget is `nameprocessor`, and the actual text of the PI (the instructions) is `SELECT * FROM blah`.

PIs are pretty rare, and are often frowned upon in the XML community, especially when used frivolously. But if you have a valid reason to use them, go for it. For example, PIs can be an excellent place for putting the kind of information (such as scripting code), which in HTML is put in comments. While you can't assume that comments will be passed on to the application, PIs always are.

Is the XML Declaration a Processing Instruction?

At first glance, you might think that the XML declaration is a PI that starts with `xml`. It uses the same `<? ?>` notation, and provides instructions to the parser (but not the application). So is it a PI?

Actually, no: The XML declaration isn't a PI, but in most cases it really doesn't make any difference whether it is or not. The only places where you'll get into trouble are the following:

- Trying to get the text of the XML declaration from an XML parser. Some parsers erroneously treat the XML declaration as a PI, and will pass it on as if it were, but most will not. The truth is, in most cases your application will never need the information in the XML declaration; that information is only for the parser. (Even the character encoding shouldn't matter to your application, because by the time the parser passes on the text, it will be Unicode, regardless of what encoding was originally used in the document.) One notable exception might be an application that wants to display an XML document to a user, in the way that we're using IE5 to display the documents in this book.
- Including an XML declaration somewhere other than at the beginning of an XML document. Although you can put a PI anywhere you want, an XML declaration must come at the beginning of a file.

Try It Out — An Order To Be Processed

Just to see what it looks like, let's add a processing instruction to our order XML.

1. Make the following changes to `order4.xml`, and save the new file as `order5.xml`:

```
<?xml version="1.0"?>
<Orders Count="2">
  <Order ID="0000000001">
    <?SernaProcessor ManualIntervention reason:Insufficient Funds?>
    <Type>N</Type>
    <Date>Jan 1, 2004, 14:29</Date>
    <Customer>
      <SernaDirect>
        <SubscriptionType>B</SubscriptionType>
        <SubscriptionLength>12</SubscriptionLength>
      </SernaDirect>
      <Address>
        <Address1>123 Somewhere Ave.</Address1>
        <Address2/>
        <City>Some Town</City>
        <State>TA</State>
        <Zip>000000000</Zip>
```

```
        </Address>
        <CreditCard>
          <Number>4111111111111111</Number>
          <CardHolderName>John Q Public</CardHolderName>
          <Expiry>11/09</Expiry>
        </CreditCard>
        <Phone>5555555555</Phone>
        <Name>John Public</Name>
        <Email>jpublic@someprovider.com</Email>
      </Customer>
      <Number>x582n9</Number>
      <Products Count="1">
        <Product>
          <Model>X9</Model>
          <Price>129.95</Price>
          <ID>x9000059</ID>
        </Product>
      </Products>
    </Order>
    <Order ID="0000000002">
      <Type>N</Type>
      <Date>Jan 1, 2004, 16:00</Date>
      <Customer>
        <SernaDirect>
          <SubscriptionType>D</SubscriptionType>
          <SubscriptionLength>12</SubscriptionLength>
        </SernaDirect>
        <Address>
          <Address1>89 Subscriber's Street</Address1>
          <Address2>Box 882</Address2>
          <City>Smallville</City>
          <State>XQ</State>
          <Zip>000000000</Zip>
        </Address>
        <CreditCard>
          <Number>4512451245124512</Number>
          <CardHolderName>Helen P Someperson</CardHolderName>
          <Expiry>01/08</Expiry>
        </CreditCard>
        <Phone>5554443333</Phone>
        <Name>Helen Someperson</Name>
        <Email>helens@isp.net</Email>
      </Customer>
      <Number>a98f78d</Number>
      <Products Count="1">
        <Product>
          <Model>Y9</Model>
          <Price>229.95</Price>
          <ID>y9000065</ID>
        </Product>
      </Products>
    </Order>
  </Orders>
```

2. In IE, it looks like Figure 2-13.

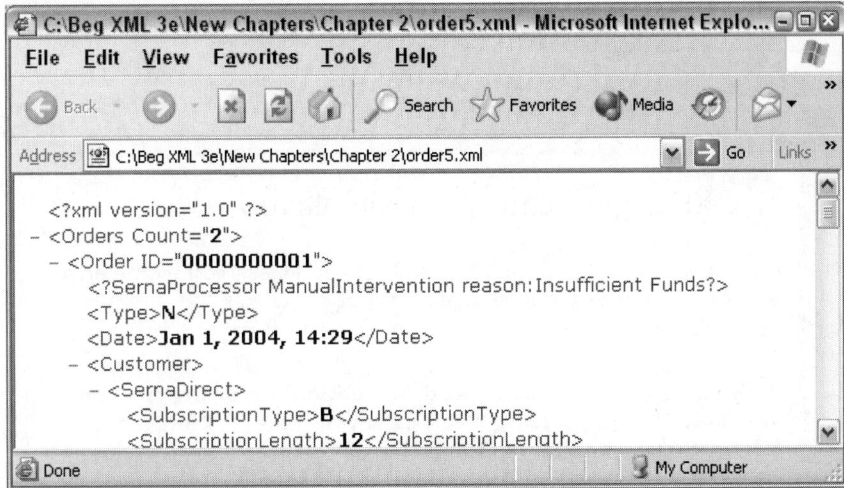

Figure 2-13

How It Works

For our example, we are targeting a *fictional* application called `SernaProcessor`, and giving it the instruction `ManualIntervention reason:Insufficient Funds`. The instruction has no meaning in the context of the XML itself, only to our `SernaProcessor` application, so it's up to the `SernaProcessor` to do something meaningful with it.

Also, since our document is UTF-16 (which the parser can infer), and since the SDD isn't doing too much for us, we've shortened the XML Declaration to the shorter syntax.

Illegal PCDATA Characters

There are some reserved characters that you can't include in your PCDATA because they are used in XML syntax: the `<` and `&` characters.

```
<!--This is not well-formed XML!-->
<comparison>6 is < 7 & 7 > 6</comparison>
```

Viewing the above XML in Internet Explorer gives the error shown in Figure 2-14.

Even if it had gotten past this, the same error would have occurred at the `&` character.

This error may seem confusing, but it could be worse. Consider the following XML:

```
<blah>Some <text in an element</blah>
```

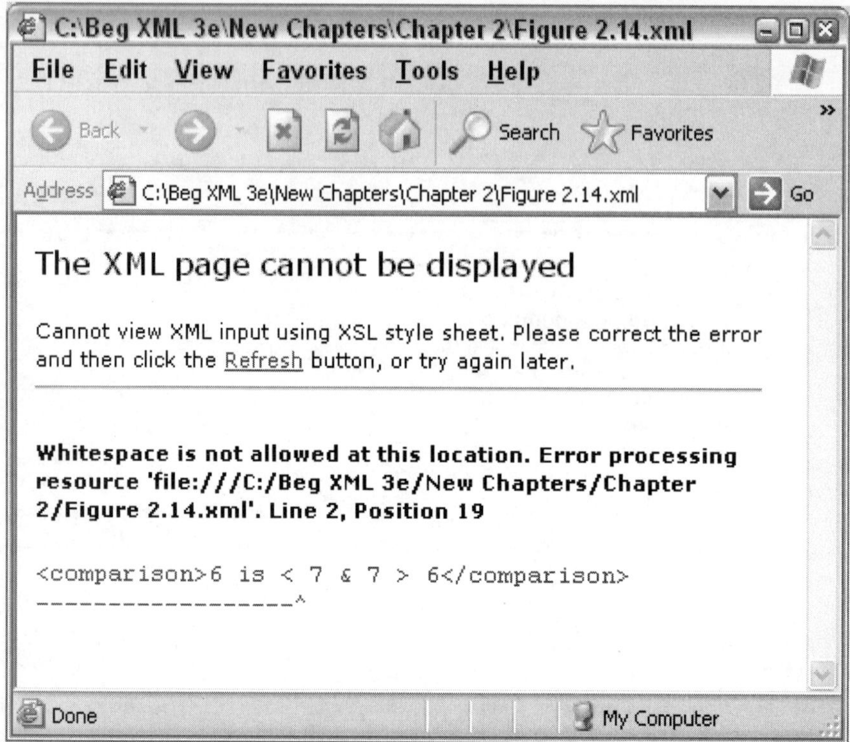

Figure 2-14

In this case an error would still be raised, but the error message would read "Missing equals sign between attribute and attribute value."

The reason for this strange error message is that the XML parser comes across the < character and expects a tag name. In the first document it found a space, which is not allowed, and in the second example it thought that "text" was the tag name, but then assumed that "in" was an attribute and expected to find an equals sign for the attribute's value.

All of this means that we can't put raw < or & characters into PCDATA. (Why & characters can't be included will become evident when the syntax for escaping characters is covered next.) There are two ways you can get around this: *escaping characters*, or enclosing text in a *CDATA section*.

Escaping Characters

To escape these two characters, you simply replace any < character with `<` and any & character with `&`. (In addition, you can also escape the > character with `>`. It isn't necessary, but it does make things more consistent, since you need to escape all of the < characters.) The previous XML example could be made well formed by doing the following:

```
<comparison>6 is &lt; 7 &amp; 7 &gt; 6 </comparison>
```

This displays properly in the browser as shown in Figure 2-15.

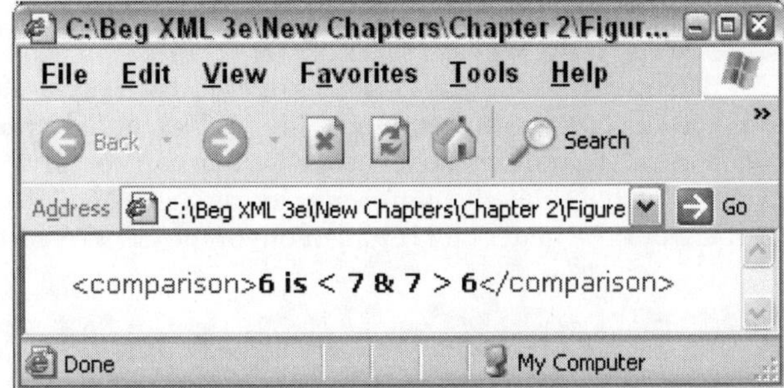

Figure 2-15

Notice that IE automatically un-escapes the characters for you when it displays the document; in other words it replaces the `<`, `&` and `>` strings with <, & and > characters. This is because the content of the `<comparison>` element really *is* `6 is < 7 & 7 > 6`—we had to escape the < and & characters so as not to confuse the parser, but once the parser has read in the markup, it knows the real content of the PCDATA.

`<` and `&` are known as *entity references*. The following entities are defined in XML:

- `&`—the & character
- `<`—the < character
- `>`—the > character
- `'`—the ' character
- `"`—the " character

Other characters can also be escaped by using *character references*. These are strings such as `&#nnn;`, where *nnn* would be replaced by the Unicode number of the character you want to insert. (Or `&#x`*nnn*`;` with an `x` preceding the number, where *nnn* is a hexadecimal representation of the Unicode character you want to insert. All of the characters in the Unicode specification are specified using hexadecimal, so allowing the hexadecimal numbers in XML means that XML authors don't have to convert back and forth between hexadecimal and decimal.)

Escaping characters in this way can be quite handy if you are authoring documents in XML that use characters your XML editor doesn't understand, or can't output, because the characters escaped are *always* Unicode characters, regardless of the encoding being used for the document. As an example, you could include the copyright symbol (©) in an XML document by inserting `©` or `©`.

CDATA Sections

If you have a lot of < and & characters that need escaping, you may find that your document quickly becomes very ugly and unreadable with all of those entity references. Luckily, there are also *CDATA sections*. CDATA is another inherited term from SGML; it stands for Character DATA. Using CDATA sections, we can tell the XML parser not to parse the text, but to let it all go by until it gets to the end of the section. CDATA sections look like this:

```
<comparison><![CDATA[6 is < 7 & 7 > 6]]></comparison>
```

Everything starting after the `<![CDATA[` and ending at the `]]>` is ignored by the parser, and passed through to the application as is. The only character sequence that can't occur within a CDATA section is "`]]>`", since the XML parser would think that you were closing the CDATA section. If you needed to include this sequence, you would be better off keeping it out of the CDATA section, like this:

```
<![CDATA[This text contains the sequence ']]>]]><![CDATA[' in it.]]>
```

Luckily, this doesn't come up very often!

In these trivial cases, CDATA sections may look more confusing than the escaping did, but in other cases it can turn out to be more readable. For example, consider the following example, which uses a CDATA section to keep an XML parser from parsing a section of JavaScript:

```
<script language='JavaScript'><![CDATA[
function myFunc()
{
    if(0 < 1 && 1 < 2)
        alert("Hello");
}
]]></script>
```

Figure 2-16 shows how this displays in IE5 or later browsers.

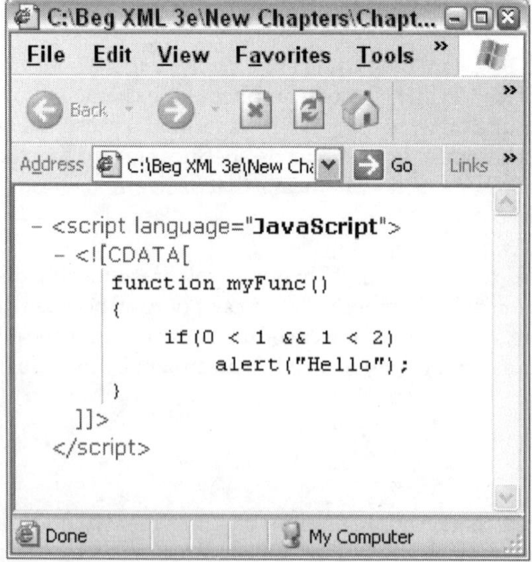

Figure 2-16

Notice the vertical line at the left-hand side of the CDATA section. This indicates that although the CDATA section is indented for readability, the actual data itself starts at that vertical line. We can visually see exactly what whitespace is included in the CDATA section.

If you're familiar with JavaScript, you'll probably find the `if` statement much easier to read than:

```
if(0 &lt; 1 &amp;&amp; 1 &lt; 2)
```

Try It Out Talking about HTML in XML

Suppose we want to create XML documentation to describe some of the various HTML tags in existence. We might develop a simple document type such as the following:

```
<HTML-Doc>
  <tag>
    <tag-name></tag-name>
    <description></description>
    <example></example>
  </tag>
</HTML-Doc>
```

In this case, we know that our `<example>` element will need to include HTML syntax, meaning that there are going to be a lot of < characters included. This makes `<example>` the perfect place to use a CDATA section, so that we don't have to search through all of our HTML code looking for illegal characters. This way we can include text like `<HTML>`, and have the parser simply treat that as six characters, rather than as a tag. To demonstrate, let's document a couple of HTML tags.

1. Create a new file (or just open up Notepad) and type this code:

```
<HTML-Doc>
  <tag>
    <tag-name>P</tag-name>
    <description>Paragraph</description>
    <example><![CDATA[
<P>Paragraphs can contain <EM>other</EM> tags.</P>
]]></example>
  </tag>
  <tag>
    <tag-name>HTML</tag-name>
    <description>HTML root element</description>
    <example><![CDATA[
<HTML>
<HEAD><TITLE>Sample HTML</TITLE></HEAD>
<BODY>
<P>Stuff goes here</P
</BODY>/HTML>
]]></example>
  </tag>
  <!--more tags to follow...-->
</HTML-Doc>
```

2. Save this document as `html-doc.xml` and view it in IE5 or later (see Figure 2-17).

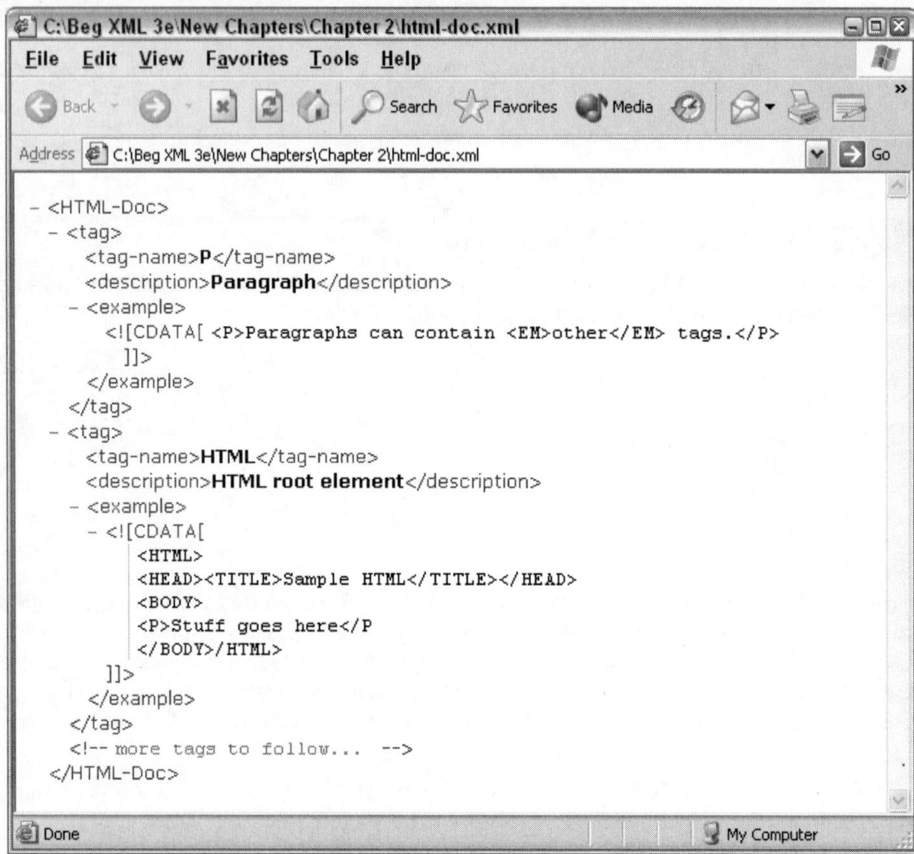

Figure 2-17

How It Works

Because of our CDATA sections, we can put whatever we want into the `<example>` elements, and don't have to worry about the text being mixed up with the actual XML markup of the document. This means that even though there are typos in the second `<example>` element (the `</P` is missing the > and `/HTML>` is missing a <), our XML is not affected.

Errors in XML

As well as specifying how a parser should get the information out of an XML document, the XML Recommendation also specifies how a parser should deal with errors in XML. There are two types of error defined: *errors* and *fatal errors*.

- An error is simply a violation of the rules in the specification, where the results are undefined; the XML processor is allowed to recover from the error and continue processing.

- Fatal errors are more serious: According to the specification, a parser is *not allowed to continue as normal* when it encounters a fatal error. (It may, however, keep processing the XML document to search for further errors.) This is called *draconian error handling*. Any error which causes an XML document to cease being well-formed is a fatal error.

The reason for this drastic handling of nonwell-formed XML is simple: It would be hard for parser writers to try and handle "well-formedness" errors, and it is extremely simple to make XML well formed. (Web browsers don't force documents to be as strict as XML does, but this is one of the reasons why web browsers are so incompatible; they must deal with *all* the errors they may encounter, and try to figure out what the person who wrote the document was really trying to code.)

But draconian error handling doesn't just benefit the parser writers; it also benefits us when we're creating XML documents. If I write an XML document that doesn't properly follow XML's syntax, I can find out my mistake right away and fix it. On the other hand, if the XML parser tried to recover from these errors, it might misinterpret what I was trying to do, but I wouldn't know about it because no error would be raised. In this case, bugs in my software would be much harder to track down, instead of being caught right at the beginning when I was creating my data. Even worse, if I sent my XML document to someone else, their parser might interpret the mistake differently.

Summary

This chapter has provided you with the basic syntax for writing well-formed XML documents.

We've seen:

- Elements and empty elements
- How to deal with whitespace in XML
- Attributes
- How to include comments
- XML declarations and encodings
- Processing instructions
- Entity references, character references, and CDATA sections

We've also learned why the strict rules of XML grammar actually benefit us in the long run, since they force us to catch our errors sooner rather than later, and how some of the rules for authoring HTML are different from the rules for authoring well-formed XML.

Unfortunately—or perhaps fortunately—you probably won't spend much of your time just authoring XML documents. You have to do something useful with the data! In the next chapters you'll learn about a very important part of XML: namespaces.

Exercise Questions

Suggested solutions to these questions can be found in Appendix A.

Question 1

For the addresses in our Order XML, we used a common format of "Address Line 1, Address Line 2, City, State, and Zip Code." Other applications need to be stricter with their addresses, and have separate elements for street number, street name, and so on. Rewrite the last version of the Order XML using the following information, instead of the Address Line 1/Address Line 2 format:

- Street Number
- Street Name
- Apt. Number
- City
- State
- Zip Code
- Additional Information

Question 2

Sometimes the syntax used by XML can be a little troublesome to figure out. The following XML document contains a few syntactical errors, preventing it from being well-formed. Correct them so that the document can be read by IE.

Hint: When I'm trying to correct a file like this, I often open it up in the browser and fix errors as the browser reports them to me. Be warned—some of the errors are a bit more difficult to figure out than others.

```
<?xml version="1"?>
<document>
  <--There are a couple of problems with this document.-->
  <Information>This document
  contains some < bold>information</bold>. Once
  it's corrected, it can be read by a parser.</Information>
</Document>
```

XML Namespaces

We have seen why XML provides some benefits over binary formats and can now create well-formed XML documents. But the time is going to come when your applications get more complex, and you need to combine elements from various document types into one XML document.

Unfortunately, you very often have cases where two document types have elements with the same name, but with different meanings and semantics. This chapter introduces *XML namespaces*, the means by which you can differentiate elements and attributes of different XML document types from each other when combining them together into other documents, or even when processing multiple documents simultaneously.

In this chapter, you will learn:

- Why you need namespaces
- What namespaces are, conceptually, and how they solve the problem of naming clashes
- The syntax for using namespaces in XML documents
- What is a URI, URL, and URN

Why Do We Need Namespaces?

Because of the nature of XML, it is possible for any company or individual to create XML document types that describe the world in their own terms. If my company feels that an `<order>` should contain a certain set of information, and another company feels that it should contain a different set of information, we can both go ahead and create different document types to describe that information. We can even both use the name `<order>` for entirely different uses, if we wish.

However, if everyone is creating personalized XML vocabularies, we'll soon run into a problem: only so many words are available in human languages, and a lot of them are going to get snapped up by people defining document types. How can I define a `<title>` element to be used to denote the title in a person's name when XHTML already has a `<title>` element used to describe the title of an HTML document? How can I then further distinguish those two `<title>` elements from the title of a book?

If all of these documents were to be kept separate, this still would not be a problem. If we saw a <title> element in an XHTML document, we'd know what kind of title we were talking about, and if we saw one in our own proprietary XML document type, we'd know what that meant too. Unfortunately, life isn't always that simple, and eventually we'll need to combine various XML elements from different document types into one XML document. For example, we might create an XML document type containing information about a person, including that person's title, but also containing the person's résumé, in XHTML form. Such a document may look similar to this:

```
<?xml version="1.0"?>
<person>
  <name>
    <title>Sir</title>
    <first>John</first>
    <middle>Fitzgerald Johansen</middle>
    <last>Doe</last>
  </name>
  <position>Vice President of Marketing</position>
  <résumé>
    <html>
    <head><title>Resume of John Doe</title></head>
    <body>
      <h1>John Doe</h1>
      <p>John's a great guy, you know?</p>
    </body>
    </html>
  </résumé>
</person>
```

If you want to type this XML into Notepad, and view the results in IE, remember to save the document using an appropriate encoding, such as Unicode or UTF-8. The "é" characters in the <résumé> element are not part of the basic ASCII character set, so they'll cause problems for the XML parser when it tries to read the document if it doesn't have an appropriate character set to work with. However, if the document is saved as one of the Unicode encodings, the parser will have no problems with it.

To an XML parser, there isn't any difference between the two <title> elements in this document. If we do a simple search of the document to find John Doe's title by looking for <title> elements, we might accidentally get Resume of John Doe instead of "Sir". Even in our application, we can't know which elements are XHTML elements and which aren't without knowing in advance the structure of the document. That is, we'd have to know that there is a <résumé> element, which is a direct child of <person>, and that all of the descendents of <résumé> are a separate type of element from the others in our document. If our structure ever changed, all of our assumptions would be lost. In the preceding document it looks like anything inside the <résumé> element is XHTML, but in other documents it might not be so obvious, and to an XML parser it isn't obvious at all.

Using Prefixes

The best way to solve this problem is for every element in a document to have a completely distinct name. For example, we might come up with a naming convention whereby every element for my proprietary XML document type gets my own prefix, and every XHTML element gets another prefix.

We could rewrite our XML document from above to something like this:

```
<?xml version="1.0"?>
<pers:person>
  <pers:name>
    <pers:title>Sir</pers:title>
    <pers:first>John</pers:first>
    <pers:middle>Fitzgerald Johansen</pers:middle>
    <pers:last>Doe</pers:last>
  </pers:name>
  <pers:position>Vice President of Marketing</pers:position>
  <pers:résumé>
    <xhtml:html>
    <xhtml:head><xhtml:title>Resume of John Doe</xhtml:title></xhtml:head>
    <xhtml:body>
    <xhtml:h1>John Doe</xhtml:h1>
    <xhtml:p>John's a great guy, you know?</xhtml:p>
    </xhtml:body>
    </xhtml:html>
  </pers:résumé>
</pers:person>
```

This is just an example to illustrate the theory: if you try to view this document in Internet Explorer, IE will give you an error about an "undeclared namespace." We'll see why as we investigate the Namespace syntax in more detail.

This is a bit uglier, but at least we (and our XML parser) can immediately tell what kind of title we're talking about: a `<pers:title>` or an `<xhtml:title>`. Doing a search for `<pers:title>` will always return `Sir`. We can always immediately tell which elements are XHTML elements, without having to know in advance the structure of our document.

By separating these elements using a prefix, we have effectively created two kinds of elements in our document: `pers` types of elements and `xhtml` types of elements. So, any elements with the `pers` prefix belong to the same "category" as each other, just as any elements with the `xhtml` prefix belong to another "category." These "categories" are called *namespaces*.

These two namespaces are illustrated in Figure 3-1.

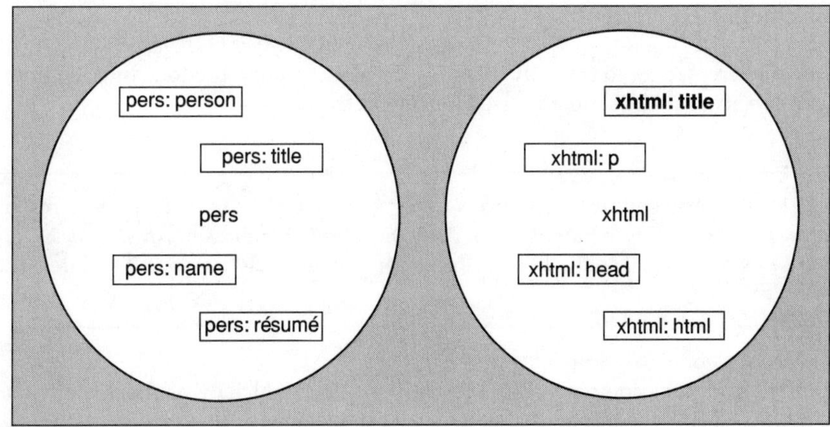

Figure 3-1

Note that namespaces are concerned with a *vocabulary*, not a *document type*. That is, the namespace distinguishes which names are in the namespace, but not what they mean or how they fit together. It is simply a "bag of names."

> **A namespace is a purely abstract entity; it's nothing more than a group of names that belong with each other conceptually.**

The concept of namespaces also exists in certain programming languages, such as Java, where the same problem exists. How can I name my Java variables whatever I want, and not have those names conflict with names already defined by others, or even by the Java library itself? The answer is that Java code is broken up into packages, where the names within a package must be unique, but the same name can be used in any package.

For example, one class defined in Java is named java.applet.Applet. The actual name of the class is just Applet; java.applet is the package which contains that class. This means that I can create my own package, and in that package I can define a class of my own, named Applet. I can even use java.applet.Applet from within my package, as long as I specify the package in which it resides, so that Java always knows which "Applet" I'm referring to.

So Why Doesn't XML Just Use These Prefixes?

Unfortunately, there is a drawback to the prefix approach to namespaces used in the previous XML: who will monitor the prefixes? The whole reason for using them is to distinguish names from different document types, but if it is going to work, the prefixes themselves also have to be unique. If one company chose the prefix `pers` and another company also chose that same prefix, the original problem still exists.

In fact, this prefix administration would have to work a lot like it works now for domain names on the Internet. A company or individual would go to the "prefix administrators" with the prefix they would like to use. If that prefix wasn't already being used, they could use it; otherwise, they would have to pick another one.

To solve this problem, we could take advantage of the already unambiguous Internet domain names in existence and specify that *URIs* must be used for the prefix names.

> **A URI (Uniform Resource Identifier) is a string of characters that identifies a resource. It can come in one of two flavors: URL (Uniform Resource Locator) or URN (Universal Resource Name). We'll look at the differences between URLs and URNs later in this chapter.**

For example, if I work for a company called Serna Ferna, Inc., which owns the domain name `sernaferna.com`, I could incorporate that into my prefix. Perhaps the document might end up looking like this:

```
<?xml version="1.0"?>
<{http://sernaferna.com/pers}person>
  <{http://sernaferna.com/pers}name>
  <{http://sernaferna.com/pers}title>
    Sir
  </{http://sernaferna.com/pers}title>
<!--etc...-->
```

Voila! We have solved our problem of uniqueness. Since our company owns the `sernaferna.com` domain name, we know that nobody else will be using that `http://sernaferna.com/pers` prefix in their XML documents, and if we want to create any additional document types, we can just keep using our domain name, and add the new namespace name to the end, such as `http://sernaferna.com/other-namespace`.

It's important to note that we need more than just the `sernaferna.com` part of the URI; we need the whole thing. Otherwise, there would be a further problem: different people could have control of different sections on that domain, and they might all want to create namespaces. For example, the company's HR department could be in charge of `http://sernaferna.com/hr` and might need to create a namespace for `names` (of employees), and the sales department could be in charge of `http://sernaferna.com/sales` and also need to create a namespace for `names` (of customers). As long as we're using the whole URI, we're fine—we can both create our namespaces (in this case `http://sernaferna.com/hr/names` and `http://sernaferna.com/sales/names`, respectively). We also need the protocol (`http`) in there because there could be yet another department that is in charge of, for example, `ftp://sernaferna.com/hr` and `ftp://sernaferna.com/sales`.

The only drawback to this solution is that our XML is no longer well formed. Our names can now include a myriad of characters that are allowed in URIs but not in XML names: `/` characters, for example. Also, for the sake of this example we used `{}` characters to separate the URL from the name, neither of which is allowed in an XML element or attribute name.

What we really need to solve all of our namespace-related problems is a way to create three-part names in XML: one part would be the name we are giving this element, the second part would be a URI associated with the name, for the element's namespace, and the third part would be an arbitrarily chosen prefix that *refers* to a URI, which specifies which namespace this element belongs to. And, in fact, this is what XML namespaces provide.

The XML namespaces specification is located at `http://www.w3.org/TR/REC-xml-names/`

How XML Namespaces Work

To use XML namespaces in your documents, elements are given *qualified names*. (In most W3C specifications *qualified name* is abbreviated to *QName*.) These qualified names consist of two parts: the *local part*, which is the same as the names we have been giving elements all along, and the *namespace prefix*, which specifies to which namespace this name belongs.

For example, to declare a namespace called `http://sernaferna.com/pers` and associate a `<person>` element with that namespace, we would do something like the following:

```
<pers:person xmlns:pers="http://sernaferna.com/pers"/>
```

The key is the `xmlns:pers` attribute (`xmlns` stands for XML NameSpace). Here we are declaring the `pers` namespace prefix and the URI of the namespace that it represents (`http://sernaferna.com/pers`). We can then use the namespace prefix with our elements, as in `pers:person`. As opposed to our previous prefixed version, the prefix itself (`pers`) doesn't have any meaning—its only purpose is to point to the namespace name. For this reason, we could replace our prefix (`pers`) with any other prefix, and this document would have exactly the same meaning.

This prefix can be used for any descendants of the `<pers:person>` element, to denote that they also belong to the `http://sernaferna.com/pers` namespace. For example:

```
<pers:person xmlns:pers="http://sernaferna.com/pers">
  <pers:name>
    <pers:title>Sir</pers:title>
  </pers:name>
</pers:person>
```

Notice that the prefix is needed on both the start and end tags of the elements. They are no longer simply being identified by their names, but by their QNames.

By now you have probably realized why colons in element names are so strongly discouraged in the XML 1.0 specification (and in this book). If you were to use a name that happened to have a colon in it with a namespace-aware XML parser, the parser would get confused, thinking that you were specifying a namespace prefix.

Internally, when this document is parsed, the parser simply replaces any namespace prefixes with the namespace itself, creating a name much like the names we used earlier in the chapter. That is, internally a parser might consider `<pers:person>` to be similar to `<{http://sernaferna.com/pers}person>`. For this reason, the `{http://sernaferna.com/pers}person` notation is often used in namespace discussions to talk about *fully qualified names*. Just remember that this is only for the benefit of easily discussing namespace issues and is not a valid XML syntax.

Try It Out — Adding XML Namespaces to Our Document

Let's see what our document would look like with proper XML namespaces. Luckily for us, there is already a namespace defined for XHTML, which is `http://www.w3.org/1999/xhtml`. We can use this namespace for the HTML we're embedding in our document.

1. Open Notepad, and type in the following XML:

```
<?xml version="1.0"?>
<pers:person xmlns:pers="http://sernaferna.com/pers"
             xmlns:html="http://www.w3.org/1999/xhtml">
  <pers:name>
    <pers:title>Sir</pers:title>
    <pers:first>John</pers:first>
    <pers:middle>Fitzgerald Johansen</pers:middle>
    <pers:last>Doe</pers:last>
  </pers:name>
  <pers:position>Vice President of Marketing</pers:position>
  <pers:résumé>
  <html:html>
```

```
      <html:head><html:title>Resume of John Doe</html:title></html:head>
      <html:body>
      <html:h1>John Doe</html:h1>
      <html:p>John's a great guy, you know?</html:p>
      </html:body>
    </html:html>
  </pers:résumé>
</pers:person>
```

2. Save this document to your hard drive as `namespace.xml`.
3. Open `namespace.xml` in IE. You should get the normal color-coded view of your XML document, similar to the Figure 3-2. (If you don't, go back and make sure you haven't made any mistakes!)

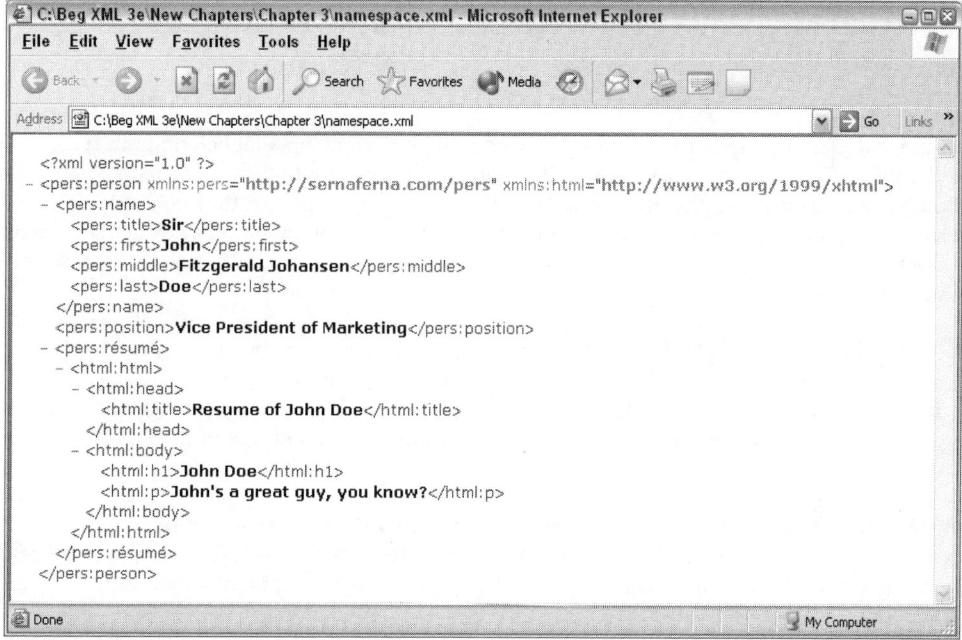

Figure 3-2

How It Works

We now have a document with elements from two separate namespaces, which we defined in the highlighted code, and any namespace-aware XML parser will be able to tell them apart. (The fact that the file opens up fine in Internet Explorer indicates that the parser bundled with this browser understands namespaces properly; if it didn't, the document might raise errors instead.) The two namespaces now look more like Figure 3-3.

The `xmlns` attributes specify the namespace prefixes we are using to point to our two namespaces:

```
<pers:person xmlns:pers="http://sernaferna.com/pers"
             xmlns:html="http://www.w3.org/1999/xhtml">
```

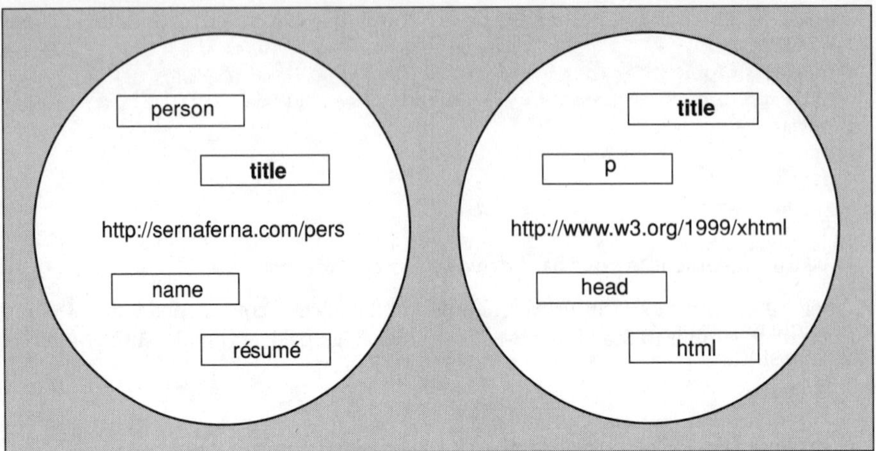

Figure 3-3

That is, we declare the `pers` prefix, which is used to specify elements that belong to the `pers` namespace, and the `html` prefix, which is used to specify elements that belong to the `xhtml` namespace. However, remember that the prefixes themselves mean nothing to the XML parser; they get replaced with the URI internally. We could have used `pers` or `myprefix` or `blah` or any other legal string of characters for the prefix; it's only the URI to which they point that the parser cares about, although using descriptive prefixes is good practice.

Because we have a way of identifying which namespace each element belongs to, we don't have to give them special, unique names. We have two vocabularies, each containing a `<title>` element, and we can mix both of these `<title>` elements in the same document. If I ever need a person's title, I can easily find any `{http://sernaferna.com/pers}title` elements I need and ignore the `{http://www.w3.org/1999/xhtml}title` elements.

However, even though my `<title>` element is prefixed with a namespace prefix, the name of the element is still `<title>`. It's just that we have now declared what namespace that `<title>` belongs to so that it won't be confused with other `<title>` elements which belong to other namespaces.

Default Namespaces

Although the previous document solves all of our namespace-related problems, it's just a little bit ugly. We have to give every element in the document a prefix to specify which namespace it belongs to, which makes the document look very similar to our first prefixed version. Luckily, we have the option of creating *default namespaces*.

> **A default namespace is exactly like a regular namespace, except that you don't have to specify a prefix for all of the elements that use it.**

It looks like this:

```
<person xmlns="http://sernaferna.com/pers">
  <name>
    <title>Sir</title>
  </name>
</person>
```

Notice that the `xmlns` attribute no longer specifies a prefix name to use for this namespace. As this is a default namespace, this element and any elements descended from it belong to this namespace, unless they explicitly specify another namespace. So the `<name>` and `<title>` elements both belong to this namespace. Note that these elements, since they don't use a prefix, are no longer called QNames, even though they are still universally unique. Many people use the generic term *universal name*, or *UName*, to describe a name in a namespace, whether it is a prefixed QName or a name in a default namespace.

We can declare more than one namespace for an element, but only one can be the default. This allows us to write XML like this:

```
<person xmlns="http://sernaferna.com/pers"
        xmlns:xhtml="http://www.w3.org/1999/xhtml">
  <name/>
  <xhtml:p>This is XHTML</xhtml:p>
</person>
```

In this case, all of the elements belong to the `http://sernaferna.com/pers` namespace, except for the `<p>` element, which is part of the `xhtml` namespace. (We've declared the namespaces and their prefixes, if applicable, in the root element so that all elements in the document can use these prefixes.) However, we can't write XML like this:

```
<person xmlns="http://sernaferna.com/pers"
        xmlns="http://www.w3.org/1999/xhtml">
```

This tries to declare two default namespaces. In this case, the XML parser wouldn't be able to figure out to what namespace the `<person>` element belongs. (Not to mention that this is a duplicate attribute, which, as we saw in Chapter 2, is not allowed in XML.)

Try It Out — Default Namespaces in Action

Let's rewrite our previous document, but use a default namespace to make it cleaner.

1. Make the following changes to `namespace.xml` and save it as `namespace2.xml`:

```
<?xml version="1.0"?>
<person xmlns="http://sernaferna.com/pers"
        xmlns:html="http://www.w3.org/1999/xhtml">
  <name>
    <title>Sir</title>
    <first>John</first>
    <middle>Fitzgerald Johansen</middle>
    <last>Doe</last>
```

```
  </name>
  <position>Vice President of Marketing</position>
  <résumé>
    <html:html>
      <html:head><html:title>Resume of John Doe</html:title></html:head>
      <html:body>
      <html:h1>John Doe</html:h1>
      <html:p>John's a great guy, you know?</html:p>
      </html:body>
    </html:html>
  </résumé>
</person>
```

2. When you view the file in Explorer, it should look like Figure 3-4.

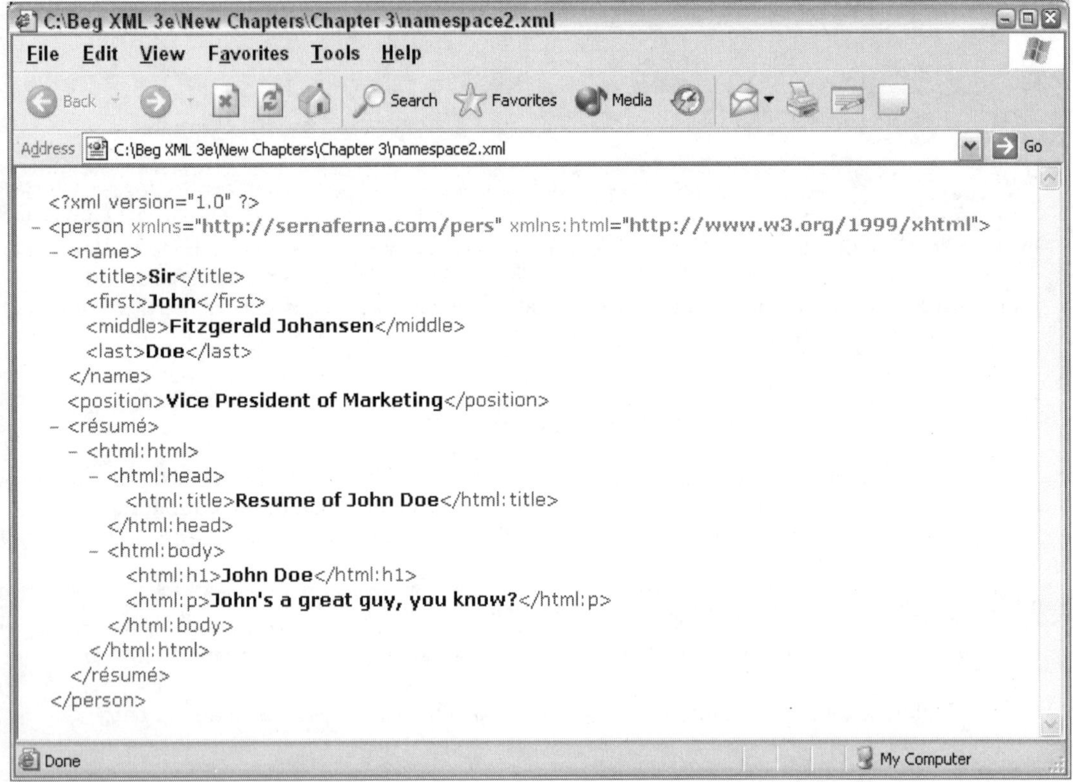

Figure 3-4

How It Works

In the <person> start tag, the first xmlns attribute doesn't specify a prefix to associate with this namespace, so this becomes the default namespace for the element, along with any of its descendents, which is why we don't need any namespace prefixes in many of the elements, such as <name>, <title>, and so on.

But since the XHTML elements are in a different namespace, we do need to specify the prefix for them, for example:

```
<html:head><html:title>Resume of John Doe</html:title></html:head>
```

Declaring Namespaces on Descendants

So far, when we have had multiple namespaces in a document, we've been declaring them all in the root element, so that the prefixes are available throughout the document. So, in our previous *Try It Out*, we declared a default namespace, as well as a namespace prefix for our HTML elements, all on the <person> element.

This means that when we have a default namespace mixed with other namespaces, we would create a document like this:

```
<person xmlns="http://sernaferna.com/pers"
        xmlns:xhtml="http://www.w3.org/1999/xhtml">
  <name/>
  <xhtml:p>This is XHTML</xhtml:p>
</person>
```

However, we don't *have* to declare all of our namespace prefixes on the root element; in fact, a namespace prefix can be declared on any element in the document. We could also have written the previous one like this:

```
<person xmlns="http://sernaferna.com/pers">
  <name/>
  <xhtml:p xmlns:xhtml="http://www.w3.org/1999/xhtml">
  This is XHTML</xhtml:p>
</person>
```

In some cases this might make our documents more readable because we're declaring the namespaces closer to where they'll actually be used. The downside to writing our documents like this is that the xhtml prefix is available only on the <p> element and its descendants; we couldn't use it on our <name> element, for example, or any other element that wasn't a descendant of <p>.

But we can take things even further and declare the XHTML namespace to be the *default* namespace for our <p> element and its descendents, like this:

```
<person xmlns="http://sernaferna.com/pers">
  <name/>
  <p xmlns="http://www.w3.org/1999/xhtml">This is XHTML</p>
</person>
```

Although `http://sernaferna.com/pers` is the default namespace for the document as a whole, `http://www.w3.org/1999/xhtml` is the default namespace for the <p> element, and any of its descendants. In other words, the `http://www.w3.org/1999/xhtml` namespace overrides the `http://sernaferna.com/pers` namespace, so that it doesn't apply to the <p> element. Again, in some cases this can make our documents more readable because we are declaring the namespaces closer to where they are used.

Try It Out Default Namespaces for Children

In the interest of readability, let's write the XML from our previous *Try It Out* again, to declare the default namespace for the <html> tag and its descendants.

1. Here are the changes to be made to namespace2.xml:

```
<?xml version="1.0"?>
<person xmlns="http://sernaferna.com/pers">
  <name>
    <title>Sir</title>
    <first>John</first>
    <middle>Fitzgerald Johansen</middle>
    <last>Doe</last>
  </name>
  <position>Vice President of Marketing</position>
  <résumé>
    <html xmlns="http://www.w3.org/1999/xhtml">
      <head><title>Resume of John Doe</title></head>
      <body>
      <h1>John Doe</h1>
      <p>John's a great guy, you know?</p>
      </body>
    </html>
  </résumé>
</person>
```

2. Save this as namespace3.xml. This looks a lot tidier than the previous version and represents the same thing.

3. Viewing the file in Explorer should look like Figure 3-5.

How It Works

Because we have completely eliminated the prefixes from our document, the element names become "cleaner." The document is no longer cluttered up with the pers: and html: prefixes everywhere, which can make it easier to read for a human reader.

Canceling Default Namespaces

Sometimes you might be working with XML documents in which not all of the elements belong to a namespace. For example, you might be creating XML documents to describe employees in your organization, and those documents might include occasional XHTML comments about the employees, such as in the following short fragment:

```
<employee>
  <name>Jane Doe</name>
  <notes>
    <p xmlns="http://www.w3.org/1999/xhtml">I've worked
    with <name>Jane Doe</name> for over a <em>year</em>
    now.</p>
  </notes>
</employee>
```

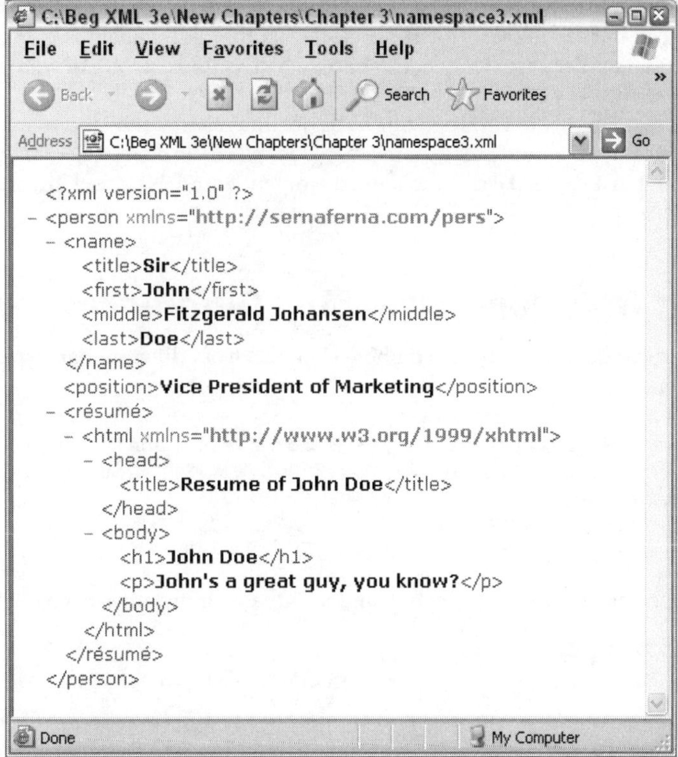

Figure 3-5

In this case, we have decided that anywhere the employee's name is included in the document it should be in a <name> element, in case the employee changes his/her name in the future, such as if Jane Doe ever gets married and becomes Jane Smith. (In this case changing the document would then be a simple matter of looking for all <name> elements that aren't in a namespace and changing the values.) Also, since these XML documents will be used only by our own application, we don't have to create a namespace for it.

However, as you see in the preceding code, one of the <name> elements occurs under the <p> element, which declares a default namespace, meaning that the <name> element also falls under that namespace. So if we searched for <name> elements that had no associated namespace, we wouldn't pick this one up. The way to get around this is to use the xmlns attribute to *cancel* the default namespace, by setting the value to an empty string. For example:

```
<employee>
  <name>Jane Doe</name>
  <notes>
    <p xmlns="http://www.w3.org/1999/xhtml">I've worked
    with <name xmlns="">Jane Doe</name> for over a <em>year</em>
    now.</p>
  </notes>
</employee>
```

Now the second <name> element is not in any namespace. Of course, if we had a namespace specifically for our <employee> document, this would become a nonissue, because we could just use the ways we've already learned to declare that an element is part of that namespace (using a namespace prefix or a default namespace). But, in this case, we're not declaring that the element is part of a namespace—we're trying to declare that it's *not* part of any namespace, which is the opposite of what we've been doing so far.

Normally, if you're going to be working with XML documents that mix and match elements from different namespaces, you would create namespaces for *all* of the elements. You wouldn't usually use elements that aren't in a namespace in the same document with UNames. However, if you ever need to, the flexibility exists.

Do Different Notations Make Any Difference?

We've now seen three different ways to combine elements from different namespaces. We can fully qualify every name, like this:

```
<pers:person xmlns:pers="http://sernaferna.com/pers"
             xmlns:xhtml="http://www.w3.org/1999/xhtml">
  <pers:name/>
  <xhtml:p>This is XHTML</xhtml:p>
</pers:person>
```

Or, we can use one namespace as the default, and just qualify any names from other namespaces, like this:

```
<person xmlns="http://sernaferna.com/pers"
        xmlns:xhtml="http://www.w3.org/1999/xhtml">
  <name/>
  <xhtml:p>This is XHTML</xhtml:p>
</person>
```

Or, we can just use defaults everywhere, like this:

```
<person xmlns="http://sernaferna.com/pers">
  <name/>
  <p xmlns="http://www.w3.org/1999/xhtml">This is XHTML</p>
</person>
```

This raises the question: Do these three fragments of XML really mean exactly the same thing?

From the pure namespaces point of view, yes, these documents mean exactly the same thing. All three documents have the same three elements, and in each instance, each element still belongs to the same namespace as it does in the other two instances.

From the point of view of most applications, these fragments also mean the same thing. When you're doing work with an XML document, you usually only care what elements you're dealing with; you don't care whether the element's namespace was declared using a default declaration or an explicit prefix any more than you care if an element with no data was written as a start tag and an end tag pair or as an empty element.

There are, however, some applications that actually do differentiate between the preceding three examples, such as an application that reads in XML and displays the source code to a user. As you may have noticed if you used IE5 or later to view the XML from the previous *Try It Outs*, it does display each one differently. Let's take a look at each of the three preceding code examples in Figures 3-6, 3-7, and 3-8, respectively:

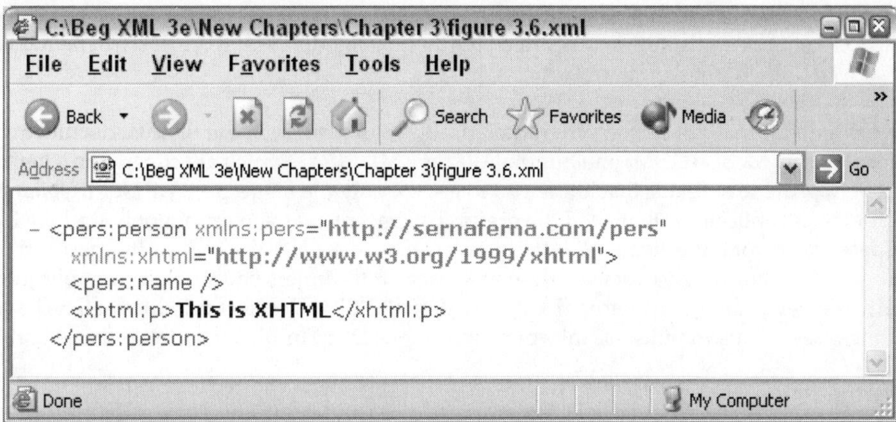

Figure 3-6

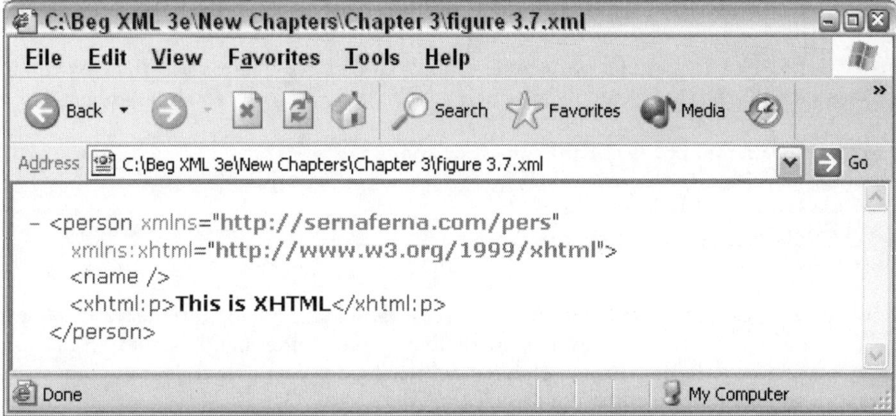

Figure 3-7

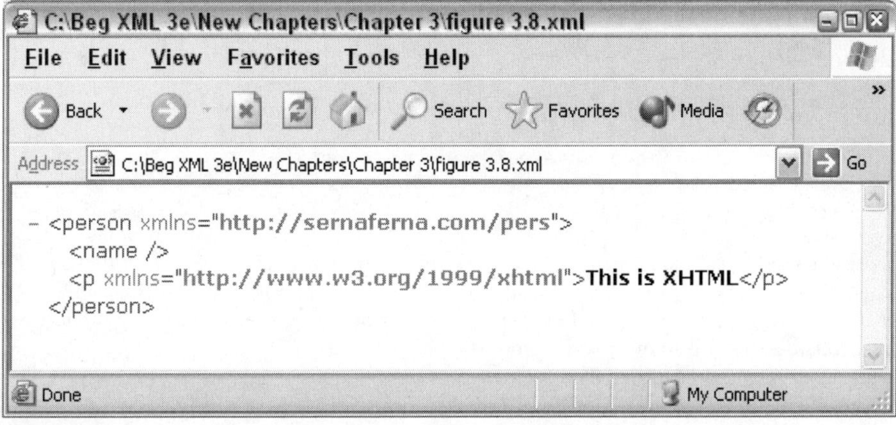

Figure 3-8

As you can see, the browser displays the documents exactly as they were written, so if we declare our namespaces using defaults, the browser displays them using defaults; if we declare them with prefixes, the browser displays them with prefixes.

The two dominant technologies to programmatically get information out of XML documents, the Document Object Model (DOM) and Simple API for XML (SAX), which are covered in Chapters 11 and 12 respectively, provide methods that allow you to get not only the namespace URI for a QName but also the prefix for those applications that need the prefix. This means that you cannot only find the fully qualified namespace names for these elements, but can go so far as to see *how* the XML author wrote those names. In real life, however, you hardly ever need the namespace prefix, unless you are writing applications to display the XML as entered to a user. Internet Explorer's default XSL style sheet can differentiate between the preceding cases because it pulls this information from the DOM implementation shipped with the browser.

Namespaces and Attributes

So far all of our discussions have been centered on elements, and we've been pretty much ignoring attributes. Do namespaces work the same for attributes as they do for elements?

The answer is no, they don't. In fact, attributes usually don't have namespaces the way elements do. They are just "associated" with the elements to which they belong. Consider the following fragment:

```
<person xmlns="http://sernaferna.com/pers">
  <name id="25">
    <title>Sir</title>
  </name>
</person>
```

We know that the <person>, <name>, and <title> elements all belong to the same namespace, which is declared in the <person> start tag. The `id` attribute, on the other hand, is not part of this namespace; it's simply associated with the <name> element, which itself is part of that default namespace. We could use a notation like this to identify it, for discussion:

```
"{http://sernaferna.com/pers}name:id"
```

That is, the `id` attribute is attached to the <name> element, which is in the `http://sernaferna.com/pers` namespace.

However, if we used prefixes, we *could* specify that `id` is in a namespace like so:

```
<a:person xmlns:a="http://sernaferna.com/pers">
  <a:name a:id="25">
    <a:title>Sir</a:title>
  </a:name>
</a:person>
```

Unfortunately, the namespaces specification leaves a bit of a gray area concerning attributes. For example, consider the following two fragments:

```
<a:name id="25">
<a:name a:id="25">
```

Are these two fragments identical? Or are they different? Well, actually, programmers can make up their own minds whether these two cases are the same or different. (In XSLT, for example, the two cases would be considered to be different.) For this reason, if you need to be sure that the XML processor will realize that your attributes are part of the same namespace as your element, you should include the prefix. On the other hand, most applications treat the two situations identically.

Consider the case where you want to perform some processing on every attribute in the `http://sernaferna.com/pers` namespace. If an application considers both of the preceding cases to be the same, then in both cases the `id` attribute gets processed. On the other hand, if the application doesn't consider both of the preceding to be the same, you get only the second `id` attribute because it is specifically declared to be in the namespace we're looking for, whereas the first one isn't.

Is this purely theoretical? Well, yes, in most cases it is. Applications don't usually look for attributes on their own; they look for particular elements, and then process the attributes on those elements.

However, attributes from a particular namespace can also be attached to elements from a different namespace. Attributes that are specifically declared to be in a namespace are called *global attributes*. A common example of a global attribute is the XHTML `class` attribute, which might be used on any XML element, XHTML or not. This would make things easier when using *Cascading Style Sheets* (CSS) to display an XML document.

Try It Out — Adding Attributes

To see this in action, let's add an `id` attribute to our <name> element and add a `style` attribute to the HTML paragraph portion of our résumé.

1. Change `namespace2.xml` to the following, and save it as `namespace4.xml`:

```
<?xml version="1.0"?>
<person xmlns="http://sernaferna.com/pers">
  <name id="1">
    <title>Sir</title>
    <first>John</first>
    <middle>Fitzgerald Johansen</middle>
    <last>Doe</last>
  </name>
  <position>Vice President of Marketing</position>
  <résumé>
    <html:html xmlns:html="http://www.w3.org/1999/xhtml">
    <html:head><html:title>Resume of John Doe</html:title></html:head>
    <html:body>
    <html:h1>John Doe</html:h1>
    <html:p html:style="FONT-FAMILY: Arial">
      John's a great guy, you know?
    </html:p>
    </html:body>
    </html:html>
  </résumé>
</person>
```

Because we want the `style` attribute to be specifically in the XHTML namespace, we have gone back to using prefixes on our XHTML elements instead of a default namespace. Another alternative would be to declare the XHTML namespace twice: once as the default, for `<html>` and all of its descendents, and once with a prefix, which could be attached to the `style` attribute.

2. Open the document in IE to view the results. It should look like Figure 3-9.

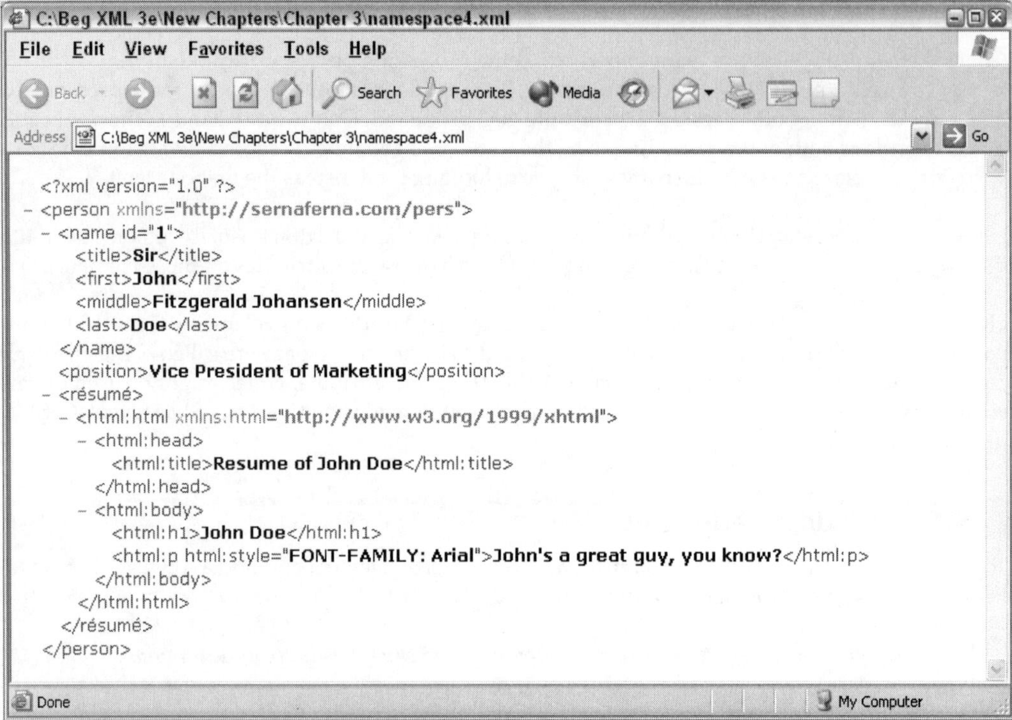

Figure 3-9

How It Works

The `id` attribute that we added is associated with the `<name>` element, but it doesn't actually have a namespace.

Similarly, the `style` attribute is associated with the `<p>` element, but in this case the attribute is specifically in the XHTML namespace.

Again, applications may or may not treat both of these the same and consider them to be in the same namespace as the elements to which they are attached. All applications will treat the `style` attribute as being in the XHTML namespace, because we have specifically said so, but some will think `id` is in the same namespace as `<name>`, and some won't.

What Exactly Are URIs?

We have mentioned that namespaces are specified using URIs, and most of the examples shown so far have been URLs. To really understand namespaces, we'll have to look at this concept a little further.

Because so much of the work done on the Internet somehow involves finding and retrieving *resources*, much thought has been put into this process. So what is a resource? Well, simply put, a resource is anything that has identity. It could be a tangible item, such as a `.gif` file or a book, or it could be a conceptual item, like the current state of the traffic in Toronto. It could be an item that is retrievable over the Internet, such as an HTML document, or an item which is not retrievable over the Internet, such as the person who wrote that HTML document.

Recall our earlier definition of a URI.

> **A URI (Uniform Resource Identifier) is a string of characters that identifies a resource. It can come in one of two flavors: URL (Uniform Resource Locator), or URN (Universal Resource Name).**

There is a document which formally describes the syntax for URIs at the IETF (Internet Engineering Task Force) website, located at `http://www.ietf.org/rfc/rfc2396.txt`*; one which describes the syntax for URNs, located at* `http://www.ietf.org/rfc/rfc2141.txt`*; and one which describes the syntax for URLs, located at* `http://www.ietf.org/rfc/rfc1738.txt`*.*

URLs

If you have been on the Internet for any length of time, you are probably already familiar with URLs, and most Internet-savvy people understand how URLs work. The first part of the URL specifies the *protocol*, `http` being the most common, with `mailto` and `ftp` also being used frequently, and others (such as `gopher`, `news`, `telnet`, `file`, and so on) being used on occasion. (Officially, the protocol part of the URL is called a *scheme*.)

The protocol is followed by a colon, and after the colon comes a path to the resource being identified.

For example, here's a URL to a web page on the Internet:

```
http://sernaferna.com/default/home.htm
```

This URL contains information that can be used to retrieve a file named `home.htm` from a server on the Internet named `sernaferna.com`. It specifies that the file is in the `default` directory (or virtual directory) and that the file should be retrieved via the HTTP protocol.

We can also create a URL to an e-mail account, like so:

```
mailto:someone@somewhere.com
```

Of course, there is a limitation on the resources that can be retrieved via URLs: obviously they must be resources of a type that is retrievable from a computer! (The resource identified in the `mailto:` URL is a bit of an exception, since it isn't actually *retrieved*; instead, a mail client is usually triggered, and a new email is created to the given address.)

URNs

URNs are not as commonly seen as URLs. In fact, most people, even those who have been using the Internet their whole lives, have never seen a URN. They exist to provide a persistent, location-independent name for a resource.

For example, a person's name is similar to a URN, because the person has the same name, no matter where they are. Even after a person dies, the name still refers to the person who used to have it when they were alive. A name is different from a URN, though, because more than one person can have the same name, whereas URNs are designed to be unique across time and space.

A URN looks something like this:

```
urn:foo:a123,456
```

First comes the string `urn`, upper- or lowercase, and a colon. After the first colon comes the *Namespace Identifier*, or *NID*, (`foo` in this case) followed by another colon. And finally comes the *Namespace Specific String*, or *NSS* (`a123,456`, for example). As you can see from the terminology, URNs were designed with namespaces already in mind. (Not necessarily XML namespaces, but namespaces in general.)

The NID portion of the URN declares what type of URN this is. For example, to create URNs for Canadian citizens, we might declare an NID of `Canadian-Citizen`.

The NSS portion of the URN is the part that must be unique and persistent. In Canada, all citizens are assigned unique Social Insurance Numbers. So, a URN for a Canadian citizen with a Social Insurance Number of 000-000-000 might look like this:

```
urn:Canadian-Citizen:000-000-000
```

Why Use URLs for Namespaces, Not URNs?

The XML namespace specification states that namespaces are identified with URIs, which leaves us the possibility of using either URLs or URNs. It seems that URNs are better suited for naming namespaces than URLs—after all, a namespace is a *conceptual* resource, not one that can be retrieved via the Internet; so why are most namespaces named using URLs instead?

Some people find it easier to create unique namespace names using URLs, since they are already guaranteed to be unique. If I own the `sernaferna.com` domain name, I can incorporate it into my namespace names and know that they will be unique.

Of course, this is still by convention; nothing stops someone at another company, say Malicious Names, Inc., from stealing Serna Ferna, Inc.'s, domain name and maliciously using it as the name for a namespace. But if everyone follows the convention, then we can be sure that there won't be *accidental* collisions, which is good enough for our purposes. You could still construct a URN like `urn:SernaFernaHR:name`, but many people feel that things are just simpler if you use URLs.

And there can also be side benefits of using URLs as namespace names. If we wanted to, we could put a document at the end of the URL that describes the elements in that namespace. For example, we have been using `http://sernaferna.com/pers` as a fictional namespace. If Serna Ferna, Inc., wanted to make the `pers` namespace public, for use in public document types, it might put a document at that location that describes the various XML elements and attributes in that namespace.

But regardless of what people are doing, the possibility of using a URN as a namespace identifier still exists, so if you have a system of URNs that you feel is unique, it is perfectly legal. URNs provide no benefits over URLs, except for the conceptual idea that they're a closer fit to what namespace names are trying to do—that is, *name* something, not *point to* something.

What Do Namespace URIs Really Mean?

Now that we know how to use namespaces to keep our element names unique, what exactly do those namespace URIs mean? In other words what does `http://sernaferna.com/pers` really represent?

The answer, according to the XML namespaces specification, is that it doesn't mean anything. The URI is simply used to give the namespace a name, but doesn't mean anything on its own. In the same way the words *John Doe* don't mean anything on their own—they are just used to identify a particular person.

Many people feel that this isn't enough for XML. In addition to keeping element names distinct, they would also like to give those elements meaning—that is, not just distinguish `<my:element>` from `<your:element>`, but also define what `<my:element>` means. What is it used for? What are the legal values for it? If we could create some kind of "schema" that would define our document type, the namespace URI might be the logical place to declare this document as adhering to that schema.

The XML Namespaces specification (`http://www.w3.org/TR/REC-xml-names/`) states "it is not a goal that [the namespace URI] be directly useable for retrieval of a schema (if any exists)." (A *schema* is a document that formally describes an XML document type. There are a number of languages available for creating schemas, such as *DTDs* and the *XML Schema* language from the W3C, which will be covered in Chapters 4 and 5.) In other words, as we've been saying, the URI is just a name or identifier; it doesn't have any kind of meaning. However, it is not strictly forbidden for it to have a meaning. For this reason, someone creating an application could legally decide that the URI used in a namespace actually does indicate some type of documentation, whether that is a prose document describing this particular document type or a technical schema document of some sort. But, in this case, the URI still wouldn't mean anything to the XML parser; it would be up to the higher-level application to read the URI and do something with it.

As an example of where this might be useful, consider a corporate information processing system where users are entering information to be stored in XML format. If different namespaces are defined for different types of documents, and those namespaces are named with URLs, then you could put a help file at the end of each URL. If users are viewing a particular type of XML document in the special application you have written for them, all they have to do is hit *F1* to get help and find out about this particular type of document. All your application has to do is open a web browser and point it to the URL that defines the namespace.

RDDL

So, in addition to providing human-readable documentation for your namespace, the options of providing schemas also exist. However, there are a number of these languages available (a few of which are covered in this book)—how do we decide what to put at the end of a URL we use for a namespace name? Do we put human-readable documentation that describes the namespace? Or do we put a document in one of these machine-readable formats? One answer is to use the *Resource Directory Description Language*, or *RDDL* (the RDDL specification can be found at `http://www.openhealth.org/RDDL/`).

RDDL was created to combine the benefits of human-readable documentation with the benefits of providing machine-readable documentation for an XML namespace. An RDDL document is actually an XHTML document, which makes it human-readable. However, since XHTML is XML, other machine-readable resources can be included in the document, using a technology called *XLink* to link the various documents together. In this way, human-readable documentation can be provided on an XML namespace, while at the same time providing links to as many other resources as needed, such as machine-readable documents on the namespace, executable code, and so on.

When Should I Use Namespaces?

By this point in the chapter, we've covered everything that we need to know about namespaces from a technical standpoint. We know what they mean, how to use them, and how to combine them. So let's sit back for a while, put our feet up, and talk philosophy. When should we create a new namespace, and when should we add new elements to an existing one?

In the course of this chapter, we have created the `http://sernaferna.com/pers` namespace, for use by our fictional company called Serna Ferna, Inc. We decided to use one namespace, to cover all of the elements that are used to create an XML document about a person. We could have split our namespace up, instead, and created separate namespaces for each element, or we could have created one namespace for the overall document, and another for the résumé. Why did I choose to do it this way?

Remember that a namespace is just a "bag of names," that is, it's a group of element names that belong together and that are distinct from element names in other namespaces. The key is the phrase *belong together*. You might think of the elements in a namespace as being the vocabulary for a language, the same way that English words are in the English vocabulary. Any words that belong to that language would go in that namespace, and words from other languages would go into other namespaces. It's up to you to decide which elements belong in the same vocabulary, and which ones should go in different vocabularies.

> *The W3C went through this process when creating XHTML, the HTML language "redone" in XML. The problem is that XHTML is based on HTML 4, which has three flavors: Frameset (which includes support for HTML frames), Strict (which is designed for clean structural markup, free from all layout tags), and Transitional (which allows formatting markup for older browsers, such as a* `bgcolor` *attribute on the <body> tag). Some HTML elements, such as <p>, appear in all three flavors, while others, such as* `<frameset>`*, may only appear in certain flavors.*
>
> *This led the W3C, in the initial specifications for XHTML, to indicate that there would be three different namespaces used, one for each flavor. However, the web community strongly disagreed with this approach. Most people consider HTML (or XHTML) to be one language—even though there may be more than one "flavor" or "dialect" of that language—so they argued that XHTML should have only one namespace associated with it. In the end, the W3C decided to go with the one-namespace approach (the namespace they*

chose is `http://www.w3.org/1999/xhtml`, which is why we've been using it for our XHTML examples).

Summary

This chapter introduced the concept of namespaces, along with their implementation in XML. We've seen:

- What benefit namespaces can potentially give us in our documents
- How to declare and use namespaces
- How to effectively use a URI as the name of a namespace

The idea behind namespaces may not seem all that relevant, unless you're combining elements from various vocabularies into one XML document. You may be thinking, "If I'm just going to create XML documents to describe my data, why mess around with all of this namespace stuff?" However, when you remember that you will be using other XML vocabularies, such as XSLT, to transform your documents or XHTML to display your data, namespaces become much more relevant. Learning the concepts behind namespaces will help you combine your documents with these other document types, in addition to any further document types you may create yourself.

Exercise Questions

Suggested solutions to these questions can be found in Appendix A.

Question 1

Earlier we had the following XML document, in which we had to cancel the default namespace:

```
<employee>
  <name>Jane Doe</name>
  <notes>
    <p xmlns="http://www.w3.org/1999/xhtml">I've worked
    with <name xmlns="">Jane Doe</name> for over a <em>year</em>
    now.</p>
  </notes>
</employee>
```

Assuming that this document is for the fictional Serna Ferna, Inc., company we've been using, create a namespace for employees and use it in this document. Be sure to keep the XHTML elements in their namespace.

Question 2

Since Serna Ferna, Inc., has been going through their employee records, they've realized that they don't have a good unique way to identify each employee. Create a global `id` attribute that can be attached to any XML element in the employee namespace you created earlier.

Put this attribute into effect by modifying the XML you created in Question 1, and marking the Jane Doe employee as employee number x125.

Question 3

Create a new XML file for an employee named Alfred Neuman, with employee number x393. In the notes for Alfred mention that he has worked closely with Jane Doe, being sure to use the `<name>` element to refer to her.

Part II: Validation

Chapter 4: Document Type Definitions

Chapter 5: XML Schemas

Chapter 6: RELAX NG

Document Type Definitions

As we have seen in the first few chapters, the rules for XML are straightforward. It doesn't take much to create well-formed XML documents to describe any information that you want. We have also learned that when we create our XML documents, we can categorize our documents into groups of similar document types, based on the elements and attributes they contain. We learned that the elements and attributes that make up a document type are known as the document's vocabulary. In Chapter 3, we learned how to use multiple vocabularies within a single document using namespaces. However, by this time, you may be wondering how to define your own types of documents and be able to check whether certain documents follow the rules of your vocabulary.

Suppose you are developing an Internet site that utilizes our `<name>` sample from Chapter 1. In our `<name>` sample, we created a simple XML document that allowed us to enter the first, middle, and last name of a person. In our sample, we used the name *John Fitzgerald Johansen Doe*. Now suppose that users of your Internet site are sending you information that does not match the vocabulary you developed. How could you verify that the content within the XML document is valid? You could write some code within your web application to check whether each of the elements is correct and in the correct order, but what if you want to modify the type of documents you can accept? You would have to update your application code, possibly in many places. This isn't much of an improvement from the text documents we discussed in Chapter 1.

The need to validate documents against a vocabulary is common in markup languages. In fact, it is so common that the creators of XML included a method for checking validity in the XML Recommendation. An XML document is *valid* if its content matches its definition of allowable elements, attributes, and other document pieces. By utilizing special *Document Type Definitions*, or DTDs, you can check the content of a document type with special parsers. The XML Recommendation separates parsers into two categories—validating and nonvalidating. Validating parsers, according to the Recommendation, must implement validity checking using DTDs. Therefore, if we have a validating parser, we can remove the content-checking code from our application and depend on the parser to verify the content of our XML document against our DTD.

> *Although you will learn everything you need to know about DTDs in this chapter, you may like to see the XML Recommendation and its discussion of DTDs for yourself. If so, you can look it up at `http://www.w3.org/TR/REC-xml#dt-doctype`.*

In this chapter, we will learn:

- How to create DTDs
- How to validate an XML document against a DTD
- How to use DTDs to create XML documents from multiple files

Running the Samples

We have talked about some of the benefits of DTDs, but it will probably help us if we look at an example DTD before we move on. To see how the DTD works, we will define a vocabulary for our `<name>` example from Chapter 1.

Preparing the Ground

We need a program that can validate an XML document against a DTD. Throughout this chapter and the next, we will be using the Topologi Schematron Validator. While this validator runs only on Windows, it allows us to use a single tool for working with many different kinds of documents. If you are not using Windows, then you should download the Sun Multi-Schema Validator.

The Topologi Schematron Validator can be downloaded from `http://www.topologi.com/products/validator/index.html`. Simply follow the download instructions on the page. Once installed, run the program and click the Options button to change the default configuration (see Figure 4-1).

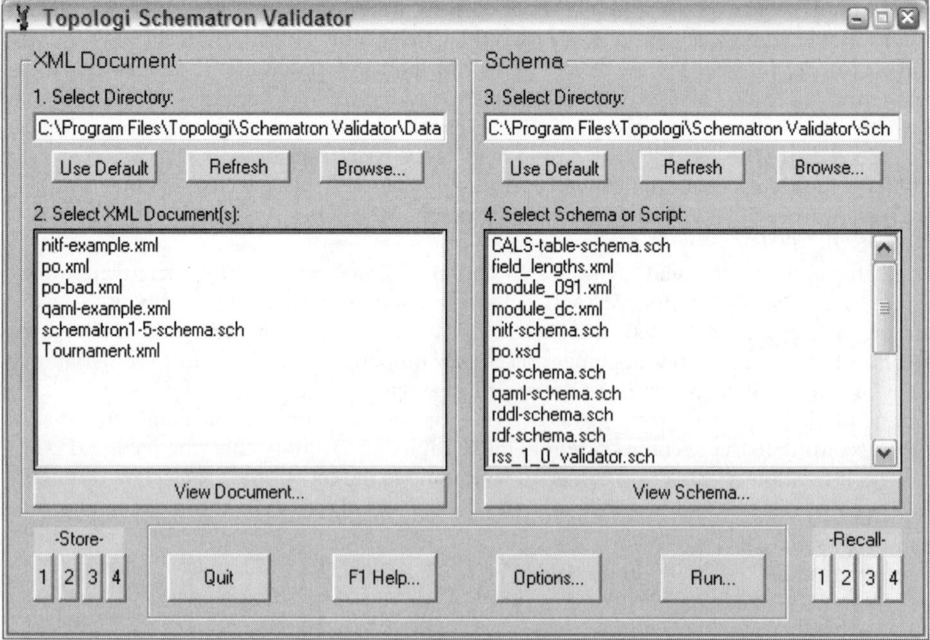

Figure 4-1

In the configuration, mark the checkbox Validate with DTD (see Figure 4-2). (In older versions, the checkbox has the text DTDValidation.) Click the Save button, and then click OK.

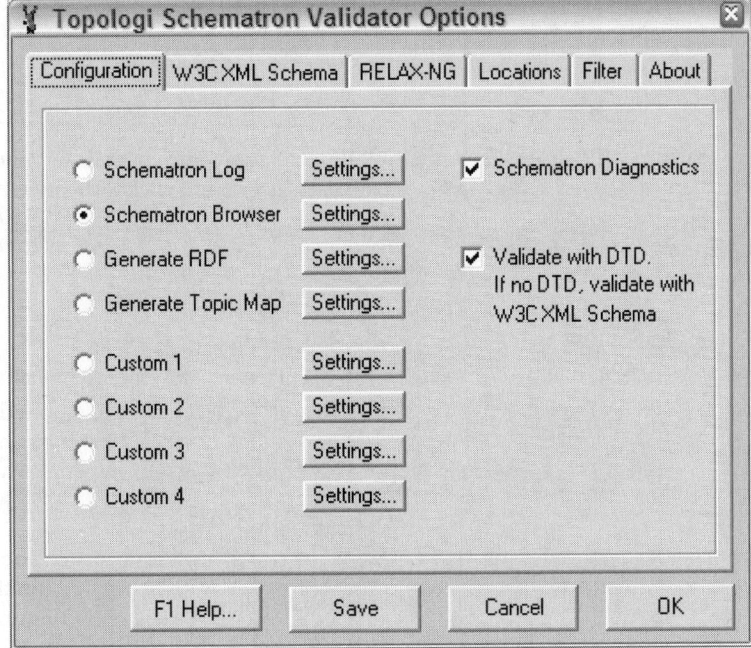

Figure 4-2

The Sun Multi-Schema Validator can be downloaded from `http://wwws.sun.com/software/xml/developers/multischema/`. It is a command-line utility, and instructions can be found in the download.

We are now ready to validate our XML documents against a DTD—all we need is a DTD.

Try It Out What's in a Name?

In this example, we embed a DTD that defines our `<name>` vocabulary directly within our XML document. Later, we will see how separating the definition from our XML document can be useful in distributed environments.

1. Open a text editor, such as Notepad, and type in the following document, making sure you include the spaces as shown. It may be easier to open the `name.xml` sample from Chapter 1 and modify it, because much of the content will remain the same:

```
<?xml version="1.0"?>
<!DOCTYPE name [
  <!ELEMENT name (first, middle, last)>
  <!ELEMENT first (#PCDATA)>
  <!ELEMENT middle (#PCDATA)>
  <!ELEMENT last (#PCDATA)>
```

```
]>
<name>
  <first>John</first>
  <middle>Fitzgerald Johansen</middle>
  <last>Doe</last>
</name>
```

Save the file as name2.xml.

2. We are ready to validate our document. Within the Topologi Schematron Validator, browse to the folder where you saved name2.xml. Select name2.xml and click the Run button (see Figure 4-3).

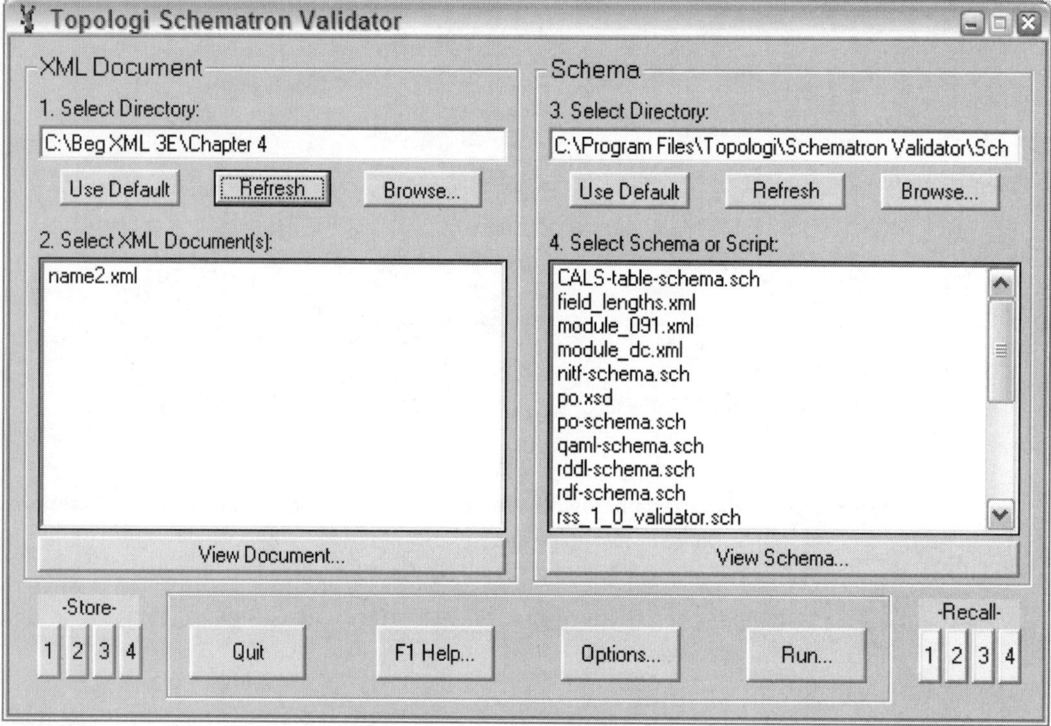

Figure 4-3

You should see the output shown in Figure 4-4.

If the output suggests that the validation completed but that there was an error in the document, correct the error (the parser will report the line number and column number of the error) and try again. When editing XML manually, it is common to make errors when you first begin. Soon you will be able to see an error and correct it preemptively.

3. Change the name of the <first> element to <given> within the name2.xml document:

```
<?xml version="1.0"?>
<!DOCTYPE name [
  <!ELEMENT name (first, middle, last)>
  <!ELEMENT first (#PCDATA)>
```

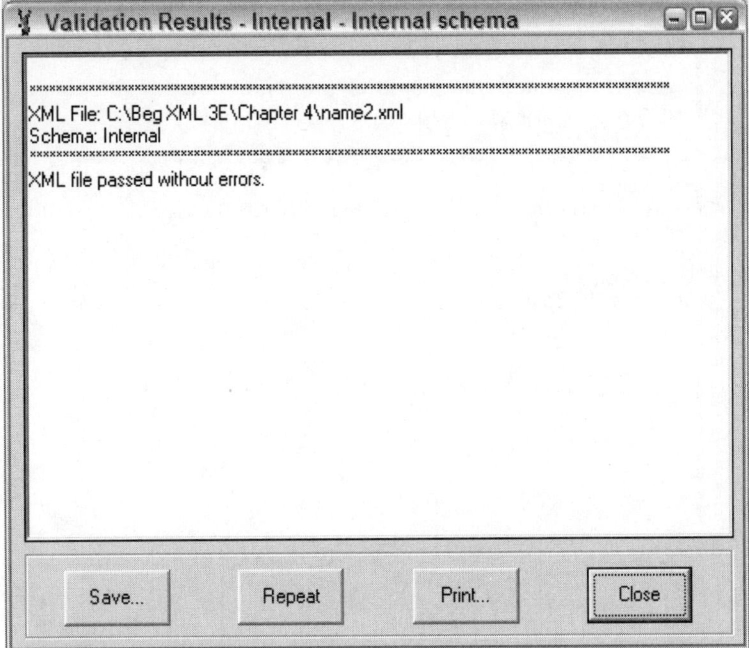

Figure 4-4

```
  <!ELEMENT middle (#PCDATA)>
  <!ELEMENT last (#PCDATA)>
]>
<name>
   <given>John</given>
   <middle>Fitzgerald Johansen</middle>
   <last>Doe</last>
</name>
```

Save the file as `name3.xml` and try validating again. This time the program should tell us that there were errors (see Figure 4-5).

The program told us that the element `<given>` was undeclared and that the content of our XML document didn't match what we specified in the DTD.

How It Works

This Try It Out used our DTD to check whether the content within our XML document matched our vocabulary. Internally, parsers handle these checks in different ways. At the most basic level, the parser reads the DTD declarations and stores them in memory. Then, as it is reading the document, it validates each element that it encounters against the matching declaration. If it finds an element or attribute that does not appear within the declarations or appears in the wrong position, or if it finds a declaration that has no matching XML content, it raises a validity error.

Let's break the DTD down into smaller pieces so that we can see some of what we will be learning later:

```
<?xml version="1.0"?>
```

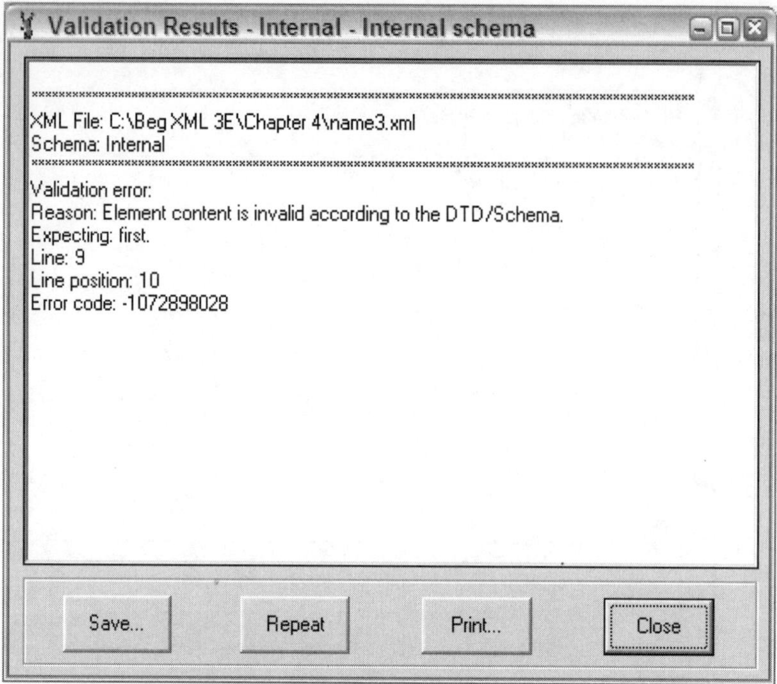

Figure 4-5

As we have seen in all of our XML documents, we begin with the XML declaration. Again, this is optional but it is highly recommended that you include it to avoid XML version conflicts later.

```
<!DOCTYPE name [
```

Immediately following the XML header is the *Document Type Declaration*, commonly referred to as the DOCTYPE. This informs the parser that there is a DTD associated with this XML document.

> **You may have noticed that the acronym for Document Type Declaration is also DTD. This is a source of confusion for many new XML users. Luckily, you will almost never see the acronym *DTD* used in reference to the Document Type Declaration. Whenever you see the acronym DTD in this book, it refers to the Document Type Definition as a whole.**

If the document contains a DTD, the Document Type Declaration must appear at the start of the document (preceded only by the XML header)—it is not permitted anywhere else within the document. The `DOCTYPE` declaration has an exclamation mark (`!`) at the start of the element name. If you remember your well-formedness rules from Chapter 2, you may already be telling anyone who will listen that you have discovered an error in your XML book. This is not an error, as the XML Recommendation indicates that *declaration elements* must begin with an exclamation mark. Declaration elements may appear only as part of the DTD. They may not appear within the main XML content. The syntax for DTDs is entirely different from the XML syntax that we have already learned. As we progress through this chapter, you will need to learn many new rules for creating your DTDs.

At this point, you may begin to notice that the syntax for DTDs is very different from the rules for basic XML documents. The primary reason for this is their foundation in Standard Generalized Markup Language (SGML). To maintain compatibility with SGML, the designers of XML decided to keep the declaration language similar. In fact, the DTD syntax in XML is a simpler form of its SGML counterpart.

In our example, we created a relatively simple `DOCTYPE` declaration; we will look at some more advanced `DOCTYPE` declaration features later.

```
<!ELEMENT name (first, middle, last)>
<!ELEMENT first (#PCDATA)>
<!ELEMENT middle (#PCDATA)>
<!ELEMENT last (#PCDATA)>
```

Directly following the `DOCTYPE` declaration is the body of the DTD. This is where we declare elements, attributes, entities, and notations. In this DTD, we have declared several elements, because that is all we needed for the vocabulary of our <name> document. Like the `DOCTYPE` declaration, the element declarations must start with an exclamation mark.

```
]>
```

Finally, we close the DTD using a closing bracket and a closing angle bracket. This effectively ends our definition and our XML document immediately follows.

Now that you have seen a DTD and a validating parser in action, you may feel ready to create DTDs for all of your XML documents. It is important to remember, however, that validation uses more processing power, even for a small document. Because of this, you may have many circumstances where you do not want to use a DTD. For example, if you are using only XML documents that are created by your company, or are machine generated (not hand typed), you can be relatively sure that they follow the rules of your vocabulary. In such cases, checking validity may be unnecessary. In fact, it may negatively affect your overall application performance.

The Document Type Declaration

The Document Type Declaration declares that we are specifying a DTD and tells the parser where to find the rest of the definition. In our first example, our Document Type Declaration was simple.

```
<!DOCTYPE name [...]>
```

The basic structure of the Document Type Declaration will always begin in the same way, with `<!DOCTYPE`. There must be some whitespace following the word `DOCTYPE` as there is after all element names. Also, whitespace is not allowed to appear in between `DOCTYPE` and the opening "`<!`".

After the whitespace, the name of the XML document's root element must appear. It must appear *exactly* as it will in the document, including any namespace prefix. Because our document's root element is `<name>`, the word `name` follows the opening `<!DOCTYPE` in our declaration.

Remember, XML is case sensitive. Therefore, any time you see a name in XML, it is case sensitive. When we say the name must appear exactly as it will in the document, this includes character case. We will see this throughout our DTD; any reference to XML names implies case sensitivity.

Following the name of the root element, you have several options for specifying the rest of the Document Type Declaration. In our `<name>` example, our element declarations appeared between the `[` and `]` of our Document Type Declaration. When declarations appear between the `[` and `]`, as in our sample, they are called *internal subset declarations*. It is also possible to have some or all of your declarations in a separate document. DTD declarations that appear in external documents are *external subset declarations*. You can refer to an external DTD in one of the following two ways:

- System identifiers
- Public identifiers

System Identifiers

A *system identifier* allows you to specify the physical location of a file accessible by your 0system. It is comprised of two parts: the keyword `SYSTEM` and a URI reference to a document with a physical location.

```
<!DOCTYPE name SYSTEM "name.dtd" [...]>
```

This can be a file on your local hard drive, a file on your intranet or network, or even a file available on the Internet. You must type the word `SYSTEM` after the name of the root element in your declaration. Immediately following the `SYSTEM` keyword is the URI reference to the location of the file in quotation marks. Some valid system identifiers include the following:

```
<!DOCTYPE name SYSTEM "file:///c:/name.dtd" [...]>

<!DOCTYPE name SYSTEM "http://sernaferna.com/hr/name.dtd" [...]>

<!DOCTYPE name SYSTEM "name.dtd">
```

Notice that in the last example we have omitted the `[` and `]`. This is perfectly normal. Specifying an internal subset is optional. You can use an external and internal subset at the same time. We will look into this later in this chapter. If you do specify an internal subset, it will appear between the `[` and `]`, immediately following the system identifier.

When used in the Document Type Declaration, a system identifier allows you to refer to an external file containing DTD declarations. We will see how to use an external DTD in our next Try It Out but before we do, we'll look at public identifiers.

Public Identifiers

Public identifiers provide a second mechanism to locate DTD resources.

```
<!DOCTYPE name PUBLIC "-//Beginning XML//DTD Name Example//EN">
```

Much like the system identifier, the public identifier begins with a keyword `PUBLIC`, followed by a specialized identifier. However, instead of a reference to a file, public identifiers are used to identify an entry in a catalog. According to the XML specification, public identifiers can follow any format; however, a commonly used format is called *Formal Public Identifiers*, or *FPIs*. The syntax for a FPI is defined in the document ISO 9070. ISO 9070 also defines the process for registration and recording of formal public identifiers.

The International Organization for Standardization, or ISO, is a group that designs government approved standards. These standards are numbered and available from the ISO for a fee. Often, you can find interpretations of the standards in books or online. You can learn more about the ISO by going to their website at `http://www.iso.ch/`.

The syntax for FPIs matches the following basic structure:

```
-//Owner//Class Description//Language//Version
```

At the most basic level, public identifiers function similarly to namespace names. Public identifiers, however, cannot be used to combine two different vocabularies in the same document. Because of this, namespaces are much more powerful and are the preferred method.

Following the identifier string, we may include an optional system identifier as well. This allows the processor to find a copy of the document if it cannot resolve the public identifier (most processors cannot resolve public identifiers). When including the optional system identifier, the `SYSTEM` keyword we saw earlier is not required. A valid document type declaration that uses a public identifier might look like:

```
<!DOCTYPE name PUBLIC "-//Beginning XML//DTD Name Example//EN" "name.dtd">
```

To summarize, the preceding declaration assumes we are defining a document type for a document whose root element is `<name>`. The definition has the following public identifier:

```
-//Beginning XML//DTD Name Example//EN
```

In case this cannot be resolved, we have provided a relative URI to a file called `name.dtd`. In the preceding example, we haven't included an internal subset.

We have mentioned catalogs, registered, and unregistered public identifiers, but are these concepts commonly used in XML development? Yes. In fact, many web browsers, when identifying the versions of an XHTML document, utilize the public identifier mechanism. For example, many XHTML web pages will utilize the public identifier `-//W3C//DTD XHTML 1.0 Strict//EN` to identify the DTD associated with the document. When the web browser reads the file, it may use a built-in DTD that corresponds to the public identifier instead of downloading a copy from the Web. This allows web browsers to cache the DTD locally, reducing processing time. When you are developing your applications, you can use the same strategy. Using public identifiers simply gives you a way to identify a vocabulary, just as namespaces do.

Now that we have learned how to use public and system identifiers, let's try to create an external DTD file and associate it with our XML document. Remember, we said that we may have an internal subset, an external subset, or both. When using an internal subset, our DTD declarations will appear within our XML document. When using an external subset, our DTD declarations will appear in a separate external file.

Try It Out The External DTD

By utilizing an external DTD, we can easily share our vocabulary with others in our company, or even our own industry. Likewise, we can utilize vocabularies that others have already developed, by referring to external files they have created. Therefore, let's reconfigure our <name> example so that our DTD is defined external to our XML document.

1. We will begin by creating a new document to form our external DTD. Open Notepad and type in the following:

```
<!ELEMENT name (first, middle, last)>
<!ELEMENT first (#PCDATA)>
<!ELEMENT middle (#PCDATA)>
<!ELEMENT last (#PCDATA)>
```

   Save the file as `name4.dtd`. Save it in the same folder where you saved your `name3.xml` document.

2. Now let's reopen our `name3.xml` document. Modify it as follows:

```
<?xml version="1.0"?>
<!DOCTYPE name PUBLIC "-//Beginning XML//DTD Name Example//EN" "name4.dtd">
<name>
  <first>John</first>
  <middle>Fitzgerald Johansen</middle>
  <last>Doe</last>
</name>
```

   Make sure you have also changed the element <given> back to <first> after our last Try It Out. Save the modified file as `name4.xml`.

3. We are ready to validate our document again. Within the Topologi Schematron Validator, browse to the folder where you saved `name4.xml`. Select `name4.xml` and click the Run button.

You should see the output shown in Figure 4-6, which shows that our validation has been successful.

If you received any errors, check whether you have typed everything correctly and try again.

How It Works

In this Try It Out, we used an external DTD to check our XML content. As you may have guessed, the syntax for the DTD changed very little. The main difference between the internal DTD and external DTD was that there was no `DOCTYPE` declaration within the external DTD. The `DOCTYPE` declaration is always located within the main XML document. In addition, within our `name4.xml` document, there was no internal subset. Instead, we used a public identifier and system identifier to indicate which DTD our validation program should use.

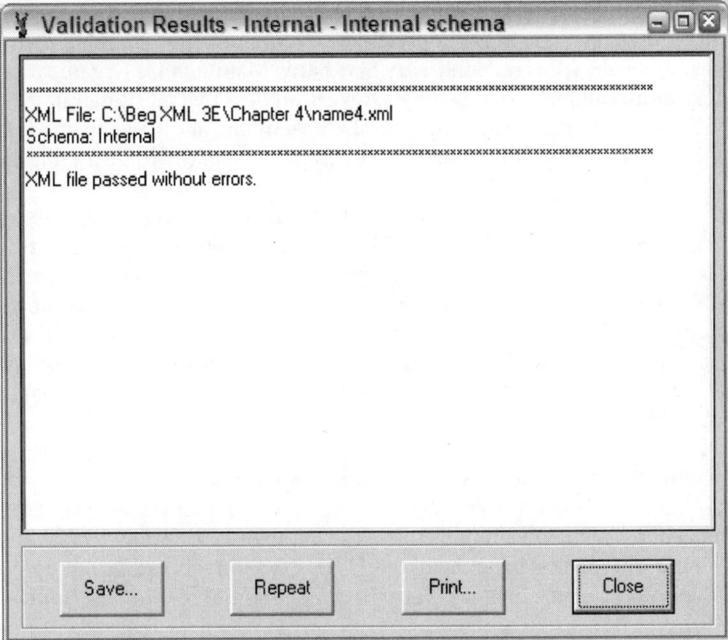

Figure 4-6

In this case, our validation program had no way to resolve public identifiers. The processor instead used the optional URI reference that we included to find the correct DTD for validation. In our example, the XML parser had to find the file identified as `name4.dtd`. Because this is a relative URL reference (it does not contain a website address or drive letter), the parser began looking in the current directory—where the XML document it was parsing was located. The XML Recommendation does not specify how parsers should handle relative URL references; however, most XML parsers will treat the path of the XML document as the base path, just as ours has done. It is important that you check your XML parser's documentation before you use relative URL references.

Using external DTDs can be very beneficial in many situations. For example, because the DTD appears in a single separate document it is easier to make changes. If the same DTD is repeated in each XML file, upgrading can be much more difficult. Later in the chapter, we will look at XML documents and DTDs that consist of many files using entities. You must remember, however, that looking up the DTD file will take extra processing time. In addition, if the DTD file is located on the Internet, you will have to wait for it to download. Often, it is better to keep a local copy of the DTD for validation purposes. If you are maintaining a local copy, you should check for changes to the DTD at the original location.

Sharing Vocabularies

In reality, most DTDs will be much more complex than our first example. Because of this, it is often better to share vocabularies and use DTDs that are widely accepted. Before you start creating your own DTDs, it is good to know where you can find existing ones. Sharing DTDs not only removes the burden of having to create the declarations, but it also allows you to more easily integrate with other companies and XML developers that use the shared vocabularies.

Many individuals and industries have developed DTDs that are de facto standards. Scientists use the Chemical Markup Language (CML) DTD to validate documents they share. In the mortgage industry, many businesses utilize the Mortgage Industry Standards Maintenance Organization's (MISMO) DTD when exchanging information. XHTML, the XML version of HTML 4.01, maintains three DTDs: Transitional, Strict, and Frameset. These three DTDs specify the allowed vocabulary for XHTML. Using these, browser developers can ensure that XHTML content is valid, before attempting to display it.

You can check several good places when trying to find a DTD for a specific industry. The first place to look is, of course, your favorite search engine. Most often, this will turn up good results. Another great place to check is the *Cover Pages*. *Cover Pages* is a priceless resource of XML information maintained by Robin Cover and can be found at `http://xml.coverpages.org/`. In addition, you might also want to check the Dublin Core Metadata Initiative, which is an online resource dedicated to creating interoperable standards. The address is `http://www.dublincore.org`. RosettaNet is a consortium of companies that are also working on developing e-business standards. You can learn more at `http://www.rosettanet.org`.

The xml-dev mailing list is another excellent resource. You can subscribe to the mailing list at `http://lists.xml.org/archives/`. Be warned, however, that the list is not for the faint of heart; hundreds of mails per week go through this list. The archives of xml-dev are full of announcements from companies and groups that have developed DTDs for widespread use. If you can't find a DTD for your application, create one. If you feel it may be useful to others in your industry, announce it on the list.

Anatomy of a DTD

Now that we have seen a DTD, let's look at each of the DTD declarations in more detail. DTDs consist of four basic parts:

- Element declarations
- Attribute declarations
- Notation declarations
- Entity declarations

To explore the more complex aspects of DTDs, we will need a more interesting example. Imagine that you are a famous paleontologist. You have been given the task of creating a list of all known dinosaurs, along with specific information about each dinosaur. You decide to use XML because of its natural structure and interoperability. Of course, you want your paleontologist colleagues to be able to add information about newly discovered dinosaurs to your list. To facilitate this you decide to create a DTD for your dinosaur vocabulary.

Just as you can create new dinosaurs by following their DNA, you can build new XML documents by simply following the instructions in the DTD. DTDs are the DNA of XML documents. Quite like a dinosaur's skeleton, the DTD structure allows us to build a complete example of a valid XML document.

We will begin creating our dinosaur vocabulary as we learn about each aspect of DTDs.

Element Declarations

Throughout the beginning of this chapter, we have seen element declarations in use, but have not yet looked at an element declaration in detail. When using a DTD to define the content of an XML document, you must declare each element that appears within the document. As we will soon see, DTDs can also include declarations for optional elements, elements that may or may not appear in the XML document.

```
<!ELEMENT dinosaurs (carnivore, herbivore, omnivore)>
```

Element declarations consist of three basic parts:

- The ELEMENT declaration
- The element name
- The element content model

As we have seen with the DOCTYPE declaration, the ELEMENT declaration is used to indicate to the parser that we are about to define an element. Much like the DOCTYPE declaration, the ELEMENT declaration begins with an exclamation mark. The declaration can appear only within the context of the DTD.

Immediately following the ELEMENT keyword is the name of the element that you are defining. Just as we saw in the DOCTYPE, the element name must appear exactly as it will within the XML document, including any namespace prefix.

The fact that you must specify the namespace prefix within DTDs is a major limitation. Essentially this means that the user is not able to choose his or her own namespace prefix but must use the prefix defined within the DTD. This limitation exists because the W3C completed the XML Recommendation before finalizing how namespaces would work. As we will see in the next chapter, XML Schemas are not limited in this way.

The content model of the element appears after the element name. An element's *content model* defines the allowable content within the element. An element may be empty, or it may contain text, element children, or a combination of children and text. This is essentially the crux of the DTD, where the entire document's structure is defined. As far as the XML Recommendation is concerned, four kinds of content models exist:

- Empty
- Element
- Mixed
- Any

Let's look at each of these content models in more detail.

Empty Content

If you remember, from Chapter 2 we learned that some elements may or may not have content:

```
<middle></middle>
<middle/>
```

The <middle> element, from Chapter 2, sometimes had content and sometimes was empty. Some elements within our XML documents may *never* need to contain content. In fact, in many cases it wouldn't make sense for an element to contain text or elements. Consider the <br/> tag in XHTML (it functions in the same way as a <br> tag within HTML). The <br/> tag allows you to insert a line break in a web page. It would not make much sense to include text within the <br/> element. Moreover, no elements would logically fit into a <br/> tag. This is a perfect candidate for an empty content model.

To define an element with an empty content model, simply include the word EMPTY following the element name in the declaration:

```
<!ELEMENT br EMPTY>
```

It is important to remember that this requires that the element be empty within the XML document. You should not declare elements that *may* contain content, using the EMPTY keyword. For example, the <middle> element may or may not contain other elements. As we will see, elements that are not declared with an empty content model may still be empty. Because the <middle> element may contain elements, we had to declare the element by using an element content model rather than the EMPTY keyword. Within our dinosaur list, we don't have any elements that will always be empty.

Element Content

As we have already seen, many elements in XML contain other elements. In fact, this is one of the primary reasons for creating XML. We have already seen an element declaration that has element content.

```
<!ELEMENT carnivore (species, length, height, speed, discoverer, location)>
```

In our dinosaur list, our <carnivore> element will have as its children a <species>, <length>, <height>, <weight>, <speed>, <discoverer>, and <location> element. When defining an element with element content you simply include the allowable elements within parentheses. Therefore, if our <carnivore> element was allowed to contain only a <species> element, our declaration would read:

```
<!ELEMENT carnivore (species)>
```

Each element that we specify as a child within our element's content must also be declared within the DTD. Therefore, in our preceding example, we would also need to define the <species> element later for our DTD to be complete. The processor needs this information so that it knows how to handle the <species> element when it is encountered. You may put the ELEMENT declarations in any order you like. As you may have guessed, the element name in our content model must appear exactly as it will in the document, including a namespace prefix, if any.

Of course, even in our small example at the start of the chapter our element had more than one child. This will often be the case. There are two fundamental ways of specifying the element children:

- ❑ Sequences
- ❑ Choices

Sequences

Often the elements within our documents must appear in distinct order. If this is the case, we define our content model using a *sequence*. When specifying a sequence of elements, we simply list the element names separated by commas. Again, this will be within the parentheses that immediately follow the name of the element we are declaring. All of our examples that had more than one element have used a sequence when declaring the content model:

```
<!ELEMENT name (first, middle, last)>
<!ELEMENT carnivore (species, length, height, weight, speed, discoverer,
location)>
```

In the preceding example, our declaration indicates that the `<name>` element must have exactly three children: `<first>`, `<middle>`, and `<last>` and that they must appear in this order. Likewise, the `<carnivore>` element must have exactly seven children in the order specified. Just as we saw with a single element content model, each of the elements that we specify in our sequence must also be declared in our DTD.

If our XML document were missing one of the elements within our sequence, or if our document contained more elements, the parser would raise an error. If all of the elements were included within our XML document, but appeared in another order such as `<last>`, `<middle>`, `<first>`, our processor would raise an error.

It is also important to note that in an element-only content model, whitespace doesn't matter. Therefore, using the above declaration, the allowable content for our `<dinosaur>` element might appear as follows:

```
<carnivore>
  <species>Tyrannosaurus Rex</species>
  <length>42 feet</length>
  <height>18 feet</height>
  <weight>5-7 tons</weight>
  <speed>25 mph</speed>
  <discoverer>
    <name>Osborn</name>
    <date>1905</date>
  </discoverer>
  <location>
    <country>Canada</country>
  </location>
</carnivore>
```

Because the whitespace within our element's content doesn't matter, we could also have the content appear as follows:

```
  <carnivore><species>Tyrannosaurus Rex</species><length>42 feet</length>
<height>18 feet</height><weight>5-7 tons</weight><speed>25
mph</speed><discoverer><name>Osborn</name><date>1905</date></discoverer>
<location><country>Canada</country></location></carnivore>
```

The spacing of the elements in an element-only content model is only for readability. It has no significance to the validation program.

Choices

Although we have used sequences throughout this chapter, in many circumstances a sequence doesn't allow us to model our element content. Suppose we needed to allow one element or another, but not both.

Obviously, we would need a choice mechanism of some sort. Consider our <location> element, where we specify where our dinosaur fossils were found:

```
<!ELEMENT location (country)>
```

Instead of requiring one element, we could require a choice between two elements:

```
<!ELEMENT location (GPS | country)>
```

This declaration would allow our <location> element to contain one <country> or one <GPS> element. If our <location> element were empty, or if it contained more than one of these elements, the parser would raise an error.

The choice content model is very similar to the sequence content model. Instead of separating the elements by commas, however, you must use the vertical bar (|) character. The vertical bar functions as an exclusive OR. An exclusive OR allows one and only one element out of the possible choices.

Combining Sequences and Choices

We have learned enough to create a DTD for the examples we have seen so far in this chapter. Many XML documents will need to leverage much more complex rules. In fact, using a simple choice or sequence might not allow us to model our document completely. Suppose we wanted to add a <region> element to our <location> content model. This would allow us to specify the country and region of the fossil find, which would be more exact.

When creating our <location> declaration, we would need to specify that the content can include either a <GPS> element *or* the <country> and <region> sequence of elements, but not both. The XML Recommendation allows us to mix sequences and choices. Because of this, we can declare our model as follows:

```
<!ELEMENT location (GPS | (country, region))>
```

As in our earlier examples, we have enclosed the entire content model within parentheses. In the preceding example, however, we have a second set of parentheses within the content model. It is good to think of this as a content model within a content model. The inner content model, in the preceding example, is a sequence specifying the elements <country> and <region>. The XML Recommendation allows us to have content models within content models within content models, and so on, infinitely.

The processor handles each inner content model much like a simple mathematical equation. Because the processor handles each model individually, it can treat each model as a separate entity. This allows us to use models in sequences and choices. In the preceding example, we had a choice between an element and a sequence content model. You could easily create a sequence of sequences, or a sequence of choices, or a choice of sequences—almost any other combination you can think of.

Mixed Content

The XML Recommendation specifies that any element with text in its content is a *mixed content model* element. Within mixed content models, text can appear by itself, or it can be interspersed between elements.

In everyday usage, people will refer to elements that can contain only text as text-only elements or text-only content.

The rules for mixed content models are similar to the element content model rules that we learned in the last section. We have already seen some examples of the simplest mixed content model—text only:

```
<!ELEMENT first (#PCDATA)>
```

In the preceding declaration we have specified the keyword `#PCDATA` within the parentheses of our content model. You may remember from Chapter 2 that `PCDATA` is an abbreviation for Parsed Character DATA. This keyword simply indicates that the parsed character data will be within our content model. An example element that adheres to this declaration might look like the following:

```
<first>John</first>
```

Mixed content models can also contain elements interspersed within the text. Suppose we wanted to include a description of our dinosaurs in our XML Document. We could create a new `<description>` element that allows us to create italic and bold sections:

```
<description>The Tyrannosaurus Rex was the <b>king</b> of the terrible
  lizards.Though many now believe it was a hunter <i>and</i> a scavenger it is
  no less fearsome.</description>
```

In this sample, we have a `<description>` element. Within the `<description>` element, we have interspersed the text with elements such as the `<i>` (indicating italic text) and the `<b>` (indicating a bold section of text).

> *If you are familiar with HTML (or XHTML) you may recognize the* `<i>` *and* `<b>` *elements. HTML frequently uses mixed content models to specify parts of the document.*

There is only one way to declare a mixed content model within DTDs. In the mixed content model, we must use the choice mechanism when adding elements. This means that each element within our content model must be separated by the vertical bar (|) character:

```
<!ELEMENT description (#PCDATA | i | b)*>
```

In the preceding sample, we have declared the new `<description>` element. Notice that we have used the choice mechanism to describe our content model; a vertical bar separates each element. We cannot use commas to separate the choices.

When including elements in the mixed content model, the `#PCDATA` keyword must always appear first in the list of choices. This allows validating parsers to immediately recognize that it is processing a mixed content model rather than an element content model. In contrast to element-only content models, we are not allowed to have inner content models in a mixed declaration.

You should also notice that we have included the `'*'` outside of the parentheses of our content model. When we are including elements within our mixed content model, we are required to include the `'*'` at the end of our content model, which tells the parser to repeat the content model. The `'*'` character is known as a *cardinality indicator*. We will learn more about cardinality indicators shortly.

Because we are using a repeated choice mechanism, we have no control over the order or number of elements within our mixed content. We can have an unlimited number of `<b>` elements, an unlimited number of `<i>` elements, and any amount of text. All of this can appear in any order within our `<description>` element. This is a major limitation of DTDs. In the next chapter, you will learn how XML Schema has improved validation of mixed content models.

To simplify, every time we declare elements within a mixed content model, they *must* follow four rules:

- They must use the choice mechanism (the vertical bar | character) to separate elements.
- The `#PCDATA` keyword must appear first in the list of elements.
- There must be no inner content models.
- If there are child elements the `'*'` cardinality indicator *must* appear at the end of the mode.

Any Content

Finally, we can declare our element utilizing the ANY keyword. The ANY keyword allows us to be even less restrictive about our content model. If we wanted, we could declare the `<description>` element using the ANY keyword.

```
<!ELEMENT description ANY>
```

In the preceding example, the ANY keyword indicates that any elements declared within the DTD can be used within the content of the `<description>` element and that they can be used in any order any number of times. The ANY keyword does not allow us to include in our XML document elements that are not declared within the DTD. In addition, any character data can appear within the `<description>` element. However, because DTDs are used to restrict content, the ANY keyword is not very popular because it does very little to restrict the allowed content of the element you are declaring.

Try It Out "When Dinosaurs Ruled the Earth"

You are probably ready to try to build a much more complex DTD with all of this newfound knowledge—you are also probably eager to see a more complete dinosaur example. In this Try It Out, we will start with the basics and add more features in following examples.

1. Open Notepad, or another text editor and input the following document:

```
<?xml version="1.0"?>
<!DOCTYPE dinosaurs PUBLIC "-//Beginning XML//DTD Dinosaurs Example//EN"
  "dinosaurs.dtd">
<dinosaurs>
  <carnivore>
    <species>Tyrannosaurus Rex</species>
    <length>42 feet</length>
    <height>18 feet</height>
    <weight>5-7 tons</weight>
    <speed>25 mph</speed>
    <weapon>
      <part-of-body>Teeth</part-of-body>
      <description>Though the Tyrannosaurus had many different sizes of teeth,
all were razor sharp and some grew to lengths of <b>9-13 inches</b>. Broken
teeth were replaced frequently by newer teeth. The powerful jaw exerted in
excess of 3000 pounds of pressure!</description>
    </weapon>
    <discoverer>
      <name>Osborn</name>
      <year>1905</year>
```

```
    </discoverer>
    <location>
      <country>Canada</country>
      <region>Alberta</region>
    </location>
    <description>The Tyrannosaurus Rex was the <b>king</b> of the terrible
lizards. Though many now believe it was a hunter <i>and</i> a scavenger it is
no less fearsome.</description>
  </carnivore>
  <herbivore>
    <species>Stegosaurus Armatus</species>
    <length>25-40 feet</length>
    <height>14 feet</height>
    <weight>2-4 tons</weight>
    <speed/>
    <weapon>
      <part-of-body>Spikes</part-of-body>
      <description>The Stegosaurus had two long rows of armor along its back.
At the end of its tail <b>four large spikes</b> were an excellent
defense.</description>
    </weapon>
    <discoverer>
      <name>Marsh</name>
      <year>1877</year>
    </discoverer>
    <location>
      <country>United States</country>
      <region>Colorado</region>
    </location>
    <description>The Stegosaurus Armatus was, perhaps, the most heavily
armored of all dinosaurs. It is very possible though that it was not very
smart, it's brain is believed to have been the <b>size of a walnut!
</b></description>
  </herbivore>
  <omnivore>
    <species>Gallimimus Bullatus</species>
    <length>18 feet</length>
    <height>8 feet</height>
    <weight>1000 pounds</weight>
    <speed>35-60 mph</speed>
    <weapon/>
    <discoverer>
      <name>Roniewicz</name>
      <year>1972</year>
    </discoverer>
    <location>
      <country>Mongolia</country>
      <region>Nemegtskaya Svita</region>
    </location>
    <description>The Gallimimus Bullatus, or <i>Chicken Mimic</i> was very
fast, perhaps even the fastest of all dinosaurs.</description>
  </omnivore>
</dinosaurs>
```

Save the file as dinosaurs.xml.

Notice that we have added a document type declaration that refers to an external system file called dinosaurs.dtd. Also, notice that the root element in our document and the element name within our declaration are the same.

2. Open a new file in Notepad and save it in the same folder where you have saved dinosaurs.xml. This file will be where we define our DTD in the same way we did earlier with dinosaurs.dtd.

3. Let's begin writing our DTD. Because we have a sample XML document, we can base most of our declarations on the text that we have. Many of us were taught that when programming we should plan and design first, and then implement. Building a DTD based on an existing sample, however, is by far the easiest method available. When designing a DTD, it is much easier to create a sample and let the document evolve before the vocabulary is set in stone. Of course, you must remember that some elements might not appear in your sample (such as some elements in choice content models).

   In our XML document, <dinosaurs> is the root element. This is the easiest place to start, so we will begin by declaring it in our DTD:

```
<!ELEMENT dinosaurs ()>
```

   We haven't specified a content model. Looking at our sample document, we can see that the <dinosaurs> element contains a <carnivore> element, followed by a <herbivore> element, and followed by an <omnivore> element. This looks just like an element sequence, so this content model should be easy to define:

```
<!ELEMENT dinosaurs (carnivore, herbivore, omnivore)>
```

   Specifying the kinds of dinosaurs as we have done is a little clumsy, especially because we don't know how many carnivores, how many herbivores, or how many omnivores to expect in our dinosaur list. For now, we are allowing only one of each type, but we'll improve this content model a little later.

4. Of course, because we have specified carnivore, herbivore, and omnivore in our content model, we know that we must declare it in our DTD. Let's start with carnivore:

```
<!ELEMENT carnivore (species, length, height, weight, speed, weapon,
  discoverer, location, description)>
```

   We also need to declare the <herbivore> and <omnivore> elements. These elements will have the same content model as our <carnivore> element.

```
<!ELEMENT herbivore (species, length, height, weight, speed, weapon,
  discoverer, location, description)>
<!ELEMENT omnivore (species, length, height, weight, speed, weapon,
  discoverer, location, description)>
```

5. Even though we have repeated the children elements within our <carnivore> content model, they are functioning the same. Because of this, we declare the children elements, such as the <species> element, only once. In fact, the XML Recommendation does not allow you to declare two elements with the same name inside a DTD.

   Let's declare each of these children elements within our DTD:

```
<!ELEMENT species (#PCDATA)>
<!ELEMENT length (#PCDATA)>
```

```
<!ELEMENT height (#PCDATA)>
<!ELEMENT weight (#PCDATA)>
<!ELEMENT speed (#PCDATA)>
```

The first five elements describe some of the physical characteristics of each dinosaur. They are all text-only elements, so we have declared that they can contain only `#PCDATA`. Remember that this qualifies as a mixed content model even though there are no element children.

6. Apart from the length, height, and weight, some dinosaurs had very powerful weapons for defending themselves, or for attacking other dinosaurs. Because of this, we want to include an element to describe the dinosaurs' weapons:

```
<!ELEMENT weapon (part-of-body, description)>
```

7. The `<weapon>` element contained two children that must also be declared in our DTD:

```
<!ELEMENT part-of-body (#PCDATA)>
<!ELEMENT description (#PCDATA | b | i)*>
```

We have decided to use a truly mixed content model for our description. This allows our XML document to contain a mix of text and elements but still allows the DTD to be restrictive about which child elements can be used.

Of course, we must include declarations for the `<b>` and `<i>` elements:

```
<!ELEMENT b (#PCDATA)>
<!ELEMENT i (#PCDATA)>
```

At this point, declaring the elements should begin to feel repetitive.

8. Our `<discoverer>` element contains two children elements:

```
<!ELEMENT discoverer (name, date)>
<!ELEMENT name (#PCDATA)>
<!ELEMENT date (#PCDATA)>
```

9. Finally, we must declare our `<location>` element. Remember that we wanted to include a choice in the declaration, allowing an option of describing the location by using GPS coordinates or by specifying a country and region. So, even though there is no `<GPS>` element in our sample document, we will include it in our DTD:

```
<!ELEMENT location (GPS | (country, region))>
<!ELEMENT GPS (#PCDATA)>
<!ELEMENT country (#PCDATA)>
<!ELEMENT region (#PCDATA)>
```

10. At this point we have completed the DTD. All of the children that were listed in content models now have their own element declarations. The final DTD should look like the following:

```
<!ELEMENT dinosaurs (carnivore, herbivore, omnivore)>
<!ELEMENT carnivore (species, length, height, weight, speed, weapon,
  discoverer, location, description)>
<!ELEMENT herbivore (species, length, height, weight, speed, weapon,
  discoverer, location, description)>
```

```
<!ELEMENT omnivore (species, length, height, weight, speed, weapon,
  discoverer, location, description)>

<!ELEMENT species (#PCDATA)>
<!ELEMENT length (#PCDATA)>
<!ELEMENT height (#PCDATA)>
<!ELEMENT weight (#PCDATA)>
<!ELEMENT speed (#PCDATA)>

<!ELEMENT weapon (part-of-body, description)>
<!ELEMENT part-of-body (#PCDATA)>
<!ELEMENT description (#PCDATA | b | i)*>
<!ELEMENT b (#PCDATA)>
<!ELEMENT i (#PCDATA)>

<!ELEMENT discoverer (name, year)>
<!ELEMENT name (#PCDATA)>
<!ELEMENT year (#PCDATA)>

<!ELEMENT location (GPS | (country, region))>
<!ELEMENT GPS (#PCDATA)>
<!ELEMENT country (#PCDATA)>
<!ELEMENT region (#PCDATA)>
```

Save the file as `dinosaurs.dtd`.

11. We are ready to validate our document again. Within the Topologi Schematron Validator, browse to the folder where you saved `dinosaurs.xml`. Select `dinosaurs.xml` and click the Run button. If you typed everything correctly, you should have received the error shown in Figure 4-7.

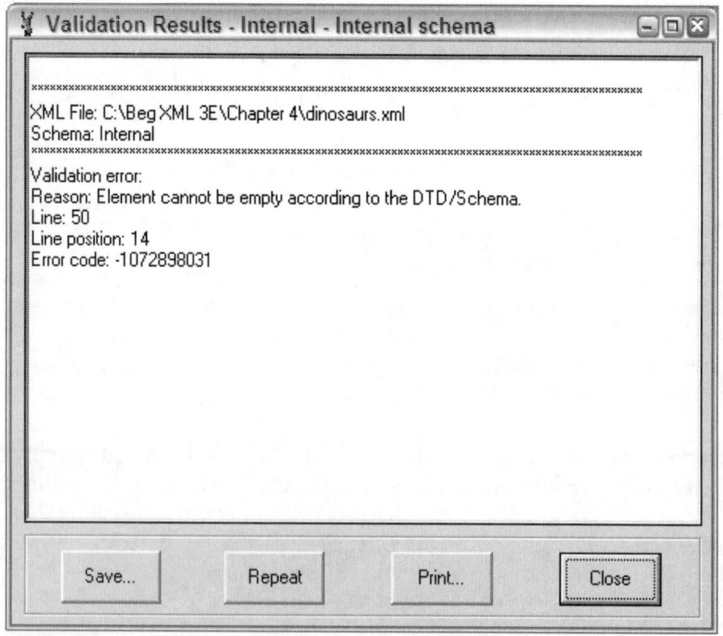

Figure 4-7

How it Works

Why did we get this error? Looking back at our XML document reveals the problem: in our <omnivore> element, our Gallimimus had no weapon. Because there was no weapon, we didn't include a <part-of-body> or <description> element. Our processor raised an error because it was expecting to see <part-of-body> and <description> elements. It expected to see these elements because we included them in the sequence content model in our weapon element declaration.

How can we fix the problem? Unfortunately, we can't yet. What we need is a way to tell the processor that the (part-of-body, description) sequence may appear once or not at all. We must learn how to tell the processor how many times the elements will appear.

Cardinality

An element's *cardinality* defines how many times it will appear within a content model. Each element within a content model can have an indicator of how many times it will appear following the element name. DTDs allow four indicators for cardinality:

Indicator	Description
[none]	As we have seen in all of our content models thus far, when no cardinality indicator is used, it indicates that the element must appear once and only once. This is the default behavior for elements used in content models.
?	Indicates that the element may appear either once or not at all.
+	Indicates that the element may appear one or more times.
*	Indicates that the element may appear zero or more times.

Let's look at these indicators in action:

```
<!ELEMENT weapon (part-of-body?, description?)>
```

Suppose we used cardinality indicators when declaring the content for our <weapon> element. By including a '?' when specifying our <part-of-body> and <description> elements, we inform the processor that these elements can appear once or not at all within our content model. If we were to validate the document again, the parser would not raise validity errors if the <part-of-body> element and <description> elements were missing. With our new declaration, the only allowable <weapon> elements include the following:

```
<weapon>
  <part-of-body>Any weapon...</part-of-body>
  <description>Any description...</description>
</weapon>
```

```
<weapon>
  <part-of-body>Any weapon...</part-of-body>
</parody>
```

```
<weapon>
  <description>Any description...</description>
</weapon>
```

```
<weapon></weapon>
```

In each of the preceding cases, we can see that the `<part-of-body>` element may or may not appear. In addition, the `<description>` element may or may not appear. In the final example, we see that the `<weapon>` element can be completely empty, with neither element appearing. An important point to remember is that because we used the '?' cardinality indicator, both the `<part-of-body>` and `<description>` elements can appear within our `<weapon>` element at the most once. Also notice that when both elements do appear, they must be in the order that we defined within our sequence.

> **Remember that the cardinality indicator affects only the content model where it appears. Even though we specify that the `<description>` element within the `<weapon>` content model can appear once or not at all, this does not affect the declaration of the `<description>` element, or any other use of the `<description>` element in our DTD. It helps to remember that when you use no cardinality indicator, it means that you are using the default (once and only once). The `<description>` element is used in four places within our DTD, but the only place where it may appear once or not at all is within our `<weapon>` content model.**

We could now get our example working by changing our content model as we have seen. Does the new model really represent what we wanted though? Of course, because it lets us have an empty `<weapon>` element and solves the problem at hand. In reality though, are there any circumstances where we would want to know only the part of the body or only the description of the weapon? Probably not. We need to define our content model so that we will get either both the `<part-of-body>` and `<description>` elements or none.

Luckily for us, the XML Recommendation allows us to apply cardinality indicators to content models as well. Remember, that earlier we said that a content model would appear within parentheses and that content models can contain inner content models. Because of this, we can change our `<weapon>` declaration one more time:

```
<!ELEMENT weapon (part-of-body, description)?>
```

The `?` indicator is functioning exactly as it did earlier. This time, however, we are indicating that the entire sequence may appear once or not at all. When we declare the `<weapon>` element using this new model, the only allowable `<weapon>` elements include the following:

```
<weapon>
  <part-of-body>Any weapon...</part-of-body>
  <description>Any description...</description>
</weapon>
```

```
<weapon></weapon>
```

This solves our problem completely, as it represents our desired content model perfectly. Before we go back to our example though, let's look at some other ways we could spruce up our dinosaur DTD.

While designing our dinosaur list, we cited only one discoverer of Gallimimus Bullatus. In fact, three discoverers were working together on a team. This inaccuracy was a major problem. Of course, in our DTD we were permitted to list only one name as discoverer. We can now fix this problem using a cardinality indicator.

Let's examine what it is that we want to accomplish. We know that every dinosaur we document will have at least one discoverer. We also know that each dinosaur might have more than one discoverer. We don't know how many discoverers each dinosaur will have. We need to use a cardinality indicator specifying that the `<name>` element can appear one or more times within our `<discoverer>` element. The '+' indicator does just that:

```
<!ELEMENT discoverer (name+, year)>
```

With the above declaration, we can document one or more discoverers for each dinosaur, which is exactly what we want to do.

Perhaps the largest deficiency remaining in our dinosaur DTD is that we can't list very many dinosaurs. Currently our DTD allows only one `<carnivore>` element, one `<herbivore>` element, and one `<omnivore>` element to appear as a child of the `<dinosaurs>` element. This won't let us get very far in documenting all known dinosaurs. We need to indicate that the elements can appear zero, one, or many times. Fortunately, the '*' cardinality indicator does just that. We could improve our DTD by changing our earlier `<dinosaur>` declaration:

```
<!ELEMENT dinosaurs (carnivore*, herbivore*, omnivore*)>
```

This might be good enough but it would be nice to have some more options for the order. With the preceding declaration we would have to list all of the carnivores, followed by all of the herbivores, and then all of the omnivores. We could use a choice content model instead:

```
<!ELEMENT dinosaurs (carnivore* | herbivore* | omnivore*)>
```

Unfortunately, this declaration gives us the choice of *one list of* `<carnivore>` or *one list of* `<herbivore>` or *one list of* `<omnivore>` elements within our list. Consider the following declaration:

```
<!ELEMENT dinosaurs (carnivore | herbivore | omnivore)*>
```

We have placed the '*' outside of the parentheses. This indicates that we want the entire content model to appear zero or more times. In this case, though, we have a choice content model. This means that we will have the choice between these three elements zero or more times. This definition allows us to have as many `<carnivore>`, `<herbivore>`, and `<omnivore>` elements as we want—and they can appear in any order.

How many dinosaurs are there? Actually, the number of "official" dinosaurs changes very often as new species of dinosaurs are discovered and as duplicate species are removed. At the time of this writing there are approximately 700 known species of dinosaurs.

Try It Out "When Dinosaurs Ruled the Earth"—Part 2

Now that we have learned how to correct and improve our DTD, let's get down to business and integrate the changes we have been going over.

1. Open the file dinosaurs.dtd and modify the highlighted sections:

```
<!ELEMENT dinosaurs (carnivore | herbivore | omnivore)*>
<!ELEMENT carnivore (species, length, height, weight, speed, weapon,
  discoverer, location, description)>
<!ELEMENT herbivore (species, length, height, weight, speed, weapon,
  discoverer, location, description)>
<!ELEMENT omnivore (species, length, height, weight, speed, weapon,
  discoverer, location, description)>

<!ELEMENT species (#PCDATA)>
<!ELEMENT length (#PCDATA)>
<!ELEMENT height (#PCDATA)>
<!ELEMENT weight (#PCDATA)>
<!ELEMENT speed (#PCDATA)>

<!ELEMENT weapon (part-of-body, description)?>
<!ELEMENT part-of-body (#PCDATA)>
<!ELEMENT description (#PCDATA | b | i)*>
<!ELEMENT b (#PCDATA)>
<!ELEMENT i (#PCDATA)>

<!ELEMENT discoverer (name+, year)>
<!ELEMENT name (#PCDATA)>
<!ELEMENT year (#PCDATA)>

<!ELEMENT location (GPS | (country, region))>
<!ELEMENT GPS (#PCDATA)>
<!ELEMENT country (#PCDATA)>
<!ELEMENT region (#PCDATA)>
```

Save the file as dinosaurs2.dtd.

2. Of course, now that we have created a new DTD file, we will need to update our XML document to refer to it. Open dinosaurs.xml and modify the DOCTYPE declaration so that it refers to our new DTD:

```
<!DOCTYPE dinosaurs PUBLIC "-//Beginning XML//DTD Dinosaurs Example//EN"
  "dinosaurs2.dtd">
```

We also need to list all of the discoverers of the Gallimimus Bullatus:

```
<omnivore>
  <species>Gallimimus Bullatus</species>
  <length>18 feet</length>
  <height>8 feet</height>
  <weight>1000 pounds</weight>
  <speed>35-60 mph</speed>
  <weapon/>
  <discoverer>
    <name>Osm&#x00F3;lska</name>
    <name>Roniewicz</name>
    <name>Barsbold</name>
    <year>1972</year>
```

```
    </discoverer>
    <location>
      <country>Mongolia</country>
      <region>Nemegtskaya Svita</region>
    </location>
    <description>The Gallimimus Bullatus, or <i>Chicken Mimic</i> was very fast,
perhaps even the fastest of all dinosaurs.</description>
  </omnivore>
```

Notice that the first name looks strange. We had to use a character entity reference to refer to *Osmólska* because of the *ó* character. We will look at character entities in much greater detail later in the chapter. For now, save the file as `dinosaurs2.xml`.

3. We are ready to validate our document again. Within the Topologi Schematron Validator, browse to the folder where you saved `dinosaurs2.xml`, select it, and click the Run button.

Your output should show a complete validation without errors. If you received any errors this time, check whether you have typed everything correctly and try again.

How It Works

This Try It Out implements much of what we learned throughout this section. To sum it up, we set out to design a DTD that described a list of all known dinosaurs. We used an assortment of complex content models so that our DTD would reflect various XML documents. Of course, when we first began designing our DTD, we didn't include many options (in fact, there were even a couple of errors). After we had the basic structure designed, we modified our DTD to correct some problems and to add some features. The design strategy is very common among XML developers.

> **Some XML designers have taken this design strategy a step further. Instead of relying only on an example XML document, they will use complex Unified Modeling Language (UML) diagrams or other types of visual aid. As we will see in the next chapter, new syntaxes have evolved based on this strategy of using an example document to describe the vocabulary. For instance, Examplotron uses a syntax in which the example essentially is the declaration. More information on Examplotron can be found at `http://examplotron.org/`.**

Now that we have a firm grasp on how to declare elements within our DTD, we will turn our attention to attributes.

Attribute Declarations

Attribute declarations are similar to element declarations in many ways. Instead of declaring content models for allowable elements, however, DTDs allow you to declare a list of allowable attributes for each element. These lists are called `ATTLIST` declarations.

```
<!ELEMENT dinosaurs (carnivore | herbivore | omnivore)*>
<!ATTLIST dinosaurs source CDATA #IMPLIED>
```

In the preceding example, we have the element declaration for our <dinosaurs> element from our dinosaur list example. Following the element declaration, we have an ATTLIST declaration that declares the allowable attributes of our <dinosaurs> element. This particular ATTLIST declares only one attribute, source, for the <dinosaurs> element.

An ATTLIST declaration consists of three basic parts:

- The ATTLIST keyword
- The associated element's name
- The list of declared attributes

Just as we have seen in all of our other declarations, the ATTLIST declaration begins with an exclamation mark to indicate that it is part of the DTD. Immediately following the ATTLIST keyword is the name of the associated element. In our example, the name of our associated element is dinosaurs. By specifying this, we indicated that we were building a list of attributes only for a <dinosaurs> element.

Following the ATTLIST name, we declared each attribute in the list. An ATTLIST declaration can include any number of attributes. Each attribute in the list consists of three parts:

- The attribute name
- The attribute type
- The attribute value declaration

Let's look at each section of the source attribute declaration:

```
source CDATA #IMPLIED
```

In the preceding declaration, the name of the attribute is source. We have declared that our source attribute can contain character data by using the CDATA keyword—this is our attribute's type. Finally, we have declared that our attribute has no default value, and further, that this attribute does not need to appear within our element using the #IMPLIED keyword. The third part of this attribute declaration is known as the *value declaration*; it controls how the XML parser will handle the attribute's value. We will look at value declaration options in more detail a little later.

Attribute Names

We learned in Chapter 2 that attribute names are very similar to element names. We must follow the basic XML naming rules when declaring an attribute. In addition to the basic naming rules, we must also make sure that we don't have duplicate names within our attribute list. Remember, duplicate attribute names are not allowed within a single element.

> **As far as DTDs are concerned, namespace declarations, such as xmlns:dino="http://sernaferna.com/dinosaurs", are also treated as any other attributes. Although the Namespace Recommendation treats xmlns attributes only as declarations, DTDs must declare them in an ATTLIST declaration if they are used. Again, this is because the W3C finalized the syntax for DTDs before the Namespace Recommendation was completed.**

To declare an attribute name, simply type the name exactly as it will appear in the XML document, including any namespace prefix.

Attribute Types

When declaring attributes, you can specify how the processor should handle the character data that appears in the value. So far, we haven't seen anything like this in DTDs. Within our element declarations, we could specify that an element contained text, but we couldn't specify how the processor should treat the text value. To solve this problem, several powerful new features are available using attributes.

Let's look at the different attribute types:

Type	Description
CDATA	Indicates that the attribute value is character data
ID	Indicates that the attribute value uniquely identifies the containing element
IDREF	Indicates that the attribute value is a reference, by ID, to a uniquely identifiable element
IDREFS	Indicates that the attribute value is a whitespace-separated list of IDREF values
ENTITY	Indicates that the attribute value is a reference to an external unparsed entity (we will learn more about entities later). The unparsed entity might be an image file or some other external resource such as an MP3 or some other binary file
ENTITIES	Indicates that the attribute value is a whitespace-separated list of ENTITY values
NMTOKEN	Indicates that the attribute value is a name token. An NMTOKEN is a string of character data consisting of standard name characters
NMTOKENS	Indicates that the attribute value is a whitespace-separated list of NMTOKEN values
Enumerated List	Apart from using the default types, you can also declare an enumerated list of possible values for the attribute

As we saw in our example, the attribute type immediately follows the attribute name. Let's look at each of these types in more detail.

CDATA

CDATA is the default attribute type. It specifies that the attribute value will be character data. A processor will do no additional type checking on a CDATA attribute, because it is the most basic of the data types. Of course, the XML well-formedness rules still apply, but as long as the content is well formed, a validating parser will accept any text as CDATA.

ID, IDREF, and IDREFS

Attributes of type ID can be used to uniquely identify an element within an XML document. Once we have uniquely identified the element, we can later use an IDREF to refer to that element. Identifying elements is paramount in many XML technologies, as we will soon see when we learn XPath in Chapter 7 and XSLT in Chapter 8. Many of you may have already seen an ID mechanism in action. Within HTML, many elements can be identified with an ID attribute. Often JavaScript code accesses the elements by their ID.

Remember several rules when using ID attributes:

- The value of an ID attribute must follow the rules for XML names.
- The value of an ID attribute must be unique within the entire XML document.
- Only one attribute of type ID may be declared per element.
- The attribute value declaration for an ID attribute must be #IMPLIED or #REQUIRED.

Suppose we added an ID attribute to our <carnivore> element:

```
<!ATTLIST carnivore kind ID #REQUIRED>
```

Then in our document we could add the unique ID:

```
<carnivore kind="Tyrannosaurus_Rex">
```

Is the value for the kind attribute valid? We have declared the kind attribute as an ID attribute. The first thing we can notice about our ID value is that there is an underscore (_) between "Tyrannosaurus" and "Rex". Remember that XML names cannot have spaces. If we had simply used the species name (with a space in between), it would have been an invalid ID because of this. Replacing each space in the value with an underscore makes the value legal.

Using the species name as the basis for our kind attribute ensures that each one is different. Remember that *any* attribute value of type ID must be unique—even if the attribute is part of an element with a different name (such as a kind attribute on a <herbivore> element). We haven't declared more than one ID attribute type in a single element. When we did declare our kind attribute, we chose to include the #REQUIRED keyword.

When we use IDREF attributes, the rules are similar:

- The value of an IDREF attribute must follow the rules for XML names.
- The value of an IDREF attribute must match the value of some ID within the XML document.

Often we need to refer to a list of elements. For example, imagine that we want to create a prey. attribute for our <carnivore> element. We might want to use an IDREFS attribute store with a list of whitespace-separated IDREF values that refer to the kind ID attributes defined for each of our dinosaurs.

ENTITY and ENTITIES

Attributes can also include references to *unparsed entities*. An unparsed entity is an entity reference to an external file that the processor cannot parse. For example, in external images are unparsed entities;

instead of actually including the image inside the document, we use special attributes to refer to the external resource. In XML we can declare *reusable* references inside our DTD using an `ENTITY` declaration. We haven't seen `ENTITY` declarations yet, so we will cover this in more detail a little later in this chapter.

For now, let's cover the rules for `ENTITY` attribute types. In `ENTITY` attributes, you must refer to an `ENTITY` that has been declared somewhere in the DTD. In addition, because you are referring to an `ENTITY`, the value must follow the rules for XML names. Consider the following attribute declaration:

```
<!ATTLIST weapon image ENTITY #IMPLIED>
```

After declaring an `image` attribute as we have done, we can then refer to an `ENTITY` within our XML document:

```
<weapon image="PictureOfTyrannosaurusTooth">
```

Our image attribute refers to an `ENTITY` that is named `PictureOfTyrannosaurusTooth`. This assumes that we have declared the `ENTITY` somewhere in our DTD. Also notice that our value follows the rules for XML names; it begins with a letter and contains valid name characters.

The `ENTITIES` attribute type is simply a whitespace-separated list of `ENTITY` values. Therefore, we could declare the following:

```
<!ATTLIST weapon images ENTITIES #IMPLIED>
```

A valid use of the above declaration might look like the following:

```
<weapon images="PictureOfTyrannosaurusTooth-Small
   PictureOfTyrannosaurusTooth-Large">
```

The `ENTITY` names are still valid (remember it is legal to use a dash in an XML name) and they are separated by whitespace. In fact, a line feed and several spaces appear between the two values. This is legal—the XML processor doesn't care *how much* whitespace separates two values. The processor considers any number of spaces, tabs, line feeds, and carriage return characters as whitespace.

NMTOKEN and NMTOKENS

Often we will need to have attributes that refer to a name or single word. This might be a reference to an element name, an entity name, an attribute name, or even a person's name. In fact, the value doesn't even have to be a real name. The `NMTOKEN` type allows us to create an attribute value that, as long as the value follows the rules for an XML name, the processor will treat as valid. You do not need to declare the name that an `NMTOKEN` attribute uses anywhere in the DTD; it only has to follow the rules for XML names.

When we learned the rules for XML names, we learned that our names are not allowed to begin with a numerical digit. `NMTOKEN` values are not required to adhere to this rule. An `NMTOKEN` value may begin with any name character, including numbers.

Suppose we added a `habitat` attribute to our `<carnivore>` element to allow us to specify what kind of environment our carnivore lived in:

```
<!ATTLIST carnivore habitat NMTOKEN #IMPLIED>
```

The following value would be allowable:

```
<carnivore habitat="forest">
```

As we have seen with other attribute types, NMTOKENS is simply a whitespace-separated list of NMTOKEN values. We could declare the habitat attribute to allow multiple habitat values as follows:

```
<!ATTLIST carnivore habitat NMTOKENS #IMPLIED>
```

The following value would be allowable:

```
<carnivore habitat="forest swamp jungle">
```

We haven't declared any of these values within our DTD; they simply follow the rules for NMTOKEN values.

Enumerated Attribute Types

Clearly, the ability to check types within attribute values is indispensable. Suppose we want to allow only a certain set of values in our attribute? We could use our existing types to restrict our attribute value, but it might not give us enough control. Suppose we want to add a period attribute. We could use this attribute to specify in which time period dinosaurs lived. We might expect to see the values Triassic, Jurassic, and Cretaceous. All of these values are character data, so we could use the CDATA type. Of course, if we did this, someone could also input the value 42, because it also is character data. This isn't what we want at all. Instead, we could use the NMTOKEN attribute type because all of our choices are valid NMTOKEN values. Of course, this would also allow values like Precambrian. We need to limit the values that are allowed for our attribute with even greater control.

An *enumerated list* allows us to do just that. When we declare our attribute, we can specify a list of allowable values. Again, the whitespace within the declaration does not matter. We can use as much or as little whitespace before and after each enumerated value as we want. Each value must be a valid XML name (except that it can start with any name character, including numeric digits). Because of this, the value itself cannot contain spaces. Let's see what a declaration for our period attribute would look like using an enumerated list:

```
<!ATTLIST carnivore period (Triassic | Jurassic | Cretaceous) #IMPLIED>
```

Here we see that we have listed out all our possible values within parentheses. All these possible values are separated by the vertical bar character (|). This declaration indicates that the value of our period attribute must match one (and only one) of the listed values. Each item in the list must be a valid NMTOKEN value. Remember the NMTOKEN type functions much like an XML name, but NMTOKEN values can begin with numerical digits.

Some *valid* uses of the new period attribute would be as follows:

```
<carnivore period="Jurassic">
```

or

```
<carnivore period="Triassic">
```

Some *invalid* values would be as follows:

```
<carnivore period="Precambrian">
```

or

```
<carnivore period="JURASSIC">
```

The first value is invalid because it attempts to use a value that is not in the list. The second value is not valid because although `Jurassic` appears in the list of allowed values, `JURASSIC` does not. Remember that because XML is case sensitive, the values in your list will be case sensitive as well.

Within the XML Recommendation, two kinds of enumerated attribute types exist. The first, as we have just seen, uses valid names for the list of possible values. The second uses valid `NOTATION` values for the list. Much like an `ENTITY`, a `NOTATION` must be declared within the DTD. `NOTATION` declarations are often used in conjunction with external files, as they are typically used to identify file types. We will look into `NOTATION` declarations at the end of this chapter. For now, just be aware that this type of declaration is allowed:

```
<!ATTLIST weapon image-format NOTATION (jpg | gif | bmp | png) #REQUIRED>
```

Again, we list the possible values within the parentheses. In a `NOTATION` enumeration though, simply insert the keyword `NOTATION` before the list of possible values. This indicates to the processor that it should check that each value within the list is a valid `NOTATION` that has been declared within the DTD. This example assumes that our DTD contains declarations for the four notation types `jpg`, `gif`, `bmp`, and `png`. By using a `NOTATION` enumeration, the parser can pass along additional information about the enumerated type. Again, we will see some of the benefits of using notations later in the chapter.

Attribute Value Declarations

Within each attribute declaration, you must also specify how the value will appear in the document. Often, we will want to provide a default value for our attribute declaration. At times, we might simply require that the attribute be specified in the document. Still other times, we might require that the value of the attribute be fixed at a given value. Each attribute can be declared with these properties.

The XML Recommendation allows us to specify that the attribute

- Has a default value
- Has a fixed value
- Is required
- Is implied

Default Values

Sometimes we need to provide a value for an attribute even if it hasn't been included in the XML document. By specifying a *default value* for our attributes, we can be sure that it is included in the final output. As the document is being processed, a validating parser automatically inserts the attribute with the default value if the attribute has been omitted. If the attribute has a default value but a value has also been included in the document, the parser uses the attribute included in the document rather than the default. Remember, only validating parsers make use of the information within the DTD, and therefore, the default value is used only by a validating parser. The ability to specify default values for attributes is one of the most valuable features within DTDs.

Specifying a default attribute is easy; simply include the value in quotation marks after the attribute type:

```
<!ATTLIST carnivore period (Triassic | Jurassic | Cretaceous) "Jurassic">
```

We have modified our period attribute so that it uses a default value. The default value we have selected is Jurassic. When a validating parser is reading our <carnivore> element, if the period attribute has been omitted, the parser will automatically insert the attribute period with the value Jurassic. If the parser does encounter a period attribute within the <carnivore> element, it will use the value that has been specified within the document.

When specifying a default value for your attribute declarations, you must be sure that the value you specify follows the rules for the attribute type that you have declared. For example, if your attribute type is NMTOKEN, then your default value must be a valid NMTOKEN. If your attribute type is CDATA, then your default value can be any well-formed XML character data.

You are not permitted to specify a default value for attributes of type ID. This might seem strange at first, but actually makes a good deal of sense. If a validating parser inserted the default value into more than one element, the ID would no longer be unique throughout the document. Remember, an ID value must be unique—if two elements had an ID attribute with the same value, the document would not be valid.

Fixed Values

In some circumstances, an attribute's value must always be fixed. When an attribute's value can never change, we use the #FIXED keyword followed by the *fixed value*. Fixed values operate much like default values. As the parser is validating the file, if the fixed attribute is encountered, then the parser checks whether the fixed value and attribute value match. If they do not match, the parser will raise a validity error. If the parser does not encounter the attribute within the element, it will insert the attribute with the fixed value.

A common use of fixed attributes is specifying version numbers. Often DTD authors will fix the version number for a specific DTD:

```
<!ATTLIST dinosaurs version CDATA #FIXED "1.0">
```

As with default values, when specifying values in fixed attribute declarations, you must be sure that the value you specify follows the rules for the attribute type you have declared. In addition, you might not specify a fixed value for an attribute of type ID.

Required Values

When you specify that an attribute is *required*, it must be included within the XML document. Often a document must have the attribute to function properly; at other times, it is simply a matter of exercising control over the document content. Suppose you require the period attribute:

```
<!ATTLIST carnivore period (Triassic | Jurassic | Cretaceous) #REQUIRED>
```

In the preceding example, we have specified that the period attribute must appear within every <carnivore> element in the document. If our parser encounters an <carnivore> element without a period attribute as it is processing the document, it raises an error.

To declare that an attribute is required, simply add the keyword `#REQUIRED` immediately after the attribute type. When declaring that an attribute is required, you are not permitted to specify a default value.

Implied Values

In most cases the attribute you are declaring won't be required and often won't even have a default or fixed value. In these circumstances, the attribute might or might not occur within the element. These attributes are called *implied attributes*, because sometimes no explicit value is available. When the attributes do occur within the element, a validating parser simply checks whether the value specified within the XML document follows the rules for the declared attribute type. If the value does not follow the rules, the parser raises a validity error.

When declaring an attribute, you must always specify a value declaration. If the attribute you are declaring has no default value, has no fixed value, and is not required, then you must declare that the attribute is *implied*. You can declare that an attribute is implied by simply adding the keyword `#IMPLIED` after the attribute's type declaration:

```
<!ATTLIST weapon image-format NOTATION (jpg | gif | bmp | png) #IMPLIED>
```

Specifying Multiple Attributes

So far, our `ATTLIST` declarations have been limited. In each of the preceding examples, we have declared only a single attribute. This is good, but many elements need more than one attribute. No problem—the `ATTLIST` declaration allows you to declare more than one attribute. For example:

```
<!ATTLIST dinosaurs version CDATA #FIXED "1.0"
                    source CDATA #IMPLIED>
```

In the preceding `ATTLIST` declaration for our `<dinosaurs>` element, we have included a `version` and a `source` attribute. Our `version` attribute is a fixed character data attribute; our `source` attribute is also a character data attribute but is optional. When declaring multiple attributes, as we have in this example, simply use whitespace to separate the two declarations. In this example, we have used a line feed and have aligned the attribute declarations with some extra spaces. This type of formatting is common when declaring multiple attributes. In addition to being able to declare more than one attribute within an `ATTLIST` declaration, you are also permitted to declare more than one `ATTLIST` for each `ELEMENT` declaration.

```
<!ATTLIST dinosaurs version CDATA #FIXED "1.0">
<!ATTLIST dinosaurs source CDATA #IMPLIED>
```

Either style for declaring multiple attributes is legal.

Try It Out "When Dinosaurs Ruled the Earth"—Part 3

Now that we have seen some common attribute declarations, let's revisit our dinosaur list example and add some improvements. As we can now declare attributes, we'll include several that can be used within our list. We will add a `version` attribute, a `source` attribute, a `kind` attribute, a `habitat` attribute, and a `period` attribute.

1. Let's begin by opening our `dinosaurs2.xml` file. We will modify our `DOCTYPE` declaration again, add some attributes, and then save the file as `dinosaurs3.xml`:

```
<?xml version="1.0"?>
<!DOCTYPE dinosaurs PUBLIC "-//Beginning XML//DTD Dinosaurs Example//EN"
 "dinosaurs3.dtd">
<dinosaurs version="1.0" source="Beginning XML 3E">
  <carnivore kind="Tyrannosaurus_Rex" habitat="forest swamp jungle">
    <species>Tyrannosaurus Rex</species>
    <length>42 feet</length>
    <height>18 feet</height>
    <weight>5-7 tons</weight>
    <speed>25 mph</speed>
    <weapon>
      <part-of-body>Teeth</part-of-body>
      <description>Though the Tyrannosaurus had many different sizes of teeth,
all were razor sharp and some grew to lengths of <b>9-13 inches</b>. Broken
teeth were replaced frequently by newer teeth. The powerful jaw exerted in
excess of 3000 pounds of pressure!</description>
    </weapon>
    <discoverer>
      <name>Osborn</name>
      <year>1905</year>
    </discoverer>
    <location>
      <country>Canada</country>
      <region>Alberta</region>
    </location>
    <description>The Tyrannosaurus Rex was the <b>king</b> of the terrible
lizards. Though many now believe it was a hunter <i>and</i> a scavenger it is
no less fearsome.</description>
  </carnivore>
  <herbivore kind="Stegosaurus_Armatus" habitat="forest swamp"
   period="Jurassic">
    <species>Stegosaurus Armatus</species>
    <length>25-40 feet</length>
    <height>14 feet</height>
    <weight>2-4 tons</weight>
    <speed/>
    <weapon>
      <part-of-body>Spikes</part-of-body>
      <description>The Stegosaurus had two long rows of armor along its back.
At the end of its tail <b>four large spikes</b> were an excellent
defense.</description>
    </weapon>
    <discoverer>
      <name>Marsh</name>
      <year>1877</year>
    </discoverer>
    <location>
      <country>United States</country>
      <region>Colorado</region>
    </location>
    <description>The Stegosaurus Armatus was, perhaps, the most heavily
armored of all dinosaurs. It is very possible though that it was not very
```

```
smart, it's  brain is believed to have been the <b>size of a
walnut!</b></description>
  </herbivore>
  <omnivore kind="Gallimimus_Bullatus" habitat="lakeshore prairie">
    <species>Gallimimus Bullatus</species>
    <length>18 feet</length>
    <height>8 feet</height>
    <weight>1000 pounds</weight>
    <speed>35-60 mph</speed>
    <weapon/>
    <discoverer>
      <name>Osm&#x00F3;lska</name>
      <name>Roniewicz</name>
      <name>Barsbold</name>
      <year>1972</year>
    </discoverer>
    <location>
      <country>Mongolia</country>
      <region>Nemegtskaya Svita</region>

    </location>
    <description>The Gallimimus Bullatus, or <i>Chicken Mimic</i> was very
fast, perhaps even the fastest of all dinosaurs.</description>
  </omnivore>
</dinosaurs>
```

2. Now that we have modified our XML document, let's declare these new attributes within our DTD. Open `dinosaurs2.dtd`, make the following modifications, and save the file as `dinosaurs3.dtd`:

```
<!ELEMENT dinosaurs (carnivore | herbivore | omnivore)*>
<!ATTLIST dinosaurs version CDATA #FIXED "1.0"
                    source CDATA #IMPLIED>

<!ELEMENT carnivore (species, length, height, weight, speed, weapon,
discoverer, location, description)>
<!ATTLIST carnivore kind ID #REQUIRED
                    habitat NMTOKENS #REQUIRED
                    period (Triassic | Jurassic | Cretaceous) "Cretaceous">

<!ELEMENT herbivore (species, length, height, weight, speed, weapon,
discoverer, location, description)>
<!ATTLIST herbivore kind ID #REQUIRED
                    habitat NMTOKENS #REQUIRED
                    period (Triassic | Jurassic | Cretaceous) "Cretaceous">

<!ELEMENT omnivore (species, length, height, weight, speed, weapon,
discoverer, location, description)>
<!ATTLIST omnivore kind ID #REQUIRED
                   habitat NMTOKENS #REQUIRED
                   period (Triassic | Jurassic | Cretaceous) "Cretaceous">

<!ELEMENT species (#PCDATA)>
<!ELEMENT length (#PCDATA)>
```

```
<!ELEMENT height (#PCDATA)>
<!ELEMENT weight (#PCDATA)>
<!ELEMENT speed (#PCDATA)>

<!ELEMENT weapon (part-of-body, description)?>
<!ATTLIST weapon images ENTITIES #IMPLIED>

<!ELEMENT part-of-body (#PCDATA)>
<!ELEMENT description (#PCDATA | b | i)*>
<!ELEMENT b (#PCDATA)>
<!ELEMENT i (#PCDATA)>

<!ELEMENT discoverer (name+, year)>
<!ELEMENT name (#PCDATA)>
<!ELEMENT year (#PCDATA)>

<!ELEMENT location (GPS | (country, region))>
<!ELEMENT GPS (#PCDATA)>
<!ELEMENT country (#PCDATA)>
<!ELEMENT region (#PCDATA)>
```

3. We are ready to validate our document again. Within the Topologi Schematron Validator, browse to the folder where you saved `dinosaurs3.xml`, select it, and click the Run button.

Your output should show a complete validation without errors. If you received any errors this time, check whether you have typed everything correctly and try again.

How It Works

In this Try It Out example, we added several `ATTLIST` declarations to our DTD. We added the attributes `version` and `source` to our `<dinosaurs>` element. We could use the `version` attribute to indicate to an application what version of the DTD this dinosaur list matches. Using the `source` attribute, we can provide a friendly description of who provided the information.

We also added attributes for the kind of dinosaur its habitat and the period it lived in. Notice that we had to declare the `ATTLIST` for these attributes separately for the `<carnivore>`, the `<herbivore>`, and the `<omnivore>` element.

The `kind` attribute allowed us to specify a unique name for each dinosaur. We created this name by simply using the species name and replacing all the whitespace with underscores (so that it was a valid XML name). The `habitat` attribute allowed us to list the types of environments in which each dinosaur lived.

We also added a `period` attribute that provided a list of possible time periods for each dinosaur. Because there were only three choices for the value of the `period` attribute, we decided to use an enumerated list. We also set the default value to `Cretaceous` because many of the dinosaurs we listed were from that period and we didn't want to type it repeatedly. You should notice that we didn't include the `period` attribute when describing our Tyrannosaurus Rex. Because we have omitted the `period` attribute, a processor, as it is parsing our document, will automatically insert the attribute with the default value. When we described our Stegosaurus Armatus, however, we needed to include the `period` attribute because it lived in the Jurassic period, and the default value was `Cretaceous`. It is also important to notice that, even when an attribute is defaulted to a specific value in the DTD, it is still allowable to have that same value appear in the XML document as we have done with the description of the Gallimimus Bullatus.

Finally, we added an `images` attribute to our <weapon> element. The `images` attribute was designed to be type `ENTITIES`. We haven't learned how to declare `ENTITIES` yet, so we didn't use these attributes in our `dinosaurs3.xml` document. For this reason, we declared that the `images` attribute is implied, as it may or may not appear within our document.

Entities

In Chapter 2, we learned that we could escape characters or use entity references to include special characters within our XML document. We learned that five *entities* are built into XML that allow us to include characters that have special meaning in XML documents. In addition to these built-in entities, we also learned that we could utilize character references to include characters that are difficult to type, such as the © character:

```
<dinosaurs version='1.0' source='Beginning XML 3E&apos;s Dinosaur List'>
<copyright>&#169; 2004 Wiley Publishing</copyright>
```

In our first example, we have included an `'` entity reference within our attribute content. This allows us to include a `'` character without our XML parser treating it as the end of the attribute value. In our second example, we have included an `©` character reference within our element content. This allows us to include the © character by specifying the character's Unicode value.

In fact, entities are not limited to simple character references within our XML documents. Entities can be used throughout the XML document to refer to sections of replacement text, other XML markup, and even external files. We can separate entities into four primary types, each of which may be used within an XML document:

- Built-in entities
- Character entities
- General entities
- Parameter entities

Let's look at each of these in more detail.

In fact, technically, each part of an XML document is an entity. For example, the root element within an XML document is called the document entity, the DTD is another entity, and so on. Of course, you cannot use these entities as you can use the four entity types we have listed; their usefulness is, therefore, limited.

Built-In Entities

We have already seen that there are five entities that can be used within an XML document by default.

- `&`—the & character
- `<`—the < character
- `>`—the > character

- `'`—the ' character
- `"`—the " character

These five entities are often called *built-in entities*, because, according to the XML Recommendation, all XML parsers must support the use of these five entities by default. You are not required to create declarations for them in the DTD. We will soon see that there are other kinds of entities that are required to be declared first within the DTD, before they are used within the document.

References to Built-In Entities

To use an entity, we must include an entity reference within our document. An *entity reference*, as the name implies, *refers* to an entity that represents a character, some text, or even an external file. A reference to a built-in entity follows the following pattern:

```
&apos;
```

The reference begins with the ampersand (`&`) character. Immediately following the ampersand is the name of the entity to which we are referring, in this case `apos`. At the end of the reference is a semicolon (`;`). Whitespace is not allowed anywhere within the reference.

In general, you can use entity references anywhere you could use normal text within the XML document. For example, you can include entity references within element contents and attribute values. You can also use entity references within your DTD within text values, such as default attribute values. Although the built-in entities allow you to include characters that are used in markup, they cannot be used in place of XML markup. For example, the following is *legal*:

```
<part-of-body>Teeth &amp; Jaw</part-of-body>
```

Here, we use the `&` built-in entity so that we can include an ampersand "`&`" in the content of our `<part-of-body>` element. This is allowed because it is within the element's text content. On the other hand, the following would be *illegal*:

```
<dinosaurs version=&quot;1.0&quot;>
```

In this example, the `"` entity is used in place of actual quotation marks. As an XML parser processes the element, it would encounter the "`&`" after the "=" and immediately raise a well-formedness error. The XML within the document is first checked for well-formedness errors, *and then* entity references are resolved. Many XML parsers will check the well-formedness of a specific section of an XML document and then begin replacing entities within that section. This can be very useful in large documents. You should consult your XML parser's documentation for more information. Also note that you cannot use entities within the names of elements or attributes.

Character Entities

Character entities, much like the five built-in entities, are not declared within the DTD. Instead, they can be used in the document within element and attribute content without any declaration. References to character entities are often used for characters that are difficult to type, or for non-ASCII characters.

References to Character Entities

Again, to utilize a character entity within your document, you must include an entity reference. The syntax for character entity references is very similar to syntaxes for the five built-in entities. In fact, we have already used a character entity reference to include the ó character in the discoverer name *Osmólska*. Consider the following character entity reference:

```
&#243;
```

As you can see from the example, the primary difference in character entity references is that there is no entity name. The reference begins with the ampersand (&) character. However, instead of an entity name, we have a hash mark (#) followed by a number, in this case 243, which is the Unicode value for the ó character. At the end of the reference is a semicolon (;). Just as we saw in our references to built-in entities, whitespace is not allowed anywhere within the character entity reference.

You can also refer to a character entity by utilizing the hexadecimal Unicode value for the character:

```
&#x00F3;
```

Here, we have used the hexadecimal value 00F3 in place of the decimal value 243. When the value you are specifying is hexadecimal, you must include a lowercase x before the value, so that the XML parser knows how it should handle the reference. In fact, it is much more common to utilize the hexadecimal form because the Unicode specification lists characters using hexadecimal values.

Where do you find the hexadecimal values for characters? The best place to start is the Unicode technical reports found at `http://www.unicode.org/charts`. *For example, the character ó that we used in our document can be found in the document* `http://www.unicode.org/charts/PDF/U0080.pdf`.

Just as we saw with built-in entity references, character entity references can be used anywhere you could use normal text, such as element content and attribute values. You can also use them within your DTD. Like the built-in entities, you cannot use character entities in place of actual XML markup or as part of the names of elements or attributes.

Does this mean that by using character references you can include any Unicode character in your XML document? Not exactly. Actually, you are permitted to include only those characters that are specified within the XML Recommendation, which was based on Unicode 3.0. As the Unicode specification has evolved, the need to utilize more characters in XML has also grown. A new version of XML, version 1.1, that will allow you to use any Unicode character that has not been forbidden is currently under development. This is why it is important that you include the XML version in the header at the start of your documents—to ensure that they are backwards compatible. The current list of allowable XML 1.0 characters can be found in the XML Recommendation at `http://www.w3.org/TR/REC-xml/#NT-Char` and `http://www.w3.org/TR/REC-xml/#CharClasses`. If an XML parser encounters a character (or character entity reference) that is not allowed, the parser should immediately raise a fatal error. Illegal characters are considered well-formedness errors.

General Entities

General entities function very similar to the five built-in entities; however, general entities must be declared within the DTD before they can be used within the XML document. Most commonly, XML developers use *general entities* to create reusable sections of *replacement text*. Instead of representing only a single character, general entities can represent characters, paragraphs, and even entire documents. Throughout this section, we learn the many uses of general entities.

You can declare general entities within the DTD in two ways. You can specify the value of the entity directly in the declaration, or you can refer to an external file. Let's begin by looking at an *internal entity declaration*:

```
<!ENTITY source-text "The source of this dinosaur list is Beginning XML 3E">
```

Just as we have seen with our earlier ELEMENT and ATTLIST declarations, the ENTITY declaration begins with an exclamation mark. Following the ENTITY keyword is the name of the entity, in this case source-text. We use this name when referring to the entity elsewhere in the XML document. The name must follow the rules for XML names, just as we have seen throughout this chapter. After the entity name, in the preceding declaration, is a line of replacement text. Whenever an XML parser encounters a reference to this entity, it substitutes the replacement text at the point of the reference. This example is an internal entity declaration because the replacement text appears directly within the declaration in the DTD.

In the preceding example, our replacement text value is The source of this dinosaur list is Beginning XML 3E. General entity values are not limited to simple characters or text values, however. Within a general entity, the replacement text can consist of any well-formed XML content. The only exception to this rule is that you are not required to have one root element within the replacement text. All of the following are examples of *legal* general entity values:

```
<!ENTITY speed-not-known "The speed for this dinosaur is & quot;Unknown& quot;">
<!ENTITY weapon-not-known "<weapon></weapon>">
<!ENTITY weapon-horns "<weapon>
                        <part-of-body>horns</part-of-body>
                        <description>Many dinosaurs had horns, they belong to
                        a special group called <i>Ceratopia</i></description>
                        </weapon>">
```

Notice that we have included entity references within our replacement text. Just as we said, entity references can be used within your DTDs in place of normal text (default attribute values and entity replacement text values). Also, notice that our values might or might not have a root element, or might have no elements at all. Although we have included entity references within our replacement text, we should note that an entity is not permitted to contain a reference to itself either directly or indirectly. The following declarations are *not legal*:

```
<!ENTITY weapon-start "<weapon>">
<!ENTITY weapon-end "</weapon>">
<!ENTITY speed-not-known "The speed for this dinosaur is &speed-not-known;">
```

The first two examples are not legal because they are not well formed. In the first declaration, we have specified the start of a <weapon> element but have not included the closing tag. In the second declaration, we have only the closing tag of a <weapon> element. You are not permitted to begin an element in one entity and end it in another—each entity must be well formed on its own. The third entity contains a reference to itself within its replacement text. When an entity refers to itself, it is known as a *recursive entity reference*.

Because there are no limits on the length of replacement text, your DTD can quickly become cluttered by sections of replacement text, making it more difficult to read. You might want to store your replacement text in an external file instead of including it within the DTD. This can be very useful when you have a large section of replacement text. When declaring your entities, instead of declaring the replacement text internally you can refer to external files. When the replacement text for an entity is stored externally, the entity is declared using an *external entity declaration*. For example, we could declare our entities as follows:

```
<!ENTITY tyrannosaurus SYSTEM "tyrannosaurus.txt">
```

or

```
<!ENTITY tyrannosaurus PUBLIC
  "-//Beginning XML//Tyrannosaurus textual description//EN" "tyrannosaurus
.txt">
```

Just as we saw with our Document Type Declaration, when referring to external files, we can use a system identifier or a public identifier. When we use a public identifier, we can also include an optional URI reference, which we have done in our example. In each of these declarations, we have referred to an external file named `tyrannosaurus.txt`. As an XML parser is processing the DTD, if it encounters an external entity declaration it *might* open the external file and parse it. If the XML parser is a validating parser it *must* open the external file, parse it, and be able to utilize the content when it is referenced. If the XML parser is not a validating parser then it might or might not attempt to parse the external file.

> **The XML Recommendation makes the distinction between validating and nonvalidating parsers primarily to make it easier to create XML parsers that conform to the XML specification. Many XML parsers don't include the ability to validate a document against a DTD because of the additional processing or programming time it requires. Many of these same parsers include the ability to use external entities, however, because of the added functionality. If you are using a nonvalidating parser, you should check the documentation to see if it can parse external entities.**

Remember, just as we saw with our internal entity declaration, the replacement text must be a well-formed XML (with the exception of requiring a single root element). If the parser encounters a well-formedness error within the external file, it will raise the error and discontinue parsing.

Sometimes, you need to refer to an external file that you do not want the XML parser to parse. For example, if the external file you are referring to is a binary file, such as an image or an MP3, the parser will surely raise an error when it attempts to parse it. You can indicate that an external entity declaration should not be parsed, by including the `NDATA` keyword and notation type at the end of the declaration:

```
<!ENTITY PictureOfTyrannosaurusTooth SYSTEM
  "http://www.destinationeducation.com/images/dinosaurs/image_longtrextooth
   .jpg"
  NDATA jpg>
<!ENTITY PictureOfTyrannosaurusTooth PUBLIC
  "-//Beginning XML//Tyrannosaurus tooth image//EN"
  "http://www.destinationeducation.com/images/dinosaurs/image_longtrextooth
   .jpg"
  NDATA jpg>
```

Notice that within the preceding ENTITY declarations we have again used the external entity declaration form by including either a system or a public identifier. In addition, we have included the keyword NDATA and the notation type jpg. The keyword NDATA is an abbreviation for notation data. It is used to indicate that the entity will not be parsed; instead, the entity is simply used to provide a reference, or *notation*, to the external file. Following the NDATA keyword was the notation type jpg. The notation type is used to indicate the kind of file we are referring to. The type must be declared within the DTD using a NOTATION declaration, which we will learn about in detail later in this chapter.

References to General Entities

Now that we have seen how to declare entities within our DTD, let's look at how to refer to them within our document:

```
&tyrannosaurus;
```

The entity reference looks very similar to the built-in entity references we learned about earlier. Again, the reference begins with the ampersand (&) character. Immediately following the ampersand is the name of the entity to which we are referring, in this case tyrannosaurus. At the end of the reference is a semicolon (;). Whitespace is not allowed anywhere within the reference, but hyphens (-) and underscores (_) are. You can refer to any general entity that you have declared within your DTD, as we have in the preceding example. When the parser encounters the reference, it will include the replacement text that is declared within the DTD or the external file to which the entity declaration refers.

The only exception to this rule is that you cannot create an entity reference to an unparsed external entity, such as an image or MP3 file. Obviously, if the external data is not parsed, it cannot be used as replacement text within the XML document.

Now that we have seen the basics of how to declare and refer to general entities, let's look at an example that uses them.

Try It Out "When Dinosaurs Ruled the Earth"—Part 4

Let's rework our dinosaur example so that each of our dinosaur descriptions can be stored in external files. In our example, we'll create text files for our descriptions and save them in the same folder as our XML document.

1. Let's begin by creating an external file for the Tyrannosaurus Rex description. Type in the following file, and save it as tyrannosaurus.txt:

```
The Tyrannosaurus Rex was the king of the terrible lizards. Though many now
believe it was a hunter and a scavenger it is no less fearsome.
```

2. Next we'll create a description file for the Stegosaurus Armatus. Instead of using plain text, we will mix in some XML elements. Type in the following file, and save it as stegosaurus.txt:

```
The Stegosaurus Armatus was, perhaps, the most <i>heavily armored</i> of all
dinosaurs. It is very possible though that it was not very smart, it's brain
is believed to have been the <b>size of a walnut!</b>
```

3. Finally, let's create a description file for the Gallimimus Bullatus. This time, we'll create a complete XML file, including the <description> element. Type in the following file, and save it as gallimimus.xml:

```
<description>The Gallimimus Bullatus, or <i>Chicken Mimic</i> was very fast,
perhaps even the fastest of all dinosaurs.</description>
```

4. We'll also need to declare the new entities within our DTD. Open dinosaurs3.dtd and add the following declarations to the end of the file. Save the file as dinosaurs4.dtd:

```
<!ENTITY speed-not-known "The speed for this dinosaur is &quot;Unknown&quot;">

<!ENTITY tyrannosaurus PUBLIC
  "-//Beginning XML//Tyrannosaurus textual description//EN"
   "tyrannosaurus.txt">
<!ENTITY stegosaurus PUBLIC
  "-//Beginning XML//Stegosaurus textual description//EN" "stegosaurus.txt">
<!ENTITY gallimimus PUBLIC
  "-//Beginning XML//Gallimimus textual description//EN" "gallimimus.xml">
```

Notice that we also added in a general entity that can be used when the speed of the dinosaur, such as the Stegosaurus, is not known.

5. Next, open dinosaurs3.xml from our last example. We will utilize the references to our newly defined entities. We will also need to change our Document Type Declaration to refer to our new DTD. Once you have completed these modifications, save the file as dinosaurs4.xml:

```
<?xml version="1.0"?>
<!DOCTYPE dinosaurs PUBLIC "-//Beginning XML//DTD Dinosaurs Example//EN"
  "dinosaurs4.dtd">
<dinosaurs version="1.0" source="Beginning XML 3E">
  <carnivore kind="Tyrannosaurus_Rex" habitat="forest swamp jungle">
    <species>Tyrannosaurus Rex</species>
    <length>42 feet</length>
    <height>18 feet</height>
    <weight>5-7 tons</weight>
    <speed>25 mph</speed>
    <weapon>
      <part-of-body>Teeth</part-of-body>
      <description>Though the Tyrannosaurus had many different sizes of teeth,
all were razor sharp and some grew to lengths of <b>9-13 inches</b>. Broken
teeth were replaced frequently by newer teeth. The powerful jaw exerted in
excess of 3000 pounds of pressure!</description>
    </weapon>
    <discoverer>
      <name>Osborn</name>
      <year>1905</year>
    </discoverer>
    <location>
      <country>Canada</country>
      <region>Alberta</region>
    </location>
```

```
    <description>&tyrannosaurus;</description>
  </carnivore>
  <herbivore kind="Stegosaurus_Armatus" habitat="forest swamp"
   period="Jurassic">
    <species>Stegosaurus Armatus</species>
    <length>25-40 feet</length>
    <height>14 feet</height>
    <weight>2-4 tons</weight>
    <speed>&speed-not-known;</speed>
    <weapon>
      <part-of-body>Spikes</part-of-body>
      <description>The Stegosaurus had two long rows of armor along its back.
At the end of its tail <b>four large spikes</b> were an excellent
defense.</description>
    </weapon>
    <discoverer>
      <name>Marsh</name>
      <year>1877</year>
    </discoverer>
    <location>
      <country>United States</country>
      <region>Colorado</region>
    </location>
    <description>&stegosaurus;</description>
  </herbivore>
  <omnivore kind="Gallimimus_Bullatus" habitat="lakeshore prairie">
    <species>Gallimimus Bullatus</species>
    <length>18 feet</length>
    <height>8 feet</height>
    <weight>1000 pounds</weight>
    <speed>35-60 mph</speed>
    <weapon/>
    <discoverer>
      <name>Osm&#x00F3;lska</name>
      <name>Roniewicz</name>
      <name>Barsbold</name>
      <year>1972</year>
    </discoverer>
    <location>
      <country>Mongolia</country>
      <region>Nemegtskaya Svita</region>
    </location>
    &gallimimus;
  </omnivore>
</dinosaurs>
```

6. We are ready to validate our document again. Within the Topologi Schematron Validator, browse to the folder where you saved `dinosaurs4.xml`, select it, and click the Run button.

Your output should show a complete validation without errors. If you received any errors this time, check whether you have typed everything correctly and try again.

Just to prove that the text has been retrieved from the external files and inserted into our XML document, open up `dinosaurs4.xml` in Internet Explorer. Figure 4-8 shows a section of what you should see.

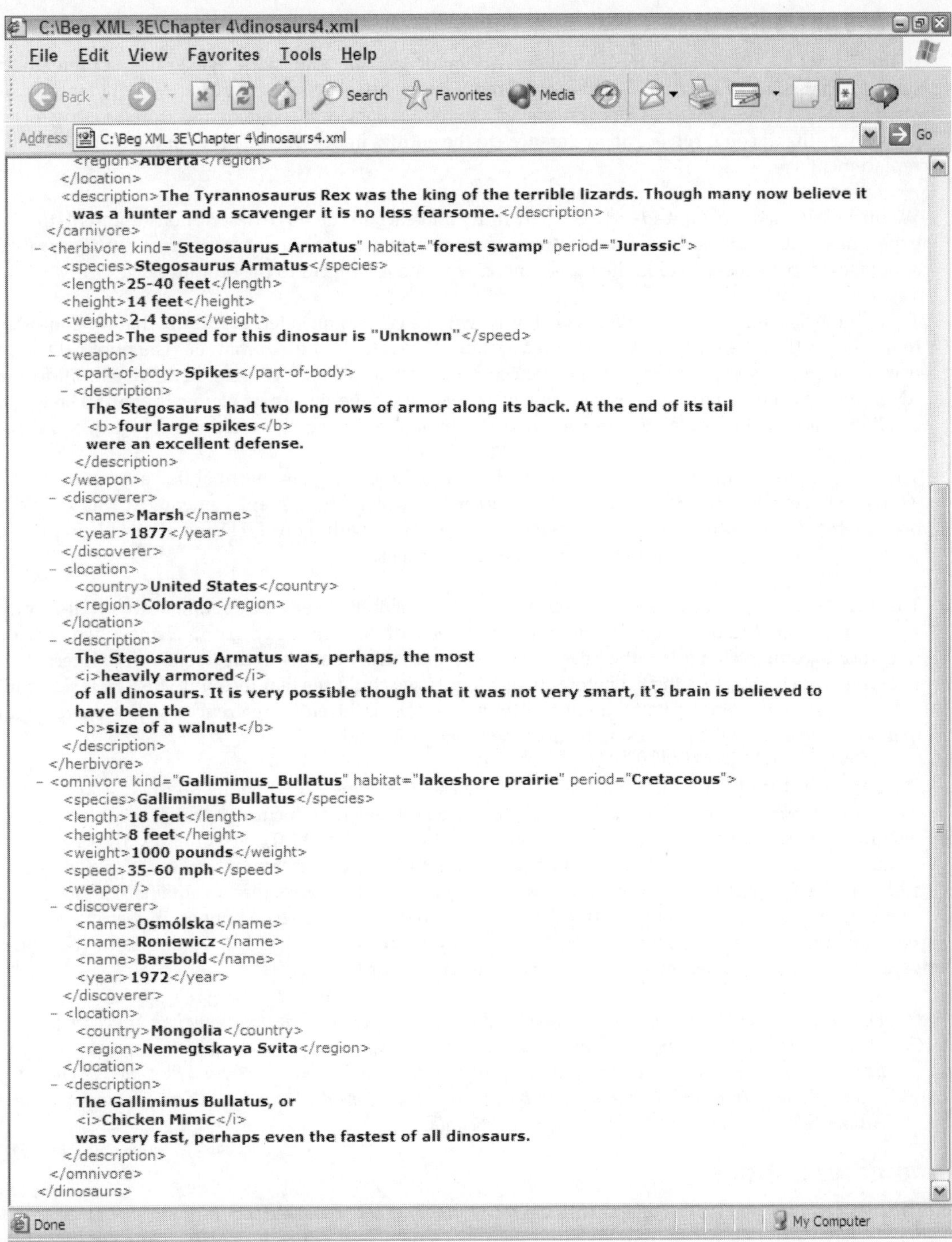

```
      <region>Alberta</region>
    </location>
    <description>The Tyrannosaurus Rex was the king of the terrible lizards. Though many now believe it
      was a hunter and a scavenger it is no less fearsome.</description>
  </carnivore>
- <herbivore kind="Stegosaurus_Armatus" habitat="forest swamp" period="Jurassic">
    <species>Stegosaurus Armatus</species>
    <length>25-40 feet</length>
    <height>14 feet</height>
    <weight>2-4 tons</weight>
    <speed>The speed for this dinosaur is "Unknown"</speed>
  - <weapon>
      <part-of-body>Spikes</part-of-body>
    - <description>
        The Stegosaurus had two long rows of armor along its back. At the end of its tail
        <b>four large spikes</b>
        were an excellent defense.
      </description>
    </weapon>
  - <discoverer>
      <name>Marsh</name>
      <year>1877</year>
    </discoverer>
  - <location>
      <country>United States</country>
      <region>Colorado</region>
    </location>
  - <description>
      The Stegosaurus Armatus was, perhaps, the most
      <i>heavily armored</i>
      of all dinosaurs. It is very possible though that it was not very smart, it's brain is believed to
      have been the
      <b>size of a walnut!</b>
    </description>
  </herbivore>
- <omnivore kind="Gallimimus_Bullatus" habitat="lakeshore prairie" period="Cretaceous">
    <species>Gallimimus Bullatus</species>
    <length>18 feet</length>
    <height>8 feet</height>
    <weight>1000 pounds</weight>
    <speed>35-60 mph</speed>
    <weapon />
  - <discoverer>
      <name>Osmólska</name>
      <name>Roniewicz</name>
      <name>Barsbold</name>
      <year>1972</year>
    </discoverer>
  - <location>
      <country>Mongolia</country>
      <region>Nemegtskaya Svita</region>
    </location>
  - <description>
      The Gallimimus Bullatus, or
      <i>Chicken Mimic</i>
      was very fast, perhaps even the fastest of all dinosaurs.
    </description>
  </omnivore>
</dinosaurs>
```

Figure 4-8

How It Works

In this Try It Out, we replaced the textual description of each dinosaur with a general entity reference. As our XML parser processed the file, it encountered the entity declarations, read the system identifier, and attempted to retrieve the files. Once it retrieved the files, it parsed the content and stored a copy in memory so that it could replace any references to the entities in our document with the correct replacement text.

We purposely made the `speed-not-known` entity and each of the three descriptions different, to experiment with some of the various features of entities. In the `speed-not-known` entity, we created a simple text replacement. Within the replacement, we used references to the built-in `quot` entity.

Though the `tyrannosaurus` entity was simply text, we created an external text file that we could refer to from our DTD. We used a public ID and a system ID to refer to the external file. The public ID was not used by our processor and, in fact, was not necessary. The simple text we used qualified as well-formed XML content even though there was no root element (in fact, there were no elements at all). The text was a valid replacement because the `<description>` element could legally contain simple text, or `#PCDATA`.

The `stegosaurus` entity value was a mix of elements and text. Again, this qualified as well-formed XML content even though there was no root element. Additionally, the replacement text was valid because the `<b>` element and the `<i>` element were declared within our DTD and allowable in the `<description>` element where the entity reference was used.

The `gallimimus` entity value was an actual XML document. By itself, the document was well-formed XML content. Instead of using the entity reference inside of the `<description>` element, we used the reference to completely replace the `<description>` element. Looking at the document in Internet Explorer (which processes the file before displaying it), we could see that the entire `gallimimus` entity value was placed where we had our entity reference. Once all the entity references were replaced with their entity values by the processor, the document was still valid.

It is important to note that we could also have used files that were stored on the Internet. However, just as we saw with our local text files, the parser must parse each external document and check it for well-formedness. Most HTML files on the web are not well-formed XML; we chose text files because we wanted to make sure that the file would not create a well-formedness error when it was parsed. In addition, the `ELEMENT` declaration for our description element specifies that it contains `#PCDATA` or `<b>` elements or `<i>` elements. If our XML parser encountered an `<html>` element within the `<description>` element, even as the result of an entity's replacement text, it would raise a validity error because we have not declared an `<html>` element within our DTD.

Earlier we mentioned that validation uses more processing power and that this might be a drawback to using DTDs. Likewise, using external entities can also decrease your application performance. You might have noticed a significant performance decrease in our last example. Because external files must be opened and read, and often downloaded from the Internet, you should consider the pros and cons of using external entities before dividing your DTD into separate modules.

Parameter Entities

Parameter entities, much like general entities, allow you to create reusable sections of replacement text. So far, we have seen that we can refer to entities within element and attribute content, within specific places inside the DTD, such as default attribute values, and within entity replacement text. Parameter entities, however, cannot be used in general content; you can refer to parameter entities only within the DTD.

Unlike other kinds of entities, the replacement text within a parameter entity can be made up of DTD declarations or pieces of declarations.

Parameter entities can also be used to build DTDs from multiple files. This is often helpful when different groups work on DTDs. In addition, as we mentioned at the beginning of the chapter, this allows you to reuse DTDs and portions of DTDs in your own XML documents. When XML documents or DTDs are broken up into multiple files, they are said to be *modular*.

Parameter entity declarations are very similar to general entity declarations:

```
<!ENTITY % defaultPeriod "Cretaceous">
```

Here we have declared an internal parameter entity named `defaultPeriod`. We can tell that this is a parameter entity because of the percent sign (`%`) before the name of the entity. This is the primary difference between the format of parameter entity declarations and that of general entity declarations. Notice the space between the `ENTITY` keyword and the percent sign, and between the percent sign and the name of the entity. This whitespace is required.

Like general entities, parameter entities can also refer to external files utilizing a system or public identifier. For example:

```
<!ENTITY % moreDeclarations SYSTEM "module.dtd">
```

or

```
<!ENTITY % moreDeclarations PUBLIC "-//Beginning XML 3E//DTD External
module//EN" "module.dtd">
```

Parameter entity declarations that refer to external files must refer to files that can be parsed by the XML parser. Earlier in this chapter we learned that general entity declarations can use the keyword `NDATA` to indicate that the external file should not be parsed. Parameter entity declarations cannot use the `NDATA` keyword.

References to Parameter Entities

When referring to a parameter entity within a DTD, the syntax changes slightly. Instead of using an ampersand (`&`) you must use a percent sign (`%`). For example:

```
%moreDeclarations;
```

As we can see, the reference consists of a percent sign (`%`), followed by the entity name, followed by a semicolon (`;`). References to parameter entities are permitted only within the DTD.

Consider our `<dinosaurs>` example, in which we declared the content models for our `<carnivore>`, `<herbivore>`, and `<omnivore>` elements:

```
<!ELEMENT carnivore (species, length, height, weight, speed, weapon,
discoverer, location, description)>
<!ELEMENT herbivore (species, length, height, weight, speed, weapon,
discoverer, location, description)>
```

```
<!ELEMENT omnivore (species, length, height, weight, speed, weapon,
discoverer, location, description)>
```

The content model for each of these element declarations is the same. Likewise, the attribute declarations for each of these elements are the same:

```
<!ATTLIST carnivore kind ID #REQUIRED
                    habitat NMTOKENS #REQUIRED
                    period (Triassic | Jurassic | Cretaceous) "Cretaceous">

<!ATTLIST herbivore kind ID #REQUIRED
                    habitat NMTOKENS #REQUIRED
                    period (Triassic | Jurassic | Cretaceous) "Cretaceous">

<!ATTLIST omnivore kind ID #REQUIRED
                   habitat NMTOKENS #REQUIRED
                   period (Triassic | Jurassic | Cretaceous) "Cretaceous">
```

We could save ourselves some typing by utilizing a parameter entity for the content model and attribute declarations.

```
<!ENTITY % dinoContentModel "(species, length, height, weight, speed, weapon,
  discoverer, location, description)">
```

In the preceding example, we have declared a parameter entity called `dinoContentModel`. We can tell that this is a parameter entity because of the percent sign in between the keyword `ENTITY` and the name. We know that this is an internal parameter entity because our replacement text is included in the declaration.

```
<!ENTITY % dinoAttributes "kind ID #REQUIRED
                           habitat NMTOKENS #REQUIRED
                           period (Triassic | Jurassic | Cretaceous)
                           &#34;Cretaceous&#34;">
```

Like the `dinoContentModel` entity, here we have declared a parameter entity called `dinoAttributes` for our repeated attribute declarations. Unfortunately, we can't use the built-in entity `"` because general entities that appear in parameter entity values are not expanded as they are in general entity values. Because of this, we instead use character entities for the quotation marks. This is perfectly legal.

Utilizing parameter entity references, we can modify our earlier declarations:

```
<!ELEMENT carnivore %dinoContentModel;>
<!ATTLIST carnivore %dinoAttributes;>
<!ELEMENT herbivore %dinoContentModel;>
<!ATTLIST herbivore %dinoAttributes;>
<!ELEMENT omnivore %dinoContentModel;>
<!ATTLIST omnivore %dinoAttributes;>
```

In a simple case such as this one, our DTD becomes much easier to read. We can quickly see that all three of these elements have exactly the same content model and exactly the same attribute declarations. In addition, if we need to make change to the content model, we have to modify only the `ENTITY` declaration.

Try It Out "When Dinosaurs Ruled the Earth"—Part 5

Let's take what we have just learned and use it within our dinosaur DTD. This will allow us to reduce the number of repeated content models within our DTD.

1. Let's begin by making the appropriate modifications to our DTD file. Open `dinosaurs4.dtd`, make the highlighted modifications, and save the file as `dinosaurs5.dtd`:

```
<!ELEMENT dinosaurs (carnivore | herbivore | omnivore)*>
<!ATTLIST dinosaurs version CDATA #FIXED "1.0"
                    source CDATA #IMPLIED>

<!ENTITY % dinoContentModel "(species, length, height, weight, speed, weapon,
  discoverer, location, description)">

<!ENTITY % dinoAttributes "kind ID #REQUIRED
                           habitat NMTOKENS #REQUIRED
                           period (Triassic | Jurassic | Cretaceous)
                           &#34;Cretaceous&#34;">

<!ELEMENT carnivore %dinoContentModel;>
<!ATTLIST carnivore %dinoAttributes;>
<!ELEMENT herbivore %dinoContentModel;>
<!ATTLIST herbivore %dinoAttributes;>
<!ELEMENT omnivore %dinoContentModel;>
<!ATTLIST omnivore %dinoAttributes;>

<!ELEMENT species (#PCDATA)>
<!ELEMENT length (#PCDATA)>
<!ELEMENT height (#PCDATA)>
<!ELEMENT weight (#PCDATA)>
<!ELEMENT speed (#PCDATA)>

<!ELEMENT weapon (part-of-body, description)?>
<!ATTLIST weapon images ENTITIES #IMPLIED>

<!ELEMENT part-of-body (#PCDATA)>
<!ELEMENT description (#PCDATA | b | i)*>
<!ELEMENT b (#PCDATA)>
<!ELEMENT i (#PCDATA)>

<!ELEMENT discoverer (name+, year)>
<!ELEMENT name (#PCDATA)>
<!ELEMENT year (#PCDATA)>

<!ELEMENT location (GPS | (country, region))>
<!ELEMENT GPS (#PCDATA)>
<!ELEMENT country (#PCDATA)>
<!ELEMENT region (#PCDATA)>

<!ENTITY speed-not-known "The speed for this dinosaur is &quot;Unknown&quot;">
```

```
<!ENTITY tyrannosaurus PUBLIC
  "-//Beginning XML//Tyrannosaurus textual description//EN"
"tyrannosaurus.txt">
<!ENTITY stegosaurus PUBLIC
  "-//Beginning XML//Stegosaurus textual description//EN" "stegosaurus.txt">
<!ENTITY gallimimus PUBLIC
  "-//Beginning XML//Gallimimus textual description//EN" "gallimimus.xml">
```

2. Next, we need to change our XML file to refer to our new DTD. This is the only change we need to make within our XML document. Open `dinosaurs4.xml` from our last example, change the Document Type Declaration to refer to our new DTD, and save the file as `dinosaurs5.xml`:

```
<!DOCTYPE dinosaurs PUBLIC "-//Beginning XML//DTD Dinosaurs Example//EN"
"dinosaurs5.dtd">
```

3. We are ready to validate our document again. Within the Topologi Schematron Validator, browse to the folder where you saved `dinosaurs5.xml`, select it, and click the Run button.

Your output should show a complete validation without errors. If you received any errors this time, check whether you have typed everything correctly and try again.

How It Works

In this last Try It Out, we were able to simplify several of our `ELEMENT` and `ATTLIST` declarations by utilizing a parameter entity for the content model and a parameter entity for the attribute declarations. Just as we have seen throughout this section, parameter entities allow us to reuse DTD declarations or pieces of declarations. As the parser attempts to process the content model for our `<carnivore>` declaration, it encounters the parameter entity reference. It replaces the entity reference with the replacement text specified in the `ENTITY` declaration.

It is important to note that the declaration of a parameter entity must occur in the DTD before any references to that entity.

Notation Declarations

Throughout this chapter, we have seen references to *notation declarations*. So far, we have seen how to use notations within specialized `ATTLIST` declarations. We have also seen that we can use notations when declaring unparsed entities. Often, we need to refer to external resources such as image files and databases that cannot be processed by an XML parser. To make use of the external files, we need an application that can utilize the data. Notation declarations allow us to associate types of external resources with external applications that can handle them.

The basic format of a notation declaration is as follows:

```
<!NOTATION jpg SYSTEM "iexplore.exe">
```

In the preceding example, we have indicated that this is a notation declaration by beginning our element with an exclamation mark and by using the `NOTATION` keyword. Following the `NOTATION` keyword is the name of our notation, in this case `jpg`. Notation names must follow the same rules as other XML names. Immediately after the notation name, we must include a `SYSTEM` or `PUBLIC` identifier that allows the processor to locate an external application for handling the notation. In this case, we have used a `SYSTEM` identifier that refers to `iexplore.exe`.

A notation, such as the one we have declared, could be used whenever we need to refer to a JPEG file. Because our XML processor cannot parse JPEG files, we need to use an external program for displaying or editing them. The external program could be any program you like, even web applications. When the parser encounters a usage of the notation name, it will simply provide the path to the application.

Try It Out "When Dinosaurs Ruled the Earth"—Part 6

Let's look at our dinosaur example one last time. Now that we understand entities and notations we should be able to complete our DTD.

1. Let's begin by opening our `dinosaurs5.dtd` file. Add the following declarations to the end of the file, and save it as `dinosaurs6.dtd`.

```
<!NOTATION jpg SYSTEM "iexplorer.exe">
<!ENTITY PictureOfTyrannosaurusTooth SYSTEM
  "http://www.destinationeducation.com/images/dinosaurs/image_longtrextooth.
  jpg" NDATA jpg>
<!ENTITY PictureOfStegosaurusSpike SYSTEM
  "http://www.destinationeducation.com/images/dinosaurs/image_stegospike.jpg"
  NDATA jpg>
<!ENTITY PictureOfStegosaurusPlate SYSTEM
  "http://www.destinationeducation.com/images/dinosaurs/image_stegoplate.jpg"
  NDATA jpg>
```

2. Now that we have modified our DTD, let's use the changes within our XML document. Open `dinosaurs5.xml`, make the following modifications, and the save the file as `dinosaurs6.xml`:

```
<?xml version="1.0"?>
<!DOCTYPE dinosaurs PUBLIC "-//Beginning XML//DTD Dinosaurs Example//EN"
  "dinosaurs6.dtd">
<dinosaurs version="1.0" source="Beginning XML 3E">
  <carnivore kind="Tyrannosaurus_Rex" habitat="forest swamp jungle"
    <species>Tyrannosaurus Rex</species>
    <length>42 feet</length>
    <height>18 feet</height>
    <weight>5-7 tons</weight>
    <speed>25 mph</speed>
    <weapon images="PictureOfTyrannosaurusTooth">
      <part-of-body>Teeth</part-of-body>
      <description>Though the Tyrannosaurus had many different sizes of teeth,
all were razor sharp and some grew to lengths of <b>9-13 inches</b>. Broken
teeth were replaced frequently by newer teeth. The powerful jaw exerted in
excess of 3000 pounds of pressure!</description>
    </weapon>
    <discoverer>
      <name>Osborn</name>
      <year>1905</year>
    </discoverer>
    <location>
```

```
        <country>Canada</country>
        <region>Alberta</region>
      </location>
      <description>&tyrannosaurus;</description>
    </carnivore>
    <herbivore kind="Stegosaurus_Armatus" habitat="forest swamp"
period="Jurassic">
      <species>Stegosaurus Armatus</species>
      <length>25-40 feet</length>
      <height>14 feet</height>
      <weight>2-4 tons</weight>
      <speed>&speed-not-known;</speed>
      <weapon images="PictureOfStegosaurusSpike PictureOfStegosaurusPlate">
        <part-of-body>Spikes</part-of-body>
        <description>The Stegosaurus had two long rows of armor along its back.
At the end of its tail <b>four large spikes</b> were an excellent
defense.</description>
      </weapon>
      <discoverer>
        <name>Marsh</name>
        <year>1877</year>
      </discoverer>
      <location>
        <country>United States</country>
        <region>Colorado</region>
      </location>
      <description>&stegosaurus;</description>
    </herbivore>
    <omnivore kind="Gallimimus_Bullatus" habitat="lakeshore prairie">
      <species>Gallimimus Bullatus</species>
      <length>18 feet</length>
      <height>8 feet</height>
      <weight>1000 pounds</weight>
      <speed>35-60 mph</speed>
      <weapon/>
      <discoverer>
        <name>Osm&#x00F3;lska</name>
        <name>Roniewicz</name>
        <name>Barsbold</name>
        <year>1972</year>
      </discoverer>
      <location>
        <country>Mongolia</country>
        <region>Nemegtskaya Svita</region>
      </location>
      &gallimimus;
    </omnivore>
</dinosaurs>
```

3. We are ready to validate our document again. Within the Topologi Schematron Validator, browse to the folder where you saved `dinosaurs6.xml`, select it, and click the Run button.

Your output should show a complete validation without errors. If you received any errors this time, check whether you have typed everything correctly and try again.

How It Works

We have finally completed a DTD for our list of dinosaurs. Although it is short, it uses some very complex features of DTDs. In this final Try It Out example, we added a `NOTATION` and several `ENTITY` declarations to our DTD; we also modified our XML document to utilize these new features.

We began by adding a notation declaration to our DTD. The notation declaration allowed us to refer to external JPEG files for the covers. We also associated JPEG files with `iexplorer.exe`, because we know that `iexplorer.exe` can open and display the external files. Whenever this notation is used, the parser will report the associated program as well. Our application or parser can use this information to provide a view of the external files, or it can ignore this information. Once we had created a notation declaration for JPEG images, we were able to create an unparsed entity that referred to an external image file.

Developing DTDs

Most of the DTDs we developed within this chapter were relatively simple. As you begin developing DTDs for your XML documents, you might find it is difficult to present the DTDs in a linear order. Most of our declarations flowed in order, but often you will not be sure in what order your DTD declarations should occur. Don't worry; apart from entities that are used within the DTDs, declarations can appear in any order. While you have ample freedom in the order you choose, it is common to keep associated declarations near one another. For example, in most DTDs, an `ATTLIST` declaration immediately follows the `ELEMENT` declaration with which it is associated.

As the flow of the DTDs becomes difficult to follow, it is important to document your declarations. You can use XML comments and processing instructions within a DTD, following rules similar to usage in XML content. Comments and processing instructions can appear in the internal or external subsets, but they cannot appear within markup declarations.

For example, the following is valid:

```
<!-- source : allows you to describe who provided the dinosaur list -->
<!ATTLIST dinosaurs source CDATA#IMPLIED>
```

The following is not valid:

```
<!ATTLIST dinosaurs
  <!-- source : allows you to describe who provided the dinosaur list -->
  source CDATA #IMPLIED>
```

When developing DTDs you should also note that comments and processing instructions are never declared.

As we have already seen, developing a DTD is easiest when you have an example XML document. What should you do if you have a very long example file with many elements? A good strategy is to divide the DTD into pieces or modules. The best way to do this is by using external parameter entities. Instead of designing the whole DTD at once, try to create DTDs for subsections of your vocabulary and then use parameter entity references when testing. Once you have your DTD working, you can combine the modules to increase performance. By dividing your DTD in this way, you can quickly identify and fix errors.

DTD Limitations

Throughout this chapter, we have seen some of the many benefits of using DTDs. They allow us to validate our content without application-specific code, allow us to supply default values for attributes, and even create modular XML documents. Throughout your XML career, you will use existing DTDs and often design your own. Because of XML's strong SGML foundation, much of the early XML development focused on the markup of technical documents. Since that time, XML has been used in areas no one ever expected. While this was a great achievement for the XML community, it began to reveal some limitations of DTDs.

Some limitations of DTDs include the following:

- Differences between DTD syntax and XML syntax
- Poor support for XML namespaces
- Poor data typing
- Limited content model descriptions

Before we look at these limitations in more detail, it is important to reiterate that even with their limitations, DTDs are a fundamental part of the XML Recommendation. DTDs will continue to be used in many diverse situations, even as other methods of describing documents emerge.

DTD Syntax

The syntax for expressing DTD declarations is different from the generic XML syntax we learned in the first few chapters. Why is the syntax so different? Early on, we learned that XML is based on SGML. Because many of the developers turning to XML used SGML, the creators of XML chose to adopt the DTD syntax that was originally developed for SGML.

This proved to be both a benefit and a limitation within XML. Initially, this made migration from SGML to XML a snap. Many users had already developed DTDs for their SGML documents. Instead of having to completely redesign their vocabularies, they could reuse what they had already done, with minimal changes. As support for XML grew, new XML tools and standards were developed that allowed users to manipulate their XML data. Unfortunately, these tools were meant for generic XML, not for DTDs.

XML Namespaces

Whenever element or attribute names are declared within a DTD, the namespace prefix and colon must be included in the declaration. In addition to this limitation, DTDs must treat namespace declarations as attributes. This is because the completion of the XML Recommendation occurred before the syntax for XML namespaces was finalized. Forcing users to declare namespace prefixes in advance defeats the purpose of namespace prefixes altogether. Merging documents from multiple namespaces when the prefixes are predefined can be problematic and confusing.

Data Typing

As XML developers began using DTDs to model more complex data (such as databases and programming objects), the need for stronger data types emerged. The only available data types within

DTDs are limited to use in attribute declarations, and even then the data types provide only a fraction of the needed functionality. No method exists for constraining the data within a text-only element to a specific type. For example, if you were modeling a database and needed to specify that data within a specific element needed to be numeric, you couldn't do so using DTDs.

Limited Content Model Descriptions

In addition to needing more advanced data types, limitations in content model descriptions became apparent soon after the XML Recommendation was published. Developers wanted the capability to mimic object inheritance in their XML content models. Developers also found the cardinality operators limiting. For example, because DTDs lack strict control on the number of times an element occurs, it is difficult to require that a specific element have more than one but less than ten occurrences.

Summary

By utilizing DTDs, we can easily validate our XML documents against a defined vocabulary of elements and attributes. This reduces the amount of code needed within our application. Instead, a validating XML parser can be used to check whether the contents of our XML document are valid according to the declarations within our DTD. DTDs allow us to exercise much more control over our document content than simple well-formedness checks do.

In this chapter, we learned:

- How to validate a document against a DTD
- How to create element declarations
- How to create attribute declarations
- How to create entity declarations
- How to create notation declarations
- How to specify an XML document and DTD using external files

We also learned that DTDs have several limitations. In the next two chapters, we will see how these limitations have been addressed in newer standards, such as XML Schemas and RELAX NG.

Exercise Questions

Suggested solutions to these questions can be found in Appendix A.

Question 1

Add another dinosaur, Triceratops Horridus, to the list of dinosaurs, based on the declarations in the dinosaurs DTD. Once you have added the new dinosaur validate your document to ensure that it is correct.

Question 2

Add a `feathers` attribute declaration for the `<carnivore>`, `<herbivore>`, and `<omnivore>` elements. The attribute should allow two possible values: *yes* and *no*. Make the attribute have a default value of *no*. If you would like to add a dinosaur that had feathers, to your document, add definitions for the Avimimus Portentosus or for the Archaeopteryx Lithographica.

Question 3

Add a `prey` attribute declaration for the `<carnivore>` and `<omnivore>` elements. Make the attribute type `IDREFS` and make the attribute `#IMPLIED`. Once you have completed this, add a `prey` attribute to the Tyrannosaurus Rex and refer to one of the dinosaur `ID`s found in your dinosaur document.

XML Schemas

In the last chapter, we learned that many people use Document Type Definitions (DTDs) to validate their XML documents. This keeps us from needing to write application-specific code to check whether our documents are valid. We also saw some of the limitations of DTDs. Since the inception of XML, several new formats have been developed that allow us to define the content of our vocabulary.

In 1999, the W3C began to develop XML Schemas in response to the growing need for a more advanced format for describing XML documents. Already, work had begun on several efforts that were intended to better model the types of document that were being created by XML developers. The W3C's effort took the best of these early technologies and then added additional features. During the development, several members of the W3C designed simpler schema languages with fewer features outside of the W3C. Perhaps the most important effort is RELAX NG, which we will discuss in depth in Chapter 6.

Today, XML Schemas are a mature technology used in a variety of XML applications. Apart from their use in validation, XML Schemas are used in XQuery, which we will cover in Chapter 9. Additionally XML Schemas can be used in conjunction with web services and SOAP, as we will see in Chapters 14 and 15, respectively.

So, what is a schema? A schema is any type of model document that defines the structure of something, such as databases structures or documents. In this case, our *something* is an XML document. In fact, DTDs are a type of schema. Throughout this book, we have been using the term *vocabulary* where we could have used the word *schema*. So, what is an XML Schema? This is where it gets confusing. The term XML Schema is used to refer to the specific W3C XML Schema technology. W3C XML Schemas, much like DTDs, allow you to describe the structure for an XML document. When referring to W3C XML Schemas, the *S* in *Schema* should be capitalized. XML Schema definitions are also commonly referred to as XSD.

In this chapter, we will learn:

- The benefits of XML Schemas
- How to create and use XML Schemas

- Some features of XML Schemas
- How to document our XML Schemas

Benefits of XML Schemas

At this point you have already invested time in learning DTDs. You know the syntax and can create complex, even modular, definitions for your vocabulary. Although XML Schemas are the next great thing, it may be helpful for you to understand some of the benefits of XML Schemas before jumping in.

- XML Schemas are created using basic XML, while DTDs utilize a separate syntax.
- XML Schemas fully support the Namespace Recommendation.
- XML Schemas allow you to validate text element content based on built-in and user-defined data types.
- XML Schemas allow you to more easily create complex and reusable content models.
- XML Schemas allow you to model concepts such as object inheritance and type substitution.

Let's look at some of these benefits in more detail.

XML Schemas Use XML Syntax

In the last chapter, we spent most of our time learning the DTD syntax. The syntax, as we learned, adds a lot to the basic rules for XML well-formedness. When defining an XML Schema, the syntax is entirely in XML; although you still have to learn the rules for which elements and attributes are required in given declarations, you can use generic XML tools—even those that have no understanding of the rules specific to XML Schema documents. As we learn new XML technologies through this book, we will see how to apply them to any XML document. For example, powerful tools such as Extensible Stylesheet Language Transformations (XSLT) can be used to work with XML Schemas, but cannot be used on DTDs. In the next chapter we will see how RELAX NG, another schema language, has two syntaxes.

XML Schema Namespace Support

Because XML Schemas were finalized after the Namespace Recommendation, the XML Schema specification was designed around their use (for a refresher on namespaces, review Chapter 3). Unlike DTDs, which do not support the full functionality of namespaces, XML Schemas enable you to define vocabularies that utilize namespace declarations. More importantly, XML Schemas allow you to mix namespaces in XML documents with less rigidity. For example, when designing an XML Schema, it is not necessary to specify namespace prefixes as you must in DTDs. Instead, the XML Schema leaves this decision to the end-user.

XML Schema Data Types

When we were developing our DTDs, we could specify that an element had mixed content, element content, or empty content. Unfortunately, when our elements contained only text, we couldn't add any constraints on the format of the text. Attribute declarations gave us some control, but even then, the types we could use in attribute declarations were very limited.

> **XML Schema divides data types into two broad categories: simple and complex. Elements that may contain attributes or other elements are declared using complexTypes. Attribute values and text content within elements are declared using simpleTypes.**

XML Schemas allow you to specify the type of textual data allowed within attributes and elements, using simpleType declarations. For example, by utilizing these types you could specify that an element may contain only date values, only positive numbers, or numbers within a certain range. Many commonly used simpleTypes are built into XML Schemas. This is, perhaps, the single most important feature within XML Schemas. By allowing you to specify allowable type of data within an element or attribute, XML Schemas enable you to more rigidly control documents. This allows you to easily create documents that are intended to represent databases, programming languages, and objects within programming languages. We will look at simpleTypes and complexTypes later in this chapter.

XML Schema Content Models

To reuse a content model within a DTD, we had to utilize parameter entities. This can lead to situations that make it difficult to reuse parts of the DTD. XML Schemas provide several mechanisms for reusing content models. In addition to the simple models that we created in DTDs, XML Schemas can model complex programming concepts. The advanced features of XML Schemas allow you to build content models upon content models, modifying the definition in each step.

Do We Still Need DTDs?

Wait a second. Why did we spend all of Chapter 4 learning about DTDs if we were just going to turn around and teach you a better way to validate documents? Don't worry—DTDs are extremely useful even with the advent of XML Schemas. Although XML Schemas provide better features for describing documents—as well as a more common syntax—they provide no `ENTITY` functionality. In many XML documents and applications, the `ENTITY` declaration is of paramount importance. On the merits of this feature alone, DTDs will live a long and happy life.

DTDs also have a special prominence because they are the only definition and validation mechanism that is embedded within the XML Recommendation. This allows DTDs to be embedded directly in the XML documents they are describing. All other syntaxes require a separate file. Parsers that support DTDs are trained to use the embedded declarations, while nonvalidating parsers are allowed to ignore the declarations. XML programming tools, such as Document Object Model (DOM) and Simple Application Programming Interface (API) for XML (SAX)—which we will learn about in Chapters 11 and 12—have special features for DTD types.

Because DTDs inherit most of their behavior from Standard Generalized Markup Language (SGML), much of the work of describing XML document types has been and will be done using DTDs.

XML Schemas

As we progress through this chapter, you should begin to see more benefits of XML Schemas, which provide many features that were never possible using DTDs. Throughout this chapter, we will focus on the basic parts of XML Schemas that are similar to DTDs. We will also learn about some of the data type mechanisms.

Unfortunately, XML Schemas cannot be covered completely in one chapter. The advanced features of XML Schemas add significant confusion and complexity. Often these features are not supported correctly within different validators, and many experts recommend against their usage. This chapter will cover the basic features—those that everyone agrees upon and recommends.

Although you will learn how to design and use XML Schemas in this chapter, you may like to see the XML Schema Recommendation for yourself. The XML Schema Recommendation is divided into three parts: an introduction to XML Schema concepts at `http://www.w3.org/TR/xmlschema-0/`*; a document that defines all of the structures used in XML Schemas at* `http://www.w3.org/TR/xmlschema-1/`*; and a document that describes XML Schema data types at* `http://www.w3.org/TR/xmlschema-2/`*.*

The XML Schema Document

Most XML Schemas are stored within a separate XML document. In this respect, XML Schemas function very similarly to external DTDs; an XML document contains a reference to the XML Schema that defines its vocabulary. An XML document that adheres to a particular XML Schema vocabulary is called an XML Schema *instance* document.

> **As we saw in the last chapter, validating a document against its vocabulary requires the use of a special parser. The XML Schema Recommendation calls these parsers *schema validators*. Not only do schema validators render a verdict on the document's schema validity, but many also provide type information to the application. This set of type information is called the *Post Schema Validation Infoset (PSVI)*. The PSVI contains all of the information in the XML document and a basic summary of everything declared in the schema. For example, PSVI output is used by XQuery and XPath2.**

Running the Samples

We have talked about some of the benefits of XML Schemas, but it will probably help us if we see an entire XML Schema before we look at each part in detail. To see how the XML Schema works we will modify our name example from the previous chapter. Throughout this chapter, we will be using the Topologi Schematron Validator to validate our documents. This is the same program that we used in Chapter 4. In addition to being able to work with DTDs, Topologi Schematron Validator is capable of checking an XML Schema instance document against its XML Schema. If you need more information on where to download the Topologi Schematron Validator from, please refer to Chapter 4.

> **At the time of this writing, support for XML Schemas is almost as widespread as the support for DTDs. A list of XML Schema tools can be found on the XML Schema homepage at `http://www.w3.org/XML/Schema#Tools`.**

Try It Out — What's in a Name?

In this example, we will create an XML Schema that defines our name vocabulary. We will also see how to refer to the XML Schema from the instance document. At the end of this example, we will break down each step to see how it works.

1. Let's begin by creating the XML Schema. Simply open a text editor, such as Notepad, and copy the following. When you are finished, save the file as `name5.xsd`.

```
<?xml version="1.0"?>
<schema xmlns="http://www.w3.org/2001/XMLSchema"
 xmlns:target="http://www.example.com/name"
 targetNamespace="http://www.example.com/name"
 elementFormDefault="qualified">
  <element name="name">
    <complexType>
      <sequence>
        <element name="first" type="string"/>
        <element name="middle" type="string"/>
        <element name="last" type="string"/>
      </sequence>
      <attribute name="title" type="string"/>
    </complexType>
  </element>
</schema>
```

2. Next, we'll need to create the instance document. This document will be very similar to our `name4.xml` example from the previous chapter. Instead of referring to a DTD, we will be referring to our newly created XML Schema. Copy the following; when you are finished, save the file as `name5.xml` in the same folder as `name5.xsd`.

```
<?xml version="1.0"?>
<name
  xmlns="http://www.example.com/name"
  xmlns:xsi="http://www.w3.org/2001/XMLSchema-instance"
  xsi:schemaLocation="http://www.example.com/name name5.xsd"
  title="Mr.">
   <first>John</first>
   <middle>Fitzgerald Johansen</middle>
   <last>Doe</last>
</name>
```

3. We are ready to validate our XML instance document against our XML Schema. Open the Topologi Schematron Validator and browse to the folder where you saved you files. Select `name5.xml` on the left side as shown in Figure 5-1.

   Because we refer to our XML Schema within `name5.xml`, we do not need to select it within the validator. Once you have highlighted `name5.xml`, click the Run button and observe the output results, as shown in Figure 5-2.

   If the output suggests that the validation completed, but that there was an error in the document, correct the error and try again.

4. If you would like to see what happens if there is an error, simply modify your `name5.xml` document and try validating again.

How It Works

In this *Try It Out* example, we created an XML Schema for our name vocabulary. Let's look at each part of our schema briefly, to get an idea of what to expect throughout the chapter.

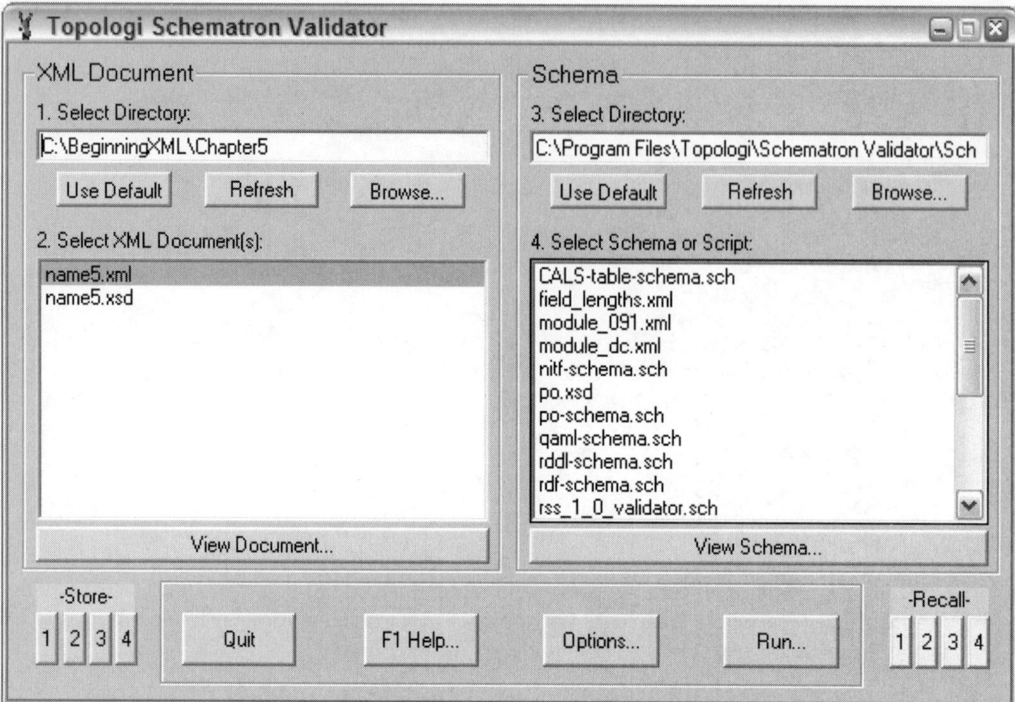

Figure 5-1

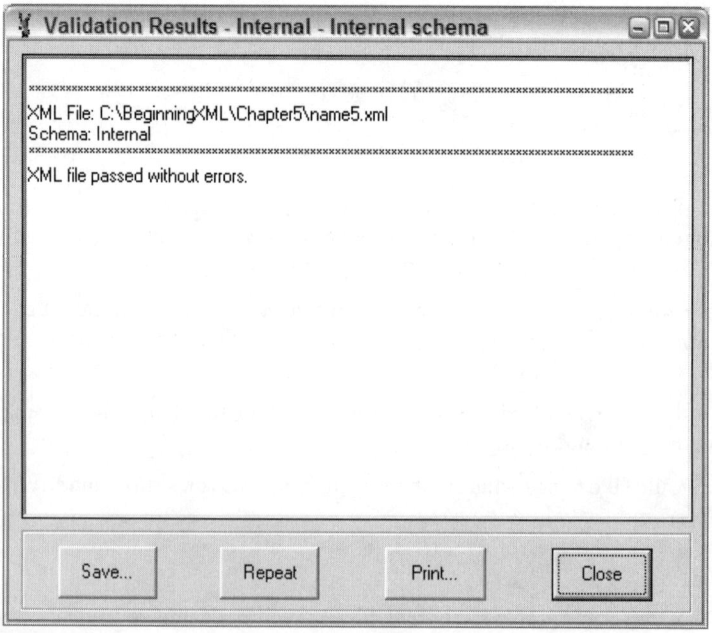

Validation Results - Internal - Internal schema

XML File: C:\BeginningXML\Chapter5\name5.xml
Schema: Internal

XML file passed without errors.

Save... Repeat Print... Close

Figure 5-2

We used the XML Schema to check if our instance document was schema valid. To connect the two documents we included a reference to the XML Schema within our instance document. The internal process by which schema validators compare the document structure against the vocabulary varies greatly. At the most basic level, the schema validator reads the declarations within the XML Schema. As it is parsing the instance document, it validates each element that it encounters against the matching declaration. If it finds an element or attribute that does not appear within the declarations, or if it finds a declaration that has no matching XML content, it raises a schema validity error.

Let's break the XML Schema down into smaller pieces so that we can see some of what we will be learning later:

```
<?xml version="1.0"?>
```

As we have seen in all of our XML documents, we begin with the XML declaration. Again, this is optional but it is highly recommended that you include it to avoid XML version conflicts later.

```
<schema xmlns="http://www.w3.org/2001/XMLSchema"
 xmlns:target="http://www.example.com/name"
 targetNamespace="http://www.example.com/name"
 elementFormDefault="qualified">
```

The root element within our XML Schema is the `<schema>` element. Within the `<schema>` element, we have our namespace declaration. We indicated that the namespace of our `<schema>` element is `http://www.w3.org/2001/XMLSchema`. Within the `<schema>` element, we have also included a `targetNamespace` attribute that indicates that we are developing a vocabulary for the namespace `http://www.example.com/name`. Remember this is just a unique name that we chose; the URL does not necessarily point to anything. We also declared a namespace that matches our `targetNamespace` with the prefix `target`. If we need to refer to any declarations within our XML Schema, we will need this declaration, so we have included it just in case. Again, you are not required to use `target` as your prefix; you could choose any prefix you like.

We also included the attribute `elementFormDefault` with the value `qualified`. Essentially, this controls the way namespaces are used within our corresponding XML document. For now, it is best to get into the habit of adding this attribute with the value `qualified`, as it will simplify our instance documents. We will look at what this means a little later in the chapter.

```
<element name="name">
```

Within our `<schema>` element, we have an `<element>` declaration. Within this `<element>` declaration, we specified that the name of the element is `name`. In this example, we have chosen to specify our content by including a `<complexType>` definition within our `<element>` declaration.

```
<complexType>
  <sequence>
    <element name="first" type="string"/>
    <element name="middle" type="string"/>
    <element name="last" type="string"/>
  </sequence>
  <attribute name="title" type="string"/>
</complexType>
```

Because our <name> element, in our example, contains the elements <first>, <middle>, and <last>, it is known as a complexType. Our <complexType> definition allows us to specify the allowable elements and their order as well as any attribute declarations.

Just as we did in our DTD, we must declare our content using a content model. In DTDs we could use sequences and choices when specifying our content model. In our example, we have indicated that we are using a sequence by including a <sequence> element. Our <sequence> declaration contains three <element> declarations. Within these declarations, we have specified that their type is string. This indicates that the elements must adhere to the XML Schema simpleType string, which allows any textual content.

In addition, within our <complexType> definition, we included an <attribute> declaration. This <attribute> declaration appears at the end of the <complexType> definition, after any content model information. By declaring a title attribute, we can easily specify how we should address the individual described by our <name> XML.

Before we move on, let's just take a quick look at our instance document:

```
<name
  xmlns="http://www.example.com/name"
  xmlns:xsi="http://www.w3.org/2001/XMLSchema-instance"
  xsi:schemaLocation="http://www.example.com/name name5.xsd"
  title="Mr.">
```

Within the root element of our instance document, we have two namespace declarations. The first indicates that our default namespace is http://www.example.com/name. This namespace matches the targetNamespace that we declared within our XML Schema. We also declare the namespace http://www.w3.org/2001/XMLSchema-instance. The XML Schema Recommendation allows you to include several attributes from this namespace within your instance document.

Our instance document includes the attribute schemaLocation. This attribute tells our schema validator where to find our XML Schema document for validation. The schemaLocation attribute is declared within the namespace http://www.w3.org/2001/XMLSchema-instance, so we have prefixed the attribute with the prefix xsi. The value of schemaLocation attribute is http://www.example.com/name name5.xsd. This is known as a namespace/file location pair; it is the namespace of our XML document and the URL of the XML Schema that describes our namespace. In this example we have used a very simple relative URL—name5.xsd. The XML Schema Recommendation allows you to declare several namespace/file location pairs within a single schemaLocation attribute—simply separate the values with whitespace. This is useful when your XML document uses multiple namespaces.

The schemaLocation attribute is only a hint for the processor to use—the processor may not use the provided location at all. For example, the validator may have a local copy of the XML Schema that it uses instead of loading the file specified, to decrease processor usage. If your XML Schema has no targetNamespace, you must refer to the XML Schema using the noNamespaceSchemaLocation attribute within our instance document.

This has been an extremely brief overview of some difficult concepts in XML Schemas. Don't worry; this *Try It Out* is intended to give you an overall context for what we will be learning throughout the chapter. We will cover each of these concepts in much greater detail.

This chapter won't list all of the elements available with XML Schemas, but will introduce the more common ones that you're likely to encounter. Furthermore, not all of the attributes are listed for some of the elements, but again, only the more common ones are. For in-depth coverage of all of the XML Schema features and their use, see Professional XML Schemas *by Jon Duckett et al. (Wrox Press 2001).*

<schema> Declarations

As we have already seen, the `<schema>` element is the root element within an XML Schema. The `<schema>` element allows us to declare namespace information as well as defaults for declarations throughout the document. The XML Schema Recommendation also allows us to include a `version` attribute that can help to identify the XML Schema and the version of our vocabulary.

```
<schema targetNamespace="URI"
  attributeFormDefault="qualified or unqualified"
  elementFormDefault="qualified or unqualified"
  version="version number">
```

The XML Schema Namespace

In our first example, we declared the namespace `http://www.w3.org/2001/XMLSchema` within our `<schema>` element. This allows us to indicate that the `<schema>` element is part of the XML Schema vocabulary. Remember, because XML is case sensitive, namespaces are case sensitive. If the namespace does not match `http://www.w3.org/2001/XMLSchema`, the schema validator should reject the document. For example, you could use any of the following `<schema>`:

```
<schema xmlns="http://www.w3.org/2001/XMLSchema">
```

or

```
<xs:schema xmlns:xs="http://www.w3.org/2001/XMLSchema">
```

or

```
<xsd:schema xmlns:xsd="http://www.w3.org/2001/XMLSchema">
```

As we learned in Chapter 3, the namespace prefix is insignificant—it is only a shortcut to the namespace declaration. You will usually see one of these three variations. The XML Schema Recommendation itself uses the prefix `xs`, and this is by far the most common usage. Using no prefix, as we have shown in the first of the preceding examples, is also very common. Because of its relative simplicity we will use this form in our examples throughout the chapter. Which prefix you use is a matter of personal preference.

Target Namespaces

The primary purpose of XML Schemas is to declare vocabularies. These vocabularies can be identified by a namespace that is specified in the `targetNamespace` attribute. It is important to realize that not all XML Schemas will have a `targetNamespace`. Many XML Schemas define vocabularies that will be reused in another XML Schema, or vocabularies that will be used in documents where the namespace is not necessary.

When declaring a `targetNamespace`, it is important to include a matching namespace declaration. Like the XML Schema namespace, you can choose any prefix you like, or you can use a default namespace declaration. The namespace declaration will be used when you are referring to declarations within the XML Schema. We will see what this means in more detail later in the section *Referring to an Existing Global Element.*

Some possible `targetNamespace` declarations include the following:

```
<schema xmlns="http://www.w3.org/2001/XMLSchema"
 targetNamespace="http://www.example.com/name"
 xmlns:target="http://www.example.com/name">
```

or

```
<xs:schema xmlns:xs="http://www.w3.org/2001/XMLSchema"
 targetNamespace="http://www.example.com/name"
 xmlns="http://www.example.com/name">
```

Notice that in the first declaration the `<schema>` element is using the default namespace, while the target namespace `http://www.example.com/name` requires the use of a prefix. However, in the second declaration we see the exact opposite; the `<schema>` element requires the use of a prefix while the target namespace `http://www.example.com/name` uses the default. Again, user preference is the only difference.

Declaration Defaults

The `<schema>` element also allows us to modify the defaults for the declarations that appear within the XML Schema. We can modify these defaults by including the following attributes:

- `elementFormDefault`
- `attributeFormDefault`

The `elementFormDefault` and `attributeFormDefault` attributes allow you to control the default qualification form for elements and attributes in the instance documents. Wait a second, what's a qualification form? Within the instance document, elements and attributes may be `qualified` or `unqualified`. An element or attribute is *qualified* if it has an associated namespace Uniform Resource Identifier (URI). For example, the following elements are qualified:

```
<name xmlns="http://www.example.com/name">
   <first>John</first>
   <middle>Fitzgerald</middle>
   <last>Doe</last>
</name>

<n:name xmlns:n="http://www.example.com/name">
   <n:first>John</n:first>
   <n:middle>Fitzgerald</n:middle>
   <n:last>Doe</n:last>
</n:name>
```

Even though our first example doesn't have a namespace prefix, it still has an associated namespace URI, `http://www.example.com/name`, and so it is qualified *but not* prefixed. Each of the children elements is also qualified because of the default namespace declaration in the <name> element. Again, these elements have no prefixes. In the second example, all of the elements are qualified *and* prefixed.

Unqualified elements have no associated namespace. For example:

```
<n:name xmlns:n="http://www.example.com/name">
   <first>John</first>
   <middle>Fitzgerald</middle>
   <last>Doe</last>
</n:name>
```

The <name> element is qualified, but the <first>, <middle>, and <last> elements are not. The <first>, <middle>, and <last> elements have no associated namespace declaration (default or otherwise), and therefore, they are unqualified. This mix of qualified and unqualified elements may seem strange; nevertheless, it is the default behavior. The default value for both `elementFormDefault` and `attributeFormDefault` is `unqualified`.

Even though the value of the `elementFormDefault` attribute is `unqualified`, some elements must be qualified regardless. For example, the <name> element must *always* be qualified in the instance document. This is because it was declared globally within our XML Schema (we will look at global and local declarations in detail in the next section). In the preceding example, this is exactly what we have done. We have qualified the <name> element with a namespace, but not the <first>, <middle>, and <last> elements.

In some cases, you will need to create a document that uses both qualified and unqualified elements. For example, XSLT and SOAP documents may contain both qualified and unqualified elements. However, most of your documents should qualify all of their elements. Without this, someone who is creating an XML document based on your vocabulary will need in-depth knowledge of your XML Schema to determine which elements should be qualified and which elements should be unqualified. Therefore, it is considered best practice that, unless you have a very specific need to mix qualified and unqualified elements, you should always include the `elementFormDefault` attribute with the value `qualified`.

<element> Declarations

When declaring an element, we are actually performing two primary tasks: specifying the element name and defining the allowable content.

```
<element
  name="name of the element"
  type="global type"
  ref="global element declaration"
  form="qualified or unqualified"
  minOccurs="non negative number"
  maxOccurs="non negative number or 'unbounded'"
  default="default value"
  fixed="fixed value">
```

According to the XML Schema Recommendation, an element's allowable content is determined by its *type*. As we have already seen, element types are divided into simpleTypes and complexTypes. XML Schemas allow you to specify an element's type in one of two ways:

- Creating a local type
- Using a global type

In addition to these two methods, you may also reuse elements by referring to an existing global element. In this case, you include a reference to the global element declaration. Of course, you do not need to specify a type in your reference; the type of the element is included in the global element declaration.

Global versus Local

Before we can understand these different methods for declaring elements, we must learn the difference between global and local declarations. XML Schema declarations can be divided into two broad categories: global declarations and local declarations.

- *Global declarations* are declarations that appear as direct children of the `<schema>` element. Global element declarations can be reused throughout the XML Schema.
- *Local declarations* do not have the `<schema>` element as their direct parent and are valid only in their specific context.

Let's look at our first example again:

```
<?xml version="1.0"?>
<schema xmlns="http://www.w3.org/2001/XMLSchema"
 xmlns:target="http://www.example.com/name"
 targetNamespace="http://www.example.com/name"
 elementFormDefault="qualified">
  <element name="name">
    <complexType>
      <sequence>
        <element name="first" type="string"/>
        <element name="middle" type="string"/>
        <element name="last" type="string"/>
      </sequence>
      <attribute name="title" type="string"/>
    </complexType>
  </element>
</schema>
```

In this XML Schema, we have four element declarations. The first declaration, our `<name>` element, is a global declaration because it is a direct child of the `<schema>` element. The declarations for the `<first>`, `<middle>`, and `<last>` elements are considered local because the declarations are not direct children of the `<schema>` element. The declarations for the `<first>`, `<middle>`, and `<last>` elements are valid only within the `<sequence>` declaration—they cannot be reused elsewhere in the XML Schema.

Creating a Local Type

Of the two methods of element declaration, creating a local type should seem the most familiar. We used this model when we declared our `<name>` element in our example. To create a local type, you simply include the type declaration as a child of the element declaration:

```
<element name="name">
  <complexType>
    <!-- type information -->
  </complexType>
</element>
```

or

```
<element name="name">
  <simpleType>
    <!-- type information -->
  </simpleType>
</element>
```

In these examples, we see that an element declaration may contain a `<complexType>` definition or a `<simpleType>` definition, but it cannot contain both at the same time. We will look at the details of these declarations a little later.

Using a Global Type

Often, many of our elements will have the same content. Instead of declaring duplicate local types throughout our schema, we can create a global type. Within our element declarations, we can refer to a global type by name. In fact, we have already seen this:

```
<element name="first" type="string"/>
```

Here, the `type` attribute refers to the built-in data type `string`. XML Schemas have many built-in data types that we will look at later in the chapter. You can also create your own global declarations and refer to them. For example, suppose we had created a global type for the content of the `<name>` element:

```
<schema xmlns="http://www.w3.org/2001/XMLSchema"
 xmlns:target="http://www.example.com/name"
 targetNamespace="http://www.example.com/name"
 elementFormDefault="qualified">
  <complexType name="NameType">
    <!-- type information -->
  </complexType>
  <element name="name" type="target:NameType"/>
</schema>
```

Even though the type is global, it is still part of the target namespace. Because of this, when referring to the type we must include the target namespace prefix (if any). In this example we used the prefix `target` to refer to the target namespace. However, it is equally correct to do the following:

```
<xs:schema xmlns:xs="http://www.w3.org/2001/XMLSchema"
 xmlns="http://www.example.com/name"
 targetNamespace="http://www.example.com/name"
 elementFormDefault="qualified">
  <xs:complexType name="NameType">
    <!-- type information -->
  </xs:complexType>
  <xs:element name="name" type="NameType"/>
</xs:schema>
```

In this example the XML Schema namespace is declared using the prefix xs and the target namespace has no prefix. Therefore, to refer to the global type NameType, we do not need to include any prefix.

Try It Out Creating Reusable Global Types

Creating global types within our XML Schema is straightforward. Let's convert our <name> example to use a named global type rather than a local type.

1. We will begin by making the necessary changes to our XML Schema. Open the file name5.xsd and make the following changes. When you are finished, save the file as name6.xsd.

```
<?xml version="1.0"?>
<schema xmlns="http://www.w3.org/2001/XMLSchema"
 xmlns:target="http://www.example.com/name"
 targetNamespace="http://www.example.com/name"
 elementFormDefault="qualified">
  <complexType name="NameType">
    <sequence>
      <element name="first" type="string"/>
      <element name="middle" type="string"/>
      <element name="last" type="string"/>
    </sequence>
    <attribute name="title" type="string"/>
  </complexType>
  <element name="name" type="target:NameType"/>
</schema>
```

2. Before we can schema validate our document, we must modify it so that it refers to our new XML Schema. Open the file name5.xml and change the xsi:schemaLocation attribute, as follows. When you are finished, save the file as name6.xml.

```
xsi:schemaLocation="http://www.example.com/name name6.xsd"
```

3. We are ready to validate our XML instance document against our XML Schema. Open the Topologi Schematron Validator and browse to the folder where you saved you files. Select name6.xml on the left side and click the Run button. This should validate with no errors just as we saw in the last *Try It Out*.

How It Works

We had to make minor modifications to our schema in order to create a reusable complexType. First, we moved our <complexType> definition from within our <element> declaration to our <schema> element. Remember, a declaration is global if it is a direct child of the <schema> element. Once we had made our <complexType> definition global, we needed to add a name attribute so that we could refer to it later. We named our <complexType> definition NameType so it would be easy to identify.

Once we declared our NameType <complexType>, we modified our <name> element declaration to refer to it. We added a type attribute to our element declaration with the value target:NameType. Keep in mind; we had to include the namespace prefix target when referring to the type, so the validator knew which namespace it should look in.

Referring to an Existing Global Element

Referring to global types allows us to easily reuse content model definitions within our XML Schema. Often, we may want to reuse entire element declarations instead of just the type. XML Schemas allow you to reuse global element declarations within your content model. To refer to a global element declaration, simply include a `ref` attribute and specify the name of the global element as the value.

```
<element ref="target:first"/>
```

Again, the name of the element must be qualified with the namespace prefix. The preceding example is an element reference to a global element named `first` that has been declared in the target namespace. Notice that when we refer to a global element declaration, we have no `type` attribute and no local type declaration. Our element declaration will use the type of the `<element>` declaration to which we are referring.

Try It Out Referring to Global Element Declarations

Let's modify our last example so that we can see how to create and refer to global element declarations.

1. Again, we will begin by making the necessary changes to our XML Schema. Open the file `name6.xsd` and make the following changes. When you are finished, save the file as `name7.xsd`.

```
<?xml version="1.0"?>
<schema xmlns="http://www.w3.org/2001/XMLSchema"
 xmlns:target="http://www.example.com/name"
 targetNamespace="http://www.example.com/name"
 elementFormDefault="qualified">
  <element name="first" type="string"/>
  <element name="middle" type="string"/>
  <element name="last" type="string"/>
  <complexType name="NameType">
    <sequence>
      <element ref="target:first"/>
      <element ref="target:middle"/>
      <element ref="target:last"/>
    </sequence>
    <attribute name="title" type="string"/>
  </complexType>
  <element name="name" type="target:NameType"/>
</schema>
```

2. Before we can schema validate our XML document, we must modify it so that it refers to our new XML Schema. Open the file `name6.xml` and change the `xsi:schemaLocation` attribute, as follows. When you are finished, save the file as `name7.xml`.

```
xsi:schemaLocation="http://www.example.com/name name7.xsd"
```

3. We are ready to validate our XML instance document against our XML Schema. Within the Topologi Schematron Validator, select `name7.xml` on the left side and click the Run button. This should validate with no errors just as we saw in the last *Try It Out*.

How It Works

In this *Try It Out*, we utilized references to global element declarations within our content model. First, we moved the declarations for our <first>, <middle>, and <last> elements from within our <complexType> definition to our <schema> element making them global. After we had created our global declarations, we inserted references to the elements within our <complexType>. In each reference, we prefixed the global element name with the prefix target.

At this point, it might help to examine what our schema validator is doing, in more detail. As our schema validator is processing our instance document, it will first encounter the root element, in this case <name>. When it encounters the <name> element, it will look it up in the XML Schema. When attempting to find the declaration for the root element, the schema validator will look through only the global element declarations.

> **In this case, we have four global element declarations: <first>, <middle>, <last>, and <name>. Any one of these could be used as the root element within an instance document; in our example, we are using the <name> element as our instance document root element. Although the XML Schema Recommendation allows us to have multiple global <element> declarations, we are still allowed to have only one root element in our instance document.**

Once the schema validator finds the matching declaration, it will find the associated type (in this case it is a global <complexType> definition NameType). It will then validate the content of the <name> element within the instance against the content model defined in the associated type. When the schema validator encounters the <element> reference declarations, it will import the global <element> declarations into the<complexType> definition, as if they had been included directly.

Now that we have seen some of the basics of how elements are declared, let's look briefly at some of the features element declarations offer. Later in the chapter, we will look at complexType definitions and content models in more depth.

Naming Elements

Specifying a name in your element declaration is very straightforward. Simply include the name attribute and specify the desired name as the value. The name must follow the rules for XML names that we have already learned. In the last chapter, when creating names in DTDs we saw that we had to include any namespace prefix in the element declaration. Because XML Schemas are namespace aware, this is unnecessary. Simply specify the name of the element; the schema validator will be able to understand any prefix that is used within the instance document. The following are examples of *valid* element names:

```
<element name="first" type="string"/>
<element name="speed" type="string"/>
```

The following are examples of *invalid* element names:

```
<element name="2ndElement" type="string"/>
<element name="target:middle" type="string"/>
```

The first of these examples is invalid because it begins with a number. Remember, XML names may include numerical digits, periods (.), hyphens (-), and underscores (_), but they must begin with a letter or an underscore (_). The second of these examples is invalid because it contains a colon (:). Since the inception of namespaces, the colon may be used only to indicate a namespace prefix. As we said earlier, the prefix must not be included as part of the name in the element declaration.

Element Qualified Form

The form attribute allows you to override the default for element qualification. Remember, if an element is qualified it must have an associated namespace when it is used in the instance document. You can specify whether the element must be qualified, by setting the value of the form attribute to qualified or unqualified. If you do not include a form attribute, the schema validator will use the value of the elementFormDefault attribute declared in the <schema> element.

Cardinality

In the last chapter, we learned that when we are specifying elements in our content models we could modify their cardinality. Cardinality represents the number of occurrences of a specific element within a content model. In XML Schemas, we can modify an element's cardinality by specifying the minOccurs and maxOccurs attributes within the element declaration.

> **It is important to note that the minOccurs and maxOccurs attributes are not permitted within global element declarations. Instead, you should use these attributes within the element references in your content models.**

Within DTDs, we had very limited options when specifying cardinality. Using cardinality indicators, we could declare that an element would appear once and only once, once or not at all, one or more times, or zero or more times. This seems to cover the basics, but many times we need more control. XML Schemas improved the model by allowing you to specify the minimum and maximum separately.

Some possible uses of the minOccurs and maxOccurs attributes include the following:

```
<element name="element1" type="string" minOccurs="2" maxOccurs="2"/>

<element ref="target:element2" maxOccurs="10"/>

<element name="element3" type="string" minOccurs="0" maxOccurs="unbounded"/>
```

In the first of the preceding examples we have declared that the element <element1> must appear within our instance document a minimum of two times and a maximum of two times. In the second example, we have declared our element using a reference to the global <element2> declaration. Even though it is declared using the ref attribute, we are permitted to use the minOccurs and maxOccurs attributes to specify the element's cardinality. In this case, we have included a maxOccurs attribute with the value 10. We have not included a minOccurs attribute, so a schema validator would use the default value, 1. In the final example, we have specified that <element3> may or may not appear within our instance document because the minOccurs attribute has the value 0. We have also indicated that it may appear an infinite number of times because the value of maxOccurs is unbounded.

The default value for the minOccurs attribute and the maxOccurs attribute is 1. This means that, by default, an element must appear only once. You can use the two attributes separately or in conjunction. The maxOccurs attribute allows you to enter the value unbounded, which indicates that there is no limit to the number of occurrences. The only additional rule you must adhere to when specifying minOccurs and maxOccurs is that the value of maxOccurs must be greater than or equal to the value for minOccurs.

Default and Fixed Values

When designing the DTD for our dinosaur list in the last chapter, we made use of attribute default and fixed values. In XML Schemas, we can declare default and fixed values for elements as well as attributes. When declaring default values for elements, we can specify only a text value. You are not permitted to specify a default value for an element whose content model will contain other elements, unless the content model is mixed. By specifying a default value for your element, you can be sure that the schema validator will treat the value as if it were included in the XML document—even if it is omitted.

To specify a default value, simply include the default attribute with the desired value. Suppose our <name> elements were being used to design the Doe family tree. We might want to make "Doe" the default for the last name element:

```
<element name="last" type="string" default="Doe"/>
```

In this example, we have declared that our element <last> will have the default value "Doe". Because of this, when a schema validator encounters the <last> element in the instance document, it will insert the default value if there is no content. For example, if the schema validator encounters

```
<last></last>
```

or

```
<last/>
```

it would treat the element as follows:

```
<last>Doe</last>
```

It is important to note that the element must appear within the document, and it must be empty. If the element does not appear within the document, or if the element already has content, the default value will not be used.

In the last chapter, in addition to default values, we also learned that attributes may have fixed values. Again, in XML Schemas elements and attributes may have fixed values. In some circumstances, you may want to make sure that an element's value does not change, such as an element whose value is used to indicate a version number. When an element's value can never change, simply include a fixed attribute with the fixed value. As the schema validator is processing the file, if an element that was declared to have a fixed value is encountered, then the parser will check whether the content and fixed attribute value match. If they do not match, the parser will raise a schema validity error. If the element is empty then the parser will insert the fixed value.

To specify a fixed value, simply include the `fixed` attribute with the desired value:

```
<element name="version" type="string" fixed="1.0"/>
```

In the preceding example, we have specified that the `<version>` element, if it appears, must contain the value `1.0`. The fixed value is a valid `string` value (the type of our `<version>` element is `string`). Therefore, the following elements would be *legal*:

```
<version>1.0</version>

<version></version>

<version/>
```

As the schema validator is processing the file it will accept the latter of these examples. Because they are empty elements, it will treat them as if the value `1.0` had been included. The following value is *not legal*:

```
<version>2.0</version>
```

When specifying fixed or default values you must ensure that the value you specify is an allowable content for the type that you have declared for your element declaration. For example, if you specified that an element had the type `positiveInteger`, you could not use `"Doe"` as a default value because it is not a positive integer. Again, default and fixed values are not permitted to contain element content. Therefore, your element must have a simpleType or a mixed content declaration. You are not permitted to use default and fixed values at the same time within a single element declaration.

Element Wildcards

Often we will want to include elements in our XML Schema without exercising as much control. Suppose we wanted our element to contain any of the elements declared in our namespace. Suppose we wanted to specify that our element can contain any elements from another namespace. This is common when designing XML Schemas. Declarations that allow you to include any element from a namespace are called *element wildcards*.

To declare an element wildcard, use the <any> declaration:

```
<any
  minOccurs="non negative number"
  maxOccurs="non negative number or 'unbounded'"
  namespace="allowable namespaces"
  processContents="lax or skip or strict">
```

The <any> declaration can appear only within a content model. You are not allowed to create global <any> declarations; instead, you must use them within content models. When specifying an <any> declaration you can specify the cardinality just as you would specify an `<element>` declaration. By specifying the `minOccurs` or the `maxOccurs` attributes, you can control the number of wildcard occurrences that are allowed within your instance document.

The <any> declaration allows you to control which namespace or namespaces the elements are allowed to come from, which is controlled by including the namespace attribute. The namespace attribute allows several values:

Value	Description
##any	Allows elements from all namespaces to be included as part of the wildcard.
##other	Allows elements from namespaces other than the targetNamespace to be included as part of the wildcard.
##targetNamespace	Allows elements from only the targetNamespace to be included as part of the wildcard.
##local	Allows any well-formed elements that are not qualified by a namespace to be included as part of the wildcard.
Whitespace-separated list of allowable namespace URIs	Allows elements from any listed namespaces to be included as part of the wildcard. Possible list values also include ##targetNamespace and ##local.

For example, suppose that we wanted to allow any well-formed XML content from any namespace within our <name> element. Within the content model for our NameType complexType we could include an element wildcard:

```
<complexType name="NameType">
  <sequence>
    <element ref="target:first"/>
    <element ref="target:middle"/>
    <element ref="target:last"/>
    <!-- allow any element from any namespace -->
    <any namespace="##any"
         processContents="lax"
         minOccurs="0"
         maxOccurs="unbounded"/>
  </sequence>
  <attribute name="title" type="string"/>
</complexType>
```

In the preceding example, we have included an <any> element wildcard. By setting the namespace attribute to ##any, we have specified that elements from all namespaces can be included as part of the wildcard. We have also included cardinality attributes to indicate the number of allowed wildcard elements. In this case, we have specified any number of elements because we have set the value of maxOccurs to unbounded. We have also indicated that there may be none at all by setting the value of the minOccurs attribute to 0. Therefore, our content model must contain a <first>, <middle>, and <last> element in sequence, followed by any number of elements from any namespace.

When the schema validator is processing an element that contains a wildcard declaration, it will validate the instance documents in one of the three following ways.

- If the value of the `processContents` attribute is set to `skip`, the processor will skip any wildcard elements in the instance document.
- If the value of `processContents` attribute is set to `lax`, then the processor will attempt to validate the wildcard elements if it has access to an XML Schema that defines them.
- If the value of the `processContents` attribute is set to `strict` (the default), the processor will attempt to validate the wildcard elements if it has access to an XML Schema that defines them. However, in contrast to using the `lax` setting, the schema validator raises a validity error if the XML Schema for the wildcard elements cannot be found and the `processContents` attribute is set to `strict`.

<complexType> Declarations

So far we have seen the basics of declaring elements. In each of our examples we utilized a `<complexType>` definition. Let's look at our type definitions in more detail. As we have already learned, our element content is controlled by `<simpleType>` and `<complexType>` definitions. Within our `<complexType>` definition we can specify the allowable element content for our declaration.

```
<complexType
mixed="Boolean expression"
name="Name of complexType">
```

All of our examples so far have used either a local or a global `<complexType>` to specify the content model for our `<name>` element declaration.

```
<element name="name">
  <complexType>
    <sequence>
      <element name="first" type="string"/>
      <element name="middle" type="string"/>
      <element name="last" type="string"/>
    </sequence>
    <attribute name="title" type="string"/>
  </complexType>
</element>
```

When we created a local declaration, we did not include a `name` attribute in our `<complexType>` definition. Local `<complexType>` definitions are *never* named; in fact, they are called *anonymous complex types*. As we have already seen, however, global `<complexType>` definitions are *always* named, so that they can be identified later.

Apart from the content models we have seen, `<complexType>` definitions can also be used to create mixed and empty content models. Mixed content models allow you to include both text and element content within a single content model. To create a mixed content model in XML Schemas, simply include the `mixed` attribute with the value `true` in your `<complexType>` definition.

```
<element name="description">
  <complexType mixed="true">
    <choice minOccurs="0" maxOccurs="unbounded">
      <element name="b" type="string"/>
```

```
      <element name="i" type="string"/>
    </choice>
  </complexType>
</element>
```

In this example, we have declared a <description> element, which can contain an infinite number of <b> and <i> elements. Because we declared the complexType as mixed, text can be interspersed throughout these elements. An allowable <description> element might look like the following:

```
<description>The Tyrannosaurus Rex was the <b>king</b> of the terrible
lizards. Though many now believe it was a hunter <i>and</i> a scavenger it is
no less fearsome.</description>
```

In this <description> element, we have textual content interspersed throughout the elements that we have declared within our content model. As the schema validator is processing the preceding example, it will ignore the textual content and instead perform standard validation on the elements. The schema validator will not perform any validation on the text. Because the elements <b> and <i> may appear repeatedly, the example is valid.

To declare an empty content model in a <complexType> definition, you simply create the <complexType> definition without any <element> or content model declarations. Consider the following declarations:

```
<element name="emptyElement">
  <complexType>
  </complexType>
</element>

<element name="emptyElement">
  <complexType/>
</element>
```

Each of these declares an element named `emptyElement`. In both cases, the <complexType> definition is empty, indicating that `emptyElement` will not contain text or element children. When used in our instance document <emptyElement> must be empty. For example, the following elements would be valid instances of the preceding declarations:

```
<emptyElement/>

<emptyElement></emptyElement>
```

Although we haven't looked at attribute declarations in XML Schemas, it should be mentioned that <complexType> definitions can also contain <attribute> declarations. Even when you are declaring an empty element, attribute declarations may still appear within the complexType. We will look at this in more detail later in this chapter.

<group> Declarations

Within our XML Schema, we can declare our elements within <complexType> definitions as we have done. In addition to <complexType> definitions, XML Schemas also allow you to define reusable groups of elements. By creating a global <group> declaration, you can easily reuse and combine entire content models.

```
<group
  name="name of global group">
```

Just as we have seen with global <complexType> definitions, all global <group> declarations must be named. Simply specify the name attribute with the desired name. Again, the name that you specify must follow the rules for XML names and it should not include a prefix. The basic structure of a global <group> declaration follows:

```
<group name="NameGroup">
  <!-- content model goes here -->
</group>
```

Try It Out Using a Global Group

Let's redesign our schema so that we can create a reusable global <group> declaration.

1. Again, we will begin by making the necessary changes to our XML Schema. Open the file name7.xsd and make the following changes. When you are finished, save the file as name8.xsd.

```
<?xml version="1.0"?>
<schema xmlns="http://www.w3.org/2001/XMLSchema"
 xmlns:target="http://www.example.com/name"
 targetNamespace="http://www.example.com/name"
 elementFormDefault="qualified">
  <group name="NameGroup">
    <sequence>
      <element name="first" type="string"/>
      <element name="middle" type="string"/>
      <element name="last" type="string"/>
    </sequence>
  </group>
  <complexType name="NameType">
    <group ref="target:NameGroup"/>
    <attribute name="title" type="string"/>
  </complexType>
  <element name="name" type="target:NameType"/>
</schema>
```

2. Before we can schema validate our XML document, we must modify it so that it refers to our new XML Schema. Open the file name7.xml and change the xsi:schemaLocation attribute, as follows. When you are finished, save the file as name8.xml.

```
xsi:schemaLocation="http://www.example.com/name name8.xsd"
```

3. We are ready to validate our XML instance document against our XML Schema. Within the Topologi Schematron Validator, select name8.xml on the left side and click the Run button. This should validate with no errors just as we saw in the last *Try It Out*.

How It Works

In this *Try It Out*, we have modified our XML Schema to use a global <group> declaration. First, we created a global <group> declaration named NameGroup. Within our declaration, we specified the allowable content model for our <name> element. Within the <complexType> definition for our <name> element, instead of including element declarations, we created a <group> reference declaration. When referring to the global <group> declaration, we included a ref attribute with the value target:NameGroup.

Notice that our <attribute> declaration still appeared within our <complexType> definition and not within our <group> declaration. This should give you some indication of the difference between a <group> and a <complexType> definition. A <complexType> definition defines the allowable content for a specific element or type of element. A <group> declaration simply allows you to create a reusable group of elements that can be used within content model declarations in your XML Schema.

As the schema validator is processing the instance document, it will process the <name> element similarly to our earlier examples. When it encounters the <name> element, it will look it up in the XML Schema. Once it finds the declaration, it will find the associated type (in this case it is a local <complexType> definition). When the schema validator encounters the <group> reference declaration, it will treat the items within the group as if they had been included directly within the <complexType> definition.

Content Models

We have already seen that we can use <complexType> and <group> declarations to specify an element's allowable content. What we haven't seen is how to build more advanced content models. Luckily, XML Schemas provide greater flexibility than DTDs when specifying an element's content model. In XML Schemas you can specify an element's content model using the following:

- A <sequence> declaration
- A <choice> declaration
- A reference to a global <group> declaration
- An <all> declaration

By using these four primary declarations, we can specify the content model of our type in a variety of ways. Each of these declarations may contain

- Inner content models
- Element declarations
- Element wildcards

Let's look at these in more detail.

<sequence> Declarations

Just as we saw in our DTD content models, specifying our content model using a sequence of elements is very simple. In fact, our first example used a <sequence> declaration when defining the allowable children of our <name> element.

```
<sequence
  minOccurs="non negative number"
  maxOccurs="non negative number or 'unbounded'">
```

The <sequence> declaration allows you to specify `minOccurs` and `maxOccurs` attributes that apply to the overall sequence. You can modify the cardinality (how many of this sequence of elements will occur) by changing the values of these attributes. The `minOccurs` and `maxOccurs` attributes function exactly as they did within our element declarations.

We have already seen that the <sequence> declaration may contain <element> declarations within it. In addition to <element> declarations, it may contain element wildcards or inner <sequence>, <choice>, or <group> references. We may have sequences within sequences within sequences, or we may have choices within sequences that are in turn within groups—almost any combination you can imagine.

A sample sequence might appear as follows:

```
<complexType>
  <sequence>
    <element name="first" type="string"/>
    <element name="middle" type="string"/>
    <element name="last" type="string"/>
  </sequence>
  <attribute name="title" type="string"/>
</complexType>
```

By utilizing a <sequence> to specify your content model, you indicate that the elements must appear within your instance document in the *sequence*, or order, specified. For example, because our `complexType` definition utilizes a sequence, the following would be *legal*:

```
<first>John</first>
<middle>Fitzgerald Johansen</middle>
<last>Doe</last>
```

The following would be *illegal*:

```
<last>Doe</last>
<middle>Fitzgerald</middle>
<first>John</first>
```

This example would not be allowable because the elements do not appear in the order that we have specified within our <sequence>.

<choice> Declarations

The basic structure of our <choice> declaration looks very much like the <sequence> declaration.

```
<choice
  minOccurs="non negative number"
  maxOccurs="non negative number or 'unbounded'">
```

Again, we can specify minOccurs and maxOccurs attributes to modify the cardinality of a <choice> declaration. The <choice> declaration is also similar to its DTD counterpart. Like the <sequence> declaration, you can specify multiple child declarations within a <choice> declaration. In an instance document, however, only one of the declarations may be used. For example, suppose we had declared the content model of our <name> element using a <choice> declaration:

```
<element name="name">
  <complexType>
    <choice>
      <element name="first" type="string"/>
      <element name="middle" type="string"/>
      <element name="last" type="string"/>
    </choice>
    <attribute name="title" type="string"/>
  </complexType>
</element>
```

If we had declared our content model as we have in the preceding example, then within our instance document we could include only the <first> element, only the <middle> element, or only the <last> element. We could not include more than one of the elements within the instance.

Just as we saw in our <sequence> declaration, our <choice> declaration may contain <element> declarations, element wildcards, and inner <sequence>, <choice>, or <group> references.

<group> References

The <group> *reference* declaration allows us to refer to global element groups within our content model. Don't confuse a <group> reference, which appears within a content model, with a global <group> declaration that defines a reusable group of elements. We have already seen that global element groups function very similarly to global type definitions; they allow us to define content models that can be grouped together and reused within other content models. Within a content model, the <group> reference declaration is used by creating a reference to one of these already declared groups.

```
<group
  ref="global group definition"
  minOccurs="non negative number"
  maxOccurs="non negative number or 'unbounded'">
```

This can be done by including a ref attribute and specifying the name of the global <group> declaration. As we saw with element references, the global group reference must be prefixed with the appropriate namespace prefix.

An example could be

```
<group name="NameGroup">
  <sequence>
    <element name="first" type="string"/>
    <element name="middle" type="string"/>
    <element name="last" type="string"/>
  </sequence>
</group>
```

```
<element name="name">
  <complexType>
    <group ref="target:NameGroup"/>
    <attribute name="title" type="string"/>
  </complexType>
</element>
```

Here the group reference within our `<complexType>` definition has a `ref` attribute with the value `target:NameGroup`. This refers to the global group declaration named `NameGroup`. We must prefix the name with a namespace prefix, in this case `target`, so that we can identify the namespace in which the `NameGroup` declaration appears.

Again, we can specify `minOccurs` and `maxOccurs` attributes to modify the cardinality of our `<group>` reference. However, the `<group>` reference may not contain element children. Of course, as we have already seen, the global `<group>` declaration that it is referring to will contain the content model and element children that define the content model.

<all> Declarations

The `<all>` declaration allows us to declare that the elements within our content model may appear in any order.

```
<all
  minOccurs="0 or 1"
  maxOccurs="1">
```

To use the `<all>` mechanism, however, we must adhere to several rules.

- First, the `<all>` declaration must be the only content model declaration that appears as a child of a `<complexType>` definition.
- Secondly, the `<all>` declaration may contain only `<element>` declarations as its children. It is not permitted to contain `<sequence>`, `<choice>`, or `<group>` declarations.
- Finally, the `<all>` declaration's children may appear once each in the instance document. This means that within the `<all>` declaration the values for `minOccurs` are limited to `0` or `1`.

Is the `<all>` declaration useful? Even though there are additional restrictions, the `<all>` declaration can be very useful. The `<all>` declaration is commonly used when the expected content is known, but not the order.

The `<all>` element has many limitations, as we have mentioned. These limitations ensure that schema validators could easily understand and process the `<all>` element. Without these restrictions, it would be very difficult to write software to validate XML Schemas that contained `<all>` declarations. In Chapter 6, we will learn about the interleave pattern, which was introduced in RELAX NG and has fewer limitations.

Suppose we had declared our `<name>` content model using the `<all>` mechanism:

```
<element name="name">
  <complexType>
    <all>
      <element name="first" type="string"/>
```

```
        <element name="middle" type="string"/>
        <element name="last" type="string"/>
      </all>
      <attribute name="title" type="string"/>
    </complexType>
  </element>
```

Notice that the <all> element is the only content model declaration within our <complexType> (<attribute> declarations do not count as content model declarations). Also, notice that our <all> declaration contains only <element> declarations as its children. Because the default value for minOccurs and maxOccurs is 1, each element can appear in the instance document once and only once. By declaring our content model as we have in the preceding example, we can validate our element content but still allow our elements to appear in any order. The allowable content for a <name> element might include

```
<first>John</first>
<middle>Fitzgerald</middle>
<last>Doe</last>
```

or

```
<first>John</first>
<last>Doe</last>
<middle>Fitzgerald</middle>
```

As long as all of the elements we have specified appear, they can appear in any order. In the second example, the <middle> element was added last (maybe it wasn't known initially). Because we have declared our content model using <all>, this is still allowable.

Try It Out Dinosaur DNA

Once again, our knowledge has surpassed our early examples. To use all of the XML Schema features that we have learned, we will turn to a more complex subject. Let's create an XML Schema for our dinosaur listing. Not only will this provide ample opportunity to use the functionality we have learned thus far, but it will also allow us to compare and contrast a DTD and its XML Schema counterpart.

1. Let's begin by creating the XML Schema. Simply open a text editor, such as Notepad, and copy the following. When you are finished, save the file as dinosaurs7.xsd.

```
<?xml version="1.0"?>
<schema xmlns="http://www.w3.org/2001/XMLSchema"
 xmlns:dino="http://www.example.com/dinosaurs"
 targetNamespace="http://www.example.com/dinosaurs"
 elementFormDefault="qualified">

  <element name="dinosaurs">
    <complexType>
      <choice minOccurs="0" maxOccurs="unbounded">
        <element name="carnivore">
          <complexType>
            <group ref="dino:DinosaurGroup"/>
```

```
          </complexType>
        </element>
        <element name="herbivore">
          <complexType>
            <group ref="dino:DinosaurGroup"/>
          </complexType>
        </element>
        <element name="omnivore">
          <complexType>
            <group ref="dino:DinosaurGroup"/>
          </complexType>
        </element>
      </choice>
    </complexType>
  </element>

  <group name="DinosaurGroup">
    <sequence>
      <element name="species" type="string"/>
      <element name="length" type="string"/>
      <element name="height" type="string"/>
      <element name="weight" type="string"/>
      <element name="speed" type="string"/>
      <element name="weapon" type="dino:WeaponType"/>
      <element name="discoverer" type="dino:DiscovererType"/>
      <element name="location" type="dino:LocationType"/>
      <element name="description" type="dino:DescriptionType"/>
    </sequence>
  </group>

  <complexType name="WeaponType">
    <sequence minOccurs="0">
      <element name="part-of-body" type="string"/>
      <element name="description" type="dino:DescriptionType"/>
    </sequence>
  </complexType>

  <complexType name="DiscovererType">
    <sequence>
      <element name="name" type="string" maxOccurs="unbounded"/>
      <element name="year" type="string"/>
    </sequence>
  </complexType>

  <complexType name="LocationType">
    <choice>
      <element name="GPS" type="string"/>
      <sequence>
        <element name="country" type="string"/>
        <element name="region" type="string"/>
      </sequence>
    </choice>
  </complexType>

  <complexType name="DescriptionType" mixed="true">
```

```
    <choice minOccurs="0" maxOccurs="unbounded">
      <element name="i" type="string"/>
      <element name="b" type="string"/>
    </choice>
  </complexType>
</schema>
```

2. Next, we'll need to create the instance document. This document will be very similar to our dinosaur samples from Chapter 4. Instead of referring to a DTD, we will be referring to our newly created XML Schema. To start with, we will not include any attributes; we will add them in later examples in this chapter. Also, the only entity we will use is the character entity `ó`. Copy the following; when you are finished, save the file as `dinosaurs7.xml`.

```
<?xml version="1.0"?>
<dinosaurs
  xmlns="http://www.example.com/dinosaurs"
  xmlns:xsi="http://www.w3.org/2001/XMLSchema-instance"
  xsi:schemaLocation="http://www.example.com/dinosaurs dinosaurs7.xsd">
  <carnivore>
    <species>Tyrannosaurus Rex</species>
    <length>42 feet</length>
    <height>18 feet</height>
    <weight>5-7 tons</weight>
    <speed>25 mph</speed>
    <weapon>
      <part-of-body>Teeth</part-of-body>
      <description>Though the Tyrannosaurus had many different sizes of teeth,
all were razor sharp and some grew to lengths of <b>9-13 inches</b>. Broken
teeth were replaced frequently by newer teeth. The powerful jaw exerted in
excess of 3000 pounds of pressure!</description>
    </weapon>
    <discoverer>
      <name>Osborn</name>
      <year>1905</year>
    </discoverer>
    <location>
      <country>Canada</country>
      <region>Alberta</region>
    </location>
    <description>The Tyrannosaurus Rex was the <b>king</b> of the terrible
lizards. Though many now believe it was a hunter <i>and</i> a scavenger it
is no less fearsome.</description>
  </carnivore>
  <herbivore>
    <species>Stegosaurus Armatus</species>
    <length>25-40 feet</length>
    <height>14 feet</height>
    <weight>2-4 tons</weight>
    <speed/>
    <weapon>
      <part-of-body>Spikes</part-of-body>
      <description>The Stegosaurus had two long rows of armor along its back.
```

```
At the end of its tail <b>four large spikes</b> were an excellent
defense.</description>
    </weapon>
    <discoverer>
      <name>Marsh</name>
      <year>1877</year>
    </discoverer>
    <location>
      <country>United States</country>
      <region>Colorado</region>
    </location>
    <description>The Stegosaurus Armatus was, perhaps, the most heavily
armored of all dinosaurs. It is very possible though that it was not very smart,
it's brain is believed to have been the <b>size of a walnut!</b></description>
  </herbivore>
  <omnivore>
    <species>Gallimimus Bullatus</species>
    <length>18 feet</length>
    <height>8 feet</height>
    <weight>1000 pounds</weight>
    <speed>35-60 mph</speed>
    <weapon/>
    <discoverer>
      <name>Osm& #x00F3;lska</name>
      <name>Roniewicz</name>
      <name>Barsbold</name>
      <year>1972</year>
    </discoverer>
    <location>
      <country>Mongolia</country>
      <region>Nemegtskaya Svita</region>
    </location>
    <description>The Gallimimus Bullatus, or <i>Chicken Mimic</i> was very
fast, perhaps even the fastest of all dinosaurs.</description>
  </omnivore>
</dinosaurs>
```

3. We are ready to validate our XML instance document against our XML Schema. Within the Topologi Schematron Validator, select `dinosaurs7.xml` on the left side and click the Run button. This should validate with no warnings and no errors just as we saw in the last *Try It Out*. If there is a validation error, correct it and try validating again.

How It Works

Let's break down each section of our `<schema>`, to figure out what is going on:

```
<schema xmlns="http://www.w3.org/2001/XMLSchema"
 xmlns:dino="http://www.example.com/dinosaurs"
 targetNamespace="http://www.example.com/dinosaurs"
 elementFormDefault="qualified">
```

As we have seen in our earlier examples, our XML Schema begins with the `<schema>` element. Again, we are careful to specify the correct namespace for XML Schemas. We have also included a targetNamespace attribute to indicate the namespace for our vocabulary. We added a namespace declaration so that we can refer to items in our targetNamespace later. This time, instead of using he prefix *target* we used the prefix *dino*. Finally, we have included the attribute elementFormDefault with the value qualified.

```
<element name="dinosaurs">
  <complexType>
    <choice minOccurs="0" maxOccurs="unbounded">
      <element name="carnivore">
        <complexType>
          <group ref="dino:DinosaurGroup"/>
        </complexType>
      </element>
      <element name="herbivore">
        <complexType>
          <group ref="dino:DinosaurGroup"/>
        </complexType>
      </element>
      <element name="omnivore">
        <complexType>
          <group ref="dino:DinosaurGroup"/>
        </complexType>
      </element>
    </choice>
  </complexType>
</element>
```

Next, we created a global <element> declaration for our <dinosaurs> element. Remember, the <dinosaurs> element must be declared globally because we will be using it as our root element within our instance document. As our schema validator processes our instance document, it will encounter the <dinosaurs> element. The schema validator will then open our XML Schema document based on the xsi:schemaLocation attribute hint and find the global declaration for the <dinosaurs> element.

We specified the type of our <dinosaurs> element by declaring a local <complexType> within our <element> declaration. Within our <complexType> definition, we used a <choice> content model. We specified that the choice could occur an unbounded amount of times or not occur at all. The possible element choices within our content model included <carnivore>, <herbivore>, and <omnivore>. Because each of the elements had identical content models, we simply created local <complexType> definitions that referred to a global <group> declaration named DinosaurGroup.

```
<complexType>
  <group ref="target:DinosaurGroup"/>
</complexType>
```

To refer to the global <group> declaration, we needed to prefix the group name with the namespace prefix for our targetNamespace. In reality, we could have used a global complexType or global group to specify the content of the <carnivore>, <herbivore>, and <omnivore> elements. In the example we used a global group. Global groups can be more easily combined and reused, but global complexTypes are more useful when using type-aware tools such as XPath2 and XQuery. When designing your own schemas it is really a matter of personal preference.

```
<group name="DinosaurGroup">
  <sequence>
    <element name="species" type="string"/>
    <element name="length" type="string"/>
    <element name="height" type="string"/>
    <element name="weight" type="string"/>
    <element name="speed" type="string"/>
    <element name="weapon" type="dino:WeaponType"/>
    <element name="discoverer" type="dino:DiscovererType"/>
    <element name="location" type="dino:LocationType"/>
    <element name="description" type="dino:DescriptionType"/>
  </sequence>
</group>
```

The <group> declaration for our DinosaurGroup was very straightforward. It listed the allowable elements for the content model within a <sequence> declaration. When declaring our <weapon> element, we specified its type by referring to the global <complexType> definition named WeaponType. We also specified global complexTypes for the <discoverer>, <location>, and <description> elements.

```
<complexType name="WeaponType">
  <sequence minOccurs="0">
    <element name="part-of-body" type="string"/>
    <element name="description" type="dino:DescriptionType"/>
  </sequence>
</complexType>
```

Our WeaponType <complexType> definition was very simple. We listed the allowable elements within its content model using a sequence. Because not all dinosaurs have weapons, we specified that the minimum number of occurrences for the whole sequence was 0. We again specified the type of the <description> element by referring to a global <complexType> definition.

```
<complexType name="DiscovererType">
  <sequence>
    <element name="name" type="string" maxOccurs="unbounded"/>
    <element name="year" type="string"/>
  </sequence>
</complexType>
```

Our DiscovererType <complexType> definition introduced nothing new. We did remember to specify that the <name> element can occur an unbounded number of times.

```
<complexType name="LocationType">
  <choice>
    <element name="GPS" type="string"/>
    <sequence>
      <element name="country" type="string"/>
      <element name="region" type="string"/>
    </sequence>
  </choice>
</complexType>
```

In the LocationType <complexType> definition we used a choice declaration to allow either the element "GPS" or the sequence of elements including "country" and "region".

```
<complexType name="DescriptionType" mixed="true">
  <choice minOccurs="0" maxOccurs="unbounded">
    <element name="i" type="string"/>
    <element name="b" type="string"/>
  </choice>
</complexType>
```

The DescriptionType <complexType> definition was a mixed declaration. To specify this, we added a mixed attribute with the value true. Within our mixed content model, we wanted to allow an unbounded number of <i> and <b> elements to be interspersed within the text, so we used a <choice> declaration.

```
</schema>
```

This completed the XML Schema for our dinosaur listing. We will continue to add features to this XML Schema as we work our way through the rest of the chapter.

<attribute> Declarations

We have spent most of this chapter looking at how to create element declarations. Of course, this is only the very first step when creating an XML Schema. Within XML Schemas, attribute declarations are similar to element declarations. In the examples for our <name> element, we have already seen an attribute declaration for the title attribute. Attribute declarations have the following format:

```
<attribute
  name="name of the attribute"
  type="global type"
  ref="global attribute declaration"
  form="qualified or unqualified"
  use="optional or prohibited or required"
  default="default value"
  fixed="fixed value">
```

As we saw with element declarations, there are two primary methods for declaring attributes:

- Creating a local type
- Using a global type

Unlike elements, which are divided into simpleTypes and complexTypes, attribute declarations are restricted to simpleTypes. Remember, complexTypes are used to define types that will contain attributes or elements; simpleTypes are used to restrict text-only content. Because an attribute can contain text only, we can use simpleTypes only to define their allowable content.

In addition to these two methods, you may also reuse attributes by referring to an existing global attribute. In this case, you include a reference to the global attribute declaration. Just as we saw with element references, you do not need to specify a type in your attribute reference; the type of the attribute is included in the global attribute declaration.

Creating a Local Type

Creating a local type for an `<attribute>` declaration is similar to creating a local type for an `<element>` declaration. To create a local type, you simply include the type declaration as a child of the `<attribute>` element:

```
<attribute name="title">
  <simpleType>
    <!-- type information -->
  </simpleType>
</element>
```

In this example, we see that an attribute declaration may contain only a `<simpleType>` definition. We will look at the details of these declarations a little later in this chapter.

Using a Global Type

Just as we saw with our `<element>` declarations, many of our attributes will have the same type of value. Instead of declaring duplicate local types throughout our schema, we can create a global `<simpleType>` definition. Within our attribute declarations, we can refer to a global type by name. This type can be one of the built-in XML Schema data types:

```
<element name="first" type="string"/>
```

You can also create your own global declarations and refer to them. For example, suppose we had created a global type for the content of the `period` attribute:

```
<schema xmlns="http://www.w3.org/2001/XMLSchema"
  xmlns:dino="http://www.example.com/dinosaurs"
  targetNamespace="http://www.example.com/dinosaurs"
  elementFormDefault="qualified">
  <simpleType name="PeriodType">
    <!-- type information -->
  </simpleType>
  <element name="carnivore">
    <complexType>
      <!-- content model information -->
      <attribute name="period" type="dino:PeriodType"/>
    </complexType>
  </element>
</schema>
```

Even though the type is global, it is still part of the target namespace. Because of this, when referring to the type, we must include the target namespace prefix (if any). In the preceding example we used the prefix `dino` to refer to the target namespace. However, it is equally correct to do the following:

```
<xs:schema xmlns:xs="http://www.w3.org/2001/XMLSchema"
 xmlns="http://www.example.com/dinosaurs"
 targetNamespace="http://www.example.com/dinosaurs"
```

```
    elementFormDefault="qualified">
  <xs:simpleType name="PeriodType">
    <!-- type information -->
  </xs:simpleType>
  <xs:element name="carnivore">
    <xs:complexType>
      <!-- content model information -->
      <xs:attribute name="period" type="PeriodType"/>
    </xs:complexType>
  </xs:element>
</xs:schema>
```

In this example the XML Schema namespace is declared using the prefix `xs`, and the target namespace has no prefix. Therefore, to refer to the global type `PeriodType`, we do not need to include any prefix.

Referring to an Existing Global Attribute

Referring to global `<simpleType>` definitions allows us to reuse attribute types within our XML Schema. Often, we may want to reuse entire attribute declarations, instead of just the type. XML Schemas allow you to reuse global attribute declarations within your `<complexType>` definition. To refer to a global attribute declaration, include a `ref` attribute in your declaration and specify the name of the global attribute as the value.

```
<attribute ref="dino:period"/>
```

Again, the name of the attribute must be qualified with the namespace prefix. Notice that when we refer to a global attribute declaration, we have no `type` attribute and no local type declaration. Our attribute declaration will use the type of the `<attribute>` declaration to which we are referring.

Unfortunately, reusing global attribute declarations can create problems in your instance documents because of namespaces. Each attribute that you declare globally *must* be qualified by a namespace in your instance document. Remember, default namespace declarations do not apply to attributes. Because of this, you *must* have a namespace prefix for attributes in your instance document that have been declared globally in your XML Schema. Instead of dealing with these issues, most XML Schema authors utilize global attributeGroups when they need to reuse declarations. We will look at attributeGroups a little later in this chapter.

Naming Attributes

Just as we saw in our element declarations, attribute names must follow the rules for XML names that we have already learned. In the last chapter, when creating names in DTDs, we saw that we had to include a namespace prefix if one were going to be used in the instance document. Because XML Schemas are namespace aware, this is unnecessary. Simply specify the name of the attribute; the schema validator will be able to understand any prefix that is used within the instance document.

Attribute Qualified Form

The `form` attribute allows you to override the default for attribute qualification. Attribute qualification functions very similarly to element qualification. If an attribute is qualified, it must have an associated namespace when it is used in the instance document. Remember, default namespaces do not apply to attributes in your instance document. Therefore, you can qualify an attribute only with a namespace prefix.

You can specify whether the attribute must be qualified by setting the value of the `form` attribute to `qualified` or `unqualified`. If you do not include a `form` attribute, the schema validator will use the value of the `attributeFormDefault` attribute declared in the `<schema>` element. Again, any attribute that is declared globally must be qualified, regardless of the `form` and `attributeFormDefault` values. Unlike elements, it is very common to have unqualified attributes within an instance document.

Attribute Use

When declaring an attribute, we can specify that it is `required`, `optional`, or `prohibited` in the instance document. To control how an attribute will be used, simply include the `use` attribute within the `<attribute>` declaration and specify the appropriate value. It should also be noted that you cannot include a `use` attribute in a global `<attribute>` declaration.

By setting the value of the `use` attribute to `prohibited`, you can ensure that an attribute may not appear within your instance document. Developers commonly use prohibited attribute declarations in conjunction with attribute wildcards. By using this model, you can specify that you want to allow a large group of attributes and subsequently disallow specific attributes within the group. If you specify that an attribute is required, it must appear within the instance document. If the attribute is omitted the schema validator will raise a validity error.

Most attributes are optional—therefore, the default value for `use` is optional. By declaring that an attribute is `optional`, you indicate that it may or may not appear in the instance document. If you specify a `default` in your attribute declaration, the value of `use` cannot be `required` or `prohibited`.

Default and Fixed Values

We have already seen that XML Schemas allow you to declare default and fixed values for elements. Declaring default and fixed values for attributes functions in exactly the same way. To specify a default value, simply include the `default` attribute with the desired value.

```
<attribute name="period" type="dino:PeriodType" default="Cretaceous"/>
```

In the preceding declaration, we have specified that the default value for the `period` attribute is `"Cretaceous"`. If the schema validator finds that the period attribute has been omitted, it will insert the attribute and set the value to `"Cretaceous"`.

Fixed values operate much like default values. As the schema validator is processing the file, if it encounters a `fixed` attribute, then the parser will check whether the attribute value and `fixed` value match. If they do not match, the parser will raise a schema validity error. If the attribute or attribute value is omitted, the parser will insert the attribute with the `fixed` value.

To specify a fixed value, simply include the `fixed` attribute with the desired value:

```
<attribute name="version" type="string" fixed="1.0"/>
```

When specifying fixed or default values, you must ensure that the value you specify is allowable content for the type that you have declared for your attribute declaration. For example, if you specified that an attribute had the type `decimal`, you could not use `"1.0 Beta"` as a default value because it is not a decimal value. Moreover, you are not permitted to use default and fixed values at the same time within a single attribute declaration.

Attribute Wildcards

Earlier in the chapter, we learned about element wildcards—declarations that allowed us to include any elements from a specific namespace or list of namespaces within our content model. We often want to declare similar behavior for attributes. Declarations that allow you to include any attribute from a namespace are called *attribute wildcards*.

To declare an attribute wildcard, use the <anyAttribute> declaration:

```
<anyAttribute
  namespace="allowable namespaces"
  processContents="lax or skip or strict">
```

The <anyAttribute> declaration can appear only within a <complexType> or <attributeGroup> declaration. You are not allowed to create global <anyAttribute> declarations. The <anyAttribute> declaration allows you to control which namespaces may be used. Allowable namespaces are specified by including the namespace attribute. The namespace attribute allows several values:

Value	Description
##any	Allows attributes from all namespaces to be included as part of the wildcard.
##other	Allows attributes from namespaces other than the targetNamespace to be included as part of the wildcard.
##targetNamespace	Allows attributes from only the targetNamespace to be included as part of the wildcard.
##local	Allows attributes that are not qualified by a namespace to be included as part of the wildcard.
Whitespace separated list of allowable namespace URIs	Allows attributes from any listed namespaces to be included as part of the wildcard. Possible list values also include ##targetNamespace and ##local.

Suppose that we wanted to allow any unqualified attributes, as well as any attributes from the http://www.w3.org/XML/1998/namespace namespace:

```
<complexType>
  <sequence>
    <!-- content model -->
  </sequence>
  <anyAttribute namespace="##local http://www.w3.org/XML/1998/namespace"
                processContents="lax"/>
</complexType>
```

By including an attribute wildcard we can achieve this. Notice that the value of the namespace attribute is a whitespace-separated list with the values ##local and http://www.w3.org/XML/1998/namespace.

The namespace `http://www.w3.org/XML/1998/namespace` contains the `xml:lang` and `xml:space` attributes. These attributes are commonly used to add information about the language or spacing of an XML document.

When the schema validator is processing an element that contains an attribute wildcard declaration, it will validate the instance documents in one of three ways:

- If the value of the `processContents` attribute is set to `skip`, the processor will skip any wildcard attributes in the element.
- If the value of `processContents` attribute is set to `lax`, then the processor will attempt to validate the wildcard attributes if it has access to an XML Schema that defines them.
- If the value of the `processContents` attribute is set to `strict` (the default), the processor will attempt to validate the wildcard attributes if it has access to an XML Schema that defines them. However, in contrast to using the lax setting, the schema validator raises a validity error if the XML Schema for the wildcard elements cannot be found.

Try It Out Dinosaur DNA—Adding Attributes

Now that we have seen all of the various options for attribute declarations, let's update our dinosaurs schema. In this example we will add two attributes to our `<dinosaurs>` element.

1. We will begin by making the necessary changes to our XML Schema. Open the file `dinosaurs7.xsd` and make the following changes. Because we need to change only the declaration for the `<dinosaurs>` element, that is all we have shown. We will add two attribute declarations after the content model. The rest of the XML Schema will remain the same. When you are finished, save the file as `dinosaurs8.xsd`.

```
<element name="dinosaurs">
  <complexType>
    <choice minOccurs="0" maxOccurs="unbounded">
      <element name="carnivore">
        <complexType>
          <group ref="dino:DinosaurGroup"/>
        </complexType>
      </element>
      <element name="herbivore">
        <complexType>
          <group ref="dino:DinosaurGroup"/>
        </complexType>
      </element>
      <element name="omnivore">
        <complexType>
          <group ref="dino:DinosaurGroup"/>
        </complexType>
      </element>
    </choice>
    <attribute name="version" type="string" fixed="1.0" />
    <attribute name="source" type="string"/>
  </complexType>
</element>
```

2. Before we can validate our instance document, we must modify it so that it refers to our new XML Schema. We will also need to add attributes to our <dinosaurs> element. Open the file dinosaurs7.xml and make the following changes to the <dinosaurs> element—the rest of the file will remain the same. When you are finished, save the file as dinosaurs8.xml.

```
<dinosaurs
  xmlns="http://www.example.com/dinosaurs"
  xmlns:xsi="http://www.w3.org/2001/XMLSchema-instance"
  xsi:schemaLocation="http://www.example.com/dinosaurs dinosaurs8.xsd"
  source="Beginning XML 3E"
  version="1.0">
```

3. We are ready to validate our XML instance document against our XML Schema. Within the Topologi Schematron Validator, select dinosaurs8.xml on the left side and click the Run button. This should validate with no warnings and no errors just as we saw in the last *Try It Out*. If there was a validation error, correct it and try validating again.

How It Works

In this *Try It Out* we added two attributes to our <dinosaurs> element. We did this by adding the attribute declarations after the content model of the local complexType definition. Let's look at each of these attribute declarations in more detail.

```
<attribute name="version" type="string" fixed="1.0"/>
```

Our first attribute declaration defined the version attribute. We indicated that its value must be type string—meaning that any text value is allowed. In our DTD we used the type CDATA. No CDATA exists in XML Schemas, so wherever you would have used CDATA, you should instead use string. When we declared the attribute, we included a fixed attribute with the value 1.0. This means that if the version attribute appears within our document then it must have the value 1.0. If the version attribute is omitted, our schema validator will insert the attribute with the value 1.0.

```
<attribute name="source" type="string"/>
```

In our second attribute declaration, we defined the name attribute. Again, we have indicated that the attribute value must be type string.

Remember, within the instance document attributes may appear in any order. In addition, no attribute may appear more than once in a single element.

<attributeGroup> Declarations

We have seen that by creating a global <group> declaration we can define reusable groups of elements. In addition to element groups, XML Schema also allows us to define attribute groups.

```
<attributeGroup
  name="name of global attribute group">
```

Often we will need to use the same set of attributes for many elements. In such a case, it is easier to create a global attribute group that can be reused in our <complexType> definitions. In DTDs this was not possible without using parameter entities.

The <attributeGroup> declaration is very similar to the <group> declaration. Like <group> declarations, all global <attributeGroup> declarations must be named. Simply specify the name attribute with the desired name. Again, the name that you specify must follow the rules for XML names, and it should not include a prefix. The basic structure of a global <attributeGroup> declaration follows:

```
<attributeGroup name="DinoAttributes">
  <!-- attribute declarations go here -->
</attributeGroup>
```

Instead of allowing content model declarations like the <group> declarations we saw earlier in the chapter, the <attributeGroup> declaration allows <attribute> declarations as children. It also allows attribute wildcards and references to global <attribute> and <attributeGroup> declarations.

Although <attributeGroup> declarations may include references to other global <attributeGroup> declarations as part of the content model, group declarations may not recursively refer to themselves. For example, the following is an illegal <attributeGroup> declaration:

```
<attributeGroup name="AttGroup1">
  <attributeGroup ref="target:AttGroup1"/>
</attributeGroup >
```

This is illegal as well:

```
<attributeGroup name="AttGroup1">
  <attributeGroup ref="target:AttGroup2"/>
</attributeGroup >
<attributeGroup name="AttGroup2">
  <attributeGroup ref="target:AttGroup1"/>
</attributeGroup >
```

This second declaration is illegal because the declaration indirectly refers to itself.

To use an <attributeGroup>, simply include an <attributeGroup> reference declaration within a <complexType> or global <attributeGroup> declaration. To specify which <attributeGroup> you are referring to, include the ref attribute with the name of the global <attributeGroup> declaration as the value. Just as we have seen with our other references, you need to specify the namespace when referring to the global declaration. To do this, include the namespace prefix in the value.

Try It Out — Dinosaur DNA—Using a Global Attribute Group

Let's redesign our schema so that we can create a reusable global <attributeGroup> declaration. We will add our dinosaur attribute declarations into our attribute group. This way, we can reuse the global attribute declaration for the <carnivore>, <herbivore>, and <omnivore> elements.

1. We will begin by making the necessary changes to our XML Schema. Open the file dinosaurs8.xsd and make the following changes. When you are finished, save the file as dinosaurs9.xsd.

```
<element name="dinosaurs">
  <complexType>
    <choice minOccurs="0" maxOccurs="unbounded">
      <element name="carnivore">
        <complexType>
          <group ref="dino:DinosaurGroup"/>
          <attributeGroup ref="dino:DinoAttributes"/>
        </complexType>
      </element>
      <element name="herbivore">
        <complexType>
          <group ref="dino:DinosaurGroup"/>
          <attributeGroup ref="dino:DinoAttributes"/>
        </complexType>
      </element>
      <element name="omnivore">
        <complexType>
          <group ref="dino:DinosaurGroup"/>
          <attributeGroup ref="dino:DinoAttributes"/>
        </complexType>
      </element>
    </choice>
    <attribute name="version" type="string" fixed="1.0" />
    <attribute name="source" type="string"/>
  </complexType>
</element>

<attributeGroup name="DinoAttributes">
  <attribute name="kind" type="ID" use="required"/>
  <attribute name="habitat" type="NMTOKENS" use="required"/>
  <attribute name="period" type="string" default="Cretaceous"/>
</attributeGroup>
```

2. Before we can validate our XML document against our schema, we must modify it so that it refers to our new XML Schema. Open the file dinosaurs8.xml and change the xsi:schemaLocation attribute, as follows. Also, add in the newly declared attributes. When you are finished, save the file as dinosaurs9.xml.

```
<?xml version="1.0"?>
<dinosaurs
  xmlns="http://www.example.com/dinosaurs"
  xmlns:xsi="http://www.w3.org/2001/XMLSchema-instance"
  xsi:schemaLocation="http://www.example.com/dinosaurs dinosaurs9.xsd"
  source="Beginning XML 3E"
  version="1.0">
  <carnivore kind="Tyrannosaurus_Rex" habitat="forest swamp jungle"
  period="Cretaceous">
    <species>Tyrannosaurus Rex</species>
    <length>42 feet</length>
```

```
    <height>18 feet</height>
    <weight>5-7 tons</weight>
    <speed>25 mph</speed>
    <weapon>
      <part-of-body>Teeth</part-of-body>
      <description>Though the Tyrannosaurus had many different sizes of teeth,
all were razor sharp and some grew to lengths of <b>9-13 inches</b>. Broken
teeth were replaced frequently by newer teeth. The powerful jaw exerted in
excess of 3000 pounds of pressure!</description>
    </weapon>
    <discoverer>
      <name>Osborn</name>
      <year>1905</year>
    </discoverer>
    <location>
      <country>Canada</country>
      <region>Alberta</region>
    </location>
    <description>The Tyrannosaurus Rex was the <b>king</b> of the terrible
lizards. Though many now believe it was a hunter <i>and</i> a scavenger it
is no less fearsome.</description>
  </carnivore>
  <herbivore kind="Stegosaurus_Armatus" habitat="forest swamp" period=
"Jurassic">
    <species>Stegosaurus Armatus</species>
    <length>25-40 feet</length>
    <height>14 feet</height>
    <weight>2-4 tons</weight>
    <speed/>
    <weapon>
      <part-of-body>Spikes</part-of-body>
      <description>The Stegosaurus had two long rows of armor along its back.
At the end of its tail <b>four large spikes</b> were an excellent
defense.</description>
    </weapon>
    <discoverer>
      <name>Marsh</name>
      <year>1877</year>
    </discoverer>
    <location>
      <country>United States</country>
      <region>Colorado</region>
    </location>
    <description>The Stegosaurus Armatus was, perhaps, the most heavily
armored of all dinosaurs. It is very possible though that it was not very smart,
it's brain is believed to have been the <b>size of a walnut!</b></description>
  </herbivore>
  <omnivore kind="Gallimimus_Bullatus" habitat="lakeshore prairie">
    <species>Gallimimus Bullatus</species>
    <length>18 feet</length>
    <height>8 feet</height>
    <weight>1000 pounds</weight>
    <speed>35-60 mph</speed>
    <weapon/>
```

```
      <discoverer>
        <name>Osm&#x00F3;lska</name>
        <name>Roniewicz</name>
        <name>Barsbold</name>
        <year>1972</year>
      </discoverer>
      <location>
        <country>Mongolia</country>
        <region>Nemegtskaya Svita</region>
      </location>
      <description>The Gallimimus Bullatus, or <i>Chicken Mimic</i> was very
fast, perhaps even the fastest of all dinosaurs.</description>
  </omnivore>
</dinosaurs>
```

3. We are ready to validate our XML instance document against our XML Schema. Within the Topologi Schematron Validator, select `dinosaurs9.xml` on the left side and click the Run button. This should validate with no warnings and no errors just as we saw in the last *Try It Out*. If there is a validation error, correct it and try validating again.

How It Works

In this *Try It Out*, we have modified our XML Schema to use a global `<attributeGroup>` declaration. We created a global `<attributeGroup>` declaration named `DinoAttributes`. Within our declaration we included the declarations for the `kind`, the `habitat`, and the `period` attribute. Within the `<complexType>` definitions for the `<carnivore>`, `<herbivore>`, and `<omnivore>` elements we added an `<attributeGroup>` reference declaration. When referring to the global `<attributeGroup>` declaration, we included a `ref` attribute with the value `dino:DinoAttributes`.

As our schema validator is processing our instance document, it will process the `<carnivore>` element similar to our earlier examples. When it encounters the `<carnivore>` element, it will look it up in the XML Schema. Once it finds the declaration, it will find the associated type (in this case it is a local `<complexType>` definition). When the schema validator encounters the `<attributeGroup>` reference declaration, it will treat the `kind` `<attribute>` declaration within the group as if it had been included directly within the `<complexType>` definition. It will do this for each attribute declaration in the group.

Notice that we did not include a `period` attribute in our description of the Gallimimus Bullatus. Because the Gallimimus Bullatus lived in the Cretaceous period, and we set the default value for `period` attribute to `Cretaceous`, we do not need to include it. As the document is being processed, the schema validator adds in the default value from the XML Schema if no value is specified in the XML document.

Data Types

Throughout this chapter, we have seen how to declare elements and attributes using `<complexType>` definitions. At the start of the chapter, however, we promised that we would see how to define the allowable content for text-only elements and attribute values. It's time that we made good on that promise.

The XML Schema Recommendation allows you to use

- ❑ Built-in data types
- ❑ User-defined data types

Built-In Data Types

In our examples throughout this chapter, we have used the `string` type for our text-only content. The `string` type is a primitive data type that allows any textual content. XML Schemas provide a number of simpleTypes that allow you to exercise greater control over textual content in your XML document. The following table lists all of the simpleTypes built into XML Schemas:

Type	Description
`string`	Any character data
`normalizedString`	A whitespace normalized string where all spaces, tabs, carriage returns, and line feed characters are converted to single spaces
`token`	A string that does not contain sequences of two or more spaces, tabs, carriage returns, or line feed characters
`byte`	A numeric value from `-128` to `127`
`unsignedByte`	A numeric value from `0` to `255`
`base64Binary`	Base64 encoded binary information
`hexBinary`	Hexadecimal encoded binary information
`integer`	A numeric value representing a whole number
`positiveInteger`	An integer whose value is greater than 0
`negativeInteger`	An integer whose value is less than 0
`nonNegativeInteger`	An integer whose value is 0 or greater
`nonPositiveInteger`	An integer whose value is less than or equal to 0
`int`	A numeric value from `-2147483648` to `2147483647`
`unsignedInt`	A numeric value from `0` to `4294967295`
`long`	A numeric value from `-9223372036854775808` to `9223372036854775807`
`unsignedLong`	A numeric value from `0` to `18446744073709551615`
`short`	A numeric value from `-32768` to `32767`
`unsignedShort`	A numeric value from `0` to `65535`
`decimal`	A numeric value that may or may not include a fractional part

Continues

Type	Description
`float`	A numeric value that corresponds to the IEEE single-precision 32-bit floating-point type defined in the standard IEEE 754-1985. (IEEE 754-1985 can be found at `http://standards.ieee.org/reading/ieee/std_public/description/busarch/754-1985_desc.html`). `-0`, `INF`, `-INF`, and `NaN` are also valid values.
`double`	A numeric value that corresponds to the IEEE double-precision 64-bit floating-point type defined in the standard IEEE 754-1985. `-0`, `INF`, `-INF` and `NaN` are also valid values.
`boolean`	A logical value, including `true`, `false`, 0, and 1
`time`	An instant of time that occurs daily as defined in section 5.3 of ISO 8601. For example, `15:45:00.000` is a valid `time` value.
`dateTime`	An instant of time including both a date and a time value as defined in section 5.4 of ISO 8601. For example, `1998-07-12:16:30:00.000` is a valid `dateTime` value.
`duration`	A span of time as defined in section 5.5.3.2 of ISO 8601. For example, `P30D` is a valid `duration` value indicating a duration of 30 days.
`date`	A date according to the Gregorian Calendar as defined in section 5.2.1 of ISO 8601. For example, `1995-05-25` is a valid `date` value.
`gMonth`	A month in the Gregorian Calendar as defined in section 3 of ISO 8601. For example, `--07` is a valid `gMonth` value.
`gYear`	A year in the Gregorian Calendar as defined in section 5.2.1 of ISO 8601. For example, `1998` is a valid `gYear` value.
`gYearMonth`	A specific month and year in the Gregorian Calendar as defined in section 5.2.1 of ISO 8601. For example, `1998-07` is a valid `gYearMonth` value.
`gDay`	A recurring day of the month as defined in section 3 of ISO 8601, such as the 12th day of the month. For example, `---12` is a valid `gDay` value.
`gMonthDay`	A recurring day of a specific month as defined in section 3 of ISO 8601, such as the 12th day of July. For example, `--07-12` is a valid gMonthDay value.
`Name`	An XML name
`QName`	A qualified XML name as defined in the Namespaces Recommendation
`NCName`	A noncolonized XML name that does not include a namespace prefix or colon as defined in the Namespaces Recommendation
`anyURI`	A valid Uniform Resource Identifier
`language`	A language constant as defined in RFC 1766, such as `en-US` (RFC 1766 can be found at `http://www.ietf.org/rfc/rfc1766.txt`)

In addition to the types listed, the XML Schema Recommendation also allows the types defined within the XML Recommendation. These types include `ID`, `IDREF`, `IDREFS`, `ENTITY`, `ENTITIES`, `NOTATION`, `NMTOKEN`, and `NMTOKENS`. These types were covered in the last chapter.

Although we have used the `string` type throughout most of our examples, any of the preceding types can be used to restrict the allowable content within your elements and attributes. Suppose we wanted to modify the declarations of our `<length>` and `<height>` elements within our dinosaurs XML Schema to ensure that the users of our XML Schema enter valid values. We could modify our declarations as follows:

```
<element name="length" type="nonNegativeInteger"/>
<element name="height" type="nonNegativeInteger"/>
```

Now, instead of allowing any textual content, we require that the user specify a numeric value that is greater than or equal to zero. For a more in-depth look at these types, see Appendix F or see the XML Schema Recommendation at `www.w3.org/TR/xmlschema-2/`.

Try It Out — Dinosaur DNA—Using the Built-In XML Schema Data Types

Let's modify our dinosaurs example so that we can take advantage of the built-in XML Schema data types:

1. We will begin by making the necessary changes to our XML Schema. Open the file `dinosaurs9.xsd` and make the following changes. When you are finished, save the file as `dinosaurs10.xsd`.

```
<?xml version="1.0"?>
<schema xmlns="http://www.w3.org/2001/XMLSchema"
  xmlns:dino="http://www.example.com/dinosaurs"
  targetNamespace="http://www.example.com/dinosaurs"
  elementFormDefault="qualified">

   <element name="dinosaurs">
    <complexType>
      <choice minOccurs="0" maxOccurs="unbounded">
        <element name="carnivore">
          <complexType>
            <group ref="dino:DinosaurGroup"/>
            <attributeGroup ref="dino:DinoAttributes"/>
          </complexType>
        </element>
        <element name="herbivore">
          <complexType>
            <group ref="dino:DinosaurGroup"/>
            <attributeGroup ref="dino:DinoAttributes"/>
          </complexType>
        </element>
        <element name="omnivore">
          <complexType>
            <group ref="dino:DinosaurGroup"/>
            <attributeGroup ref="dino:DinoAttributes"/>
          </complexType>
        </element>
      </choice>
      <attribute name="version" type="decimal" fixed="1.0" />
```

```
        <attribute name="source" type="normalizedString"/>
      </complexType>
    </element>

    <attributeGroup name="DinoAttributes">
      <attribute name="kind" type="ID" use="required"/>
      <attribute name="habitat" type="NMTOKENS" use="required"/>
      <attribute name="period" type="token" default="Cretaceous"/>
    </attributeGroup>

    <group name="DinosaurGroup">
      <sequence>
        <element name="species" type="string"/>
        <element name="length" type="nonNegativeInteger"/>
        <element name="height" type="nonNegativeInteger"/>
        <element name="weight" type="string"/>
        <element name="speed" type="string"/>
        <element name="weapon" type="dino:WeaponType"/>
        <element name="discoverer" type="dino:DiscovererType"/>
        <element name="location" type="dino:LocationType"/>
        <element name="description" type="dino:DescriptionType"/>
      </sequence>
    </group>

    <complexType name="WeaponType">
      <sequence minOccurs="0">
        <element name="part-of-body" type="string"/>
        <element name="description" type="dino:DescriptionType"/>
      </sequence>
    </complexType>

    <complexType name="DiscovererType">
      <sequence>
        <element name="name" type="string" maxOccurs="unbounded"/>
        <element name="year" type="gYear"/>
      </sequence>
    </complexType>

    <complexType name="LocationType">
      <choice>
        <element name="GPS" type="string"/>
        <sequence>
          <element name="country" type="string"/>
          <element name="region" type="string"/>
        </sequence>
      </choice>
    </complexType>

    <complexType name="DescriptionType" mixed="true">
      <choice minOccurs="0" maxOccurs="unbounded">
        <element name="i" type="string"/>
        <element name="b" type="string"/>
      </choice>
    </complexType>
  </schema>
```

2. Before we can schema validate our XML document, we must modify it so that it refers to our new XML Schema. Open the file `dinosaurs10.xml` and change the `xsi:schemaLocation` attribute. When you are finished, save the file as `dinosaurs10.xml`.

```
xsi:schemaLocation="http://www.example.com/dinosaurs dinosaurs10.xsd"
```

3. We are ready to validate our XML instance document against our XML Schema. Within the Topologi Schematron Validator, select `dinosaurs10.xml` on the left side and click the Run button:

   You should see the output as shown in Figure 5-3.

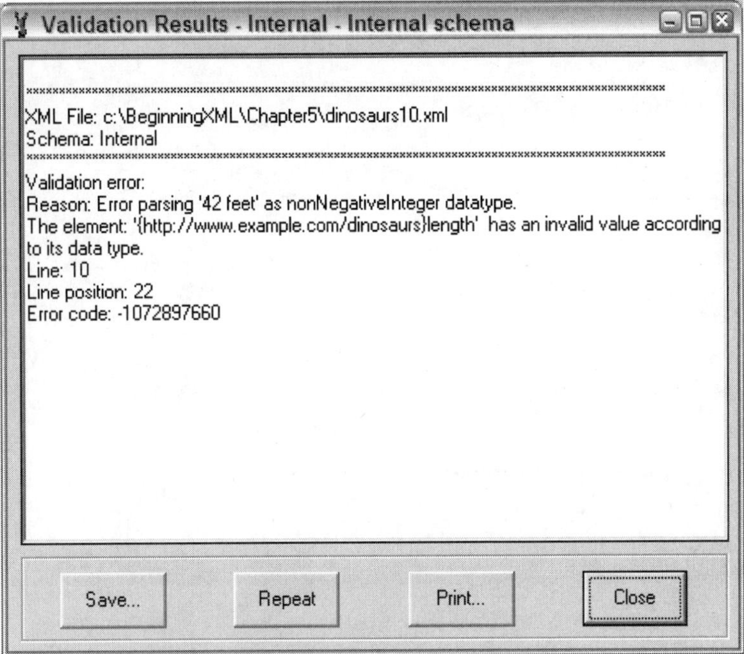

Figure 5-3

Why did we get an error? Because we are using more restrictive types, we will need to update our instance document.

4. Open the file `dinosaurs10.xml` and modify the `<length>` and `<height>` elements. We need to remove the text `"feet"` from each value. When you are finished, save the file.

```
<length>42</length>
<height>18</height>
```

or

```
<length>25</length>
<height>14</height>
```

or

```
<length>18</length>
<height>8</height>
```

5. Now that we have fixed the error, we are ready to validate our XML instance document against our XML Schema. Within the Topologi Schematron Validator, click the Run button.

   You should see the output as shown in Figure 5-4.

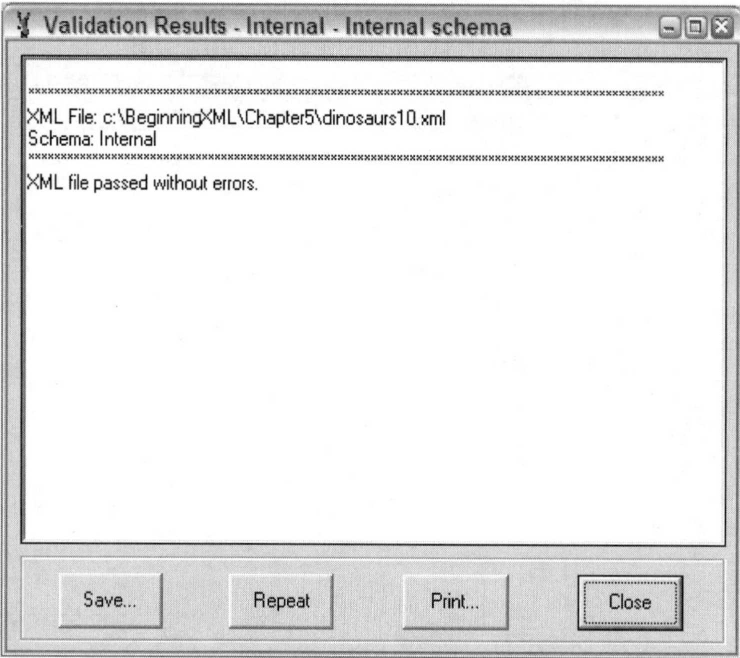

Figure 5-4

How It Works

In this *Try It Out* we used some of the XML Schema built-in data types. These data types allow us to exercise more control over the textual content within our instance documents. As we saw in the last chapter, DTDs were not capable of advanced data typing. Let's look at some of the types we used, in a little more detail.

```
<attribute name="version" type="decimal" fixed="1.0"/>
```

We began by changing the type of our `version` attribute from `string` to `decimal`. This is a perfect fit because our version number must always be a valid decimal number.

```
<attribute name="source" type="normalizedString"/>
```

We modified the `<source>` attribute declaration to use the `normalizedString` type. This type allows us to guarantee that no extra spaces or line feeds will be there within the content of our `source` attribute.

```
<attribute name="period" type="token" default="Cretaceous"/>
```

Because our `period` must be a single value, we decided to use the `token` type. The `token` type is somewhat less restrictive than the `name` type, but more restrictive than the `string` type. In reality though, the `token` type is not restrictive enough. It allows any token value including `Precambrian`—which is not really what we want. We will learn how to make this declaration more restrictive in the next section.

```
<element name="length" type="nonNegativeInteger"/>
<element name="height" type="nonNegativeInteger"/>
```

We modified our `<length>` and `<height>` elements so that they used the built-in type `nonNegativeInteger`. What we didn't do was modify our instance document right away, and it caused an error when we schema validated our document the first time. To fix the error we had to remove the text `"feet"` from each value.

This is actually a pretty big change. Because we are using a numeric type, we can't include any of the units of measurement (in this case `"feet"`). This happens quite often when designing XML Schemas. Typically, the best way to handle this is to use a more restrictive type, such as `nonNegativeInteger`, and add an attribute for the unit type. So

```
<length>42 feet</length>
```

would become

```
<length units="feet">42</length>
```

This allows your XML Schemas to be more complete while still validating numeric values.

```
<element name="year" type="gYear"/>
```

We modified the `<year>` element so that it used the built-in type `gYear`. Because the `gYear` value is based on the international standard ISO 8601, we must follow specific rules when including the value. As we saw in the example in the data types table earlier in the chapter, simple `gYear` values follow the format:

```
CCYY
```

where `CC` is the hundreds of years in the Gregorian calendar and `YY` represents the year. Therefore, our values, such as `1877`, were valid.

As our schema validator processes our document, not only is it checking whether the element content models we have specified are correct, it is also checking whether the textual data we have included in our elements is valid based on the type we specified.

User-Defined Data Types

Although the XML Schema Recommendation includes a wealth of built-in data types, it doesn't include everything. As we are developing our XML Schemas, we will run into many elements and attribute values that require a type not defined in the XML Schema Recommendation. Consider the `period` attribute declaration. Although we restricted its value to the `token` type, it will still accept unwanted values such as the following:

```
period="Precambrian"
```

According to our declaration, the value `Precambrian` is valid because it is a single token. Is this really what we wanted? What we need is to create a list of allowable values as we did in our DTD. No such built-in type exists within the XML Schema Recommendation, so we must create a new type using a `<simpleType>` definition.

<simpleType> Declarations

Often, when designing our XML Schemas we will need to design our own data types. We can create custom user-defined data types using the `<simpleType>` definition.

```
<simpleType
  name="name of the simpleType"
  final="#all or list or union or restriction">
```

When we declare a simpleType, we must always base our declaration on an existing data type. The existing data type may be a built-in XML Schema data type, or it may be another user data type. Because we must derive every `<simpleType>` definition from another data type, `<simpleType>` definitions are often called *derived types*. There are three primary derived types:

- Restriction types
- List types
- Union types

In this section, we learn the basics of `<simpleType>` declarations and user-defined types. In addition, Appendix F covers data types in detail. If you are looking for an in-depth treatment of all of the features and options, see *Professional XML Schemas* by Jon Duckett et al. (Wrox Press 2001).

<restriction> Declarations

The most common `<simpleType>` derivation is the restriction type. Restriction types are declared using the `<restriction>` declaration.

```
<restriction
  base="name of the simpleType you are deriving from">
```

Fundamentally, a derived type declared using the `<restriction>` declaration is a subset of its base type. Facets control all simpleTypes within XML Schemas. A *facet* is a single property or trait of a simpleType. For example, the built-in numeric type `nonNegativeInteger` was created by setting the facet `minInclusive` to zero. This specifies that the minimum value allowed for the type is zero. By constraining the facets of existing types, we can create our own more restrictive types.

There are 12 constraining facets:

Facet	Description
`minExclusive`	Allows you to specify the minimum value for the type that excludes the value you specify
`minInclusive`	Allows you to specify the minimum value for the type that includes the value you specify
`maxExclusive`	Allows you to specify the maximum value for the type that excludes the value you specify
`maxInclusive`	Allows you to specify the maximum value for the type that includes the value you specify
`totalDigits`	Allows you to specify the total number of digits in a numeric type
`fractionDigits`	Allows you to specify the number of fractional digits in a numeric type (for example, the number of digits to the right of the decimal point)
`length`	Allows you to specify the number of items in a list type or the number of characters in a string type
`minLength`	Allows you to specify the minimum number of items in a list type or the minimum number of characters in a string type
`maxLength`	Allows you to specify the maximum number of items in a list type or the maximum number of characters in a string type
`enumeration`	Allows you to specify an allowable value in an enumerated list
`whiteSpace`	Allows you to specify how whitespace should be treated within the type
`pattern`	Allows you to restrict string types using regular expressions

Not all types use every facet. In fact, most types can be constrained only by a couple of facets. For a complete list of what constraining facets can be used when restricting the built-in XML Schema types, see Appendix F.

Within a `<restriction>` declaration you must specify the type you are restricting using the `base` attribute. The value of the `base` attribute is a reference to a global simpleType, or built-in XML Schema data type. As we have seen with all references in our XML Schema, the reference is a namespace qualified value and, therefore, may need to be prefixed. The `<restriction>` declaration also allows you to derive your type from a local `<simpleType>` definition.

A good example of a restriction type that uses enumeration facets is a type that restricts the allowable values for the `period` attribute in our dinosaur listing:

```
<attribute name="period">
  <simpleType>
    <restriction base="string">
```

```
        <enumeration value="Triassic"/>
        <enumeration value="Jurassic"/>
        <enumeration value="Cretaceous"/>
      </restriction>
    </simpleType>
  </attribute>
```

In this declaration, we have created a <restriction> declaration with the base type string. Within our restriction, we have specified multiple enumeration facets to create a list of all of the allowable values for our type.

Try It Out Dinosaur DNA—Creating a Restriction simpleType

As we saw in the *User-Defined Data Types* section earlier in the chapter, the period attribute should be more restrictive. Now that we know how to create our own <simpleType> definitions, let's create a <restriction> type for the period attribute:

1. We will begin by making the necessary changes to our XML Schema. Open the file dinosaurs10.xsd and make the following changes. We need to modify only the <attribute> declaration for the period attribute. The rest of the XML Schema remains the same. When you are finished, save the file as dinosaurs11.xsd.

```
<attributeGroup name="DinoAttributes">
  <attribute name="kind" type="ID" use="required"/>
  <attribute name="habitat" type="NMTOKENS" use="required"/>
  <attribute name="period" default="Cretaceous">
    <simpleType>
      <restriction base="string">
        <enumeration value="Triassic"/>
        <enumeration value="Jurassic"/>
        <enumeration value="Cretaceous"/>
      </restriction>
    </simpleType>
  </attribute>
</attributeGroup>
```

2. Before we can schema validate our XML document, we must modify it so that it refers to our new XML Schema. Open the file dinosaurs10.xml and change the xsi:schemaLocation attribute, as follows. When you are finished, save the file as dinosaurs11.xml.

```
xsi:schemaLocation="http://www.example.com/dinosaurs dinosaurs11.xsd"
```

3. We are ready to validate our XML instance document against our XML Schema. Within the Topologi Schematron Validator, select dinosaurs11.xml on the left side and click the Run button. This should validate with no warnings and no errors just as we saw in the last *Try It Out*. If there is a validation error, correct it and try validating again.

How It Works

In this *Try It Out*, we modified the period attribute declaration. We created an internal <simpleType> definition that was a restriction derived from nonNegativeInteger. This allowed us to limit the values that could be used within the period attribute.

```
<attribute name="period" default="Cretaceous">
  <simpleType>
    <restriction base="string">
      <enumeration value="Triassic"/>
      <enumeration value="Jurassic"/>
      <enumeration value="Cretaceous"/>
    </restriction>
  </simpleType>
</attribute>
```

To declare the attribute's type, we created a local simpleType declaration. Because we changed our attribute's type to a local simpleType, we had to remove the original type by removing the `type` attribute.

<list> Declarations

Often we will need to create a list of items. Using a `<list>` declaration, we can base our list items on a specific simpleType.

```
<list
  itemType="name of simpleType used for items">
```

When creating our `<list>` declaration, we could specify the type of items in our list by including the `itemType` attribute. The value of the `itemType` attribute should be a reference to a global `<simpleType>` definition or built-in XML Schema data type. Again, the reference is a namespace qualified value and, therefore, may need to be prefixed. The `<list>` declaration also allows you to specify your `itemType` by creating a local `<simpleType>` definition.

When choosing the `itemType`, you must remember that you are creating a whitespace-separated list. Because of this, your items cannot contain whitespace. Therefore, types that include whitespace cannot be used as `itemTypes`. A side effect of this limitation is that you cannot create a list whose `itemType` is itself a list.

For example:

```
<element name="length">
  <simpleType>
    <list itemType="nonNegativeInteger"/>
  </simpleType>
</element>
```

In the preceding declaration, we have created a list of `nonNegativeInteger` values. A valid `<length>` element might appear as follows:

```
<length>25 42</length>
```

If we used this within our dinosaur XML Schema, it would allow us to specify multiple lengths within our instance document, but still require that they be valid non-negative numbers.

<union> Declarations

Finally, when creating your derived types, you may need to combine two or more types. By declaring a `<union>` type, you can validate your type against the allowable values in multiple types.

```
<union
  memberTypes="whitespace separated list of types">
```

When creating our <union> declaration, we could specify the types we are combining by including the memberTypes attribute. The value of the memberTypes attribute should be a whitespace-separated list of references to global <simpleType> definitions or built-in XML Schema data types. Again, these references are namespace qualified values and, therefore, may be needed to be prefixed. The <union> declaration also allows you to specify your memberTypes by creating local <simpleType> definitions.

Suppose you wanted to allow the value "Unknown" in the <length> and <height> elements. To do this you could use a union of a type that allows a list of nonNegativeIntegers and a type that allows the string "Unknown".

```
<simpleType name="IntegerList">
  <list itemType="nonNegativeInteger"/>
</simpleType>

<simpleType name="UnknownString">
  <restriction base="string">
    <enumeration value="Unknown"/>
  </restriction>
</simpleType>
```

In the preceding example, we have created two <simpleType> definitions that allow our desired values. Now, we could modify the <length> element so that it would allow you to specify either a list of lengths or the string "Unknown":

```
<element name="length">
  <simpleType>
    <union memberTypes="dino:IntegerList dino:UnknownString"/>
  </simpleType>
</element>
```

In this declaration, we have created a union of our two simpleTypes IntegerList and UnknownString. With this declaration, our <length> element can contain one of the values available within either IntegerList or UnknownString. Some *valid* <length> elements include

```
<length>25 42</length>
<length>Unknown</length>
```

Some *invalid* <length> elements include

```
<length>unknown</length>
<length>Unknown 42</length>
```

The first two <length> elements both contain valid values. The third <length> element is invalid because the value unknown is not listed in either of our unioned types—the values are case sensitive. The fourth <length> element is invalid because the schema validator will treat this as a single value. Although "Unknown" and "42" are allowable by themselves, the value "Unknown 42" is not listed in either of our unioned types.

Try It Out Dinosaur DNA—More simpleTypes

Let's add these new types into our dinosaur listing:

1. We will begin by making the necessary changes to our XML Schema. Open the file `dinosaurs11.xsd` and make the following changes. We first need to add the new `<simpleType>` declarations.

```
<simpleType name="IntegerList">
  <list itemType="nonNegativeInteger"/>
</simpleType>

<simpleType name="UnknownString">
  <restriction base="string">
    <enumeration value="Unknown"/>
  </restriction>
</simpleType>
```

2. We also need to modify the `<length>` and `<height>` element declarations. The rest of the XML Schema will remain the same. When you are finished, save the file as `dinosaurs12.xsd`:

```
    <element name="length">
      <simpleType>
        <union memberTypes="dino:IntegerList dino:UnknownString"/>
      </simpleType>
    </element>
    <element name="height">
      <simpleType>
        <union memberTypes="dino:IntegerList dino:UnknownString"/>
      </simpleType>
    </element>
```

3. Before we can schema validate our XML document, we must modify it so that it refers to our new XML Schema. Open the file `dinosaurs11.xml` and change the `xsi:schemaLocation` attribute, as follows. When you are finished, save the file as `dinosaurs12.xml`.

```
xsi:schemaLocation="http://www.example.com/dinosaurs dinosaurs12.xsd"
```

4. We are ready to validate our XML instance document against our XML Schema. Within the Topologi Schematron Validator, select `dinosaurs12.xml` on the left side and click the Run button. This should validate with no warnings and no errors just as we saw in the last *Try It Out*. If there is a validation error, correct it and try validating again.

How It Works

In this *Try It Out*, we added some more complex `<simpleType>` declarations in our schema. We first created two global `<simpleType>` declarations that allowed us to specify a list of non-negative numbers or use the string `"Unknown"`. We then modified the `<length>` and `<height>` elements to use our new declarations.

```
<element name="length">
  <simpleType>
    <union memberTypes="dino:IntegerList dino:UnknownString"/>
  </simpleType>
</element>
```

To declare the element's type, we created a local simpleType declaration. Because we changed our element's type to a local simpleType, we had to remove the original type by removing the `type` attribute.

Creating Elements with <simpleType> Content and Attributes

At this point we have learned two ways to specify the allowable content for an element. We first learned how to construct complex element declarations, which can contain both elements and attributes using the `<complexType>` declaration. In the last section, we learned how to restrict the content of our elements using the `<simpleType>` declaration. To create an element with simple content *and* attributes we must put together some of what we have already learned.

We will again start with a basic element declaration, such as in the following example:

```
<element name="length">
  <!-- Specify type here -->
</element>
```

Within the element declaration we will include a `<complexType>` declaration where we will specify that we want our element to have simple content, such as text. We can do this by creating a `<complexType>` declaration that contains a `<simpleContent>` element, such as in the following example:

```
<element name="length">
  <complexType>
    <simpleContent>
      <!-- Specify type here -->
    </simpleContent>
  </complexType>
</element>
```

We will also need to specify what kind of data type should be used to validate our simple content. Within the `<simpleContent>` element we can create an `<extension>` declaration. We must use an `<extension>` declaration because we will be extending an existing data type by adding attribute declarations. Take the following for example:

```
<element name="length">
  <complexType>
    <simpleContent>
      <extension base="string">
        <attribute name="units" type="string" default="feet" />
      </extension>
    </simpleContent>
  </complexType>
</element>
```

When we created the <extension> declaration, we added a base attribute where we specified the data type to use as the basis for our element's content. In the preceding example we used the built-in string type as our base. We are not limited to using the built-in data types however; we can also refer to any global <simpleType> in our XML Schema. For example, we could refer to IntergerList type we created in the previous section as shown in the following example:

```
<element name="length">
  <complexType>
    <simpleContent>
      <extension base="dino:IntegerList">
        <attribute name="units" type="string" default="feet" />
      </extension>
    </simpleContent>
  </complexType>
</element>
```

After specifying the extension base type, we then declared the attributes. Just as we saw in our <complexType> declarations earlier in the chapter, we can include <attribute> and <attributeGroup> declarations inside the <extension> element.

Any of the following examples are allowable <length> elements based on the previous declaration:

```
<length units="meters">25 42</length>
<length>25</length>
<length />
```

In the first of the preceding examples, the <length> element contained two integer values and a units attribute. In the second example, we omitted the units attribute. If a schema validator encountered this element, it would use the default value "feet" that we specified in our attribute declaration. We also included a single integer value in the element content. In the final example we omitted the units attribute and didn't include any integer values.

The following examples would be invalid:

```
<length>25-42 feet</length>
<length units="feet" value="25"/>
```

The first was invalid because the element content was not a list of integers as we specified in our declaration. The second was invalid because we included a value attribute that we never declared.

Creating a Schema from Multiple Documents

When declaring our XML Schemas, we have used a single schema document to keep things simple. The XML Schema Recommendation introduces mechanisms for combining XML Schemas and reusing definitions. As we saw in Chapter 4, reusing existing definitions is good practice—it saves us time when creating the documents and increases our document's interoperability.

Several XML Schema authors have already begun developing libraries of commonly used types that can be reused in your XML Schemas. The W3C type library can be found at http://www.w3.org/2001/03/XMLSchema/TypeLibrary.xsd.

The XML Schema Recommendation provides two primary declarations for use with multiple XML Schema documents:

- `<import>`
- `<include>`

Let's look at each of these features in more detail:

<import> Declarations

The `<import>` declaration, as the name implies, allows us to import global declarations from other XML Schemas. The `<import>` declaration is used primarily for combining XML Schemas that have different `targetNamespaces`. By importing the declarations, the two XML Schemas can be used in conjunction within an instance document. It is important to note that the `<import>` declaration allows us to *refer* to declarations only within other XML Schemas. In the next section we will learn about the `<include>` declaration, which *includes* the declarations as if they had been declared. The `<include>` declaration can be used only for XML Schemas with the same `targetNamespace`.

```
<import
  namespace="URI"
  schemaLocation="URI">
```

The `<import>` declaration is always declared globally within an XML Schema (it must be a direct child of the `<schema>` element). This means that the `<import>` declaration applies to the entire XML Schema. When importing declarations from other namespaces, the schema validator will attempt to look up the namespace declaration based on the `schemaLocation` attribute specified within the corresponding `<import>` declaration. Of course, as we saw earlier in this chapter, the `schemaLocation` attribute serves only as a hint to the processor. The processor may elect to use another copy of the XML Schema. If the schema validator cannot locate the XML Schema for any reason, it may raise an error or proceed with lax validation.

To get a better idea of how this works, we need a sample XML Schema that uses the `<import>` declaration. Let's combine the examples that we have been working with in the past two chapters. Within the XML Schema for our dinosaur listing, we will import the declarations from our `<name>` vocabulary. We will use the imported `<name>` declarations to better define our dinosaur discoverers.

Try It Out Dinosaur DNA—Importing XML Schema Declarations

In this example we will take our dinosaur listing and introduce an `<import>` declaration. We will import the name vocabulary that we have been developing. We will need to modify our instance document to reflect the changes in our XML Schemas.

1. Let's begin by modifying our dinosaur vocabulary. We will need to import the name vocabulary and use the imported types. Open the file `dinosaur12.xsd` and make the following changes.

```
<?xml version="1.0"?>
<schema xmlns="http://www.w3.org/2001/XMLSchema"
 xmlns:dino="http://www.example.com/dinosaurs"
```

```
xmlns:name="http://www.example.com/name"
targetNamespace="http://www.example.com/dinosaurs"
elementFormDefault="qualified">

  <import namespace="http://www.example.com/name"
    schemaLocation="name8.xsd"/>
```

2. We also need to modify the declaration of the <discoverer> element. When you are finished, save the file as dinosaur13.xsd.

```
<complexType name="DiscovererType">
  <sequence>
    <element ref="name:name" maxOccurs="unbounded"/>
    <element name="year" type="gYear"/>
  </sequence>
</complexType>
```

3. Now that we have modified our XML Schema document, let's create an instance document that reflects the changes. This document will appear to be very similar to our dinosaurs12.xml document. Only the <name> elements will change. Open the file dinosaurs12.xml and make the following changes. When you are finished, save the file as dinosaurs13.xml.

```
<?xml version="1.0"?>
<dinosaurs
  xmlns="http://www.example.com/dinosaurs"
  xmlns:name="http://www.example.com/name"
  xmlns:xsi="http://www.w3.org/2001/XMLSchema-instance"
  xsi:schemaLocation="http://www.example.com/dinosaurs dinosaurs13.xsd"
  source="Beginning XML 3E"
  version="1.0">
  <carnivore kind="Tyrannosaurus_Rex" habitat="forest swamp jungle"
    period="Cretaceous">
    <species>Tyrannosaurus Rex</species>
    <length>25 42</length>
    <height>18</height>
    <weight>5-7 tons</weight>
    <speed>25 mph</speed>
    <weapon>
      <part-of-body>Teeth</part-of-body>
      <description>Though the Tyrannosaurus had many different sizes of teeth,
all were razor sharp and some grew to lengths of <b>9-13 inches</b>. Broken
teeth were replaced frequently by newer teeth. The powerful jaw exerted in
excess of 3000 pounds of pressure!</description>
    </weapon>
    <discoverer>
      <name:name title="Mr.">
        <name:first>Henry</name:first>
        <name:middle>Fairfield</name:middle>
        <name:last>Osborn</name:last>
      </name:name>
      <year>1905</year>
    </discoverer>
    <location>
```

```
      <country>Canada</country>
      <region>Alberta</region>
    </location>
    <description>The Tyrannosaurus Rex was the <b>king</b> of the terrible
lizards. Though many now believe it was a hunter <i>and</i> a scavenger it
is no less fearsome.</description>
  </carnivore>
  <herbivore kind="Stegosaurus_Armatus" habitat="forest swamp" period=
"Jurassic">
    <species>Stegosaurus Armatus</species>
    <length>25</length>
    <height>14</height>
    <weight>2-4 tons</weight>
    <speed/>
    <weapon>
      <part-of-body>Spikes</part-of-body>
      <description>The Stegosaurus had two long rows of armor along its back.
At the end of its tail <b>four large spikes</b> were an excellent
defense.</description>
    </weapon>
    <discoverer>
      <name:name title="Mr.">
        <name:first>Othniel</name:first>
        <name:middle>Charles</name:middle>
        <name:last>Marsh</name:last>
      </name:name>
      <year>1877</year>
    </discoverer>
    <location>
      <country>United States</country>
      <region>Colorado</region>
    </location>
    <description>The Stegosaurus Armatus was, perhaps, the most heavily
armored of all dinosaurs. It is very possible though that it was not very smart,
it's brain is believed to have been the <b>size of a walnut!</b></description>
  </herbivore>
  <omnivore kind="Gallimimus_Bullatus" habitat="lakeshore prairie">
    <species>Gallimimus Bullatus</species>
    <length>18</length>
    <height>8</height>
    <weight>1000 pounds</weight>
    <speed>35-60 mph</speed>
    <weapon/>
    <discoverer>
      <name:name title="Ms.">
        <name:first>Halszka</name:first>
        <name:middle/>
        <name:last>Osm&#x00F3;lska</name:last>
      </name:name>
      <name:name title="Ms.">
        <name:first>Ewa</name:first>
        <name:middle/>
        <name:last>Roniewicz</name:last>
      </name:name>
```

```
        <name:name title="Mr.">
          <name:first>Rinchen</name:first>
          <name:middle/>
          <name:last>Barsbold</name:last>
        </name:name>
        <year>1972</year>
      </discoverer>
      <location>
        <country>Mongolia</country>
        <region>Nemegtskaya Svita</region>
      </location>
      <description>The Gallimimus Bullatus, or <i>Chicken Mimic</i> was very fast,
perhaps even the fastest of all dinosaurs.</description>
    </omnivore>
</dinosaurs>
```

4. We are ready to validate our XML instance document against our XML Schema. Within the Topologi Schematron Validator, select dinosaurs13.xml on the left side and click the Run button. This should validate with no warnings and no errors just as we saw in the last *Try It Out*. If there is a validation error, correct it and try validating again.

How It Works

In this *Try It Out*, we imported one XML Schema into another. We used the <import> declaration because the two XML Schemas were designed for different targetNamespaces. Within our first XML Schema, we had already declared a single global element that could be used to describe names. In our second XML Schema, we were forced to do some more work:

```
<schema xmlns="http://www.w3.org/2001/XMLSchema"
 xmlns:dino="http://www.example.com/dinosaurs"
 xmlns:name="http://www.example.com/name"
 targetNamespace="http://www.example.com/dinosaurs"
 elementFormDefault="qualified">
```

The first addition that we had to make was an XML namespace declaration in the root element. We added a namespace declaration for the namespace http://www.example.com/name. We needed to add this declaration so that we could refer to items declared within the namespace later in our XML Schema.

Secondly, we added an <import> declaration.

```
  <import namespace="http://www.example.com/name"
    schemaLocation="name8.xsd"/>
```

This <import> declaration is straightforward. We are importing the declarations from the http://www.example.com/name namespace, which is located in the file name8.xsd. This declaration allows us to reuse the declarations from our name8.xsd XML Schema within our dinosaurs13.xsd XML Schema. If you are using another schema validator, you should check the documentation for special rules when referring to external files. For example, the Xerces parser handles relative URL references differently in older versions.

Finally, we modified the name element declaration within our <discoverer> declaration.

```
<element ref="name:name" maxOccurs="unbounded"/>
```

Notice that we used the namespace prefix we declared within the root element when referring to the name element declaration from our name8.xsd file. Instead of using an element reference, we could have also referred to the global type NameType.

Once we made these changes, we had to create a new, compliant instance document. The major difference (apart from the schemaLocation) was the modified content of our <discoverer> elements.

```
<discoverer>
  <name:name title="Mr.">
    <name:first>Henry</name:first>
    <name:middle>Fairfield</name:middle>
    <name:last>Osborn</name:last>
  </name:name>
  <year>1905</year>
</discoverer>
```

This might seem a little more confusing than you would expect. Because we declared that the elementFormDefault of both XML Schemas was qualified, we are required to qualify all our elements with namespace prefixes (or a default namespace declaration).

The title attribute doesn't need to be qualified because we didn't modify the attributeFormDefault within our XML Schemas—so it uses the default value unqualified. The <first>, <middle>, and <last> elements are all declared within the http://www.example.com/name namespace; therefore, we must qualify them with the name prefix we declared in the root element of our instance document.

<include> Declarations

The <include> declaration functions very similarly to the <import> declaration. Unlike the <import> declaration, however, the <include> declaration allows us to combine XML Schemas that are designed for the same targetNamespace (or no targetNamespace) much more effectively. When a schema validator encounters an <include> declaration, it treats the global declarations from the included XML Schema as if they had been declared in the XML Schema that contains the <include> declaration. This subtle distinction makes quite a difference when you are using many modules to define your targetNamespace.

```
<include
  schemaLocation="URI">
```

Notice, within the <include> declaration, there is no namespace attribute. Again, unlike the <import> declaration, the <include> declaration can be used only on documents with the same targetNamespace, or no targetNamespace. Because of this, a namespace attribute would be redundant. Just as we saw before, the schemaLocation attribute allows you to specify the location of the XML Schema you are including. The schemaLocation value again functions as a validator hint. If the schema validator cannot locate a copy of the XML Schema for any reason, it may raise an error or proceed with lax validation.

To demonstrate the <include> declaration we are going to need an example that utilizes two XML Schema documents with the same `targetNamespace`. To do this we will break our dinosaur list into two parts—moving all of the type declarations to a new XML Schema that can be included.

Try It Out Dinosaur DNA—Including XML Schema Declarations

In this *Try It Out* we will divide our XML Schema into two parts and include one in the other. This is known as dividing an XML Schema into modules—separate files that make up the overall XML Schema.

1. We will begin by creating a new XML Schema that declares the all of the types used in our dinosaur listing. To create the declarations, you can simply copy and paste the declarations from `dinosaurs13.xsd`. Once you have created the file, save it as `dinosaur-types.xsd` in the same folder where you have saved your other XML Schemas.

```
<?xml version="1.0"?>
<schema xmlns="http://www.w3.org/2001/XMLSchema"
 xmlns:dino="http://www.example.com/dinosaurs"
 xmlns:name="http://www.example.com/name"
 targetNamespace="http://www.example.com/dinosaurs"
 elementFormDefault="qualified">

  <import namespace="http://www.example.com/name"
    schemaLocation="name8.xsd"/>

  <complexType name="WeaponType">
    <sequence minOccurs="0">
      <element name="part-of-body" type="string"/>
      <element name="description" type="dino:DescriptionType"/>
    </sequence>
  </complexType>

  <complexType name="DiscovererType">
    <sequence>
      <element ref="name:name" maxOccurs="unbounded"/>
      <element name="year" type="gYear"/>
    </sequence>
  </complexType>

  <complexType name="LocationType">
    <choice>
      <element name="GPS" type="string"/>
      <sequence>
        <element name="country" type="string"/>
        <element name="region" type="string"/>
      </sequence>
    </choice>
  </complexType>

  <complexType name="DescriptionType" mixed="true">
    <choice minOccurs="0" maxOccurs="unbounded">
      <element name="i" type="string"/>
      <element name="b" type="string"/>
```

```
    </choice>
  </complexType>

  <simpleType name="IntegerList">
    <list itemType="nonNegativeInteger"/>
  </simpleType>

  <simpleType name="UnknownString">
    <restriction base="string">
      <enumeration value="Unknown"/>
    </restriction>
  </simpleType>

</schema>
```

2. Now that we have created our dinosaur-types.xsd XML Schema, we need to make some modifications to the dinosaurs13.xsd XML Schema. We will begin by inserting an <include> declaration. We can remove our <import> declaration because it was moved into the new dinosaur-types.xsd XML Schema. We can also remove the type declarations that we moved into the new schema. Open the file dinosaurs13.xsd, make the following modifications, and save the file as dinosaurs14.xsd.

```
<?xml version="1.0"?>
<schema xmlns="http://www.w3.org/2001/XMLSchema"
 xmlns:dino="http://www.example.com/dinosaurs"
 targetNamespace="http://www.example.com/dinosaurs"
 elementFormDefault="qualified">

  <include schemaLocation="dinosaur-types.xsd"/>

  <element name="dinosaurs">
    <complexType>
      <choice minOccurs="0" maxOccurs="unbounded">
        <element name="carnivore">
          <complexType>
            <group ref="dino:DinosaurGroup"/>
            <attributeGroup ref="dino:DinoAttributes"/>
          </complexType>
        </element>
        <element name="herbivore">
          <complexType>
            <group ref="dino:DinosaurGroup"/>
            <attributeGroup ref="dino:DinoAttributes"/>
          </complexType>
        </element>
        <element name="omnivore">
          <complexType>
            <group ref="dino:DinosaurGroup"/>
            <attributeGroup ref="dino:DinoAttributes"/>
          </complexType>
        </element>
      </choice>
      <attribute name="version" type="decimal" fixed="1.0" />
```

```
      <attribute name="source" type="normalizedString"/>
    </complexType>
  </element>

  <attributeGroup name="DinoAttributes">
    <attribute name="kind" type="ID" use="required"/>
    <attribute name="habitat" type="NMTOKENS" use="required"/>
    <attribute name="period" default="Cretaceous">
      <simpleType>
        <restriction base="string">
          <enumeration value="Triassic"/>
          <enumeration value="Jurassic"/>
          <enumeration value="Cretaceous"/>
        </restriction>
      </simpleType>
    </attribute>
  </attributeGroup>

  <group name="DinosaurGroup">
    <sequence>
      <element name="species" type="string"/>
      <element name="length">
        <simpleType>
          <union memberTypes="dino:IntegerList dino:UnknownString"/>
        </simpleType>
      </element>
      <element name="height">
        <simpleType>
          <union memberTypes="dino:IntegerList dino:UnknownString"/>
        </simpleType>
      </element>
      <element name="weight" type="string"/>
      <element name="speed" type="string"/>
      <element name="weapon" type="dino:WeaponType"/>
      <element name="discoverer" type="dino:DiscovererType"/>
      <element name="location" type="dino:LocationType"/>
      <element name="description" type="dino:DescriptionType"/>
    </sequence>
  </group>

  <!-- Types moved into dinosaur-types.xsd -->

</schema>
```

3. Before we can schema validate our document, we must modify it so that it refers to our new XML Schema. Open the file `dinosaurs13.xml` and change the `xsi:schemaLocation` attribute, as follows. When you are finished, save the file as `dinosaurs14.xml`.

```
xsi:schemaLocation="http://www.example.com/dinosaurs dinosaurs14.xsd"
```

4. We are ready to validate our XML instance document against our XML Schema. Within the Topologi Schematron Validator, select `dinosaurs14.xml` on the left side and click the Run button. This should validate with no warnings and no errors just as we saw in the last *Try It Out*. If there is a validation error, correct it and try validating again.

How It Works

Dividing complex XML Schemas into modules can be an excellent design technique. In this *Try It Out*, we divided our dinosaur vocabulary into two modules. We declared these modules in separate XML Schema documents each with `http://www.example.com/dinosaurs` as the `targetNamespace`. Because the two documents utilized the same `targetNamespace`, we simply used an `<include>` declaration to combine them.

```
<include schemaLocation="dinosaur-types.xsd" />
```

As the schema validator processes `dinosaurs14.xsd`, it includes the declarations from `dinosaur-types.xsd` with the declarations for `dinosaurs14.xsd` as if they had been declared in one document. Because of this, we were able to use all of the types as if they were declared within `dinosaurs14.xsd`. Because we didn't introduce any namespace complexities, there was no need to change the instance document to support the new modular design.

> *What happens when the XML Schema you are including has no `targetNamespace`? Declarations within XML Schemas that have no `targetNamespace` are treated differently. These declarations are known as Chameleon Components. Chameleon Components take on the `targetNamespace` of the XML Schema that includes them. So, even though they were declared with no `targetNamespace`, when they are included they take the `targetNamespace` of the XML Schema that is including them.*

Documenting XML Schemas

Throughout your programming career, and even in this book, you have heard that documenting your code is one of the best habits you can develop. The XML Schema Recommendation provides several mechanisms for documenting your code:

- Comments
- Attributes from other namespaces
- Annotations

Let's look at each of these documenting methods in more detail.

Comments

In Chapter 2, we learned that XML allows you to introduce comments in your XML documents. Because the XML Schema is an XML document, you can freely intersperse XML comments throughout the declarations, as long as you follow the rules for XML well-formedness.

```
<!-- This complexType allows you to describe the physiological
  attributes of the dinosaur that allowed them to better attack
  other dinosaurs or defend themselves. -->
<complexType name="WeaponType">
  <!-- You may include the children elements or omit them -->
  <sequence minOccurs="0">
```

```
      <element name="part-of-body" type="string"/>
      <element name="description" type="dino:DescriptionType"/>
    </sequence>
  </complexType>
```

In the preceding XML Schema fragment, we have placed two comments. The first comment simply introduces our complexType and when it should be used. If someone were reading our XML Schema, this would surely give the user some guidance when creating his or her instance documents. We used the second comment to inform the user that the sequence may or may not appear.

While these comments are useful for someone reading our XML Schema, many processors will not report XML comments. Therefore, the document must be read by a human for the comments to be useful in all cases.

Attributes from Other Namespaces

The XML Schema Recommendation provides a second mechanism for documenting your XML Schemas. All of the elements defined within the XML Schema vocabulary allow you to include any attribute from another namespace. You can use the alternative attributes to introduce descriptive data that is included with your element.

Suppose you declared an attribute for comments within the namespace `http://www.example.com/documentation`. You could use this attribute throughout your XML Schema to include comments that are embedded within your elements.

```
<?xml version="1.0"?>
<schema
  xmlns="http://www.w3.org/2001/XMLSchema"
  targetNamespace="http://www.example.com/dinosaurs"
  xmlns:dino="http://www.example.com/dinosaurs"
  elementFormDefault="qualified"
  xmlns:doc="http://www.w3.org/documentation">
  <complexType name="WeaponType"
   doc:comments="This complexType allows you to describe the physiological
   attributes of the dinosaur that allowed them to better attack
   other dinosaurs or defend themselves.">
    <sequence minOccurs="0"
     doc:comments="You may include the children elements or omit them">
      <element name="part-of-body" type="string"/>
      <element name="description" type="dino:DescriptionType"/>
    </sequence>
  </complexType>
 ...

</schema>
```

In this example, we have included a namespace declaration for a fictitious vocabulary for documentation. We assumed that within our fictitious namespace there was a declaration for the `comments` attribute. Throughout our XML Schema document, we introduced descriptions of the items we were declaring by including the `comments` attribute from the documentation vocabulary.

As a schema validator processes the document, it will ignore all of the `comments` attributes because they are declared in another namespace. The attributes can still be used to pass information on to other applications. In addition, the comments provide extra information for those reading our XML Schema.

Annotations

The primary documenting features introduced in the XML Schema Recommendation are called annotations. *Annotations* allow you to provide documentation information, as well as additional application information.

```
<annotation
  id="ID">
```

The <annotation> declaration can appear as a child of most XML Schema declarations. The <annotation> declaration allows you to add two forms of information to your declarations:

- Application information
- Documentation information

Each <annotation> declaration may contain the elements <appinfo> and <documentation>. These elements may contain *any* XML content from *any* namespace. Each of these elements may also contain a `source` attribute. The `source` attribute is used to refer to an external file that may be used for application information or documentation information. Typically, <appinfo> declarations are used to pass information such as example files, associated images, or additional information for validation. Annotations usually include <documentation> declarations to describe the features, or uses, of a particular declaration within the XML Schema.

Consider the following example:

```
<?xml version="1.0"?>
<schema xmlns="http://www.w3.org/2001/XMLSchema"
targetNamespace="http://www.example.com/name"
xmlns:target="http://www.example.com/name"
elementFormDefault="qualified">
  <annotation>
    <appinfo source="name-instance.xml"/>
    <documentation xmlns:html="http://www.w3.org/1999/xhtml">
      <html:p>
        The name vocabulary was created for a Chapter 2 sample. We have
upgraded it to an <html:strong>XML Schema</html:strong>. The appinfo of this
<html:pre>&lt;annotation&gt;</html:pre> element points to a sample XML file.
The sample should be used <html:i>only as an example</html:i>
      </html:p>
    </documentation>
  </annotation>
  <element name="name">
    <annotation>
      <documentation source="name.html"/>
    </annotation>
    <complexType>
```

```
        <sequence>
          <element name="first" type="string"/>
          <element name="middle" type="string"/>
          <element name="last" type="string"/>
        </sequence>
        <attribute name="title" type="string"/>
      </complexType>
    </element>
  </schema>
```

Within this example XML Schema, we have two <annotation> declarations. Our first <annotation> declaration is contained within our <schema> element. It is used to add information that is applicable to the entire XML Schema document.

Within our first <annotation> declaration, we have included both <appinfo> and <documentation> element. We didn't include any content within our <appinfo> element. Instead, we included a `source` attribute that pointed to an example XML instance document. Of course, schema validators must be programmed to utilize the <appinfo> declaration. Many programs define different behavior for the <appinfo> declaration. Often the <appinfo> declaration contains additional validation information, such as other schema languages.

> **Schematron is another language for defining your vocabulary. Schematron definitions, because they offer additional features, are often embedded directly within the `<appinfo>` declaration. Several processors that can use Schematron in conjunction with XML Schemas have been written. The Topologi Schematron Validator that we have been using throughout our examples is written specifically for this purpose. This is covered in detail within *Professional XML Schemas* by Jon Duckett et al. (Wrox Press 2001).**

The <documentation> declaration within our first annotation contains an HTML fragment that could be used when generating a user's manual for our XML Schema. Our second annotation included only a <documentation> declaration. Unlike the first <documentation> declaration, the second declaration was empty and instead used the `source` attribute to refer to an external file called `name.html`.

Summary

In this chapter, we've learned how to create XML Schemas that can be used to schema validate our XML documents. We started again with our simple name examples and then progressed to our more complex dinosaur examples.

We've learned:

- The advantages of XML Schemas over Document Type Definitions
- How to associate an XML Schema with an XML document
- How to declare element and attribute types
- How to declare groups and attribute groups

- ❑ How to specify allowable XML content using simpleTypes and complexTypes
- ❑ How to create an XML Schema using multiple documents and namespaces
- ❑ How to document your XML Schema

While we have not discussed all of the options available within XML Schemas, we have established a foundation upon which you can build many XML Schemas.

> *Now that you understand the basics of XML Schemas, you are ready to create your own vocabularies. Even with the basics, however, you have many styles and choices when designing your XML Schemas. Roger Costello, with the help of many volunteers, has created an XML Schemas Best Practices document that gives advice on what the best choice or style is for many different situations. This document can be found at* `http://www.xfront.com/BestPracticesHomepage.html`.

Exercise Questions

Suggested solutions to these questions can be found in Appendix A.

Question 1

Add a `units` attribute to the `<length>` and `<height>` element declarations. Once you have added the attribute declaration, add the `units` attribute in your instance document and specify the value `"feet"`.

Question 2

Add a `feathers` attribute declaration for the `<carnivore>`, `<herbivore>`, and `<omnivore>` elements. The attribute should allow two possible values: `yes` and `no`. Make the attribute have a default value of `no`.

Question 3

Modify the `<description>` declaration to include an element wildcard. Within the wildcard, specify that the description element can accept any elements from the namespace `http://www.w3.org/1999/xhtml`. Set the `processContents` attribute to `lax`.

6

RELAX NG

RELAX NG is a very powerful, yet easy to understand XML Schema technology that can be used to validate XML instance documents. Like W3C XML Schema (XSD), which we studied in the previous chapter, RELAX NG is grammar-based. We define the structure of a valid XML instance document in a RELAX NG schema document. We then use the RELAX NG schema document to validate XML instance document(s). It is possible for many XML instance documents to be valid, according to a single RELAX NG schema document. Alternatively, it is possible for a single XML instance document to be valid with respect to multiple RELAX NG schema documents.

RELAX NG takes a different approach to validating XML documents, when compared to XML schemas. RELAX NG schemas are based on patterns, whereas XML schemas are based on simpleTypes and complexTypes. The power of RELAX NG centers around its use of patterns. RELAX NG does not have the type hierarchy of XML schemas and does not support type inheritance. As we will see later, RELAX NG schemas use pattern composition and named patterns to support pattern reuse, instead of inheritance. While type inheritance is not supported, datatyping is. RELAX NG supports the data types provided by the W3C XML Schema part II, datatypes specification. For example, RELAX NG schemas have full use of XML Schema data types, like `xsd:int`, `xsd:double`, and `xsd:decimal`, as well as the XML Schema facets that were previously discussed. In fact, RELAX NG was designed with pluggable data types in mind. That is, users can invent their own type system, and RELAX NG schemas can be built using user-defined types, instead of, or in addition to, using the XML Schema data types.

Here are some of the key features of RELAX NG:

- It's simple and easy to learn.
- It has two different syntaxes: XML Syntax and Compact Syntax.
- It supports XML Schema data types.
- It supports user-defined data types.
- It supports XML namespaces.
- It's highly composable.
- It uses pattern-based grammar with a strong mathematical foundation.
- It employs regular treatment for both elements and attributes.

As mentioned previously, RELAX NG has two different syntaxes: an XML syntax and a compact syntax. The compact syntax is, well, compact, and tailored for the (human) user that will be creating and modifying RELAX NG schemas. The XML syntax is machine-processable. The Trang program can convert the compact syntax to the XML Syntax and back. Trang can also convert RELAX NG schemas into DTDs or XML schemas. Most RELAX NG validators today need the XML syntax in order to validate the document, but some are becoming available that can validate directly off the compact syntax.

Since the compact syntax of RELAX NG is easier for humans to read and write, we'll use that syntax in this book to describe RELAX NG. For every compact syntax schema we show, you can convert it to the XML Syntax using Trang.

In this chapter, we will cover the following:

- Basic RELAX NG patterns, which are the building blocks of RELAX NG schemas.
- Composing and combining patterns into higher-level components for reuse, as well as full schema grammars.
- The remaining features of RELAX NG, including namespaces, name-classes, datatyping, and some common design patterns.

Basic RELAX NG Patterns

RELAX NG employs patterns as a core schema development concept. We can describe patterns of XML elements and attributes, including sequencing and choice. As we will see, patterns of simple data enumerations can also be described. Patterns can be nested, allowing the schema author to describe the entire XML structure from top to bottom, starting from a single top-level pattern. In this section we'll look at the patterns that are common to all RELAX NG schemas. In the next section, we'll see how patterns can be given names, enabling reuse.

Introduction to Patterns and Element Patterns

Let's start our discussion of RELAX NG by taking a quick look at some of the patterns. There are many different kinds of patterns you can use, and, additionally, you can combine patterns in various ways.

Pattern Name	Pattern
element pattern	`element` *nameClass* {*pattern*}
attribute pattern	`attribute` *nameClass* {*pattern*}
text pattern	`text`
sequence pattern	*pattern* [,*pattern*]+
zero or more pattern	*pattern**

The square brackets indicate an optional part of the grammar. Note that patterns are recursive in nature. That is, the element and attribute patterns are defined by placing another pattern inside the curly braces (`{}`). This recursive ability is very powerful but does take some getting used to.

The preceding patterns show three RELAX NG (compact syntax) keywords: `element`, `attribute`, and `text`. NameClasses are a nice feature of RELAX NG that we will discuss later. For starters, you can think of the element or attribute *nameClass* as simply being the element or attribute name.

Let's take a look at a simple XML instance document and work our way into a RELAX NG schema. Here is a sample XML instance document for an address book, `addressBook.xml`. For simplicity, we'll only track first and last names.

```
<addressBook>
    <entry>
        <firstName>Maria</firstName>
        <lastName>Knapik</lastName>
    </entry>
    <entry>
        <firstName>Anne</firstName>
        <lastName>Hughes</lastName>
    </entry>
</addressBook>
```

Here is a complete RELAX NG compact schema document (`addressBook.rnc`):

```
element addressBook {
    element entry {
         element firstName { text },
         element lastName  { text }
    }*
}
```

Using XMLDistilled's Xmlde editor (`http://www.xmldistilled.com`), simply create the RNC file and save it as `addressBook.rnc`. Next, create a new XML document with the editor. The Xmlde editor is free, easy to set up and install, and supports color syntax highlighting of XML documents. Most importantly for our use, the Xmlde editor supports validation against an RNC schema using the RNV processor. When using the Xmlde editor, you do not have to convert your RELAX NG compact syntax schemas into the RELAX NG XML Syntax form of the schema. You can validate the XML instance document directly against the compact syntax RNC file. (The Topologi editor does not support the RELAX NG compact syntax.)

Figure 6-1 shows the `addressBook` XML file using the Xmlde editor. Simply choose the menu: Tools ➪ Validate Using RNC to validate your XML document against any RNC schema. When you validate, "No Errors Found" will be displayed in the bottom pane if your XML file is valid, as shown in Figure 6-1.

In Figure 6-2, the first set of `<firstName/>` and `<lastName/>` elements were reversed, causing a validation error. In the bottom pane, you can see the error message, which displays the line and column number—in this example, (4,8)—to help you locate the error.

The Xmlde editor can also validate an RNC schema file stand-alone, and check XML files for simple well-formedness. It can also autodetect the schema you wish to use, depending on the XML file you are currently editing.

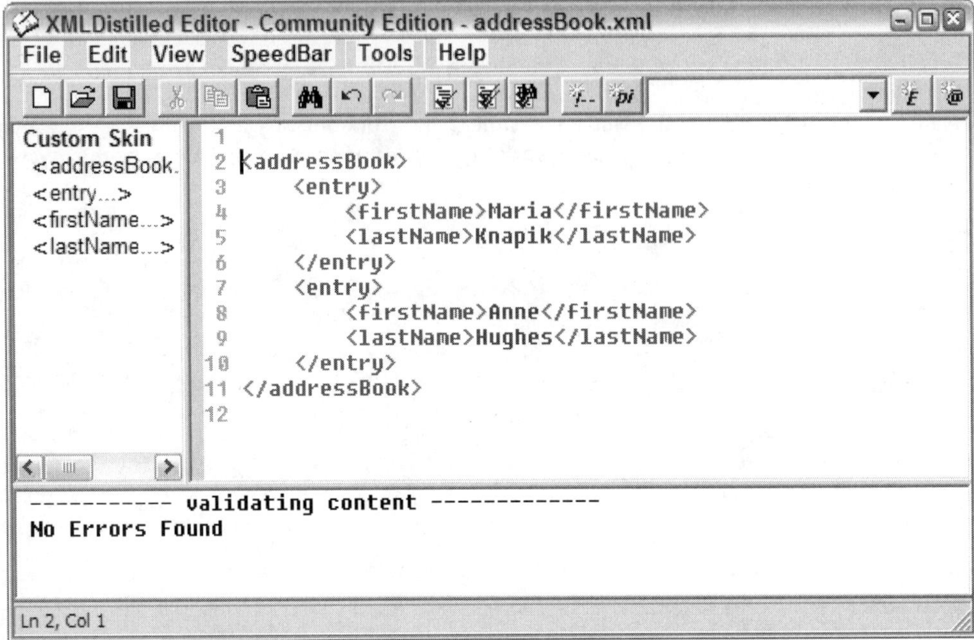

Figure 6-1

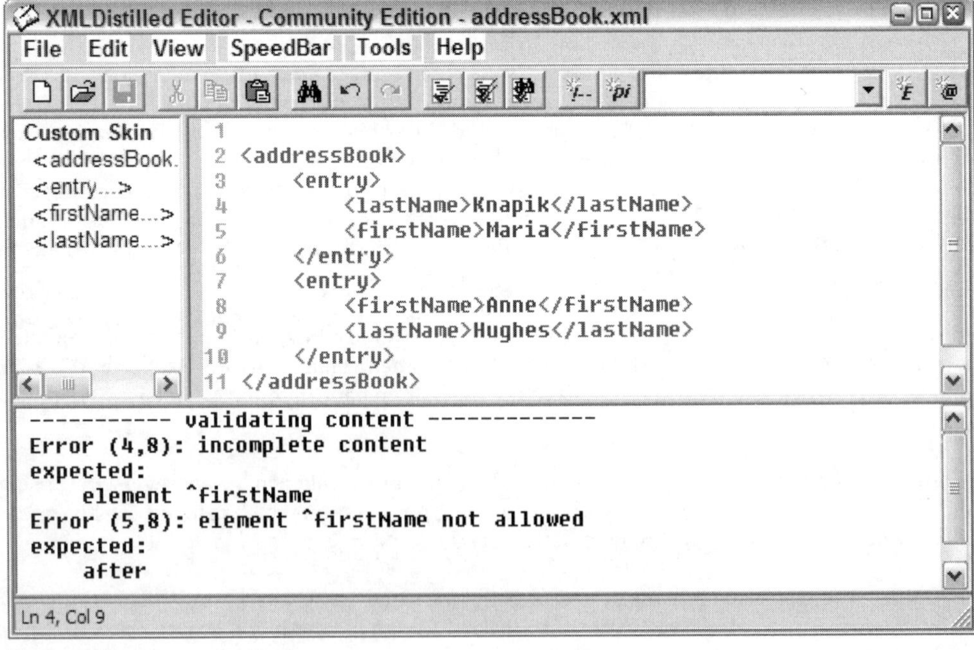

Figure 6-2

Note: Unlike DTD or XML Schema, RELAX NG does not define a technique for an XML instance document to reference the schema document. It is up to the user (via editing tools, command-line arguments, or processing code) to select the schema at runtime. A conscious decision was made by the RELAX NG committee to not provide such a mechanism. Some reasons for this include security issues as well as the fact that it is quite possible that a particular instance document may need to be validated against different schemas, at different times, for different reasons.

I hope you find this syntax easy to read. Note that it is not an XML Syntax, it is a compact syntax. This small snippet is also a complete RELAX NG schema. Converting this RELAX NG schema to words: An `addressBook` element can have zero or more (due to the `*` sign) `entry` elements. Each `entry` element must have one `firstName` element, followed by one `lastName` element. The `firstName` element contains text, and the `lastName` element contains text. (It is okay for the instance document to have empty `firstName` and/or `lastName` elements, as in `<firstName></firstName>` or `<firstName/>`)

If not specified, the cardinality is one, so one `firstName` and one `lastName` element is expected to occur, for each entry, once in the instance document. Please refer to Chapter 4 on DTDs for a discussion of cardinality. The comma (`,`) represents a sequence, and for element patterns, this dictates the order in which the elements must occur: `firstName` must come before `lastName` in this case.

If you wanted to change the cardinality on, say `firstName` and `lastName`, you would use the same symbols you saw earlier in Chapter 4 on DTDs. The question mark symbol (`?`) defines an optional pattern, the plus sign (`+`) designates one or more, and the asterisk (`*`) designates zero or more. Therefore, if you wanted the `firstName` to be optional, and `lastName` to occur one or more times, inside each `entry` element, a possible schema would be as follows:

```
element addressBook {
    element entry {
         element firstName { text }?,
         element lastName  { text }+
    }*
}
```

Attribute Patterns

Now, let's add some attributes to the instance document. Say we had two attributes: `type`, which specifies whether an entry is friend or family, and `dateOfBirth`, on each `entry` element. A sample instance document would be as follows:

```
<addressBook>
   <entry type="family" dateOfBirth="8/14/59">
       <firstName>Maria</firstName>
       <lastName>Knapik</lastName>
   </entry>
   <entry type="friend" dateOfBirth="3/15/62">
       <firstName>Joe</firstName>
       <lastName>Hughes</lastName>
   </entry>
</addressBook>
```

In RNC notation, the attribute pattern is formed much like the element pattern. Here is the RNC schema that will validate the previous XML:

```
element addressBook {
    element entry {
         attribute type { text },
         attribute dateOfBirth { text },
         element firstName { text } ?,
         element lastName  { text } +
    }*
}
```

Notice that attribute and element patterns are treated as equals, as far as RNC syntax is concerned. There are a few differences between element and attribute patterns though. One difference is that the order of the attribute patterns does not matter, as, in XML, attributes can appear in any order. Another difference is that you would not find cardinality indicators of one or more (+) or zero or more (*) on attributes. Attributes can be optional, but they cannot appear more than once on an individual element. This means that the following RNC schema, with `type` and `dateOfBirth` attributes reversed, would be identical to the previous one:

```
element addressBook {
    element entry {
         attribute dateOfBirth { text },
         attribute type { text },
         element firstName { text }?,
         element lastName  { text }+
    }*
}
```

However, if we switched the `firstName` and `lastName` element patterns, the schema would be different, as element order is significant in a sequence. The concept of "similar syntax" for elements and attributes is very nice in that you don't need to carry around the "heavier syntax" used in XML schemas. Namely, in RNC, there is no need to specify simpleTypes, complexTypes, groups versus attribute groups, and the special-case syntax needed in XML schemas or DTD for declaring attributes versus elements.

Moreover, since RELAX NG is based on patterns and tree automata, you can specify more complex and flexible validation concepts in RELAX NG, when compared to XML schemas. For example, in RELAX NG, you can specify that an element `<foo>` has element `<e1>` and attribute `a1`, or put in another way: element `<e2>` and attribute `a2`. The complete schema for this combination would be as follows:

```
element foo {
          ( attribute a1 { text }, element e1 { text }) |
          ( attribute a2 { text }, element e2 { text } )
    }
```

The pipe symbol (|) specifies a choice combination. Here are the choice and group patterns, which are used in the preceding schema:

Pattern Name	Pattern
choice pattern	*pattern* [|*pattern*]+
group pattern	(*pattern*)

Here is one XML instance document that would be *valid* using the previous schema (combining `a1` and `e1` is ok):

```
<foo a1="hello">
          <e1>data</e1>
</foo>
```

Here is another (combining `a2` and `e2` is ok):

```
<foo a2="hello">
         <e2>data</e2>
</foo>
```

However, this XML instance would be *invalid*, because element `e2` is combined with attribute `a1`:

```
<foo a1="hello">
         <e2>data</e2>
</foo>
```

Enumerated Values

In an earlier schema, we had a `type` attribute that contained either the string friend or `family`. However, our schema used the `text` pattern, which allows any string. Like XML Schema validation (and even DTD validation), RELAX NG allows enumerated values to be defined in the schema, then it is used to verify that the instance documents contain those values. (DTDs only support enumerated values in attribute content.) Here is our sample XML document:

```
<addressBook>
    <entry type="family" dateOfBirth="8/14/59">
        <firstName>Maria</firstName>
        <lastName>Knapik</lastName>
    </entry>
    <entry type="friend" dateOfBirth="3/15/62">
        <firstName>Joe</firstName>
        <lastName>Hughes</lastName>
    </entry>
</addressBook>
```

If we wanted to use enumerated values in a RELAX NG, we would use the following pattern:

Pattern Name	Pattern
Enumeration pattern	`dataTypeValue`

With the addition of this new pattern, we can construct the following schema. The `dataTypeValue` is any literal string inside single or double quotes:

```
element addressBook {
    element entry {
```

```
            attribute dateOfBirth { text },
            attribute type { 'family' | 'friend' },
            element firstName { text } ?,
            element lastName  { text }+
      }*
}
```

Instead of using the RNC keyword `text`, we used a choice of two literal values, family or friend. Validating against enumerated values is a very common and useful validation technique. Enumerated value validation is also possible for use in element content. For example, if you only wanted to allow people with first names of Joe or Maria, you could define your `firstName` element this way:

```
element firstName { 'Joe' | 'Maria' }
```

As we shall see later, RELAX NG supports *datatype validation*, like validating against numeric values, date, time, or even regular expressions.

Co-Occurrence Constraints

Because RELAX NG is built on patterns and allows flexible pattern combinations, you can construct schemas that support what is called *co-occurrence* constraints. (These constraints are not legal in XML Schema or DTD.) Suppose we had to specify that a particular element had either child element `<A>` or child element `<B>`, depending on the value of an attribute. Here is a sample XML instance to illustrate this concept:

```
<transportation>
     <vehicle type="Automobile" >
          <make>Ford</make>
     </vehicle>
     <vehicle type="Trolley">
          <fare>2.50</fare>
          <tax>1.00</tax>
     </vehicle>
</transportation>
```

The idea is that the content allowed for the `<vehicle>` element depends on the *value* of the `type` attribute. If the value `Automobile` is found, a `<make>` element is allowed, if the value `Trolley` is found, then `<fare>` and `<tax>` must be present. Here is the RNC schema:

```
element transportation {
     element vehicle {
          ( attribute type { 'Automobile' },
            element make { text }
          ) |
          ( attribute type { 'Trolley' },
            element fare { text },
            element tax { text }
          )
     }*
}
```

Mixed Content Pattern

DTD and XML Schema syntax both contain special constructs to handle mixed content. Mixed content allows you to mix text and other child elements freely when declaring the content model of a particular element. In RELAX NG, there is the mixed pattern that handles mixed content:

Pattern Name	Pattern
mixed pattern	`mixed` {*pattern*}

Let's see an example for using the mixed pattern. Let's use the paragraph tag (<p>) of HTML as an example. Inside an HTML paragraph, you can place a mixture of text and bold (<b>) or italic (<i>) tags. For simplicity, we'll assume the <b> and <i> tags can only contain text. Here is an example XML instance:

```
<html>
     <body>
            <p>The rain in <b>Spain</b> falls <i>mainly</i> in the
<b>plain</b>.</p>
     </body>
</html>
```

As you can see, text is scattered in and around the <b> and <i> child elements. The following RNC schema will handle the previous document:

```
element html {
     element body {
          element p { mixed { element b { text} | element i { text } }* }
     }
}
```

By placing the * and | symbols, the preceding schema allows zero or more occurrences of <b> and/or <i> to be used as children of the <p> element, mixed in with text. This is a common design pattern for mixed content models. Note that DTD and XML schemas are limited to this particular use of mixed content, but RELAX NG is not. You can utilize other patterns with mixed content, as any pattern can go inside the two curly braces of the mixed pattern. For example, you could have a mixed pattern for paragraphs that required one <b> tag, followed by an optional <i> tag, followed by zero or more <em> tags, and in that order. The RNC schema for this new content model would be as follows:

```
element p { mixed { element b {text}, element i{text}?, element em {text}* } }
```

Note that in the new content model, the <em> tag can occur multiple times, but <b> and <i> cannot.

The Empty Pattern

XML has the concept of an *empty* element—that is, an element that contains no content, no child elements, and no text content. Empty elements *may* contain attributes, however. To provide for empty elements, RELAX NG has an empty pattern.

Pattern Name	Pattern
empty pattern	`Empty`

Here is an example using the empty pattern. Suppose we have an element, called `<br>` that has no attributes or child elements. That is, the `<br>` element is completely empty. Here is the XML:

```
<br/> <!-- or <br></br> -->
```

Here is the schema:

```
element br { empty }
```

Here's another example. If you had an element called `<file>` that was empty, but allowed `name` and `size` attributes, the XML would look like this:

```
<file name="abc.txt" size="2000" />
```

The schema then would be as follows:

```
element file { attribute name { text }, attribute size { text }, empty }
```

Connector Patterns and Grouping

RELAX NG has three connector patterns: *sequence, choice,* and *interleave.* We'll get to interleave in a moment, but, for now, let's review sequence and choice, and how these connector patterns can be grouped. We have seen the sequence and choice patterns earlier in this chapter, but we'll repeat them here:

Pattern Name	Pattern
sequence pattern	*Pattern* [, *pattern*]+
choice pattern	*Pattern* [| *pattern*]+

Elements, attributes, or other patterns can be combined with sequence or choice connectors. Therefore, you can have multiple patterns connected. For example:

```
element point3D { element x{text}, element y{text}, element z{text} }
```

In the preceding example, the comma connector represents sequence, so the order of the elements in the instance document must be `<x>` first, then `<y>`, then `<z>`, as shown in the following:

```
<point3D>
            <x>5</x><y>6</y><z>7</z>
</point3D>
```

Note that due to the way the connector patterns are described, you cannot combine sequence and choice in the same group. That is, we are allowed to have a sequence in a group, like this:

```
element x{text} , element y{text} , element z{text}
```

Or, we can have a choice used in a group:

```
element x{text} | element y{text} | element z{text}
```

But we cannot have a mixture of choice and sequence:

```
element x{text} , element y{text} | element z{text}
```

This last example tries to mix sequence and choice in a single group, which is not allowed. If you wish to use more than one kind of connector, you must group your content model using the parenthesis in the group pattern:

Pattern Name	Pattern
group pattern	(*pattern*)

The following shows how sequence and choice could be used together to describe a content model:

```
element x { text } , ( element y { text } | element z { text } )
```

As long as the same connector is used inside the parenthesis, all is well. You can also nest parentheses to any level, as in the following:

```
(element a {text}, (element b{text} | (element c {text} , element d
{text} ) ) )
```

Remember also that grouping patterns supports cardinality, allowing you to add `*`, `?`, and `+` symbols to the pattern as follows:

```
(element a{text}, (element b{text} | (element c{text},element d{text} ) * ) ? ) +
```

The Interleave Pattern

The third connector pattern we have available is the *interleave* pattern, which is quite powerful. As we've seen, the sequence connector requires that elements be ordered. The choice connector allows a choice between, say, two or more elements or other patterns. At a high level, interleave allows child elements (or other patterns) to occur in any order. For example, let's say we had to account for a person's name and phone number, as in the following XML instance:

```
<person>
        <name>Julie Gaven</name>
        <phone>555-1234</phone>
</person>
```

We could use the sequence connector if we wanted to force <name> to come before <phone>, but let's say that we really don't care about the order of the child elements <name> and <phone>. Instead we want to require that both <name> and <phone> are present. The choice connector would not work in this case, because we require both to be there; it's not an either/or situation. Hence, the interleave connector (&) is used as shown in the following:

```
element person { element name{text} & element phone { text } }
```

The interleave pattern is as follows:

Pattern Name	Pattern
interleave pattern	*pattern* [& *pattern*]+

The most common use of the interleave connector is to allow single element patterns to occur in any order. However, since two patterns can appear on either side of the interleave connector, and not just a single element pattern, you could make other types of content models possible. For example, let's say you had three elements: <a/>, <b/>, and <c/>, and they had to occur, in that order underneath a parent element. You would also need another element (say, an <id/> element) that could occur anywhere underneath that parent element, but you don't care where it occurred. This following would be a valid instance:

```
<root>
     <a/>
     <id>54643</id>
     <b/>
     <c/>
</root>
```

Here, we can use two separate patterns, connected via the interleave connector, as follows:

```
element root {
     element id { text } &
     ( element a { text }, element b { text}, element c { text } )
}
```

Here, the sequence: a,b,c is *interleaved* with id. You could add a + to id to allow multiple id elements to be interleaved in between the a,b,c sequence.

Try It Out Dinosaur Sample

In this example, we will create a RELAX NG compact syntax schema for an example XML document we saw back in Chapter 4 on DTDs.

1. Let's begin by creating the XML instance document. Simply open the Xmlde text editor, and enter the following. When you are finished, save the file as dinosaur.xml.

```
<carnivore>
  <species>Tyrannosaurus Rex</species>
  <length>42 feet</length>
  <height>18 feet</height>
```

```
    <weight>5-7 tons</weight>
    <speed>25 mph</speed>
    <discoverer>
      <name>Osborn</name>
      <date>1905</date>
    </discoverer>
    <location>
      <country>Canada</country>
    </location>
  </carnivore>
```

2. Next, we'll need to create the RNC schema document. Some of the rules we will go by will be as follows: All elements with content contain text. All elements will have a cardinality of one, except <country/>, which can occur one or more times. Copy the following into the Xmlde editor, and save the file as `dinosaur.rnc` in the same folder as `dinosaur.xml`.

```
element carnivore {
   element species { text },
   element length  { text },
   element height  { text },
   element weight  { text },
   element speed   { text },
   element discoverer {
        element  name { text },
        element  date { text }
   },
   element location {
        element country { text }+
   }
}
```

3. We are ready to validate our XML instance document against our RNC schema. Open the Xmlde editor, load the `dinosaur.xml` file, and choose Tools ➪ Validate Using RNC.

How It Works

In this *Try It Out* example, we created an XML instance document for the dinosaur vocabulary, then we created an RNC schema. The dinosaur XML has a root element, called `carnivore`, which contains seven different child elements, so we begin our schema this way:

```
element carnivore {
   element species { text },
   element length  { text },
   element height  { text },
   element weight  { text },
   element speed   { text },
   element discoverer {

   },
   element location {

   }
}
```

The `discoverer` element has two child elements, `name` and `date`, so we will add in those patterns:

```
element discoverer {
     element name { text },
     element date { text }
},
```

Lastly, we have to build out the `location` element by adding the `country` child element.

```
element location {
     element country { text }+
}
```

Note the + sign after the closing curly brace on `country`, signaling that `country` can occur one or more times.

Combining and Reusing Patterns and Grammars

In this section, we'll take a look at building patterns and entire grammars for reuse. We'll see how to break down patterns so that they can be reused and recombined in various ways. In addition, we'll take a look at breaking our RELAX NG grammars down into multiple physical files and how to redefine included patterns.

Named Patterns

All the RNC schemas we have shown thus far have been valid and complete RNC schemas. It is perfectly legal to create RNC schemas with one top-level (a.k.a. *root*) element, adding nested patterns, to any level, as needed. However, instead of creating one huge nested pattern, RELAX NG also allows you to construct complex schemas out of smaller pieces called *named pattern definitions*. Breaking one large pattern into multiple pieces (or named pattern definitions) makes it easier to manage complex schemas, as well as enabling reuse. It can also make your schema smaller, more flexible and easier to understand. Let's construct a schema for the following XML instance (the XML snippet shown is part of a fictional purchase order):

```
<purchaseOrder>
     <poNumber>123-7YUY</poNumber>
     <orderDate>3/18/2004</orderDate>
     <shipTo>
          <name>Marissa Evers</name>
          <address1>123 Main St</address1>
          <address2>Apt 14-A</address2>
          <city>Round Hill</city>
          <state>VA</state>
          <zip>20145</zip>
     </shipTo>
     <billTo>
          <name>Gregory Hughes</name>
          <address1>456 High St</address1>
          <city>Alexandria</city>
```

```
            <state>VA</state>
            <zip>20745</zip>
        </billTo>
</purchaseOrder>
```

Assuming the <address2> element is optional and all others are required, here is a possible RNC schema for the purchaseOrder XML, as shown previously:

```
element purchaseOrder {
            element poNumber { text },
            element orderDate { text },
            element shipTo {
                        element name { text },
                        element address1 { text },
                        element address2 { text }?,
                        element city { text },
                        element state { text },
                        element zip { text }
             },
            element billTo {
                        element name { text },
                        element address1 { text },
                        element address2 { text }?,
                        element city { text },
                        element state { text },
                        element zip { text }
             }
}
```

Note that this schema has some repeating patterns of elements. Unfortunately, if we choose to design our schema with one root element pattern, we need to repeat these nested elements. Let's add named pattern definitions as an alternate schema design. First, we'll add a named pattern definition called NameAddressDef, which will hold the six reusable element definitions:

```
NameAddressDef = ( element name { text }, element address1 { text },
                   element address2 { text }?, element city { text },
                   element state { text }, element zip { text } )
```

Note: The parenthesis around the entire element list is not required. Also be aware that recursive and reentrant patterns are allowed. A pattern reference can reference the current pattern name, either directly (recursive) or indirectly (reentrant).

NameAddressDef is a named pattern identifier and can be any name you choose. It does not have to start with an uppercase letter. Now that we've defined the sequence of reusable elements, we can reference the NameAddressDef definition from *inside* other patterns, as shown here:

```
ShipToDef = element shipTo { NameAddressDef }
BillToDef = element billTo { NameAddressDef }
```

Pattern reuse could not be any easier! You can simply use the named pattern identifier anywhere a pattern is allowed. The NameAddressDef on the right-hand side of the equals sign (=) references the original NameAddressDef definition, which appears to the left of the equals sign. Again, it is important to realize that NameAddressDef, ShipToDef, and BillToDef are named pattern names; they are not element or attribute names. Only named pattern names can appear to the left of the = sign.

Note: If you use one of the RNC keywords as your pattern name, you must precede it with a \, as in: \element = element hello {text}.

Next, we'll add definitions for <poNumber> and <orderDate>, as follows:

```
PONumberDef  = element poNumber   { text }
OrderDateDef = element orderDate { text }
```

Lastly, we can add a definition for the root element, <purchaseOrder>, as follows:

```
start = element purchaseOrder {
            PONumberDef, OrderDateDef, ShipToDef, BillToDef
}
```

This last pattern name is special in that it uses RNC's start keyword, which calls out the root element of the XML instance. The order in which you list the definitions in your schema is your choice. Putting it all together, here is the complete schema, with a top-down layout:

```
start          = element purchaseOrder {
                     PONumberDef, OrderDateDef, ShipToDef, BillToDef
                 }
PONumberDef    = element poNumber   { text }
OrderDateDef   = element orderDate { text }
ShipToDef      = element shipTo { NameAddressDef }
BillToDef      = element billTo { NameAddressDef }
NameAddressDef =  ( element name {text}, element address1 {text},
                    element address2 {text}?, element city {text},
                    element state {text}, element zip {text} )
```

One additional feature about pattern names is very important to understand. RNC grammar syntax was designed so that you don't have to worry about name collisions between pattern names and element (or attribute) names. You cannot place an element name to the left of the = sign. Due to this feature, many RNC schema designers use the same name for both the element (or attribute) and the pattern that defines that element. Why bother creating new unique names when you don't need to? The following is the same schema as shown previously, with the pattern names renamed to match the element names:

```
start = element purchaseOrder {
                     poNumber, orderDate, shipTo, billTo
        }
poNumber    = element poNumber   { text }
orderDate   = element orderDate { text }
shipTo      = element shipTo { NameAddress }
billTo      = element billTo { NameAddress }
NameAddress = ( element name {text}, element address1 {text},
                element address2 {text}?, element city {text},
                element state {text}, element zip {text} )
```

Named patterns are quite useful and important for schema designers, making our RELAX NG schemas easy to create, maintain, understand, and reuse! It is common to create named patterns for reusable components, or groups of attributes and/or elements. It's completely up to you how you want to expand your patterns into one or more pattern definitions, by employing the group pattern discussed earlier. For example, take a look at the following RNC snippet:

```
start = element purchaseOrder {
                    poNumber, orderDate, shipTo, billTo
        }
```

We can break this down into the following:

```
start = purchaseOrder
purchaseOrder = element purchaseOrder ( headerInfo, locationInfo )
headerInfo   = ( poNumber, orderDate )
locationInfo = ( shipTo, billTo )
```

It really depends on how you want to break down the reuse of your patterns and how much granularity and flexibility you need when combining and redefining multiple named patterns. We'll look at combining pattern definitions next.

assignMethod and Combining Named Pattern Definitions

Up till this point, we have been using the = assign method for our named patterns. That is, we assign a name to a pattern using the equals sign. This technique works fine, as long as our pattern names are unique. Using additional assign methods, RELAX NG gives you complete control over how identically named patterns combine. The full notation for creating named patterns is as follows:

```
namedPatternName assignMethod  pattern
```

Where `assignMethod` is one of the following symbols: =, |=, or &=. The term `assignMethod` is not a keyword. In RELAX NG, it is possible to have two or more named patterns with the same name; however, one must take some care when defining pattern names. Consider the following invalid schema:

```
start        = element entry { info }
info         = element name {text}
info         = element name {text}, element phone {text}
```

You cannot have two identically named patterns (`info` in this case) that use the = `assignMethod`. Though RELAX NG allows two identically named patterns, you must choose up front which technique to use when combining the named patterns. There are two combinations possible: choice or interleave.

Note: When combining patterns of elements, choice is common. Interleave is often used when combining patterns of attributes, since ordering does not matter. You can also place the various `assignMethod` *symbols on the special start pattern. This would allow you to combine multiple grammars that had different root elements.*

Let's make the preceding schema valid by using the choice `assignMethod`:

```
start          = element entry { info }
info           |= element name {text}
info           |= element firstName {text}, element lastName {text}
```

This basically says that element `<entry>` can have either a `<name>` child element or `<firstName>` followed by `<lastName>`. You are not allowed to mix |= and & = on identically named patterns. However, the following is legal:

```
start          = element entry { info }
info           = element name {text}
info           |= element firstName {text}, element lastName {text}
```

Here, we used = on the first `info`, and |= on the second. This has the same meaning as if they had both used |=.

> *Note: While using identically named patterns in a single schema file is rare, it is common for one schema file to include another, and here is a case where you might have to pay some extra attention to the `assignMethod` you choose to employ on your named patterns. For example, in the preceding schema, the first `info` pattern may come from `schema1.rnc`. The preceding `start` pattern and `second info` pattern may be found in `schema2.rnc`, which includes `schema1.rnc`.*

Schema Modularization Using the Include Directive

RELAX NG is extremely flexible when it comes to schema modularization. You are free to break down large schema files into smaller, reusable chunks. You can then combine these smaller files in various ways to develop your complete vocabulary. Schema files are allowed to include other schema files and at various levels. We'll use the `purchaseOrder` schema we saw earlier to illustrate some of the ways we can modularize our schema design:

```
purchaseOrder1.rnc:

start = element purchaseOrder {
                   poNumber, orderDate, shipTo, billTo
        }
poNumber    = element poNumber { text }
orderDate   = element orderDate { text }
shipTo      = element shipTo { NameAddress }
billTo      = element billTo { NameAddress }
NameAddress = ( name, address1, address2?, city, state, zip )
name        = element name {text}
address1    = element address1 {text}
address2    = element address2 {text}
city        = element city {text}
state       = element state {text}
zip         = element zip {text}
```

Let's say we wanted to modularize this schema by moving the `NameAddress` pattern into a separate schema file, `NameAddress.rnc` as follows:

```
NameAddress.rnc:

NameAddress = ( name, address1, address2?, city, state, zip )
name         = element name {text}
address1     = element address1 {text}
address2     = element address2 {text}
city         = element city {text}
state        = element state {text}
zip          = element zip {text}
```

Here is the new, modularized `purchaseOrder` schema:

```
purchaseOrder2.rnc:

include "NameAddress.rnc"
start = element purchaseOrder {
                 poNumber, orderDate, shipTo, billTo
        }
poNumber    = element poNumber { text }
orderDate   = element orderDate { text }
shipTo      = element shipTo { NameAddress }
billTo      = element billTo { NameAddress }
```

The `include` directive enables us to merge multiple physical schemas into one. A file name or URL may be specified. When we merge two or more schemas using the `include` directive, the named patterns in these schemas are all combined into one schema. The `assignMethod` that was discussed earlier will become more important here if there are identically named patterns in the included schemas.

Note: Recursive includes are not allowed. It is up to you to ensure that a single schema file is only included once, either directly or indirectly.

Redefining Included Named Patterns

When multiple grammars are merged into one, all the named patterns are combined. When you merge grammars like this, the *including* grammar has the ability to redefine one or more of the named patterns in the included grammar(s). For example, let's say we wanted to create a U.K. version of the purchase order, replacing the `<state>` element with `<region>` and the `<zip>` element with `<postalCode>`. Using the same `NameAddress.rnc` file as shown previously, let's construct a new `purchaseOrderUK.rnc` for U.K. purchase orders. (Note that the root element name was also modified to be `<purchaseOrderUK>`, although this change was not required.) Here is the new schema with two redefined patterns:

```
purchaseOrderUK.rnc:

include "NameAddress.rnc" {
              state = element region {text}
              zip = element postalCode {text}
        }

start = element purchaseOrderUK {
                 poNumber, orderDate, shipTo, billTo
        }
```

```
poNumber    = element poNumber { text }
orderDate   = element orderDate { text }
shipTo      = element shipTo { NameAddress }
billTo      = element billTo { NameAddress }
```

The curly braces that follow the include directive contain a list of named patterns that will replace the originals found in the `NameAddress.rnc` file. No need to worry about `assignMethod` here; since there is no combination of patterns taking place, it is a total replacement. You can also replace the `start` pattern, if one exists, in the included grammar.

Here is the modified XML instance document that will validate against the new U.K. version of the schema:

```
<purchaseOrderUK>
     <poNumber>123-7YUY</poNumber>
     <orderDate>3/18/2004</orderDate>
     <shipTo>
          <name>Rachel Maria</name>
          <address1>123 Main St</address1>
          <address2>Apt 14-A</address2>
          <city>Round Hill</city>
          <region>Bristol</region>
          <postalCode>78E7Y</postalCode>
     </shipTo>
     <billTo>
          <name>Max Jones</name>
          <address1>456 High St</address1>
          <city>Stratford</city>
          <region>Bristol</region>
          <postalCode>73U34I</postalCode>
     </billTo>
</purchaseOrderUK>
```

This granular redefining capability was enabled due to the fact that the developer of the original `NameAddress` schema had the forethought to create separate named patterns for each piece of the `NameAddress` content model, allowing other schemas to use `NameAddress` and redefine patterns as needed.

It is important to note that the `purchaseOrderUK` schema could have replaced the `state` and `zip` patterns with any RELAX NG pattern. For example, it was not required that the replacement had to be one element (`zip`) for one element (`postalCode`). Remember, you are replacing patterns, not elements. `purchaseOrderUK` could have replaced the Zip pattern with an attribute pattern, or a pattern with three attributes, or a pattern with a choice of two elements and an attribute.

Removing Patterns with the notAllowed Pattern

RELAX NG has a `notAllowed` pattern. One use of the `notAllowed` pattern is to effectively remove patterns of an included schema. This can be especially useful when one schema includes another, and there are name collisions. Let's say `mainSchema` has a grammar with a `start` pattern, and so does `subSchema`. If `mainSchema` includes `subSchema` at the top level, then the two `start` patterns have a name conflict. You would have to decide how to combine the two `start` patterns. However, this may be problematic. Perhaps you wish to effectively throw away the `start` pattern in the `subSchema`, instead of being forced to combine with it. The `notAllowed` pattern can be used for this, as follows:

```
subSchema.rnc:
start = a
a = element a { s1,s2 }
s1 = element s1 { text }
s2 = element s2 { text }
```

Here `mainSchema` includes `subSchema` but redefines the `start` pattern from `subSchema` to be `notAllowed`. This effectively removes the `start` pattern in `subSchema`.

```
mainSchema.rnc:
include "subSchema.rnc" {
               start = notAllowed
        }
start |= element main { s1, s2, s3 }
s3 = element s3 { text }
```

Extending Schemas with Composition

Commonly a feature needed by schema designers, schema *extension* takes a reusable, shared, content model and customizes it. In the last section, we saw how to redefine patterns as well as how to combine multiple schemas using the `include` directive. We can also extend existing content models, that is, add new elements and attributes as needed to extend the base definition. Even though RELAX NG does not support object-oriented style inheritance, extension is supported in many different ways. In fact, you saw one way in the last section using RELAX NG's redefine capability. Another common way that RELAX NG supports extension is through *composition*, which is simply one pattern's ability to reference another.

Let's create a new `purchaseOrder`, but this time, we want to extend the `NameAddress` pattern and add in a few more elements, for example, `<email>` and `<homePage>`. This is different than our earlier discussion in that we are not redefining any of the existing elements in the existing `NameAddress` pattern; we only want to extend it by appending more elements. Here is the new `purchaseOrder` schema:

```
purchaseOrderExt.rnc:

include "NameAddress.rnc"

start = element purchaseOrderUK {
                   poNumber, orderDate, shipTo, billTo
        }
poNumber    = element poNumber { text }
orderDate   = element orderDate { text }
shipTo      = element shipTo { NameAddressExt }
billTo      = element billTo { NameAddressExt }
NameAddressExt = ( NameAddress, email?, homePage? )
email       = element email { text }
homePage    = element homePage { text }
```

In the new schema, the content models for <shipTo> and <billTo> now reference a newly created `NameAddressExt` pattern, which with composition extends the `NameAddress` pattern by appending a simple sequence of two additional elements. Of course, we aren't limited to appending a sequence of elements; we can use any RELAX NG pattern.

We could, for example, build a choice of `NameAddress` and other elements or attributes, as shown in the following:

```
NameAddressExt = NameAddress | GPSLocation
GPSLocation = element GPSLocation {text}, attribute timeZone{text}
```

We could also allow text strings between `NameAddress` elements, by interleaving `NameAddress` with text:

```
NameAddressExt = NameAddress & text
```

Or, we could add elements before the `NameAddress` pattern, instead of after it as follows:

```
NameAddressExt = AgencyInfo, NameAddress
AgencyInfo = element agencyName { text }, element agencyType { text }
```

Extensibility in RELAX NG

In the previous chapter on XML schemas, you saw how XML Schema supports object-oriented inheritance features as a means for schema reuse. XML schemas have simple and complex types that can be extended and/or restricted as a means to support schema extensions. RELAX NG is quite a bit different than XML Schema in this regard because it doesn't have the concept of types and instead is based on patterns. While RELAX NG does not support inheritance, this does not mean that reuse and extendability are impossible. In fact, as we have already seen, RELAX NG patterns can be composed, extended, redefined, and combined in very flexible ways. With RELAX NG, *the power is in the patterns!*

Here is yet another way to create a RELAX NG schema framework that is designed to be *extendable.* Assume we need to create a large, interconnected vocabulary, and we want others to be able to automatically extend different parts of our grammar via custom, user-defined patterns. While RELAX NG does not allow inheritance, you can, with a little forethought, add some *placeholder* patterns, utilizing the `notAllowed` pattern. These `placeHolder` patterns can then be combined with user-defined *extension* patterns. Let's see how this would work.

First, here is a tiny snippet of the large, heavily interconnected vocabulary:

```
start = element shipTo { NameAddress }
...
NameAddress = ( name, street, city, NameAddress.ext )
name = element name { text }
street = element street { text }
city = element city { text }
NameAddress.ext |= notAllowed
...
```

Again, assume that this vocabulary is highly interconnected, where many of the other patterns reference the previous NameAddress pattern. The NameAddress.ext pattern in the previous schema has no effect on the base-level NameAddress pattern, since it is currently set to notAllowed.

Now, let's construct the user extension schema, which will simply define a new NameAddress.ext pattern, effectively *extending* the original NameAddress pattern:

```
NameAddress.ext |= ( email, url )
email = element email { text }
url = element url { text }
```

When both schemas are included into one grammar, the combination will validate the following XML:

```
<shipTo>
     <name>Rachel Maria</name>
     <street>123 Main St</street>
     <city>Round Hill</city>
     <email>rachel@maria.com</email>
     <url>http://abc.com</url>
</shipTo>
```

More importantly, all the pattern references to NameAddress in the original schema, in addition to shipTo, will now support the extended version.

Nested Grammars and the RELAX NG Grammar Pattern

RELAX NG also supports nested grammars via the grammar pattern. Let's say we had an XML document with some grammar, which we'll call *outer* (outer, title, before, and after elements), and we wanted to embed another grammar, say an HTML document, in the middle. In our example, outer is the root element, and the HTML document is embedded between the before and after elements, as follows:

```
<outer>
   <title>Outer Document Title</title>
   <before>some before text here</before>
   <html>
       <title>My Web Page</title>
       <body>hello</body>
       <!-- rest of html goes here -->
   </html>
   <after>some after text here</after>
</outer>
```

It is quite reasonable that the outer grammar elements and the html grammar elements would be in separate namespaces as well, but that is not a requirement. A single RELAX NG grammar can consist of any number of namespaces. We'll learn how RELAX NG supports namespaces later in this chapter. Here is a single schema that contains the outer grammar including a nested grammar that defines the HTML elements:

```
start = outer
outer = element outer { title, before, embeddedHTML, after }
title = element title { text }
```

```
before = element before { text }
after = element after { text }

embeddedHTML = grammar {
                   start = html
                   html = element html { title, body }
                   title = element title { text }
                   body = element body { text }
               }
```

The `grammar` pattern allows you to nest named pattern declarations. Every nested grammar pattern must have at least one `start` pattern, which designates the start of the nested grammar.

It is important to realize that when you have nested grammars, you have a nested set of named pattern declarations. The five named patterns in the outer grammar (*start, outer, title, before,* and *after*) do not combine with the four named patterns (*start, html, title,* and *body*) in the nested grammar. This means that we do not have to be concerned about how the two title patterns will combine. This is quite a bit different than the way the `include` directive operated earlier. Earlier, we saw how a top-level `include` directive could combine all the named patterns from multiple physical files into one grammar. When this happened, we had to be concerned about named-pattern name collisions and how the named patterns would combine. With nested grammars, we do not have this concern.

In the preceding example, the named patterns in the outer and HTML grammars are completely separate. For example, the schema below would generate an error, because the content model for the HTML grammar's title pattern is referencing named patterns `before` and `after`, which are in the outer grammar and not in scope:

```
start = outer
outer = element outer { title, before, embeddedHTML, after }
title  = element title  { text }
before = element before { text }
after  = element after  { text }

embeddedHTML = grammar {
                   start = html
                   html  = element html { title, body }
                   title = element title { before, text, after } # error here
                   body  = element body  { text }
               }
```

It is possible to allow patterns in nested grammars to refer to named patterns in their *parent grammar* by using the `parent` pattern, as shown here:

```
start = outer
outer = element outer { title, before, embeddedHTML, after }
title  = element title   { text }
before = element before  { text }
after  = element after   { text }

embeddedHTML = grammar {
```

```
                        start = html
                        html  = element html { title, body }
                        title = element title {
                                    parent before, # references outer grammar
                                    text,
                                    parent after } # references outer grammar
                        body = element body { text }
                   }
```

It is also possible to keep the outer grammar and the nested grammar in separate physical files, using a nested `include` directive. Here is the outer grammar schema file, which includes the nested HTML grammar:

```
start = outer
outer = element outer { title, before, embeddedHTML, after }
title  = element title   { text }
before = element before  { text }
after  = element after   { text }

embeddedHTML = grammar {
                    include "htmlgrammar.rnc"
               }
```

Here is the nested HTML grammar, `htmlgrammar.rnc`:

```
start = html
html  = element html { title, body }
title = element title { parent before, text, parent after }
body  = element body  { text }
```

Try It Out   Dinosaurs, Version 2

In this example, we will redo our previous dinosaur example, only with named patterns. Instead of creating one nested pattern, we will design named patterns for reuse and use pattern references.

1. Here is a new version of the dinosaur XML instance document, `dynosaur2.xml`. Note that `dinosaurs` is the new root element. We will also allow multiple `herbivore` child elements in addition to `carnivore`, with this new version of the schema.

```
<dinosaurs>
   <carnivore>
     <species>Tyrannosaurus Rex</species>
     <length>42 feet</length>
     <height>18 feet</height>
     <weight>5-7 tons</weight>
     <speed>25 mph</speed>
     <discoverer>
       <name>Osborn</name>
       <date>1905</date>
     </discoverer>
```

```
      <location>
        <country>Canada</country>
      </location>
    </carnivore>
</dinosaurs>
```

2. Next, we'll need to create a new version of a RNC schema document with named patterns. Copy the following into the Xmlde editor, and save the file as `dinosaur2.rnc` in the same folder as `dinosaur2.xml`.

```
start = dinosaurs
dinosaurs = element dinosaurs { (carnivore | herbivore)* }

carnivore = element carnivore { dinoInfo }
herbivore = element herbivore { dinoInfo }

dinoInfo = ( species, length, height, weight, speed, discoverer, location )

species     = element species { text }
length      = element length  { text }
height      = element height  { text }
weight      = element weight  { text }
speed       = element speed   { text }

discoverer = element discoverer { name, date }
name        = element name { text }
date        = element date { text }

location    = element location { country+ }
country     = element country { text }
```

3. We are ready to validate our XML instance document against our new RNC schema. Open the Xmlde editor, load the `dinosaur2.xml` file, and choose Tools ➪ Validate Using RNC.

How It Works

In this *Try It Out* example, we created a new RNC schema for our existing dinosaur XML instance. We created named patterns for the various pieces of the schema. Initially, we created a start pattern that calls out the root element, `dinosaurs`:

```
start = dinosaurs
dinosaurs = element dinosaurs { (carnivore | herbivore)* }
```

Next, we define named patterns for `carnivore` and `herbivore`. The + sign on item indicates a one or more occurrence for that pattern:

```
version = attribute version { text }
carnivore = element carnivore  { dinoInfo }
herbivore = element herbivore  { dinoInfo }
```

Lastly, we can create a reusable `dinoInfo` pattern, and supporting element patterns:

```
dinoInfo = ( species, length, height, weight, speed, discoverer, location )

species     = element species { text }
length      = element length { text }
height      = element height { text }
weight      = element weight { text }
speed       = element speed { text }

discoverer = element discoverer { name, date }
name        = element name { text }
date        = element date { text }

location    = element location { country+ }
country     = element country { text }
```

Additional RELAX NG Features

We'll complete our discussion of RELAX NG by looking at some additional features. These include namespaces, name-classes and wildcards, data types, list pattern, comments, and divisions.

Namespaces

XML allows instance documents to contain elements and attributes that are tied to one or more namespaces. For starters, we will keep it simple and start out with an XML document that is tied to a single namespace:

```
<zoo xmlns="http://www.ZOO.com" >
    <tiger>Maggie</tiger>
    <emu>Rachel</emu>
</zoo>
```

In the preceding document, all the elements belong to the `http://www.zoo.com` namespace. Adding the default namespace declaration to the schema specifies the namespace used for any unprefixed element names (see `zoo`, `tiger`, and `emu` below). The following schema will validate the document:

```
default namespace = "http://www.zoo.com"
start = zoo
zoo   = element zoo { tiger , emu }
tiger = element tiger { text }
emu   = element emu { text }
```

Note: There are many differences in the way XML schemas handle namespaces and the way RELAX NG does it. RELAX NG doesn't have the concept of XML schema's single `targetNamespace`. In RELAX NG, as we will see shortly, we can have one schema document that describes many elements and/or attributes from many different namespaces. I think you will find that RELAX NG handles namespaces with elegance and simplicity.

Now we'll make it more complex by modifying the previous XML document so that it has multiple namespaces. We'll keep the root element <zoo> in the http://www.zoo.com namespace, but we will move the child elements <tiger> and <emu> into a different namespace: http://www.animal.com.

```
<zoo   xmlns="http://www.zoo.com" xmlns:animal="http://www.animal.com" >
     <animal:tiger>Maggie</animal:tiger>
     <animal:emu>Rachel</animal:emu>
</zoo>
```

Note: Refer back to the chapter on namespaces, as there are many ways to construct this document, using different combinations of default namespace declarations and prefixes.

With the addition of RELAX NG's namespace declaration, we can support multiple namespaces. In the following schema, note that zoo is unprefixed, leaving zoo tied to the default namespace, http://www.zoo.com, while tiger and emu are prefixed, tying them to the http://www.animal.com namespace:

```
default namespace = "http://www.zoo.com"
namespace animal = "http://www.animal.com"
start = zoo
zoo   = element zoo {  tiger , emu }
tiger = element animal:tiger { text }
emu   = element animal:emu   { text }
```

In RELAX NG, element or attribute names can be assigned namespaces, not pattern names. Also, it is not necessary that the schema document use the same prefix strings as the instance document. Prefixes (animal in our case) are user-defined. You can add as many namespace declarations as you want to your schema, allowing a single schema to support as many namespaces as you wish. Alternatively, you may elect to have a different default namespace for each schema document you create, then combine the schemas via the include directive, producing a final logical schema that allows multiple namespaces. Either way, RELAX NG makes using namespaces quite easy and flexible.

RELAX NG can also handle null namespaces, using a null URI string. Let's assume we wanted the <emu> element to belong to the null namespace, as in:

```
<zoo   xmlns="http://www.zoo.com" xmlns:animal="http://www.animal.com" >
    <animal:tiger>Maggie</animal:tiger>
    <emu xmlns="">Rachel</emu>
</zoo>
```

To support this, use a null namespaces URI, as in the following:

```
default namespace = "http://www.zoo.com"
namespace animal = "http://www.animal.com"
namespace local = ""
start = zoo
zoo   = element zoo {  tiger , emu }
tiger = element animal:tiger  { text }
emu   = element local:emu     { text }
```

Note: The prefix `local` is not a RELAX NG keyword; we can use any identifier we wish.

When you declare a default namespace, that namespace takes effect for the entire schema.

Name-Classes

RELAX NG uses name-classes to describe the legal names that you can use for elements and attributes. It is important to realize that with RELAX NG, modeling the name of a particular element or attribute is distinct from modeling the content model that is allowed for that element or attribute. We have already seen some features of name-classes, but now let's take a look at all the possibilities. Here are the element and attribute patterns we saw at the beginning of this chapter:

Pattern Name	Pattern
element pattern	`element` *nameClass {pattern}*
attribute pattern	`attribute` *nameClass {pattern}*

RELAX NG has four possibilities you can choose from when establishing a name-class for your element and attribute patterns:

1. Name (includes namespaces)
2. Name-class Choice and Grouping
3. NameSpace with wildcard
4. AnyName

Let's take a look at some examples of these four possibilities.

Note: Name-classes are available for both element and attribute patterns, however, in the examples that follow, we will only provide examples using element patterns.

Name (includes namespaces)

The first kind of name-class, Name, includes simple element and attribute names, with or without namespace prefixes. Every schema example presented so far in this chapter used this version of name-class.

Here is an element that uses the Name name-class, without a prefix:

```
tiger = element tiger { text }
```

And here is an example with a prefix:

```
tiger = element animal:tiger { text }
```

Most of the element (and attribute) patterns you will develop for your RELAX NG schemas will utilize this version of name-class.

Name-Class Choice and Grouping

This second form allows you to provide a choice of names to use for your elements and attributes. Here is an example using a choice:

```
start = zoo
zoo = element zoo { animal* }
animal = element tiger | emu | elephant { text }
```

This schema will validate the following instance:

```
<zoo>
     <elephant/>
     <tiger/>
</zoo>
```

Optionally, you can add parentheses around the choice list:

```
animal = element ( tiger | emu | elephant ) { text }
```

Of course, you can add names with namespaces to the list of names, assuming you had the appropriate namespace declarations, as in:

```
animal = element ( animal:tiger | local:emu | elephant ) { text }
```

Using this choice feature of name-classes can make your schemas easier to read, but it only works if all the element names in the list have the same content model, text in this case. If any of the element names listed had different content models, you would need separate element patterns for each one.

Using Namespaces with Wildcards

This third name-class feature allows you to use wildcards for the names of elements (or attributes), which are attached to a particular namespace. Let's take the following XML instance:

```
<zoo xmlns="http://www.zoo.com" xmlns:animal="http://www.animal.com">
     <!-- allow any element from any "http://www.animal.com" namespace -->
     <animal:tiger/>
     <animal:emu/>
</zoo>
```

Here is the schema, using the namespace with wildcard feature:

```
default namespace = "http://www.zoo.com"
namespace animal = "http://www.animal.com"
start = zoo
zoo   = element zoo { anyAnimal* }
anyAnimal = element animal:* { text }
```

The last line in the previous schema says: the `anyAnimal` pattern matches any child element, containing text, as long as that child element is from the `http://www.animal.com` namespace. Notice that we do not have to add additional named patterns to describe the `<emu>` or `<tiger>` elements, or any other elements that might suddenly appear under `<zoo>`. All we are saying is that we will accept any element, with text content, from the `http://www.animal.com` namespace.

In addition to using namespace wildcards, you can optionally add *exceptions*, which allow you to remove one or more names from the wildcard. For example, let's say we wanted to allow any animal except `<animal:tiger>`. We use a minus sign to designate what names are disallowed. Here is the syntax:

```
anyAnimal = element animal:* - animal:tiger { text }
```

You could disallow both `<animal:tiger>` and `<animal:emu>` with this syntax:`anyAnimal =`

```
element animal:* - ( animal:tiger | animal:emu ) { text }
```

While namespace wildcards are a nice feature, you may have noticed one severe limitation with all the preceding schemas. All the `animal` elements—`<tiger>`, `<emu>`, and so on—must have `text` content. This is a big limitation! What if we wanted to really open up the content model to allow any animal element with any element (or attribute) content? We will see how to accomplish this using the last name-class feature, `AnyName`.

Using AnyName

The `AnyName` name-class feature opens up many different kinds of patterns involving wildcards. The `*` symbol for the name-class enables this feature, as the following illustrates:

```
start= zoo
zoo = element zoo { anyElementWithText* }
anyElementWithText = element * { text }
```

The preceding last line allows any element, from any namespace, as long as it has text content. Here is a valid instance document, notice the addition of some new tags:

```
<zoo xmlns:animal="http://www.animal.com">
     <animal:dog>Dollie</animal:dog>
     <animal:tiger>Pumpkin</animal:tiger>
     <poNumber>TR783</poNumber>
     <animal:emu>Pepper</animal:emu>
     <p>Some text here </p>
</zoo>
```

Using the `AnyName` name-class pattern, and mixing in some pattern recursion, we can finally get rid of the text content limitation. Here is a pattern that will allow any element, with any child elements, to any depth:

```
anyElement = element * { anyElement | text }*
```

This single pattern can be used to validate any XML document, as long as there are no attributes. If we want to add any attributes to the mix, then we can use the following pattern:

```
anyElement = element * { anyAttribute | anyElement | text }*
anyAttribute = attribute * { text }
```

This pattern can be compressed into the following:

```
any = element * { attribute * {text} | any | text }*
```

Note: `any`, `anyElement`, and `anyAttribute` are NOT RELAX NG keywords, feel free to use any identifier you wish.

The `AnyName` name-class also allows exceptions. We can disallow certain names from the `AnyName` wildcard, as we saw earlier. We can also combine the four different name-class features to create flexible patterns. Following are some example patterns that employ exceptions.

Any element from any namespace, except elements with the local name of `emu`:

```
anyExample1 = element * - *:emu { text }
```

Any element from any namespace, except elements with the local names `emu` or `tiger`:

```
anyExample2 = element * - (*:emu | *:tiger ) { text }
```

Any element from any namespace, except element with the local name `emu` from the `animal` namespace:

```
anyExample3 = element * - animal:emu { text }
```

Any element from any namespace, except any element from the `animal` namespace:

```
anyExample4 = element * - animal:* { text }
```

Any element from any namespace, except elements from the null namespace:

```
namespace local = ""
anyExample5 = element * - local:* { text }
```

Finally, any element from the `animal` namespace, or any element from any namespace with the local name `alien`, except elements with local name `emu` or elements from the `zoo` namespace:

```
anyExample6 = element (animal:* | *:alien ) - (*:emu | zoo:* ) { text }
```

Again, all the preceding samples are shown with text content, but we can open up the content models as needed.

Data Types

RELAX NG supports data type validation through external data types. RELAX NG has a mechanism defined by which users can add their own datatype library systems. Of course, to use a datatype library, you need to have a RELAX NG validator that implements that library system. Most available RELAX NG validators ship with support for the XML Schema data types, including XML Schema *facets*. The datatype prefix `xsd` is used to reference the XML Schema data types, and is pre-defined in RELAX NG.

For example, here is a complete schema that uses the XML Schema `integer` data type:

```
start = root
root= element root { xsd:integer }
```

This schema would validate the following instance document:

```
<root>1234</root>
```

And the following would not be valid, because the data is not of type `integer`:

```
<root>hello</root>
```

If you are employing a custom user-defined datatype library, then your schema would use the datatypes declaration:

```
datatypes color = "http://www.rainbow.com/datatypes"
start = house
house = element house { color:beige }
```

Again, in this case, you would need to rely on a RELAX NG validator that understood the data types URI, as well as the `beige` type.

Let's revisit the `purchaseOrder` schema, and we can see data types and facets in use. Here is the `purchaseOrder` XML instance document:

```
<purchaseOrder>
     <poNumber>123-7yuy</poNumber>
     <orderDate>2004-11-26</orderDate>
     <shipTo>
          <name>Marissa Evers</name>
          <address1>123 Main St</address1>
          <address2>Apt 14-A</address2>
          <city>Round Hill</city>
          <state>VA</state>
          <zip>20145</zip>
     </shipTo>
     <billTo>
          <name>Gregory Hughes</name>
          <address1>456 High St</address1>
          <city>Alexandria</city>
          <state>VA</state>
          <zip>20745</zip>
     </billTo>
</purchaseOrder>
```

In our earlier schema, all the non-leaf elements were defined using RELAX NG's `text` patterns, as in the following:

```
orderDate = element orderDate { text }
```

Let's modify the schema so that we employ the following datatype checking:

- `poNumber` must have three digits, followed by a dash (-), one digit, then three lowercase letters.
- `orderDate` must be a date format.

- name, address1, address2, and city can be strings up to 25 characters in length.
- zip must be a five-digit numeric value.
- state must be two uppercase letters.

Here is the schema that accomplishes these datatype constraints:

```
start = element purchaseOrder {
                      poNumber, orderDate, shipTo, billTo
         }
poNumber    = element poNumber   { strPO }
orderDate   = element orderDate { xsd:date }
shipTo      = element shipTo { NameAddress }
billTo      = element billTo { NameAddress }
NameAddress = ( name, address1, address2?, city, state, zip )
name        = element name      { str25 }
address1    = element address1 { str25 }
address2    = element address2 { str25 }
city        = element city      { str25 }
state       = element state     { strState }
zip         = element zip       { strZip   }

# datatype patterns                                          sample patterns:
strPO       = xsd:string { pattern="\d{3}-\d[a-z]{3}" }    #999-9aaa
str25       = xsd:string { maxLength="25" }
strState    = xsd:string { pattern="[A-Z]{2}" }             #AA
strZip      = xsd:string { pattern="\d{5}" }                #99999
```

Note: In RNC notation, everything to the right of a # sign is a comment. In sample patterns, 9 = number, A = uppercase letter, and a = lowercase letter.

In the preceding schema, we employ the xsd:date and xsd:string types. The xsd:string types are further restricted by the XML Schema pattern and maxLength facets. You are free to use any XML Schema facets except for whitespace and enumeration.

List Patterns

List patterns allow you to validate a whitespace-separated list of tokens. For example, let's say we wanted to provide data for an array of three-dimensional points, each point consisting of an x, y, and z value. The XML instance would look like this:

```
<points3D>
     4     6     7
    13    20    33
    15     2    99
</points3D>
```

Note that the data can be all on one line or even one number per line. The individual items need to be separated by whitespace. Here is the schema, utilizing the list pattern:

```
start = points3D
points3D = element points3D { list { (xsd:int, xsd:int, xsd:int)+ } }
```

We aren't limited to integral data types; we can also have, say, the following:

```
<someData>
Monday          6      77.3
Tuesday         7      88.8
Wednesday       8      99.9
</someData>
```

Then we can validate with the following:

```
start = someData
someData = element someData { list { (weekday, xsd:int, xsd:double)+ } }
weekday = "Monday" | "Tuesday" | "Wednesday" | "Thursday" | "Friday"
```

Comments and Divisions

You can add comments to your schemas, and you can also break an individual schema into parts (called *divisions*). The following schema was divided into three divisions, one for includes, one for header information, and one for detail information. Comments start with a # and continue to the end of line. Here is an example of using both comments and divisions:

```
div {
     # top-level includes
     include "aaa.rnc"
     include "bbb.rnc"
}

div {
    # header-level patterns
    start = po
    po = element po { header, detail }
    header = element header { text }
    ...
}

div {
    # detail-level patterns
    detail = element detail { text }
    ...
}
```

Useful Resources

Here is a list of some RELAX NG-related URLs that you might find helpful:

- Main specifications: `http://www.relaxng.org/`
- Validating parsers/processors:
    - Jing: `http://www.thaiopensource.com/relaxng/jing.html`
    - Trang: `http://thaiopensource.com/relaxng/trang.html`

    - MSV: `http://wwws.sun.com/software/xml/developers/multischema/`
    - Topologi: `http://www.topologi.com`
    - RNV: `http://www.davidashen.net/rnv.html`
- Editors:
    - Xmlde: `http://www.xmldistilled.com`
    - Topologi: `http://www.topologi.com/products/tme/index.html`
    - Oxygen: `http://www.oxygenxml.com/`
    - Nxml mode for GNU Emacs: `http://www.thaiopensource.com/download/`

Summary

In this chapter, we've learned how to create RELAX NG compact schemas that can be used to validate our XML instance documents.

We've learned the basic RELAX NG patterns, including element, attribute, and enumerations, as well as pattern grouping and connectors (sequence, choice, and interleave). Then we covered how to create named patterns for reuse and how to modularize schemas into multiple files using the include directive. Next, we discussed how to use nested grammars to avoid named pattern collisions, as well as how to create RNC schemas with extendability in mind. Lastly, we learned how to use namespaces and name-classes in RNC schemas, and how to employ datatype validation, lists, comments, and divisions.

While we have not discussed every single option available with RELAX NG schemas, we have certainly covered the vast majority of features. I hope you have as much fun as I do using this fabulous technology!

Exercise Questions

Suggested solutions to these questions can be found in Appendix A.

Question 1

Break the `dinosaur2.rnc` schema file into two schemas. In `dinosaur3Main.rnc`, place the main schema elements. In `dinoInfo.rnc`, place the `dinoInfo` pattern. At the top level, place an include directive in `dinosaur3Main.rnc` to include `dinoInfo.rnc`.

Question 2

Add a wildcard extension to the `dinoInfo` pattern, so that the users can extend the dinosaur schema by adding any elements they desire to `dinoInfo`.

Part III: Processing

XPath

When writing code to process XML, you often want to select specific parts of an XML document to process in a particular way. For example, you might want to select some invoices that fit a date range of interest. Similarly, you may want to specifically exclude some part(s) of an XML document from processing. For example, if you make basic human resources data available on your corporate intranet, you probably want to be sure not to display confidential information such as salary for an employee. To achieve those basic needs, it is essential to have an understanding of a technology that allows you to select a part or parts of an XML document to process. The XML Path Language, XPath, is designed to allow the developer to select specific parts of an XML document.

XPath was designed specifically for use with Extensible Stylesheet Language Transformations (XSLT), which is described in more detail in Chapter 8, and with XML Pointer (XPointer), which is not discussed in detail in this book. More recently, XForms 1.0 (described in Chapter 19) makes use of XPath 1.0, too.

XPointer was intended for use with the XML Link Language, XLink. Xlink, which became a W3C recommendation in 2001, has seen limited adoption to date. As a result, XPointer is currently also not widely used. Therefore, XPath in this chapter is described primarily in the context of how it is used with XSLT, and the code examples in the chapter use XSLT. To run XSLT code using the Saxon XSLT processor, see the information provided in Chapter 8.

The use of XForms, which includes XPath expressions that bind a form control to the instance data of an XForms document, is discussed in Chapter 19.

We will cover the following:

- Ways of looking at an XML document, including the XPath Data Model
- How to visualize XPath and how the component parts of XPath syntax fit together to allow you to navigate around the XPath data model
- The XPath axes—the "directions" that are available to navigate around the XPath data model

- XPath 1.0 functions
- Looking ahead to XPath 2.0

To understand what XPath is and how it is used we will first consider ways in which an XML document can be represented.

Ways of Looking at an XML Document

In the early chapters of this book you saw how an XML document can be written as a nested structure of start tags and end tags, possibly together with processing instructions, comments, attributes, namespace declarations, and text content of elements. An XML document written in that way is simply a sequence of Unicode characters. When XML is expressed in that way, it is said to be *serialized*.

However, although serialized XML is convenient for the human reader, a serialized document is not the only way an XML document can be represented. It is often more useful to model the logical structure of an XML document in a way that describes the logical components that make up the XML document and exposes those components for programmatic manipulation. For example, read the following XML markup:

```
<Paragraph>Some text.</Paragraph>
```

You probably think of it logically as a `Paragraph` element with some text content, rather than as a left-angled bracket followed by an uppercase P, and so on. Similarly, to process XML, you need some formal model of the logical content of the document.

The W3C has developed three specifications—XPath, the XML Document Object Model (DOM), and the XML Information Set—each of which represents a logical model of an XML document in similar but distinct ways.

This chapter focuses on the XPath 1.0 data model because that underlies how XPath is used. Representing an XML document using the XML DOM is discussed briefly here and in more detail in Chapter 11. A fourth way in which an XML document can be represented, the XML Information Set, often abbreviated as the XML *infoset*, is also described briefly.

Serialized Document

In a serialized XML document we write start and end tags and, except in XML documents of trivial length, there is a nested structure of elements, such as in the following simple document:

```
<?xml version="1.0" encoding="UTF-8"?>
<!-- This is a comment. -->
<Book>
<Chapter>Some content</Chapter>
<Appendix>Some appendix content.</Appendix>
</Book>
```

By now, you should be familiar with such XML documents and how to write well-formed XML. But how are these documents represented in the XPath data model?

XPath Data Model

The XPath data model represents most parts of a serialized XML document as a tree of nodes. Most parts, but not all, of an XML document are represented as nodes in the XPath data model. A root node represents the document itself. An element node represents each element in an XML document. Each attribute is represented by an attribute node and so on, for comments and processing instructions. A text node represents an element's text content. In-scope namespaces are represented by namespace nodes. We will look in more detail at each type of node in a moment.

A few parts of an XML document are not represented in the XPath data model. An XML declaration, if present, is not represented in any way in the XPath data model, nor is a document type declaration (DOCTYPE declaration) represented. In addition, while comments and processing instructions can be represented by comment nodes and processing instruction nodes, any comments and processing instructions contained in the document type declaration are not represented at all in the XPath data model.

The Document Object Model

Like the XPath data model, the Document Object Model represents an XML document as a hierarchical tree of nodes. The types of nodes used in the DOM are different from those used in XPath. The nodes used in the DOM and writing code to manipulate the DOM are described in Chapter 11.

The XML Information Set

The XML Information Set (infoset) represents an XML document as a hierarchical tree but uses a different approach from both the XPath model and the DOM.

> *The XML Information Set recommendation is located at* `http://www.w3.org/TR/xml-infoset/`. *At the time of writing, a second edition of the XML Information Set recommendation is in preparation. If the URL given does not display the second edition, I suggest you visit* `http://www.w3.org/tr/` *and do a search on the text "info," and you should locate a link to the XML Infoset Second Edition recommendation.*

The infoset represents an XML document as a tree of *information items*. Each information item is similar in concept to a node in the XPath model. Each information item has *properties,* which store values that describe one of the item's characteristics.

Our focus in this chapter is XPath, so let's try to get a handle on it.

Visualizing XPath

XPath can be a very abstract and confusing topic. One of the ways of visualizing XPath, which newcomers to XPath often find helpful, is to think of XPath as street directions around the hierarchical tree of nodes that make up the XPath data model.

In real life, you can give street directions in two ways: relative to a fixed point, or relative to the current position. In XPath, you can write *absolute* XPath expressions, which always start from a standard point, the root node. Alternatively, you can write *relative* XPath expressions, which vary depending on where you start. In XPath, the starting point is called the *context*.

All legal XPath code can be called an expression. An XPath expression that returns a node-set is called a location path.

When giving street directions, you have four basic directions: North, South, East, and West. In XPath, there are 13 directions. In XPath, a direction is called an *axis*. Just as you might give someone street directions such as "Starting from the square, head East for one block and it's the first building on the right with a red door," in XPath, you might write something like this:

```
/Book/Chapter[@number=2]
```

If we were to express that XPath expression in English, we might say, "Starting from the root node, take the `child` axis and look for element nodes called `Book`; then, for each of those `Book` element nodes, look for element nodes called `Chapter`; then select only those `Chapter` element nodes that have a `number` attribute whose value is 2." We can refer to a `child` axis when it isn't actually mentioned because the `child` axis is the default axis in XPath. The part of the expression in square brackets is a *predicate*, which acts to filter nodes selected by the earlier part of the expression. Axes, predicates, and other XPath constructs are explored in more detail later.

A relative location path could be written as follows:

```
Chapter[@number=2]
```

This could be expressed in English as, "Starting from where you are currently located, take the `child` axis, select `Chapter` element nodes, and then filter those nodes to retain only `Chapter` element nodes that possess a `number` attribute whose value is 2." You will likely immediately realize that the result you get depends on your starting position (the XPath context). So it's important to understand just what context means in XPath.

Context

In XPath, the context indicates the location of the node where a processor is currently situated, so to speak. That node is called the *context node.*

However, the context consists of more than just the context node. It also includes a *context position* and a *context size.* Consider the following XML document:

```
<Book>
 <Chapter number="1">This is the first chapter</Chapter>
 <Chapter number="2">This is the second chapter</Chapter>
 <Chapter number="3">This is the third chapter</Chapter>
 <Chapter number="4">This is the fourth chapter</Chapter>
 <Chapter number="5">This is the fifth chapter</Chapter>
</Book>
```

Suppose the context node is the node that represents the `Chapter` element node for the second chapter. We can use the `position()` and `last()` functions, which are described in more detail later in this chapter, to show the position of the context node and the context size.

```
<xsl:stylesheet
 version="1.0"
 xmlns:xsl="http://www.w3.org/1999/XSL/Transform" >

<xsl:template match="/">
 <html>
  <head>
   <title>This shows the context position and context size.</title>
  </head>
  <body>
   <h3>Context position and context size demo.</h3>
   <xsl:apply-templates select="/Book/Chapter" />
  </body>
 </html>
</xsl:template>

<xsl:template match="Chapter">
 <xsl:if test="position()=2">
 <p>When the context node is the second <b>Chapter</b> element node then</p>
 <p>the context position is <xsl:value-of select="position()" /></p>
 <p>and the context size is <xsl:value-of select="last()" />.</p>
 <p>The text the <b> Chapter</b> element node contains is
'<xsl:value-of select="." />'.</p>
 </xsl:if>
</xsl:template>

</xsl:stylesheet>
```

The simple HTML document created by the stylesheet is shown in Figure 7-1.

The files `Books.xml`, `Books.xsl`, and `Books.html` are included in the code download. The instructions to run the code are described in Chapter 8 on XSLT.

Notice that in the value of the `select` attribute of the `xsl:value-of` element you see the `position()` function and the `last()` function. As you see in Figure 7-1, the context position is 2 and the context size is 5.

In addition to the context node, the context position, and the context size, the context also includes variable bindings that are in scope, namespace declarations that are in scope, and a function library (the XPath 1.0 function library).

What Is a Node?

A node is a representation in the XPath data model of a logical part of an XML document.

In XPath 1.0 there are seven types of nodes:

- ❑ Root node
- ❑ Element node
- ❑ Attribute node
- ❑ Text node

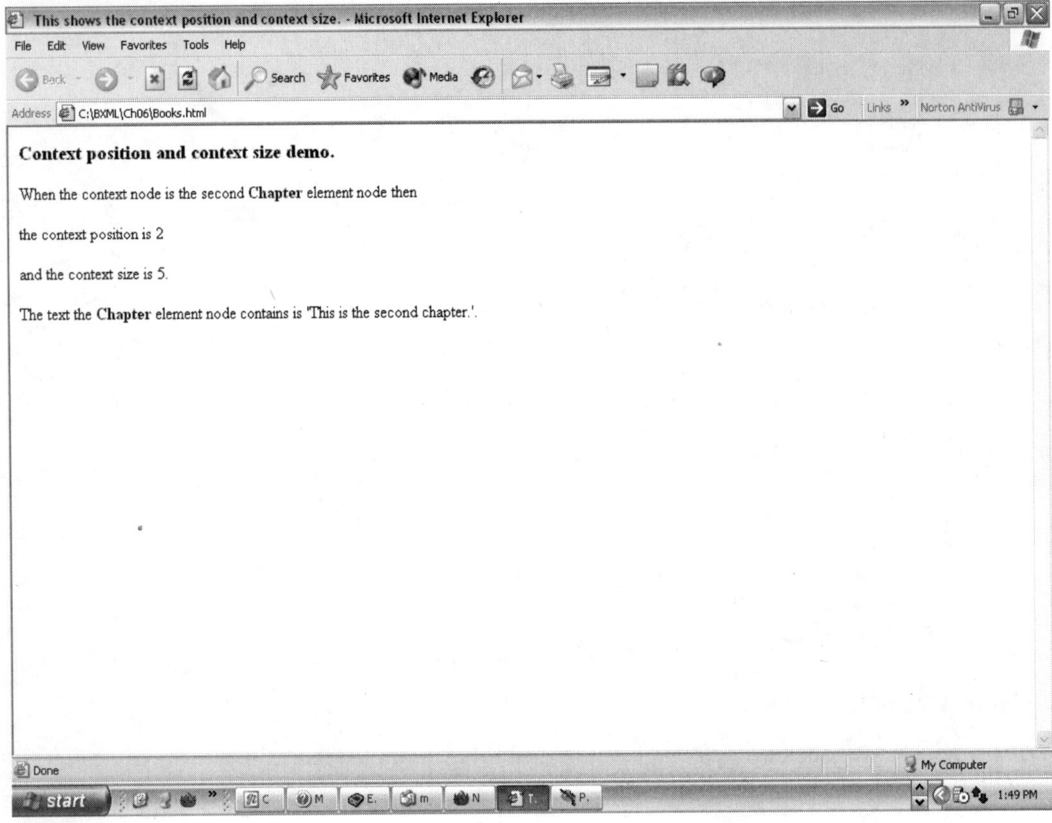

Figure 7-1

- Namespace node
- Comment node
- Processing Instruction node

Each node type is described in more detail in the following sections.

Root Node

The root node represents the document itself, independent of any content it has. The root node is the apex of the hierarchy of nodes that represents an XML document. The element node, which represents the document element, is a *child node* of the root node. The root node may also have child nodes, which are processing instruction nodes or comment nodes that correspond to any processing instructions or comments in the prolog of the serialized XML document.

The XML declaration and the document type declaration are not children of the root node. Neither of those features of a serialized XML document is represented in the XPath data model.

The root node's text value is the concatenation of the values of all descendant text nodes of the root node, in document order. Examine the following XML document:

```
<MixedContent>
Mary had a <Emphasis>little</Emphasis> lamb.
</MixedContent>
```

The text value of this document is `Mary had a little lamb.`

The root node does not have a name.

Element Node

Each element in an XML document is represented as an *element node* in the XPath data model.

Element nodes have a name made up of the namespace URI of the element and the local part of its name. For developers it is easier to work with a *qualified name*, also called a *QName*, which is a namespace prefix followed by a colon character followed by the local part of the element type name:

```
prefix:localpart
```

The string value of an element node is the concatenation of the values of all its descendant text nodes, in document order.

An element node may represent an element that possesses a unique ID attribute. If it does, the `id()` function can be used to access that element node.

Attribute Node

Each attribute in an XML document is represented in the XPath model as an *attribute node*. The element node with which the attribute node is associated is said to be the parent node of the attribute node.

Attribute nodes have a name and a string value.

Text Node

Text content of an element node is represented in the XPath data model as a *text node*.

The string value of a text node is its character data. A text node does not have a name.

Namespace Node

All in-scope namespaces of an element node are represented as *namespace nodes*. XPath takes an extravagant approach to namespace nodes. Each element node has its own namespace node for *all* in-scope namespaces. For example, imagine the XPath model of the following code:

```
<Book xmlns="http://www.XMML.com/booknamespace">
 <Chapter number="1">Some text content.</Chapter>
 <Chapter number="2">Some different text content.</Chapter>
</Book>
```

The `Book` element node has a namespace node associated with the namespace URI `http://www.XMML.com/booknamespace`. Each of the `Chapter` element nodes also has its own namespace node associated with the same namespace URI, `http://www.XMML.com/booknamespace`. This simple document has three separate namespace nodes associated with the same namespace URI. In complex documents, large numbers of namespace nodes can be associated with a single URI and some elements deep in the hierarchy can have several namespace nodes.

The `name()` function returns the namespace prefix associated with the namespace node. The `self:: node()` expression (which can be abbreviated to a period character) returns the namespace URI of the namespace node.

Comment Node

A comment node represents a comment in the XML document. Comments in the document type declaration are not represented in the XPath data model.

Processing Instruction Node

A processing instruction node in the XPath model represents a processing instruction in the corresponding XML document. Processing instructions in the document type declaration are not represented in the XPath data model.

The name of a processing instruction node is its target (turn to Chapter 2 for more on processing instructions). The string value of a processing instruction node is its content, excluding the target.

XPath 1.0 Types

XPath 1.0 has four expression types:

- boolean
- node-set
- number
- string

Booleans

In an XPath 1.0 expression a boolean value is written as one of the values `true()` or `false()`. You may wonder why we don't simply use the values `true` and `false`. It is possible that an XML developer might choose to have a structure like this:

```
<true>
 ... some content
</true>
```

`true` is a legal XML name, and can be used to name an element.

As you'll see later, the XPath way to select the `true` element node is indistinguishable from the value `true`. By using the syntax `true()` and `false()`, which technically are XPath functions, we remove the possible ambiguity.

Node-Sets

A node-set is a set of XPath nodes. Technically, an XPath 1.0 node-set is unordered. However, when used in XSLT, which is currently XPath's main use, processing of a node-set is always in the document order of the nodes for forward axes and in reverse document order for reverse axes. XPath axes are discussed later. Most axes, including the `child` axis, are forward axes.

Consider what document order means by examining the following simple document:

```
<PurchaseOrder>
 <Date>2005-01-01</Date>
 <To>XMML.com</To>
 <ShippingAddress>
  <Street>123 Any Street</Street>
  <City>Anytown</City>
  <State>AZ</State>
 </ShippingAddress>
 <ZipCode>12345</ZipCode>
</PurchaseOrder>
```

The `PurchaseOrder` element is first in document order. Document order among the children of the `PurchaseOrder` element is then `Date`, `To`, `ShippingAddress`, and `ZipCode`. All the child nodes of `ShippingAddress` come earlier in document order than the `ZipCode` element.

Numbers

In XPath, numbers are floating point numbers. There is no way to directly represent an integer in XPath, although numeric functions will typically return a whole number from, for example, the `count()` function, which counts the number of nodes in a node-set.

Strings

A string value in XPath is a sequence of Unicode characters. Generally, like XML, XPath is not limited to ASCII characters but uses the much more extensive Unicode character set (turn to Chapter 2 for more on Unicode).

XPath 1.0 has no type corresponding to a date. All dates are treated in XPath as strings. So, for example, manipulation of strings that represent dates to extract the month from a date depends on knowing exactly how the string is written, and on using various XPath string manipulation functions.

So far, we have talked about XPath in a pretty abstract way. How is XPath written?

Abbreviated and Unabbreviated Syntax

XPath syntax is not written in XML, one reason being that we often use an XPath expression as the value of an attribute. For example, if we wanted to select the value of a `Section` element node, we might write the following:

```
<xsl:value-of select="/Book/Chapter/Section" />
```

If XPath were written using XML, there would be problems in achieving well-formedness. For example, we couldn't use left or right-angled brackets inside the `select` attribute. The syntax used in XPath is similar to the path syntax used for UNIX and Linux directories. The `xsl:value-of` element, by the way, is an XSLT element, which is described in Chapter 8.

The most common tasks you will want to perform using XPath, the selection of elements and attributes, can be written using an *abbreviated syntax*, such as shown in the previous example. The *unabbreviated syntax* with the same meaning is written as follows:

```
<xsl:value-of select="/child::Book/child::Chapter/child::Section" />
```

To select an attribute using unabbreviated syntax, we can write the following:

```
attribute:: attributename
```

Or, in the abbreviated form, simply write the following:

```
@attributename
```

When using XPath, use the abbreviated syntax where possible. For the two most common tasks—selecting element nodes and attribute nodes using the `child` and `attribute` axes—it can achieve the same functionality as the unabbreviated syntax.

XPath 1.0 Axes

XPath 1.0 has a total of 13 axes, which are used to navigate the node tree of the XPath data model. In the following list, notice that the first letter of the name of an axis is always lowercase. Because XPath, like XML, is case sensitive, using an uppercase initial letter for the name of an axis will cause unexpected results.

- child Axis
- attribute Axis
- ancestor Axis
- ancestor-or-self Axis
- descendant Axis
- descendant-or-self Axis
- following Axis
- following-sibling Axis
- namespace Axis
- parent Axis
- preceding Axis
- preceding-sibling Axis
- self Axis

The following sections look more closely at each axis in turn. First, we'll look at the `child` and `attribute` axes, because they are the axes you will use most often.

Note that the name of each axis is case sensitive. All axis names are lowercase only.

Child Axis

The `child` axis is the default axis in XPath. The `child` axis selects nodes that are immediate child nodes of the context node. Thus, consider a structure like this in an XML document:

```
<Invoice>
<Date>2004-01-02</Date>
<Item quantity="4">QD123</Item>
<Item quantity="5">AC345</Item>
</Invoice>
```

If the context node is the `Invoice` element node, the location path,

```
child::Item
```

or, in abbreviated syntax,

```
Item
```

will return a node-set containing both `Item` element nodes, which are child nodes of the `Invoice` element.

To select both the `Date` element node and `Item` element nodes, which are child nodes of the `Invoice` element node (which is also the context node), you can write the following:

```
child::*
```

Or, in abbreviated syntax, the following:

```
*
```

The `*` indicates any name, and the only nodes in the `child` axis that have names are element nodes.

If you want to select all child nodes, including comment nodes, processing instruction nodes, and text nodes you can write the following:

```
child::node()
```

Or, in abbreviated syntax, the following:

```
node()
```

If you want to specifically select text node children of a context node, you can write the following:

```
child::text()
```

Or, in abbreviated syntax, the following:

```
text()
```

Because it is the default axis, it is not necessary to express the `child` axis when using abbreviated syntax. Thus, the location paths

```
/child::Book/child::Chapter/child::Section
```

and

```
/Book/Chapter/Section
```

both mean the same thing. Starting at the root node, there are three location steps, each of which uses the `child` axis. In the first example, which uses the unabbreviated syntax, the `child` axis is expressed explicitly. In the second example, the `child` axis is not explicitly expressed.

At the end of the following section, the *Try It Out* example will demonstrate the use of the `child` axis and the `attribute` axis.

attribute Axis

The `attribute` axis is used to select the attribute nodes associated with an element node. If the context node is an element node, the location paths

```
attribute::*
```

or

```
@*
```

each will return all the attribute nodes associated with that element node.

Alternatively, if you want to select a specific attribute node named `security`, you write either

```
attribute::security
```

or

```
@security
```

Remember that the `@` character is an abbreviation for the `attribute` axis.

If the context node is not an element node, the `attribute` axis returns an empty node-set.

The following example shows use of the `child` and `attribute` axes in a simple XSLT stylesheet. If you have no experience with XSLT, you may need to take a look at Chapter 8 for basic information.

Try It Out — Using child and attribute Axes

In this example we will use both the child and attribute axes. First, let's look at using XPath in XSLT to create a very simple HTML web page. The source XML document, `PersonData.xml`, is shown here:

```
<?xml version='1.0'?>
<PersonData>
<Name DOB="1920/11/25">
```

```
  <FirstName>Jack</FirstName>
  <LastName>Slack</LastName>
 </Name>
</PersonData>
```

The XSLT stylesheet, `PersonData.xsl`, is shown here:

```
<?xml version='1.0'?>
<xsl:stylesheet
 xmlns:xsl="http://www.w3.org/1999/XSL/Transform"
 version="1.0"
>

<xsl:template match="/">
 <html>
  <head>
    <title>Information about <xsl:value-of select="/PersonData/Name/FirstName"/>
    <xsl:text> </xsl:text>
    <xsl:value-of select="/PersonData/Name/LastName" />
    </title>
  </head>
 <body>
 <p><xsl:value-of select="/PersonData/Name/FirstName" /><xsl:text>
 </xsl:text>
 <xsl:value-of select="/PersonData/Name/LastName" /> was born on
 <xsl:value-of select="/PersonData/Name/@DOB" /></p>
 </body>
</html>

</xsl:template>

</xsl:stylesheet>
```

The following instructions assume that you have installed the Saxon XSLT processor, as described in Chapter 8.

1. Open a command window.
2. Navigate to the directory where the files `PersonData.xml` and `PersonData.xsl` are located.
3. Enter the following command at the command line:

```
java -jar saxon7.jar -o PersonData.html PersonData.xml PersonData.xsl
```

   If all has worked correctly, you should see no error messages. If you see error messages from Saxon, review how you installed Saxon in light of the instructions in Chapter 8.

4. Double-click `PersonData.html`, and you should see a very simple web page, which has the following code:

```
<html>
  <head>
    <meta http-equiv="Content-Type" content="text/html; charset=UTF-8">
    <title>Information about Jack Slack</title>
```

```
    </head>
    <body>
       <p>Jack Slack was born on 1920/11/25</p>
    </body>
  </html>
```

How It Works

First, let's look at how the content of the title element is created. The XSLT xsl:value-of element (as shown in the following) uses the child axis three times to select the value of the FirstName element:

```
<xsl:value-of select="/PersonData/Name/FirstName"/>
```

The location path is an absolute location path, which uses abbreviated syntax. So, from the root node the PersonData element in the child axis is selected. Then with the PersonData element node as context node, the Name element is selected, and finally, with the Name element node as context node, the FirstName element node is selected. The xsl:value-of element does what it says—it selects the value of the node specified which in this case is the FirstName element node.

Similarly, the following code retrieves the person's last name, also using the child axis three times:

```
<xsl:value-of select="/PersonData/Name/LastName" />
```

The date of birth displayed in the web page is retrieved using both the child axis and the attribute axis as follows:

```
<xsl:value-of select="/PersonData/Name/@DOB" />
```

The context node is the root node. First the child axis is used, and the PersonData element node is selected. In the next location step, the child axis is again used and the Name element node is selected. Finally, the attribute axis is used and the DOB attribute node is selected. This selects the value of the DOB attribute node.

ancestor Axis

The ancestor axis selects the parent node of the context node, the parent of that node, its parent, and so on until the root node of the document is selected. If the context node is the root node, the ancestor axis returns an empty node-set.

If we had an XML document like this,

```
<Book>
 <Chapter number="1">
  <Section>This is the first section.</Section>
  <Section>This is the second section.</Section>
 </Chapter>
 <Chapter number="2">
  <!-- and so on -->
 </Chapter>
</Book>
```

and the context node was the element node corresponding to the second `Section` element node in Chapter 1, then the location path

```
ancestor::*
```

would return the `Chapter` element node, which has a `number` attribute node with a value of 1, the `Book` element node, and the root node.

Note that there is no way to express the `ancestor` axis using abbreviated syntax.

ancestor-or-self Axis

The `ancestor-or-self` axis includes all nodes in the `ancestor` axis plus the context node (which is in the `self` axis).

Using the document in the `ancestor` axis section and the same context node, the location path,

```
ancestor::Section
```

returns an empty node-set because no `ancestor` element node is named `Section`, but the location path,

```
ancestor-or-self::Section
```

would return the `Section` element node, which is the context node.

descendant Axis

The `descendant` axis selects the child nodes of the context node, the child nodes of those child nodes, and so on.

Consider the following XML document:

```
<Invoices>
 <Invoice>
  <Date>2004-01-01</Date>
  <Item>KDH987</Item>
  <Item>DSE355</Item>
 </Invoice>
<Invoice>
  <Date>2004-01-01</Date>
  <Item>RAH198</Item>
  <Item>DJE385</Item>
 </Invoice>
</Invoices>
```

If the `Invoices` element node was the context node, the location path,

```
descendant::*
```

would select both the `Invoice` element nodes, both the `Date` element nodes, and all the `Item` element nodes. Location paths that use the `descendant` axis can be expressed only in unabbreviated syntax.

Examine the following, which uses the `descendant` axis with an absolute location path:

```
/descendant::Item
```

All the `Item` element nodes in the document that contain the context node would be selected.

descendant-or-self Axis

The `descendant-or-self` axis includes all the nodes in the `descendant` axis plus the context node (which is contained in the `self` axis).

following Axis

The `following` axis contains all nodes that come after the context node in document order, but excludes all descendant nodes and any attribute nodes and namespace nodes associated with the context node.

It's probably easiest to demonstrate the use of the `following` axis using an example. (We will use the same XML document, `Employees.xml`, to demonstrate the use of the `following-sibling` axis, the `preceding` axis, and the `preceding-sibling` axis a little later in this section.)

Here is the source XML document:

```
<Employees>
 <Person>
  <FirstName>Lara</FirstName>
  <LastName>Farmer</LastName>
  <DateOfBirth>1944-12-12</DateOfBirth>
 </Person>
 <Person>
  <FirstName>Patrick</FirstName>
  <LastName>Stepfoot</LastName>
  <DateOfBirth>1955-11-11</DateOfBirth>
 </Person>
 <Person>
  <FirstName>Angela</FirstName>
  <LastName>Paris</LastName>
  <DateOfBirth>1980-10-10</DateOfBirth>
 </Person>
</Employees>
```

Here is the XSLT stylesheet (`Employees.xsl`) that shows the element nodes in the `following` axis:

```
<xsl:stylesheet
 version="1.0"
 xmlns:xsl="http://www.w3.org/1999/XSL/Transform" >

<xsl:template match="/">
 <html>
  <head>
   <title>This demonstrates the following axis.</title>
  </head>
```

```
    <body>
     <h3>Following axis demo.</h3>
     <xsl:apply-templates select="/Employees/Person[1]/FirstName" />
    </body>
   </html>
  </xsl:template>

  <xsl:template match="FirstName">
   <xsl:for-each select="following::*">
    <p><xsl:value-of select="name(.)" /> which contains the text
  "<xsl:value-of select='.' />".</p>
   </xsl:for-each>
  </xsl:template>
  </xsl:stylesheet>
```

Notice the use of the `following` axis in the `xsl:for-each` element toward the end of the XSLT:

```
  <xsl:for-each select="following::*" />
```

The element nodes in the `following` axis are shown in Figure 7-2. Alongside each element node is its text content. Notice that for the `Person` elements all the text content of its child elements is shown.

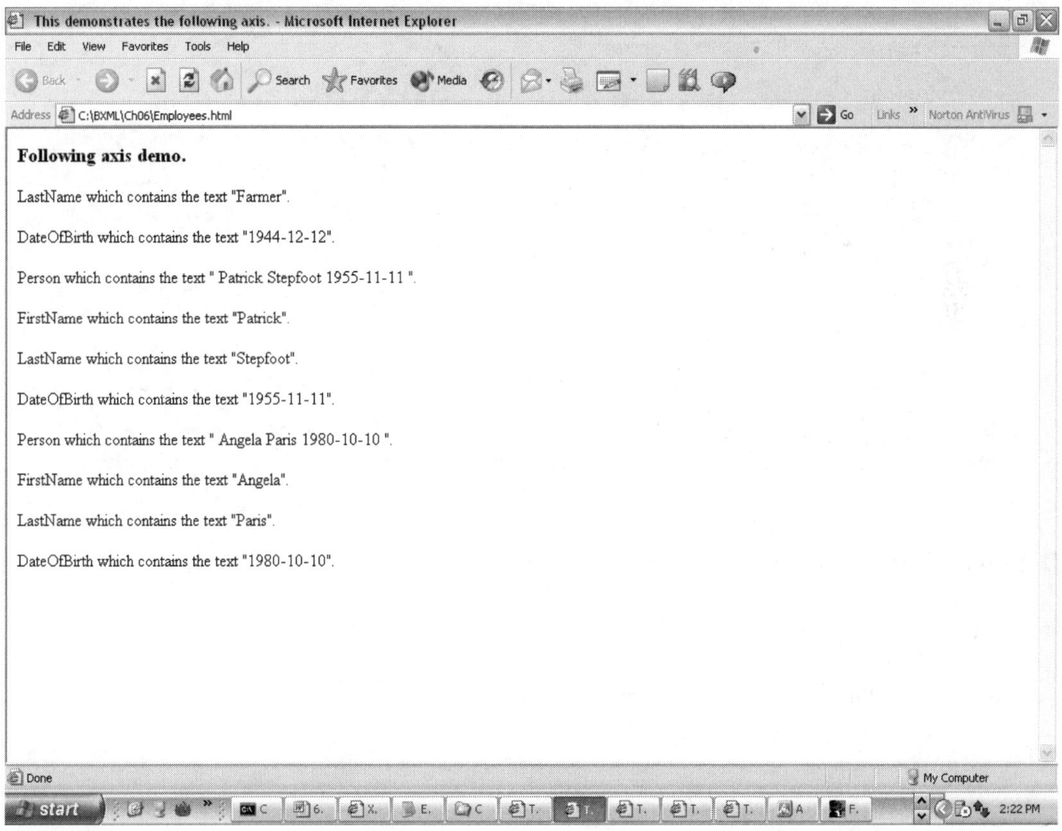

Figure 7-2

following-sibling Axis

The definition of the following-sibling axis is that it includes those nodes in the following axis that share their parent node with the context node. Again, a demo may help you grasp the concept. We will use the same XML document, Employees.xml, as in the example for the following axis together with this XSLT stylesheet (Employees2.xsl):

```
<xsl:stylesheet
 version="1.0"
 xmlns:xsl="http://www.w3.org/1999/XSL/Transform" >

<xsl:template match="/">
 <html>
  <head>
   <title>This demonstrates the following-sibling axis.</title>
  </head>
  <body>
   <h3>Following-sibling axis demo.</h3>
   <xsl:apply-templates select="/Employees/Person[1]/FirstName" />
  </body>
 </html>
</xsl:template>

<xsl:template match="FirstName">
 <xsl:for-each select="following-sibling::*">
  <p><xsl:value-of select="name(.)" /> which contains the text
"<xsl:value-of select='.' />".</p>
 </xsl:for-each>
</xsl:template>

</xsl:stylesheet>
```

Notice the use of the following-sibling axis in the xsl:for-each element toward the end of the code:

```
<xsl:for-each select="following-sibling::*">
```

As you can see in Figure 7-3, there are only two element nodes, the LastName and DateOfBirth element nodes for the same person whose FirstName element node was the context node.

namespace Axis

The namespace axis is used to select namespace nodes. An element node has a separate namespace node for each in-scope namespace.

Examine the following XML source document (xmmlBooks.xml):

```
<xmml:Book xmlns:xmml="http://www.XMML.com/namespaces">
 <xmml:Chapter number="1">Some text.</xmml:Chapter>
 <xmml:Chapter number="2">Some more text.</xmml:Chapter>
</xmml:Book>
```

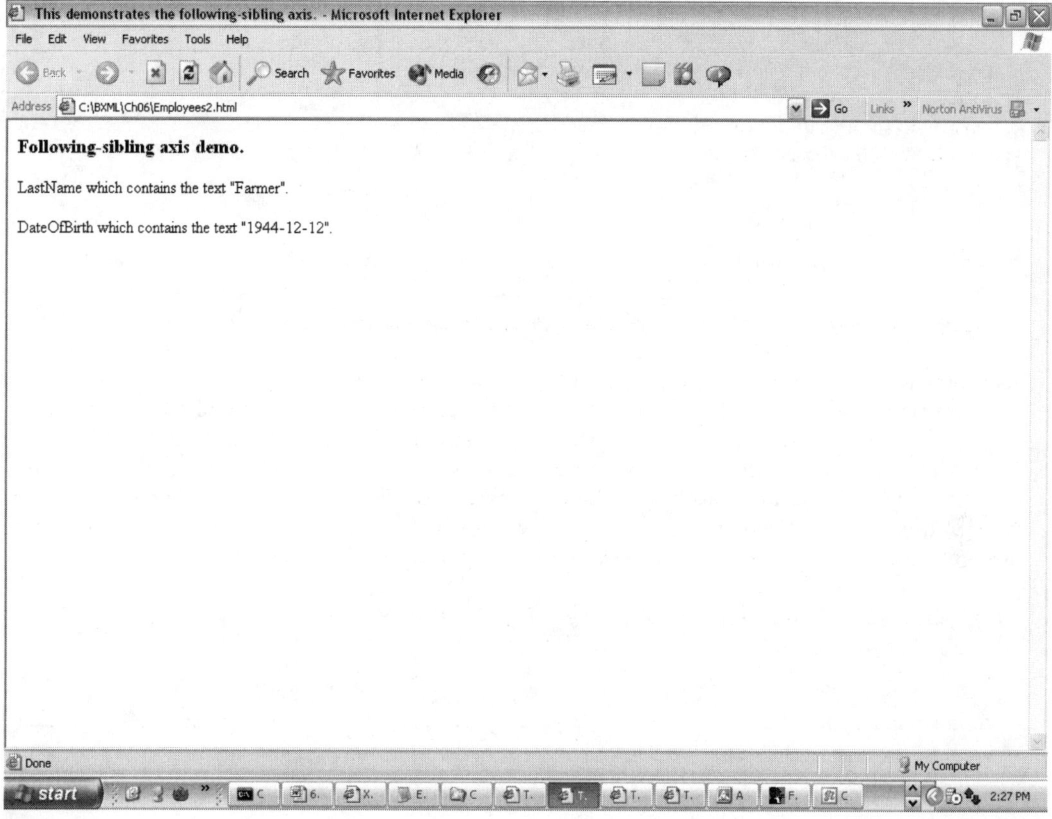

Figure 7-3

We can apply the following stylesheet (`xmmlBooks.xsl`) to show the namespace nodes that exist on the `xmml:Book` element node:

```
<xsl:stylesheet
 version="1.0"
 xmlns:xsl="http://www.w3.org/1999/XSL/Transform"
 xmlns:xmml="http://www.XMML.com/namespaces" >

<xsl:template match="/">
 <html>
  <head>
   <title>This shows namespace nodes.</title>
  </head>
  <body>
   <h3>Namespace nodes of the xmml:Book element.</h3>
   <xsl:apply-templates select="/xmml:Book" />
  </body>
 </html>
</xsl:template>

<xsl:template match="xmml:Book">
```

```
  <xsl:for-each select="namespace::node()">
  <p><xsl:value-of select="position()" />. The namespace prefix
 <b><xsl:value-of select="name(.)" /></b>
  has the namespace URI <b><xsl:value-of select="." /></b>. </p>
  </xsl:for-each>
 </xsl:template>

 </xsl:stylesheet>
```

Notice the namespace declaration using the `xmml` namespace prefix on the `xmml:Book` element:

```
 <xmml:Book xmlns:xmml="http://www.XMML.com/namespaces">
```

As shown in Figure 7-4, two namespace nodes are associated with the `xmml:Book` element node. The namespace node with the URI of `http://www.XMML.com/namespaces` will likely not be a surprise, because it was explicitly declared in a namespace declaration. The namespace node with the URI of `http://www.w3.org/XML/1998/namespace` may be unexpected. It is present because all XML element nodes have a namespace node with that namespace URI associated with them. Remember that you can use `xml:lang` and `xml:space` attributes on any XML element, so the `xml` namespace must be declared; in this case, the namespace declaration is built into all XML processors.

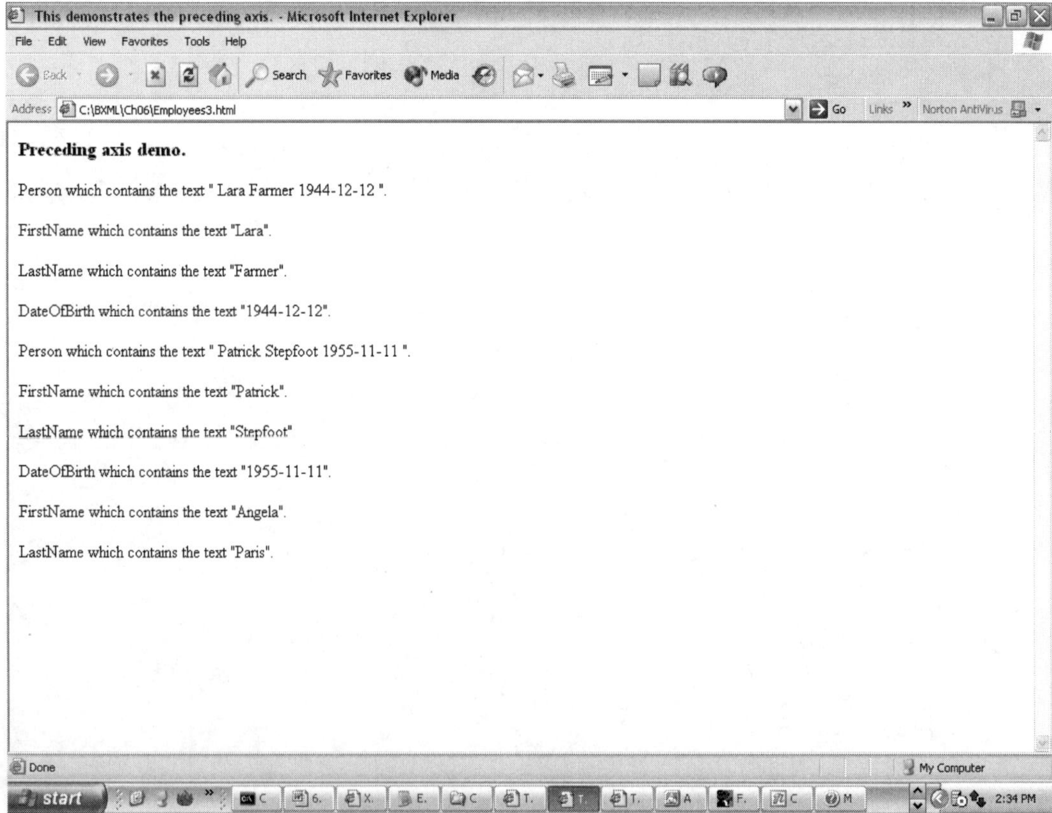

Figure 7-4

parent Axis

The `parent` axis is used to select the parent node of the context node. Examine the following document:

```
<Parts>
 <Part number="ABC123" />
 <Part number="DEF234" />
</Parts>
```

If the context node was a `Part` element node, then the following location path selects the parent node, which is the `Parts` element node:

```
parent::node()
```

There is an abbreviated syntax for the `parent` axis:

```
..
```

This is probably familiar to you from encountering the same usage in directory paths on your hard disk.

If, however, the context node was the `Parts` element node, the same location path would select the root node of the document.

preceding Axis

The `preceding` axis contains all nodes that come before the context node in document order, excluding nodes in the `ancestor` axis and attribute and namespace nodes.

To demonstrate the `preceding` axis, we will again use `Employees.xml` as the source XML document. The stylesheet (`Employees3.xsl`) is shown here:

```
<xsl:stylesheet
 version="1.0"
 xmlns:xsl="http://www.w3.org/1999/XSL/Transform" >

<xsl:template match="/">
 <html>
  <head>
   <title>This demonstrates the preceding axis.</title>
  </head>
  <body>
   <h3>Preceding axis demo.</h3>
   <xsl:apply-templates select="/Employees/Person[3]/DateOfBirth" />
  </body>
 </html>
</xsl:template>

<xsl:template match="DateOfBirth">
 <xsl:for-each select="preceding::*">
```

```
  <p><xsl:value-of select="name(.)" /> which contains the text
  "<xsl:value-of select='.' />".</p>
 </xsl:for-each>
</xsl:template>

</xsl:stylesheet>
```

Notice the use of the `preceding` axis in the `xsl:for-each` element:

```
<xsl:for-each select="preceding::*">
```

Figure 7-5 shows the element nodes in the `preceding` axis with their contained text. The HTML output file (`Employees3.html`) is included in the code download for this book.

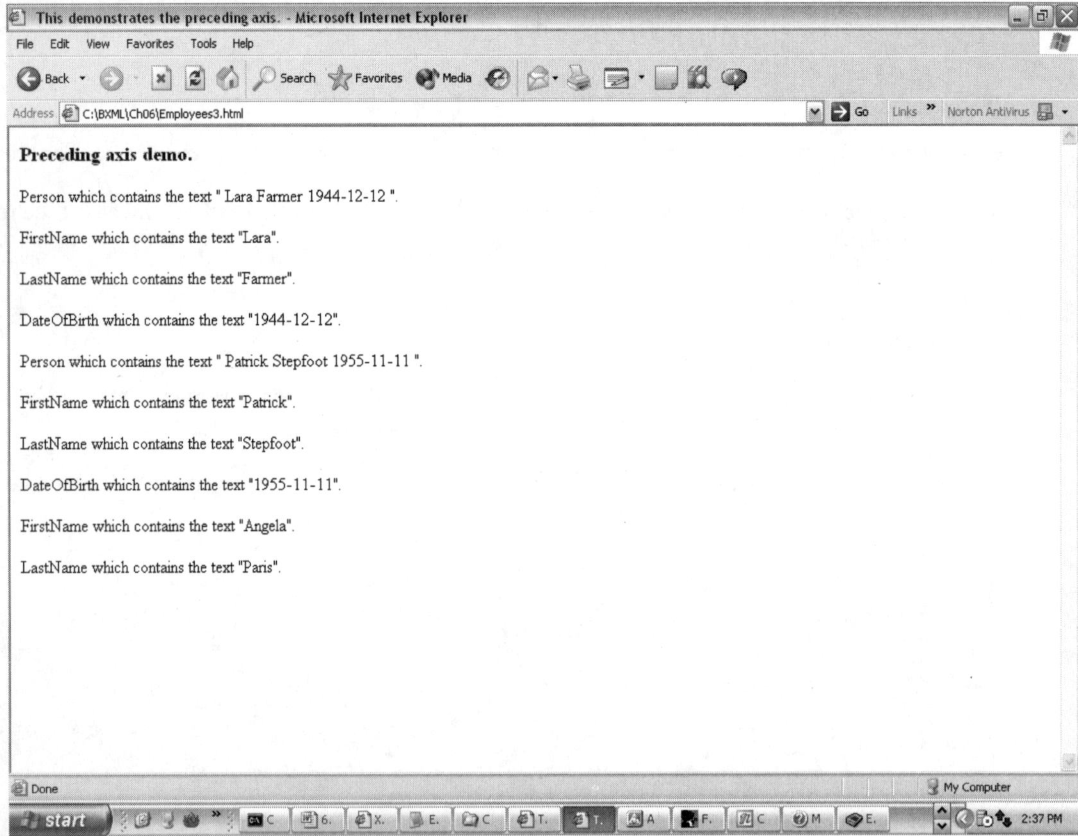

Figure 7-5

preceding-sibling Axis

The `preceding-sibling` axis includes those nodes that are in the `preceding` axis and that also share a parent node with the context node.

The following stylesheet (`Employees4.xsl`) displays the preceding siblings of the `DateOfBirth` element node of the third person in the source XML document.

```
<xsl:stylesheet
 version="1.0"
 xmlns:xsl="http://www.w3.org/1999/XSL/Transform" >

<xsl:template match="/">
 <html>
  <head>
   <title>This demonstrates the preceding-sibling axis.</title>
  </head>
  <body>
   <h3>Preceding axis demo.</h3>
   <xsl:apply-templates select="/Employees/Person[3]/DateOfBirth" />
  </body>
 </html>
</xsl:template>

<xsl:template match="DateOfBirth">
 <xsl:for-each select="preceding-sibling::*">
  <p><xsl:value-of select="name(.)" /> which contains the text
"<xsl:value-of select='.' />".</p>
 </xsl:for-each>
</xsl:template>

</xsl:stylesheet>
```

Figure 7-6 shows the element nodes in the `preceding-sibling` axis with their text content.

self Axis

The `self` axis selects the context node. The unabbreviated syntax for the `self` axis is as follows:

```
self::node()
```

The abbreviated syntax for the context node is the period character. Thus, if we wanted to select the value of the context node using the `xsl:value-of` element, we would write the following:

```
<xsl:value-of select="." />
```

The unabbreviated syntax is as follows:

```
<xsl:value-of select="self::node()" />
```

XPath allows you to filter nodes selected from an axis using *predicates*. Predicates frequently used XPath functions, so next we'll look at the functions available in XPath 1.0, and at how predicates can be used to filter node-sets.

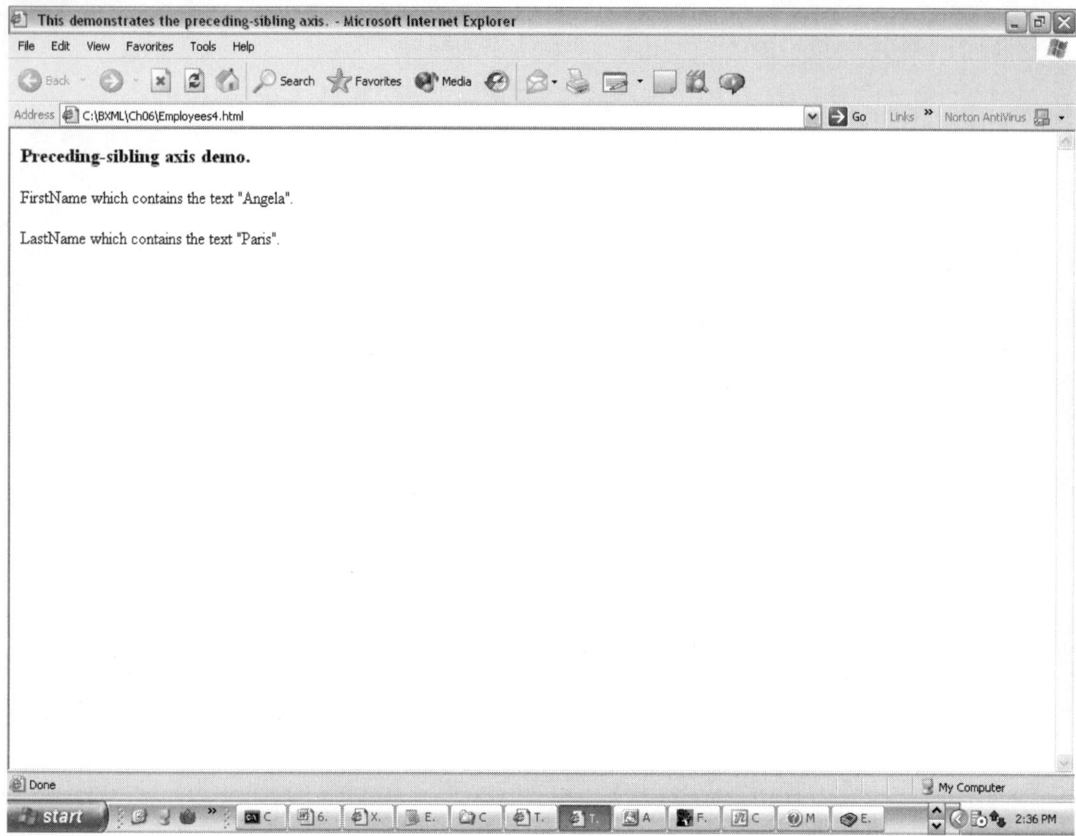

Figure 7-6

XPath 1.0 Functions

The XPath 1.0 specification defines a core function library. The functions making up the function library are listed here; some will be used in XSLT examples in Chapter 8.

Boolean Functions

The XPath 1.0 boolean functions are as follows:

- `boolean()`—Takes an object as its argument and returns a boolean value. If the argument is a number, true is returned if the number is not zero or NaN. If the argument is a node-set, true is returned if the node-set is not empty. If the argument is a string, true is returned if the string is not empty.
- `false()`—Takes no argument and returns the boolean value false.
- `lang()`—Takes a string argument. Returns true if the language of the context node is the language indicated by the string argument or one of its sublanguages.

- `not()`—Takes a boolean expression as its argument; it returns true if the argument evaluates to false, and returns false if the argument evaluates to true.
- `true()`—Has no argument and returns the boolean value true.

Node-Set Functions

The XPath 1.0 functions are as follows:

- `count()`—Takes a node-set argument and returns a value equal to the number of nodes in the node-set.
- `id()`—Takes a string as its argument and returns a node-set containing any node that has an ID attribute equal to the function's argument.
- `last()`—Returns a value equal to the context size.
- `local-name()`—Takes zero or one node-sets as its argument and returns the local part of the element name, if it exists or if no argument node-set exists it returns the local part of the name of the context node.
- `name()`—Takes zero or one node-set arguments and returns the name of the node in prefix:localpart format.
- `namespace-uri()`—Takes zero or one node-sets as its argument and returns the namespace URI of the argument node-set or if there is no argument the namespace URI of the context node is returned.
- `position()`—Returns a value equal to the context position.

Numeric Functions

The number functions of XPath 1.0 are as follows:

- `ceiling()`—Takes a number as its argument and returns the integer that is closest to negative infinity but which is larger than the value of the function's argument.
- `floor()`—Takes a number as its argument and returns the integer that is closest to positive infinity but which does not exceed the value of the function's argument.
- `number()`—Takes a string, boolean or node-set as its argument and returns a number. If there is a string argument and it contains characters that constitute a number, that number is returned; otherwise, NaN is returned. If the argument is the boolean true, 1 is returned. If the argument is boolean false, 0 is returned. If the argument is a node-set, it is as if the string() function is applied to the node-set, and then the number() function is applied to the string value that results.
- `round()`—Takes a number as its argument and returns the integer that is closest to the number argument.
- `sum()`—Takes a node-set as its argument and returns the number of nodes in the node-set.

String Functions

The string functions of XPath 1.0 are as follows:

- `concat()`—Takes two or more string arguments and returns the concatenation of those strings.
- `contains()`—Takes two string arguments and returns a boolean value that is true if the first string argument contains the second string argument.
- `normalize-space()`—Takes a single string argument. Adjacent whitespace characters are replaced by single-space characters.
- `starts-with()`—Takes two string arguments and returns a boolean value that is true if the first argument string starts with the second argument string.
- `string()`—Takes a boolean, node-set, or number as its argument and returns a string value.
- `string-length()`—Takes a single string argument and returns a number that indicates the length of the string.
- `substring()`—Can take two or three arguments. When it takes two arguments, the first is a string (of which we select a substring) and the second is a number. It then returns a string beginning at the character of the first argument as indicated by the number argument and continuing to the end of the string. If a third argument is present, that indicates the character at which the returned string ends.
- `substring-after()`—Takes two string arguments and returns the part of the first string that occurs after the first occurrence of the second string argument in the first string argument.
- `substring-before()`—Takes two string arguments and returns the part of the first string that occurs before the first occurrence of the second string.
- `translate()`—Takes three string arguments.

Predicates

Predicates are used to filter node-sets selected using an axis and location step. A predicate is optional in each location step of an XPath expression. There can also be more than one predicate in any one location step.

If we had a document with various security levels assigned in a `security` attribute on a `Section` element, we could use predicates to decide which sections to display.

```
//Section[@security="confidential"]
```

This would select `Section` element nodes that possessed a `security` attribute whose value was the string `confidential`.

If the `Section` element also had a `version` attribute that identified draft or final sections, we could choose public, final sections using two predicates, like this:

```
//Section[@security="public"][@version="final"]
```

Each predicate selects only from nodes that are already selected.

Now that we have looked at each of the parts of XPath expressions, let's put the pieces together so you have a solid appreciation of what is and is not allowed in an XPath expression.

Structure of XPath Expressions

Most complex XPath expressions select node-sets, therefore those expressions are also location paths.

A location path is made up of *location steps*. Depending on the context node and the complexity of the document, location paths can have many location steps.

Each location step is potentially made of three parts:

- An axis
- A node test
- An optional predicate

Examine the following location path:

```
child::Paragraph[position()=2]
```

The axis is `child`, the node test is `Paragraph`, and the predicate (there is one predicate in this example) is `[position()=2]`.

An axis is present in every location path. However, when the `child` axis is used in abbreviated syntax, the axis is not actually expressed in the surface syntax of the location path.

The node test is used to specify what type of node in the axis should be selected. For example, to select all `child` element nodes of `Book` element nodes that are `Chapter` element nodes, we could write the following:

```
/Book/Chapter
```

This location path has two location steps. The initial `/` character indicates that the context node is the root node. The next location step, `Book`, selects all `Book` element nodes in the `child` axis. The second `/` character is a separator between location steps. The second location step is `Chapter`, which selects `Chapter` element nodes in the `child` axis. The same location path would be written in unabbreviated syntax like this:

```
/child::Book/child::Chapter
```

You may find that this shows the parts of the location path more clearly.

The first location step starts at the root node and selects all `Book` element nodes that are children of the root node. If the document element is a `Book` element, a single `Book` element node is present in the node-set selected by the first location step (with any other document element, the node-set is empty and processing of the location path stops with an empty node-set being returned). Starting at that node, the next location step then looks for `Chapter` element nodes that are child element nodes of the `Book` element node returned by the first location step.

Suppose the location path had another location step, as shown here:

```
/child::Book/child::Chapter/child::Section
```

Then, after finding all the `Chapter` element nodes that are selected by the second location step, any `Section` element nodes of each of the selected `Chapter` element nodes are chosen in turn.

Suppose the location path is modified to include a predicate, as shown here:

```
/child::Book/child::Chapter[position()=3]/child::Section
```

Then only the `Chapter` element node that is in the third position in document order would be selected by the second location step. Processing of all other `Chapter` element nodes would stop and those nodes would not be included in the returned node-set. For the `Chapter` element node in third position, all its `Section` element node children would be selected.

The only type of node in the `child` axis that has a name is the element node. But other nodes, such as comment nodes and text nodes, can also be present in the `child` axis. To select all nodes in the `child` axis that are child nodes of the `Book` element node, we would write the following:

```
/Book/node()
```

This location path would select all nodes in the child axis that are child nodes of `Book` element nodes, which are children of the root node.

Predicates are optional. Suppose we have a more complex structure that included `Chapter` elements, `Section` elements, and `Paragraph` elements, and we want to select the third paragraph in the second section in the first chapter. We could use a location path like this:

```
/Book/Chapter[1]/Section[2]/Paragraph[3]
```

The second, third, and fourth location steps each include a predicate. The same location path could be written in unabbreviated syntax, like this:

```
/child::Book/child::Chapter[position()=1]/child::Section[position()=2]/
child::Paragraph[position()=3]
```

Predicates can also be multiple for any location step. Suppose we want to select the third paragraph in the second section in the first chapter only if the first `Chapter` element has a `security` attribute whose value is `public`; we could write this:

```
/Book/Chapter[1][@security="public"]/Section[2]/Paragraph[3]
```

Or, using unabbreviated syntax, we could write the following:

```
/child::Book/child::Chapter[position()=1][attribute::security="public"]/
child::Section[position()=2]/child::Paragraph[position()=3]
```

Notice that the second location step has two predicates, `[1][@security="public"]`. Both predicates must be satisfied before a `Chapter` element node can be selected. The order of predicates can also influence the node-set returned.

Be careful when using predicates such as `[@security="public"]` as the values of XSLT attributes, such as the select attribute of the `xsl:value-of` element. Make sure you use different paired quotes or apostrophes for the value inside the predicate than those used to delimit the attribute value. You could write the following:

```
<xsl:value-of select="/Book/Chapter[@security='public']" />
```

Alternatively, you could write the following:

```
<xsl:value-of select='/Book/Chapter[@security="public"]' />
```

In other words, if you use paired quotes to delimit the value of the `select` attribute, use paired apostrophes inside the predicate; or if you use paired apostrophes to delimit the attribute value, use paired quotes inside the predicate.

Before we move on to Chapter 8 and look at how XPath is used with XSLT, let's briefly look ahead to the upcoming XPath version 2.0.

Looking Forward to XPath 2.0

At the time of writing, the development of XPath 2.0 is fairly far advanced, and XPath 2.0 is likely to be finalized a few months after this book is published.

The latest version of the XPath 2.0 specification is located at `http://www.w3.org/tr/xpath20/`. *Functions for XPath 2.0 are specified in a separate document located at* `http://www.w3.org/TR/xpath-functions/`.

At the time of writing, further general information on XPath 2.0 is found at `http://www.w3.org/XML/Query`. *Currently, the XPath link from* `http://www.w3.org/` *describes only XPath 1.0.*

XPath 2.0 is a much more powerful language than XPath 1.0 and is also significantly more complex. Unlike the XPath 1.0 specification, which is described in a single document, the XPath 2.0 specification is described in several supporting documents in addition to the XPath 2.0 specification itself.

There are several supporting documents for the XPath 2.0 specification. The XPath 2.0 Requirements document is located at `http://www.w3.org/TR/xpath20req`. *The formal semantics of XPath 2.0 is described at* `http://www.w3.org/TR/xquery-semantics/`.

XPath 2.0 can be described as an expression language for processing *sequences*. A sequence is a generalization of the XPath 1.0 concept of a node-set to also include atomic values. Unlike an XPath 1.0 node-set, an XPath 2.0 sequence is ordered.

XPath 2.0 is a syntactic subset of the XML Query Language (XQuery), which is described in Chapter 9. So reading Chapter 9 on XQuery will give you a good overview of XPath 2.0 too.

Revised XPath Data Model

The data model underlying XPath 2.0 is significantly different from the XPath 1.0 model. Some highlights of differences are described here.

Every XPath 2.0 expression returns a sequence. A sequence in XPath 2.0 is ordered, whereas a node-set in XPath 1.0 is not ordered. In XPath 1.0 a node-set is not allowed to contain duplicates. By contrast, an XPath 2.0 sequence may contain duplicates.

> *The XPath 2.0 Data Model is described at* `http://www.w3.org/TR/xpath-datamodel/`.

W3C XML Schema Data Types

In XPath 1.0, a node has a pretty primitive type system, which really doesn't intrude much into the developer's consciousness. In XPath 2.0 typing of nodes becomes much more formal and complex. Typing of nodes and items in XPath 2.0 uses W3C XML Schema. (W3C XML Schema was described in Chapter 5.)

XPath 2.0 adds the W3C XML Schema data types for date-time values. Because many XML documents, such as invoices and purchase orders, include date-time data, the ability to automatically validate values in XPath 2.0 is a potentially significant advantage, compared to the absence of date-time types in XPath 1.0.

Additional XPath 2.0 Functions

XPath 2.0 shares its function library with XQuery 1.0. Many more functions are provided in XPath 2.0 than were specified in XPath 1.0. In fact, in XPath 2.0, there are so many functions that a separate specification describes them.

> *The document specifying XPath 2.0 functions is located at* `http://www.w3.org/TR/xpath-functions`.

This has given you a very brief overview of XPath 2.0. Further information on XPath 2.0 is included in Chapter 9. About 75 percent of XQuery 1.0 is identical to XPath 2.0.

Summary

This chapter covered version 1.0 of the XML Path Languge, XPath. We were introduced to the concept of the XPath model and the important concept of the context was discussed. The XPath axes and the functions in the XPath 1.0 function library were described.

Exercise Questions

Suggested solutions to these questions can be found in Appendix A.

Question 1

Name two XPath axes which, respectively, can be used to select element nodes and attribute nodes. If the context node is an element node, give the XPath location path, which selects the `number` attribute node of that element node. Show the answer in both abbreviated and unabbreviated syntax.

Question 2

XPath 1.0 allows wildcards to be used when selecting child nodes of the context node. What is the location path, which selects all child nodes of the context node? Give the answer in both abbreviated and unabbreviated syntax.

XSLT

XSLT, Extensible Stylesheet Language Transformations, is a very important XML language in many XML workflows. In many business situations, data is either stored as XML or can be made available from a database as XML. XSLT is important because, typically, the way XML is stored needs to be changed before it is used. Wherever the data comes from, the XML might need to be presented to end-users or might need to be shared with business partners in a format that is convenient for those business partners. XSLT plays a key role in converting XML to its presentation formats and restructuring XML to fit the structures useful to business partners.

In this chapter we will learn:

- How XSLT can be used to convert XML for presentation or restructure XML for business-to-business data interchange.
- How XSLT differs from conventional procedural languages.
- An XSLT transformation is described in terms of a source document and a result document. However, under the hood, the transformation taking place is a source tree (which uses the XPath data model) to a result tree (which also uses the XPath data model).
- How the elements that make up an XSLT stylesheet are used. For example, we look at how to use the `xsl:value-of` element to retrieve values from the source tree which is being transformed, and look at the `xsl:copy` and `xsl:copy-of` elements which, respectively, shallow copy and deep copy nodes from the source tree.
- How to use XSLT variables and parameters.

What Is XSLT?

XSLT is a declarative programming language, written in XML, for converting XML to some other output. Often the output is XML or HTML, but in principle, XSLT can produce arbitrary output from any given XML source document. For example, an XML document can be restructured to conform to a business partner's schema, or a selection from an XML document can be made to correspond to specified criteria, such as selecting invoices from a specified period.

Alternatively, XML data can be transformed so that the data is part of an HTML document, XHTML document, WML (Wireless Markup Language) page, or other presentation format. Just as it is efficient to store relational data once to avoid data inconsistencies, so having one XML data source that can then be converted to multiple presentation formats is an efficient and effective workflow when multiple formats, which may themselves be evolving, need to be produced.

XSLT uses XPath, to which you were introduced in Chapter 7, to select the parts of the source XML document that are used in the result document. All the XPath 1.0 functions are available to an XSLT processor, and XSLT 1.0 has a few functions of its own.

XSLT is a declarative language. Often newcomers to XSLT find it difficult to adapt from the mindset that they use while programming in procedural languages such as Java or JavaScript. Therefore, we will take the first code examples slowly to help you understand the difference between a declarative language and a procedural one.

Restructuring XML

One of the major uses of XSLT is to restructure XML for use by another user, for example, a business partner. A common scenario is that two companies who need to exchange XML documents electronically have, for historical reasons, differences in the structures of basic documents such as invoices and purchase orders.

XSLT can copy selected parts of the source XML unchanged into the result document or can create new elements or attributes in the result document. The name of elements and attributes can be changed. Elements or attributes present in the source document can be selectively omitted from the result document. By combining these options, any arbitrary change can typically be achieved between the source document and the result document.

Presenting XML Content

XML is often presented as HTML or XHTML on the desktop, as well as various other options on mobile devices. XSLT is often used to transform select parts of the XML document for display. For example, you might create a linked set of HTML pages, each of which contains data from a specified time period. Using XSLT, appropriate data for each HTML page can be selected from the same XML document.

How Does an XSLT Processor Work?

Before we start writing code, it is helpful to understand how, in general terms, an XSLT processor works. At its simplest, we can look on an XSLT processor as a piece of software that accepts an XML document (the *source document*), applies an XSLT stylesheet to it, and produces another document called the *result document* that can be XML, HTML or plain text.

If you have read Chapter 7 on XPath, then you will likely already be able to guess that that isn't the whole story. A slightly more detailed description of an XSLT processor is that it accepts a source document and creates an in-memory tree representation of that source document, according to the XPath data model, called the *source tree*. The XSLT processor processes the source tree according to the *templates* that are contained in the XSLT stylesheet. A *result tree* is created. The creation of a result tree from a source tree is called *transformation*. After the result tree is created, a process called *serialization* takes place that creates a familiar, serialized XML (or other) document from the result tree.

Strictly speaking, an XSLT 1.0 processor is responsible only for the transformation of the source tree to the result tree. However, most XSLT processor software also contains an XML parser that creates the source tree and a serializer component that serializes the result tree.

Running the Examples

The examples used in this chapter are standard XSLT 1.0 code. Therefore, you should be able to run them using any reputable XSLT processor. XSLT processors that you might want to consider as alternatives to the Saxon XSLT processor that we use in this chapter are the Xalan XSLT processor from the Apache Foundation and MSXML from Microsoft Corporation.

> **Information on the Java 2 and C++ versions of the Xalan XSLT processor are available at `http://xml.apache.org/`. Information on the MSXML software, which is also called Microsoft XML Core Services, is available at `http://msdn.microsoft.com/library/default.asp?url=/library/en-us/xmlsdk/htm/sdk_intro_6g53.asp`. Useful support information on MSXML is available at `http://www.netcrucible.com/`.**

In this chapter, step-by-step instructions are supplied for using the Saxon XSLT processor.

Introducing the Saxon XSLT Processor

All examples in this chapter will use the Saxon XSLT processor, which is written by Michael Kay, editor of the XSLT 2.0 specification. General information on the latest version of Saxon is located at `http://saxon.sourceforge.net/`. The version I used when writing this chapter is Saxon 7.8, which incorporates both XSLT 1.0 and XSLT 2.0 functionality. If you want to explore only XSLT 1.0 functionality, you can use Saxon 6.5.3. I am using Saxon 7.8 since I will make use of its XQuery 1.0 functionality in Chapter 9.

At the time of writing, the Saxon processor is being updated on an ongoing basis to add ever more complete XPath 2.0 and XSLT 2.0 functionality. Therefore, it is likely that the latest version when you read this will be a version other than 7.8 or 6.5.3. Take time to read the descriptions of the available versions at the Saxon web page to ensure that you choose a version that supports XSLT 1.0 (all versions currently do) and that is stable (from time to time quasi-experimental versions are released).

Installing the Saxon XSLT Processor

To run the Saxon XSLT processor, you need to have a Java Virtual Machine, JVM, installed on your machine. To check whether you have a Java Virtual Machine correctly installed, open a command window and type the following:

```
java -version
```

If Java is installed, then you will see a message similar to the following:

```
java version "1.4.2"
Java (TM)2 Runtime Environment, Standard Edition (build 1.4.2-b28)
Java HotSpot (TM) Client VM (build 1.4.2-b28, mixed mode)
```

If Java is not installed, you will need to obtain a suitable version of Java and install it.

You can obtain a Java Virtual Machine either by installing a Java Runtime Environment (JRE) or a Java Software Development Kit (SDK). If you don't already have a JVM installed, then information on the current version of Java (you need J2SE, Java 2 Standard Edition version 1.4 or higher, to run Saxon 7.8) is available at `http://java.sun.com`. Look for a link to further information on J2SE.

Assuming that you have downloaded a Java 2 version 1.4 SDK, launch the installer and follow the onscreen installation instructions to install it.

After you have completed the installation, open a command prompt window. Add the command prompt type

```
java -version
```

and hit Enter. If a Java virtual machine has been successfully installed, then a message similar to the one shown earlier will be displayed.

You also need to install the selected version of Saxon to an appropriate directory. Launch the Saxon Zip file that you downloaded and extract the files to the desired directory using a tool such as WinZip.

If you want to be able to run `saxon7.jar` from any directory you will need to add the file, giving its full path, to your `CLASSPATH` environment variable.

To create or edit the `CLASSPATH` environment variable on Windows XP, click Start, select Control Panel, and select the System option. On the System Properties window, select the Advanced tab and click the Environment Variables button toward the bottom of that tab. The Environment Variables window opens.

In the System Variables section look at the existing environment variables to see if `CLASSPATH` or `classpath` (it isn't case sensitive) is already present. If it is, then click the Edit button; the Edit System Variable window opens. Edit the Variable Value text box to reflect the location where you installed Saxon and the version that you chose to install. Once you are sure that you correctly typed the location click OK.

If there is no `CLASSPATH` variable in the System Variables section, then look at the User Variables section to check whether it isn't there. Assuming that it isn't, click the New button in the System Variables section. The New System Variable window opens. Enter `CLASSPATH` (either case) in the Variable Name text box and enter the location of Saxon in the Variable Value text box. Figure 8-1 shows the New System Variable window with the `CLASSPATH` variable added. Click OK.

If you have a command prompt window open, you need to restart it so that the changes you made to the environment variables are applied to it.

Now you can test if the installation of Saxon is working correctly. Navigate to the directory where you intend to install your XML source files and your XSLT stylesheets. For the purposes of this chapter, they

Figure 8-1

are installed on my machine at `c:\BXML\Ch08`. At the command prompt type the following:

```
java -jar saxon7.jar
```

If everything is working correctly, you will see the default Saxon error message, which includes information about how to use the command-line switches, shown in Figure 8-2 indicating that you haven't entered a full command to make Saxon carry out a transformation. At the moment we don't need to do anything more because the display of that error message is an indication that Saxon is installed correctly.

We are almost ready to run our first XSLT example, but next we will look briefly at how procedural and declarative programming languages differ.

Procedural versus Declarative Programming

Many newcomers to XSLT find it tough to adjust to the difference in approach when using XSLT compared to using procedural programming languages. The following brief sections highlight the differences between the two approaches.

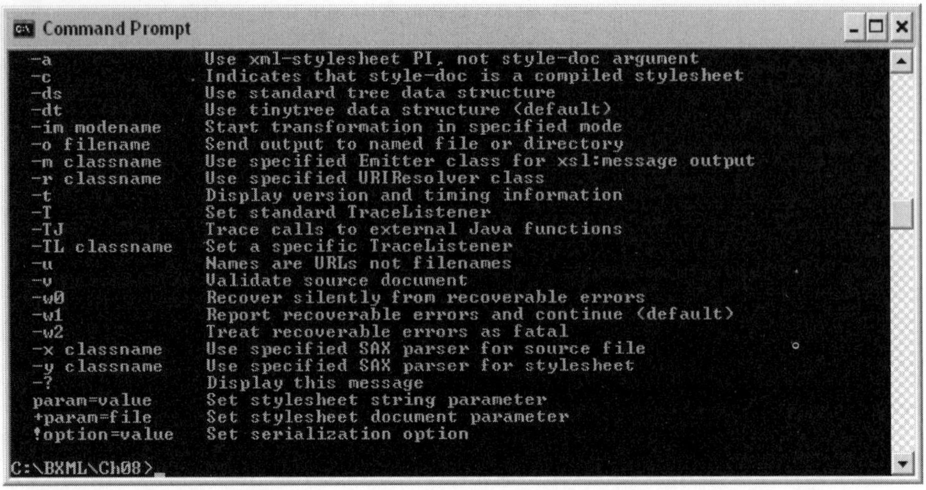

```
Command Prompt
-a                  Use xml-stylesheet PI, not style-doc argument
-c                  Indicates that style-doc is a compiled stylesheet
-ds                 Use standard tree data structure
-dt                 Use tinytree data structure (default)
-im modename        Start transformation in specified mode
-o filename         Send output to named file or directory
-m classname        Use specified Emitter class for xsl:message output
-r classname        Use specified URIResolver class
-t                  Display version and timing information
-T                  Set standard TraceListener
-TJ                 Trace calls to external Java functions
-TL classname       Set a specific TraceListener
-u                  Names are URLs not filenames
-v                  Validate source document
-w0                 Recover silently from recoverable errors
-w1                 Report recoverable errors and continue (default)
-w2                 Treat recoverable errors as fatal
-x classname        Use specified SAX parser for source file
-y classname        Use specified SAX parser for stylesheet
-?                  Display this message
param=value         Set stylesheet string parameter
+param=file         Set stylesheet document parameter
!option=value       Set serialization option

C:\BXML\Ch08>_
```

Figure 8-2

Procedural Programming

When using a procedural programming language such as JavaScript, you tell the computer step by step what you want to do. You might define a function, and then you define each thing that the computer is supposed to do, assigning a variable, iterating through a loop, and so on. The mental picture of what the function is supposed to achieve exists only in your mind.

Declarative Programming

The procedural programming approach contrasts with declarative programming where you tell the computer what you want to achieve. XSLT resembles SQL in that respect. For example, in SQL you tell the relational database management system (RDBMS) to SELECT certain columns, but you don't expect to tell it *how* to retrieve the desired data. XSLT is similar. You specify what the XSLT processor is to create each time it comes across a particular *pattern* in the source tree.

To specify what the XSLT processor is to do you frequently use the `xsl:template` element with a `match` attribute that contains the relevant pattern.

So if you wanted to create certain output for every `Chapter` element in a source XML document you would have code like this:

```
<xsl:template match="Chapter">
 <!-- The content of the <xsl:template> element defines what is to be added -->
 <!-- to the result tree. -->
</xsl:template>
```

Notice how the pattern `Chapter` appears as the value of the `match` attribute of the `xsl:template` element.

Let's move on and create a simple XSLT stylesheet and look at how it works.

Foundational XSLT Elements

We will create an example that makes a simple HTML web page from the XML source document shown here:

```
<People>
<Person>
 <Name>George H.W. Bush</Name>
 <Description>George Bush was a late 20th century politician who was elected
as President of the United States.</Description>
</Person>
<Person>
 <Name>Winston Churchill</Name>
 <Description>Winston Churchill was a mid 20th Century British politician who
became famous as Prime Minister during the Second World War.</Description>
</Person>
<Person>
 <Name>John F. Kennedy</Name>
 <Description>JFK, as he was affectionately known, was a United States
President who was assassinated in Dallas, Texas.</Description>
</Person>
</People>
```

As you can see the file, `People.xml`, contains brief information about three famous twentieth-century politicians.

The following stylesheet, `People.xsl`, creates a simple HTML web page, `People.html`, which contains the name and description information about the politicians.

```
<xsl:stylesheet
 xmlns:xsl="http://www.w3.org/1999/XSL/Transform"
 version="1.0" >

<xsl:template match="/">
 <html>
  <head>
   <title>Information about <xsl:value-of select="count(/People/Person)" />
people.</title>
  </head>
  <body>
  <h3>Information about <xsl:value-of select="count(/People/Person)" />
people.</h3>
  <br />
   <xsl:apply-templates select="/People/Person" />
  </body>
</html>
</xsl:template>

<xsl:template match="Person">
 <h3><xsl:value-of select="Name" /></h3>
 <p><xsl:value-of select="Description" /></p>
```

```
<br />
</xsl:template>

</xsl:stylesheet>
```

The HTML page created by the transformation is shown in Figure 8-3.

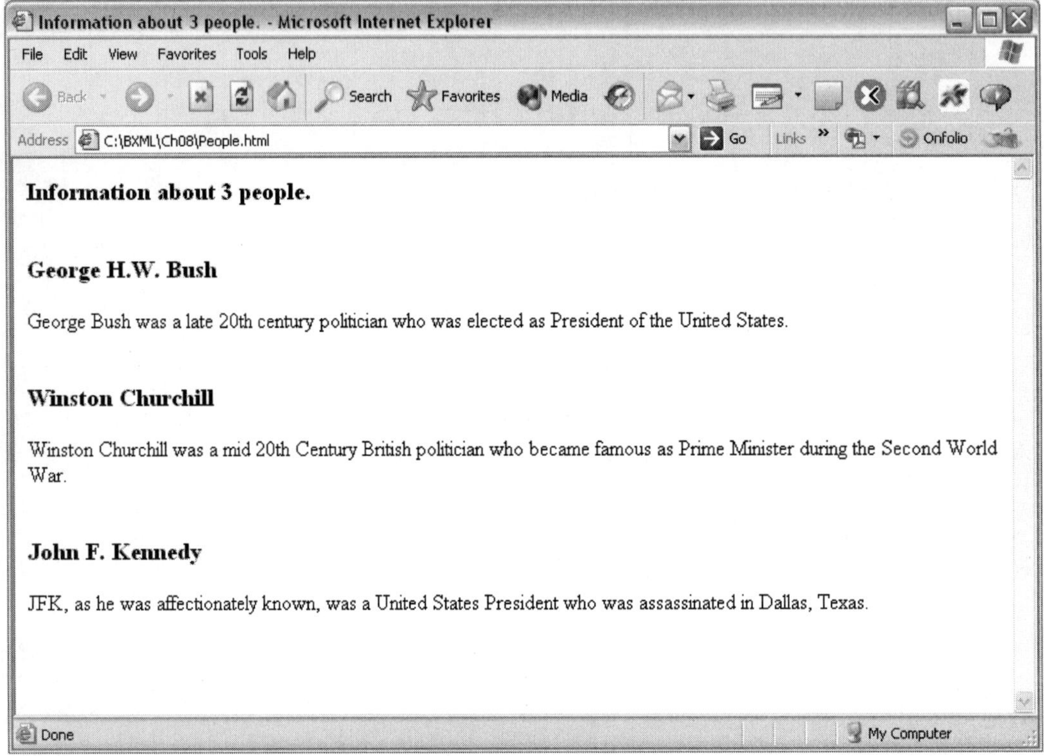

Figure 8-3

The HTML code produced by the listing, with white space tidied for display, is shown in the following block:

```
<html>
 <head>
  <meta http-equiv="Content-Type" content="text/html; charset=UTF-8">
  <title>Information about 3 people.</title>
 </head>
 <body>
  <h3>Information about 3 people.</h3>
  <br>
  <h3>George H.W. Bush</h3>
  <p>George Bush was a late 20th century politician who was elected as
President of the United States.</p>
```

```
    <br>
    <h3>Winston Churchill</h3>
    <p>Winston Churchill was a mid 20th Century British politician who became
  famous as Prime Minister during the Second World War.</p>
    <br>
    <h3>John F. Kennedy</h3>
    <p>JFK, as he was affectionately known, was a United States President who
  was assassinated in Dallas, Texas.</p>
    <br>
   </body>
  </html>
```

Next, we will analyze the stylesheet `People.xsl` while we look at the XSLT elements that were used in it.

The <xsl:stylesheet> Element

Every full XSLT stylesheet has as its document element either an `xsl:stylesheet` element or an `xsl:transform` element.

> **For very simple XSLT stylesheets it is possible to omit the `xsl:stylesheet` element and have, for example, an HTML document that includes elements from the XSLT namespace scattered inside it, in a way similar to Active Server Pages (ASP) or JavaServer Page (JSP) code. Since these simplified XSLT stylesheets are very limited in what they can do, they won't be discussed further here.**

Both the `xsl:stylesheet` and `xsl:transform` elements mean the same, and apart from the requirement that you have matching start and end tags, you can use whichever you prefer.

> **The `<xsl:stylesheet>` element is semantically identical to the `<xsl:transform>` element. You can use the elements interchangeably in your XSLT stylesheets. Most XSLT stylesheets that you are likely to see will use the `<xsl:stylesheet>` element, so that element is used in this chapter.**

The start tag of the `xsl:stylesheet` element has a mandatory `version` attribute. The only allowed value for the `version` attribute in an XSLT 1.0 stylesheet is `1.0`. You can see this in the following excerpt from the `People.xsl` example stylesheet:

```
<xsl:stylesheet
 xmlns:xsl="http://www.w3.org/1999/XSL/Transform"
 version="1.0" >
```

You can also see in the preceding excerpt from the stylesheet that the `xsl:stylesheet` element must also have a namespace declaration for the XSLT namespace. The XSLT namespace has the URI `http://www.w3.org/1999/XSL/Transform`. Any other URI in a namespace declaration identifies elements that are not XSLT. You can use any namespace prefix that you want for XSLT elements; some people use an `xslt` namespace prefix, but the indicative namespace prefix for the XSLT namespace is `xsl`.

The <xsl:template> Element

An XSLT processor looks in a stylesheet for an `xsl:template` element that has a `match` attribute with value of `/` (which matches the root node of the XPath model of the source tree). The following excerpt from the `People.xsl` example stylesheet shows the `xsl:template` element with the `match` attribute of `/`.

```
<xsl:template match="/">
 <html>
  <head>
   <title>Information about <xsl:value-of select="count(/People/Person)" />
people.</title>
  </head>
  <body>
  <h3>Information about <xsl:value-of select="count(/People/Person)" />
people.</h3>
  <br />
   <xsl:apply-templates select="/People/Person" />
  </body>
 </html>
</xsl:template>
```

Each time the XSLT processor finds a node in the source tree that is a root node, the structure corresponding to the content of this template is added to the result tree. Of course, you have only one root node in an XPath model, so the nodes are added only once to the result tree.

Many of the elements in the template that match the root node are likely to be familiar to you as HTML/XHTML elements. These elements are added to the result tree literally, and so are called *literal result elements*. However, in the template there are also several elements from the XSLT namespace. Those elements are called *instructions*.

A frequently used instruction is the `xsl:apply-templates` element.

The <xsl:apply-templates> Element

In the `People.xsl stylesheet`, there is one `xsl:apply-templates` element inside the template that matches the root node:

```
<xsl:apply-templates select="/People/Person" />
```

The `xsl:apply-templates` element causes the XSLT processor to look for matching nodes in the source tree. In this case, the nodes to be looked for are specified by the XPath location path `/People/Person`, which specifies `Person` element nodes that are child nodes of a `People` element node, which is, in turn, a child node of the root node. In the source document, `People.xml`, there are three `Person` elements (as is shown by the highlighted code lines in the following excerpt):

```
<People>
<Person>
 <Name>George H.W. Bush</Name>
 <Description>George Bush was a late 20th century politician who was elected
as President of the United States.</Description>
```

```
</Person>
<Person>
 <Name>Winston Churchill</Name>
 <Description>Winston Churchill was a mid 20th Century British politician who
became famous as Prime Minister during the Second World War.</Description>
</Person>
<Person>
 <Name>John F. Kennedy</Name>
 <Description>JFK, as he was affectionately known, was a United States
President who was assassinated in Dallas, Texas.</Description>
</Person>
</People>
```

The XSLT processor then looks for a template that matches such a `Person` element node. The example stylesheet we've been using, `People.xsl`, has such a template as follows:

```
<xsl:template match="Person">
 <h3><xsl:value-of select="Name" /></h3>
 <p><xsl:value-of select="Description" /></p>
 <br />
</xsl:template>
```

The preceding template has an `xsl:template` element with a `match` attribute that matches the XPath pattern `Person`, so it provides a match for the value of the `select` attribute of the `xsl:apply-templates` element. So each time the XSLT processor finds a `Person` element node that corresponds to the location path `/People/Person`, the content of this template is processed and content is added to the result tree. Since three such nodes exist, the content specified by the template is added to the result tree three times.

The content of the template consists partly of literal result elements that are HTML/XHTML elements and partly of elements in the XSLT namespace, specifically, the `xsl:value-of` element.

Getting Information from the Source Tree

When you are writing a stylesheet, it is often important to be able to use literal result elements, but typically, you will often also want to use information contained in the source tree. XSLT provides a number of ways to use information from the source tree. A frequently used XSLT instruction to achieve that is the `xsl:value-of` element.

The <xsl:value-of> Element

The `xsl:value-of` element, as its name implies, provides the value of a part of the source tree that represents the source XML document. The `xsl:value-of` element has a mandatory `select` attribute, whose value is an XPath location path.

In the template that matched the root node, we used the `xsl:value-of` element to provide the content of the title and `h3` elements:

```
 <html>
  <head>
   <title>Information about <xsl:value-of select="count(/People/Person)" />
people.</title>
```

```
  </head>
  <body>
  <h3>Information about <xsl:value-of select="count(/People/Person)" />
people.</h3>
```

The value of the `select` attribute uses the XPath `count()` function. The argument to the `count()` function is itself an XPath location path, `/People/Person`. That location path again matches each `Person` element node in the source tree, which has a `People` element node as its parent, which, in turn, has the root node as its parent. As you saw a short time ago there are three such `Person` elements in the source document and therefore three corresponding `Person` element nodes in the source tree. Not surprisingly, the `count()` function counts how many such nodes are there and the XSLT processor replaces the `xsl:value-of` XSLT instruction with the literal value 3. For example in the `title` element, the following

```
    <title>Information about <xsl:value-of select="count(/People/Person)" />
people.</title>
```

in the stylesheet is replaced by

```
    <title>Information about 3 people.</title>
```

in the result document.

Similarly, in the template that matches a `Person` element node (like the following one from the sample stylesheet),

```
<xsl:template match="Person">
 <h3><xsl:value-of select="Name" /></h3>
 <p><xsl:value-of select="Description" /></p>
 <br />
</xsl:template>
```

the `xsl:value-of` elements are replaced in the result document by text corresponding, respectively, to the `Name` element node and the `Description` element node that are child nodes of the `Person` element node that matches the value of the `match` attribute of the `xsl:template` element.

To clarify further, the value of the `select` attribute is the relative location path `Name`, which matches a `Name` element node that is a child node of the context node. When the template that matches the pattern `Person` is instantiated, the context node is defined by the `select` attribute of the `xsl:apply-templates` element, as indicated in the following excerpt from the sample stylesheet:

```
    <xsl:apply-templates select="/People/Person" />
```

So, the relative location path `Name` in

```
    <h3><xsl:value-of select="Name" /></h3>
```

could be written as the following absolute location path:

```
 /People/Person/Name
```

That path matches any of the three Name element nodes in the source tree, but by using the relat... location path, we ensure that only the value of the Name element node that is the child of the present Person element node is added to the result tree.

The xsl:value-of element is the simplest XSLT element that extracts information from the source tree. It simply selects the value of a node-set, which might be only a single node, specified by the location path that is the value of the select attribute of the xsl:value-of element. If there is more than one node in the node-set then the xsl:value-of element uses the value of the first node in document order only, not the values of all nodes. The xsl:value-of element is useful particularly when producing output for presentation, as in the example you have just seen, but it can also be used when XML is being restructured.

The next two elements we discuss, the xsl:copy and xsl:copy-of elements, are useful primarily when XML is being restructured.

The <xsl:copy> Element

The xsl:copy element copies a node to the result tree, but it doesn't copy any descendant nodes nor, if the context node is an element node, does it cause any attribute nodes to be copied. This can be useful when, for example, you want to use an element but change the structure of its content or add or remove attributes from it.

Try It Out — Using the xsl:copy Element

Let's look at how the xsl:copy element can be used. First, let's look at how we can convert an element-based structure to one where child elements in the source document are expressed in the result document as attributes.

The source XML, Persons.xml, is shown here:

```
<Persons>
 <Person>
  <FirstName>Jill</FirstName>
  <LastName>Harper</LastName>
 </Person>
 <Person>
  <FirstName>Claire</FirstName>
  <LastName>Vogue</LastName>
 </Person>
 <Person>
  <FirstName>Paul</FirstName>
  <LastName>Cathedral</LastName>
 </Person>
</Persons>
```

Notice that the first and last names are held as child elements of the Person element.

Suppose we want to restructure this so that the Person element has a FirstName attribute and a LastName attribute instead of the child elements shown previously. The stylesheet, Persons.xsl, can restructure the XML to achieve that.

```
<xsl:stylesheet
 xmlns:xsl="http://www.w3.org/1999/XSL/Transform"
 version="1.0" >

<xsl:template match="/">
 <Persons>
  <xsl:apply-templates select="/Persons/Person" />
 </Persons>
</xsl:template>

<xsl:template match="Person">
 <xsl:copy>
  <xsl:attribute name="FirstName"><xsl:value-of select="FirstName"/>
</xsl:attribute>
  <xsl:attribute name="LastName"><xsl:value-of select="LastName"/>
</xsl:attribute>
 </xsl:copy>
</xsl:template>

</xsl:stylesheet>
```

1. Navigate to the directory where `Persons.xml` and `Persons.xsl` are stored.
2. To carry out the transformation, type the following at the command line:

```
java -jar saxon7.jar -o PersonsOut.xml Persons.xml Persons.xsl
```

How It Works

Let's look at how this stylesheet works. As before, there is a template that matches the root node of the source document. Instead of creating HTML/XHTML literal result elements as we did in the first example, we add a `Persons` literal result element. The `xsl:apply-templates` element is used with the absolute location path `/Persons/Person`. There is a template that has a `match` attribute with value of `Person`, which matches the value of the `select` attribute of the `xsl:apply-templates` element. So, for each `Person` node in the source document, that template specifies how it is processed.

First, notice how the `xsl:copy` element is used inside the template:

```
<xsl:template match="Person">
 <xsl:copy>
  <xsl:attribute name="FirstName"><xsl:value-of select="FirstName"/>
</xsl:attribute>
  <xsl:attribute name="LastName"><xsl:value-of select="LastName"/>
</xsl:attribute>
 </xsl:copy>
</xsl:template>
```

The `xsl:copy` element is used when the context node is a `Person` element node. Therefore, a node that is the same as the context node is added to the result tree. In other words, a `Person` element node is added to the result tree, but its child nodes—the `FirstName` element node and the `LastName` element node—are not copied.

If we serialized the result document at this point when only the `xsl:copy` element has been processed, then it would look like this:

```
<Persons>
 <Person />
 <Person />
 <Person />
</Person>
```

However, the template uses the `xsl:attribute` element to add a new attribute to the `Person` element node in the result tree. The `name` attribute of the `xsl:attribute` element specifies that the name of the new attributes are called `FirstName` and `LastName`.

```
<xsl:template match="Person">
 <xsl:copy>
  <xsl:attribute name="FirstName"><xsl:value-of select="FirstName"/>
</xsl:attribute>
  <xsl:attribute name="LastName"><xsl:value-of select="LastName"/>
</xsl:attribute>
 </xsl:copy>
</xsl:template>
```

The `xsl:value-of` element is used to specify the value of the newly created attributes. For the `FirstName` attribute, the value is the value of the `FirstName` element in the source document. For the `LastName` attribute, the value selected is the value of the `LastName` element in the source document. Figure 8-4 shows the result document displayed in Internet Explorer.

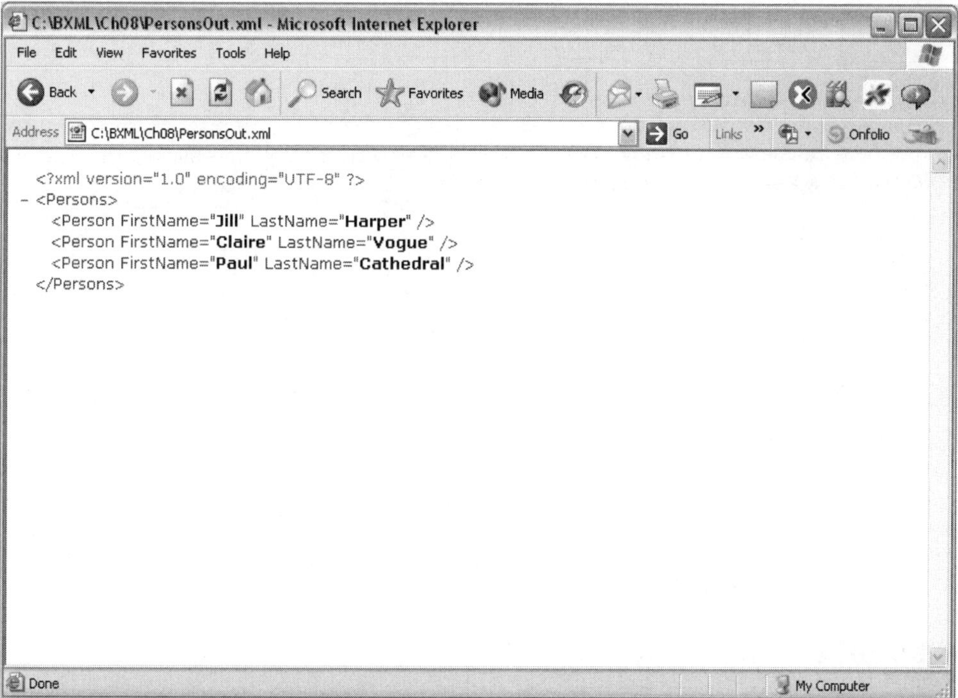

Figure 8-4

The result document, PersonsOut.xml, tidied for on-page presentation, is shown here:

```
<?xml version="1.0" encoding="UTF-8"?>
<Persons>
 <Person FirstName="Jill" LastName="Harper"/>
 <Person FirstName="Claire" LastName="Vogue"/>
 <Person FirstName="Paul" LastName="Cathedral"/>
</Persons>
```

Notice that the Person elements are now empty elements and that each Person element now has a FirstName attribute and a LastName attribute.

Try It Out Adding Child Elements

Sometimes we need to do the opposite when restructuring an element. We can reverse the process, again using the xsl:copy element. We can use PersonsOut.xml as the source document. We will remove the FirstName and LastName attributes and add new FirstName and LastName child elements to the Person element. The stylesheet Persons2.xsl is shown here:

```
<xsl:stylesheet
 xmlns:xsl="http://www.w3.org/1999/XSL/Transform"
 version="1.0" >

<xsl:template match="/">
 <Persons>
  <xsl:apply-templates select="/Persons/Person" />
 </Persons>
</xsl:template>

<xsl:template match="Person">
 <xsl:copy>
  <xsl:element name="FirstName"><xsl:value-of select="@FirstName"/>
</xsl:element>
  <xsl:element name="LastName"><xsl:value-of select="@LastName"/>
</xsl:element>
 </xsl:copy>
</xsl:template>

</xsl:stylesheet>
```

1. Navigate to the directory containing the PersonsOut.xml and Persons2.xsl files.
2. To run the transformation, type the following at the command line:

```
java -jar saxon7.jar -o PersonsBack.xml PersonsOut.xml Persons2.xsl
```

3. Open PersonsBack.xml in your favorite editor to see the structure created using the Persons2.xsl stylesheet.

How It Works

The stylesheet Persons2.xsl differs from the previous stylesheet, Persons.xsl, only in the content of the template that matches the Person element node:

```
<xsl:template match="Person">
 <xsl:copy>
  <xsl:element name="FirstName"><xsl:value-of select="@FirstName"/>
</xsl:element>
  <xsl:element name="LastName"><xsl:value-of select="@LastName"/>
</xsl:element>
 </xsl:copy>
</xsl:template>
```

The `xsl:copy` element, as before, adds a `Person` element node to the result tree. Each `xsl:element` element adds a child element node to the `Person` element node. The name of the new element node is specified in the `name` attribute of the `xsl:element` element. The value of the new element is specified using the `xsl:value-of` element:

```
<xsl:value-of select="@FirstName" />
```

The location path in the `select` attribute specifies that the value of the newly created `FirstName` element node is the value of the `FirstName` attribute in the source tree.

The preceding examples have given you an idea of how to use the `xsl:copy` element. However, sometimes you will want to copy an entire structure from the source XML document to the result document. In that case, the `xsl:copy-of` element comes into play.

The <xsl:copy-of> Element

The `xsl:copy-of` element causes a deep copy to take place. In other words, a node together with all its attribute nodes and descendant nodes is copied to the result tree.

Suppose you receive a purchase order (`PurchaseOrder.xml` shown here) as a source document:

```
<PurchaseOrder>
 <From>Example.org</From>
 <To>XMML.com</To>
 <Address>
  <Street>234 Any Street</Street>
  <City>Any Town</City>
  <State>MO</State>
  <ZipCode>98765</ZipCode>
 </Address>
 <!-- Other purchase order information would go here. -->
</PurchaseOrder>
```

The stylesheet, `PurchaseOrder.xsl`, to create an Invoice, `Invoice.xml`, from the purchase order is shown here:

```
<xsl:stylesheet
 xmlns:xsl="http://www.w3.org/1999/XSL/Transform"
 version="1.0" >

<xsl:template match="/">
 <Invoice>
```

```
    <xsl:apply-templates select="/PurchaseOrder/To" />
    <xsl:apply-templates select = "/PurchaseOrder/From" />
    <xsl:apply-templates select="/PurchaseOrder/Address" />
    <xsl:comment>The rest of the Invoice would go here.</xsl:comment>
  </Invoice>
</xsl:template>

<xsl:template match="To">
  <xsl:element name="From"><xsl:value-of select="." /></xsl:element>
</xsl:template>

<xsl:template match="From">
  <xsl:element name="To"><xsl:value-of select="." /></xsl:element>
</xsl:template>

<xsl:template match="Address">
  <xsl:copy-of select="." />
</xsl:template>

</xsl:stylesheet>
```

To run the transformation enter the following at the command line:

```
java -jar saxon7.jar -o Invoice.xml PurchaseOrder.xml PurchaseOrder.xsl
```

Now, let's walk through what the stylesheet does. The template that matches the root node creates an `Invoice` element as a literal result element. Then three `xsl:apply-templates` element are used to create the content of the `Invoice` element.

```
<xsl:template match="/">
  <Invoice>
    <xsl:apply-templates select="/PurchaseOrder/To" />
    <xsl:apply-templates select = "/PurchaseOrder/From" />
    <xsl:apply-templates select="/PurchaseOrder/Address" />
    <xsl:comment>The rest of the Invoice would go here.</xsl:comment>
  </Invoice>
</xsl:template>
```

The first `xsl:apply-templates` element selects `To` element nodes in the source tree and matches this template:

```
<xsl:template match="To">
  <xsl:element name="From"><xsl:value-of select="." /></xsl:element>
</xsl:template>
```

A new element node, `From`, is created using the value of the `To` element node in the source tree. Remember that the value of the select attribute of `xsl:value-of`,

```
<xsl:value-of select="." />
```

is the abbreviated syntax for the context node, which is the `To` element node.

Similarly, the second `xsl:apply-templates` element matches `From` element nodes.

```
<xsl:template match="From">
 <xsl:element name="To"><xsl:value-of select="." /></xsl:element>
</xsl:template>
```

A new element, `To`, is created in the result tree and given the value of the `From` element node in the source tree.

The result of those two templates simply switches the From and To parties, which you would expect to be switched between a purchase order and an invoice.

The `Address` element in the source document can be used unchanged in the invoice.

```
  <Address>
   <Street>234 Any Street</Street>
   <City>Any Town</City>
   <State>MO</State>
   <ZipCode>98765</ZipCode>
  </Address>
```

So, the third `xsl:apply-templates` element in the stylesheet selects the location path `/PurchaseOrder/Address`, and the following template matches:

```
<xsl:template match="Address">
 <xsl:copy-of select="." />
</xsl:template>
```

The `xsl:copy-of` element copies the `Address` element node from the source tree to the result tree, together with all its descendant nodes (and attribute nodes, if it had any).

The result document, `Invoice.xml`, is shown here:

```
<?xml version="1.0" encoding="UTF-8"?>
<Invoice>
 <From>XMML.com</From>
 <To>Example.org</To>
  <Address>
   <Street>234 Any Street</Street>
   <City>Any Town</City>
   <State>MO</State>
   <ZipCode>98765</ZipCode>
   </Address><!--The rest of the Invoice would go here.-->
</Invoice>
```

Influencing the Output with the <xsl:output> Element

XSLT can be used to produce XML, HTML, or text output. The developer makes a choice among these options by using the `xsl:output` element.

XML output is the default, and it is not necessary to specify XML as an output method. If you want to do it explicitly, then this code is used:

```
<xsl:output method="xml" />
```

The value of the method attribute is case sensitive and must be all lowercase.

HTML output is specified like this:

```
<xsl:output method="html" />
```

Text output is specified like this:

```
<xsl:output method="text" />
```

In XSLT 1.0, there is no way to specify XHTML output. Still, using the HTML output method, using all lowercase element names, and otherwise ensuring well-formedness will produce code that is essentially XHTML, which most modern browsers will display.

Conditional Processing

So far you have seen pretty simple XSLT stylesheets that carry out a transformation in only one way each time a template is instantiated. At times, you will want to apply conditions when processing. The xsl:if and xsl:choose elements allow conditional processing in XSLT.

The <xsl:if> Element

The xsl:if element tests whether a boolean condition is true or false. If it is true, then the content of the xsl:if element is instantiated. If it is false, then nothing specified inside the xsl:if element is added to the result tree.

Suppose we wished to test whether the age data on some historical or fictional characters corresponded to an imposed upper realistic age limit of 110 years. The source document, Characters.xml, is shown here:

```
<Characters>
 <Character age="99">Julius Caesar</Character>
 <Character age="23">Anne Boleyn</Character>
 <Character age="41">George Washington</Character>
 <Character age="45">Martin Luther</Character>
 <Character age="800">Methuselah</Character>
 <Character age="119">Moses</Character>
 <Character age="50">Asterix the Gaul</Character>
</Characters>
```

A quick glance at a short document like this reveals that two characters have unusually high ages. When you have thousands or tens of thousands of Character elements, it is more appropriate to automate the checks.

The stylesheet, Characters.xsl, uses the xsl:if element to add to the result tree only when the value of the age attribute exceeds the specified upper age limit of 110.

```
<xsl:stylesheet
 xmlns:xsl="http://www.w3.org/1999/XSL/Transform"
 version="1.0" >

<xsl:template match="/">
 <html>
  <head>
   <title>Age check on Characters.</title>
  </head>
  <body>
  <h3>The recorded age is unusually high. Please check original data.</h3>
  <xsl:apply-templates select="/Characters/Character" />
  </body>
 </html>
</xsl:template>
<xsl:template match="Character">
 <xsl:if test="@age &gt; 110 " >
 <p><b><xsl:value-of select="." /></b> is older than expected. Please check if
this character's age, <b><xsl:value-of select="@age" /></b>, is correct.</p>
 </xsl:if>
</xsl:template>

</xsl:stylesheet>
```

The `xsl:apply-templates` element in the template that matches the root node selects `Character` element nodes for which the following template matches:

```
<xsl:template match="Character">
 <xsl:if test="@age &gt; 110 " >
 <p><b><xsl:value-of select="." /></b> is older than expected. Please check if
 this character's age, <b><xsl:value-of select="@age" /></b>, is correct.</p>
 </xsl:if>
</xsl:template>
```

Notice that the `xsl:if` element is a child element of the `xsl:template` element. Therefore, if the `test` attribute of the `xsl:if` element returns the boolean value `false`, then nothing is output from the template for that `Character` element.

The output from the transformation is shown in Figure 8-5.

As you can see in the figure, only those characters whose age exceeds 110 are displayed in the web page created by the transformation.

While the `xsl:if` element either outputs something or outputs nothing, the `xsl:choose` element is intended to allow alternate output options.

The <xsl:choose> Element

Suppose that we want to indicate whether the age of a character is suspicious or acceptable. Using the same XML source document used in the previous section, `Characters.xml`, we can use the following stylesheet, `CharactersChoose.xsl`, to indicate an assessment for each character:

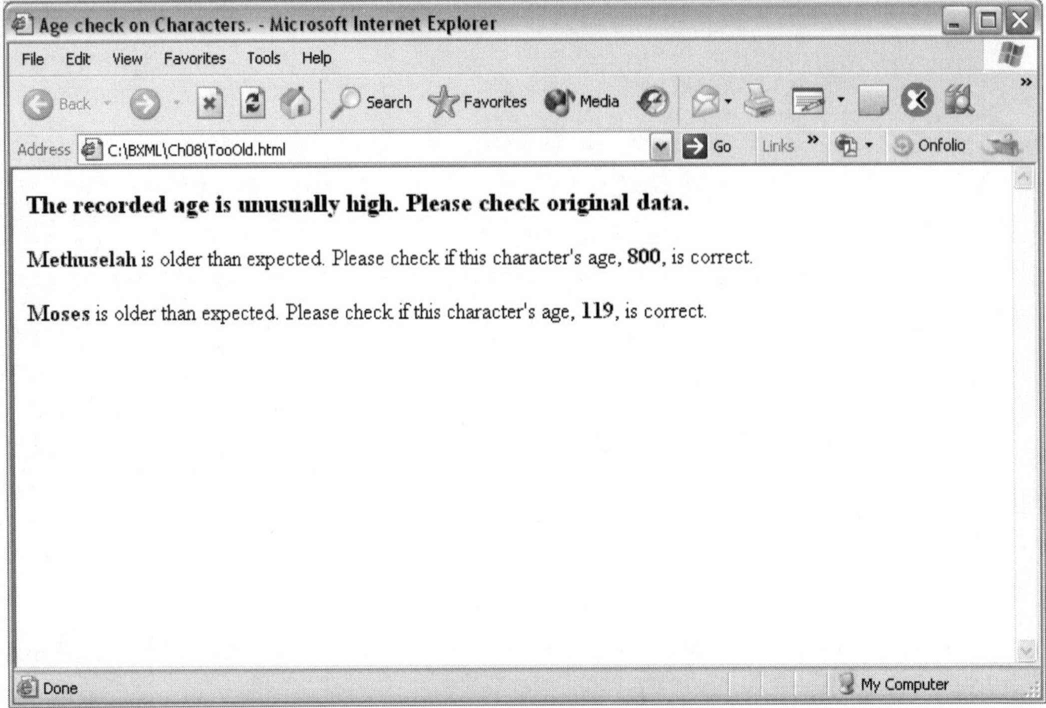

Figure 8-5

```
<xsl:stylesheet
 xmlns:xsl="http://www.w3.org/1999/XSL/Transform"
 version="1.0" >

<xsl:template match="/">
 <html>
  <head>
   <title>Age check on all Characters.</title>
  </head>
  <body>
  <h3>The following is the assessment of the age data.</h3>
  <xsl:apply-templates select="/Characters/Character" />
  </body>
 </html>
</xsl:template>

<xsl:template match="Character">
 <xsl:choose>
  <xsl:when test="@age &gt; 110 " >
   <p><b><xsl:value-of select="." /></b> - too high. Please check if this
   character's age, <b><xsl:value-of select="@age" /></b>, is correct.</p>
  </xsl:when>
  <xsl:otherwise>
  </xsl:otherwise>
```

```
  </xsl:choose>
 </xsl:template>

 </xsl:stylesheet>
```

To run the transformation, enter the following at the command line:

```
java -jar saxon7.jar -o AgeAssessed.html Characters.xml CharactersChoose.xsl
```

The key part of this transformation is in the template that matches `Character` element nodes:

```
<xsl:template match="Character">
 <xsl:choose>
  <xsl:when test="@age &gt; 110 " >
   <p><b><xsl:value-of select="." /></b> - too high. Please check if this
   character's age, <b><xsl:value-of select="@age" /></b>, is correct.</p>
  </xsl:when>
  <xsl:otherwise>
   <p><b><xsl:value-of select="." /></b> - ok</p>.
  </xsl:otherwise>
 </xsl:choose>
</xsl:template>
```

Notice how the `xsl:choose` element is nested immediately inside the `xsl:template` element. So the output from that template is entirely controlled by the `xsl:choose` element.

Nested inside the `xsl:choose` element are an `xsl:when` element and an `xsl:otherwise` element. On the `xsl:when` element is a `test` attribute whose value is a boolean value. If the value of the `test` attribute is the boolean value `true`, then the content of the `xsl:when` element is output. If the value of the `test` attribute of the `xsl:when` attribute is `false`, then none of the content of the `xsl:when` element is output; the content of the `xsl:otherwise` element is output instead.

The HTML output, `AgeAssessed.html`, tidied for on page display, is shown here:

```
<html>
 <head>
  <meta http-equiv="Content-Type" content="text/html; charset=UTF-8">
   <title>Age check on all Characters.</title>
 </head>
 <body>
  <h3>The following is the assessment of the age data.</h3>
  <p><b>Julius Caesar</b> - ok</p>
  <p><b>Anne Boleyn</b> - ok</p>
  <p><b>George Washington</b> - ok</p>
  <p><b>Martin Luther</b> - ok</p>
  <p><b>Methuselah</b> - too high. Please check if this character's age,
  <b>800</b>, is correct.</p>
  <p><b>Moses</b> - too high. Please check if this character's age, <b>119
  </b>, is correct.</p>
  <p><b>Asterix the Gaul</b> - ok</p>
 </body>
</html>
```

Output is created for every Character element node in the source tree. If the value of the age attribute is greater than 110, then a message asking the user to check that character's age is output, as indicated by the content of the xsl:when element. Otherwise an *ok* message is output, as specified in the xsl:otherwise element.

The result web page is shown in Figure 8-6.

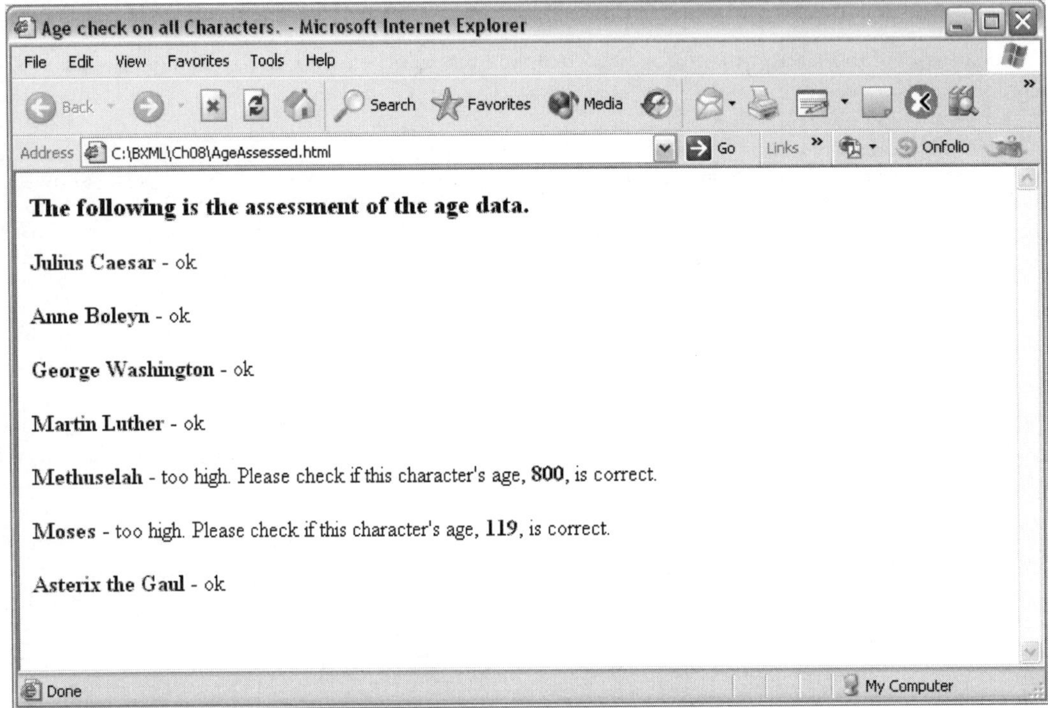

Figure 8-6

In the preceding example, the xsl:choose element had only one xsl:when element. However, it can have an arbitrary number of xsl:when elements as its children, each with a boolean test specified in the test attribute. The content of the first xsl:when element that has a test attribute that evaluates to the boolean value true is output. All other xsl:when elements generate no output, and the xsl:otherwise is ignored. However, if none of the xsl:when elements has a test attribute that evaluates to the boolean value true, then the content of the xsl:otherwise element, if one is present, is output.

Having looked at how we can make choices between processing options, we will now move on to look at how we can process several nodes with each being processed in the same way.

The <xsl:for-each> Element

The xsl:for-each element allows iteration across a node-set, with each node being processed according to the XSLT instructions nested inside the xsl:for-each element.

For example, consider a source document, `Objects.xml`, that shows some characteristics of an object.

```
<?xml version='1.0'?>
<Objects>
 <Object name="Car">
  <Characteristic>Hard</Characteristic>
  <Characteristic>Shiny</Characteristic>
  <Characteristic>Has 4 wheels</Characteristic>
  <Characteristic>Internal Combustion Engine</Characteristic>
 </Object>
</Objects>
```

The `xsl:for-each` element can be used to iterate across this node-set and create some specified output for each node in the node-set. We could, for example, use the `xsl:for-each` element to create an HTML list item, `li` element, for each characteristic of an object. The following code, `object.xsl`, shows a stylesheet that does this.

```
<?xml version='1.0'?>
<xsl:stylesheet
 xmlns:xsl="http://www.w3.org/1999/XSL/Transform"
 version="1.0"
 >

<xsl:template match="/">
 <html>
  <head>
   <title>Object Characteristics</title>
  </head>
  <body>
  <h3>Characteristics of <xsl:value-of select="Objects/Object/@name" /></h3>
  <xsl:apply-templates select="/Objects/Object" />
  </body>
 </html>
</xsl:template>

<xsl:template match="Object">
 <ul>
 <xsl:for-each select="Characteristic">
  <li><xsl:value-of select="." /></li>
 </xsl:for-each>
 </ul>
</xsl:template>

</xsl:stylesheet>
```

The interesting part of this stylesheet is the template that matches `Object` element nodes:

```
<xsl:template match="Object">
 <ul>
 <xsl:for-each select="Characteristic">
  <li><xsl:value-of select="." /></li>
 </xsl:for-each>
 </ul>
</xsl:template>
```

Inside the template, the start and end tags of an unordered list are specified using literal result elements. Between those tags we use the xsl:for-each element to create a list item for each Characteristic element node child of the context node, which is an Object element node.

The xsl:for-each element and the xsl:apply-templates elements allow us to process nodes in document order. However, you may need to output data in an order, which differs from the order in the source document. The xsl:sort element provides the functionality to sort XML data during a transformation.

The <xsl:sort> Element

The xsl:sort element is used to specify sort order for node-sets. The xsl:sort element can be used together with the xsl:apply-templates element and the xsl:for-each element. The following example shows both usages.

Suppose we have a larger group of objects that we want to describe in an HTML web page. The source XML, Objects2.xml, is shown in the following code.

```
<?xml version='1.0'?>
<Objects>
 <Object name="Car">
  <Characteristic>Hard</Characteristic>
  <Characteristic>Shiny</Characteristic>
  <Characteristic>Has 4 wheels</Characteristic>
  <Characteristic>Internal Combustion Engine</Characteristic>
 </Object>
  <Object name="Orange">
  <Characteristic>Fruit</Characteristic>
  <Characteristic>Juicy</Characteristic>
  <Characteristic>Dimpled skin</Characteristic>
  <Characteristic>Citrus</Characteristic>
 </Object>
  <Object name="Giraffe">
  <Characteristic>Tall</Characteristic>
  <Characteristic>Four legs</Characteristic>
  <Characteristic>Big spots</Characteristic>
  <Characteristic>Mammal</Characteristic>
 </Object>
  <Object name="Prawn Cracker">
  <Characteristic>Crisp</Characteristic>
  <Characteristic>Savoury</Characteristic>
  <Characteristic>Off white</Characteristic>
  <Characteristic>Edible</Characteristic>
 </Object>
</Objects>
```

Suppose we want to sort the data before display. The objects are to be sorted in ascending alphabetical order, and the characteristics are to be sorted in descending alphabetical order. The stylesheet, Objects3.xsl, creates an HTML file with those sort orders applied.

```
<?xml version='1.0'?>
<xsl:stylesheet
```

```
  xmlns:xsl="http://www.w3.org/1999/XSL/Transform"
  version="1.0"
  >

<xsl:template match="/">
 <html>
  <head>
   <title>Object Characteristics</title>
  </head>
  <body>
  <xsl:apply-templates select="/Objects/Object" >
   <xsl:sort select="@name" />
  </xsl:apply-templates>
  </body>
 </html>
</xsl:template>

<xsl:template match="Object">
  <h3>Characteristics of <xsl:value-of select="@name" /></h3>
 <ul>
 <xsl:for-each select="Characteristic">
 <xsl:sort select="." order="descending" />
  <li><xsl:value-of select="." /></li>
 </xsl:for-each>
 </ul>
</xsl:template>

</xsl:stylesheet>
```

First, look at the use of `xsl:sort` in association with the `xsl:apply-templates` element:

```
<xsl:apply-templates select="/Objects/Object" >
 <xsl:sort select="@name" />
</xsl:apply-templates>
```

As normal, we use the `select` attribute of the `xsl:apply-templates` element to specify a node-set. Unlike earlier examples, the `xsl:apply-templates` element is not an empty element, instead it has an `xsl:sort` element nested inside it. The value of the `select` attribute of the `xsl:sort` element specifies the value by which the node-set is to be sorted. In this case the value of the `select` attribute is a relative location path, `@name`, which specifies the `name` attribute node whose parent is an `Object` element node.

The default sort order is ascending so you don't need to specify that to produce the desired sort order for objects. However, when we come to sort the `Characteristic` element nodes the desired sort order is descending, so that needs to be specified using the `order` attribute on the `xsl:sort` element.

```
<xsl:template match="Object">
  <h3>Characteristics of <xsl:value-of select="@name" /></h3>
 <ul>
 <xsl:for-each select="Characteristic">
 <xsl:sort select="." order="descending" />
  <li><xsl:value-of select="." /></li>
 </xsl:for-each>
 </ul>
</xsl:template>
```

Notice how the unordered list is created in the preceding template. The start and end tags of the `ul` element come outside the `xsl:for-each` element. The `xsl:sort` element is nested inside the `xsl:for-each` element, coming immediately after its start tag. The node-set selected by the `xsl:for-each` element are `Characteristic` element nodes. It is the value of those nodes that we want to sort by, so we use the period character as the value of the `select` attribute of the `xsl:sort` element. Remember the period character selects the context node itself, being an abbreviation for the location path `self::node()`. To sort the characteristics in descending order, we specify the value of the `order` attribute of the `xsl:sort` element as `descending`.

XSLT Modes

You have learned how you can select, for example, element nodes in the source tree and produce output corresponding to their content. So far in the examples that you have seen, a node in the source tree has either been processed once or not at all. But at times we will need to use a node in the source tree more than once. A classic situation is using a chapter title in the source document at the top of its own page and also using the same information in a table of contents for the document.

The XSLT solution to this need to process certain nodes more than once is the *mode*. An XSLT mode is expressed using a `mode` attribute on an `xsl:apply-templates` element, like this:

```
<xsl:apply-templates select="/Book/Chapter" mode="TOC" />
```

Suppose the stylesheet had two templates, one with this start tag

```
<xsl:template match="Chapter" >
```

and the other with this start tag

```
<xsl:template match="Chapter" mode="TOC" >
```

Both templates match as far as the value of the `match` attribute is concerned. However, if the `xsl:apply-templates` element has a `mode` attribute, a template is instantiated only if it has both a matching value in the `match` attribute and in the `mode` attribute of the `xsl:template` element.

Let's show this in operation to solve our problem of having to process chapter titles so that they are used in a table of contents and also displayed as the title of the chapter when the chapter is displayed. The content of a very abbreviated version of this book, `BegXML.xml`, is stored as XML and is shown here:

```
<?xml version='1.0'?>
<Book>
<Title>Beginning XML, 3rd Edition</Title>
<Authors>
 <Author>David Hunter</Author>
 <Author>Andrew Watt</Author>
 <Author>Jeff Rafter</Author>
 <Author>Kurt Cagle</Author>
 <Author>John Duckett</Author>
</Authors>
<Year>2004</Year>
<Chapters>
```

```
<Chapter number="1" title="What is XML?">XML is a markup language, derived
 from SGML.</Chapter>
<Chapter number="2" title="Well-formed XML">To be well-formed an XML document
 must satisfy several rules about its structure.</Chapter>
<Chapter number="3" title="Namespaces">To help unambiguously identify the
 names of elements and attributes the notion of an XML namespace is
 used.</Chapter>
<Chapter number="4" title="DTD">A document type definition, DTD, is a way to
 specify the permitted structure of an XML document.</Chapter>
<Chapter number="5" title="Schemas">W3C XML Schema and Relax NG are two schema
 languages to specify the structure of XML documents.</Chapter>
</Chapters>
</Book>
```

The aim is to create an HTML document with a table of contents and the chapter text, as in Figure 8-7.

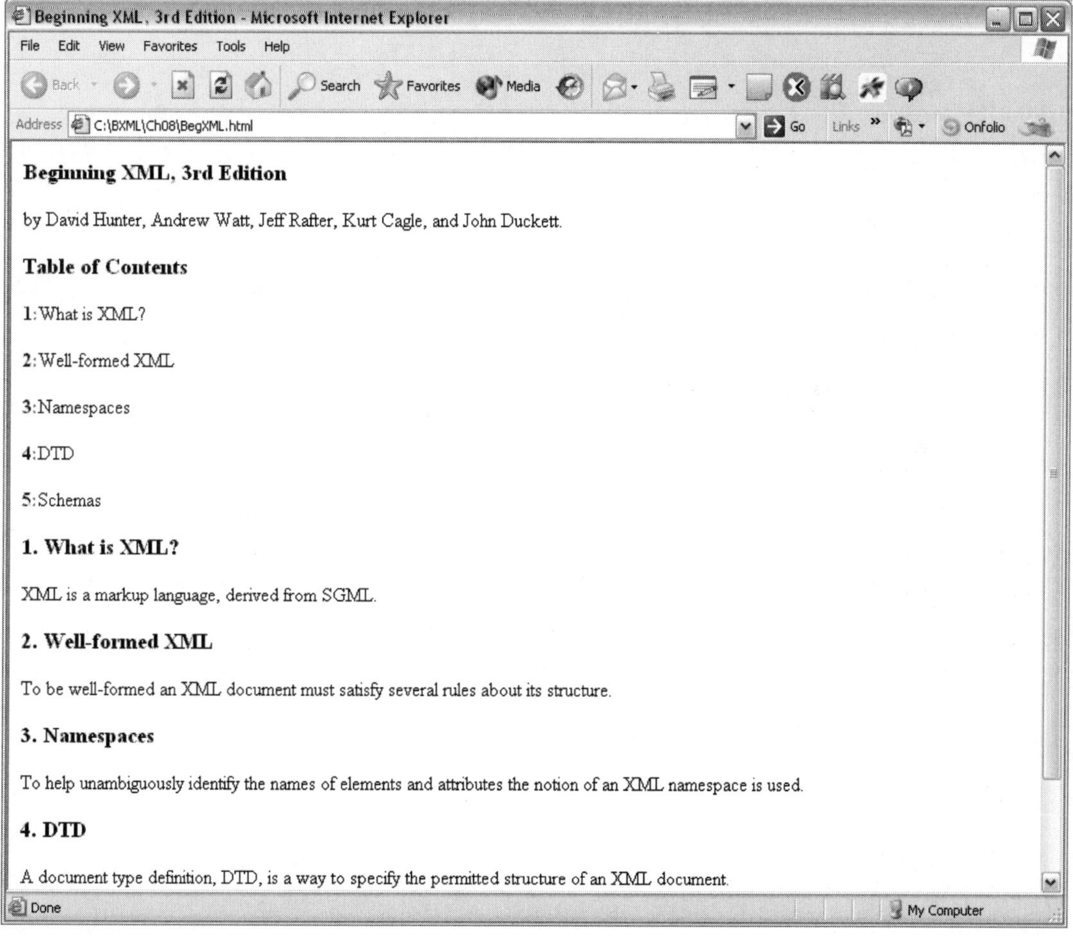

Figure 8-7

The stylesheet, `BegXML.xsl`, to create the HTML web page is shown here:

```
<?xml version='1.0'?>
<xsl:stylesheet
 xmlns:xsl="http://www.w3.org/1999/XSL/Transform"
 version="1.0"
 >

<xsl:template match="/">
 <html>
  <head>
   <title><xsl:value-of select="/Book/Title" /></title>
  </head>
  <body>
  <h3><xsl:value-of select="/Book/Title" /></h3>
  <p>by <xsl:apply-templates select="/Book/Authors/Author" />
  </p>
  <h3>Table of Contents</h3>
  <xsl:apply-templates select="/Book/Chapters/Chapter" mode="TOC" />
  <xsl:apply-templates select="/Book/Chapters/Chapter" mode="fulltext" />
  </body>
 </html>
</xsl:template>

<xsl:template match="Author">
<xsl:value-of select="." />
<xsl:if test="position() != last()"><xsl:text>, </xsl:text></xsl:if>
<xsl:if test="position() = last()-1"><xsl:text>and </xsl:text></xsl:if>
<xsl:if test="position() = last()"><xsl:text>.</xsl:text></xsl:if>
</xsl:template>

<xsl:template match="Chapter" mode="TOC">
 <p><b><xsl:value-of select="@number" />:</b> <xsl:value-of select="@title" />
</p>
</xsl:template>

<xsl:template match="Chapter" mode="fulltext">
<h3><xsl:value-of select="@number" />. <xsl:value-of select="@title" /></h3>
<p><xsl:value-of select="." /></p>
</xsl:template>

</xsl:stylesheet>
```

You can note several differences from stylesheets that you have already seen. The template that matches the root node has three `xsl:apply-templates` elements in it:

```
<xsl:template match="/">
 <html>
  <head>
   <title><xsl:value-of select="/Book/Title" /></title>
  </head>
  <body>
  <h3><xsl:value-of select="/Book/Title" /></h3>
  <p>by <xsl:apply-templates select="/Book/Authors/Author" />
```

```
    </p>
    <h3>Table of Contents</h3>
    <xsl:apply-templates select="/Book/Chapters/Chapter" mode="TOC" />
    <xsl:apply-templates select="/Book/Chapters/Chapter" mode="fulltext" />
    </body>
   </html>
  </xsl:template>
```

The first `xsl:apply-templates` element matches this template:

```
<xsl:template match="Author">
<xsl:value-of select="." />
<xsl:if test="position() != last()"><xsl:text>, </xsl:text></xsl:if>
<xsl:if test="position() = last()-1"><xsl:text>and </xsl:text></xsl:if>
<xsl:if test="position() = last()"><xsl:text>.</xsl:text></xsl:if>
</xsl:template>
```

The `xsl:value-of` element simply outputs an author's name. But punctuation is controlled using the `xsl:if` element and the XPath `position()` function and `last()` function. The first `xsl:if` element causes a comma followed by a space character to be output. This is done when the position of the `Author` element node is not last in document order among the `Author` element nodes in the node-set selected by the first of the three `xsl:apply-templates` elements in the template matching the root node.

The second `xsl:if` element produces output only if the `Author` element node is the second last `Author` element node in the node-set. The third `xsl:if` element produces a period character only when the `Author` element node is the last one.

Taken together, all this gives a correctly punctuated author list:

```
<p>by David Hunter, Andrew Watt, Jeff Rafter, Kurt Cagle, and John
Duckett.</p>
```

The `xsl:text` element was used in each of the `xsl:if` elements. It is not needed here, and we could have obtained the same output without using it. However, the `xsl:text` element is essential if we want to output whitespace literally, either a space character or a newline character, for example. To output a space character, we could write the following:

```
<xsl:text> </xsl:text>
```

To output a newline character, we could write the following:

```
<xsl:text>
</xsl:text>
```

The second and third `xsl:apply-templates` from the `BegXML.xsl` stylesheet demonstrate the use of modes:

```
<xsl:apply-templates select="/Book/Chapters/Chapter" mode="TOC" />
<xsl:apply-templates select="/Book/Chapters/Chapter" mode="fulltext" />
```

The first `xsl:apply-templates` element matches this template, as is shown in the following:

```
<xsl:template match="Chapter" mode="TOC">
 <p><b><xsl:value-of select="@number" />:</b> <xsl:value-of
select= "@title" /></p>
</xsl:template>
```

Notice that the value of the `select` attribute of the `xsl:apply-templates` element matches the value of the `match` attribute of the `xsl:template` element, and at the same time the values of the two `mode` attributes are the same.

The content added to the result tree is straightforward using the `xsl:value-of` element that you have seen several times before. Importantly, by using a mode attribute on both the `xsl:apply-templates` and `xsl:template` element, it leaves us free to process the `Chapter` nodes a second time, using another `xsl:apply-templates` element:

```
<xsl:apply-templates select="/Book/Chapters/Chapter" mode="fulltext" />
```

The preceding `xsl:apply-templates` element matches the following template:

```
<xsl:template match="Chapter" mode="fulltext">
<h3><xsl:value-of select="@number" />. <xsl:value-of select="@title" /></h3>
<p><xsl:value-of select="." /></p>
</xsl:template>
```

Note that the `match` attribute of the `xsl:template` element matches the `select` attribute of the `xsl:apply-templates` element, and the two `mode` attributes also match.

The HTML document, `BegXML.html`, that the stylesheet produces is shown here after tidying for on-page presentation:

```
<html>
 <head>
  <meta http-equiv="Content-Type" content="text/html; charset=UTF-8">
  <title>Beginning XML, 3rd Edition</title>
 </head>
 <body>
  <h3>Beginning XML, 3rd Edition</h3>
  <p>by David Hunter, Andrew Watt, Jeff Rafter, Kurt Cagle, and John
  Duckett.</p>
  <h3>Table of Contents</h3>
  <p><b>1:</b>What is XML?</p>
  <p><b>2:</b>Well-formed XML</p>
  <p><b>3:</b>Namespaces</p>
  <p><b>4:</b>DTD</p>
  <p><b>5:</b>Schemas</p>
  <h3>1. What is XML?</h3>
  <p>XML is a markup language, derived from SGML.</p>
  <h3>2. Well-formed XML</h3>
  <p>To be well-formed an XML document must satisfy several rules about its
  structure.</p>
```

```
    <h3>3. Namespaces</h3>
    <p>To help unambiguously identify the names of elements and attributes the
    notion of an XML namespace is used.</p>
    <h3>4. DTD</h3>
    <p>A document type definition, DTD, is a way to specify the permitted
    structure of an XML document.</p>
    <h3>5. Schemas</h3>
    <p>W3C XML Schema and Relax NG are two schema languages to specify the
    structure of XML documents.</p>
  </body>
</html>
```

As you have seen, modes allow multiple processing of nodes in the source tree for different purposes.

XSLT Variables and Parameters

XSLT allows variables and parameters to be specified by the `xsl:variable` and `xsl:parameter` elements, respectively. Both variables and parameters are referenced using `$VariableName` or `$ParameterName` syntax.

Suppose we want to be able to enter the name of a person and find their age. A source document, `Ages.xml`, is shown here:

```
<?xml version='1.0'?>
<Ages>
 <Person name="Peter" age="21" />
 <Person name="Angela" age="12" />
 <Person name="Augustus" age="92" />
 <Person name="George" age="44" />
 <Person name="Hannah" age="30" />
</Ages>
```

Next, we show the stylesheet. Note the `xsl:param` element as a child element of the `xsl:stylesheet` element.

```
<?xml version='1.0'?>
<xsl:stylesheet
 xmlns:xsl="http://www.w3.org/1999/XSL/Transform"
 version="1.0"
 >
<xsl:param name="person" />

<xsl:template match="/">
 <html>
  <head>
   <title>Finding an age using an XSLT parameter</title>
  </head>
  <body>
   <xsl:apply-templates select="/Ages/Person[@name=$person]" />
  </body>
 </html>
```

```
</xsl:template>

<xsl:template match="Person">
<p>The age of <xsl:value-of select="$person" /> is <xsl:value-of
  select="@age"/> </p>
</xsl:template>

</xsl:stylesheet>
```

To pass in a parameter from the command line, we use syntax like this:

```
java -jar saxon7.jar -o Ages.html Ages.xml Ages.xsl person="Peter"
```

This passes in `Peter` as the value of the `person` parameter. If we pass in the name `Hannah` to the stylesheet, the HTML output is as follows:

```
<html>
 <head>
  <meta http-equiv="Content-Type" content="text/html; charset=UTF-8">
  <title>Finding an age using an XSLT parameter</title>
 </head>
 <body>
  <p>The age of Hannah is 30</p>
 </body>
</html>
```

The `person` parameter is used twice in the stylesheet. First, it is used in a predicate in the value of the `select` attribute of the `xsl:apply-templates` element:

```
<xsl:apply-templates select="/Ages/Person[@name=$person]" />
```

Later, it is used inside the matching template to display the value of the `person` parameter using the `xsl:value-of` element:

```
<xsl:template match="Person">
<p>The age of <xsl:value-of select="$person" /> is <xsl:value-of
  select="@age"/></p>
</xsl:template>
```

XSLT variables behave in the same way as parameters but with one difference. Parameters can be passed into a transformation from outside. Variables are defined inside an XSLT stylesheet. There are two ways to specify an XSLT variable: the first way uses the `select` attribute of the `xsl:variable` element as shown in the following:

```
<xsl:variable name="variableName" select="someExpression" />
```

The second way to specify an XSLT variable is to supply content between the start tag and the end tag of the `xsl:variable` element as shown in the following:

```
<xsl:variable name="variableName">
 <!-- Some content goes here which can define the value of the variable. -->
</xsl:variable>
```

The variable can then be employed by using the `$variableName` notation at an appropriate place in the stylesheet.

Named Templates and the <xsl:call-template> Element

The `xsl:apply-templates` element that you have seen in use several times in this chapter allows addressing of selected parts of the source tree of nodes. However, at times you may want to use a template in a way similar to using a function in, for example, JavaScript. *Named templates* in XSLT allow you to do this.

Named templates are identified, not surprisingly, by a `name` attribute on an `xsl:template` element:

```
<xsl:template name="TemplateName">
<!-- The template content goes here. -->
</xsl:template>
```

Named templates are called using the `xsl:call-template` element.

The simplest use of `xsl:call-template` is when no parameter is passed to the named template:

```
<xsl:call-template name="TemplateName" />
```

However, you will often want to pass one or more parameters to a named template, and that is done using the `xsl:with-param` element, like this:

```
<xsl:call-template name="TemplateName" >
 <xsl:with-param name="ParameterName" />
 <!-- More <xsl:with-param> elements can go here. -->
</xsl:call-template>
```

The `xsl:with-param` element can optionally have a `select` attribute whose value is an expression, which can specify how the value to be passed is selected.

When a parameter is passed to a named template, the template is written like this:

```
<xsl:template name="TemplateName">
 <xsl:with-param name="ParameterName" />
 <!-- Rest of template goes here. -->
</xsl:template>
```

The content of a template called using `xsl:call-template` can use any of the XSLT elements that we have discussed in this chapter.

XSLT Functions

All of the XPath 1.0 functions that were described in Chapter 7 are available to an XSLT processor. In addition to those functions, XSLT 1.0 provides a limited number of additional functions to provide functionality specifically relevant to XSLT, several of which are listed here.

- The `document()` function enables access to documents other than the document that contains the context node. This allows the use of multiple documents as source XML documents.

- The `key()` function can be used with the `xsl:key` element to provide an indexing mechanism for XML source documents.
- The `format-number()` function can be used with the `xsl:decimal-format` element to provide fine control of how numeric values are displayed in a result document.
- The `generate-id()` function allows the generation of `ID` attribute nodes in the result tree.

Looking Forward to XSLT 2.0

The development of XSLT 2.0, like that of XPath 2.0, is likely to be complete a few months after this book is published.

> **The latest version of the XSLT 2.0 specification is located at `http://www.w3.org/tr/xslt20/`.**

Some of the main features of XSLT 2.0 will include the following:

- **New data model**—The data model for XSLT 2.0 is the same data model that is used for XPath 2.0 and for the XML Query Language, XQuery. XQuery is described in Chapter 9.
- **W3C XML Schema data types**—W3X XML Schema data types replace the data types used in XPath 1.0 and in XSLT 1.0.
- **New elements**—Several new elements are added in XSLT 2.0, including elements that help with grouping tasks, which are difficult to accomplish in XSLT 1.0.
- **New functions**—XSLT 2.0 uses the additional functions that form part of XPath 2.0. This provides a much bigger function library than is available, as standard, in XSLT 1.0.

XSLT 2.0 provides a significantly more powerful language than XSLT 1.0. As well as the changes listed previously, it allows dates to be stored as dates, rather than as strings, which adds convenience when handling documents that include many dates, particularly if those dates are expressed in formats used in different countries. The downside of XSLT 2.0 is that it is significantly more complex than XSLT 1.0 for users unfamiliar with the W3C XML Schema data types.

Summary

In this chapter, we learned that XML documents can be restructured for data interchange or transformed for presentation using XSLT. An XSLT transformation changes a source tree into a result tree. We saw how an XSLT stylesheet is created and how elements are available to retrieve values from a source tree, copy nodes from the source tree to the result tree, carry out conditional processing, iterate over nodes, and sort nodes.

Exercise Questions

Suggested solutions to these questions can be found in Appendix A.

Question 1

If you need to process a node in the source tree more than once but in different ways each time, what technique does XSLT provide to achieve this?

Question 2

What are the two XSLT elements that provide conditional processing? Describe how the functionality provided by these two elements differs.

Part IV: Databases

XQuery, the XML Query Language

Large amounts of information are now being stored as XML or can be made available as XML from relational and other databases with XML functionality. As the volume of XML-based information increases, the need for a query language to efficiently query and make use of that XML data is obvious. At the time of writing the W3C, the World Wide Web Consortium, is developing an XML query language called XQuery. This chapter will introduce you to using XQuery and walk you through several working examples using XQuery's features.

XQuery is, in my opinion, likely to become as important in the XML world as SQL has become in the relational database world. In the near future any self-respecting developer who uses XML will be expected to have at least a basic understanding of XQuery and the skill to use it to carry out frequently used queries. Those who work routinely with large volumes of XML data will be expected to have significant expertise in using XQuery as they create programmatic solutions to XML data handling business issues.

In this chapter you will learn:

- Why XQuery was created to complement languages such as SQL and XSLT
- How to get started with XQuery using the prototype XQuery tools which are already available
- How to query an XML document using XQuery and how to create new elements in the result using element constructors
- About the XQuery data model and how to use the different types of expression in XQuery, including the important FLWOR (for, let, where, order by, return) expressions
- How to use some XQuery functions
- What further developments are likely in future versions of XQuery including full text searching and update functionality

> **At the time of writing, the specification of XQuery is not yet finalized at the World Wide Web Consortium. However, much of the XQuery language is now stable. In light of XQuery's anticipated importance many examples of how to use XQuery syntax is included here. Most of what is described and demonstrated in this chapter is likely to continue to work unchanged in the final XQuery specification. However, it is possible that some components of XQuery syntax will change and you are advised to check the W3C website for the current status of XQuery and information about any late changes in the details of XQuery. General XQuery information is located at `http://www.w3.org/XML/Query`, including links to each of the several XQuery specification documents.**

Why XQuery?

First, let's briefly look at a few of the factors that led to the creation of XQuery at the W3C.

Historical Factors

The expansion in storage of data as XML and the different approaches to storing that XML data—in conventional relational databases which are XML-enabled, in native XML databases, and so on—meant that the ways to access XML data could potentially splinter, with no single language being accepted as *the* XML query language. This would mean that an important advantage of XML, that it can be processed using standard tools, would potentially be lost. The realization that several vendors and experts were working on the development of XML query languages resulted in an effort at the W3C to create a single, standard XML query language, which will be called XQuery.

When relational databases became a standard technology for enterprise and desktop databases, the advantages of having a common language for retrieving, inserting, deleting, or updating data in a relational data store were recognized and applied when the Structured Query Language (SQL) was created. Due, perhaps, to intercompany rivalry and the timescale of the development of the SQL standard compared to commercial need, significant differences in how individual relational products implemented SQL developed and still exist. Similar processes to develop distinct XML-targeted query languages were underway but have, in the end, been brought together to support the development of XQuery at the W3C.

Despite these efforts at cooperation, XQuery may still be at risk of suffering partial splintering into proprietary approaches, in part because XQuery 1.0 won't have all the necessary functionality that is needed in an XML query language for an enterprise data handling system. XQuery 1.0 will be able to query XML data, but will have no functionality to delete, update, or insert XML data. The XQuery working group is, of course, well aware of those additional needs but took a pragmatic decision that it is better to get the most commonly used part of an XML query language—the capacity to retrieve data—finished as a W3C Recommendation in a reasonable time frame, rather than attempt to do everything in XQuery 1.0 but risk the timelines slipping out substantially. The data model which is used by XQuery has been designed with the future needs for deletion, updating, and inserting in mind, so hopefully once development of the XQuery 1.0 specification is complete, users of XQuery shouldn't have to wait too long for an update with the additional functionality just mentioned.

Technical Factors

The technical factors for XQuery can be split into several components, some of which are briefly described here.

Storing the huge volumes of business data that are around today as lengthy sequences of Unicode characters as serialized XML documents is potentially a very inefficient way to store that data, and retrieval would be difficult, too. So, under the hood, the data that can be made available as XML is likely to be stored in some binary format, whether in an enterprise relational database management system or in a native XML database.

> **Databases that can store or emit XML data are discussed in Chapter 10.**

XQuery is designed primarily around a data model that has the property of being able to be serialized as XML. So when developing a query language for XML, significant effort was focused on defining a data model appropriate for use in large data stores.

XML data, like any other data which is stored in large quantity and which typically is at least partially confidential, requires many of the features already available in relational database management systems. For example, indexing of XML data is needed to enable speedy retrieval of XML. Security capabilities are also essential in any real-life scenario.

Current Status

At the time of writing, the XQuery specifications are still at Working Draft status at the W3C. However, some of those specifications are Last Call Working Drafts, meaning that the working group thinks that the XQuery specification is close to being completed. It also means that enough of XQuery is stable, that we have several prototype implementations that we can use to explore the XQuery language. It is likely that the XQuery specification will be completed and published as a W3C Recommendation some months after this book is published.

Developing XQuery, XSLT 2.0, and XPath 2.0

This section briefly describes why XQuery, XPath 2.0, and XSLT 2.0 have been developed in the ways that they have at the W3C. In addition, similarities and differences are briefly described.

Work on XSLT 1.0 and on the predecessor prototypes for XQuery started as separate processes. The background of XSLT, and of XPath, is in document processing. The historical background of XQuery is in querying databases. Of course, XML can express both documents and data, a notion often expressed by referring to document-centric XML and data-centric XML. At the time that the various efforts started, the extent of the potential for common ground in querying document-centric XML and data-centric XML was very likely not fully appreciated.

In the XSLT 1.0 specification it was specifically stated that XSLT was not intended as a general-purpose transformation language. So several potentially useful features were not included in XSLT 1.0, and XSLT was targeted primarily at producing result documents for human consumption. So it was reasonable that that XSLT processing should attempt to produce some output, rather than failing completely if a source document wasn't structured quite as expected. Since at that time it was often assumed that XSLT processing would be carried out on the client side, it was rightly assumed that it was inappropriate to deliver some error message to an end-user who had no control over the stylesheet producing the error.

Because of the refusal to attempt a general-purpose transformation language, some potentially useful functionality such as strong math support and text manipulation did not feature in XSLT 1.0. Developers of XSLT might also plausibly have been assumed to be working with XML, to be using XML tools, and so would be comfortable using a language expressed in XML. Therefore, a language expressed in XML made a lot of sense.

The background to the need for XQuery differed significantly. XQuery was intended for retrieval of data from large collections of XML documents, in contrast to the common scenario where XSLT is used to process a single source XML document or a small number of XML documents. Unlike source documents to be processed by XSLT, the XML to be processed by XQuery would be unlikely to be held in memory at one time; single documents or collections of documents would be simply too large to allow a *Document Object Model* (DOM) tree to be constructed in memory. The large size of XML documents to be queried increased the importance of optimizing queries, including indexing of the XML to be queried. Potential users of XQuery would likely come from a database background where they would expect document structure to be defined by a schema, in contrast to the pretty permissive approach that can be accepted when using XSLT to process document-centric XML. Error handling would appropriately be rigorous in the context of a large datastore and so error handling is much stricter in XQuery than it was in XSLT 1.0.

As you can probably appreciate, despite the differences that I have highlighted, there is considerable overlap in what the two, initially separate communities wanted to do with XML using XSLT and XQuery, respectively. Both XSLT and XQuery have XML as input and create a result that takes nodes from the source XML tree(s) and combines and filters the source and often adds arbitrary literal content (supplied either statically or dynamically) to the result. Both XSLT and XQuery provide a library of functions (much more extensive in XSLT 2.0 than XSLT 1.0) and allow the creation of user-defined functions. Both languages allow nested iteration—using the `xsl:for-each` element in XSLT and the FLWOR expression (described later in this chapter) in XQuery. Both XSLT and XQuery take a similar approach to variables, in that the value of variables may not be changed once the variable is created, a characteristic that many newcomers to XSLT find surprising. Both XSLT and XQuery are declarative functional languages without a full assignment statement, although XQuery does have a limited assignment-like `let` clause available.

Given a different history, it is quite possible that only one XML query language rather than two would have been developed at the W3C. Even if that had been the case, sufficient flexibility to accommodate the differing emphases that I have briefly described would likely have been necessary.

Using XSLT 1.0 and XQuery

XSLT 1.0 is probably used most for converting XML documents to HTML (and to a lesser extent XHTML) for display. XSLT 1.0 is also used to create other XML-based presentation formats such as Scalable Vector Graphics (SVG), which is described in Chapter 18, and PDF files (using as intermediary the other part of XSL, XSL Formatting Objects). The final part of XSLT 1.0 usage is in the conversion of one XML document structure to another XML document structure in business-to-business (B2B) transactions. It seems likely that the latter usage will continue to increase significantly.

XQuery, on the other hand, will likely be used more in querying databases, a task that can be accomplished using XSLT (at least where the data is exposed as XML) but may most appropriately be carried out using XQuery. The practical needs associated with use of XQuery mean that it is likely to be used generally either in an enterprise-level database management system or programmatically using C#,

Java, or similar programming language. The absence of XML syntax in XQuery makes it easier to use XQuery with other programming languages. An XML-based alternative syntax for XQuery, named XQueryX, is under development but it is very verbose and initial uptake looks likely to be slow.

Comparing XSLT, XPath, and XQuery

XSLT is written using XML syntax. By contrast, XQuery uses a non-XML syntax. The fact that XSLT stylesheets are written in XML means that XSLT stylesheets can be generated by or modified by XML tools including other XSLT stylesheets. Such use of XSLT is not rare in large-scale usage. XQuery cannot be sculpted using such tools, because it uses a non-XML syntax.

Both XSLT and XQuery can be used to add nodes to a result tree. XSLT requires XPath to work at all. The roles of the two languages can be broadly summarized as follows: XPath selects nodes from a source tree (which models an XML document), and XSLT causes nodes to be added to a result tree. Similarly, much of XQuery depends on its XPath 2.0 subset.

Despite the differences between XQuery and XSLT syntax, you also have similarities. In XSLT the value of some attributes is an *attribute value template,* which is an expression enclosed in paired curly brackets. This resembles the syntax used in XQuery for expressions. So the following code:

```
<a href="{@URL}">Click for further information</a>
```

can be written in both XSLT and XQuery. The paired curly brackets are used in XSLT to indicate an attribute value template. In XQuery paired curly brackets enclose an XQuery expression. In XQuery it is possible to nest expressions, which, given the XML syntax limitations of XSLT, is not possible in XSLT.

XPath 1.0 has been adapted in version 2.0 to form a subset of XQuery 1.0. The use of XPath 2.0 to select nodes in XQuery is not surprising, because XQuery needs to carry out similar retrieval of specified XML data. You will see in a moment that you can use XPath expressions in XQuery to retrieve nodes. In XQuery the retrieved nodes (and values, if present, that are also allowed) are called a *sequence,* rather than the XPath 1.0 term, node-set.

XQuery Tools

Despite the fact that XQuery is not yet completed as a W3C specification, a large number of software companies and independent developers have developed partial or more complete implementations of XQuery. That proliferation of XQuery tools is an indication of the fact that many software vendors see XQuery as an important XML standard with significant commercial potential.

> **The W3C updates on an ongoing basis a web page where links to XQuery implementations and other sources of useful XQuery information are mentioned. Visit `http://www.w3.org/XML/Query` and follow the link to Products to explore XQuery implementations.**

Because, at the time of writing, XQuery has not been finalized, none of the prototype XQuery tools can yet be finalized. Tools are being updated on different schedules with some prototypes now being visibly outdated (at least in publicly available versions) compared to the most recent XQuery draft specification documents.

To run examples in this chapter, we will use the Saxon processor, which is free and is a very up-to-date implementation of both XSLT and XQuery. The creator of Saxon is a member of the working groups that are creating XQuery, XPath 2.0, and XSLT 2.0. Therefore, Saxon is typically among the most up-to-date implementations, although at the time of writing not all aspects of the XQuery language had been implemented.

Saxon

If you chose to download Saxon version 7.*x* in Chapter 8, then you are in good shape to use Saxon to process XQuery queries. If not, then to use Saxon to process XQuery queries, visit `http://saxon.sourceforge.net/` again and look for the currently available versions of Saxon that support XQuery. Versions after Saxon 7.6 have some XQuery support. At the time of writing, Saxon 7.8 is the latest version and it includes a substantial amount of XQuery functionality. If there is a later version available at the time you visit the site it is likely to have more up-to-date and complete XQuery functionality. However, sometimes experimental versions of Saxon are offered for download, so carefully read the descriptions of the available versions to check which is suitable for your needs.

First, if necessary, install the Saxon processor, following the instructions given in Chapter 8.

To test if Saxon XQuery functionality is present, type the following at the command line:

```
java net.sf.saxon.Query
```

and if everything is working correctly, you should receive an error message as shown in Figure 9-1 indicating that no source file name was specified.

```
Command Prompt
C:\BXML\Ch09>java net.sf.saxon.Query
No source file name
SAXON 7.8 from Michael Kay
Usage:  java net.sf.saxon.Query [options] style-doc {param=value}...
Options:
  -ds               Use standard tree data structure
  -dt               Use tinytree data structure (default)
  -e                Explain optimized query expression
  -noext            Disallow calls to Java methods
  -o filename       Send output to named file
  -r classname      Use specified URIResolver class
  -strip            Strip whitespace text nodes
  -t                Display version and timing information
  -T                Trace query execution
  -TJ               Trace calls to external Java functions
  -u                Names are URLs not filenames
  -wrap             Wraps result sequence in XML elements
  -?                Display this message
  param=value       Set stylesheet string parameter
  +param=value      Set stylesheet document parameter
  !option=value     Set serialization option

C:\BXML\Ch09>_
```

Figure 9-1

Remember that Java is case-sensitive and a mistaken uppercase or lowercase character entered at the command line will likely lead to an error message when `java.exe` runs.

If you used Saxon in Chapter 8 to carry out XSLT transformations, you will notice that the command-line syntax to access Saxon's XQuery functionality is significantly different from the syntax used when using XSLT.

Saxon comes with extensive help files. Typically, installation of Saxon creates a `doc` directory, which includes several HTML help files. Look for a file labeled `using-xquery.html`, or similar, and check the latest information about which parts of XQuery are supported.

Several other online XQuery demos are available, and several other products or prototypes support XQuery. Some are mentioned in the following sections.

X-Hive.com Online

You can find a very user-friendly XQuery demonstration online at `http://www.x-hive.com/xquery/`. An example query and its result are shown in Figure 9-2. You can use one of the pre-built queries that were used in the XQuery use cases document or edit them to test out your increasing understanding of XQuery, and the results or, if you get things wrong, lengthy Java error messages are displayed in the right panel. If you get the syntax hopelessly wrong as you try to adapt existing queries, then you can restore a query with correct syntax simply by re-selecting it from a drop-down list.

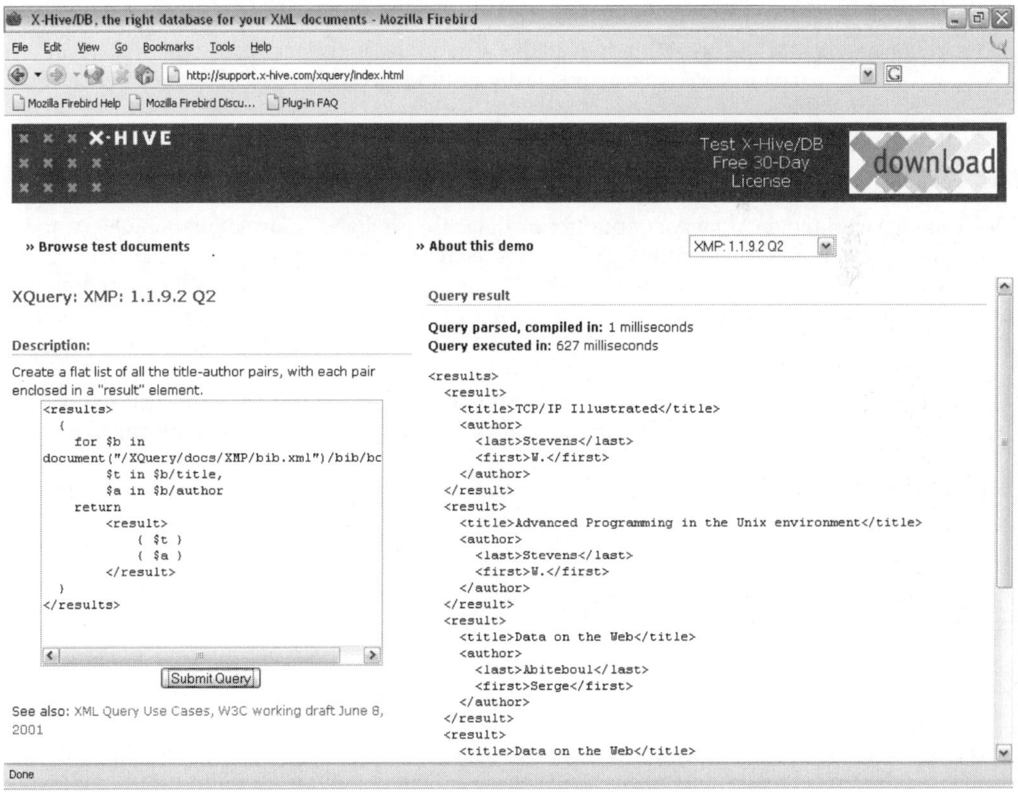

Figure 9-2

At the time of writing, the X-Hive online demo had not been updated for some time and some minor differences existed between the syntax it uses and the latest XQuery draft. Nonetheless, it gives a very nice interactive interface to explore the creation of XQuery queries.

X-Hive Database

The X-Hive database that underpins the X-Hive.com database also supports XQuery. Further information is located at `http://www.x-hive.com`.

Tamino Database

You can find an online demo of XQuery using Software AG's Tamino database located at `http://tamino.demozone.softwareag.com/demoXQuery/XQueryDemo/index.jsp`.

Microsoft SQL Server 2005

Microsoft's enterprise relational database management system, SQL Server, will include XQuery support in the version likely to be released during 2005. At present this version is in beta and has the codename "Yukon." By visiting the web pages at `http://www.microsoft.com/sql/yukon` and `http://msdn.microsoft.com/xml/`, you will likely find a considerable amount of information about Yukon and its XML support. If you read this around the suggested likely release date, information about SQL Server Yukon will likely be accessible by visiting `http://www.microsoft.com/sql/`.

Oracle

Oracle is also working on XQuery support for its database products. Information on XQuery and a technology preview available for the Oracle database are accessible from `http://otn.oracle.com/sample_code/tech/xml/xmldb/xmldb_xquerydownload.html`. If the preceding URL is not available when you are reading this chapter, then visiting `http://otn.oracle.com/` and inserting XQuery in the Search text box is likely to find the current information about XQuery in Oracle.

The implementations mentioned in the preceding sections are only a few of many. Visit `http://www.w3.org/XML/Query` to check for further implementations and for links to current information about them.

Let's now move on to run some simple XQuery examples, so that you begin to have a feel for what XQuery queries look like.

Some XQuery Examples

Saxon can run XQuery queries from Java applications. However, for the purposes of this chapter we will run queries from the command line.

One difference between the Saxon syntax for XSLT processing and for XQuery processing is that the location of the XML document to be queried is not specified on the command line. Rather, it is specified using one of XQuery's input functions.

Input Functions

At the time of writing, the XQuery input functions are the `doc()` function and the `collection()` function and both are implemented in Saxon 7.8.

The doc() Function

The `doc()` function is used to specify the XML document that we want to query. To demonstrate basic XQuery functionality we will query the following simple XML document, `SimpleBooks.xml`. It is used here and later in the chapter as a source XML document.

```
<?xml version='1.0'?>
<Books>
 <Book>Beginning XML, 3rd Edition</Book>
 <Book>Beginning Red Hat Linux 9</Book>
 <Book>Professional XML Development with Apache Tools</Book>
</Books>
```

For convenience, we will specify XQuery queries in documents with a `.xquery` suffix, but you can use another suffix if you prefer. Using Saxon from the command line, you simply specify the filename that contains the XQuery query.

The first query we will run is contained in the file `SimpleBooks.xquery`, and contains the following one line of code:

```
doc("SimpleBooks.xml")/Books/Book
```

The query consists of the `doc()` function, whose single string argument specifies that the XML document `SimpleBooks.xml` is to be used as the source document for the query. The remaining part of the query should remind you of XPath location paths that you were introduced to in Chapter 7, since that is exactly what they are. Remember, I said earlier that XPath 2.0 is a subset of XQuery. The expression `/Books/Book` is an XQuery expression that could also be an XPath 2.0 expression—the syntax and semantics is the same in both XQuery and XPath 2.0. This means that you can apply your understanding of XPath 1.0, gained in Chapter 7, to some parts of XQuery syntax.

The expression is evaluated from left to right. The initial `/` character indicates that evaluation starts at the document node of `SimpleBooks.xml`, that a `Books` element node (there can be only one element node child of the document node in a well-formed XML document) that is a child node of the document node is selected, and then using that node as context, its `Book` child element node(s) are selected.

> **The XQuery `doc()` function is similar to the XSLT `document()` function. The `doc()` function returns a single document. The `document()` function processes a sequence of URIs allowing multiple XML documents to be processed.**

To have Saxon run the query and display the output to the command window, you enter:

```
java net.sf.saxon.Query SimpleBooks.xquery
```

at the command line. The filename `SimpleBooks.xquery` is supplied to the Saxon XQuery processor. The output of the query is shown in Figure 9-3.

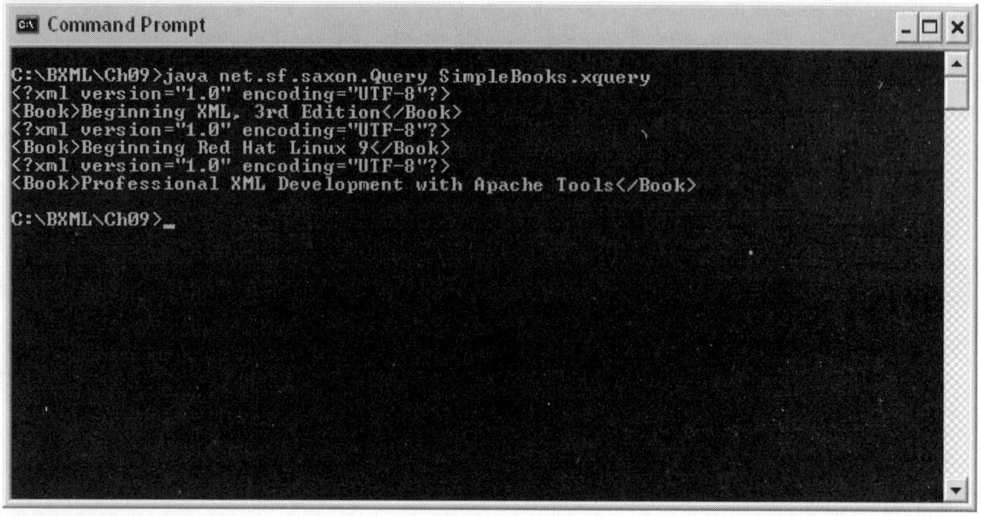

```
Command Prompt
C:\BXML\Ch09>java net.sf.saxon.Query SimpleBooks.xquery
<?xml version="1.0" encoding="UTF-8"?>
<Book>Beginning XML, 3rd Edition</Book>
<?xml version="1.0" encoding="UTF-8"?>
<Book>Beginning Red Hat Linux 9</Book>
<?xml version="1.0" encoding="UTF-8"?>
<Book>Professional XML Development with Apache Tools</Book>

C:\BXML\Ch09>_
```

Figure 9-3

Notice that there are three XML declarations output to the command window, each of which is followed by a `Book` element and its text content. The reason for that behavior is that all XQuery queries return a *sequence* of *items*. Each `Book` element node selected by the XPath expression `/Books/Book` is in the sequence returned by the query. Saxon's default behavior is to output each item in the sequence with its own XML declaration, a behavior that we often will not want. We will look at how to take control of that in a moment.

The collection() Function

The `collection()` function is used to process several XML documents at a time. The `collection()` function takes as its argument a string that is an `xsd:anyURI` value. The `collection()` function can be used to access a collection of nodes in a database, for example.

Because we are primarily using individual XML documents as the target of queries in this chapter, we will focus on the use of the `doc()` function.

Retrieving Nodes

As you have seen, in XQuery we can retrieve nodes in a fairly straightforward way using XPath expressions.

However, XQuery 1.0 has a few limitations when compared to XPath. All XQuery processors lack the XPath `namespace` axis. In addition, some XQuery processors lack support for the following XPath axes:

- `ancestor`
- `ancestor-or-self`
- `following`

- `following-sibling`
- `preceding`
- `preceding-sibling`

XQuery implementations that support the preceding axes are said to support the *full axis feature*, but even those XQuery processors are not "full" in a certain sense, because the `namespace` axis is not supported. The decision in XQuery, at least as currently drafted, to drop these axes seems to have arisen from a difference in view between those familiar with XPath and those who think more in terms of relational databases. In any case, unless later drafts change the situation, it will be necessary to accept the absence of the axes mentioned in some XQuery processors and code accordingly.

Try It Out — Retrieving Nodes

1. Let's carry out some more queries using a source XML document adapted from the W3C's use case sample data. It is shown here and contained in the file `BibAdapted.xml`. Note that this data will be used as the source XML in several example queries.

```
<?xml version='1.0'?>
<bib>
 <book year="1994">
  <title>TCP/IP Illustrated</title>
  <author><last>Stevens</last><first>W.</first></author>
  <publisher>Addison-Wesley</publisher>
  <price> 65.95</price>
 </book>

 <book year="1992">
  <title>Advanced Programming in the Unix environment</title>
  <author><last>Stevens</last><first>W.</first></author>
  <publisher>Addison-Wesley</publisher>
  <price>65.95</price>
 </book>

 <book year="2000">
  <title>Data on the Web</title>
  <author><last>Abiteboul</last><first>Serge</first></author>
  <author><last>Buneman</last><first>Peter</first></author>
  <author><last>Suciu</last><first>Dan</first></author>
  <publisher>Morgan Kaufmann Publishers</publisher>
  <price>39.95</price>
 </book>

 <book year="1999">
  <title>The Economics of Technology and Content for Digital TV</title>
  <editor>
   <last>Gerbarg</last><first>Darcy</first>
   <affiliation>CITI</affiliation>
  </editor>
  <publisher>Kluwer Academic Publishers</publisher>
  <price>129.95</price>
 </book>
```

```
  <book year="2004">
   <title>Beginning XML, 3rd Edition</title>
   <author><last>Hunter</last><first>David</first></author>
   <author><last>Watt</last><first>Andrew</first></author>
   <author><last>Rafter</last><first>Jeff</first></author>
   <author><last>Cagle</last><first></first>Kurt</author>
   <author><last>Duckett</last><first>John</first></author>
   <publisher>Wrox Press</publisher>
   <price>TBA</price>
  </book>

</bib>
```

As you can see the document element is a `bib` element, inside which are nested several `book` elements, each of which has some basic data such as year of publication and authors or editors.

2. Let's select all book elements in `BibAdapted.xml` using the following query, which is contained in the file `BibQuery1.xquery`:

```
doc("BibAdapted.xml")/bib/book
```

3. We will send the result of the query to an output file `BibQuery1Out.xml`, by typing the following at the command line:

```
java net.sf.saxon.Query -o BibQuery1Out.xml BibQuery1.xquery
```

4. Notice that the name of the output file is specified by the `-o` switch followed by the output filename, before the name of the file that contains the XQuery query. Part of that result document is shown here (it was snipped to reduce on page length, only two of the five `book` elements are shown):

```
<?xml version="1.0" encoding="UTF-8"?>
<book year="1994">

   <title>TCP/IP Illustrated</title>

   <author>
      <last>Stevens</last>
      <first>W.</first>
   </author>

   <publisher>Addison-Wesley</publisher>

   <price> 65.95</price>
 </book>

<?xml version="1.0" encoding="UTF-8"?>
<book year="1992">

   <!-- THERE IS A BIG SNIP HERE -->

<?xml version="1.0" encoding="UTF-8"?>
<book year="2004">
```

```
    <title>Beginning XML, 3rd Edition</title>
    <author>
      <last>Hunter</last>
      <first>David</first>
    </author>

    <author>
      <last>Watt</last>
      <first>Andrew</first>
    </author>

    <author>
      <last>Rafter</last>
      <first>Jeff</first>
    </author>

    <author>
      <last>Cagle</last>
      <first/>Kurt</author>

    <author>
      <last>Duckett</last>
      <first>John</first>
    </author>

    <publisher>Wrox Press</publisher>

    <price>TBA</price>
  </book>
```

How It Works

One important thing to observe here is that XQuery can output a document that is not well-formed XML. Notice you have three XML declarations in the snipped output document (there are others in the unsnipped version) and no single document element in the file called `BibQuery1.xml`.

This contrasts with XSLT, which assuming you use the `xml` output method, will not let you create a stylesheet to output markup that is not well-formed. In XQuery the responsibility of producing well-formed XML lies very much with the creator of the query.

Creating a well-formed result in this case is straightforward. We simply add an element constructor to the query and ensure that the XQuery expression is nested inside it. So let's introduce element constructors and look at how they are used.

Element Constructors

In XSLT 1.0 new elements can be added to the result document using *literal result elements*. In XQuery we can similarly create new XML elements by including literal start tags and end tags in appropriate places in the XQuery query.

A very simple example of using an element constructor is the following query, which is contained in the file `SimpleBooks2.xquery`:

```
<Books>
{doc("SimpleBooks.xml")/Books/Book}
</Books>
```

The element constructor has a literal start tag for a `Books` element, followed by the expression we saw earlier that retrieves `Book` element nodes from the file `SimpleBooks.xml`. Then, once all the selected `Book` element nodes have been found, it adds a literal end tag for the `Books` element.

To display the output to the command window, we can enter the following at the command line:

```
java net.sf.saxon.Query -o SimpleBooks2Out.xml SimpleBooks2.xquery
```

The output file, `SimpleBooks2Out.xml`, is shown here:

```
<?xml version="1.0" encoding="UTF-8"?>
<Books>
   <Book>Beginning XML, 3rd Edition</Book>
   <Book>Beginning Red Hat Linux 9</Book>
   <Book>Professional XML Development with Apache Tools</Book>
</Books>
```

Notice that in the preceding query the XQuery expression `doc("SimpleBooks.xml")/Books/Book` is contained inside paired curly brackets. If you omit the paired curly brackets, then the XPath expression will be treated just as text. The XPath expression is displayed literally, and the carriage return is shown as a character reference `
`. The output document when you make that error is `SimpleBooks2WRONGOut.xml`, shown here:

```
<?xml version="1.0" encoding="UTF-8"?>
<Books>&#xD;
doc("SimpleBooks.xml")/Books/Book&#xD;
</Books>
```

We can create well-formed XML from the `BibAdapted.xml` file using the following query:

```
<myNewBib>{
doc("BibAdapted.xml")/bib/book
}</myNewBib>
```

that is contained in the file `BibQuery2.xquery`. The query creates the start tag for a new element named `myNewBib`, then uses an XQuery expression similar to those you have used before to select all the `book` elements, and then outputs the end tag of the newly created `myNewBib` element.

The output document, `BibQuery2Out.xml` (a little snipped for presentation) is shown here:

```
<?xml version="1.0" encoding="UTF-8"?>
<myNewBib>
   <book year="1994">

      <title>TCP/IP Illustrated</title>

      <author>
         <last>Stevens</last>
         <first>W.</first>
```

```
      </author>

      <publisher>Addison-Wesley</publisher>

      <price> 65.95</price>

   </book>
   <book year="1992">

      <title>Advanced Programming in the Unix environment</title>

      <author>
         <last>Stevens</last>
         <first>W.</first>
      </author>

      <publisher>Addison-Wesley</publisher>

      <price>65.95</price>

   </book>
  <!-- AGAIN A BIG SNIP HERE -->
   <book year="2004">

      <title>Beginning XML, 3rd Edition</title>

      <author>
         <last>Hunter</last>
         <first>David</first>
      </author>

      <author>
         <last>Watt</last>
         <first>Andrew</first>
      </author>

      <author>
         <last>Rafter</last>
         <first>Jeff</first>
      </author>

      <author>
         <last>Cagle</last>
         <first/>Kurt</author>

      <author>
         <last>Duckett</last>
         <first>John</first>
      </author>

      <publisher>Wrox Press</publisher>

      <price>TBA</price>

   </book>
</myNewBib>
```

Up to this point we have used simple XPath expressions to output content based only on the structure of the source XML. In practice we will want to manipulate or filter that XML in various ways. One option is simply to filter using an XPath predicate.

We can use XPath predicates in an XQuery query, as in the following code:

```
<myNewBib>{
doc("BibAdapted.xml")/bib/book[@year>2002]
}</myNewBib>
```

which is contained in the file `BibQuery3.xquery`. The predicate `[@year>2002]` tests if the value of the `year` attribute of a `book` element in `BibAdapted.xml` is greater than `2002`, and if it is, then that `book` element is selected and it together with its content is output.

That query filters out all but one book in `BidAdapted.xml`, and the output it produces, in `BibQuery3Out.xml`, is shown here:

```
<?xml version="1.0" encoding="UTF-8"?>
<myNewBib>
   <book year="2004">

      <title>Beginning XML, 3rd Edition</title>

      <author>
         <last>Hunter</last>
         <first>David</first>
      </author>

      <author>
         <last>Watt</last>
         <first>Andrew</first>
      </author>

      <author>
         <last>Rafter</last>
         <first>Jeff</first>
      </author>

      <author>
         <last>Cagle</last>
         <first/>Kurt</author>

      <author>
         <last>Duckett</last>
         <first>John</first>
      </author>

      <publisher>Wrox Press</publisher>

      <price>TBA</price>

   </book>
</myNewBib>
```

As you can see, even a very simple answer like this takes up quite a bit of space. How do we get control of whitespace? That is done in the *prolog* of an XQuery query, which we will consider next.

The XQuery Prolog

The prolog of an XQuery document is used to provide the XQuery processor with pieces of information that might be necessary for correct processing of a query. The prolog is written before the main part of an XQuery query.

Strictly speaking, the version declaration and module declaration come before the prolog proper. But I would expect most developers to treat them as effectively part of the prolog. The important thing to remember is the following order:

- The version declaration, if present, must always come first
- Next is the module declaration (if there is one)
- Then comes the rest of the prolog

The XQuery Version Declaration

First, you might want to specify the version of XQuery being used. It is optional, but if it is present, it must come first. At the time of writing that is a little redundant because only a single version—version 1.0—exists. But once a version of XQuery with update and other functionality is added, then it is likely that other XQuery versions will also be available.

To specify that the query is XQuery 1.0 use the following code:

```
xquery version "1.0";
```

Notice the `xquery` keyword (all lowercase), followed by `version`, and then the version number as a string contained in paired quotes or paired apostrophes. The declaration is completed by a semicolon character. Notice that unlike XML, there is no = character between `version` and the version number. If you are used to writing XML code, it's an easy mistake to make.

XQuery Modules

XQuery queries may be made up of one or more modules. The examples in this chapter consist of a single module. However, reuse of XQuery code is likely to be common in the construction of complex queries.

The prolog of an XQuery module contains the following declaration:

```
module namespace XMML = "http://www.XMML.com/XQueryModule/";
```

The `module` declaration identifies the module as a library module. In the preceding declaration the namespace prefix `XMML` is associated with the Uniform Resource Identifier (URI) `http://www.XMML.com/XQueryModule/`. An XQuery module declaration is similar to an XML namespace declaration in that a namespace prefix is associated with a namespace URI.

In a library module, as in stand-alone XQuery documents, the version declaration, if present, comes first, and then the module declaration precedes the rest of the prolog.

Having looked at the version declaration and module declaration, let's move on to look at the other parts of the prolog. These can be written in any convenient order.

The base-uri Declaration

URIs can be relative or absolute. Relative URIs are resolved in relation to a base URI. The `base-uri` is declared in XQuery using the `base-uri` declaration similar to the following:

```
declare base-uri "http://someRelevantURI.com";
```

The namespace Declaration

Also included in the prolog are the relevant namespace declarations. In an XQuery that is, for example, creating output that includes elements that are namespace-qualified, it is necessary to declare the namespace to which those elements belong. Like an XML namespace declaration, an XQuery namespace declaration associates a namespace prefix with a namespace URI. If you intended to use XQuery to create an XSLT stylesheet you might include a namespace declaration like this:

```
declare namespace xsl = "http://www.w3.org/1999/XSL/Transform"
```

And later, in the body of the query, you might see:

```
<xsl:stylesheet version = "1.0" xmlns:xsl="http://www.w3.org/1999/XSL/Transform">
```

indicating the start of an XSLT 1.0 stylesheet.

Default namespace Declarations

Any default namespace declarations are also included in the prolog. For reasons of convenience you may want to write element or function names without a namespace prefix. This is done using the default namespace declarations.

To declare a default namespace for elements you use the following syntax:

```
declare default element namespace "http://someRelevantURI.com"
```

To declare a default namespace for functions use the following syntax:

```
declare default function namespace "http://someRelevantURI.com"
```

Schema Imports

You may want to have access to element, attribute, or type definitions from a particular schema and this, too, is expressed in the prolog. This schema can be imported using the following syntax:

```
import schema namespace xhtml = "http://www.w3.org/1999/xhtml"
```

to import the schema for an XHTML document. If you want to specify a URL at which the schema is located you can use a schema import of the following type:

```
import schema namespace xhtml = "http://www.w3.org/1999/xhtml"
at "http://ActualSchemaLocation.com/xhtml.xsd"
```

which specifies a URL from which the schema can be accessed.

Variable Declarations

You may want to declare XQuery variables. If so, that too is done in the prolog. To declare a variable `$seven` and specify that its value is the integer 7 you can use the following syntax:

```
declare variable $seven as xsd:integer {7};
```

assuming that you had a namespace declaration associating the namespace prefix `xsd` with the namespace URI for the W3C XML Schema.

Validation Declaration

Also in the prolog, you may wish to specify how validation is to be carried out. Permitted values are `lax`, `skip`, or `strict`. To specify strict validation you can write a validation declaration like this:

```
declare validation strict;
```

The xmlspace Declaration

One of the prolog's declarations indicates whether to strip or preserve whitespace, as shown in the following query, `BibQuery4.xquery`:

```
xquery version "1.0";
declare xmlspace = strip;
(: The above line is the XQuery way to strip whitespace :)
<myNewBib>{
doc("BibAdapted.xml")/bib/book[@year>2002]
}</myNewBib>
```

Whitespace in XQuery is handled a little differently from whitespace in XML. In XQuery the concept of *boundary whitespace* indicates whitespace that occurs at the boundaries of elements (before the start tag or after the end tag) or expressions. Such boundary whitespace can be useful in laying out complex queries neatly. If you want to strip extraneous boundary whitespace, you can use the construct shown in the second line of the preceding code.

At the time of this writing, Saxon seems to ignore the declaration to strip boundary whitespace using the syntax just shown.

If you wish explicitly to specify that boundary whitespace is preserved, use the following construct:

```
declare xmlspace = preserve;
```

You saw earlier how to use element constructors to add XML elements literally to the output of a query. Now let's look at how to create computed constructors.

Computed Constructors

In earlier examples we saw how literal start and end tags can be used to construct elements in the result of a query. Another syntax allows elements and attributes to be constructed at runtime.

Let's create a simple library using element and attribute constructors. For clarity we will use string literals to provide the values of the created attributes and elements. Of course, you can substitute any arbitrary XQuery expression in place of the string literals to achieve similar but more complex things. The query, `Library.xquery`, is shown here:

```
element library{

 element book {
  attribute year {2004},
  element title {
   "Beginning XML, 3rd Edition"
   }
  },

 element book {
  attribute year {2003},
  element title {
   "Beginning Red Hat Linux 9"
   }
  },

 element book {
  attribute year {2003},
  element title {
   "Beginning ASP.NET 1.1 with VB.NET 2003"
   }
 }

}
```

The `library` element, which is the document element of the output XML document, is created using the following construct:

```
element library {
 ...
}
```

All attributes and descendants are created inside that construct.

When creating a single child element of the `library` element, the `book` element, a similar syntax is followed:

```
element book {
 attribute year {2004},
 element title {
  "Beginning XML, 3rd Edition"
  }
 }
```

Any attributes that belong to the `book` element are specified first, using a comma as the separator between attribute specifications. Then any child elements of the `book` element are added in the order in which they are to be included in the output document.

If you have a sequence of elements that have to be constructed, a comma is added after the relevant closing curly bracket.

The output document, `LibraryOut.xml`, is shown here:

```
<?xml version="1.0" encoding="UTF-8"?>
<library>
   <book year="2004">
      <title>Beginning XML, 3rd Edition</title>
   </book>
   <book year="2003">
      <title>Beginning Red Hat Linux 9</title>
   </book>
   <book year="2003">
      <title>Beginning ASP.NET 1.1 with VB.NET 2003</title>
   </book>
</library>
```

When creating queries of this type, once you get beyond fairly simple queries, like the preceding one, it is very easy to make mistakes by failing to correctly pair up curly braces or to omit the crucial comma that separates attributes and child elements. If you make such basic mistakes in long queries, you can be subjected to a cascade of error messages due, for example, to omitting a single comma fairly early in the query. I find that the best way to avoid such errors is to create the elements and attributes from the outside in, pairing up curly brackets as I add an element or attribute.

Syntax

In the following two sections I will briefly introduce a couple of aspects of XQuery syntax of which you need to be aware when writing XQuery code.

XQuery Comments

In XQuery comments are written using scowly and smiley faces to start and end the comment, respectively:

```
(: After the scowl, we smile when the comment ends. :)
```

This notation is used only to define comments inside the query. Unlike HTML comments, for example, it is permissible to nest XQuery comments, which can be useful when using comments to comment out suspect code when debugging by hand.

No syntax to create a "to end of line" comment, equivalent to the `//` notation in JavaScript, for example, exists in XQuery.

Delimiting Strings

Strings in XQuery are delimited by paired double quotes or by paired apostrophes, as you saw in the example where we created elements and supplied their content as string literals. For example, a `Paragraph` element with text content can be written in either of the two following ways:

```
element Paragraph {
 "Some content contained in paired double quotes"
}
```

or

```
element Paragraph {
  'Some content contained in paired apostrophes.'
}
```

The XQuery Data Model

The XQuery data model is significantly different from the XPath 1.0 data model to which you were introduced in Chapter 7. But it also has similarities to the XPath 1.0 data model.

Shared Data Model with XPath 2.0 and XSLT 2.0

The XQuery data model and XPath 2.0 and XSLT 2.0 data models are the same. So, once you have learned the data model for one of these technologies you know the foundations of the other two. In Chapter 8 I mentioned that XSLT transformations use a source tree as input to a transformation. Similarly, all XQuery queries use an instance of the XQuery data model as input and another instance of the data model as output. Each of those instances of the data model is represented as a tree-like hierarchy broadly similar to an XSLT source tree.

Many parts of an XML document can be represented by nodes in the XQuery data model. Let's move on to look briefly at each of the node kinds available in XQuery.

Node Kinds

Node kinds in XQuery are similar to the types of node available in XPath 1.0. The one notable change is that the root node of XPath 1.0 is replaced by the document node in XQuery 1.0. The XQuery 1.0 node kinds are document, element, attribute, namespace, text, comment, and processing instruction. Each node represents the corresponding part of an XML document indicated by its name. Every XQuery node has identity that distinguishes it from all other nodes, including nodes with the same name and content.

Sequences cf Node-Sets

In XQuery the XPath 1.0 node-set is replaced by a sequence. A sequence can contain nodes or atomic values or a mixture of nodes and atomic values. The term *item* is the collective term in XQuery for nodes and atomic values. An atomic value corresponds to a W3C XML Schema simple-Type.

Sequences are written inside paired parentheses and items are separated by commas. Sequences cannot be nested, so the sequence:

```
(1,2, (3, 4, 5), 6)
```

is equivalent to writing:

```
(1, 2, 3, 4, 5, 6)
```

Document Order

In XQuery all nodes created when parsing an XML document are in an order, called document order. Attributes associated with an element are considered to occur after the element in document order and before any child elements.

Comparing Items and Nodes

The XQuery data model generalizes the idea of a node-set that was present in XPath 1.0. In XQuery the result of an expression is a *sequence*. A sequence can include nodes (just like XPath 1.0) but can also include atomic values.

Types in XQuery

In XQuery the W3C XML Schema type system is used. You were introduced to W3C XML Schema types in Chapter 5.

Axes in XQuery

As mentioned earlier in the chapter, XQuery processors do not support the XPath `namespace` axis. Only XQuery processors that support the full-axis feature support processing of the `ancestor`, `ancestor-or-self`, `following`, `following-sibling`, `preceding` or `preceding-sibling` axes. All XQuery processors support the `child`, `parent`, `descendant`, `descendant-or-self` axes.

XQuery Expressions

As mentioned earlier, XQuery expressions include XPath expressions, which tend to principally focus on path expressions. However, XQuery adds a rich feature set on top of the XPath functionality. The FLWOR expression adds significant power to queries which cannot be expressed by traditional XPath path expressions.

FLWOR Expressions

The FLWOR expression is a pivotal part of the power of XQuery. It owes much to the `SELECT` statement in SQL. A FLWOR expression binds variables to sequences of values in the `for` and `let` clauses and then uses those variables in the construction of the output of the query. Because binding is an essential part of a FLWOR expression, every FLWOR expression must have either a `for` clause or a `let` clause, but many FLWOR expressions will have both.

A FLWOR expression has the following components, not all of which occur in any one expression:

- `for`
- `let`
- `where`
- `order by`
- `return`

The first four components of FLWOR can be expressed in XSLT using, respectively, the `xsl:for-each`, `xsl:variable`, `xsl:if`, and `xsl:sort` elements to produce similar results. So many XQuery FLOWR expressions could be expressed in XSLT with very similar semantics.

> **Remember that XQuery is case sensitive. So use `for` (lowercase) not `FOR` (uppercase) and so on in FLWOR expressions, or you will get some puzzling error messages.**

If you make the error of using the wrong case for any of the keywords `for`, `let`, `where`, `order by`, and `return`, you can expect to get some very puzzling error messages from the Saxon XQuery processor, perhaps mentioning odd characters beyond the end of the query. If you, for example, use uppercase `FOR` instead of the correct lowercase `for`, then among the error messages you are likely to get is an indication that a variable is undeclared, since any variable declared in the `for` statement in which you mistakenly used uppercase `FOR` is not recognized as having been declared. If you see mention of an undeclared variable, it is worth checking the case of either `for` or `let` in your query, since `for` clauses bind multiple variables and `let` clauses bind single variables and a case error would lead the relevant variable or variables not being bound. However, other XQuery processors, or indeed later versions of Saxon, may give more informative error messages.

for Expressions

One version of the `for` expression is the `for ... in` expression, as shown in `ForIn.xquery`:

```
<items>
{for $i in (1,2,3,4)
return <item>{$i}</item>}
</items>
```

If we run the preceding query from the command line, the output in file `ForInOut.xml` is shown here:

```
<?xml version="1.0" encoding="UTF-8"?>
<items>
  <item>1</item>
  <item>2</item>
  <item>3</item>
  <item>4</item>
</items>
```

The query contains an element constructor that is a literal start tag of the enclosing `items` element in the output document. The `for` statement binds the items in the sequence `(1, 2, 3, 4)` to the variable `$i`. Because the `in` keyword is used in the `for` statement, each individual item in the sequence is, in turn, considered to be represented by `$i`, in much the same way as we could use an XPath expression to return a sequence of nodes (in XPath 1.0 a node-set of nodes).

The `return` statement specifies that for each item in `$i` an `item` start tag is created, an expression `$i` is evaluated and inserted as text, and a literal end tag for the `item` element is added. Once all possible values for the `$i` variable have been processed, the end tag for the `items` element is added.

It doesn't matter whether items are values or nodes, because both values and nodes are *items*, as the following example demonstrates. The source XML is `Products.xml`, shown here:

```
<?xml version='1.0'?>
<Products>
 <Product>Widget</Product>
 <Product>Gadget</Product>
 <Product>Knife</Product>
 <Product>Spoon</Product>
</Products>
```

The query, `ForIn2.xquery`, is shown here:

```
<items>
{for $i in (1,2, doc("Products.xml")/Products/Product/text(), 3, 4)
return <item>{$i}</item>}
</items>
```

Notice that between the first pair of items in the sequence in the `for` statement and the last pair of items in the sequence an XPath expression `doc("Products.xml)/Products/Product/text()` has been inserted. For each value in `$i`, whether it is a value or a text node selected by the XPath expression, the value of `$i` is inserted between the start and end tags of an `item` element.

The output document, `ForIn2Out.xml`, is shown here:

```
<?xml version="1.0" encoding="UTF-8"?>
<items>
    <item>1</item>
    <item>2</item>
    <item>Widget</item>
    <item>Gadget</item>
    <item>Knife</item>
    <item>Spoon</item>
    <item>3</item>
    <item>4</item>
</items>
```

Items supplied as literal values in the sequence in the `for` statement of the query and items selected by the XPath expression are treated the same.

The `for` statement also has a `for ... in ... to` option. So instead of writing:

```
for $i in (1,2,3,4,5)
```

we can write:

```
for $i in 1 to 5
```

So if we run `ForIn3.xquery`, as here:

```
<items>
{for $i in 1 to 5
return <item>{$i}</item>}
</items>
```

we produce the output in ForIn3Out.xml, shown here:

```
<?xml version="1.0" encoding="UTF-8"?>
<items>
   <item>1</item>
   <item>2</item>
   <item>3</item>
   <item>4</item>
   <item>5</item>
</items>
```

We can use this structure in combination with other literal values, as here in ForIn4.xquery:

```
<items>
{for $i in (1 to 5, 7, 8)
return <item>{$i}</item>}
</items>
```

with the second line being a convenient shorthand for:

```
{for $i in (1, 2, 3, 4, 5, 7, 8)
```

The output is in the code download in the file ForIn4Out.xml. An item element is created which contains a value contained in the input sequence.

It is also possible to nest for statements, as here in ForNested.xquery:

```
<items>
{for $i in (1 to 5, 7, 8) return
 <group>{ for $a in (1 to ($i - 2))
 return<item>{$a}</item>}
 </group>
 }
</items>
```

The output, ForNestedOut.xml, is shown here:

```
<?xml version="1.0" encoding="UTF-8"?>
<items>
   <group/>
   <group/>
   <group>
      <item>1</item>
   </group>
   <group>
      <item>1</item>
      <item>2</item>
   </group>
   <group>
      <item>1</item>
      <item>2</item>
      <item>3</item>
```

```
    </group>
    <group>
        <item>1</item>
        <item>2</item>
        <item>3</item>
        <item>4</item>
        <item>5</item>
    </group>
    <group>
        <item>1</item>
        <item>2</item>
        <item>3</item>
        <item>4</item>
        <item>5</item>
        <item>6</item>
    </group>
</items>
```

The variable `$i` is specified in the outer `for` statement and is equivalent to the sequence `(1, 2, 3, 4, 5, 7, 8)`. For each value of `$i`, a `group` element is created.

The content of each group element is defined by the nested `for` expression:

```
{ for $a in (1 to ($i - 2))
return<item>{$a}</item>}
```

When `$i` is 1 or 2 no `item` elements are added to the corresponding `group` elements since the value `$i` - 2 is less than 1.

When `$i` is 3, then a single item element is generated since:

```
for $a in (1 to ($i - 2))
```

is equivalent to:

```
for $a in 1 to 1
```

so one `item` element is output. As `$i` becomes larger, then additional `item` elements are nested in subsequent `group` elements.

Often you will want to filter the output of a FLWOR statement, using a `where` clause.

Filtering with the where Clause

The `where` clause is used in `for` expressions to filter what is returned in the result. For example, suppose we wanted to find any books in `BibAdapted.xml` that were published in the year 2004. The query shown here, `Year.xquery`, can do that.

```
<books>{
for $book in doc("BibAdapted.xml")/bib/book
 where $book/@year = "2004"
 return
```

```
    element book {
     attribute year {$book/@year},
     element title {$book/title/text()}
     }
   }
</books>
```

A books element is created literally, and its content is defined using a FLWOR expression. The `where` clause selects only books where the `year` attribute has the value `2004`. The content of such books, of which there is only one in the example, is specified using this expression:

```
element book {
 attribute year {$book/@year},
 element title {$book/title/text()}
 }
```

which constructs a `book` element and uses XPath expressions to assign a value to its `year` attribute and its title `child` element.

Sorting Using the order by Clause

The `order by` clause, allows the sorting of the output in a specified order. The following query, `OrderByTitle.xquery`, shows how the `order by` clause can be used.

```
<books>{
 for $book in doc("BibAdapted.xml")/bib/book
 let $t := $book/title/text()
 order by $t
 return
  <book><title>{$t}</title></book>
  }
</books>
```

The `order by` clause:

```
order by $t
```

specifies that the output is to be ordered by the value of the text content of the `title` element of book elements in the source XML document. In other words, the output is sorted alphabetically by title, as demonstrated in the output of the query `OrderByTitleOut.xml` shown here:

```
<?xml version="1.0" encoding="UTF-8"?>
<books>
   <book>
      <title>Advanced Programming in the Unix environment</title>
   </book>
   <book>
      <title>Beginning XML, 3rd Edition</title>
   </book>
   <book>
      <title>Data on the Web</title>
```

```
    </book>
    <book>
       <title>TCP/IP Illustrated</title>
    </book>
    <book>
       <title>The Economics of Technology and Content for Digital TV</title>
    </book>
</books>
```

If we wanted to order in reverse alphabetical order, we could write the `order by` clause as follows:

```
order by $t descending
```

The FLWOR expression lets us iterate over a sequence of items. However, sometimes we need to process nodes only in certain circumstances using XQuery's support for conditional processing.

Conditional Expressions

Conditional expressions in XQuery use the `if` keyword.

Let's produce a query on `BibAdapted.xml` that outputs a book's title and a count of its authors only if the number of authors exceeds two. The query, `MultiAuthor.xquery`, is shown here:

```
<MultiAuthor>
{for $book in doc("BibAdapted.xml")/bib/book
return
 if (count($book/author) > 2)
  then <book>
        <title>{$book/title/text()}</title>
        <NumberOfAuthors>{count($book/author)}</NumberOfAuthors>
       </book>
  else ()
}
</MultiAuthor>
```

The query uses a `for` statement to associate the variable `$book` with each book element in `BibAdapted.xml`. All of the `return` statement is governed by the conditional statement

```
if (count($book/author) > 2)
```

The `count()` function counts how many `author` elements are child elements of `$book`.

So, if the number of `author` elements that are child elements of `$book` exceeds two then the `then` clause specifies the corresponding output:

```
then <book>
     <title>{$book/title/text()}</title>
     <NumberOfAuthors>{count($book/author)}</NumberOfAuthors>
    </book>
```

But if the number of author elements does not exceed two, then the `else` clause comes into play:

```
else ()
```

In this case producing the empty sequence signified by `()`.

The output, `MultiAuthorOut.xml`, is shown here:

```
<?xml version="1.0" encoding="UTF-8"?>
<MultiAuthor>
   <book>
      <title>Data on the Web</title>
      <NumberOfAuthors>3</NumberOfAuthors>
   </book>
   <book>
      <title>Beginning XML, 3rd Edition</title>
      <NumberOfAuthors>5</NumberOfAuthors>
   </book>
</MultiAuthor>
```

XQuery Functions

XQuery provides a huge range of functions to allow an extensive set of tools to manipulate and filter data. You saw a simple use of the `count()` function to count the number of `author` element nodes in an earlier example describing conditional processing. A couple of commonly used functions are described here.

A full description of the XQuery functions is contained in a lengthy, separate W3C document located at `http://www.w3.org/tr/xpath-functions`. The URL describes the functions common to XPath 2.0 (hence the final part of the URL) and XQuery 1.0.

The concat() Function

The `concat()` function is used to concatenate strings. The following shows a simple example. The source XML, `Parts.xml`, contains two strings that we want to join together.

```
<?xml version='1.0'?>
<Parts>
 <Part>To be or not to be,</Part>
 <Part>that is the question!</Part>
</Parts>
```

The query, `ASaying.xquery`, is shown here:

```
<ASaying>{
 for $a in doc("Parts.xml")/Parts/Part[1]
 for $b in doc("Parts.xml")/Parts/Part[2]
 return
 concat($a, $b)
}
</ASaying>
```

Notice that we declare two variables, `$a` and `$b`, using XPath path expressions to select relevant parts of the source XML document. In the return statement, the `concat()` function is used to concatenate the strings, and the output, `ASayingOut.xml`, is shown here:

```
<?xml version="1.0" encoding="UTF-8"?>
<ASaying>To be or not to be,that is the question!</ASaying>
```

The count() Function

Let's use the `count()` function to calculate the number of `Book` elements that are present in `SimpleBooks.xml`, which you saw earlier in the chapter. The query is contained in the file, `Count.xquery`, whose content is shown here:

```
<library count="{count(doc('SimpleBooks.xml')/Books/Book)}">
 {
 for $b in doc("SimpleBooks.xml")/Books/Book
 return <book>{$b/text()}</book>
 }
</library>
```

To run the query, type the following at the command line:

```
java net.sf.saxon.Query -o CountOut.xml Count.xquery
```

Notice that the `count()` function is used inside the value of the `count` attribute of the element `library`, which is created literally. The expression used to create the value of the `count` attribute, `count(doc('SimpleBooks.xml')/Books/Book)`, uses the `count()` function with the argument `doc('SimpleBooks.xml')/Books/Book`. That expression selects all the `Book` elements in `SimpleBook.xml` and returns them in a sequence. At the risk of stating the obvious, there are three `Book` element nodes in the sequence. The `count()` function then counts those nodes and returns the value `3` in the `count` attribute.

The query uses two nested expressions to create the content of the `library` element. The `for` statement is used to iterate over `Book` element nodes.

The result of the query is shown in `CountOut.xml`, which is displayed here:

```
<?xml version="1.0" encoding="UTF-8"?>
<library count="3">
   <book>Beginning XML, 3rd Edition</book>
   <book>Beginning Red Hat Linux 9</book>
   <book>Professional XML Development with Apache Tools</book>
</library>
```

Using Parameters with XQuery

External parameters may be passed to an XQuery query. In XQuery a parameter is considered to be a variable that is declared as external.

To pass a string `"Hello World!"` to an XQuery, `ParameterExample.xquery`, and display the output on the console we use the following syntax at the command line:

```
java net.sf.saxon.Query ParameterExample.xquery input="Hello World!"
```

The query is shown here:

```
declare variable $input as xs:string external;
<output>
 {$input}
</output>
```

Notice the variable declaration specifies that the variable `$input` is external and is of type `xs:string`. In the absence of a namespace declaration to the contrary, the namespace prefix `xs` is treated as the namespace prefix for the W3C XML Schema namespace.

In this simple example we simply use an element constructor to create an `output` element and specify that the element's content is an XQuery expression `$input`. The output is shown in Figure 9-4.

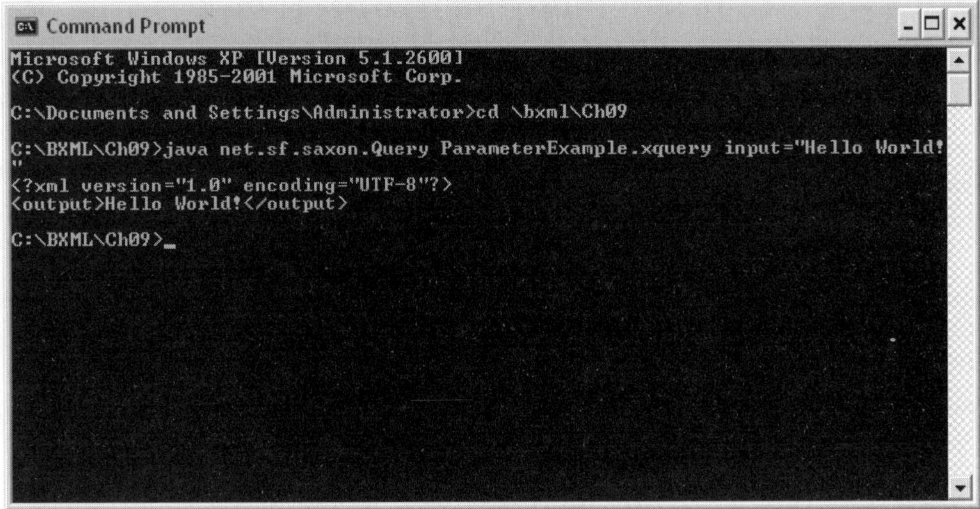

Figure 9-4

Proprietary Extensions to XQuery

The lack of update, delete, and insert functionality in XQuery 1.0 makes it inevitable that commercial database products such as SQL Server from Microsoft and the Oracle product will provide some nonstandard syntax to achieve these crucial aspects of a full-fledged XML query language. The brief discussion in this section will be based on Microsoft's SQL Server 2005 database management system, which is currently in beta. Detail is, of course, subject to change as the product goes through its beta development. Microsoft refers to these extensions as DML, presumably to leave open the option of adding future official XQuery insert, update, or delete functionality to a future version of SQL Server.

Insert Functionality

In SQL Server 2005 the `insert` keyword can be used to add content as descendant node(s) to a specified node, to add sibling nodes before or after existing nodes, or to add an attribute to an existing element node.

Suppose you wanted to insert a `Part` element as a child node of a `Parts` element node in a parts library; you might write code like this:

```
insert <Part>A widget</Part>
 into (/PartsLibrary/Parts)[1]
```

To insert a new `Part` after all the other parts you might write:

```
insert <Part>The last widget</Part>
after (/PartsLibrary/Parts/Part) [last()]
```

To add a `year` attribute to a `Book` element in a catalog you might write:

```
insert attribute year {"2004"}
into Catalog[1]/Book[1]
```

Delete Functionality

The `delete` keyword in the Microsoft DML is used to delete specified node(s). For example, to delete the last step in a set of instructions you might write:

```
delete /Instructions/Step[last()]
```

Update Functionality

The `update` functionality updates a node in the data model. For example, to update the last step in a set of instructions you might write:

```
replace value of /Instructions/Step[last()]/text()[1]
to "Now you are finished"
```

It seems likely that a future version of XQuery will provide an `update` keyword that will, in time, replace the above syntax.

Looking Ahead

As mentioned earlier in the chapter, it is likely that the XQuery specification will be finalized shortly after this book is published. However, almost everyone who has taken an interest in XQuery during its development recognizes that XQuery 1.0 is only a step toward a full-featured XQuery language. Two important aspects of the future of XQuery are mentioned here.

Update Functionality (as Part of XQuery)

Any XML data store that relies on XQuery as its primary query language must, like XML, be able to insert, delete, and update arbitrary parts of XML content. XQuery 1.0 has no such functionality, but the W3C working group has made it clear that such functionality is very much in its plans for XQuery after version 1.0. At the time of writing no drafts relating to this functionality have been issued by the W3C. If you are interested in this kind of functionality as a W3C standard specification, then visit `http://www.w3.org/XML/query`, navigate to specifications, and check for any requirements documents or working drafts that indicate a version of XQuery greater than 1.0.

Full-Text Search

At the time of writing, W3C has issued preliminary drafts that indicate that full-text search functionality will be developed soon for XQuery. Because the drafts are at a very early stage of development at the time of writing, it is likely that substantial changes may take place and therefore no examples are given in this chapter. Visit `http://www.w3.org/XML/query` and check for the up-to-date specifications for full-text search.

Summary

In this chapter, we learned about some foundational aspects of the upcoming XML query language, XQuery. XQuery is based on XPath 2.0 and has a number of similarities to XSLT 2.0, which is also under development at the W3C. The XQuery prolog defines a number of components that determine how an XQuery will be processed. XQuery uses XPath path expressions for simple data retrieval but adds the very flexible and powerful FLWOR expressions to add a new dimension to querying of XML data.

Exercise Questions

Suggested solutions to these questions can be found in Appendix A.

Question 1

What notation is used in an XQuery expression to indicate that its content is created dynamically?

Question 2

What are the component parts of a FLWOR expression and what do they each do?

XML and Databases

The volume of XML used by businesses is increasing as enterprises send increasing numbers of messages as XML.. Many websites use XML as a data store, which is transformed into HTML or XHTML for online display. The diversity of sources of XML data is increasing, too. For example, a new generation of forms products and technologies, such as Microsoft's InfoPath and W3C XForms, is also beginning to supply XML data directly to data stores such as Microsoft Access or SQL Server from forms filled in by a variety of information workers.

To monitor business activity, you need to be able to store or exchange possibly huge amounts of data as XML and to recognize the benefits of the flexibility that XML provides to reflect the structure of business data and to process or interchange it further. In addition, XML is being used increasingly for business-critical data, some of which is particularly confidential and needs to be secured from unauthorized eyes. This situation throws up many issues that need to be considered when storing XML in a production setting. It isn't enough that data is available as XML; other issues such as security and scalability come into the picture, too.

In Chapter 9 we looked at XQuery, the XML query language under development at the W3C. In this chapter we will look at broader issues that relate to the use of XML with databases. These issues will be illustrated by some examples of using XML with a native XML database and an XML-enabled enterprise database management system.

In this chapter you will learn:

- Why XML-enabled database systems are needed
- How to perform foundational tasks using a native XML database, the Xindice database from the Apache Foundation
- How to use some of the XML functionality in a full-fledged enterprise relational database management system that also has XML functionality

The Need for Efficient XML Data Stores

Efficiency is an important criterion when considering how to store data as XML. If XML is stored *as* XML how can it be processed efficiently? When data is measured in gigabytes, creating an

Document Object Model (DOM) becomes impractical in many situations and alternative must be explored.

When volumes of XML data grow, the efficiency of searching becomes important. However, the XML is actually stored, the addition of indexes to speed up search of that XML becomes increasingly necessary. Efficiency of data retrieval is important in many practical settings. For example, when XML data is used in web-based user interaction or in XML Web services, performance is of great importance if the user is to feel that the system is sufficiently responsive.

If data is stored as something other than XML, the issue of how fast, say, data held in relational form can be transformed into XML comes into play. Can an individual database product supply data as XML fast enough for users or other business processes to use, without imposing unacceptable delays?

Issues of reliability also come into play. You may have designed an XML database that works well. At least it works well when it's working, but if it doesn't stay online almost 100 percent of the time when it is needed and if it has evident dips in performance in certain circumstances, then that database may simply be unacceptable in a production setting.

Increase in Amount of XML

I first started using XML in early 1999 and first wrote about using it about a year later. When I first began working with XML, it was, I think, seen as a pretty specialized, abstract topic that I suspect many people failed to see as relevant. I remember thinking when I first used XML that it could be an important technology. While I expected XML use to grow enormously, I don't think I had any idea just how much and how fast it would grow. XML's growth in five years has been astonishing.

Of course, XML has its limitations. I see XML as the paper clip of business communication. It helps bring the organization where it wasn't possible or wasn't easy before. And, it's going to continue growing as its value in connecting all sorts of data becomes clearer to business users.

Diverse Data

One of the underlying factors that supports the increasing use of XML is that XML has enormous flexibility in representing data. It can represent data structures that are difficult or inefficient to represent as relational data. So, in some settings, native XML databases that handle XML that a relational database might not easily handle may carve out a niche. But the situation is fluid and fuzzy. You will find no universally accepted definition of a native XML database. Perhaps the most practical definition of a native XML database is a database designed primarily or only to handle XML data.

Structured Data

People who come from a relational database background tend to refer to relational data as *structured data*, overlooking the reality that many other types of data are also structured, but structured in a different, more complex or more variable way. However, I will use the term *structured data* to refer primarily to relational data, although it is also relevant to keep in mind that relational data is, in a real sense, simply structured data.

Semi-Structured Data

The terms *semi-structured data* and *loosely structured data* have no clear boundaries. Semi-structured data is a term used often by relational database folks to refer to nonrelational data, very often XML data.

Loosely Structured Data

Loosely structured data is a term that tends to be applied to document-centric XML. XML documents, such as XHTML web pages or DocBook documents, can be enormously varied in structure. They are, of course, still structured and, assuming they are correctly written, correspond to a schema. A big difference between a relational mindset and an XHTML or DocBook document is that there is much more flexibility in the XHTML document and much more variation allowed than can be allowed in a relational database.

Whether you view relational data as inflexibly and simply structured data or simply as "structured data" (as if there were no other kind) is as much a matter of philosophy or perspective as anything else. Similarly, whether you view XML documents as loosely structured data (the relational viewpoint) or as richly structured, flexibly structured data is again a matter of perspective.

Comparing XML-Based Data and Relational Data

Before we move on to examine approaches to using XML in modern databases, let's take a very brief look at how the structure of relational data and XML compare. If you don't appreciate these simple differences, then much of what follows may be hard for you to understand.

In a relational database, data is stored in tables that consist of rows and columns. In a column, data of a particular kind is stored for all records in the table. Each record in the table is represented as a row. The order of rows in a relational table does not indicate any ordering of the data. This contrasts with XML where document order is intrinsically present and affects, for example, the data that is returned by an XPath function such as `position()`.

Only the simplest relational data can be stored in a single table and a typical relational database will have multiple tables with complex logical relationships between tables. Data in different tables is associated by the use of keys. For example, a `CustomerID` field (or column) may exist in a `Customers` table. Identification of orders for that customer is likely to be facilitated by the existence of a corresponding value in the `CustomerID` column of an `Orders` table.

Relationships between data can be one-to-one (think of son to father), one-to-many (think of son to parents or customer to orders), or many-to-many (think of products to orders—one product can appear in many orders, and one order can contain many products). Each of these types of relationships can be represented by storing data in two or more relational tables.

Relational databases, as typically structured, have no hierarchy as such, unlike XML documents, which are intrinsically hierarchical, as exemplified in the XPath data model, Document Object Model, and the XML Infoset.

XML data is intrinsically ordered, as in this simple example.

```
<Orders>
 <Order Customer="Acme Industries" Date="2003-12-11" Value="1234.56"
 Currency="US Dollars" />
 <Order Customer="Fiction Fabricators" Date="2004-02-11" Value="4300.12"
 Currency="US Dollars" />
<Order Customer="Aspiring Assemblers" Date="2005-07-11" Value="10000.00"
 Currency="US Dollars" />
</Orders>
```

XML is intrinsically hierarchical, a condition imposed by the criteria that define a well-formed XML document. Storing even simple data like this in a relational table would lose the ordering of orders. Whether that matters or not depends on whether you need to assemble the data in XML at a later date to recapture the original structure.

Approaches to Storing XML

The need to store XML doesn't occur in a vacuum. Huge amounts of data had already been stored for years before XML was invented, much of it in conventional relational database management systems.

Producing XML from Relational Databases

Large numbers of HTML and XHTML websites are created, directly or indirectly, from relational data. Widely used combinations are PHP with the MySQL database or ASP or ASP.NET with SQL Server or Microsoft Access. Data is stored conventionally as relational tables, and the programmer writes code to create HTML or XHTML, sometimes using XML as an intermediate stage. XHTML is an XML application language. Creating XHTML web pages from relational data demonstrates one way in which relational data can be used to produce a presentation-oriented form of XML. What that common activity demonstrates is that it is possible to map relational data to hierarchical XML structures and return those hierarchical structures to a user.

For example, when using PHP to query data from a couple of tables in MySQL to present it to a user of a web page, it is unlikely that the developer will want to present the data only in tables similar to the structures in the database. More likely, the developer will convert the nonordered, nonhierarchical structure of relational data into something with at least some order and hierarchy, since that fits well into HTML and XHTML web pages, which are themselves hierarchical.

If individual programmers can figure out ways to convert relational data to XML, then it is not surprising that vendors of database products also recognized the opportunity to get into a growing XML market that the ability to export XML from a relational data store would bring. So, many relational databases allow XML to be returned to the user from data held in relational tables.

Moving XML to Relational Databases

Similarly, many relational database management systems now have the ability to accept XML data from a user, convert it into a relational form, and then store that latter data in relational tables.

Depending on whether any meta data about ordering is captured in the process of shredding XML into parts that a relational database can handle, it may be possible to reconstitute the original XML document. In many situations such precise reconstitution is not needed.

The ability to shred and glue together bits of data to mimic XML functionality is fine, not least since it works for many situations. But it's not the only approach. Enter native XML databases.

Native XML Databases

So what is a native XML database? You'll find no single, universally agreed definition. A simple and reasonably helpful definition is that a native XML database is designed to store XML. But, if it also stores data structures other than XML, does it then stop being a native XML database?

A native XML database might choose to implement XML using a model like the XML Infoset, the XML DOM, XPath, or *Simple API for XML* (SAX) events. It is also likely to capture aspects of an XML document like document order.

Relational database technology is now pretty mature, having a sound theoretical basis and a couple of decades of practical experience in widely used products. By contrast, native XML databases are recent introductions; they don't have the same kind of theoretical underpinning as relational databases do, and they are evolving and are likely to continue to evolve for some years to come.

Whatever the underlying storage mechanism, a native XML database product also maps an XML document to the storage model. The mapping differs substantially, perhaps, from the detail of the shredding of an XML document into a relational database.

Native XML databases often store XML documents in collections. Queries can be made across a collection. Depending on the product, a collection may be defined by a schema or may contain documents of differing structure. The latter approach is likely to be greeted with horror by those used to the predictability of a relational model.

At the time of writing, many native XML databases use XPath 1.0 as the query language. However, in the next year or so it is likely that XQuery-enabled native XML databases will become more common. XPath 1.0 lacks, for example, grouping constructs and the ability to type data using W3C XML Schema.

Updates to native XML databases currently lack standardization. Whereas the querying limitations of XPath 1.0 will be alleviated by the upcoming introduction of XQuery 1.0, the lack of insert, delete, and update functionality in XQuery 1.0 means that nonstandard update mechanisms are likely to persist in the native XML database world for some time to come.

In practice, the boundary between native XML databases and XML-enabled relational databases looks likely to become progressively blurred. For example, Microsoft's upcoming version of SQL Server, codenamed "Yukon," will add the ability to store a new `xml` data type without discarding its traditional strengths as a relational database management system.

For many practical purposes it won't matter whether you are using a native XML database or an XML-enabled relational database product. You, as the user or developer, send XML into both types and you get XML back, so why should you worry what is under the hood? Quite often you needn't. Making a choice about XML-enabled relational database versus native XML database is similar to making any other software choice. You should define clearly what your needs are and go and find the best fit for those functional needs depending on price, supported operating system(s), and a host of other criteria.

In the rest of this chapter we will look at using two very different database products as examples of native XML databases and XML-enabled database management systems. Xindice is a native XML database from the Apache Software Foundation. SQL Server is a Microsoft enterprise-capable relational database management system with some XML functionality.

Using Native XML Databases

As mentioned earlier, native XML databases can differ in their approach. Individual databases in the native XML database category vary significantly in their capabilities. I will use the Apache Software Foundation's Xindice to explore how one native XML database works.

I chose Xindice partly because it is free and can be downloaded so that you can work through the code examples if you want to. I would encourage you to do that because there is no substitute in understanding a piece of software for actually installing it, getting it working and then writing code to make it do what you want it to do.

Obtaining and Installing Xindice

The Xindice native XML database is one of several XML projects under development at the Apache Software Foundation. Those XML projects are described at `http://xml.apache.org`. The Xindice project pages are accessible from that URL. Downloads are available as source code, web archive (`.war`), and jar files.

The instructions given here assume that you will install and run Tomcat and Xindice on your local machine. They refer to the installation and configuration of Xindice 1.1 beta 3. If you are installing on a separate server modify paths and URLs accordingly.

By contrast to earlier versions of Xindice, Xindice 1.1 runs in a servlet container such as Apache Tomcat. If you don't already have a servlet container installed, visit `http://jakarta.apache.org` and select the latest stable build of Tomcat appropriate to your operating system. At the time of writing, the latest stable build was Tomcat 5.0.18.

To run Tomcat and Xindice you will need a Java Runtime Environment installed. A Java Runtime Environment can be downloaded from `http://java.sun.com`. Look for information about J2SE and download either a Java Runtime Environment or a Java SDK (if you also want to do Java development). At the time of writing, Java version 1.4.2 works with Xindice 1.1 beta 3. Check the latest documentation for Xindice and Tomcat for any compatibility issues at the time you download the pieces of software.

Install the Java Runtime Environment, following the installation instructions available at the `java.sun.com` site. I installed to `c:\j2sdk1.4.2_03`.

The Tomcat server can be downloaded from `http://jakarta.apache.org/tomcat/`. An `.exe` installer was available at the time of writing for installing on the Windows platform. Tomcat has extensive documentation that provides full installation instructions.

Install Tomcat. I chose to install Tomcat at `c:\Tomcat 5.0.18`. Double-clicking the installer gave a straightforward install. If you choose another directory then adjust the paths in the following description accordingly. Make sure that you select, during the Tomcat install, a sufficiently up-to-date Java Runtime, since Xindice won't run on a J2SDK or Java Runtime before 1.3. At the end of the Windows install of Tomcat, you will be offered an option to start Tomcat. After starting Tomcat you should be able to access the Tomcat welcome page at the URL `http://localhost:8080`. Adjust the URL for your servername if you haven't installed Tomcat on your own local development machine. If Tomcat runs correctly, you should see an appearance similar to that shown in Figure 10-1.

The following procedure describes how I succeeded in getting Xindice 1.1 beta 3 to install. Installation is likely to be more fully documented closer to final release of Xindice 1.1. Visit `http://xml.apache.org/xindice/index.html` and check the Documentation part of the navigation bar and the How-Tos tab on the same page for installation information.

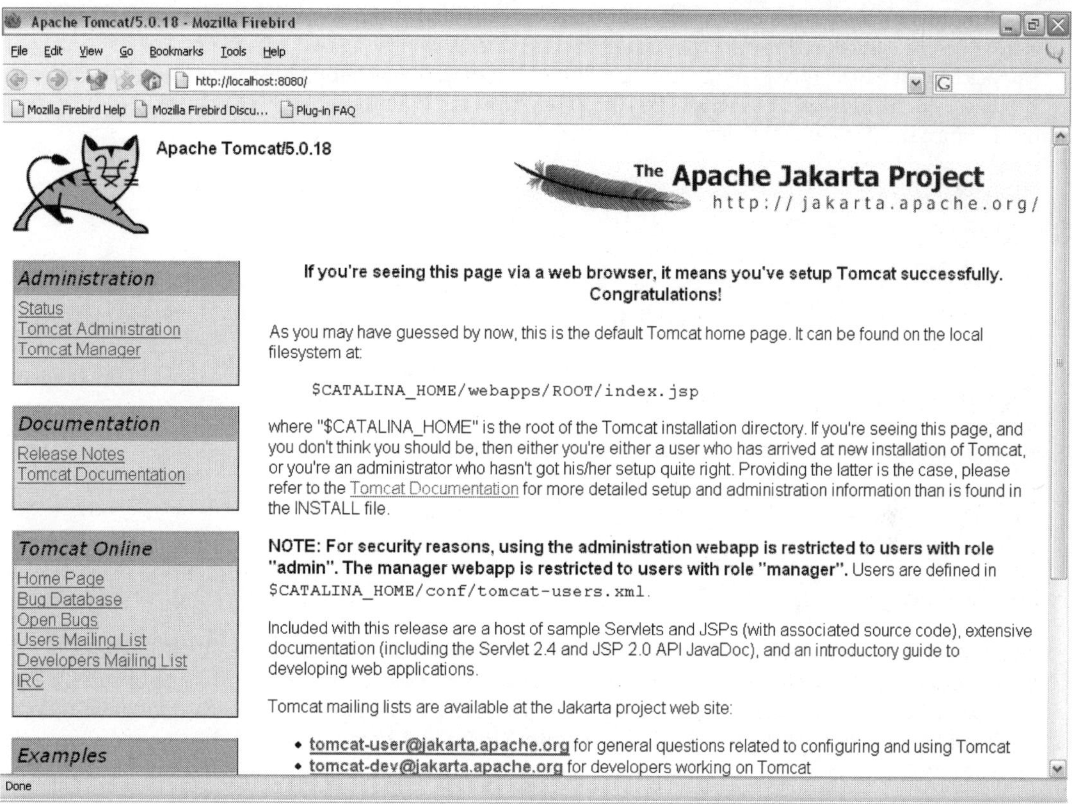

Figure 10-1

I elected to download the zipped web archive option for Xindice. The version current at the time of writing was Xindice 1.1 beta 3. You will need to use WinZip or some similar program to unzip the download. By default, Xindice 1.1 beta 3 uses the directory xindice-1.1b3 as its installation directory. For convenience, I installed on C:\, which resulted in the installation being installed in the directory C:\xindice-1.1b3. Remember to ensure that the Use Folder Names option is checked in WinZip before you extract files otherwise the files will be installed in a single directory with the possibility of name clashes.

The next step is to install Xindice on the Tomcat server. If you are using Tomcat 5.0.18 in its default configuration, which unpacks a `.war` file as soon as it is pasted into the `webapps` directory, you must stop Tomcat before you copy the `Xindice-1.1b3.war` file; otherwise, it will be unpacked to a directory `Xindice-1.1b3` and things won't work correctly. To stop Tomcat on Windows XP, select Start, go to Control Panel, choose Administrative Tools, and then choose Services. In the Services window you should see Apache Tomcat early in the list of Windows services. If you chose to run Tomcat at the end of the installation process, it may not show as started in the Services window. If that is the case, start it again in the Services window. When Apache Tomcat shows as "started," then stop the Tomcat Service. You are now ready to copy the Xindice web archive to Tomcat.

In `C:\xindice-1.1b3` or the directory where you installed Xindice, look for the file `Xindice-1.1b3.war` or a similar name if you installed a later version. Copy that file. Navigate to `C:\Tomcat 5.0.18\webapps` (or the webapps directory of your Tomcat installation if you installed in another directory) and paste `Xindice-1.1b3.war` into that directory. Rename the web archive to `xindice.war`. Restart Tomcat. The `xindice.war` file (formerly named `xindice-1.1b3.war`) will be unpacked and a directory named xindice will be created in the webapps directory. Enter the URL `http://localhost:8080/xindice/` in a web browser. If all has gone well, then you should see an appearance similar to that shown in Figure 10-2.

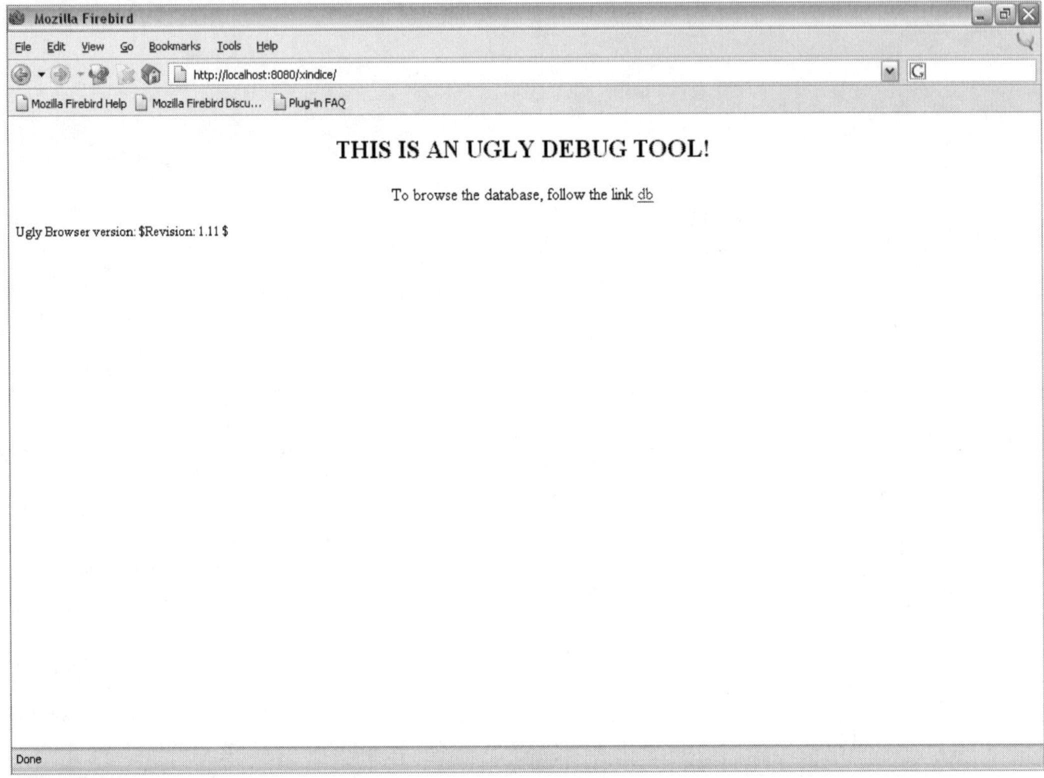

Figure 10-2

If you overlooked the step to stop Tomcat before pasting `xindice-1.1b3.war`, you will likely end up with a nonworking installation. Stop Tomcat. If you don't, you won't be allowed to delete the `.war` file or the xindice-1.1b3 directory. Delete the xindice-1.1b3 directory, rename `xindice-1.1b3.war` to `xindice.war`, and restart Tomcat. And you should be able to reproduce Figure 10-2.

The visual appearance isn't impressive but it does demonstrate that Xindice is correctly installed, at least as far as obtaining access through the browser is concerned. From that browser window move into the database by clicking the `db` link, then click `system`, then click `SysConfig`, and then click `database.xml`. You should see an appearance similar to Figure 10-3.

As you can perhaps see in Figure 10-3, the XML database in Xindice at installation consists of the following XML document:

```
<?xml version="1.0"?>
<database name="db"/>
```

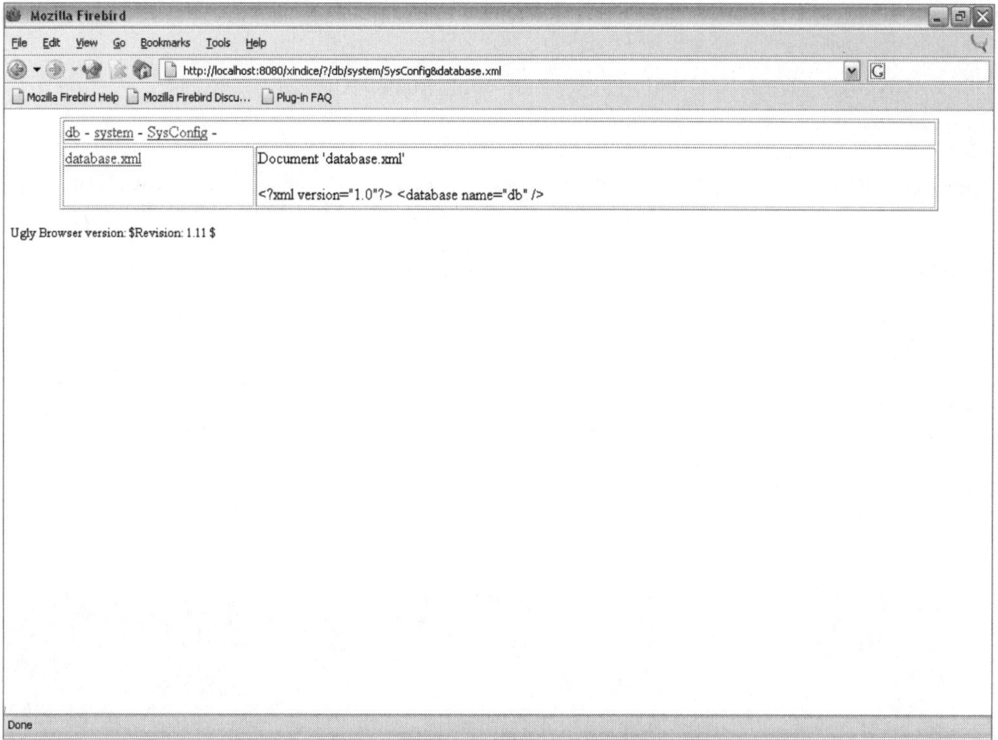

Figure 10-3

So far so good. We have access to the native XML data store using a URL in a web browser. But, to create a worthwhile data store we need to be able to add XML data to the data store. This requires that we use a command-line Xindice tool. At the time of writing, the configuration of that tool was undocumented. So what is described here may not be the only or best way to configure it, but it did work for me.

> **Documentation of the beta was sparse at the time of writing. Check `http://xml.apache.org/xindice/community/howto/index.html` to see the current documentation. In addition, the Xindice project has just added a Wiki, which will include FAQ information. Visit `http://wiki.apache.org/xindice` to check out the current Wiki content.**

Remember you have already downloaded and unzipped the zipped web archive file. I also downloaded and unzipped to `C:\xindice-1.1b3` the zipped jar file and the zipped source file to the same directory; in other words, both downloads were installed in one directory. There were one or more missing files in some of the zip files so it seemed that no single binary download had all the files needed.

You will also need to set three environment variables:

- **JAVA_HOME**—The directory where you installed the Java Runtime that you selected to use with Tomcat, in my case `C:\j2sdk1.4.2_03`

- **CATALINA_HOME**—The directory where you installed Tomcat, in my case `C:\Tomcat 5.0.18`
- **XINDICE_HOME**—The directory where you installed Xindice, in my case `C:\xindice-1.1b3`

Open a command window and navigate to `C:\xindice-1.1b3\bin` (or equivalent). If the environment variables have been set correctly then you should be able to run Xindice from any directory.

Assuming that you have followed this step by step you should be able to type,

```
xindice
```

at the command line, that runs `xindice.bat`, which is located in the `C:\xindice-1.1b3\bin` directory and a fairly lengthy error message telling you that you have omitted parameters and listing a couple of screens of Xindice parameters should be displayed, similar to the appearance in Figure 10-4.

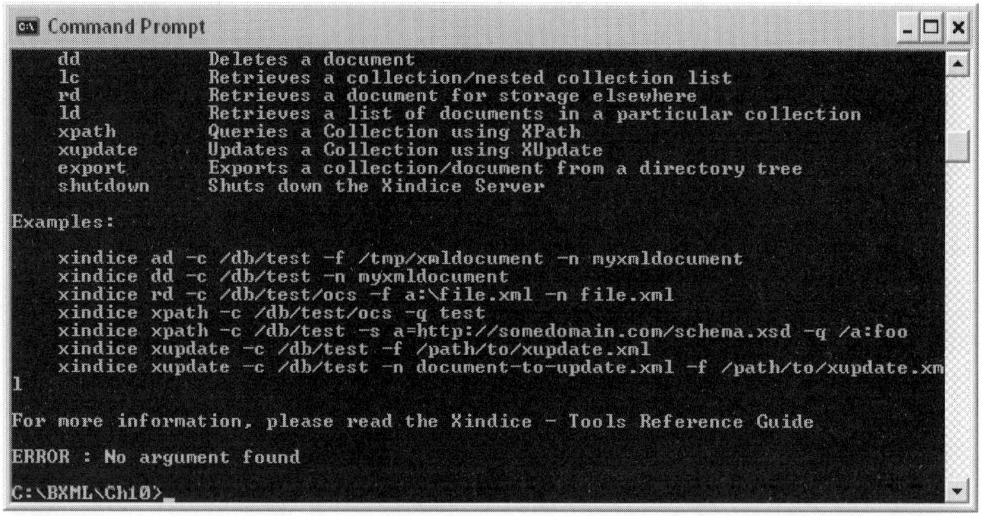

```
Command Prompt
    dd            Deletes a document
    lc            Retrieves a collection/nested collection list
    rd            Retrieves a document for storage elsewhere
    ld            Retrieves a list of documents in a particular collection
    xpath         Queries a Collection using XPath
    xupdate       Updates a Collection using XUpdate
    export        Exports a collection/document from a directory tree
    shutdown      Shuts down the Xindice Server

Examples:

    xindice ad -c /db/test -f /tmp/xmldocument -n myxmldocument
    xindice dd -c /db/test -n myxmldocument
    xindice rd -c /db/test/ocs -f a:\file.xml -n file.xml
    xindice xpath -c /db/test/ocs -q test
    xindice xpath -c /db/test -s a=http://somedomain.com/schema.xsd -q /a:foo
    xindice xupdate -c /db/test -f /path/to/xupdate.xml
    xindice xupdate -c /db/test -n document-to-update.xml -f /path/to/xupdate.xm
l

For more information, please read the Xindice - Tools Reference Guide

ERROR : No argument found

C:\BXML\Ch10>_
```

Figure 10-4

Having configured Xindice, let's move on and use it.

Adding Information

As you saw earlier in Figure 10-3, the Xindice database after installation is empty. So if you want to explore how to retrieve and manipulate information, you first need to put some XML data into the Xindice database.

The Xindice database, at least when viewed in a browser, presents its content as an XML document. The basic structure of the Xindice database is as follows:

```
<?xml version="1.0"?>
<database name="db"></database>
```

With the `database` element being the document element in the Xindice data store.

Xindice, at least in version 1.1 beta 3, assumes from the command line that Xindice is accessible by default on port 8888. If you are running Tomcat in its default configuration, then the port number is 8080. That means you need to specify the server name and port explicitly in all Xindice command-line commands, unless you are running on port 8888.

To add data to the Xindice database, you first need to create a collection, which is represented in the data store as a `collection` element. At the command line enter the following command, assuming you have Tomcat (or equivalent application server) running on port 8080:

```
xindice ac -c xmldb:xindice://localhost:8080/db -n Test
```

to create a collection called `test`. The `ac` component of the command line signifies add collection, and is an abbreviation for `add_collection`. The `-c` component refers to the collection context, which can be a canonical name of the collection or, as shown previously, a complete `xmldb` URL. Notice how the URL is constructed. The protocol is `xmldb:xindice`, which is followed by the `://` separators that you will be familiar with when accessing a web page. In this example and all later examples I spell out the host and port, `localhost:8080`, for clarity. If your server is not `localhost`, adjust this accordingly and similarly make an adjustment if your application server is not using port 8080. Notice, too, that when you use the `xmldb:xindice` protocol that you can omit the `xindice` part of the URL, compared to the HTTP URL shown here:

```
http://localhost:8080/xindice/?/db/
```

which displays the `database` element of the Xindice database. In other words, when you use the `xmldb:xindice` protocol, you don't need to insert `xindice` in the URL after `localhost:8080/`. The `-n` switch, in the earlier command, signifies the name, in this case of the collection that we want to be added to the database.

Add a second collection named `People`, which we will use in later examples, by entering this at the command line:

```
xindice ac -c xmldb:xindice://localhost:8080/db -n People
```

You will use the `test` collection to show examples of deletion in Xindice.

When you connect to the data in the browser, using the URL `http://localhost:8080/xindice/?/db/system/SysConfig&database.xml`, you should see an XML structure displayed corresponding to the following (which has been tidied to aid clarity):

```
<?xml version="1.0"?>
<database name="db">
 <collections>
  <collection compressed="true" name="test">
    <filer class="org.apache.xindice.core.filer.BTreeFiler" />
```

```
      <indexes />
    </collection>
    <collection compressed="true" name="People">
      <filer class="org.apache.xindice.core.filer.BTreeFiler" />
      <indexes />
    </collection>
  </collections>
</database>
```

Two `collection` elements have been added as children of the `database` element. The browser appearance is shown in Figure 10-5.

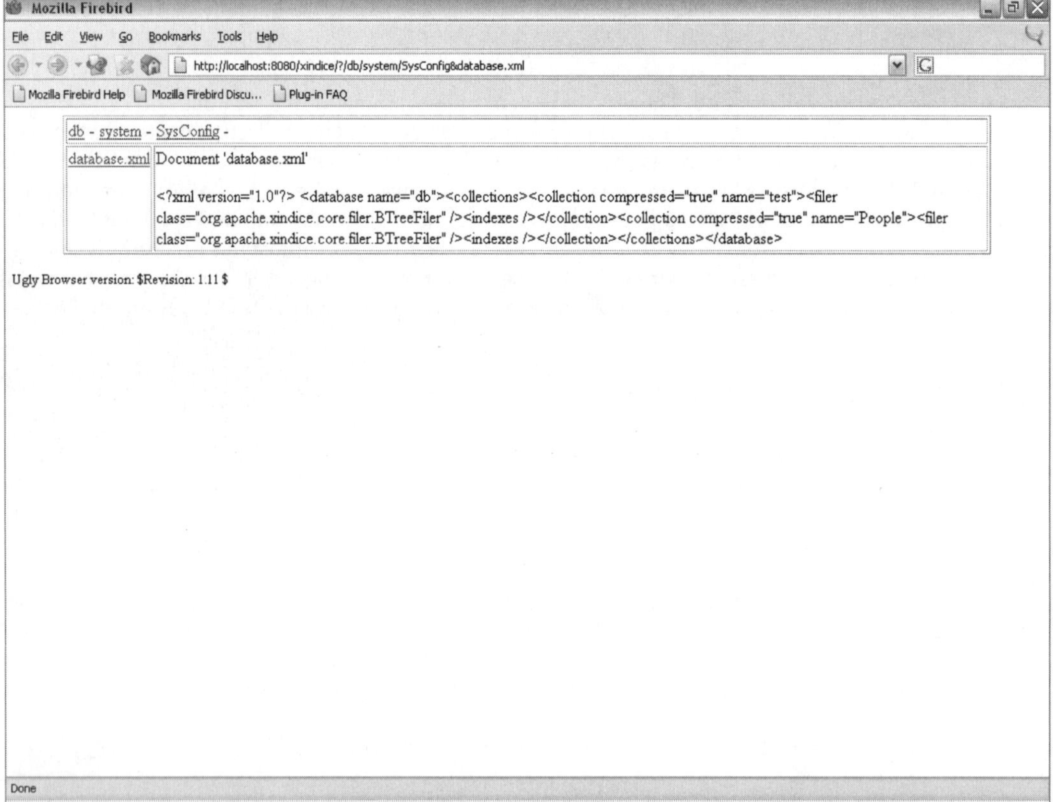

Figure 10-5

From the command line you can similarly confirm that the `test` and `People` collections exist by typing the following:

```
xindice lc -c xmldb:xindice://localhost:8080/db
```

If everything is working well, then you should see an appearance similar to that shown in Figure 10-6.

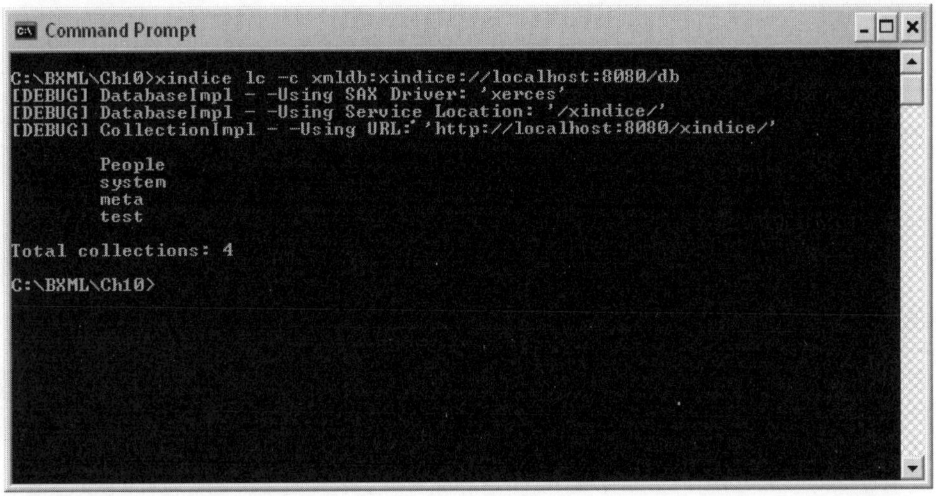

```
Command Prompt

C:\BXML\Ch10>xindice lc -c xmldb:xindice://localhost:8080/db
[DEBUG] DatabaseImpl - -Using SAX Driver: 'xerces'
[DEBUG] DatabaseImpl - -Using Service Location: '/xindice/'
[DEBUG] CollectionImpl - -Using URL: 'http://localhost:8080/xindice/'

        People
        system
        meta
        test

Total collections: 4

C:\BXML\Ch10>
```

Figure 10-6

In addition to, hopefully, confirming that you have successfully created the `test` and `People` collections, you will see that two system collections, `system` and `meta`, are also listed.

Collections in Xindice provide a container inside which you can add an XML document. Now you will add a simple XML document, `Person1.xml`, to the `People` collection. Its content is shown here.

```
<?xml version='1.0'?>
<Person>
<FirstName>John</FirstName>
<LastName>Smith</LastName>
<DoB>1970-12-22</DoB>
</Person>
```

To add `Person1.xml` to the Xindice database, assuming that it is stored in the same directory from which you are issuing the command, type this at the command line:

```
xindice ad -c xmldb:xindice://localhost:8080/db/People -f Person1.xml
-n Person1
```

The `ad` command is an abbreviation for `add_document`. You can use whichever form you prefer. The `-c` switch defines the context, as previously explained. Notice that since you want to add the document `Person1.xml` to the `People` collection that the name of the `People` collection is included in the context. The `-f` switch is used to define the path to the desired document, in this case, simply the file name. The `-n` switch defines the name to be given to the XML document in the Xindice database.

You will also add a second XML document, `Person2.xml`, shown here.

```
<?xml version='1.0'?>
<Person>
<FirstName>Jane</FirstName>
```

```
<LastName>Doe</LastName>
<DoB>1961-12-09</DoB>
</Person>
```

To add it, enter the following at the command line:

```
xindice ad -c xmldb:xindice://localhost:8080/db/People -f Person2.xml -
n Person2
```

To confirm that both documents have been correctly added to the database, enter the following at the command line:

```
xindice ld -c xmldb:xindice://localhost:8080/db/People
```

Figure 10-7 shows the confirmation that the documents `Person1` and `Person2` have been added to the database.

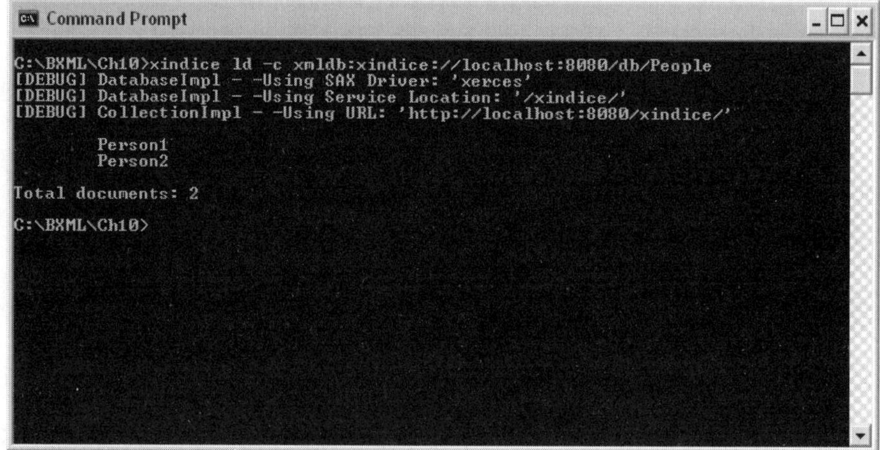

Figure 10-7

Now that you know you have some data in the Xindice database, you can look at how to retrieve or query the data.

Retrieving Information

If you put XML data into a Xindice database, inevitably you will want to retrieve information, too. One simple way is to use the `retrieve_document` command.

To retrieve the `Person1.xml` document that you added earlier to the database and create a new file named `Person1Out.xml`, you can use the following command:

```
xindice rd -c xmldb:xindice://localhost:8080/db/People -n Person1 -f
Person1Out.xml
```

The `rd` command is an abbreviation for `retrieve_document`. Since the `Person1.xml` document was stored in the `People` collection with the name `Person1`, you use the `-c` switch to fully specify the context, the `-n` switch to specify the name of the document you want to retrieve, and the `-f` switch to specify the name of the file to which we wish the XML to be written.

If you look in Windows Explorer, assuming you are using Windows, you should see that `Person1Out.xml` has been added to the directory. Opening the file shows the document contains this XML:

```
<?xml version="1.0"?>
<Person>
 <FirstName>John</FirstName>
 <LastName>Smith</LastName>
 <DoB>1970-12-22</DoB>
</Person>
```

which, happily, is the same as the XML document that we stored in the database a little earlier.

Searching for Information

Xindice also allows you to search for information using XPath 1.0 queries. If you wanted to retrieve both documents that you have stored in the database, you can do using the following command:

```
xindice xpath_query -c xmldb:xindice://localhost:8080/db/People -q /Person
```

Notice the `xpath_query` parameter that must follow `xindice`. The context is specified, as before, using the `-c` switch and the full URL for the `People` collection. The XPath query is specified using the `-q` switch and, in this case, is simply `/Person`.

Figure 10-8 shows the output from the query.

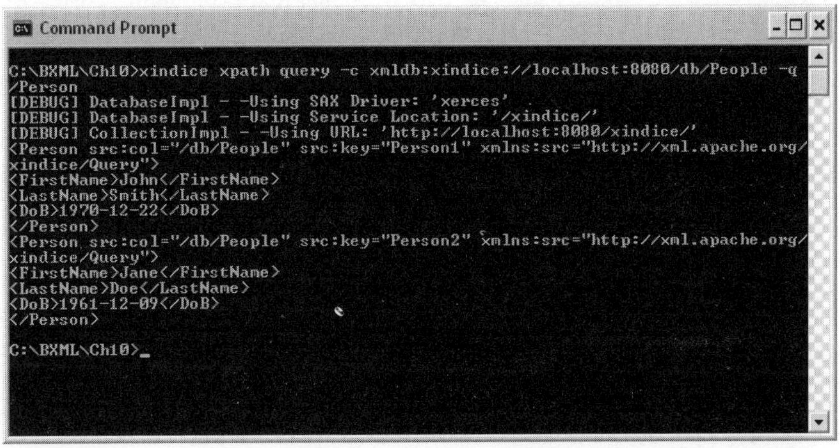

```
Command Prompt
C:\BXML\Ch10>xindice xpath query -c xmldb:xindice://localhost:8080/db/People -q
/Person
[DEBUG] DatabaseImpl - -Using SAX Driver: 'xerces'
[DEBUG] DatabaseImpl - -Using Service Location: '/xindice/'
[DEBUG] CollectionImpl - -Using URL: 'http://localhost:8080/xindice/'
<Person src:col="/db/People" src:key="Person1" xmlns:src="http://xml.apache.org/
xindice/Query">
<FirstName>John</FirstName>
<LastName>Smith</LastName>
<DoB>1970-12-22</DoB>
</Person>
<Person src:col="/db/People" src:key="Person2" xmlns:src="http://xml.apache.org/
xindice/Query">
<FirstName>Jane</FirstName>
<LastName>Doe</LastName>
<DoB>1961-12-09</DoB>
</Person>

C:\BXML\Ch10>_
```

Figure 10-8

Notice in the figure that a namespace declaration associating the namespace prefix with the namespace URI `http://xml.apache.org/xindice/Query` is added to each `Person` element that has been retrieved, together with `src:col` and `src:key` attributes indicating where in the Xindice database the data was retrieved from.

In Xindice 1.1 beta 3, there is a discrepancy between the on-screen help that specifies `xpath` as the parameter for an XPath query, whereas it is in fact `xpath_query`. If you download a later version of Xindice, be sure to check the syntax appropriate to that version.

Programming Xindice

The focus of this brief description of Xindice has been to show you some of its XML functionality and show how it can be used to add, retrieve, and query data to and from a Xindice database. In practice, in a production project you are more likely to use Xindice programmatically. As you have seen, XPath 1.0 is used to query a Xindice database. Xindice has both DOM and SAX programming interfaces. The Document Object Model (DOM) and how to use it is introduced in Chapter 11 and the Simple API for XML (SAX) is introduced in Chapter 12. It is beyond the scope of this chapter to show you how to use these application program interfaces (APIs) specifically to program Xindice.

Information on how a developer should use Xindice is found in the Xindice Developer's Guide, currently located at `http://xml.apache.org/xindice/guide-developer.html`. If you have installed Xindice, a copy of the Developer's Guide will be installed in the `docs` directory, including a PDF version if you wish to print the documentation.

Having looked at Xindice as an example of a native XML database, let's move on to look at how XML can be manipulated in an example commercial relational database management system.

XML in RDBMS

The practical reality is that huge volumes of data are currently stored in relational database management systems (RDBMS). Moving that data to native XML storage, even if it were desirable and possible, would be a huge logistical task. In reality, for reasons similar to the continuing existence of the COBOL language in many enterprises, the task will never be carried out. Relational data works well for many practical business purposes, and many business processes depend critically on at least some of that relational data. So, it would be folly to risk breaking something that works by moving all relational data to XML.

However, there is also an opposite pressure, the desire to use data derived from those traditional relational data stores in modern XML-based business processes, either within an enterprise or between enterprises. The question then becomes how can additional XML-relevant functionality be added to existing relational databases.

The vendors of major enterprise relational database management systems such IBM's DB2, Oracle, and Microsoft's SQL Server have taken differing approaches. In this section we will look briefly at the XML functionality in SQL Server 2000, which can be considered as a first generation XML-enabled relational database management system, and we will also take a peek ahead at the enhancements in XML-targeted functionality that will be available in SQL Server "Yukon," which is likely to be released by Microsoft a few months after this book is published.

One reason for choosing to describe SQL Server is that, typically, a 120-day evaluation is available for free download. At the time of writing, the evaluation version is available at `http://www.microsoft.com/sql/evaluation/trial/default.asp`. If you possess a 180-day evaluation edition CD for SQL Server be aware that that version is likely to be old and have a vulnerability to the Slammer worm.

XML Functionality in SQL Server 2000

SQL Server 2000 was the first version of SQL Server to have any XML functionality. Microsoft describes SQL Server 2000 as an XML-enabled database. When you are introduced a little later to the XML functionality in SQL Server Yukon, you will see that, in comparison, SQL Server 2000 is a partly XML-enabled database. The functionality in SQL Server 2000 that leads to that designation of XML-enabled database includes:

- Support for XDR schemas (later upgraded to XSD schemas)
- HTTP access to SQL Server 2000
- SQLXML functionality (added in SQLXML 1.0)
- A SOAP component (added in SQLXML 3.0)
- Retrieval of XML using the `SELECT` statement and `FOR XML` clause
- Writing XML using the `OPENXML` rowset provider
- Retrieval of XML data using XPath 1.0

SQL keywords are not case-sensitive. Many people who code in SQL use uppercase for SQL keywords, but that is a convention only.

XDR and XSD Schema Support

XML Data Reduced (XDR) is a schema language expressed in XML that was widely used by Microsoft prior to the development of W3C XML Schema. XDR is now essentially outdated and Microsoft is recommending all users to write SQL Server schemas only in XSD (W3C XML Schema) schemas going forward. XSD is an abbreviation for XML Schema Definition language, a term once applied to what became W3C XML Schema.

XDR schema documents constrain XML instance documents in ways similar to W3C XML Schema documents. XDR was used by Microsoft in SQL Server 2000 because the W3C XML Schema specification was not yet final.

The advantages of schema-defined data include facilitation of indexing and scope for optimizing processing of queries.

HTTP Access to SQL Server 2000

At the time that SQL Server 2000 was released, a common expectation was that XML would be sent to client browsers and transformed there, using Extensible Stylesheet Language Transformations (XSLT), to create HTML. Perhaps with that use for XML in mind, as well as dynamic data driven websites, HTTP access was added to SQL Server 2000. For reasons of security and scalability, the HTTP access wasn't directly to SQL Server 2000 but via an Internet Server Application Programming Interface (ISAPI) extension to Microsoft's Internet Information Services (IIS) web server. In other words, in a three-tier application, the handling of HTTP requests takes place on the middle tier. The ISAPI filter can recognize and process requests intended for SQL Server and, after authentication, can forward the request via a SQL OLEDB provider to SQL Server 2000. SQL Server returns the requested data, which may or may not be XML and returns that to the middle tier. In the middle tier, post-processing may occur, and the data is then returned to the web browser client or other client application.

There are four kinds of queries that can be passed in a URL to SQL Server. Each is briefly described here. For these queries to work, you will need to customize IIS virtual directories, as described in the SQL Server documentation.

URL Query

The URL query allows an SQL statement to be incorporated into a URL, including SQL statements that specify that XML is to be returned. So, if I have IIS running as localhost, I can retrieve data from the Employees table of the sample NorthWind database and display it as XML using the following URL (which should be typed in the browser without a line break, which was necessary for printing):

```
http://localhost/nwind?sql=SELECT+FirstName,+LastName+FROM+Employees+FOR+XML+
AUTO&root=root
```

The `nwind` part of the URL is a virtual root, mapped to a physical location by IIS configuration. The result of the query in Internet Explorer is shown in Figure 10-9.

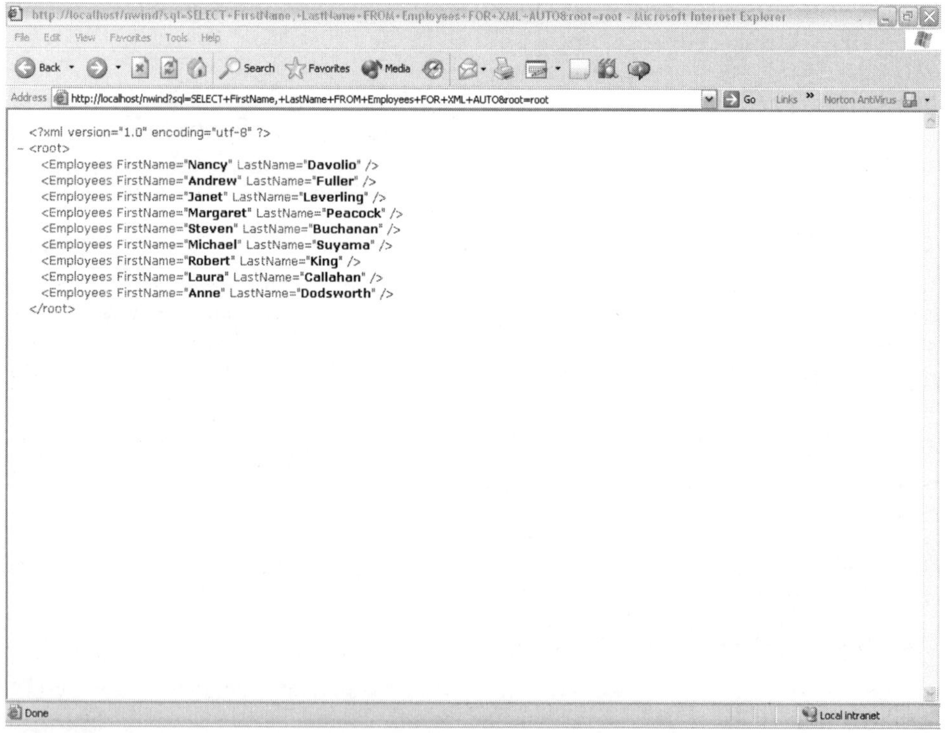

Figure 10-9

The URL query uses the `FOR XML` clause in the `SELECT` statement, which is described later. The document element is specified as a `root` element, as you can see in Figure 10-9. The data for each employee is displayed in an `Employees` (plural) element. If we were hand crafting the XML we would probably call that an `Employee` (singular) element, but the `FOR XML` clause uses the name of the table as the name of the element it creates.

The following lists the allowed parameters:

- **sql**—Uses an SQL statement, as you have seen
- **xsl**—Specifies an XSLT stylesheet on the middle tier to transform XML after the query has executed against the SQL Server
- **contenttype**—Specifies the content type of what is returned
- **encoding**—Specifies the encoding of the result, for example, `UTF-8`
- **root**—Specifies the name of the element which is the document element of the returned XML

Because, in principle, any SQL statement can be included in a URL, make sure that you don't open a production SQL Server to malicious SQL code by omitting to set appropriate permission settings for users who access the database from the web. Also, make sure that your browser or other application can handle the data that is sent to it.

Direct Query

A direct query takes the form:

```
http://servername/vroot/dbobject/xpath
```

where `vroot` is a virtual root whose physical location is specified by configuring IIS. The `dbobject` part of the URL signifies that the following part of the URL is an object access. XPath syntax is used in the final part of the URL to access the data.

Direct queries are often used to retrieve images, for example, to use in web pages. The XPath syntax can be used only to retrieve a single column from the database. In the XPath expression, the table or view is expressed as an element and the column name as an attribute.

So, retrieving a specified image from the Images column of an Employees table we might write `/Employees[@EmployeeID="35"]/@Image` as the XPath part of the URL.

XML Templates

XML templates allow you to conceal the structure of your database and, therefore are from a security point of view a preferred approach.

The URL when using XML templates takes the form:

```
http://servername/vroot/vname?params
```

where `servername` is the name of the server, `vroot` is a virtual root, and vname is the name of a template to which parameters can be passed.

When using XML templates be sure that you check the XML template for well-formedness. If the XML is not well-formed, you are likely to get a 404 error in the browser that might cause you to waste time checking virtual directories or other browser settings when the problem is a simple syntax error in the XML template.

Implementation-defined parameters that can be passed to an XML template are `xsl`, `encoding`, and `contenttype`. Developers may add additional parameters that are referenced inside the templates.

An XML template has a structure like this:

```
<root
 xmlns:sql="urn:schemas-microsoft-com:xml-sql">
 <sql:header>
 <!-- parameters can go here, if desired. -->
 </sql:header>

 <sql:query>
  SELECT FirstName, LastName
  FROM Employees
  FOR XML AUTO
 </sql:query>
</root>
```

The `sql:header` element can contain one or more `sql:parameter` elements whose `name` attribute specifies the name of a parameter and whose value specifies the parameter's default value. The SQL statement is contained in an `sql:query` element and is similar to the query using the URL query approach. On this occasion, there is no need to specify the document element—the document element of the template is echoed with the results of the query nested inside it.

If the preceding code is saved as a file `TestTemplate.xml` in the template subdirectory of the `nwind` virtual root, then you can query the Northwind database using the following URL:

```
http://localhost/nwind/template/TestTemplate.xml
```

This better conceals the database structure from a user and so provides additional security protection by providing protection from maliciously edited URLs. The query returns the data shown in Figure 10-10, which is similar in appearance to Figure 10-9. Notice, however, that a template XML file is used in the URL.

You can easily provide a more informative document element to the XML produced by using a different element name in the template. For example, the document element in `TestTemplate2.xml`, shown here:

```
<?xml version='1.0'?>
<myEmployees
 mlns:sql="urn:schemas-microsoft-com:xml-sql">
 <sql:header>
 </sql:header>
```

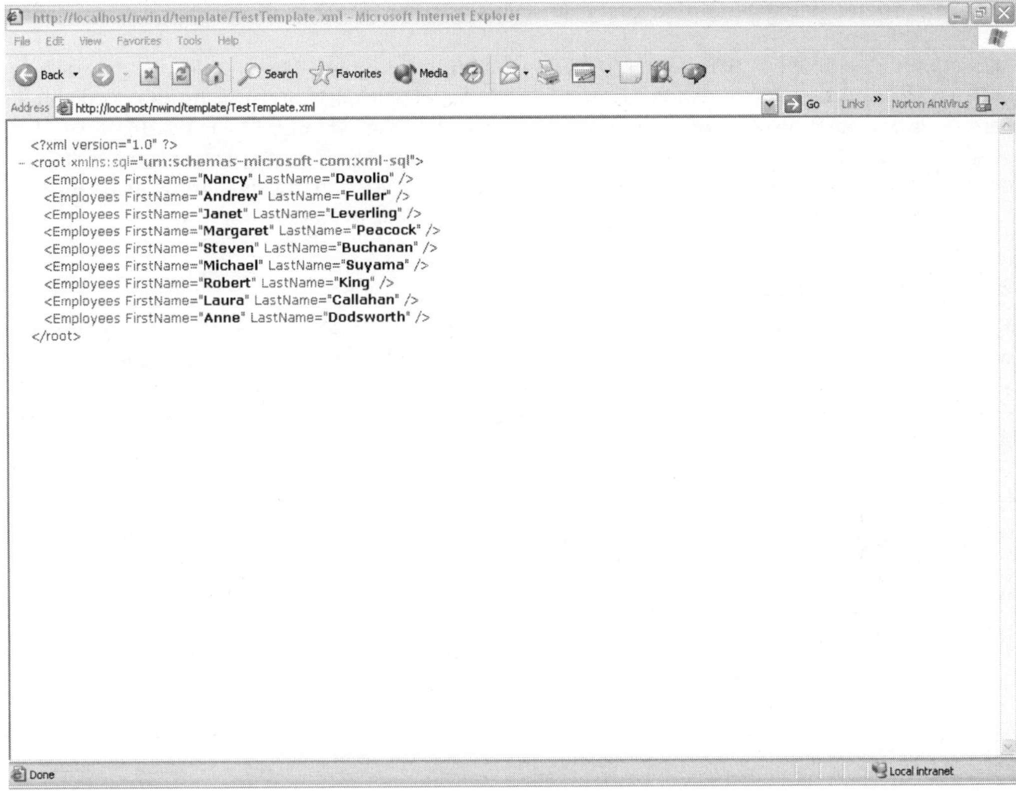

Figure 10-10

```
  <sql:query>
   SELECT FirstName, LastName
   FROM Employees
   FOR XML AUTO
  </sql:query>
</myEmployees>
```

is the `myEmployees` element, which is more informative than calling it `root` element. We will discuss the `FOR XML` clause in more detail shortly and discuss how you can take greater control of the structure of the XML that the template query generates.

An additional advantage of the template approach is that the SQL statements can be of arbitrary complexity, allowing powerful queries to be executed across the web.

XML Views

SQL Server 2000 also provides XML views. An XML view can be thought of as providing a way for developers who understand XML (but who may not understand SQL) to provide an XML view of relational data. In the initial release of SQL Server 2000, XDR schemas were used to specify a schema that mapped the relational data to the XML view. Later releases of SQLXML added XSD schema functionality as an additional, and preferred, option.

XPath 1.0 location paths are used to query the XML view.

Note that to benefit from XSD schemas to produce XML views you will need to install the latest version of SQLXML, which can be downloaded from the Microsoft website. Currently, the SQLXML version 3 Service Pack 1 can be downloaded from `http://www.microsoft.com/downloads/details.aspx?FamilyID=4023deea-f179-45de-b41d-84e4ff655a3b&displaylang=en`. Before downloading that version, you may wish to search for SQLXML downloads in the Search box on `http://www.microsoft.com/` to ensure you locate the latest version.

The FOR XML Clause

The `FOR XML` clause allows relational result sets to be presented to the user as XML. The `FOR XML` clause was introduced in SQL Server 2000 and is used as an extension to the SQL `SELECT` statement. This approach allows SQL Server developers to apply their existing SQL knowledge in retrieving data from relational tables, while also extending that knowledge to provide a syntax to create XML structures from relational data.

Data retrieved using the `FOR XML` clause is structured into a well-formed XML document. Its structure, being XML, is hierarchical rather than the (possibly multiple) tabular structure in which the data was stored, although the degree to which the `FOR XML` clause produces a hierarchy depends on the mode used with `FOR XML`.

The `FOR XML` clause can be used in the following four modes, which give varying degrees of developer control over the structure of the XML produced from an SQL query:

- `raw`
- `auto`
- `explicit`
- `nested` (this was not in the initial release but was added in an SQLXML release)

Using raw Mode

When you use `raw` mode, the XML produced from a database query is very similar to the row-based structure in which the data existed in the SQL Server table. A `row` element is created for each row in the result set. Nested XML structures are not produced. Values of columns in the result set are expressed as attribute names and value on the `row` elements.

Using auto Mode

In `AUTO` mode, the table or view name is used as the element name. In the default version of `AUTO` mode, column names are expressed as attributes. The following query is included in the XML template `FORXMLAuto1.xml`:

```
SELECT Customers.CustomerID, OrderID
FROM Customers, Orders
WHERE Customers.CustomerID = Orders.CustomerID
ORDER BY Customers.CustomerID
FOR XML AUTO
```

The template is used by specifying the URL:

```
http://localhost/nwind/template/FORXMLAuto1.xml
```

The result of the template query is shown in Figure 10-11.

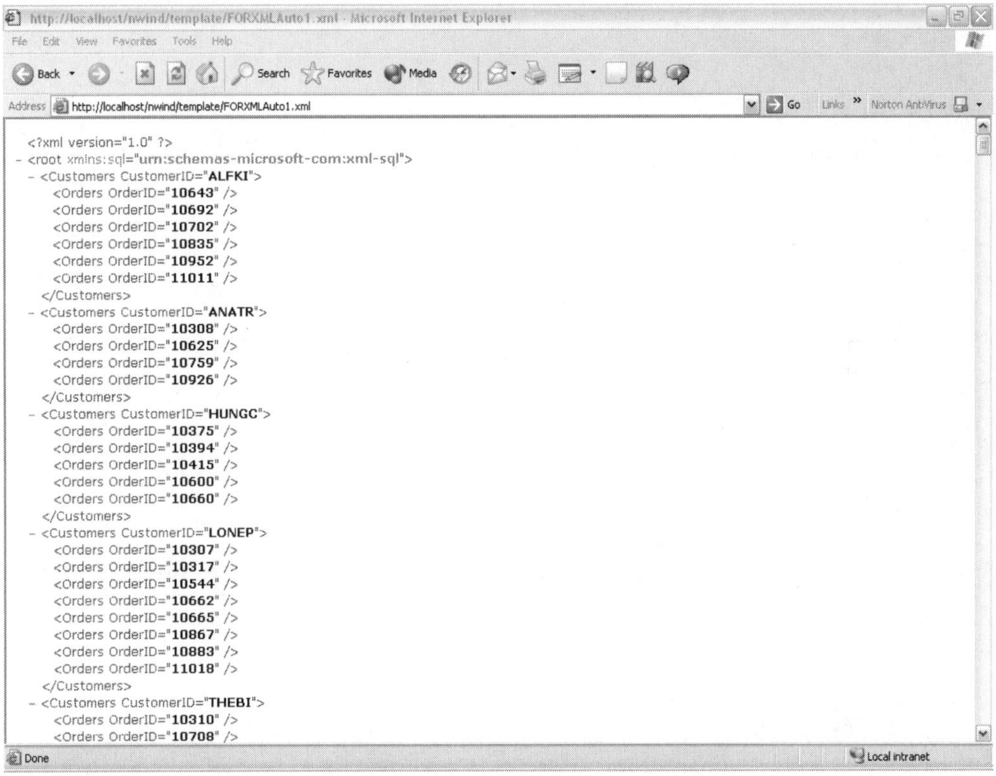

Figure 10-11

Notice that the `OrderID` is displayed as an attribute of an `Orders` element.

However, you also have an `ELEMENTS` option for `FOR XML AUTO` that allows column names to be expressed as elements nested inside the element name that corresponds to the name of the table. The order of nested elements can be specified by the ordering of column names in the `SELECT` statement in the SQL.

The following SQL code, which is included in the file `FORXMLAuto2.xml`, uses the `ELEMENTS` option. The output is shown in Figure 10-12. Notice how an `OrderID` element is a child element of the `Orders` element when the `ELEMENTS` option is used.

```
SELECT Customers.CustomerID, OrderID
FROM Customers, Orders
WHERE Customers.CustomerID = Orders.CustomerID
FOR XML AUTO, ELEMENTS
```

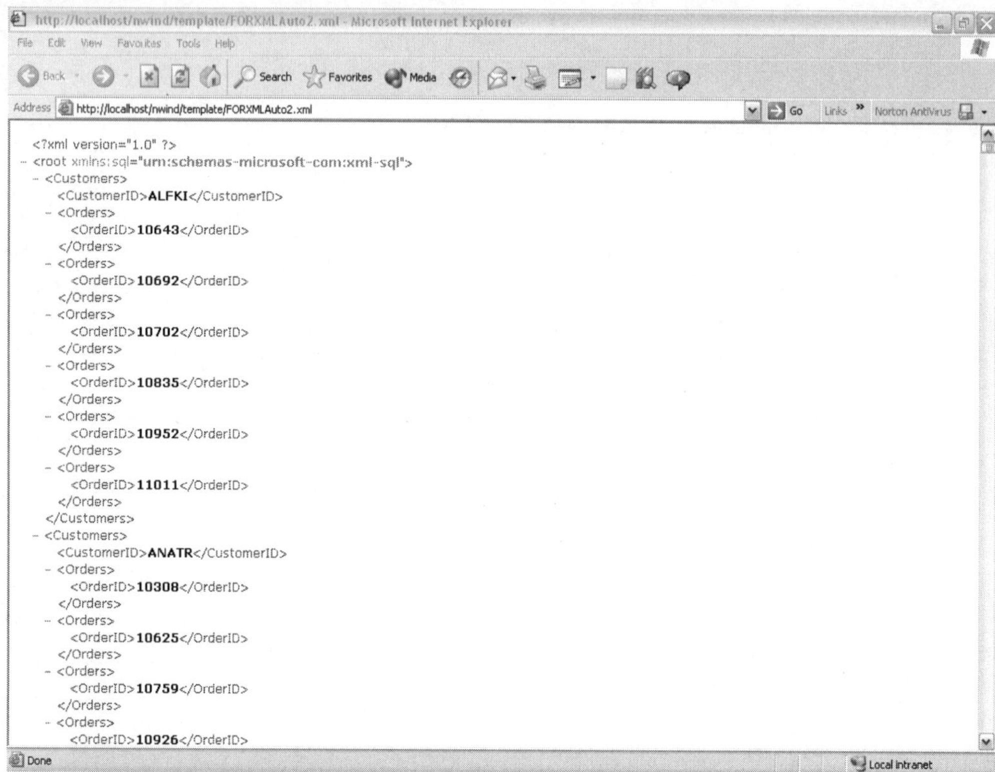

Figure 10-12

> **When you are testing XML templates, simple SQL syntax errors can cause a 500, internal server error. Internet Explorer 6 seems to have a bug that may fail to recognize a corrected file when a failed page is refreshed.**

It is also possible to change the names of elements using table and column aliases.

Using explicit Mode

The `explicit` mode of the `FOR XML` clause provides the developer with complete control in specifying the XML structure to be produced from the data returned from the query. For example, columns can be individually mapped to elements or attributes, according to the developer's needs. The `explicit` mode also allows creation of XML CDATA sections and ID/IDREF pairs, if needed.

Using nested Mode

In the original SQL Server 2000 release, there were only three modes for the `FOR XML` clause. The `nested` mode, which was first made available in an SQL Server Service Pack, specifies that XML formatting is carried out on what the SQL Server documentation calls the client-side, meaning the middle tier, which is a client to SQL Server.

OPENXML

The OPENXML statement provides a relational view of XML data, so allowing XML data to be sent to SQL Server 2000 and shredded into components that correspond to the relational data model and, therefore, can be stored in SQL Server's relational tables.

The OPENXML statement can be used in T-SQL stored procedures. Rows and columns are specified using XPath 1.0.

The OPENXML statement works pretty much as follows. A system stored procedure sp_xml_preparedocument parses XML into a DOM tree. The OPENXML statement specifies how the content of that DOM tree is shredded into relational tables, rows, and columns. The shredded (now relational) data is inserted into the appropriate part of the SQL Server database.

Developers should use the sp_xml_remove document stored procedure to clean up the DOM.

XML Functionality in SQL Server "Yukon"

Likely to be released early in 2005, SQL Server "Yukon", which will be called SQL Server 2005, is the version of SQL Server that follows SQL Server 2000.

Because SQL Server 2005 is currently in beta, then potentially anything I write about it is subject to change. I have tried to pick aspects that I guess are less likely to change, but be sure to check the SQL Server Books Online, which is part of the download, if you choose to download Yukon once a public beta or final version is available.

First, let's look at one of Yukon's most fundamental innovations in terms of XML support— the ability to store XML in columns, variables, or parameters.

The xml Data Type

SQL Server Yukon adds a new xml data type. That means that XML documents can be stored in an SQL Server Yukon database without—as has been the only option in SQL Server 2000—being shredded into parts and stored in multiple relational tables that conform with the relational data model or stored simply as a sequence of characters, which loses the logical content of the XML document. XML data stored as the xml data type can, in effect, be treated as if it were still an XML document. In reality, the xml data type is stored in a proprietary binary format under the hood, but as far as the developer is concerned it is accessible as XML with its logical structure intact.

This is a significant improvement over the situation in SQL Server 2000 where XML documents were either shredded using OpenXML as described earlier or, alternatively, saved as a text format that could be retrieved only as a series of characters. Queries on the latter documents could not necessarily rely on well-formedness or validity of the text cum XML that was being retrieved, and all XML-specific processing would need to take place outside the database, often in the middle tier of a three-tier application.

The existence of the xml data type means that XML documents stored, for example, in an SQL Server Yukon column can be treated as if they are collections of XML documents sitting on your hard drive. Of course, the details of the interface to that XML is specific to SQL Server Yukon, just as there were aspects specific to Xindice when you accessed XML stored in it.

Among the general advantages of storage in SQL Server 2005 is that XML storage benefits from the security, scalability, and other aspects of an enterprise-level database management system.

XML documents stored in Yukon can be treated as XML in any other setting. One practical effect of that is that you can use XQuery, to which you were introduced in Chapter 9, to query XML columns in Yukon. Perhaps surprisingly, two XML document instances cannot be compared in this release, in part because of the flexibility of XML Syntax. Consider for example the subtleties of trying to compare two lengthy XML documents that can, for example, have paired apostrophes or paired quotes to contain attribute values, can have differently ordered attributes, can have different namespace prefixes although the namespace URI may be the same, and can have empty elements written with start and end tags or with the empty element tag.

Documents stored as the `XML` data type can optionally be validated against a specified W3C XML Schema document. XML data that is not associated with a schema document is termed *untyped,* and XML associated with a schema documented is termed *typed.*

Let's look at how to create a simple table to contain XML documents in SQL Server Yukon. The graphical interface in Yukon has changed significantly from SQL Server 2000. The SQL Server Management Studio is the main graphical tool for manipulating database objects and writing SQL code. The SQL Management Studio is based on Microsoft's Visual Studio product and, in Yukon, developers can create solutions and projects in ways that are likely to be familiar to them if they are users of Visual Studio. It is possible that details of the user interface may change in the final release of Yukon.

Connect to the instance of SQL Server Yukon that is of interest. In the Object Explorer, expand the nodes so that User Databases is shown. Right-click and select the New Database option. A dialog box opens into which you insert the name of the database. I called the database `XMLDocTest`.

Next, create a table called `Docs` using the following SQL:

```
CREATE TABLE Docs (
 DocID INTEGER IDENTITY PRIMARY KEY,
 XMLDoc XML
 )
```

The column `XMLDoc` is of type `xml`. Since this is an SQL statement, the data type is not case-sensitive. Now we have an empty table.

For the purposes of this example, you will add simple XML documents with the following structure:

```
<Person>
 <FirstName></FirstName>
 <LastName></LastName>
</Person>
```

You can insert XML documents using SQL `INSERT` statement, as follows, which shows insertion of a single XML document:

```
INSERT Docs
VALUES ('<Person><FirstName>John</FirstName>,
<LastName>Smith</LastName></Person>'
)
```

After adding a few documents to the XMLDoc column, you can confirm that retrieval works correctly using the SQL statement:

```
SELECT XMLDoc
FROM Docs
```

The result of that SQL Query is shown in Figure 10-13.

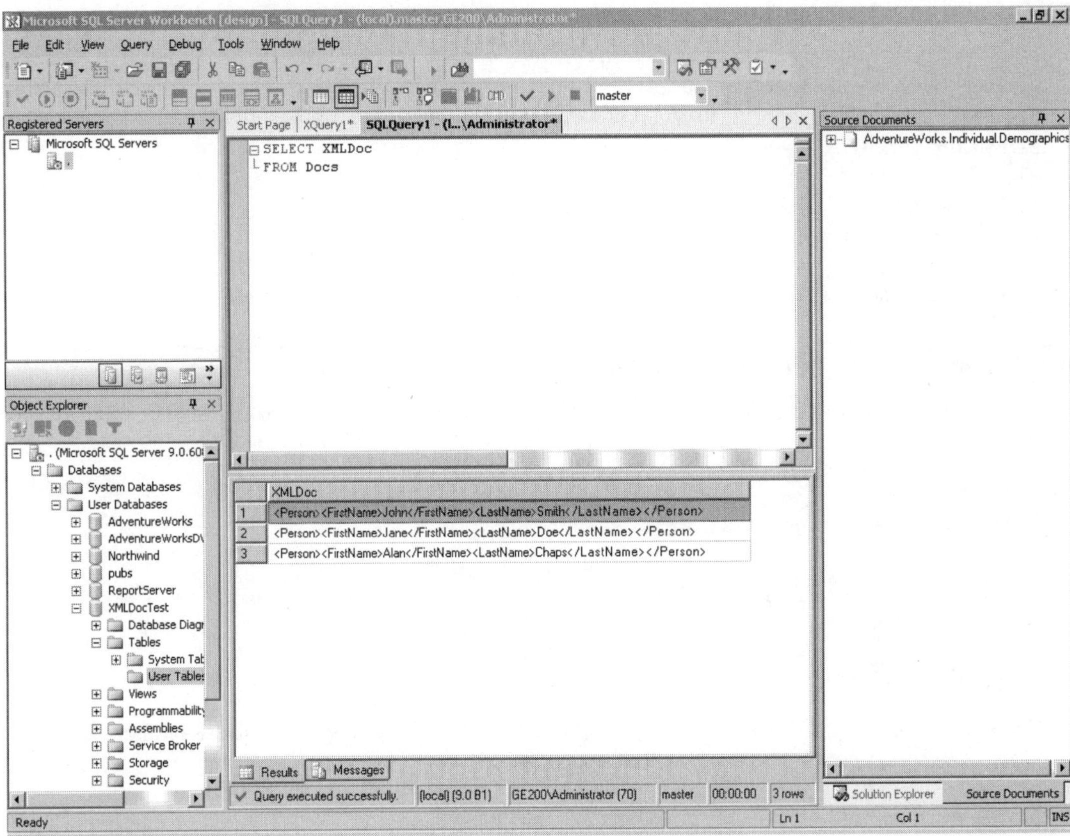

Figure 10-13

The values contained in the `XMLDoc` column are displayed in the lower-middle pane in the figure. A little later you will create some simple XQuery queries.

XML documents in Yukon can be indexed for more efficient retrieval, and optionally a full-text index can be created. To create a full-text index on a document, you use a command like the following:

```
CREATE FULLTEXT INDEX ON docs(xDoc)
```

The `xml` data type allows the following methods to be used: `query()`, `value()`, `exist()`, `modify()`, and `nodes()`.

XQuery in SQL Server Yukon

The `xml` data type can be queried using the XQuery language, which you were introduced in Chapter 9. In SQL Server Yukon, XQuery expressions are embedded inside Transact-SQL. Transact-SQL is the flavor of the SQL language used in SQL Server.

First, we will look at the proprietary extensions to XQuery in the XML Data Modification Language. Then, we will look at the `query()` method that is used to allow XQuery queries inside SQL `SELECT` statements.

Extensions to XQuery in SQL Server Yukon

The W3C XQuery specification is limited in that it can only query an XML (or XML-enabled) data source. There is no facility in XQuery 1.0 to carry out deletions, to insert new data, or (combining those actions) to modify data. In SQL Server Yukon, the XML Data Modification Language (DML) adds three keywords to the functionality available in XQuery 1.0:

- `delete`
- `insert`
- `replace value of`

Try It Out — Deleting with XML DML

First, let's look at using the `delete` keyword. The following code shows an example of how it can be used.

```
declare @myDoc XML
SET @myDoc = '<Person><FirstName>John</FirstName>
 <LastName>Smith</LastName></Person>
 '
SELECT @myDoc
SET @myDoc.modify('
 delete /Person/*[2]
')
SELECT @myDoc
```

If you have access to SQL Server 2005, then follow these steps. The steps describe the things needed when using SQL Server beta 1. It is possible that details may change in later betas or the release version of SQL Server 2005.

1. Open the SQL Server Workbench.
2. Connect to the default instance.
3. From the Start Page, select New SQL Server Query.
4. Enter the preceding code.
5. Hit F5 to run the SQL code. If you have typed in the code correctly, the original document should be displayed, and the modified document should be displayed below it.
6. You will need to adjust the width of the columns to display the full XML.

How It Works

The first line of the code declares a variable `myDoc` and specifies the data type as `xml`. The `SET` statement:

```
SET @myDoc = '<Person><FirstName>John</FirstName>
 <LastName>Smith</LastName></Person>
 ')
```

specifies a value for the `myDoc` variable. It's a familiar `Person` element with `FirstName` and `LastName` child elements and corresponding text content.

The `SELECT` statement following the `SET` statement causes the value of `myDoc` to be displayed.

Next, the `modify` function is used to modify the value of the `xml` datatype:

```
SET @myDoc.modify('
 delete /Person/*[2]
')
```

The Data Modification Language statement inside the `modify` function is, like XQuery, case-sensitive. The `delete` keyword is used to specify which part of the XML document is to be deleted. In this case the XPath expression `/Person/*[2]` specifies that it is the second child element of the `Person` element that is to be deleted, which is the `LastName` element.

The final `SELECT` statement shows the value of `myDoc` after the deletion has taken place. Figure 10-14 shows the results of both `SELECT` statements.

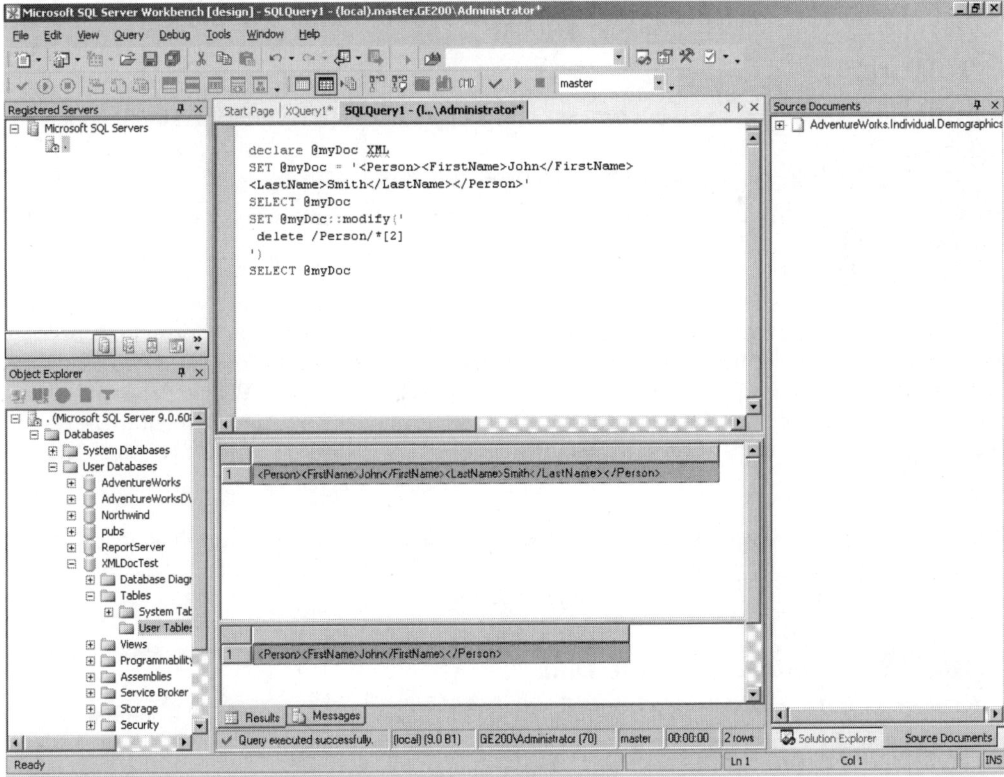

Figure 10-14

Try It Out Inserting with XML DML

Next, let's look at an example of using the `insert` keyword. The Transact-SQL code is shown here:

```
declare @myDoc XML
SET @myDoc = '<Person><LastName>Smith</LastName></Person>'
SELECT @myDoc
SET @myDoc::modify('
 insert <FirstName>John</FirstName>
 as first
 into /Person[1]
')
SELECT @myDoc
```

1. Open the SQL Server Workbench.
2. Connect to the default instance.
3. From the Start Page select New SQL Server Query.
4. Enter the preceding code.
5. Hit F5 to run the SQL code. If you have typed in the code correctly, the original document should be displayed, and the modified document should be displayed below it.
6. You will need to adjust the width of the columns to display the full XML.

How It Works

In the first line you declare a variable `myDoc` and specify it has the data type `xml`. In the code:

```
SET @myDoc = '<Person><LastName>Smith</LastName></Person>'
```

we set the value of the `myDoc` variable and specify a `Person` element that contains only a `LastName` element, which contains the text `Smith`.

The `modify` function is used to contain the XQuery extension that you want to use. The `insert` keyword specifies that the modification is an insert operation. The XML to be inserted follows the `insert` keyword. Notice that it is not enclosed by apostrophes or quotes. The clause `as first` specifies that the inserted XML is to be inserted first, and the `into` clause uses an XPath expression, `/Person`, to specify that the `FirstName` element and its content is to be added as a child element to the `Person` element. Given the `as first` clause, you know that the `FirstName` element is to be the first child of the `Person` element.

When you run the Transact-SQL, then the first `SELECT` statement causes the original XML to be displayed, and the second `SELECT` statement causes the XML to be displayed after the `insert` operation has completed. Both results are shown in Figure 10-15.

Try It Out Updating with XML DML

In the final example of using the Data Modification Language, you will update the content of an XML variable so that the value of the `FirstName` element is changed from `John` to `Jane`. The code is shown here:

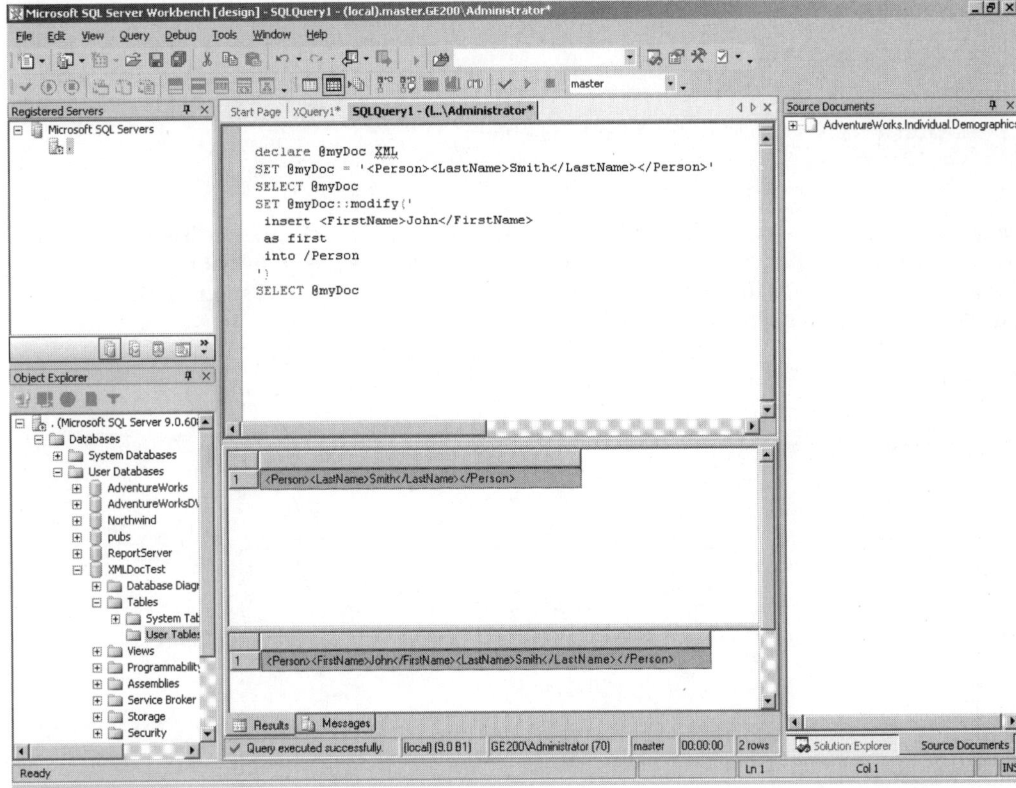

Figure 10-15

```
declare @myDoc XML
SET @myDoc = '<Person><FirstName>John</FirstName>
 <LastName>Smith</LastName></Person>
SELECT @myDoc
SET @myDoc.modify('
 replace value of /Person/FirstName
 to "Jane"
 ')
SELECT @myDoc
```

1. Open the SQL Server Workbench.
2. Connect to the default instance.
3. From the Start Page select New SQL Server Query.
4. Enter the preceding code.
5. Hit F5 to run the SQL code. If you have typed in the code correctly, the original document should be displayed, and the modified document should be displayed below it.
6. You will need to adjust the width of the columns to display the full XML.

How It Works

Notice the `modify` function:

```
SET @myDoc.modify('
 replace value of /Person/FirstName/text()
 to "Jane"
 ')
```

where the `replace value of` keyword indicates an update and an XPath expression indicates which part of the XML the update is to be applied to. In this case it is the text node that is the child of the `FirstName` element, in other words, the value of the `FirstName` element, specified by the XPath expression `/Person/FirstName/text()`.

The results of the two `SELECT` statements are shown in Figure 10-16.

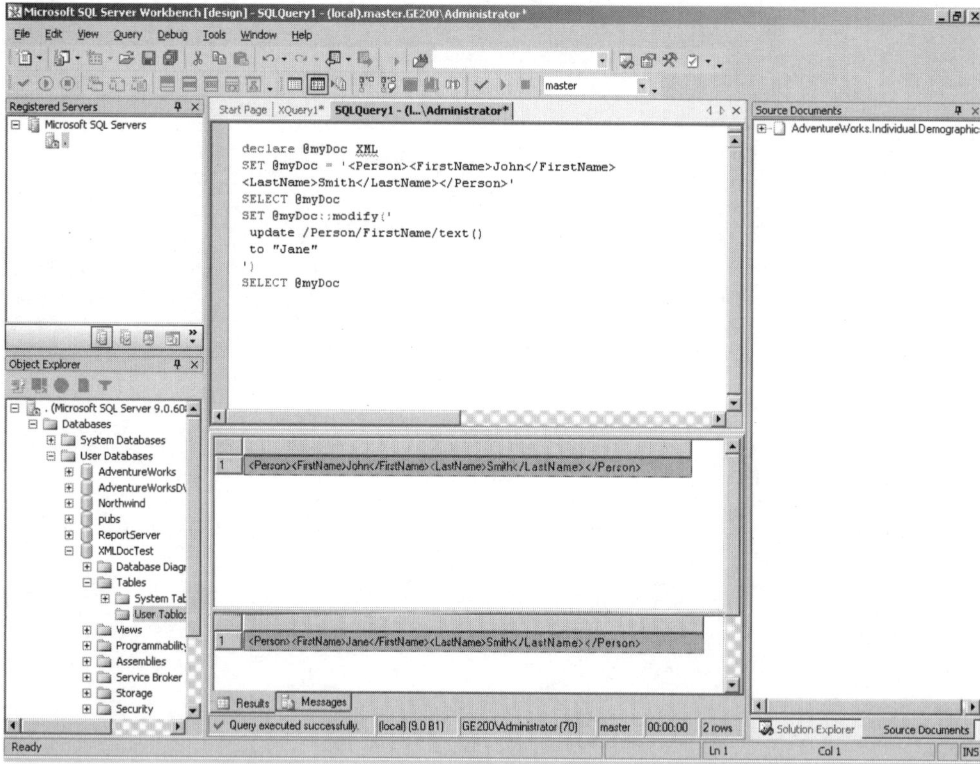

Figure 10-16

The query() Method

The `query()` method allows you to construct XQuery statements in SQL Server Yukon.

The following query uses the `query()` method to output the names of each person in a newly constructed `Name` element with the value of the `LastName` element followed by a comma and then the value of the `FirstName` element. The code is shown here:

```
SELECT XMLDoc.query('
 for $p in /Person
 return
 <Name>{$p/LastName/text()},{$p/FirstName/text()}
')
FROM Docs
```

The first line indicates that a selection is being made using the `query()` method applied to the `XMLDoc` column (which, of course, is of data type `xml`).

The `for` clause specifies that the variable `$p` is bound to the `Person` element node.

The `return` clause specifies that a `Name` element is to be constructed using an element constructor. The first part of the content of each `Name` element is created by evaluating the XQuery expression `$p/LastName/text()`, which, of course, is the text content of the `LastName` element. A literal comma is output, and then the XQuery expression `$p/FirstName/text()` is evaluated.

Figure 10-17 shows the output when the `SELECT` statement containing the XQuery query is run.

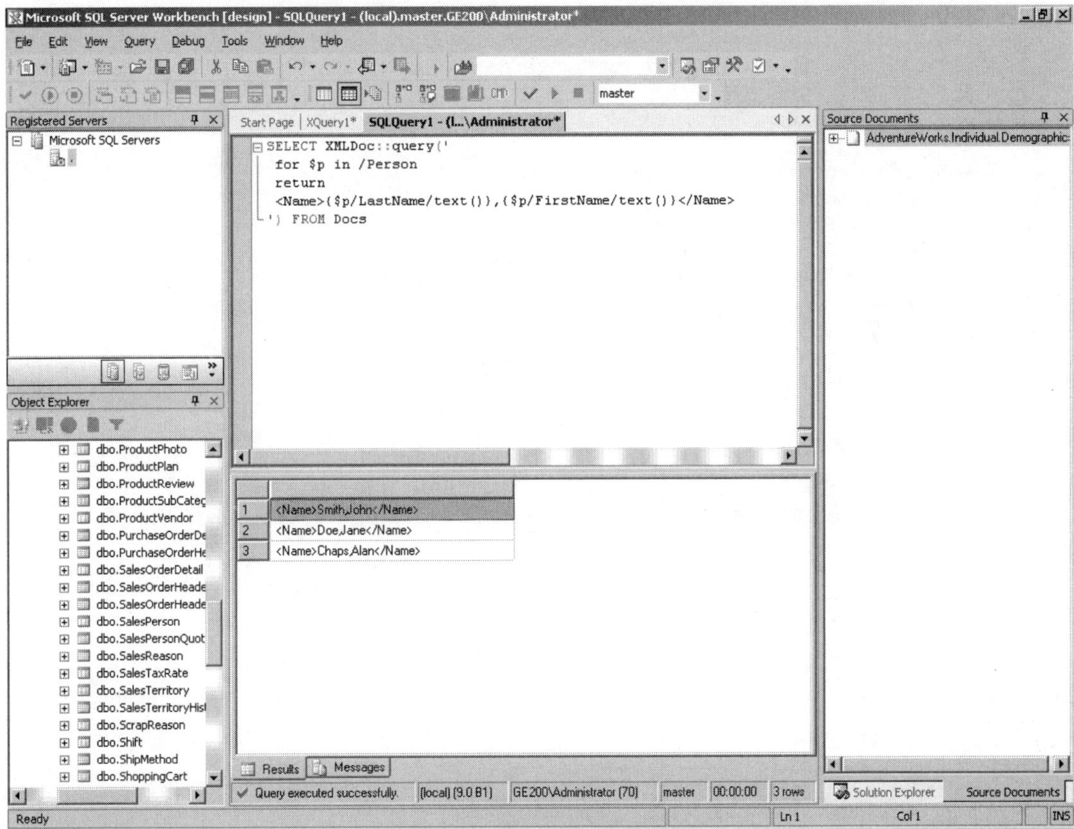

Figure 10-17

W3C XML Schema in SQL Server Yukon

I mentioned earlier that the new `xml` data type is now a first-class data type in Yukon. The `xml` data type can be used to store untyped and typed XML data. Therefore, it shouldn't be surprising that, just as relational data is specified by a schema, so the new `xml` data type can be associated with a W3C XML Schema document to specify its structure. The XDR schema language that was used in SQL Server 2000 has been replaced by W3C XML Schema in SQL Server Yukon.

> **It seems likely that in SQL Server Yukon beta 2 the functionality described in this section will change significantly.**

First, let's look at how you can specify a schema for data of type `xml`. A W3C XML Schema document can be specified using the `CREATE XMLSCHEMA` statement. Paired apostrophes surround the W3C XML Schema document itself. So, if you wanted to create a very simple schema for a document that could contain a `Person` element and child elements named `FirstName` and `LastName` you could do so using the following syntax:

```
CREATE XMLSCHEMA '
<xsd:schema xmlns:xsd="http://www.w3.org/2001/XMLSchema"
 targetNamespace="http://www.XMML.com/SampleNamespace"
 xmlns="http://www.XMML.com/SampleNamespace">
 <xsd:element name="Person">
  <xsd:complexType>
   <xsd:sequence>
    <xsd:element name="FirstName" />
    <xsd:element name="LastName" />
   </xsd:sequence>
  </xsd:complexType>
 </xsd:element>
</xsd:schema>
'
```

If you want to drop the XML Schema, then we can do so using a `DROP XMLSCHEMA` statement, like the following:

```
DROP XMLSCHEMA NAMESPACE "http://www.XMML.com/SampleNamespace"
```

When you use the `DROP XMLSCHEMA` statement to drop a namespace, remember that the namespace is an XML namespace URI, so it is case-sensitive.

Untyped and typed `xml` data can be used in an SQL Server column, variable, or parameter. If you want to create a `Docs` table and associate it with a W3C XML Schema document, you can do so using code like the following:

```
CREATE TABLE Docs (
 DocID INTEGER IDENTITY PRIMARY KEY,
 XMLDoc XML('http://www.XMML.com/SampleNamespace')
 )
```

For reasons of optimization XML Schemas are shredded and stored internally in a proprietary
Most of the schema can be reconstructed as an XML document from this proprietary format usi
`xml_schema_namespace` intrinsic function. So, if you had imported the schema shown earlier, you could retrieve it using the following code:

```
SELECT xml_schema_namespace('http://XMML.com/SampleNamespace')
```

Remember, too, that there can be multiple ways of writing a functionally equivalent W3C XML Schema document, for example, using references, named types, or anonymous types. SQL Server will not respect such differences when reconstituting a schema document.

In addition, parts of the schema that are primarily documentation—for example, annotations and comments—are not stored in SQL Server's proprietary format. Therefore, to ensure precise recovery of an original W3C XML Schema document, it is necessary to store the serialized XML Schema document separately. One possibility is to store it in a column of type `xml` or `varchar(max)` in a separate table.

Choosing a Database to Store XML

At the end of the day knowing a little of the theory of XML and databases isn't the direction from which most businesses will approach storage of XML. They are likely to have large amounts of existing data in conventional relational database management systems and will want to leverage the skills and knowledge that their database administrators and other employees have of such RDBMS. So, I would expect much of the enterprise attention on XML and databases to be focused on adding XML support to existing RDBMS such as IBM's DB2, Oracle, or Microsoft's SQL Server. Of course, as XML functionality is added to such products, it becomes a little fuzzy whether they remain an RDBMS or become some other hybrid entity. For most businesses, that will be an academic point. They want a database that works, that is secure, that scales as business volume grows, that is easy to manage, and so on.

On the other hand, for some business uses, a custom application that uses a native XML database such as Xindice may be an appropriate approach.

Looking Ahead

At present there is no standard update technique for native XML databases, and there is unlikely to be one until a version of XQuery after version 1.0 is released. In an ideal world we would have a standard update language in the way that XQuery looks like being pretty tightly standardized across different commercial database products. That tight standardization of the query aspect of XQuery contrasts with the significant impact of proprietary aspects of the implementation of SQL in many relational database management systems. SQL Server Yukon provides one proprietary solution to fill this gap. In time it is likely that the W3C will produce a standard data modification language either as part of a later version of XQuery or to accompany it. Meanwhile, users of native XML databases and enterprise XML-enabled relational database management systems will have to make a choice of which proprietary data modification language they use.

Summary

In this chapter, we learned about the increasing business need to store or expose data as XML. The characteristics of a viable XML-enabled database were discussed, and two different examples of XML-enabled databases were shown. First, Xindice, a native XML database, was explored. Finally,

Microsoft's SQL Server 2000 was explored together with a preliminary look at the upcoming SQL Server 2005 ("Yukon") to see how additional XML functionality is being added to one commercial enterprise grade relational database management system.

Exercise Questions

Suggested solutions to these questions can be found in Appendix A.

Question 1

List some reasons why adding XML functionality to a relational database management system may be preferable to using a native XML database.

Question 2

What methods are available in SQL Server 2005 to manipulate data in a database column that is of type `xml`?

Part V: Programming

The XML Document Object Model (DOM)

In this chapter we will explore the XML Document Object Model, often called the XML DOM or simply the DOM, and look at how it can be manipulated in various ways. The XML DOM is primarily used by programmers as a way to manipulate the content of an XML document. The XML DOM is useful for tasks as diverse as manipulating data to animating part of an SVG graphic.

Although many XML programmers refer to the XML DOM simply as the DOM, the term *DOM* can also be used to refer to the HTML Document Object Model, the XML Document Object Model or both. In this chapter the focus will be on the XML DOM.

In this chapter, you will learn:

- What is the purpose of the XML Document Object Model
- How the DOM specification was developed at W3C
- About important XML DOM interfaces and objects, such as the `Node` and `Document` interfaces
- How to add and delete elements and attributes from a document object model and manipulate a DOM tree in other ways
- How the XML DOM is used under the covers in Microsoft InfoPath 2003

What Is an XML Document Object Model For?

The XML Document Object Model provides an interface for programmers to create XML documents, to navigate them, and to add, modify, or delete parts of those XML documents while they are held in memory. For an XML document to be represented in computer memory, a serialized XML document must have been processed by an XML parser. An XML parser, not surprisingly, *parses* the Unicode characters that are found in an XML document and then, in one option, creates a logical *model* of the XML document in memory—at least that is how it looks to the developer. Parsing also means that entities are not represented in the XML DOM, since any entities referenced in the XML would be expanded by an XML parser before the DOM tree was constructed. For example, in the XML DOM the predefined entity `&` would be represented by the single character, `&`. This raises corresponding issues when serializing an XML DOM. The character `&` in a DOM node would need to be expanded to `&` to avoid constructing an XML document that was not well formed.

The DOM provides a logical view on the in-memory structure that represents an XML document. Like the XPath document model, introduced in Chapter 7, the XML DOM represents an XML document in a way that is equivalent to a hierarchical tree-like structure consisting of *nodes*. A DOM implementation isn't obliged to create a tree as long as it appears to a developer to be equivalent to an in-memory tree.

The XML document itself is represented as a `Document` node. Like the root node in XPath 1.0 a DOM `Document` node is always situated at the apex of a tree. However, the `Document` node differs significantly from an XPath root node in its characteristics and its descendant nodes are also significantly different representations of parts of an XML document compared to XPath 1.0 nodes.

An XML document might typically be parsed by an XML parser, which checks for well-formedness and, optionally, for validity of the document. The XML DOM may then be constructed as an in-memory representation of the XML document. However, this doesn't happen in a vacuum. Typically, the XML DOM will be associated with some other application. In many of the examples later in this chapter, for the sake of illustrating principles relating to the XML DOM, that other application will be a web browser, but the options are almost limitless given the increase in use of XML in all types of business process. In the latter part of this chapter we will look briefly at how the XML DOM is used in an enterprise XML forms product from Microsoft called InfoPath 2003.

In the Microsoft MSXML component the XML parser, a DOM implementation, and several other XML technologies are implemented in one component.

Interfaces and Objects

Often you will read about interfaces and objects as if the two terms were pretty much interchangeable, but that is not really the case. An interface is a more abstract concept than an object.

Outside the programming world we might, loosely speaking, have a class of person characterized by success in an electoral process and residence at 1600 Pennsylvania Avenue. Very probably you would guess that the class of person we are talking about is a President of the United States. Apart from electoral information, a President would have assorted other properties such as name, inauguration date, political party represented, and so on. If the general concept of a President is an interface, we can view a specific *instance* of a President as corresponding to an object. If we refer to John Fitzgerald Kennedy, we have particular values for that individual, for example Democratic Party as the value of the party represented characteristic.

The class of person, President, has a set of characteristics and a set of actions for which he has authority such as appointing a cabinet and signing Acts of Congress. Similarly, an interface describes the properties and behavior of a class of objects. Characteristics of the interface are termed *properties* and actions or capacities of the interface are termed *methods*.

In general terms, if you think of parts of an XML document, you know that an element has certain characteristics, for example, a name and an optionally empty nonordered set of attributes. However, any particular XML element—any particular instance of the class element—has particular values for the characteristics of that class.

An interface can be considered as being a contract. The properties defined in the interface are available on all objects that are instances of that class. The methods specified in the interface are also present on all objects in the class.

There is a `Document` interface defined in the XML DOM. One of the properties of that interface is the `documentElement` property, which specifies the document element of the document. For any particular document there is a `Document` node, which is an object that implements the `Document` interface. Since the `Document` interface has a `documentElement` property, you can be sure that the `Document` object also has such a property, and you can query or assign a value to the `documentElement` property on that particular object. Whatever properties and methods the `Document` interface has (we will look in detail at those later in the chapter) a `Document` object has the same.

Since an object is an instance of an interface and has all the characteristics (properties and methods) that the interface has, it is very easy to slip from describing an interface to describing an instance of it—an object. It isn't easy in natural writing to be technically wholly consistent in separating interfaces from objects, a difficulty that the creators of the DOM also seem to have found since, arguably, what they created was a Document Interface Model rather than a Document Object Model.

The Document Object Model at the W3C

The official specifications of the XML Document Object Model have been developed by the World Wide Web Consortium (W3C). The various editions of the DOM specification have been referred to as *Levels*. So the first DOM specification was finalized as the Document Object Model Level 1 recommendation in October 1998. The recommendation is located at `http://www.w3.org/TR/1998/REC-DOM-Level-1-19981001/`. DOM Level 1 provided an approach both to the DOM for HTML and for XML. This chapter will focus only on those aspects of DOM Level 1 that apply to XML. The HTML interfaces are not described.

The XML DOM, like XPath 1.0, is a *logical* model of an XML document. An implementer of the XML DOM is free to implement the DOM in any way that presents the interface to the developer as if it, logically, corresponded to a hierarchical tree-like structure. The DOM Level 1 specification also left the technique and syntax to achieve creation of a `Document` node up to the creators of DOM implementations. Similarly, serialization of an XML DOM was not defined in the Level 1 recommendation.

The XML DOM, Level 1, provides an interface for developers to use to manipulate XML documents. Equally, the DOM can be presented as an interface to proprietary structures that themselves allow manipulation of structures representing XML, so providing a common means across programs to manipulate models of XML. The big advantage of the XML DOM is that as far as users are concerned, they appear to have a standard interface to allow manipulation of XML.

Having a shared interface potentially improves a programmer's productivity, since a developer need only be familiar with one common interface. Of course, in practice, that hasn't always been delivered, in part because the DOM Level 1 specification provided no common interface to create a representation of XML documents. Therefore that basic functionality had to be essentially proprietary.

The DOM also failed to provide a universal interface in the sense that it is not ideal or suitable for larger XML documents. The DOM, although useful for relatively small-scale XML programming, becomes impractical once you think of handling very large XML documents, since the DOM requires a single tree (or equivalent structure) to be created in memory. For really large XML documents the Simple API for XML (SAX), which is described in Chapter 12, provides an approach that scales better than the XML DOM. So, in practice, many XML developers will need to be familiar with both the XML DOM and with SAX.

DOM Level 1 did not include a way to create an XML document. In addition, it did not include a specification of XML events. DOM Level 1 specified language bindings for Java and ECMAScript, is still often colloquially referred to as JavaScript.

DOM Level 2 added some new functionality, which resulted in the XML DOM specification being split into several modules. The Core module had few changes from DOM Level 1.

The DOM Level 2 specification documents and their location are listed here:

- **Document Object Model (DOM) Level 2 Core**—`http://www.w3.org/TR/2000/REC-DOM-Level-2-Core-20001113/`
- **Document Object Model (DOM) Level 2 Events**—`http://www.w3.org/TR/2000/REC-DOM-Level-2-Events-20001113/`
- **Document Object Model (DOM) Level 2 Style**—`http://www.w3.org/TR/2000/REC-DOM-Level-2-Style-20001113/`
- **Document Object Model (DOM) Level 2 Traversal and Range**—`http://www.w3.org/TR/2000/REC-DOM-Level-2-Traversal-Range-20001113/`
- **Document Object Model (DOM) Level 2 Views**—`http://www.w3.org/TR/2000/REC-DOM-Level-2-Views-20001113/`
- **Document Object Model (DOM) Level 2 HTML**—`http://www.w3.org/TR/DOM-Level-2-HTML/`

The Style specification refers to the DOM of Cascading Style Sheets and the HTML specification applies only to HTML documents. Neither of those specifications will be considered further in this chapter.

XML DOM Implementations

A DOM implementation will provide all interfaces described in a particular level of the DOM specification. However, an implementer is free to provide additional interfaces. For example, in DOM Level 1 it was essential that implementers provided some additional interfaces since DOM Level 1 provided no standard mechanism for creating an XML DOM `Document` object.

Similarly, implementers may use the XML DOM for specialized purposes that benefit from specialized functionality. The Adobe SVG Viewer version 3, which is a widely used SVG viewer at the time of writing, provides several additional properties and methods for manipulation of objects in the SVG DOM in addition to those required to comply with the XML DOM specifications.

Two Ways to View DOM Nodes

The XML DOM provides two ways in which you can look at DOM nodes. We will briefly look at each of these in turn.

- One way of looking at a DOM tree is that it is a hierarchy of `Node` objects, some of which expose specialized interfaces. Viewed in this way all XML DOM objects are `Node` objects. This way of viewing an XML DOM is particularly useful when we identify properties and methods that are common to all DOM nodes.
- The alternative way to view a DOM tree is to view the root of the tree as a `Document` node (or object) whose descendant nodes are objects of different specialized types. For example, the child nodes of the `Document` object may be a `DocumentType` object (which represents a `DOCTYPE` declaration), an `Element` object (which represents the document element of the document), and zero or more `ProcessingInstruction` objects and `Comment` objects (which represent any processing instructions and comments in the prolog of the XML document). If you recall the permitted structure of an XML document and, specifically, its prolog, the allowed objects should be fairly self-explanatory. Remember that an XML declaration is not, strictly speaking, a processing instruction, and therefore, it is not represented as a `ProcessingInstruction` node in the XML DOM.

I find the second viewpoint more intuitive when trying to visualize the effect that my code is having or intended to have on nodes within the DOM, so I will mostly use that approach in the descriptions of the DOM that follow.

Overview of the XML DOM

In this section I will briefly describe the objects or interfaces that make up the XML DOM so that you can get the general picture of how an XML document is represented. Each of the node types will be briefly mentioned here, but several of the node types will be discussed in more detail and demonstrated in example code later in the chapter.

As I describe the allowed node types, you will likely find it helpful to think how those node types correspond to parts of serialized XML documents.

As mentioned earlier, the root of the DOM hierarchy is always a `Document` node, if an XML document is being represented. The child nodes of the `Document` node are the `DocumentType` node, `Element` node, `ProcessingInstruction` nodes, and `Comment` nodes. The `DocumentType`, `Comment`, and `ProcessingInstruction` node types may not have child nodes.

If the DOM tree represents a fragment of an XML document, for example, snipped from an existing DOM tree or newly created, then the root of the hierarchy is a `DocumentFragment` node. Given the circumstances in which it is used, it is not surprising that the child nodes of a `DocumentFragment` node need not conform to XML's well-formedness rules, although once the nodes in the document fragment have been added to a full XML DOM tree the equivalent of well-formedness rules apply again. The most common child node of the `DocumentFragment` node is likely to be `Element` nodes but other allowed child node types are `Comment`, `ProcessingInstruction`, `Text`, `CDATASection`, and `EntityReference`.

`Element` nodes represent the document element of an XML document and all other elements in the document. The permitted child node types of an `Element` node are `Element`, `Comment`, `ProcessingInstruction`, `Text`, `CDATASection`, and `EntityReference`. Notice that the permitted child nodes of the `Element` node are the same as the allowed child nodes of the `DocumentFragment` node.

Attributes in an XML document are represented by the `Attr` node type. An `Attr` node is associated with an `Element` node but is not considered to be a child node of the `Element` node. In the DOM an `Attr` node is not a child node of the `Element` node and therefore is not considered part of the DOM tree, despite the `Attr` node implementing the `Node` interface. Thus, the `parentNode`, `previousSibling`, and `nextSibling` attributes of the `Attr` node have a `Null` value. The text content of an attribute is represented in a `Text` node.

> **The DOM representation of attributes differs significantly from the representation of attributes in the XPath data model, which was described in Chapter 7. In XPath an attribute node is considered not to be a child of the element node with which it is associated, but seemingly paradoxically, in the XPath model the element node is considered to be the parent node of the attribute node.**

Most of the code you write to manipulate the XML DOM is likely to include the `Document`, the `Element`, the `Attr`, and the `Text` node types.

The `CDATASection` and the `Notation` node types correspond to the similarly named structures in an XML document. The `Entity` node type represents a parsed or unparsed entity in an XML document. An `Entity` node may have child nodes of the following node types: `Element`, `Comment`, `ProcessingInstruction`, `Text`, `CDATASection`, and `EntityReference`.

An `EntityReference` node may have the following child node types: `Element`, `Comment`, `ProcessingInstruction`, `Text`, `CDATASection`, and `EntityReference`.

In the examples in this chapter we won't look further at the use of `CDATASection`, `Entity`, and `EntityReference` node types. If you want to explore those node types further, they are described in the DOM Core specification at the URL given earlier in the chapter.

Now that you have an overview of the node types that make up an XML DOM document or document fragment, let's move on to look at the tools you will need to run the examples.

Tools to Run the Examples

To run the DOM examples in this chapter that are to be run in a web browser you need access to Internet Explorer version 5.0 or greater. An installation of Internet Explorer 5.0 or greater is likely to have version 3 of Microsoft XML Core Services, also called MSXML3, already installed. You can check which versions of MSXML are already installed on your machine by using Search, making sure that hidden files and folders are to be searched, and performing a search for `msxml*.dll`. This should detect all versions of MSXML on your machine. Depending on your language settings, which version of Internet Explorer you have installed, and other installed Microsoft programs with XML functionality (for example, Office 2003 installs `msxml5.dll`), you are likely to have multiple versions of MSXML installed.

If you don't have `msxml3.dll` already installed, then visit `http://www.microsoft.com/downloads/details.aspx?FamilyID=c0f86022-2d4c-4162-8fb8-66bfc12f32b0&displaylang=en` to download MSXML3 SP4. If you need functionality specific to MSXML 4, which you won't need to run the examples in this chapter, then visit `http://www.microsoft.com/downloads/details.aspx?displaylang=en&FamilyID=3144b72b-b4f2-46da-b4b6-c5d7485f2b42` to download MSXML 4 SP2. Those service packs are current at the time of writing. Since further service packs may have been issued, it is probably also sensible to visit Google.com and search for "MSXML download site:microsoft.com" to identify the latest MSXML downloads, since service packs often include security patches.

Browser-based examples will use Microsoft JScript, Microsoft's flavor of ECMAScript, to manipulate the XML DOM. In the following two examples, since you may not have done any JScript programming, I will show you some very basic scripting techniques before we move on to look at the XML DOM in more detail.

> **When creating variable names it is often useful to use a prefix to indicate what type of value the variable holds. For example, use the prefix `str` to indicate a string variable or an `obj` prefix to indicate that the variable refers to an object.**

Try It Out Checking if MSXML3 Is Installed

The following example allows you to check directly whether MSXML3 is already installed on your computer. Note that in this code, we are scripting XML inside an HTML document.

1. Enter the following code and save it as `MSXMLTest.html`:

```
<html>
 <head>
  <title>Test MSXML Install</title>
 </head>
 <body>
 <script language="JScript" type="text/javascript">
  try {
    var strXML = "<?xml version='1.0' ?><AnyElement>Some text</AnyElement>"
    var objXMLDOM = new ActiveXObject("Msxml2.DOMDocument.3.0");
    objXMLDOM.loadXML(strXML);

    // If no exception is raised MSXML 3 must be installed.
    document.write("MSXML 3 is installed on your machine.");

  }
    // If there is an exception it could be a coding error but
    // it is likely that MSXML 3 is not installed.
  catch (e)
   {
    document.write("MSXML 3 is NOT installed on your machine.");
   }
  </script>
 </body>
</html>
```

2. Navigate in Windows Explorer to the directory containing the `MSXMLTest.html` file.

3. In Windows Explorer, double-click `MSXMLTest.html` to open the HTML file in the default browser.
4. Observe in the web page whether MSXML3 is installed or not on your machine.

The JScript code includes a `try ... catch` construct. This means that if the code inside the `try` block executes without raising an exception, then only the code in the `try` statement is executed. If an exception is raised by the code in the `try` block, then processing of the remaining statements in the `try` block stops, the exception is caught, and the code in the `catch` block is executed.

How It Works

The first line of JScript code in the `try` block (as shown in the following code) initializes a string variable, `strXML`, and assigns to that variable a string value, `<?xml version='1.0'?><AnyElement> Some text</AnyElement>`, which happens to be a very simple well-formed XML document:

```
var strXML = "<?xml version='1.0' ?><AnyElement>Some text</AnyElement>"
```

The next line initializes an object, `objXMLDOM`, and assigns to that newly created variable a new ActiveX object, which is an XML DOM object created using MSXML3, as shown in the following:

```
var objXMLDOM = new ActiveXObject("Msxml2.DOMDocument.3.0");
```

If the MSXML3 DLL, `msxml3.dll`, is present on your machine, then the final code line in the `try` block is executed as follows:

```
document.write("MSXML 3 is installed on your machine.");
```

Now the text `MSXML 3 is installed on your machine.` is written to the otherwise blank HTML page.

If MSXML3 is not present on your machine, then an exception will be raised when attempting to run this line of code and processing of the `try` block will stop:

```
var objXMLDOM = new ActiveXObject("Msxml2.DOMDocument.3.0");
```

The code in the `catch` block will be executed so the text `MSXML 3 is NOT installed on your machine.` will be displayed on the HTML web page:

```
catch (e)
  {
   document.write("MSXML 3 is NOT installed on your machine.");
  }
```

If `msxml3.dll` is present on your machine, execution of the code continues in the `try` block:

```
objXMLDOM.loadXML(strXML);
```

The `loadXML()` method is used to load the string variable `strXML` into the XML DOM object `objXMLDOM`.

If no exception is raised by any of the code we have discussed, execution continues in the `try` block:

```
// If no exception is raised MSXML 3 must be installed.
document.write("MSXML 3 is installed on your machine.");
```

The string `MSXML 3 is installed on your machine.` is written to the HTML page, using the `write()` method of the HTML `document` object.

Try It Out Navigating to the Document Element

Now that we know we have MSXML3 available to us, let's extend this simple example to navigate to the document element of our simple XML document and display it in an alert box.

The modified code, `MSXMLTest2.html`, is shown here:

```
<html>
 <head>
  <title>Test MSXML Install</title>
  <script>
   function showXML(){
   alert(objXMLDOM.documentElement.nodeName);
   }
  </script>
 </head>
<body>
 <script language="JScript" type="text/javascript">
  try {
   var strXML = "<?xml version='1.0' ?><AnyElement>Some text</AnyElement>"
   var objXMLDOM = new ActiveXObject("Msxml2.DOMDocument.3.0");
   objXMLDOM.loadXML(strXML);

   // If no exception is raised MSXML 3 must be installed.
   document.write("MSXML 3 is installed on your machine.");

 }
  // If there is an exception it could be a coding error but
  // it is likely that MSXML 3 is not installed.
  catch (e)
  {
    document.write("MSXML 3 is NOT installed on your machine.");
  }
 </script>
 <br /><br />
 <input type="button" value="Click here to show XML" onclick="showXML()" />
 </body>
</html>
```

1. Navigate in Windows Explorer to the directory that contains the `MSXMLTest2.html` file, and double-click the file.
2. Click on the "Click here to show XML" button.
3. Observe the name of the document element of the XML document.

How It Works

The following HTML `input` element creates a simple button that has an `onclick` attribute:

```
<input type="button" value="Click here to show XML" onclick="showXML()" />
```

When the button is clicked the `showXML()` function, specified as the value of the `onclick` attribute, is called. The `showXML()` function defined in the head of the HTML document is then called as shown in the following:

```
<script>
 function showXML(){
 alert(objXMLDOM.documentElement.nodeName);
 }
</script>
```

The JScript `alert()` function can be used to display a modal dialog box (also called an alert box or message box).

The argument supplied to the `alert()` function is `objXMLDOM.documentElement.nodeName`. The syntax of the argument uses the period character to indicate properties or methods of an object. Remember that the `objXMLDOM` variable was declared to hold an XML DOM object—a `Document` node. So, in plain English, the argument to the `alert()` function is the name of the node that is the document element of the XML DOM object that is assigned to the variable `objXMLDOM`.

Since we assigned the following string variable, `strXML`:

```
objXMLDOM.loadXML(strXML);
```

that contained the following value:

```
<?xml version='1.0' ?><AnyElement>Some text</AnyElement>
```

to the `objXMLDOM` object using the `loadXML()` method, we can see that the name of the document element of the XML document is `AnyElement`.

If we open `MSXMLTest2.html` in a web browser and click the button, we can display that name, as shown in Figure 11-1.

Now that we know we have a working setup, we can proceed to take a look at four node types that are of broad importance in the XML DOM—the `Node` interface, the `NamedNodeMap` interface, the `NodeList` interface, and the `DOMException` interface. As mentioned earlier, keeping the idea of interface and node strictly separated is a little artificial, and I will slip from using one term to the other. After all, all `Node` objects have the properties and methods defined in the `Node` interface.

The Node Object

I mentioned earlier that one way of viewing nodes in an XML DOM is as specializations of the `Node` object. One very good reason for viewing an XML DOM in that way is that the `Node` object has properties

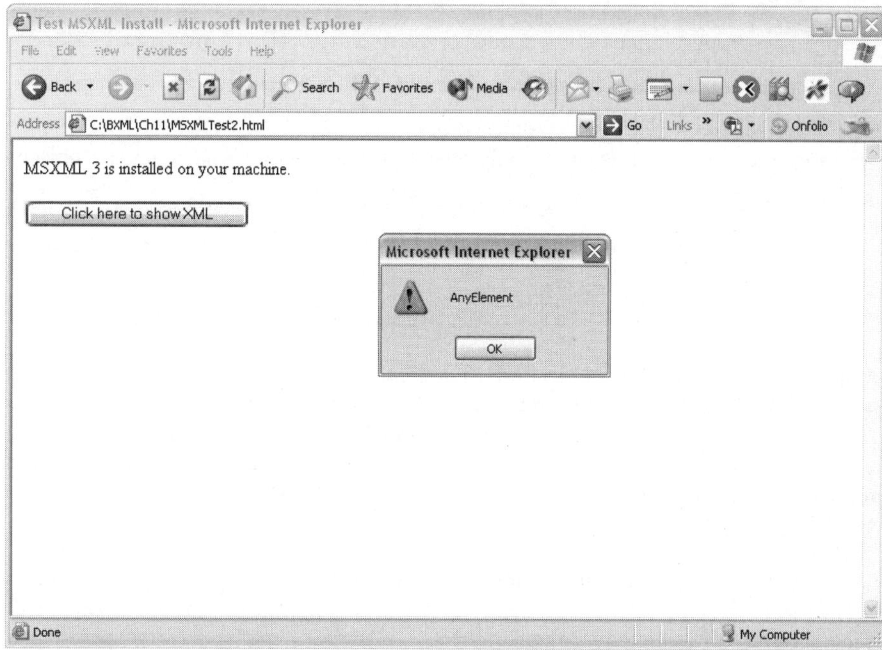

Figure 11-1

and methods that are also available on all other types of XML DOM node that you will meet in this chapter. XML DOM programming consists of retrieving and setting some of these properties directly or using the methods defined in an interface to manipulate the object that instantiates that interface or related objects.

I will list and describe these properties and methods briefly here to give you an impression of the range of properties and methods that are available to a developer whatever type of DOM node is being used.

Properties of the Node Object

The `Node` object in DOM Level 2 has 14 properties, which are listed here:

- `attributes`—This is a read-only property whose value is a `NamedNodeMap` object.
- `childNodes`—This is a read-only property whose value is a `NodeList` object.
- `firstChild`—This is a read-only property whose value is a `Node` object.
- `lastChild`—This is a read-only property whose value is a `Node` object.
- `localName`—This is a read-only property that is a `String`.
- `namespaceURI`—This is a read-only property whose value is a `String`.
- `nextSibling`—This is a read-only property whose value is a `Node` object.
- `nodeName`—This is the name of the node, if it has one, and its value is a `String` type.

- nodeType—This is a read-only property that is of type number. The number value of the nodeType property maps to the names of the node types that I mentioned earlier.
- nodeValue—This property is of type String. When the property is being set or retrieved, a DOMException can be raised.
- ownerDocument—This is a read-only property whose value is a Document object.
- parentNode—This is a read-only property whose value is a Node object.
- prefix—This property is a String. When the property is being set, a DOMException can be raised.
- previousSibling—This is a read-only property whose value is a Node object.

These properties allow the developer to find out a great deal about the node itself and about the XML DOM surrounding the currently selected node. Depending on the particular node object, there may be no retrievable useful value for some properties made available by the Node interface. For example, a Document object does not have a parent node, and a Comment node has no attributes or child nodes. For Element nodes it is frequently of interest to know what child nodes it has and so the childNodes property is of significance for that node type.

We can retrieve several pieces of information about the node using the Node object's properties. We can retrieve its name in the nodeName property. If the name of the node is namespace-qualified, we can retrieve the local part of its qualified name in the localName property, its namespace prefix in the prefix property and the namespace URI in the namespaceURI property. If the node is an Element node and has attributes, then they are retrieved from the attributes property. And, of course, if the node has a value, the nodeValue property gives us the necessary information.

In addition to accessing information about the current node itself, we can find out useful information about that node's surroundings in the DOM. For example, we can obtain a list of the child nodes of the currently selected node using the childNodes property. Within that list of child nodes we can specify the first node using the firstChild property and the last child using the lastChild property. We can get information about its parent node using the parentNode property and about its adjacent sibling nodes using the previousSibling property and the nextSibling property. In a broader context the ownerDocument property tells us what document the node belongs to.

Try It Out Exploring Child Nodes

Let's use the techniques we have already seen to navigate around a simple XML document.

1. Enter the following code and save it as ChildNodes.html:

```
<html>
 <head>
  <title>Retrieve information about child nodes.</title>
 </head>
 <body>
  <script language="JScript" type="text/javascript">
   try {
   var strXML = "<?xml version='1.0' ?><Book><Chapter>This is Chapter
   1.</Chapter><Chapter>This is Chapter 2.</Chapter><Chapter>This is Chapter
   3.</Chapter></Book>"
```

```
    var objXMLDOM = new ActiveXObject("Msxml2.DOMDocument.3.0");
    objXMLDOM.loadXML(strXML);

    var strDisplay;
    strDisplay = "";
    strDisplay += "The value of the first child node is: "
     + objXMLDOM.documentElement.firstChild.nodeName + "\n";
    strDisplay += "Its text content is: "
    + objXMLDOM.documentElement.firstChild.firstChild.nodeValue + "\n";
    strDisplay += "The value of the last child node is: "
    + objXMLDOM.documentElement.lastChild.nodeName + "\n";
    strDisplay += "Its text content is: "
    + objXMLDOM.documentElement.lastChild.firstChild.nodeValue + "\n";
    alert(strDisplay);

   }

   catch (e)
    {
     alert("An exception has occurred.");
    }
  </script>
  </body>
</html>
```

2. In Windows Explorer navigate to the directory containing the file `ChildNodes.html`, and double-click the file to open it in your default browser.
3. Observe the information displayed in the alert box. Figure 11-2 shows the on-screen result when `ChildNodes.html` is run.

How It Works

On this occasion we are assigning a slightly more complicated string to the `strXML` variable:

```
var strXML = "<?xml version='1.0' ?><Book><Chapter>This is Chapter
1.</Chapter><Chapter>This is Chapter 2.</Chapter><Chapter>This is
Chapter 3.</Chapter></Book>"
```

In the original code all of the preceding code was on one line. In a later example we will return to that point and demonstrate why it can be important.

To make the XML document's structure clearer I have rewritten it here:

```
<?xml version='1.0' ?>
 <Book>
  <Chapter>This is Chapter 1.</Chapter>
  <Chapter>This is Chapter 2.</Chapter>
  <Chapter>This is Chapter 3.</Chapter>
</Book>
```

Next, we construct a display string in the `strDisplay` variable:

```
var strDisplay;
strDisplay = "";
```

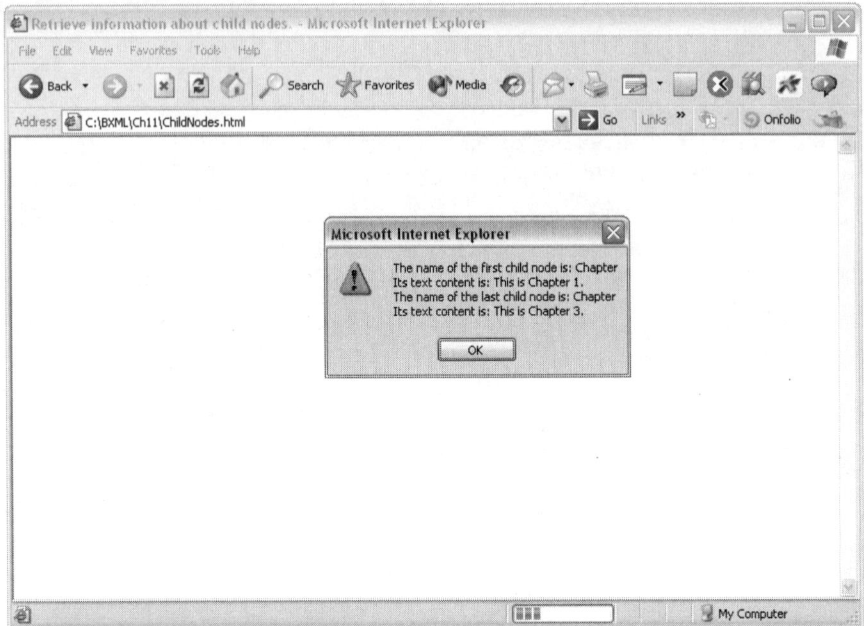

Figure 11-2

After declaring the `strDisplay` variable, its value is set to the empty string.

Next, we use a JScript shorthand += operator to add new string content to the existing content of the string:

```
strDisplay += "The value of the first child node is: "
    + objXMLDOM.documentElement.firstChild.nodeName + "\n";
```

The preceding line of code uses the `documentElement` and `firstChild` properties to retrieve the name of the node that is the first child of the document element (a `Book` element) of the document and adds it with explanatory text to the `strDisplay` variable. The `\n` enables us to indicate a newline character.

We then continue to add more text to the `strDisplay` variable:

```
strDisplay += "Its text content is: "
+ objXMLDOM.documentElement.firstChild.firstChild.nodeValue + "\n";
```

The preceding code retrieves the value (contained in the `nodeValue` property) of the first child node (using the `firstChild` property again, this time retrieving a `Text` node, which is the first child of a `Chapter Element` node) of the first child (retrieves a `Book Element` node using the `firstChild` property) of the document element node in the document.

```
strDisplay += "The value of the last child node is: "
+ objXMLDOM.documentElement.lastChild.nodeName + "\n";
+ objXMLDOM.documentElement.lastChild.firstChild.nodeValue + "\n";
```

The preceding code retrieves the name and text content of the last child node (using the `lastChild` property) of the document element. As before, the values retrieved from the XML DOM are appended to the `strDisplay` variable together with explanatory text.

```
alert(strDisplay);
```

And, finally, we display the value of the `strDisplay` variable that we have built up step by step by retrieving information from the XML DOM.

A couple of the properties mentioned in the preceding material introduce objects that we haven't met before, the `NamedNodeMap` object and the `NodeList` object. After we look at the methods of the `Node` object we will look at both those interfaces.

Methods of the Node Object

The `Node` object has nine methods. These methods include some that you will use frequently in XML DOM programming. In the list that follows the names of arguments of the methods will, in working programs, be replaced by variables that you define in your script or other code.

- `appendChild(newChild)`—This method returns a `Node` object. The `newChild` argument is a `Node` object. This method can raise a `DOMException` object.
- `cloneNode(deep)`—This method returns a `Node` object. The `deep` argument is a `Boolean` value.
- `hasAttributes()`—This method returns a `Boolean` value. It has no arguments.
- `hasChildNodes()`—This method returns a `Boolean` value. It has no arguments.
- `insertBefore(newChild, refChild)`—This method returns a `Node` object. The `newChild` and `refChild` arguments are each `Node` objects. This method can raise a `DOMException` object.
- `isSupported(feature, version)`—This method returns a `Boolean` value. The `feature` and `version` arguments are each `String` values.
- `normalize()`—This method has no return value and takes no arguments.
- `removeChild(oldChild)`—This method returns a `Node` object. The `oldChild` argument is a `Node` object. This method can raise a `DOMException` object.
- `replaceChild(newChild, oldChild)`—This method returns a `Node` object. The `newChild` and `oldChild` arguments are each `Node` objects. This method can raise a `DOMException` object.

The names of most of the methods of the `Node` object are pretty self-explanatory. The `insertBefore()` method, for example, allows a new child node to be inserted before a specified existing child node. The `appendChild()` method allows a new child node to be added. The `removeChild()` method allows a specified node to be removed from the XML DOM tree. The `cloneNode()` method allows a node to be copied.

Just as the properties of the `Node` object tell us a lot about the node and its DOM environment, so the methods of the `Node` object allow the developer to manipulate the XML DOM tree by adding and removing nodes and so on. Later in the chapter we will use these properties and methods of the `Node` object as well as the more specialized properties and methods of more specialized types of node.

Before we look at examples using the methods of the `Node` object, let's first look at how to load an existing XML document.

Loading an XML Document

If we don't supply literal characters equivalent to a well-formed XML document using the `loadXML()` method, we have the option to load an existing XML document using the `load()` method of the `Document` object.

We will load the following short XML document, `SimpleDoc.xml`:

```
<?xml version='1.0'?>
<MyDocument>
 <Paragraph>
 The XML DOM is a hierarchical representation of an XML document.
 </Paragraph>
 <Paragraph>
 For large documents the DOM can be problematic since the entire tree must
 be constructed in memory. For those situations SAX may be preferred
 or necessary.
 </Paragraph>
</MyDocument>
```

We will load `SimpleDoc.xml` and display the document element of the XML document using the following code:

```
<html>
 <head>
  <title>MSXML Load Example</title>
  <script>
   function showXML(){
   alert("The document element of the document is named: \n" +
   objXMLDOM.documentElement.nodeName);
   }
  </script>
 </head>
<body>
<p>This example tests the <b>load()</b> method.</p>
 <script language="JScript" type="text/javascript">
  try {
   var objXMLDOM = new ActiveXObject("Msxml2.DOMDocument.3.0");
   objXMLDOM.load("c:\\ BXML\\ Ch11\\SimpleDoc.xml");
 }
  catch (e)
  {
    document.write("An exception was raised.");
  }
 </script>
 <br />
 <input type="button" value="Click here to show XML information"
 onclick="showXML()" />
 </body>
</html>
```

In the `try` block of the script element inside the body element, we create an XML DOM document object as before:

```
var objXMLDOM = new ActiveXObject("Msxml2.DOMDocument.3.0");
```

At this stage we have a DOM `Document` node with no descendant nodes. When the following statement is executed:

```
objXMLDOM.load("c:\\BXML\\ Ch11\\SimpleDoc.xml");
```

the XML document `SimpleDoc.xml` is loaded, its XML is parsed, and the appropriate node tree is created as the markup inside the `objXMLDOM` object. Notice that we need to *escape* backslash characters that we want to occur literally in the string. We do that simply by using two successive backslash characters to represent a single literal backslash character in the path to the XML file.

We can confirm that the `SimpleDoc.xml` document has loaded correctly by accessing and displaying the name of the document element of the file, `SimpleDoc.xml`, which was loaded:

```
alert("The document element of the document is named: \n" +
objXMLDOM.documentElement.nodeName);
```

The `documentElement` property of the `Document` node allows us to retrieve the `Element` node that represents the `MyDocument` element. We use the `nodeName` property to retrieve the name of that `Element` node.

The result of clicking the button is shown in Figure 11-3.

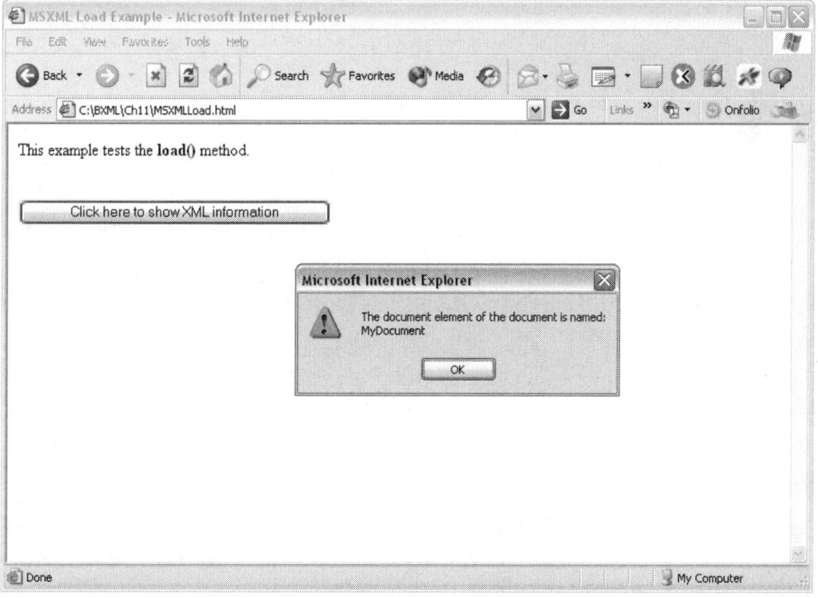

Figure 11-3

As you can see, we have successfully retrieved the name of the document element of `SimpleDoc.xml`.

Try It Out — Deleting a Node

A common task in DOM programming is to delete an existing node. In the following example we will delete the first child node in the XML document.

1. For this example we will use the code shown here and name it `DeleteNode.html`:

```
<html>
 <head>
<title>Delete a child node.</title>
 </head>
 <body>
  <script language="JScript" type="text/javascript">
   try {
   var strXML = "<?xml version='1.0' ?><Book><Chapter>This is Chapter
   1.</Chapter><Chapter>This is Chapter 2.</Chapter><Chapter>This is Chapter
   3.</Chapter></Book>"
   var objXMLDOM = new ActiveXObject("Msxml2.DOMDocument.3.0");
   objXMLDOM.loadXML(strXML);

   alert(objXMLDOM.xml);
   var objToBeDeleted = objXMLDOM.documentElement.firstChild;
   alert(objToBeDeleted.firstChild.nodeValue);
   objXMLDOM.documentElement.removeChild(objToBeDeleted);
   alert(objXMLDOM.xml);
  }

  catch (e)
   {
    alert("An exception has occurred.");
   }
  </script>
 </body>
</html>
```

2. Navigate in Windows Explorer to the directory that contains the file `DeleteNode.html`, and double-click the file.
3. Observe the information in the alert box, which displays when the web page is opened in the browser, and compare it to the XML document.
4. Click OK in the following alert boxes and observe the change in the XML structure when the element has been deleted.

How It Works

In this example we first display in an alert box the XML document originally created from the `strXML` variable. This time we use a proprietary property of the `Document` object, the `xml` property, which allows us easily to display the XML content of the XML DOM:

```
alert(objXMLDOM.xml);
```

Next, we declare a variable `objToBeDeleted` and assign as its value the node defined here:

```
var objToBeDeleted = objXMLDOM.documentElement.firstChild;
```

which is the first child node of the document element node—in other words, the first of the three `Chapter Element` nodes in the document.

Next, we use an alert box:

```
alert(objToBeDeleted.firstChild.nodeValue);
```

to display the text content of the selected `Element` node to confirm that it is indeed the first `Chapter Element` node that has been assigned to the variable `objToBeDeleted`.

```
objXMLDOM.documentElement.removeChild(objToBeDeleted);
alert(objXMLDOM.xml);
```

And, finally, we use the `removeChild()` method to delete the first `Chapter` node and again use the `xml` property in an `alert` statement to display the XML structure remaining in the XML DOM. Figure 11-4 confirms that the first `Chapter` element has been removed.

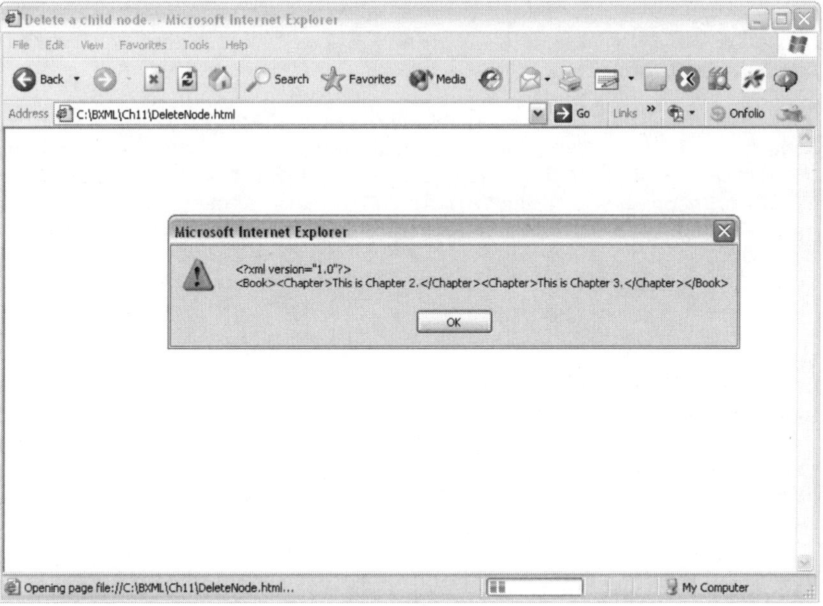

Figure 11-4

Try It Out Adding New Nodes

The `Node` object possesses the `appendChild()`, `insertBefore()`, and `replaceNode()` methods all of which can be used to either add a new node or in the case of `replaceNode()` remove an old node and add a new node in one operation.

1. First, let's add new nodes using the `appendChild()` and `insertBefore()` methods. Enter the following code and save it as `AddNodes.html`:

```
<html>
 <head>
  <title>Add nodes.</title>
 </head>
 <body>
  <script language="JScript" type="text/javascript">
   try {
   var strXML = "<?xml version='1.0' ?><Book><Chapter>This is Chapter
   1.</Chapter><Chapter>This is Chapter 2.</Chapter><Chapter>This is Chapter
   3.</Chapter></Book>"
   var objXMLDOM = new ActiveXObject("Msxml2.DOMDocument.3.0");
   objXMLDOM.loadXML(strXML);

   alert(objXMLDOM.xml);
   // First use the insertBefore(newChild, refChild) method to insert
   // an Introduction element
   var objOriginalFirst = objXMLDOM.documentElement.firstChild;
   var strNewText = "This is new text added using XML DOM programming.";
   var objTextNode = objXMLDOM.createTextNode(strNewText);
   var objToBeInserted = objXMLDOM.createElement("Introduction");
   objToBeInserted.appendChild(objTextNode);
   objXMLDOM.documentElement.insertBefore(objToBeInserted, objOriginalFirst);
   alert(objXMLDOM.xml);

   // Also add an Appendix element using appendChild() method
   strNewText = "This is a new appendix added using XML DOM programming.";
   objTextNode = objXMLDOM.createTextNode(strNewText);
   var objToBeAdded = objXMLDOM.createElement("Appendix");
   objToBeAdded.appendChild(objTextNode);
   objXMLDOM.documentElement.appendChild(objToBeAdded);
   alert(objXMLDOM.xml);
  }

  catch (e)
   {
    alert("An exception has occurred.");
   }
  </script>
 </body>
</html>
```

2. Navigate in Windows Explorer to the directory that contains the file `AddNodes.html`, and double-click the file.
3. Examine the structure of the XML in the initial alert box.
4. Click OK and observe the changes in the structure of the XML as the JavaScript code is processed.

How It Works

The first block of new code uses the `insertBefore()` method to insert an `Introduction` element before the first `Chapter` element.

First, we use the `alert()` method to display the original XML using the `xml` property:

```
alert(objXMLDOM.xml);
```

Next, we declare a variable `objOriginalFirst` and assign it the first `Element` node child of the document element, which represents the first `Chapter` element:

```
// First use the insertBefore(newChild, refChild) method to insert
// an Introduction element
var objOriginalFirst = objXMLDOM.documentElement.firstChild;
```

Then, we declare a string variable `strNewText`:

```
var strNewText = "This is new text added using XML DOM programming.";
```

Then, we come to a couple of important techniques that will be new to you. First, we use the `createTextNode()` method of the `Document` object to create a new `Text` node and assign the string variable `strNewText` as the value of the newly created `Text` node:

```
var objTextNode = objXMLDOM.createTextNode(strNewText);
```

At this stage we have a new `Text` node that is not part of the XML DOM but that does have a value assigned to it.

Next, we declare a variable `objToBeInserted` and use the `createElement()` method of the `Document` object to create a new `Element` node that represents an `Introduction` element and assigns that new `Element` node as the value of the `objToBeInserted` variable:

```
var objToBeInserted = objXMLDOM.createElement("Introduction");
```

At this point we have two object variables, `objTextNode` and `objToBeInserted`, but nothing has yet been added to the XML DOM. We next need to add these nodes to the XML DOM.

First, we add the new `Text` node as a child of the newly created `Introduction Element` node:

```
objToBeInserted.appendChild(objTextNode);
```

At this stage we have a document fragment with an `Element` node that has a single child node, a `Text` node, which has the `nodeValue` property of `This is new text added using XML DOM programming.`

Then, we add that document fragment to the XML DOM using the `insertBefore()` method of the `Node` object:

```
objXMLDOM.documentElement.insertBefore(objToBeInserted, objOriginalFirst);
```

Our new `Introduction` element and its text content have now been added to the XML DOM. We can use the `alert()` method to show that the newly created `Introduction` element has been successfully added:

```
alert(objXMLDOM.xml);
```

Figure 11-5 shows the result after the Introduction element and its text content have been added.

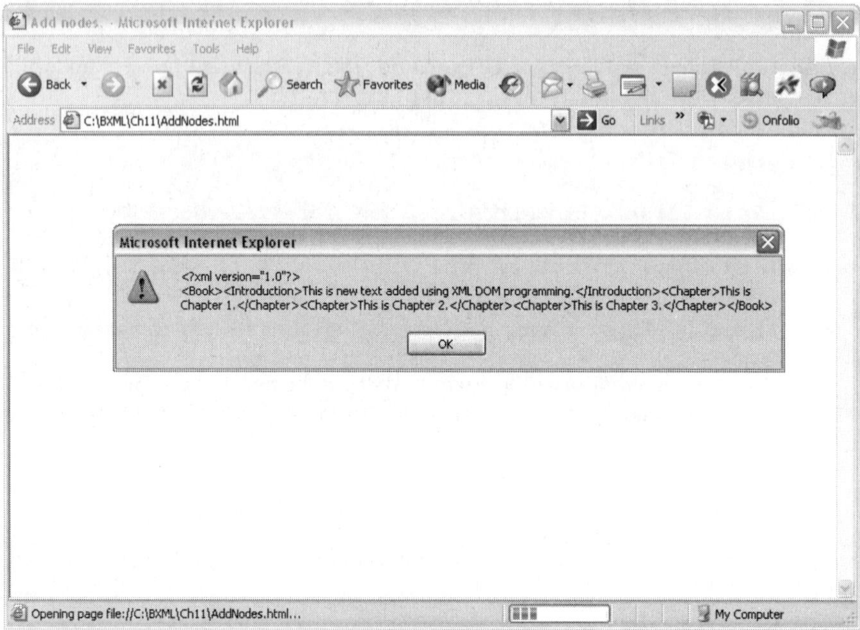

Figure 11-5

Next, we use the appendChild() method in a different way to add an Appendix element to the XML document.

First, we assign a new String value to the strNewText variable:

```
// Also add an Appendix element using appendChild() method
strNewText = "This is a new appendix added using XML DOM programming.";
```

Then, assign a newly created Text node to the objTextNode variable:

```
objTextNode = objXMLDOM.createTextNode(strNewText);
```

Then, we use the createElement() method of the Document object to create a new Element node representing an Appendix element.

```
var objToBeAdded = objXMLDOM.createElement("Appendix");
```

Next, we add the Text node to the newly created Element node using the appendChild() method:

```
objToBeAdded.appendChild(objTextNode);
```

If you understood the earlier part of this example where we used the insertBefore() method you will hopefully realize that at this stage nothing has yet been added to the XML DOM.

Then, we use the appendChild() method to add the new Appendix Element node to the XML DOM.

```
objXMLDOM.documentElement.appendChild(objToBeAdded);
```

The default behavior of the appendChild() method is to add the new Element node after any sibling nodes. So if a node has no child nodes, the appendChild() method adds its only child node. If a node already has child nodes, then the appendChild() node adds a new child node after all the existing child nodes.

Finally, we use the alert() method to display the new structure of our XML:

```
alert(objXMLDOM.xml);
```

As you can see in Figure 11-6, the XML now has an Appendix element with the text content previously described.

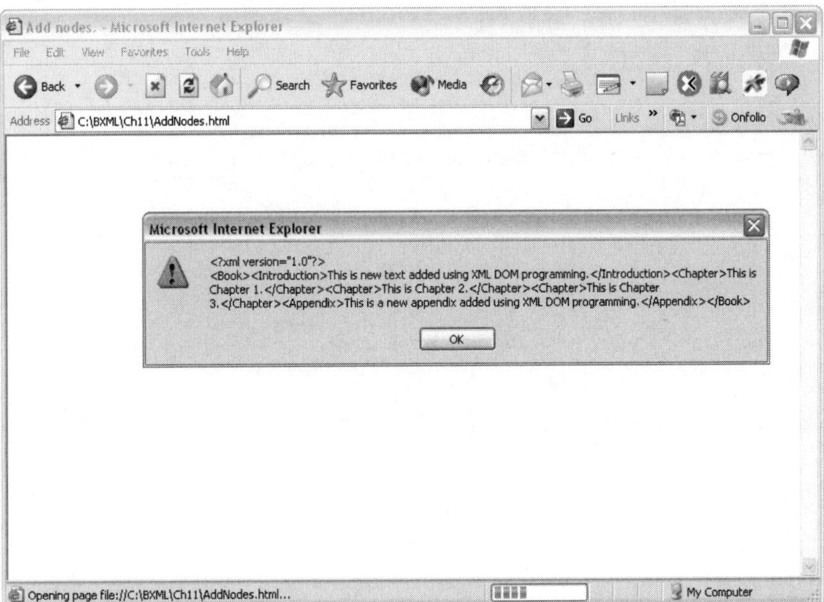

Figure 11-6

The Effect of Text Nodes

A common technique is to iterate through the child nodes of a specified Element node and retrieve or set information of some type. However, the issue of whitespace (or in XML DOM terms Text nodes) becomes important if we don't want to get some unexpected surprises.

Instead of using the loadXML() method to load a string into the XML DOM we will load an XML document, Book.xml:

```
<?xml version='1.0'?>
<Book xml:space="preserve">
 <Chapter>This is Chapter 1.</Chapter>
```

```
  <Chapter>This is Chapter 2.</Chapter>
  <Chapter>This is Chapter 3.</Chapter>
</Book>
```

The following HTML document, `Whitespace.html`, shows the child nodes of the `Book` element using the `childNodes()` property of the `Node` object. This time we will run the code and view the result in the browser before analyzing the code in detail. Read the code carefully and see if you can work out what will be displayed in the browser.

```
<html>
 <head>
  <title>Child Nodes and Whitespace Example</title>
  <script>
   function showChildNodes(){
  var strDisplay = "";
  var objDocElem = objXMLDOM.documentElement;
  strDisplay += "There are " + objXMLDOM.documentElement.childNodes.length + "
  child nodes of the " + objXMLDOM.documentElement.nodeName + " element.\n";
  for (i=0; i<objXMLDOM.documentElement.childNodes.length; i++)
 {
   strDisplay += "The name of the child node in position " + i + " is " +
   objDocElem.childNodes.item(i).nodeName + "\n";
 } // end for loop
  alert(strDisplay);
   }
  </script>
 </head>
<body>
<p>Text nodes and the childNodes property.</p>
 <script language="JScript" type="text/javascript">
  try {
   var objXMLDOM = new ActiveXObject("Msxml2.DOMDocument.3.0");
   objXMLDOM.load("c:\ \BXML\ \ Ch11\ \Book.xml");

}
  catch (e)
  {
    document.write("An exception was raised.");
  }
 </script>
 <br />
 <input type="button" value="Click here to show XML information"
onclick="showChildNodes()" />
 </body>
</html>
```

The result of running the code is shown in Figure 11-7.

You may have expected to see three child nodes being displayed, each of which has the `nodeName` of `Chapter`. Instead, we see that the `Element` node representing the `Book` element has seven child nodes, only three of which have their `nodeName` property with value of `Chapter`.

Where have the extra child nodes come from? The answer lies in `Book.xml`.

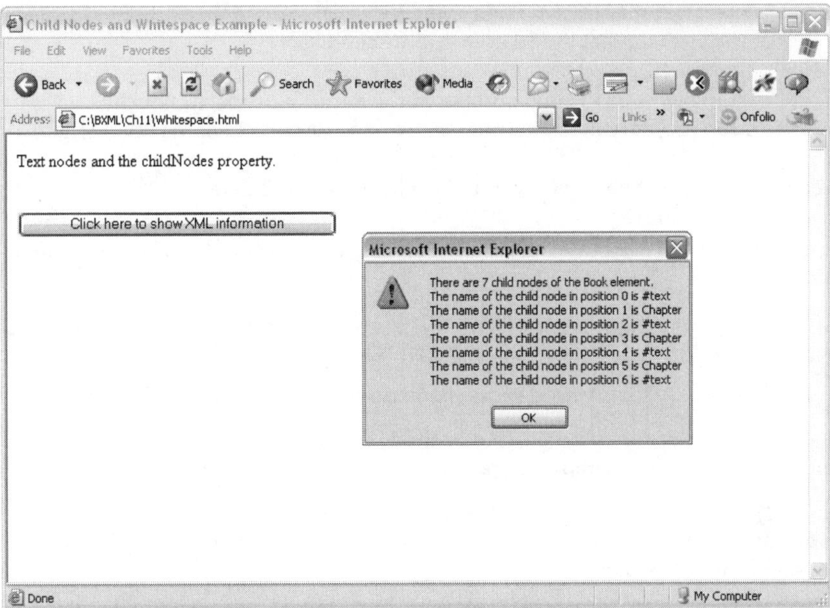

Figure 11-7

When using the MSXML parser, it is necessary to specify that whitespace is preserved using the `xml:space` attribute. On many other XML parsers the whitespace between tags is preserved as the default.

After the end tag of the `Book` element there is a newline character that is a child node of the `Book` node. It is a `Text` node and has the `nodeName` property of `#text` as you see in Figure 11-7. Its value would include a newline character and the space characters at the beginning of the following line. The next child node represents a `Chapter` element. Just as whitespace occurred after the end tag of the `Book` element, so there is similar whitespace after the end tag of the first `Chapter` element. So, another `Text` node follows.

The issue of whitespace can trip you up if you use software that by default preserves whitespace and you try to access one particular child node, likely an `Element` node, using the `item()` method of the `NodeList` object with a numeric index. Depending on circumstances you get no output, an error, or unexpected output. Being aware of the potential issues with whitespace will hopefully help prevent you getting into such problems. It is also prudent to reduce the chance of errors or unexpected behavior by inserting a conditional statement to test if a child node is of a particular node type before processing it.

The NamedNodeMap Object

A little earlier I introduced the `attributes` property of the `Node` object and indicated that its value was a `NamedNodeMap` object. A named node map is an unordered set of objects. As you probably remember, the attributes of an XML element are unordered, so we can't use ordered constructs such as lists to refer to attributes.

When the Node object is an Element node, then the attributes property holds information about all the attributes of the element that the Element node represents.

The NamedNodeMap object has a single property, the length property, which is a Number value. The value of the length property indicates how many nodes are in the named node map.

The NamedNodeMap object has seven methods, which are listed here:

- getNamedItem(name)—This method returns a Node object. The name argument is a String value.
- getNamedItemNS(namespaceURI, localName)—This method returns a Node object. The namespaceURI and localName arguments are String values.
- item(index)—This method returns a Node object. The index argument is a Number value.
- removeNamedItem(name)—This method returns a Node object. The name argument is a String value. This method can raise a DOMException object.
- removeNamedItemNS(namespaceURI, localName)—This method returns a Node object. The namespaceURI and localName arguments are String values. This method can raise a DOMException object.
- setNamedItem(name)—This method returns a Node object. The name argument is a String value. This method can raise a DOMException object.
- setNamedItemNS(arg)—This method returns a Node object. The arg argument is a String value. This method can raise a DOMException object.

A NamedNodeMap object is used to retrieve the attributes of an element, and, typically, we use a name corresponding to the attribute's name. Therefore, for example, the getNamedItem() method has a name as its argument.

Notice, too, that there are separate pairs of methods for getting and setting nodes in the named node map depending on whether or not the Node objects in the named node map are or are not in a namespace. When the nodes are not in a namespace, the getNamedItem(), removeNamedItem(), and setNamedItem() methods are used. For nodes in a namespace the getNamedItemNS(), removeNamedItemNS(), and setNamedItemNS() methods are used.

Try It Out Adding and Removing Attributes

In this example we will use some of the methods of the NamedNodeMap interface to alter the values of attributes to reflect a change in the structure of our XML.

1. Enter the following code and save it as AlterValue.html:

```
<html>
 <head>
  <title>Retrieve a named node and change its value</title>
 </head>
 <body>
  <script language="JScript" type="text/javascript">
   try {
```

```
 var strXML = "<?xml version='1.0' ?><Book><Chapter number='1'>This is
 Chapter 1.</Chapter><Chapter number='2'>This is Chapter 2.</Chapter>
<Chapter number='3'>This is the original Chapter 3.</Chapter></Book>"
 var objXMLDOM = new ActiveXObject("Msxml2.DOMDocument.3.0");
 objXMLDOM.loadXML(strXML);

 alert(objXMLDOM.xml); // Show the original XML
 // First use the insertBefore(newChild, refChild) method to insert
 // another Chapter element
 objOriginalThird = objXMLDOM.documentElement.childNodes.item(2);
 alert(objOriginalThird.firstChild.nodeValue); // Confirm we have the
 right Chapter node

 var strNewText = "This is the new Chapter 3.";
 var objTextNode = objXMLDOM.createTextNode(strNewText);
 var objToBeInserted = objXMLDOM.createElement("Chapter");
 objToBeInserted.appendChild(objTextNode);
 objXMLDOM.documentElement.insertBefore(objToBeInserted, objOriginalThird);
 alert("A Chapter element has been inserted before the original third
 Chapter.\n\n" + objXMLDOM.xml); // Display intermediate state of XML

 // Remove and replace number attribute on old Chapter 3
 var objNewNumberAttribute = objXMLDOM.createAttribute("number");
 objNewNumberAttribute.nodeValue = 4;
 var mapChapterAttributes = objXMLDOM.documentElement.lastChild.attributes ;
 mapChapterAttributes.removeNamedItem("number");
 mapChapterAttributes.setNamedItem(objNewNumberAttribute) ;
 alert("The old number attribute of the final chapter has been removed and a
 new number \nattribute with value of 4 replaces it\n\n" + objXMLDOM.xml);
 // Display intermediate state of the XML

 // Add a number attribute to the inserted Chapter 3
 var objAddedNumberAttribute = objXMLDOM.createAttribute("number");
 objAddedNumberAttribute.nodeValue = 3;
 mapChapterAttributes = objXMLDOM.documentElement.childNodes.item(2)
 .attributes;
 mapChapterAttributes.setNamedItem(objAddedNumberAttribute);
 alert("A number attribute has been added (with value of 3) to the inserted
 Chapter element.\n\n" + objXMLDOM.xml);
}

catch (e)
 {
  alert("An exception has occurred.");
 }
</script>
</body>
</html>
```

2. Navigate in Windows Explorer to the directory that contains `AlterValue.html`, and double-click the file to open it in the default browser.
3. Examine the XML structure shown in the alert box.
4. Click the OK button to see the steps of how the XML structure is changed.

How It Works

What the code does is to insert a new `Chapter` node into the XML. We then have a fourth `Chapter` whose `number` attribute has the value of `3`. We need to change that. Then, we add a `number` attribute to the inserted `Chapter` node.

We are going to insert the new `Chapter` node before the last child node of the document element:

```
    objOriginalThird = objXMLDOM.documentElement.childNodes.item(2);
    alert(objOriginalThird.firstChild.nodeValue); // Confirm we have the right
Chapter node
```

The preceding `alert()` method is primarily for debugging to confirm that the correct child node has been selected using the `item()` method.

Next, we use the `insertBefore()` method to insert a new `Chapter` node:

```
    var strNewText = "This is the new Chapter 3.";
    var objTextNode = objXMLDOM.createTextNode(strNewText);
    var objToBeInserted = objXMLDOM.createElement("Chapter");
    objToBeInserted.appendChild(objTextNode);
    objXMLDOM.documentElement.insertBefore(objToBeInserted, objOriginalThird);
    alert("A Chapter element has been inserted before the original third
Chapter.\n\n" + objXMLDOM.xml); // Display intermediate state of XML
```

You have seen use of the `insertBefore()` method a little earlier. Refer back to that explanation if the preceding code isn't clear. An `alert()` method shows that the new element has been added (see Figure 11-8).

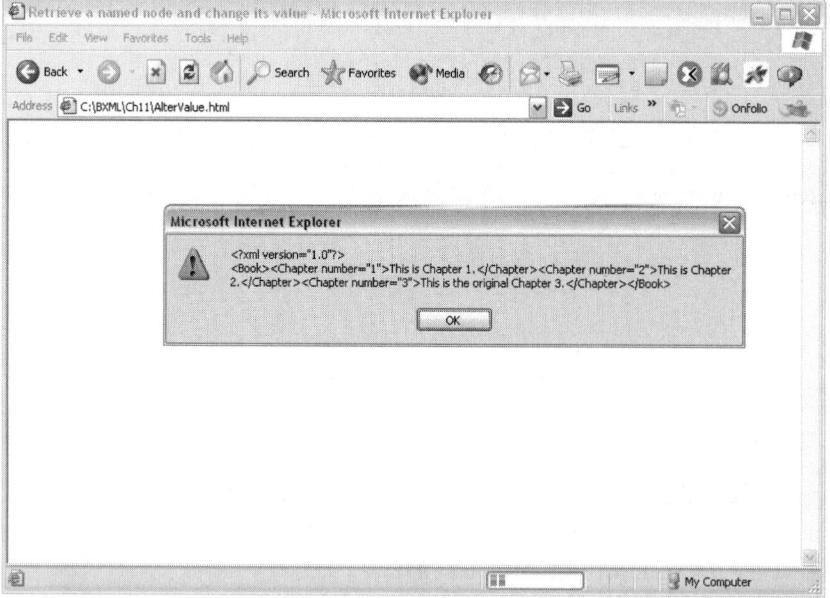

Figure 11-8

Then we need to change the value of the number attribute of what was originally the third chapter. The methods of the NamedNodeMap interface don't allow us to do that directly. We need to remove the old number attribute and add a new one.

First, we use the createAttribute() method of the Document object to create a number node:

```
var objNewNumberAttribute = objXMLDOM.createAttribute("number");
```

Then, we assign the number 4 to the nodeValue property of the newly created Attr node:

```
objNewNumberAttribute.nodeValue = 4;
```

Then, we declare a mapChapterAttributes variable to which we assign the value of the attributes property of the last Chapter Element node:

```
var mapChapterAttributes = objXMLDOM.documentElement.lastChild.attributes ;
```

Using the removeNamedItem() method of the mapChapterAttributes variable, we remove the old number attribute from the last chapter:

```
mapChapterAttributes.removeNamedItem("number");
```

Then, we use the setNamedItem() method of the NamedNodeMap interface to add in the number node we created a little earlier:

```
mapChapterAttributes.setNamedItem(objNewNumberAttribute) ;
```

And, finally in this stage, we display the XML to confirm that the value of the number attribute of the final Chapter element has been, as desired, changed from 3 to 4, to reflect the insertion of the additional Chapter element.

```
alert("The old number attribute of the final chapter has been removed and a
new number \nattribute with value of 4 replaces it\n\n" + objXMLDOM.xml); //
Display intermediate state of the XML
```

We still need to add a new number attribute to the Chapter node we inserted earlier. The technique we use is similar to the way we created a number node in the previous part of the code.

```
// Add a number attribute to the inserted Chapter 3
var objAddedNumberAttribute = objXMLDOM.createAttribute("number");
objAddedNumberAttribute.nodeValue = 3;
mapChapterAttributes = objXMLDOM.documentElement.childNodes.item(2).attributes;
mapChapterAttributes.setNamedItem(objAddedNumberAttribute);
alert("A number attribute has been added (with value of 3) to the inserted
Chapter element.\n\n" + objXMLDOM.xml);
```

We use the createAttribute() method of the Document object to create a new Attr node, assign its nodeValue property a value, and then use the setNamedItem() method of the NamedNodeMap interface to add the new number attribute to the Chapter node that was inserted a little earlier.

As you can see in Figure 11-9, we now have a document with the added `Chapter` element where each `Chapter` element has a `number` attribute with an appropriate value.

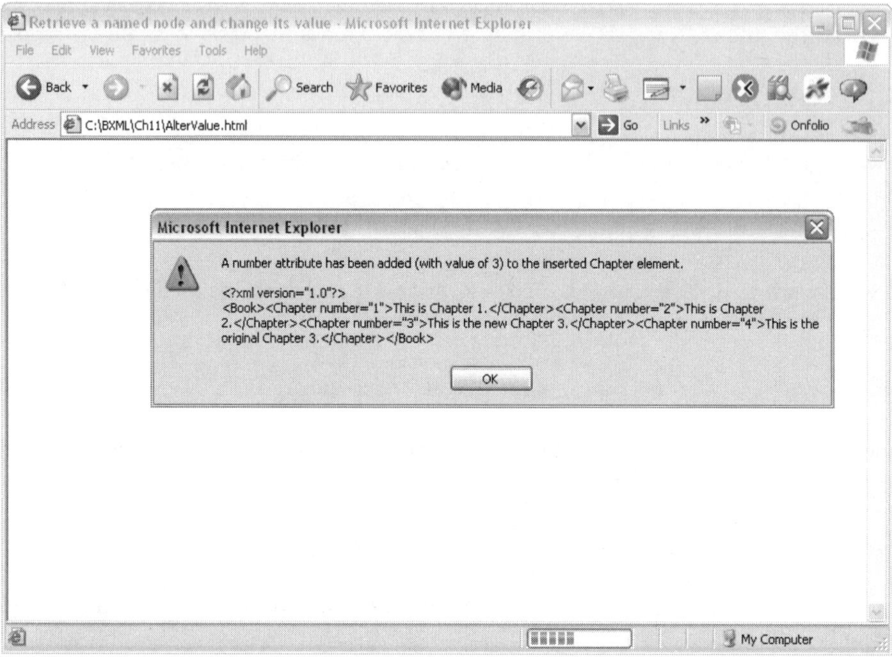

Figure 11-9

The NodeList Object

When introducing the `childNodes` property of the `Node` object, I indicated that the `childNodes` property has a value that is a `NodeList`. The `NodeList` object can be used to process all child nodes of a specified node.

The `NodeList` object has one property, the `length` property, that is, a read-only property of type `Number`. The `length` property tells us how many nodes are present in the list of nodes. Knowing that can be useful when, for example, creating a `for` loop to process all child nodes of a particular node.

The `NodeList` object has one method, the `item()` method. The `item()` method takes a single argument, which is a `Number` value, and returns a `Node` object. The code `item(3)` returns the *fourth* child node, since the first child node is returned by `item(0)`. The `item()` method was used in an earlier example.

The DOMException Object

In almost any programming situation something can go wrong, perhaps because you type some syntax incorrectly, you get a property or method name wrong, or you forget that a property is read-only and try to change it. Or, you simply try to do something that isn't allowed. In programming of the XML DOM when an error occurs, an exception is said to be thrown. The exception is then caught by an exception handler.

Let's create a simple example to deliberately cause a `DOMException` object to be raised. The following code is contained in `DOMException.html`.

```
<html>
 <head>
  <title>Raising a DOMException</title>
 </head>
 <body>
  <p>Deliberately raising a DOMException by trying to add a second
  child element to the Document node.</p>
  <script language="JScript" type="text/javascript">
  try {
    var strXML = "<?xml version='1.0' ?><AnyElement>Some text</AnyElement>"
    var objXMLDOM = new ActiveXObject("Msxml2.DOMDocument.3.0");
    objXMLDOM.loadXML(strXML);

    var strXML2 = "DisallowedElement";
    var newElement = objXMLDOM.createElement(strXML2);
    alert("Everything is working nicely until now.");
    objXMLDOM.appendChild(newElement);

}
    // If there is an exception it must be in the preceding statement
    // since the first alert box displayed correctly.
    catch (e)
    {
      alert("An exception was raised.");
    }
  </script>
  </body>
</html>
```

As before, we use the string variable `strXML` and the `loadXML()` method to create a simple XML DOM. Then, we create a second string variable, `strXML2`:

```
var strXML2 = "DisallowedElement";
```

which is a string that we will use when we create a new `Element` node using the `createElement()` method of the `Document` object:

```
var newElement = objXMLDOM.createElement(strXML2);
```

We will use the value of the `strXML2` variable to provide the name of the new `Element` node.

Next, an alert box is displayed to indicate that no exception has been raised until that point:

```
alert("Everything is working nicely until now.");
```

Then, we attempt to add the newly created `Element` node that had been assigned to the `newElement` variable as a child node of the `Document` node:

```
objXMLDOM.appendChild(newElement);
```

which is obviously illegal. Since a well-formed XML document can have only one document element, it is therefore illegal to attempt to add the `DissallowedElement` node as a child node to the `Document` object because we had earlier used the `loadXML()` method to provide an `AnyElement` node as the document element node.

When an exception is raised, the `catch` block is used to specify code to be run in response to that exception. However, in this example we simply specify that an alert box is displayed with a message that indicates that an exception has been raised, as shown in Figure 11-10.

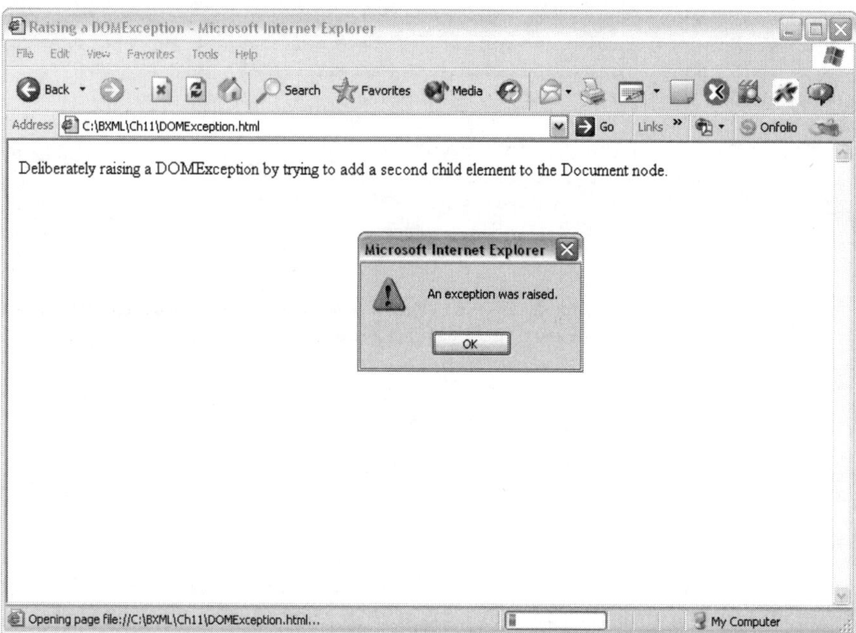

Figure 11-10

The Document Interface

The `Document` interface has featured in several examples earlier in this chapter. That is inevitable since all XML DOMs have a `Document` object.

The `Document` interface has three properties:

- `documentElement`—This read-only property returns an `Element` object.
- `doctype`—This read-only property is a `DocumentType` object, corresponding to a `DOCTYPE` declaration, if present, in the XML document.
- `implementation`—This read-only property is a `DOMImplementation` object.

As you have seen in earlier examples, the documentElement property is very useful to get a handle on the document element of the XML. From there, we can navigate around the XML DOM.

The Document interface has 14 methods:

- createAttribute(name)—This method returns an Attr object. The name argument is a String value. This method can raise a DOMException object.
- createAttributeNS(namespaceURI, qualifiedName)—This method returns an Attr object. The namespaceURI and qualifiedName arguments are String values. This method can raise a DOMException object.
- createCDATASection(data)—This method returns a CDATASection object. The data argument is a String value. This method can raise a DOMException object.
- createComment(data)—This method returns a Comment object. The data argument is a String value.
- createDocumentFragment()—This method takes no argument and returns a DocumentFragment object.
- createElement(tagName)—This method returns an Element object. The tagName argument is a String value. This method can raise a DOMException object.
- createElementNS(namespaceURI, qualifiedName)—This method returns an Element object. The namespaceURI and qualifiedName arguments are String values. This method can raise a DOMException object.
- createEntityReference(name)—This method returns an EntityReference object. The name argument is a String value. This method can raise a DOMException object.
- createProcessingInstruction(target, data)—This method returns a ProcessingInstruction object. The target and data arguments are each of type String. This method can raise a DOMException object.
- createTextNode(data)—This method returns a Text object. The data argument is a String value.
- getElementById(elementId)—This method returns an Element object. The elementId argument is a String value.
- getElementsByTagName(tagname)—This method returns a NodeList object. The tagname argument is a String value.
- getElementsByTagNameNS(namespaceURI, localName)—This method returns a NodeList object. The namespaceURI and localName arguments are String values. This method can raise a DOMException object.
- importNode(importedNode, deep)—This method returns a Node object. The importedNode argument is a Node object. The deep argument is a Boolean value. This method can raise a DOMException object.

The methods of the Document object are pivotal to the process of adding new nodes to a document. You saw in earlier examples how the createElement(), createTextNode(), and createAttribute() methods of the Document object can be used to create new nodes of the specified type, which can later be appended to or inserted into the XML DOM at the desired place. The createElement() and createAttribute() methods take an argument of type String, but you will need to make sure that the string is also a legal XML name.

When you are creating new Element and Attr nodes that are in a namespace, for example, when manipulating SVG, then you must use the createElementNS() and createAttributeNS() methods to achieve the correct results.

You will likely use the createCDATASection(), createComment(), and createProcessingInstruction() methods less often, but they are there if you need to add the corresponding components to an XML document.

The getElementsByTagName() method is useful to retrieve all elements that are not in a namespace and that have a particular element name. For example, to retrieve all Chapter nodes in a DOM you would use code like this:

```
objXMLDOM.getElementsByTagName("Chapter");
```

You would then have a NodeList object containing all such Chapter nodes for further processing.

If you are retrieving Element nodes that are in a namespace, for example SVG, you will need to use the getElementsByTagNameNS() method. Remember that namespace URIs must match character for character if you are to successfully retrieve the intended node(s).

If you are manipulating XML documents that had ID attributes, then you can use the getElementById() method to retrieve a specific Element node.

A full listing of the DOM Level 2 interfaces is available in Appendix B, but hopefully, having worked through the examples, you now feel that you have the knowledge to manipulate the XML DOM, for example, to add and remove nodes and to alter their value.

As I indicated earlier, the XML DOM is typically embedded in an application and forms at least part of the way in which XML is used in an application. To briefly illustrate this I will introduce InfoPath 2003 and discuss how the XML DOM is used in it.

How the XML DOM Is Used in InfoPath 2003

InfoPath 2003 is an enterprise XML-based forms tool from Microsoft that is designed to produce XML data from forms without requiring the end-user to have any understanding or awareness of XML. At the heart of InfoPath 2003 are several XML technologies including the Microsoft implementation of the XML DOM in MSXML 5.

A free trial of InfoPath is described at http://www.microsoft.com/office/infopath/prodinfo/trial.mspx. Unfortunately, the free trial is available only by ordering a CD, so shipping charges of a few dollars are unavoidable given the present distribution options. At the time of writing, no download option exists.

The data of an InfoPath form is held as XML in a DOM. As far as the InfoPath developer is concerned this is exposed as a "data source" that reflects the node hierarchy in the XML DOM but without requiring, for simple forms at least, the developer to have an understanding of how the XML DOM works. The data source for an InfoPath form is shown in Figure 11-11.

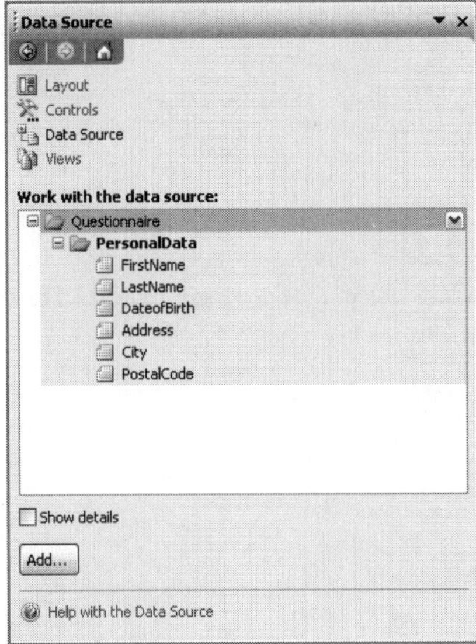

Figure 11-11

The simplest InfoPath forms use a single XML DOM to hold the data returned from a query or that is to be submitted to a relational database or XML Web service. However, many forms will have multiple XML DOMs in a single InfoPath solution. The values available in, for example, drop-down list form controls are secondary XML DOMs and can be retrieved from XML documents or from relational data sources.

I mentioned earlier that many DOM implementations have proprietary extensions. The manipulation of the InfoPath XML DOM depends on proprietary Microsoft methods that allow XPath strings to be used as arguments to those methods. The W3C is also working on proposals to facilitate interoperability of XPath and DOM, but those are not finalized at the time of writing.

The use of the XML DOM in InfoPath serves to illustrate how the DOM can be used as part of a larger application, whether custom coded or, with InfoPath 2003, a commercial application with XML DOM under the covers.

Summary

In this chapter, we learned what the XML DOM is and a little about its history at the W3C. The differences between interfaces and nodes were discussed. Several of the most commonly used DOM interfaces and objects were described and a number of examples were demonstrated using the Microsoft MSXML3 XML parser.

Exercise Questions

Suggested solutions to these questions can be found in Appendix A.

Question 1

Describe an important difference between the `NamedNodeMap` object and the `NodeList` object.

Question 2

List the methods of the `Document` object that are used to add `Element` nodes, which are, first, in no namespace and, second, in a namespace.

Simple API for XML (SAX)

In the last chapter we learned about the Document Object Model (DOM) and how it can be used to work with our XML document. The DOM is great when we work with relatively small documents that can easily fit into memory. But what do we do when we need to read an XML file that is several megabytes or even several gigabytes large? Loading this kind of data into memory can be very slow, and in many cases not possible. Luckily, we have another way to get the data out of an XML document.

In this chapter, we will learn:

- What is SAX
- Where to download SAX and how to set it up
- How and when to use the primary SAX interfaces

Because SAX is a programming application program interface (API), we will need to cover some in-depth programming concepts within this chapter. As we did in the last chapter, we will take it step by step; however, we will have to assume some programming experience. We will also be working through many examples. So you can try out the examples, we will explain how to download and install the Java Development Kit (JDK). If you do not plan on programming applications for XML, but rather plan to use XML for its design and document driven nature, you may want to skip this chapter.

What Is SAX and Why Was It Invented?

The *Simple API for XML*, or *SAX*, was developed as a standardized way to parse an XML, to enable more efficient analysis of large XML documents. The problem with the DOM is that before we can use it to traverse a document it has to build up a massive in-memory map of the document. This takes up space, and—more importantly—time. If you're trying to extract a small amount of information from the document, this can be extremely inefficient.

Let's illustrate this by a simple analogy.

A Simple Analogy

Parsing an XML document using SAX is very similar to watching a train pass by. It is very easy to catalog certain events of the train's passing. For example, you might observe the start of the train and the end of the train. You also might note the start of each car and the end of each car. Ideally, you would note the contents and characteristics of each car: color, length, engineer, baggage, passengers and so on. Using this method you could survey every part of the train.

SAX treats XML documents in much the same way. As the XML parser parses the documents, it reports a stream of events back to the application. We have events for the start of the document, the end of the document, the start and end of each element, the character contents of each element, and so on.

Unfortunately or fortunately depending on your point of view, receiving the events emitted by a SAX parser is like watching a runaway train. Once started, you cannot interrupt the parser to go back and look at an earlier part of the document. Unlike DOM, which gives you access to the entire document at once, SAX stores little or nothing from event to event. Although this seems like a major limitation, it is this very fact that gives SAX its speed and power.

> **What if we want to pause the stream of events from a SAX parser and come back to it later? Because SAX parsers push the data back to the application, they are generally referred to a push processors. The DOM model, which allows our application to retrieve the information when ready, is more generally a pull process. Some SAX parsers have emerged that allow us to pull the events when we're ready. These parsers work by allowing us to pause and resume the parsing process. Although it still does not allow us to go backward, it adds greater flexibility in the design of applications. In addition, a new pull-based API for handling XML streams called StAX, the Streaming API for XML, has emerged as an excellent solution.**

A Brief History of SAX

The extraordinary thing about SAX is that it isn't owned by anyone. It doesn't belong to any consortium, standards body, company, or individual. So it doesn't survive because so-and-so says that you must use it to comply with standard X, or because company Y is dominant in the marketplace. It survives because it's simple and it works.

SAX arose out of discussions on the XML-DEV mailing list (now hosted by OASIS at `http://www.oasis-open.org/`, and you can read the archives at `http://lists.xml.org/archives/xml-dev/`) aimed at resolving incompatibilities between different XML parsers (this was back in the infancy of XML in late 1997). David Megginson took on the job of coordinating the process of specifying a new API and then declared the SAX 1.0 specification frozen on May 11, 1998. A whole series of SAX 1.0-compliant parsers then began to emerge, both from vast corporations (IBM and Sun, for example) and from enterprising individuals (such as James Clark). All of these parsers were freely available for public download.

Eventually, a number of shortcomings in the specification became apparent, and David Megginson and his colleagues got back to work, finally producing the SAX 2.0 specification on May 5, 2000. The improvements centered on added support for namespaces and tighter adherence to the XML specification. Since that time several enhancements were made to expose additional information in the XML document, but the core of SAX was very stable. On April 27, 2004, these changes were finalized and released as version 2.0.2.

SAX is specified as a set of Java interfaces, which, initially, meant that if you were going to do any serious work with it, you were going to be looking at doing some Java programming, using JDK 1.1 or later. Now, however, a wide variety of languages have their own version of SAX. We will discuss some of these later in the chapter. In deference to the SAX tradition, however, we're going to start with some Java examples.

Where to Get SAX

All of the latest information about SAX can be found at `http://www.saxproject.org`. It is currently maintained by David Brownell and remains a public domain open source project hosted by SourceForge. To download SAX you can go to the home page and then browse for the latest version, or you can go directly to the SourceForge project page at `http://sourceforge.net/project/showfiles.php?group_id=29449`.

In the distribution you will find all of the Java interfaces, the extension interfaces, some helper files, and the documentation. You will not, however, find a SAX parser. To actually use SAX, you need to download one of the many XML parsers that have been developed to work with SAX.

Some popular Java SAX parsers include:

Parser	Driver identifier	Description
Xerces-J	org.apache.xerces.parsers.SAXParser	The Xerces parser, which we will be using throughout this chapter, is maintained by the Apache group. It is available at `http://xml.apache.org/xerces-j`
Ælfred2	gnu.xml.aelfred2.XmlReader	The Ælfred2 parser is highly conformant as it was written and modified by the creators of SAX. It is available as part of the GNUJAXP project at `http://www.gnu.org/software/classpathx/jaxp/`
Crimson	org.apache.crimson.parser.XMLReaderImpl	The Crimson parser was originally part of the Crimson project at `http://xml.apache.org/crimson/`. It is now included as part of Sun's Java API for XML Parsing available at `http://java.sun.com/xml`
Oracle	oracle.xml.parser.v2.SAXParser	Oracle maintains a SAX parser as part of its XML toolkit. It can be

Continues

Parser	Driver identifier	Description
		downloaded from the Oracle Technology Network at `http://otn.oracle.com/tech/xml/index.html`
XP	com.jclark.xml.sax.SAX2Driver	XP is an XML 1.0 parser written by James Clark. A SAX2 driver was created for use with the latest versions of SAX. More information can be found at `http://www.xmlmind.com/_xpforjaxp/docs/`

Setting Up SAX

I don't know about you, but I'm itching to try all this out. However, before we can do anything, we need to get hold of some software. Here's what we need:

- For our parser, we're going to use the latest Java version of Apache Xerces. This is available from `http://xml.apache.org/xerces-j`.
- We'll also need the Java Development Kit, release 1.1 or later. If you don't happen to have one lying around, your best bet is to download the latest edition of the Sun Java 2 Platform, Standard Edition from `http://java.sun.com/j2se/`. However, this is pretty massive download, and if you're pushed for bandwidth, JDK 1.1 is quite acceptable. This is still available from `http://java.sun.com/products/archive/index.html`, although even this is still a large download, so you might want to get this ready well in advance.

Receiving SAX Events

You may be wondering how we're going to be receiving these events. Remember the discussion on *interfaces* in the last chapter? If not, it might be a good time to take a look again to refresh your memory. What we're going to do is write a Java class that *implements* one of the SAX interfaces, which means our class will have all of the same functions as the interface.

We specify that a class implements an interface by declaring it like this:

```
public class MyClass implements ContentHandler
```

`MyClass` is the name of my new class, and `ContentHandler` is the name of the interface. Actually, this is the most important interface in SAX, as it is the one that defines the callback methods for content related events (that is, events about elements, attributes, and their contents). So what we're doing here is creating a class that contains methods that a SAX-aware parser knows about.

The `ContentHandler` interface contains a whole series of methods, most of which in the normal course of events we don't really want to be bothered with. Unfortunately, when we implement an interface, we have to provide implementations of *all* the methods defined in that interface. However, SAX provides us with a default, empty implementation of them, called DefaultHandler. So rather than *implement* ContentHandler, we can instead *extend* DefaultHandler, like this:

```
public class MyClass extends DefaultHandler
```

We can then pick and choose which methods we want to provide our own implementations, to trap specific events. This is called *overriding* the methods, and it works like this.

If you leave things as they are, the base class (DefaultHandler in this case) provides its own implementation of them for use by MyClass. So if, for example, there's a method in the ContentHandler interface called startDocument, whenever another piece of code invokes the startDocument method of MyClass's implementation of ContentHandler, the method invoked is actually DefaultHandler.startDocument. This is because DefaultHandler is providing a default implementation of startDocument. This is called "inheriting an implementation."

However, if we provide our own implementations of the methods, then they are used instead. In the preceding example, the method invoked would now be MyClass.startDocument. This might do something totally different from DefaultHandler's implementation.

Actually, DefaultHandler is a really hard-working class because it also provides default implementations of the three other core SAX interfaces: ErrorHandler, DTDHandler, and EntityResolver. We'll come across them in a little while, but for the time being, we'll focus on ContentHandler.

ContentHandler Interface

The ContentHandler interface, as the name implies, is designed to control the reporting of events for the content of the document. This includes information about the text, attributes, processing instructions, elements, and even the document itself. Here is a quick summary of methods that a ContentHandler must implement:

Event	Description
StartDocument	Event to notify the application that the parser has read the start of the document.
EndDocument	Event to notify the application that the parser has read the end of the document.
StartElement	Event to notify the application that the parser has read an element start tag.
EndElement	Event to notify the application that the parser has read an element end tag. Note: This event will be fired immediately after the startElement event for empty elements where the ending tag is implicit.
Characters	Event to notify the application that the parser has read a block of characters. Multiple characters events may be fired for a single section of text.

Continues

Event	Description
`IgnorableWhitespace`	Event to notify the application that the parser has read a block of whitespace that can probably be ignored, such as formatting and spacing of elements. Multiple `ignorableWhitespace` events may be fired for a single section of whitespace.
`SkippedEntity`	Event to notify the application that the parser has skipped an external entity.
`ProcessingInstruction`	Event to notify the application that the parser has read a processing instruction.
`StartPrefixMapping`	Event to notify the application that the parser has read an XML namespace declaration, and that a new namespace prefix is in scope.
`EndPrefixMapping`	Event to notify the application that a namespace prefix mapping is no longer in scope.
`SetDocumentLocator`	Event that allows the parser to pass a `Locator` object to the application.

We will cover each of these events in more detail. Let's try a small example to see how it works.

Try It Out The Start of Something Big

1. Let's begin by creating a sample XML document that we can use throughout this chapter—we'll continue to use the train example that we used as an analogy toward the start of the chapter:

```
<?xml version="1.0"?>
<train>
  <car type="Engine">
    <color>Black</color>
    <weight>512 tons</weight>
    <length>60 feet</length>
    <occupants>3</occupants>
  </car>
  <car type="Baggage">
    <color>Green</color>
    <weight>80 tons</weight>
    <length>40 feet</length>
    <occupants>0</occupants>
  </car>
  <car type="Dining">
    <color>Green and Yellow</color>
    <weight>50 tons</weight>
    <length>50 feet</length>
    <occupants>18</occupants>
```

```
  </car>
  <car type="Passenger">
    <color>Green and Yellow</color>
    <weight>40 tons</weight>
    <length>60 feet</length>
    <occupants>23</occupants>
  </car>
  <car type="Pullman">
    <color>Green and Yellow</color>
    <weight>50 tons</weight>
    <length>60 feet</length>
    <occupants>23</occupants>
  </car>
  <car type="Caboose">
    <color>Red</color>
    <weight>90 tons</weight>
    <length>30 feet</length>
    <occupants>4</occupants>
  </car>
</train>
```

It may not be a very long train, but so long as it has a caboose, it's complete. A better example of SAX's power, however, would be much larger. Save this file as `Train.xml` in a directory that you can use for your project.

2. Now you need to create a Java class that does the work of starting the parser and handling the events. You begin the class by telling the compiler that you will be using the SAX library by importing several packages.

```
import javax.xml.parsers.SAXParserFactory;
import javax.xml.parsers.SAXParser;
import org.xml.sax.*;
import org.xml.sax.helpers.*;
```

3. You can now begin your class, which will be called `TrainReader`.

```
public class TrainReader extends DefaultHandler
{

  public static void main(String[] args)
    throws Exception
  {
    System.out.println("Running train reader...");
    TrainReader readerObj = new TrainReader();
    readerObj.read(args[0]);
  }
```

The `main` method declaration is standard Java: this is the piece of code that will be executed when you start the class. It prints out a message, creates a new instance of the class that it resides in, and invokes a method called `read()`.

The `void` part of the declaration, incidentally, means that the method doesn't return a value to its caller, and the `throws Exception` part means that if anything happens that it can't cope with, it passes the exception back so the caller can deal with it. You'll see more of exceptions later.

```
public void read(String fileName)
  throws Exception
{
  XMLReader reader =
    XMLReaderFactory.createXMLReader("org.apache.xerces.parsers.SAXParser");
  reader.setContentHandler(this);
  reader.parse(fileName);
}
```

The first line of this method creates an `XMLReader` object using a factory helper object. This is, in fact, the only place in the code where you explicitly refer to the fact that it's the Xerces parser that you're using. So you could in fact substitute the qualified name of another parser here if you happened to have another one handy.

4. Now you can start working with the events themselves, the whole reason you are writing the class. You will start with the simplest of events, the start of the document and the end of the document.

```
public void startDocument()
  throws SAXException
{
  System.out.println("Start of the train");
}
```

5. Now you can create a function to catch the event that the parser has reached the end of the train.

```
public void endDocument()
  throws SAXException
{
  System.out.println("End of the train");
}
```

6. Finally, you can add the closing of the class.

```
}
```

Save this as file `TrainReader.java` in the same folder that you saved `Train.xml`. In these examples, we will assume you are compiling and executing our Java classes from a command prompt. If you are on Windows, you can find a shortcut to open a command prompt in the Start Menu in the Accessories folder. You may already be using a Java Development Environment (JDE), which is fine as long as you have access to view the console output.

At the command prompt, change to the directory where you have saved `TrainReader.java` and compile:

```
javac TrainReader.java
```

If you received an error such as:

```
'javac' is not recognized as an internal or external command,
operable program or batch file.
```

then it is likely that you have not added your Java bin folder to your `PATH` environment variable. Check your setup and try again. If you received another error compiling, check that you typed the code correctly and try again.

If you have added the SAX and Xerces packages to your `CLASSPATH` environment variable you can run your `TrainReader` program:

```
java TrainReader Train.xml
```

If you did not want to modify your `CLASSPATH` variable, you could simply copy the `xercesImpl.jar` file and `sax2r2.jar` files into your project directory and type:

```
java -cp sax2r2.jar;xercesImpl.jar TrainReader Train.xml
```

You should see:

```
Running train reader...
Start of the train
End of the train
```

Though this may not seem like groundbreaking output, the code behind our `TrainReader` class is the basis of any SAX project. From here you can quickly expand your code to examine any part of any XML document, regardless of the size.

If you saw an error, check that you typed in `Train.xml` correctly and try again. We will discuss possible errors in more detail later in the chapter.

How It Works

Before you move onto another example, let's break down some important parts of the `TrainReader` class. In the `main()` function you created an `XMLReader` object by sending a registered parser name to a factory function.

```
      XMLReader reader =
XMLReaderFactory.createXMLReader("org.apache.xerces.parsers.SAXParser");
```

Before you parsed, you made sure to tell the `XMLReader` that your class should receive events about the content of the XML document.

```
      reader.setContentHandler(this);
```

Then you started the parsing, passing the name of the file you wanted to parse.

```
      reader.parse(fileName);
```

At that point, the SAX parser took over. As it parsed the document, it made sure to call the event handlers that were registered. So, when the parser encountered the start of the document it reported a `startDocument` event to the registered `ContentHandler`, our `TrainReader` class. It did this by executing the `startDocument` function.

```
public void startDocument()
  throws SAXException
{
   System.out.println("Start of the train ");
}
```

And when it reached the end of the document, it called the similar `endDocument` function.

```
public void endDocument()
  throws SAXException
{
   System.out.println("End of the train ");
}
```

Handling Element Events

Now that you have learned the basics of handling events using the `ContentHandler` interface, let's look at how to handle element events. Let's look at the `startElement` function first:

```
public void startElement(String uri, String localName, String qName,
Attributes atts)
  throws SAXException
```

The first three parameters help to identify the element that the parser encountered—they allow you to identify the element based on its namespace name and local name, or by its prefix. If you remember our discussion of namespaces from Chapter 3, this behavior allows you to uniquely identify similar elements in different vocabularies.

So, if the parser encountered the following:

```
<myPrefix:myElement xmlns:myPrefix="http://example.com">
```

Then it would fire an event for the start of the element with the following values:

Parameter	Value
`Uri`	`http://example.com`
`LocalName`	MyElement
`Qname`	myPrefix:myElement

As you can see, the `uri` parameter represents the namespace URI associated with the element. The `localName` parameter contains part of the element name after the ":". The `qName` parameter is the qualified name—or the local name and the namespace prefix. If there is no prefix for the element name (for example, if there is no namespace or a default namespace), then the `localName` and `qName` should be the same.

> **Though most SAX parsers will report identical strings for the `localName` and `qName` parameters when there is no prefix, some do not. By default, some parsers may report an empty string for the `qName` parameter if the element has a namespace. For this reason it is recommended that you first check the `uri` parameter for null. If the `uri` paramter is not null, then you should use the combination of the `uri` and the `localName` instead of the `qName` parameter. You may be wondering why this is preferred. Remember, that any prefix can be used to refer to a namespace, and this may change from document to document. Using the namespace URI directly is more reliable.**

Attributes

The `startElement` event also provides a fourth parameter—the attributes. The `Attributes` interface gives us the ability to easily lookup the attributes and their values at the start of each element. The default `Attributes` interface provides us with the following functions:

Method	Description
`getLength`	Determine the number of attributes available in the `Attributes` interface.
`getIndex`	Retrieve the index of a specific attribute in the list. The `getIndex` function allows you to look up the index by using the attribute's qualified name or by using both the local name and namespace URI.
`getLocalName`	Retrieve a specific attribute's local name by sending the index in the list.
`getQName`	Retrieve a specific attribute's qualified name by sending the index in the list.
`getURI`	Retrieve a specific attribute's namespace URI by sending the index in the list.
`getType`	Retrieve a specific attribute's type by sending the index in the list, by using the attribute's qualified name, or by using both the local name and namespace URI. If there is no Document Type Definition (DTD), this function will always return `CDATA`.
`getValue`	Retrieve a specific attribute's value by sending the index in the list, by using the attribute's qualified name, or by using both the local name and namespace URI.

Like the element parameters, you are able to access the attributes through their qualified names or through the local names and namespace URIs. It is important to note that namespace declarations (the xmlns declarations we learned about in Chapter 3) will not be reported as attributes by default.

In the latest version of SAX, some parsers expose extended behavior through an interface called `Attributes2`, which allows you to check whether an attribute was declared in a DTD, and to check whether or not the attribute value appeared in the XML document or if it appeared because of a DTD or XML Schema attribute default declaration. We will cover the extension interfaces a little later in the chapter.

Let's look at an example of working with elements and attributes:

Try It Out — Element and Attribute Events

In this example, we will simply try to report the type of each train car, as your SAX parser fires the appropriate events. We'll use the same XML document, `Train.xml`, from the first example and modify the Java program a little.

1. Begin by opening `TrainReader.java` and adding the following function just after the `endDocument` function:

```
public void startElement(String uri, String localName, String qName,
  Attributes atts)
  throws SAXException
{
  if (localName.equals("car")) {
    if (atts != null) {
      System.out.println("Car: " + atts.getValue("type"));
    }
  }
}
```

2. Save this as file `TrainReader.java` in the same folder that you saved `Train.xml`. At the command prompt, change to the directory where you have saved `TrainReader.java` and compile:

```
javac TrainReader.java
```

3. Once you have compiled the class, you can run the program:

```
java TrainReader Train.xml
```

You should see:

```
Running train reader...
Start of the train
Car: Engine
Car: Baggage
Car: Dining
Car: Passenger
Car: Pullman
Car: Caboose
End of the train
```

How It Works

The core of this *Try It Out* is exactly the same as the first example. The only thing you did differently was to create an event handler for the start of each element.

```
if (localName.equals("car")) {
```

The first thing you did in your handler was to check the element's local name. Because you are using Xerces, you know that the `localName` and `qName` parameters are always reliable and always the same for documents without namespaces—you just chose to use `localName` to get in the habit. If the element name was `"car"`, you proceeded with the attribute code.

```
if (atts != null) {
  System.out.println("Car: " + atts.getValue("type"));
}
```

Your first step was to check whether the passed in `Attributes` interface was not `null`. According to the SAX specification, it should never be `null`. However, some early parsers did not follow this constraint. Then, you simply print out the value of the `"type"` attribute. It is important to note that if the `"type"` attribute is not found in the `Attributes` list, the `getValue` function will return `null`. In a more complete application, where the source XML documents vary, it would be a good idea to check for this case.

Handling Character Content

Now that you have worked with the elements and the attributes, you should look at how to work with the character content in our document. Working with the `characters` event is very similar to the events you have already seen:

```
public void characters(char[] ch, int start, int len)
  throws SAXException
```

Notice that the characters are delivered as a buffer, rather than a string. This allows for parser designers to more easily reuse internal buffers, which can effectively reduce the number of memory allocations and increase the overall performance. Passing in the start position and length to copy from the buffer can also help to increase performance. Luckily, it is very easy to create strings in Java with these parameters.

Unfortunately, working with the `characters` function is not quite as straightforward as it might seem. There is no obligation on the parser writer to deliver all the character data between two tags as a single block. (If you think about it, this is actually quite reasonable—after all, the string might turn out to be extremely long, and it could make for a very clumsy parser implementation.) From an application point of view, this just means that you may need to build up your string over a number of `character` events.

Try It Out Adding Colorful Characters

Though we are sticking with the trains again, we will add quite a bit in this *Try It Out*. We'll try to output the color of each car and its car type.

1. For starters we will add some private variables to our class.

```
import javax.xml.parsers.SAXParserFactory;
import javax.xml.parsers.SAXParser;
import org.xml.sax.*;
import org.xml.sax.helpers.*;

public class TrainReader extends DefaultHandler
{
```

```
  private boolean isColor;
  private String trainCarType = "";
  private StringBuffer trainCarColor = new StringBuffer();

  public static void main(String[] args)
    throws Exception
  {
    System.out.println("Running train reader...");
    TrainReader readerObj = new TrainReader();
    readerObj.read(args[0]);
  }

  public void read(String fileName)
    throws Exception
  {
    XMLReader reader =
      XMLReaderFactory.createXMLReader("org.apache.xerces.parsers.SAXParser");
    reader.setContentHandler(this);
    reader.parse(fileName);
  }

  public void startDocument()
    throws SAXException
  {
    System.out.println("Start of the train");
  }

  public void endDocument()
    throws SAXException
  {
    System.out.println("End of the train");
}
```

2. Next, we will modify the `startElement` function to record some of the data before the parser continues. Just because the SAX parser doesn't remember data from event to event doesn't mean our application can't. We'll set the `isColor` flag to tell us if we have started a color element. We'll also record the car type instead of just outputting it immediately as we did in our last example.

```
public void startElement(String uri, String localName, String qName,
Attributes atts)
  throws SAXException
{
  if (localName.equals("car")) {
    if (atts != null) {
      trainCarType = atts.getValue("type");
    }
  }

  if (localName.equals("color"))
  {
    trainCarColor.setLength(0);
```

```
      isColor = true;
    } else
      isColor = false;
  }
```

Notice that we are again working with the `localName` parameter instead of the `qName` parameter. If the `localName` is `"color"`, we set our flag to `true`; otherwise, we set it to `false`. We also make sure to reset our `trainCarColor StringBuffer` to be empty at the start of each new `color` element.

3. We can now add our `characters` event handler:

```
public void characters(char[] ch, int start, int len)
  throws SAXException
{
  if (isColor)
  {
    trainCarColor.append(ch, start, len);
  }
}
```

Remember, the parser may report the characters for an element in multiple chunks (even if the character data is very small). For this reason, we collect all of the `characters` events into a single `StringBuffer`, appending the data with each new call. We also check to make sure that we are appending the data only from `"color"` elements by checking the `isColor` flag we set in the `startElement` event.

4. Finally, we need to add an event handler to catch the end of the color element.

```
public void endElement(String uri, String localName, String qName)
 throws SAXException
{
 if (isColor)
 {
    System.out.println("The color of the " + trainCarType + " car is " +
      trainCarColor.toString());
 }
 isColor = false;
}
```

Here we output a message including the `StringBuffer` that we built up in the `characters` event. We also set the `isColor` flag back to `false` so that we don't collect unneeded character data in our `characters` event.

Again, save this as file `TrainReader.java` in the same folder that you saved `Train.xml` and compile the class:

```
javac TrainReader.java
```

Once you have compiled the class, you can run the program:

```
java TrainReader Train.xml
```

You should see:

```
Running train reader...
Start of the train
The color of the Engine car is Black
The color of the Baggage car is Green
The color of the Dining car is Green and Yellow
The color of the Passenger car is Green and Yellow
The color of the Pullman car is Green and Yellow
The color of the Caboose car is Red
End of the train
```

How It Works

The examples are now beginning to hint at the power, and difficulty, of SAX. As you can see, retrieving the data out of the SAX model is fairly simple. However, the complexity of the application grows very quickly when you need to associate and store data between event callbacks.

Just as we have seen throughout the chapter, the process began very simply. As the SAX parser began parsing the document, it called our `startDocument` function. Then, for each new element it called our `startElement` function. When the parser encountered a `"car"` element and fired the event, we stored the `type` attribute for later use.

```
trainCarType = atts.getValue("type");
```

Until the parser encountered another `"car"` element, the `trainCarType` variable remained unchanged. When the parser encountered the start of a `"color"` element, we set a flag to alert our application to append any character data to our `trainCarColor StringBuffer`:

```
if (isColor)
{
  trainCarColor.append(ch, start, len);
}
```

Instead of outputting the train car's color immediately, we waited until the `endElement` event. We did this to ensure that we had collected all of the character content in the color element. For example, if the parser had fired the following events:

```
Start of element: color
 Character data: Green and
 Character data: Yellow
 End of element: color
```

If we had simply assigned the `trainCarColor` instead of appending the data each time, we would overwrite `"Green and"` with `"Yellow"` during the second `characters` event.

When to Ignore ignorableWhitespace

The `ignorableWhitespace` event is very similar to the `characters` event. In fact, the parameter lists for the two functions are identical:

```
public void ignorableWhitespace(char[] ch, int start, int len)
  throws SAXException
```

Not only are the parameters identical, but also the functionality is very similar. Parsers may call the `ignorableWhitespace` function multiple times within a single element.

So, why have the `ignorableWhitespace` event? Whitespaces, such as spaces, tabs, and line feeds, which are used to make an XML document more readable, are often not important to the application, even though they are part of the XML content. For example, the line feed and spaces between the end of the `color` element and the start of the `weight` element has no meaning, whereas the space between `"512"` and `"tons"` within the `weight` element is very meaningful.

```
<car type="Engine">
 <color>Black</color>
 <weight>512 tons</weight>
 <length>60 feet</length>
 <occupants>3</occupants>
</car>
```

The only way a SAX parser can know that the whitespace is ignorable is when an element is declared as in a DTD to not contain `PCDATA`. For this reason, only validating parsers can report this event. If the parser has no knowledge of the DTD then it must assume that all character data, including whitespace, is important, and it must report it in the `characters` event.

Skipped Entities

The `skippedEntity` event, much like the `ignorableWhitespace` event, alerts the application that the SAX parser has encountered information it believes the application can or must skip. In the case of the `skippedEntity` event, the SAX parser has not expanded an entity reference it encountered in the XML document. An entity might be "skipped" for several reasons:

- The entity is a reference to an external resource that cannot be parsed or cannot be found
- The entity is an external general entity and the `http://xml.org/sax/features/external-general-entities` feature is set to false
- The entity is an external parameter entity and the `http://xml.org/sax/features/external-parameter-entities` feature is set to false

We'll talk about the `external-general-entities` and `external-parameter-entities` features later in this chapter. The `skippedEntity` event is declared as follows:

```
public void skippedEntity(String name)
  throws SAXException
```

The `name` parameter is the name of the entity that was skipped. The `name` parameter will begin with `"%"` in the case of a parameter entity. SAX considers the external DTD subset an entity. Therefore, if the `name` parameter is `"[dtd]"` it means that the external DTD subset was not processed.

Handling Special Commands with Processing Instructions

Processing instructions, as you may remember from Chapter 2, allow XML document authors to pass specific instructions to applications. SAX allows you to receive these special instructions in your application through the `processingInstruction` event:

```
public void processingInstruction(String target, String data)
  throws SAXException
```

Consider the following processing instruction:

```
<?instructionForTrainPrograms blowWhistle?>
```

Here the `target` would be `"instructionForTrainPrograms"` and the `data` would be `"blowWhistle"`. Using the `processingInstruction` event, adding special functionality to your application becomes relatively easy. In reality, though, processing instructions are seldom used. In fact, many people argued against the inclusion of processing instructions in the XML specification. With that said, however, processing instructions are legal and intended for use within processing applications.

You probably don't need to be reminded at this point that the XML declaration at the start of an XML document is *not* really a processing instruction, and as such it won't cause you to receive a `processingInstruction` event. Or at least, if it does, then you should switch to another parser, quickly.

Namespace Prefixes

When working with the element events, we saw that it is best to use the namespace URI and local name instead of the prefix. But what do you do if you want keep track of the prefixes used for each namespace? SAX processors will fire a `startPrefixMapping` event and `endPrefixMapping` event for any namespace declaration.

```
public void startPrefixMapping(String prefix, String uri)
  throws SAXException

public void endPrefixMapping(String prefix)
  throws SAXException
```

The `prefix` parameter is the namespace prefix that is being declared. In the case of a default namespace declaration, the prefix should be an empty string. The `uri` parameter is the namespace URI that is being declared. So for the namespace declaration:

```
xmlns:example=http://example.com
```

the `prefix` parameter would be "`example`" and the `uri` parameter would be "`http://example.com`." A `startPrefixMapping` event will occur immediately before the `startElement` event for the element where a namespace declaration appears. Likewise, an `endPrefixMapping` event will occur immediately after the corresponding `endElement` event. Keep in mind that the `xml` prefix is built-in. Because of this a SAX parser will not fire `startPrefixMapping` and `endPrefixMapping` events when an attribute or declaration with the `xml` prefix is encountered.

Stopping the Process in Exceptional Circumstances

In Chapters 4, 5, and 6, we learned how to validate our documents against a DTD, XML Schema, or RELAX NG schema. But what should we do if we have a rule that is so complex that it cannot be expressed in one of these languages? Again, the designers of SAX considered this problem. As you may have noticed, all of the event functions that we have used so far have declared that they may throw a `SAXException`. This allows us to create a new `SAXException` when we want to stop the processing.

Let's try another example:

Try It Out Pulling the Brakes

We will make a small modification to our last example. We will add a new rule to require that our caboose be `"Red"`. After all, nobody likes a train with a caboose that isn't red.

1. The only change that we'll make is in our `endElement` function—we'll check the `trainCarType` for `"Caboose"` and then check the color:

```
public void endElement(String uri, String localName, String qName)
  throws SAXException
{
  if (isColor)
  {
    System.out.println("The color of the " + trainCarType + " car is " +
      trainCarColor.toString());
    if ((trainCarType.equals("Caboose")) & &
      (!trainCarColor.toString().equals("Red")))
    {
      throw new SAXException("The caboose is not red!");
    }
  }
  isColor = false;
}
```

This is all we need to do to stop the parsing process. Save this as file `TrainReader.java` in the same folder that you saved `Train.xml` and compile the class:

```
javac TrainReader.java
```

Once you have compiled the class, you can run the program:

```
java TrainReader Train.xml
```

You should see:

```
Running train reader...
Start of the train
The color of the Engine car is Black
The color of the Baggage car is Green
The color of the Dining car is Green and Yellow
The color of the Passenger car is Green and Yellow
The color of the Pullman car is Green and Yellow
The color of the Caboose car is Red
End of the train
```

Of course, our caboose is red, so we did not receive an error. Let's change the color of our caboose in `Train.xml`:

```
<car type="Caboose">
  <color>Green</color>
  <weight>90 tons</weight>
  <length>30 feet</length>
  <occupants>4</occupants>
</car>
```

Let's try running our `TrainReader` again:

```
java TrainReader Train.xml
```

You should see:

```
Running train reader...
Start of the train
The color of the Engine car is Black
The color of the Baggage car is Green
The color of the Dining car is Green and Yellow
The color of the Passenger car is Green and Yellow
The color of the Pullman car is Green and Yellow
The color of the Caboose car is Green
Exception in thread "main" org.xml.sax.SAXException: The caboose is not red!
        at TrainReader.endElement(TrainReader.java:80)
        at org.apache.xerces.parsers.AbstractSAXParser.endElement
        (Unknown Source)
        at org.apache.xerces.impl.XMLNSDocumentScannerImpl.scanEndElement
        (Unknown Source)
        at org.apache.xerces.impl.XMLDocumentFragmentScannerImpl$
        FragmentContentDispatcher.dispatch(Unknown Source)
        at org.apache.xerces.impl.XMLDocumentFragmentScannerImpl.scanDocument
        (Unknown Source)
        at org.apache.xerces.parsers.XML11Configuration.parse(Unknown Source)
        at org.apache.xerces.parsers.DTDConfiguration.parse(Unknown Source)
        at org.apache.xerces.parsers.XMLParser.parse(Unknown Source)
        at org.apache.xerces.parsers.AbstractSAXParser.parse(Unknown Source)
        at TrainReader.read(TrainReader.java:29)
        at TrainReader.main(TrainReader.java:20)
```

Notice that when the exception was raised it stopped the whole application. This is because we are not handling the exception anywhere. Let's add that to our application now.

2. Add a `try..catch` block around the call to the `parse` function where we start reading the document.

```
public void read(String fileName)
  throws Exception
{
  XMLReader reader =
    XMLReaderFactory.createXMLReader("org.apache.xerces.parsers.SAXParser");
  reader.setContentHandler(this);
```

```
    try
    {
      reader.parse(fileName);
    }
    catch (SAXException e)
    {
      System.out.println("Parsing stopped : " + e.getMessage());
    }
}
```

Once this is complete, you can again compile `TrainReader.java`:

```
javac TrainReader.java
```

Once you have compiled the class, you can run the program:

```
java TrainReader Train.xml
```

You should see:

```
Running train reader...
Start of the train
The color of the Engine car is Black
The color of the Baggage car is Green
The color of the Dining car is Green and Yellow
The color of the Passenger car is Green and Yellow
The color of the Pullman car is Green and Yellow
The color of the Caboose car is Green
Parsing stopped : The caboose is not red!
```

How It Works

Taking advantage of the exception mechanism built into SAX allows us to quickly stop the parsing process if we deem necessary. This means that we can add additional validation for more complex constraints that cannot be modeled using DTDs or XML Schemas. In the example we used the exception mechanism to ensure that the caboose was red, but this same concept can be used to model any type of business rules needed in your application including complex calculations or specialized lookups.

Once the exception was thrown, we didn't receive any more SAX events, even though the parser had not completed parsing the document. Many SAX parsers are designed to fire an `endDocument` event even when there is an exception or error in the document. This design allows applications a guaranteed time to do any miscellaneous cleanup such as release memory. At the time of this writing, however, the Xerces parser, the Crimson Parser, and the Oracle parser do not fire the `endDocument` event if an error or exception is encountered. Because of this, it is safest to assume that the `endDocument` function will not be called, which means you should always have a `try..finally` block surrounding calls to the `parse` function if you need to ensure that certain actions are taken even when there is an exception.

Providing the Location of the Error

Although we have provided an error message for our problem XML document, we haven't given the author of the XML document very much information to go and fix the error. It would be helpful to provide the line number and the column position of the error. SAX allows us to pass this information along in our message.

The only event callback we haven't used from the `ContentHandler` so far in this chapter is `setDocumentLocator`. The `setDocumentLocator` callback allows the parser to pass the application a `Locator` interface. Using this interface you can easily determine the line number and column position at any time within your application. The methods of the `Locator` object include:

Method	Description
`GetLineNumber`	Retrieves the line number for the current event.
`GetColumnNumber`	Retrieves the column number for the current event.
`GetSystemId`	Retrieves the system identifier of the document for the current event. Because XML documents may be composed of multiple external entities, this may change throughout the parsing process.
`GetPublicId`	Retrieves the public identifier of the document for the current event. Because XML documents may be composed of multiple external entities, this may change throughout the parsing process.

The latest version of SAX has also introduced an extended version of the `Locator` interface, called `Locator2`. The `Locator2` interface allows you to retrieve the XML version and encoding declaration. We will talk about the extension interfaces later in the chapter.

The `setDocumentLocator` callback, if it is called, will occur before any other event callbacks. It may not be called at all, or it may be passed a `null` locator object. Because of this, you must always check for `null` before using the locator. All of the parsers listed in the beginning of the chapter except XP provide locator information that can be used throughout the parsing process.

Try It Out Which Stop Is This?

Let's add some information to that exception we created using the document locator. If the parser provides a locator, we'll display the document name, the line number, and the column position when the exception is thrown.

1. To start with, let's add a private variable to hold on to the locator object when it is passed in the callback. We'll call this `trainLocator`.

```
public class TrainReader extends DefaultHandler
{

  private boolean isColor;
  private String trainCarType = "";
  private StringBuffer trainCarColor = new StringBuffer();
  private Locator trainLocator = null;
```

2. Next, we need to add the handler for our `setDocumentLocator` event:

```
public void setDocumentLocator(Locator loc)
{
  trainLocator = loc;
}
```

Notice that this function does not declare that a `SAXException` can be thrown. Until the `startDocument` event has been fired, error information is unreliable.

3. Finally, we need to modify our exception message in the `endElement` event handler:

```
public void endElement(String uri, String localName, String qName)
  throws SAXException
{
  if (isColor)
  {
    System.out.println("The color of the " + trainCarType + " car is " +
      trainCarColor.toString());
    if ((trainCarType.equals("Caboose")) & &
      (!trainCarColor.toString().equals("Red")))
    {
      if (trainLocator != null)
        throw new SAXException("The caboose is not red at line " +
          trainLocator.getLineNumber() + ", column " +
          trainLocator.getColumnNumber() );
      else
        throw new SAXException("The caboose is not red!");
    }
  }
  isColor = false;
}
```

As we said before, we must check that the locator is not null before we can use it. Let's compile `TrainReader.java`:

```
javac TrainReader.java
```

Once you have compiled the class, you can run the program:

```
java TrainReader Train.xml
```

You should see:

```
Running train reader...
Start of the train
The color of the Engine car is Black
The color of the Baggage car is Green
The color of the Dining car is Green and Yellow
The color of the Passenger car is Green and Yellow
The color of the Pullman car is Green and Yellow
The color of the Caboose car is Green
Parsing stopped : The caboose is not red at line 34, column 25
```

How It Works

By handling the `setDocumentLocator` event, we were able to access the `Locator` object supplied by our XML parser. This allowed us to easily notify the user where the error occurred in the XML document. In a small document, such as the sample that we are working with, the benefit may not be very obvious. In a multi-gigabyte document, however, this information would be invaluable.

The information provided by the `Locator` is not always absolute. Some parsers are better than others at determining the location in the document. For the most part, the line number is accurate. The reported column position can vary wildly between parsers, however. Because of this, it is probably best to use the `Locator` information in situations where the exact position is not critical.

ErrorHandler Interface

We still haven't finished with errors. What if we want to do our own handling of parser errors? It probably won't come as a great surprise to find out that what we do is implement some methods of an interface. However, these new methods aren't part of `ContentHandler`; they're part of another interface altogether, called `ErrorHandler`. As it happens, the `DefaultHandler` class provides us with a rudimentary implementation of this interface as well, although it doesn't actually do anything apart from throw a `SAXException` to print out a trace of the call stack, like the one we saw in the earlier example.

Event	Description
`warning`	Allows the parser to notify the application of a warning it has encountered in the parsing process. Though the XML Recommendation provides many possible warning conditions, very few SAX parsers actually produce warnings.
`error`	Allows the parser to notify the application that it has encountered an error. Even though the parser has encountered an error, parsing can continue. Validation errors should be reported through this event.
`fatalError`	Allows the parser to notify the application that it has encountered a fatal error and cannot continue parsing. Well-formedness errors should be reported through this event.

To receive error events, you must call `setErrorHandler` and pass a reference to the `TrainReader` object. This is the exact analog of the call to `setContentHandler` that we used to tell the parser where to send the content related events.

Try It Out To Err Is Human, To Handle Errors Is Divine

In this example we'll extend the `TrainReader` class so that we catch parser errors and report their location. So, as well as overriding some of `DefaultHandler`'s implementation of `ContentHandler`, we're going to be overriding some of its implementation of `ErrorHandler`. We will also upgrade our sample by creating a DTD for our `Train` vocabulary and validating our XML document. This will allow us to see how the `ErrorHandler` works with different kinds of errors.

1. Let's begin by modifying the sample XML document. We'll add an internal DTD so that we can validate the document:

```
<?xml version="1.0"?>
<!DOCTYPE train [
  <!ELEMENT train (car*)>
  <!ELEMENT car (color, weight, length, occupants)>
  <!ATTLIST car type CDATA #IMPLIED>
  <!ELEMENT color (#PCDATA)>
  <!ELEMENT weight (#PCDATA)>
  <!ELEMENT length (#PCDATA)>
  <!ELEMENT occupants (#PCDATA)>
]>
```

   Again, save this file as `Train.xml` in the directory that we are using for our project.

2. Now, we will need to modify our `TrainReader` class. First, we will add the call to `setErrorHandler` and set the validation feature to `true` to turn on validation:

```
public void read(String fileName)
  throws Exception
{
  XMLReader reader =
      XMLReaderFactory.createXMLReader("org.apache.xerces.parsers.SAXParser");
  reader.setContentHandler(this);
  reader.setErrorHandler(this);
  try
  {
     reader.setFeature("http://xml.org/sax/features/validation", true);
  }
  catch (SAXException e)
  {
     System.err.println("Cannot activate validation");
  }
  try
  {
   reader.parse(fileName);
  }
  catch (SAXException e)
  {
    System.out.println("Parsing stopped : " + e.getMessage());
  }
}
```

   Notice that we set the validation feature within a `try..catch` block. We will talk more about features and properties later in the chapter.

3. Next, we need to add the error-handling functions to our `TrainReader` class. These will override the minimal implementations provided by `DefaultHandler`:

```
public void warning (SAXParseException exception)
  throws SAXException {
```

```
    System.err.println("[Warning] " +
      exception.getMessage() + " at line " +
      exception.getLineNumber() + ", column " +
      exception.getColumnNumber() );
  }

  public void error (SAXParseException exception)
    throws SAXException {
    System.err.println("[Error] " +
      exception.getMessage() + " at line " +
      exception.getLineNumber() + ", column " +
      exception.getColumnNumber() );
  }

  public void fatalError (SAXParseException exception)
    throws SAXException {
    System.err.println("[Fatal Error] " +
      exception.getMessage() + " at line " +
      exception.getLineNumber() + ", column " +
      exception.getColumnNumber() );
  throw exception;
  }
```

All we're doing here is printing out the location of the error, taken from the incoming `SAXParseException` object, and then—in the case of `fatalError`—rethrowing the error back to the parser. In most parsers rethrowing the exception is unnecessary, but it ensures that regardless of the parser chosen, parsing will stop when a fatal error is encountered. It's worth noting that if the parser doesn't support `Locator`, it's not going to provide us with anything meaningful in these methods on `SAXParseException`.

Let's compile `TrainReader.java`:

```
javac TrainReader.java
```

Once you have compiled the class, you can run the program:

```
java TrainReader Train.xml
```

You should see:

```
Running train reader...
Start of the train
The color of the Engine car is Black
The color of the Baggage car is Green
The color of the Dining car is Green and Yellow
The color of the Passenger car is Green and Yellow
The color of the Pullman car is Green and Yellow
The color of the Caboose car is Green
Parsing stopped : The caboose is not red at line 34, column 25
```

We have the same output we had in the last example. Obviously, we didn't change the color of our caboose back to `Red`. What is important to note is that the exception thrown by the application was not passed through any of our new error-handling methods. When you create an exception to stop parsing, it is immediate.

4. Let's insert a couple of errors into our XML document so that we can see the new error functions in action. First, rename the `occupants` element inside of the `"Engine"` to be a `conductors` element. Then, delete the ">" on the closing `car` tag. Finally, we need to change the caboose color to "`Red`":

```
<?xml version="1.0"?>
<!DOCTYPE train [
  <!ELEMENT train (car*)>
  <!ELEMENT car (color, weight, length, occupants)>
  <!ATTLIST car type CDATA #IMPLIED>
  <!ELEMENT color (#PCDATA)>
  <!ELEMENT weight (#PCDATA)>
  <!ELEMENT length (#PCDATA)>
  <!ELEMENT occupants (#PCDATA)>
]>
<train>
  <car type="Engine">
    <color>Black</color>
    <weight>512 tons</weight>
    <length>60 feet</length>
    <conductors>3</conductors>
  </car
  <car type="Baggage">
    <color>Green</color>
    <weight>80 tons</weight>
    <length>40 feet</length>
    <occupants>0</occupants>
  </car>
  <car type="Dining">
    <color>Green and Yellow</color>
    <weight>50 tons</weight>
    <length>50 feet</length>
    <occupants>18</occupants>
  </car>
  <car type="Passenger">
    <color>Green and Yellow</color>
    <weight>40 tons</weight>
    <length>60 feet</length>
    <occupants>23</occupants>
  </car>
  <car type="Pullman">
    <color>Green and Yellow</color>
    <weight>50 tons</weight>
    <length>60 feet</length>
    <occupants>23</occupants>
  </car>
  <car type="Caboose">
    <color>Red</color>
    <weight>90 tons</weight>
    <length>30 feet</length>
    <occupants>4</occupants>
  </car>
</train>
```

Again, save this file as `Train.xml` and run the program:

```
java TrainReader Train.xml
```

You should see:

```
Running train reader...
Start of the train
The color of the Engine car is Black
[Error] Element type "conductors" must be declared. at line 16, column 17
[Fatal Error] The end-tag for element type "car" must end with a '>'
delimiter. at line 18, column 3
Parsing stopped : The end-tag for element type "car" must end with a '>'
delimiter.
```

How It Works

By handling the errors reported by the parser, we are able to provide useful error messages back to the application, and ultimately, the user. The three levels of errors allow us to report the information even when parsing can continue, or if we decide, stop parsing for all errors and warnings. Let's look at our output in more detail:

```
Running train reader...
Start of the train
The color of the Engine car is Black
```

The process begins as it has in every other example, firing off events normally.

```
[Error] Element type "conductors" must be declared. at line 16, column 17
```

Then, we encounter our first error, the `conductors` element that we added. The Xerces parser raised an error when it encountered the `conductors` element because it was not declared in the DTD we provided with our document. Some parsers will also raise an error about the missing `occupants` element. The error that was raised was only a validation error, which meant that parsing could continue because the document could still be well formed even if it was not valid.

```
[Fatal Error] The end-tag for element type "car" must end with a '>'
delimiter. at line 18, column 3
```

The parsing, and events, continued until it reached the well-formedness error we introduced. Once the parser encounters a well-formedness error, it cannot continue trying to parse the document according to the XML specification. After outputting the message, our application rethrew the exception that was then caught by the exception handler around the call to the `parse` function:

```
Parsing stopped : The end-tag for element type "car" must end with a '>'
delimiter.
```

Again, we output a message about the error. Of course, with our newly added error-handling code, the message was redundant.

DTDHandler Interface

Now that we have added a DTD to our document you may want to receive some events about the declarations. The logical place to turn is the `DTDHandler` interface. Unfortunately, the `DTDHandler` interface provides us with very little information about the DTD itself. In fact it allows us to see the declarations only for notations and unparsed entities.

Event	Description
`NotationDecl`	Allows the parser to notify the application that it has read a notation declaration.
`UnparsedEntityDecl`	Allows the parser to notify the application that it has read an unparsed entity declaration.

When parsing documents that make use of notations and unparsed entities to refer to external files—such as image references in XHTML or embedded references to non-XML documents—the application must have access to the declarations of these items in the DTD. This is why the creators of SAX made them available through the `DTDHandler`, one of the default interfaces associated with an `XMLReader`.

The declarations of elements, attributes, and internal entities, however, are not required for general XML processing. These declarations are more useful for XML editors and validators. For this reason, the events for these declarations were made available in one of the extension interfaces, `DeclHandler`. We'll look at the extension interfaces in more detail later in the chapter.

Using the `DTDHandler` interface is very similar to using the `ContentHandler` and `ErrorHandler` interfaces. The `DefaultHandler` class we used as the base class of the `TrainReader` also implements the `DTDHandler` interface. So, working with the events is simply a matter of overriding the default behavior, just as we did with the `ErrorHandler` and `ContentHandler` events. To tell the `XMLReader` to send the `DTDHandler` events to our application, we can simply call the `setDTDHandler` function, as shown in the following:

```
reader.setDTDHandler(this);
```

You may be wondering if there is an interface for receiving XML Schema events. Surprisingly, there isn't. In fact, there are no events fired for XML Schema declarations either. The creators of SAX wanted to ensure that all of the information outlined in the XML specification was available through the interfaces. Remember, DTDs are part of the XML specification, but XML Schemas are defined in their own, separate specification.

EntityResolver Interface

The `EntityResolver` interface allows us to control how a SAX parser behaves when it attempts to resolve external entity references within the DTD. So, much like the `DTDHandler`, it is frequently not used. However, when an XML document utilizes external entity references, it is highly recommended that you provide an EntityResolver.

The EntityResolver interface defines only one function:

Event	Description
resolveEntity	Allows the application to handle the resolution of entity lookups for the parser.

Just as we have seen with your other default interfaces, the EntityResolver interface is implemented by the DefaultHandler class. Therefore, to handle the event callback, we simply need to override the resolveEntity function in the TrainReader class and make a call to the setEntityResolver function:

```
reader.setEntityResolver(this);
```

Consider the following entity declaration:

```
<!ENTITY train PUBLIC "-//TRAINS//images PNG 1.0//EN"
  "http://example.com/train.jpg">
```

In this case the resolveEntity function would be passed "-//TRAINS//images PNG 1.0//EN" as the public identifier and "http://example.com/train.jpg" as the system identifier. The DefaultHandler class's implementation of the resolveEntity function returns a null InputSource by default. When handling the resolveEntity event, however, your application can take any number of actions. It could create an InputSource based on the system identifier. Or it could create an InputSource based on a stream returned from a database, hashtable, or catalog lookup that used the public identifier as the key. Or it could simply return null. These options and many more allow your application to control how the processor opens and connects to external resources.

Features and Properties

As we have already seen in this chapter, some of the behavior of SAX parsers is controlled through setting features and properties. For example, to activate validation we needed to set the "http://xml.org/sax/features/validation" feature to true. In fact, all features in SAX are controlled this way, by setting a flag true or false. The feature and property names in SAX are full URIs so that they can have unique names—much like namespace names.

Working with Features

To change the value of a feature in SAX, you must simply call the setFeature function of the XMLReader.

```
public void setFeature(String name, boolean value)
  throws SAXNotRecognizedException, SAXNotSupportedException
```

When doing this, however, it is important to remember that parsers may not support, or even recognize, every feature. If a SAX parser does not recognize the name of the feature, the `setFeature` function will raise a `SAXNotRecognizedException`. If it recognizes the feature name but does not support a feature (or does not support changing the value of a feature at a certain time) the `setFeature` function will raise a `SAXNotSupportedException`. For example, if a SAX parser does not support validation, it would raise a `SAXNotSupportedException` when you attempted to change the value.

The `getFeature` function allows you to check the value of any feature.

```
public boolean getFeature(String name)
  throws SAXNotRecognizedException, SAXNotSupportedException
```

Like the `setFeature` function, the `getFeature` function may raise exceptions if it does not recognize the name of the feature or does not support checking the value at certain time (such as before, during, or after the `parse` function has been called). For this reason, it is good to place all of your calls to the `setFeature` and `getFeature` functions within a `try..catch` block to handle any exceptions.

All SAX parsers should recognize, but may not support, the following features:

Feature	Default	Description
`http://xml.org/sax/features/validation`	unspecified	Controls whether or not the parser will validate the document as it parses. In addition to controlling validation, it also affects certain parser behaviors. For example, if the feature is set to `true`, all external entities must be read.
`http://xml.org/sax/features/namespaces`	`true`	In the latest version of SAX, this feature should always be `true`, meaning that namespace URI and prefix values will be sent to the element and attribute functions when available.
`http://xml.org/sax/features/namespace-prefixes`	`false`	In the latest version of SAX, this feature should always be `false`. It means that names with colons will be treated as prefixes and local names. If this flag is set to `true` then raw XML names will be sent to the application.
`http://xml.org/sax/features/xmlns-uris`	`false`	Allows you to control whether or not xmlns declarations are reported as having the namespace URI `http://www.w3.org/2000/xmlns/`.

Continues

Feature	Default	Description
		By default, SAX conforms to the original Namespaces in XML Recommendation and will not report this URI. The 1.1 Recommendation and an erratum to the 1.0 edition modified this behavior.
`http://xml.org/sax/features/resolve-dtd-uris`	`true`	Controls whether or not the SAX parser will "absolutize" system IDs relative to the base URI before reporting them. Parsers will use the Locator's `systemID` as the base URI. This feature does not apply to `EntityResolver.resolveEntity`, nor does it apply to `LexicalHandler.startDTD`.
`http://xml.org/sax/features/external-general-entities`	unspecified	Controls whether or not external general entities should be processed. If the validation feature is set to `true`, this feature will always be true.
`http://xml.org/sax/features/external-parameter-entities`	unspecified	Controls whether or not external parameter entities should be processed. If the validation feature is set to `true`, this feature will always be true.
`http://xml.org/sax/features/lexical-handler/paramater-entities`	unspecified	Controls the reporting of start and end of parameter entity inclusions in the `LexicalHandler`.
`http://xml.org/sax/features/is-standalone`	none	Allows you to determine whether or not the stand-alone flag was set in the XML declaration. This feature can be accessed only after the `startDocument` event has completed. The feature is read-only and will return true only if the stand-alone flag in the XML declaration has a value of `yes`.
`http://xml.org/sax/features/use-attributes2`	unspecified	Check this read-only feature to determine whether or not the `Attributes` interface passed to the `startElement` event supports the `Attributes2` extensions. The `Attributes2` extensions allow you to examine additional information about the declaration of the attribute in the DTD. For more information on the `Attributes2` interface see

Feature	Default	Description
		Appendix G on this book's website (http://www.wrox.com). Because this feature was introduced in a later version of SAX, some SAX parsers will not recognize it.
`http://xml.org/sax/features/use-locator2`	unspecified	Check this read-only feature to determine whether or not the `Locator` interface passed to the `setDocumentLocator` event supports the `Locator2` extensions. The `Locator2` extensions allow you determine the XML version and encoding declared in an entity's XML declaration. For more information on the `Locator2` interface, see Appendix G on this book's website (http://www .wrox.com). Because this feature was introduced in a later version of SAX, some SAX parsers will not recognize it.
`http://xml.org/sax/features/use-entity-resolver2`	`true` (if recognized)	Set this feature to true (the default) if the `EntityResolver` interface passed to the `setEntityResolver` function supports the `EntityResolver2` extensions. If it does not support the extensions set this feature to false. The `EntityResolver2` extensions allow you to receive callbacks for the resolution of entities and the external subset of the DTD. For more information on the `EntityResolver2` interface, see Appendix G on this book's website (http://www.wrox.com). Because this feature was introduced in a later version of SAX, some SAX parsers will not recognize it.
`http://xml.org/sax/features/string-interning`	unspecified	Allows you to determine if the strings reported in event callbacks were interned using the Java function `String.intern`. This allows for fast comparison of strings.
`http://xml.org/sax/features/unicode-normalization-checking`	`false`	Controls whether the parser reports Unicode normalization errors as described in section 2.13 and Appendix B of the XML 1.1 Recommendation. Because these errors are not fatal, if encountered they will be reported using the `ErrorHandler.error` callback.

Continues

Feature	Default	Description
`http://xml.org/sax/features/xml-1.1`	unspecified	Read-only property that returns true if the parser supports XML 1.1 and XML 1.0. If the parser does not support XML 1.1 then this feature will be false.

Working with Properties

Working with properties is very similar to working with features. Instead of boolean flags, however, properties may be any kind of object. The property mechanism is most often used to connect helper objects to an `XMLReader`. For example, SAX comes with an extension set of interfaces called `DeclHandler` and `LexicalHandler` that allow you to receive additional events about the XML document. Because these interfaces are considered extensions, the only way to register these event handlers with the `XMLReader` is through the `setProperty` function.

```
public void setProperty(String name, Object value)
  throws SAXNotRecognizedException, SAXNotSupportedException

public Object getProperty(String name)
  throws SAXNotRecognizedException, SAXNotSupportedException
```

As we saw with the `setFeature` and `getFeature` functions, all calls to `setProperty` and `getProperty` should be safely placed in `try..catch` blocks as they may raise exceptions. Some of the default property names include:

Property Name	Description
`http://xml.org/sax/properties/declaration-handler`	Specifies the `DeclHandler` object registered to receive events for declarations within the DTD.
`http://xml.org/sax/properties/lexical-handler`	Specifies the `LexicalHandler` object registered to receive lexical events, such as comments, CDATA sections, and entity references.
`http://xml.org/sax/properties/document-xml-version`	Read-only property that describes the actual version of the XML Document, such as "1.0" or "1.1". This property can only be accessed during the parse and after the `startDocument` callback has been completed.

Extension Interfaces

The two primary extension interfaces are the `DeclHandler` and the `LexicalHandler`. Using these interfaces, you can receive events for each DTD declaration and specific items such as comments, CDATA sections, and entity references as they are expanded. It is not required by the XML specification that these items be passed to the application by an XML processor. All the same, the information can be very useful at times, and for this reason the creators of SAX wanted to ensure that they could be accessed.

The `DeclHandler` interface declares the following events:

Event	Description
`AttributeDecl`	Allows the parser to notify the application that it has read an attribute declaration
`ElementDecl`	Allows the parser to notify the application that it has read an element declaration.
`ExternalEntityDecl`	Allows the parser to notify the applicatio.n that it has read an external entity declaration.
`InternalEntityDecl`	Allows the parser to notify the application that it has read an internal entity declaration.

The `LexicalHandler` interface declares the following events:

Event	Description
`comment`	Allows the parser to notify the document that it has read a comment. The entire comment will be passed back to the application in one event call; it will not be buffered as it may be in the `characters` and `ignorableWhitespace` events.
`startCDATA`	Allows the parser to notify the document that it has encountered a CDATA section start marker. The character data within the CDATA section will always be passed to the application through the `characters` event.
`endCDATA`	Allows the parser to notify the document that it has encountered a CDATA section end marker.
`startDTD`	Allows the parser to notify the document that it has begun reading a DTD.
`endDTD`	Allows the parser to notify the document that it has finished reading a DTD.
`startEntity`	Allows the parser to notify the document that it has started reading or expanding an entity.
`endEntity`	Allows the parser to notify the document that it has finished reading or expanding an entity.

Because these are extension interfaces, they must be registered with the `XMLReader` using the property mechanism, as we just learned. For example, to register a class as a handler or `LexicalHandler` events you might do the following:

```
reader.setProperty("http://xml.org/sax/properties/lexical-handler", this);
```

It is important to note that the `DefaultHandler` class, which we used as the basis of the `TrainReader` class, does not implement any of the extension interfaces. In the latest version of SAX, however, an extension class was added called `DefaultHandler2`. This class not only implements the core interfaces, but the extension interfaces as well. So, if you want to receive the `LexicalHandler` and `DeclHandler` events, it is probably a good idea to descend from `DefaultHandler2` instead of the `DefaultHandler` class.

Good SAX and Bad SAX

Now that we're thoroughly familiar with SAX, this is a good point to review what SAX is good at and what it isn't so good at, so that we can decide when to use it and when to use another approach, such as the DOM.

As we've seen, SAX is great for analyzing and extracting content from XML documents. Let's look at what makes it so good:

- It's simple: you need to implement only three or perhaps four interfaces to get going.
- It doesn't load the whole document into memory, so it doesn't take up vast amounts of space. Of course, if your application is using SAX to build up its own in-memory image of the document, it's likely to end up taking a similar amount of space as the DOM would have done (unless your in-memory image is a lot more efficient than the DOM!).
- The parser itself typically has a smaller footprint than that of its DOM cousin. In fact, DOM implementations are often built on top of SAX.
- It's quick, because it doesn't need to read in the whole document before you start work on it.
- It focuses on the real content rather than the way that it's laid out.
- It's great at filtering data and letting you concentrate on the subset that you're interested in.

So why don't we use it for everything? Here are a few drawbacks:

- You get the data in the order that SAX gives it to you. You have absolutely no control over the order in which the parser searches. As we have seen in our *Try It Outs*, this means that you may need to build up the data that you need over several event invocations. This can be a problem if you're doing particularly complex searches.
- SAX programming requires fairly intricate state keeping, which is prone to errors.
- If you're interested in analyzing an entire document, DOM is much better, because you can traverse your way around the DOM in whichever direction you want, as many times as you want.

Consumers, Producers, and Filters

Throughout this chapter we have covered the basics of SAX. We created an application that receives, or *consumes*, SAX events. Although this is the most common usage of SAX, it is important to note that you can use it in other ways. In addition to consuming events from an `XMLReader`, it is possible to write classes that *produce* SAX events. For example, you might want to write a class that reads a comma-delimited file and fires SAX events, similar to an `XMLReader`. You could then have a single application that was able to receive events from either an XML document or a comma-delimited file.

Instead of producing or consuming events, you may want to simply *filter* events as they pass from `XMLReader` to event handler. A SAX filter acts as a middleman between the parser and application. Filters can insert, remove, or even modify events before passing them on to the application. If we returned to the earlier train analogy, we could say that a filter is very similar to a tunnel that the train passes through. While in the tunnel, the train might be painted, new cars might be added in, or cars may be removed.

In fact, many filters already exist for SAX, which allow you to do anything from specialized validation to document transformation. Many filters can be chained together, creating a SAX *pipeline*. Included in SAX is an `XMLFilter` interface that is intended for standardizing how filters are created.

Considering the many ways to use SAX will enable you to create more complex and more powerful applications.

Other Languages

Because the SAX model works so well for processing XML documents, the Java interfaces have been translated to many programming languages and environments. Currently, the most widely accepted are:

Language	Available Interfaces
C++	Xerces-C++, the counterpart to the Xerces-J toolkit we are using from Apache, defines a set of C and C++ bindings available at `http://xml.apache.org/xerces-c`. MSXML, the Microsoft XML toolkit, provides C++ and COM interfaces (including ActiveX wrappers) available at `http://msdn.microsoft.com/library/en-us/xmlsdk30/htm/sax2_reference.asp`. Arabica toolkit provides C++ bindings that make more extensive use of C++ language features, available at `http://www.jezuk.co.uk/cgi-bin/view/Arabica`. ElCel Technology provides C++ bindings, available at `http://www.elcel.com/products/xmltoolkit.html`. GNU Compiler for Java has derived C++ bindings available at `http://gcc.gnu.org/java`.
Perl	SAX bindings for Perl can be found at `http://cvs.sourceforge.net/viewcvs.py/perl-xml/libxml-perl/doc/sax-2.0.html?rev=HEAD`.

Continues

Language	Available Interfaces
Python	Python 2.0 includes support for SAX processing in its markup toolkit as part of the default distribution available at `http://www.python.org/`.
Pascal	SAX for Pascal bindings can be found at `http://saxforpascal.sourceforge.net/`.
Visual Basic	MSXML, the Microsoft XML toolkit, provides Visual Basic interfaces available at `http://msdn.microsoft.com/library/en-us/xmlsdk30/htm/sax2_reference.asp`.
.NET	The `System.Xml` classes distributed with .NET provide implementations usable in various .NET languages.
Curl	Curl is a web content management system with its own SAX bindings, available at `http://www.curl.com/`.

In general, these versions of SAX have stayed within the spirit of the original Java interfaces while making good use of their own individual language features. Many new projects such as SAX.NET at `http://sourceforge.net/projects/saxdotnet` are also underway to provide additional bindings for SAX.

Summary

SAX is an excellent API for analyzing and extracting information from large XML documents without incurring the time and space overheads associated with the DOM. In this chapter, you learned how to use SAX to catch events passed to you by a parser, by implementing a known SAX interface, `ContentHandler`. You used this to extract some simple information from an XML document.

You also looked at error handling, and found out how to implement sophisticated intelligent parsing, reporting errors as we did so. In addition you looked at how to supplement the error-handling mechanisms in the parser by using the `Locator` object. Finally, you read about the strengths and weaknesses of SAX.

Now that you are well versed in the APIs used to work with XML in applications, you can look closer at how XML can be used to communicate between multiple applications.

Exercise Questions

Suggested solutions to these questions can be found in Appendix A.

Question 1

Calculate the weight, length, and total number of occupants on the entire train. Once the document has been parsed, print out the result of the calculations.

Question 2

Print out a list of all elements declared in the DTD. To do this, descend the `TrainReader` class from `DefaultHandler2` instead of `DefaultHandler`. Register the `TrainReader` class with the parser so that you can receive `DeclHandler` events. (Hint: you will need to use a property.)

Part VI: Communication

RSS and Content Syndication

One of the interesting characteristics of the web is the way that certain ideas seem to arise spontaneously, without any centralized direction. Content syndication technologies definitely fall into this category, and they have emerged as a direct consequence of the linked structure of the web and general standardization on the use of XML.

This chapter is focused on a number of aspects of content syndication, including the RSS and Atom formats and their role in such areas as blogs, news services, and the like. There is no doubt these technologies will play a major role in the next logical leap in the connectedness of the web, and so it's useful to understand them not just from an XML-format standpoint but also in terms of how they are shaping the future Internet.

In this chapter we will:

- Introduce the concepts and technologies of content syndication and meta data
- Briefly look at the history of RSS, Atom, and related languages
- See what the feed languages have in common, and how they differ
- See how a simple newsreader/aggregator can be implemented using Python
- See examples of XSLT used to generate and display newsfeeds

There is a lot more to RSS and content syndication than could be covered in a single chapter, so the aim here is to give you a good grounding in the basic ideas, and then give you a taste of how XML tools such as SAX and XSLT can be used in this rapidly expanding field.

Syndication and Meta Data

Turn on your TV and you'll see spontaneous snapshots of the current state of the TV "space," one channel at a time. Information is transmitted to the box in front of you, mostly appearing in the form of shows. Some shows will be instantly familiar to you (the ill-fated man in a red shirt jumping in front of the Klingon phaser—you'd think these guys would learn!), and some may require you a little bit of time to figure out what's going on. If you're lucky, you'll jump to a commercial break and see the transitional title, but some programming will remain mystifying no matter how long you watch (any public cable access channel, for instance).

One of the largest circulated magazines on the planet is *TV Guide*. Although it has some editorial content, people typically do not buy the magazine for that content. They are interested in the listings—what channel transmits what show at what time. *TV Guide* listings will provide a certain amount of information for each such show beyond this, such as abstracts describing the show itself, the stars, a family rating, and a key number used by automated video recorders to set them to record the show automatically.

The deployment of resources on a network (whether television or computer) is called *syndication*. The TV guide provides description of the shows, information about information. Stepping down into the less human-friendly computer world, we have something very similar, meta data, which is data about data. The essence of RSS and related formats is found where these two ideas join: syndication and meta data.

A syndication feed is simply an XML file comprised of meta data elements and in most cases some content as well. There are several distinct standard formats, notably RSS 1.0, RSS 2.0, and Atom. As XML formats these (and various other RSS x.x dialects) are largely incompatible, having different document structures and element definitions, though they each share a common basic model of a syndication feed. There is the feed itself, which will have characteristics, such as a title and publication date. The feed carries a series of discrete blocks of data, known as items or entries, each of which will also have a set of individual characteristics, again such as title and date. These items are little chunks of information, which either describe a resource on the web (a link will be provided) or are a self-contained unit, carrying content along with them.

Syndication Systems

Like most other web systems, syndication systems are generally based around the client-server model. At one end you have a web server delivering data using the Hypertext Transfer Protocol (HTTP), and at the other end a client application receiving it. On the web, the server will use a piece of software like Apache or IIS, and the client will use a browser like Internet Explorer or Mozilla Firefox. HTML-oriented web systems tend to have a clear distinction between the roles and location of the applications: the server is usually part of a remote system, and the client appears on the user's desktop. HTML data is primarily intended for immediate rendering and display for the user to read it on their home computer.

However, syndication material is intended for machine-readability first, and there will be at least one extra stage of processing before the content appears on the user's screen. Machine-readability means that it is possible to pass around and process the data relatively easily, allowing a huge amount of versatility in systems. The net result is that applications that produce material for syndication purposes can appear either server-side or client-side (desktop), as can applications that consume this material.

Perhaps the key to understanding the differences between syndication and typical web pages is the notion of time. A syndicated resource (an item in a feed) is generally only available for a short period of time at a given point in the network, at which stage it will disappear from the feed, although there is likely to be an archived version of the information on the publisher's site.

The different kinds of syndication software components can roughly be split into four categories: server-producer, server-consumer, client-producer, and client-consumer. In practice software products may combine these different pieces of functionality, but it will help to look at these parts in isolation.

Here is an overview of each, with the more familiar systems first.

Server-Producer

A server-side producer of syndication material is in essence no different from that used to publish regular HTML web pages. At minimum this would be a static XML file in one of the syndication formats placed on a web server. More usefully the XML data will be produced from some kind of content management system. The stereotypical content management systems in this context are weblog (blog) tools. The main page of the (HTML) website will feature a series of diary-like entry, with the most recent entry appearing first. Behind the scenes there will be some kind of a database containing the entry material, and the system will present this in reverse-chronological order on a nicely formatted web page. In parallel with the HTML-generating subsystems of the application will be syndication feed format (RSS and/or Atom) producing subsystems. These two subsystems are likely to be very similar, as the end result usually only differs in format. Many blogging systems, such as Movable Type, include a common templating system to produce either HTML or syndication format XML.

Client-Consumer

Although it is possible to view certain kinds of syndicated feeds in a web browser, one of the major benefits of syndication comes into play with so-called newsreaders or aggregator tools. The reader application will allow the user to subscribe to a large number of different feeds and present the material from these feeds in an integrated fashion. There are two common styles of feed-reader user interface:

- Single pane presents items from the feeds in sequence as they might appear on a weblog.
- Multipane styles are often modeled on e-mail applications and present a selectable list of feeds in one panel and the content of the selected feed in another.

The techniques used to process and display this material vary considerably. Many pass the data directly to display, whereas others incorporate searching and filtering, and at least two systems (NewsMonster and Haystack) use Semantic Web technologies to enable powerful handling of feed data. Several newsreaders (for example, Radio and Amphetadesk) use a small web server running on the client machine to render content in a standard browser. There are also wide variations in the sophistication of these tools. Some may provide presentation of each feed as a whole; others will do it item-by-item by date, through user-defined categories or any combination of these and other alternatives. You will see the code for a very simple aggregator later in this chapter.

Client-Producer

Ok, so the server-producer puts content on a web server, and the client-consumer processes and displays this content. But where does the content come from in the first place? Again blogging tools are the stereotype. Let's say there's an author of a weblog who uses a tool to compose posts containing his thoughts for the day and cat photos. Clicking a button will submit this data to a content management system that will typically load the content into its database, for subsequent display as in the preceding server-producer. The four categories presented here break down a little at this point, as many blogging tools actually operate from the web server as well, with the user being presented a web form in which to enter his content. Where the client-producer category fits best is with desktop blogging clients, which run as conventional applications. When the user clicks Submit (or whatever), the material will be sent over the web to the content management system.

There is a technical issue that should be mentioned at this point. When it comes to communications, the server-producer and client-consumer systems generally operate in exactly the same way as

HTML-oriented web servers and clients using the HTTP protocol directly. The feed material will be delivered in one of the syndication formats: RSS or Atom.

However, when it comes to posting material to a management system, then other strategies are commonly used. In particular, developers of the Blogger blogging service designed a specification for transmitting blog material from the author's client to the online service. Although the specification was only intended as a prototype, the "Blogger API" became the de facto standard for posting to blogging and similar content management systems. The Blogger API defines a small set of XML-RPC elements to encode the material and pass it to the server. There were certain limitations of this specification, which led to MetaWeblog API from Userland, which extends the elements in a way that makes it possible to send all the most common pieces of data that might be required. There was a partial recognition in the MetaWeblog API that there was a degree of redundancy in the specifications. The data that is passed from an authoring tool is essentially the same in structure and content as the material passed from the server to newsreaders, so the MetaWeblog API uses some of the vocabulary of RSS 2.0 to describe the structural elements.

Since the XML-RPC blogging APIs came out, there has been a growing realization in the developer community that not only is there redundancy at the level of naming parts of the messages being passed around, but also in the fundamental techniques used to pass them around. To transfer syndicated material from a server to a client, the client sends an HTTP `GET` message to the server, and the server responds with a bunch of RSS/Atom-formatted data. On the other hand, when transferring material from the client to the server, the blogging APIs wrap the content in XML-RPC messages and use a HTTP `POST` to send that. The question is why use XML-RPC format when there is already a perfectly good RSS or Atom format? Recent developments have seen a gradual shift from XML-RPC to the passing of XML data directly over HTTP, and also more use of the less familiar HTTP verbs, such as `PUT` (to place an XML document on the web) and `DELETE` (to delete a document).

Server-Consumer

There are two ways of looking at the server-producer kind of syndication component. Firstly, there's the functionality needed to receive material sent from a client-producer, blog posts, and the like. Secondly, there's the possibility to take material from other syndication servers (for example, server-producers) and do interesting things with that. The latter approach still isn't all that common, though it offers considerable potential for the future. There are glimpses of what is possible in the form of online aggregators, which combine the feeds from many different sources and either display the result as a single web page (not unlike a client-side aggregator). There are online services like Technorati, which use syndicated data to provide enhanced search. Another online service, PubSub, allows you to register a search query and then subscribe to a feed of the results, which are extracted from among more than a million feeds.

It's worth noting that the distinction between server-consumer as the recipient of a single author's blog posts and server-consumer as an online information aggregator is likely to blur as HTTP + syndication format client-producer systems become more widespread.

The Origin of RSS Species

So, where and when did these systems and the formats they use originate? The metadata side of RSS can be said to have begun in the mid-1990s, with the development of the Meta Content Framework at Apple, essentially a table of contents for a website. The notion of building a syndication network for the Internet came about in large part due to the idea of a "Push" model for publication. In this model, syndication documents, written in XML, would be pushed to the client from the server, describing a set of "channels" and their associated web content, including when this content was to be published and when it would expire. By doing this, the thinking went, large concerns could *push* their content specifically through these channels, establishing the traditional media notion of brand-naming channels and turning the Internet into something with properties more similar to a television set than the document server that had characterized the web up to that point.

Microsoft's Content Definition Format

XML syndication formats really began when Microsoft entered the fray with a push technology. The *Content Definition Format* (CDF) was specifically targeted to be a comprehensive syndication format that would appeal to "traditional" broadcasters, and the roster of companies that provided content initially read like a who's who of the entertainment industry. The CDF format and Active Channel, the Windows-based component within Internet Explorer that supported it, was more oriented toward a true syndication model, with the publishers being the big names. The Channel bar would periodically download content based upon the syndication schedule within the CDF format, caching the content that would then make it available immediately upon demand. Here is an example of CDF:

```
<CHANNEL BASE="http://www.intertwingly.net/blog/" HREF="index.html"
  LASTMOD="2004-04-15T10:12:16-04:00">

  <TITLE>Sam Ruby</TITLE>
  <ABSTRACT>It's just data</ABSTRACT>

  <ITEM HREF="1760.html"
    LASTMOD="2004-04-14T11:23:26-04:00">
    <TITLE>Survival guide to I18n</TITLE>
    <ABSTRACT>In the next installment of the atom guide,
    I tackle what may very well
    be the number one issue in ill-formed feeds:
    character encoding in
    general, and smart quotes in particular.
    &amp;#160; In the process of
    producing this documentation, I am struck...</ABSTRACT>
  </ITEM>

  <ITEM HREF="1759.html"
    LASTMOD="2004-04-08T16:27:42-04:00">
    <TITLE>GRDDL</TITLE>
    <ABSTRACT>DanBri pointed me to a specification named GRDDL.&amp;#160;
    It looks like exactly what I was looking for last August.&amp;#160;
    Any XML file is one
    namespace declaration, one attribute definition,
    and one XSLT file away
    from RDF. Oddly, it defines a...</ABSTRACT>
  </ITEM>

</CHANNEL>
```

You may be wondering why a sample of format dating from the 1990s is presented in a 21st century book on XML. There are two reasons: firstly, the model of a feed and its items is essentially the same model in use today, and it contains features that found their way into RSS and have stayed there ever since—channel, item, title, and so on. Secondly, this format is still supported by Microsoft software. If you are using Internet Explorer you may be surprised to find out that you're already in possession of a CDF reader. If you point your browser at `http://www.intertwingly.net/blog/index.cdf` you will be asked if you want to add this channel to your list of favorites. If you say yes then you can read the items in that channel. Unfortunately, there isn't much CDF material around these days.

The Great Push Revolution that was supposed to herald a complete reshaping of the web more or less failed to materialize. A big part of the reason for this may have been the fact that although push technology makes a great deal of sense to marketers—you deliver your message to your customers rather than have your customers come to you—it held far less value to the people who were the recipients of such push technology.

Userland and scriptingNews

The content management company Userland has played a prominent role in the history of XML syndication, a notable move being their introduction of the scriptingNews format. This followed experiments by the company with Apple's MCF and Microsoft's CDF; in fact, the syntax of scriptingNews was very similar to CDF.

Netscape and RSS 0.9

Netscape submitted their XML version of the Meta Content Framework to the W3C not long after Microsoft's submission of CDF, but their real entrance to the syndication arena came with their introduction of the RDF Site Summary (RSS) 0.9 language. This format used the fledgling *Resource Description Framework* (RDF) language, and RSS defined a simple structure for collecting linked information and publishing it into a customized part of their browser section. RDF evolved from MCF and various other sources, and also played an important role in the internal workings of the Netscape Navigator browser. The syntax of RSS 0.9 appeared very much like that of the scriptingNews and CDF formats, yet its RDF base made a significant conceptual difference.

Simply RDF

RDF is not surprisingly all about describing resources and is described in a suite of six specifications from the W3C. Although very simple in principle, RDF took a lot of material to describe in full because of its theoretical grounding in logic and various practical requirements. It forms the basis for the W3C's Semantic Web initiative, which is based on a vision of how the existing web can be improved with the help of meta data and a little logic. Anyone working with syndication feeds or interested in the future of the web should at least read the RDF Primer (`http://www.w3.org/TR/rdf-primer/`). The interchange format for RDF is known as RDF/XML, which forms the basis of RSS 0.9 and 1.0. An example of the XML syntax of RSS 0.9 will be shown in just a moment, but we will need a little more information to be able to interpret it correctly for there's more to it than meets the eye.

The key to RDF is the concept of a resource. A resource is usually something that can be identified on the web. Many resources have a universal identifier (URI), which in the case of web pages will be the same as their address (URL). Pretty much anything else (people, places, and concepts) can be identified in this way by assigning URIs. Descriptions are made in RDF using statements, which have the following three parts:

- The thing being described
- The characteristic of interest
- The value of that characteristic

For example, the thing being described might be a book, say, *A Christmas Carol*, the characteristic of interest (property) could be the author, and the value would be the name of the author, Charles Dickens. In RDF jargon these three parts are the subject, predicate, and object, and together they form a triple. This grouping roughly corresponds to the English sentence structure of subject, verb, and object. Each triple corresponds to a single statement. The subject is a resource, the predicate is a special kind of resource used to denote a property, and the object can either be another resource or literal text. As resources, the predicates are identified using URIs, and the same predicates are often reused—when we ask who the author of a book is, we are asking the same question regardless of the book we are talking about or whoever happens to be the author. However, a lot of the time it isn't convenient or even possible to give everything we want to talk about a URI (what is the URI of *A Christmas Carol*?), and in these circumstances RDF uses a stand-in for the URI called a blank node. So you can say in effect resourceX has author Charles Dickens, and resourceX has the title *A Christmas Carol*. Those two properties in combination make it pretty unambiguous about which resource is under discussion.

Now take look at the RSS 0.9 as shown in the following:

```
<?xml version="1.0"?>
<rdf:RDF
   xmlns:rdf="http://www.w3.org/1999/02/22-rdf-syntax-ns#"
   xmlns="http://my.netscape.com/rdf/simple/0.9/">

   <channel>
        <title>The Metaphorical Web</title>
        <link>http://www.metaphoricalweb.com</link>
        <description>Kurt Cagle's Metaphorical Web site, filled with information
        on XML, XSLT, SVG and other things X-related.</description>
   </channel>
   <item>
        <title>The Metaphorical Web #23: The Shape of Things to Come</title>
        <link>http://www.metaphoricalweb.com/?method=showPage&amp;
        src=metaphorical23.xml
</link>
        <description>Resolutions and Reflections on the State of Tech in
        2004</description>
   </item>

   <item>
        <title>SVG 1.2: Into the interface</title>
        <link>http://www.metaphoricalweb.com/?
        method=showPage&amp;src=svg12.xml</link>
        <description>A look at the recently announced SVG 1.2
        specification.</description>
   </item>

</rdf:RDF>
```

Ok, it's got a root `<rdf:RDF>` element, and a couple of namespaces are declared. But it certainly isn't obvious how it has anything to do with the triple things. Take a look again at the first two lines inside the outer element:

```
...
<channel>
       <title>The Metaphorical Web</title>
...
```

What this is saying in the RDF interpretation is that there is a resource of the *type* "channel," which has a property called *title* and whose value is "The Metaphorical Web". *Type* here refers to an RDF term that expresses class membership—another way of saying the resource in question is a member of the class `channel`. The channel resource isn't associated with a URI, so it's a blank node. Through the standard XML namespaces interpretation, both `channel` and `title` are qualified with the namespace `http://my.netscape.com/rdf/simple/0.9/`, which means both these terms are unambiguously associated with URIs. Expressed as triples (giving the blank node the temporary identifier `id0`), the preceding two lines become the following:

```
subject: id0
predicate: http://www.w3.org/1999/02/22-rdf-syntax-ns#type
object: http://my.netscape.com/rdf/simple/0.9/channel

subject: id0
predicate: http://my.netscape.com/rdf/simple/0.9/title
object: "The Metaphorical Web"
```

It's no coincidence that the RSS 0.9 RDF/XML syntax look similar to the plain XML CDF material. It's conveying much the same kind of information, except in a form, which can be interpreted by a computer as globally unambiguous logical statements. However, another important point about the use of RDF/XML is that this is no longer merely about the language of syndication. Defined using RDF Schema and each having their own namespace, different vocabularies can be used together in the same document. Alongside the channels, items, and titles, it's also possible to use terms defined elsewhere. The item might actually be a *book*, with the *author* Charles Dickens. The RDF model allows such terms to be incorporated and interpreted in exactly the same way as the core RSS vocabulary. This is a major boon for extensibility.

If you refer back to the full example, you can see that the structure is broken up into a channel and multiple items. The *human* meaning of a channel is a little ambiguous—you could associate it with an organizational entity (CNN, Netscape, Microsoft, and so on) or with a specific website. The *link* associated with the channel can consequently point to the main web page of that organization's website, or to a specific RSS-oriented channel page that pulls the appropriate relevant meta data. The channel's *description* provides the abstract or rationale for this particular channel, telling the receiver a little more about itself.

Each of the item elements in turn has a similar structure, describing a title, a link, and an abstract description. The original 0.9 specification included a few other primary fields, including links to icons and posting dates, but these were very much secondary to what amounted to a collection of editorial links.

The RSS 0.9 specification has proven to be fairly robust and is still in use as something of a baseline RSS specification. It is also the immediate precursor of the RSS 1.0 format. It's rather confusing, but the RSS 0.91–0.94 specifications are very different than RSS 0.9 and 1.0. The growth of syndication has been marred by political battles over the best approach to take—in a nutshell the conflict centers around whether it is more important for the format to be easily read by humans or machines.

Netscape, Userland, and RSS 0.9x

Netscape backed away from its original RDF-oriented approach to RSS, and influenced by Userland's scriptingNews and the way people were actually using the format, Netscape dropped the RDF approach in RSS 0.91. Along with RDF, out went namespaces and in came a DTD and a new name: Rich Site Summary. Not long after this Netscape dropped RSS altogether. It was picked up by Userland, and further minor changes were made (the DTD was discarded, and a *different* version of RSS 0.91 was released). The format was effectively promoted by Userland, who also introduced some of the first software applications dedicated to blogging and syndication. The following is a typical example of RSS 0.91:

```
<rss version="0.91">
  <channel>
    <title>The Metaphorical Web</title>
    <link>http://www.metaphoricalweb.com/</link>
    <description>Kurt Cagle's Metaphorical Web site, filled with
       information on XML, XSLT, SVG and other things X-related.
    </description>
    <language>en-us</language>
    <item>
      <title>The Metaphorical Web #23: The Shape of Things to Come</title>
      <link>http://www.metaphoricalweb.com/metaphorical23.xml
</link>
      <description>Resolutions and Reflections on the State of Tech
        in 2004
      </description>
    </item>
    <item>
       <title>SVG 1.2: Into the interface</title>
       <link>http://www.metaphoricalweb.com/svg12.xml</link>
       <description>A look at the recently announced
         SVG 1.2 specification.
       </description>
    </item>
  </channel>
</rss>
```

On the surface the syntax is fairly similar to the 0.90 version, and if you ignore the removal of the `rdf:RDF` element and namespaces, the biggest difference is that the channel is now a container of various items, rather than being a sibling.

RSS 0.91's greatest strength was that it was simple. As a straightforward XML format, its greatest weakness was that it was rather weakly specified with several ambiguous element definitions, and the lack of namespace support meant that its use with other XML languages was severely impaired. One advantage "vanilla" XML has over RDF/XML is that simple DTDs can be used for validation, but the DTD Netscape had provided with their version 0.91 was removed when the spec was adopted by Userland.

Still a large proportion of syndicated feeds are to this day RSS 0.91, and this Userland style of RSS evolved through versions 0.92, 0.93, and (briefly) 0.94 before becoming RSS 2.0, which we will see in a moment. But first, we return to RDF.

RSS-DEV and RSS 1.0

Despite being relatively simple and reasonably popular, the Userland versions of RSS came under increasing criticism for ambiguities in the specifications and the practical limitations inherent in a namespace-free XML format. The additional 0.9x numbered versions of RSS were seen as painting over cracks and had also served to further fragment the already fractious marketplace.

An informal mailing list sprang up, RSS-DEV, to address these problems, and the result was the RSS 1.0 specification. Unfortunately, the RSS-DEV proposal, which was essentially an RDF-oriented revision of RSS 0.9, clashed with the RDF/namespace-free 0.91 approach followed by Userland. Agreement wasn't forthcoming on a way forward, and as a result, RSS forked. One thread carried the banner of simplicity; the other had the banner of interoperability. This is the source of considerable confusion to newcomers to RSS, as both forms are designed for the same primary purpose, yet they differ considerably in their construction. The rebranding of Userland's RSS as Really Simple Syndication helps a little in contrast to RSS-DEV's RDF Site Summary.

The RSS-DEV reintroduced the RDF basis, taking advantage of the modularity offered by that language, and made it possible to reuse terms from the Dublin Core metadata standard (`http://dublincore.org`) and add "modules" (RDF vocabularies) for content and syndication-specific terms. This is what RSS 1.0 looks like:

```
<?xml version="1.0" encoding="iso-8859-1"?>
<rdf:RDF xmlns:rdf="http://www.w3.org/1999/02/22-rdf-syntax-ns#"
                xmlns:dc="http://purl.org/dc/elements/1.1/"
                xmlns:sy="http://purl.org/rss/1.0/modules/syndication/"
                xmlns="http://purl.org/rss/1.0/">

  <channel rdf:about="http://journal.dajobe.org/journal/index.rdf">
    <title>Dave Beckett - Journalblog</title>
    <link>http://journal.dajobe.org/journal/</link>
    <description>Semantic web and free software hacking.</description>
    <language>en</language>
    <dc:date>2004-04-16T08:22:58+00:00</dc:date>
    <sy:updatePeriod>hourly</sy:updatePeriod>
    <sy:updateFrequency>1</sy:updateFrequency>

    <items>
      <rdf:Seq>
        <rdf:li
 rdf:resource="http://journal.dajobe.org/journal/2004_03.html#001678" />
        <rdf:li
 rdf:resource="http://journal.dajobe.org/journal/2004_03.html#001677" />
      </rdf:Seq>
    </items>
  </channel>

 <item rdf:about="http://journal.dajobe.org/journal/archives/
   2004_03.html#001678">
   <title>MySQL lifts restrictive licensing terms</title>
   <description> MySQL lifts restrictive licensing terms (Silicon.com)
     by Stephen Shankland. Reports the adding of a Free and Open Source
   Software...</description>
   <link>http://journal.dajobe.org/journal/archives/2004_03.html#001678</link>
   <dc:subject>comment</dc:subject>
   <dc:creator>dajobe</dc:creator>
   <dc:date>2004-03-16T20:56:39+00:00</dc:date>
 </item>

 <item rdf:about="http://journal.dajobe.org/journal/archives/
   2004_03.html#001677">
```

```
    <title>The trouble with Rover is revealed</title>
    <description> The trouble with Rover is revealed by Ron Wilson, EE Times
      on how the Spirit Mars rover got stuck...</description>
    <link>http://journal.dajobe.org/journal/archives/2004_03.html#001677</link>
    <dc:subject>link</dc:subject>
    <dc:creator>dajobe</dc:creator>
    <dc:date>2004-03-08T18:06:35+00:00</dc:date>
  </item>

</rdf:RDF>
```

To a human with a text editor, this format appears considerably more complex than RSS 0.91. It restores the role of RDF as the namespace that provides descriptive content, and a valid RSS 1.0 document is also a valid RDF document (and not coincidentally a valid XML document). To a computer (for example, either a namespace-aware XML parser or an RDF tool), it contains the same kind of information as "simple" RSS expressed in a less ambiguous and more interoperable form.

Like RSS 0.9, the XML has an outer `<rdf:RDF>` element (which incidentally is no longer a requirement of RDF/XML). After the namespace declarations, there is a channel block, which first describes the channel feed itself and then lists the individual items found in the feed. The channel resource is identified with a URI, which makes the information portable. There's no doubt what the title, description and so on refer to. Title, link, description, and language are all defined in the core RSS 1.0 specification. XML namespaces (with the RDF interpretation) are employed to provide properties defined in the Dublin Core (`dc:date`) and Syndication (`sy:updatePeriod`, `sy:updateFrequency`) modules.

The channel has an `items` property, which has the `rdf:Seq` type. The RSS 1.0 specification describes this as sequence used to contain all the items and to denote item order for rendering and reconstruction. The items contained in the feed are then listed, each identified with a URI. So the channel block describes this feed, specifying which items it contains.

The items themselves are listed separately: each is identified by a URI, and the channel block has associated these resources with the channel, so there's no need for XML element nesting to group them together. Each item has its own set of properties, a title, and description as seen in the preceding RSS formats, along with a link which is defined as the item's URL. Usually, this will be the same as the URI given in the item's own `rdf:about` attribute. Again, terms from Dublin Core are used for the subject, creator (author), and date. This makes it much more suited for broad scale syndication as well, since Dublin Core has become adopted as the de facto standard for dealing with document-descriptive content.

Looking again from an RDF point of view, note that the object of the statements which list the `item` URIs become the subject of the statements that describe the items themselves. In most XML languages this kind of connection is made through element nesting, and it's clear that tree structures can be built up this way. However, the use of identifiers for the points of interest (the resource URIs) in RDF also makes it possible for any resource to be related to any other resource, allowing arbitrary node and arc graph structures. Loops and self-references can occur. This versatility is one of the important features of RDF, and is very similar to the arbitrary hyperlinking of the web. The downside is that there isn't any elegant way of representing graph structures in a tree-oriented syntax like XML, which is one big reason why RDF/XML syntax can be hard on the eye.

Reliable statistics on the deployment of the different formats on the web are hard to come by, but according to the Syndic8 service (`http://www.syndic8.com`), RSS 1.0 accounts for approximately half, and the other half is mostly shared between RSS 0.91 and RSS 2.0.

Userland and RSS 2.0

After a period of simmering unrest in the syndication world, and several 0.x releases in the Simple Syndication thread each making minor modifications, Userland released an RSS 2.0 specification. This followed the RSS 0.91 side of the fork, and the syntax is completely incompatible with RSS 1.0. Most of the changes from RSS 0.91 are relatively minor, although two are significant: the introduction of the `<guid>` element and (limited) namespace support. You can see in the following code example how similar the syntax appears to the earlier "simple" version. There are small differences that prevent true backward compatibility, but in practice this is unlikely to be a problem as a high degree of flexibility is needed for a tool to support *any* version of RSS!

The `<guid>` element is defined as being a (optional) globally unique identifier for each item. The specification doesn't prescribe what this should be, other than a string. In practice, people tend to use URIs, which are the global identifiers of the web. This also makes sense because if the `isPermalink` attribute has a value of `true`, then the `<guid>` will contain the URL of an archived (usually HTML) version of the item.

```
<rss version="2.0">
 <channel>
        <title>inessential.com</title>
        <link>http://inessential.com/</link>
        <description>Brent Simmons' weblog.</description>
        <language>en-us</language>
        <managingEditor>Brent Simmons (brent@ranchero.com)</managingEditor>
        <webMaster>Brent Simmons (brent@ranchero.com)</webMaster>
        <pubDate>Thu, 15 Apr 2004 19:56:13 GMT</pubDate>
        <lastBuildDate>Thu, 15 Apr 2004 19:56:13 GMT</lastBuildDate>
        <item>
               <title>Bowie</title>
               <link>http://inessential.com/?comments=1&amp;postid=2836</link>
               <description>Sheila and I saw David Bowie at the Key Arena last
               night. He was great, the band rocked&amp;mdash;and Sheila and I
               both have &amp;ldquo;All the Young Dudes&amp;rdquo; stuck in
               our head.&lt;br /&gt;&lt;br /&gt;</description>

        <guid isPermaLink="true">http://inessential.com/?comments=1&amp;
        postid=2836</guid>
               <pubDate>Thu, 15 Apr 2004 19:56:13 GMT</pubDate>
               </item>
        <item>
               <title>Socializing at WWDC</title>
               <link>http://inessential.com/?comments=1&amp;postid=2835</link>
               <description>Buzz Andersen proposes a &lt;a href=&quot;
               http://www.scifihifi.com/weblog/wwdc2004/Socializing-
               at-WWDC.html&quot;&gt;weblogger get-together at WWDC&lt;/a&gt;.
               Good thinking. Count me in.</description>
               <guid isPermaLink="true">http://inessential.com/?
               comments=1&amp;
               postid=2835</guid>
               <pubDate>Fri, 02 Apr 2004 00:53:57 GMT</pubDate>
               </item>
        </channel>
</rss>
```

XML namespace support in RSS 2.0 is limited in the sense that although material from other namespaces can be included within an RSS 2.0 feed, the format doesn't have a namespace of its own, which precludes use of RSS 2.0 elements in other XML languages.

The principle differences between the 1.0 and 2.0 versions ultimately come back to whether or not RDF is used as the foundation. In general, RSS 2.0 suffers from much the same problem that the various 0.9x standards did. Because the schema is essentially arbitrary and not formally documented, there is a great deal of ambiguity in this spec that makes it all too susceptible to being "extended" out of existence. That is to say, the moment that someone writes a "standard" extension to the set of tags, the two versions are no longer completely compatible.

It wasn't long after the RSS 2.0 specification was published that further unrest in the syndication world started to emerge. Despite the namespace support, it turned out not to be that straightforward to extend the base format, something developers were keen to do. The problem is that, unlike RSS 1.0, RSS 2.0 lacks a general framework (RDF) into which extensions can be placed. You can more or less add whatever you like to RSS 2.0, but you have to rely completely on tool developers to support those extensions. Any material added to RSS 1.0 has to be in the RDF/XML syntax, and as such, the material can be unambiguously interpreted as relationships between resources. More than likely it will still be necessary to get the support of tool developers to do useful things with the extensions, but there is at least a common semantic language that provides RDF tools with partial understanding of the data.

There followed other significant changes of a political nature with RSS 2.0. First, the RSS 2.0 specification was frozen and has in effect been declared the last in the line of Really Simple Syndication formats.

That was by no means the end of the story. One particular aspect of extensibility probably caused the greatest upheaval since RSS 2.0. The original syndication specifications were metadata-oriented and pointed to content elsewhere on the web. The `<description>` element was intended to describe that remote resource. However, with the growth in blogging and newsreader tools, a demand for *content* within feeds grew. RSS 1.0 responded with the addition of the Content module. In the RSS 2.0 thread the response manifested itself as a shift in the semantics of the `<description>` element. It no longer describes some other piece of content; it *contains* that content.

The demand for content in feeds highlighted a significant problem with the RSS 2.0 specification: it says that the `<description>` element may contain HTML, and that's all it says. There is no way for applications to distinguish HTML from plain text, so how do you tell what content is markup and what is just talking about markup? The spec was now frozen, so developers started to work around the problem using namespace-qualified extensions, such as `xhtml:body`, to insert well-defined markup. Soon after this there was controversy over the use of extensions with RSS 2.0, specifically the use of Dublin Core element to express information that could appear in core elements. Where previously there had been criticism of "simple" RSS from the RSS-DEV camp, dissent was now appearing amongst supporters of the "simple" standard. This led to another open community initiative being launched with the aim of fixing the problems of RSS 2.0 and hopefully unifying the syndication world, including the RSS 1.0 developers. Accepting the roadmap for RSS presented in the RSS 2.0 specification meant the name RSS couldn't be used, and after lengthy discussion the new project got a name: Atom.

The RSS 1.0 specification gained a lot of support in part because it was a grassroots community-built specification, whereas the 0.9x thread was seen as being comparatively proprietary thanks to Userland's ownership. In a bid for street legitimacy, the specification was placed in the Berkman Center for Internet & Society at Harvard Law School repository under the Creative Commons license, with the explicit caveat that the document is considered normative and *final*. The move to Berkman was welcomed though doubts have been expressed about the wisdom of freezing the specification at this point. On the political level this runs counter to the typical community development process, and so it's debatable as to whether this will enshrine RSS 2.0 as *the* syndication standard or simply lead to its demise. Whatever happens to RSS, the Atom project has gained enough momentum to produce two draft specifications.

Atom

It's not an exaggeration to say that the RSS space is rather a mess right now. Though the space is tending to converge on either RSS 1.0 or RSS 2.0, there are actually nine different RSS standards in current use. The highly fluid and decentralized nature of blog space itself contributes to uncertainty as well, but being optimistic, Atom does offer an opportunity for the two main syndication camps to unite.

Anyone can contribute to the Atom project, and hence the way the project is managed is unusual. There is a public mailing list, but much of the proposal/counter-proposal discussion takes place on a Wiki, a kind of website that anyone can edit. One of the first things to happen was the separation of the format specification from the protocol that specifies how the data should be moved around. As mentioned earlier, the primary protocol is that of the web, HTTP, with the payload being Atom format XML. In parallel with this direct approach there is also development of a SOAP-based protocol to enable greater interoperability with the web services world.

The format is structurally and conceptually very much like its RSS predecessors, and its practical design comes somewhere between the RSS 1.0 and 2.0 versions. Though the syntax isn't RDF/XML, full namespace support is included, and work is under way to provide a mapping to the RDF model. Most of the elements are direct descendants of those found in RSS, although considerable work has been done to give it robust support for inline content, using a new `<content>` element.

Atom format is currently only on version 0.3 and not really intended for public use in its present form. However even in this early version, support has been included in many of the leading blogging and syndication tool creators. Bear in mind that although radical changes aren't anticipated, the material presented in the following section may be very different than what makes it to the full release version 1.0.

The first thing you'll probably notice about the upcoming example is that Atom is rather verbose! It pretty well includes all the features that have ever been seen in feed formats, along with a few new ones. Most of the elements should be recognizable from the previous listings or are self-explanatory. The naming of parts differs from RSS, so an Atom `entry` corresponds to an RSS `item` and so on.

The first real enhancement is the `<id>` element, which roughly corresponds to the `<guid>` of RSS 2.0 and the `rdf:about` attribute found in RSS 1.0 to identify entities. Rather than leaving it to chance that this will be a unique string, the specification makes this a URI, which by definition will be unique. In effect, the identifiers (URIs) and locators (URLs) of entities within the format have been separated. This was a slightly controversial move, as many would argue that the two should be interchangeable. Time will tell whether this is a good idea or not. Where the `<id>` element identifies, the `<link>` element locates. This element is modeled on its namesake in HTML, to provide a link and information about related resources.

The `<info>` element is another innovation. The feed-level metadata elements, such as `title`, are intended to provide information about the feed, which will be passed to subsequent machine processing. The `<info>` element, on the other hand, is designed as a more immediate, human-readable description of the feed. It is possible in modern web browsers to associate XML data with stylesheets, so the idea is that when someone opens an Atom feed in a regular browser, they will see an informative message nicely formatted, rather than the mess of XML source that is usually presented to a browser in RSS.

The `content` element is designed to allow virtually anything that can be passed over XML. In this example the `type` attribute of this element is given the mime type of XHTML (`application/xhtml+xml`), so any tool reading the feed will know what it's looking at. Here's a piece of Atom format as generated by the (commercial) TypePad blogging system:

```
<feed version="0.3" xmlns="http://purl.org/atom/ns#"
xmlns:dc="http://purl.org/dc/elements/1.1/">
  <id>tag:typepad.com,2003:weblog-1105</id>
  <title>Finally Atom</title>
  <link rel="alternate" type="text/html" href="http:
  //danja.typepad.com/fecho/" />
  <link rel="service.post"
      type="application/x.atom+xml"
      href="http://www.typepad.com/t/atom/weblog/blog_id=1105"
      title="Finally Atom" />
  <modified>2004-04-15T08:35:05Z</modified>
  <tagline>following the development of the syndication framework
      formerly known as Pie, then Echo...</tagline>
  <generator url="http://www.typepad.com/" version="1.1.4">TypePad</generator>
  <info type="application/xhtml+xml">
      <div xmlns="http://www.w3.org/1999/xhtml">
        This is an Atom formatted XML site feed. It is intended to be viewed
        in a Newsreader or syndicated to another site. Please visit
        <a href="http://www.example.com/">example.com</a> for more info.
      </div>
  </info>
  <entry>
    <title>Survival guide to i18n</title>
    <id>tag:typepad.com,2003:post-1215348</id>
    <issued>2004-04-15T10:35:05+02:00</issued>
    <modified>2004-04-15T08:35:26Z</modified>
    <created>2004-04-15T08:35:05Z</created>
    <summary>Sam Ruby has published the second part of his practical
      Atom Guide, with a quick overview of Internationalization (i18n)
      issues : Survival guide to i18n...</summary>

    <author>
      <name>danja</name>
    </author>
    <content type="application/xhtml+xml"
      xml:lang="en-gb"
      xml:base="http://danja.typepad.com/fecho/">
        <div xmlns="http://www.w3.org/1999/xhtml">
        <p>Sam Ruby has published the second part of his practical
        <a href="http://intertwingly.net/stories/2004/04/08/atomguide.html">
        Atom Guide</a>, with a quick overview of Internationalization (i18n)
        issues :
        <a title="Survival guide to i18n"
          href="http://intertwingly.net/stories/2004/04/14/i18n.html">
        Survival guide to i18n</a></p></div>
```

```
</content>
  </entry>

  <entry>
    <title>An Atom-Powered Wiki |  2004-04-14 |  BitWorking</title>
    <link rel="alternate"
        type="text/html"
        href="http://danja.typepad.com/fecho/2004/04/an_atompowered_.html" />

    <link rel="service.edit"
        type="application/x.atom+xml"
        href="http://www.typepad.com/t/atom/weblog/blog_id=1105/entry_id
        =1215337" title="An Atom-Powered Wiki | 2004-04-14 | BitWorking" />
    <id>tag:typepad.com,2003:post-1215337</id>
    <issued>2004-04-15T10:30:07+02:00</issued>

    <modified>2004-04-15T08:30:22Z</modified>
    <created>2004-04-15T08:30:07Z</created>
    <summary>An article (with code) called An Atom-Powered Wiki from
        Joe Gregorio, at xml.com. (live demo - errm, just like a Wiki)...
    </summary>
    <author>
      <name>danja</name>
    </author>
    <dc:subject>Implementations</dc:subject>

    <content type="application/xhtml+xml"
      xml:lang="en-gb" xml:base="http://danja.typepad.com/fecho/">
        <div xmlns="http://www.w3.org/1999/xhtml"><p>An article (with code)
        called <a title="XML.com: An Atom-Powered Wiki"
        href="http://www.xml.com/lpt/a/2004/04/14/atomwiki.html">
        An Atom-Powered Wiki</a> from
        <a href="http://bitworking.org/news/An_Atom_Powered_Wiki">
        Joe Gregorio</a>, at xml.com.<br />
        (<a href="http://piki.bitworking.org/piki.cgi">live demo</a> -
        errm, just like a Wiki)<br />
        </p></div>
</content>

  </entry>
</feed>
```

Working with News Feeds

Over the course of the 20th century, newspapers evolved into news organizations with the advent of each new medium. Initially, most newspapers operated independently, and the coverage of anything beyond local information was usually handled by dedicated reporters in major cities. However, for most newspapers, such reporters were typically very costly to maintain. Consequently, these news organizations would pool their resources together to create syndicates, feeding certain articles (and columns) to the syndicates who would then license them out to other publishers. These news syndicates or services specialized in certain areas. Associated Press (AP) and United Press International (UPI) handled syndication within the United States, while Reuters evolved as a source for European news, especially financial news. Similarly, comic strips were usually handled by separate syndicates (such as King Features Syndicates).

In this sense these news services act as *aggregators*: they aggregate news from a wide variety of different sources into a stream of abstracts that are then passed to their subscribing news-media. Depending upon the service, the media outlet pays either a set fee for a block of stories (some of which may never get used) or they pay on a per-piece basis. Moreover, often only headlines and abstracts rather than the whole article are sent over the wire through the newsfeed; the media has to call the syndicate to actually get the article itself.

One way of thinking about these aggregations is that they bundle related content together, regardless of the initial source. For instance, a sports-dedicated aggregation feed may very well pull together all articles on baseball, football, and basketball, but the feed wouldn't include high finance articles unless they were sports-related. In essence, such a syndication service provides a perspective or viewpoint on the data made available—it creates an *editorial* judgment that all of the articles in the bundle will target a particular type of user.

This has made RSS news feeds ideal for creating highly targeted bundles of related content. For instance, it's possible for a website that promotes XML technology to generate an RSS feed about articles that deal with XML in some fashion. Some of these may be in-house articles, and some may be press releases, articles, or white papers from other locations on the web. By combining them, the website is able to act in the role of an aggregator.

Newsreaders

Aggregation isn't a phenomenon that just occurs with distributors of content; indeed, most newspapers tend to work with multiple distributors for various sections (financials, sports, comics, and columnists) and act as the aggregator to shape the news content for a specific region or audience. The web makes it possible to do the same thing with an audience of one—content that can be aggregated from a wide range of different sources and filtered into an e-newspaper that users can set up for themselves.

These "local" aggregators are usually known as *newsreaders*, applications that let you both add (and otherwise manage) RSS feeds into a general "newspaper" of articles. Such newsreaders typically pull from a wide number of XML feeds, letting you specify which feeds you wish to use and, in some cases, permitting you to add or remove feeds. Although there may be new newsreaders out by the time this book sees print, there are a number of RSS readers that have rapidly become the de facto leaders in this burgeoning realm.

Data Quality

Whenever we work with material on the web, there is an issue that should be borne in mind. Not all data purporting to be XML actually *is* XML. It's relatively common to find RSS feeds that are not well formed. One of the most common failings is that the characters in the XML document aren't from the declared encoding (UTF-8, ISO-8859-1, or something similar). Another likely corruption is that characters within the textual content of the feed are incorrectly escaped. A stray < instead of a `<` is plenty to trip up a standard XML processor. Unfortunately, many of the popular blogging tools make it extremely easy to produce an ill-formed feed, a factor not really taken into account by the "simple" philosophy of syndication.

There was considerable discussion by the Atom developers on this issue, and responses ranged from the creation of an "ultra-liberal" parser that does its best to read *anything*, to the suggestion that aggregation tools simply reject ill-formed feeds to discourage their production. The approach that found most support was (as you might expect) a compromise—the parser should attempt to display the data as intended, but notify the end-user that the feed contained errors and encourage him or her to notify the feed producer. In addition, a proposal for an entirely optional HTTP-based error notification system looks likely to appear in the Atom API.

A Simple Aggregator

The application described here is a simple newsreader, which will aggregate news items from several channels. It will be provided with a list of feed addresses in a text file, and when run, the newsreader will present the most recent five items from all those feeds. To keep things simple the reader only has a command-line user interface and won't remember what it has read from the feeds previously.

Modeling Feeds

The programmer has many options for dealing with XML data, and the choice of approach will often depend on the complexity of the data structures. In many circumstances the data can be read directly into a DOM model and processed from there. However, there is a complication with syndicated material—the source data can be in one of three completely different syntaxes: RSS 1.0, RSS 2.0 and its predecessors and Atom. As the application will only be a simple newsreader, the sophistication offered by the RDF model behind RSS 1.0 isn't needed, but there is a simple model implicit in news feeds: a feed comprises a number of items, and each of those items has a set of properties. So at the heart of the aggregator presented here is an object-oriented version of that model. A feed will be represented by a `Feed` object, and items will be represented by `Item` objects. Each `Item` object will have member variables to represent the various properties of that item. To keep things simple the code here only uses three properties of each item in the feeds: the title, date, and content. The item itself and these three properties can each be mapped to an XML element in each of the three main syntaxes, as shown in the following table.

Model	RSS 1.0	RSS x.x	Atom
Item	`rss:item`	`item`	`atom:entry`
Title	`dc:title`	`title`	`atom:title`
Date	`dc:date`	`pubDate`	`atom:issued`
Content	`dc:description,` `content:encoded`	`description,` `xhtml:body`	`atom:content`

Here the namespaces of the elements are identified by their usual prefixes as follows (note that the "simple" RSS dialects don't have a namespace):

- ❑ `rss` is RSS 1.0 (`http://purl.org/rss/1.0/`)
- ❑ `dc` is Dublin Core (`http://purl.org/dc/elements/1.1/`)

- `xhtml` is XHTML (`http://www.w3.org/1999/xhtml`)
- `content` is the content module for RSS 1.0 (`http://purl.org/rss/1.0/modules/content/`)
- `atom` is, you guessed it, Atom (`http://purl.org/atom/ns#`)

Note that the namespaces are only strings used for identification; there's no guarantee of finding anything useful at `http://purl.org/rss/1.0/` and so on if you use it as an address in a web browser (in practice, you'll usually find the spec or a RDF Schema, but this varies).

The correspondence between the different syntaxes is only approximate. Each version has its own definitions, and although they don't coincide exactly, they are close enough in practice to be used in a basic newsreader.

Syntax Isn't Model

Though there's a reasonable alignment between the elements of different kinds listed in the preceding table, this doesn't hold for the overall structure of the different syndication syntaxes. In particular, both plain XML RSS and Atom use element nesting to associate the items with the feed. If you look back to the sample of RSS 1.0, it's clear that something different is going on. RSS 1.0 uses the interpretation of RDF in XML to say that the `channel` resource has a property called `items` which points to a `Seq` (sequence) of `item` instances. The `item` instances in the `Seq` are identified with URIs, as are the individual `item` entries themselves, which enables an RDF processor to tell that the same resources are being referred to. In short, the structural interpretation is completely different.

All of this sounds very complicated, but it is still essentially the same subject-predicate-object triple structure discussed earlier, with the object of one triple (channel-items-Seq) appearing as the subject in others (Seq-li-resource).

There are actually two pieces of information implicit in the XML structure of simple RSS that are made explicit in RSS 1.0. In addition to the association between the feed and its component items, there is also the order of the items. The use of a `Seq` in RSS 1.0 and the document order of the XML elements in Atom and the RSS x.x dialects provide an ordering, though there hasn't been any common agreement on what this ordering signifies.

To keep the code simple in the aggregator presented here, two assumptions have been made about the material being represented in the various syntaxes as follows:

- Firstly, the items in the file obtained from a particular location are all part of the same conceptual feed. This may seem obvious; in fact, it has to be the case in plain XML RSS as there can only be one root `<rss>` element, but there is potential in RDF/XML (on which RSS 1.0 is based) for representing practically anything in an individual file. In practice though, it's a relatively safe assumption.
- The second assumption is that in a news-reading application, the end-user won't be interested in the arbitrary order of the items in the feed (element or `Seq` order) but the dates on which the items were published.

The first assumption means there is no need to check where in the document structure individual items appear, and the second means there is no need to interpret the `Seq` or remember the element order. There is little or no cost to these assumptions in practice, yet it enables considerable code simplification.

All that is needed is to recognize when an element corresponding to an item (`rss:item`, `item`, or `atom:entry`) occurs within a feed and to start recording its properties. In all the syntaxes the main properties are provided in child elements of the item element, so only a very simple structure has to be managed.

So what you have here are different syntaxes, but a part of the structure is common to all three despite differences in element naming. An object model can be constructed from a simple one-to-one mapping from each set of elements. On encountering a particular element in the XML, a corresponding action needs to be carried out on the objects. There is an XML programming tool that is ideally suited to this kind of situation: SAX.

SAX2 the Rescue!

As you saw in Chapter 12, SAX works by responding to method calls generated when various different entities with the XML document are encountered. The entities of interest for this simple application are the following:

- The elements correspond to items.
- The elements correspond to the properties of the items and the values of those properties.

Three SAX methods can provide all the relevant information: `startElement`, `characters`, and `endElement`. The first of these will signal which element has been encountered, providing its name and namespace (if it has one). It's easy enough to tell if that element corresponds to an item. From the previous table, we know its name will either be `item` or `entry`. Similarly, each of the three kinds of properties elements can be identified. The data sent to characters is the text content of the elements, which will be the values of the properties. A call to the `endElement` method will signal that the element's closing tag has been encountered, so the program can deal with whatever's been encountered inside it.

Again using the previous table, we can derive the following simple rules that determine the nature of the elements encountered:

- `rss:item` | `item` | `atom:entry` = item
- `dc:title` | `title` | `atom:title` = title
- `dc:date` | `pubDate` | `atom:issued` = date
- `dc:description` | `content:encoded` | `description` | `xhtml:body` | `atom:content` = content

If `startElement` has been called, any subsequent calls matching the last three elements will pass on the values of that particular property of that element, until the `endElement` method is called. There may be calls to the property elements outside of an item block, and we can reasonably assume that those properties apply to the feed as a whole. This makes it straightforward to extract the title of the feed.

You may notice that the element names are pretty well separated between each meaning—there is little likelihood of the title data being purposefully published in an element called `<date>`, for example. This makes the coding of these rules somewhat easier, though, in general, it is good practice to make it possible to get at the namespace of elements to avoid naming clashes.

Program Flow

When the main application is run, the list of feeds is picked up from the text file. Each of the addresses in turn will be passed to an XML parser. The aggregator then needs to read the data found on the web at that address. In more sophisticated aggregators, you will find a considerable amount of code devoted to the reading of data over HTTP in a way that both respects the feed publisher and makes the system as efficient as possible, but the parsers in PyXML are capable of reading data directly from a web address. So to keep things simple, that's what's shown in Figure 13-1.

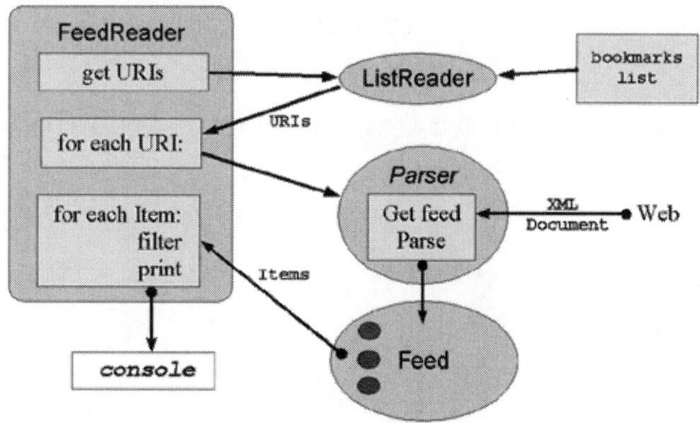

Figure 13-1

Implementation

The aggregator is written in Python, a language that has reasonably sophisticated XML support (PyXML), and everything we'll need to run it is available for free download from `http://www.python.org`. If you're not familiar with Python, don't worry—it's a very simple language, and the code is self-explanatory to a great extent. All you really need to know is that it uses indentation to separate functional blocks rather than braces {}. Oh yes, and the # character means the rest of the line is a comment.

Note that it would be very straightforward to port the code given here to any other languages with good XML support, such as Java or C#.

The code is contained in the following four files:

- `feed_reader.py` controls the operation.
- `feed.py` models the feed and items.
- `feed_handler.py` constructs objects from the content of the feed.
- `list_reader.py` reads a list of feed addresses.

Address List Reader: ListReader

We will also need the addresses of the feeds we'd like to aggregate. At its simplest this can be a text file containing the URIs, like the following:

```
http://danja.typepad.com/fecho/atom.xml
http://www.ftrain.com/xml/feed/rss.rdf
http://www.intertwingly.net/blog/index.rss2
```

An aggregator should be able to deal with all the major formats. Here we have a selection: the first feed is in Atom format, the second is RSS 2.0, and the third RSS 1.0. A text list is the simplest format the URIs can be supplied in. For convenience, a little string manipulation makes it possible to use Internet Explorer or Netscape/Mozilla bookmarks file to supply the list of URIs. The addresses of the syndication feeds should be added to a regular bookmark folder in the browser. With IE it's possible to export a single bookmark folder to use as the URI list, but with Netscape/Mozilla all the bookmarks are exported in one go. The following code is set up to read the links only in the first folder in such a bookmarks file.

The `list_reader.py` source file contains a single class, `ListReader`, with a single method, `get_uris` as follows:

```
import re

class ListReader:
    """ Reads URIs from file """

    def get_uris(self, filename):
        """ Returns a list of the URIs contained in the named file """
        file = open(filename, 'r')
        text = file.read()
        file.close()

        # get the first block of a Netscape file
        text = text.split('</DL>')[0]

        # get the uris
        pattern = 'http://\S*\w'
        return re.findall(pattern,text)
```

Try It Out — Reading a List of URIs

The purpose of this exercise is really just to check that our Python installation is working correctly. If you're not familiar with Python, then this also demonstrates how useful command-line interaction with the interpreter can be. Before we start we'll need to download and install Python (it's available from `http://python.org`).

> *Python comes in a complete package as a free download, available for most platforms—as its enthusiasts say, batteries are included. Installation is very straightforward; there's an MS Windows installer. In the standard package you get the Python interpreter, which may be run interactively or from a command line or even a web server. There's also a basic Integrated Development Environment tool called IDLE and plenty of documentation.*

Once Python is installed, you can try out the following:

1. Open a text editor and type in the previous listing and save it as `list_reader.py`.

2. Open a new text editor window and type in the following three URIs:

```
http://danja.typepad.com/fecho/atom.xml
http://www.ftrain.com/xml/feed/rss.rdf
http://www.intertwingly.net/blog/index.rss2
```

3. Save this as `feeds.txt` in the same folder as `list_reader.py`.
4. Open a common prompt and **cd** to the folder containing these files.
5. Type in the command **python** and press Enter. You should see something like this:

```
D:\rss-samples\test>python
Python 2.3.3 (#51, Dec 18 2003, 20:22:39) [MSC v.1200 32 bit (Intel)] on win32
Type "help", "copyright", "credits" or "license" for more information.
>>
```

You are now in the Python interpreter.

6. Type in the following lines and press Enter after each line (the interpreter will display the >>> prompt):

```
>>> from list_reader import ListReader
>>> reader = ListReader()
>>> print reader.get_uris("feeds.txt")
```

After the last line, the interpreter should respond with the following:

```
['http://danja.typepad.com/fecho/atom.xml', 'http://www.ftrain
.com/xml/feed/rss.rdf', 'http://www.intertwingly.net/blog/index.rss2']
>>>
```

How It Works

The first line you gave the interpreter was this:

```
from list_reader import ListReader
```

This makes the class `ListReader` in the package `list_reader` available to the interpreter (the package is contained in the file `list_reader.py`). The next line was:

```
reader = ListReader()
```

This creates a new instance of the `ListReader` class and assigns it to the variable reader. The next line you asked to be interpreted was:

```
print reader.get_uris("feeds.txt")
```

This calls the `get_uris` method of the reader object, passing it a string, which corresponds to the filename of interest. The `print` method was used to display the object (on the command line) returned by the `get_uris` method. The object returned was displayed as this:

```
['http://danja.typepad.com/fecho/atom.xml','http://www.ftrain.com/xml/feed/rss.
rdf', 'http://www.intertwingly.net/blog/index.rss2']
```

This is the syntax for a standard Python list, here containing three items, which are the three URIs extracted from `feeds.txt`.

Now for an explanation of how `list_reader.py` worked internally, here's the source again:

```
import re

class ListReader:
    """ Reads URIs from file """

    def get_uris(self, filename):
        """ Returns a list of the URIs contained in the named file """
        file = open(filename, 'r')
        text = file.read()
        file.close()

        # get the first block of a Netscape file
        text = text.split('</DL>')[0]

        # get the uris
        pattern = 'http://\S*\w'
        return re.findall(pattern,text)
```

The `get_uris` method is called with a single parameter. This will be the name of the file that contains the list of URIs (the `self` parameter is an artifact of Python's approach to methods and functions, and refers to the `method` object). The file opens as read-only (`r`), and its contents are read into a string called `text` and then closed. To trim down a Netscape bookmarks file, the built-in `split` string method divides the string up into a list, with everything before the first occurrence of the `</DL>` tag going into the first part of the list, which is accessed with the index `[0]`. The `text` variable will then contain this trimmed block or the whole of the text if there aren't any `</DL>` tags in the file. A regular expression is then used to find all the occurrences within the string of the characters `http://` followed by any number of nonwhitespace characters (signified by `\S*`) and terminated by an alphanumeric character. It's crude, but it works well enough for text and bookmark files. The URIs are returned from this method as another list.

Application Controller: FeedReader

The list of URIs is the starting point for the main control block of the program, which is the `FeedReader` class contained in `feed_reader.py`. If you refer back to Figure 13-1, you should be able to see how the functional parts of the application are tied together. Here are the first few lines of `feed_reader.py`, which acts as the overall controller of the application:

```
import urllib2
import xml.sax
import list_reader
import feed_handler
import feed

feedlist_filename = 'list-bookmarks.txt'
```

```
def main():
    """ Runs the application """
    FeedReader().read(feedlist_filename)
```

The code starts with the library imports. `urllib2` and `xml.sax` are only used here to provide error messages if something goes wrong with HTTP reading or parsing. `list_reader` is the previous URI list reader code (in `list_reader.py`), `feed_handler` contains the custom SAX handler (which you'll see shortly), and `feed` contains the class which models the feeds.

The name of the file containing the URI list is given as a constant. You can either save your list with this filename or change it here. Because Python is an interpreted language, any change will take effect next time you run the program. The `main()` function runs the application by creating a new instance of the `FeedReader` class and telling it to read the named file. When the new instance of `FeedReader` is created the `init` method is automatically called, which is used here to initialize a list, which will contain all the items obtained from the feeds:

```
class FeedReader:
    """ Controls the reading of feeds """
    def __init__(self):
        """ Initializes the list of items """
        self.all_items = []
```

The `read` method looks after the primary operations of the aggregator and begins by obtaining a parser from a local helper method `create_parser`, then getting the list of URIs contained in the supplied file as shown in the following:

```
    def read(self, feedlist_filename):
        """ Reads each of the feeds listed in the file """
        parser = self.create_parser()

        feed_uris = self.get_feed_uris(feedlist_filename)
```

The next block of code selects each URI in turn and does what is necessary to get the items out of that feed, which is to create a SAX handler and attach it to the parser to be called as the parser reads through the feed's XML. The magic of the SAX handler code will appear shortly, but it's a risky business reading data from the web and parsing it, so the single command that initiates these actions, `parser .parse(uri)`, is wrapped in a `try...except` block to catch any errors. Once the reading and parsing has happened, the `feed_handler` instance will contain a `feed` object, which in turn will contain the items found in the feed (you will see the source to these classes in a moment). To give some indication of the success of the reading/parsing, the number of items contained in the feed is then printed. The items are available as a list of `handler.feed.items`, the length of this list (`len`) will be the number of items, and the standard `str` function is used to convert this number to a string for printing to the console.

```
        for uri in feed_uris:
            print 'Reading '+uri,
            handler = feed_handler.FeedHandler()
            parser.setContentHandler(handler)
            try:
                parser.parse(uri)
```

```
                print ' : ' + str(len(handler.feed.items)) + ' items'
                self.all_items.extend(handler.feed.items)

            except xml.sax.SAXParseException:
                print '\n XML error reading feed : '+uri
                parser = self.create_parser()
            except urllib2.HTTPError:
                print '\n HTTP error reading feed : '+uri
                parser = self.create_parser()
        self.print_items()
```

If an error occurs while either reading from the web or parsing, a corresponding exception will be raised, and a simple error message will then be printed to the console. The parser is likely to have been trashed by the error, so a new instance is created. Whether or not the reading/parsing was successful, the program will now loop back and start work on the next URI on the list. Once all the URIs have been read, a helper method (shown in an upcoming code example) `print_items` will be called to show the required items on the console. The following methods in `FeedReader` are all helpers that are used by the `read` method in the previous listing.

The `get_feed_uris` method creates an instance of the `ListReader` class we saw earlier, and its `get_uris` method returns a list of the URIs found in the file as shown in the following:

```
    def get_feed_uris(self, filename):
        """ Use the list reader to obtain feed addresses """
        lr = list_reader.ListReader()
        return lr.get_uris(filename)
```

The `create_parser` method makes standard calls to Python's SAX library to create a fully namespace-aware parser as follows:

```
    def create_parser(self):
        """ Creates a namespace-aware SAX parser """
        parser = xml.sax.make_parser()
        parser.setFeature(xml.sax.handler.feature_namespaces, 1)
        parser.setFeature(xml.sax.handler.feature_namespace_prefixes, 1)
        return parser
```

The next method is used in the item sorting process and uses the built-in `cmp` function to compare two values, in this case the `date` properties of two items. Given the two values x and y, the return value is a number less than zero if $x < y$, zero if $x = y$, and greater than zero if $x > y$. The `date` properties are represented as the number of seconds since a preset date (usually the 1st of January, 1970), so a newer item here will actually have a larger numeric date value. Here is the code that does the comparison:

```
    def newer_than(self, itemA, itemB):
        """ Compares the two items """
        return cmp(itemB.date, itemA.date)
```

The `get_newest_items` method uses the `sort` method built into Python lists to reorganize the contents of the `all_items` list. The comparison used in the sort is the `newer_than` method from earlier, and a Python "slice" (`[:5]`) is used to obtain the last five items in the list. When we put this together, we have the following:

```
    def get_newest_items(self):
        """ Sorts items using the newer_than comparison """
        self.all_items.sort(self.newer_than)
        return self.all_items[:5]
```

Note that the slice is a very convenient piece of Python syntax and selects a range of items in a sequence object. For example, `z = my_list[x:y]` *would copy the contents of* `my_list` *from index* `x` *to index* `y` *into list* `z`*.*

The `print_items` method applies the sorting and slicing previously mentioned and then prints the resultant five items to the console, as illustrated in the following code:

```
    def print_items(self):
        """ Prints the filtered items to console """
        print '\n*** Newest 5 Items ***\n'
        for item in self.get_newest_items():
            print item
```

The final part of `feed_reader.py` is a Python idiom used to call the initial `main()` function when this file is executed as shown in the following:

```
if __name__ == '__main__':
    """ Program entry point """
    main()
```

Model: Feed and Item

The preceding `FeedReader` class uses a SAX handler to create representations of feeds and their items. Before looking at the handler code, here is the `feed.py` file, which contains the code that defines those representations. It contains two classes, `Feed` and `Item`. The plain XML RSS dialects generally use the older RFC 2822 date format used in e-mails, whereas RSS 1.0 and Atom use a specific version of the ISO 8601 format used in many XML systems known as W3CDTF. As mentioned earlier, the dates will be represented within the application as the number of seconds since a specific date, so libraries which include methods for conversion of the e-mail and ISO 8601 formats to this number are included in the imports. The significance of `BAD_TIME_HANDICAP` will be explained in a moment, but first, let's take a look at the `feed.py` file:

```
import email.Utils
import xml.utils.iso8601
import time

BAD_TIME_HANDICAP = 43200
```

The `Feed` class in the following listing is initialized with a list called `items` to hold individual items found in a feed and a string called `title` to hold the title of the feed (with the title being initialized to an empty string):

```
class Feed:
    """ Simple model of a syndication feed data file """
    def __init__(self):
```

```
        """ Initialize storage """
        self.items = []
        self.title = ''
```

Although items are free-standing entities in a sense, they are initially derived from a specific feed, and this is reflected in the code by having the `Item` instances created by the `Feed` class. The `create_item` method creates an `Item` object and then passes the title of the feed to the `Item` object's source property. Once initialized in this way, the `Item` is added to the list of items maintained by the `Feed` object as shown in the following:

```
    def create_item(self):
        """ Returns a new Item object """
        item = Item()
        item.source = self.title
        self.items.append(item)
        return item
```

To make testing easier, the `Feed` object overrides the standard Python `__str__` method to provide a useful string representation of itself. All the method here does is run through each of the items in its list and adds the string representation of them to a combined string as follows:

```
    def __str__(self):
        """ Custom 'toString()' method to pretty-print """
        string =''
        for item in self.items:
            string.append(item.__str__())
        return string
```

The `item` class essentially wraps up four properties that will be extracted from the XML: `title`, `content`, `source` (the title of the feed it came from), and `date`. Each of these is maintained as an instance variable, the values of the first three being initialized to an empty string. It's not uncommon to encounter `date` values in feeds that aren't well formatted, so it's possible to initialize the `date` value to the current time (given by `time.time()`). The only problem with this approach is that any items with bad `date` values will appear newer than all the others. So as a little hack to prevent this without excluding the items altogether, a `handicap` value is subtracted from the current time. The constant `BAD_TIME_HANDICAP` was set to 43,200 at the start, which as the time is represented here in seconds corresponds to 12 hours. So any item with a bad date will be considered 12 hours old as shown in the following:

```
class Item:
    """ Simple model of a single item within a syndication feed """
    def __init__(self):
        """ Initialize properties to defaults """
        self.title = ''
        self.content = ''
        self.source = ''
        self.date = time.time() - BAD_TIME_HANDICAP # seconds from the Epoch
```

The next two methods make up the setter for the value of the date. The first, `set_rfc2822_time`, uses methods from the e-mail utility library to convert a string (like `Sat, 10 Apr 2004 21:13:28 PDT`) to the number of seconds since 01/01/1970 (`1081656808`). Similarly, the `set_w3cdtf_time` method converts an ISO 8601-compliant string (for example, `2004-04-10T21:13:28-00:00`) into seconds. If either conversion fails, then an error message is printed, and the value of `date` will stay at its initial (handicapped) value as illustrated in the following:

```
    def set_rfc2822_time(self, old_date):
        """ Set email-format time """
        try:
            temp = email.Utils.parsedate_tz(old_date)
            self.date = email.Utils.mktime_tz(temp)
        except ValueError:
            print "Bad date : %s" % (old_date)

    def set_w3cdtf_time(self, new_date):
        """ Set web-format time """
        try:
            self.date = xml.utils.iso8601.parse(new_date)
        except ValueError:
            print "Bad date : %s" % (new_date)
```

The `get_formatted_date` method uses the e-mail library again to convert the number of seconds into a human-friendly form, for example, `Sat, 10 Apr 2004 23:13:28 +0200`), as follows:

```
    def get_formatted_date(self):
        """ Returns human-readable date string """
        return email.Utils.formatdate(self.date, True)
    # RFC 822 date, adjusted to local time
```

Like the `Feed` class, `Item` also has a custom `__str__` method to give a nice representation of the object. This is simply the title of the feed it came from and the title of the item itself, followed by the content of the item and finally the date as shown in the following:

```
    def __str__(self):
        """ Custom 'toString()' method to pretty-print """
        return (self.source + ' : '
            + self.title +'\n'
            + self.content + '\n'
            + self.get_formatted_date() + '\n')
```

So that's how feeds and items are represented, and you will soon see the tastiest part of the code, the SAX handler that will build `Feed` and `Item` objects based on what appears in the feed XML document. This file (`feed_handler.py`) contains a single class `FeedHandler`, which is a subclass of `xlm.sax.ContentHandler`. An instance of this class is passed to the parser every time a feed document is to be read, and as the parser encounters appropriate entities in the feed three specific methods will automatically be called: `startElementNS`, `characters`, and `endElementNS`. The namespace-enhanced versions of these methods are used because the elements in feeds can come from different namespaces.

XML Markup Handler: FeedHandler

As discussed earlier, there isn't much structure to deal with—just the feed and contained items, but there is a complication not mentioned earlier. The title and content elements of items may contain markup. This shouldn't happen with RSS 1.0; the value of `content:encoded` is enclosed in a CDATA section or the individual characters escaped as needed. However, the parent RDF/XML specification does describe XML Literals, and the material found in the wild often veers wildly from the spec. In any case, the rich content model of Atom is designed to allow XML, and the RSS 2.0 specification is unclear on the issue. So markup should be expected. If the markup is, for example, HTML 3.2 and isn't escaped, then the whole document won't be well formed and by definition won't be XML—a different kettle of fish. However, if the markup is a well-formed XML (for example, XHTML), then there will be a call to the SAX start and end element methods for each element within the content.

So the code has an instance variable `state` to keep track of where the parser is within an XML document's structure. This variable can take the value of one of the three constants. If its value is `IN_ITEM`, then the parser is reading somewhere inside an element that corresponds to an item. If its value is `IN_CONTENT`, then the parser is somewhere inside an element that contains the body content of the item. If neither of these is the case, then the variable will have the value `IN_NONE`.

The code itself begins with imports from several libraries, including the SAX material you might have expected as well as the regular expression library `re` and `codecs`, which contain tools that will be used for cleaning up the content data. There is then a constant `TRIM_LENGTH`, which will determine the maximum amount of content text to include for each item. For the purposes of demonstration and to save paper, this is set to a very low 100 characters. This constant is followed by the three alternate state constants as shown in the following:

```
import xml.sax
import xml.sax.saxutils
import feed
import re
import codecs

# Maximum length of item content
TRIM_LENGTH = 100

# Parser state
IN_NONE = 0
IN_ITEM = 1
IN_CONTENT = 2
```

The content will be stripped of markup, and a regular expression is provided to match any XML-like tag (for example, `<this>`). However, if the content is HTML, then it's desirable to retain a little of the original formatting, so another regular expression is used to recognize `<br>` and `<p>` tags, which will be replaced with `newline` characters as shown in the following:

```
# Regular expressions for cleaning data
TAG_PATTERN = re.compile("<(.|\n)+?>")
NEWLINE_PATTERN = re.compile("(<br.*>)|(<p.*>)")
```

The `FeedHandler` class itself begins by creating a new instance of the `Feed` class to hold whatever data is extracted from the feed being parsed. The `state` variable begins with a value of `IN_NONE` and an instance variable `text` is initialized to the empty string. The `text` variable will be used to accumulate text encountered between the element tags as shown in the following:

```
# Subclass from ContentHandler in order to gain default behaviors
class FeedHandler(xml.sax.ContentHandler):
    """ Extracts data from feeds, in response to SAX events """
```

```
    def __init__(self):
        "Initialize feed object, interpreter state and content"
        self.feed = feed.Feed()
        self.state = IN_NONE
        self.text = ''
        return
```

The next method, `startElementNS`, is called by the parser whenever an opening element tag is encountered and receives values for the element name—the prefix-qualified name of the element along with an object containing the element's attributes. The name variable actually contains two values (it's a Python tuple), which are the namespace of the element and its local name. These values are extracted into the separate `namespace`, `localname` strings. If the feed being read was RSS 1.0, then a `<title>` element would cause the method to be called with the values `name = ('http://purl.org/rss/1.0/', 'title'), qname = 'title'`. (If the element uses a namespace prefix, like `<dc:title>`, then the `qname` string would include that prefix, such as `dc:title` in this case.) In this simple application the attributes aren't used, but SAX makes them available as an `NSAttributes` object.

> **A tuple is an ordered set of values. A pair of geographic coordinates is one example, an RDF triple another. In Python, a tuple can be expressed as a comma-separated list of values, usually surrounded in parentheses, for example, (1, 2, 3, "go"). In general, the values within tuples don't have to be of the same type. It's common to talk of n-tuples, where n is the number of values—the example here is a 4-tuple.**

The `startElementNS` method checks to see whether the parser is inside content, by determining whether the state is `IN_CONTENT`. If this isn't the case, then the content accumulator `text` is emptied by setting it to an empty string. If the name of the element is one of those that corresponds to an item in the simple model (`item` or `entry`), then a new item is created, and the state changes to reflect the parser's position within an item block. The last check here tests whether the parser is already inside an item block, and if it is then whether the element is one that corresponds to the content. The actual string comparison is done by a separate method to keep the code tidy as there are quite a few alternatives. If the element name matches, then the state is switched into `IN_CONTENT` as shown in the following:

```
    def startElementNS(self, name, qname, attributes):
        "Identifies nature of element in feed (called by SAX parser)"
        (namespace, localname) = name

        if self.state != IN_CONTENT:
            self.text = '' # new element, not in content

        if localname == 'item' or localname == "entry": # RSS or Atom
            self.current_item = self.feed.create_item()
            self.state = IN_ITEM
            return

        if self.state == IN_ITEM:
            if self.is_content_element(localname):
            self.state = IN_CONTENT
        return
```

The characters method merely adds any text encountered within the elements to the text accumulator as illustrated in the following:

```
    def characters(self, text):
        "Accumulates text (called by SAX parser)"
        self.text = self.text + text
```

The endElementNS method is called when the parser encounters a closing tag, like </this>. It receives the values of the element name and qname, and once again the name tuple is split into its component namespace, localname parts. What follows are a lot of statements, which are conditional on the name of the element and/or the current state (which corresponds to the parser's position in the XML). This essentially carries out the matching rules between the different kinds of elements that may be encountered in RSS 1.0, 2.0, or Atom, and the Item properties in the application's representation. You may want to refer back to the table of near equivalents and the examples of feed data to get an idea of why the choices are made where they are. Here is the endElementNS method:

```
    def endElementNS(self, name, qname):
        "Collects element content, switches state as appropriate
        (called by SAX parser)"
        (namespace, localname) = name
```

Ok, first choice—has the parser come to the end of an item? If so, revert to the IN_NONE state as shown in the following:

```
        if localname == 'item' or localname == 'entry': # end of item
            self.state = IN_NONE
            return
```

Next up, are we in content? If so, is the tag the parser just encountered one of those classed as the end of content? If both of the answers are yes, then the content accumulated from characters in text is cleaned up and passed to the current item object. As it's the end of content, the state also needs shifting back down to IN_ITEM. Whatever the answer to the second question, if the first answer was yes, then we're done here as shown in the following:

```
        if self.state == IN_CONTENT:
            if self.is_content_element(localname): # end of content
                self.current_item.content = self.cleanup_text(self.text)
                self.state = IN_ITEM
            return
```

Now that the content is out of the way with its possible nested elements, the rest of the text that makes it this far will be the simple content of an element. We clean it up as outlined in the following:

```
        # cleanup text - we probably want it
        text = self.cleanup_text(self.text)
```

At this point, if the parser isn't within an item block and the element name is title, then what we have here is the title of the feed. We pass it on as follows:

```
        if self.state != IN_ITEM: # feed title
            if localname == "title":
                self.feed.title = self.text
            return
```

The parser must now be within an item block thanks to the last choice. So if there's a title element here, it must refer to the item. We pass that on too as follows:

```
        if localname == "title":
            self.current_item.title = text
            return
```

Now we get on to the tricky issue of dates. If the parser has found an RSS 1.0 date (dc:date) or an Atom date (atom:issued), then it will be in ISO 8601 format, so we need to pass it to the item through the appropriate converter as shown in the following:

```
        if localname == "date" or localname == "issued":
            self.current_item.set_w3cdtf_time(text)
            return
```

RSS 2.0 and most of its relatives use a pubDate element in RFC 2822 e-mail format, so pass *that* through the appropriate converter as shown in the following:

```
        if localname == "pubDate":
            self.current_item.set_rfc2822_time(text)
            return
```

Handler Helpers

Ok, that's the rules logic dealt with, and the rest of feed_handler.py is devoted to helper methods. The first, is_content_element, checks the alternatives to see if the local name of the element corresponds to that of an item:

```
    def is_content_element(self, localname):
        "Checks if element may contain item/entry content"
        return (localname == "description" or # most RSS x.x
            localname == "encoded" or # RSS 1.0 content:encoded
            localname == "body" or # RSS 2.0 xhtml:body
            localname == "content") # Atom
```

The next three methods are all about tidying up text nodes (which may include escaped markup) found within the content. Cleaning up the text begins by stripping whitespace from each end. This is more important than it might seem, because depending on the layout of the feed data there may be a host of newlines and tabs to make the feed look nice but which only get in the way of the content. These unnecessary newlines should be replaced by a single space.

Next, a utility method unescape in the SAX library is used to unescape characters like <this> to <this>. This is followed by a class to another helper method process_tags to do a little more stripping. If this application used a browser to view the content, then this step wouldn't be needed (or even desirable), but markup displayed to console just looks bad, and `<a href="...">`*hyperlinks* `</a>` won't work.

The next piece of cleaning is a little controversial. The content delivered in feed can be Unicode, with characters from any international character set, but most consoles are ill-prepared to display such material. The standard string encode method is used to flatten everything down to plain old ASCII. This is rather drastic, and there may well be characters that don't fit in this small character set. The second value determines what should happen in this case—possible values are `strict` (default) `ignore`, or `replace`. The `replace` alternative swaps the character for a question mark, hardly improving legibility. The `strict` option throws an error whenever a character won't fit, and it's not really appropriate here either. The third option, `ignore`, simply leaves out any characters that can't be correctly represented in the chosen ASCII encoding. This isn't a great move for internationalization, as any language that uses a lot of non-ASCII characters will be decimated, but as an anglo-centric hack, it does mean that most of the time something meaningful will be presented at the console. The following code shows the sequence of method calls used to make the text more presentable:

```
    def cleanup_text(self, text):
        "Strips material that won't look good in plain text"
        text = text.strip()
        text = text.replace('\n', ' ')
        text = xml.sax.saxutils.unescape(text)
        text = self.process_tags(text)
        text = text.encode('ascii','ignore')
        text = self.trim(text)
        return text
```

The `process_tags` method (called from `cleanup_text`) uses regular expressions to first replace any `<br>` or `<p>` tags in the content with `newline` characters, then replace any remaining tags with a single space character as shown in the following:

```
    def process_tags(self, string):
        """ Turns <br/> into \n then removes all <tags> """
        re.sub(NEWLINE_PATTERN, '\n', string)
        return re.sub(TAG_PATTERN, ' ', string)
```

The cleaning done by the last method in the `FeedHandler` class is really a matter of taste. The amount of text found in each post varies greatly between different sources. You may not want to read whole essays through your newsreader. So the `trim` method cuts the string length down to a preset size determined by the `TRIM_LENGTH` constant. However, just counting characters and chopping will result in some words being cut in half, so this method looks for the first space character in the text after the `TRIM_LENGTH` index and cuts there. If there aren't any spaces in between that index and the end of the text, then the method chops anyway. It is a matter of taste, and other strategies are possible such as looking for paragraph breaks and cutting there. Although it's fairly crude, the end result is quite effective. The code that does the trimming is as follows:

```
    def trim(self, text):
        "Trim string length neatly"
        end_space = text.find(' ', TRIM_LENGTH)
        if end_space != -1:
```

```
            text = text[:end_space] + " ..."
        else:
            text = text[:TRIM_LENGTH] # hard cut
        return text
```

Ok, that's it, the whole of the aggregator application. There isn't a lot of code, but that's largely thanks to libraries taking care of the details.

Try It Out Running the Aggregator

To run the code, you'll need to have Python installed (see the note with the *Reading a List of URIs Try it Out* earlier in the chapter) and be connected to the Internet.

1. Download and install the latest version of the PyXML package, which is a small download (`http://pyxml.sourceforge.net/`) and a simple install (PyXML is a very popular Python XML library which implements the standard SAX and DOM APIs).
2. Open a command prompt window, and **cd** to the folder containing the source files.
3. Then type the following:

```
python feed_reader.py
```

An alternative way to run the code is to use IDLE. This is a very simple IDE with a syntax-coloring editor and various debugging aids. You should start IDLE by double-clicking its icon, and then using its File menu, open the `feed_reader.py` file in a new window. Pressing the F5 key when the code is in the editor window will run the application.

Whichever way you run the application, you should see something like this:

```
Reading http://danja.typepad.com/fecho/atom.xml : 15 items
Reading http://www.ftrain.com/xml/feed/rss.rdf : 20 items
Reading http://www.intertwingly.net/blog/index.rss2 : 5 items

*** Newest 5 Items ***

Ftrain.com : The Spy
Protecting myself, and others, from my own geek nature.
Tue, 13 Apr 2004 02:00:00 +0200

Ftrain.com : Pepsitilting
The Gray Album and carbonated soda.
Mon, 12 Apr 2004 02:00:00 +0200

Ftrain.com : Age of X
What time is it?
Fri, 09 Apr 2004 02:00:00 +0200
Finally Atom : Atom in the press
Alongside RSS, presented quite favourably. MediaDailyNews 04-08-04
Thu, 08 Apr 2004 22:24:44 +0200

Sam Ruby : GRDDL
DanBri pointed me to a specification named GRDDL. It looks like exactly
```

```
what I was looking for last August. ...
Thu, 08 Apr 2004 21:27:42 +0200
```

How It Works

You've already seen the details of how this works, but to remind you of the overall picture:

- A list of feed addresses is loaded from a text file.
- Each of the addresses is visited in turn, and the data is passed to a SAX handler.
- The handler creates objects corresponding to the feed and items within the feed.
- The individual items from all feeds are combined into a single list and sorted.
- The items are printed in the command window.

Extending the Aggregator

There are obviously a thousand and one things that could be done to improve this application, but whatever the enhancement in the processing or user interface, you will still be dependent on the material pumped out to feeds. XML is defined by its acronym as extensible, and what this means in practice is that elements outside of the core language can be included with the aid of XML namespaces. According to the underlying XML namespaces specification, the producer can potentially put material from other namespaces pretty much where he likes, but this isn't as simple as it sounds because the consumer then has to know what to do with them. So far two approaches have been taken to extensibility in syndication.

RSS 2.0 leaves the specification of extensions entirely up to developers. This sounds desirable but has significant drawbacks because there is nothing within the specification to say how an element from an extension relates to other elements in a feed. One drawback is that each extension appears like a completely custom application, needing all-new code at both the producer and consumer ends. Another drawback is that without full cooperation between developers, there's no way of guaranteeing that the two extensions will work together.

The RSS 1.0 approach is to fall back on RDF, specifically the structural interpretation of RDF/XML. The structure in which elements and attributes appear within an RDF/XML document gives an unambiguous interpretation according to the RDF model, irrespective of the namespaces. You can tell that certain elements/attributes correspond to resources, and that others correspond to relationships between those resources. The advantage here is that much of the lower-level code for dealing with feed data can be reused across extensions, as the basic interpretation will be the same. It also means independently developed extensions for RSS 1.0 will automatically be compatible with each other.

At the time of writing, the approach to extensions in Atom is still under discussion. The likelihood is that it will define certain relationships based on XML structure to avoid ambiguity. However, the RDF/XML syntax allows the same thing to be said in many ways. This is a blessing if you want to give an existing XML language an RDF interpretation, but a curse if you don't need that versatility and just want a simple parser. Versatility of this kind isn't needed in Atom, so chances are a more restrictive syntax will be used.

Assuming you still want to use extensions in this aggregator, here's one way of doing it.

There is a growing class of tools that take material from one feed (or site) and quote it directly in another feed (or site). Of particular relevance here are online aggregators, such as the "Planet" sites: Planet Gnome, Planet Debian, Planet RDF, and so on. These are weblog-like sites, the posts of which come directly from the syndication feeds of existing blogs or news sites. They each have syndication feeds of their own. You may like to take a moment to look at Planet RDF: the human-readable site is at `http://planetrdf.com`, and it has an RSS 1.0 feed at `http://planetrdf.com/index.rdf`. There is a list of the source feeds from which the system aggregates on the main page. The RSS is very much like regular feeds, except the developers behind it have played nice and included a reference back to the original site the material came from. This appears in the feed as a per-item element from the Dublin Core vocabulary as shown in the following:

```
...
<dc:source>Lost Boy by Leigh Dodds</dc:source>
...
```

The text inside this element is the title of the feed from which the item was extracted. It's pretty easy to capture this in the aggregator described here. To include the material from this element in the aggregated display, two things are needed: a way of extracting the data from the feed and a suitable place to put it in the display.

Like the other elements the application uses, the local name of the element is enough to recognize it. It is certainly possible to have a naming clash on "source," though unlikely. This element is used to describe an item, and the code already has a way to handle this kind of information. Additionally, the code picks out the immediate source of the item (the title of feed from whence it came) and uses this in the title line of the displayed results. So all that is needed is another conditional, inserted at the appropriate point, and the source information can be added to the title line of the results.

Try It Out Extending Aggregator Element Handling

This is only a very simple example, but it should demonstrate how straightforward it can be to make aggregator behavior more interesting.

1. Open the file `feed_handler.py` in a text editor.
2. At the end of the `endElementNS` method, insert the following code:

```
...
        if localname == "pubDate":
            self.current_item.set_rfc2822_time(text)
            return

        if localname == "source":
            self.current_item.source = '('+self.current_item.source+') '+text
            return

    def is_content_element(self, localname):
        "Checks if element may contain item/entry content"
...
```

3. Open `feeds.txt` in the editor and add the following feed URI:

```
http://danja.typepad.com/fecho/atom.xml
http://www.ftrain.com/xml/feed/rss.rdf
http://www.intertwingly.net/blog/index.rss2
http://planetrdf.com/index.rdf
```

4. Run the application again (see the previous *Try It Out*).

How It Works

Amongst the items that the aggregator shows you, you should see something like this:

```
(Planet RDF) Lost Boy by Leigh Dodds : XML Processing Model
The W3C have posted a Note discussing requirements for an XML Processing
Model.
This is good news, ...
Tue, 13 Apr 2004 14:14:09 +0200
```

The name of the aggregated feed from which the item has been extracted is in brackets, followed by the title of the original feed from which it came.

Transforming RSS with XSLT

Because syndicated feeds are usually XML, you can process them using XSLT directly (turn to Chapter 8 for more on XSLT). There are three common situations in which you might want to do this:

- Generating a feed from existing data
- Processing feed data for display
- Pre-processing feed data for other purposes

The first situation assumes you have some XML available for transformation, although as this could be XHTML from cleaned-up HTML, it isn't a major assumption. The other two situations are similar to each other, taking syndication feed XML as input. The difference is that the desired output of the second is likely to be something suitable for immediate rendering, whereas the third situation will translate data into a format appropriate for subsequent processing.

Generating a Feed from Existing Data

One additional application that is worth mentioning is that an XSLT transformation can be used to generate other feed formats when only one is available. So if your blogging software only produces RSS 1.0, a standard transformation can provide your site with feeds for Atom and RSS 2.0. A web search will provide you with several examples (names like `rss2rdf.xsl` are popular!).

Be warned that the different formats may carry different amounts of information. For example, in RSS 2.0 most elements are optional, in Atom most elements are mandatory, and there isn't one-to-one correspondence of many elements. So a conversion from one to the other may be lossy or may demand that you artificially create values for elements. For demonstration purposes the examples here only use RSS 0.91, a particularly undemanding specification.

The following is an XSLT transformation that will generate RSS from an XHTML document:

```
<xsl:stylesheet version="1.0"
    xmlns:xsl="http://www.w3.org/1999/XSL/Transform"
    xmlns:xhtml="http://www.w3.org/1999/xhtml">

<xsl:output method="xml" indent="yes"/>

<xsl:template match="/xhtml:html">
  <rss version="0.91">
    <channel>
    <description>This will not change</description>
    <link>http://example.org</link>
    <xsl:apply-templates />
    </channel>
  </rss>
</xsl:template>

<xsl:template match="xhtml:title">
  <title>
    <xsl:value-of select="." />
  </title>
</xsl:template>

<xsl:template match="xhtml:body/xhtml:h1">
  <item>
    <title>
      <xsl:value-of select="." />
    </title>
    <description>
      <xsl:value-of select="following-sibling::xhtml:p" />
    </description>
  </item>
</xsl:template>

<xsl:template match="text()" />

</xsl:stylesheet>
```

Try It Out Generating RSS from XHTML

1. Open a text editor and type in the previous listing.
2. Save the file as xhtml2rss.xsl.
3. Type the following into the text editor:

```
<?xml version="1.0" encoding="UTF-8"?>
<!DOCTYPE html PUBLIC "-//W3C//DTD XHTML 1.0 Strict//EN"
        "http://www.w3.org/TR/xhtml1/DTD/xhtml1-strict.dtd">
```

```
<html xmlns="http://www.w3.org/1999/xhtml">
    <head>
        <title>My Example Document</title>
    </head>
    <body>
 <h1>A first discussion point</h1>
        <p>Something related to the first point.</p>
 <h1>A second discussion point</h1>
        <p>Something related to the second point.</p>
    </body>
</html>
```

4. Save that as `document.html` in the same folder as `xhtml2rss.xsl`.
5. Use an XSLT processor to apply the transformation to the document.

   Refer to the XSLT chapter for details of how to do this. A suitable processor is Saxon, available from `http://saxon.sourceforge.net/`.

   The command line for Saxon with `saxon7.jar` and the data and XSLT file in the same folder is:

```
java -jar saxon7.jar -o document.rss document.html xhtml2rss.xsl
```

6. Open the newly created `document.rss` in the text editor. You should see the following RSS 0.9 document:

```
<?xml version="1.0" encoding="UTF-8"?>
<rss version="0.91" xmlns:xhtml="http://www.w3.org/1999/xhtml">
   <channel>
      <description>This will not change</description>
      <link>http://example.org</link>
      <title>My Example Document</title>
      <item>
         <title>A first discussion point</title>
         <description>Something related to the first point.</description>
      </item>
      <item>
         <title>A second discussion point</title>
         <description>Something related to the second point.</description>
      </item>
   </channel>
</rss>
```

How It Works

The root element of the stylesheet declares the prefixes for the required namespaces, `xsl:` and `xhtml:`. The output element is set to deliver indented XML:

```
<xsl:stylesheet version="1.0"
    xmlns:xsl="http://www.w3.org/1999/XSL/Transform"
    xmlns:xhtml="http://www.w3.org/1999/xhtml">

<xsl:output method="xml" indent="yes"/>
```

The first template in the XSLT is designed to match the root `html` element of the XHTML document. In that document the XHTML namespace is declared as the default, but in the stylesheet, it's necessary to refer explicitly to the elements using the `xhtml:` prefix to avoid conflicts with the no-namespace RSS. The template looks like this:

```
<xsl:template match="/xhtml:html">
  <rss version="0.91">
    <channel>
    <description>This will not change</description>
    <link>http://example.org</link>
    <xsl:apply-templates />
    </channel>
  </rss>
</xsl:template>
```

This will output the `rss` and `channel` start tags followed by preset `description` and `link` elements, and then it'll apply the rest of the templates to whatever's inside the root `xhtml:html` element. The template then closes the `channel` and `rss` elements.

The next template is set up to match any `xhtml:title` elements:

```
<xsl:template match="xhtml:title">
  <title>
    <xsl:value-of select="." />
  </title>
</xsl:template>
```

There is just one matching element in the XHTML document, which contains the text `My example document`. This gets selected and placed in a `title` element. Note that the input element is in the XHTML namespace, and the output has no namespace, to correspond to the RSS 0.91 specification.

The next template is a little more complicated. The material in the source XHTML document is considered to correspond to an item is of the form:

```
<h1>Item Title</h1>
       <p>Item Description</p>
```

To pick these blocks out, the stylesheet matches on `xhtml:h1` elements that are contained in an `xhtml:body`, as we can see here:

```
<xsl:template match="xhtml:body/xhtml:h1">
  <item>
    <title>
      <xsl:value-of select="." />
    </title>
    <description>
      <xsl:value-of select="following-sibling::xhtml:p" />
    </description>
  </item>
</xsl:template>
```

An outer no-namespace <item> element wraps everything produced in this template. It contains a <title> element which will be given the content of whatever's in the context node, which is the xhtml:h1 element. So the header text is passed into the item's title element. Next, the content for the RSS <description> element is extracted by using the following-sibling::xhtml:p selector. This addresses the next xhtml:p element after the xhtml:h1.

The final template is needed to mop up any text not directly covered by the other elements, which would otherwise appear in the output:

```
  <xsl:template match="text()" />
</xsl:stylesheet>
```

Note that the stylesheet presented here assumes the source document will be well-formed XHTML, with a heading/paragraph structure following that of the example. In practice, the XSLT will have to be modified to suit the document structure. If the original document isn't XHTML (HTML 3.2, for example), then a tool such as HTML Tidy (http://www.w3.org/People/Raggett/tidy/) can be used to convert it before applying the transformation.

If the authoring of the original XHTML is under your control, then you can take more control over the conversion process. You can add markers to the document to say which parts correspond to items, descriptions, and so on (for example, <div class="item">). An online service is available that follows this approach can be found at http://www.w3.org/2000/08/w3c-synd/.

One final point: Although this general technique for generating a feed has a lot in common with "screenscraping" techniques (which generally break when the page author makes a minor change to the layout), it's most useful when the authors of the original document *are* involved. The fact that the source document is XML greatly expands the possibilities. Research is ongoing into methods of embedding more general meta data in XHTML and other XML documents, with a couple of recent proposals being available at the following sites:

- http://www.w3.org/MarkUp/2004/02/xhtml-rdf.html
- http://www.w3.org/2004/01/rdxh/spec

Processing Feed Data for Display

What better way to follow a demonstration of XHTML-to-RSS conversion than an RSS-to-XHTML stylesheet. This isn't quite as perverse as it may sound—it's useful to be able to render your own feed for browser viewing, and this conversion offers a simple way of viewing other people's feeds. Though it is relatively straightforward to display material from someone else's syndication feed on your own site this way, it certainly isn't a good idea without obtaining permission first. Aside from copyright issues, every time your page is loaded it will call the remote site, adding to their bandwidth load. There are ways around this, basically caching the data locally, but that's beyond the scope of this chapter.

Generating XHTML from RSS isn't very different than the other way around, as you can see in this listing:

```
<xsl:stylesheet version="1.0"
    xmlns:xsl="http://www.w3.org/1999/XSL/Transform"
    xmlns="http://www.w3.org/1999/xhtml">

<xsl:output method="html" indent="yes"/>
```

```
<xsl:template match="rss">
  <xsl:text disable-output-escaping="yes">
    &lt;!DOCTYPE html PUBLIC "-//W3C//DTD XHTML 1.0 Strict//EN"
    "http://www.w3.org/TR/xhtml1/DTD/xhtml1-strict.dtd"&gt;
  </xsl:text>
  <html>
    <xsl:apply-templates />
  </html>
</xsl:template>

<xsl:template match="channel">
  <head>
    <title>
      <xsl:value-of select="title" />
    </title>
  </head>
  <body>
    <xsl:apply-templates />
  </body>
</xsl:template>

<xsl:template match="item">
  <h1><xsl:value-of select="title" /></h1>
  <p><xsl:value-of select="description" /></p>
</xsl:template>

<xsl:template match="text()" />

</xsl:stylesheet>
```

Try It Out — Generating XHTML from an RSS Feed

1. Enter the previous listing into a text editor.
2. Save as `rss2xhtml.xsl` in the same folder as `document.rss`.
3. Apply the stylesheet to `document.rss`. The command line for Saxon with `saxon7.jar` and the data and XSLT file in the same folder is:

```
java -jar saxon7.jar -o document.xml document.rss rss2xhtml.xsl
```

4. Open the newly created `document.xml` in the text editor. You should see the following XHTML document:

```
<!DOCTYPE html PUBLIC "-//W3C//DTD XHTML 1.0 Strict//EN"
 "http://www.w3.org/TR/xhtml1/DTD/xhtml1-strict.dtd">
<html xmlns="http://www.w3.org/1999/xhtml">
   <head>
      <title>My Example Document</title>
   </head>
   <body>
```

```
        <h1>A first discussion point</h1>
        <p>Something related to the first point.</p>
        <h1>A second discussion point</h1>
        <p>Something related to the second point.</p>
    </body>
</html>
```

As you can see, it closely resembles the XHTML original (document.html) used to create the RSS data.

How It Works

As in the previous stylesheet, the namespaces in use are those of XSLT and XHTML. This time though the output method is html. The xml output method can be used to produce equally valid data as XHTML is XML, but the syntax turns out a little tidier (this is likely to vary between XSLT processors).

```
<xsl:stylesheet version="1.0"
    xmlns:xsl="http://www.w3.org/1999/XSL/Transform"
    xmlns="http://www.w3.org/1999/xhtml">

<xsl:output method="html" indent="yes"/>
```

The first template here matches the root <rss> element of the RSS 0.91 document. The template puts in place an appropriate DOCTYPE declaration, which is wrapped in an xsl:text element with escaping disabled to allow the end <...> characters to appear in the output without breaking this XML's well-formedness. The root element of the XHTML document is put in position, and the other templates are applied to the rest of the feed data. Here is the first template:

```
<xsl:template match="rss">
  <xsl:text disable-output-escaping="yes">
    &lt;!DOCTYPE html PUBLIC "-//W3C//DTD XHTML 1.0 Strict//EN"
    "http://www.w3.org/TR/xhtml1/DTD/xhtml1-strict.dtd"&gt;
  </xsl:text>
  <html>
    <xsl:apply-templates />
  </html>
</xsl:template>
```

The next template matches the <channel> element. This actually corresponds to two separate sections in the desired XHTML, the head and the body. All that's needed in the head is the content of the title element, which appears as an immediate child of channel. The material that has to go into the body of the XHTML document is a little more complicated, so other templates are applied to sort that out. Here then is the channel template:

```
<xsl:template match="channel">
  <head>
    <title>
      <xsl:value-of select="title" />
    </title>
  </head>
  <body>
    <xsl:apply-templates />
  </body>
</xsl:template>
```

For each item element that appears in the feed, a pair of <h1> and <p> elements are created, corresponding to the RSS <title> and <description>. Here is the template, and you can see how the content is transferred from the RSS kinds of element to their XHTML mappings:

```
<xsl:template match="item">
  <h1><xsl:value-of select="title" /></h1>
  <p><xsl:value-of select="description" /></p>
</xsl:template>
```

Once more a utility template is included to mop up any stray text, before the closing `xsl:stylesheet` element closes this document:

```
<xsl:template match="text()" />

</xsl:stylesheet>
```

Browser Processing

A bonus feature of modern web browsers, such as Mozilla and Internet Explorer, is that they have XSLT engines built in. This means it's possible to style a feed format document in the browser. All that's needed is a XML Processing Instruction that points toward the stylesheet. This is very straightforward, as you can see here, modifying `document.rss`:

```
<?xml version="1.0"?>
<?xml-stylesheet type="text/xsl" href="rss2xhtml.xsl"?>
<rss version="0.91">
   <channel>
...
```

If we save this modified version as `document.xml` and open it with our browser, we'll see a rendering that's exactly the same as what we see with the XHTML version listed earlier.

Note that browsers aren't that smart at figuring out what kind of document they're being presented with, and so when saved and loaded locally, the filename extension has to be something the browser will recognize. If you try loading a file `document.rss` into a browser, chances are it'll ask you where you want to save it.

When it comes to displaying XML (such as RSS and Atom) in a browser, the world's your oyster—you can generate XHTML using a stylesheet, and the resulting document can be additionally styled using CSS. There's no real need for anyone to see raw XML in his or her browser. This is one reason the Atom group has created the <info> element, which can be used along with client-side styling to present an informative message about the feed alongside a human-readable rendering of the XML.

Pre-Processing Feed Data

Another reason we might want to process feed data with XSLT would be to interface easily with existing systems. For example, if we wanted to store the feed items in a database, we could set up a transformation to extract the content from a feed and format it as SQL statements, as follows:

```
INSERT INTO feed-table
   VALUES (item-id, "This is the title", "This is the item description");
```

One particularly useful application of XSLT is to use transformation to "normalize" the data from the various formats into a common representation, which can then be passed on to subsequent processing.

This is in effect the same technique used in the aggregator application we've just seen, except there the normalization is to the application's internal representation of a feed model.

A quick web search should yield something suitable for most requirements like this, or at least something that you can modify to fit your specific needs. A couple of examples of existing work are Morten Frederickson's anything-to-RSS 1.0 converter (`http://purl.org/net/syndication/subscribe/feed-rss1.0.xsl`) and Aaron Cope's Atom-to-RSS 1.0 and -2.0 stylesheets (`http://www.aaronland.info/xsl/atom/0.3/`).

Reviewing the Different Formats

There are at least three different syndication formats for a feed consumer to deal with, and you may want to build different subsystems to deal with each individually. Even when XSLT is available this can be desirable, as no single feed model can really do justice to all the variations. So how do you tell what format a feed is? Here are the addresses of some syndication feeds:

```
http://news.bbc.co.uk/rss/newsonline_world_edition/front_page/rss091.xml
http://blogs.it/0100198/rss.xml
http://purl.org/net/morten/blog/feed/rdf/
http://swordfish.rdfweb.org/people/libby/rdfweb/webwho.xrdf
http://icite.net/blog/?flavor=atom&smm=y
```

You might suppose a rough rule of thumb may be to examine the filename. It is, but this is pretty unreliable for *any* format on the web. A marginally more reliable approach (and one which counts as good practice against the web specifications) is to examine the MIME type of the data. A convenient way of doing this is to use the `wget` command-line application to download the files (this is a standard Unix utility, an MS Windows version is available from `http://unxutils.sourceforge.net/`).

In use, `wget` looks like this:

```
D:\rss-samples>wget http://blogs.it/0100198/rss.xml
--16:23:35--  http://blogs.it/0100198/rss.xml
           => 'rss.xml'
Resolving blogs.it... 213.92.76.66
Connecting to blogs.it[213.92.76.66]:80... connected.
HTTP request sent, awaiting response... 200 OK
Length: 87,810 [text/xml]

100%[====================================>] 87,810        7.51K/s    ETA 00:00

16:23:48 (7.91 KB/s) - 'rss.xml' saved [87810/87810]
```

It provides a lot of useful information: the IP address of the host called, the HTTP response (200 OK), the length of the file in bytes (87,810), and then the part of interest: `[text/xml]`. If we run `wget` with each of the previous addresses, we will see the MIME types are as follows:

```
[text/xml] http://news.bbc.co.uk/rss/
                newsonline_world_edition/front_page/rss091.xml
[text/xml] http://blogs.it/0100198/rss.xml
[application/rdf+xml] http://purl.org/net/morten/blog/feed/rdf/
[text/plain] http://swordfish.rdfweb.org/people/libby/rdfweb/webwho.xrdf
[application/atom+xml] http://icite.net/blog/?flavor=atom&smm=y
```

As well as the preceding MIME types, it's not uncommon to see `application/rss+xml` used, although that has no official standing.

So has that helped decide what formats these are? Well, hardly. The only reliable way to find out is to look inside the files and see what it says there, and even then it can be tricky. So run `wget` to get the previous files, and have a look inside with a text editor. Snipping off the XML prolog (and irrelevant namespaces), the data files begin like this (this one's from `http://news.bbc.co.uk/rss/newsonline_world_edition/front_page/rss091.xml`):

```
<rss version="0.91">
   <channel>
   <title>BBC News | News Front Page | World Edition</title>
...
```

Ok, that's clearly RSS, flagged by the root element. It even tells you that it's version 0.91. Here's another from `http://blogs.it/0100198/rss.xml`:

```
<rss version="2.0">
<channel>
   <title>Marc&apos;s Voice</title>
...
```

Again, a helpful root tells you it's RSS 2.0. Now here's one from `http://purl.org/net/morten/blog/feed/rdf/`:

```
<rdf:RDF
 xmlns="http://purl.org/rss/1.0/"
 xmlns:rdf="http://www.w3.org/1999/02/22-rdf-syntax-ns#">

<channel rdf:about="http://purl.org/net/morten/blog/rdf">
 <title>Binary Relations</title>
...
```

The `rdf:RDF` root suggests it, and the `rss:channel` element confirms it—this is RSS 1.0. However, the following from `http://swordfish.rdfweb.org/people/libby/rdfweb/webwho.xrdf` is less clear:

```
<rdf:RDF
    xmlns:rdf="http://www.w3.org/1999/02/22-rdf-syntax-ns#"
    xmlns:foaf="http://xmlns.com/foaf/0.1/">
...>

<rdf:Description rdf:about="">
  <foaf:maker>
    <foaf:Person>
      <foaf:name>Libby Miller</foaf:name>
...
```

The `rdf:RDF` root and a lot of namespaces could indicate that this is RSS 1.0 using a bunch of extension modules. We could have to go a long way through this file to be sure. The interchangeability of RDF vocabularies means that RSS 1.0 terms can crop up almost anywhere, whether or not we wish to count any document as a whole as a syndication feed is another matter. As it happens there aren't any RSS elements in this particular file, it's a FOAF (Friend-of-a-Friend) Personal Profile Document. It's perfectly valid data; it's just simply not a syndication feed as such.

Now for a last example from `http://icite.net/blog/?flavor=atom&smm=y`:

```
<feed version="0.3"
     xmlns="http://purl.org/atom/ns#"
     xmlns:dc="http://purl.org/dc/elements/1.1/"
     xml:lang="en">

     <title>the iCite net development blog</title>
...
```

The `<feed>` gives this away from the start: this is Atom. The version is only 0.3, but chances are it'll make it to version 1.0 without changing that root element.

These examples have been chosen because they are all *good* examples, that is to say they conform to their individual specifications. In the wild, things might get messy, but at least the preceding checks give you a place to start.

Useful Resources

Here's a selection of some additional resources for further information on the topics discussed in this chapter.

The following sites are good specifications resource:

- RSS 1.0: `http://purl.org/rss/1.0/spec`
- RSS 2.0: `http://blogs.law.harvard.edu/tech/rss`
- Atom (pre-draft): `http://www.mnot.net/drafts/draft-nottingham-atom-format-02.html`
- Atom Wiki: `http://www.intertwingly.net/wiki/pie/FrontPage`
- RDF: `http://www.w3.org/RDF/`
- Dublin Core Metadata Initiative: `http://dublincore.org/`
- W3CDTF (Date and Time Formats): `http://www.w3.org/TR/NOTE-datetime`

These sites offer tutorials:

- RDF Primer: `http://www.w3.org/TR/rdf-primer/`
- Atom Enabled: `http://www.atomenabled.org/`
- Syndication Best Practices: `http://www.ariadne.ac.uk/issue35/miller/`

- The Absolute Minimum Every Software Developer Absolutely, Positively Must Know About Unicode and Character Sets (No Excuses!), Joel Spolsky: `http://www.joelonsoftware.com/articles/Unicode.html`

There are dozens of newsreader/aggregator tools available; the following are two lists of these consumer tools:

- Weblogs Compendium: `http://www.lights.com/weblogs/rss.html`
- RSS Info: `http://blogspace.com/rss/readers`

The following offer information on producer tools:

- WordPress (blogging tool): `http://wordpress.org/`
- Bloglines (online aggregator): `http://www.bloglines.com/`
- PubSub (information monitor): `http://pubsub.com/`
- Syndic8 (feed portal): `www.syndic8.com`
- RSS at Open Directory: `http://dmoz.org/Reference/Libraries/Library_and_Information_Science/Technical_Services/Cataloguing/Metadata/RDF/Applications/RSS/`
- Open Source Content Management Systems: `http://www.opensourcecms.com/`

Here are some miscellaneous resources:

- Feed Validator: `http://feeds.archive.org/validator/`
- RDF Validator: `http://www.w3.org/RDF/Validator/`
- RDF Resource Guide: `http://www.ilrt.bris.ac.uk/discovery/rdf/resources/`
- rss-dev Mailing List: `http://groups.yahoo.com/group/rss-dev/`

Summary

At the start of this chapter we saw how the current ideas of content syndication grew out of "push" technologies and early meta data efforts, the foundations laid by CDF and MCF followed by Netscape's RSS 0.9 and scriptingNews format. We discussed how the components of syndication systems carry out different roles: Server-Producer, Client-Consumer, Client-Producer, and Server-Consumer. The chapter then covered the basic ideas behind the Resource Description Framework (RDF) on which RSS 1.0 is built, as well as the relatively straightforward syntax of RSS 2.0. This was followed by discussion of Atom, an open language that hopes to get beyond political divisions that have been the bane of the RSS community and concentrate on advancing the technology.

There then followed a brief discussion of some of the practical issues of syndication, which led into description of an aggregator written in Python. Hopefully, you will have tried the application and undoubtedly thought of ways in which it can be extended. Most of the development around syndication has been from the grassroots, and it's a fertile area for new ideas. It really is worthwhile putting your ideas into practice.

The chapter then briefly covered some of the things that can be achieved by using XSLT with feed formats, such as generation of feed data from XHTML and rendering to a browser. The topic of RSS and content syndication is wide and deep, and a single chapter cannot do justice to it. However, we have seen the fundamental concepts, a small sample of the techniques that can be applied, and one or two of the problems developers face. We have also seen how XML is central to content syndication. You are now equipped to change the world—or at least a geeky corner of it.

Exercise Questions

Suggested solutions to these questions can be found in Appendix A.

Question 1

At the end of the description of the simple Python aggregator, it was demonstrated how it was relatively simple to extend the range of the elements covered, by adding support for `dc:source`. Your first challenge is to extend the application so that it also displays the author of a feed entry, if that information is available.

You should check the specs and some real-world feeds yourself, but the elements used for identifying the author of an item are usually one of the following: `author`, `dc:creator`, `atom:name`, or `foaf:name`. The `author` element appears in the "simple" RSS versions (0.9x, 2.0) and has no namespace. However, there is a slight complication, as there is also an element in RSS 2.0 called `name`, which is used for the name of the text object in a text input area (the text input area elements are rarely encountered in practice, but it does make for a more interesting exercise). So part of this exercise is to ensure that this element won't be mistaken for the name of the author.

Question 2

We saw toward the end of the chapter how the most common syndication formats show themselves, and earlier in the chapter we saw how it was possible to run an XSLT stylesheet over RSS feeds to produce an XHTML rendering. The exercise here is to apply the second technique to the first task. Try to write an XSLT transformation that will tell us the format of the feed, together with its title.

Web Services

So far we've covered what XML is and how to create well-formed and valid XML documents, and we've even seen a couple of programmatic interfaces into XML documents in the form of DOM and SAX. We also discussed the fact that XML isn't really a language on its own; it's a meta language, to be used in the creation of other languages.

This chapter will take a slightly different turn. Rather than discussing XML itself, we'll discuss an application of XML: *Web services* allow objects on one computer to call and make use of objects on other computers. In other words, Web services are a means of performing distributed computing.

In this chapter we'll learn:

- What a Remote Procedure Call (RPC) is, and what RPC protocols exist currently
- Why Web services can provide more flexibility than previous RPC protocols
- How XML-RPC works
- Why most Web services implementations should use HTTP as a transport protocol, and how HTTP works under the hood
- How the specifications that surround Web services fit together

What Is an RPC?

It is often necessary to design *distributed systems*, where the code to run an application is spread across multiple computers. For example, to create a large transaction processing system, you might have a separate server for business logic objects, one for presentation logic objects, a database server, and so on, all of which need to talk to each other (see Figure 14-1).

In order for a model like this to work, code on one computer needs to call code on another computer. For example, the code in the web server might need a list of orders for display on a web page, in which case it would call code on the business objects server to provide that list of orders. That code in turn might need to talk to the database. When code on one computer calls code on another computer, this is called a *Remote Procedure Call*, usually abbreviated as RPC.

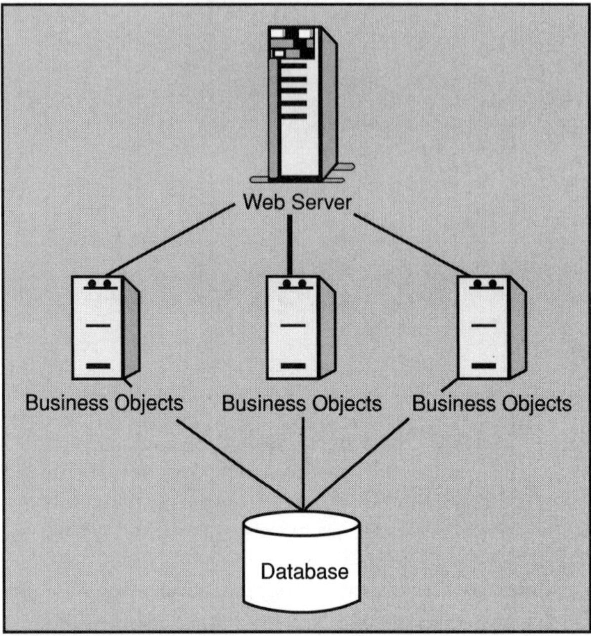

Figure 14-1

In order to make an RPC, you need to know the following things:

- Where does the code you want to call reside? If you want to execute a particular piece of code, you need to know where that code is!
- Does the code need any parameters? If so, what type of parameters? For example, if you want to call a remote procedure to add two numbers together, that procedure would need to know what numbers it's adding.
- Will the procedure return any data? If so, in what format? For example, a procedure to add two numbers would probably return a third number, which would be the result of the calculation.

In addition, you need to deal with networking issues, packaging any data for transport from computer to computer, and a number of other issues. For this reason, a number of RPC *protocols* have been developed.

> **A protocol is a set of rules that allow different applications, or even different computers, to communicate. For example, TCP (Transmission Control Protocol) and IP (Internet Protocol) are protocols that allow computers on the Internet to talk to each other, because they set up rules about how data should be passed, how computers are addressed, and so on.**

These protocols specify how to provide an address for the remote computer, how to package up data to be sent to the remote procedures and how to get back a response, how to initiate the call, how to deal with errors, and all of the other details that need to be addressed to allow multiple computers to communicate with each other. (Such RPC protocols often piggyback on other protocols; for example, an RPC protocol might specify that TCP/IP must be used as its network transport.)

RPC Protocols

There are a number of protocols that exist for performing remote procedure calls, but the most common are DCOM and IIOP (both of which are extensions of other technologies: COM and CORBA, respectively), and Java RMI. Each of these protocols provides the functionality that you need to perform remote procedure calls, although each also has its drawbacks.

The following sections will discuss these protocols, and those drawbacks, although we won't really go too much into technical details. We'll just take it for granted that these protocols provide the functionality needed to perform remote procedure calls.

DCOM

Microsoft developed a technology called the *Component Object Model*, or *COM* (see `http://www.microsoft.com/com/default.asp`), to help facilitate *component-based software*. That is, software that can be broken down into smaller, separate, components, which can then be shared across an application, or even across multiple applications. COM provides a standard way of writing objects so that they can be discovered at runtime and used by any application running on the computer. What's more, COM objects are language-independent. That means that you can write a COM object in virtually any programming language—C, C++, Visual Basic, and so on—and that object can talk to any other COM object, even if it was written in a different language.

A good example of COM in action is Microsoft Office: because much of the functionality in Office has been provided through COM objects, it is easy for one Office application to make use of another. For example, since Excel's functionality is exposed through COM objects, we might create a Word document that contains an embedded Excel spreadsheet.

However, this functionality is not limited to Office applications; we could also write our own application that makes use of Excel's functionality to perform complex calculations, or uses Word's spell-checking component. This would allow us to write our applications quicker, since we wouldn't have to write the functionality for a spell-checking component or a complex math component ourselves. By extension, we could also write our own shareable components for use in others' applications.

COM is a handy technology to use when creating reusable components, but it doesn't tackle the problem of distributed applications. In order for our application to make use of a COM object, that object must reside on the same computer as our application. For this reason, Microsoft developed a technology called *Distributed COM*, or *DCOM* (see `http://www.microsoft.com/com/tech/dcom.asp`). DCOM extends the COM programming model and allows applications to call COM objects that reside on remote computers. To an application, calling a remote object from a server using DCOM is just as easy as calling a local object on the same PC using COM—as long as the necessary configuration has been done ahead of time.

However, as handy as COM and DCOM are for writing component-based software and distributed applications, they have one major drawback: both of these technologies are Microsoft-specific. The COM objects we write, or that we want to use, will only work on computers running Microsoft Windows. And, even though we can call remote objects over DCOM, those objects also must be running on computers using Microsoft Windows.

> *There have been DCOM implementations written for other non-Microsoft operating systems, but they haven't reached large acceptance. In practice, when someone wants to develop a distributed application on non-Microsoft platforms, they use one of the other RPC protocols.*

For some people, this may not be a problem. For example, if I'm developing an application for my company, and we have already standardized on Microsoft Windows for our employees, then using a Microsoft-specific technology might be fine. For others, however, this limitation means that DCOM is just not an option.

IIOP

Prior even to Microsoft's work on COM, the *Object Management Group* (OMG, see `http://www.omg.org/`) had developed a technology to solve the same problems that COM and DCOM try to solve but in a platform-neutral way. They called this technology the *Common Object Request Broker Architecture* (CORBA, see `http://www.corba.org/`). Just as with COM, CORBA objects can be written in virtually any programming language, and any CORBA object can talk to any other, even if it was written in a different language. CORBA works similarly to COM, the main difference being who supplies the underlying architecture for the technology.

For COM objects, the underlying COM functionality is provided by the operating system (Windows), whereas with CORBA, an *Object Request Broker* (ORB) provides the underlying functionality (see Figure 14-2). In fact, the processes for instantiating COM and CORBA objects are similar.

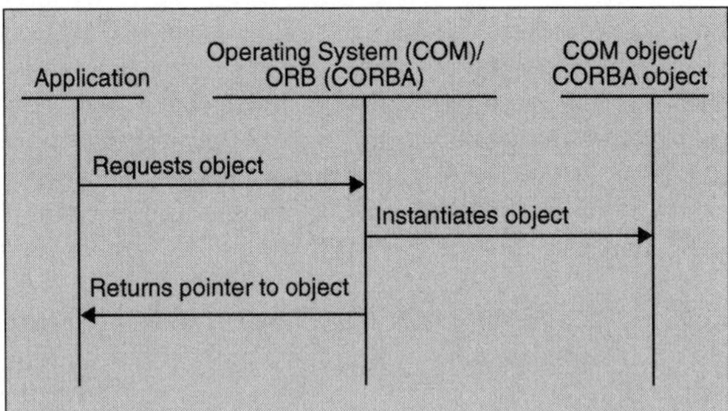

Figure 14-2

But while the concepts are the same, using an ORB instead of the operating system to provide the base object services gives one important advantage: it makes CORBA platform-independent. Any vendor who creates an ORB can create versions for Windows, Unix, Linux, and so on.

Furthermore, the OMG created the *Internet Inter-ORB Protocol* (IIOP), which allows communication between different ORBs. This means that you not only have platform-independence, you also have ORB-independence. You can combine ORBs from different vendors and have remote objects talking to each other over IIOP (as long as you stay away from any vendor-specific extensions to IIOP).

Java RMI

Both DCOM and IIOP provide similar functionality: they provide a language-independent way to call objects that reside on remote computers. IIOP goes a step further than DCOM and allows for components to be run on different platforms. However, there is already a language that is specifically designed to enable you to "write once, run anywhere": Java.

Java provides the *Remote Method Invocation* (RMI, see `http://java.sun.com/products/jdk/rmi/`) system for distributed computing. Since Java objects can be run from any platform, the idea behind RMI is to just write everything in Java and then have those objects communicate with each other.

Although Java can be used to write CORBA objects that can be called over IIOP, or even to write COM objects using certain nonstandard Java language extensions, using RMI for distributed computing can provide a smaller learning curve because the programmer isn't required to learn about CORBA and IIOP. Since all of the objects involved are using the same programming language, any data types are simply the built-in Java data types, and Java exceptions can be used for error handling. Finally, Java RMI can do one thing DCOM and IIOP can't: it can transfer code with every call. That is, even if the remote computer we're calling doesn't have the code it needs, we can send it and still have the remote computer perform the processing.

However, the obvious drawback to Java RMI is that it ties the programmer to one programming language, Java, for all of the objects in the distributed system.

The New RPC Protocol: Web Services

With the Internet fast becoming the platform on which applications run, it's no surprise that a truly language- and platform-independent way of creating distributed applications has become the Holy Grail of software development. As of now, it looks as though that Holy Grail has made itself known in the form of *Web services*.

Technically, a "web service" is any information that can be requested over the web. Of course, that means that even a simple request for a web page is technically a "web service," but when we talk about Web services, that's generally not what we're talking about.

Web services are a means for requesting information over the Internet all right, but they typically involve the encoding of both the request and the response in XML. Along with using standard Internet protocols for transport, this encoding makes messages universally available. That means that a Perl program running on Linux can call a .NET program running on Windows.NET, and nobody will be the wiser. (For more on how .NET and XML can work together, check out Chapter 20.)

Of course, nothing's ever quite that simple, at least this early in the game. In order to make these Web services available, there have to be standards so that everyone knows what information can be requested, how to request it, and what form the response will take.

In the following pages, we'll take a look at XML-RPC, a simple form of Web services. We'll then expand the discussion to look at the more heavy-duty protocols and how they fit together. In the next chapter, we'll take a closer look at two of the most commonly used protocols, SOAP and WSDL.

XML-RPC

One of the easiest ways to see Web services in action is to look at the XML-RPC protocol. Designed to be simple, it provides a means for calling a remote procedure by specifying the procedure to call and the parameters to pass. The client sends a command, encoded as XML, to the server, which performs the Remote Procedure Call and returns a response, also encoded as XML.

The protocol is simple, but the process—sending an XML request over the web and getting back an XML response—is the foundation of Web services, so understanding how it works will help you understand more complex protocols such as SOAP.

The service we'll look at is The Internet Topic Exchange, a set of "channels" that list postings on particular topics. For example, when SernaFerna, Inc. adds music news to their website, they can add an entry to the "music" channel.

Let's start by looking at the API we're going to be calling.

The Target API

The Internet Topic Exchange has only two available methods. The first is as follows:

```
struct topicExchange.getChannels()
```

This method does exactly what it says it does; it returns a list of existing channels. (Don't worry about the `struct` yet.) It doesn't have any parameters, so calling it will be very simple.

Now let's take a look at the second method:

```
struct topicExchange.ping(string topicName, struct details)
```

This method is used to add a new entry to a particular topic, as defined by the `topicName`. We'll look at actually making the request in a moment, but first let's look at how to construct an XML Web services message.

A Simple Request

The simplest XML-RPC request would be one that executes a method with no parameters. In this example, that would be the `topicExchange.getChannels()` method as shown in the following:

```
<methodCall>
    <methodName>topicExchange.getChannels</methodName>
</methodCall>
```

In this case, the process is straightforward; we're simply calling the `topicExchange.getChannels()` method, as specified in the `methodName` element. When we send this XML snippet to the service, the service returns an XML document that lists existing channels. We'll look at that response in a moment, but first let's look at a more complex request.

Passing Parameters

Most of the time the method you want to call requires parameters, so XML-RPC includes a way to specify them within the XML request. For example, the `topicExchange.ping()` method requires a `string` and a `struct`.

The string is easy to specify, as shown in the following:

```
<methodCall>
  <methodName>topicExchange.ping</methodName>
  <params>
    <param>
      <value><string>music</string></value>
    </param>
  </params>
</methodCall>
```

Here we're specifying a set of parameters using the `params` element, and then a single parameter using the `param` element. Within the `param` element we're specifying the first parameter, the channel name, noting that it is to be treated as a string. XML-RPC actually specifies seven types of scalar values: `<i4>` (or `<int>`, a 4-byte signed integer), `<boolean>` (0 for false or 1 for true), `<string>`, `<double>`, `<dateTime.iso8601>` (a date/time value, such as 20040422T16:12:04), and `<base64>` (base64-encoded binary data).

In some cases, the parameter is not a single scalar value, but a group of values, known as a `struct`.

Using a struct

A `struct` is a set of named values passed as you might pass an object. For example, the Internet Topic Exchange expects the information on the posting to which you're linking to come as a single `struct` as follows:

```
<methodCall>
  <methodName>topicExchange.ping</methodName>
  <params>
    <param>
      <value><string>music</string></value>
    </param>
    <param>
      <value>
        <struct>
          <member>
            <name>blog_name</name>
            <value><string>SernaFerna Today</string></value>
          </member>
          <member>
            <name>title</name>
            <value><string>Today's specials</string></value>
          </member>
          <member>
            <name>url</name>
            <value>
              <string>http://www.sernaferna.com/news/041204.html</string>
```

```
            </value>
          </member>
          <member>
            <name>excerpt</name>
            <value><string>Serna Ferna music announced some new specials
                   today, including some never-before-heard artists along
                   with the classics.</string></value>
          </member>
        </struct>
      </value>
    </param>
  </params>
</methodCall>
```

In this case, the `details` parameter consists of a single value, but that value is a `struct`. The `struct` consists of four `members`, with each member having a `name` and a `value`. As before, the value is a scalar of one of the seven types, but that's not actually a requirement. A `struct` can have a `struct` as one or more of its members, as you can see in the response we get from the `getChannels()` method:

```
<methodResponse>
  <params>
    <param>
      <value>
        <struct>
          <member>
            <name>channels</name>
            <value>
              <struct>
                <member>
                  <name>dance</name>
                  <value>
                    <struct>
                      <member>
                        <name>url</name>
                        <value>
                          <string>http://topicexchange.com/t/dance/</string>
                        </value>
                      </member>
                    </struct>
                  </value>
                </member>
                <member>
                  <name>logic</name>
                  <value>
                    <struct>
                      <member>
                        <name>url</name>
                        <value>
                          <string>http://topicexchange.com/t/logic/</string>
                        </value>
                      </member>
                    </struct>
                  </value>
                </member>
...
```

```
                </struct>
              </value>
            </member>
          </struct>
        </value>
      </param>
    </params>
  </methodResponse>
```

This response has been snipped for brevity's sake, but the structure is just as it would be for the dozens of other channels. And that's it, as far as XML-RPC syntax is concerned. Now we just have to look at how to actually send a request.

The Network Transport

Generally, Web services specifications allow you to use any network transport to send and receive messages. For example, you could use IBM MQSeries or Microsoft Message Queue (MSMQ) to send SOAP messages asynchronously over a queue, or even use SMTP to send SOAP messages via e-mail. However, the most common protocol used will probably be HTTP. In fact, the XML-RPC specification requires it, so that is what we'll concentrate on in this chapter.

HTTP

Many readers may already be somewhat familiar with the HTTP protocol, since it is used every time we request a web page in our browsers. Most Web services implementations will use HTTP as their underlying protocol, so we should take a look at how it works under the hood.

The *Hypertext Transfer Protocol* (HTTP) is a request/response protocol. This means that when we make an HTTP request, at its most basic, the following steps occur:

- The client (in most cases, the browser) opens a connection to the HTTP server.
- The client sends a request to the server.
- The server does some processing.
- The server sends back a response.
- The connection is closed.

An HTTP message contains two parts: a set of *headers*, followed by an optional *body*. The headers are simply text, where each header is separated from the next by a new line character, while the body might be text or binary information. The body is separated from the headers by two new line characters.

For example, suppose we attempt to load an HTML page, located at `http://www.sernaferna.com/samplepage.html`, into our browser, which in this case is Internet Explorer 5.5. The browser sends a request similar to the following to the `www.sernaferna.com` server:

```
GET /samplepage.htm HTTP/1.1
Accept: */*
```

```
Accept-Language: en-ca
Accept-Encoding: gzip, deflate
User-Agent: Mozilla/4.0 (compatible; MSIE 5.5; Windows NT 5.0)
Host: www.sernaferna.com
```

The first line of our request specifies the method that is to be performed by the HTTP server. HTTP defines a few types of requests, but we have specified `GET`, indicating to the server that we want to get the resource indicated, which in this case is `/samplepage.html`. (Another common method is `POST`, which we'll discuss in a moment.) This line also specifies that we're using the HTTP/1.1 version of the protocol. There are a number of other headers there as well, which specify to the web server a few pieces of information about the browser, such as what types of information it can receive. Those are as follows:

- `Accept` tells the server what MIME types this browser accepts. (In this case, `*/*`, meaning any MIME types.)
- `Accept-Language` tells the server what language this browser is using. Servers can potentially use this information to customize the content sent back. In this case, the browser is specifying that it is the Canadian (`ca`) dialect of the English (`en`) language.
- `Accept-Encoding` specifies to the server if the content can be encoded before being sent to the browser. In this case, the browser has specified that it can accept documents that are encoded using `gzip` or `deflate`.

For a `GET` request, there is no body in the HTTP message.

In response, the server sends something similar to the following:

```
HTTP/1.1 200 OK
Server: Microsoft-IIS/5.0
Date: Fri, 06 Jul 2001 15:30:52 GMT
Content-Type: text/html
Last-Modified: Thu, 05 Jul 2001 15:19:57 GMT
Content-Length: 98

<html>
<head><title>Hello world</title></head>
<body>
<p>Hello world</p>
</body>
</html>
```

Again, there is a set of HTTP headers, this time followed by the body. In this case, some of the headers sent by the HTTP server were as follows:

- A status code, `200`, indicating that the request was successful. The HTTP specification (`ftp://ftp.isi.edu/in-notes/rfc2616.txt`) defines a number of valid status codes that can be sent in an HTTP response, such as the famous (or infamous) 404 code, which means that the resource being requested could not be found.
- A `Content-Type` header, indicating what type of content is contained in the body of the message. A client application (such as a web browser) uses this header to decide what to do with

the item; for example, if the content type were that of a `.wav` file, the browser might load an external sound program to play it, or give the user the option of saving it to the hard drive instead.

- A `Content-Length` header, which indicates how long the body of the message will be.

The `GET` method is the most common HTTP method used in regular everyday surfing. The second most common is the `POST` method. When you do a `POST`, information is sent to the HTTP server in the body of the message. For example, when you fill out a form on a web page and click the Submit button, the web browser will usually `POST` that information to the web server, which processes it before sending back the results.

Suppose we create an HTML page that includes a form like this:

```
<html>
<head>
<title>Test form</title>
</head>
<body>
<form action="acceptform.asp" method="POST">
  Enter your first name: <input name="txtFirstName" /><br />
  Enter your last name: <input name="txtLastName" /><br />
  <input type="submit" />
</form>
</body>
</html>
```

This form will `POST` any information to a page called `acceptform.asp`, in the same location as this HTML file, similar to the following:

```
POST /acceptform.asp HTTP/1.1
Accept: */*
Referer: http://www.sernaferna.com/myform.htm
Accept-Language: en-ca
Content-Type: application/x-www-form-urlencoded
Accept-Encoding: gzip, deflate
User-Agent: Mozilla/4.0 (compatible; MSIE 5.5; Windows NT 5.0)
Host: www.sernaferna.com
Content-Length: 33

txtFirstName=John& txtLastName=Doe
```

So, while the `GET` method provides for surfing the Internet, it's the `POST` method that allows for things like e-commerce, since information can be passed back and forth.

As we'll see later in the chapter, the `GET` method can also send information by appending it to the URL, but, in general, `POST` is used wherever possible.

Why HTTP for Web Services?

Earlier we mentioned that most Web services implementations would probably use HTTP as their transport. Why is that? Here are a few reasons:

- HTTP is already a widely implemented, and well understood, protocol.
- The request/response paradigm lends itself to RPC well.

- Most firewalls are already configured to work with HTTP.
- HTTP makes it easy to build in security by using Secure Sockets Layer (SSL).

Widely Implemented

One of the primary reasons for the explosive growth of the Internet was the availability of the World Wide Web, which runs over the HTTP protocol. There are millions of web servers in existence, serving up HTML and other content over HTTP, and many, many companies using HTTP for e-commerce.

HTTP is a relatively easy protocol to implement, which is one of the reasons that the web works as smoothly as it does. If HTTP had been hard to implement, a number of implementers would have probably gotten it wrong, meaning that some web browsers wouldn't have worked with some web servers.

Using HTTP for Web services implementations will therefore be easier than other network protocols would have been. This is especially true because Web services implementations can piggyback on existing web servers; in other words, use their HTTP implementation. This means that you don't have to worry about the HTTP implementation at all.

Request/Response

Most of the time, when a client is making an RPC call, it needs to receive some kind of response. For example, if we make a call to the `getChannels()` method, we would need to get a list of channels back, or it wouldn't be a very useful procedure to call. In other instances, such as submitting a new entry to a topic, we may not need data back from the RPC call, but we may still need confirmation that the procedure executed successfully. For example, if we are submitting an order to a back-end database, there may not be data to return, but we should know whether the submission failed or succeeded.

HTTP's request/response paradigm lends itself easily to this type of situation. For our "add entry" remote procedure, we must do the following;

- Open a connection to the server providing the XML-RPC service
- Send the information on the entry to be added
- Process the addition
- Get back the result, including an error code if it didn't work, and a ping identifier if it did
- Close the connection

In some cases, such as in the SOAP specification, messages are one-way instead of two-way. This would mean that there would have to be two separate messages sent: one from the client to the server with, say, numbers to add, and one from the server back to the client with the result of the calculation. In most cases, however, when a specification requires the use of two one-way messages, it also says that when a request/response protocol, such as HTTP, is used, these two messages can be combined in the request/response of the protocol.

Firewall-Ready

Most companies protect themselves from outside hackers by placing a *firewall* between their internal systems and the external Internet. Firewalls are designed to protect a network by blocking certain types of network traffic. Most firewalls allow HTTP traffic (the type of network traffic which would be generated by browsing the web) but disallow other types of traffic.

These firewalls protect the company's data, but they also make it more difficult to provide web-based services to the outside world. For example, consider a company selling goods over the web. This web-based service would need certain information, such as which items are available in stock, which it would have to get from the company's internal systems. In order to provide this service, the company would probably have to create an environment such as the one shown in Figure 14-3.

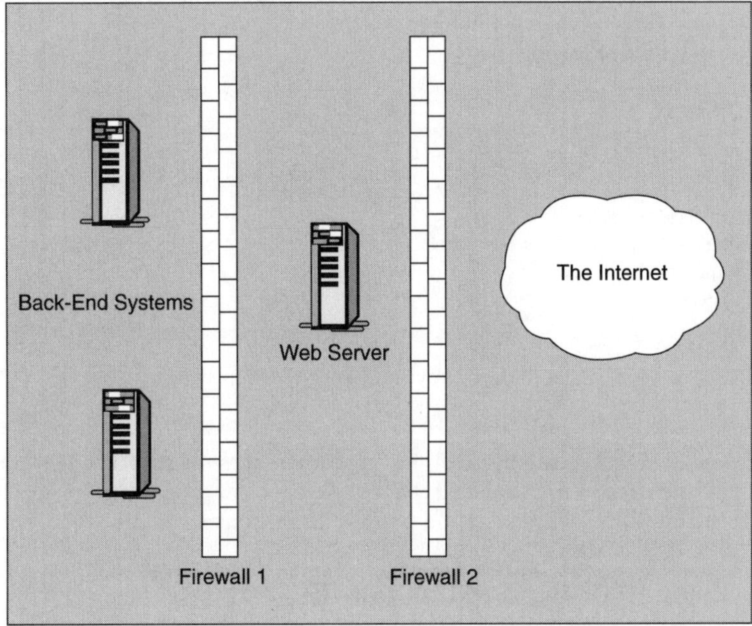

Figure 14-3

This is a very common configuration, in which the web server is placed between two firewalls. (This section, between the two firewalls, is often called a *Demilitarized Zone*, or *DMZ*.) Firewall 1 protects the company's internal systems and must be carefully configured to allow the proper communication between the web server and the internal systems, without letting any other traffic get through. Firewall 2 is configured to let traffic through between the web server and the Internet, but no other traffic.

This arrangement protects the company's internal systems, but because of the complexity added by these firewalls—especially for the communication between the web server and the back-end servers—it makes it a bit more difficult for the developers who are creating this web-based service. However, because firewalls are configured to let HTTP traffic go through, it is much easier to provide the necessary functionality if all of the communication between the web server and the other servers uses this protocol.

Security

Because there is already an existing security model for HTTP, the *Secure Sockets Layer* (SSL), it is very easy to make transactions over HTTP secure. SSL encrypts traffic as it passes over the web to protect it from prying eyes, so it's perfect for web transactions, such as credit card orders. In fact, SSL is so common that there are even hardware accelerators available to speed up SSL transactions.

Using HTTP for XML-RPC

Using HTTP for XML-RPC messages is very easy. There are only two things you need to do with the client:

- For the HTTP method, use `POST`.
- For the body of the message, include an XML document comprising the XML-RPC request.

For example, consider the following:

```
POST /RPC2 HTTP/1.1
Accept: */*
Accept-Language: en-ca
Content-Type: application/x-www-form-urlencoded
Accept-Encoding: gzip, deflate
User-Agent: Mozilla/4.0 (compatible; MSIE 5.5; Windows NT 5.0)
Host: www.sernaferna.com
Content-Length: 79

<methodCall>
    <methodName>topicExchange.getChannels</methodName>
</methodCall>
```

The headers define the request, and the XML-RPC request makes up the body. The server knows how to retrieve that body and process it. In the next chapter, we'll look at processing the actual request, but for now we'll just send an XML-RPC request and process the response.

Try It Out — Using HTTP POST to Call Our RPC

We'll write a simple HTML page to test this. This page will use MSXML to post the information to the Internet Topic Exchange, so it will need IE 5 or higher to run.

1. Enter the following code. Note that the important code, the JavaScript, is highlighted in the following:

```
<html><head><title>POST Tester</title>
  <script language="JavaScript">
function doPost()
{
    var xdDoc, xhHTTP, sXML

    sXML = "<methodCall>"+
           "<methodName>topicExchange.ping</methodName>"+
           "<params><param><value><string>test</string></value></param>"+
           "<param><value><struct>"+
           "<member><name>blog_name</name>"+
                "<value><string>"+pingForm.blog_name.value+"</string></value>"+
           "</member><member><name>title</name>"+
```

```
                "<value><string>"+pingForm.title.value+"</string></value>"+
            "</member><member><name>url</name>"+
                "<value><string>"+pingForm.url.value+"</string></value>"+
            "</member><member><name>excerpt</name>"+
                "<value><string>"+pingForm.excerpt.value+"</string></value>"+
            "</member></struct></value>"+
            "</param></params>"+
            "</methodCall>";

    xdDoc = new ActiveXObject("MSXML.DOMDocument");
    xdDoc.loadXML(sXML);

    xhHTTP = new ActiveXObject("MSXML2.XMLHTTP");
    xhHTTP.open("POST", "http://topicexchange.com/RPC2", false);
    xhHTTP.send(xdDoc);

    xdDoc = xhHTTP.responseXML;

    if(xdDoc.selectSingleNode("//member[name='flError']/value").text == "1")
    {
        var msg = "Error: \n"+
              xdDoc.selectSingleNode("//member[name='message']/value").text;
        alert(msg);
    }
    else
    {
        var msg = "Success! Ping "+
             xdDoc.selectSingleNode("//member[name='pingid']/value").text+
             " successfully added to URL "+
             xdDoc.selectSingleNode("//member[name='topicUrl']/value").text;
        alert(msg);
    }
}
  </script>
  </head>
<body>
  <form name="pingForm" id="pingForm">
  <table width="100%">
    <tr><td>Blog name:</td>
        <td><input id="blog_name" name="blog_name" size="45"></td></tr>
    <tr><td>Post title:</td>
        <td><input id="title" name="title" size="45" ></td></tr>
    <tr><td>Post url:</td>
        <td><input id="url" name="url" size="45"></td></tr>
    <tr><td>Post excerpt:</td>
        <td><textarea rows="6" cols="34" id="excerpt"
               name="excerpt"></textarea></td></tr>
  </table>
  <input type="button" value="Send The Ping" id="btnPost" name="btnPost"
            onclick="doPost()">
  </form>
</body>
</html>
```

2. Save this as `posttester.html`, and then open it up in IE. Fill in the text boxes, with sample information—the actual text doesn't matter, since this is a "test" channel—and click the POST button to perform the POST and get back the results. For example, Figure 14-4 shows a successful result.

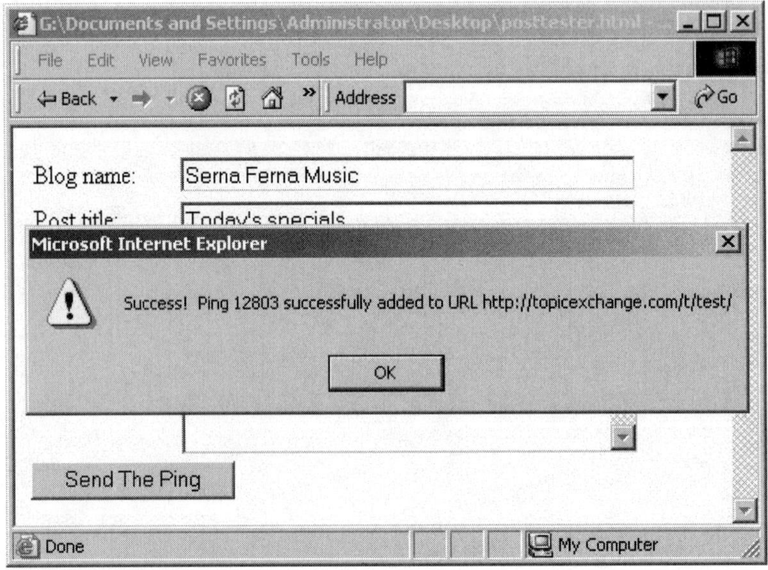

Figure 14-4

If, however, you were to try sending a ping that already existed, you would see the error message shown in Figure 14-5.

How It Works

This example makes use of MSXML's `XMLHTTP` object, which can make HTTP requests. To start, we needed to open the connection, which we did using the following line of code:

```
xhHTTP.open("POST", "http://topicexchange.com/RPC2", false);
```

We passed the following three parameters to the `open()` method:

- The HTTP method we wish to use—in this case, `POST`.
- The URL to which we're sending the request.
- A Boolean parameter, to indicate if this should be an asynchronous operation. We specified `false`, meaning that we want `XMLHTTP` to make the request synchronously.

Next, we called the `send()` method to POST our information, and we passed it a `DOMDocument` object (`xdDoc`) containing our information, pulled from the HTML form and packaged up in XML.

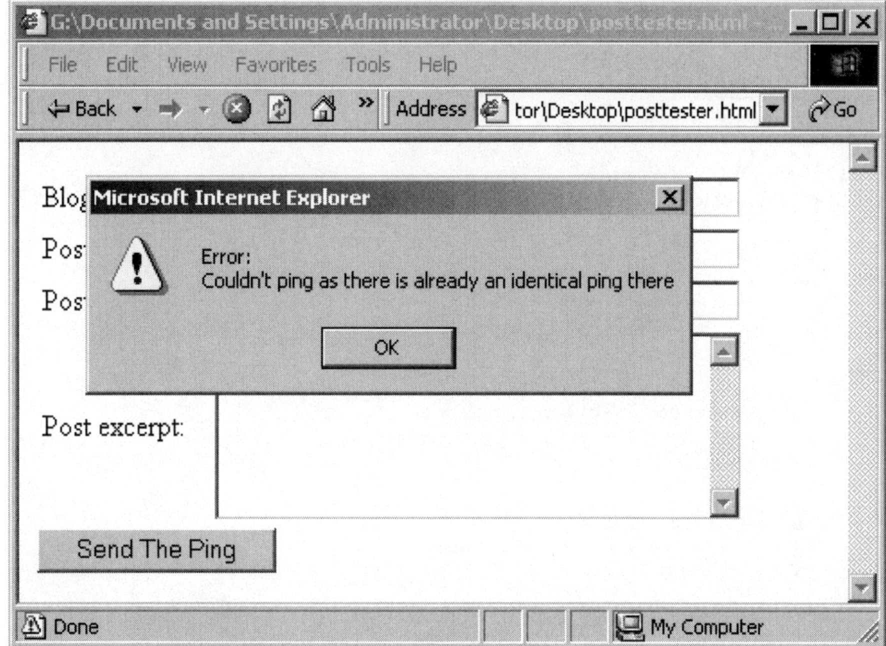

Figure 14-5

Once the `send()` method returned, we pulled the HTTP response from the `responseXML` property, which returns a `DOMDocument`. (There is also a `responseText` property, which would return us the raw text. This text would only include the body of the HTTP response, though, not the headers. In this case, the text would be an XML stream.)

The information is being posted to the server in a format similar to this:

```
POST /RPC2 HTTP/1.1
Accept:*/*
Accept-Language: en-ca
Content-Type: application/x-www-form-urlencoded
Accept-Encoding: gzip, deflate
User-Agent: Mozilla/4.0 (compatible; MSIE 5.5; Windows NT 5.0)
Host: www.sernaferna.com
Content-Length: 649

<methodCall><methodName>topicExchange.ping</methodName><params><param><value>
<string>test</string></value></param><param><value><struct><member>
<name>blog_name</name><value><string>Serna˜Ferna˜Music</string></value>
</member><member><name>title</name><value><string>Today's˜Specials</string>
</value></member><member><name>url</name><value><string>http://www.sernaferna
.com/news/041204.html</string></value></member><member><name>excerpt</name>
<value><string>Serna Ferna music announced some new specials today, including
some never-before-heard artists along with the classics.</string></value>
</member></struct></value></param></params></methodCall>
```

Meanwhile, the information is being returned in a format similar to this:

```
HTTP/1.1 200 OK
Server: Microsoft-IIS/5.0
Date: Fri, 06 Jul 2001 17:48:34 GMT
Content-Length: 48
Content-Type: text/xml

<methodResponse>
  <params>
    <param>
      <value>
        <struct>
          <member>
            <name>topicUrl</name>
            <value><string>http://topicexchange.com/t/test/</string></value>
          </member>
          <member>
            <name>flError</name>
            <value><boolean>0</boolean></value>
          </member>
          <member>
            <name>editkey</name>
            <value><string>cqvq9v20805830945mv0a9w4850239185932850</string>
            </value>
          </member>
          <member>
            <name>errorCode</name>
            <value><int>0</int></value>
          </member>
          <member>
            <name>pingId</name>
            <value><string>12793</string></value>
          </member>
          <member>
            <name>message</name>
            <value><string>New ping added.</string></value>
          </member>
          <member>
            <name>topicName</name>
            <value><string>test</string></value>
          </member>
        </struct>
      </value>
    </param>
  </params>
</methodResponse>
```

So far we have created a system in which messages are passed back and forth, via HTTP POST, in which all of the data is encoded in XML. This is very handy but really only a very small part of the overall picture.

Taking a REST

So far we've been working exclusively with the POST method. Now I'd like to talk about using Web services with the GET method. In fact, I want to say a few words about a Web service that in some circles is not considered a Web service at all. Early in this chapter, I said that technically, a "web service" was any information requested over the web. For example, back in 1996, I built a Java applet that retrieved a calculation from a remote URL. At the time there was no XML involved. The numbers involved in the calculation were simply included as part of the URL, and the response consisted of the result of the calculation. That, in a nutshell, is REST.

Short for *REpresentational State Transfer*, REST is not a specification, but rather an architecture, which asserts that all resources should be directly addressable by URL. For example, our XML-RPC implementation would not be RESTful because we use a single URL for both the `getChannels()` and `ping()` methods; you can't tell the difference between requests just by the URL.

On the other hand, if we were to request an XML document from Amazon.com using the following URL, that would be an example of REST, because all of the necessary information is part of the URL:

```
http://xml.amazon.com/onca/xml3?t=thevanguardsc-20&dev-t=xxxxxxxxxxxxxx&Key
wordSearch=web+services&mode=books&type=lite&page=1&f=xml
```

In fact, many developers who think they're using Web services are actually using REST. Amazon.com provides access to its database and functionality via Web services, but they also allow developers the option to simply include all the relevant information as part of the URL rather than sending a SOAP message. According to some reports, the overwhelming majority of requests to the Amazon API use this method. Now let's try an example and see how this works.

Try It Out Calling a Web Service Using REST

Rather than using POST to execute a Remote Procedure Call, we're going to use GET to request an XML response. In this case, we'll create a simple web page that accepts a topic and returns the number of books Amazon has listed for that particular topic.

1. Start by creating an HTML form to take in the information:

```
<html>
  <head>
      <title>GET Tester</title>
  </head>
  <body>
    <form name="searchForm" id="searchForm">
      <p>
        What topic would you like to research? <br />
        <input id="keyword" name="keyword" size="45">
      </p>
      <input type="button" value="Send The Request">
    </form>
  </body>
</html>
```

2. Next, add the JavaScript that takes the form information and constructs a URL:

```
<html>
  <head>
      <title>GET Tester</title>
  <script language="JavaScript">
function doGet()
{

    var keyword = searchForm.keyword.value;

    sRequest = "http://xml.amazon.com/onca/xml3?t=webservices-20"+
                     "&dev-t=xxxxxxxxxxxxxxxx&KeywordSearch="+keyword+
                     "&mode=books&type=lite&page=1&f=xml";
}
  </script>
  </head>
  <body>
    <form name="searchForm" id="searchForm">
      <p>
        What topic would you like to research? <br />
        <input id="keyword" name="keyword" size="45">
      </p>
      <input type="button" value="Send The Request" onclick="doGet()">
    </form>
 </body>
</html>
```

3. Finally, send the request and analyze the results:

```
<html>
  <head>
      <title>GET Tester</title>
  <script language="JavaScript">
function doGet()
{
    var xdDoc, xhHTTP, sXML

    var keyword = searchForm.keyword.value;

    sRequest = "http://xml.amazon.com/onca/xml3?t=webservices-20"+
                     "&dev-t=xxxxxxxxxxxxxxxx&KeywordSearch="+keyword+
                     "&mode=books&type=lite&page=1&f=xml";

    xdDoc = new ActiveXObject("MSXML.DOMDocument");

    xhHTTP = new ActiveXObject("MSXML2.XMLHTTP");
    xhHTTP.open("GET", sRequest, false);
    xhHTTP.send();

    xdDoc = xhHTTP.responseXML;
    numResults = xdDoc.selectSingleNode("/ProductInfo/TotalResults").text;

    alert("Amazon lists "+numResults+" books on "+keyword+".");
```

```
}
  </script>
  </head>
  <body>
    <form name="searchForm" id="searchForm">
      <p>
        What topic would you like to research? <br />
        <input id="keyword" name="keyword" size="45">
      </p>
      <input type="button" value="Send The Request" onclick="doGet()">
    </form>
  </body>
</html>
```

4. Enter a topic and click the Send The Request button to see the results as shown in Figure 14-6.

Figure 14-6

How It Works

Whereas in the first *Try It Out* we created an XML document to send to the remote Web Service, all we actually have to do here is construct the URL correctly. The URL consists of seven name/value pairs such as `type=lite`, each separated by an ampersand (&). For example, the mode of the search is books. The browser actually pulls the keyword information from the web form and uses it to construct the URL.

In fact, you could construct virtually any request this way. For example, we might have posted to the TopicExchange without creating an XML-RPC message just by calling the URL:

```
http://topicexchange.com/t/music/?blog_name=Serna+Ferna&title=Todays+Specials
&url=http://www.sernaferna.com/news/041204.html&excerpt=Serna+Ferna+music+
today...
```

We didn't do that, however, because it goes against the way the web was designed. `GET` requests are only to be used for requests that have no "side effects." Otherwise, you're supposed to use `POST`. In other words, you can request the number of books Amazon carries using `GET`, but if you're going to actually place an order, use `POST`.

Once we've constructed the URL, we can send it to the server. This process is much the same as a `POST` request, but there is no body sent with the request. The response is a pure XML document—to see it, add the command `alert(xdDoc.text)` to the script—from which we can pull a particular node or nodes.

So is REST a form of Web services? Many (including those who have first espoused REST) would disagree with me, but I say yes. True, you're not sending an XML request, but most of the time you are getting an XML response.

The moral of the story? Be careful when you say "web services." There are plenty of specifications to go around; make sure you know which one you're talking about. In fact, Web-services-related standards abound, so before you go any further into using any of them, you should understand how they fit together.

The Web Services Stack

If you've been having trouble keeping track of all of the Web services-related specifications out there and just how they all fit together, don't feel bad, it's not just you. The fact is that there are literally dozens of specs out there, with a considerable amount of duplication as companies jockey for position in this nascent field. Lately it's gotten so bad that even Don Box, one of the creators of the major Web services protocol, SOAP, commented at a conference that the proliferation in standards has led to a "cacaphony" in the field and that developers should writer fewer specs and more applications.

Not that some standardization isn't necessary, of course. That's the whole purpose of the creation of "web services" as an area of work, to find a way to standardize communications between systems. In this section, I'm going to talk about the major standards you must know in order to implement most Web services systems. I'll then go on to talk about some of the emerging standards and how they all fit together.

SOAP

If you can learn only one Web-services-related protocol, *SOAP* is probably your best bet. Originally conceived as the Simple Object Access Protocol, SOAP has now been adapted for so many different uses that it's been stripped of its acronym.

SOAP is an XML-based language that provides a way for two different systems to exchange information relating to a Remote Procedure Call or other operation. SOAP messages consist of a `Header`, which contains information about the request, and a `Body`, which contains the request itself. Both the `Header` and `Body` are contained within an `Envelope`.

SOAP calls are more robust than, say, XML-RPC calls, because you can use arbitrary XML. This enables you to structure the call in a way that's best for your application. For example, if your application will ultimately need an XML node such as the following:

```
<totals>
  <dept id="2332">
    <gross>433229.03</gross>
```

```
      <net>23272.39</net>
    </dept>
    <dept id="4001">
      <gross>993882.98</gross>
      <net>388209.27</net>
    </dept>
  </totals>
```

then rather than trying to squeeze your data into an arbitrary format such as XML-RPC, you can create a SOAP message such as the following:

```
<?xml version="1.0" encoding="UTF-8"?>
<SOAP:Envelope xmlns:SOAP="http://www.w3.org/2003/05/soap-envelope">

  <SOAP:Header></SOAP:Header>
  <SOAP:Body>

    <totals xmlns="http://www.sernaferna.com/SOAP/accounting">
      <dept id="2332">
        <gross>433229.03</gross>
        <net>23272.39</net>
      </dept>
      <dept id="4001">
        <gross>993882.98</gross>
        <net>388209.27</net>
      </dept>
    </totals>

   </SOAP:Body>
</SOAP:Envelope>
```

SOAP also has the capability to take advantage of technologies such as XML-Signature for security. You can also use attachments with SOAP, so a request could conceivably return, say, a document or other information. In the next chapter, we'll create a complete SOAP server and client, and we'll look at the syntax of a SOAP message.

Of course, this opens up another problem: how do you know what a SOAP request should look like, and what it will return as a result? As we'll see next, WSDL solves that problem.

WSDL

The *Web Services Description Language* (WSDL) is an XML-based language that provides a contract between a Web Service and the outside world. To understand this better, let's go back to our discussion of COM and CORBA.

The reason that COM and CORBA objects can be so readily shared is that they have defined contracts with the outside world. This contract defines the methods an object provides, as well as the parameters to those methods and their return values. Interfaces for both COM and CORBA are written in variants of the *Interface Definition Language* (IDL). Code can then be written to look at an object's interface and figure out what functions are provided. In practice, this dynamic investigation of an object's interface often happens at design time, as a programmer is writing the code that calls another object. A programmer would find out what interface an object supports and then write code that properly calls that interface.

Web services have a similar contract with the outside world, except that the contract is written in WSDL, instead of IDL. This WSDL document outlines what messages this SOAP server expects in order to provide services, as well as what messages it returns. Again, in practice, WSDL would probably be used at design time. A programmer would use WSDL to figure out what procedures are available from the SOAP server and what format of XML is expected by that procedure, and then write the code to call it.

Or, to take things a step further, programmers might never have to look at WSDL directly or even deal with the underlying SOAP protocol. There are already a number of SOAP toolkits available, which can hide the complexities of SOAP from us. If we point one of these toolkits at a WSDL document, it can automatically generate code to make the SOAP call for us! At that point, working with SOAP is as easy as calling any other local object on your machine.

> *Two popular SOAP toolkits are the Web Services Toolkit from IBM, available from their developerWorks website (`http://www.ibm.com/developerworks`), and the SOAP Toolkit from Microsoft, available from their Microsoft Developer Network website (`http://msdn.microsoft.com`).*

In the next chapter, we'll look at the syntax for a WSDL document. But once you've built it, how do you let others know that it's out there? Enter UDDI.

UDDI

The *Universal Discovery, Description, and Integration* protocol (UDDI) allows Web services to be registered so that they can be discovered by programmers and other Web services.

For example, if I'm going to create a Web Service that serves a particular function, such as providing up-to-the-minute traffic reports by GPS coordinates, I can register that service with a UDDI registry. The global UDDI registry system consists of a number of different servers that all mirror each other, so by registering your company with one, you add it to all the others.

The advantage of registering with the UDDI registry is twofold. First, your company's contact information is available, so if another company is going to do business with you, it can use the "white pages" type of lookup to get the necessary contact information. A company's listing not only includes the typical name, phone number, and address type of information, but also information on the services available. For example, it might include a link to a WSDL file that describes the traffic reporting system.

The UDDI registry system also enables companies to find each other based on the types of Web services they offer. This is called a "green pages" type of listing. For example, you could use the green pages to find a company that uses Web services to take orders for widgets. The listing would also include information on what the widget order request should look like and the structure of the order confirmation, or at the very least, a link to that information.

Many of the SOAP toolkits available, such as IBM's Web Services Toolkit, provide tools to work with UDDI.

Surrounding Specifications

So far we've described a landscape in which you can use a UDDI registry to discover a Web Service for which a WSDL file describes the SOAP messages used by the service. For all practical purposes, you could stop right there, because you have all of the pieces that are absolutely necessary, but as you start building your applications, you will discover there are other issues that need to be addressed.

For example, just because a Web Service might be built using such specifications as SOAP and WSDL doesn't mean that your client is going to flawlessly interact with it. Interoperability continues to be a challenge between systems, from locating the appropriate resource to making sure types are correctly implemented. Numerous specifications have emerged in an attempt to choreograph the increasingly complex dance web between service providers and consumers. Finally, any activity that involves business eventually needs security.

In this section, we'll look at some of the many specifications that have been working their way into the marketplace. Only time will tell which will survive and which will ultimately wither, but it helps to understand what's out there and how it all fits together.

Interoperability

At the time of this writing, the big name in interoperability is the Web Services Interoperability Organization, or WS-I (`http://www.ws-i.org`). This industry group includes companies such as IBM, Microsoft, and Sun Microsystems, and the purpose of the organization is to define specific "profiles" for Web services and provide testing tools so that companies can be certain that their implementations don't contain any hidden "gotchas." WS-I has released a Basic Profile as well as a number of use cases and sample implementations.

Some other interoperability-related specifications include the following:

- WS-Addressing (`http://msdn.microsoft.com/ws/2003/03/ws-addressing/`), provides a way to specify the "location" of a Web Service. Remember, we're not always talking about HTTP. W-Addressing defines an XML document that tells you how to "find" a service, no matter how many firewalls, proxies, or other devices and gateways lie between you and that service.
- WS Inspection Language, or WSIL (`http://www-106.ibm.com/developerworks/webservices/library/ws-wsilspec.html`), provides a way for you to specify what Web services you have available and where developers can find information. For example, you might have published specifications as XML on your website. WSIL tells you how to let people know where they are.
- WS-Eventing (`http://msdn.microsoft.com/webservices/understanding/specs/default.aspx?pull=/library/en-us/dnglobspec/html/ws-eventing.asp`) and WS-Notification (`http://www-106.ibm.com/developerworks/library/specification/ws-notification/`), both describe protocols that involve a publish/subscribe pattern, in which Web services subscribe to or provide event notifications.

Coordination

For a while, it looked like the winner in the coordination and choreography space was going to be ebXML (`http://www.ebxml.org`), a Web services version of Electronic Data Interchange (EDI), in which companies become "trading partners" and define their interactions individually. ebXML consists of a number of different modules specifying the ways in which businesses can define not only what information they're looking for and the form it should take, but the types of messages that should be sent from a multiple-step process. Although ebXML is very specific and seems to work well in the arena for which it was designed, it doesn't necessarily generalize well in order to cover Web services outside the EDI realm.

As such, Business Process Execution Language for Web Services (BPEL4WS) (`http://msdn.microsoft.com/library/default.asp?url=/library/en-us/dnbiz2k2/html/bpel1-0.asp`) has been proposed by a coalition of companies, including Microsoft and IBM. BPEL4WS defines a notation for specifying business process ultimately implemented as Web services. Business processes fall into two categories: *executable business processes* and *business protocols*. Executable business processes are actual actions performed in an interaction, while business protocols describe the effects (for example, orders placed) without specifying how they're actually accomplished. When BPEL4WS was introduced in 2002, it wasn't under the watchful eye of any standards body, which was a concern for many developers, so work is currently ongoing within the Web Services Business Process Execution Language (WS-BPEL) (`http://www.oasis-open.org/committees/tc_home.php?wg_abbrev=wsbpel`) group at the OASIS standards body.

Not to be outdone, the World Wide Web Consortium has opened the WS-Choreography (`http://www.w3.org/2002/ws/chor/`) activity, which is developing a way for companies to describe their interactions with trading partners. In other words, they're not actually defining how data gets exchanged, but rather the language to describe how data gets exchanged. In fact, Choreography Definition Language is one of the group's deliverables.

In the meantime, Microsoft, IBM, and BEA are also proposing WS-Coordination (`http://www-106.ibm.com/developerworks/library/ws-coor/`), which is also intended to provide a way to describe these interactions. This specification also involves the WS-AtomicTransaction specification for describing individual components of a transaction.

Security

Given its importance, perhaps it should come as no surprise that security is another area that is hotly contested at the time of this writing. In addition to the basic specifications set out by the World Wide Web Consortium, such as XML Encryption (`http://www.w3.org/Encryption/2001/`) and XML Signature (`http://www.w3.org/Signature/`), the industry is currently working on standards for identity recognition, reliable messaging, and overall security policies.

Both the Liberty Alliance (`http://www.projectliberty.org`), which includes Sun Microsystems, and WS-Federation (Web Services Federation Language) (`http://www-106.ibm.com/developerworks/webservices/library/ws-fedworld/`) espoused by IBM and Microsoft are trying to specify a means for creating a "federated identity." In other words, you should be able to sign on to one site with your username and password, smart card, fingerprint, or any other form of identification, and be recognized wherever you go, even if it's to another site and another application.

Perhaps the most confusing competition is between WS Reliable Messaging (`http://www.oasis-open.org/committees/tc_home.php?wg_abbrev=wsrm`) and WS-ReliableMessaging (`http://www-106.ibm.com/developerworks/webservices/library/ws-rm/`). In essence, both specifications are trying to describe a protocol for reliably delivering messages between distributed applications within a particular tolerance, or Quality of Service. These specifications deal with message order, retransmission, and ensuring that both parties to a transaction are aware of whether or not a message has been successfully received.

Two other specifications to consider are WS-Security and WS-Policy.

- WS-Security (`http://www-106.ibm.com/developerworks/webservices/library/ws-secure/`) is designed to provide enhancements to SOAP that make it easier to control issues such as message integrity, message confidentiality, and authentication, no matter what security model or encryption method you use.
- WS-Policy (`http://www-106.ibm.com/developerworks/webservices/library/ws-polfram/`) is a specification meant to help people writing other specifications, and it provides a way to specify the "requirements, preferences, and capabilities" of a Web Service.

Summary

In this chapter, we have looked at Web services, a group of XML-based protocols for performing remote procedure calls. We have studied how Web services can be used, and even put them into practice by creating an XML-RPC client using the Internet Explorer browser.

Because Web services are based on easy-to-implement and standardized technologies such as XML and HTTP, they have the potential to become a universal tool. In fact, most of the hype surrounding Web services concerns its interoperability. At least initially, companies providing Web services software are concentrating on making their software as interoperable as possible with the software from other companies, instead of creating proprietary changes to the standards, but they're also creating a good number of new standards.

In general, Web services are XML messages sent as the body of an HTTP `POST` request. The response is XML, which we can then analyze. We can also request a Web services response via an HTTP `GET` request. For any level more complex than that, standards are still being shaken out.

In the next chapter, we'll take a deeper look at two of the most important Web services specifications, SOAP and WSDL.

Exercise Questions

Suggested solutions to these questions can be found in Appendix A.

Question 1

Imagine you are trying to contact an XML-RPC-based Web Service to submit a classified ad for a lost dog. The required information includes your name, phone number, and the body of the ad. What might the XML request look like?

Question 2

You are trying to call a REST-based Web Service to check on the status of a service order. The service needs the following information:

```
cust_id: 3263827
order_id: THX1138
```

What might the request look like?

SOAP and WSDL

In the last chapter, we talked about Web services and examined an overall view of how they work toward enabling disparate systems to communicate. Of course, if everyone just chose their own formats in which to send messages back and forth, that wouldn't do much good in the interoperability area, so a standard format is a must. XML-RPC is good for remote procedure calls, but it's limited in what you can do with it. SOAP overcomes that problem by enabling rich XML documents to be transferred easily between systems, even allowing for the possibility of attachments. Of course, this flexibility means that you'll need a way to describe your SOAP messages, and that's where Web Services Description Language comes in (WSDL). WSDL provides a standard way of describing where and how to make requests to a SOAP-based service.

In this chapter we'll take our examinations a step further. First, we'll create a simple Web service using a method called REST (which was covered in the previous chapter), and then we'll expand our horizons by creating a SOAP service and accessing it via SOAP messages. We'll then look at describing it using WSDL so that other developers can make use of it if desired.

In this chapter we'll learn:

- Why SOAP can provide more flexibility than previous RPC protocols
- How to format SOAP messages
- When to use GET versus POST in an HTTP request
- What are SOAP intermediaries
- How to describe a service using WSDL
- The difference between SOAP styles

Laying the Groundwork

Any Web services project requires planning, so before we jump into installing software and creating files, let's take a moment to look at what we're trying to accomplish. Ultimately, we want to look at sending and receiving SOAP messages, and describing them using WSDL. To do that, we'll need to have the following in place:

- The client. In the last chapter, we created an XML-RPC client in Internet Explorer. In this chapter we'll use a lot of the same techniques to create a SOAP client.
- The server. We're going to create two kinds of SOAP services in this chapter, and they'll both use Active Server Pages. Because of differences in what various systems can run, we'll look at both "classic" ASP and at ASP.NET, but the idea is to show you the mechanics of a Web service, and not to teach you how to use one particular language.

In order to run some of the examples in this chapter, you will need *Internet Information Server* (IIS), or *Personal Web Server* (PWS) installed on your machine. The good news is that if you're running most modern versions of Windows, you can install one or the other for free. PWS is fine for testing and for internal intranet websites, but it's definitely not suitable for high-use Internet websites as it's not robust or secure enough. However, it is great for developing a server-side script before deploying it to IIS, the full Windows web server. The version you choose also depends on what operating system you're running.

Running Examples in Windows 2003, XP, and 2000

The steps needed to install a web server on Windows depend on which operating system is being used. A version of IIS comes with Windows 2003, Windows XP Professional Edition, and Windows 2000. In most cases, it will be installed by default, but if it's not, you'll need to go to Control Panel, Add/Remove programs, and select Add/Remove Windows Components, under which you'll find the option to install Internet Information Services (IIS).

Unfortunately, IIS doesn't come with Windows XP Home Edition, and neither IIS nor PWS can be installed on it. (See the section under *Other Operating Systems* a little later in this chapter if you still want to run the examples.)

Running Examples in Windows NT and Windows 95

Windows NT 4 Server and Workstation users already have a version of IIS installed, but if your machine still has the preinstalled version, you will need to upgrade it by installing the *NT Option Pack*. For Windows NT 4 Server users, this installs the full IIS server version, while Workstation and Windows 95 users will have the PWS version installed. The NT Option pack can be obtained both on the Windows NT CD and from the Microsoft website at `http://www.microsoft.com/ntserver/nts/downloads/recommended/NT4OptPk/default.asp`.

Next, we'll look at all the steps necessary to install PWS on a Windows 98 machine. You should find that most of the steps are similar on other versions of Windows, with just a few minor variations.

Running Examples in Windows 98

For Windows 98 users, the setup files for PWS are on the Windows 98 CD in the directory `\add-ons\pws\`. We need to copy these files from the PWS directory on the CD to the local hard drive—the `C:\Temp` directory would be a good place.

Due to changes in Windows 98 operating system, one of the files, `MtsSetup.dll`, is out-of-date and needs to be replaced with one downloaded from the Microsoft website. (This step only needs to be performed for Windows 98 users.) This file can be downloaded from: `http://download.microsoft.com/download/transaction/Patch/1/W95/EN-US/Mtssetup.exe`.

Save the executable file to your hard drive in the `C:\Temp` directory, and then run it. First, the license agreement will appear. Read it, and if you agree, click Yes to start the install.

Next, in the text box that appears, as shown in Figure 15-1, either enter or browse to the directory into which the PWS directory was copied from the CD, and then click OK.

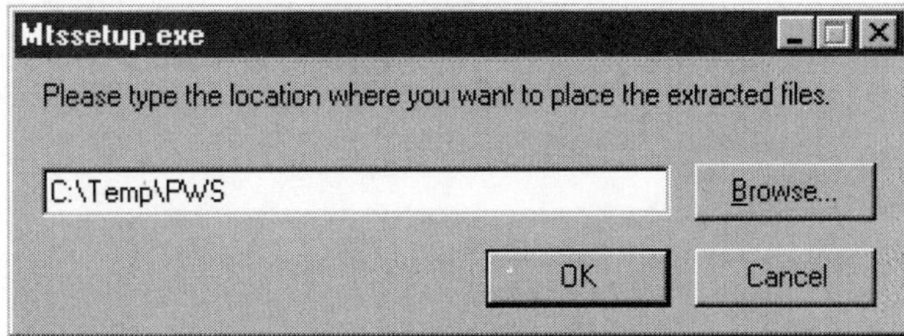

Figure 15-1

When the box shown in Figure 15-2 pops up asking if you want to overwrite the existing `Mtssetup.dll` file with the new one you just downloaded, click Yes.

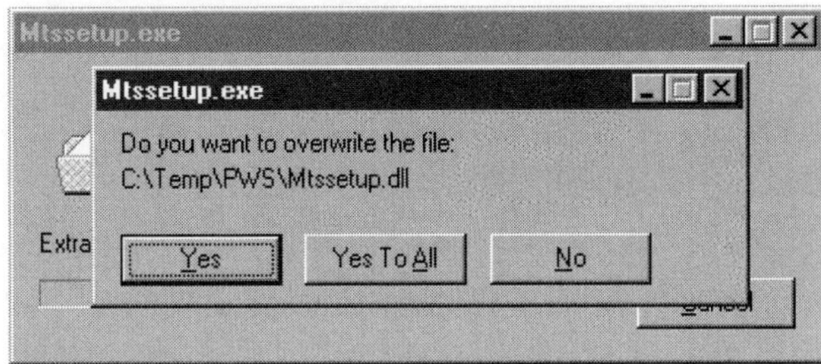

Figure 15-2

That completes the update. Now we can start the PWS installation process by running `setup.exe` in `C:\Temp\PWS` from Run on the Start menu.

You should then see an introductory screen. Click the Next button and you'll be given a choice of whether you want a Minimum, Typical or Custom install. Unless hard drive space is at a premium (that is, you have less than 50MB free), then go for the Typical install, which requires about 32MB of hard drive space.

In the next screen (see Figure 15-3), you can choose the directory where the web directories and web pages for the server will be stored. The default directory is fine unless you have limited space on your `C:` drive, in which case any hard drive is acceptable. Once you've selected the directory, click Next and the PWS installation will commence.

Once the install has finished, click Finish and restart the computer.

Running Examples in the .NET Framework

If you are using Windows 2003, you have the .NET Framework built in to your operating system, and if you are using Windows NT or later, you have the option to install it. The .NET Framework changes the way that Active Server Pages work.

If you choose to install it, you can download the .NET Framework Redistributable from `http://www.asp.net/download.aspx?tabindex=0&tabid=1`. Installing according to the instructions configures IIS to run ASP.NET pages.

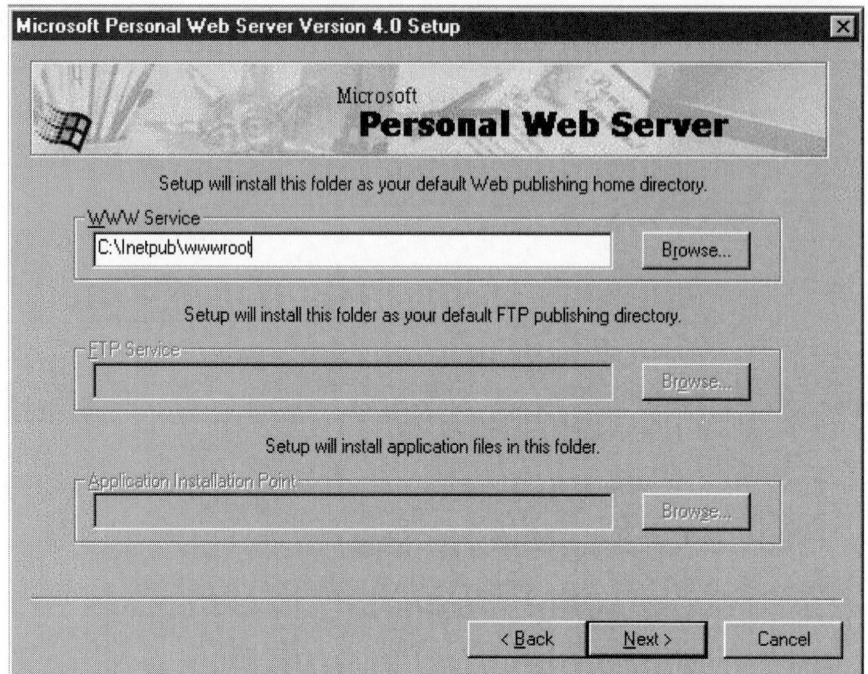

Figure 15-3

Because this chapter is about SOAP and WSDL, we won't talk about it, but .NET does simplify the creation of Web services by providing a layer of abstraction between you and the actual code. For more on how XML and .NET can work together, see Chapter 20.

Running Examples in Other Operating Systems

If you're using an operating system for which PWS and IIS are unavailable (such as Linux, for example), you have two options. Your first option is to check out Mono, an open-source version of the .NET Framework designed to work on other operating systems. (See `http://www.go-mono.com/` for more information.) You can also purchase a product, such as Java System Active Server Pages (formerly Chilisoft ASP), in order to add support for Active Server Pages and work the examples as you go. If that's not your style, however, you can just go ahead and use whatever language is comfortable for you. The concepts are fairly simple, so any environment, such as Java Servlets or a Perl script, will work. Hooray for interoperability!

The New RPC Protocol: SOAP

According to the current SOAP specification, SOAP is "a lightweight protocol for exchange of information in a decentralized, distributed environment." In other words, it is a standard way to send information from one computer to another using XML to represent the information.

At the time of writing, you can find information on the current version of SOAP, SOAP 1.2, at `http://www.w3.org/2000/xp/Group/`.

In a nutshell, the SOAP specification defines a protocol where all information sent from computer to computer is marked up in XML, with the information transmitted via HTTP in most cases.

Technically, SOAP messages don't have to be sent via HTTP. Any networking protocol, such as SMTP or FTP, could be used. However, for the reasons we discussed in the last chapter, in practice, HTTP will probably continue to be the most common protocol used for SOAP for some time.

Let's take a look at some of the advantages of SOAP over other protocols such as DCOM or Java RMI:

- It's platform-, language-, and vendor-neutral. Because SOAP is implemented using XML and (usually) HTTP, it is easy to process and send SOAP requests in any language, on any platform, without having to depend on tools from a particular vendor.
- It's easy to implement. SOAP was designed to be less complex than the other protocols. Even if it has gotten away from that a bit in recent years, a SOAP server can still be implemented using nothing more than a web server and an ASP page or a CGI script.
- It's firewall-safe. Assuming that you use HTTP as your network protocol, you can pass SOAP messages across a firewall without having to perform extensive configuration.

In this chapter, we'll look at creating part of a hypothetical music order service.

Try It Out — Creating an RPC Server in ASP

Before we start creating SOAP messages, we need to look at the process of creating an RPC server that receives a request and sends back a response. I've chosen to start with a fairly simple procedure to write: one that takes a unit price and quantity and returns the appropriate discount along with the total price.

To start with, we're going to create a simple ASP page that accepts two numbers, evaluates them, and returns the results in XML.

1. To begin with, we need to create our ASP page. Call the page `updateTotal1.asp`.

   This page pulls information from the *query string*. This is the information that is appended to the end of a URL. For example, in the URL `http://localhost/SOAP/updateTotal1.asp?quantity=12&unitPrice=14.99`, the URL itself is `http://localhost/SOAP/updateTotal1.asp`, while `?quantity=12& unitPrice=14.99` is the query string. The ASP object model makes getting this information easy. The main code for the page will be as follows:

```
Response.ContentType = "text/xml"

Dim quantity, unitPrice
Dim discount, extPrice

On Error Resume Next

quantity = Request.QueryString.Item("quantity")
unitPrice = Request.QueryString.Item("unitPrice")

discount = QuantityDiscount(quantity)
extPrice = (CDbl(quantity) * CDbl(unitPrice))*(1 - (discount/100))
```

```
If Err.number <> 0 Then
   Response.Write (ErrorXML())
Else
   Response.Write (SuccessXML(discount, extPrice))
End If
```

We've set the content type of our result to `text/xml`, which indicates to the browser calling this page that the results are XML. We've then pulled the information from the query string and stored it in a pair of variables (`quantity` and `unitPrice`). Finally, we retrieved any quantity discount and calculated the final price, checking to make sure that there is no error.

If there is an error, we call a function called `ErrorXML()`, and send the results to the output. Otherwise, we call a function called `SuccessXML()`, passing it the results of our calculations, and send that to the output.

2. Finally, we just need to add the three functions, `QuantityDiscount()`, `ErrorXML()`, and `SucessXML()` as shown in the following:

```
Function QuantityDiscount(quantity)
    'For the sake of the example, just return a fixed amount
    QuantityDiscount = 10
End Function

Function ErrorXML()
   Dim sXML

   sXML = "<Error><Reason>Invalid numbers</Reason></Error>"

   ErrorXML = sXML
End Function

Function SuccessXML(sDiscount, sExtprice)
   Dim sXML

   sXML = "<updateTotalResponse>" & vbNewLine
   sXML = sXML & " <discount>" & sDiscount & "</discount>" & vbNewLine
   sXML = sXML & " <extPrice>" & sExtprice & "</extPrice>" & vbNewLine
   sXML = sXML & "</updateTotalResponse>"

   SuccessXML = sXML
End Function
```

3. Our final ASP page will look like this:

```
<%@ Language="VBScript" %>
<%
Response.ContentType = "text/xml"

Dim quantity, unitPrice
Dim discount, extPrice

On Error Resume Next

quantity = Request.QueryString.Item("quantity")
```

```
unitPrice = Request.QueryString.Item("unitPrice")

discount = QuantityDiscount(quantity)
extPrice = (CDbl(quantity) * CDbl(unitPrice))*(1 - (discount/100))

If Err.number <> 0 Then
   Response.Write (ErrorXML())
Else
   Response.Write (SuccessXML(discount, extPrice))
End If

Function QuantityDiscount(quantity)
    'For the sake of the example, just return a fixed amount
    QuantityDiscount = 10
End Function

Function ErrorXML()
   Dim sXML

   sXML = "<Error><Reason>Invalid numbers</Reason></Error>"

   ErrorXML = sXML
End Function

Function SuccessXML(sDiscount, sExtprice)
   Dim sXML

   sXML = "<updateTotalResponse>" & vbNewLine
   sXML = sXML & "    <discount>" & sDiscount & "</discount>" & vbNewLine
   sXML = sXML & "    <extPrice>" & sExtprice & "</extPrice>" & vbNewLine
   sXML = sXML & "    </updateTotalResponse>"

   SuccessXML = sXML
End Function
%>
```

If you're using ASP.NET, you'll want to make two small changes. First of all, save the page as `updateTotal1.aspx` rather than `updateTotal1.asp`. Second, use VB syntax rather than VBScript syntax. The page should look like this:

```
<script language="VB" runat="server">
Sub Page_Load(Src As Object, E As EventArgs)

Response.ContentType = "text/xml"

Dim quantity, unitPrice
Dim discount, extPrice

On Error Resume Next

quantity = Request.QueryString.Item("quantity")
unitPrice = Request.QueryString.Item("unitPrice")

discount = QuantityDiscount(quantity)
```

```
extPrice = (CDbl(quantity) * CDbl(unitPrice))*(1 - (discount/100))

If Err.number <> 0 Then
   Response.Write (ErrorXML())
Else
   Response.Write (SuccessXML(discount, extPrice))
End If

End Sub

Function QuantityDiscount(quantity)
   'For the sake of the example, just return a fixed amount
   QuantityDiscount = 10
End Function

Function ErrorXML()
   Dim sXML

   sXML = "<Error><Reason>Invalid numbers</Reason></Error>"

   ErrorXML = sXML
End Function

Function SuccessXML(sDiscount, sExtprice)
   Dim sXML

   sXML = "<updateTotalResponse>" & vbNewLine
   sXML = sXML & " <discount>" & sDiscount & "</discount>" & vbNewLine
   sXML = sXML & " <extPrice>" & sExtprice & "</extPrice>" & vbNewLine
   sXML = sXML & "</updateTotalResponse>"

   SuccessXML = sXML
End Function

</script>
```

4. To try this page out, open a browser and type in the URL, appending the query string `?quantity=5&itemid=Item1&unitPrice=54`. For example, on my machine that URL is the one shown earlier: `http://localhost/SOAP/updateTotal1.asp?quantity=5&unit Price=54`, since the `updateTotal1.asp` file is in a `SOAP` subdirectory of my `InetPub/www root` directory, which is where the web server looks for web files. (If you're using ASP.NET, don't forget to use `updateTotal1.aspx` instead of `updateTotal1.asp`.) On your machine the URL might be slightly different, but the query string will be the same. In your browser, the results should look like Figure 15-4.

5. Now let's try it again, but this time we'll pass a nonnumeric value for one of the variables we're passing. For example, if we use `http://localhost/SOAP/updateTotal1.asp?quantity =5&unitPrice=bogus`, we will get the following results as shown in Figure 15-5. (The actual value doesn't matter, as long as it's nonnumeric so that it causes an error.)

How It Works

This page pulls two values from the query string, casts them as numbers, and performs two actions. First, it requests a quantity discount from a function, and then the page multiplies the two original numbers

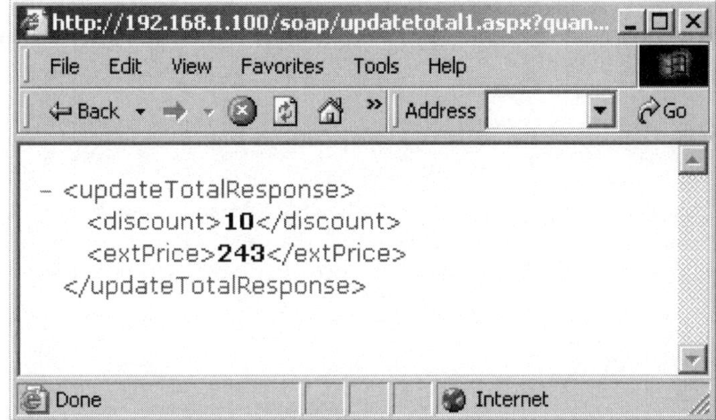

Figure 15-4

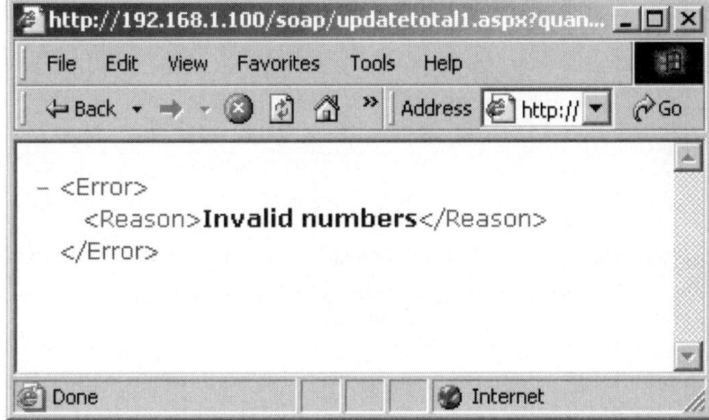

Figure 15-5

together. It finally returns the results as XML. If either of the two values isn't numeric, meaning that they can't be multiplied together, a different XML document is written back to the client, indicating that there was a problem.

Note that this ASP page isn't limited to being called from a browser. For example, we could load the XML directly and then retrieve the numbers from it, as in this VB.NET example:

```
Sub Main()
    Dim xdDoc As System.Xml.XmlDocument = new System.Xml.XmlDocument()

    xdDoc.Load ("http://localhost/soap/updatetotal1.aspx?quantity=5&unitPrice=54")

    If xdDoc.documentElement.name = "Error" Then
        MsgBox ("Unable to perform calculation")
    Else
        MsgBox (xdDoc.selectSingleNode("/updateTotalResponse/extPrice"))
    End If
End Sub
```

We pass a URL, including the query string, to the `Load()` method, and then check the results. If the root element is named `Error`, then we know something went wrong. Otherwise, we can get the results out of our XML.

Just RESTing

Technically speaking, what we just did isn't actually a SOAP transaction, but not for the reasons you might think. The issue isn't that we sent a URL rather than a SOAP message in order to make the request; SOAP actually defines just such a transaction. The problem is the fact that the response wasn't actually a SOAP message.

Let's take a look at the output:

```
<updateTotalResponse>
  <discount>10</discount>
  <extPrice>243</extPrice>
</updateTotalResponse>
```

This is a perfectly well-formed XML message, but it doesn't conform to the structure of a SOAP message. A SOAP message, as we'll see in the next section, consists of an `Envelope` element that contains a `Header` and `Body`. If this were a SOAP message, the XML we see here would have been contained in the SOAP `Body`.

So why did we just go through all that? We did it because for one thing, this is still a perfectly valid way of creating a Web service. Known as *REpresentational State Transfer* (REST), it's based on the idea that any piece of information on the World Wide Web should be addressable via a URL. In this case, that URL included a query string with parameter information.

REST is growing in popularity as people discover that it is, in many ways, much easier to use than SOAP. After all, you don't have to create an outgoing XML message, and you don't have to figure out how to POST it, as we saw in the previous chapter.

All of this begs the question: if REST is so much easier, why use SOAP at all? Aside from the fact that in some cases the request data is difficult or impossible to provide as a URL, the answer lies in the fundamental architecture of the web. We submitted this request as a `GET`, which means that any parameters were part of the URL and not the body of the message. If we were to remain true to the way the Web is supposed to be constructed, `GET` requests are only for actions that have no "side effects," such as making changes to a database. That means that we can use this method for getting information, but we couldn't use it for, say, placing an order, because the act of making that request changes something on the server.

When SOAP was still growing in popularity, some developers insisted that REST was somehow better because it was simpler. SOAP 1.2 ends the controversy by adopting a somewhat RESTful stance, making it possible to use an HTTP `GET` request to send information and parameters and get a SOAP response. Before we see that in action, though, we should look at how SOAP itself works.

Basic SOAP Messages

As we mentioned before, SOAP messages are basically XML documents, usually sent across HTTP. SOAP specifies the following:

- Rules on how the message should be sent. Although the SOAP specification says that any network protocol can be used, there are specific rules included in the specification for HTTP, as that's the protocol most people use.
- The overall structure of the XML that is sent. This is called the *envelope*. Any information to be sent back and forth over SOAP is contained within this envelope, and is known as the *payload*.
- Rules on how data is represented in this XML. These are called the *encoding rules*.

When we send data to a SOAP server, the data must be represented in a particular way, so that the server will be able to understand it. The SOAP 1.2 specification outlines a simple XML document type, which is used for all SOAP messages. The basic structure of that document is as follows:

```
<env:Envelope xmlns:env="http://www.w3.org/2003/05/soap-envelope">
  <env:Header>
    <head-ns:someHeaderElem xmlns:head-ns="some URI"
                            env:mustUnderstand="true|false"
                            env:relay="true|false"
                            env:role="some URI"/>
  </env:Header>
  <env:Body encodingStyle="http://www.w3.org/2003/05/soap-encoding">
    <some-ns:someElem xmlns:some-ns="some URI"/>
    <!-- OR -->
    <env:Fault>
     <env:Code>
       <env:Value>Specified values</env:Value>
       <env:Subcode>
         <env:Value>Specified values</env:Value>
       </env:Subcode>
     </env:Code>
     <env:Reason>
       <env:Text xml:lang="en-US">English text</env:Text>
       <env:Text xml:lang="fr">Texte français</env:Text>
     </env:Reason>
     <env:Detail>
       <!-- Application specific information -->
     </env:Detail>
    </env:Fault>
  </env:Body>
</env:Envelope>
```

As you can see, there aren't a lot of elements involved in a SOAP message itself, unless something goes wrong. There are three main elements, `<Envelope>`, `<Header>`, and `<Body>`, and starting in version 1.2, of SOAP, a number of error-related elements. Of these elements, only `<Envelope>` and `<Body>` are mandatory; `<Header>` is optional, and `<Fault>` and its child elements are only required when an error occurs. In addition, all of the attributes (`encodingStyle`, `mustUnderstand`, and so on) are optional.

<Envelope>

Other than the fact that it resides in SOAP's envelope namespace, `http://www.w3.org/2003/05/soap-envelope`, the `<Envelope>` element doesn't really need any explanation. It simply provides the root element for the XML document and is usually used to include any namespace declarations. The next couple of sections will talk about the other elements available, as well as the various attributes.

<Body>

The <Body> element contains the main body of the SOAP message. The actual RPC calls are made using direct children of the <Body> element (which are called *body blocks*). For example, consider the following:

```
<env:Envelope xmlns:env="http://www.w3.org/2003/05/soap-envelope">
    <env:Body>
        <o:addToCart xmlns="http://www.sernaferna.com/soap/ordersystem">
            <o:cartid>THX1138</cartid>
            <o:item>ZIBKA</o:item>
            <o:quantity>3</o:quantity>
            <o:extPrice>34.97</o:extPrice>
        </o:addToCart>
    </env:Body>

</env:Envelope>
```

In this case, we're making one RPC call, to a procedure called `addToCart`, in the `http://www.sernaferna.com/soap/ordersystem` namespace. (You can add multiple calls to a single message, if necessary.) The `addToCart` procedure takes four parameters, `cartid`, `item`, `quantity`, and `extPrice`. Direct child elements of the <Body> element must reside in a namespace other than the SOAP namespace. This namespace is what the SOAP server will use to uniquely identify this procedure, so that it knows what code to run. When the procedure is done running, the server uses the HTTP response to send back a SOAP message. The <Body> of that message might look similar to this:

```
<env:Envelope xmlns:env='http://www.w3.org/2003/05/soap-envelope'>

  <env:Body>
    <o:addToCartResponse xmlns:o='http://www.sernaferna.com/soap/ordersystem'>
      <o:cartid>THX1138</o:cartid>
      <o:status>OK</o:status>
      <o:quantity>3</o:quantity>
      <o:itemid>ZIBKA</o:itemid>
      </so:addToCartResponse>
    </env:Body>

</env:Envelope>
```

That is, the response is just another SOAP message, using an XML structure similar to the request, in that it has a Body in an Envelope, with the relevant information included as the payload.

Encoding Style

Before moving on I'd like to say a few words about encoding. Usually, in the realm of XML, when we talk about encoding, we're talking about esoteric aspects of passing text around, but in the SOAP world, encoding is pretty straightforward. It simply refers to the way in which you're representing the data. In our examples, we'll be using the SOAP style encoding, which means we're using plain old elements and text, with maybe an attribute or two thrown in. We can let an application know that's what we're doing by adding the optional encodingStyle attribute, as shown in the following example:

```
<env:Envelope xmlns:env='http://www.w3.org/2003/05/soap-envelope'>

  <env:Body env:encodingStyle="http://www.w3.org/2003/05/soap-encoding">
    <o:addToCartResponse xmlns:o='http://www.sernaferna.com/soap/ordersystem'>
      <o:cartid>THX1138</o:cartid>
      <o:status>OK</o:status>
      <o:quantity>3</o:quantity>
      <o:itemid>ZIBKA</o:itemid>
    </o:addToCartResponse>
  </env:Body>

</env:Envelope>
```

This is to distinguish it from other encodings, such as RDF, shown in the following:

```
<env:Envelope xmlns:env='http://www.w3.org/2003/05/soap-envelope'>
  <env:Body>
    <rdf:RDF xmlns:rdf="http://www.w3.org/1999/02/22-rdf-syntax-ns#"
          xmlns:o="http://www.sernaferna.com/soap/ordersystem'
      env:encodingStyle="http://www.w3.org/1999/02/22-rdf-syntax-ns#">
      <o:addToCartResponse
         rdf:About=
         "http://www.sernaferna.com/soap/ordersystem/addtocart.asp?cartid
          =THX1138">
        <o:cartid>THX1138</o:cartid>
        <o:status>OK</o:status>
        <o:quantity>3</o:quantity>
        <o:itemid>ZIBKA</o:itemid>
      </o:addToCartResponse>
    </rdf:RDF>
  </env:Body>

</env:Envelope>
```

The information is the same, but it's represented, or encoded, differently. We can create also our own encoding, but of course if our goal is interoperability, we'll want to use a standard encoding style.

Try It Out GETing a SOAP Message

Our last *Try It Out* gave us almost all of the benefits of SOAP. It will work easily with a firewall, and all of the information is passed over HTTP in XML, meaning that we could implement our remote procedure using any language, on any platform, and we can call it from any language, on any platform. However, our solution is still a little proprietary. In order to make our procedure more universal, we need to go one step further and use a SOAP envelope for our XML.

In this case, we're still going to be using a GET request, but rather than returning the raw XML, we're going to enclose it in a SOAP envelope, like so:

```
<env:Envelope xmlns:env="http://www.w3.org/2003/05/soap-envelope">
  <env:Body>
```

```
    <o:updateTotalResponse xmlns:o="http://www.sernaferna.com/soap/ordersystem">
      <o:discount>10</o:discount>
      <o:extPrice>243</o:extPrice>
    </o:updateTotalResponse>

  </env:Body>
</env:Envelope>
```

In this case, we'll also send the request and receive the response through an HTML form.

1. First, create an HTML file in the text editor and save it as `soapclient.html`.
2. Next, add an HTML form. Just add the following:

```
<html>
<head>
    <title>GET Tester</title>
</head>
<body>

<h1>SOAP Pricing Tool</h1>

<form name="orderForm" id="orderForm">

  Quantity: <input id="qty" name="qty" size="3" value="1" />
  <br />
  Item: <i>Zibka Smiles</i>, by The Polka Dot Zither Band <br />
  <br />
  Discount: <span id="discount"></span>
  <br />
  Unit Price: <input id="unitPrice" name="unitPrice" value="12.95" size="4"/>
  <br />
  Extended Price: <input id="extPrice" name="extPrice" size="4" value="12.95" />

</form>
</body>
</html>
```

   Save the file and load it in the browser. (Like the example in the last chapter, this one requires Internet Explorer 5 or higher.) What we've created is a simple form as shown in Figure 15-6.

3. Next, we need to add the script that's going to make the call to the SOAP server. Fortunately, it's very similar to what we did in the last chapter. Add this script to the `soapclient.html` file:

```
<html>
<head>
   <title>GET Tester</title>

<script language="JavaScript">
function updateTotal(){

    var qty = orderForm.qty.value;
```

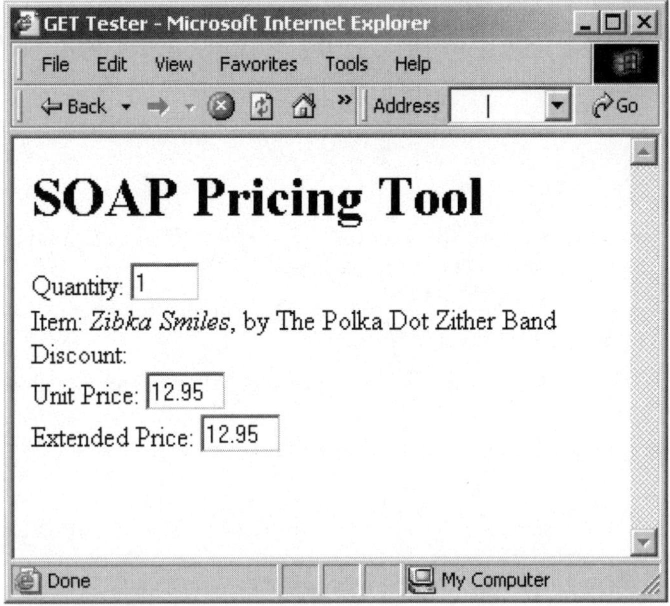

Figure 15-6

```
    var unitPrice = orderForm.unitPrice.value;

    xdDoc = new ActiveXObject("MSXML.DOMDocument");

    xhHTTP = new ActiveXObject("MSXML2.XMLHTTP");
    xhHTTP.open("GET", "http://localhost/soap/updateTotal2.asp?quantity="
                         + qty + "& unitPrice=" + unitPrice, false);
    xhHTTP.send();
    xdDoc = xhHTTP.responseXML;

    alert(xdDoc.xml);
}
</script>
</head>
<body>

<h1>SOAP Pricing Tool</h1>

<form name="orderForm" id="orderForm">

  Quantity: <input id="qty" name="qty" size="3" value="1"
                                    onChange="updateTotal();"/>
  <br />
  Item: <i>Zibka Smiles</i>, by The Polka Dot Zither Band
  <br />
  Discount: <span id="discount"></span>
  <br />
  Unit Price: <input id="unitPrice" name="unitPrice" value="12.95" size="4"/>
```

```
    <br />
    Extended Price: <input id="extPrice" name="extPrice" size="4" value="12.95" />

</form>

</body>
</html>
```

Note that we've also added a handler to the `quantity` field so that when the user changes the quantity, the `UpdateTotal()` script executes.

4. Now we need to create the ASP page to serve the content. Save a copy of `updateTotal1.asp` and call it `updateTotal2.asp`.

5. Update the `SuccessXML()` function to add the SOAP elements as follows:

```
Function SuccessXML(sDiscount, sExtprice)
   Dim sXML

   sXML = "<env:Envelope xmlns:env='http://www.w3.org/2003/05/soap-envelope'>"
   sXML = sXML & vbNewLine & "<env:Body>"
   sXML = sXML & vbNewLine & "<o:updateTotalResponse "
   sXML = sXML & "xmlns:o='http://www.sernaferna.com/soap/ordersystem'>"
   sXML = sXML & vbNewLine & " <o:discount>" & discount & "</o:discount>"
   sXML = sXML & vbNewLine & " <o:extPrice>" & extPrice & "</o:extPrice>"
   sXML = sXML & vbNewLine & "</o:updateTotalResponse>"
   sXML = sXML & vbNewLine & "</env:Body>"
   sXML = sXML & vbNewLine & "</env:Envelope>"

   SuccessXML = sXML
End Function
```

Note that we've left the `ErrorXML()` function alone for now, but it's not a legitimate SOAP error message; we'll look at those in the next section.

6. Now let's test the page. Reload the `soapclient.html` page in the browser, change the quantity, and press the Tab key or click outside the box. We should see an alert box with the returned SOAP message as shown in Figure 15-7.

Figure 15-7

7. Now we just have to add the result to the page. Make the following additions to the `soapclient.html` page:

```
<script language="JavaScript">
function updateTotal(){

    var qty = orderForm.qty.value;
    var unitPrice = orderForm.unitPrice.value;

    xdDoc = new ActiveXObject("MSXML.DOMDocument");

    xhHTTP = new ActiveXObject("MSXML2.XMLHTTP");
    xhHTTP.open("GET", "http://localhost/soap/updateTotal2.asp?quantity="
                    + qty + "& unitPrice=" + unitPrice, false);

    xhHTTP.send();
    xdDoc = xhHTTP.responseXML;

    var discount, extPrice;
    discount = xdDoc.selectSingleNode("//o:discount").text + "% off";
    extPrice = xdDoc.selectSingleNode("//o:extPrice").text;

    document.getElementById("discount").innerHTML = discount;
    orderForm.extPrice.value = extPrice;
}
</script>
```

What we've done here is to extract the returned information from the SOAP message and use it to update the page. Refresh the `soapclient.html` page in the browser and once again update the quantity as shown in Figure 15-8.

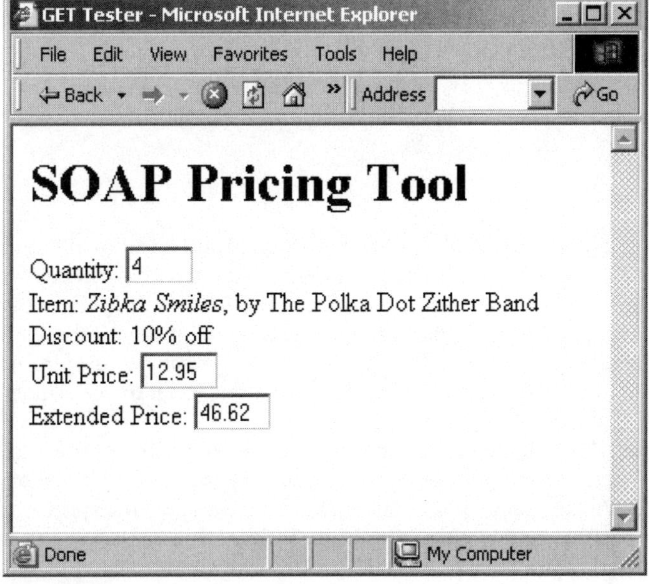

Figure 15-8

This time, rather than displaying a window with the resulting SOAP message, the page displays the appropriate information directly on the page.

How It Works

In this *Try It Out* we've shown a practical (if a bit contrived) example of working with a SOAP server. Using the browser, we created a simple SOAP client that retrieved information from the user interface (the quantity and unit price), sent a request to a SOAP server (the GET request), and displayed the results (the discount and extended price).

In this case, we've created a client using the browser, so we had to use a MIME type that the browser understands: `text/xml`. Under other circumstances, however, we'd want to use the actual SOAP MIME type, `application/soap+xml`. In other words, the ASP page would begin with the following:

```
Response.ContentType = "application/soap+xml"
```

This way, administrators can configure their firewalls to allow packets with this MIME type to pass through, even if they are blocking other types of content.

It's important to understand that we've only scratched the surface of what SOAP can do. Let's take a look at some more detailed uses.

More Complex SOAP Interactions

So far we've gotten the basics of how SOAP works, but now it's time to delve a little more deeply. SOAP messages can consist of not just a `Body`, which contains the payload, or data to be processed, but also a `Header` element containing information about the payload. The `Header` also gives you a good deal of control of how its information is processed.

In this section, we'll also look at the structure of a SOAP `Fault`, and we'll look at using SOAP in a `POST` operation rather than a `GET` operation.

First, let's look at the rest of the SOAP `Envelope`'s structure.

<Header>

The `<Header>` element comes into play when you need to add additional information to your SOAP message. For example, suppose you created a system whereby orders can be placed into your database using SOAP messages, and you have defined a standard SOAP message format that anyone communicating with your system must use. You might use a SOAP header for authentication information, so that only authorized persons or systems can make use of your system. These elements, called *header blocks*, are specifically designed for *meta information*, or information about the information contained in the body.

When there is a `<Header>` element, it must be the first element child of the `<Envelope>` element. Functionally, the `<Header>` element works very much like the `<Body>` element; it's simply a placeholder for other elements, in namespaces other than the SOAP envelope namespace, each of which is a SOAP message to be evaluated in conjunction with the main SOAP message(s) in the body. In general, however, it doesn't contain information to be processed.

The SOAP 1.2 Recommendation also defines optional attributes we can include on those header entries: mustUnderstand, role, and relay.

The mustUnderstand Attribute

The mustUnderstand attribute specifies whether it is absolutely necessary for the SOAP server to process a particular header block. A value of true indicates that the header entry is mandatory, and that the server must either process it or indicate an error. For example, consider the following:

```
<soap:Envelope xmlns:soap="http://www.w3.org/2003/05/soap-envelope">
  <soap:Header xmlns:some-ns="http://www.sernaferna.com/soap/headers/">
    <some-ns:authentication mustUnderstand="true">
      <UserID>User ID goes here...</UserID>
      <Password>Password goes here...</Password>
    </some-ns:authentication>

    <some-ns:log mustUnderstand="false">
      <additional-info>Info goes here...</additional-info>
    </some-ns:log>

    <some-ns:log>
      <additional-info>Info goes here...</additional-info>
    </some-ns:log>
  </soap:Header>
  <soap:Body xmlns:body-ns="http://www.sernaferna.com/soap/rpc">
    <body-ns:mainRPC>
      <additional-info/>
    </body-ns:mainRPC>
  </soap:Body>
</soap:Envelope>
```

This SOAP message contains three header entries: one for authentication and two for logging purposes.

For the <authentication> header entry, we specified a value of true for mustUnderstand. (In SOAP 1.1, we would have specified it as 1.) This means that the SOAP server must process the header block. If the SOAP server doesn't understand this header entry, it must reject the entire SOAP message—the server is not allowed to process the entries in the SOAP body. In this way, we're forcing the server to use proper authentication.

In the second header entry, we specified a value of false for mustUnderstand, which makes this header entry optional. This means that if the SOAP server doesn't understand this particular header entry, it can still go ahead and process the SOAP body anyway.

Finally, in the third header entry the mustUnderstand attribute was left out. In this case, the header entry is optional, just as if we had specified the mustUnderstand attribute with a value of false.

The role Attribute

In some cases a SOAP message may pass through a number of applications on a number of computers before it gets to its final destination. We might send a SOAP message to Computer A, which might then send that message on to Computer B. Computer A would be called a *SOAP intermediary*.

In these cases you can specify that some SOAP headers must be processed by a specific intermediary by using the `role` attribute. The value of the attribute is a URI, which uniquely identifies each intermediary. The SOAP specification also defines the following three roles:

- `http://www.w3.org/2003/05/soap-envelope/role/next` applies to the next intermediary in line, wherever it is.
- `http://www.w3.org/2003/05/soap-envelope/role/ultimateReceiver` only applies to the very last stop.
- `http://www.w3.org/2003/05/soap-envelope/role/none` effectively "turns off" the header block.

When an intermediary processes a header entry, it must remove that header from the message before passing it on. On the other hand, the SOAP specification also says that a similar header entry could be inserted in its place; so you could process the SOAP header entry, and then put in another, identical, header block.

The relay Attribute

The SOAP specification also requires a SOAP intermediary to remove any headers it doesn't process, which presents a problem. What if we wanted to add a new feature and target it at any intermediary that might understand it? The answer lies in the `relay` attribute. By setting the `relay` attribute to `true`, we can instruct any intermediary that encounters it to either process it or leave it alone. (If the intermediary does process the header, the intermediary still must remove it.)

The default value for the relay attribute is `false`.

<Fault>

Any time computers are involved, things can go wrong, and there may be times when a SOAP server is not able to process a SOAP message, for whatever reason. Perhaps a resource needed to perform the operation isn't available, or invalid parameters were passed, or the server doesn't understand the SOAP request in the first place. In these cases, the server will return fault codes to the client to indicate these errors.

Fault codes are sent using the same format as other SOAP messages. However, in this case the `<Body>` element will have only one child, a `<Fault>` element. Children of the `<Fault>` element contain details of the error. A SOAP message indicating a fault might look similar to this:

```
<env:Envelope xmlns:env="http://www.w3.org/2003/05/soap-envelope"
              xmlns:rpc="http://www.w3.org/2003/05/soap-rpc">
  <env:Body>
   <env:Fault>
     <env:Code>
       <env:Value>env:Sender</env:Value>
       <env:Subcode>
         <env:Value>rpc:BadArguments</env:Value>
       </env:Subcode>
     </env:Code>
     <env:Reason>
       <env:Text xml:lang="en-US">Processing error</env:Text>
       <env:Text xml:lang="fr">Erreur de traitement </env:Text>
```

```
      </env:Reason>
      <env:Detail>
        <o:orderFaultInfo xmlns:o="http://www.sernaferna.com/soap/ordersystem">
          <o:errorCode>WA872</o:errorCode>
          <o:message>Cart doesn't exist</o:message>
        </o:OrderFaultInfo>
      </env:Detail>
    </env:Fault>
  </env:Body>
</env:Envelope>
```

The `<Code>` element contains a `<Value>` that consists of a unique identifier that identifies this particular type of error. The SOAP specification defines five such identifiers in the following table.

Fault Code	Description
`VersionMismatch`	A SOAP message was received that specified a version of the SOAP protocol that this server doesn't understand. (This would happen, for example, if you sent a SOAP 1.2 message to a SOAP 1.1 server.)
`MustUnderstand`	The SOAP message contained a mandatory header that the SOAP server didn't understand.
`Sender`	Indicates that the message was not properly formatted. That is, the client made a mistake when creating the SOAP message. This identifier also applies if the message itself is well formed, but doesn't contain the correct information. For example, if authentication information were missing, this identifier would apply.
`Receiver`	Indicates that the server had problems processing the message, even though the contents of the message were formatted properly. For example, perhaps a database was down.
`DataEncodingUnknown`	Indicates that the data in the SOAP message is organized, or encoded, in a way the server doesn't understand.

Keep in mind that the identifier is actually namespace-qualified, using the `http://www.w3.org/2003/05/soap-envelope` namespace.

You also have the option of adding information in different languages, as you can see in this example's `<Text>` elements, as well as application-specific information as part of the `<Detail>` element. Note that application-specific information in the `<Detail>` element must have its own namespace.

Try It Out POSTing a SOAP message

Our last two *Try It Outs* were devoted to simply getting information from the SOAP server. Because we weren't actually changing anything on the server, we could use the `GET` method and simply pass all of the information as part of the URL. (Remember, you're only supposed to use `GET` when there are no side effects from calling the URL.)

Now let's examine a situation for which that isn't the case. In this *Try It Out*, we'll look at a SOAP procedure that adds the item to a hypothetical shopping cart. Because this is not an "idempotent" process—it causes side effects, in that, it adds an item to the order—we'll have to submit our information via the `POST` method, and that means creating a SOAP message within the client.

To call the `addToCart` procedure, we'll use the following SOAP message, with placeholders shown in italics:

```
<env:Envelope xmlns:env="http://www.w3.org/2003/05/soap-envelope">
<env:Body>
  <o:addToCart xmlns:o="http://www.sernaferna.com/soap/ordersystem">
    <o:cartId>CARTID</o:cartId>
    <o:item itemId="ITEMID">
      <o:quantity>QUANTITY</o:quantity>
      <o:extPrice>PRICE</o:extPrice>
    </o:item>
  </o:addToCart>
</env:Body>
</env:Envelope>
```

For our response, we'll send the following XML back to the client:

```
<env:Envelope xmlns:env="http://www.w3.org/2003/05/soap-envelope">
  <env:Body>
    <o:addToCartResponse xmlns:o="http://www.sernaferna.com/soap/ordersystem">
      <o:cartId>CARTID</o:cartId>
      <o:status>STATUS</o:status>
      <o:quantity>QUANTITY</o:quantity>
      <o:itemId>ITEMID</o:itemId>
    </o:addToCartResponse>
  </env:Body>
</env:Envelope>
```

Also, we need to handle our errors using a SOAP envelope as well. We'll use the following format for our errors:

```
<env:Envelope xmlns:env="http://www.w3.org/2003/05/soap-envelope"
              xmlns:rpc="http://www.w3.org/2003/05/soap-rpc">
  <env:Body>
   <env:Fault>
     <env:Code>
       <env:Value>env:FAULTCODE</env:Value>
       <env:Subcode>
         <env:Value>SUBVALUE</env:Value>
       </env:Subcode>
     </env:Code>
     <env:Reason>
       <env:Text>ERROR DESCRIPTION</env:Text>
     </env:Reason>
     <env:Detail>
       <o:orderFaultInfo xmlns:o="http://www.sernaferna.com/soap/ordersystem">
```

```
        <o:errorCode> APPLICATION-SPECIFIC ERROR CODE</o:errorCode>
        <o:message> APPLICATION-SPECIFIC ERROR MESSAGE</o:message>
      </o:OrderFaultInfo>
    </env:Detail>
  </env:Fault>
 </env:Body>
</env:Envelope>
```

1. To start, create a new ASP page called `addToCart.asp`.
2. Next, create the basic page by retrieving the submitted SOAP message and extracting the appropriate information:

```
<%@ Language="VBScript" %>
<%
Response.ContentType = "text/xml"

Dim xdRequestXML
Dim sCartid, sItemid, sQuantity, sProcedure
Dim sStatus

Set xdRequestXML = Server.CreateObject("MSXML.DOMDocument")

xdRequestXML.load Request

sCartid = xdRequestXML.selectSingleNode("//o:cartId").firstChild.nodeValue
sItemid = xdRequestXML.selectSingleNode("//o:item/@itemId").nodeValue
sQuantity = xdRequestXML.selectSingleNode("//o:quantity").firstChild.nodeValue
sProcedure = xdRequestXML.documentElement.firstChild.firstChild.nodeName

%>
```

As before, when we add a SOAP message as the request, it comes through to the ASP and is ready to load as an XML Document.

3. Next, add the `SuccessXML()` function. If the procedure successfully adds the item to the specified cart, we'll return a SOAP message to that effect, so modify the page as follows:

```
Function SuccessXML(sCartid, sItemid, sQuantity)
   Dim sXML

   sXML = "<env:Envelope xmlns:env="
   sXML = sXML & "'http://www.w3.org/2003/05/soap-envelope'>"
   sXML = sXML & vbNewLine & "<env:Body>" & vbNewLine
   sXML = sXML & "<o:addToCartResponse "
   sXML = sXML & "xmlns:o='http://www.sernaferna.com/soap/ordersystem'>"
   sXML = sXML & vbNewLine
   sXML = sXML & "<o:cartId>"& sCartid& "</o:cartId>" & vbNewLine
   sXML = sXML & "<o:status>OK</o:status>" & vbNewLine
   sXML = sXML & "<o:quantity>"& sQuantity & "</o:quantity>" & vbNewLine
   sXML = sXML & "<o:itemId>" & sItemid & "</o:itemId>" & vbNewLine
   sXML = sXML & "</o:addToCartResponse>" & vbNewLine
```

```
    sXML = sXML & "</env:Body>" & vbNewLine
    sXML = sXML & "</env:Envelope>"

    SuccessXML = sXML
End Function
```

4. In addition, we also need to return a proper SOAP envelope when an error occurs. The `ErrorXML()` function will have to provide information as to where the error came from as well as any application-specific information, so add it as follows:

```
Function ErrorXML(sFaultCode, sSubvalue, sReason, sErrorCode, sMessage)
    Dim sXML

    sXML = "<env:Envelope xmlns:env="
    sXML = sXML & "'http://schemas.xmlsoap.org/soap/envelope/'>"
    sXML = sXML & vbNewLine & "<env:Body>"
    sXML = sXML & "<env:Fault>" & vbNewLine
    sXML = sXML & "  <env:Code>" & vbNewLine
    sXML = sXML & "    <env:Value>env:"& sFaultCode& "</env:Value>" & vbNewLine
    sXML = sXML & "    <env:Subcode>" & vbNewLine
    sXML = sXML & "      <env:Value>"& sSubvalue& "</env:Value>" & vbNewLine
    sXML = sXML & "    </env:Subcode>" & vbNewLine
    sXML = sXML & "  </env:Code>" & vbNewLine
    sXML = sXML & "  <env:Reason>" & vbNewLine
    sXML = sXML & "    <env:Text>"& sReason& "</env:Text>" & vbNewLine
    sXML = sXML & "  </env:Reason>" & vbNewLine
    sXML = sXML & "  <env:Detail>" & vbNewLine
    sXML = sXML & "    <o:orderFaultInfo "
    sXML = sXML & "    xmlns:o='http://www.sernaferna.com/soap/ordersystem'>"
    sXML = sXML & vbNewLine
    sXML = sXML & "     <o:errorCode>"& sErrorCode& "</o:errorCode>" & vbNewLine
    sXML = sXML & "     <o:message>"& sMessage& "</o:message>" & vbNewLine
    sXML = sXML & "     </o:orderFaultInfo>" & vbNewLine
    sXML = sXML & "   </env:Detail>" & vbNewLine
    sXML = sXML & "</env:Fault>" & vbNewLine
    sXML = sXML & "</env:Body>" & vbNewLine
    sXML = sXML & "</env:Envelope>"
    ErrorXML = sXML
End Function
```

Notice that because some of the information in this XML is dynamic, based on the type of error that occurred, the `ErrorXML()` function takes a number of parameters. This will be a lot more useful to users of our procedure than a response that simply provides a single message no matter what's wrong.

5. Finally, we need to add the code that processes the input and determines whether to return a success or failure message. For our purposes, we won't actually process the data, but we will check for common errors. The final page looks like this:

```
<%@ Language="VBScript" %>
<%
Response.ContentType = "text/xml"

Dim xdRequestXML
```

```
Dim sCartid, sItemid, sQuantity, sProcedure
Dim sStatus

Set xdRequestXML = Server.CreateObject("MSXML.DOMDocument")

xdRequestXML.load Request

sCartid = xdRequestXML.selectSingleNode("//o:cartId").firstChild.nodeValue
sItemid = xdRequestXML.selectSingleNode("//o:item/@itemId").nodeValue
sQuantity = xdRequestXML.selectSingleNode("//o:quantity").firstChild.nodeValue
sProcedure = xdRequestXML.documentElement.firstChild.firstChild.nodeName

On Error Resume Next
'In the production system, we'd add the item to the cart here.

If Err.number <> 0 Then
  Response.Write ErrorXML("Sender", "rpc:BadArguments", "Improper arguments", _
                              "1000", "Unknown cart or item")
ElseIf sProcedure <> "o:addToCart" Then
  Response.Write ErrorXML("Sender", "rpc:ProcedureNotPresent", _
                    "Procedure not supported", "0000", "Unknown procedure")
Else
  Response.Write SuccessXML(sCartid, sItemid, sQuantity)
End If

Function ErrorXML(sFaultCode, sSubvalue, sReason, sErrorCode, sMessage)
   Dim sXML

   sXML = "<env:Envelope xmlns:env="
   sXML = sXML & "'http://schemas.xmlsoap.org/soap/envelope/'>"
   sXML = sXML & vbNewLine & "<env:Body>" & vbNewLine
   sXML = sXML & "<env:Fault>" & vbNewLine
   sXML = sXML & "  <env:Code>" & vbNewLine
   sXML = sXML & "    <env:Value>env:"& sFaultCode& "</env:Value>" & vbNewLine
   sXML = sXML & "    <env:Subcode>" & vbNewLine
   sXML = sXML & "      <env:Value>"& sSubvalue& "</env:Value>" & vbNewLine
   sXML = sXML & "    </env:Subcode>" & vbNewLine
   sXML = sXML & "  </env:Code>" & vbNewLine
   sXML = sXML & "  <env:Reason>" & vbNewLine
   sXML = sXML & "    <env:Text>"& sReason& "</env:Text>" & vbNewLine
   sXML = sXML & "  </env:Reason>" & vbNewLine
   sXML = sXML & "  <env:Detail>" & vbNewLine
   sXML = sXML & "    <o:orderFaultInfo "
   sXML = sXML & "    xmlns:o='http://www.sernaferna.com/soap/ordersystem'>"
   sXML = sXML & vbNewLine
   sXML = sXML & "      <o:errorCode>"& sErrorCode& "</o:errorCode>" & vbNewLine
   sXML = sXML & "      <o:message>"& sMessage& "</o:message>" & vbNewLine
   sXML = sXML & "    </o:orderFaultInfo>" & vbNewLine
   sXML = sXML & "  </env:Detail>" & vbNewLine
   sXML = sXML & "</env:Fault>" & vbNewLine
   sXML = sXML & "</env:Body>" & vbNewLine
   sXML = sXML & "</env:Envelope>"
   ErrorXML = sXML
End Function
```

```
Function SuccessXML(sCartid, sItemid, sQuantity)
   Dim sXML

   sXML = "<env:Envelope xmlns:env="
   sXML = sXML & "'http://www.w3.org/2003/05/soap-envelope'>"
   sXML = sXML & vbNewLine & "<env:Body>" & vbNewLine
   sXML = sXML & "<o:addToCartResponse "
   sXML = sXML & "xmlns:o='http://www.sernaferna.com/soap/ordersystem'>"
   sXML = sXML & vbNewLine
   sXML = sXML & "<o:cartId>"& sCartid& "</o:cartId>" & vbNewLine
   sXML = sXML & "<o:status>OK</o:status>" & vbNewLine
   sXML = sXML & "<o:quantity>"& sQuantity & "</o:quantity>" & vbNewLine
   sXML = sXML & "<o:itemId>" & sItemid & "</o:itemId>" & vbNewLine
   sXML = sXML & "</o:addToCartResponse>" & vbNewLine
   sXML = sXML & "</env:Body>" & vbNewLine
   sXML = sXML & "</env:Envelope>"

   SuccessXML = sXML
End Function
%>
```

6. Finally, we need to modify our HTML test page to pass the proper SOAP message to `addtocart.asp`. Open `soapclient.html` and add the `sendOrder()` function as follows:

```
<html>
<head>
   <title>GET Tester</title>

<script language="JavaScript">

function updateTotal(){

    var qty = orderForm.qty.value;
    var unitPrice = orderForm.unitPrice.value;

    xdDoc = new ActiveXObject("MSXML.DOMDocument");

    xhHTTP = new ActiveXObject("MSXML2.XMLHTTP");
    xhHTTP.open("GET", "http://localhost/soap/updateTotal2.asp?quantity="
                    + qty + "& unitPrice=" + unitPrice, false);

    xhHTTP.send();
    xdDoc = xhHTTP.responseXML;

    var discount, extPrice;
    discount = xdDoc.selectSingleNode("//o:discount").text + "% off";
    extPrice = xdDoc.selectSingleNode("//o:extPrice").text;

    document.getElementById("discount").innerHTML = discount;
    orderForm.extPrice.value = extPrice;

 }
```

```
function sendOrder(){
    var xdDoc, xhHTTP, sXML
    sXML = "<env:Envelope xmlns:env="
    sXML = sXML + "'http://www.w3.org/2003/05/soap-envelope'>"
    sXML = sXML + "<env:Body>"
    sXML = sXML + "<o:addToCart "+
            "xmlns:o='http://www.sernaferna.com/soap/ordersystem'>";
    sXML = sXML + " <o:cartId>"+orderForm.cartId.value+"</o:cartId>";
    sXML = sXML + " <o:item itemId='"+orderForm.itemId.value+"'>";
    sXML = sXML + "    <o:quantity>"+orderForm.qty.value+"</o:quantity>";
    sXML = sXML + "    <o:extPrice>"+orderForm.extPrice.value+"</o:extPrice>";
    sXML = sXML + " </o:item>";
    sXML = sXML + "</o:addToCart>";
    sXML = sXML + "</env:Body>";
    sXML = sXML + "</env:Envelope>";

    xdDoc = new ActiveXObject("MSXML.DOMDocument");
    xdDoc.loadXML(sXML);

    xhHTTP = new ActiveXObject("MSXML2.XMLHTTP");
    xhHTTP.open("POST", "http://localhost/soap/submitOrder1.asp", false);
    xhHTTP.send(xdDoc);

    xdDoc = xhHTTP.responseXML;

    var responseName;
    responseName = xdDoc.selectSingleNode("//env:Body").firstChild.nodeName;

    if (responseName == "env:Fault") {
       var reason, message
       reason =
           xdDoc.selectSingleNode("//env:Reason/env:Text").firstChild.nodeValue;
       message = xdDoc.selectSingleNode("//o:message").firstChild.nodeValue;

       alert(reason+":\n"+message);

    } else {
       var orderNumber, status, total;
        cartId = xdDoc.selectSingleNode("//o:cartId").firstChild.nodeValue;
        status = xdDoc.selectSingleNode("//o:status").firstChild.nodeValue;
        itemId = xdDoc.selectSingleNode("//o:itemId").firstChild.nodeValue;

        submitDiv.innerHTML = "<b>Item "+itemId+" added to cart
        #"+ cartId+"</b>";
    }

}

</script>
</head>
<body>

<h1>SOAP Pricing Tool</h1>

<form name="orderForm" id="orderForm">

  <input type="hidden" name="itemId" id="itemId" value="ZIBKA" />
```

```
    <input type="hidden" name="cartId" id="cartId" value="THX1138" />

    Quantity: <input id="qty" name="qty" size="3" onChange="updateTotal();"
                 value="0" />
    <br />
    Item: <i>Zibka Smiles</i>, by The Polka Dot Zither Band
    <br />
    Discount: <span id="discount"></span>
    <br />
    Unit Price: <input id="unitPrice" name="unitPrice" value="12.95" size="4"/>
    <br />
    Extended Price: <input id="extPrice" name="extPrice" size="4" value="0" />

    <div id="submitDiv">
    <input type="button" value="Add to cart" id="submitButton" name="submitButton"
           onclick="sendOrder()">
    </div>
  </form>

  </body>
  </html>
```

There really isn't anything new here, when you come right down to it. When the user clicks the Submit button, the browser creates a SOAP message with the data from the form. It then uses `POST` to send that SOAP message to the server, which processes it and sends back either a success or a failure message. If it sends back a failure message, as indicated by the `<Fault>` element, the browser pops up an alert box showing the reason. If it sends back a success message, the browser extracts the appropriate information from it and uses it to replace the Submit button.

7. Save your changes and open `soapclient.html` in IE. Add some quantity of items and click the Add to Cart button. You should see something like the following (see Figure 15-9)

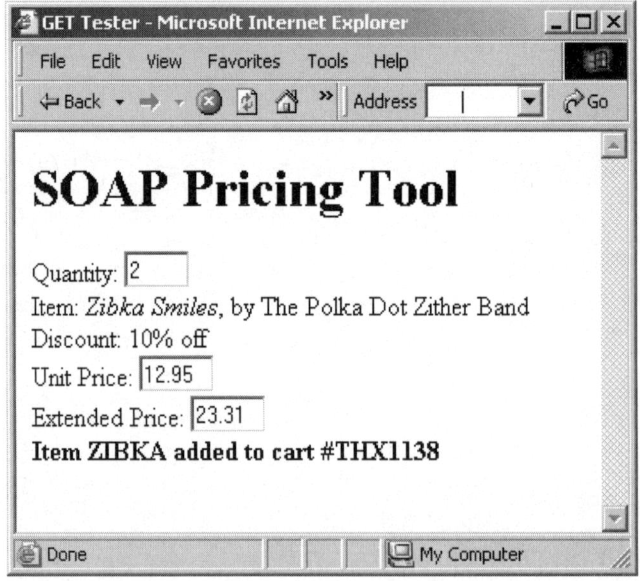

Figure 15-9

How It Works

Here we used the same techniques we were using for raw XML messages to put together valid SOAP messages both on the incoming and outgoing streams. We used the data entered by the user on a form to create a SOAP message that was sent to a server. The server extracted information from that SOAP message using typical XML tactics, evaluated the data, and then determined whether to send a success or failure message. The success message is another SOAP message that simply includes a payload, which was then interpreted by the browser and displayed on the page. The failure message, or fault, was also analyzed by the browser. A SOAP 1.2 `Fault` can include a wealth of information, related to both SOAP and to the application itself.

Of course, this seems like a lot of work for a very simple operation! However, realize that we have created, from scratch, all of the plumbing necessary to create an entire SOAP service. Implementing a more difficult SOAP service, such as some type of order-processing system, would require the same level of plumbing, even though the functionality being provided would be much more difficult.

In addition, there are a number of SOAP toolkits available, meaning that you won't necessarily have to generate the SOAP messages by hand like this every time you want to use SOAP to send messages from one computer to another. However, now, when you use those toolkits, you'll understand what's going on under the hood. While vendors get their respective acts together, that will come in handy when the inevitable inconsistencies and incompatibilities appear.

Defining Web Services: WSDL

You've built a Web service. Now what?

Hopefully, the "now what" is that other people and organizations start using the service you've built. In order to do that, however, they need to know two things:

- How to call the service
- What to expect as a response from the service

Fortunately, there's an easy way to give them the answer to both questions: Web Services Description Language (WSDL). WSDL provides a standardized way to describe a Web service. That means you can create a WSDL file that describes your service, make the file available, and sit back and let people use it.

Of course, a WSDL file isn't just for people. Remember when I talked about toolkits that take most of the work out of creating SOAP messages? They're built on the principle that they can automatically generate a client for your Web service just by analyzing the WSDL file. In this way, WSDL helps to make Web services truly platform- and language-independent.

How's that, you ask? It's simple. A WSDL file is written in XML, describing the data to be passed and the method for passing it, but it doesn't lean toward any particular language. That means that a Web services client generator can use the WSDL information to generate a client in any language. For example, a code generator for Java could create a client to access our ASP-based service. And the best part is that the client is pure Java. A developer writing an application around it doesn't have to know the details of the service, just the methods of the proxy class that actually accesses the service. The proxy sits between the client and the actual service, translating messages back and forth.

At the time of this writing, WSDL 2.0 was still at Working Draft status at the World Wide Web Consortium, so we'll concentrate on the version currently in widespread use, WSDL 1.1, and talk about some of the likely changes afterwards.

You can read the current specification for WSDL, WSDL 1.1, at `http://www.w3.org/TR/wsdl`.

<definitions>

In this chapter we'll use WSDL to describe a service that sends SOAP messages over HTTP, but in actuality WSDL is designed to be much more general. First, you define the data that will be sent, then you define the way it will be sent. In this way, a single WSDL file can describe a service that's implemented as SOAP over HTTP as well as, say, SOAP over e-mail or even a completely different means.

In our case, though, we'll stick with a look at SOAP over HTTP, because that's by far the most common usage right now.

A WSDL file starts with a `<definitions>` element as follows:

```
<?xml version="1.0"?>
<definitions name="temperature"
    targetNamespace="http://www.example.com/temperature"
    xmlns:typens="http://www.example.com/temperature"
    xmlns:xsd="http://www.w3.org/2000/10/XMLSchema"
    xmlns:soap="http://schemas.xmlsoap.org/wsdl/soap/"
    xmlns="http://schemas.xmlsoap.org/wsdl/">

</definitions>
```

The first task in a WSDL file is to define the information that will be sent to and from the service. A WSDL file builds the service up in levels. First, it defines the data to be sent and received, and then it uses that data to define messages.

<types>

Remember, there's no way to know for sure that the service will use SOAP, or even that the information will be XML, but WSDL enables you to define the *information set*—in other words, the information itself, regardless of how it's ultimately represented—using XML Schemas. For example, consider a simple service that takes in a postal code and date and returns an average temperature. The service would have two types of data to deal with, as shown in the following:

```
<types>
   <xsd:schema xmlns=""
        xmlns:xsd="http://www.w3.org/2000/10/XMLSchema"
        targetNamespace="http://www.example.com/temperature">
      <xsd:complexType name="temperatureRequestType">
         <xsd:sequence>
            <xsd:element name="where" type="xsd:string" />
            <xsd:element name="when" type="xsd:date"/>
         </xsd:sequence>
      </xsd:complexType>
```

```
        <xsd:complexType name="temperatureResponseType">
            <xsd:sequence>
                <xsd:element name="temperature" type="xsd:integer"/>
            </xsd:sequence>
        </xsd:complexType>
    </xsd:schema>
</types>
```

Just as in a normal schema document, we've defined two types, `temperatureRequestType` and `temperatureResponseType`. We can use them to define messages.

<messages>

When you define a message in a WSDL file, you're defining the content, rather than the representation. Sure, when we send SOAP messages, we'll be sending XML in a SOAP envelope, but that doesn't matter when we define the messages in the WSDL file. All we care about is what the message is, what it's called, and what kind of data it holds. Take the following example:

```
<message name="TemperatureRequestMsg">
    <part name="getTemperature" type="typens:temperatureRequestType"/>
</message>
<message name="TemperatureResponseMsg">
    <part name="temperatureResponse" type="typens:temperatureResponseType"/>
</message>
```

Looking at the first message, we've defined a message that consists of an element called `getTemperature` of the type `temperatureRequestType`. This translates into the following SOAP message:

```
<env:Envelope xmlns:env="http://www.w3.org/2003/05/soap-envelope">
   <env:Body>
      <getTemperature>
         <where>POSTAL CODE</where>
         <when>DATE</when>
      </getTemperature>
   </env:Body>
</env:Envelope>
```

Notice that the namespace for the payload is still missing. We'll take care of that later in the WSDL file.

<portTypes>

One of the major improvements coming in WSDL 2.0 is the likely change of the `<portTypes>` element to the `<interfaces>` element, and that's fortunate. Although `portType` seems to make sense from a structural point of view—later, we'll reference it when we define an actual port—it really is more of an interface, as it defines the various operations you can carry out with the service. These operations come in two varieties, input and output, and are made up of the messages we defined earlier. Let's look at the following example:

```
<portType name="TemperatureServicePortType">
    <operation name="GetTemperature">
        <input message="typens:TemperatureRequestMsg"/>
```

```
        <output message="typens:TemperatureResponseMsg"/>
    </operation>
</portType>
```

This `portType` shows that we're dealing with a request-response pattern; the user sends an input message, the structure of which is defined as a `TemperatureRequestMsg`, and the service returns an output message in the form of a `TemperatureResponseMsg`.

Next, we have to define how those messages are sent.

<binding>

Up until this point, we actually haven't said anything that has anything to do with SOAP. We've defined messages and put them together into operations, but we haven't said anything about the protocol we'll use to send them. The binding element sets up the first part of this process. In our case, we're going to bind the operations to SOAP as follows:

```
<binding name="TemperatureBinding" type="typens:TemperatureServicePortType">
    <soap:binding style="rpc" transport="http://schemas.xmlsoap.org/soap/http"/>
    <operation name="GetTemperature">
        <soap:operation />
        <input>
            <soap:body use="encoded"
                       encodingStyle="http://www.w3.org/2003/05/soap-encoding"
                       namespace="http://www.example.com/temperature" />
        </input>
        <output>
            <soap:body use="encoded"
                       encodingStyle="http://www.w3.org/2003/05/soap-encoding"
                       namespace="http://www.example.com/temperature" />
        </output>
    </operation>
</binding>
```

Notice that the `soap:` namespace finally comes into play at this point. Let's take this one step at a time.

<soap:binding>

The `<soap:binding>` element specifies that we are, in fact, dealing with a SOAP message, but it does more than that. The `transport` attribute is easy; it simply specifies that we're sending the message via HTTP. The `style` attribute is a little more complex. (But just a little.)

Both, in this chapter and the previous one, we've concentrated on the use of Web services as another means of performing remote procedure calls, but that's not their only use. In fact, in many cases, information is simply passed to the service, which acts upon the data, rather than having the data determine what is to be done.

The `style` attribute has two possible values: `rpc` and `document`. The `rpc` value is a message in which you simply have a method name and parameters. For example, in our message, the payload represents a call to the `getTemperature` method with the parameters `34652` and `2004-5-23`, as shown in the following:

```
<env:Envelope xmlns:env="http://www.w3.org/2003/05/soap-envelope">
  <env:Body>
```

```
      <getTemperature>
        <where>34652</where>
        <when>2004-05-23</when>
      </getTemperature>
    </env:Body>
  </env:Envelope>
```

The data is contained in an outer element (getTemperature), which is itself contained within the <env:Body> element.

When you use the document style, however, the situation is slightly different. In that case, the entire contents of the <env:Body> element are considered to be the data in question. For example, we might have created a SOAP message of the following:

```
<env:Envelope xmlns:env="http://www.w3.org/2003/05/soap-envelope">
  <env:Body>
    <where>34652</where>
    <when>2004-05-23</when>
  </env:Body>
</env:Envelope>
```

The document style also enables you to send more complex documents that might not fit into the RPC mold.

Notice that neither of these examples shows the namespaces for the payload. That gets set in the soap:body element, which we'll cover shortly.

<soap:operation>

If the <soap:operation> element looks out of place just sitting there with no attributes, it's because in many ways it is out of place. The SOAP 1.1 specification required all services to use a SOAPAction header that defined the application that was supposed to execute it. This was an HTTP header, so you'd see something like this:

```
POST /soap.asp HTTP/1.1
Accept: image/gif, image/x-xbitmap, image/jpeg, image/pjpeg, */*
Accept-Language: en-us
Content-Type: application/x-www-form-urlencoded
Accept-Encoding: gzip, deflate
User-Agent: Mozilla/4.0 (compatible; MSIE 5.5; Windows NT 5.0)
Host: www.example.com
Content-Length: 242
SOAPAction: "http://www.example.org/soap/TemperatureService.asp"

<env:Envelope xmlns:env="http://www.w3.org/2003/05/soap-envelope">
  <env:Body>
    <getTemperature>
      <where>34652</where>
      <when>2004-05-23</when>
    </getTemperature>
  </env:Body>
</env:Envelope>
```

The SOAP 1.2 specification did away with the SOAPAction header, but it's still necessary to specify that this is a SOAP message, hence the soap:operation element.

<soap:body>

The binding element references an operation, which, in this case, is already defined as having an input and an output message. Within the binding element, we'll define how those messages are to be presented using the soap:body element. For example, we've specified the following:

```
                <soap:body use="encoded"
                           encodingStyle="http://www.w3.org/2003/05/soap-encoding"
                           namespace="http://www.example.com/temperature" />
```

For the input message, we're specifying that it's a SOAP message. Like the style attribute, the use attribute has two possible values: literal, and encoded. When the use is specified as literal, it means that the server is not to assume any particular meaning in the XML, but to take it as a whole. Normally, we'll use the literal use with the document style. If we specify the use as encoded, we have to specify the encodingStyle. In this case, we specify the SOAP style, but we could use other encodings, such as RDF or even an entirely new encoding style. Finally, we specify the namespace of the payload, so we wind up with a complete message as follows:

```
<env:Envelope xmlns:env="http://www.w3.org/2003/05/soap-envelope">
  <env:Body>
    <t:getTemperature xmlns:t="http://www.example.com/temperature">
      <t:where>34652</t:where>
      <t:when>2004-05-23</t:when>
    </t:getTemperature>
  </env:Body>
</env:Envelope>
```

Now we just need to know where to send it.

<service>

The final step in creating a WSDL file is to specify the service that we're creating by putting all of these pieces together, as shown in the following:

```
<service name="TemperatureService">
   <port name="TemperaturePort" binding="typens:TemperatureBinding">
      <soap:address location="http://www.example.com/temp/getTemp.asp"/>
   </port>
</service>
```

When we create a service, we're specifying where and how to send the information. In fact, the port element you see here will likely be renamed to endpoint in WSDL 2.0, because that's what it is: the endpoint for the connection between the server and a client. First, we reference the binding we just created, and then we send it as a SOAP message to the address specified by the location attribute. That's it. Now let's try it out.

Try It Out Specifying the Order Service via WSDL

In this *Try It Out* we'll create a WSDL file that describes the service we created earlier in the chapter.

1. Open a new text file and name it `SernaFernaMusic.wsdl`.
2. Start by creating the overall structure for the file:

```
<?xml version="1.0"?>
<definitions name="SernaFerna"
    targetNamespace="http://www.sernaferna.com/soap/ordersystem"
    xmlns:typens="http://www.sernaferna.com/soap/ordersystem"
    xmlns:xsd="http://www.w3.org/2000/10/XMLSchema"
    xmlns:soap="http://schemas.xmlsoap.org/wsdl/soap/"
    xmlns:soapenc="http://schemas.xmlsoap.org/soap/encoding/"
    xmlns:wsdl="http://schemas.xmlsoap.org/wsdl/"
    xmlns="http://schemas.xmlsoap.org/wsdl/">

</definitions>
```

3. Add definitions for the XML in the messages to be passed:

```
<types>
        <xsd:schema xmlns=""
           xmlns:xsd="http://www.w3.org/2000/10/XMLSchema"
           targetNamespace="http://www.sernaferna.com/soap/ordersystem">
               <xsd:complexType name="addToCartType">
                  <xsd:sequence>
                     <xsd:element name="cartId" type="xsd:string" />
                     <xsd:element name="item">
                         <xsd:complexType>
                            <xsd:sequence>
                               <xsd:element name="quantity"
                                                  type="xsd:string"/>
                               <xsd:element name="extPrice"
                                                  type="xsd:string"/>
                            </xsd:sequence>
                            <xsd:attribute name="itemId"
                                                  type="xsd:string" />
                         </xsd:complexType>
                     </xsd:element>
                  </xsd:sequence>
               </xsd:complexType>
               <xsd:complexType name="addToCartResponseType">
                  <xsd:sequence>
                     <xsd:element name="cartId" type="xsd:string"/>
                     <xsd:element name="status" type="xsd:string"/>
                     <xsd:element name="quantity" type="xsd:string"/>
                     <xsd:element name="itemId" type="xsd:string"/>
                  </xsd:sequence>
               </xsd:complexType>
        </xsd:schema>
</types>
```

4. Next, define the messages to be sent to and from the service:

```
<message name="AddToCartRequestMsg">
   <part name="addToCart" type="typens:addToCartType"/>
</message>
<message name="AddToCartResponseMsg">
   <part name="addToCartResponse" type="typens:addToCartResponseType"/>
</message>
```

5. Now define the portType, or interface that will use the messages:

```
<portType name="SernaFernaPort">
   <operation name="AddToCart">
      <input message="typens:AddToCartRequestMsg"/>
      <output message="typens:AddToCartResponseMsg"/>
   </operation>
</portType>
```

6. Next, bind the portType to a particular protocol, in our case SOAP:

```
<binding name="SernaFernaBinding"
                         type="typens:SernaFernaPort">
   <soap:binding style="rpc"
      transport="http://schemas.xmlsoap.org/soap/http"/>
   <operation name="AddToCart">
      <soap:operation />
         <input>
            <soap:body use="encoded"
                  namespace="http://www.sernaferna.com/soap/ordersystem"
                  encodingStyle="http://schemas.xmlsoap.org/soap/encoding/"/>
         </input>
         <output>
            <soap:body use="encoded"
                  namespace="http://www.sernaferna.com/soap/ordersystem"
                  encodingStyle="http://schemas.xmlsoap.org/soap/encoding/"/>
         </output>
   </operation>
</binding>
```

7. Finally, define the actual service by associating the binding with an endpoint. This gives you the following final file:

```
<?xml version="1.0"?>
<definitions name="SernaFerna"
    targetNamespace="http://www.sernaferna.com/soap/ordersystem"
    xmlns:typens="http://www.sernaferna.com/soap/ordersystem"
    xmlns:xsd="http://www.w3.org/2000/10/XMLSchema"
    xmlns:soap="http://schemas.xmlsoap.org/wsdl/soap/"
    xmlns:soapenc="http://schemas.xmlsoap.org/soap/encoding/"
    xmlns:wsdl="http://schemas.xmlsoap.org/wsdl/"
    xmlns="http://schemas.xmlsoap.org/wsdl/">
```

```
<types>
         <xsd:schema xmlns=""
            xmlns:xsd="http://www.w3.org/2000/10/XMLSchema"
            targetNamespace="http://www.sernaferna.com/soap/ordersystem">
                <xsd:complexType name="addToCartType">
                   <xsd:sequence>
                      <xsd:element name="cartId" type="xsd:string" />
                      <xsd:element name="item">
                         <xsd:complexType>
                            <xsd:sequence>
                               <xsd:element name="quantity"
                                                  type="xsd:string"/>
                               <xsd:element name="extPrice"
                                                  type="xsd:string"/>
                            </xsd:sequence>
                            <xsd:attribute name="itemId"
                                                  type="xsd:string" />
                         </xsd:complexType>
                      </xsd:element>
                  </xsd:sequence>
               </xsd:complexType>
               <xsd:complexType name="addToCartResponseType">
                  <xsd:sequence>
                     <xsd:element name="cartId" type="xsd:string"/>
                     <xsd:element name="status" type="xsd:string"/>
                     <xsd:element name="quantity" type="xsd:string"/>
                     <xsd:element name="itemId" type="xsd:string"/>
                  </xsd:sequence>
               </xsd:complexType>
        </xsd:schema>
</types>

<message name="AddToCartRequestMsg">
        <part name="addToCart" type="typens:addToCartType"/>
</message>
<message name="AddToCartResponseMsg">
        <part name="addToCartResponse" type="typens:addToCartResponseType"/>
</message>

<portType name="SernaFernaPort">
        <operation name="AddToCart">
               <input message="typens:AddToCartRequestMsg"/>
               <output message="typens:AddToCartResponseMsg"/>
        </operation>
</portType>
<binding name="SernaFernaBinding"
                     type="typens:SernaFernaPort">
        <soap:binding style="rpc"
              transport="http://schemas.xmlsoap.org/soap/http"/>
        <operation name="AddToCart">
               <soap:operation/>
               <input>
                       <soap:body use="encoded"
namespace="http://www.sernaferna.com/soap/ordersystem"
encodingStyle="http://schemas.xmlsoap.org/soap/encoding/"/>
```

```
                </input>
                <output>
                        <soap:body use="encoded"
namespace="http://www.sernaferna.com/soap/ordersystem"
encodingStyle="http://schemas.xmlsoap.org/soap/encoding/"/>
               </output>
        </operation>
</binding>
<service name="SernaFernaService">
        <port name="SernaFernaPort" binding="typens:SernaFernaBinding">
               <soap:address location="http://localhost/soap/submitOrder1.asp"/>
        </port>
</service>

</definitions>
```

How It Works

In this *Try It Out* we created a simple WSDL file describing the SOAP messages sent to and from the hypothetical Serna Ferna Music Service. First, we created the data types for the messages to be sent. We then combined them into messages, created operations out of the messages, and finally bound them to a protocol and a service.

Other Bindings

It's important to understand that WSDL doesn't necessarily describe a SOAP service. Earlier in this chapter we looked at a situation in which messages were passed by HTTP without benefit of a SOAP wrapper. These REST messages can also be defined via WSDL by adding the HTTP binding.

The basic process is the same as it was for SOAP: define the data types, group them into messages, create operations from the messages and `portTypes` from the operations, and then create a binding that ties them all in to a particular protocol, as shown in the following:

```
<?xml version="1.0"?>
<definitions name="SernaFerna"
    targetNamespace="http://www.sernaferna.com/soap/ordersystem"
    xmlns:typens="http://www.sernaferna.com/soap/ordersystem"
    xmlns:xsd="http://www.w3.org/2000/10/XMLSchema"
    xmlns:soap="http://schemas.xmlsoap.org/wsdl/soap/"
    xmlns:soapenc="http://schemas.xmlsoap.org/soap/encoding/"
    xmlns:wsdl="http://schemas.xmlsoap.org/wsdl/"
    xmlns:http="http://schemas.xmlsoap.org/wsdl/http/"
    xmlns:mime="http://schemas.xmlsoap.org/wsdl/mime/"
    xmlns="http://schemas.xmlsoap.org/wsdl/">

<types>
        <xsd:schema xmlns=""
           xmlns:xsd="http://www.w3.org/2000/10/XMLSchema"
           targetNamespace="http://www.sernaferna.com/soap/ordersystem">
               <xsd:complexType name="addToCartType">
                        <xsd:sequence>
```

```
                    <xsd:element name="cartId" type="xsd:string" />
                      <xsd:element name="itemId" type="xsd:string"/>
                  <xsd:element name="quantity" type="xsd:string"/>
                  <xsd:element name="extPrice" type="xsd:string"/>
            </xsd:sequence>
            </xsd:complexType>
            <xsd:complexType name="addToCartResponseType">
            <xsd:sequence>
                  <xsd:element name="cartId" type="xsd:string"/>
                  <xsd:element name="status" type="xsd:string"/>
                  <xsd:element name="quantity" type="xsd:string"/>
               <xsd:element name="itemId" type="xsd:string"/>
            </xsd:sequence>
      </xsd:complexType>
      <xsd:complexType name="updateTotalsResponseType">
            <xsd:sequence>
                  <xsd:element name="discount" type="xsd:string" />
                          <xsd:element name="extPrice"
type="xsd:string"/>
            </xsd:sequence>
      </xsd:complexType>

        </xsd:schema>
</types>

<message name="AddToCartRequestMsg">
        <part name="addToCart" type="typens:addToCartType"/>
</message>
<message name="AddToCartResponseMsg">
        <part name="addToCartResponse" type="typens:addToCartResponseType"/>
</message>

<message name="UpdateTotalsRequestMsg">
        <part name="quantity" type="xsd:number"/>
        <part name="untPrice" type="xsd:number"/>
</message>
<message name="UpdateTotalsResponseMsg">
        <part name="updateTotalsResponse" type="typens:
         updateTotalsResponseType"/>
</message>

<portType name="SernaFernaPort">
        <operation name="AddToCart">
                <input message="typens:AddToCartRequestMsg"/>
                <output message="typens:AddToCartResponseMsg"/>
        </operation>
</portType>

<portType name="SernaFernaRESTPort">
        <operation name="updateTotal1.aspx">
                <input message="typens:UpdateTotalsRequestMsg"/>
                <output message="typens:UpdateTotalsResponseMsg"/>
        </operation>
</portType>
```

```
<binding name="SernaFernaBinding"
                         type="typens:SernaFernaPort">
        <soap:binding style="rpc"
              transport="http://schemas.xmlsoap.org/soap/http"/>
        <operation name="AddToCart">
               <soap:operation/>
               <input>
                        <soap:body use="encoded"
namespace="http://www.sernaferna.com/soap/ordersystem"
encodingStyle="http://schemas.xmlsoap.org/soap/encoding/"/>
                </input>
                <output>
                        <soap:body use="encoded"
namespace="http://www.sernaferna.com/soap/ordersystem"
encodingStyle="http://schemas.xmlsoap.org/soap/encoding/"/>
                </output>
         </operation>
</binding>

<binding name="SernaFernaRESTBinding"
                         type="typens:SernaFernaRESTPort">
        <http:binding verb="GET"/>
        <operation name="updateTotals1.aspx">
               <http:operation location="updateTotals1.aspx"/>
               <input>
                       <http:urlEncoded/>
               </input>
               <output>
                       <mime:content type="text/xml"/>
               </output>
        </operation>
</binding>

<service name="SernaFernaService">
        <port name="SernaFernaPort" binding="typens:SernaFernaBinding">
               <soap:address location="http://localhost/soap/submitOrder1.asp"/>
        </port>
        <port name="SernaFernaRESTPort" binding="typens:SernaFernaRESTBinding">
               <http:address location="http://localhost/soap/"/>
        </port>

</service>
</definitions>
```

In this way, we can define a service that uses any protocol using WSDL.

Summary

In this chapter, we have looked at SOAP, an XML-based protocol for performing remote procedure calls and passing information between computers. We have studied how this protocol is used and even put it to practice by creating a SOAP-based shopping cart system.

Because SOAP is based on easy-to-implement and standardized technologies, such as XML and HTTP, it has the potential to become a very universal protocol indeed. In fact, most of the hype surrounding SOAP concerns its interoperability. At least initially, companies providing SOAP software are concentrating on making their software as interoperable as possible with the software from other companies, instead of creating proprietary changes to the standard.

With the backing of companies such as Microsoft, IBM, DevelopMentor, Lotus, UserLand Software, Sun Microsystems, and Canon, SOAP is already a widely implemented technology. The Web services built on top of SOAP also have huge potential for creating widely accessible functionality over the web.

That said, SOAP is not the only game in town. We also looked at a simpler form of Web service, REST, which is currently growing in popularity.

We then looked at Web Services Definition Language, or WSDL, which is designed to enable you to provide another developer with all of the information he or she might need in order to access your service. WSDL can be used with any protocol but is particularly well suited to SOAP. We looked at the various parts of a WSDL document and created one for the SOAP and REST services we built earlier in the chapter.

Exercise Questions

Suggested solutions to these questions can be found in Appendix A.

Question 1

Create a SOAP message that fulfills the following requirements:

1. It corresponds to an RPC called `getRadioOperators()`.
2. It passes the following information:
    - City and State or Postal Code
    - Radius
    - License Class
3. The server must receive and verify a call sign from the sender.

Question 2

Create a WSDL file that describes the document in Question 1.

Part VII: Display

XHTML

When people say XHTML is the new HTML, it is not in the sense that fashion pundits might say brown is the new black; it is the W3C's replacement for HTML. Rather than creating HTML 5, the W3C made XHTML, which is akin to when Macromedia created Flash MX instead of Flash 6, or when Microsoft released Windows XP instead of Windows 2001. XHTML is actually the reformulation of HTML 4 written in XML, and therefore you have a few new rules to learn, the first of which is that it shall be XML-compliant.

The good news is that the elements and attributes available to you in XHTML are almost identical to those in HTML 4 (after all, XHTML 1.0 is a version of HTML 4 written in XML), so you won't need to learn a new vocabulary in this chapter. There are, however, a few changes in how you are supposed to construct documents, which is what you will learn in this chapter.

While XML is finding its way into many aspects of programming, data storage and document authoring, it was primarily designed for use on the web. It is hardly surprising, therefore, that the W3C wanted to make these changes to HTML (which is the most widely used language on the web) to make it an application of XML.

So, why do you need to learn a new version of HTML? After all, existing browsers will continue to support HTML, as we know it, for the foreseeable future (and there are many sites on the Internet that may never be upgraded). There are several reasons for upgrading which will be covered in this chapter, including the following:

- It can make our page size smaller and our code clearer to read.
- Our code can be used with all XML-aware processors (from authoring tools and validators through to XSLT, DOM, and SAX processors).
- It addresses issues regarding creating web pages so that they can be viewed on all the new devices that can now access the Internet, from phones to fridges, without each type of device requiring its own different language.
- XHTML processors can require less memory and power (which is essential for smaller devices).
- Some new browsers and devices are being written to only support XHTML.

XHTML is probably the most popular application of XML today, and if you are familiar with HTML, you will be writing XHTML pages in no time at all.

There are two versions of XHTML you need to look at: XHTML 1.0 and XHTML 1.1, both of which are covered in this chapter. You need to understand XHTML 1.0 in order to learn XHTML 1.1, so try to avoid the urge to skip through.

Before you even look at XHTML, however, you may not be aware that in HTML 4.1 all stylistic markup (such as the `<font>` element and `bgcolor` attribute, which is used to indicate how a document should appear) was marked as *deprecated*, indicating that it was going to be phased out in future versions of the specifications, and it is essential to address the removal of the stylistic markup before we start on XHTML.

So, in this chapter, you will learn the following:

- How to keep style and content separate, and the benefits of doing so.
- The different versions and document types of XHTML.
- How to write XHTML 1.0 documents.
- What modularized XHTML is, and how it will allow us to write pages for many different devices.

This chapter assumes you have a basic knowledge of HTML. If you do not, there are plenty of free tutorials available on the web.

Separating Style from Content

All of the stylistic markup in HTML—markup such as the `<font>` element for indicating which typeface to use or the `bgcolor` attribute for indicating background colors—was deprecated in HTML 4.1, with the expressed purpose that document authors should stop using such markup to indicate how pages should be displayed. Anything that indicated how a document should appear, rather than being about the structure or content of the document, was marked for removal from future versions of the specification, with the exception of the `<style>` element and `style` attribute (both of which contained CSS rules or a link to a CSS style sheet). To understand why this markup was deprecated, you need to take a trip back in time.

The web was originally created for transmitting scientific documents between researchers, to make the work more easily and widely available. Web page authors used markup to describe the structure of a document, identifying which parts of the document should be headings, paragraphs, bulleted or numbered lists, and tables. The browser would then use these tags to render the document correctly. The problem was that it all looked fairly boring.

As we all know, the rise of the web was phenomenal. Very soon all kinds of people found new uses for the web, and new users wanted far greater control over how their web pages looked. As a result, both the W3C and browser manufacturers introduced all kinds of markup that allowed web page authors to control how the pages appeared in browsers.

The problem with all this stylistic markup was that documents became much longer and more complicated. Whereas the first HTML documents only described the structure of a page, the addition of stylistic markup resulted in pages that were littered with markup that affected the presentation of the document. `<font>` tags were used to specify typefaces, sizes, and the color of text. Tables were used to specify the layout for a page rather than to describe tabular data. Background colors and images were set for several types of element.

> *Other stylistic markup that has been deprecated includes* `align`, `border`, `color`, `cellpadding`, `cellspacing`, `size`, `style`, `valign`, *and* `width` *attributes and the* `<s>`, `<strike>`, `<basefont>`, `<u>`, *and* `<center>` *elements. The rule of thumb is: If it just indicates how the item should appear, it has been deprecated.*

HTML markup no longer just described the structure and content of a document—its headings, paragraphs, lists, and so on—it also described how it should appear on a desktop PC web browser. Not only did this result in more complex documents, but also there was a new problem: the desktop PC was no longer the only device that accesses the Internet, and pages designed to work on a desktop PC would not work on all other devices.

Therefore, it was decided that all stylistic markup should be removed and put in a separate stylesheet, linked from the HTML document. The language for this is Cascading Style Sheets, which you may already be familiar with—if not, the next chapter covers CSS in detail.

Splitting of style from content has several advantages over including style rules in the document, some of which are listed here:

- Pages are simpler because they do not contain tables to control presentation as well as markup.
- Pages are smaller because each page does not have to repeat the instructions for how the page should be styled, rather the whole site (or several pages) can use the same stylesheet. Therefore, once the stylesheet has been downloaded, pages are quicker to load, and you do not have to send as much data from your server.
- If you (or your boss) want to change the color of all pages in your site, you can do so by just changing the stylesheet rather than changing each page individually.
- The same HTML document could be used with different stylesheets for different purposes—for example, you could have one stylesheet for browsing on-screen and another for printing out information. This makes documents more reusable, rather than having to be recreated for different mediums.
- Markup just describes documents structure and content once more (as it was originally intended).
- Web users with visual impairments would be able to more effectively view pages, because they would not contain fixed sizes for fonts, making them easier to read and navigate. Furthermore, devices like screen readers would not have to contend with markup that was incorrectly used—such as the use of tables to control layout.

The next chapter looks at styling XML using CSS, and as you will see, many of the same rules and constraints apply when styling XHTML as any other application of XML. Because CSS is not covered until the next chapter, the examples in this chapter will look rather plain, but you know to avoid using stylistic markup in your XHTML documents.

Learning XHTML 1.0

Having seen that XHTML is taking a step toward removing stylistic markup, instead of relying on stylesheets to control the presentation of documents, it is time to look at the other differences between the

HTML and XHTML. As I already mentioned, the elements and attributes available to you in XHTML are virtually identical to those in other versions of HTML; so, there is no need to learn a whole new vocabulary for XHTML documents. The key topics introduced in this section are as follows:

- The three document types of XHTML 1.0, Strict, Transitional, and Frameset, and when to use each one.
- The basic changes to the elements are attributes of HTML to make them XML compliant.
- The advantages of having a stricter language.
- How to validate your XHTML documents, and why this is important. You will also see some pitfalls that you might come across when trying to validate XHTML documents.

The first thing to cover is the three document types of XHTML 1.0, each of which is different, but don't let this put you off. Even though you may not have known it, there were three versions of HTML 4 too!

The Strict, Transitional, and Frameset DTDs of XHTML 1.0

Like many other XML vocabularies, each version of XHTML has a DTD that defines markup and allowable structure of conforming documents (more recently these have also been made available in XML Schema). There are actually three XHTML 1.0 *Document Type Definitions* you can follow when writing XHTML 1.0 pages:

- Transitional—This DTD allows deprecated markup from HTML 4.1.
- Strict—This DTD does not allow deprecated markup from HTML 4.1.
- Frameset—You'd use this DTD when creating pages that use frames.

As you shall see later in the chapter, XHTML 1.1 has only one document type to choose from.

The idea of removing all stylistic markup may have raised some alarm bells for some of you. Without the stylistic markup we are used to, it is going to be very hard to create visually attractive pages. Even the latest browsers do not fully and perfectly support CSS2, which we are now supposed to use to style documents, never mind the older browsers that are still used to access your sites. Therefore, the *transitional* document type still allows you to use deprecated markup from HTML 4.

All of the element and attribute names, and allowable uses of them, are the same in transitional XHTML 1.0 as they are in HTML 4.01—even the root element of the document is still `<html>` (rather than `<xhtml>`). However, there are some minor changes you need to look at because you are writing a document conforming to the rules of XML, which will be addressed in the following section.

The *strict* form of XHTML 1.0, as its name suggests, is stricter than transitional XHTML; it does not allow use of the deprecated markup, in particular, the deprecated styling markup (leaving only the `<style>` element and `style` attribute). This helps to fulfill one of the aims of XHTML: splitting style from content. Also, you should not use tables for layout purposes in strict XHTML 1.0, as this is using a table to control the presentation of the document rather than its intended use of displaying tabular data.

The *frameset* document allows us to create documents that utilize frames to show multiple pages in a single window. This technique is still mainly used to create a navigation frame separate from the documents that are being shown.

Because the transitional document type still allows you to use markup that was deprecated in HTML 4.1, it is common with web developers moving across to XHTML, whose pages need to be viewed in older browsers that do not support CSS. It also helps those who still want to use tables for layout.

Basic Changes in Writing XHTML

Because we are now writing XML documents, we have to make some changes from the way we used to write HTML. Specifically, we need to do the following:

- Consider starting each document with the XML declaration.
- Include a `DOCTYPE` declaration.
- Only use lowercase characters for element and attribute names.
- Provide values for all attributes. These should be written inside double quotation marks.
- Make sure our document is well formed.
- Close empty elements with a forward slash after the tag name but before the closing angled bracket.
- Use `id` attributes instead of `name` attributes to uniquely identify fragments of documents.
- Specify the language the document is written in. This should be specified using an ISO 639 language code (for example, `en` for English, `us-en` for US English, or `fr` for French).
- Specify the character encoding the document is saved in (as you will see this is particularly important if you are using characters not included in the ASCII character set).

The following sections will address each of these sections in turn, and as you will see you do not *have* to do *all* of these things, but it is advised to get into good habits early.

XML Declaration

Seeing as our XHTML documents are indeed XML documents, it is recommended that they start with the following XML declaration:

```
<?xml version="1.0" encoding=" ISO-8859-1" ?>
```

This should be right at the very start of the document, there should not even be a space before it. (We will come back to the `encoding` attribute at the end of this section when we look at specifying character encoding for a document.)

This can cause a problem, however, because some of the older browsers have problems with the XML declaration and will have one of the two following reactions:

- They will ignore it.
- They will display the declaration as if it were part of the text for the document.

The following browsers have problems with the XML declaration:

- Netscape Navigator 3.04 and earlier
- Internet Explorer 3.0 and earlier

If your documents need to be viewed by these browser versions, you may choose to ignore the XML declaration.

DOCTYPE Declaration

Immediately following the XML declaration (or at the start of the document if the XML declaration is not present), you should put the *DOCTYPE declaration*. This indicates what kind of document you are writing.

Because there are three XHTML 1.0 document types (strict, transitional, and frameset), there are three possible options for the `DOCTYPE` declaration as discussed in the following sections.

Transitional Documents

For transitional XHTML 1.0 documents (which can include the deprecated markup from HTML 4.1—in particular, the stylistic markup), we would use the following declaration:

```
<!DOCTYPE html PUBLIC "-//W3C//DTD XHTML 1.0 Transitional//EN"
  "http://www.w3.org/TR/xhtml1/DTD/xhtml1-transitional.dtd">
```

Strict Documents

For strict XHTML 1.0 documents (with none of the markup deprecated in HTML 4.1—in particular, the stylistic markup), we would use the following declaration:

```
<!DOCTYPE html PUBLIC "-//W3C//DTD XHTML 1.0 Strict//EN"
  "http://www.w3.org/TR/xhtml1/DTD/xhtml1-strict.dtd">
```

A strictly conforming XHTML document must contain the `DOCTYPE` declaration before the root element, although a transitional or frameset document may leave it out.

Frameset Documents

For frameset XHTML 1.0 documents, we would use the following declaration:

```
<!DOCTYPE html PUBLIC "-//W3C//DTD XHTML 1.0 Frameset//EN"
  "http://www.w3.org/TR/xhtml1/DTD/xhtml1-frameset.dtd">
```

Case Sensitivity

As XML is case sensitive, it is hardly surprising to learn that XHTML is too. All element names and attributes in the XHTML vocabulary must be written in lowercase, as shown in the following example:

```
<body onclick="someFunction();">
```

Of course, the element content or value of an attribute does not have to be lowercase; you can write what you like between the opening and closing tags of an element and within the quotes of an attribute (except quotation marks, which would close the attribute).

The decision to make XML case-sensitive was largely driven by internationalization efforts. Whereas you can easily convert English characters from uppercase to lowercase, some languages do not have such a direct mapping. There may be no equivalent in a different case, or it might depend upon the region. So that the specification could use different languages, it was therefore decided to make XML case-sensitive.

Attribute Values

There are two points we need to be aware of when writing XHTML attributes as follows:

- All attributes must be enclosed in double quotation marks.
- A value must be given for each attribute.

In some versions of HTML, you could write attributes without giving the value in quotes, as shown in the following example:

```
<TD align=center>
```

This is not allowed in XHTML documents. After all our XHTML documents are XML documents, and putting attribute values in quotes is a basic requirement for a document to be well formed.

Furthermore, HTML also allowed some attributes to be written without a value. It was known as attribute minimization, and where a value was not given, a default would be used. For example, in an HTML form, when using the `<option>` element to create a drop-down list box, you could use the `selected` attribute without a value to indicate that this option should be shown when the page loads and act as the default value as shown in the following:

```
<OPTION selected value="option1">
```

Even if the value is left blank, all attributes in XHTML must be given a value enclosed in double quotation marks, like this:

```
<option selected="selected" value="option1">
```

You should also note that any trailing whitespace at the end of an attribute value would be stripped out of the document, and any line breaks or multiple spaces between words would be collapsed into one space, rather like most processors treat spaces in HTML.

Well-Formedness and Validity of Documents

As with all XML documents, all XHTML documents must be *well formed*. The basic requirements for a well-formed document were covered in Chapter 2—a well-formed document is one that meets the syntactic rules of XML. With regard to this, we should look at the following:

- The unique root element; the `<html>` element
- Empty elements, because every start tag must have a corresponding end tag
- The correct nesting of elements

To be understood by an XHTML processor, such as a web browser, a document instance should also be able to be validated using the DTD specified in the DOCTYPE declaration; we will look at validation later in the chapter.

Unique Root HTML Element

In order to be well formed, an XML document must have a unique root element. In the case of XHTML documents, you might think that this would be <xhtml>, but it is not—the root element remains <html>.

This shows us that XHTML really is the new version of HTML, not some alternative. It also means that older browsers will still display XHTML documents.

You can use a namespace on the root element to indicate which namespace the markup belongs to. This is required in strictly conforming documents but is not necessary in transitional or frameset documents unless you are mixing different vocabularies within the same document (for example, using SVG inside an XHTML document).

Here is an example using namespace defaulting on the root element to indicate the markup belongs to the strict XHTML 1.0 document type:

```
<!DOCTYPE html PUBLIC "-//W3C//DTD XHTML 1.0 Strict//EN"
  "http://www.w3.org/TR/xhtml1/DTD/xhtml1-strict.dtd">
<html xmlns=" http://www.w3.org/1999/xhtml">
...
</html>
```

Empty Elements

An element that has no character content between its opening and closing tags is known as an *empty element.* In HTML, the <img>, <hr> and <br> elements are examples of empty elements.

As with all XML documents, you cannot just use an opening tag for empty elements; you must add a forward slash before the closing angled bracket of the tag. So, the correct way of writing elements, such as img in XHTML, is:

```
<img src="MyCompanyLogo.gif" alt="My Company Logo" />
```

Similarly, we would write hr and br elements like the following:

```
<br />
<hr />
```

Note how I have left a space between the hr and the forward slash character, rather than writing <br/>. This is because some older browsers will not understand the tag unless this space is there and will therefore ignore it. If you add the space before the closing slash, it will be displayed.

Correct Nesting of Elements

In XHTML all elements must nest correctly within each other. Most browsers would forgive the following HTML and show it on-screen:

```
<p>Here is some text in a paragraph. <em>And here is some emphasized text in a
 paragraph.</p></em>
```

This would not be allowed in XHTML, as it would not meet the requirements for the document to be considered well formed. Rather it should be written like this:

```
<p>Here is some text in a paragraph. <em>And here is some emphasized text in a
 paragraph.</em></p>
```

Names and IDs

In HTML the <a>, <applet>, <form>, <frame>, <iframe>, <img>, and <map> elements could carry the name attribute, in order to identify a fragment of a document. One popular use of the name attribute is with anchor elements so links can be created that take you to a particular subsection of a page. For example, you might add the following to the top of your page so that you could create back to top links further down the page.

```
< a name="top"></a>
```

In XHTML the name attribute is replaced by another attribute, the id attribute. This is because fragment identifiers in XML must be of type ID, and each element can only have one attribute whose value is of type ID. So the id attribute in XHTML is of type ID as shown in the following:

```
<a id="top"></a>
```

This can cause a problem if you wanted to create links to a specific part of a page or within a page, as older browsers will still expect the name attribute to be used with a elements, including the following:

- Netscape Navigator 4.79 and earlier
- Internet Explorer 4.0 and earlier

For maximum browser-compatibility when writing XHTML documents, you can therefore use transitional XHTML 1.0 and include both the name and id attributes on the same element, although name has been deprecated in XHTML 1.0.

Remember, because the id attribute is of XML ID type, therefore its value must be unique within the document.

Specifying Language

It might seem perfectly obvious to you which language your web page is written in, but HTML 4 and XHTML 1.0 allow you to specify the language either for the whole documents or the language used in specific elements. This is done using the lang attribute. Browsers could use this information to display the page using language-specific ways, such as the correct use of hyphenating characters, other applications could use it to check whether they could display or process the document, and screen readers would be able to read different languages in different voices if they needed to.

The value of the lang attribute should be an ISO 639 language code (for example, en for English, fr for French, ja for Japanese, and so on). You can find a full list of these language codes at http://www.oasis-open.org/cover/iso639a.html.

XHTML 1.1 replaces the lang attribute with the xml:lang attribute. Because xml:lang can be used in any XML document it can also be used in XHTML 1.0 documents.

Currently there is very little support for either `lang` or `xml:lang`, but it is good practice to include the `xml:lang` attribute.

Character Encoding

A character encoding is a table that defines a numeric value for each character. We need these encodings because a computer does not store characters in the way you see them on the screen.

As we learned in Chapter 2, XML processors, by default, are expected to understand at least two encodings: *UTF-8* and *UTF-16*. UTF-8 is a character encoding that supports the first 128 ASCII characters as well as additional characters from languages other than English that feature accents, as well a wide range of other symbols. UTF-16, is even larger than UTF-8 and supports characters from many other languages such as Chinese and Japanese.

> *The key advantages of UTF-8 and UTF-16 are that programs written to support these character encodings will be able to handle different languages without needing to be rewritten, and documents can easily be created that contain characters from several languages.*

By default, if you do not specify an encoding, XML documents are assumed to be written in UTF-8. If the tool you are writing in, however, uses a different encoding, then you can end up with characters that do not display properly.

In order to support characters from different languages, UTF-16 requires two or more bytes for each character, whereas ASCII and UTF-8 only require 1 byte for each character. This means that some text editors and browsers do not support UTF-16.

It is also important to remember that while we can often view XHTML documents in older browsers if they use the `text/html` mime type, these older processors do not contain XML processors and do not all support UTF-16 by default. Therefore, your documents written in UTF-16 may not display correctly.

> *You will also commonly see the character encoding set to `ISO-8859-1`, which is an ISO character encoding for the Latin alphabet for the U.K., North America, Western Europe, Latin America, The Caribbean, Canada, and Africa. Many document authoring programs, such as Macromedia Dreamweaver and Microsoft FrontPage use this setting.*

How to Specify Character Encoding in XHTML

XHTML allows two ways to specify the character set your document uses (for the best chance of success, you should use both):

- The XML declaration
- The `meta` element

We have already seen the XML declaration at the beginning of most of the XML documents we have written in this book. Plenty of these examples have included the encoding attribute, like the following:

```
<?xml version="1.0" encoding="UTF-8">
```

Remember, some browsers may either ignore the XML Declaration or display the declaration as if it were part of the text for the document. Browsers that will do this include Netscape Navigator 3.04 and earlier and Internet Explorer 3.0 and earlier.

Even if the browser does not display the XML declaration as text, it does not necessarily mean that it understands it. Therefore, you should also declare your encoding in a `meta` element like so:

```
<meta http-equiv="Content-Type" content="text/html; charset=UTF-8" />
```

Using the `<meta>` tag with the `http-equiv` attribute set to `Content-Type` tells the browser what type of content this document contains. In our preceding example, the document type is set to `text/html`, and the encoding is given as `UTF-8`.

The mime type `text/html` actually means the browser will treat our page as if it were HTML. This is good news for older browsers, which will be able to display it.

XHTML also introduced the mime type `application/xhtml+xml`, which was supposed to be used on XHTML 1.0; however, there are some points you should note if you are tempted to use it:

- Internet Explorer will not be able to handle this mime type, so you need to serve it as `text/html` to most browsers.
- It must be valid XHTML, or Mozilla-based browsers will display an error.
- When using CSS selectors with XML documents the selectors are case-sensitive, so you must match the case of the selector to that of the element.

Some people avoid using the XML Declaration in XHTML documents as it can be ignored by older browsers or treated as part of the text of the document.

When a document contains both the XML Declaration and the `meta` element, the encoding value in the XML declaration takes precedence. Browsers that do not understand the XML Declaration, however, will still use the `meta` element.

Server-Side Content Types

If you are using a server-side technology—such as ASP, PHP, or JSP—to create XHTML documents, the best way to specify an encoding is by using the HTTP header `Content-Type`. The implementations are specific to the server-side environment you choose (so you should refer to documentation for your chosen language), and it is not always an option, but where possible this is the most reliable way to specify the encoding.

Summary of Changes Between Writing XHTML and HTML

We have already met all of the changes we need to know about writing XHTML rather than HTML. If you are familiar with HTML, writing XHTML documents should be a breeze! There are very few changes, and the elements and attributes remain the same (although you should avoid presentational mark up where possible).

So, when writing an XHTML 1.0 document, we must be aware of the following:

- We can include the optional XML Declaration.
- We should include a `DOCTYPE` declaration, indicating whether you are writing a document according to the Transitional, Strict, or Frameset DTD.

- We must write all element and attribute names in lowercase.
- We must close all elements.
- We must make sure all elements nest correctly.
- We should consider using `id` attributes instead of `name` attributes.
- We should indicate the language our documents are written in using the `lang` or `xml:lang` attributes.
- We should specify the character encoding the document is written in.

In order to demonstrate these simple changes, we should look at an example of an XHTML page.

Try It Out Creating an XHTML 1.0 Document

In this example, you are going to create a strict XHTML 1.0 page that documents how to write lists in XHTML. It will look very similar to the type of HTML document that you're probably used to writing, but the example will highlight the differences in writing XHTML.

1. Start you favorite web page editor, or text editor, and create a file called `eg01.html`.
2. Add the following XML declaration and encoding :

```
<?xml version="1.0" encoding="UTF-8" ?>
```

3. Next, we add the `DOCTYPE` declaration, which indicates that the document is written according to the Strict XHTML 1.0 DTD.

```
<?xml version="1.0" encoding="UTF-8" ?>
<!DOCTYPE html PUBLIC "-//W3C//DTD XHTML 1.0 Strict//EN"
  "http://www.w3.org/TR/xhtml1/DTD/xhtml1-strict.dtd">
```

4. Add the `<html>` element, and use namespace defaulting to indicate that it is part of the XHTML 1.0 namespace.

```
<?xml version="1.0" encoding="UTF-8" ?>
<!DOCTYPE html PUBLIC "-//W3C//DTD XHTML 1.0 Strict//EN"
  "http://www.w3.org/TR/xhtml1/DTD/xhtml1-strict.dtd">
<html xmlns="http://www.w3.org/1999/xhtml">
</html>
```

5. Add the `<head>` element, with a `<title>` element just as you would have in any HTML document. Also add a `meta` element, to specify the content type of the document and the character encoding you are using. The document needs to work in IE 6 and older browsers, so you should stick with the `text/html` mime type in the `content` attribute.

```
<head>
  <meta http-equiv="Content-Type" content="text/html; charset=UTF-8" />
  <title>Lists in XHTML</title>
</head>
```

6. Add the <body> elements and the following headings:

```
<body>
   <h1>Lists in XHTML</h1>
   <h2>Ordered Lists</h2>
   <h2>Unordered Lists</h2>
   <h2>Definition Lists</h2>
</body>
```

   As you might use different levels of headings in a word processor, here is a main heading, with lower level headings that mark the start of subsections. So far, the document is self-describing just as XML aims—the head, title, body, and different level headings all describe the content and structure of the document.

7. Add an unordered list that introduces the types of lists available in XHTML:

```
<ul>
  <li>Ordered List</li>
  <li>Unordered List</li>
  <li>Definition Lists</li>
</ul>
```

   Note how you must close the line item element. HTML was more forgiving than this, and if you left out some closing tags, pages would still be displayed. XHTML, being an application of XML, is not so forgiving, so you must add the closing tags.

8. Ideally, you should link these list items to anchors inside each of the relevant headings.

```
<ul>
  <li><a href="#orderedList">Ordered List</a></li>
  <li><a href="#unorderedList">Unordered List</a></li>
  <li><a href="#definitionList">Definition Lists</a></li>
</ul>

<h2><a id="orderedList" />Ordered List</h2>
<h2><a id="unorderedList" />Unordered List</h2>
<h2><a id="definitionList" />Definition List</h2>
```

   As with all attributes in XML, both the value of the `href` attribute on the link and the `id` attribute must be given in double quotes.

9. You can now add in the rest of the document, which contains paragraphs describing each type of bullet. It would also be good to add a back-to-top link to the bottom of the page (inside a <div> element, because it's an inline element and therefore shouldn't appear at block level). Here is the full page:

```
<?xml version="1.0" encoding="UTF-8"?>
<!DOCTYPE html PUBLIC "-//W3C//DTD XHTML 1.0 Strict//EN"
  "http://www.w3.org/TR/xhtml1/DTD/xhtml1-strict.dtd">
<html xmlns="http://www.w3.org/1999/xhtml" lang="en">
```

```
<head>
  <meta http-equiv="Content-Type" content="text/html; charset=UTF-8" />
  <title>Lists in XHTML</title>
</head>

<body>

  <h1><a id="lists">Lists in XHTML</a></h1>
  <p>Three types of list are available to us when writing an XHTML document.
     These are:</p>

  <ul>
    <li><a href="#orderedList">Ordered List</a></li>
    <li><a href="#unorderedList">Unordered List</a></li>
    <li><a href="#definitionList">Definition Lists</a></li>
  </ul>

  <h2><a id="orderedList">Ordered List</a></h2>
  <p>An ordered list allows you to create a list of items, each of which is
     preceeded by a number. The list is automatically numbered in ascending
     order.</p>
  <p>The list is started with a <code>nl</code> tag, which indicates the
     start of a numbered list. The <code>nl</code> element is the containing
     element, for the numbered list. Each list item is then placed inside a
     <code>li</code> element. </p>

  <h2><a id="unorderedList">Unordered List</a></h2>
  <p>An unordered list is a fancy name for a list of bullet points that are
     not preceeded by numbers. The containing element for the items in an
     unordered list is the <code>ul</code> element. Again each item in the
     list is put inside the <code>li</code> element.</p>

  <h2><a id="definitionList">Definition List</a></h2>
  <p>The least common type of list is a definition list, which tends to
     comprise of words and their definitions.</p>
  <p>The containing element for a definition list is <code>dl</code>
     element.Each term that has to be defined is contained inside a & gt;DT& lt;
     element, while the definition is contained in a & gt;DL& lt; element, like
     so.</p>
  <div><a href="#lists">Back to top</a></div>
</body>
</html>
```

10. Save the file, and open it in a browser. You should see something like Figure 16-1.

How It Works

Most of this document will be very familiar to you, so I will only highlight the parts that are particularly noteworthy and different than HTML.

The example started off with the option XML declaration, followed by a DOCTYPE declaration which indicates which DTD the document obeys the rules of. In this case it was the Strict XHTML DTD.

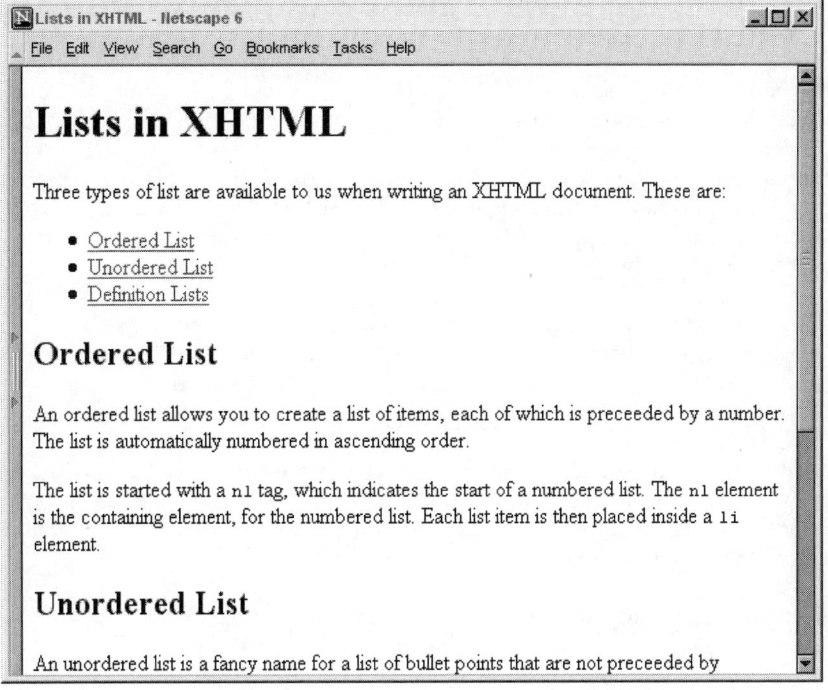

Figure 16-1

The root element was the `<html>` element, as with earlier HTML documents. However, it did carry a namespace to indicate that the markup belonged to the XHTML namespace.

Both the `<meta>` element inside the head of the document and the XML declaration carried the `encoding` attributes to indicate the character encoding that the document was written in.

Every element had to be closed properly. For example, the `<meta>` element was an example of an empty element; it had no content and therefore had a forward slash character before the closing angled bracket. Meanwhile all other elements had an opening and closing element.

All elements nested correctly to create a well-formed document, and all attribute values were given in quotes.

The bulleted list of topics covered was linked to the relevant headings using the `id` attribute rather than the `name` attribute to create destination anchors. The `id` attribute value must be of ID type, so it must be unique within the document and must obey the rules of XML 1.0 names.

Finally, there is no stylistic mark up (as suggested at the beginning of the chapter). In order to change the fonts, colors, and other presentational rules for this document, a link would be made to a CSS style sheet using the `<link>` element, as you will see in the next chapter.

As you can see, there are not too many differences in this document than there would be in an HTML document, but the rules for creating an XHTML document are stricter than those for creating HTML so you need to be clear on the few changes there are.

Stricter Documents Make Faster and Lighter Processors

As you can see, there are new constraints on how we write documents in XHTML (in particular, the strict document type). We can no longer omit closing `</li>` tags on our bullet points, line breaks, and image tags must be written as empty elements, and the values of attributes must be given in quotes.

These extra requirements might seem like a bit of a hassle. After all with HTML, you can often get away with writing documents that contain all manner of mistakes, yet they still display correctly. But there is a very good reason for the strict approach, and you only need to try to download the latest version of one of the main browsers to see why.

Mainstream browsers tend to contain a lot of code that allows us to view HTML pages that contain errors in their code, from tags that are not closed to elements that are not nested properly. While it may help people who are just learning to write pages and get them up on the Internet, the cost is bigger browsers, which take longer to download.

When we consider the range of new devices that will be able to connect to the Internet, we cannot expect all of them to support megabytes of code just to allow some people to write pages incorrectly. Imagine if a mobile phone was expected to carry a program that weighs in at 52MB, which is the amount of hard disk space you need to run Netscape 7.1.

Other benefits from being strict with our code include the following:

- Pages can be displayed faster.
- Because the stricter rules make our XHTML documents conform to the rules of XML documents, we can use all kinds of XML tools with our XHTML documents, including DOM, SAX, and XSLT processors and authoring tools.
- As we shall see shortly in this chapter, we will be able to use the same language, XHTML, on many different types of Internet-enabled devices.

So, for the sake of keeping what are good habits anyway, we get some real advantages as developers (unless we want to learn new languages for each kind of device).

XHTML Tools

We do not need any fancy new tools to write XHTML documents, a plain text editor like Windows Notepad or Mac Simple Text will suffice, providing it supports the character encoding you want to write in. Many of the latest versions of document-authoring tools you might have come across also support XHTML documents, such as Macromedia Dreamweaver and Microsoft FrontPage (but make sure you have selected the appropriate options in your program or it might continue to produce standard HTML code with some errors).

But this is just the tip of the iceberg when it comes to tools you can use with your XHTML pages. Because XHTML documents are themselves XML documents, you can use any of the tools you have already met in this book to work with your XHTML pages:

- You could use any XML editor to write your XHTML pages, and though they may not be written specifically for XHTML, they will help you close tags, check well-formedness, and show allowable elements and attributes.
- You can use DOM- and SAX-aware processors to programmatically access your code.
- You can use XSLT to perform transformations on your XHTML. For example, you could use an XSLT stylesheet to transform a document conforming to the strict XHTML 1.0 DTD into one conforming to the transitional DTD so that it has better support for older browsers. This means you still have future proofed strict XHTML documents and backward-compatible versions generated from transformations.
- You can also use any XML validation tools to validate your XHTML documents.

Validating our documents is a good practice to get into, so that is addressed next.

Validating XHTML Documents

Although browsers are unlikely to validate your XHTML documents, and browsers on a desktop PC are likely to display your page even if it contains errors, it's a good idea that you validate your documents manually when you have written them to make sure they do not contain any errors. While your desktop browser might show the XHTML page you created as you intended, validating a document is the best way to help ensure you get the results you expect when the document is used with different applications (even if these are just browsers on other operating systems).

HTML browsers have been so forgiving of our errors that most people have developed at least one or two bad habits. Even if you think you stick rigidly to standards, you might be surprised. It is particularly useful when we start to write XHTML that we check our pages (after all, if you had made a mistake, you wouldn't want to come back and change all your pages when your boss decides you are going to have to perform XSLT transforms on each document next year).

Some authoring tools will validate your XHTML documents for you, or they will have interactive debugging features such as highlighting of errors. There are a lot of other options available to us; because XHTML documents are themselves XML documents, we can use any validating XML processor to validate our XHTML documents. We have already met some validating processors in this book, in particular Chapter 4 looked at processors that validated documents against DTDs.

Probably the simplest way to check your XHTML documents, however, is to use one of the free online XHTML validation services, such as the one provided by the W3C at `http://validator.w3.org`.

Following is the example we just saw being put through the W3C validator, but I removed the quotes from this attribute before running the document through the processor to generate this error. Figure 16-2 shows the error we'll get.

```
<li><a href=#orderedList>Ordered List</a></li>
```

As you can see, we are told where our errors are found so we can correct them. In the long run this process should save you time.

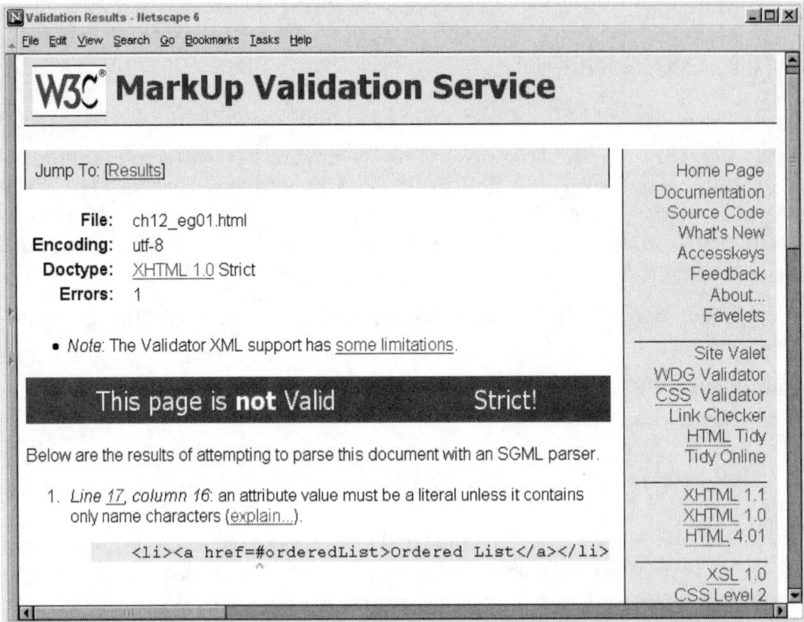

Figure 16-2

Validation Pitfalls

If you are seasoned in writing HTML pages or converting sites from HTML to XHTML, there are a couple of points we should look at which you are likely to come across; otherwise you are likely to have problems when you validate your pages. These are as follows:

- Using JavaScript in your pages
- Using content from third parties (such as advertising)

Including JavaScript in Your Page

Rather than including JavaScript in your pages, you should get into the habit of putting scripts in separate files, which are then referred to using the `script` element, as shown in the following code:

```
<script type="text/javascript" src="scripts/formValidation.js">
```

This can have great benefits, as you are likely to find that, in no time at all, you have developed a script library that you will be able to reuse, which will save you development time in the long run. It also means that, if several pages use the same script you can make alterations to just one file and they will have the same effect across the whole site without having to manually alter each page.

If, however, you must include script in your page, you must watch for the following things:

- XHTML processors can strip out anything in comment markers.
- The < and > characters will break the structure of an XHTML document unless it's placed in a CDATA section.

When writing JavaScript, you've probably gotten into the habit of putting it inside comment marks, so that older browsers that don't support JavaScript do not raise an error and can still display the page. With XHTML, however, both browsers and servers can strip out comments that they find in a document before displaying the data, which would mean JavaScript code would be lost.

To avoid your script being stripped out, you should place it within a CDATA section, as discussed in Chapter 2. This has the added advantage that you can use the < and > characters without breaking the structure of the document. For example, the following code will work with most older browsers (with the exception of Netscape Navigator 3 and below):

```
<script type="text/javascript"><![CDATA[
function validateEmail {...
... }
]]></script>
```

If your browser knows you're using XML, because you use the mime type `application/xhtml+xml` (as opposed to using `text/html` when the browser will act as if it's just HTML), you have the following additional issues to deal with:

- If you use `getElementsByTagName()` with the XML DOM, elements are returned in lowercase, whereas the HTML DOM will return them in uppercase.
- You cannot just use the `document.write()` method to write to the page; you have to create a new element in the document.
- To access contents of a document, you cannot use collections such as `document.form`; you have to use another method like the `getElementsByTagName()`.

Incorporating Content from Other People

There are many reasons why you might display content created by others within your web pages. For example, you might be syndicating some content from another content provider, or you could be showing advertisements from a third-party source.

This could be a problem because you might not be getting the latest version of XHTML. While you could ask for it in the correct format, this may not be possible with syndicated content, and it may hold you up when dealing with advertisers, hence affecting advertising revenue. If you just have to live with their versions, you have the two following options:

- Downgrade your version of XHTML to whatever the client is using. Although you might be happy to downgrade from strict XHTML 1.0 to transitional XHTML 1.0, you might be less willing to downgrade to HTML 3.2 if that is what your client uses.
- Use client-side JavaScript to include the information in the page. This ensures your base page is a valid document, and that you can display your pages in browsers that support the incorporated format and those that do not.

Having looked at some of these validation issues, hopefully you will be confident to get writing XHTML 1.0 documents. As I said at the beginning of the chapter, however, there is another version of XHTML. XHTML 1.1 takes XHTML toward the future and is based on a modularized form of XHTML.

Modularized XHTML

Having looked at XHTML 1.0 and the changes you have to make when writing HTML as an application of XML, we should now look at XHTML 1.1, which takes a much larger step forward. Before XHTML 1.1 was produced, XHTML was split into a set of modules, and you do not need to look far in order to see why.

In the past few years there have been an increasing number of different devices that connect to the Internet including mobile phones, PDAs, TVs, digital book readers, and refrigerators. Because of the inherent limitations (such as screen size) of some of these devices, not all of the HTML 4 specification is relevant to them. Furthermore, some of these devices do not have the power or memory to implement the full specification. Therefore, more compact languages have been developed specifically to support these new devices. Some examples include CHTML (Compact HTML), WML (Wireless Markup Language), and the HTML 4.0 Guidelines for Mobile Access.

If we look at the competing languages that have sprung up to support different devices, we can see that they share common features. Each language allows users to mark up the following types of information:

- Basic text, including headings, paragraphs, and lists
- Hyperlinks and links to related documents
- Basic forms
- Basic tables
- Images
- Meta information

The W3C understood that the various devices that can now access the Internet could no longer be served by one single language (HTML). Therefore, rather than have several competing languages for different devices, the W3C thought it would be much better if XHTML were split into modules, with each module covering some common functionality (such as basic text or hyperlinks). That way, these modules could be used as building blocks for the variations of XHTML developed for different devices.

Instead of reinventing the wheel, like CHTML and WML did, all languages could be built from these same basic building blocks. The new document types would be based on what is known as an *XHTML Host Language*, which is then extended with other modules. For example, the XHTML 1.1 DTD contains 21 modules that cover the functionality of the XHTML 1.0 Strict DTD. We shall also shortly meet another document type called XHTML Basic, which was designed as a host language for use on smaller devices, which uses just 11 modules.

> *When a new document type is being created and only part of a module's functionality is required, then the whole module must be included in the language (it cannot just include part of a module). This makes it easier to learn a new language because the developer can say which modules it uses, and the document author will know it supports all of the markup from that module, rather than having to check individual elements.*

In the following table, we can see the full list of XHTML *Abstract Modules* in the first column (these are like the basic functionality of HTML split into related subsets) In the second column you see the core modules required to be an application of XHTML. In the third and fourth columns you see which modules are used in the XHTML Basic DTD and the XHTML 1.1 DTD.

Module Name	Core Module	XHTML Basic DTD	XHTML 1.1 DTD
Structure	X	X	X
Text	X	X	X
Hypertext	X	X	X
List	X	X	X
Applet			
Object		X	X
Presentation			X
Edit			X
Bidirectional text			X
Frames			
IFrame			
Basic forms		X	
Forms			X
Basic tables		X	
Table			X
Image		X	X
Client-side image map			X
Server-side image map			X
Intrinsic events			X
Metainformation		X	X
Scripting			X
Stylesheet			X
Style attribute (deprecated)			X
Link		X	X
Target			
Base		X	X
Ruby annotation			X
Name identification			
Legacy			

Note that the legacy module supports elements that have been deprecated from earlier versions of HTML and XHTML, and is therefore helpful in writing code that supports older devices.

There is another additional benefit as well; modularization makes it possible to create new document types that mix XHTML with other XML languages, such as SVG or MathML, which would result in what is known as a *hybrid document type*. Indeed, when new versions of XHTML come out, extensions to the language can take the form of new modules.

This will make cross-browser development far easier, and we can finally say goodbye to deprecated features such as stylistic markup of HTML 4 that were allowed into XHTML 1.0.

Module Implementations

As we learned in Chapter 1, each document type has a DTD or XML Schema (or other schema) that defines the elements, attributes, and allowable structures of documents conforming to that document type.

A *module implementation* is a form of schema, such as a DTD or XML Schema, containing the element types, attribute-list declarations, and content model declarations that define the module. With each module having a separate implementation, it makes it far easier to create markup languages using the modules as opposed to fishing the appropriate parts from one large document.

While XHTML 1.1 was initially released with a DTD, the W3C later released an XML Schema version of the implementations.

XHTML 1.1

XHTML 1.1 uses a selection of the abstract modules defined by XHTML modularization, and the implementations of those modules, in a document type called XHTML 1.1. So, XHTML 1.1 is an example of the modules combined into a specific document type. We saw the modules that XHTML 1.1 contains in the previous table.

The modules used give the same functionality that we found in strict XHTML 1.0. The only changes we have to make from writing a strict XHTML 1.0 document are the following:

1. The `DOCTYPE` declaration must precede the root element (which should carry the `xmlns` attribute). The public identifier, if present, should be represented like the following:

```
<!DOCTYPE html PUBLIC "-//W3C//DTD XHTML 1.1//EN"
    "http://www.w3.org/TR/xhtml11/DTD/xhtml11.dtd">
```

2. The `lang` attribute has been replaced by the `xml:lang` attribute.
3. The `name` attribute has been replaced by the `id` attribute.
4. The Ruby collection of elements has been added.

   Ruby is a term for a run of small character annotations that are sometimes added to the characters of an ideographic script like Japanese to clarify the pronunciation (and/or the meaning) of those characters. In vertical text they are usually added in a very small font along the side of the ideogram, while in horizontal text they are used on the top.

5. The `style` attribute has been deprecated.

Here is an example of an XHTML 1.1-conforming document that highlights how similar the XHTML 1.1. document is to an XHTML document:

```
<?xml version="1.0" encoding="UTF-8" ?>
<!DOCTYPE html PUBLIC "-//W3C//DTD XHTML 1.1//EN"
    "http://www.w3.org/TR/xhtml11/DTD/xhtml11.dtd">

<html xmlns="http://www.w3.org/1999/xhtml" xml:lang="en" >
  <head>
    <title>Example 2</title>
  </head>
  <body>
    <a id="sampleParagraph"><p>This document conforms to XHTML 1.1.</p></a>
  </body>
</html>
```

XHTML Basic

Another good example of the use of XHTML modularization is *XHTML Basic,* a document type in itself, which was designed for devices that do not support the full set of XHTML features, such as mobile phones, PDAs, car navigation systems, digital book readers, and smart watches.

As we have already mentioned, the memory and power that would be required to implement the full HTML specification would be too high for some smaller devices. So, rather than create a whole new language for these devices from scratch, XHTML Basic takes the four core modules of XHTML and extends them with the basic forms, basic tables, image, object, meta information, link and base modules. Here is a quick summary of the modules and elements available in XHTML Basic.

Module	Elements
Structure module*	`body, head, html, title`
Text module*	`abbr, acronym, address, blockquote, br, cite, code, dfn, div, em, h1, h2, h3, h4, h5, h6, kbd, p, pre, q, samp, span, strong, var`
Hypertext module*	`A`
List module*	`dl, dt, dd, ol, ul, li`
Basic forms module	`form, input, label, select, option, textarea`
Basic tables module	`table, tr, td, th, caption`
Image module	`Img`
Object module	`object, param`
Metainformation module	`Meta`
Link module	`Link`
Base module	`Base`

** = core module*

XHTML Basic is not supposed to be the one and only language that will ever be used on small devices. Rather it is supposed to be a common base that can be extended. For example, some people might want to extend it with the addition of the bi-directional text module, or indeed create an event model to deal with things like incoming call events (which would not apply to, say, televisions).

It is this kind of subsetting and extending of XHTML that makes it a language that will form a strong basis for all kinds of future clients.

To finish this section, it is worthwhile to take a quick look at some of the markup and modules of XHTML that were not included in XHTML Basic, and why they were left out. We now know that HTML 4 contained features that not every device could support, and that there were several competing markup languages for mobile devices that recreated common functionality in each of these languages. We also know that XHTML Basic will be a base for further extensions of XHTML. So, here is some of the markup that was left out, and some of the reasons why it was left out:

- The `<style>` element was left out because you can use the `<link>` element to link external stylesheets to a document (rather than use an internal stylesheet—if you don't know the difference between the two, we shall see more in the next chapter). Therefore, browsers that support stylesheets can download them, but they are not required to support them in order to display information.
- `<script>` and `<noscript>` elements are not supported because small devices might not have the memory and CPU power to handle execution of scripts or programs. It was deemed that documents for these devices should be readable without requiring scripts.
- Event-handler attributes, which are used to invoke scripts, are not supported because events tend to be device-dependent. For example, a TV might have an `onChannelChange` event, while a phone might have an `incomingCall` event, neither of which applies to the other device. Ideally, it would be better to use a generic event-handling mechanism than hardwiring event names into the DTD.
- Whereas basic XHTML forms are supported, more complex form functions are not applicable to all small devices. For example, if a device does not have a local file system, it will not be able to use the file and image input types in forms. This is why only the basic XHTML forms module is included.
- As with forms, only basic tables are supported. Tables can be difficult to display at the best of times on small devices, so features of the tables module will not apply to all small devices (for example, the nesting of tables is left out). It is recommended that users follow the web content accessibility guidelines 1.0 for creating accessible tables.

So, while XHTML Basic can be used as is, the intention is that it be used as a host language. These features could be added in for a particular implementation that would support these features. Adding markup from other languages results in a new document type that is an extension of XHTML Basic.

Summary

In this chapter you have learned how HTML has been reformulated as an application of XML in XHTML 1.0. You have seen the three XHTML 1.0 document types, and how converting HTML to an application of XML does not require learning too much new, other than obeying rules that any well-formed XML document would, such as the following:

- The optional presence of an XML Declaration
- A required DOCTYPE declaration
- Element and attribute names are case-sensitive
- All attributes must be given values, and the values must be given in double quotes
- There must be a unique root `<html>` element
- Empty elements must be written with the closing slash before the end of the tag, for example, `<br />`.
- Elements must be correctly nested
- The `name` attribute is replaced by the `id` attribute, which is of XML ID type, for uniquely identifying a fragment (and its value must therefore be unique within the document)
- We can specify language and character encodings

In return, you saw the following improvements:

- A stricter syntax, which makes it is possible to create processors that require less memory and power and is ideal for portable devices.
- Pages that are simpler and will display quicker.
- All tools that are XML-aware can be used when working with strict XHTML 1.0 documents, such as XSLT, DOM, and SAX. In particular, you can validate documents using any XML validation tool, or using one of the free online validation resources.

Some pitfalls to validating documents were also covered, in particular, handling JavaScript (which should be placed in external files or CDATA sections) and content from other sources (which can be imported using JavaScript).

Having looked at XHTML 1.0, we went on to see how XHTML has been split into modules of related markup. These modules can be combined to create new document types for the wide range of new web-enabled devices that are coming onto the market.

We saw XHTML Basic, which is a rather minimal build of the modules designed for use on small devices, while XHTML 1.1 is an example of a larger build, avoiding the old presentation features, but offering a rich language for devices that have the required resources to support the larger language.

After going through XHTML in the next chapter, we will go on to look at CSS, which is the language that we will use to style our documents from now on. CSS can be used with any application of XML, not just the various versions of XHTML. Indeed the next chapter will look at how we can use CSS to control presentation of page markup languages without relying on tricks like tables for positioning parts of a document.

Exercise Questions

Suggested solutions to these questions can be found in Appendix A.

Question 1

Take the following HTML 3.2 example, and create a version in strict XHTML 1.0 without any stylistic markup.

```
<HTML>
<HEAD>
   <TITLE>Excerise One</TITLE>
</HEAD>
<BODY bgcolor=white>

<A NAME="top"></A>
<H1 align=center>XHTML</H1>

<FONT face=arial size=2>
  XHTML 1.0 is the reformulation of HTML in XHTML. There are three XHTML 1.0
  document types:

  <UL>
    <LI>Transitional
    <LI>Strict
    <LI>Frameset
  </UL>

  XHTML has also been split into <b>modules</b>, from which document types
  such as XHTML 1.1 and XHTML Basic have been formed.
</FONT>

<A href="#top">Back to top</a>
</BODY>
</HTML>
```

Question 2

Take the same HTML 3.2 example, and create a second version that uses transitional XHTML and can work in most legacy browsers.

Once you have written your documents, validate them using the W3C validator at `http://validator.w3.org/`.

Cascading Style Sheets (CSS)

This chapter takes a look at *Cascading Style Sheets* (CSS) as a means of styling our XML documents for use on the web. You may well have already used CSS with HTML or XHTML; indeed the first example you will see shows how to style XHTML documents using CSS (this will get you started if you are new to CSS). Dealing with other XML document types, however, requires some different techniques that you will read in this chapter.

As we saw in the last chapter, when the W3C released HTML 4 they *deprecated* stylistic markup (such as the `<center>` and `<font>` elements and the `bgcolor` and `width` attributes), which meant that such markup would not be featured in future versions. (Indeed, by XHTML 1.1—the latest incarnation of HTML at the time of writing—stylistic markup had been completely removed.) Rather we are encouraged to use a style language, such as CSS, to style our documents.

Yet even when you remove stylistic markup from an XHTML document, the browser still knows how to display elements, such as tables, lists of different levels of headings, and so on. In other XML vocabularies, we will not even have this most rudimentary help with layout. After all, a `<table>` element in your XML vocabulary might be used to describe a piece of wood with four legs. Considering that a browser will not know how any of the elements in your XML vocabulary need to be displayed, we have a lot more work to do when styling XML documents with CSS than XHTML documents.

If you know that your XML documents will be displayed on the web, some of the points you learn in this chapter might even affect the way in which you write your vocabulary or schema. For example, by the end of the chapter you will see how CSS is much more suited to displaying element content than attribute values.

In this chapter you will learn the following:

- ❑ How CSS relies upon a box model for styling documents, whereby the content of each element inhabits a box.
- ❑ How to use CSS to style HTML and XHTML documents rather than relying on stylistic markup.

- How to give your XML documents a visual structure, so that they can look like XHTML documents with features such as tables, lists, links, and images even though the browser does not know how to present any of the elements.

Before you start looking at CSS, however, it is important to reiterate the reasons why we need style sheets.

This chapter uses Internet Explorer 6 and Netscape 6 (or higher). Some features described and demonstrated are not available in all browsers yet.

Why Style Sheets?

In the last chapter we looked at why strict XHTML 1.0 and XHTML 1.1 (the W3C's replacement for HTML) no longer contain markup to indicate how a document should be styled (except the `<style>` element and the deprecated `style` attribute). Before XHTML was created, HTML contained the following three types of markup:

- *Structural markup*, which describes the structure of a document, the headings, paragraphs, line breaks, and lists using elements such as `<h1>`, `<p>`, `<br>`, `<ul>`, and `<li>` elements.
- *Semantic markup*, which tells us something about the document we are marking up; for example, the `<meta>` and `<title>` elements.
- *Stylistic markup*, which indicates how the document should be presented on a browser, using elements such as `<font>` and `<s>`, and attributes such as `bgcolor`.

There is an odd-one-out here: the stylistic markup. The other two tell us something about the content of the document, whereas the stylistic markup just tells us how the document should be presented for one medium (the desktop PC browser), not about the document itself. While a `<font>` element might tell us in which typeface a designer wanted a line of a page to be shown, the `<font>` element does not tell us anything about the structure of the document in the same way a heading or paragraph element does—and the same designer might want a different font for the same text in a different medium.

Remembering that applications of XML are supposed to create self-describing documents, we can see that styling doesn't tell anything about the content of the document and should not be included in most of our documents. Rather than using stylistic markup in our documents, we can use another language in a separate document to indicate how our documents should be rendered, and we can even have different style sheets for different mediums—one each for PC browsers, browsers in set top boxes for TVs, printer-friendly versions of pages, and so on, which all have different types of display (in particular, different resolutions).

Remember that most XML languages do not include markup that indicates how the document should be styled. Indeed, many XML languages will never even be styled as they are to transfer data between applications.

This chapter addresses how we can use this separate language, CSS, to style XML documents. Some of the things we will see in this chapter are only starting to be supported in the version 6 and 7 browsers, so the chapter will not only take you to the limits of what is possible with CSS in browsers now, but also whet your appetite for what will be possible in the near future.

The topics covered in this chapter include:

- How CSS works
- How to style XML documents with CSS
- Using CSS selectors to indicate which elements a CSS rule applies to
- The box model that CSS is based upon
- Positioning schemes that allow CSS to control layouts of pages
- Laying out tabular XML data with CSS
- Linking between XML documents
- Adding images to XML documents
- Adding text to our documents from the style sheet
- Using attribute values in documents

The first thing to do is make sure you are familiar with writing a basic CSS style sheet, and how the presentational or stylistic CSS rules are applied to a document.

There have actually been two versions of CSS already published by the W3C called CSS1 and CSS2. CSS2 built upon the functionality of CSS1, and both will be covered in this chapter under the general term CSS.

Introducing CSS

CSS allows us to style a document by associating presentation rules with the elements that appear in the document we want to style; these rules indicate how the content of those elements should be rendered. Here is an example of a CSS rule (see Figure 17-1). Rather than using a `<font>` element to specify typefaces, this rule indicates that all `<h1>` elements should use the Arial typeface.

Figure 17-1

The rule is split into two parts, as follows:

- The *selector* indicates which element or elements the declaration applies to (you can have a comma-separated list of several elements).
- The *declaration* sets out how the elements should be styled. In this case, the content of the `<h1>` elements should be in the Arial typeface.

The declaration is also split into two parts, separated by a colon as follows:

- A *property*, which is the property of the selected element(s) that we want to affect; in Figure 17-1 we have been setting the `font-family` property.
- A *value*, which is a specification for this property; in this case it is the `Arial` typeface.

Although you do not need to add a semicolon at the end of a single declaration, a declaration can consist of several property-value pairs, and each property-value pair within a rule must be separated by a semicolon. Therefore, it is good practice to start adding them from the beginning in case you want to add another later, because if you forget to add the semicolon, any further property-value pairs will be ignored.

Following is an example of a CSS rule that applies to several elements (the `<h1>`, `<h2>` and `<h3>` elements) where each element's name is separated by a comma. It also specifies several properties for these elements, where each rule is separated by a semicolon. All the properties are kept inside the curly braces as shown in the following:

```
h1, h2, h3 { color:#000000;
             background-color:#FFFFFF;
             font-family:arial, verdana, sans-serif;
             font-weight:bold;}
```

This should be fairly straightforward; the content of each heading element will be written in a bold, black, Arial typeface (unless the computer does not have it, in which case it will look for Verdana, then any Sans-serif font), with a white background.

If you have done any HTML work at all, this should be quite familiar to you. Rather than using the `bgcolor` attribute on an element, you use the `background-color` property in CSS. Rather than use a `<font>` element to describe the typeface we want to use, we add the `font-family` property to the rule for that element. Rather than using `<b></b>` tags, you use the `font-weight` property.

CSS Properties

The following table shows the main properties available to us from CSS1 and CSS2 (there are some other properties in these specifications, but they are rarely used and are not supported yet by the major browsers):

FONT
font
font-family
font-size
font-size-adjust
font-stretch
font-style
font-variant
font-weight

TEXT
color
direction
letter-spacing
text-align
text-decoration
text-indent
text-shadow
text-transform
unicode-bidi
white-space
word-spacing

BACKGROUND
background
background-attachment
background-color
background-image
background-position
background-repeat

BORDER
border
border-bottom
border-bottom-color
border-bottom-style
border-bottom-width
border-color
border-left
border-left-color
border-left-style
border-left-width
border-right
border-right-color
border-right-style
border-right-width
border-style
border-top
border-top-color
border-top-style
border-top-width
border-width

MARGIN
margin
margin-bottom
margin-left
margin-right
margin-top

PADDING
padding
padding-bottom
padding-left
padding-right
padding-top

DIMENSIONS
height
line-height
max-height
max-width
min-height
min-width
width

POSITIONING
bottom
clip
left
overflow
right
top
vertical-align
z-index

OUTLINES
outline
outline-color
outline-style
outline-width

TABLE
border-collapse
border-spacing
caption-side
empty-cells
table-layout

LIST and MARKER
list-style
list-style-image
list-style-position
list-style-type
marker-offset

GENERATED CONTENT
content
counter-increment
counter-reset
quotes

CLASSIFICATION
clear
cursor
display
float
position
visibility

Inheritance

There is a good reason why the word "cascading" comes at the beginning of the name for CSS. Many of the CSS properties can be inherited by child elements, so once you have declared a rule, that rule will apply to all child elements of the element to which it was applied. For example, if you set up a rule on the `<body>` element in an XHTML document, it will apply to all elements in the body of the document. For example, if you indicated a `font-family` property for the `<body>` element, all of the text in the document should appear in that font. You can override the rule, by creating a more specific rule for certain child elements; for example, you might want all headings in a different font than the rest of the page.

Take another look at the following CSS rule (which we met earlier in the chapter):

```
h1, h2, h3 { color:#000000;
             background-color:#FFFFFF;
             font-family:arial, verdana, sans-serif;
             font-weight:bold;}
```

Imagine that you now want the <h3> element to be italic as well, then you can just add the following rule:

```
h1, h2, h3 {color:#000000; background-color:#FFFFFF;
            font-family:arial, verdana, sans-serif;
            font-weight:bold;}
h3          {font-style:italic;}
```

This saves writing all the property-value pairs out again that the <h3> element has in common with other heading elements. The more specific a rule within the style sheet, the greater precedence it has in the cascade. For example, if you don't want the h3 element to be bold, you could just add the following into the rule:

```
h3              {font-weight:normal;}
```

This would override the `font-weight:bold;` declaration before it. The order in which rules appear within the style sheet, however, does not matter.

There is also another reason CSS style sheets have "cascading" in the title: you can use rules from several style sheets by importing one into another or using several style sheets with the same document. You might use multiple style sheets if, for example, you wanted to include all styles common to the whole site in one CSS document (such as company colors and fonts), and all the styles just for a subsection of the site in another (such as specific layout for a certain section of the site).

Try It Out   Styling an XHTML Document with CSS

The first type of XML document to look at styling is an XHTML document. If you have ever used CSS with an HTML document, this should be quite straightforward. The document you will be styling is the XHTML example from the previous chapter that described lists in XHTML. There will not be anything too adventurous in this first example—just some basic rules about how this document should be presented to get you into the swing of writing CSS.

1. Open the file `ch16_eg01.html` from the previous chapter, and add the following line with the `link` element (which is the only highlighted line) then save it as `ch17_eg01.xml`:

```
<?xml version="1.0" encoding="UTF-8"?>
<!DOCTYPE html PUBLIC "-//W3C//DTD XHTML 1.0 Strict//EN"
    "http://www.w3.org/TR/xhtml1/DTD/xhtml1-strict.dtd">
<html xmlns="http://www.w3.org/1999/xhtml" lang="en">

<head>
  <meta http-equiv="Content-Type" content="text/html; charset=UTF-8" />
  <title>Lists in XHTML</title>
  <link rel="stylesheet" type="text/css" href="ch17_eg01.css" />
</head>
```

```
<body>

  <h1><a id="lists" />Lists in XHTML</h1>
  <p>Three types of list are available to us when writing an XHTML document.
     These are:</p>

  <ul>
    <li><a href="#orderedList">Ordered List</a></li>
    <li><a href="#unorderedList">Unordered List</a></li>
    <li><a href="#definitionList">Definition Lists</a></li>
  </ul>

  <h2><a id="orderedList" />Ordered List</h2>
  <p>An ordered list allows you to create a list of items, each of which is
     preceeded by a number. The list is automatically numbered in ascending
     order.</p>
  <p>The list is started with a <code>nl</code> tag, which indicates the start
     of a numbered list. The <code>nl</code> element is the containing
     element, for the numbered list. Each list item is then placed inside a
     <code>li</code>element. </p>

  <h2><a id="unorderedList" />Unordered List</h2>
  <p>An unordered list is a fancy name for a list of bullet points that are
     not preceeded by numbers. The containing element for the items in an
     unordered list is the <code>ul</code> element. Again each item in the
     list is put inside the <code>li</code> element.</p>

  <h2><a id="definitionList" />Definition List</h2>
  <p>The least common type of list is a definition list, which tends to
     comprise of words and their definitions.</p>
  <p>The containing element for a definition list is <code>dl</code> element.
     Each term that has to be defined is contained inside a <code>&lt;DT&gt;
     </code> element, while the definition is contained in a <code>&lt;DL&gt;
     </code> element, like so.</p>
  <div><a href="#lists">Back to top</a></div>
</body>
</html>
```

2. Using your favorite web or text editor, create a file called ch17_eg01.css for your style sheet.
3. The first rules you should write indicate the settings for the whole document, so the first selector should indicate that we want to apply rules to the <body> element.

```
body {}
```

4. Having written the selector, you need to add the declarations that say the background of the document should be white and the text should be black—and while you're at it, specify a typeface. To do this, add the following to the rule:

```
body {
  color:#000000;
  background-color:#FFFFFF;
  font-family:arial, verdana, sans-serif;}
```

5. Next, indicate that the level 2 headings should be italicized, while the code elements should have a gray background so that these elements stick out.

```
h2 {font-style:italic;}
code {background-color:#CCCCCC;}
```

6. Save the CSS file you have just written and open the HTML document in a browser. You should end up with something that looks like Figure 17-2.

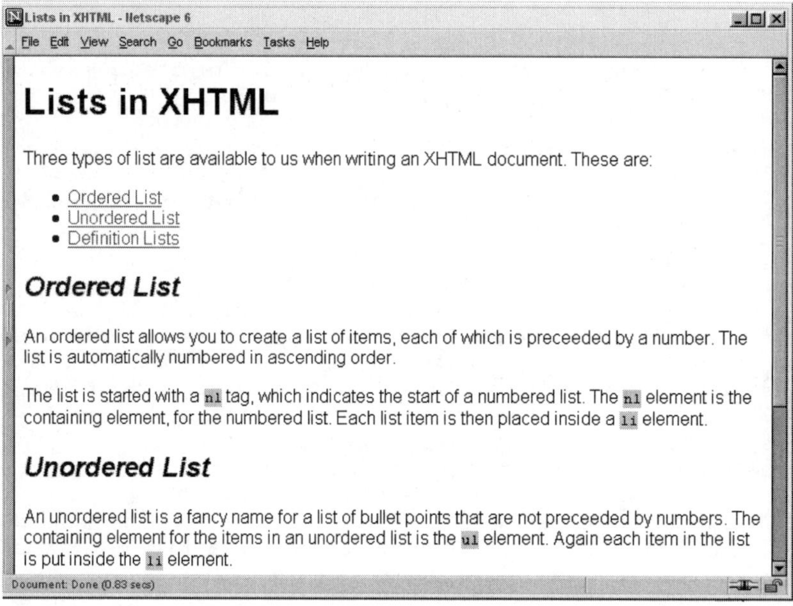

Figure 17-2

How It Works

Firstly, the `<link>` element in the source XHTML document indicates that there is a CSS style sheet available that can be applied to the document.

```
<link rel="stylesheet" type="text/css" href="ch17_eg01.css" />
```

Remember that there are two parts to a CSS rule: the selector, which indicates which element(s) the rule applies to, and the declarations (which are made up of properties and their values). Looking at the first rule in the style sheet, the selector applies to the <body> element, and because the rules cascade, the declarations for the <body> element also applies to all other child elements (unless there is a more specific rule).

```
body {
  color:#000000;
  background-color:#FFFFFF;
  font-family:arial, verdana, sans-serif;}
```

The first two rules, setting the `color` property to black and the `background-color` to white, are the same as the default values for these settings in most browsers. The third, `font-family`, indicates that the computer should try to render text in an Arial typeface. If it cannot find Arial, it should look for Verdana, failing which it should use any Sans-serif font.

The other two rules act on specific elements, the first indicates that all `<h2>` elements should be italicized, while the contents of a `<code>` element should have a gray background.

```
h2 {font-style:italic;}
code {background-color:#CCCCCC;}
```

Something interesting is going on here, however. The list items appear indented with bullet points to the left of them, and the contents of the `<code>` elements are in a monospace font (probably of the Courier family). Yet the style sheet did not specify that either of these things should happen. The reason they appear like this is because we are using XHTML, and the browser is programmed to know how some elements in XHTML should be displayed. For instance, the browser knows that items in an unordered list should be prefaced with a bullet point, and that contents of `<code>` elements should be displayed in a monospace font. There are more obvious examples too: the headings are all different sizes of text, but we did not specify the sizes for these headings.

Browsers tend to have default ways of displaying XHTML elements if they are not otherwise told. We can see this happening alongside the rules we have specified in CSS here.

Using CSS with XHTML versus Other XML Vocabularies

The first example got you styling a simple XHTML document with CSS. Alongside the rules that were specified in the CSS, the browser took it upon itself to control how some of the elements should appear; the size of text in heading elements, the bullets in unordered lists, and the typeface of `code` elements were all controlled by the browser. If the example had contained a `<table>` element, the browser would have known to start displaying tabular data; if it had contained an ordered list, the browser would have created numbered bullets, and any text inside an `<em>` element would have been italicized.

With most other XML vocabularies, however, the browser will have no idea how to display individual elements (except perhaps languages such as SVG, MathML, or XUL which are languages specifically for presentation). If you create an XML vocabulary, it may well have an element called `heading1`, but the browser will not know its content should be in a larger font than anything else in the document. There could be an element called `<bulletPoint>`, but the browser would not know to display a bullet point.

The rest of the examples in this chapter will therefore look at displaying vocabularies other than XHTML, because the browser will not have any idea how to display them. Before going any further, however, it is important to take a quick look at some more of the basics of CSS.

Attaching the Style Sheet to an XML Document

When you use CSS with HTML or XHTML, the CSS rules can be put inside a `<style>` element contained within the head of the document rather than in a separate document. In other XML vocabularies, however, we *must* use a stand-alone style sheet.

In the preceding XHTML example, the `<link>` element was used to associate the style sheet with the XHTML document, because it is part of the XHTML vocabulary that XHTML-aware browsers will understand. For other XML vocabularies we must use a processing instruction to link a style sheet to a document instance—after all a `<link>` element may mean all kinds of other things in different vocabularies.

We link a style sheet to an XML document using a processing instruction, like the following:

```
<?xml-stylesheet type="text/css" href="ch17_eg13.css" ?>
```

The processing instruction requires the following attributes:

Attribute	Description
`href`	Indicates the location of the style sheet—its value is a URL.
`type`	Indicates the MIME type of the style sheet, which is text/css for CSS style sheets. If the user agent does not understand the type (perhaps it's a non CSS-aware mobile phone), it will not need to download it.

The processing instruction can also take the following optional attributes:

Attribute	Description
`Title`	The name or title of the style sheet.
`Media`	Indicates which media the specified style sheet has been written to work with. Values include the `screen` (primarily for color computer screens), as well as `aural`, `Braille`, `handheld`, and `tv`.
`Charset`	Indicates the character set used.
`Alternate`	Indicates whether the style sheet is the preferred style sheet. It can take the values `yes` or `no`; if not supplied, the default value is `no`.

You can include as many style sheets as you like by adding further processing instructions for each of the style sheets you want to use with the document. You can also add processing instructions to include an XSLT stylesheet, as we saw in Chapter 8.

Selectors

As we have already seen, the selector is the portion of the CSS rule that indicates which elements the rule should apply to.

In addition to providing the element name as a selector, you can use the following as selectors. Firstly, there is the *universal selector*, which is an asterisk, indicating a wildcard and matching all element types in the document.

```
*{}
```

Then there is a *type selector*, which matches all of the elements specified in the comma-delimited list. The following would match all page, heading, and paragraph elements.

```
page, heading, paragraph {}
```

A *child selector* will match an element that is a direct child of another. In this case it matches child elements that are direct children of parent elements.

```
parent > child {}
```

A *descendant selector* matches an element type that is a descendant of another specified element, at any level of nesting—not just a direct child. In this case it matches <a> elements that are contained within a <p> element.

```
p a {}
```

An *adjacent sibling* selector matches an element type that is the next sibling of another. Here it matches <second> elements that have the same parent as a <first> element and appear immediately after the <first> element (it would not match a <second> element that comes after another <second> element).

```
first + second
```

There are also a series of selectors called attribute selectors, which we will look at later in the chapter in the section called *Attribute Selectors*.

You might have used the class selector, which matches the value of a class attribute, in HTML and XHTML documents, but it only works with these languages because the browser already knows the meaning of the class attribute for these vocabularies. Even if your XML contained a class attribute, the browser would not associate it with the class selector.

There is also a selector called the ID selector, which works like the class attribute but only works with attributes of ID type. Although the browser will understand this for HTML and XHTML elements, for other XML vocabularies, the browser would need to know that an attribute was of type ID. This would require a DTD or schema that specified the attribute's type. Because the browser is not forced to validate with a DTD or schema, even if one is specified for the XML document, you cannot rely on it knowing when an attribute is of type ID.

Using CSS for Layout of XML Documents

While the first example in this chapter showed the browser knew something about how to display XHTML documents, we have noted that the same is not true of other XML vocabularies (with the noted exception of other presentation languages such as SVG or MathML). Even if your XML vocabulary has an element called <p> or <b>, the browser will not know you want its content to be displayed as a paragraph or in bold. Similarly, if you have an <img> element in your XML vocabulary, the browser will not know you want it to display an image, and if you had a <ul> element, the browser will not know it should add bullet points. Therefore, you need to address the following issues:

- How to create sophisticated layouts without the use of tables, as web designers often rely on tables to create layouts they require.
- How to present tabular data in XML.

- How to link between XML documents.
- How to display bullet points.
- How to display images in our documents.

Furthermore, in order to evaluate when it is best to use CSS, and when looking at another technology (such as XSLT) might be better (to transform our documents into HTML or XHTML), we also need to look at the following:

- The extent to which we can reorder the content so that elements are presented in a different sequence to the one in which they appear in the original XML document.
- How we can add content that is not in the XML document, such as new headings that explain the content of the element (after all, in the XML file the element's name describes its content, but the element name is not viewed in the browser).
- How we can display attribute content, since many XML files contain important data we may wish to view in attribute values.

One of the great things about using CSS with XHTML is that you can start to get results very quickly. You do not need to understand everything about how CSS works in order to get started: Attach styles to elements and off you go. When you work with XML, however, in particular when it comes to positioning and layout, it is important to understand how CSS renders a page. CSS operates on something known as *the box model*, so you need to learn how this works before looking at how it's implemented when laying out pages in this model.

Understanding the Box Model

When displaying a document, CSS treats each element in the document as a *rectangular box*. Each box is made up of four components: *content* surrounded by *padding*, a *border*, and *margins.*

Each boxes' margins are transparent, borders can have styles (for example, solid or dashed), and backgrounds apply to the area inside the border, which includes padding and content. The padding is the area between the border and the content. (See Figure 17-3.)

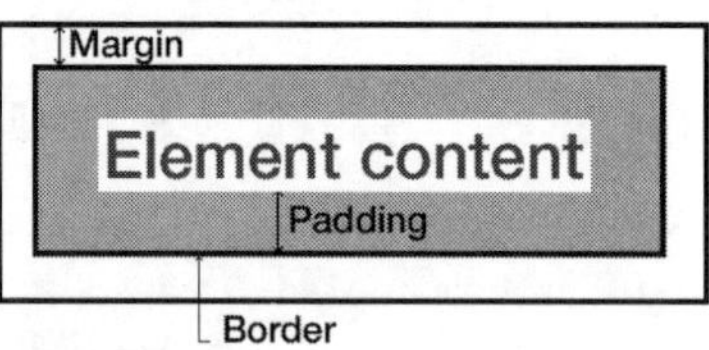

Figure 17-3

The default width for margins, borders, and padding is zero. However, the width can be specified using CSS—in fact, different widths can be given for each side of the box. For example, you might have a wider border on the top and more padding to the right.

> *If you specify a width and height for a box, you are actually setting the width and height of the content area, although some versions of Internet Explorer actually read width and height values as measuring the height and width of the content plus padding plus border.*

Block and Inline Boxes

Each box can contain other boxes, corresponding to elements that are nested inside of it. There are two types of boxes in CSS: *block* and *inline*. In HTML, block boxes are created by elements, such as `<p>`, `<div>`, or `<table>`, while inline boxes are created by tags, such as `<b>`, `<em>`, and `<span>`, as well as content, such as text and images. Block boxes deal with a block of content (each paragraph is treated as if it has a carriage return before and after its content), while the contents of inline boxes can flow together, without the carriage returns (such as a reference being italicized or an important statement being in bold text in the middle of a sentence).

Some elements in HTML such as lists and tables have other types of boxes, but the browser treats them as a block or inline box when it comes to positioning, so we will not go into that here.

When styling XML with CSS the browser does not know which elements should be displayed as block and which as inline, so we need to specify this as a property of the element. To do this we use the `display` property, which takes a value of either `block` or `inline`. As we shall see, the way in which we lay out our document and the style of a parent box can affect these properties (for example, an absolutely positioned element is always treated as a block-level element even if it has a `display` property whose value is `inline`).

You can also set the `display` property to have a value of `none`, in which case the browser will act as if neither the element, nor any of its children exist (even if those children have declared `display` values of `block` or `inline`).

Try It Out Block and Inline Boxes

To demonstrate the box model, a paragraph of text is all that is needed. This paragraph will be a block level element and will contain some inline elements.

1. Create a document called `ch17_eg02.xml`. Start your document with the XML processing instruction, and then add the processing instruction to attach a style sheet called `ch17_eg02.css`, which is in the same folder:

```
<?xml version="1.0" encoding="UTF-8" ?>
<?xml-stylesheet type="text/css" href="ch17_eg02.css" ?>
```

2. Add the following fragment of XML:

```
<paragraph>This book is called <reference>Beginning XML</reference>, it will
 help you to learn <keyword>XML</keyword>.</paragraph>
```

3. Open a blank document to create your CSS style sheet, write selectors for each element of the fragment of XML, and put curly braces next to each element:

```
paragraph {}
reference {}
keyword {}
```

4. Add whether each element should be a block or inline element with the `display` property (don't forget to add the semicolon at the end; you will be adding more declarations to the rule in a moment):

```
paragraph {
   display:block;}
reference {
   display:inline;}
keyword {
   display:inline;}
```

5. Finally, you add other rules for how you want that box to be presented. Note the use of gray borders for each element so that you can see where the edges of the box are:

```
paragraph {
   display:block;
   padding:10px;
   border:solid; border-width:4px; border-color:#CCCCCC;}

reference {
   display:inline;
   font-style:italic;
   color:#CC3333;
   border:solid; border-width:2px; border-color:#CCCCCC;}

keyword {
   display:inline;
   font-weight:bold;
   color:#990000;
   border:solid; border-width:2px; border-color:#CCCCCC;}
```

The result should look something like Figure 17-4.

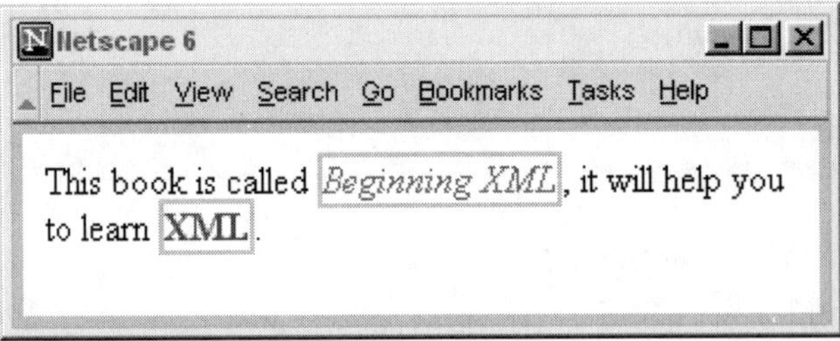

Figure 17-4

How It Works

In this example, the `<paragraph>` element is a block-level element that acts as the containing element for the inline `<reference>` and `<keywords>` elements.

Because the `<paragraph>` element is given a `display` property with a value of `block`, nothing will appear to the left or right of it, as if there was a carriage return before or after the content of this element. Meanwhile, the `<reference>` and `<keywords>` elements have been given a `display` property with a value of `inline`, which means they will appear in the flow of the rest of the sentence, rather than in a block box standing on its own.

You will see later in the chapter how to get two block-level elements to be displayed next to each other, which, for example, you could use to create two columns of text.

In the same way that an element containing another element is called a containing element, a box that contains another box, or several boxes, is known as a containing box or containing block.

Anonymous Boxes

In order to simplify the way CSS positioning works, the direct children of a block box will either be all inline boxes or all block boxes. So, when the children of an element, which is supposed to be displayed as a block level element, are to be displayed as both block and inline, then an *anonymous box* is created to make the inline element a block-level element.

To illustrate this, take the paragraph from the last example and put it inside a `<page>` element. You can also add an inline `vpageNumber>` element inside it at the same level as the `<paragraph>` element, like the following example (this file is available with the downloadable code for this chapter and is called `ch17_eg03.xml`):

```
<?xml version="1.0" encoding="UTF-8" ?>
<?xml-stylesheet type="text/css" href="ch17_eg03.css" ?>
<page>
   <pageNumber>1</pageNumber>
   <paragraph>This book is called <reference>Beginning XML</reference>,
   it will help you to learn <keywords>XML</keywords>.</paragraph>
</page>
```

Then add the following styles to the style sheet from the previous example and rename it `ch17_eg03.css`:

```
page {
   display:block;
   padding:10px;
   margin:10px;
   border-style:solid; border-width:4px; border-color:#000000;}

pageNumber {
   display:inline;
   font-style:italic;
   border-style:solid; border-width:4px; border-color:#CCCCCC;}
```

Here you can see that the `<page>` element has two direct children: the inline `<pageNumber>` element and the block-level `<paragraph>` element. Although the `<pageNumber>` element has its display `property` set to `inline`, it behaves like a block box because an anonymous block box is created around it. This is just an invisible container for the inline element so that it gets treated as a block box.

There is no need to set rules for anonymous boxes; rather we would make the element a block-level box in the first place.

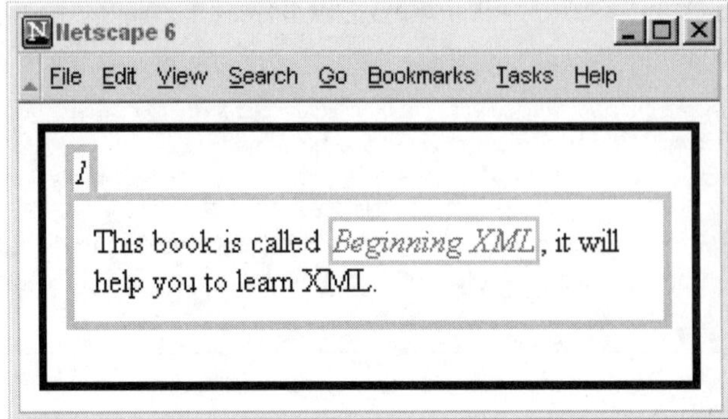

Figure 17-5

Positioning in CSS

We have already established that, in order to lay out XML documents using CSS, you need to understand the box model.

Knowing that the content of each element can be displayed as a box, the layout process becomes a case of deciding which type of box you want an element to be in (inline or block) and where you want that box to appear on the page.

CSS 2 has three types of positioning: *normal flow*, *float positioning (or floated for short)*, and *absolute positioning*. It is important to see how we can use these to position the boxes that correspond to each element.

Normal Flow

Normal flow is the default type of positioning that you get without specifying any other type of positioning; *block boxes* flow from the *top to the bottom* of the page in the order they appear in the source document, starting at the top of their containing block, while *inline boxes* flow horizontally from *left to right*.

Try It Out Normal Flow

All you need to do to really see normal flow working is add another paragraph to the XML of the simple example we have been using so far.

1. Add the following line to the XML in the previous example, and save it as `ch17_eg04.xml`:

```
<?xml version="1.0" encoding="UTF-8" ?>
<?xml-stylesheet type="text/css" href="ch17_eg03.css" ?>
<page>
   <pageNumber>1</pageNumber>
   <paragraph>This book is called <reference>Beginning XML</reference>,
   it will help you to learn <keyword>XML</keyword>.</paragraph>
   <paragraph>The current chapter focuses on using CSS to display
   XML documents.</paragraph>
</page>
```

2. Open the new XML document in a browser, and it should look something like Figure 17-6.

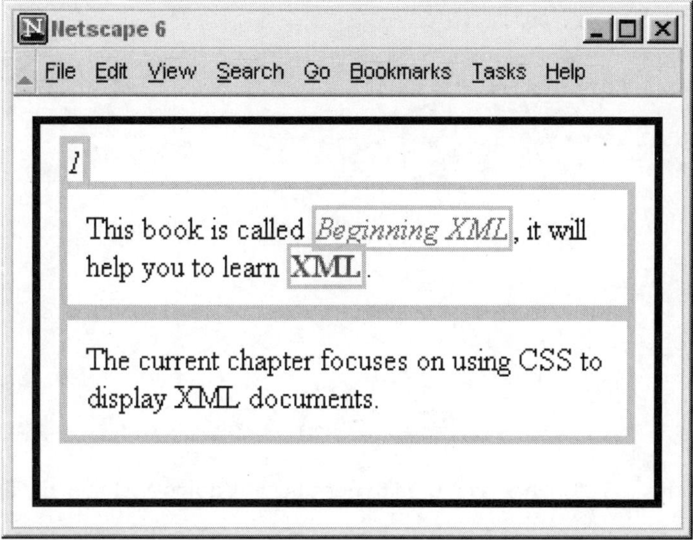

Figure 17-6

How It Works

The `<page>` and `<paragraph>` elements are block-level elements, and the `<pageNumber>` element is treated as a block-level element because it is put in an anonymous box. Each of these block-level items is treated as if it has a carriage return before and after it; the items appear to flow from top to bottom within the page.

The `<keyword>` and `<reference>` elements, meanwhile, flow within the normal text of the paragraph, left to right. Inline boxes are wrapped as needed, moving down to a new line when the available width is exceeded.

Vertical Margins Collapse in Normal Flow

You should also note here that vertical margins of boxes collapse in the normal flow. So, instead of adding the bottom margin of a block box to create the distance between their respective borders, only the larger of the two values is used.

Horizontal margins, however, are never collapsed.

Relative Positioning

There is another type of positioning that falls under the banner of normal positioning: *relative positioning*. This renders the page just like normal flow but then offsets the box by a given amount.

You indicate that a box should be relatively positioned by giving the `position` property a value of `relative`. Then you use the `left`, `right`, `top`, and `bottom` properties to specify the offset values.

One example of where this is particularly useful is when rendering subscript or superscript text. Here we'll add a <footnoteNumber> after the <reference> element in the example (ch17_eg05.xml):

```
<page>
   <pageNumber>1</pageNumber>
   <paragraph>This book is called <reference>Beginning XML</reference>
   <footnoteNumber>3</footnoteNumber>, it will help you to learn
   <keywords>XML</keywords>.</paragraph>
</page>
```

And here is the rule for the <footnoteNumber> element (ch17_eg05.css):

```
footnoteNumber {
   position:relative; top:3px;
   display:inline;
   font-size:9pt; font-weight:bold;
   color:#990000;
   border-style:solid; border-width:2px; border-color:#CCCCCC;}
```

You can see how the top offset has been used to push the box down as shown in Figure 17-7.

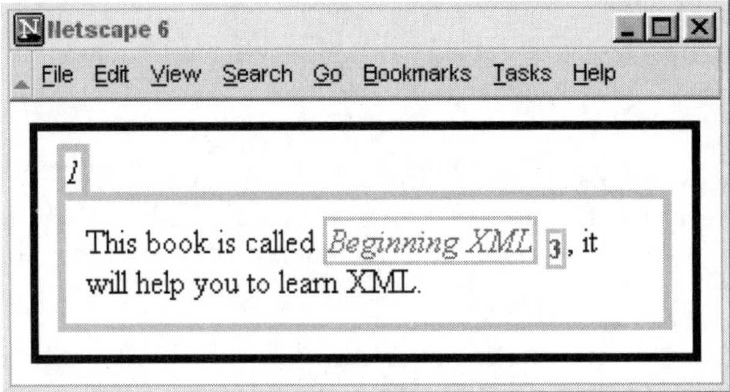

Figure 17-7

You should only specify a left or right offset and a top or bottom offset. If you specify both, one must be the absolute negative of the other (for example, top:3px; bottom:-3px;). If you have top and bottom or left and right, and they do not have absolute negative values of each other, the right or bottom offset will be ignored.

Overlapping Relative Positioning

When you use relative positioning, you can end up with some boxes overlapping others. Because you are offsetting a box relative to normal flow, one box will end up on top of another if the offset is large enough. This may create an effect you are looking for; however, there are a couple of pitfalls you should be aware of:

- Unless you set a background for a box (either a background color or image) it will, by default, be transparent, so when the overlapping of text occurs, you would get an unreadable mess.

- The CSS specification does not say which element should appear on top when relatively positioned elements overlap each other; therefore, there can be differences between browsers.

To illustrate this possibility, the file `ch17_eg06.css` (for use with `ch17_eg06.xml`) contains a relative positioned `<keywords>` element, and the background is set to white:

```
keywords {
   display:inline;
   position:relative; right:45px;
   background-color:#ffffff;
   color:#990000;
   font-weight:bold;
   border:solid; border-width:2px; border-color:#CCCCCC;}
```

Here you can see the result in Figure 17-8.

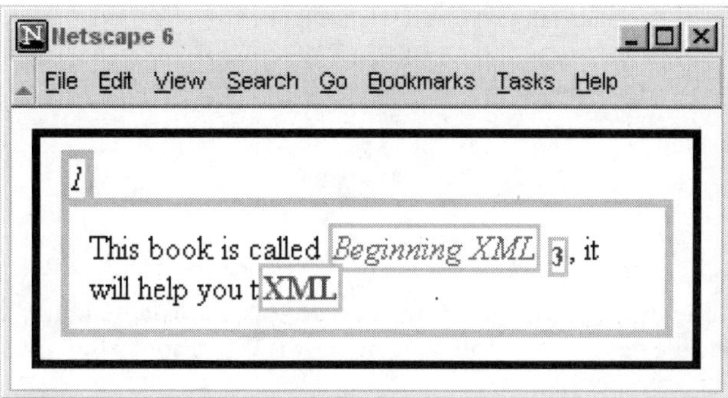

Figure 17-8

In IE and Netscape the relatively positioned element will appear at the front; in Opera the order in which the elements appear in the document will determine which one appears on the top.

Float Positioning

The second type of positioning you need to look at creates a box that *floats*, allowing other content to *flow around it*.

A box that is floated is shifted as far to the left or right of the containing box as is possible within that block's padding. (Its vertical margins, however, will not be collapsed above or below it like block boxes in normal flow can; rather it will be aligned with the top of the containing box.)

To indicate that you want a box floated either to the left or the right of the containing box, you set the `float` property to have a value of either `left` or `right`. Even if these boxes are defined as inline boxes, they will be treated as block-level boxes.

Whenever you specify a `float` property, you should also set a `width` property too, indicating the width of the containing box that the floating box should take up, otherwise it will automatically take up 100 percent of the width of the containing box (leaving no space for things to flow around it, therefore it is just like a plain block-level element).

Try It Out — Creating a Floating Box

1. Create a file called `ch17eg_07.xml`. Then add the XML declaration and a link to a style sheet called `ch17_eg07.css` like so:

```
<?xml version="1.0" encoding="UTF-8" ?>
<?xml-stylesheet type="text/css" href="ch17_eg06.css" ?>
```

2. Add the following XML, which contains a `<pullQuote>` element we will float, to the file:

```
<review>
    <title>The Wrox Review</title>
    <pullQuote>If you want to learn XML, this is the book.</pullQuote>
    <paragraph>Extensible Markup Languages is a rapidly maturing technology
      with powerful real-world applications, particularly for the management,
      display, and transport of data. Together with its many related
      technologies, it has become the standard for data and document delivery
      on the web. <reference>Beginning XML</reference> is for any developer
      who is interested in learning to use <keyword>XML</keyword> in web,
      e-commerce, or data storage applications. Some knowledge of mark up,
      scripting, and/or object oriented programming languages is
      advantageous, but not essential, as the basis of these techniques is
      explained as required.</paragraph>
</review>
```

3. Create another file called `ch17_eg07.css`, and add the element names that are in the XML document you have just created. While you do this, indicate whether you want each element to be a block-level element or an inline element (the exception is the `<pullQuote>` element, which we'll get to in a moment):

```
review {display:block;}
title {display:block;}
pullQuote {}
paragraph {display:block;}
keyword {display:inline;}
```

4. You want to make the `<pullQuote>` element float to the left of the paragraph, so add the `float` property with a value of `left` and a `width` property with a value of 20 percent. Remember, if you do not add the `width` property, the floated element will display just like any other block-level element.

```
pullQuote {
    float:left;
    width:20%;}
```

5. Now add the rest of the rules for how the document will be styled. The title of the book should be in a black box with white text, and each box should have a border to illustrate where the edges of the box are, as shown:

```
review {
    display:block;
    padding:10px;
```

```
   margin:10px;
   border-style:solid; border-width:4px; border-color:#000000;}

title {
   display:block;
   font-size:24px;
   padding:5px;
   color:#FFFFFF; background-color:#000000;}

pullQuote {
   float:left;
   width:20%;
   font-style:italic;
   padding:10px; margin:10px;
   border:solid; border-width:4px; border-color:#CCCCCC;}

paragraph {
   display:block;
   padding:10px;
   border:solid; border-width:4px; border-color:#CCCCCC;}

keyword {
   display:inline;
   font-weight:bold;
   color:#990000;
   border:solid; border-width:2px; border-color:#CCCCCC;}
```

6. Open the XML file in your browser, and you should see something like that shown in Figure 17-9.

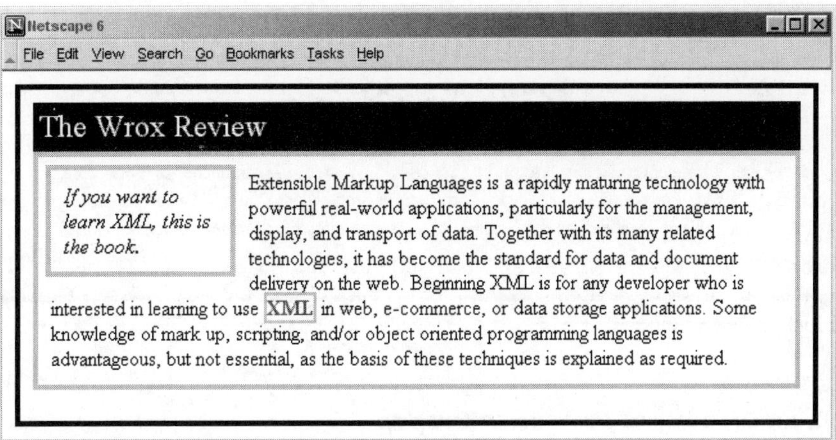

Figure 17-9

How It Works

The `<pullQuote>` element has been given a property of `float`, with a value of `left`, which indicates that the box should be floated to the left of the containing `review` element. Remember the `width` property is vital when adding a float; otherwise the whole content of the element would be treated like any block-level element and take up the full width of the containing box.

It is interesting to note that no matter whether the <pullQuote> element appears before or after the paragraph element, it will still be in the same place. This has important implications for the ability to present the contents of an XML document in a different sequence than the one it follows in the XML source. A float can be used to bring the content of any element to the top of a document.

Overlapping Floated Boxes

Floated boxes can cause overlap problems just like relatively positioned ones. A floated box can overlap block-level boxes that are in normal flow mode. Figure 17-10 shows what would happen if you added another <paragraph> element and increased the length of the <pullQuote> so it is long enough to overlap (there is an example in the download code for this chapter in the file ch17_eg08.xml).

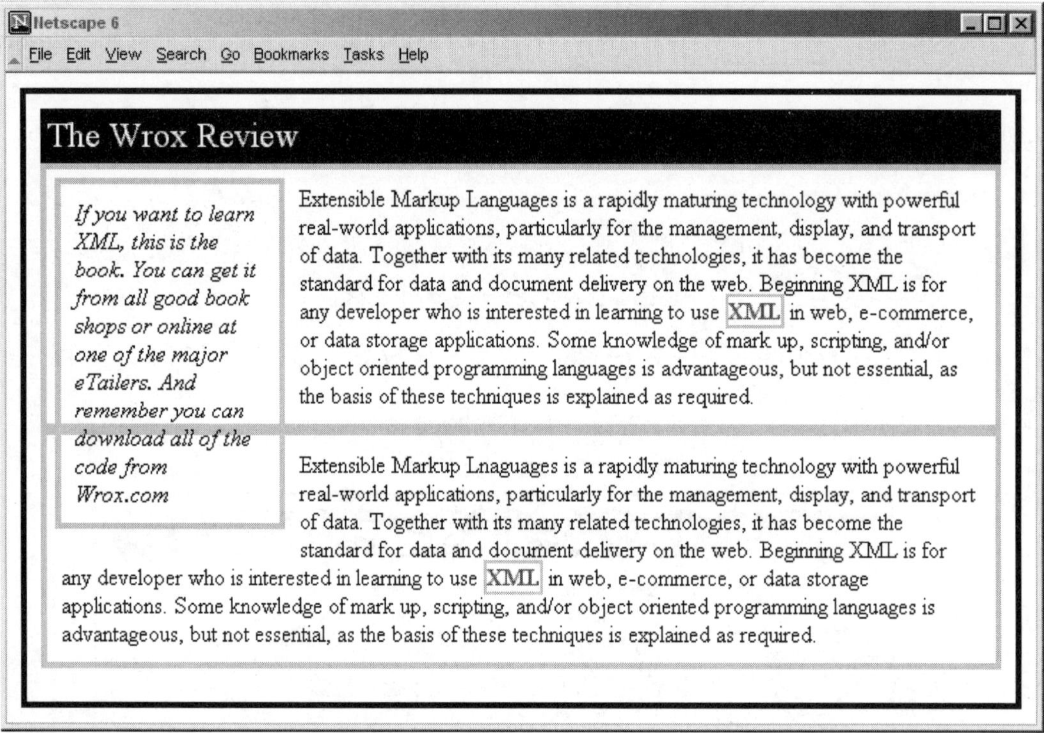

Figure 17-10

Using the Clear Property to Prevent an Overlap

If you do not want the content of an element to wrap around the content of a floated element, you can use the clear property. In the example we just saw, we would use the clear property on the second paragraph element like so:

```
paragraph2 {clear:left;}
```

The value of the property can be any of the following:

Value	Description
`Left`	The left side of box must not be adjacent to an earlier floating box
`Right`	The right side of box must not be adjacent to an earlier floating box
`Both`	Neither the left nor right side of box may be adjacent to an earlier floating box
`None`	The default setting where content is placed adjacent to the floated element on either side
`Inherit`	Inherits the parent element's property

You can see how `clear` works in Figure 17-11 (`ch17_eg09.xml` and `ch17_eg09.css` illustrate this in the code download).

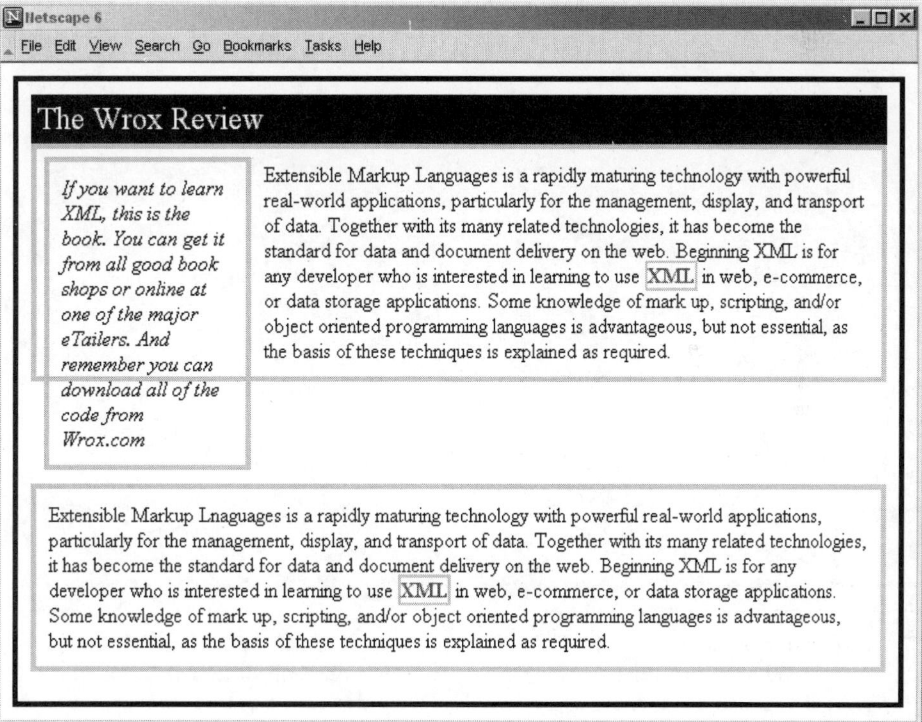

Figure 17-11

Absolute Positioning

The third method of positioning is *absolute positioning*. Absolutely positioned elements are completely removed from the normal flow. They are always treated as block-level elements and are positioned within their containing block using offset values for the `left`, `top`, `right`, and `bottom` properties. For example, you might want a `<page>` element to appear 10 pixels in from the left of the browser window and 20 pixels from the top of the window, and the <title> within the <page> element to be 10 pixels from the top of the <page> and 5 pixels in from the left.

You indicate that an element's content should be absolutely positioned using the `position` property with a value of `absolute`. It is important to remember, however, that the content of the containing element will not float around the absolutely positioned box like it does with a floated box, rather it will appear above or be placed on top of the containing box.

> *Version 6 of Internet Explorer and Opera will not correctly display offset values given for the* `right` *and* `bottom` *properties, although Netscape 6 handles them correctly. Therefore it is best to rely on the* `left` *and* `top` *properties.*

Try It Out — Using Absolute Positioning to Create Columns of Text

In this example, we are going to create a page with two columns of text. The XML file will contain a root element called <page> and will have two child elements, <column1> and <column2>, each of which will contain a paragraph of text. Here is the XML file called `ch17_eg10.xml`:

```
<?xml version="1.0" encoding="UTF-8" ?>
<?xml-stylesheet type="text/css" href="ch17_eg10.css" ?>
<page>
   <column1>
      <paragraph>This is a paragraph...</paragraph>
      <paragraph>This is a paragraph...</paragraph>
      <paragraph>This is a paragraph...</paragraph>
   </column1>
   <column2>
      <paragraph>This is a paragraph...</paragraph>
      <paragraph>This is a paragraph...</paragraph>
      <paragraph>This is a paragraph...</paragraph>
   </column2>
</page>
```

1. Start a style sheet called `ch17_eg10.css` and add these elements to it:

```
page{}
column1{}
column2{}
paragraph{}
```

2. Now you need to decide which elements are to be absolutely positioned and which elements are block-level or inline. When doing this, remember that all absolutely positioned elements are treated as block-level elements, so you do not need to add a `display` property to them:

```
page{display:block;}
column1{position:absolute;}
column2{position:absolute;}
paragraph{display:block;}
```

3. Now you can decide where you want to have your absolutely positioned elements. The <page> element is the containing element, then <column1> can be the left-hand column, and <column2> can be the right-hand column.

You often need to specify the `width` or `height` of boxes when using absolute positioning; after all you use offsets to position boxes, and if you do not set widths of boxes, you might cause overlap. The columns should therefore be set to be 200 pixels wide, so we can position the second column 250 pixels in from its containing element as follows:

```
page {
  display:block;
  width:470px;}

column1 {
  position:absolute;
  left:10px; top:10px;
  width:200px;}

column2 {
  position:absolute;
  left:250px; top:10px;
  width:200px;}

paragraph {
  display:block;
  padding-bottom:10px;}
```

4. The only thing left to do is add in some padding and borders so you can see where the boxes' borders are:

```
page {
  display:block;
  width:470px;
  padding:10px;
  border-style:solid; border-width:2px; border-color:#000000;}

column1 {
  position:absolute;
  left:10px; top:10px;
  width:200px;
  padding:10px;
  border-style:solid; border-width:2px; border-color:#CCCCCC;}

column2 {
  position:absolute;
  left:250px; top:10px;
  width:200px;
  padding:10px;
  border-style:solid; border-width:2px; border-color:#CCCCCC;}

paragraph {
  display:block;
  padding-bottom:10px;}
```

5. Finally, open up the XML page in your browser to see how it looks; you should end up with something like that shown in Figure 17-12.

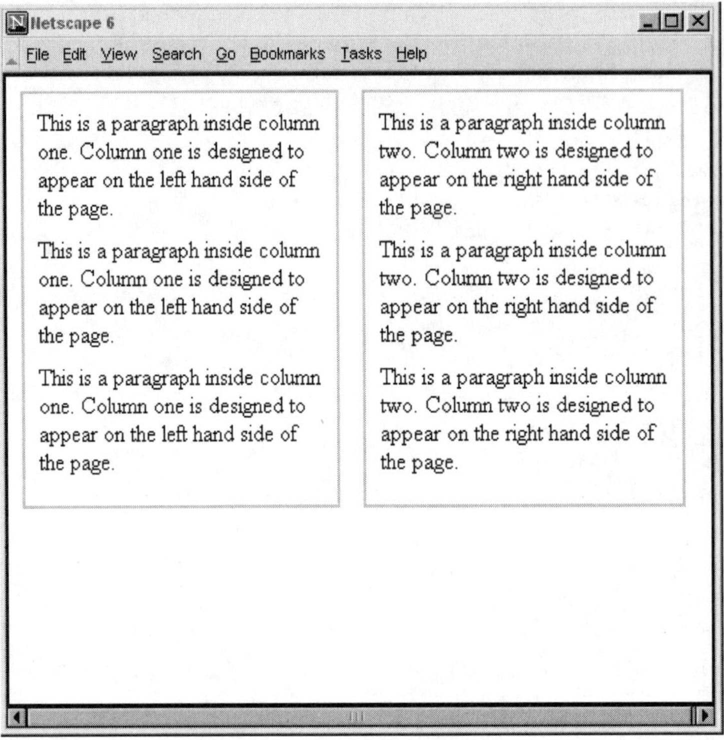

Figure 17-12

How It Works

This example created two columns of text by using absolute positioning to position the `<column1>` and `<column2>` elements. The `<column1>` element was positioned 10 pixels in from the left of the browser window and 10 pixels from the top. It was given a width of 200 pixels. Meanwhile, the `<column2>` element was positioned 250 pixels in from the left and 10 pixels from the top; it was also 200 pixels wide.

Because the width of these column elements had been specified, it was possible to position them next to each other in the browser window using the top and left offsets.

The content of these elements is then positioned using normal flow inside their respective containing blocks.

Fixed Positioning

Fixed positioning is a special subset of absolute positioning, where the box does not move when users scroll down the page. To give a box fixed positioning, you add the `position` property with a value of `fixed`. To position the box, you use offsets just as you would with absolute positioning, although the box is positioned relative to the browser window, not its containing element.

Netscape 6.1 and Opera 6 support fixed positioning, as does IE 5.5 on a Mac, but IE 6 on Windows does not support fixed positioning.

Try It Out Fixed Positioning

In this exercise you will add a new element to the last example. The new element will be a heading for the page.

1. Open the last example and add the following <heading> element just after the opening <page> tag. Call the file ch17_eg11.xml:

```
<page>
   <heading>This is a Heading</heading>
   <column1>
```

2. Then change the value for the href attribute on the <link> element to point to the new style sheet, which will be called ch17_eg11.css:

```
<?xml-stylesheet type="text/css" href="ch17_eg11.css" ?>
```

3. Open the style sheet ch17_eg10.css, add the following rule for the heading element, and then save it as ch17_eg11.css:

```
heading {
  position:fixed;
  width:100%; padding:20px;
  top:0px; left:0px;
  color:#FFFFFF; background-color:#666666;
  font-family:arial, verdana, sans-serif; font-size:22px;}
```

4. 4. Save the file and open it in the browser. If your browser supports fixed positioning, you should see something like that shown in Figure 17-13.

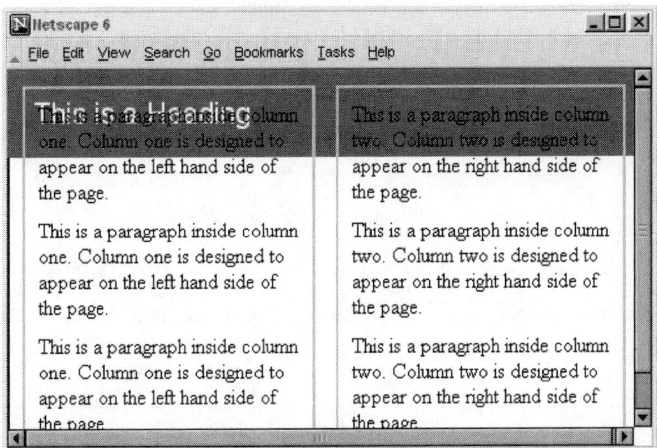

Figure 17-13

How It Works

As you can see in the style sheet, the `<heading>` element has been given the `position` property with a value of `fixed` to make sure the heading stays in the same place. The `width` property makes sure the heading goes across the whole page, and the `top` and `left` offsets indicate that it should be positioned at the top left-hand corner of the browser window.

There is a bit of a problem here, however, as you can see; the columns inside the page overlap the heading. Furthermore, if they did not overlap the heading, they would be masked by it. There are two things you would need to address this issue. Firstly, you need to add an offset to the columns so that they appear below the `<heading>` element. Secondly, you would need to arrange the order of the elements so that the columns were not displayed above the heading when the user scrolls down the page.

Overlapping Absolutely Positioned Elements and Z-Index

Absolutely positioned elements have a tendency to overlap each other and nonpositioned elements. When this happens, the default behavior is to place the first elements underneath later ones. This is known as *stacking context*. You can, however, control which element appears on top using the `z-index` property. If you are familiar with graphic design packages, it is similar to using the "bring to top" and "send to back" features.

The value of the `z-index` property is a number, and the higher the number the nearer the top that element should be displayed.

Laying Out Tabular Data

The problem when you look at laying out tabular data in XML is pretty obvious: you don't have the `<table>` element, and related row and cell elements, you had in HTML and XHTML.

If you knew how many rows and columns of data there were going to be, you could use absolute positioning to position each cell (but your style sheet would only accommodate this number of columns and rows). Luckily, the `display` property can take a value of `table`, which helps us in this matter.

The `display` property takes the following values (whose use corresponds with HTML meanings for `<table>`, `<tr>`, `<td>` and `<caption>` elements) designed specifically for laying out tabular data:

Value of Display	Description
`display:table;`	Indicates that an element's content represents a table
`display:table-row;`	Indicates that an element's content represents a table row
`display:table-cell;`	Indicates that an element's content represents a table cell
`display:table-caption;`	Indicates that an element's content represents a table caption

The CSS table properties do not work in IE 6 on Windows or IE 5 on Mac, although they do work with Netscape 6 and Opera 6 browsers.

Try It Out — Using Display Property to Display Tabular Data

In this example, you are going to create a tabular presentation of the following XML data. Although the element names in this example match the tabular content, they could equally be some other data structure.

```
<?xml version="1.0" encoding="UTF-8" ?>
<?xml-stylesheet type="text/css" href="ch17_eg12.css" ?> <page>
  <table>
    <tableRow>
      <tableCell1>One</tableCell1>
      <tableCell2>Two</tableCell2>
      <tableCell3>Three</tableCell3>
    </tableRow>
    <tableRow>
      <tableCell1>Four</tableCell1>
      <tableCell2>Five</tableCell2>
      <tableCell3>Six</tableCell3>
    </tableRow>
  </table>
</page>
```

1. Create a new style sheet document called `ch17_eg12.css`, and add element names and their appropriate display properties to each element like so:

```
page {display:block;}
table {display:table;}
tableRow {display:table-row;}
tableCell1, tableCell2, tablecell3 {display:table-cell;}
```

2. Add some padding and shading so you can see where each element begins and ends:

```
page {
  display:block;
  color:#000000; background-color:#EFEFEF;
  border-style:solid; border-width:2px; border-color:#000000; }

table {
  display:table;
  padding:20px;
  color:#000000; background-color:#CCCCCC;
  border-style:solid; border-width:2px; border-color:#000000; }

tableRow {display:table-row;}

tableCell1, tableCell2, tableCell3 {
  display:table-cell;
  padding:10px;
  color:#000000; background-color:#EFEFEF;
  border-style:solid; border-width:2px; border-color:#000000; }
```

3. Save the style sheet and open the XML file in a browser. In Netscape or Opera, you should end up with a result similar to Figure 17-14.

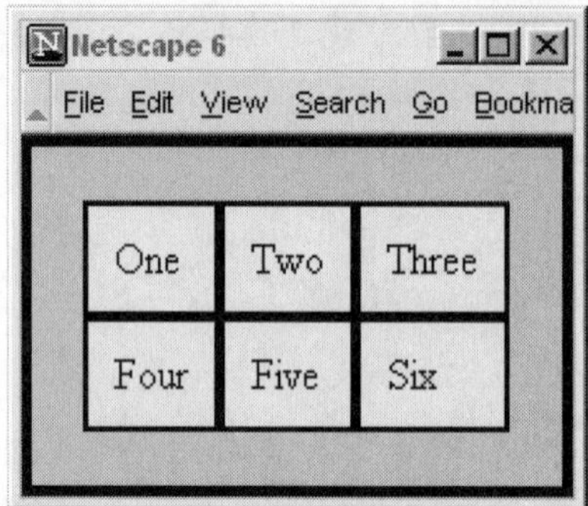

Figure 17-14

How It Works

Obviously, the key to this example is the special values for the `display` property that allow us to indicate to the browser which elements indicate rows or cells of a table.

There is an issue, however, which is quite limiting to this approach. The whole technique relies on the XML file having a structure like the one in our example XML. The element that corresponds to the row must contain the elements that correspond to cells. So you need a repeating structure for this technique to work.

The cells could have the same name. I just chose to give them different names to illustrate that they could have different names, as more real-life uses of XML are likely to follow this structure. However, you cannot miss an element in any row; it must be present even if its content is empty. Nor can you have any extra elements in any of the rows, or the table will not display properly.

So, your XML must have a strict structure if you are going to display it as a table.

Having seen how to display tables, we should move onto another type of markup that we will miss from HTML, namely links.

Links in XML Documents

In the XML 1.0 Recommendation, there is no equivalent of the `<a>` element to create hyperlinks. So, if we are going to use CSS to display our XML documents, we need a way of indicating which element should be a link.

While the XML Recommendation itself does not offer a way to create links in XML documents, another W3C recommendation, *XLink*, provides a mechanism for linking that goes far beyond that we are used to with HTML links.

Netscape 6 (and later) supports a limited subset of XLink, and it is enough to reproduce the functionality of the `<a>` and `<img>` tags in HTML. Opera and Internet Explorer have yet to add any implementation of XLink (although Opera did have a proprietary extension to CSS to allow you to define a link).

XLink is a powerful and complicated technology that provides users with advanced features, such as allowing an author to offer multiple destinations from a single link and the ability to define links in separate link documents or databases rather than the source files. There is not enough space to cover XLink in full in this chapter, although we will look at the subset of it implemented by Netscape 6 (no new XLink features were added in Netscape 7).

XLink Support in Netscape

The limited support for XLink introduced in Netscape 6 allows users to create links with the same functionality as those of HTML. It allows you to embed an XLink into the document, and the document the link points to can replace the current document (just like a normal link in HTML) or open the document in a new window (which is similar to using `target="_new"` on a link in HTML). You can even open a link automatically when a page loads, which lets you create popup windows when the page loads or replace the content of the current page that is loading.

Any element in an XML document can be a linking element. You simply add attributes from the XLink namespace to that element to indicate that the element should be treated as a link. These attributes are listed in the following table.

Attribute	Description
`xlink:type`	Indicates whether the link is a *simple* or *extended* link. Netscape 6 only supports simple links so we give it a value of `simple`. Simple links are just like those we are familiar with using in HTML: they link from one document to another. The URL of the document we are linking to will be given as a value of the `href` attribute.
`xlink:href`	Indicates the target of the link, just as it does in HTML, and its value is a URI.
`xlink:title`	Allows you to provide a title that describes what the user might find in the destination document for the link and is similar to the `title` attribute on HTML links.
`xlink:show`	Indicates where the target document should appear and can take the following values: `new` if the document should appear in a new window `replace` if the document should replace the content of this window `embed` if the document should be inserted at the current point in the document
`xlink:actuate`	Allows you to specify when the link should be activated. There are two possible values: `onRequest` to wait for the user to activate the link `onLoad` to activate the link when the page loads

As you can see, the attributes are shown here with a namsespace prefix of `xlink:` because attributes without prefixes are assumed to belong to the same namespace as the element that carries them. As these attributes belong to the XLink namespace, we add the following namespace declaration to the root element of our documents:

```
xmlns:xlink="http://www.w3.org/1999/xlink"
```

Try It Out Using XLink in Netscape

In this example we will create a simple link that takes the user from one page to a new page. We need to pay special attention to the XML as that is where the real work is being done with the XLink.

1. Create a file called `ch17_eg13.xml`, and add the XML declaration and a style sheet link to a style sheet called `ch17_eg13.css` like so:

```
<?xml version="1.0" encoding="UTF-8" ?>
<?xml-stylesheet type="text/css" href="ch16_eg13.css" ?>
```

2. Next, put in a root element called `<page>`. This element must contain the namespace declaration, like so:

```
<page xmlns:xlink="http://www.w3.org/1999/xlink">
```

3. Now there are a couple of paragraphs to explain the example. The interesting part is the `<link>` element, with the `xlink` attributes that actually create the link:

```
<paragraph>The following link uses XLink to replicate the functionality of
HTML hyperlinks between pages:</paragraph>

<paragraph><link xlink:type="simple"
   xlink:show="replace"
   xlink:actuate="onRequest"
   xlink:title="This link is like a link between pages in HTML"
   xlink:href="http://www.wrox.com">
     Click here</link>
   to be taken to a new page</paragraph>
```

4. Finish up the XML page with the closing root element's tag:

```
</page>
```

5. Next create a simple style sheet called `ch17_eg13.css` with the following rules. Note how the link is made blue and underlined to indicate that it is a link:

```
page {
  display:block;
  padding:10px;
  color:#000000; background-color:#FFFFFF;
  border-style:solid; border-width:2px; border-color:#000000;}
```

```
paragraph {
  display:block;
  font-family:arial, verdana, sans-serif; font-size:20px;
  padding:20px;
  color:#000000; background-color:#FFFFFF;}

link {
  display:inline;
  color:#0000FF;
  text-decoration:underline;}
```

6. Open the XML file in Netscape 6+, and you should see something like Figure 17-15.

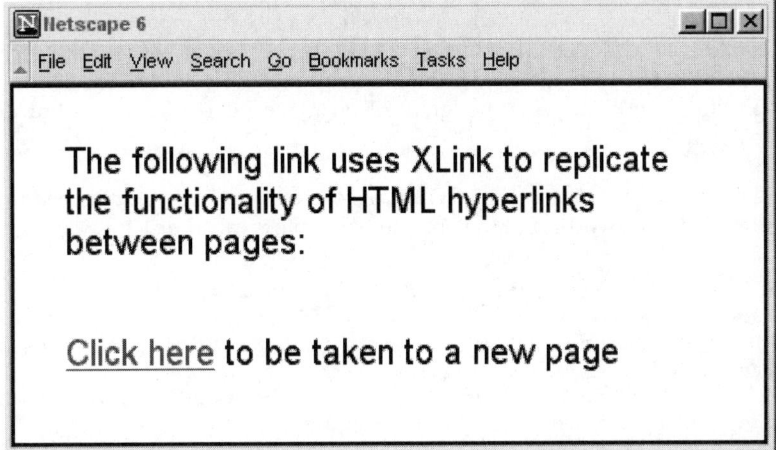

Figure 17-15

How It Works

As you can see, the example works just like a link in an HTML document, but if you go view the source, you will see that it is still XML. The really interesting parts here are the XLink attributes, not the CSS.

The equivalent in HTML would be the following:

```
<a href="http://www.wrox.com" title="This is the title of the link" >
```

In the case of XLink, not only do you have the `href` and `title` attributes, you also have a couple of new ones. First, you have to indicate whether it is a simple or complex link (although Netscape only supports simple links):

```
xlink:type="simple"
```

Then, you have the `actuate` attribute, to indicate when the link should be activated:

```
xlink:actuate="onRequest"
```

The show attribute indicates that we want the target of the link to replace this page:

```
xlink:show="replace"
xlink:title="This link is like a link between pages in HTML"
xlink:href="http://www.wrox.com">
```

Just like a links in HTML, the content of the element used as a link will be what the user can click on. If there is no element content then the user will have nothing to click on, although this is not a problem if the actuate attribute has a value of onLoad.

Forcing Links Using the HTML Namespace

There is an alternative to using XLink, which suffers from a lack of support in browsers. You can embed HTML syntax into your XML documents using the HTML namespace, so your browser will pick up on the meaning of HTML elements and render them appropriately. This technique works fine on Opera 5+, Netscape 6+ and IE 6+ on Windows, although IE 5.5 on a Mac will not follow the link even though it is displayed like a link.

To rework the example you just saw using HTML instead of XLink, you would need to change the lines that are highlighted (this reworking of the previous example is called ch17_eg14.xml):

```
<page xmlns:html="http://www.w3.org/TR/REC-html40">
   <paragraph>The following link uses XLink to replicate the functionality of
    HTML hyperlinks between pages:</paragraph>
   <paragraph>
   <html:a href="http://www.wrox.com">Click here</html:a>
    to be taken to a new page</paragraph>
</page>
```

While this works, it is not the ideal approach because it forces you to use HTML elements in a document that otherwise would not contain elements like these.

Images in XML Documents

Having looked at using XLink to create links in our XML documents, we should have a fair idea of how images can be included in XML documents; by giving the xlink:show attribute a value of embed, so that the image file is embedded in the document where the link appears. Unfortunately, however, IE 6, Netscape 7, and Opera 6 do not support embedding of images in documents using XLink.

You can see how this should work in theory in the following piece of code (ch17_eg15.xml); note how the actuate attribute needs a value of onLoad so that it loads with the rest of the page.

```
<link xlink:type="simple"
   xlink:show="embed"
   xlink:actuate="onLoad"
   xlink:title="An image inserted using XLink"
   xlink:href="wrox_logo.gif"></link>
```

You could also use a value of `replace` for the `show` attribute if you wanted an image to replace the whole document (which would work in Netscape 6+).

One way around the lack of browser support for images in XML documents is through the use of the CSS `background-image` property.

An element in the XML document can be associated with a CSS rule that uses the `background-image` property with a value of `url(file_name)`. This example contains an element called `<logo />` (`ch17_eg17.xml`):

```
<page>
  <logo />
  <paragraph>You should see an image above this paragraph, which was inserted
   into the page using the background-image property in a CSS style
   sheet.</paragraph>
</page>
```

The CSS rule associated with this element should then look something like this (`ch17_eg17.css`):

```
logo {
  display:block;
  background-image:url(wrox_logo.gif);
  margin:5px;
  width:615px; height:25px;}
```

The benefit of this technique is that it works with IE 5+, Netscape 6+, and Opera 5+. The problem, however, is that the source XML document must include a separate element for each image you want in the resulting document (until attribute selectors are better supported in browsers—we'll meet attribute selectors later in the chapter). You must also have a rule in your CSS for each of these elements/images.

Using CSS to Add Content to Documents

Having seen how XSLT works in Chapter 8, you might wonder how you can add new text or images into your XML documents from the CSS file. In truth, the ways in which you can add to XML documents using CSS are very limited. Although there are four pseudo-elements introduced in CSS2 that give us some helpful results:

Pseudo-element	Description
`:before`	Allows you to insert content before an element
`:after`	Allows you to insert content after an element
`:first_letter`	Allows you to add special styles to the first letter of the selector
`:first-line`	Allows you to add special styles to the first line of the text in a selector

The syntax for pseudo-elements is as follows:

```
selector:pseudo-element {property:value;}
```

So, you might make the first letter of a paragraph larger than the rest by adding a rule like this:

```
paragraph:first-letter {font-size:42px;}
```

Making bulleted lists is another particularly helpful application of these pseudo-elements.

Try It Out Creating a Bulleted List Using the :before Pseudo-Element

In this example you are going to create a CSS that deals with different levels of bulleted lists. The XML document we will work with looks like this (`ch17_eg17.xml`):

```
<?xml version="1.0" encoding="UTF-8" ?>
<?xml-stylesheet type="text/css" href="ch17_eg17.css" ?>
<page>
  <paragraph>The effect of a bulleted list is created using CSS.</paragraph>

  <list>
    <bulletPoint>Item one</bulletPoint>
    <bulletPoint>Item two</bulletPoint>
    <bulletPoint>Item three</bulletPoint>
     <list>
        <bulletPoint>Item three point one</bulletPoint>
        <bulletPoint>Item three point two</bulletPoint>
     </list>
     <bulletPoint>Item four</bulletPoint>
  </list>

</page>
```

1. Add the element names and their `display` properties. Each element will be a block-level element, including each bullet point, as each point should start on a new line:

```
page {display:block;}
paragraph {display:block;}
list {display:block;}
bulletPoint {display:block;}
```

2. Add another selector for the `<bulletPoint>` element, and use the `:before` psuedo-element with it so we can add a + sign to indicate our bullet point:

```
bulletPoint:before {content:"+ ";}
```

3. Finally, add in some other styles, borders, fonts, colors, and padding, to make the page complete:

```
page {
  display:block;
  padding:10px;
  color:#000000; background-color:#FFFFFF;
  border-style:solid; border-width:2px; border-color:#000000;}

paragraph {
  display:block;
```

```
  font-family:arial, verdana, sans-serif; font-size:20px;
  padding:20px;
  color:#000000; background-color:#FFFFFF;}

list {
  display:block;
  padding-left:20px;}

bulletPoint {display:block;}
bulletPoint:before {content:"+ ";}
```

4. Save this file as ch17_eg17.css and take a look at it in a browser. The result should be something like Figure 17-16.

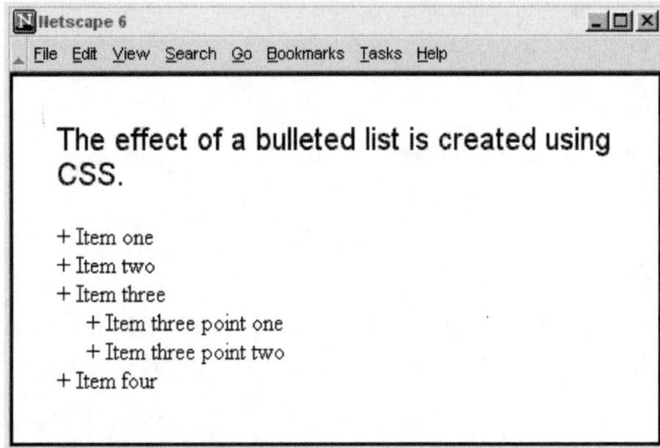

Figure 17-16

How It Works

This example illustrates the three steps that make a bulleted list work with an XML document. First, the containing element for the list needs to be displayed as a block-level element. In this case it is the <list> element:

```
list {display:block;}
```

Just as a <ul> or <ol> element in HTML can contain another <ul> or <ol> element to create a nested list, we can do the same with this list element. The padding to the left of this block-level element makes it clear that it is a nested list:

```
list {
  display:block;
  padding-left:20px;}
```

Secondly, the <bulletPoint> element, which represents an item in the list, is set to be a block-level element. This will make each item appear on a new line using normal flow:

```
bulletPoint {display:block;}
```

Finally, the use of the `:before` pseudo element adds the marker (or bullet point) before each item in the list. This inserts the + symbol before each item as shown in the following:

```
bulletPoint:before {content:"+ ";}
```

CSS2 also introduced counters, which will allow us to create numbered lists using this approach, although they are not yet supported by the major browsers.

Attribute Content

You may well have noticed that throughout the chapter so far the examples have only displayed and talked about displaying element content. To wrap up this topic, you need to first look at how to use attributes in selectors and then how to display attribute values.

Attribute Selectors

CSS2 introduced the ability to use attributes and their values in conjunction with element names as the selector for a CSS rule.

Selector	Matches
`myElement[myAttribute]`	An element called `myElement` carrying an attribute called `myAttribute`
`myElement[myAttribute="myValue"]`	An element called `myElement` carrying an attribute called `myAttribute` whose value is `myValue`
`myElement[myAttribute~="myValue"]`	An element called `myElement` carrying an attribute called `myAttribute`, whose value is a list of space-separated words, one of which is exactly the same a `myValue`
`myElement[myAttribute|="myValue"]`	An element called `myElement` carrying an attribute called `myAttribute` whose value begins with `myValue`

Unfortunately, none of these work in IE 6 or Opera 6, and only the first two work in Netscape 6. When they do become supported, however, they will be powerful tools for allowing you to apply a style to an element based on the presence of, or value of, an attribute.

Using Attribute Values in Documents

One of the biggest drawbacks of working with XML and CSS is that there is no simple method for displaying attribute values from our documents. You might have noticed that all of our examples so far concentrated on element content, and the reason is that CSS is designed to style element content, not attribute values.

There is, however, a trick you can employ enabling you to display values of attributes. The trick relies on the `:before` and `:after` pseudo-elements we saw earlier in the chapter. Using these pseudo-elements, you can add attribute values before or after the element that carries that attribute—unfortunately, however, you cannot display an attribute value before or after any element other than the one that carries it.

The secret lies in a property called `content`, whose value can be set to `attr(`*`attributeName`*`)` where *`attributeName`* is the name of the attribute whose content we want to add before or after the element.

The drawback to this trick is that it only works in Netscape 6+ and Opera 5+, not IE 6.

Try It Out — Displaying Attribute Values

In this example, we are going to go back to an earlier example, `ch17_eg07.xml`, and add an `author` attribute to the `<title>` element.

1. Open `ch17_eg07.xml`, change the style sheet to point to `ch17_eg18.css`, and save the file as `ch17_eg18.xml`.

   Then add in the following line, and save the file:

```
<?xml version="1.0" encoding="UTF-8" ?>
<?xml-stylesheet type="text/css" href="ch17_eg18.css" ?>
<review>
   <title author="Tom Bishop">The Wrox Review</title>
   <pullQuote>If you want to learn XML, this is the book.</pullQuote>
   <paragraph>Extensible Markup Languages is a rapidly maturing technology
     with powerful real-world applications, particularly for the management,
     display, and transport of data. Together with its many related
     technologies, it has become the standard for data and document delivery
     on the web. <reference> Beginning XML</reference> is for any developer
     who is interested in learning to use <keyword>XML</keyword> in web,
     e-commerce, or data storage applications.Some knowledge of mark up,
     scripting, and/or object oriented programming languages is advantageous,
     but not essential, as the basis of these techniques is explained as
     required.</paragraph>
</review>
```

2. Open the style sheet `ch17_07.css` and add the following rule:

```
title:after {
   display:block;
   font-size:14px;
   color:#efefef; font-weight:bold; font-style:italic;
   content:"Written by: " attr(author);}
```

3. Save this file as `ch17_eg18.css`.

4. Open `ch17_eg18.xml` in your browser, and you should end up with a page something like the one shown in Figure 17-17.

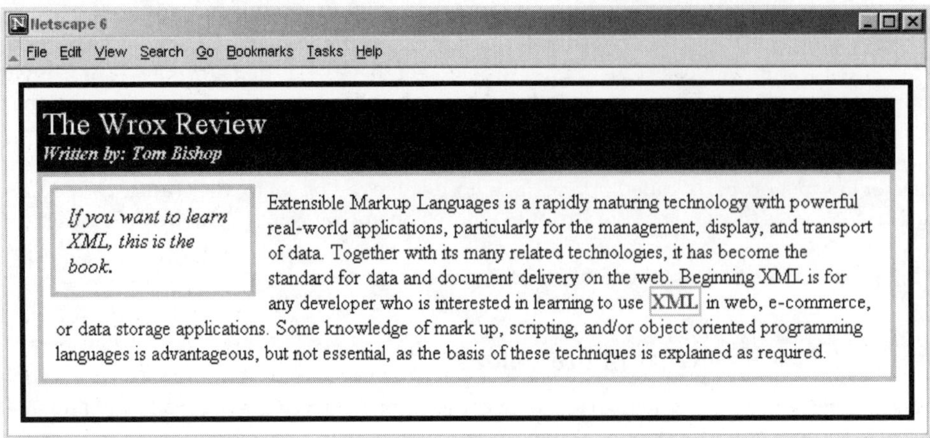

Figure 17-17

How It Works

This example not only takes an attribute value and displays it on-screen, but it also writes some additional text beforehand.

As noted, there is the restriction that we can only write attribute values before or after the element that carries them. So, this example used the `:after` psuedo-element to display the value of the `<author>` attribute after the `<title>` element. The psuedo-element is used in the selector, like so:

```
title:after {
```

While the `content` property writes the attribute value to the screen as follows:

```
content:"Written by: " attr(author);}
```

As you can see, this example not only added the attribute value, but also some text saying "Written by:" so that the attribute value did not just appear from the blue.

Summary

This chapter started out by introducing you to CSS and how it can be used with XHTML. As you saw, however, a web browser already knows how to deal with many of the elements in XHTML, such as `table`, `ul`, and `b`. When you write your own XML vocabularies, however, the browser will not know how to interpret any of the elements, which means you have to lay out your documents from scratch.

The box model of CSS puts the content of every element in either an inline or block box, and by positioning these boxes carefully, you can achieve complex layouts. You have seen that normal flow, relative positioning, float positioning, absolute positioning, and fixed positioning allow you to control where the elements appear.

The chapter also covered how to create tables and bulleted lists, and how to display links and images in our XML documents.

You saw, on the way, that three of CSS's significant weaknesses are the following:

- There is still very little support for some of the more advanced features, such as table layout properties and complex positioning.
- It is very difficult to reorder element content from the order presented in the original XML document.
- To display attribute values, you need to use a workaround that is not supported in Internet Explorer.

These drawbacks may encourage you to look at transforming your XML using XSLT into either XHTML or another XML vocabulary that is easier to present. Transforming your content into XHTML would also give you the advantage of being able to add images and links to your documents that would work in most browsers.

Alternatively, you may have the luxury of being able to write a vocabulary that will be easy to display using CSS now that you know where its strengths and weaknesses regarding presenting XML lie.

Exercise Questions

Suggested solutions to these questions can be found in Appendix A.

Question 1

The exercises for this chapter focus on one example: a purchase order. You will slowly build up a more complex style sheet for the following XML file (`ch17_ex01.xml`):

```
<?xml version="1.0" encoding="UTF-8" ?>
<?xml-stylesheet type="text/css" href="ch17_ex01.css" ?>

<purchaseOrder orderID="x1129001">

<buyer>
   <companyName>Woodland Toys</companyName>
   <purchaserName>Tom Walter</purchaserName>
   <address>
     <address1>The Business Centre</address1>
     <address2>127 Main Road</address2>
     <town>Albury</town>
     <city>Seaforth</city>
     <state>BC</state>
     <zipCode>22001</zipCode>
  </address>
</buyer>

<orders>
   <item>
      <sku>126552</sku>
```

```
        <product>People Carrier</product>
        <description>Childs pedal operated car</description>
    </item>
    <item>
        <sku>122452</sku>
        <product>BubbleBaby</product>
        <description>Bean filled soft toy</description>
    </item>
    <item>
        <sku>129112</sku>
        <product>My First Drum Kit</product>
        <description>Childs plastic drum kit</description>
    </item>
</orders>

</purchaseOrder>
```

First, create a rule to put the purchase order in a box, with a 1 pixel black border, 20 pixels of padding inside, and a 20-pixel margin to separate the box from the browser window.

Question 2

Create a rule that writes "Purchase Order Number" in a large, bold, Arial typeface as the heading (in case the user does not have Arial, you should add Verdana as a second option and the default Sans-serif font as the third option), and that collects the purchase order number from the `orderID` attribute.

Question 3

Add the buyer's details to the purchase order, with the company name in bold and each part of the address on a new line in a smaller Arial font (and if the user does not have Arial it should look for Verdana or the default Sans-serif font).

Question 4

Write out the items ordered in a table.

Scalable Vector Graphics (SVG)

Simple things should be simple. Complex things should be possible.
—Alan Kay

In this chapter we will introduce Scalable Vector Graphics (SVG), which is an extremely versatile 2-D graphics format designed primarily for the web. Its specification is maintained by the World Wide Web Consortium (W3C), and it offers an open alternative to proprietary graphics systems.

Here we will introduce the core concepts together with some of the most commonly used features, with corresponding practical code. The SVG specification is brimming with features—far too many to describe in a single chapter—but to get to grips with the language, we'll need to see how to write practical code and have a general idea of the kind of things SVG can do.

So this chapter is divided into four sections:

- First, we will be given an overview of SVG, the kind of things it's good for and what tools are available to the developer.
- Next is a hands-on section in which we will see some of the basics of SVG demonstrated in code examples.
- We will then learn how a simple but complete browser-based SVG application can be constructed using XHTML and SVG, as well as a script manipulating the XML DOM.
- The last part of this chapter is a section-by-section summary of the contents of the SVG specification.

The information in this chapter is quite densely packed, but once you start playing with SVG yourself, you will discover that not only is it easier to work with than it looks on the printed page, it's also a lot of fun.

What Is SVG?

SVG is primarily a language for creating graphic documents. The language uses simple, intuitive terms like "circle" and "line," which makes it easy to learn. It's an XML language, which means it is possible to generate and process using standard XML tools. SVG's use of XML's structural features makes it straightforward to construct complex diagrams based on simpler, modular parts. It has

been designed with the web in mind, and the documents can be viewed in browsers with the appropriate plug-in. In addition to offering animation and scripting capabilities, SVG also supports sophisticated graphic filtering, processing, and geometry, though none of these advanced features are necessary to get started creating useful images.

Scalable, Vector, Graphics

Rather than defining images pixel-by-pixel as in bitmapped formats such as JPEG and GIF, SVG defines how images should be drawn using a series of statements. This approach has several advantages. SVG image files tend to be significantly smaller than their bitmap equivalents, a desirable characteristic on the web. Secondly, parts of an image can be treated as separate objects and manipulated independently. This means complex diagrams can be built from simpler components, and that dynamic effects (for example, animation) are relatively straightforward. Vector graphic images can easily be resized—this is one of the reasons for the "Scalable" in the name—which is particularly useful on devices with small screens, such as mobile phones. Most viewers also allow you to *zoom* (enlarge and reduce) and *pan* (move side to side and up and down) the graphics, but on top of the versatility of vector graphics, SVG has an ace card—it's true XML. All the benefits described in this book of using XML apply to SVG. Tools such as XSLT (covered in Chapter 8), programming models such as DOM (covered in Chapter 11), interoperability, and internationalization—all of these are there for SVG, thanks to its definition as XML. That's still not all, though. You can not only draw graphics, but you can also write applications—SVG has a powerful scripting facility built in.

Since the end product of SVG is visual, there is a lot of geometry and color theory involved. Most of the theory is either trivial or makes intuitive sense, but some of the mathematics can seem daunting. Fortunately, there are websites with coverage of this kind of theory, either specific to SVG or more general. Remember, the search engine is your friend.

There are parts of SVG that are difficult to describe in words alone. Fortunately, as a visual language it's straightforward to demonstrate these features. There isn't space in this chapter to go into great depth, but there are many examples available on the web. The starting point is the W3C specification, which contains code for most things, but a search engine is likely to give you more complex, practical examples. As with XHTML (covered in Chapter 16), if you're not sure how something's been done, view source and find out.

Putting SVG to Work

The uses of SVG can loosely be divided into three categories as follows:

- Static graphics rendering, where the code is used to define a fixed image
- Self-contained applications, where the animation and scripting capabilities of SVG are used to provide dynamic, interactive graphics
- Server-based applications, where SVG provides the front end for bigger and more complex systems

Static Graphics

There are many situations where traditional web graphics formats, such as GIF and JPEG, are unsuitable. For example, you might have a large and complex engineering drawing. There would be a problem with the size of the image file taking a long time to download, and once you had the image in your browser, it would be very difficult to navigate around. Being vector-based means that SVG diagrams can have much smaller file sizes, and the ability to zoom and pan means that navigation is straightforward.

Self-Contained Applications

Most SVG viewers support client-side scripting, and this combined with SVG's animation facilities make it an extremely versatile tool for creating applications that will run in the browser. There are several other systems available for building this kind of thing, such as Macromedia Flash and Java Applets, but Flash is a proprietary system whereas SVG is an open standard built on existing web standards, such as XML, ECMAScript (Javascript), and Cascading Style Sheets (CSS). The advantage SVG has over applets is that the focus on graphics makes it considerably easier to create visually appealing browser-based applications.

Server-Based Applications

SVG's web standards base means it's perfectly suited for the construction of rich user interfaces to server-side systems. Where a graphic front end is needed for a system that handles a large amount of data or complex processing, SVG is a good solution. A typical example would be Geographic Information Systems, where the server can produce maps on the fly based on client requests. All the facilities available to client-side applications and static graphics are available to build browser-based clients that are as rich as the system demands. Because SVG is XML, it is relatively easy to generate from other XML data—generating graphs to dynamically include in reports is a typical example.

An SVG Toolkit

Thanks to the openness and versatility of SVG it's practically impossible to recommend any single set of tools. To hand-build SVG files, you'll need some kind of editing tool, and to see the result, you'll need a viewer. The simplest of these would be a text editor and a browser plug-in, though there are considerably more sophisticated editors available. If you want to build more dynamic systems or integrate with existing systems, then you'll need to look at what tools are available for the programming languages that you want to work with. For each of these jobs there is a wide range of options; some of the better-known alternatives are listed in the following sections. The W3C maintains an official list of SVG implementations (`http://www.w3.org/Graphics/SVG/SVG-Implementations`), although with a web search, you may find more up-to-date tools suited to your particular needs. Here are a few specific suggestions; most are free, and some are open source.

Viewers

The most popular way of viewing SVG files on a desktop computer is to use a browser plug-in. Microsoft's Internet Explorer web browser together with Adobe's plug-in (available from `http://www.adobe.com/svg/`) is one option. At the time of writing, the release version 3.0 is available for most platforms and languages, though there is a version 6.0 beta for MS Windows, English only, available from `http://www.adobe.com/svg/viewer/install/beta.html`. If you right-click with your mouse over an SVG graphic in the plug-in you get a menu of actions—zoom, pan, view source, and so on.

Corel also provides a free browser plug-in: `http://www.smartgraphics.com`.

Batik, the Java toolkit for SVG, includes a cross-platform viewer called Squiggle (see `http://xml.apache.org/batik`.) Squiggle is a good choice while you're developing with SVG as it gives more useful error messages than the browser plug-ins.

Support for SVG on Mozilla-based browsers (Netscape, Firefox, and others) is less than perfect—the Adobe plug-in version 3.0 has known bugs in this environment. However, considerable work has already been done on native support for SVG in these browsers, and this has been declared as one of the Mozilla project's priorities.

Editors

It depends on what you want to do with SVG, but a text editor is certainly adequate for simple hand-coding. To check your code the W3C have produced an SVG Validator that can be used online or downloaded and run locally (go to `http://jiggles.w3.org/svgvalidator/`).

Also from the W3C is Amaya, a combined web browser and editor with support for SVG and rather a lot more, available at `http://www.w3.org/Amaya/` (the OpenGL version provides better SVG support).

A generic XML editor like Butterfly (`http://www.butterflyxml.org/`) can make life easier by checking the validity of your data as you go along, and can also advise which attributes are available for particular elements.

If you're interested in drawing, then Inkscape (`http://www.inkscape.org/`) is an open source editor, and the commercial JASC WebDraw (`http://www.jasc.com/products/webdraw/`) offers editing with animation support. Adobe Illustrator and GoLive are other commercial alternatives (`http://www.adobe.com/svg`).

Programming Tools

If you're working with self-contained SVG applications, then pretty well any Javascript editor can help, and many general-purpose text editors, like the open source jEdit (`http://www.jedit.org/`), offer syntax highlighting along with other conveniences.

There are SVG-specific programming libraries available for most languages. For instance, there's the librsvg (`http://librsvg.sourceforge.net`) for Linux applications, several Perl modules at CPAN, and SVGDraw for Python (`http://www2.sfk.nl/svg`). There's a fairly new project for open source SVG on .NET called SVG# (`http://www.sharpvectorgraphics.org/`). Probably the most sophisticated programmer's toolkit is Apache Batik (`http://xml.apache.org/batik/`), which provides just about everything you're likely to need for SVG work in Java.

The list of tools that can generate SVG is actually very, very long thanks to its use of XML. Any tool that can create or modify XML can be applied to SVG. In particular, DOM (and similar) libraries for any language offer a straightforward way of dynamically generating SVG data. XSLT makes it possible to transform data from other XML formats into SVG for a graphic representation.

It's beyond the range of this chapter to describe how to use SVG with other programming languages, but remember the material in the rest of this book on using XML applies exactly the same when it comes to working with SVG as any other XML language.

Getting Started

Getting started with SVG is very easy, as simple things really are simple. Most XML elements in the SVG format correspond to graphics elements, and most XML attributes correspond to attributes (or properties) of the elements. The names of elements and attributes are fairly self-explanatory: `circle` will draw a circle, `rect` will draw a rectangle, and so on. Here is a minimal example:

```
<svg xmlns="http://www.w3.org/2000/svg">
  <rect x="100" y="10" width="100" height="100" fill="green" />
</svg>
```

The <svg> element clearly marks the boundaries of the SVG material, in this case the whole document. The namespace declaration is also needed to unambiguously identify the element and attribute names—SVG document fragments like this can be embedded in other XML documents, and without a namespace, clashes between element and attribute names might occur.

The `rect` element defines a rectangle with its characteristics given as attributes. The `x` and `y` values are the coordinates of the top left-hand corner of the rectangle, measured in pixels across and down from the top left-hand corner of the viewing area. Yes, it is upside-down compared to regular coordinates, but in most web browsers that top left-hand corner is the only fixed point. The width and height are both 100 pixels, giving us a square. The `fill` attribute here says to color the inside of the shape green.

If you type the preceding example into a text editor, save it and open the resulting file in an SVG viewer (here using Batik Squiggle), you should see a green square like the one shown in Figure 18-1.

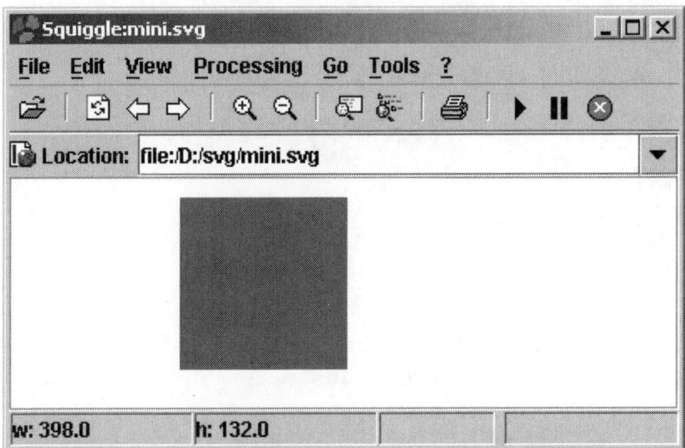

Figure 18-1

The previous example included the SVG namespace, but there is more information we can pass on to XML systems. Saying that the data is XML is a good start, and specifying a `DOCTYPE` will allow a processor to check whether or not the content is valid against a DTD. Here is the same fragment filled out to be a more complete XML document:

```
<?xml version="1.0" standalone="yes"?>
<!DOCTYPE svg PUBLIC "-//W3C//DTD SVG 1.1//EN"
        "http://www.w3.org/Graphics/SVG/1.1/DTD/svg11.dtd">

<svg xmlns="http://www.w3.org/2000/svg" version="1.1">
    <rect x="100" y="10" width="100" height="100" fill="green" />
</svg>
```

The XML version specified here is 1.0; though there is XML 1.1, it's unlikely that it will be in common use with languages like SVG in the foreseeable future. The version of SVG is stated as 1.1, the latest W3C Recommendation. Most SVG viewers won't care very much about these niceties, but it's good practice to include them. This is especially true if you are working on the web where there's no way of telling what might consume your data.

Try It Out Basic Shapes in SVG

There are a handful of basic shapes available in SVG from which we can build more complex images: rectangles (including ones with optional rounded corners), circles, ellipses, lines, polygons (enclosed areas), and polylines (line segments joined together). So let's see how these basic shapes are used.

1. Obtain and install an SVG viewer. If you're using Internet Explorer, then the SVG viewer plug-in from Adobe is a good choice: `http://www.adobe.com/svg/`.
2. Open a text editor and type in the following code:

```
<?xml version="1.0"?>
<!DOCTYPE svg PUBLIC "-//W3C//DTD SVG 1.1//EN"
    "http://www.w3.org/Graphics/SVG/1.1/DTD/svg11.dtd">

<svg xmlns="http://www.w3.org/2000/svg" version="1.1">

  <rect x="1" y="1" width="100" height="100"
        fill="none" stroke="blue" stroke-width="10" />

  <line x1="10" y1="10" x2="90" y2="90"
                      stroke="green" stroke-width="4" />

  <circle cx="50" cy="50" r="30" fill="red" />
</svg>
```

3. Save this document to your hard drive as `shapes.svg`.
4. Open `shapes.svg` in IE. Double-clicking the file in Windows Explorer should launch IE showing the shapes, as shown in Figure 18-2.

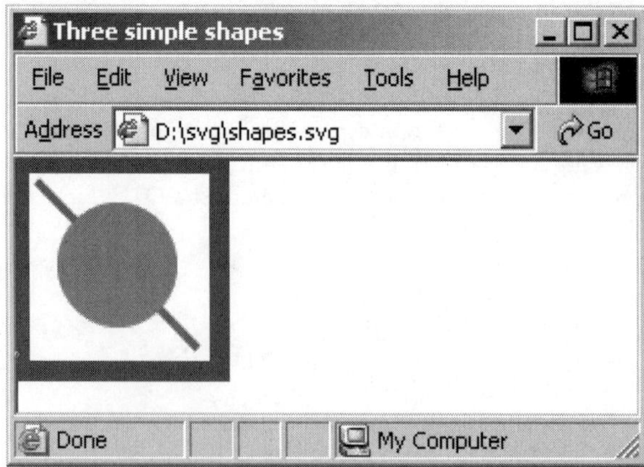

Figure 18-2

How It Works

The code starts with XML information, and then we have the SVG-specific material contained in the root `<svg>` element. The first child element is `rect`, and this will draw a rectangle as in the previous example. The `x` and `y` coordinates position this shape on the screen, just inside the top-left corner of the viewing area. This time the value of `fill` has been set as `none`, so the inside of this shape will be the color of whatever's underneath. This `rect` element has two more attributes, `stroke` and `stroke-width`. The stroke draws the lines that define the shape, in this case the outline of the rectangle. The value of the `stroke` attribute, determines the color of the outline, and here it's blue. The `stroke-width` attribute says how thick the outline should be, in this case 10 pixels.

Next, we have a line element. Lines are *straight*, going from one point on screen to another. Those points are given as two sets of coordinates, the start point being (x1, y1) and the end point (x2,y2). So in the previous code the line starts at a point 10 pixels from the left-hand side of the viewing area (`x1="10"`) and 10 pixels down from the top (`y1="10"`). The line runs to the point 90 pixels across (`x2="90"`) and 90 pixels down from the top left-hand corner of the viewing area (`y2="90"`). A simple line doesn't enclose any space, so there is no `fill` attribute here. But a line can be stroked, and here the color is given as green and the width of the line given as 4 pixels.

The third shape element is a circle. Circles are defined in SVG using the coordinates of their center point and their radius. The center point is expressed as the value of the `cx` and `cy` attributes, and the radius is in the `r` attribute.

The Painter's Model

In the previous example, the square outline defined by the `rect` element is clearly visible, as is the circle, but the middle section of the line has been obscured by the circle. This is a feature, not a bug! If you refer back to the source, inside the root `svg` element, there are three child elements at the same level: `rect`, `line`, and `circle`. The coordinates of these elements locate them in more or less the same area of screen. The order in which the elements appear is significant; it is the order in which the visual objects will be rendered. This is commonly referred to as the *Painter's Model*. The `rect` comes first, so a rectangle is painted on the "canvas." Next, the line gets drawn on the canvas on top of whatever's already there. Finally, the circle gets drawn on top of everything else.

If we rearrange the source data so that the elements appear in the reverse order, we can see the difference as shown in Figure 18-3.

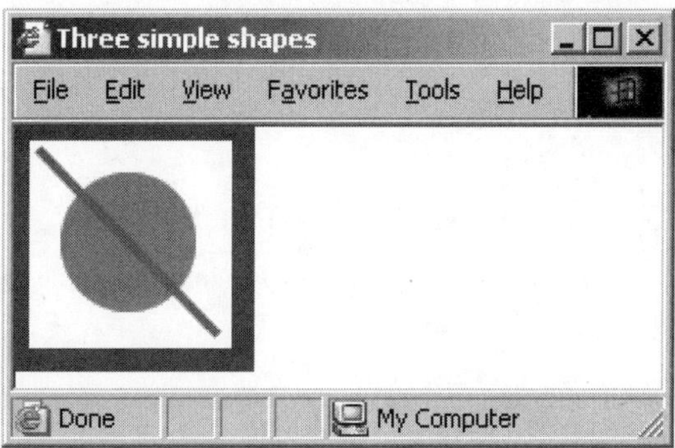

Figure 18-3

```
...
  <circle cx="50" cy="50" r="30" fill="red" />

  <line x1="10" y1="10" x2="90" y2="90"
        stroke="green" stroke-width="4" />

  <rect x="1" y="1" width="100" height="100"
        fill="none" stroke="blue" stroke-width="10" />

...
```

The circle is now painted first, followed by the line, and finally the rectangle. The line comes after the circle in the same location, so it's painted on top. Although the rectangle was painted last, we can still see the line and the circle as the `fill` attribute of `rect` is `none`. We are in effect looking through the square outline at the other objects.

Try It Out Painter's Model

There are a handful of basic shapes available in SVG from which we can build more complex images: rectangles (including ones with optional rounded corners), circles, ellipses, lines, polygons (enclosed areas), and polylines (line segments joined together). So let's see how these basic shapes are used.

1. Open the example in a text editor again, and add the following:

```
<?xml version="1.0"?>
<!DOCTYPE svg PUBLIC "-//W3C//DTD SVG 1.1//EN"
    "http://www.w3.org/Graphics/SVG/1.1/DTD/svg11.dtd">

<svg xmlns="http://www.w3.org/2000/svg" version="1.1">

  <rect x="1" y="1" width="100" height="100"
       fill="none" stroke="blue" stroke-width="10" />

  <line x1="10" y1="10" x2="90" y2="90"
                  stroke="green" stroke-width="4" />

  <polygon points="60,0 75,46 120,46 84,74
                  97,120 60,93 23,120 36,74
                  0,46 45,46"
          stroke="orange" fill="yellow" />

  <circle cx="50" cy="50" r="30" fill="red" />
</svg>
```

2. Save this document to your hard drive as `shapes.svg`.
3. Open `shapes.svg` in IE. Double-clicking the file in Windows Explorer should launch IE showing the shapes.

You will now see the red circle on top of a yellow star, below which you can see the rectangle and line as before.

How It Works

The polygon is another of SVG's Basic Shapes, though it's rather like a path in that the shape is described as a series of (absolute) points where a straight line will be drawn from point to point. The coordinates of the points are specified in the `points` attribute of the `polygon` element. The polygon here defines the lines that make up the outline of the five-pointed start.

In the previous listing, the `polygon` (star) comes after the `rect` and `line` elements, so it will be painted on top of them. However, the circle appears after the polygon, so it gets painted on top. You may like to experiment with the order of the elements to confirm that the image is appearing as if each is being painted on its predecessors.

Grouping

The `g` element allows you to group together related elements using the hierarchical structure of XML. For example, if you wanted a circle and a line to behave as if they were a single element, you could wrap them in a `g` element like this:

```
...
<g stroke="green" stroke-width="4">

   <circle cx="50" cy="50" r="30" fill="red" />
   <line x1="10" y1="10" x2="90" y2="90" />
</g>
...
```

This is convenient if you want various elements to share the same properties—here the `stroke` and `stroke-width` attributes in the `g` element will be applied to both the circle and the line. If either of these child elements had `stroke` or `stroke-width` attributes of its own, they would override the defaults inherited from the parent `g` element.

Transformations

The `transform` attribute allows modification of a shape or set of shapes defined in a group. There are several simple expressions that can go into the attribute. These are as follows:

- `translate`: to display the shapes shifted across and down by specified distances
- `rotate`: to rotate the shapes by a given angle around a specified point
- `scale`: to make the shapes larger or smaller by a specified ratio
- `skewX`: to *lean* the shapes along the x-axis
- `skewY`: to lean the shapes along the y-axis

These operators can be used individually in attributes or in combination. For example, the following will have the effect of drawing the rectangle starting from the point (101, 101) and rotated by 45 degrees:

```
<rect x="1" y="1" width="100" height="100"
      fill="none" stroke="blue" stroke-width="10"
      transform="translate(100,100) rotate(45)"/>
```

You can also use a transformation matrix to apply to a shape or set of shapes, which can give any arbitrary shifting and twisting of the shapes, though to use this successfully you'll need some knowledge of matrix arithmetic.

Paths

The basic shape elements are a convenient way of drawing common figures, but not the only way. Each of the shapes and a whole lot more can be created using a more fundamental drawing device, the path. An SVG `path` element describes the behavior of a virtual pen, which can be used to create practically any shape you like. The pen can be moved without drawing, and it can draw straight-line segments and curves. What the pen should draw is given in an attribute of the path element named `d`, for data. As an example we can duplicate the shapes drawn in the previous example using paths, starting with the following line where we had:

```
<line x1="10" y1="10" x2="90" y2="90" stroke="green" stroke-width="4" />
```

This instructed the SVG renderer to paint a 4-pixel-wide green line between the points (10, 10) and (90, 90). This can be expressed as pen movements in a similar fashion as follows:

```
<path d="M 10,10 L 90,90" stroke="green" stroke-width="4" />
```

Inside the `d` attribute there are two commands: the first is `M 10,10` and the second `L 90,90`. The first command says to move (`M`) the virtual pen to the point (10, 10), and the second says to paint a line *from the current point* to the point (90, 90). The concept of *current point* is very important when using paths, though it isn't altogether obvious in this example, but we can make a small change to the example, which should emphasize the significance of the *current point*:

```
<path d="M 10,10 l 80,80" stroke="green" stroke-width="4" />
```

The difference is that the `L` is now lowercase, and the two values have each been reduced by 10. In an SVG viewer the lines will appear exactly the same, because the path commands are case-sensitive, which determines the meaning of the coordinates given. Uppercase letters (`L`, `M`, and so on) are used to signify that *absolute* coordinates should be used, and lowercase letters signify that *relative* coordinates should be used. In the preceding first version, `L 90,90` indicates the drawing of a line to the point (90, 90) measured from the top left-hand corner (0, 0). In the second version, `l 80,80` indicates drawing a line to the point (80, 80) measured from the current point. Thanks to the initial movement of `M 10,10` the current point is positioned 10 pixels down and 10 pixels to the right of the top left-hand corner of the screen, so the target point is that much closer. Relative to the point (10, 10), the required target is 80 pixels to the right and 80 down.

In this example we only have one move followed by one line—paths can be as long as you like, put together as a sequence of commands.

Here are the commands that can appear in paths. The specification uses shorthand names as shown in the following table.

M	Moveto	Moves to a new starting point.
L	Lineto	Draws a line from the current position to a new point.
H	horizontal lineto	Draws a horizontal line from the current point to line up with a new point.
V	vertical lineto	Draws a vertical line from the current point to line up with a new point.
Z	Closepath	Draws a straight line from the current point to current path's starting point.
A	elliptical arc	Draws an elliptical arc from the current point to a new point. Other values in the data define the exact shape.
Q	Quadratic Bézier curveto	Draws a quadratic Bézier curve from the current point to a new point. Other values in the data define the exact shape.
T	smooth quadratic Bézier curveto	Draws a quadratic Bézier curve from the current point to a new point. Values in a preceding curve's data define the exact shape.
C	curveto (cubic Bézier)	Draws a cubic Bézier curve from the current point to a new point. Other values in the data define the exact shape.
S	smooth curveto (cubic Bézier)	Draws a cubic Bézier curve from the current point to a new point. Values in a preceding curve's data define the exact shape.

Note that each of the commands can appear in uppercase (absolute coordinates) or lowercase (relative coordinates).

The first two we have already seen in the line example—`M` (moveto) changes the current point to a new location without drawing anything, and `L` (lineto) draws a straight line from the current point to the specified coordinates. The horizontal and vertical lineto commands `H` and `V` aren't followed by a pair of coordinates, just a single value (x for horizontal, y for vertical). The other value will remain the same as it is for the current point.

The `Z` command, closepath, is used when we want to draw a closed shape, something that encloses an area. The command draws a straight line from the current point back to the initial starting point of the current subpath (for example, where the pen first went down in this particular part).

We can see how this works if we draw the rectangle part of the example using paths. The basic shape version looks like this:

```
<rect x="1" y="1" width="100" height="100" fill="none" stroke="blue"
stroke-width="10" />
```

The top left-hand corner of the rectangle is specified, along with its dimensions. The path approach isn't anywhere near as easy to read:

```
<path d="M 1,1 L 1,100 L 100,100 L 100,1 z" fill="none" stroke="blue"
stroke-width="10" />
```

The data starts with a command to move to the point (1, 1), which is followed by a line to the point (1, 100). Next, there is another line *from the current point* to the absolute position (100, 100), followed by a line from there to (100, 1). Finally, a `z` command (note lowercase) closed the square, drawing a line from the current point (100, 1) back to the point where the pen last started drawing in this part of the path, which was (1, 1).

The remainder of the path commands (`A`, `Q`, `T`, `C`, and `S`) draw curves, based on different mathematical formula applied to various values you supply. You don't actually need to know anything about the formula to be able to use these commands to draw curves, the SVG specification (section 8.2) has examples of each kind of curve. We can use the elliptical arc command to make a path version of the circle in the basic shape example.

Once again here is the easy-to-read version as follows:

```
<circle cx="50" cy="50" r="30" fill="red" />
```

The coordinates of the center of the circle are given along with its radius. There are several ways the circle could be drawn, none of which are particularly straightforward. The series of values that follow the elliptical arc command are listed in the spec as `rx ry x-axis-rotation large-arc-flag sweep-flag x y`. The first two values give the radius in the x and y directions, for a circle they're equal values. The arc is drawn from the current point to the point given by the coordinates (x, y). Here we've used the relative version of the command, drawing the arc around to the point (1, 1). If (0, 0) is specified, the shape disappears altogether, presumably a feature of the rendering algorithm. The other values give further information on how the arc is to be drawn.

```
<path d="M30,70.7 a30,30 1 1,1 1,1" fill="red" />
```

In this section we've only been using paths to paint very simple shapes. They really only come into their own when more complex drawings are needed. To show this in a very limited fashion, consider what we've seen so far: a virtual pen has drawn a line, another virtual pen has drawn a square, and a third virtual pen has drawn a circle. If we don't care about changing the pen's ink (the `fill` and `stroke` attributes), we can draw the whole lot in one go as shown in the following code:

```
<path d="M1 1L1 100L100 100L100 1z M10 10l80 80M30 70.7a30 30 1 1 1 1 1"
        stroke="pink" stroke-width="5" />
```

If you look at the data line carefully you can see how each part has been taken from the preceding three single path elements. The syntax here is a little different—there's no reason why the commas and spaces shouldn't have appeared as in the individual examples, but there are alternatives. Commas and/or whitespace can be used to separate the numbers in a path, as can the command letters themselves. Here we've opted for a concise version. The resulting image looks like Figure 18-4.

Paths are an extremely versatile way of drawing shapes with SVG, but that versatility comes at the cost of it being considerably more difficult to write the code manually and make sense of existing code. In practice, you probably won't want to write paths any more complex than the last example here without the help of tools.

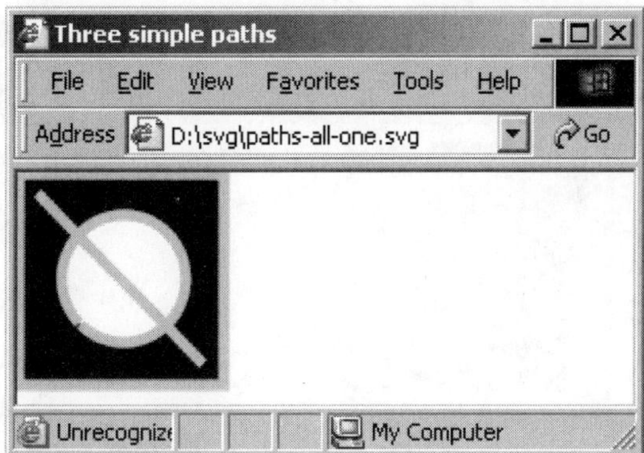

Figure 18-4

Images

Bitmap images such as GIFs and JPEGs can easily be incorporated into SVG documents using the `image` element. The following snippet draws a yellow rectangle with a green border, and places a picture of a flag on top of that:

```
<svg version="1.1"
     xmlns="http://www.w3.org/2000/svg"
     xmlns:xlink="http://www.w3.org/1999/xlink">

   <rect x="10" y="10" width="120" height="120"
         fill="yellow" stroke="green" stroke-width="4" />

  <image xlink:href="http://www.jpeg.org/images/flag_fr.jpg"
         type="image/jpeg" x="20" y="20" width="100" height="100" />

</svg>
```

The `image` element uses an attribute from the XLink namespace, so the namespace prefix `xlink` is declared in the root `svg` element. The MIME (Internet Media) type of the image is given as an attribute (`image/jpeg`) along with the required position and dimensions of the image (see Figure 18-5).

Note that the flag is distorted—the original image is actually smaller than the `width` and `height` values given in the `image` element, so the viewer stretched it to fit.

Text

The first thing we need to know about text in SVG is that it is *real* text. Any kind of image can contain text, but try copying and pasting text from a JPEG image. In SVG, text is a first class citizen. We can copy it from the rendered graphics and employ tools that can read the text from the source code or modify it in the DOM tree.

Support for text in SVG 1.1 is very sophisticated, yet lacking in one particular respect. The sophistication extends to using different character sets, styles, and orientations—virtually any written language can be

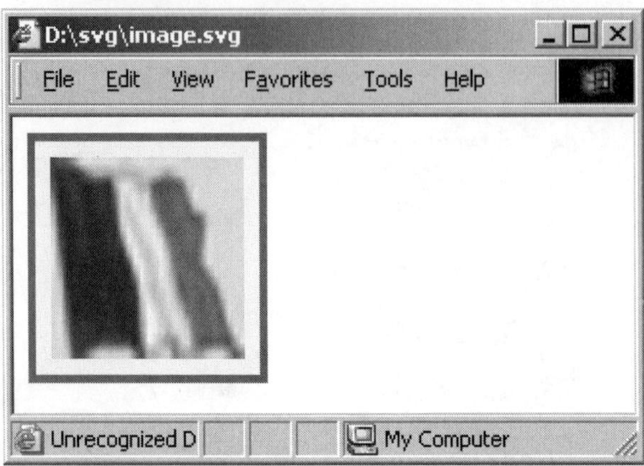

Figure 18-5

rendered in SVG without much difficulty. You can even create your own character sets (a font is defined as a set of "glyphs"). Where SVG 1.1 falls short is in support for multiline text. You can write a series of lines of text easily enough, but a single block of text cannot be made to wrap on to the next line as you might expect. This is a feature promised for SVG 1.2.

In its basic form, as you are likely to want to use it most of the time, there's not a lot to learn about SVG text. Here is an example of some text, which will appear in a little frame, the same as in the image example:

```
<svg version="1.1" xmlns="http://www.w3.org/2000/svg">

   <rect x="10" y="10" width="120" height="120"
         fill="yellow" stroke="green" stroke-width="4" />

   <text x="15" y="70" font-size="20" fill="red">SVG is XML</text>

</svg>
```

The text is defined using a text element. The x and y attributes here give the point at which to start writing the text. In this simple example this refers to the bottom left-hand side of the first character. The color of the text is given by the `fill` attribute, and the size of the letters by the `font-size` attribute, which is defined by CSS2. Virtually all the CSS2 properties can be applied to SVG text (see Figure 18-6).

Comments, Annotation, and Meta Data

A key benefit of SVG as XML is its machine readability. A computer can read and interpret the content of an SVG file beyond what's needed for the graphics display. Your SVG files may be read by different software than straightforward viewers, for example, robots building indexes for search engines. Even with viewers there are places to put information outside of the graphics display such as the title bar of the viewer window, or in popup tooltips.

Three elements within SVG are available specifically for providing this kind of extra information: `title`, `desc`, and `metadata`. The first two of these are used in the following example:

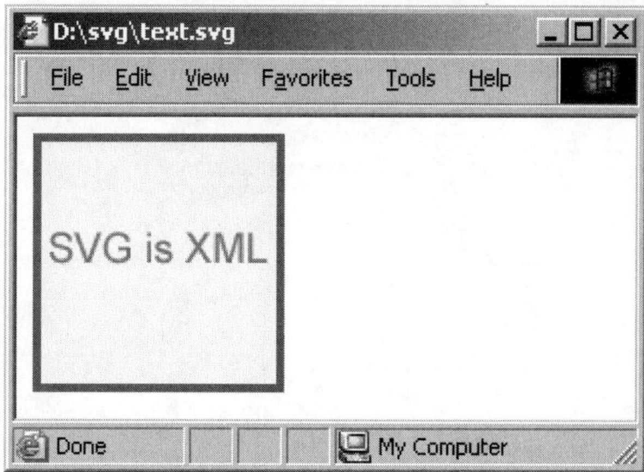

Figure 18-6

```
<svg version="1.1" xmlns="http://www.w3.org/2000/svg">

   <!-- This is an XML comment-->

   <title>This is the title of the document</title>
   <desc>This is the description of the document</desc>
   <g>
      <title>This is a circle</title>
      <desc>Its color is red.</desc>
      <circle cx="60" cy="60" r="50" fill="red"/>
   </g>
</svg>
```

First of all, there is a regular XML comment. These should only be included to assist anyone reading the source code, so don't put anything too valuable in a comment. Next come a `title` and `desc` element as children of the root element. In this position these are giving the title and a description of the document itself. We then have a `g` element, which contains a `title`, `desc`, and a `circle`. The title and description in this case refer to this group of elements.

Unlike the graphics elements, what the user agent (the software reading the document) does with the data in these elements is not mandated in the specification, although none of it will display directly as part of the graphics. As you might expect, this has led to some variation in what's been implemented in the viewers. The Squiggle viewer is ahead of the field in its treatment of these elements, and Figure 18-7 shows the previous file in that viewer.

You can see that the document title ("This is the title of the document") is shown in the title bar. The mouse pointer is over a part of the group of elements, and Squiggle has displayed a popup note showing the contents of the `title` and `desc` elements.

The `metadata` element allows more complex machine-readable data to be included in the document. The W3C has been leading initiatives to make material on the web more useful by adding as much machine-readable information as possible. There are others, but the leading metadata standard is the Resource Description Framework (`http://w3.org/RDF`). This makes it possible to say anything about

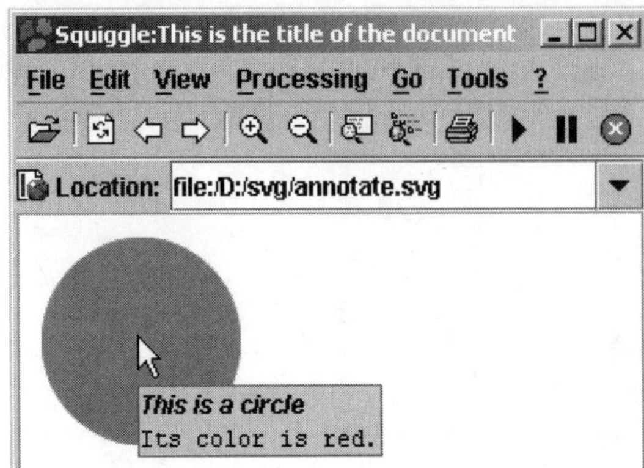

Figure 18-7

virtually anything in a form that computers can use. The framework is really a data model, but the format used for interchange of this data is an XML language, RDF/XML. There has been considerable industry support for the W3C initiative, for example, all of Adobe's tools now embed RDF in their data files—JPEGs, PDF, and of course SVG. A good place to start finding out more about using SVG and RDF together is the "Codepiction" site (`http://rdfweb.org/2002/01/photo/`), which is part of the FOAF (Friend-of-a-friend) project.

Remember that under most circumstances the contents of the `title`, `desc`, and `metadata` elements won't be visible as part of the SVG graphics. However, some web browsers without a plug-in will display these as plain text.

> **Different web users have different requirements, and there are many people who can't use a browser in the regular fashion because of disabilities such as poor eyesight. Several features of SVG make it particularly good for communication in such circumstances, which are discussed in the W3C note "Accessibility Features of SVG" (`http://www.w3.org/TR/SVG-access/`. For example, being able to zoom in on images makes SVG images more accessible to people with impaired vision. Providing text equivalents of images in `title` and `desc` elements can also allow the information to be conveyed using text-to-speech screenreaders.**

Scripting

SVG has a scripting facility very similar to that of HTML. The language usually available is ECMAScript, which is the international standard version of Javascript. It's beyond the scope of this book to provide an introduction to ECMAScript/Javascript, but the examples we will be using are relatively self-explanatory.

If the code shown in Figure 18-8 (`script.svg`) is opened in a viewer, you will see a green triangle. Clicking the mouse on the triangle will make it turn red.

The code is really in two parts. The first is an SVG element, which defines the triangle shape, and the second part is a piece of ECMAScript, which responds to the mouse click and changes the triangle's color.

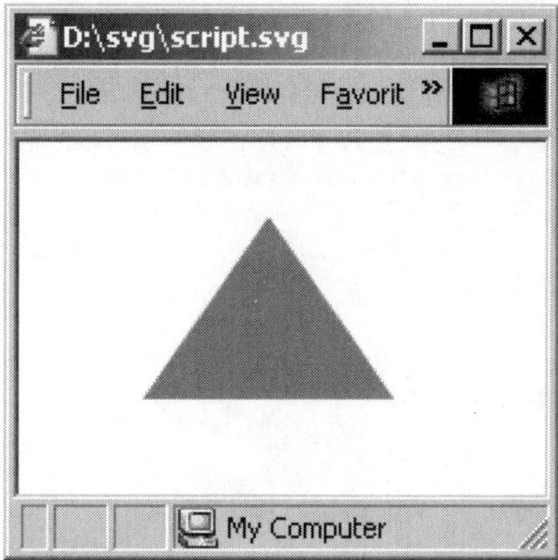

Figure 18-8

```
<?xml version="1.0" standalone="no"?>
<!DOCTYPE svg PUBLIC "-//W3C//DTD SVG 1.1//EN"
  "http://www.w3.org/Graphics/SVG/1.1/DTD/svg11.dtd">
<svg xmlns="http://www.w3.org/2000/svg" version="1.1">

   <polygon points="150,100, 50,100 100,29.3" fill="green"
          onclick="handleClick(evt)" />

   <script type="text/ecmascript">
      <![CDATA[

        function handleClick(evt) {
           var polygon = evt.target;
           polygon.setAttribute("fill", "red");
        }

      ]]>
   </script>
</svg>
```

The triangle is defined as a polygon. A triangle has three corners, hence we have three sets of x,y coordinates. The `fill` attribute for the polygon is `green`, so it will appear shaded in that color.

The `onclick` attribute is a special attribute that associates the element with an event and part of the script. In this example the event is a mouse click, and the part of the script is a user-defined function called `handleClick`. That function will be passed an object (`evt`) that carries information relating to the mouse click event.

Scripts in SVG are included using a `<script>` element. As you will see later in this chapter it is possible to point to an external script file, but there isn't much code here, so it's included in the SVG document file itself.

The script listing is wrapped in a `CDATA` section, as there may be characters in the script (for example, <) that would break XML's well-formedness rule. Here the script comprises a single function, `handleClick`, which will be called when the user clicks the triangle.

The first statement of the function creates a new variable called `polygon` (the name isn't important) and sets this to the value of the `target` attribute of the `evt` object. The target is the object on which the event occurred, in this case the `polygon` element in the SVG part of the code. The next line uses a DOM method to set the `polygon` element's value to the `red` string. This has the effect of changing the value in memory of that part of the SVG to be equivalent to the following:

```
<polygon points="150,100, 50,100 100,29.3" fill="red"
        onclick="handleClick(evt)" />
```

Note that the actual source code doesn't change, only the in-memory representation, which is the DOM tree, but the end result is the same: the triangle becomes red.

SVG on Your Website

Publishing SVG material on the web is nearly as straightforward as publishing XHTML. Bear in mind that people who visit your site will need an SVG-capable viewer—having a link on one of your XHTML pages to one of the browser plug-ins is a good idea.

Even if the visitor is using an SVG-capable browser, the browser may not realize that the material it's seeing is SVG. If you point your browser at one of your newly uploaded SVG masterpieces and all you see is XML code, don't be dismayed. There are two ways to give the browser a hint. The first is to give the file an appropriate extension—svg for regular SVG files and `.svgz` for gzip compressed files. Secondly (and more importantly), you should ensure that the web server delivers the document with the right MIME type. At the time of writing, most web servers *don't*. Depending on your setup you may have to ask the server administrator to add the MIME type to the configuration for you. With most Apache-based services it's possible to add the MIME type yourself. Simply create a file called `.htaccess` (note the initial dot) in the top-level directory below which your SVG files will appear and enter the following text:

```
AddType image/svg+xml svg
AddType image/svg+xml svgz
AddEncoding gzip svgz
```

To check whether the material's being served correctly, you'll need a download tool such as *wget* (a GNU tool, Win32 ports are available), which will tell you what the MIME type is (for SVG it should be `image/svg+xml`).

Tangram: A Simple Application

To give you a taste of how an SVG application fits together, here is a little toy. Tangram is a jigsaw-like Chinese puzzle based on seven flat geometric pieces, which can be arranged (without overlap) to make various shapes, the simplest of which is a square. In the toy application shown in Figure 18-9, we begin with all the pieces in a square box and click a Scramble button to scatter them out of the box. The goal is to fit the pieces back into the box.

The application is composed of the following three files:

- `tangram.html`—an XHTML file which will display the puzzle together with some instructions
- `tangram.svg`—an SVG file which defines the graphics, including control buttons
- `tangram.es`—an ECMAScript file which looks after movement of the pieces

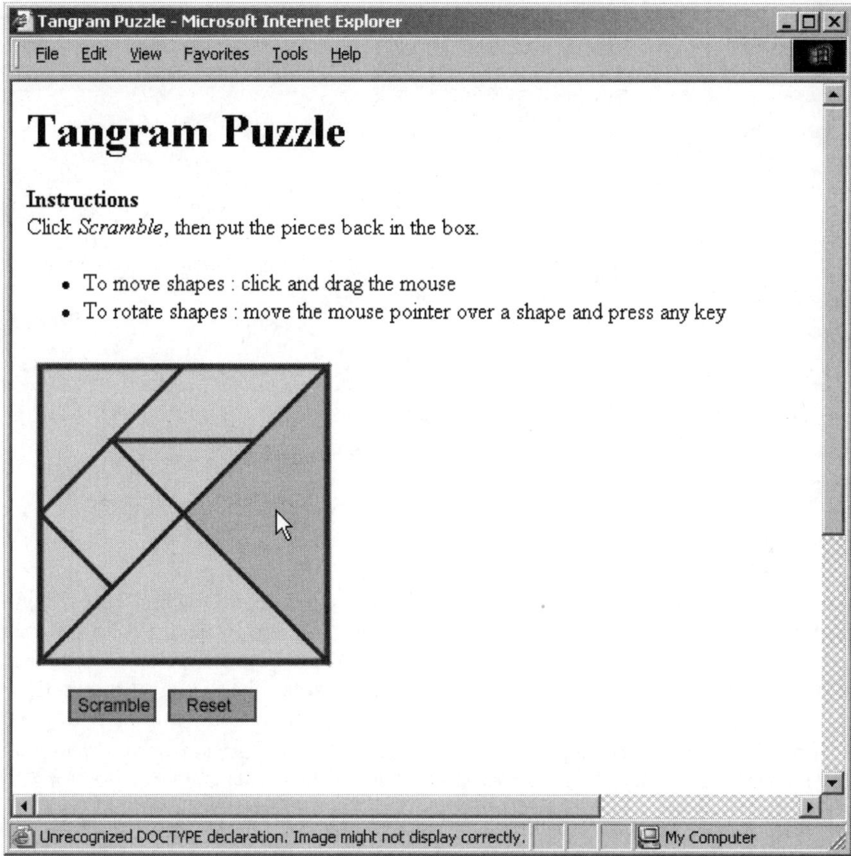

Figure 18-9

XHTML Wrapper

SVG files can be viewed directly in capable browsers, or they can form part of a regular XHTML page. The first file on the preceding list is standard XHTML, using the *Transitional* DOCTYPE. You will probably recognize most of its elements; they were all tags in legacy HTML, though the object element deserves some additional explanation.

```
<?xml version="1.0"?>
<!DOCTYPE html PUBLIC "-//W3C//DTD XHTML 1.0 Transitional//EN"
    "http://www.w3.org/TR/xhtml1/DTD/xhtml1-transitional.dtd">

<html xmlns="http://www.w3.org/1999/xhtml">
<head>
 <title>Tangram Puzzle</title>
</head>

<body>
 <h1>Tangram Puzzle</h1>
```

```
<p>
        <strong>Instructions</strong><br/>
        Click <em>Scramble</em>, then put the pieces back in the box.<br/>

</p>

 <ul>

        <li>To move shapes : click and drag the mouse</li>
        li>To rotate shapes :
           move the mouse pointer over a shape and press any key</li>

 </ul>

 <object data="tangram.svg" type="image/svg+xml" width="750" height="550">
    <embed src="tangram.svg" type="image/svg+xml" width="750" height="550" />
  </object>

</body>

</html>
```

The document leads in with conventional XML/XHTML material, and the body begins with a heading, then a small paragraph of text (`p`) featuring some emphasis (`em` and `strong`), followed by an unnumbered list (`ul`) containing two items (`li`), which make up the instructions. After the instructions comes the interesting part—the `object` element that will display the SVG graphics in the XHTML page.

> *Note: Historically, it's not been easy to display things like this in web pages in a consistent fashion as different browsers supported different approaches. The additional nonstandard `<embed>` tag is included here for maximal browser support. At the time of writing, the code here works with Internet Explorer 6 with the Adobe plug-in.*

The data attribute contains a relative URI pointing to the SVG file (it's in the same directory as this XHTML file). The `width` and `height` attributes of the `object` element determine the size of the area into which the SVG graphics will be drawn. The `type` attribute supplies the browser with the officially registered MIME (Internet Media) type of SVG data, so the browser knows how to handle the content of the linked file.

SVG Shapes

The SVG part of the application is relatively straightforward. Essentially, what we have is the box that the puzzle pieces start in, and the pieces themselves are represented as polygons and two labeled buttons. When the source code is stripped down to its elements, we can see the overall structure:

```
<svg>
    <script/>

    <title>Tangrams</title>
    <desc>An old Chinese puzzle</desc>

    <rect/> <!-- the pieces box -->
```

```
        <g> <!-- the pieces -->
            <polygon/>
            <polygon/>
            <polygon/>
            <polygon/>
            <polygon/>
            <polygon/>
            <polygon/>
        </g>

        <g><!-- "Scramble" button -->
             <rect/>
             <text>Scramble</text>
        </g>

        <g><!-- "Reset" button -->
             <rect/>
             <text>Reset</text>
        </g>
    </svg>
```

As well as the basic shapes and text, there is also a `script` element to link to an external ECMAScript file, which will look after mouse and keyboard interaction. A `title` and `desc` element provides machine-readable annotation. The `g` elements are used to provide common attributes to their child elements and simplify event listening.

We need to be able to move the pieces around. Therefore a mouse click-and-drag gesture is used, and we need listeners for various mouse events. To make the puzzle a little more interesting, we will also want to rotate the pieces to get them the right way around. This is done by selecting a piece and then pressing any key. A piece is selected by simply moving the mouse cursor over it. When the mouse cursor is over a piece, it will change color to indicate it has been selected.

There is some more behavior to look after: responding to mouse clicks on the buttons. A click on the Scramble button will scatter the pieces around, and a click on the Reset button will return them to their starting positions.

All this behavior has introduced a minor complication: the various elements have to respond to mouse and keyboard events. So there are hooks in the code to call appropriate functions in the ECMAScript, though the keyboard event handling is set up in the script itself.

```
<?xml version="1.0" standalone="no" ?>
<!DOCTYPE svg PUBLIC "-//W3C//DTD SVG 1.1//EN"
"http://www.w3.org/Graphics/SVG/1.1/DTD/svg11.dtd">

<svg version="1.1"
     xmlns="http://www.w3.org/2000/svg"
     xmlns:xlink="http://www.w3.org/1999/xlink"
     width="750px" height="550px"
     viewBox="-10 -10 740 540"
     onload="init(evt)">
```

After the XML prolog and DOCTYPE declaration, we have the document's root `svg` element. As well as declaring the SVG namespace and version, this also has attributes to position and scale the graphics in a suitably sized area (the viewBox) within the initial viewport specified by the width and height attributes. Here the viewBox data is just used to shift all the graphics 10 pixels down and to the right to provide a margin. The onload attribute is one of several possible event attributes, and the effect here is that when the SVG document is loaded into the viewer, a user-defined (in the script) function called init will be called and passed an object evt that models to the onload event.

The next line links in the script, and like the element in the previous XHTML code, the type attribute gives the MIME type of the linked file so the viewer knows what to expect. Similarly, a relative link is made as the script file (tangram.es) will be in the same directory as this document. There then follows a title and description for this SVG document:

```
<script type="text/ecmascript" xlink:href="tangram.es" />

<title>Tangrams</title>
<desc>An old Chinese puzzle</desc>
```

Now we get on to the graphic elements, starting with the square container box. This rectangle is colored yellow and has a 5-pixel dark blue outline, these characteristics being set in the elements' attributes as shown in the following:

```
<rect x="0" y="0" width="200" height="200" fill="yellow"
      stroke="darkblue" stroke-width="5"/>
```

Next we have the polygon elements, which will paint the puzzle pieces. All these pieces share the same fill and outline (stroke) characteristics. Therefore, the polygon elements are grouped together in a g element, and those attributes appear with that element. The parent-child inheritance of the characteristics means that this is equivalent to adding the attributes to all the individual children. An attribute introduced here is fill-opacity. This can take a value from 0 (transparent) to 1 (opaque). Setting this at 0.8 gives the shapes an attractive translucency, rather like stained glass. As with their appearance, all the pieces share the same behavior when responding to mouse events, so the event attributes (onmouseover and others) also appear in the parent g element. Each of these attributes contains a value corresponding to a function in the script. For instance, when the mouse cursor moves over a shape, the mouseover method in the script will be called. To simplify reference in the script, we give the g element an id attribute.

```
<g id="PolyGroup" fill="lightgreen" stroke="darkblue"
   stroke-width="3" fill-opacity="0.8"
   onmouseover="mouseover(evt)"
   onmouseout="mouseout(evt)"
   onmouseup="mouseup(evt)"
   onmousemove="move(evt)"
   onmousedown="mousedown(evt)">
```

Try It Out — Tangram Shapes

Let's see what this looks like in a browser just as static shapes.

1. Open a text editor and enter the previous code, starting from:

```
<?xml version="1.0" standalone="no" ?>
<!DOCTYPE svg PUBLIC "-//W3C//DTD SVG 1.1//EN"
"http://www.w3.org/Graphics/SVG/1.1/DTD/svg11.dtd">
...
```

2. Add the following code:

```
        <polygon points="0,0 0,100 100,0"
                 transform="translate(0,0) rotate(0,0,0)" />

        <polygon points="100,0 50,50 150,50 200,0"
                 transform="translate(0,0) rotate(0,0,0)" />

        <polygon points="50,50 0,100 50,150 100,100"
                 transform="translate(0,0) rotate(0,0,0)"/>

        <polygon points="50,50 100,100 150,50"
                 transform="translate(0,0) rotate(0,0,0)"/>

        <polygon points="200,0 100,100 200,200"
                 transform="translate(0,0) rotate(0,0,0)"/>

        <polygon points="0,100 0,200 50,150"
                 transform="translate(0,0) rotate(0,0,0)"/>

        <polygon points="0,200, 200,200 100,100"
                 transform="translate(0,0) rotate(0,0,0)"/>
        </g>
        </svg>
```

3. Save the file as `tangram.svg`.

4. Open the file in a browser or SVG viewer.

After an initial error message popup, you should see the Tangram pieces all neatly positioned in a box. Moving the mouse over the pieces should also produce error messages. This is because calls are being made to a nonexistent script.

Note: If you're using IE and don't get an error message here, go into IE's Tools menu and select Internet Options. Click the Advanced tab. Under Browsing, make sure the Disable script debugging and Display a notification about every script error options are not checked. Click OK.

How It Works

The pieces themselves are defined as polygon elements, each having three (triangles) or four (quadrilaterals) pairs of coordinates. Each of the elements also has a `transform` attribute, containing a `translate` and a `rotate` part. These attributes will be used to hold the movement and rotation information of the pieces. The two values in the `translate` part say how far to shift the element across and down. The first value in the `rotate` part gives the rotation angle (in degrees), and the next two values are the x and y coordinates of the point around which the shape should be rotated. All these values are set to zero to start, because there's no translation or rotation.

Try It Out — Adding the Buttons

Next, we will see how to add the two control buttons, Scramble and Reset.

1. Open the file you just typed in, `tangram.svg`, in a text editor.

2. Delete the </svg> tag at the end, and type in the following block of code:

```
    <g onclick="scramble()">
            <rect x="20" y="220" width="60" height="20"
                      style="fill:coral;stroke:blue;stroke-width:2"/>
            <text x="20px" y="220px" transform="translate(6,14)"
      style="fill:black;font-size:12;font-family:Arial">Scramble</text>
    </g>

    <g onclick="reset()">
            <rect x="90" y="220" width="60" height="20"
                       style="fill:violet;stroke:blue;stroke-width:2"/>
            <text x="90px" y="220px" transform="translate(12,14)"
      style="fill:black;font-size:12;font-family:Arial">Reset</text>
    </g>
</svg>
```

3. Save the file again as `tangram.svg`.
4. Open the file in your browser.

Once again, you will be presented with an error message popup at the start, but you should now see the buttons defined previously due to the lack of a script.

How It Works

Each button is drawn as a colored rectangle with a stroked outline and a text label positioned in the center of the rectangle. It's convenient to use the same coordinates for both the rectangle and the text, making the small adjustment needed to center the text with a simple `translate` transformation. The behavior in response to mouse clicks is set up in `g` elements, as we want the same thing to happen whether the text or the rectangle is clicked. Clicking the first button will call the `scramble()` function in the script, and clicking the second button will call the `reset()` function. These functions haven't yet been defined, so for now the clicks produce error messages.

Tangram Script

The interactivity of the Tangram puzzle is provided by the ECMAScript (Javascript) in the file `tangram.es`. When the mouse is moved or clicked, the SVG DOM causes functions in the script to be called. Those functions will in turn make changes to the DOM to carry out the required behavior—moving the puzzle pieces. For example, Figure 18-10 shows the visual result of clicking the scramble button.

To give you an idea of how it all fits together before we look at the details of the source, here is an overview of the functions the script contains:

```
init(evt)
mousedown(evt)
mouseup(evt)
mouseover(evt)
mouseout(evt)
move(evt)
```

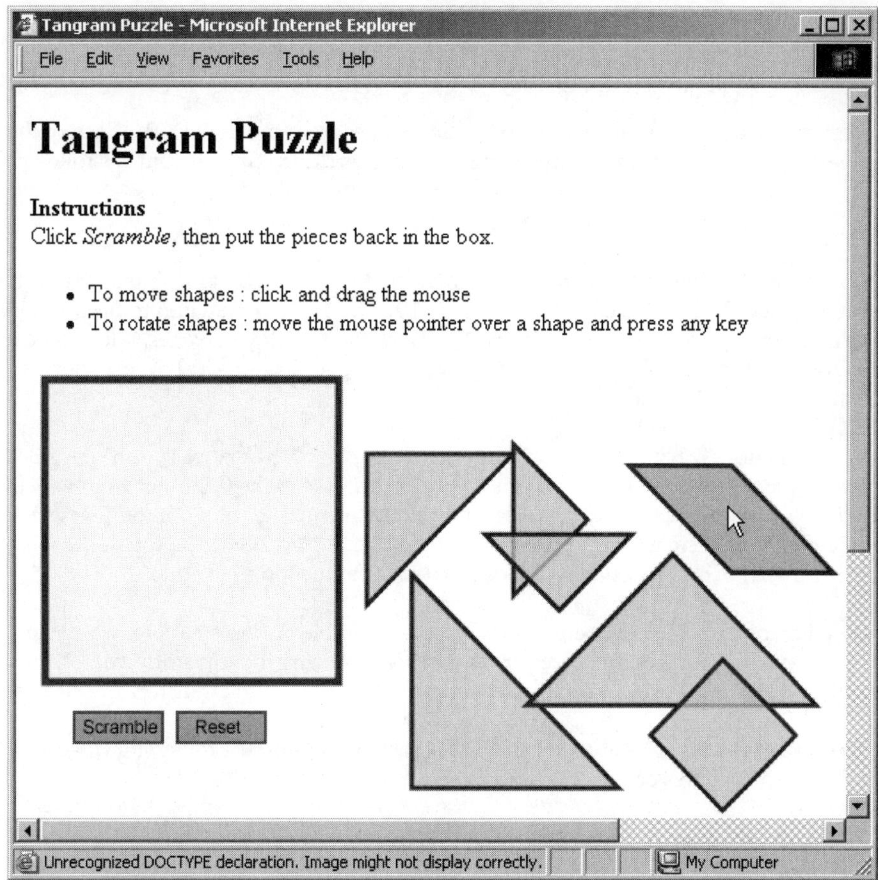

Figure 18-10

```
getTransformBlock(polygon, index)
getRotateAngle(polygon)
getCenter(polygon)

moveToFront(polygon)
rotatePolygon(evt)

scramble()
reset()
```

The first six functions are all called in response to events generated from user interaction with the SVG document. The `init(evt)` function is called when the document is initially loaded into the viewer using the `onload` attribute in its top-level `svg` element. That function initializes several variables. The rest of the functions here are called when particular mouse actions occur. For example, moving the mouse pointer over a puzzle piece will cause the `mouseover(evt)` method to be called, and the `evt` object it receives will contain a reference to that particular piece. These functions all have a hook in the SVG code in the `g` element (the parent of the pieces), where there are special attributes corresponding to each action pointing to these functions. The `mousedown(evt)` and `mouseup(evt)` functions are used to recognize the start and end of a click-and-drag gesture, which is used to move the pieces around. The actual movement is tracked by the `move(evt)` method. The `mouseover(evt)` and `mouseout(evt)` functions change the color of the piece the mouse pointer passes over.

The next set of functions are utilities to help reading values from the SVG DOM. Each of the puzzle pieces, the `polygon` elements in the preceding SVG, has a `transform` attribute as follows:

```
transform="translate(0,0) rotate(0,0,0)"
```

This attribute is a string with two distinct blocks: the first is a `translate` command and the second a `rotate` command. The `getTransformBlock(polygon, index)` function returns a string containing the whole of the command for the specified `polygon` element. If the index has value 0, the translate block is returned, and if it is 1, then the rotate block is returned. `getRotateAngle(polygon)` returns the angle specified in the rotate block.

The next two functions carry out operations on the pieces. `getCenter(polygon)` returns the coordinates of the center point of the specified polygon relative to the 0, 0 point from which it is referenced. This is used to calculate the offsets needed to line up the center of the shapes to the mouse pointer when moving them around. If there are other puzzle pieces lying on top of the piece selected, the `moveToFront(polygon)` function will move that piece to the top of the pile.

The last two functions look after operations when the Scramble or Reset buttons are clicked. The `scramble()` function scatters the pieces around by randomizing the transform values, and the `reset()` function returns all the pieces to their initial positions by setting all the transform values back to 0.

Ok, now you might like to see the code itself. It begins by declaring the following three global variables illustrated in the following code:

- `polyGroup` will refer to the object in the SVG DOM corresponding to the `g` element which is the parent of the `polygon` elements which represent the puzzle pieces.
- `selectedPoly` will be the individual `polygon` element corresponding to the piece the user has selected.
- `track` will be `true` when a piece is being dragged around the screen, and `false` otherwise.

```
var polyGroup;
var selectedPoly;
var track = false;
```

The `init(evt)` function is called when the SVG document is loaded into the viewer. It begins by getting a reference to the document itself from the event passed by the caller (the SVG DOM). From this the DOM object corresponding to the `g` element is obtained, taking advantage of the fact it has an `id` attribute `"PolyGroup"`. To handle key presses, an event listener is added to the `polyGroup` object, so whenever there's a key event, the `rotatePolygon(evt)` method will be called as shown in the following:

```
function init(evt) {
   var svgDoc = evt.getTarget().getOwnerDocument();
   polyGroup = svgDoc.getElementById("PolyGroup");
   polyGroup.addEventListener("keypress", rotatePolygon, false);
}
```

When a mouse button is pressed, the `mousedown(evt)` method gets called. The event object `evt` carries a reference to the element on which it was called, which may be a puzzle piece. The `selectedPoly` variable is given this reference. The element is checked to see if it is a puzzle piece by evaluating its name. If its name is not `polygon`, the value of `selectedPoly` is cleared, and the function returns. If it is a `polygon` element, then the `track` variable is set to `true`, as this action might mean it is about to be dragged. The selected shape is then moved in front of any other pieces, as shown in the following:

```
function mousedown(evt){
    selectedPoly = evt.getTarget();
    if(selectedPoly.nodeName != "polygon"){
        selectedPoly = null;
        return;
    }
    track = true;
    selectedPoly = moveToFront(selectedPoly);
}
```

When the mouse button is released, the `mouseup(evt)` function gets called. All this does is reset the `track` variable—as there won't be any dragging—as shown in the following:

```
function mouseup(evt){
   track=false;
}
```

The `mouseover(evt)` function checks whether the DOM element over which the mouse has been moved is a `polygon` (a puzzle piece). In that case the element has the value of its `fill` attribute changed to `orange`, changing the color of the piece on-screen, as shown in the following:

```
function mouseover(evt){
    if(evt.getTarget().nodeName == "polygon"){
        evt.getTarget().setAttribute("fill", "orange");
    }
}
```

The `mouseout(evt)` function is called when the mouse pointer moves off a visual element, and it resets the `fill` attribute and the color of the piece back to its original value of `lightgreen` as shown in the following:

```
function mouseout(evt){
   if((evt.getTarget().nodeName == "polygon")){
        evt.getTarget().setAttribute("fill", "lightgreen");
    }
}
```

The `move(evt)` function begins by checking in case the element on which it was called wasn't a `polygon`, or that the value of `track` says not to drag the element. If either is the case, then the function returns without any further operations, except for resetting the `track` variable just to be sure. If the piece is to be moved, then an object `center` is created which will contain the x,y coordinates of the current center point of the selected shape. The coordinates of the mouse pointer are then retrieved using the built-in event methods getClientX() and getClientY(). These have the corresponding values of the center variable subtracted from them to produce new values for the translate part of the shape's transform attribute. The value of the transform attribute is reconstructed from these new translate values and the existing rotate part, which is obtained using getTransformBlock with the index 1 as shown in the following:

```
function move(evt){
  if((evt.getTarget().nodeName != "polygon") || (track == false) ){
      track = false;
      return;
  }
  var center = getCenter(selectedPoly);

   var x = evt.getClientX()-center.x;
   var y = evt.getClientY()-center.y;
   translateString = "translate("+x+","+y+")";

   selectedPoly.setAttribute("transform",
         translateString+" "+getTransformBlock(selectedPoly, 1));
}
```

The getTransformBlock(poly, index) function starts by getting the transform attribute from the supplied polygon. Here again is the form that the attribute will take, with some arbitrary values as follows:

```
transform="translate(11,23) rotate(90,100,100)"
```

The function will return either the translate or rotate part of a shape's transform attribute, and to get at this, the function employs a very useful piece of ECMAScript functionality: regular expressions. Discussion of regular expressions is beyond the scope of this chapter, but if you've not encountered them already, there are plenty of tutorials on the web. Here the built-in split method is applied to the whole transform string. The / / argument is a regular expression which will match all single spaces in the string. What's returned from split is an array of strings, built from splitting the input string on whatever the regular expression matched. So applied to the previous transform string, split(/ /)[0] would give you the string translate(11,23), and split(/ /)[1] would give you rotate(90,100,100).

```
function getTransformBlock(polygon, index){
 var transformString = polygon.getAttribute("transform");
 return transformString.split(/ /)[index];
}
```

The getRotateAngle(polygon) function first uses the previous function to get the rotate(90,100,100) part, then uses another regular expression, reg, with the built-in exec function to extract the first number. The regular expression here will match any decimal number, such as 123 or 55.6, and the exec function applied to the rotateString will return the first matching value, which is our rotate angle. This value will be a string, so the built-in parseFloat(string) function is used to convert it into a floating-point number as shown in the following:

```
function getRotateAngle(polygon){
 var rotateString = getTransformBlock(polygon, 1);
 var reg = /([0-9]+)(\.?)([0-9]*)/;
 return parseFloat(reg.exec(rotateString));
}
```

The `getCenter(polygon)` is passed a polygon and returns an object containing a pair of values, the coordinates of the shape's center point relative to 0, 0. This is calculated by taking the average of the x values and the average of the y values of the polygon's corner points. The regular-expression-based `split` method is used again in the function. Here it is applied to the `points` attribute of the polygon, which will look something like `"0,200 200,200 100,100"`. Each pair of coordinates corresponds to one of the shape's corners. The pairs are separated by spaces, so we can separate each pair of numbers using `split(/ /)`. The length of the array this gives us will be the same as the number of pairs of values. The function steps through each pair of values and applies the `split` method again, this time with a regular expression that will match commas. This gives an array containing two strings, which are converted into integers and then added to the running totals `xSum` and `ySum`. The `center` object is defined as having two properties, x and y, which are then given the calculated average values of x and y. The `center` object is then returned as shown in the following:

```
function getCenter(polygon){
 var pointsString = polygon.getAttribute("points");
 var split = pointsString.split(/ /);
 var xSum = 0;
 var ySum = 0;
 var coords;
 for(var i=0;i<split.length;i++){
         coords = split[i].split(/,/);
         xSum = xSum + parseInt(coords[0]);
         ySum = ySum + parseInt(coords[1]);
 }
 var center = {
   x: 0,
   y: 0
   };

 center.x = xSum/split.length;
 center.y = ySum/split.length;
 return center;
}
```

The `moveToFront(polygon)` function modifies the SVG DOM to move the specified polygon into the foreground, above any other objects on-screen. As you saw earlier, SVG's Painter's Model means that graphic elements that appear earlier in the document get painted first. It follows that whichever shape appears last in the elements defining the puzzle pieces will be painted last, or on top. So here the function does a little element juggling using standard XML DOM methods to make the specified polygon the last of the polygon's children. This is done by first cloning a copy of the polygon of interest and appending that to its parent's (the `polyGroup`'s) list of children. The original `polygon` element is then removed from the DOM tree, and its new clone returned as shown in the following:

```
function moveToFront(polygon){
   var clone = polygon.cloneNode(true);
   polyGroup.appendChild(clone);
   polyGroup.removeChild(polygon);
   return clone;
}
```

The `rotatePolygon` function was attached to a keyboard listener in the `init()` function, and it will be called when a key is pressed. The function receives an `evt` object from which further information could be extracted, such as which key was pressed. However, as there is only one action, this is ignored, and all key presses have the same result. First the current rotation angle (in degrees) is obtained using the `helper` function `getRotateAngle(polygon)` described earlier. This has the value 22.5 added to it, which will rotate the shape 1/8th of a circle clockwise. The `getCenter(polygon)` function is reused to give the point around which the rotation should take place. A new string for the `transform` attribute is then built up, consisting of the current translate block together with a revised rotate block as shown in the following:

```
function rotatePolygon(evt){
   var rotation = getRotateAngle(selectedPoly);
   rotation = rotation + 22.5;
   var center = getCenter(selectedPoly);
   var transformString = getTransformBlock(selectedPoly, 0)
      + " rotate(" + rotation + "," + center.x + "," + center.y + ")";

   selectedPoly.setAttribute("transform", transformString);
}
```

The last two methods are called when the Scramble or Reset buttons are clicked. The code to `scramble()` looks a lot more complex than it actually is. It starts by obtaining the set of `polygon` elements through the `childNodes` DOM property of the parent `polyGroup`, then steps through these, and randomizes the values contained in the transform attribute of each shape in turn. The individual child elements are accessed using the XML DOM method `item(x)`. Note that a check is made to ensure that the item in question actually is a `polygon` element, as text nodes corresponding to whitespace in the SVG will also appear as children here. The random values are generated using the ECMAScript `Math.random` function, which are scaled and offset as needed to make the shapes appear in a suitable part of the screen (over to the right of the puzzle pieces' box). Once again the attribute strings are built up, and the value of the `transform` attribute in the DOM is set.

```
function scramble(){
 var children = polyGroup.childNodes;

 var transformString;
 var randX;
 var randY;
 var randAngle;
 var center;

 for(var i=0;i<children.length;i++){

         if(children.item(i).nodeName == "polygon"){
                center = getCenter(children.item(i));
                randX = 200+Math.floor (200*Math.random());
                randY = Math.floor (200*Math.random());
                randAngle = Math.floor (8*Math.random()) * 45;

                transformString = "translate("+randX+","+randY+") ";
                transformString = transformString
    + "rotate(" + randAngle + "," + center.x + "," + center.y + ")";
                children.item(i).setAttribute("transform", transformString);
         }
 }
   track=false;
}
```

One of the most straightforward functions, the `reset()` function steps through the shapes in exactly the same manner as `scramble()`, but this time it resets the values contained in the `transform` attribute back to 0, thus putting all the pieces back into their starting positions.

```
function reset(){
    var children = polyGroup.childNodes;
    var transformString = "translate(0,0) rotate(0,0,0)";
    for(var i=0;i<children.length;i++){
        if(children.item(i).nodeName == "polygon"){
            children.item(i).setAttribute("transform", transformString);
        }
    }
    track=false;
}
```

Try It Out Running the Tangram Application

1. Open a new window in your text editor.
2. Type in the code listed in the previous *Scripting* section.
3. Save the file as `tangram.es` in the same folder as `tangram.svg`.
4. Open `tangram.svg` in your browser.
5. Click the Scramble button.
6. Try and place the pieces back into the box.

How It Works

The application as a whole works by manipulating the in-memory DOM model of the SVG. Mouse behavior causes functions in the script to be called. Moving the mouse over a shape leads to a call to `mouseover(evt)`, which changes the color of a shape by setting the shape's fill attribute.

Clicking a piece automatically makes a call to `mousedown(evt)`, which in turn calls `moveToFront(polygon)`, which moves the `polygon` element corresponding to that shape below the others in the DOM tree, causing it to be painted last, on top of the others. Once clicked, the shape in question is remembered by using its `polygon` element as the value of `selectedPolygon`.

When a shape is clicked and dragged, the `move(evt)` function adjusts the`translate` part of the `polygon` element's `transform` attribute according to the mouse movements.

An event listener notices when a key has been pressed and automatically calls `rotatePolygon(polygon)`, which adds 22.5 degrees to the `rotate` angle in the currently selected `polygon` element's transform attribute.

A mouse click on the Scramble button leads to a call to the `scramble()` function, which randomizes the values in each `polygon` element's `transform` attribute. Clicking the Reset button leads to a call to the `reset()` function which zeros all the `transform` values.

Further Applications

This Tangram code shows how the scripting facilities of SVG can enable you to give your applications custom interactivity. There wasn't space to cover it here, but if you imagine an application like this delivered from a web server, it's relatively straightforward to use HTTP methods to pass information back to the server. Simple hyperlinking can allow other SVG documents to be loaded in response to user interactions. Relatively complex stand-alone applications can be built using SVG with scripting, and relatively rich custom clients for web applications can be created in the same way.

The SVG Specification

The requirements for 2-D graphics on the web run wide and deep, and as a result the SVG specification is a fairly long and technical document. This part of the chapter aims to provide the reader with some orientation in that document and to offer an overview of some of the powerful capabilities of the language that there wasn't space to describe in detail.

The SVG specification is maintained by the World Wide Web Consortium, and at the time of writing, the current version is SVG 1.1, which became a Recommendation on January 14, 2003. It is largely the same as version 1.0 but defined in a modular form and fixes various problems encountered in that version. The current Recommendation is at `http://www.w3.org/TR/SVG/`, and various translations and further information can be found through the SVG home page at `http://www.w3.org/Graphics/SVG/`.

At the time of writing, SVG version 1.2 is under development. There is a "Working Draft" specification available at `http://www.w3.org/TR/SVG12/`, which suggests a final "Recommendation" version shouldn't be too far off.

1. Introduction

This introduces the specification but also describes a little of how SVG can be used alongside other XML standards using modularization. SVG is broken down into chunks of functionality corresponding to each major section of the specification. There's also a handy terminology reference here.

2. Concepts

The primary concept here is the name Scalable Vector Graphics, which we've already covered. Aside from this the descriptions here are an overview of some of the characteristics of SVG covered in depth later on in the spec. A subsection here, (2.3) *Options for using SVG in Web pages,* has largely been covered by the *SVG on Your Web Site* section of this chapter.

3. Rendering Model

The rendering model is essentially the Painter's Model described earlier in this chapter. This part of the specification gives a high-level view of the model, together with an introduction to how various objects get painted.

4. Basic Data Types and Interfaces

The basic data types of SVG include *integer*, *number*, *length,* and *coordinate*. This section goes into some detail to define these types, and if you're planning on generating SVG programmatically, you will need to ensure you are using suitable type in your code.

This section also contains a handy reference table of the color keywords recognized by SVG. There are a lot of these, many of which aren't obvious: for example, the color `peachpuff` corresponds to the red, green, blue mix `rgb(255, 218, 185).`

The last part of this section describes elements and contains a list of the basic DOM interfaces for each element described. It's unlikely that you'll ever need this material, as the documentation for whatever programming tools you're using should cover whatever DOM functionality is available. That in turn is likely to be derived from specific language bindings (for ECMAScript and Java) linked from the specification appendices.

5. Document Structure

This section describes the structural parts of an SVG document, including the `svg` and `g` (grouping) elements and the `title` and `desc` (description) elements. We looked at these four elements earlier in this chapter, but there are other important elements that come under the structural heading.

As a web-oriented XML specification, various SVG elements can refer to objects using URI references. These may be local to the current document or in completely different files on the web. One use of these references is hyperlinking using the `a` element, which works in a similar way to its counterpart in XHTML. SVG also has a `defs` element, which contains elements that may be referred to elsewhere, usually later in the same document. A typical usage would be to have various special effects defined in a `defs` block at the start of a document, and then the elements to which the effects would be applied would refer back to those definitions.

The `symbol` and `use` elements together allow the definition of arbitrary symbols and the rendering of those symbols as required in the graphics. For example, an architectural drawing might have various standard building shapes defined in symbol blocks. These will be placed at appropriate positions with the `use` element, which refers back to the symbol definition by means of a URI reference, so a symbol can be used many times.

The `switch` element provides some degree of conditional processing, making it possible to customize the material displayed according to information provided by the viewer software. For example, you might want to show different text according to the language settings of the client.

The Document Structure section also specifies two attributes that may be used with any SVG element: `id` and `xml:base`. These follow the attribute definitions found in the XML 1.0 and XML Base specifications. The first attribute is used to give elements a unique name, and the second is used to provide a base URI from which relative references should be resolved.

This section of the specification also defines the elements and attributes that comprise the various modules. For example, the Basic Structure Module (5.13) includes the elements `svg`, `g`, `defs`, `desc`, `title`, `metadata`, and `use`. Each element is listed with a set of attributes that may appear with that element.

6. Styling

In the examples, we have used attributes like `fill` and `font-size` to affect how elements are rendered. These attributes are only the tip of the iceberg. SVG supports a whole range of styling attributes, many of which are shared with CSS2 and XSLT. As with XHTML, external style sheets can also be used to determine the appearance of documents. This section of the specification lists SVG's styling properties and gives advice and examples of how they can be used.

7. Coordinate Systems, Transformations, and Units

There is considerably more in the specification on how to position graphics on-screen than covered in this chapter. Information on this and the mathematical details of transforming shapes is described in this part of the specification.

8. Paths

This section describes more fully the techniques we saw earlier for drawing shapes using a virtual pen. There are clear examples provided for simple lines and movements as well as description of how curved paths can be drawn.

9. Basic Shapes

We have seen most of the basic shape elements in this chapter: `line`, `rect`, `circle`, `polygon`, `polyline` (like a polygon but not closed), and `ellipse`. This section gives the full definitions of these elements and details of how their path data attributes (`d`) are constructed.

10. Text

There is a lot that can be done using simple `text` elements with styling and transformation, but this section describes additional tricks using the `tspan` element to modify blocks within a text element and the `tref` element to reuse pieces of text in different places in your graphics.

11. Painting: Filling, Stroking, and Marker Symbols

SVG provides fine-grained control over how lines and shapes are outlined and colored in, and the details of what's available are given in this section. Marker symbols are based around the `marker` element, which makes it easy to decorate lines, for example, making them appear as arrows.

12. Color

Where the painting section deals with the details of where the paint should go, this section gives the details of how to specify what the paint should look like. In particular, it covers the `color` property and describes the use of the `color-profile` element to accurately match the required appearance with the color handling of particular viewing devices.

13. Gradients and Patterns

Gradients and patterns allow you to fill in shapes and areas with something more interesting than solid color. SVG gradients offer a variety of ways to blend shading between different colors, and patterns (as the name suggests) let you define wallpaper-like repeated patterns that can be used to fill regions of your graphics.

14. Clipping, Masking, and Compositing

Clipping and masking allow you to define the regions on which you want paint to appear. Compositing allows you to define how the colors in different layers or overlaps in your graphics should be combined. These features offer a powerful set of tools for determining exactly how the layers of your graphics should work together.

15. Filter Effects

SVG filters let you use sophisticated visual effects in your graphics. For example, if you want shadows on your text or your buttons to appear in 3-D, this is the place to look. The `filter` element is used to group combinations of 20 or so individual effect elements that do things like blur elements or give the impression of theatrical lighting.

16. Interactivity

This section lists the document, mouse, and keyboard events that can be used to make your graphics interactive. These events will generally be hooked to hyperlinks, scripts, or animations.

17. Linking

SVG linking is similar to that of XHTML and based around the XLink specification. The main types of behavior are the same as what is provided in XHTML, although there are variations and extensions described here.

18. Scripting

The scripting section gives the formal specification of the script element and (along with the last two sections) describes various details relating to interactivity.

19. Animation

SVG graphics can be animated using a set of elements and attributes that specify how parts of the graphics will behave over time. There's quite a lot to this section. However, it is relatively straightforward, and clear examples are provided.

20. Fonts

SVG font support goes way beyond the things familiar from word processors. Not only can you use international character sets, but you can even design your own from scratch.

21. Meta Data

This short section describes the use of the `metadata` element you saw earlier in this chapter, with an example of the kind RDF material that can be used inside it.

22. Backward Compatibility

This section describes two scenarios where compatibility may be a problem, the first involving the `switch` element and the second regarding the use of the `object` tag in HTML.

23. Extensibility

SVG derives a lot of extensibility from XML, though there is also an element `foreignObject` that can be used to embed material in SVG for rendering.

Appendices

Here is a list of the specification's appendices, which can help as reference for many of SVG's features:

- Appendix A: DTD
- Appendix B: SVG Document Object Model (DOM)
- Appendix C: IDL Definitions
- Appendix D: Java Language Binding

- Appendix E: ECMAScript Language Binding
- Appendix F: Implementation Requirements
- Appendix G: Conformance Criteria
- Appendix H: Accessibility Support
- Appendix I: Internationalization Support
- Appendix J: Minimizing SVG File Sizes
- Appendix K: References
- Appendix L: Element Index
- Appendix M: Attribute Index
- Appendix N: Property Index
- Appendix O: Feature Strings
- Appendix P: Index

Useful Resources

Here are some other helpful SVG resources:

SVG Wiki
`http://www.protocol7.com/svg-wiki/default.asp`

SVG Specifications and News at W3C
`http://www.w3.org/Graphics/SVG/`

Croczilla SVG Samples
`http://www.croczilla.com/svg/samples/`

SVG Developers Mailing List
`http://groups.yahoo.com/group/svg-developers/`

Adobe SVG Zone (there is also a mailing list)
`http://www.adobe.com/svg/`

Accessibility Features of SVG
`http://www.w3.org/TR/SVG-access/`

Apache Batik SVG Toolkit
`http://xml.apache.org/batik/`

Summary

In this chapter we saw how SVG is not only an extremely versatile drawing format, but thanks to XML and scripting support, SVG is also highly programmable.

The overview at the start of the chapter has given us a background on what SVG is and what it's good for. The introductory code section showed how we can use basic shapes and other core features of SVG, as well as how SVG fits into the web environment. The Tangram application demonstrated that it is relatively straightforward to build a visually appealing, interactive application for the web. The warning was given at the start that SVG is far bigger than what can be contained in one chapter, but hopefully the overview of the SVG specification will have given us a general idea of the kind of features that are available.

Finally, if you've played with the code a little, it will undoubtedly have occurred to you that SVG can be a great deal of fun!

Exercise Questions

Suggested solutions to these questions can be found in Appendix A.

Question 1

By now, it's likely that you've thought of 1,001 different things you'd like to do with SVG, but to get you moving, here is a drawing task to help familiarize you with the basic shapes. Figure 18-11 shows a picture of a stylized windmill. Your mission is to write the SVG code needed to draw it. There's some description of how it was done below, but if you like a challenge, you can try it before looking at those hints. Squared paper can help in working out the coordinates; don't forget the y-axis starts with zero at the top.

Figure 18-11

Hint

There are several different ways of doing this with SVG, but here the body of the windmill was constructed from a (yellow) `polygon` element with a (yellow) `circle` element half-overlapping on top. The four (blue) vanes are `polygon` elements with three points. The shape in the middle of the vanes is a (blue) `rect` element, with a transform to rotate it 45 degrees. At the bottom of the windmill is a (green) `line` element.

Question 2

The Tangram puzzle described in this chapter had a square as the target shape to build from the seven pieces. If you search the web, you will find many more shapes that can be constructed from them. So the challenge here is to get the application to start with the pieces organized into the stylized cat as shown in Figure 18-12. Everything else should stay the same—clicking Reset will still place all the pieces into the square box. Don't spend too much time on the details of this. Just try to figure out how you would go about doing it, bearing in mind that SVG is XML.

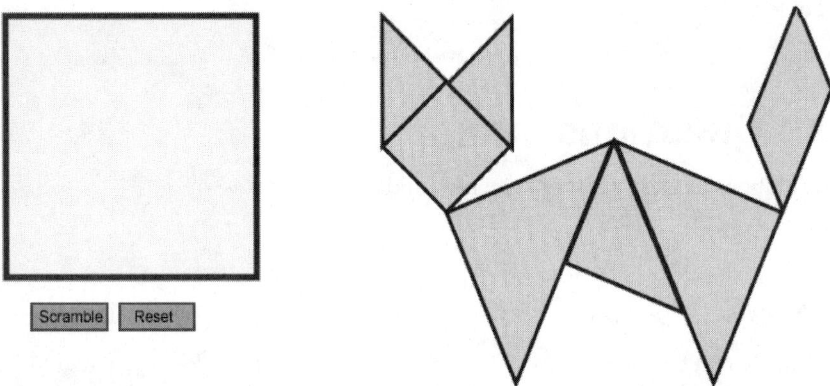

Figure 18-12

XForms

XForms is an XML-based forms technology specified by the W3C. XForms is intended to replace HTML forms, which are now around a decade old.

In several earlier chapters we have discussed how to manipulate XML using technologies such as XPath, XSLT, XQuery, and the XML DOM, but we have yet to discuss how we can collect data to form part of an XML-based workflow. XForms is an important tool in the XML developer's toolbox, since XForms submits data from forms as well-formed XML documents.

Forms are an integral part of day-to-day business activity. Filling in paper forms or electronic forms is almost inescapable for anyone who is an information worker. As XML-based workflows become more prevalent in large enterprises and progressively trickle down into smaller businesses, the advantages of submitting XML data will become more widely appreciated.

XForms isn't the only XML-based forms tool, and although the main focus of this chapter is Xforms, other proprietary solutions to XML-based forms are also described briefly toward the end of the chapter.

We will cover the following:

- How XForms improves on existing HTML forms technology
- How the XForms model is created, including a discussion and examples of using the `xforms:model`, `xforms:instance`, `xforms:submission`, and `xforms:bind` elements
- How W3C XML Schema, Xpath, and XML Namespaces are used in XForms
- How to use XForms form controls
- Commercial alternatives to XForms

How Does XForms Improve on HTML Forms?

If you are going to work with XML on the server, the fact that XForms documents submit data as well-formed XML documents is a significant advantage. Thus, if you are using an XML-based workflow, the standard XML tools can be directly applied to the data being sent across the wire.

Another advantage is that XForms has a different way of associating form controls that are visible to the end-user with the underlying data that is collected. In HTML forms a single HTML element defines the visual appearance of a form control and also accepts a value from the user. This inextricably ties together the form's appearance and the data collected which becomes undesirable as the range of browser clients becomes wider. Defining a single data structure (which is to be submitted regardless of the type of client device) can have coding maintenance benefits. One has to be realistic about how far that principle can be taken. It is very easy to create forms for a desktop browser that would not be feasible to display on, say, a mobile phone because of its limited screen real estate.

XForms uses W3C XML Schema for typing data. XForms processors can validate user-entered data and automatically identify invalid entries, often without any need for client-side scripting or for a roundtrip to the server. In addition, you can validate on both client-side and server-side using a single W3C XML Schema document, an approach which offers distinct advantages compared to, for example, validating data on the client side using JavaScript and on the server side with, say, Python or Perl. The client-side code and server-side code can both reference a single W3C XML Schema document, so the developer only has to make updates to the schema in a single place, avoiding the need for coding changes in two different languages to cope with evolving business needs.

XForms form controls incorporate labels, which increase accessibility. In addition, XForms form controls may include tooltips to improve usability by providing suggestions to help users understand what data is expected for each form control.

Assuming that these potential benefits are sufficient to tempt you into trying out XForms, what tools do you need to set up and get running?

XForms Tools

To create and test XForms documents effectively you need two types of tools, one to create an XForms document and an XForms viewer. At the time of writing, not even six months after XForms became a W3C Recommendation, there are several XForms viewers available and a couple of XForms designers. Both types of tool are listed on the W3C XForms page at `http://www.w3.org/MarkUp/Forms/#implementations`. The page is often not kept comprehensively up-to-date, so it is prudent to follow links to check on the current status of the projects.

First, let's briefly look at the XForms viewers that are available.

XForms Viewers

XForms viewers typically take one of the following three forms:

- Browser plug-ins (typically for Internet Explorer)
- Java applications
- As part of a proprietary toolset

There are several XForms processors available, as final or prototype versions, for Internet Explorer 6. The fairly widely used formsPlayer plug-in from x-port.net is a browser plug-in, which is described and available for download at a dedicated URL: `http://www.formsplayer.com/`.

An XForms document must have some way of signaling to Internet Explorer that elements in the XForms namespace (`http://www.w3.org/2002/xforms`) are to be processed by an XForms processor. In the case of the formsPlayer, this is achieved by embedding the following code in the head of an XHTML document:

```
<object id="FormsPlayer" classid="CLSID:4D0ABA11-C5F0-4478-991A-375C4B648F58"
 width="0" height="0">
<b>FormsPlayer has failed to load! Please check your installation.</b>
   <br />
   <br />
</object>
<?import namespace="xforms" implementation="#FormsPlayer"?>
```

The `object` element allows the formsPlayer to be loaded. If loading fails, the markup content of the `object` element is displayed.

Notice too, the processing instruction (go to Chapter 2 for more on processing instruction). The value of the `namespace` pseudo-attribute of the processing instruction must match the namespace prefix chosen in that document for the XForms Namespace. In other words, to successfully use the `import` processing instruction as shown previously, you must have the following namespace declaration in scope:

```
xmlns:xforms="http://www.w3.org/2002/xforms
```

Typically, the namespace declaration will be on the document element, as shown here in the `html` element for an XHTML document:

```
<html xmlns="http://www.w3.org/1999/xhtml"
  xmlns:xforms="http://www.w3.org/2002/xforms">
```

Used inside the XFormation Designer mentioned in the next section, the x-port.net formsPlayer is also used to display several of the examples in this chapter. Figure 19-1 shows the display of a simple XForms document in Internet Explorer 6. The default behavior is to display an fP logo beside each XForms form control.

Java-based XForms processors are the main alternative approach to embedding an XForms processor in a web browser. Two Java applications were widely used during the development and testing of the XForms specification—the X-Smiles browser (downloadable from `http://www.x-smiles.org`) and the Novell XForms Preview (see `http://www.novell.com/xforms`).

The X-Smiles browser is a free-standing Java browser designed to process and display elements in several XML namespaces. The XML formats that are supported include XForms, XSLT, XHTML, SVG, XSL-FO, and SMIL 2.0 Basic. Figure 19-2 shows the X-Smiles browser with links to various sample XForms documents visible.

One feature of the X-Smiles browser allows you to supply an XML instance document, which includes an `xml-stylesheet` processing instruction, and the X-Smiles browser will generate the output format (for example, a multi-namespace XHTML and XForms document) on the fly.

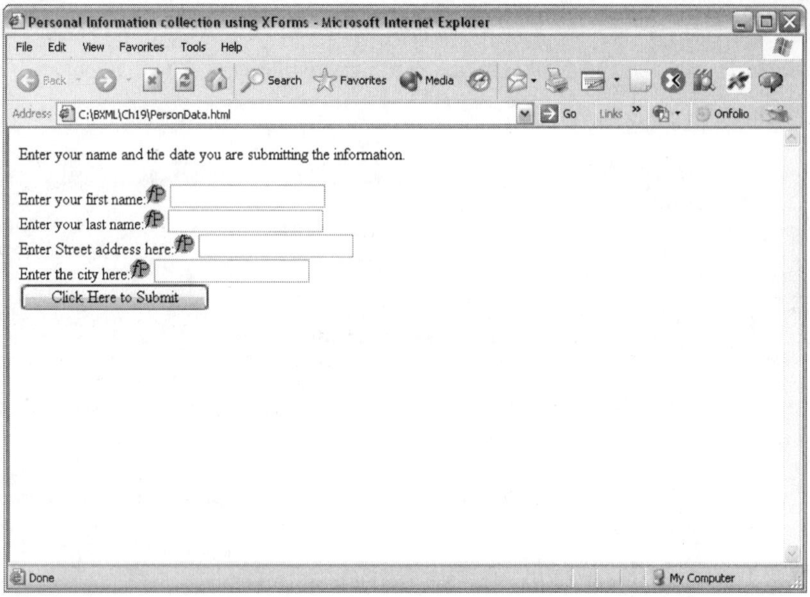

Figure 19-1

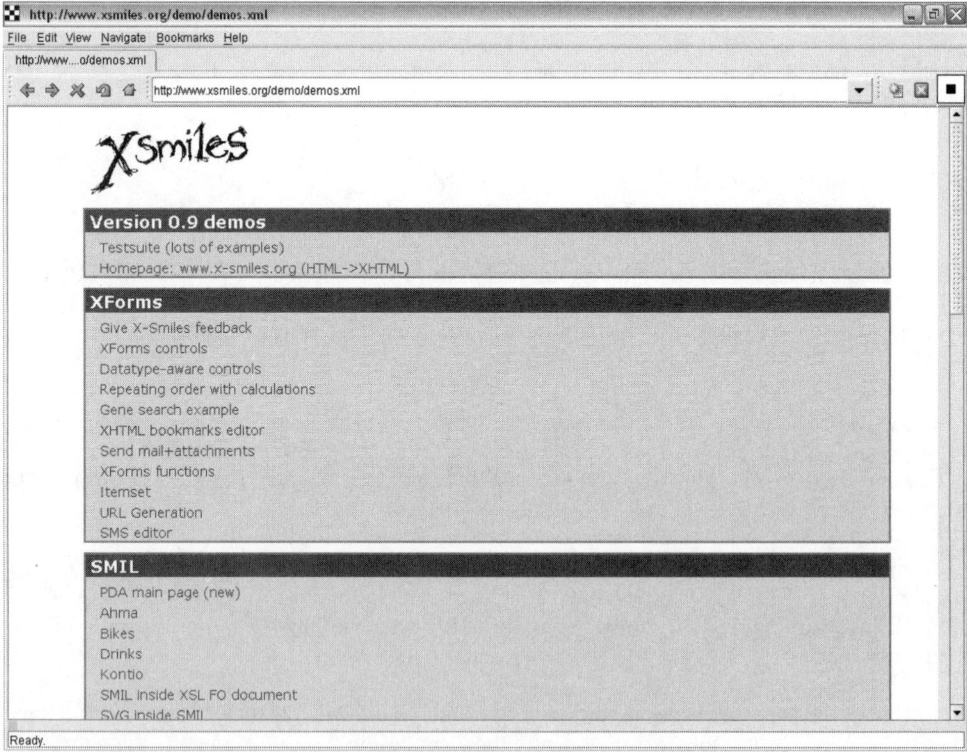

Figure 19-2

XForms Designers

The XForms specification reached Recommendation status in October 2003. At the time of writing only a few months have passed, so it is not surprising that XForms design tools are still not large in number. At the time of writing only one XForms design tool, XFormation from Focus Software, has been commercially released. A 30-day trial version of XFormation is available from `http://www.xformation.com`. Figure 19-3 shows a screenshot of XFormation during the design of an XForms document.

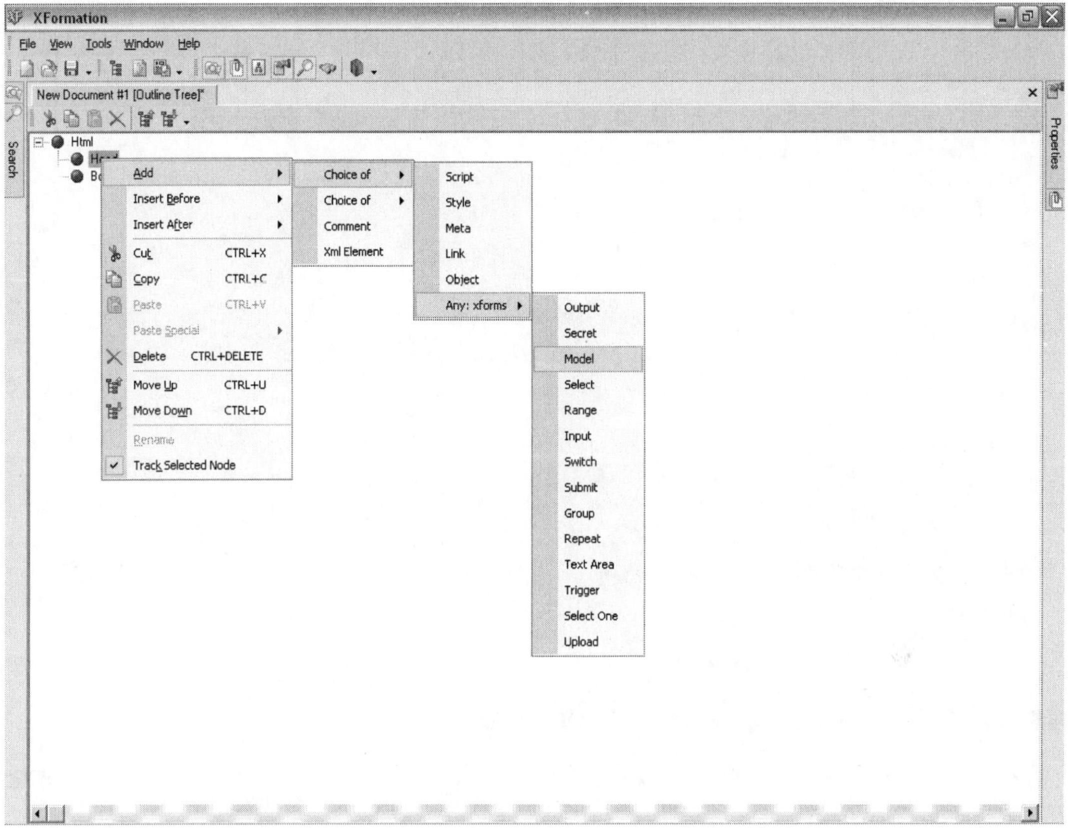

Figure 19-3

Other XForms design tools are under development, but at the time of writing, release versions have not been publicly announced. A preliminary version of onForm xPress is described at `http://www.blackdog.co.uk/pages/onform_xpress.htm`. The onForm xPress designer has a more visual drag-and-drop approach than the initial release version of XFormation. Figure 19-4 shows an early version of an XForms document using onForm xPress.

Having briefly looked at XForms tools, let's take an overview of how an XForms document is structured by creating a simple XForms example inside an XHTML web page.

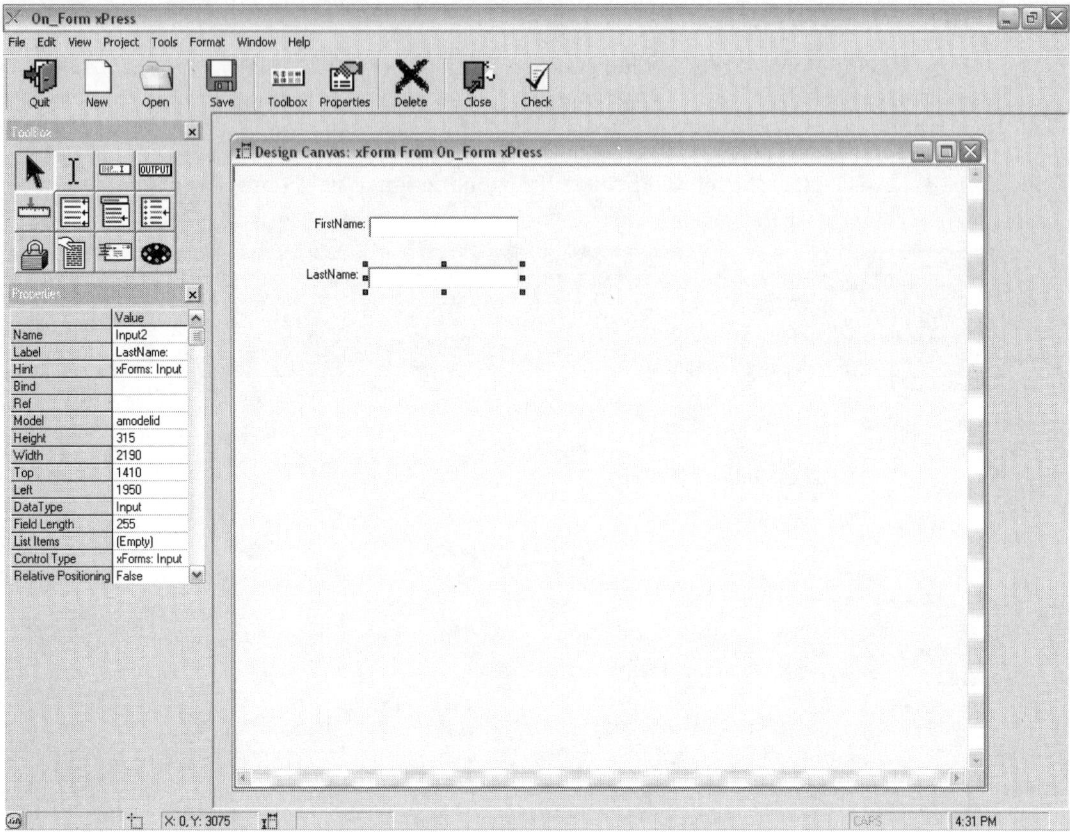

Figure 19-4

An Illustrative XForms Example

To create a working XForms document, several different parts need to be present and working together correctly. In order to focus on how XForms works, we will hand code this example.

XForms documents are not intended to be free-standing. Instead, XForms markup is intended to be combined with markup in another XML namespace (for example, the XHTML namespace or SVG namespace, as appropriate) to produce XHTML or SVG documents that have XForms functionality.

In all code in this chapter, the namespace prefix `xforms` will be used when referring to elements in the XForms Namespace (see `http://www.w3.org/2002/xforms`). In full code listings an appropriate namespace declaration will be provided. In code snippets, XForms elements will be shown with the `xforms` namespace prefix, assuming that the corresponding namespace declaration is in scope for that element.

Try It Out Creating an XForms Document

First, let's look at a simplified XForms document which demonstrates many of the fundamental techniques that you will use regularly in XForms. In this example the XForms markup is embedded inside an XHTML web page. The XHTML and XForms code, `PersonData.html`, is shown here (the XHTML page produced by rendering this example in the formsPlayer was shown in Figure 19-1):

```
<?xml version="1.0"?>

<html
 xmlns="http://www.w3.org/1999/xhtml"
 xmlns:xforms="http://www.w3.org/2002/xforms"
 xmlns:xmml="http://www.XMML.com/namespace" >
<head>
 <object id="FormsPlayer" classid="CLSID:4D0ABA11-C5F0-4478-991A-375C4B648F58">
  <b>FormsPlayer has failed to load! Please check your installation.</b>
  <br />
 </object>
<?import namespace="xforms" implementation="#FormsPlayer"?>
<title>Personal Information collection using XForms</title>
<xforms:model schema="Person.xsd" >
 <xforms:instance >
  <Person xmlns="http://www.XMML.com/namespace" >
   <FirstName></FirstName>
   <LastName></LastName>
   <Street></Street>
   <City></City>
  </Person>
 </xforms:instance>
 <xforms:submission id="PersonData" action="file://c:/BXML/Ch19/SavedPerson.xml"
 method="put" />
</xforms:model>
</head>
<body>
 <p>Enter your name and the date you are submitting the information.</p>
 <xforms:input ref="/xmml:Person/xmml:FirstName">
  <xforms:label>Enter your first name:</xforms:label>
 </xforms:input>
 <br />
 <xforms:input ref="/xmml:Person/xmml:LastName" >
  <xforms:label>Enter your last name:</xforms:label>
 </xforms:input>
 <br />
  <xforms:input ref="/xmml:Person/xmml:Street" >
  <xforms:label>Enter Street address here:</xforms:label>
 </xforms:input>
 <br />
   <xforms:input ref="/xmml:Person/xmml:City" >
  <xforms:label>Enter the city here:</xforms:label>
 </xforms:input>
 <br />
 <xforms:submit submission="PersonData" replace="all" >
```

```
    <xforms:label>Click Here to Submit</xforms:label>
  </xforms:submit>
 </body>
 </html>
```

We will use this simple example to explore the fundamental building blocks of an XForms document.

How It Works

As with any XForms document, there are many aspects to how it works, and we will look at those aspects in this section and the sections that follow.

Notice the three namespace declarations in the start tag of the html document element:

```
<html
 xmlns="http://www.w3.org/1999/xhtml"
 xmlns:xforms="http://www.w3.org/2002/xforms"
 xmlns:xmml="http://www.XMML.com/namespace" >
```

The first namespace declaration signifies that elements in the XHTML namespace will have no namespace prefix in this part of the document. Elements in the XForms namespace have the namespace prefix xforms, and elements in the XML document, which will be submitted by the XForms processor, use the namespace prefix xmml, which is associated with a specified namespace URI. (Namespace issues are discussed in more detail later in this section.)

Next, let's look at the content of the XHTML head element. We indicate that we want the formsPlayer loaded and used to process elements in the XForms namespace as follows:

```
  <object id="FormsPlayer" classid="CLSID:4D0ABA11-C5F0-4478-991A-375C4B648F58">
   <b>FormsPlayer has failed to load! Please check your installation.</b>
   <br />
  </object>
<?import namespace="xforms" implementation="#FormsPlayer"?>
```

Apart from the page title, the main part of the content of the XHTML head element relates to the XForms model for the XForms document.

The XForms Model

Let's take a look at the XForms code contained in the head section of the XHTML document, which specifies the XForms model. After looking at the markup used in this example, we will also consider some other aspects of the xforms:model element.

```
<xforms:model schema="Person.xsd" >
 <xforms:instance >
  <Person xmlns="http://www.XMML.com/namespace" >
   <FirstName></FirstName>
   <LastName></LastName>
   <Street></Street>
   <City></City>
```

```
    </Person>
   </xforms:instance>
   <xforms:submission id="PersonData" action="file://c:/BXML/Ch19/SavedPerson.xml"
   method="put" />
  </xforms:model>
```

The XForms namespace is still in scope since the `xforms:model` element is a descendant of the XHTML `html` element where the XForms namespace was declared; therefore no further namespace declaration is needed.

A `schema` attribute is present on the `xforms:model` element and specifies the URL where a W3C XML Schema document is located. The W3C XML Schema document specifies the permitted structure of the XML content of the `xforms:instance` element. If specified in the schema document, data types will give a hint to the XForms processor about how a particular component of the instance should be rendered. For example, the occurrence of an `xsd:date` data type will typically result in a date form control being used.

The `schema` attribute is optional on the `xforms:model` element. An XForms model may alternatively have a child `xsd:schema` element, assuming that the `xsd` namespace prefix has been associated with the namespace URI `http://www.w3.org/2001/XMLSchema`. Effectively, a W3C XML Schema document can be inserted into an XForms model or elsewhere in the XML document. A W3C XML Schema document used in that way would be likely to have an `id` attribute, and the name of that `id` attribute would be used with the # character as the value of the `schema` attribute.

The `xforms:model` element has two child elements in this example, an `xforms:instance` element and an `xforms:submission` element. The other permitted child elements of `xforms:model` in the XForms namespace are `xforms:bind` and elements in the XForms Action module, each of which are discussed later in this chapter.

An `xforms:model` element may, optionally, have a `functions` attribute. The value of the `functions` attribute is a space-separated list of extension function names (which are QNames) needed by the XForms model. XForms uses the rather limited function library provided by XPath 1.0. Therefore for anything other than straightforward calculations, for example, use of extension functions is likely to be needed, assuming that numeric processing is to be done client-side.

An XForms document may contain more than one `xforms:model` element. If, as in this initial example, there is only one `xforms:model` element, there is no requirement that the `xforms:model` element have an `id` attribute. Any `xforms:model` element other than the default is identified by an `id` attribute. Some developers prefer that even the default `xforms:model` has an `id` attribute, often with a convenient value of `default`, to act as disambiguating identification. Some XForms processors or designers may also require that the default `xforms:model` element have an `id` attribute.

The xforms:instance Element

The `xforms:instance` element is a child element of the `xforms:model` element. The `xforms:instance` element is optional in any particular `xforms:model` element, but in cases where there is a single XForms model, it will include an `xforms:instance` element, as here:

```
<xforms:instance >
 <Person xmlns="http://www.XMML.com/namespace" >
  <FirstName></FirstName>
```

```
    <LastName></LastName>
    <Street></Street>
    <City></City>
  </Person>
</xforms:instance>
```

The preceding code shows one of the two permitted ways to define the initial structure of *instance data*, a term I will return to in a moment. The other option is to have a `src` attribute on an empty `xforms:instance` element whose value is a URL from which a well-formed XML document can be retrieved.

```
<xforms:instance src="http://www.example.com/instancedata.xml" />
```

If retrieval of the XML document is unsuccessful, then an exception is raised.

The content of the `xforms:instance` element must itself be a well-formed XML document. If an XML document is accessed using a URL in the `src` attribute, then well-formedness is taken care of automatically, assuming retrieval is successful. If element content for the `xforms:instance` element is provided inline, it is the developer's responsibility to ensure that the `xforms:instance` element has a single element child and satisfies the other well-formedness constraints.

Why the emphasis on the well-formedness of the descendant elements of `xforms:instance`? It is from these elements contained in the `xforms:instance` element that a separate XPath data model is constructed, which, as you will remember, can only be created from an XML document when it is well formed. The separate XPath data model is the *instance data* mentioned earlier.

It is this separate XPath data model to which XForms form controls are bound. If you change values in form controls and do a View Source on the XHTML page, you won't see the changes you made in the form controls reflected there. The changes in data are reflected in the separate XPath data model—the instance data.

The separate XPath data model for the instance data, of course, has its own root node. The `Person` element shown earlier is the document element for that separate copy. Suppose we wanted to bind a form control to the `FirstName` element. To access it we could use the following XPath expression:

```
/xmml:Person/xmml:FirstName
```

If the meaning of that expression is unclear, you might want take a second look at Chapter 7 on XPath 1.0. I will return to the use of namespaces in XForms documents a little later in this section.

Now that we know where the data from an XForms document is stored while the form is open, how do we specify what happens when we choose to submit the data?

The xforms:submission Element

An XForms document needs some way to specify how and where data is to be submitted. The `xforms:submission` element, an optional child element of the `xforms:model` element, specifies that information as follows:

```
<xforms:submission id="PersonData" action="file://c:/BXML/Ch19/SavedPerson.xml"
method="put" />
```

The `action` attribute is required, and its value is a URI that specifies where the XForm instance data, after serialization, is to be sent. In the previous example we use the `file` protocol to save the data to a file on a hard disk.

The `method` attribute is required, and its value is the method by which data is to be submitted. Permitted values include `post`, `get`, and `put`.

> **Remember that XML is case-sensitive. The values of the `method` attribute are always expressed entirely in lowercase characters.**

The `xforms:submission` element must have an `id` attribute. The `id` attribute is used to bind an `xforms:submit` element (which we haven't discussed yet) in the visible part of the form to a particular `xforms:submission` element.

Following are several more attributes which can be used on the `xforms:submission` element:

- `bind`—An optional reference to an `xforms:bind` element.
- `cdata-section-elements`—An optional attribute listing elements whose content is to be serialized using CDATA sections.
- `encoding`—An optional attribute specifying the encoding of the serialized XML.
- `includenamespaceprefixes`—An optional attribute which can be used to exclude (despite its name) some namespace prefixes from serialization by listing those which are to be serialized. The default is to serialize all.
- `indent`—An optional attribute indicating whether the serializer should add whitespace to the XML to aid readability.
- `mediatype`—An optional attribute specifying the mediatype of the serialized XML.
- `omit-xml-declaration`—An optional attribute indicating whether or not the XML declaration is to be omitted from the serialized XML.
- `ref`—An optional binding expression to part of the instance data. This allows submission of only part of the instance data—the element node specified by the binding expression and all descendant elements. The default value for the `ref` attribute is `/`, indicating that all the instance data is to be submitted.
- `replace`—An optional attribute indicating how data returned after a submit is to be replaced.
- `standalone`—An optional attribute specifying whether or not to include a stand-alone attribute in the XML declaration of the serialized XML.
- `version`—An optional attribute which specifies the version of XML to be used when serializing the instance data prior to submission.

The xforms:bind Element

The `xforms:bind` element is a child element of the `xforms:model` element but isn't used in the example. The use of the `xforms:bind` element with *model item properties* is described later in this chapter.

W3C XML Schema in XForms

The data submitted from an XForms document is well-formed XML. An XForms processor has a W3C XML Schema processor built in so the option is available to validate data that a user enters against a specified schema.

Here is the schema document, `Person.xsd`, which defines the permitted structure of the content of the `xforms:instance` element:

```
<?xml version="1.0" encoding="UTF-8"?>
<xs:schema xmlns:xs="http://www.w3.org/2001/XMLSchema"
 targetNamespace="http://www.XMML.com/namespace"
 elementFormDefault="qualified"
 attributeFormDefault="unqualified">
  <xs:element name="Person">
    <xs:annotation>
      <xs:documentation>This simple form records the name and address of
      a person.</xs:documentation>
  </xs:annotation>
  <xs:complexType>
   <xs:sequence>
     <xs:element name="FirstName" type="xs:string" />
     <xs:element name="LastName" type="xs:string" />
     <xs:element name="Street" type="xs:string"/>
     <xs:element name="City" type="xs:string"/>
   </xs:sequence>
  </xs:complexType>
 </xs:element>
</xs:schema>
```

The document element defined in the schema is the `Person` element in the `http://www.XMML.com/namespace` namespace. The permitted content of that `Person` element is a sequence of child elements, `FirstName`, `LastName`, `Street`, and `City`, all in the same namespace. The value of each of those elements is of type `string`.

XPath 1.0 in XForms

XForms form controls, such as `xforms:input`, (which we will discuss in detail later) must be associated with parts of the content of the `xforms:instance` element which is nested inside an `xforms:model` element. For simplicity in this initial description, I will assume that the XForms document has a single `xforms:model` element which does not need an `id` attribute.

So, somewhere inside the `body` of an XHTML document, we have an `xforms:input` element that has a `ref` attribute which might look like this:

```
<xforms:input ref="/xmml:Person/xmml:FirstName">
 <!-- Content here. -->
</xforms:input>
```

If you are familiar with at least the basics of XPath, you will recognize that the value of the `ref` attribute on the `xforms:input` element is an XPath location path. In XPath 1.0 the initial / character in a location path indicates that the context node is the root node of a document (or more strictly the root node of an XPath model of an XML document).

So which XML document is being referred to? The answer is the XPath data model created from the content of the `xforms:instance` element. Remember that the content of the `xforms:instance` element must be a well-formed XML document, as shown in the following:

```
<xforms:instance>
 <!-- This content must have a single element which is a child
  of the xforms:instance element. In addition it must be well-formed on all
  other criteria. -->
</xforms:instance>
```

The XPath location path (the value of the `ref` attribute on the `xforms:input` element) looked like this:

```
/xmml:Person/xmml:FirstName
```

However, the content of the `xforms:instance` element showed the `FirstName` element like this:

```
<FirstName></FirstName>
```

To understand why this works, we need to quickly review the use of XML namespaces in XForms documents.

XML Namespaces in XForms Documents

All XForms documents contain multiple namespaces. Typically, there are at least three namespaces in any one document: the XForms namespace itself, the namespace of the containing display format such as XHTML and SVG and, very often, the namespace of the elements which are the content of the `xforms:instance` element.

In our simple example we had three namespace declarations on the document element, `html`:

```
<html
 xmlns="http://www.w3.org/1999/xhtml"
 xmlns:xforms="http://www.w3.org/2002/xforms"
 xmlns:xmml="http://www.XMML.com/namespace" >
```

So throughout the document these namespace declarations apply except if there are other namespace declarations in descendant elements. The `Person` element which is a child of the `xforms:instance` element had the following namespace declaration:

```
<Person xmlns="http://www.XMML.com/namespace" >
```

So, its child `FirstName` element is in the namespace `http://www.XMML.com/namespace` but is written simply as the following, since the namespace declaration on the `Person` element is in scope:

```
<FirstName></FirstName>
```

However, on the `xforms:input` element, which is in the body of the XHTML document, the namespace declaration that is in scope for that namespace is as follows:

```
xmlns:xmml="http://www.XMML.com/namespace"
```

So, an element in the namespace `http://www.XMML.com/namespace` has the namespace prefix `xmml`. Therefore, to bind to a `FirstName` element in that namespace, we need to write the XPath expression like this:

```
<xforms:input ref="/xmml:Person/xmml:FirstName" >
```

That location path references the `FirstName` element in the instance data since both the location path and the element node in the instance data are associated with the namespace `http://www.XMML.com/namespace`.

> **The use of XML namespaces in XForms can seem quite confusing at first, but it is important that you get a handle on this, since any errors in the handling of namespaces will mean that your XForms document won't work correctly (for example, data entered in a form control won't be captured in the corresponding part of the instance data) and, in all likelihood, the data will not be submitted.**

Having seen how the XForms `xforms:input` form control can be bound to instance data, let's take a closer look at the range of XForms form controls that are available in XForms 1.0.

XForms Form Controls

In principle, the XForms data model will work with a range of user interface technologies. As long as individual form controls can be bound to appropriate parts of the instance data, the data supplied by the end-user can be added to the instance data. As long as there is a binding from a submit form control to the `xforms:submission` element in the XForms model, then the XML data can be submitted to an appropriate URL endpoint.

In practice, at the time of writing, the XForms form controls are the dominant set of form controls used with an XForms data model although other sets of form controls may appear in time. This section briefly describes the XForms form controls and their characteristics.

The xforms:input Element

Specifying a text box into which a user can enter arbitrary text, the `xforms:input` element is bound to a node in the instance data using one of two techniques. First, as you saw in the earlier example, a `ref` attribute can contain an XPath 1.0 location path, which specifies a node in the instance data. The alternative technique for binding is to use a `bind` attribute whose value is of type `xsd:IDREF` and references an `xforms:bind` element. When only one XForms model is present in the document, then it isn't necessary to specify which model the `ref` attribute is pointing to. However, when there is more than one XForms model, the `model` attribute of the `xforms:input` element can be used to disambiguate the situation.

The `xforms:input` element, in common with many other XForms form controls, can optionally have an `appearance` attribute. An XForms processor must support the values `full`, `compact`, and `minimal`, but it may support other QNames, too.

An optional `navindex` attribute, whose value is an integer, can be used to specify the sequence in which form controls are navigated.

The `accesskey` attribute may, optionally, define a keyboard shortcut to access a particular form control.

The `incremental` attribute has a value, which is an `xsd:Boolean`. The default value is `false`. When the value of the `incremental` attribute is set to `true`, then a change in the value contained in an `xforms:input` element causes the `xforms-value-changed` event to fire. This then allows the XForms developer to create an event handler that can provide additional functionality or information to the user, as appropriate to the situation.

If Cascading Style Sheets styling is being used in an XForms document, then the `xforms:input` element will likely also have a `class` attribute.

The following elements are allowed in the content of the `xforms:input` element: `xforms:label`, `xforms:help`, `xforms:hint`, and `xforms:alert`. In addition, an element from the XForms Action Module (which is described later) is allowed.

The xforms:secret Element

The `xforms:secret` element has the same set of attributes and permitted element content as the `xforms:input` form control. The `xforms:secret` element is intended for use in entering passwords, and the character values entered by a user are echoed to the screen as some non-meaningful characters.

The xforms:textarea Element

The `xforms:textarea` element has the same set of attributes and the same permitted element content as the `xforms:input` element. The `xforms:textarea` element allows multiline entry of character data.

The xforms:output Element

The `xforms:output` element differs in function from those XForms controls we have discussed so far, since it does not directly accept user input. It can be used, for example, to display a date value (perhaps the current date) to ensure that a correct date is submitted with a form. Another use is to display a calculated value, for example, the total cost of a number of items in an online purchase.

The `xforms:output` element may have a `ref` or `bind` attribute, but neither is required since the value need not be stored in the instance data. The `xforms:output` element has an `appearance` attribute with permitted values as described previously, but it does not have a `navindex` or `accesskey` attribute, because users are not permitted to enter data into an `xforms:output` form control.

The `xforms:output` element may have a `value` attribute whose value is an XPath 1.0 expression. This allows display in read-only mode of a specified part of the instance data, if the `xforms:output` is displaying part of the instance data.

An `xforms:output` element may have an optional child `xforms:label` element, but no other child element content is allowed.

The xforms:upload Element

Often used to upload a file selected from the file system of the user's machine to a specified URL, the `xforms:upload` element uses either a `ref` attribute or a `bind` attribute to bind to an appropriate part of the instance data. The `appearance`, `navindex`, and `accesskey` attributes may be used as previously described.

The `xforms:upload` element may have the `xforms:label`, `xforms:help`, `xforms:hint`, and `xforms:alert` elements as child elements, as well as an element from the XForms Action Module. In addition, the `xforms:upload` element may optionally have `xforms:filename` and `xforms:mediatype` elements whose purpose is, respectively, to specify the filename for the uploaded file and its media type.

The xforms:range Element

The XForms form control elements described so far are likely to remind you of HTML forms. The `xforms:range` element has no counterpart in HTML. The purpose of the `xforms:range` element is to specify, in a way visible to the user, a permitted range of values for the characteristic represented by the form control. It might be used to specify a minimum and maximum number of a particular item to be purchased, for example, when an item is in limited supply and a ceiling on purchases needs to be imposed. Another use is to specify an allowed range of numeric values when responding to a survey.

The `xforms:range` element may have a `bind` or `ref` attribute to specify the component of the instance data to which it is bound. It may also have `appearance`, `navindex`, and `accesskey` attributes.

The allowed values displayed by the `xforms:range` form control are specified by its `start` and `end` attributes. The intermediate values to be displayed are specified using the `step` and `incremental` attributes.

The permitted content of the `xforms:range` form control are the `xforms:label`, `xforms:hint`, `xforms:help`, and `xforms:alert` elements as well as an element from the XForms Action Module.

The xforms:trigger Element

The `xforms:trigger` element is broadly equivalent to the `button` element in HTML forms. The `xforms:trigger` element can be used to respond to user action.

The `xforms:trigger` element may have a `bind` or `ref` attribute to specify the component of the instance data to which it is bound, but it does not need to be bound to any component of the instance data. It may also have `appearance`, `navindex`, and `accesskey` attributes.

The permitted content of the `xforms:trigger` form control are the `xforms:label`, `xforms:hint`, `xforms:help`, and `xforms:alert` elements as well as an element from the XForms Action Module.

The xforms:submit Element

Used to submit instance data, the `xforms:submit` element has a mandatory `submission` attribute whose value is an `IDREF` to an `xforms:submission` element in an XForms model somewhere in the same document. So, assuming that the id attribute of the corresponding xforms:submission element has the value submitsurvey, we can write an xforms:submit element like this:

```
<xforms:submit submission="submitsurvey">
 <xforms:label>Click Here to Submit the Survey</xforms:label>
</xforms:submit>
```

The submission process depends on the xforms-submit event being raised on the xforms:submit element and being despatched to the corresponding xforms:submission element.

A binding attribute, ref or bind, is not required since the xforms:submit element is not bound directly to instance data. However, the xforms:submit element may be affected by the model item properties (discussed later in this chapter) of a component of the instance data.

The xforms:submit element may have appearance, navindex, and accesskey attributes whose permitted values have been described previously.

The permitted content of the xforms:submit form control are the xforms:label, xforms:hint, xforms:help, and xforms:alert elements as well as an element from the XForms Action Module.

The xforms:select Element

The xforms:select element allows the user to make one or more choices from a set of choices. The rough equivalent in an HTML form would be checkboxes that allow multiple choices to be made. To make a choice limited to a single choice, the xforms:select1 element (described in the following section) is used. The xforms:select attribute is bound to a node in the instance data using either a ref attribute or a bind attribute.

The selection attribute of the xforms:select element defines whether or not values other than those supplied are permitted. The default value of the selection attribute is closed. If it is desired to allow users to add additional values to the selection of values available, then the value of the selection attribute must be open.

The permitted content of the xforms:select element includes the following elements: xforms:label, xforms:choice, xforms:item, xforms:itemset and an element from the XForms Action Module.

For example, to allow a selection to be made among options for pizza toppings, the xforms:select element may be used like this:

```
<xforms:select ref="/xmml:PizzaOrder/xmml:Toppings" >
 <xforms:label>Select the toppings for your pizza. You may select up
 to two toppings.</xforms:label>
 <xforms:item>
  <xforms:label>Chocolate</xforms:label>
  <xforms:value>Choc</xforms:value>
 </xforms:item>
 <xforms:item>
  <xforms:label>Pepperoni</xforms:label>
  <xforms:value>Pepp</xforms:value>
 </xforms:item>
```

```
    <xforms:item>
     <xforms:label>Ham and Pineapple</xforms:label>
     <xforms:value>HamnPin</xforms:value>
    </xforms:item>
    <xforms:item>
     <xforms:label>Chilli Beef</xforms:label>
     <xforms:value>Chil</xforms:value>
    </xforms:item>
   </xforms:select>
```

Because no value was expressed for the `selection` attribute in the previous code, the user cannot add additional options to those offered by the developer.

> **Be careful when specifying values for the `xforms:value` element. The selections made are stored as a whitespace-separated list. So if the value for the Ham and Pineapple choice had been `Ham and Pineapple` in the `xforms:value` element, this would be interpreted as a list of three choices: `Ham`, `and`, and `Pineapple`, which is almost certainly not what you or the user intended.**

The visual appearance of an `xforms:select` element may be controlled using the `appearance` attribute. Navigation to an `xforms:select` element may be specified using the `navigationindex` attribute. Direct access to an `xforms:select` element can be provided using the `accesskey` attribute.

The incremental attribute of the `xforms:select` element defines whether or not `xforms-value-changed` events are raised after each value is selected. The default value of the `incremental` attribute is `true`.

As well as providing items for possible selection literally as in the preceding code example, it is also possible to provide values for the `xforms:select` element by referencing the content of an `xforms:instance` element, whose content is not, typically, intended for submission. An example of this is shown in the `xforms:select1` section which follows.

The xforms:select1 Element

The `xforms:select1` element is intended to allow a single choice from a range of options. In HTML, forms would normally be done using a set of radio buttons. The `xforms:select1` element is bound to a node in the instance data using the `ref` or `bind` attribute. It has optional `appearance`, `navigationindex`, and `accesskey` attributes.

Like the `xforms:select` element, the `xforms:select1` element has optional `selection` and `incremental` attributes. The `selection` attribute specifies whether additional choices, other than those provided by the form author, are allowed. The possible values are `open` and `closed`. The default value is `closed`. The `incremental` attribute specifies whether an `xforms-value-changed` event is raised each time the choice is changed. The default value of the `incremental` attribute is `true`.

Let's take a look at how the selection elements can be used. The following example, `PizzaOrder.html`, uses both the `xforms:select` and `xforms:select1` elements. The full code listing is shown here. The component parts of the listing are then explained.

```
<?xml version="1.0"?>
<html
 xmlns="http://www.w3.org/1999/xhtml"
 xmlns:xforms="http://www.w3.org/2002/xforms"
 xmlns:xmml="http://www.XMML.com/namespace" >
<head>
  <object id="FormsPlayer" classid="CLSID:4D0ABA11-C5F0-4478-991A-375C4B648F58">
  <b>FormsPlayer has failed to load! Please check your installation.</b>
  <br />
 </object>
 <?import namespace="xforms" implementation="#FormsPlayer"?>
 <title>Using the &lt;xforms:itemset&gt; element.</title>

 <xforms:model id="default">
  <xforms:instance >
   <xmml:Pizza xmlns:xmml="http://www.XMML.com/namespace" >
    <xmml:Size></xmml:Size>
    <xmml:Toppings></xmml:Toppings>
   </xmml:Pizza>
  </xforms:instance>
  <xforms:submission id="mySubmit" action="file://c:/BXML/Ch19/PizzaOrder.xml"
  method="put" />
 </xforms:model>

 <xforms:model id="myToppings">
  <xforms:instance>
   <xmml:ToppingsAvailable xmlns:xmml="http://www.XMML.com/namespace" >
    <xmml:ToppingAvailable type="Choc">
     <xmml:Description>Chocolate</xmml:Description>
    </xmml:ToppingAvailable>
    <xmml:ToppingAvailable type="Pepp">
     <xmml:Description>Pepperoni</xmml:Description>
    </xmml:ToppingAvailable>
    <xmml:ToppingAvailable type="HamnPin">
     <xmml:Description>Ham and Pineapple</xmml:Description>
    </xmml:ToppingAvailable>
    <xmml:ToppingAvailable type="Chil">
     <xmml:Description>Chilli Beef</xmml:Description>
    </xmml:ToppingAvailable>
   </xmml:ToppingsAvailable>
  </xforms:instance>
 </xforms:model>

 <xforms:model id="mySizes">
  <xforms:instance>
   <xmml:SizesAvailable xmlns:xmml="http://www.XMML.com/namespace">
    <xmml:SizeAvailable type="S">
     <xmml:Description>Small</xmml:Description>
    </xmml:SizeAvailable>
    <xmml:SizeAvailable type="M">
     <xmml:Description>Medium</xmml:Description>
    </xmml:SizeAvailable>
    <xmml:SizeAvailable type="L">
     <xmml:Description>Large</xmml:Description>
```

```
      </xmml:SizeAvailable>
     </xmml:SizesAvailable>
    </xforms:instance>
   </xforms:model>
  </head>
  <body>
  <p>Choose the size and toppings for your pizza.</p>
  <xforms:select1 model="default" ref="/xmml:Pizza/xmml:Size" >
   <xforms:label>Sizes offered.</xforms:label>
   <xforms:itemset model="mySizes"
   nodeset="/xmml:SizesAvailable/xmml:SizeAvailable" >
    <xforms:label ref="xmml:Description/text()" />
    <xforms:value ref="xmml:Description/text()" />
   </xforms:itemset>
  </xforms:select1>
  <br />
  <p>Choose your toppings here. You may choose up to two toppings.</p>
   <xforms:select model="default" ref="/xmml:Pizza/xmml:Toppings" >
    <xforms:label>There are four toppings to choose from.</xforms:label>
    <xforms:itemset model="myToppings"
    nodeset="/xmml:ToppingsAvailable/xmml:ToppingAvailable" >
     <xforms:label ref="xmml:Description" />
     <xforms:value ref="xmml:Description" />
    </xforms:itemset>
   </xforms:select>
  <br /><br />
  <xforms:submit submission="mySubmit">
   <xforms:label>Click Here to submit your Order.</xforms:label>
  </xforms:submit>
  </body>
  </html>
```

You should be familiar with the use of namespace declarations and the `object` element to load the formsPlayer and the processing instruction to specify to formsPlayer the namespace prefix of the XForms namespace.

This XForms document has three XForms models in it. The purpose of the first, the default, is to contain the instance data intended for submission by the user.

```
<xforms:model id="default">
 <xforms:instance >
  <xmml:Pizza xmlns:xmml="http://www.XMML.com/namespace" >
   <xmml:Size></xmml:Size>
   <xmml:Toppings></xmml:Toppings>
  </xmml:Pizza>
 </xforms:instance>
 <xforms:submission id="mySubmit" action="file://c:/BXML/Ch19/PizzaOrder.xml"
 method="put" />
</xforms:model>
```

The document to be submitted is straightforward having an `xmml:Pizza` element as its document element and two child elements, `xmml:Size` and `xmml:Toppings`.

The `xforms:submission` element specifies that we will use the `put` method to save the instance data to an XML file at the URL `file://c:/BXML/Ch19/PizzaOrder.xml`.

The next XForms model is shown in the following:

```
<xforms:model id="myToppings">
 <xforms:instance>
  <xmml:ToppingsAvailable xmlns:xmml="http://www.XMML.com/namespace" >
   <xmml:ToppingAvailable type="Choc">
    <xmml:Description>Chocolate</xmml:Description>
   </xmml:ToppingAvailable>
   <xmml:ToppingAvailable type="Pepp">
    <xmml:Description>Pepperoni</xmml:Description>
   </xmml:ToppingAvailable>
   <xmml:ToppingAvailable type="HamnPin">
    <xmml:Description>Ham and Pineapple</xmml:Description>
   </xmml:ToppingAvailable>
   <xmml:ToppingAvailable type="Chil">
    <xmml:Description>Chilli Beef</xmml:Description>
   </xmml:ToppingAvailable>
  </xmml:ToppingsAvailable>
 </xforms:instance>
</xforms:model>
```

This model must have an `id` attribute, since it is not the default XForms model. We will see how the value of that `id` attribute is used to retrieve the data contained inside it a little later in the description of this example.

The `xforms:instance` element has as its content a well-formed XML document that provides basic information about a range of pizza toppings, which may or may not be to your taste. Here we have specified content literally. In a working environment it might be more appropriate to reference a separate XML file, using a `src` attribute on the `xforms:instance` element. By using that technique, available toppings for a range of XForms forms could then be modified, when necessary, in one place. The data in this XForms data model will be used to populate an `xforms:select` element.

The third XForms data model in the document (shown in the following code) is used to provide information about the choice of sizes of pizza available.

```
<xforms:model id="mySizes">
 <xforms:instance>
  <xmml:SizesAvailable xmlns:xmml="http://www.XMML.com/namespace">
   <xmml:SizeAvailable type="S">
    <xmml:Description>Small</xmml:Description>
   </xmml:SizeAvailable>
   <xmml:SizeAvailable type="M">
    <xmml:Description>Medium</xmml:Description>
   </xmml:SizeAvailable>
   <xmml:SizeAvailable type="L">
    <xmml:Description>Large</xmml:Description>
   </xmml:SizeAvailable>
  </xmml:SizesAvailable>
 </xforms:instance>
</xforms:model>
```

The instance data in the XPath model produced from the content of the `xforms:instance` element will be used to populate an `xforms:select1` element.

Here is the `xforms:select1` element populated from the `mySizes` XForms model:

```
<xforms:select1 model="default" ref="/xmml:Pizza/xmml:Size" >
 <xforms:label>Sizes offered.</xforms:label>
 <xforms:itemset model="mySizes"
 nodeset="/xmml:SizesAvailable/xmml:SizeAvailable" >
  <xforms:label ref="xmml:Description/text()" />
  <xforms:value ref="xmml:Description/text()" />
 </xforms:itemset>
</xforms:select1>
```

Notice on the `xforms:select1` element that there is a `model` attribute, and its value is `default`, not `mySizes` as you might have expected. The value of the `model` attribute refers to the XForms model in which the instance data is situated for submission later. That instance data is derived from the `default` XForms model. The value of the `ref` attribute references the node in the instance data to which the value of the `xforms:select1` element is bound.

The content of the `xforms:label` element simply provides a label for the `xforms:select1` element as you can see in Figure 19-5.

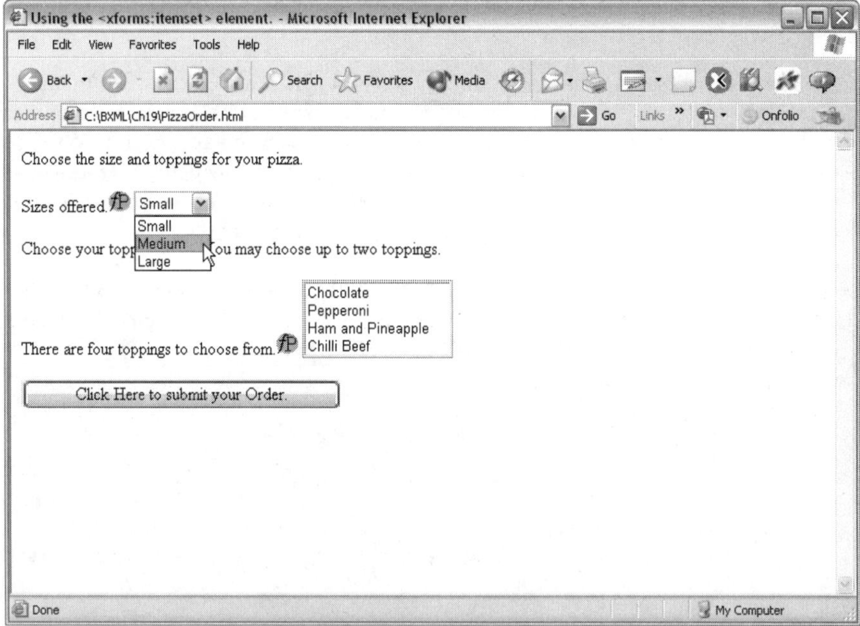

Figure 19-5

The other content of the `xforms:select1` element is an `xforms:itemset` element as follows:

```
<xforms:itemset model="mySizes"
 nodeset="/xmml:SizesAvailable/xmml:SizeAvailable" >
 <xforms:label ref="xmml:Description/text()" />
 <xforms:value ref="xmml:Description/text()" />
</xforms:itemset>
```

Notice that the `model` attribute of the `xforms:itemset` element references the `mySizes` XForms model. It is in that context that the value of the `nodeset` attribute is interpreted. The location path `/xmml:SizesAvailable/xmml:SizeAvailable` in the `nodeset` attribute selects the three `xmml:SizeAvailable` elements in that XForms model.

The label to be displayed in the `xforms:select1` form control is defined using another XPath location path in the value of the `ref` attribute of the `xforms:label` element. On this occasion we have chosen to submit the same value as the description, but we might have equally chosen to submit the value of the `type` attribute of the `xmml:SizeAvailable` element using the `@type` attribute as the value of the `ref` attribute of the `xforms:value` element.

The toppings for the chosen size of pizza are specified using the `xforms:select` element and its content shown here:

```
<xforms:select model="default" ref="/xmml:Pizza/xmml:Toppings" >
 <xforms:label>There are four toppings to choose from.</xforms:label>
 <xforms:itemset model="myToppings"
 nodeset="/xmml:ToppingsAvailable/xmml:ToppingAvailable" >
  <xforms:label ref="xmml:Description" />
  <xforms:value ref="xmml:Description" />
 </xforms:itemset>
</xforms:select>
```

Notice that on the `xforms:select` element the value of the model attribute is a reference to the `default` XForms model, since it is that XForms model which specifies the instance data. The value of the `ref` attribute references the `xmml:Toppings` node.

The `xforms:itemset` element is used in a way similar to the provision of the sizes of pizza shown earlier. The value of the `model` attribute references the `myToppings` XForms model, so the location path specified in the value of the `nodeset` attribute is interpreted in that context.

The `xforms:label` and `xforms:value` elements are used, respectively, to specify the options to be displayed and the value to be submitted.

Clicking the `xforms:submit` form control, because it is bound to the `mySubmit xforms:submission` element causes the instance data, after serialization, to be saved to the file `c:\BXML\Ch19\PizzaOrder.xml`. The saved document from one use of the form is shown here:

```
<xmml:Pizza xmlns:xmml="http://www.XMML.com/namespace">
 <xmml:Size>Medium</xmml:Size>
 <xmml:Toppings>Pepperoni</xmml:Toppings>
</xmml:Pizza>
```

We have on a few occasions earlier in the chapter mentioned model item properties without specifying what they are. Now let's look at what model item properties are and how we specify them.

XForms Model Item Properties

XForms model item properties let you do things like making a form control read-only or specifying that its value is a calculated value. At the heart of how XForms model item properties work is the `xforms:bind` element.

The xforms:bind Element

The `xforms:bind` element is a child element of the `xforms:model` element. Depending on how many form controls it is desired to specify model item properties for, there can be multiple `xforms:bind` elements in any `xforms:model` element's content.

The `nodeset` attribute of the `xforms:bind` element specifies a node-set in the instance data for which an XForms model item property is to be specified.

A model item property is specified using an attribute, identically named to the property, on an `xforms:bind` element. For example, to specify that a Name is required, we would write something like the following (depending on the path to the node of interest in the instance data):

```
<xforms:bind required="true()" nodeset="/somePath/Name" />
```

More than one property can be specified on a single `xforms:bind` element.

The XForms model items properties are listed here:

- `calculate` specifies a calculation to be performed to provide a value for the component of the instance data.
- `constraint` specifies a constraint on the value of the component of the data source.
- `p3ptype` specifies a Platform for Privacy Preferences element to be associated with the component of the instance data.
- `readonly` specifies whether or not a component of the instance data is read-only or not. The allowed values for the corresponding `readonly` attribute are `true()` and `false()`. The default value is `false()`.
- `relevant` specifies whether or not a component of the instance data is relevant in particular circumstances. For example, if an employee's gender is male, then maternity leave is unlikely to be relevant.
- `required` signifies whether or not a value is required for the bound component of the instance data.
- `type` allows a W3C XML Schema data types to be specified for a component of the instance data, in the absence of a W3C XML Schema document.

Try It Out Using Model Item Properties

Let's look at an example that uses several of the model item properties just mentioned. The following example code is in the file `ModelItemPropertiesExample.html`.

```
<?xml version="1.0"?>
<html
 xmlns="http://www.w3.org/1999/xhtml"
 xmlns:xforms="http://www.w3.org/2002/xforms"
 xmlns:xmml="http://www.XMML.com/namespace"
 xmlns:xsd="http://www.w3.org/2001/XMLSchema" >
<head>
  <object id="FormsPlayer" classid="CLSID:4D0ABA11-C5F0-4478-991A-375C4B648F58">
  <b>FormsPlayer has failed to load! Please check your installation.</b>
  <br />
 </object>
 <?import namespace="xforms" implementation="#FormsPlayer"?>
 <title>Example using Model Item Properties.</title>

 <xforms:model id="default">
  <xforms:instance >
   <xmml:Employee xmlns:xmml="http://www.XMML.com/namespace" >
    <xmml:FirstName></xmml:FirstName>
    <xmml:LastName></xmml:LastName>
    <xmml:Gender></xmml:Gender>
    <xmml:StartDate></xmml:StartDate>
    <xmml:EndDate></xmml:EndDate>
    <xmml:Comments></xmml:Comments>
    <xmml:MaternityLeave></xmml:MaternityLeave>
   </xmml:Employee>
  </xforms:instance>
  <xforms:submission id="mySubmit" action="file://c:/BXML/Ch19/EmployeeData.xml"
  method="put" />
  <xforms:bind nodeset="/xmml:Employee/xmml:FirstName" required="true()" />
  <xforms:bind nodeset="/xmml:Employee/xmml:LastName" required="true()" />
  <xforms:bind nodeset="/xmml:Employee/xmml:StartDate" required="true()"
  type="xsd:date" />
  <xforms:bind nodeset="/xmml:Employee/xmml:EndDate" type="xsd:date"
  required="false()" />
  <xforms:bind nodeset="/xmml:Employee/xmml:MaternityLeave"
  relevant="/xmml:Employee/xmml:Gender/text() = 'Female'" />
 </xforms:model>

 <xforms:model id="myEmployeeInfo">
  <xforms:instance>
   <xmml:EmployeeChoices xmlns:xmml="http://www.XMML.com/namespace" >
    <xmml:GenderChoices >
     <xmml:GenderChoice>
      <xmml:Description>Male</xmml:Description>
     </xmml:GenderChoice>
     <xmml:GenderChoice>
      <xmml:Description>Female</xmml:Description>
     </xmml:GenderChoice>
    </xmml:GenderChoices>
```

```
      <xmml:MaternityChoices >
      <xmml:MaternityChoice>
       <xmml:Description>Yes</xmml:Description>
      </xmml:MaternityChoice>
      <xmml:MaternityChoice>
       <xmml:Description>No</xmml:Description>
      </xmml:MaternityChoice>
     </xmml:MaternityChoices>
    </xmml:EmployeeChoices>
   </xforms:instance>
  </xforms:model>

 </head>
 <body>
 <p>Enter employee information here.</p>
 <xforms:input model="default" ref="/xmml:Employee/xmml:FirstName" >
  <xforms:label>First Name:</xforms:label>
 </xforms:input>
 <br />
 <xforms:input model="default" ref="/xmml:Employee/xmml:LastName" >
  <xforms:label>Last Name: </xforms:label>
 </xforms:input>
 <br />
 <xforms:select1 model="default" ref="/xmml:Employee/xmml:Gender" >
 <xforms:label>Enter the employee's gender: </xforms:label>
  <xforms:itemset model="myEmployeeInfo"
  nodeset="/xmml:EmployeeChoices/xmml:GenderChoices/xmml:GenderChoice" >
   <xforms:label ref="xmml:Description" />
   <xforms:value ref="xmml:Description" />
  </xforms:itemset>
 </xforms:select1>
 <p>Enter start and end dates of employment.</p>
 <xforms:input ref="/xmml:Employee/xmml:StartDate">
  <xforms:label>Start Date:</xforms:label>
 </xforms:input>
 <br />
 <xforms:input ref="/xmml:Employee/xmml:EndDate">
  <xforms:label>End Date: </xforms:label>
 </xforms:input>
 <br />
 <xforms:select1 model="default" ref="/xmml:Employee/xmml:MaternityLeave">
 <xforms:label>Has the employee had maternity leave?</xforms:label>
  <xforms:itemset model="myEmployeeInfo"
  nodeset="/xmml:EmployeeChoices/xmml:MaternityChoices/xmml:MaternityChoice" >
   <xforms:label ref="xmml:Description" />
   <xforms:value ref="xmml:Description" />
  </xforms:itemset>
 </xforms:select1>
 <br />
 <xforms:textarea ref="/xmml:Employee/xmml:Comments">
  <xforms:label>Enter comments here:</xforms:label>
 </xforms:textarea>

 <br />
```

```
<xforms:submit submission="mySubmit">
 <xforms:label>Click Here to submit your Order.</xforms:label>
</xforms:submit>
</body>
</html>
```

Figure 19-6 shows a filled-in form ready to submit.

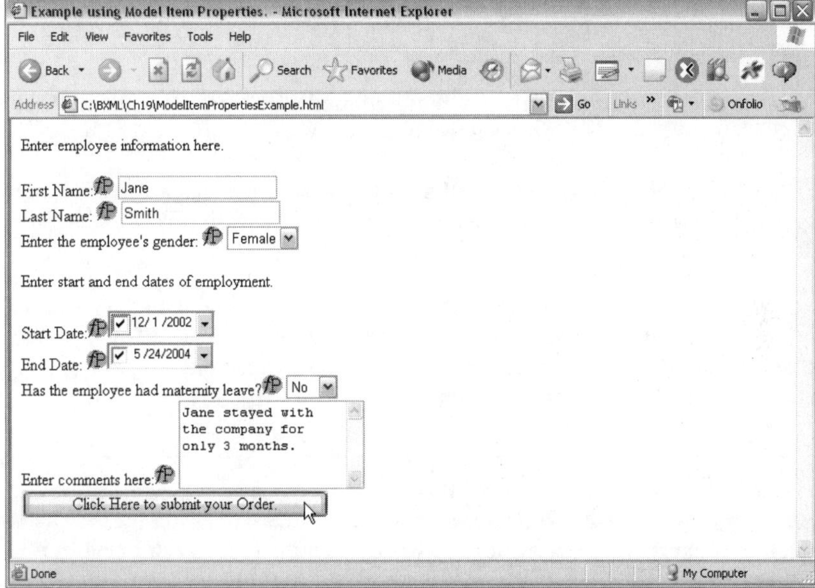

Figure 19-6

How It Works

In the default XForms model, we see that the content of the `xforms:instance` element is some basic data about an employee:

```
<xforms:instance >
 <xmml:Employee xmlns:xmml="http://www.XMML.com/namespace" >
  <xmml:FirstName></xmml:FirstName>
  <xmml:LastName></xmml:LastName>
  <xmml:Gender></xmml:Gender>
  <xmml:StartDate></xmml:StartDate>
  <xmml:EndDate></xmml:EndDate>
  <xmml:Comments></xmml:Comments>
  <xmml:MaternityLeave></xmml:MaternityLeave>
 </xmml:Employee>
</xforms:instance>
```

The remainder of that default XForms model is an `xforms:submission` element specifying where the serialized instance data is to be saved:

```
<xforms:submission id="mySubmit"
 action="file://c:/BXML/Ch19/EmployeeData.xml" method="put" />
```

The most interesting part of the XForms model is the several `xforms:bind` elements shown here:

```
<xforms:bind nodeset="/xmml:Employee/xmml:FirstName" required="true()" />
<xforms:bind nodeset="/xmml:Employee/xmml:LastName" required="true()" />
<xforms:bind nodeset="/xmml:Employee/xmml:StartDate" required="true()"
 type="xsd:date" />
<xforms:bind nodeset="/xmml:Employee/xmml:EndDate" type="xsd:date"
 required="false()" />
<xforms:bind nodeset="/xmml:Employee/xmml:MaternityLeave"
 relevant="/xmml:Employee/xmml:Gender/text() = 'Female'" />
```

The first two `xforms:bind` elements use the required model item property simply to specify that both a first name and a last name for the employee are required.

The `xforms:bind` element, which relates to the start date, specifies that a value is required for start date and that the data type is an `xsd:date` value. As you can see, this also causes a date form control to be displayed for the start date.

Since some employees will still be employed and so won't have an end date the `required` attribute on the `xforms:bind` element which binds to the end date is set to `false()`.Remember that to specify a boolean value in XPath you must use the `true()` or `false()` functions since `true` or `false` in a location path are interpreted as element type names.

> **The version of formsPlayer used for this writing did not recognize setting the `required` attribute of an `xforms:bind` element to `false()`. This means that when testing the example, you will need to provide an end date for each person for whom you enter data.**

If an employee is male, then he is, for obvious reasons, not eligible for maternity leave. So, if we set the value of gender to `Male`, you will find that you cannot set a value for maternity leave.

The remainder of the form markup uses code techniques you have seen before, so it isn't explained further here.

The submitted data, `EmployeeData.xml`, is shown here:

```
<xmml:Employee xmlns:xmml="http://www.XMML.com/namespace">
 <xmml:FirstName>Jane</xmml:FirstName>
 <xmml:LastName>Smith</xmml:LastName>
 <xmml:Gender>Female</xmml:Gender>
 <xmml:StartDate>2003-12-01</xmml:StartDate>
 <xmml:EndDate>2004-03-25</xmml:EndDate>
 <xmml:Comments>Jane stayed with the company for only 3 months.</xmml:Comments>
 <xmml:MaternityLeave>No</xmml:MaternityLeave>
</xmml:Employee>
```

There is an unexpected behavior in formsPlayer. Despite the required property for `xmml:EndDate` being set to `false()`, it appears to require a value to be submitted. It also provides error messages, seen in Figure 19-7, which don't help to identify where the validation problem lies.

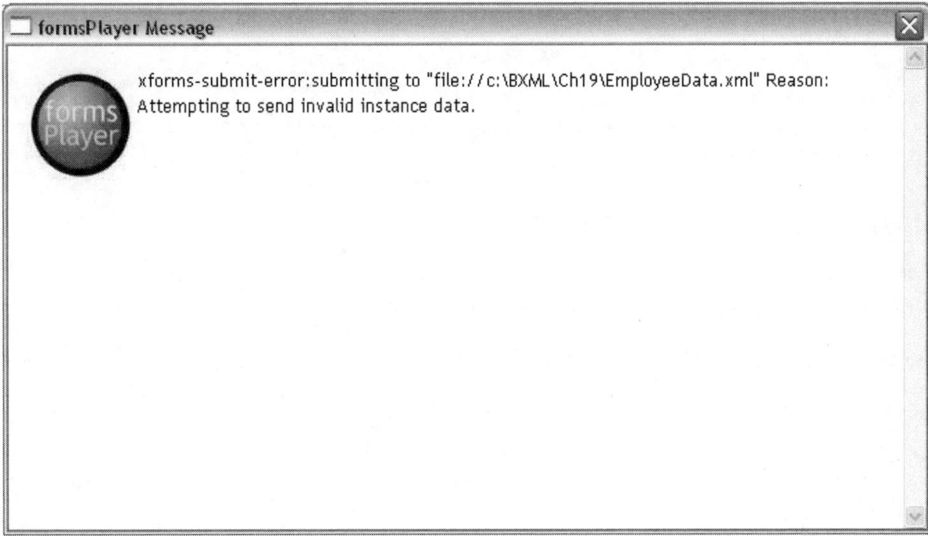
formsPlayer Message
xforms-submit-error:submitting to "file://c:\BXML\Ch19\EmployeeData.xml" Reason:
Attempting to send invalid instance data.
forms Player

Figure 19-7

XForms Events

XForms has a large number of events which are described in more detail in the XForms specification at `http://www.w3.org/TR/xforms/index-all.html#rpm-events`.

XForms events are categorized into the following four groups:

- Initialization events, which are fired when an XForms processor is starting up and loading an XForms document.
- Interaction events, which are fired in response to user actions.
- Notification events, which indicate that something has happened in the form.
- Error events, which indicate that something has gone wrong during form processing.

Creating event handlers for XForms events allows us to add custom functionality to XForms documents that we create.

The XForms Action Module

The XForms Action Module specifies XForms elements that function as declarative event handlers. XForms does not define any mechanism for scripted handling of events, leaving that to host languages, such as XHTML and SVG.

I mentioned earlier that an element from this module could be included in the content of several XForms form controls. So, if we were to mimic the reset functionality available in HTML forms by using the `xforms:trigger` element, we would use code like the following, assuming that the namespace for

XML events was declared to be associated with the namespace prefix ev:

```
<xforms:trigger>
 <xforms:label>Reset the instance data.</xforms:label>
 <xforms:reset ev:event="DOMActivate" model=''default" />
</xforms:trigger>
```

The xforms:action Element

Used to group other elements from the XForms Action Module, the `xforms:action` element typically has an event attribute as illustrated in the preceding code snippet.

The permitted element content of the `xforms:action` element is listed here: `xforms:delete`, `xforms:dispatch`, `xforms:insert`, `xforms:load`, `xforms:message`, `xforms:rebuild`, `xforms:recalculate`, `xforms:refresh`, `xforms:reset`, `xforms:revalidate`, `xforms:send`, `xforms:setfocus`,`xforms:setindex`, `xforms:setvalue`, and `xforms:toggle`. All but the `xforms:delete`, `xforms:insert`, `xforms:setindex`, and `xforms:toggle` elements are part of the XForms Action Module.

The xforms:dispatch Element

The `xforms:dispatch` element dispatches an event to an element specified by the value of the `target` attribute of `xforms:dispatch`. Like the `xforms:action` element, the `xforms:dispatch` element may have an event attribute. In addition, it may have `name`, `target`, `bubbles`, and `cancelable` attributes. The value of the `name` attribute is the name of the event to be dispatched. The value of the `target` attribute, an `xsd:IDREF` value, is the element to which the event is to be dispatched. The value of the `bubbles` attribute is a boolean value indicating whether or not the event bubbles. The value of the `cancelable` attribute indicates whether or not custom events can be cancelled. It has no effect on predefined events.

The `xforms:dispatch` element is an empty element.

The xforms:load Element

The `xforms:load` element causes an external resource to be loaded. The `xforms:load` element has `resource` and `show` attributes. The `resource` attribute is an `xsd:anyURI` value and references the external resource to be loaded. The `show` attribute, which has permitted values of `new` and `replace`, specifies how the resource is to be displayed. The `xforms:load` also has an `event` attribute in the XML events namespace whose value is an XForms event.

The `xforms:load` element is an empty element.

The xforms:message Element

The `xforms:message` element specifies a message to be displayed to the user. The `xforms:message` has an `event` attribute in the XML events namespace whose value is an XForms event. A `src` attribute, if present, has a value of type `xsd:anyURI` and identifies an external resource to be retrieved.

The content of the `xforms:message` element is either character data or one or more `xforms:output` elements. The `xforms:message` element may be an empty element if it has a `src` attribute which retrieves an external resource.

The xforms:rebuild Element

The `xforms:rebuild` element has an `event` attribute which specifies an XForms event. The `xforms-rebuild` element responds to the `xforms-rebuild` event. In addition, it has a `model` attribute whose value is of type `xsd:IDREF` and specifies the XForms model whose instance data is to be rebuilt.

The `xforms:rebuild` element has no content.

The xforms:recalculate Element

The `xforms:recalculate` element causes the `xforms-recalculate` event to be processed. The `xforms:recalculate` element has an `event` attribute in the XML events namespace. It also has a `model` attribute whose value is of type `xsd:IDREF` and specifies the XForms model whose instance data is to be recalculated.

The `xforms:recalculate` element has no content.

The xforms:refresh Element

The `xforms:refresh` element causes the `xforms-refresh` event to be processed. The `xforms:refresh` element has an `event` attribute in the XML events namespace. It also has a `model` attribute whose value is of type `xsd:IDREF` and specifies the XForms model, the display of whose instance data needs to be refreshed.

The `xforms:refresh` element has no content.

The xforms:reset Element

The `xforms:reset` element causes the `xforms-reset` event to be dispatched to a specified XForms model. The model, which is to be reset, is specified using the `model` attribute whose value is of type `xsd:IDREF`.

The `xforms:reset` element has no content.

The xforms:revalidate Element

The `xforms:revalidate` element causes the `xforms-revalidate` event to be processed. The XForms model whose instance data is to be revalidated is specified using the `model` attribute whose value is of type `xsd:IDREF`.

The `xforms:revalidate` element is an empty element.

The xforms:send Element

The `xforms:send` element can initiate submission of instance data by sending an `xforms-submit` event. The `xforms:send` element has a submission attribute whose value is of type `xsd:IDREF` and references an `xforms:submission` element which has an `id` attribute with matching value.

The `xforms:send` element has no content.

The xforms:setfocus Element

The `xforms:setfocus` element dispatches the `xforms-focus` event to a form control which is identified by means of the `control` attribute of the `xforms:setfocus` element. The value of the `control` attribute is of type xsd:IDREF.

The `xforms:setfocus` element is an empty element.

The xforms:setvalue Element

The `xforms:setvalue` element sets the value of a specified node in the instance data. The `xforms:setvalue` element has an `event` attribute in the XML events namespace. A `bind` or `ref` attribute specifies the instance data node whose value is to be set.

The value to be set on the specified instance data node can be provided by the character content of the `xforms:setvalue` element or can be specified using the `value` attribute whose value is an XPath 1.0 expression.

Developing and Debugging XForms

If you are new to XForms and also new to XML creating even simple XForms documents can be quite tough to get right at first. There are just such a large number of things that you can get wrong.

I would very much suggest that you start with really simple forms until you become familiar with creating working XForms documents, assuming you are hand coding. Be sure that you have mastered basic but essential techniques such as understanding XML namespaces. Also be sure that you understand the section that describes what instance data is and how XPath location paths are used to reference nodes inside the instance data.

You will save yourself a lot of grief by using an XML-aware editor to code. Examples of stand-alone XML editors include XMLWriter (`http://www.xmlwriter.net`) and XMLSpy (`http://www.xmlspy.com`) as well as the XML editors available with XFormation and onForm xPress. An XML-aware editor will catch those simple well-formedness errors that can be very tough to spot by eye once a form moves beyond the trivial.

If form controls aren't working correctly (for example, an `xforms:input` element loses the value you entered when you tab away from the form control), it is likely that the binding to the instance data is faulty. That failure to bind can be due, for example, to omitting a `ref` attribute, to omitting a leading / character in the value of a `ref` attribute or getting namespace declarations wrong. Another possible cause when you have multiple XForms models is not specifying a `model` attribute that has an `xsd:IDREF` to the correct XForms model.

Commercial Alternatives to XForms

Many commercial software companies are developing tools in the XML forms arena, in response to the increased used of XML in enterprise applications. In this section I will briefly introduce two tools in this space where XForms technology is not used.

Microsoft InfoPath 2003

Microsoft InfoPath 2003 is a Microsoft tool intended to be used to submit and retrieve XML from relational databases, such as Microsoft Access and SQL Server, to XML web services and to Microsoft application servers, such as Windows SharePoint Services and BizTalk Server 2004.

Microsoft InfoPath 2003 has a very nice visual designer, which allows users who are not familiar with XML to create InfoPath forms, which submit well-formed XML. For more advanced work familiarity with XSLT, JScript, VBScript or a .NET language is needed.

Figure 19-8 shows the InfoPath designer with a simple sample form open and the Controls task pane visible.

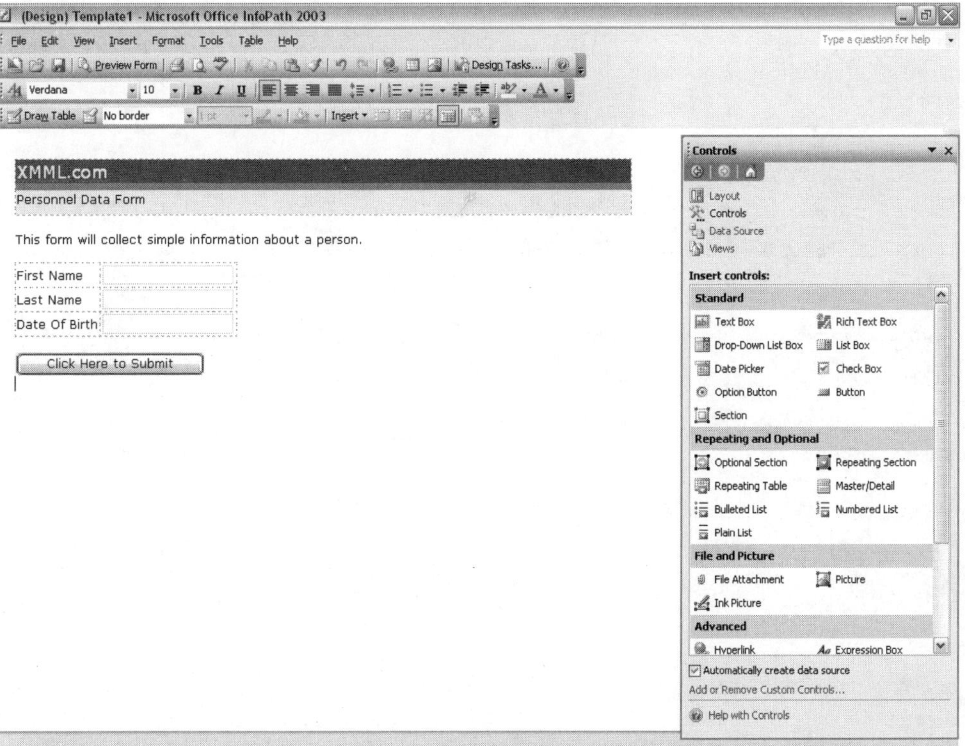

Figure 19-8

Further information about InfoPath 2003 is located at `http://office.microsoft.com/home/office.aspx?assetid=FX01085792`.

Adobe XML/PDF Forms Designer

At the time of writing, the public beta for the Adobe XML/PDF Forms Designer was just about to start, so the brief description, which follows is based on initial descriptive material of the Designer and samples of its output, which can be viewed and filled in using the Adobe Acrobat Reader.

The Adobe XML/PDF Forms Designer, like InfoPath 2003, uses a proprietary file format that bundles up several files, which are necessary for the functioning of the Acrobat form. It resembles InfoPath in that respect since Infopath uses a cabinet file with an `.xsn` extension to hold its XML files.

Like many other Adobe design tools, the Adobe XML/PDF Designer is a very polished tool in many respects. Figure 19-9 shows the Adobe XML/PDF Designer displaying one of the sample forms supplied with the Designer.

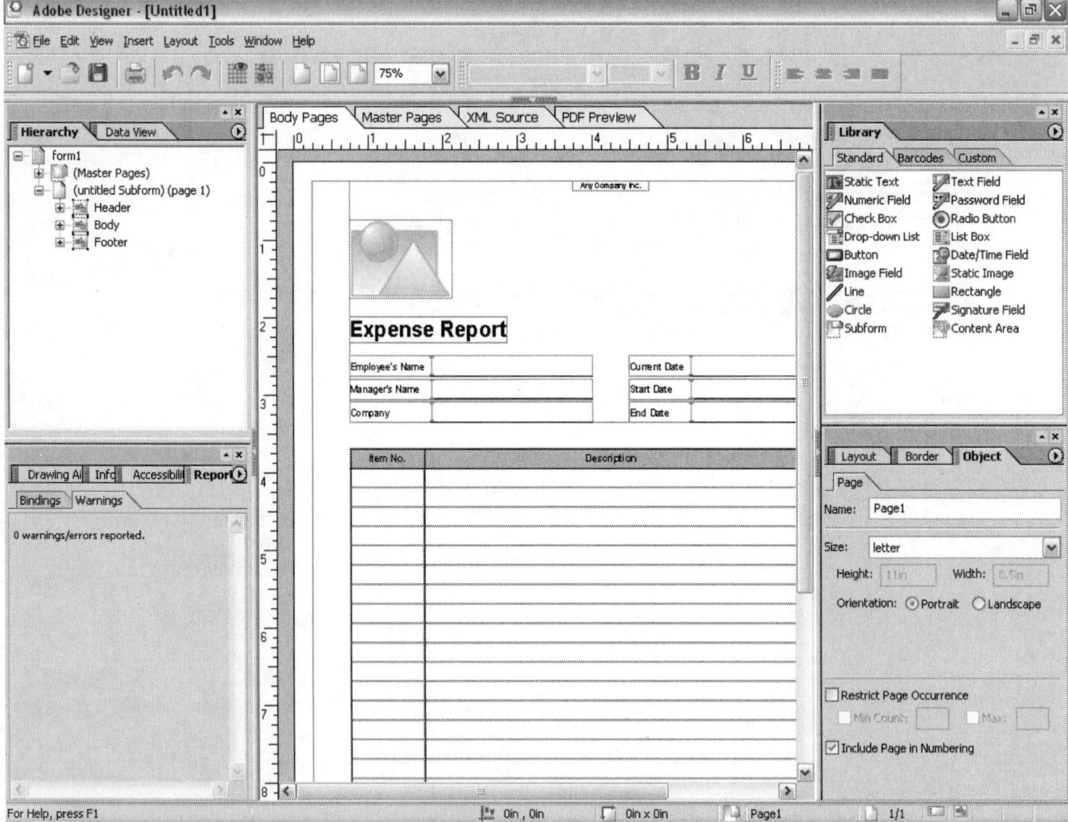

Figure 19-9

At the time of writing, the final version of the Adobe XML/PDF Designer has not been released, so there is no public URL for the product. I suggest you visit `http://www.adobe.com/` and search for further information.

Summary

In this chapter we were introduced to XForms. After discussing the XForms model, we covered how to create instance data and how to configure submission of a form. Then, we went over XForms form controls, finishing up with XForms model item properties.

Exercise Questions

Suggested solutions to these questions can be found in Appendix A.

Question 1

Experiment in the code examples given in the chapter with the effect of changing the value of the `appearance` attribute on the `xforms:select` and `xforms:select1` elements. This, particularly, when viewed in more than one XForms viewer will give you an impression of the range of visual appearances available to an XForms developer.

Question 2

Describe the differences in purpose of the `xforms:submit` and `xforms:submission` elements.

Part VIII: Case Studies

Case Study 1: .NET XML Web Services

The idea behind Web services is to provide transparent functionality exposed through a web interface. In order to do this, you must provide a service that adheres to the prevailing standards; how the actual service is implemented is of no concern to the user or the consumer. The specific code may be written in any language. All the user needs to know is the location of the service and what functionality is available.

This chapter demonstrates the creation of an XML Web service and how it can be utilized by two different clients. The development languages used are Visual Basic .NET (VB.NET), JavaScript, and C#—proof-positive of the ability to mix and match as the need requires and of the interoperability of a Web service and its clients regardless of each individual component's specific construction.

In this chapter, we will learn:

- How to create an XML Web service
- How to build a web client
- How to use C# to make a .NET client

The XML Web Service

We will develop the service itself using VB.NET. Note that this is a slightly simplified version of a service written to provide an in-house phone directory system for a medium-sized company. The basic requirement is that when given a surname or partial surname, the service would return the office phone number of any matching individuals. This is a common enough scenario and can easily be managed using any modern server-side coding (ASP, for example) without resorting to the extra complexity of a full-scale Web service. The reason to do it this way, however, is one of the prime goals of nearly all Web services: reusability. Once the service is available, it can be utilized in many circumstances, from the company intranet to the Internet, from PDAs and via a WAP-enabled phone to name but a few. All these prospective clients would be able to send and receive the necessary data, but the user interface on each would be quite different. For many years, this decoupling of functionality and user interface has been one of the foremost ambitions of modern software development.

Perhaps the easiest way to develop a .NET Web service is to use Microsoft's Visual Studio .NET. This provides a number of templates along with the customary features of an IDE (Integrated Development Environment), such as syntax highlighting, code completion, and context-sensitive help.

However, all this comes at a price, from both a monetary and a learning point of view. Using a simpler development environment means that the fundamental principles will be more exposed, and this will serve well when, in future projects, there is a need to understand the underlying plumbing, especially important when things are not working as intended. For these reasons, creating the Web service and the clients will be done using only freely available tools, a simple text editor. Windows Notepad will do just fine here, and the command-line tools, which are included in the freely downloadable .NET Framework SDK.

To complete the case study you will need to have the .NET Framework SDK installed. This is available from `msdn.com/netframework`. *It may also be necessary to first install the framework itself, which can be found at the same URL.*

> **One thing to watch out for when using Notepad is to make sure that when saving files, "All files" is selected in the Save as type drop-down box. Otherwise, Notepad will helpfully append the suffix `txt` to all your file names.**

The other main design decision is to use Microsoft Access as a back-end database. Although not suitable for an industrial strength, multi-user application, it means that we can develop without the additional overhead of something more suitable, such as SQL Server. Note that the application can be developed without the presence of Access on the computer. Microsoft Access stores all the database information in a binary formatted file with the extension `mdb`. If you don't have Access installed or don't want to bother creating the database yourself, a suitable `mdb` file can be downloaded from this book's website.

Try It Out Creating a Web Service

This service will be hosted by Microsoft's Internet Information Server (IIS). Version 5 or 6 will be necessary, as previous versions do not support ASP.NET. IIS is available with the professional editions of Windows 2000 and XP.

There are three main stages in setting up this service; firstly, configuring the web server, secondly, creating and installing the database, and finally producing, compiling, and installing the Web service code files themselves.

1. First, create a new folder named `PhoneBook` on the server. For the rest of this chapter the assumption is that development is taking place on the same machine that's running IIS. If this is not the case, replace the word `localhost` with the name of your server in all of the URLs that appear in the following code.
2. Open the management console for the web server by right-clicking the My Computer icon and choosing Manage. Navigate to Default Web Site via Services and Applications ⇨ Internet

Information Services ➪ Web Sites. Make sure the server is running by right-clicking and choosing Start. Now create a new virtual directory by right-clicking and selecting New ➪ Virtual Directory. Choose PhoneBook as the folder alias, and browse to the folder we just created when asked for the content directory.

3. Now it's time to add the Access database. You can copy `PhoneBook.mdb` from the downloaded code for this chapter to the `PhoneBook` folder that we just created. Alternatively, if you have a copy of Microsoft Access 2000 or greater you can create a new database named `PhoneBook.mdb` with one table named `tblDirectory`, which would have the following structure:

Column	Data Type
Id	AutoNumber
Forenames	Text (200)
Surname	Text (100)
Telephone	Text (100)

4. Populate a few rows of the table with some test data; make sure that you have at least two surnames beginning with the same letter. Refer to Figure 20-1 if you need inspiration.

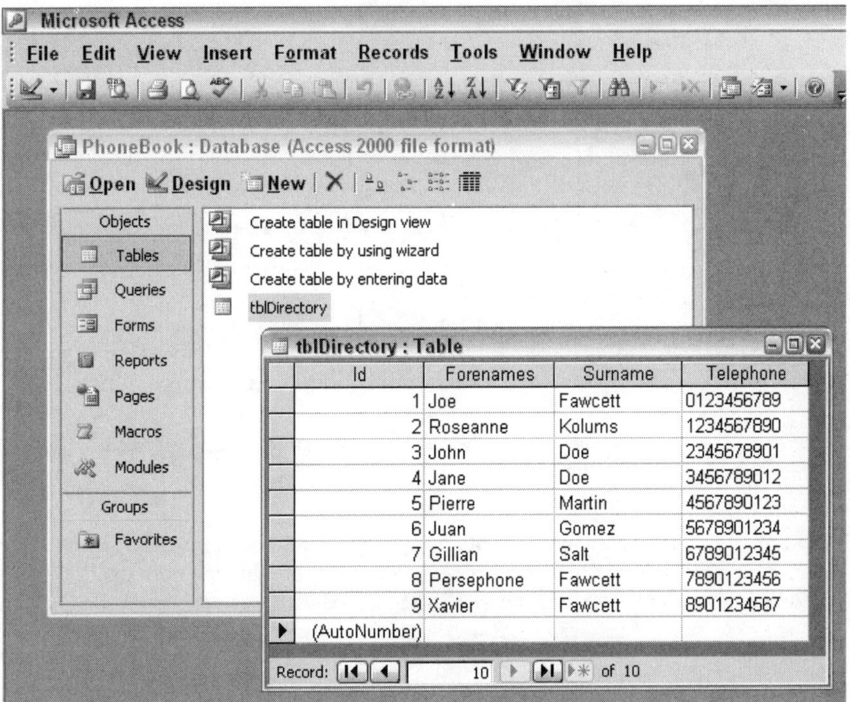

Figure 20-1

5. Finally, create the following query using SQL view and save it as `qryPhoneFromSurname`:

```
PARAMETERS [Search] Text (100);
SELECT tblDirectory.Surname, tblDirectory.Forenames, tblDirectory.Telephone
FROM tblDirectory
WHERE tblDirectory.Surname Like [Search]
ORDER BY tblDirectory.Surname, tblDirectory.Forenames;
```

Depending on your version of Access, this will look something like Figure 20-2.

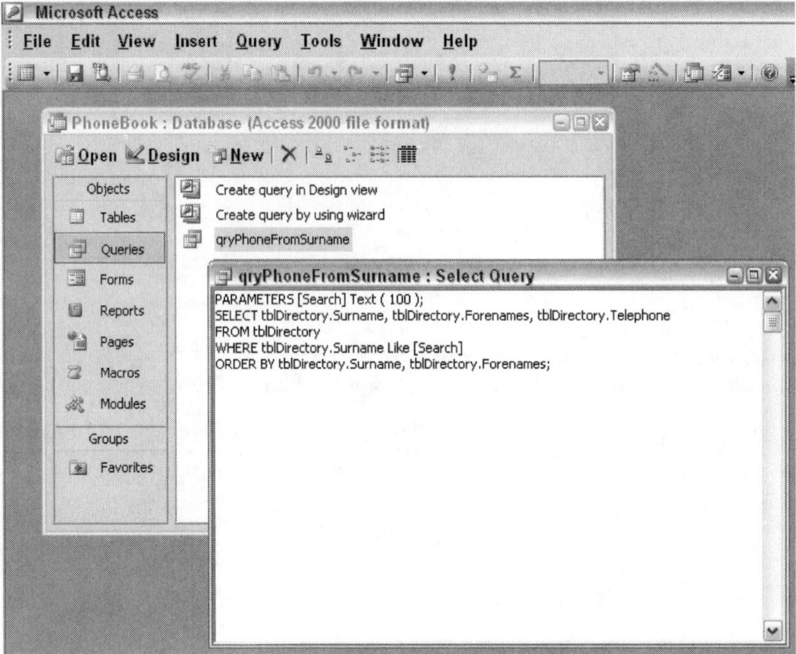

Figure 20-2

6. Now on with the actual code. Open a new file in Notepad and save it to the `PhoneBook` folder with the name `PhoneBookLookup.asmx`. This file, which will be our entry point to the service, only contains the following code, which should all be entered on one line:

```
<%@ WebService Language="vb" Codebehind="PhoneLookup.asmx.vb"
 Class="PhoneBook.PhoneBook" %>
```

7. The code, which does the work, will be kept in the file `PhoneLookup.asmx.vb` referred to by the `Codebehind` attribute in the preceding line. Create this file now using Notepad, add the following code, and save it to the `PhoneBook` folder:

```
Imports System.Data
Imports System.Data.OleDb
Imports System.Web.Services
Imports System.Configuration
```

```
<System.Web.Services.WebService _
(Namespace:="http://wrox.com/PhoneBook/PhoneLookup")> _
Public Class PhoneBook
  Inherits System.Web.Services.WebService

  <WebMethod(Description:= "Finds telephone numbers based on surname.")> _
  Public Function FindNumbers(ByVal Surname As String) As String()
    Return GetDetails(Surname)
  End Function

  Private Function GetDetails(ByVal Surname As String) As String()
    Dim sConnection As String = GetAppSetting("ConnString")
    Dim sQuery As String = GetAppSetting("FindQuery")
    Dim oConn As New OleDbConnection(sConnection)
    Dim cmd As New OleDbCommand(sQuery, oConn)
    cmd.CommandType = CommandType.StoredProcedure
    Dim oParam As OleDbParameter = __
        cmd.Parameters.Add("Surname", OleDbType.VarChar, 20)
    oParam.Value = Surname
    oConn.Open()
    Dim oDR As OleDbDataReader = cmd.ExecuteReader()
    Dim arrResult As String()
    Dim iRows As Long = -1
    Do While oDR.Read()
      iRows = iRows + 1
      ReDim Preserve arrResult(iRows)
      arrResult(iRows) = oDR.GetString(0) & _
                "|" & oDR.GetString(1) & _
                "|" & oDR.GetString(2)
    Loop
    oDR.Close()
    oConn.Close()
    Return arrResult
  End Function

  Private Function GetAppSetting(ByVal Key As String) As String
    Dim sAppSetting As String = _
      ConfigurationSettings.AppSettings(Key)
    Return sAppSetting
  End Function

End Class
```

How It Works

The first four lines of the code, containing the `Imports` keyword, make the members of these namespaces available without having to use a fully qualified name when referring to them. For example, we can use `OleDbDataReader` instead of `System.Data.OleDb.OleDbDataReader`.

Following this comes the class declaration:

```
<System.Web.Services.WebService _
(Namespace:="http://wrox.com/PhoneBook/PhoneLookup")> _
Public Class PhoneBook
  Inherits System.Web.Services.WebService
```

The class, declared `Public` so that it's available externally, inherits from `System.Web.Services.WebService`. It also has an attribute, enclosed in the <> characters. This attribute is read during compilation and instructs the compiler to inject code that provides extra functionality. These two things mean that the class will support all the necessary extra features to act as a Web service. The class will, for example, have the ability to generate its own Web Services Description Language (WSDL) file, which describes the service in a standard XML format and can be used by consumers of the service to simplify code generation. An example of this appears later in the chapter when the C# client is created.

> **The Web Services Description Language (WSDL) is yet another example of XML rearing its well-formed head. It is a standardized format describing every detail of a Web service and will include all the public methods, details of their arguments, and return values as well as what style of requests are supported. WSDL is a complicated format, and to avoid mistakes, it is usually generated automatically by various tools. The full standard is available from `http://www.w3.org/TR/wsdl`.**

Note the namespace included in the `WebService` attribute, `http://wrox.com/PhoneBook/PhoneLookup`. This does not refer to a web page, instead this namespace is simply a unique string of characters used to differentiate this service from any others. Using a domain name that you own means that the name will not clash with others; the remaining part of the string can follow your own standards but should not contain any spaces. If you don't assign a namespace, then your service will receive a temporary one, `http://www.tempuri.org`, which is unsuitable for production usage. (For more on namespaces, turn to Chapter 3.)

The Web service only exposes one method, `FindNumbers`, which accepts a string parameter and returns an array of strings. Take the following code for example:

```
<WebMethod(Description:= "Finds telephone numbers based on surname.")> _
 Public Function FindNumbers(ByVal Surname As String) As String()
   Return GetDetails(Surname)
 End Function
```

As the preceding code shows, it has also been marked with the `WebMethod` attribute, which tells the compiler to include its details in the WSDL file mentioned previously. An optional description is provided, which can be used by a client to provide help to the user; we will see this description appear in the automatic test page that we use shortly. The web method uses a helper function, `GetDetails`, to retrieve the data. The signature of `GetDetails` is shown in the following:

```
Private Function GetDetails(ByVal Surname As String) As String()
```

`GetDetails` is declared as private and does not have the `WebMethod` attribute, so this helper function is invisible to users of the service. When we pass a string to the method, it returns an array of strings detailing the forename, surname, and phone number of any matching entries in the database. Each individual item in the array is of the form `forenames|surname|telephone` with a pipe (|) character separating the columns. It may appear to be more natural to use a two-dimensional array for this type of data, but multi-dimensional arrays cannot be handled automatically by .NET Web services. Using them or returning the results as an array of objects would involve an extra layer of complexity, which would both distract from the study and make the service inaccessible from some clients. Next comes two lines, which use the `GetAppSetting` function to initialize the connection details for the database and the name of the query used for searches:

```
Dim sConnection As String = GetAppSetting("ConnString")
Dim sQuery As String = GetAppSetting("FindQuery")
```

The `GetAppSetting` function is again private with no extra attributes, as shown in the following:

```
Private Function GetAppSetting(ByVal Key As String) As String
  Dim sAppSetting As String = _
    ConfigurationSettings.AppSettings(Key)
  Return sAppSetting
End Function
```

This function simply looks up a value in the `web.config` file associated with this service. The `web.config` is another XML file that resides in the `PhoneBook` folder. The use of XML as configuration files has replaced the old style INI files in the .NET Framework. The advantage of these new style configuration files is that they are easier to create and read, and that they offer the advantage of being able to use XML's hierarchic nature to provide more detailed and context-sensitive information. You'll need to create the following file, named `web.config` and store it alongside the two code files created so far:

```
<?xml version="1.0" encoding="utf-8" ?>
<configuration>
  <appSettings>
        <add key="ConnString"
value="Provider=Microsoft.Jet.OLEDB.4.0; Data
 Source=C:\InetPub\WWWroot\PhoneBook\PhoneBook.mdb" />
        <add key="FindQuery" value="qryPhoneFromSurname" />
  </appSettings>
  <system.web>
    <compilation defaultLanguage="vb" debug="true" />
    <customErrors mode="RemoteOnly" />
    <authentication mode="Windows" />
    <authorization>
        <allow users="*" />
    </authorization>
    <trace enabled="false" requestLimit="10" pageOutput="false"
 traceMode="SortByTime" localOnly="true" />
        <sessionState
            mode="InProc"
            stateConnectionString="tcpip=127.0.0.1:42424"
     sqlConnectionString="data source=127.0.0.1;Trusted_Connection=yes"
            cookieless="false"
            timeout="20"
    />
    <globalization requestEncoding="utf-8" responseEncoding="utf-8" />
  </system.web>
</configuration>
```

You may need to change the path to the database if you have created the Web Service folder in a different location than the default or if you have put it in a separate location altogether. A version of this file is available with the code download, and this one has comments included that explain what the sections are for and what choices are available for each one.

As can be seen, the custom settings have been added to the appSettings block underneath the root element configuration. The two entries simply consist of a key and a value. One contains the connection string details, the other the name of the query or stored procedure used to find the appropriate rows in the table. The advantage of this approach is that you can change from Access to a more robust database, such as SQL Server, simply by altering the config file. You don't need to do any recompilation or even restart the web server for the changes to take effect.

Returning to the GetDetails function, the next few lines connect to our database and initialize the OleDbCommand that is used to perform our query.

```
Dim oConn As New OleDbConnection(sConnection)
Dim cmd As New OleDbCommand(sQuery, oConn)
cmd.CommandType = CommandType.StoredProcedure
```

Now the parameter object is created, its value is set to the search string, and the connection is opened:

```
Dim oParam As OleDbParameter = _
        cmd.Parameters.Add("Surname", OleDbType.VarChar, 20)
oParam.Value = Surname
oConn.Open()
```

The next step is to use an OleDbDataReader to collect the results of executing the command. Follow this by looping through the rows returned and add them to an array, as follows:

```
Dim oDR As OleDbDataReader = cmd.ExecuteReader()
Dim arrResult As String()
Dim iRows As Long = -1
Do While oDR.Read()
    iRows = iRows + 1
    ReDim Preserve arrResult(iRows)
    arrResult(iRows) = oDR.GetString(0) & _
                    "|" & oDR.GetString(1) & _
                    "|" & oDR.GetString(2)
Loop
```

The function finishes by tidying up and returning the populated array, as follows:

```
oDR.Close()
oConn.Close()
Return arrResult
```

At this stage we have all the ingredients for the Web Service. There is one more step to complete before testing, however. We need to compile PhoneLookup.asmx.vb into PhoneBook.dll using the Visual Basic compiler that comes with .NET Framework.

Create a new folder named bin directly underneath the PhoneBook directory. Then, open a command window and navigate to the PhoneBook folder. Enter the following, rather ugly-looking, statement:

```
vbc /t:library /r:System.dll /r:System.Web.dll /r:System.Web.Services.dll
 /r:System.Data.dll PhoneLookup.asmx.vb /rootnamespace:PhoneBook
 /out:bin\PhoneBook.dll
```

If the `vbc` executable does not lie in your environment path, then you will need to prefix this command with its full path. This would normally be `C:\WINDOWS\Microsoft.NET\Framework\ <version>\` where the last part is the latest version number of .NET on the machine. A batch file containing this code is included with the download for this chapter.

This command tells the compiler to do the following:

- Create a DLL rather than an EXE (`t:library`)
- Include a number of system assemblies (these are indicated by the `r:` switches)
- Call the output file `PhoneBook.dll`
- Include the class in the `PhoneBook` namespace

Now that we have completed this last step, the Web service is ready for its first outing. Enter the following URL into your browser: `http://localhost/phonebook/phonelookup.asmx`.

On this first visit you will probably notice a delay while ASP.NET creates the necessary classes. After this, provided you don't change the source files, it will reuse them, and things should be quicker.

You should be greeted with a page similar to the one shown in Figure 20-3.

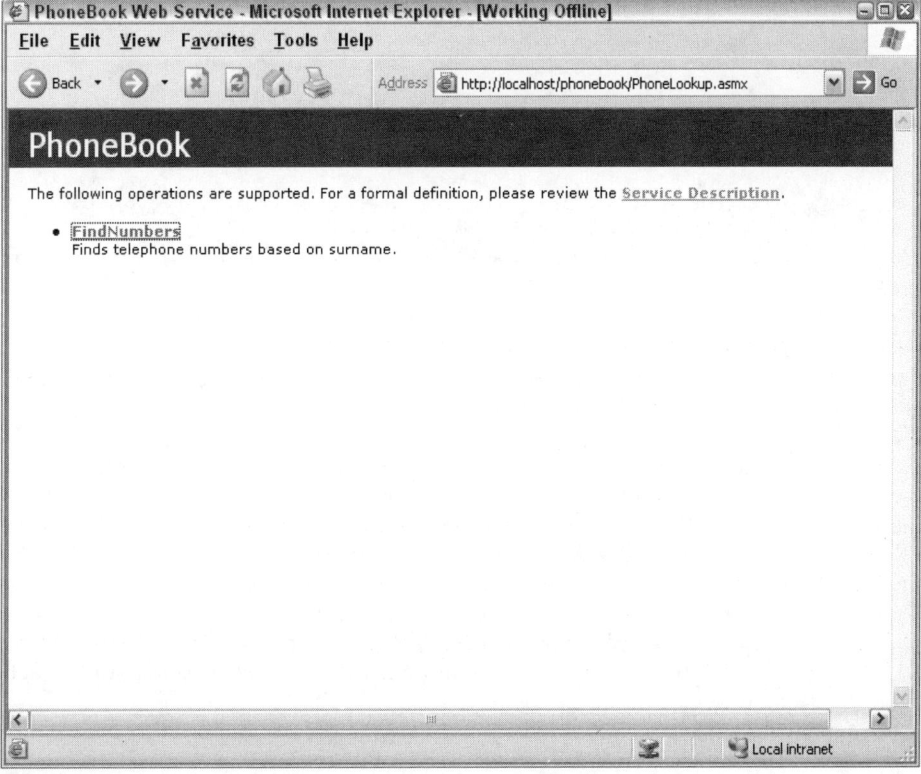

Figure 20-3

There is only the one public method shown, along with the description from the `WebMethod` attribute that was mentioned previously. The Service Description link leads to the WSDL document discussed earlier. Click the FindNumbers link, and you'll see the page displayed in Figure 20-4.

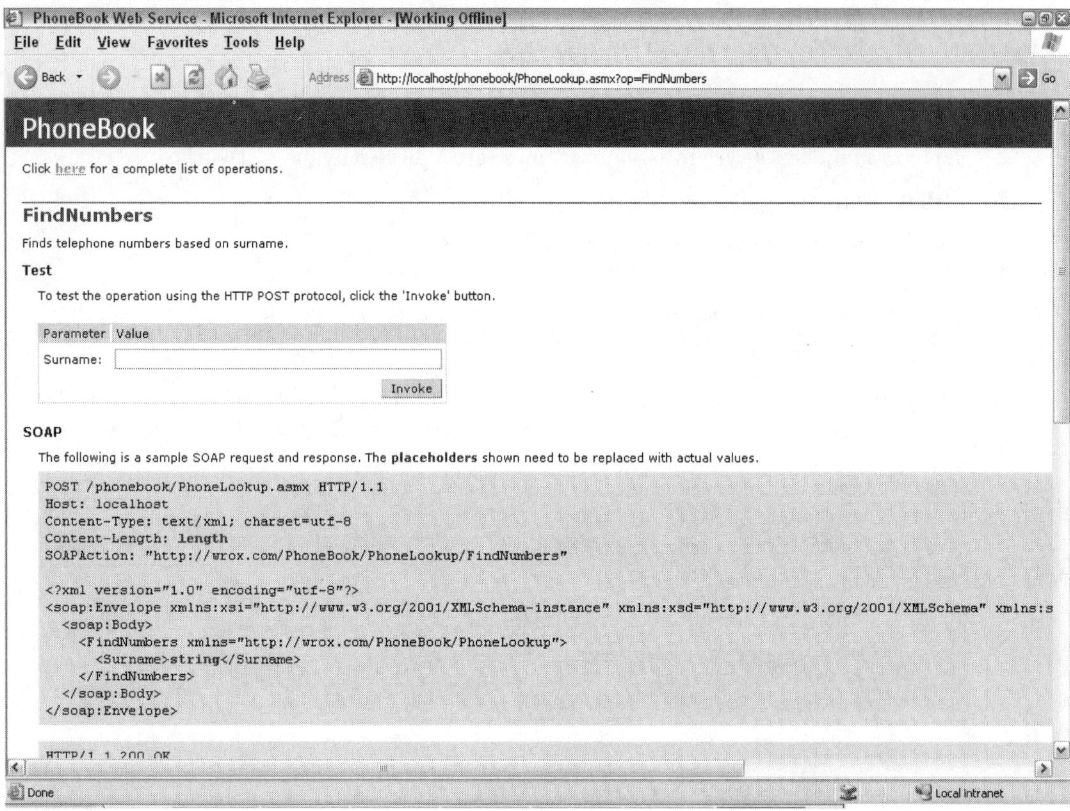

Figure 20-4

This is a complete test harness for the `FindNumbers` web method. Both this page and the previous are made possible because we both inherited our class from `System.Web.Services.WebService` and because of the attributes we attached to the code.

There are two examples on the page of how to invoke the `FindNumbers` method, one uses the `POST` protocol whereby the function arguments are sent as name-value pairs in the request header and the response is a simple XML document. This is the method used in the test page when the Invoke button is clicked. The other technique is using SOAP whereby the request is wrapped in a more complex XML document and the response is returned in a similarly structured manner. You can get the full story on SOAP by reading Chapter 15. The SOAP method has the advantage of being able to cope with more complicated arguments being passed in the request as well as giving more detailed error information should things go awry on the server. The two clients demonstrated later on in this study will both use the SOAP technique.

For a basic test of the service, enter a string into the page's text box. Remember that the method matches using SQL's LIKE comparison operator, so a percent sign (%) needs to be appended to the string for wild card matching. Using the test data shown earlier in Figure 20-1, an XML document will be returned as seen in Figure 20-5.

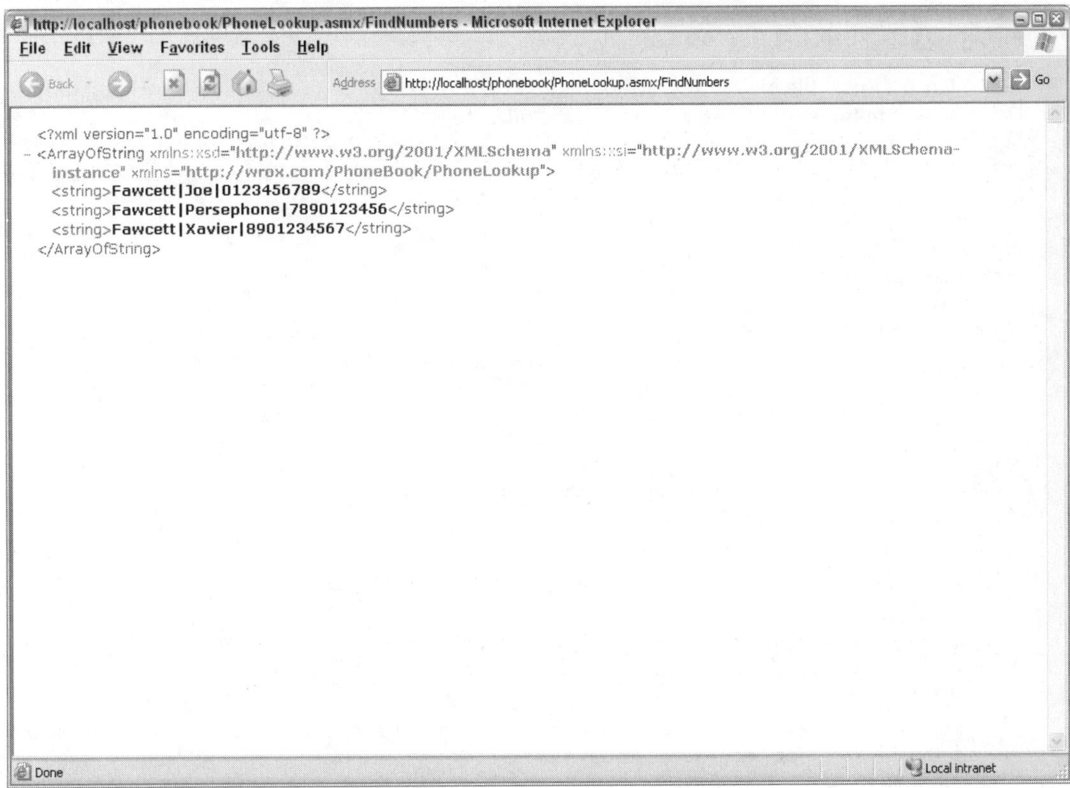

Figure 20-5

Consuming the Web Service

There are a number of ways to consume or use a Web service, and two very different clients will be constructed in the following sections. The first is a web page using standard HTML, JavaScript, and Microsoft's XML Core Services library—this is a set of COM classes that can be used to parse and transform XML as well as send and receive data to and from a web server. The other will be written in C#, Microsoft's .NET-compliant language. This example will show how to utilize virtually any service quickly and without having to worry about the low-level protocols.

The Web Page Client

Again we will rely on basic tools—our trusty text editor will suffice. We also need to ensure that we have a recent version of what Microsoft now terms *XML Core Services;* currently this is version 4.0, but for this article, version 3.0 will also work. Version 4.0 is currently available without cost from `msdn.com/xml` and includes an option to install an extensive Help file. If you are unable to install this version, 3.0 comes as standard with Windows XP and is also installed by many other applications, so chances are that it is available on your machine already. Version 3 is slightly slower and less featured than version 4 and does have some quirky features, but it will be more than able to cope with our needs.

Try It Out Creating a Web Client

1. Create a new file in your text editor named `PhoneBookClient.htm`, and for testing purposes, save it in the `PhoneBook` folder with the other files.
2. Now enter the following code:

```
<html>
<head>
<title>PhoneBook Web Client</title>
<script type="text/javascript">

var SERVICE_URL = "http://localhost/phonebook/phonelookup.asmx";

var PARSER_ID = "Msxml2.DomDocument.4.0";
var REQUESTER_ID = "Msxml2.XmlHttp.4.0"

//var PARSER_ID = "Msxml2.DomDocument.3.0";
//var REQUESTER_ID = "Msxml2.XmlHttp.3.0

"
function doSoapRequest(Surname)
{
  var sTemplateXml = '<soap:Envelope '
                   + 'xmlns:xsi="http://www.w3.org/2001/XMLSchema-instance" '
                   + 'xmlns:xsd="http://www.w3.org/2001/XMLSchema" '
                   + 'xmlns:soap="http://schemas.xmlsoap.org/soap/envelope/">'
                   + '<soap:Body>'
                   + '<FindNumbers xmlns="http://wrox.com/PhoneBook/
                      PhoneLookup">'
                   + '<Surname/></FindNumbers></soap:Body></soap:Envelope>';

  var oDom = new ActiveXObject(PARSER_ID);
  oDom.setProperty("SelectionLanguage", "XPath");
  var oHttpReq = new ActiveXObject(REQUESTER_ID);
  var bLoaded = oDom.loadXML(sTemplateXml);
  if (bLoaded)
  {
    var sNamespaces = "xmlns:soap='http://schemas.xmlsoap.org/soap/envelope/' "
                    + "xmlns:myNS='http://wrox.com/PhoneBook/PhoneLookup'";
    oDom.setProperty("SelectionNamespaces", sNamespaces);
    var sXPath = "/soap:Envelope/soap:Body/myNS:FindNumbers/myNS:Surname";
    var oParameterNode = oDom.selectSingleNode(sXPath);
    oParameterNode.text = Surname + "%";
    oHttpReq.open("POST", SERVICE_URL, false);
    var sActionHeader = "http://wrox.com/PhoneBook/PhoneLookup/FindNumbers";
    oHttpReq.setRequestHeader("SOAPAction", sActionHeader);
    oHttpReq.send(oDom);
    showMessage("request", oDom.xml);
    if (oHttpReq.status == 200)
```

```
    {
      if (oHttpReq.responseXML)
      {
        showMessage("response", oHttpReq.responseXML.xml);
        oDom.load(oHttpReq.responseXML);
        showResult(oDom);
      }
      else
      {
        showMessage("response", oHttpReq.getAllResponseHeaders() + "\n"
                                  + oHttpReq.responseText);
      }
    }
    else
    {
      showMessage("response", oHttpReq.status + " - " + oHttpReq.statusText);
    }
  }
  else
  {
    showMessage("response", oDom.parseError.reason + "\n"
                              + oDom.parseError.srcText);
  }
  oHttpReq = null;
  oDom = null;
}

function showMessage(Type, Text)
{
  var sId = (Type.toLowerCase() == "request" ? "txtRequest" : "txtResponse");
  var oText = document.getElementById(sId);
  oText.value = Text;
}

function parseResult(Text)
{
  var arrDetails = Text.split("|");
  return arrDetails[0] + ", " + arrDetails[1] + " - " + arrDetails[2] +
"<br>";
}

function showResult(Dom)
{
  var oDiv = document.getElementById("divNumbers");
  var sXPath = "/soap:Envelope/soap:Body/myNS:FindNumbersResponse/"
             + "myNS:FindNumbersResult/myNS:string";
  var colNodes = Dom.selectNodes(sXPath);
  var iResultCount = colNodes.length;
  var sResult = "";
  if (iResultCount > 0)
  {
    for (var i = 0; i < iResultCount; i++)
    {
      var oResultNode = colNodes[i];
```

```
        sResult += parseResult(oResultNode.text);
      }
    }
    else
    {
      sResult = "No numbers found.";
    }
    oDiv.innerHTML = sResult;
}

function init()
{
  document.getElementById("txtSurname").focus();
}

</script>
</head>

<body onload="init();">
<input type="text" id="txtSurname" size="20" maxlength="20">  
<input type="button" value="Send Request"
 onclick="doSoapRequest(txtSurname.value);"><br>
<div id="divNumbers" style="position: relative;border: 3px outset #c0c0c0;
 height: 150px; width: 80%;"></div>
<table cols="2" width="100%">
<tbody>
<tr><th>Request</th><th>Response</th></tr>
<tr><td><textarea id="txtRequest" cols="50" rows="25"></textarea></td>
<td><textarea id="txtResponse" cols="50" rows="25"></textarea></td></tr>
</tbody>
</table>
</body>
</html>
```

3. At the top of the file you will see the following code:

```
var SERVICE_URL = "http://localhost/phonebook/phonelookup.asmx";

var PARSER_ID = "Msxml2.DomDocument.4.0";
var REQUESTER_ID = "Msxml2.XmlHttp.4.0"

//var PARSER_ID = "Msxml2.DomDocument.3.0";
//var REQUESTER_ID = "Msxml2.XmlHttp.3.0"
```

You may need to change the `SERVICE_URL` variable, and if you only have the version 3.0 parser installed, you must remove the comment flags, `//`, from the two lines specifying the `PARSER_ID` and the `REQUESTER_ID` and move them to the lines above, like this:

```
//var PARSER_ID = "Msxml2.DomDocument.4.0";
//var REQUESTER_ID = "Msxml2.XmlHttp.4.0"

var PARSER_ID = "Msxml2.DomDocument.3.0";
var REQUESTER_ID = "Msxml2.XmlHttp.3.0"
```

4. Open the file by navigating to `http://localhost/phonebook/phonebookclient.htm` in your browser. Accept any warnings that may appear about allowing ActiveX controls. Figure 20-6 shows the resulting page.

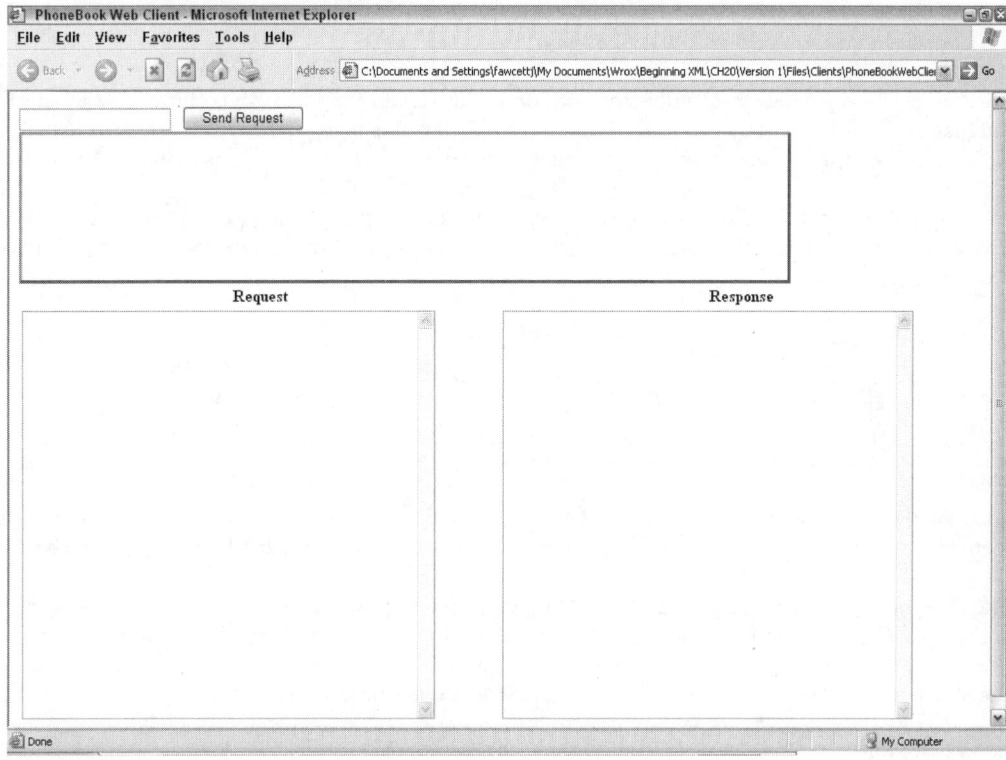

Figure 20-6

5. Test the page by typing **D%** into the text box and clicking Send Request. The actual XML sent to the service is displayed in the left-hand text area. The service's response is shown in the text area labeled Response.If all is well, then any matches are displayed in the pane at the top of the page.

How It Works

Although the page seems to contain masses of JavaScript, most of this is to do with the user interface. The bulk of the work is done by the `doSoapRequest` function as follows:

```
function doSoapRequest(Surname)
{
  var sTemplateXml = '<soap:Envelope '
                   + 'xmlns:xsi="http://www.w3.org/2001/XMLSchema-instance" '
                   + 'xmlns:xsd="http://www.w3.org/2001/XMLSchema" '
                   + 'xmlns:soap="http://schemas.xmlsoap.org/soap/envelope/">'
                   + '<soap:Body>'
                   + '<FindNumbers xmlns="http://wrox.com/PhoneBook/
                     PhoneLookup">'
                   + '<Surname/></FindNumbers></soap:Body></soap:Envelope>';
```

sTemplateXml contains the XML needed for a basic SOAP request to the FindNumbers web method. The XML string was simply copied from the page shown in Figure 20-4 except the Surname element has had its contents removed.

```
var oDom = new ActiveXObject(PARSER_ID);
oDom.setProperty("SelectionLanguage", "XPath");
```

The two preceding lines create a new instance of the XML parser, and XPath is chosen as the selection language. This is not strictly necessary if the version 4 parser is being used, but is essential for version 3 because by default version 3 uses an older dialect called XSLPattern, which has a different syntax.

Next, an instance of Msxml2.XmlHttp is created. This is confusingly named because it can be used to access any form of data delivered by a web server, not just XML. It can also send data in the form of name-value pairs or XML.

```
var oHttpReq = new ActiveXObject(REQUESTER_ID);
```

We now load the SOAP request template into the parser as shown in the following:

```
var bLoaded = oDom.loadXML(sTemplateXml);
```

A boolean is returned by this function and stored in the bLoaded variable. True means the XML is well formed, and false indicates an error whose details can be accessed via the parseError object.

The first thing to do is to let the parser know in which namespaces the nodes in the document are contained. When searching the document, matches are made on the fully qualified name, not just the prefix and the local name. You may have noticed that only two namespaces are referred to as opposed to the four declared in the document. This is because we do not need to refer to any nodes that lie in the *http://www.w3.org/2001/XMLSchema-instance* or *http://www.w3.org/2001/XMLSchema* namespaces.

We must also associate a prefix with the http://wrox.com/PhoneBook/PhoneLookup namespace. Although this is a default namespace in the SOAP request, the current version of XPath does not support these, and a dummy prefix (in this case we use myNS) is allocated to enable node selection, as shown in the following:

```
if (bLoaded)
{
  var sNamespaces = "xmlns:soap='http://schemas.xmlsoap.org/soap/envelope/' "
                  + "xmlns:myNS='http://wrox.com/PhoneBook/PhoneLookup'";
  oDom.setProperty("SelectionNamespaces", sNamespaces);
```

An XPath expression is now constructed which will access the node containing the argument for FindNumbers, and the node is retrieved via selectSingleNode. The text value of the node is set to the value entered in the text box txtSurname, and a percent sign (%) is appended to enable wild card matching

```
var sXPath = "/soap:Envelope/soap:Body/myNS:FindNumbers/myNS:Surname";
var oParameterNode = oDom.selectSingleNode(sXPath);
oParameterNode.text = Surname + "%";
```

The open method prepares the request object by specifying the method, in this case POST, whereby data is passed in the HTTP header. The URL of the service is also specified, and the third parameter specifies a boolean value indicating whether or not to proceed with any further code immediately after sending the request or to wait for a response from the server. In this case, false instructs the code to wait as follows:

```
oHttpReq.open("POST", SERVICE_URL, false);
```

ASP.NET requires that a custom request header be added to the SOAP request, which matches the soapAction attribute in the service's WSDL document. This is added using the setRequestHeader method, and then the XML document is posted to the server using the send method.

```
var sActionHeader = "http://wrox.com/PhoneBook/PhoneLookup/FindNumbers";
oHttpReq.setRequestHeader("SOAPAction", sActionHeader);
oHttpReq.send(oDom);
```

Shown in the following code, showMessage is a simple helper function that shows text in one of the text areas on the page:

```
showMessage("request", oDom.xml);
```

When a web server responds to a request, it sends back a status code. 200 means all is well; others include the famous 404 for object not found and 500 for an internal server error, often a memory exception while processing.

```
if (oHttpReq.status == 200)
{
```

If the request reaches the service, then a SOAP response will be returned in the responseXML property. Failing this, the responseBody is used to provide an error description along with any other headers that may have been returned. These are accessed via the getAllResponseHeaders method as shown in the following:

```
if (oHttpReq.responseXML)
{
  showMessage("response", oHttpReq.responseXML.xml);
  oDom.load(oHttpReq.responseXML);
  showResult(oDom);
}
else
{
  showMessage("response", oHttpReq.getAllResponseHeaders() + "\n"
                         + oHttpReq.responseText);
}
```

If the status property is not equal to 200, the status and statusDescription are shown to the user as follows:

```
else
{
  showMessage("response", oHttpReq.status + " - "
                         + oHttpReq.statusText);
}
```

If bLoaded is false because the XML request was malformed, the reason is displayed in the right-hand panel in this case as follows:

```
else
{
  showMessage("response", oDom.parseError.reason +
 "\n" + oDom.parseError.srcText);
}
```

The showResult method parses the responseXML. You may be wondering why—as this contains the raw SOAP XML response, it wasn't passed directly to this method but was first loaded into the DomDocument used for the request. The reason is that we have not specified the namespaces used in the response as we did by applying setProperty("SelectionNamespaces") on the request. By loading the XML into the original parser, we can reuse the prefixes all ready allocated.

The showResult function first obtains a reference to the div used for output. An XPath statement pointing to the part of the response document where the results are held is passed to the selectNodes method of the DomDocument. Any matching nodes are stored in the colNodes variable, as shown in the following:

```
function showResult(Dom)
{
  var oDiv = document.getElementById("divNumbers");
  var sXPath = "/soap:Envelope/soap:Body/myNS:FindNumbersResponse/"
             + "myNS:FindNumbersResult/myNS:string";
  var colNodes = Dom.selectNodes(sXPath);
```

The number of nodes found is stored in iResultCount. If this is greater than zero, then at least one match was found. By looping through the node list, we can process the individual nodes and format their text values using the parseResult function as shown in the following:

```
var iResultCount = colNodes.length;
var sResult = "";
if (iResultCount > 0)
{
  for (var i = 0; i < iResultCount; i++)
  {
    var oResultNode = colNodes[i];
    sResult += parseResult(oResultNode.text);
  }
}
```

parseResult simply uses the JavaScript split method to remove the pipe symbols and return each component as an array element. Some punctuation is then added for readability, as shown in the following:

```
function parseResult(Text)
{
  var arrDetails = Text.split("|");
  return arrDetails[0] + ", " + arrDetails[1] + " - " + arrDetails[2] +
  "<br>";
}
```

If there are no nodes found, then a simple message is displayed as shown in the following:

```
    else
    {
      sResult = "No numbers found.";
    }
      oDiv.innerHTML = sResult;
  }
```

The .NET Client

Our second client will be built using C#. It will have a simple console application rather than being forms-based. It will accept the search parameter from the command line and display the results in the same format as the web client.

Try It Out Creating a C# Client

There are two stages involved in creating the C# client; first, creating a proxy class to communicate with the Web service, and second, creating a user interface that takes advantage of the proxy and can both receive input from and display data to the user.

> **In this context a proxy class means a class that stands in for another one. Instead of having to deal directly with the Web Service and having to manipulate SOAP requests and responses directly as we did with the web client, we let the proxy deal with all the internals. All we need to do is to pass it the relevant input and read the returned values.**

Our first task is to create a *proxy class*. This will appear as a real object to the application and will behave in exactly the same way as if the `PhoneBook` class were simply residing on the client machine and accessing a local database. In reality, the method calls will be passed on to the Web service, and the response returned to the client.

1. Create a new folder named `PhoneBookCsClient` on your machine. Open a command prompt and navigate to this folder.

   We will be using the WSDL.exe tool, which comes with the .NET Framework SDK. This can create `proxy` classes in a number of .NET languages based on a WSDL file or by referring to the `asmx` directly.

   > *There is a small problem using `WSDL.exe` in that its location depends on what programs you have on your machine and in what order they were installed. It is sometimes under `C:\program files\microsoft.net\frameworksdk\bin` folder, but if you have Visual Studio, it will be under `c:\Program Files\Microsoft Visual Studio .NET\Common7\Tools\bin` or `c:\Program Files\Microsoft Visual Studio .NET 2003\Common7\Tools\bin`. If the relevant folder is not in your environment, PATH variable then you will need to specify the complete path in the following command.*

2. You can now enter the following on one line:

```
wsdl /n:PhoneBookProxy /out:PhoneBookProxy.cs
 http://localhost/phonebook/PhoneLookup.asmx
```

3. Assuming the Web service is available, `PhoneBookProxy.cs` will be created. We then compile this with the following command, again on one line:

```
csc /t:library /r:System.dll /r:System.Web.dll /r:System.Web.Services.dll
 /r:System.Data.dll /r:System.Xml.dll PhoneBookProxy.cs
```

This should result in `PhoneBookProxy.dll` being created.

4. We can now create a console application that utilizes this assembly. Create a new text file named `PhoneBookClient.cs` and save it in the same folder as the DLL you just created. Enter the following code:

```
using System;
using PhoneBookProxy;

namespace PhoneClient
{
class PhoneBookClient
{
         [STAThread]
         static void Main(string[] args)
         {
           string[] arrNumbers;
           PhoneBook pb = new PhoneBook();
           while (true)
           {
             Console.WriteLine
             ("Enter a partial surname or just press ENTER to exit:");
             string sSurname = Console.ReadLine();
             if (sSurname.Length == 0) break;
             arrNumbers = pb.FindNumbers(sSurname + "%");
             if (arrNumbers != null)
             {
               int iMatchCount = arrNumbers.Length;
               Console.WriteLine("{0} matches found:\n", iMatchCount);
               for (int i = 0; i < iMatchCount; i++)
               {
                 Console.WriteLine("{0}", parseResult(arrNumbers[i]));
               }
               Console.WriteLine();
             }
             else
             {
               Console.WriteLine("No numbers found.");
             }
           }
           pb = null;
         }
```

```
    static private string parseResult(string Text)
    {
      char[] arrDelimiters = new char[]{'|'};
      string[] arrDetails = Text.Split(arrDelimiters);
      return arrDetails[0] + ", " + arrDetails[1] + " - " + arrDetails[2];
    }
  }
}
```

5. Compile to an EXE using the command-line compiler, `csc`, once more as follows:

```
csc /t:exe /r:PhoneBookProxy.dll PhoneBookClient.cs
```

   The folder should contain `PhoneBookClient.exe`.

6. After running the file by entering `PhoneBookClient.exe`, the user is prompted to enter a partial surname. Results appear as shown in Figure 20-7.

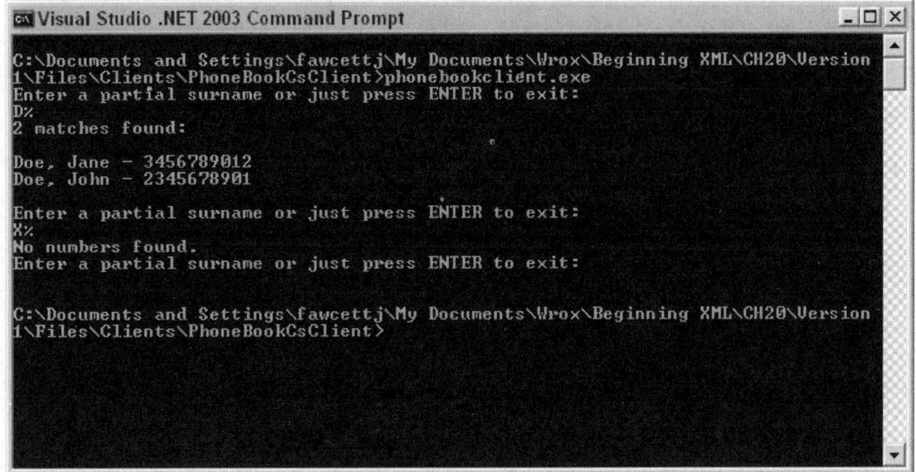

Figure 20-7

How It Works

First of all use two using statements so that classes in the `System` and `PhoneBookProxy` namespaces can be referenced without fully qualified names:

```
using System;
using PhoneBookProxy;
```

In the `Main` function (the entry point to the application), a new instance of `PhoneBook` is created as shown in the following:

```
PhoneBook pb = new PhoneBook();
```

Then, an infinite loop is set up using `while (true)`, and after outputting a message, the client waits for input, which is read into `sSurname`:

```
Console.WriteLine
            ("Enter a partial surname or just press ENTER to exit:");
string sSurname = Console.ReadLine();
```

If the entry is empty, then the `break` statement jumps to end of the loop, and the application closes after setting the reference to the `PhoneBookProxy` to null, as shown in the following:

```
if (sSurname.Length == 0) break;
```

Otherwise, the returned array is iterated again, and each item is displayed in a virtually identical manner to that used in the web page client, as follows:

```
if (arrNumbers != null)
{
  int iMatchCount = arrNumbers.Length;
  Console.WriteLine("{0} matches found:\n", iMatchCount);
  for (int i = 0; i < iMatchCount; i++)
  {
    Console.WriteLine("{0}", parseResult(arrNumbers[i]));
  }
  Console.WriteLine();
}
```

The slight difference is that if no matches are found, then null is returned rather than an empty array.

What Next?

There are a number of other clients that could take advantage of this service with perhaps the most obvious one being a WAP client running on a mobile phone. This would use Wireless Markup Language (WML), an XML version of HTML that is suited to clients with limited screen sizes and low bandwidth. As sending a full SOAP request from this sort of device is going to be difficult, it is likely that just the raw search string would be passed to a proxy client running on a server, and this client would make a SOAP request to the Web service. The results could be displayed in such a fashion as to allow the user to call one of the telephone numbers returned.

Another possibility would be to combine the service with a voice-operated telephone system (perhaps written using VoiceXML, a language used to specify prompts) that would accept voice responses and interface with external systems. You can learn more by visiting `http://www.voiceXML.org`.

Summary

In this chapter we examined some of the common techniques used to create and utilize a .NET XML Web service. We started by creating a simple but useful service that retrieved information from a database after accepting a user specified parameter. We saw how to decouple the database from the code, implementing the service by storing configuration details in the `web.config` file. This enables us to change the database used without rewriting and recompiling any code.

Next, we created two clients that took advantage of the service, the first was written in JavaScript and exposed all the underlying details right down to direct manipulation of the underlying XML SOAP request and response. The second client was written at a higher level where the low-level details were handled for us by an automatically generated proxy class.

The following list summarizes the salient points of working with .NET Web services:

- It's perfectly possible to create a Web service using freely available tools. This way the underlying structure is better understood.
- A .NET Web service needs to be marked with the `WebService` attribute.
- Any methods that are to be exposed need the `WebMethod` attribute.
- Clients can use a Web service irrespective of their own development language or that of the service.
- There is no need for the client to parse actual XML. `Proxy` classes can hide the underlying details.

Case Study 2: XML and PHP

PHP and XML have evolved in parallel. Riding the wave of the web, XML has become a standard description protocol for data structures while PHP has become a best-of-breed object-oriented programming (or scripting) language for building web applications. Current PHP support for XML uses the Expat library from James Clark (`jclark.com`). Expat is a library of C code that is available under the MIT license to better enable parsing of XML. As of this writing, PHP version 5 is in testing and will be incorporating support for the latest of XML (as found in `libxml2`).

> **PHP stands for PHP: Hypertext Preprocessor (a recursive acronym in the tradition of GNU, which stands for GNU's Not Unix). From `http://www.php.net/history`: "PHP succeeds an older product, named PHP/FI. PHP/FI was created by Rasmus Lerdorf in 1995, initially as a simple set of Perl scripts for tracking accesses to his online resume. He named this set of scripts 'Personal Home Page Tools.' As more functionality was required, Rasmus wrote a much larger C implementation, which was able to communicate with databases, and enabled users to develop simple dynamic web applications. Rasmus chose to release the source code for PHP/FI for everybody to see, so that anybody can use it, as well as fix bugs in it and improve the code." PHP was renamed but not reinitiated in a new release in 1997. For more, go to the official PHP website at `http://www.php.net/`.**

Generally used for the dynamic generation of HTML to be shipped to remote web browsers, PHP can be run from the Apache server on Linux, from other servers such as IIS from Microsoft, or even in a stand-alone batch mode. Capable of running under Windows, Linux, or a number of other operating systems, PHP is available (in source as well as in executable form) for these environments as a free download from `http://www.php.net`. PHP is also packaged with many Linux distributions.

PHP generally runs as an interpreted language, which has costs and benefits. Although it may take longer to run than a compiled equivalent, PHP gains extra power in that it has the ability to modify its own code, dynamically name variables, and so on.

Fortunately, those responsible for PHP (contributors who today are working through the Apache Foundation `http://www.apache.org/`) have seen fit to include a plethora of XML capabilities within class libraries readily accessible to the PHP programmer, even beyond what comes with Expat and `libxml2`.

Much of the strength of XML comes from the ways in which its data can be easily transformed, and here PHP becomes a versatile tool providing even more ways to transform XML than are offered through strictly XML-oriented tools (as will be seen in this case study).

The ease of use of a minimal set of PHP is also significant. Though PHP can be used to develop Web services as complicated as Yahoo, it can also be scaled down to use the least complicated application code of all: "Hello World!" (When PHP is interpreted by the server, anything in the source code file (`x.php`) not within a set of PHP tags is considered to be HTML, and therefore sent to the browser as-is!)

Hello World!

In this chapter we provide a minimal set of PHP rules and syntax very useful for setting up all kinds of transformations. Our case study here shows an example of how you can do that. We present incremental examples that ultimately build to an example XML application.

In this chapter we will cover the following:

- Elementary programming in PHP, including how to use PHP control structures, constants, variables, and operators
- How to get data from the browser screen or a file from the server's files or even another web page
- How to build a program in PHP—this is our case study

PHP is a programming language that has similarities to Perl and C++, and PHP provides its users with modularity, object orientation, and relational database connectivity. Most of its capabilities are beyond the scope of this chapter but are described in a number of other good books. In this chapter you will find what you need for a simple real-world application that accepts XML data on insider trading and builds a summary table of it. You will also find references to take you beyond this chapter's scope of discussion.

> **Whether you choose to call it a "scripting" language or a "programming" language depends more on your use and audience than the language itself. You can write simple ad hoc scripts in PHP, and you can also write very complicated programs to handle web- (and even batch-) based data processing in PHP. In this book we will use the more historical term, *programming*.**

Elementary Programming in PHP

Programming in PHP is much like programming in C++ or Perl, with some exceptions that usually serve to make the programming easier. PHP is a block-structured language which generally means that you can write semi-autonomous sections of code that live in their own little worlds if you want them to do so. It is also an object-oriented language, so if that suits your needs, it has those capabilities for you to create objects of varying levels of abstraction. To work with its XML capabilities, some minimal object-oriented work is required.

Objects are defined as *instances* of *classes*. Suppose I own a 1957 Ford Fairlane. It can be considered an instance of the class called 1957 Ford Fairlanes. In object-oriented relationships, we often refer to "is a" relationships to illustrate levels of abstraction. We can also say that a 1957 Ford Fairlane *is a* Ford, that a Ford *is a* car, that a car *is a* vehicle, and that a vehicle *is a* machine. In this case study, however, we will only be dealing with one abstraction level: a parser object that will perform the tasks of parsing our XML. It is also convenient that the PHP program lives within HTML code. You may recall that HTML stands for HyperText Markup Language and is derived from SGML, from which XML is also derived. Because of PHP's residency within HTML, all valid HTML code is also valid PHP code. Active PHP code, if included, can generate further HTML code to be output at the same time as the including HTML.

We mentioned earlier that PHP has the simplest "Hello World!" of all, but if we want to go beyond simply writing things that will be printed per se or merely as HTML, we need to enclose active PHP code within PHP tags: `<?PHP` and `?>`. Within these tags `<?PHP` and `?>` we can use PHP to control what is output, generally to the browser. Outside of these tags, whatever is present is sent directly to the browser to be interpreted as HTML.

> *Depending on the server, it may or may not be permissible to use* `<?` *instead of* `<?PHP`*, so it is not advisable to use this shorthand. Therefore, we will use* `<?PHP` *consistently here. Note that it is not permissible to embed PHP code in XML or XHTML using* `<?`*. An alternative set of tags which we will not illustrate here and is only included for reference is* `<script language="php">` *and* `</script>`*.*

Basic Information about PHP

Here we will give you a sufficient minimal set of PHP syntax to use in creating the program for the case study or other similar programs. There is far more to PHP than we have space to include in this chapter, but this is a good starting point. We will show you the basics of programming and how to use those basics in PHP to work a real example with XML data. (You should have PHP 4.3.6 or later to run all of this sample code.)

Programming Principles

A computer program (or more simply *program* or even *script*) is a sequence of statements to the computer, grouped inside of control structures and written in a specialized language, showing what the computer should do. Control structures identify the sequences, conditions, and iterations in which the statements or other control structures are performed.

The computer that is running a program does what it is told to do. Often this is consternation to those who did not realize that it does exactly what it was told to do, not what they meant it to do. First, the computer usually accepts input from the outside world. It follows directions using constants, making calculations and decisions, and changing variables. It creates output to go back to the outside world. Sometimes these things happen quickly and repeatedly in rapid iteration. Other times these things happen only once. Sometimes things are described in great detail in the program but do not happen at all when the program is run. It depends on what the runtime circumstances are and what you tell the computer to do, which will be based on what is needed as you perceive it and describe it in the programming language, not, of course, necessarily what you want.

Comments

A note about comments is in order: PHP is primarily a programming language, but it allows you to write English (or other language) text into the program to help other people (or even yourself at a later point in time) who will be looking at the program later to understand what is done. Anything enclosed within a slash-asterisk (/*) and an asterisk-slash (*/) is allowed to stand as a comment and is not interpreted as part of the program to be run. Any part of a line following a double-slash (//) or a pound-sign (#) is similarly treated except that the comment ends with the line. Following is an example:

Try It Out Putting Comments in a Program

Let's see what happens when we put comments into a program. You will see that PHP ignores them, even when the human reader does not.

1. You can run this program by first saving it to a file named `trycomments.php`:

```
<?PHP
// This simple program will add 1 to 1 and print 2, in a round-about way.
function phpfunction($something) { // define "phpfunction" for our own use
  return $something+1; # return the value of $something plus 1
/* We are jumping ahead by showing functions, variables and operators,
but don't worry about them yet - we'll cover them in more detail later. */
}

print phpfunction(1); /* this user-created function called phpfunction does
whatever it is that it does to 1 and creates another value. */
?>
```

2. Assuming you have PHP installed, enter `php trycomments.php`.
3. The program will print the number 2.

How It Works

As you can see, PHP ignores everything that we placed in any of the three comment styles that we used. The good news is that the human reader (it could be you) can see the comments and make later decisions about what to change in the program based on the information in the comments.

Control Structures

Every program is composed of control structures, which determine which part of the program has control. In the case of PHP and nearly all other programming languages, the computer starts doing what it is told to do at the beginning of the program and continues sequentially to the end unless it encounters something to change the order of command execution.

Sequences and Compound Statements

We call our first control structure a *sequence*, and the sequence's *statement*—the basic element of the sequence—typically instructs the computer to do something, such as make an assignment to a variable, perform a calculation as determined by an expression, or call a function. Statements can be grouped as compound statements and treated as one unit if enclosed by curly braces `{...}`. Each statement ends with a semicolon (`;`), a closing brace of a compound statement (`}`), or a closing tag (`?>`). Expressions will be described a little later in this chapter.

A statement can be an assignment of a variable, a call to a function, or any of a set of permissible commands, some of which we will discuss later. For now let's use a variable called `$x`. To set variables, we frequently use assignment statements, which are composed of the variable being assigned, the assignment operator (=), and the expression that will be calculated. The result of the expression calculation will be assigned to the first mentioned variable. If we want to set variable `$x` to a value of 1, we would do so as follows:

```
$x = 1;
```

Another example statement would be the following:

```
echo "x = $x"; // Print the value of $x
```

This directs that the value of x be labeled and output. (The `echo` command specifies that the string that follows is output. Strings given within double quotes are further interpreted by PHP and replacement values such as `$x` are substituted in the string. This does not happen for strings given within single quotes.)

Selections

Selection is the second basic control structure and allows a choice to be made. In PHP it can be made with an `if` (*`condition`*) *`statement`* `elseif` *`statement`* `else` *`statement`*. Selection is also made implicitly in some of the iteration control structures that we use.

```
$x = 1;
if ($x == 1) /* This is a comparison, testing to see if the variable $x is
                equal to the value of the literal constant 1. */

$y = 2; /* This is an assignment statement, setting the variable $y to
           the value of the literal constant 2.*/

elseif ($x == 2)

$y = 3; /* This is an assignment statement, setting the variable $y to
            the value of the literal constant 3. */

else

$y = 4;

echo "the result is $y"; /* will print 2. */
```

Iterations

Iteration is the third basic control structure enabling us to repeat a set of statements that we perform (this structure is also commonly called a *loop*). Typically, iteration uses a `while` loop, a `for` loop, or a `foreach` loop. Most iterative structures allow a selection decision to be made that will end the execution when a certain condition is true or false. The `while` and `do...while` loop structures require the programmer to ensure that something tested is different each time the loop is executed so that the loop will eventually terminate. The `for` and `foreach` commands directly allow for something to be changed each time we iterate, and for us to test to see if we are at the end and don't need to repeat anymore.

The `while` loop allows us to repeat a statement (or compound statement within braces: `{...}`) until a condition is no longer true. If the condition is never true, the statement is never executed. The `while` loop has the following format:

```
while (Boolean-expression)  loop-statement;
```

where the following apply:

- *`Boolean-expression`* is evaluated and tested at the beginning of each iteration of the loop; the loop is only executed if the *`Boolean-expression`* is `true`, and if the *`Boolean-expression`* is `false`, the control exits the loop. A *`Boolean-expression`* can only have a value of `true` or `false`.
- The *`loop-statement`* is executed with each iteration, provided that the *`Boolean-expression`* is `true`.

Following is an example of a `while` loop that adds the numbers from 0 to 9:

```
$x = 0; $i = 0; // we will explain these operators (=, <, ++, and +) later.
While ($i < 10) {
  $x = $x + $i;
  $i++;
}
echo "The sum of numbers from 0 to 9 is $x";
```

The `for` loop is commonly used to express a simple iteration in which an index is incremented each time we execute the loop. It consists of the keyword `for` followed by a pair of parentheses enclosing a statement, an expression, and another statement, each separated by semicolons. The first statement is executed to initialize the loop as shown in the following:

```
for (initial-statement; Boolean-expression; repetitive-statement)
loop-statement;
```

where

- *`initial-statement`* is executed at the beginning of the loop.
- *`Boolean-expression`* is evaluated and tested at the beginning of each iteration of the loop; the loop is only executed if the *`Boolean-expression`* is `true`, and if the *`Boolean-expression`* is false, control exits the loop.
- *`repetitive-statement`* is executed at the end of each iteration.
- *`loop-statement`* is executed with each iteration, provided that the *`Boolean-expression`* is true.

Following is an example of the use of a `for` loop to sum the numbers from 0 to 9.

```
$x = 0; // we will explain these operators (=, <, ++, and +) later.
for ($i = 0;   $i    < 10; $i ++) {
 $x = $x + $i;
}
echo "The sum of numbers from 0 to 9 is $x";
```

The `foreach` loop allows us to operate on each value within an array. We name the array and say where we want each key (also known as subscript) and its associated value to go. It has the following format:

```
foreach (array-name as key => value) loop-statement;
```

where

- `array-name` represents an array with values 0 through 9.
- `loop-statement` is executed with each iteration, provided that the `Boolean-expression` is true.

Let's suppose we have the integer values 0 through 9 in an array `$a`. Then we could sum them with `foreach` as follows:

```
$x = 0;
foreach ($a as $key => $value) {
 $x += $value;
}
echo "The sum of numbers from 0 to 9 is $x";
```

You can see how these iteration control structures give us real power in describing repetitive actions for the computer to take.

Constants and Variables

A *constant* represents a value that does not change during the running of the program. Typically, constants are expressed as literal values, such as `5` or `Name and Address:`. (Nonliteral constants are beyond the scope of our discussion.)

A *variable* is a value that is allowed to change over the course of program execution. It can simply be an integer, as we saw with the examples given earlier, or it can be a string or even an abstract type that we define. Variables can be any of a number of types. PHP is generally considered to be a "loosely typed" language, meaning that the programmer does not have to declare what type of variable it is before it is used. A variable in PHP is generally defined implicitly at the point at which it is first used. If it is first used as an integer, then the variable is an integer. If the variable is first used as a string, it is a string, and so on. The type can change with any new assignment.

The most significant restriction on variable naming is that the names of all variables in PHP must begin with a dollar sign (`$`). Following that must be a letter or an underscore character. After that can come an arbitrary string of letters, digits, and ASCII characters from x7F to xFF. (This author discourages you from (1) using a leading underscore because PHP will often use that designation for its own variables and (2) using the ASCII characters from x7F to xFF because they may not all print or display consistently on all output devices or even within interpretive programs.)

The assignment statement is the most basic PHP statement and consists of the following form:

```
variable = expression;
```

A variable can be a base variable, an array, an object, or a resource. A base variable can be any of the following types:

- NULL (represents that the variable has no value)
- Boolean (has a logical value of either `true` or `false`)
- integer (numbers like 1, 5, 2345, 0, or –40 which don't have a fractional part)
- floating-point (or just "floating") number (which can be fractions like 1.5, –2.0, 3.14159, and 6.022×10^23)
- double precision floating-point number (which have a greater range and precision of values than do ordinary floating numbers and can include about 14 decimal digits of precision 3.1415926535898)
- string (has a value of arbitrary text)

Precision depends on the underlying platform, so your mileage may vary slightly with different computers. Additional precision is available in an optional library that can be used with PHP. The "Binary Calculator" (BCMath Arbitrary Precision Mathematics Functions) is packaged with PHP but must be enabled when PHP is configured.

An *array* is a variable (not a base variable) that exists as a collection of variables, each identified by an index which is itself a base variable. (All arrays are also hashes and therefore are by nature sparse—you don't need to declare limits to their sizes as is often required in other programming languages.) Following is an illustration of an array:

```
$a[0]='pig';
$a[1]='cow';
$a[2]='horse';
$a[3]='dog';
for ($i = 1; $i < 4; $i++) echo "a $a[$i] is a mammal<br>";
```

Arrays of arrays can be easily constructed to form multidimensional arrays. In fact, in PHP all you need to do is to reference the subscript and the array is created as shown in the following:

```
$master_report[$issuerCik]['count']++; // counts number of transactions
for issuer
$master_report[$issuerCik]['shares']+=$shares; // totals share volume
for issuer
```

An *object* is a collection of variables and *functions* (also called *methods* in the context of being part of an object class), which work with it, giving it behavior when interacting with other objects, as follows:

- Each object is an instance of a class, which is a category of object definitions.
- You can define a class of variable that takes on new meanings and properties for use in your programs. You can define them, or you can use someone else's definition of them. You can create

instances of them that suit your immediate needs. Creating or using these classes is called *object-oriented programming*.

- Classes can be maintained in hierarchy. (Explanations of inheritance of properties from higher-level classes, as well as other subjects of object-oriented programming, are beyond the scope of this chapter.)
- Some classes are provided for you, such as the XML parser, and you can also define your own.

A *resource* is an abstract variable that allows you to point to a file, a database, etc. (You will see examples of them, but we will not dwell on any further explanation here.)

Operators

In PHP, as in most programming languages, *expressions* show operations on data to create new data. An expression can be a variable or a literal itself, and an expression can also show an operation on one or more expressions. Operators bind expressions together to show the computer which operations to perform.

First, let's look at PHP's *arithmetic* operators:

Operator	Meaning	Type	Example
+	Addition	Dyadic	$a + $b (sum of $a and $b)
–	Subtraction	Dyadic	$a – $b (difference of $a from $b)
*	Multiplication	Dyadic	$a * $b (product of $a and $b)
/	Division	Dyadic	$a / $b (floating quotient of $a divided by $b)
%	Modulus	Dyadic	$a % $b (remainder of $a divided by $b)
++	Incrementation	Monadic	$a++ (The sum of $a and 1 is placed in $a after the variable is used) ++$a (The sum of $a and 1 is placed in $a before the variable is used)
--	Decrementation	Monadic	$a-- (The algebraic sum of $a and –1 is placed in $a after the variable is used) --$a (The algebraic sum of $a and –1 is placed in $a before the variable is used)

These work as you would expect them to work from the rules of arithmetic, as you can see in this example:

```
$master_report[$issuerCik]['dollars']+=$shares*$price; /* add to total dollar
volume for issuer */
```

Casting operators are used to force a type on a variable. They are `(int)`, `(double)`, `(string)`, `(array)`, and `(object)` as shown here to change the way that a variable is interpreted:

```
<?PHP
$x=4.5;
$a=(int)$x;
echo $a; // prints 4
?>
```

The arithmetic operators won't help if you can't use the results, so we have an *assignment* operator: =. Though it may look like it means "equal to," the assignment operator indicates that the resulting value of the expression on the right should be copied to the variable on the left.

We also have some shorthand assignment operators that allow you to combine arithmetic and assignment in one operation. You effectively substitute the current value of the receiving variable into the first operand.

Operator	Meaning	Illustration
+=	Reflexive Addition	"$a+=$b" means "$a = $a + $b"
-=	Reflexive Subtraction	"$a-=$b" means "$a = $a – $b"
*=	Reflexive Multiplication	"$a*=$b" means "$a = $a * $b"
/=	Reflexive Division	"$a/=$b" means "$a = $a / $b"
%=	Reflexive Modulus	"$a%=$b" means "$a = $a % $b"

Comparison operators allow you to compare values and do things differently depending on what your comparison finds. The resulting expression from a comparison operator has a logical (otherwise known as boolean) value.

Operator	Meaning	Illustration
==	Test for Equality	$a == $b true if $a is equal to $b
!=	Test for Inequality	$a != $b true if $a is not equal to $b
<	Test less than	$a < $b true if $a is less than $b
>	Test greater than	$a > $b true if $a is greater than $b
<=	Test less than or equal to	$a <= $b true if $a is less than or equal to $b
>=	Test greater than or equal to	$a >= $b true if $a is greater than or equal to $b

Comparison operators create an expression with a Boolean (or logical) value of either `true` or `false`. They are generally used in `if`, `for`, and `while` statements, but can be used anywhere a Boolean expression is permitted. Boolean valued expressions may be compounded. Boolean operators perform operations on Boolean values and create expressions with Boolean values.

Operator	Name	Illustration
And	And	(\$a = \$b) and (\$c = \$d)
Or	Or	(\$a = \$b) or (\$c = \$d)
Xor	Exclusive or	(\$a = \$b) xor (\$c = \$d)
!	Not (The symbol `!` is sometimes referenced as "bang.")	(\$a = \$b) and !(\$c = \$d)
&&	And	(\$a = \$b) && (\$c = \$d)
||	Or	(\$a = \$b) || (\$c = \$d)

Note when you write out "`and`" instead of using `&&` or "`or`" instead of `||`, they operate at a different level of precedence, being executed after all arithmetic as shown in our later discussion of operator precedence.

PHP has an *error control operator* (`@`) that precedes functions and suppresses output of error messages. Be careful with it because you just might want that error message.

The *execution* operator can be used to provide a command to the operating system. To use it you enclose the operating system command as a string between two backticks as follows:

```
$a=`dir`;
```

Then the string `$a` will have the output of the command `dir`. Need we say that this operator's existence alone is enough reason not to allow insecure web users any access to your PHP code? Supposing a bad guy had the ability to enter PHP code on your system, he could then enter commands in this fashion to delete your files or even to use file transfer protocol to make your system accept a virus or other nasty program.

There are two *string operators*. The concatenation operator (`.`) returns a combined string consisting of a left part with the operand of the left and a right part with the operand of the right. The concatenating assignment operator (`.=`) appends the argument on the right side to the argument on the left side.

```
$a = "hello";
$b .= "world"; // puts "hello world" in $b.
$c = $b . " I want to get off"; // puts "hello world I want to get off" in $c.
```

Operator precedence refers to which operators are executed before which other operators in an expression that does not have the order of execution determined by parentheses, which force whatever is enclosed to be executed before what is outside.

The following is a list of PHP operators with the lowest precedence operators first.

,	^
or	&
xor	== != === !==
and	< <= > >=
print	<<>>
= += –= *= /= .= %= &= |= ^ = ~= <<=>>=	+ –.
? :	* / %
||	! ~ ++ – (int) (double) (string) (array) (object) @
&&	[
|	New

We will now turn to look at some simple ways to get data into our PHP program. One is from the browser screen, and the other is from a file or similar structure. (In this chapter we will not review how to access a relational database, which is out of our scope.)

Getting Data from the Browser Screen

An HTML form, when submitted to a server by a browser, will convey data to PHP by one of the two popular methods, `GET` and `POST`. In some PHP installations the data will arrive already named as a PHP variable, although this process is discouraged as it can lead to security weaknesses because it will allow the user to introduce pre-valued variables into your program that just could change what your program does in a way you didn't expect!

Your user's browser allows extra data to be placed after the URL. When the user places a question mark (`?`) after the URL and then provides *`name=value`* pairs separated by ampersands (`&`), these *`name=value`* pairs become available to your PHP program. The question is how they will be available. Depending on options defaulted by your host, the data could arrive as PHP variables with the names and values given in the *`name=value`* pairs. If this option is not selected, the data is still available, but is in the array `$_GET` subscripted by *`names`*. It is generally agreed that this option should not be selected unless you are running an old PHP program that is too difficult to upgrade.

You can undo the effects of such an option (if you are using a shared server, this option was obviously selected by someone other than yourself). Since variables from the URL line are always subscripts to the array `$_GET` as well as possibly being variables themselves, we can walk through the `$_GET` array and squash them where we find them. Put the following code in the beginning of your PHP program:

```
foreach ($_GET as $key => $value) if (isset($$key)) unset($$key);
```

The double dollar sign `$$key` tells PHP to use the variable whose name is contained in `$key`. `isset` is a function to tell you whether a variable has been set, and `unset` makes the variable go away completely as if it had never existed.

Try It Out — Getting or Posting Data from the Browser

The following is an example that you can skip if you are not familiar with HTML (and go directly to *Getting Data from a File*), but don't be afraid to try it if you want to. In this example, you can write a PHP/HTML form and watch it send data back to you.

1. First, use an editor to enter the following into a file that is accessible to your web server as `mypage.php`:

```
<?PHP
echo "
<HTML>
   <BODY>
      <FORM METHOD=POST> ".$_POST['data']."<BR>
         <INPUT TYPE=TEXT NAME='data' VALUE='".$_POST['data']."'>
         <INPUT TYPE=SUBMIT>
      </FORM>
   </BODY>
</HTML>
 ";
?>
```

2. Second, bring it up on your browser (Figure 21-1 shows a Mozilla browser on a Windows system accessing PHP on a Linux system, but you can use Windows, Linux, or even MacInstosh for either browser, or server, or both).

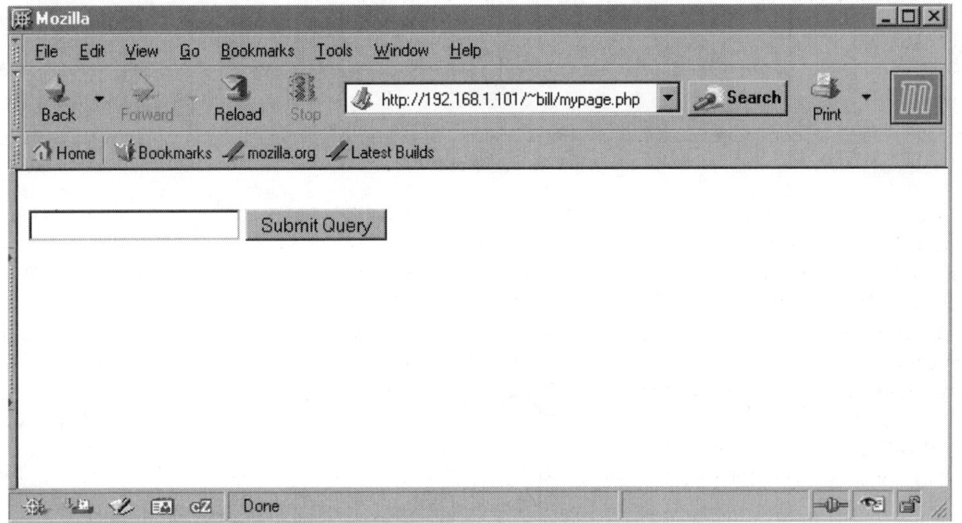

Figure 21-1

3. Now, enter some data that you want to be found by your PHP program as shown in Figure 21-2.
4. Press the Submit button, and you will see that PHP has found the data and is able to do what ever it is told to do with it, in this case just repeat it back to you and put it in the blank as shown in Figure 21-3.

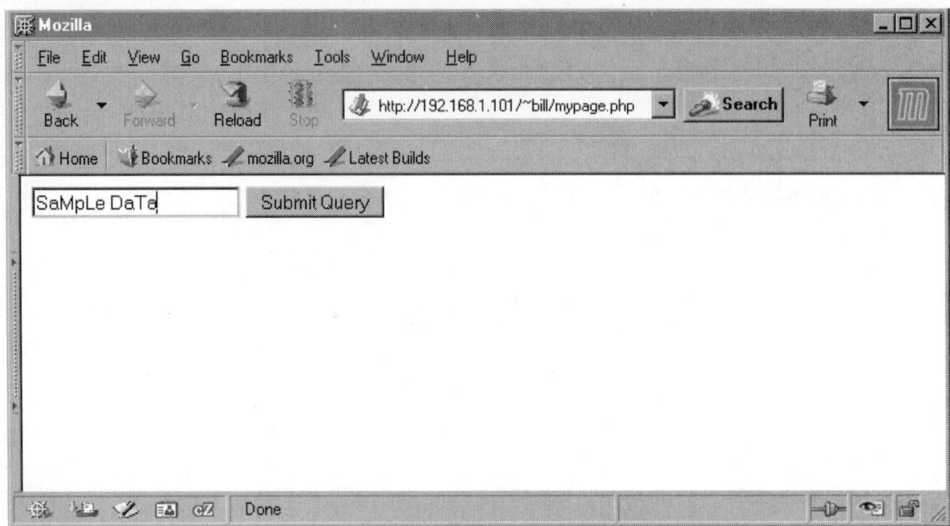

Figure 21-2

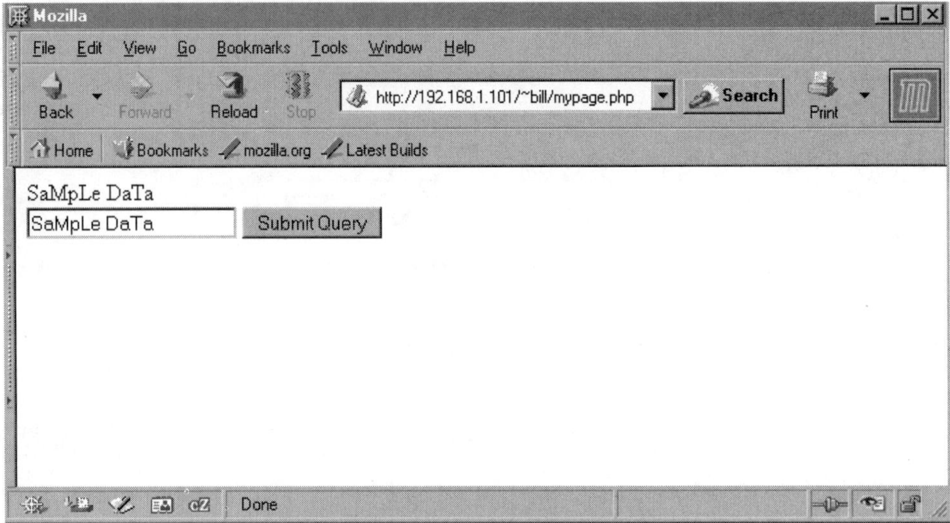

Figure 21-3

5. If we were to substitute the string `GET` for `POST` everywhere it occurs, we would have a similar result, except that the information would be turned around through the URL, and we would see what we typed in the text box duplicated in the URL as well as on the page (as shown in Figure 21-4). This alternate way of sending data can be very useful, but you need to recognize that the user can always change it.

6. Now change the data in the URL only and just hit the Enter key. The data you put in on the URL was thought to come from the form (see Figure 21-5).

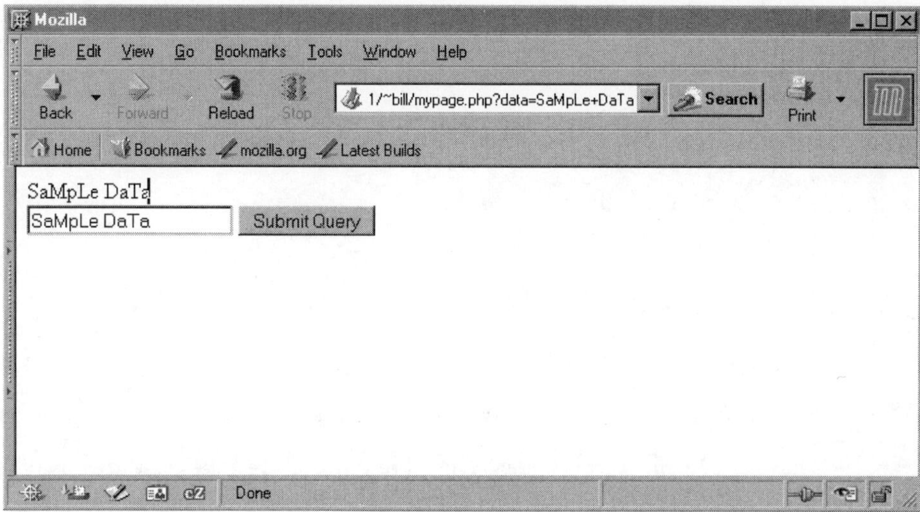

Figure 21-4

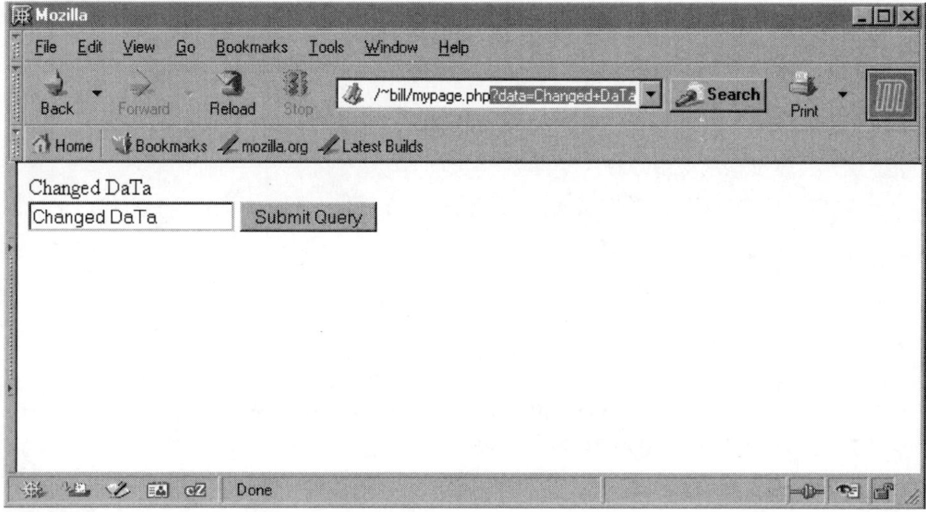

Figure 21-5

How It Works

Data that is entered through forms on the browser is available to PHP. You have noticed that you were able to use the URL to send unanticipated data to PHP. This is why we generally use `POST`ed data, as it is too easy for a user to make changes we did not anticipate when we use `GET`.

Getting Data from a File

PHP gives us some C-like functions for handling files. There are many file functions that are beyond our scope right now but can do good things for you. Most of these will also work with the URLs that point to web pages, so you can treat a remote web page much as you would treat a file. For this minimal set of PHP tools, we will examine `opendir()`, `readdir()`,`closedir()`, `fopen()`, `fgets()`, and `fclose()`.

```
resource opendir(string path)
```

`opendir` returns a handle (`resource`) to be used in a subsequent `readdir()` and `closedir()` call.

```
string readdir(resource dir_handle)
```

`readdir()` returns the name of the next file in the directory.

```
void closedir(resource dir_handle)
```

`closedir()` closes a previously opened directory.

```
resource fopen(string filename, string mode [,int use_include_path])
```

`fopen` opens a file or a URL, in effect binding a named resource (`filename`) to a stream. If the file name begins with `http://`, it is assumed to be a URL unless forbidden by your installation.

The `mode` is a string telling PHP whether you will be reading or writing, and some other things it needs to know. Usually, you will either make the mode `r` or `w` for reading or writing, respectively.

```
string fgets(resource handle [, int length])
```

`fgets()` returns a line up to a linefeed or carriage return from the file pointed to by `handle`.

```
bool fclose (resource handle)
```

`fclose()` closes a file and returns a Boolean value indicating whether the close was successful, `true` on success and `false` on failure.

```
string file_get_contents(string filename [, bool use_include_path [, resource
context]])
```

`file_get_contents()` opens, reads, and closes a file all in one function. (This function is new with PHP 4.3.0.) If you know your XML file will fit in memory and you want to process your data one file at a time, it can save steps, as shown in the following example:

```
$handle = opendir("./edgar_data");

while ($file = readdir ($handle)) {
   if (!strcasecmp($base_name=substr($file,-3),".nc")) {
      if (strlen($base_name)==0) break; /* don't get caught by a file
      merely named ".nc"*/

                  $contents = file_get_contents("./edgar_data/$file");
            // puts entire file into memory
// process file here
   }
}

closedir($handle);
```

Building a Program

The task here is to illustrate PHP by building an example that will read XML from a government database and summarize what is read. (This illustration program requires PHP 4.3.0 or later.) The specific database is the Electronic Data Gathering And Retrieval (EDGAR) system of the United States Securities and Exchange Commission (SEC). People who are considered "insiders" of public corporations must advise the SEC about their stock trades in the companies in which they are "inside." The SEC then makes this information public through its website and use of anonymous file transfer protocol (FTP).

Try It Out Getting Data from the SEC's EDGAR Database

You can set your browser to `ftp://ftp.sec.gov/edgar/Feed/` (see Figure 21-6) and indicate you want to download a file. These metafiles are named for the year, month, and day of their creation (`yyyymmdd.nc.tar.gz`). Be careful, as these metafiles can take some time to download, and the SEC would prefer that you download them after normal business hours. A smaller one recently took three minutes on a cable modem. Some are as big as 120MB and would take about 45 minutes to download over a phone line.

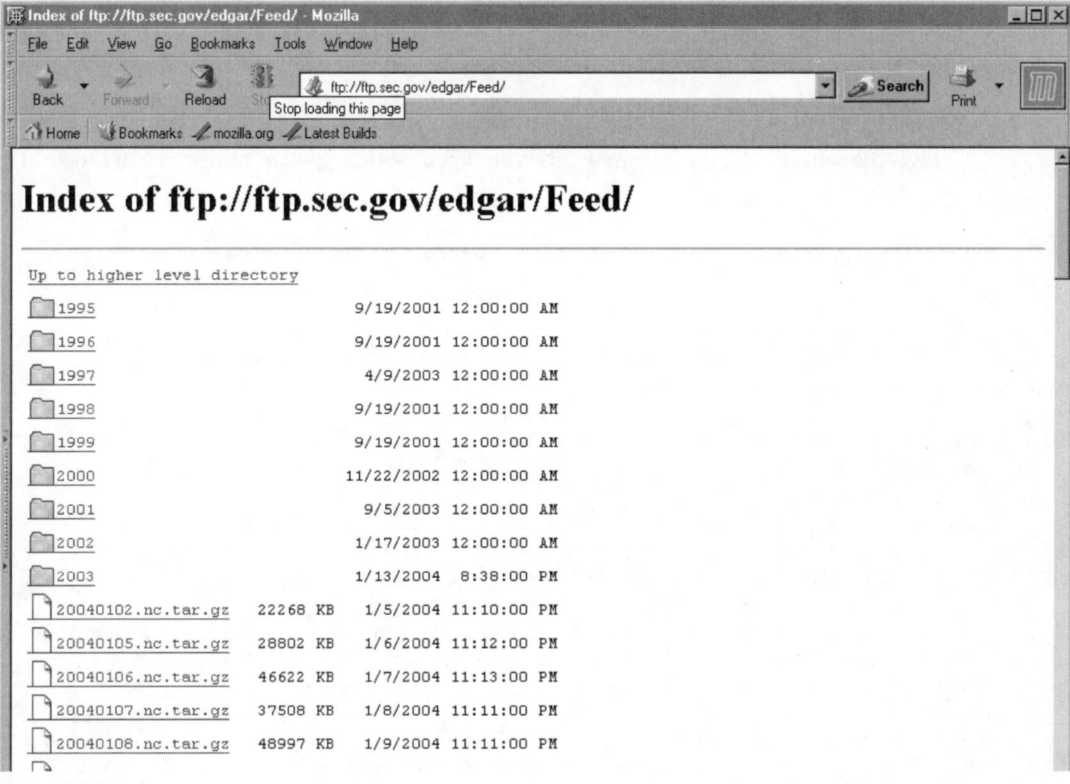

Figure 21-6

1. Double-click the file name that you want. They are named by date.
2. Once you have the file, you will have to use a utility such as Winzip to unzip the individual files so that your program can work with them. Put the files in a directory called `edgar_data`. After this you will have the data needed to run the program we are building.

Here's another way of completing the *Try It Out* with an alternative system. Using an Unix-like system such as Linux, you can use a command-line procedure, log into `ftp.sec.gov`, and directly from EDGAR, download a metafile (this is a file of files that have been combined using a compression algorithm) by clicking its name.

1. Enter ftp `ftp.sec.gov`.
2. You will get back something like this:

```
Connected to ftp.sec.gov.
220 FTP server ready.
530 Please login with USER and PASS.
530 Please login with USER and PASS.
KERBEROS_V4 rejected as an authentication type
Name (ftp.sec.gov:bill):
```

3. At this point enter the word "anonymous" as your name (not "bill"). This is perfectly legal and legitimate. This server is configured to accept anyone who wants to log on as a guest this way.
4. Now you will be asked, as a courtesy, to enter your email address as a password. This is standard on Unix systems and is just a way for the administration to see who is using their system. (Since this is the same field used for passwords, your email address will not print as you type it. This is normal.)

```
331 Guest login ok, send your complete e-mail address as password.
Password:
```

5. You are then accepted into the system and provided with an introduction.

```
230-
230-------------------------
230- Welcome to FTP.SEC.GOV!
230-------------------------
230-
230-Welcome to the Securities & Exchange Commission's Public Information
230-Server. This file contains introductory information and will be
230-periodically revised. This server features SEC public documents,
230-information of interest to the investing public, rulemaking activities,
230-and access to the Commission's electronic filing database, EDGAR. The
230-public will be able to query the EDGAR database for any company
    currently
230-filing electronically with the SEC. These filings are updated 24 hours
230-after they are filed with the Commission. This server will support WWW
230-and anonymous FTP and can be reached at "http://www.sec.gov" and
230-"ftp.sec.gov" respectively.
```

```
230-
230-Archive note: Please read /edgar/README-2000-10-04.txt as the archive
230-  structure has changed!
230-
230-Questions? Comments. Please send email to webmaster@sec.gov.
230-
230-
230-Welcome to the Securities & Exchange Commission's Public
230-Information Server. This file contains introductory information
230-and will be periodically revised. This server features SEC
230-public documents, information of interest to the investing
230-public, rulemaking activities, and access to the Commission's
230-electronic filing database, EDGAR. The public will be able to
230-query the EDGAR database for any company currently filing
230-electronically with the SEC. These filings are updated 24 hours
230-after they are filed with the Commission. This server will
230-support WWW and anonymous FTP and can be reached at
230-"http://www.sec.gov" and "ftp.sec.gov" respectively.
230-
230-Get the file named general.txt for an introduction to this data
230-archive.
230-
230-Updated 08/15/2000
230-
230-Please read the file README-1995-09-26.txt
230-  it was last modified on Tue Sep 26 05:00:00 1995 - 3171 days ago
230-Please read the file README.txt
230-  it was last modified on Tue Aug 15 14:29:31 2000 - 1387 days ago
230 Guest login ok, access restrictions apply.
Remote system type is UNIX.
Using binary mode to transfer files.
ftp>
```

6. Now we need to navigate to EDGAR. Enter **cd edgar**, then enter **cd Feed**. Remember that capitalization is significant here.

```
ftp> cd edgar
250-Please read the file README-2000-10-04.txt
250-  it was last modified on Mon Mar 3 13:01:22 2003 - 458 days ago
250 CWD command successful.
ftp> cd Feed
250 CWD command successful.
ftp>
```

7. Typing **ls** here will show you what is available. Past years' information is available in subdirectories. The current year's information is available on this directory.

8. Choose a file to download. Enter **get** followed by the file name.

```
ftp> get 20040601.nc.tar.gz
local: 20040601.nc.tar.gz remote: 20040601.nc.tar.gz
227 Entering Passive Mode (12,154,80,50,76,63)
150 Opening BINARY mode data connection for 20040601.nc.tar.gz (73523935 bytes).
```

9. When the file is completely downloaded, type **quit** to quit ftp and create a working directory (if you haven't already) called `edgar_data` and change it to your current directory with the `cd` command.

```
mkdir edgar_data
cd edgar_data
```

10. The file is actually a file of other files, packed in what is called the tar format (which originally stood for Tape ARchive). You can make it all available in the `edgar_data` directory by issuing this command:

```
tar -xzf ../20040601.nc.tar.gz
```

11. Now you have the data needed to run the program we will be building. All you need now is the program.

How It Works

We are using what have become common functions with the Internet; we are downloading and then decompressing (or "untaring," or unzipping) files that will be used on our own computer. Because the SEC saved the files in a compressed form, it not only saved itself the cost of the extra disk space, but it saved us time—it takes much less time to download a compressed file than it does a file with the same information that is not compressed.

The XML in these files is embedded within the EDGAR eXtended Forms Definition Language (XFDL); for more information you can go to `http://www.merrillcorp.com/products_services/edgar/filer_manual/Volume_I/ch5 .pdf`). By using PHP we are able to easily extract the XML from those files that have it and then examine its contents.

In the spirit of creating a practical exercise, we will choose to only look at Form 4 filings, which give us the changes to an insider's holdings. Some people would want to look at only acquisitions (buy orders) and not dispositions (sell orders) thinking that personal needs are more likely to drive a disposition of stock but that the insider would have to have special confidence in the company to buy its stock—in this vein we will select only acquisitions.

For simplicity's sake, we bypass the footnotes that are included as text embedded within the XML that could change the meaning of the numbers. The intent of this program is to identify stocks that merit further examination rather than to recommend a decision. A footnote could explain something that would throw the other entries into a different light wherein they could be misinterpreted without the footnote; for example, it could explain that a stock share's price of $0.00 is due to the stock being given as an incentive to an employee rather than begin bought outright. We will track the total dollar amount of the acquisitions by multiplying the number of shares by price per share and prepare a table that is formatted to be read by a browser. (We don't plan to present this immediately on demand but rather preprocess the data to be presented later. This is because it can take about two minutes with a 2 GHz processor to complete this processing on a single day's data and PHP will generally default to a 30-second time limit when run through a web server.) This means that when you want to use your browser to interpret the data, rather than point it to the PHP program as you might normally do, you would want to point it to an HTML file that is created by this PHP program, having previously run on its own.

This example is really only to show you the power of PHP with XML. It is written to run on PHP 4.3.6 or above including PHP 5, which we expect to have even greater XML capabilities when it is formally released.

Many programmers like to test their programs as they build them. We will work some of our examples of the preceding text into a program and test as we build.

We previously saw how to build a loop around a search of a directory for files we could examine. Now we need to put some more functionality into the loop so that it can examine the files. In our previous example we loaded a variable `$contents` with the entire contents of a file. Now we need to find the XML within it. The XML code is bracketed by `<XML>`—we will actually start with the `<?xml` that follows it because our parser will stumble over any intermediate line feeds—and `</XML>` tags. We'll not be picky and take them in a case-insensitive matter. PHP has some handy string functions. Among them is `split` which splits a string into sections, putting the sections into an array of as many pieces as you want. The function splits the string by what are called *regular expressions.* (Regular expressions are a handy shorthand for setting up a pattern to see if the pattern exists within a string. For information on regular expressions you can find something about them in nearly any book on Unix or Linux. They are explained in detail at `http://etext.lib.virginia.edu/helpsheets/regex.html`. For our example we are not getting into anything fancy with regular expressions, however. If a substring matches `<?xml`, we chop off everything before it. If a substring matches `</XML>`, we chop off everything after it.

Try It Out Getting the XML and Only the XML

Here is how we cut out everything but the XML that we want.

1. First, we take out everything before the XML that appears in the file contents as follows:

```
$split_array1=spliti("<\?xml",$contents,2);
```

2. Then, we remove everything after the XML:

```
$split_array2=spliti("</XML>",$split_array1[1],2);
```

3. And finally, we put back the leading (`<?xml`):

```
$xml="<?xml".$split_array2[0]; /* We replace the first matching string.*/
```

How It Works

The first parameter is sought, and everything up to and including it is removed. Note we have to escape the question mark (`?`) with a backslash so that it will not be accepted as a control character in a regular expression. The second parameter is obviously the contents. The third parameter is the number of fields you want in your result; if you were going to seek more of these strings you would want a higher number, but we just want two.

Some of the files we get from EDGAR do not have XML code in them. In these cases our `$xml` string is less than five characters as it is only what we have put into it. In these cases we ignore the file and do no further processing on it.

```
$len=strlen($xml);
if ($len<=5) {
        // no <?xml in file
}
else { // following is our work with XML
```

Try It Out Parsing the XML

Now we venture into the world of objects. We need to create a parser, which is an object that will parse a string for us. When we perform the function `xml_parser_create()`, the work of creating an instance of the parser class (for example, a parser) is done for us.

1. PHP's XML parsers need to know whether to use case folding, which is more commonly known as "uppercasing." There is no reason not to be case-sensitive here, so we turn this option off:

```
// set option so that case folding is not used
xml_parser_set_option($parser, XML_OPTION_CASE_FOLDING, false);
```

2. We have to designate a function to handle starting and ending of parsing of any of the XML tags that we encounter. `xml_set_element_handler` is are used for these purposes.

```
// designate functions to handle starting and ending of parsing
xml_set_element_handler($parser, "startElementHandler",
"endElementHandler"); // note that the passed function names should be in
quotes
```

3. Next, we have to designate a function to deal with the character data that we get from XML:

```
// designate a function to handle character data
xml_set_character_data_handler($parser, "cdataHandler");
```

4. Next, we do the parsing. We set this up so that if the parser has a problem, we will print out the error codes using functions `xml_get_error_code`, `xml_error_string`, `xml_get_current_line_number`, and `xml_get_current_column_number`. Remember that the work we are doing at the beginning, in between, and at the end of the tags will be done in the functions we just named before (`startElementHandler`, `endElementHandler`, and `cdataHandler`):

```
if (!xml_parse($parser, $xml, 1)) {
 printf("\n".$xml."\n");
 printf("Error code: %d <BR>\n", xml_get_error_code($parser));
 printf("Error: %s <BR>\n", xml_error_string($parser));
 die(sprintf("XML error on line %d at position %d",
 xml_get_current_line_number($parser),
 xml_get_current_column_number($parser)));
   }
```

When we are done, we free the parser so that its resources do not hang around cluttering up the computer's workspace. If your program were only parsing one string and it were ending now, you would only do this for good form, as the resources would be held for only a very short time and would be released when PHP ended processing. However, we are looping through a set of files here and are processing each file. For this reason we should conserve our processing resources and release the resources used specifically for parsing this file as follows:

```
xml_parser_free($parser);
```

How It Works

The parser that we create is an object that will do the parsing work for us. Part of that work is handing off chunks that are parsed to our own functions, `startElementHandler()` and `endElementHandler()`, which do the work that we tell them to do.

But we are not done. We have been working at a high level, just setting up the detailed work that needs to be done, which is in the functions (`startElementHandler`, `endElementHandler`, and `cdataHandler`).

Try It Out — Handling the Data

1. In our detail handling routines the simplest is the one we use for the start of the XML elements, `startElementHandler`. We want to track where we are, so we need to mark a trail, which we call `$trail`. Because this is a function, we need to declare `$trail` global in order to work with the same `$trail` that other functions are using because otherwise our function's variables would be unavailable elsewhere. Then we need to use a function called `array_push` to push the name of the tag we are at onto the `$trail` array. The push concept is often described to be like that of a stack of plates in a cafeteria—you can push plates onto the stack, and you can pop them off of the stack in exactly the reverse order in which you pushed them onto it. Because XML tags are nested, this gives us an easy way to keep track of where we are. Not just the name of the current low-level tag, but all the tags at successively higher levels will be available to us too, through the `$trail` array.

```
function startElementHandler($parser, $name, $attribs) {
      // do things you need to do at the beginning
      global $trail;
      array_push($trail,$name);
}
```

2. Handling character data is a little more involved in this application. We need to maintain several more variables as `global`. In addition to the trail, we need to globalize anything that we want to reference when we are in the `endElementHandler` function later. We globalize data that we are extracting from the XML such as shares, price, amount, and so on. We also globalize accumulating variables so that we can have summary information.

```
// the handler for character data
function cdataHandler($parser, $data) {
global $trail,$shares,$total_shares,$issuerCik,$documentType,
         $price,$amount,$total_shares_owner,$periodOfReport,
         $issuerName,$master_report,
         $transactionAcquiredDisposedCode,$tranCount;
```

3. Now we use our `$trail` information. Remember that this function is called every time any character data is processed. For every data element that is in a value tag nested within a tag that more eloquently describes it, we have to look at both the value tag and the next tag out. For example, when accessing the number of shares involved in a transaction, we check both `transactionShares` and `value`. Then if that is the character data we are processing, we capture the data for use globally.

```
if ($trail[count($trail)-2]=='transactionShares'
 && $trail[count($trail)-1]=='value') {
        $shares=$data;
}
```

4. We can do things besides just capturing this data. If need be, we can transform it as well. EDGAR gives us dates in a standard American English format. PHP is very helpful in giving us an easy way to convert it to a standard Unix timestamp (the number of seconds since midnight, universal coordinated time [UTC], January 1, 1970). The Unix timestamp is easy to add, subtract, compare, and so on, and can be easily converted back to whatever human readable format we would like. The PHP function `strtotime` will accept many different human versions of the date, including EDGAR's.

```
if ($trail[count($trail)-1]=='periodOfReport') {
        $periodOfReport=strtotime($data); /* converts date to unix timestamp
        for sorting and ranging */
```

We should be aware that this standard Unix timestamp will cease to be effective in 32-bit variables on January 18, 2038, when it will exceed the available number of bits required for storage of its value. The problems approaching that time will be not unlike the problems we had approaching the time when the decimal year rolled over on January 1, 2000.

5. The `endElementHandler` function allows us the opportunity of managing all of the data collected by the `cdataHandler` function. Whatever variables we globalized are now ready for us. First, we need to recognize that the only end tags that we want are those for the `ownershipDocument` and `documentType` of 4. We are also only going to review acquisitions, so we want the `transactionAcquiredDisposedCode` to be "A".

```
if ($name == 'ownershipDocument' and $documentType==4
     and $transactionAcquiredDisposedCode=='A') {
```

6. Next, we need to accumulate information for our report. We have praised PHP's array capabilities before, and now you will see them work well for you. We choose an array named `$master_report`. Its first dimension will be the EDGAR company identifier, `$issuerCik`. Its second dimension will accumulate values for the company, specifically a count of transactions (`'count'`), a count of shares (`'shares'`), a count of dollars we know are involved (`'dollars'`), and the name of the company (`'issuerName'`).

```
$master_report[$issuerCik]['count']++; /* counts number of transactions for
issuer */
$master_report[$issuerCik]['shares']+=$shares; /* totals share volume for
issuer */
```

```
$master_report[$issuerCik]['dollars']+=$shares*$price; /* add to total
dollar volume for issuer */
$master_report[$issuerCik]['issuerName']=$issuerName; /* set name of issuer */
```

7. We also want to track the dates of the transactions that we are reviewing. Here we will track a begin and an end for the range of dates involving this company using PHP's functions `min` and `max`:

```
if (!isset( $master_report[$issuerCik]['periodOfReport']['begin'])) {
          $master_report[$issuerCik]['periodOfReport']['begin']=
                        $periodOfReport;
}
else {
                 $master_report[$issuerCik]['periodOfReport']['begin']=
                        min($master_report[$issuerCik]
                        ['periodOfReport']['begin'],$periodOfReport);
/* take the earlier of this date and the earliest date for this company
this date */
}
$master_report[$issuerCik]['periodOfReport']['end']=
 max($master_report[$issuerCik]['periodOfReport']['end'],$periodOfReport);
/* take the later of this date and the latest date for this company before
this date */
```

8. Next, we "`unset`" the variables we have used for this ownership document. PHP's `unset` function makes PHP think that the variables never existed so that we will have a clean slate with the next ownership document:

```
unset($issuerName);
unset($issuerCik);
unset($shares);
unset($price);
```

9. Because counting transactions is a good control, we want to make an independent count of the number of transactions we have processed. Here is the place to do that.

```
$tranCount++;
```

10. At the end of this function, we want to pop the `$trail` array so that we will be ready for the next nesting that we encounter.

```
array_pop($trail);
```

How It Works

PHP's dynamic array creation capability is used to the maximum here. Simply by using an array name with a given subscript, we, in effect, create it. PHP keeps track of the arrays and doesn't need to be told whether we are using a subscript for the first time or not. We end up with an array of summary information that we can use for our reporting.

Try It Out Write the Report

We can use the accumulated data in the array `$master_report` as the source for everything we need to write HTML that can be easily read by a browser.

1. We have now defined all of our information collection efforts. We can now turn our attention to reporting on our results. First, we close our `handle` on the directory and then `echo` some HTML so that we can create a table with appropriate headings over the columns we will be filling.

```
closedir($handle);
echo "<TABLE border=1><TR><TH>Issuer</TH><TH>Number of
Transactions</TH><TH>Dollar Volume</TH><TH>Number of Shares</TH><TH>Range
of Dates</TH></TR>";
```

2. Then, we sort our report in company number order (the order of the first dimension of `$master_report`):

```
ksort($master_report); // put report in CIK order
reset($master_report); // necessary for the following "foreach" command
```

3. The `foreach` loop command allows us to walk through our `$master_report` array extracting its `issuerCik` dimension and setting up the second dimension as a first dimension for a new array called `$CIKarray`. Within this walking of the array, we take the data that we had placed in there while parsing the XML and report on its aggregations:

```
foreach ($master_report as $issuerCik=>$CIKarray) {
 $count=number_format($CIKarray['count']);
 $shares=number_format($CIKarray['shares']);
 $dollars='$'.number_format($CIKarray['dollars'],2,'.',',');
 $issuerName=$CIKarray['issuerName'];
 $beginDate=date("m/d/y",$CIKarray['periodOfReport']['begin']);
 $endDate=date("m/d/y",$CIKarray['periodOfReport']['end']);

 echo "<TR><TD>$issuerCik<BR>$issuerName</TD><TD align=right>$count</TD><TD
align=right>$dollars</TD><TD align=right>$shares</TD><TD>$beginDate -
<BR>$endDate</TD></TR>\n";
}
```

4. After that, we only need to tell HTML to end the table, put out a date to show when we did this, and a control total that we can balance against the report, if for no better reason than to assure ourselves by some manual adding that we got the same total of transactions into the array as we did when we counted XML transactions and provide a simple test of our programming.

```
echo "</TABLE>";

$date=date("Y M d H:i"); //formats an output date
echo "These $tranCount transactions were reported on $date.<BR>";
```

5. Then, to show PHP we are done, we conclude with an ending tag:

```
?>
```

At this point you want to make sure that you have saved your work (and/or copied the program from the CD provided with this text).

How It Works

Here is where it happens. We have built the program and are ready to run it to produce a viewable web page.

Ensure that your data is on the directory `edgar_data` and that the program is set up as a file with the name `process_edgar_xml.php` on your current directory (of which `edgar_data` is a subdirectory). At the command line enter the following:

```
php process_edgar_xml.php >edgar_report.html
```

After this has run, you should have a report that can be displayed on your browser. The following table shows the sample output.

Issuer	Number of Transactions	Dollar Volume	Number of Shares	Range of Dates
6769	6	$2,529.65	65	02/26/04–
APACHE CORP				2/26/04
9534	13	$0.00	73,600	02/24/04–
BANDAG INC				2/24/04
9984	5	$701,181.06	26,455	02/25/04–
BARNES GROUP INC				2/25/04
10329	6	$2,376,000.00	112,500	02/24/04–
BASSETT FURNITURE INDUSTRIES INC				2/24/04
12978	1	$2,366.57	71	02/25/04–
BOISE CASCADE CORP				2/25/04

Useful Resources

The Apache Foundation keeps current documentation on PHP live at its website `www.php.net`. PHP version 5 is expected to have significantly improved XML capabilities, but as of this writing some of the XML features are considered experimental and warnings are issued to keep people from depending on every feature.

- *Apache, MySQL, and PHP Weekend Crash Course* by Steven M. Schafer. Wiley Publishing, Inc., ISBN 0-7645-4320-2.
- *MySQL/PHP Database Applications* by Brad Bulger, Jay Greenspan, and David Wall. Wiley Publishing, Inc., ISBN 0-7645-4963-4.

- *PHP fast&easy web development* by Julie C. Meloni. PrimaTech, ISBN 0-7615-6055-X.
- *Professional PHP Programming* by Jesus Castagnetto, Harish Rawat, Sascha Schumann, Chris Scollo, and Deepak Veliath. Wiley Publishing, Inc., ISBN 1-861002-96-3.
- *Secure PHP Development* by Mohammed J. Kabir. Wiley Publishing, Inc., ISBN 0-7645-4966-9.

One great thing about PHP is that contributors are not only continually improving the language, but contributors are also providing class libraries with significant functionality. A few sources of code you can take and use are at:

- `http://phpxmlclasses.sourceforge.net/` gets you to a collection of classes and resources to process XML using PHP.
- `http://www.phpclasses.org/` provides the "PHP Classes Repository."
- `http://pear.php.net` The PHP Extension and Application Repository (PEAR) is a framework and distribution system for reusable PHP components. It can be especially useful in providing a database interface that works with multiple database management systems.

Websites that provide forums or other useful information for PHP coders include:

- The Web Monkey (`http://hotwired.lycos.com/webmonkey/programming/php/index.html`) also provides a library of articles on PHP.
- `http://www.phpgeek.com/` is "your home for resources related to using PHP on the Windows platforms."
- `http://www.phpbuilder.com` provides articles and the potential to gain from interaction with over 50,000 members.
- A website from a good group that welcomes people from outside their area: the New York PHP group at `www.nyphp.org`.

There are PHP conferences going on around the world, with archival information on PHP conventions available from `http://www.php-con.com/`.

Integrated Development Environments are being deployed and improved as this is being written. Two commercial products are the Zend Studio (`http://www.zend.com`) and NuSphere (`http://www.phped.com/`), and an open-source debugger project is hosted at SourceForge: `http://sourceforge.net/projects/dbg2/`.

Summary

We have provided a basic (if quick) introduction to programming in PHP. We have shown how to use PHP to develop most of the common programming control structures and develop your own program to accept XML data. We showed how this could be done to analyze data in XML form, and in particular, data on insider trading from the U.S. Securities and Exchange Commission.

Enjoy your venture into PHP coding. Please let me know if I can help. I can be reached at `patterson@computer.org` (and please put "[Wiley book]" in the subject heading of your email so that you get through my spam filter).

Part IX: Appendixes

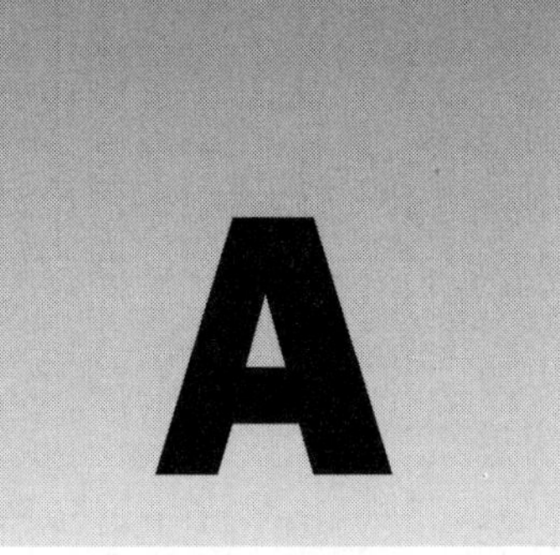

Exercise Solutions

In this appendix you'll find some suggested solutions to the exercise questions that were posed at the end of most of the chapters throughout the book.

Chapter 1

This chapter gave us an overview of XML and why it's so useful.

Question 1

Modify the "name" XML document you've been working with to include the person's title (Mr., Ms., Dr., and so on).

Solution

Because of the self-describing nature of XML, the only hard part about adding a title to our "name" example is deciding what to call it. If we call it "title," we can add it to our document as follows:

```
<name>
  <title>Mr.</title>
  <first>John</first>
  <middle>Fitzgerald Johansen</middle>
  <last>Doe</last>
</name>
```

Another way to handle it might be to treat a title as a simple prefix to the name; this would also allow us the flexibility of adding a suffix. This approach might look like the following:

```
<name>
  <prefix>Mr.</prefix>
  <first>John</first>
  <middle>Fitzgerald Johansen</middle>
  <last>Doe</last>
  <suffix>the 3rd</suffix>
</name>
```

In this case, instead of giving the data an explicit label, we're making it more generic and allowing some text to come before and after the name.

Question 2

The "`name`" example we've been using so far has been in English. However, XML is language-agnostic, so we can create XML documents in any language we wish. Therefore, create a new French document type to represent a name. You can use the following table for the names of the XML elements:

English	French
Name	identité
First	prénom
Last	nom
Middle	deuxième-prénom

Solution

Although this might seem like a trick question, it's actually not. As we'll see in Chapter 2, XML allows the special French characters required here, as well as many thousands of other characters, in our element names. That means that creating the document in French is just as easy as creating it in English. You can do it as follows:

```
<identité>
  <prénom>John</prénom>
  <deuxième-prénom>Fitzgerald Johansen</deuxième-prénom>
  <nom>Doe</nom>
</identité>
```

If you enter this into Notepad, save it using the UTF-8 encoding, and view it in Internet Explorer it will show up just as easily as the English version did, as shown in Figure A-1.

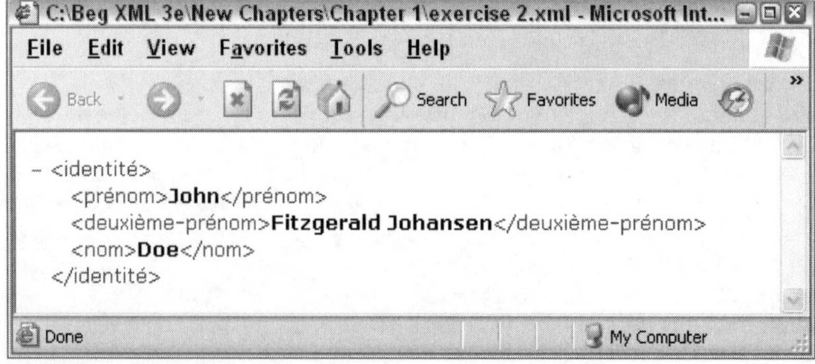

Figure A-1

When you save this document, however, be sure to specify to Notepad that you want to save the file using the UTF-8 encoding. If you use the default ANSI encoding, the document won't show up in the browser properly. Instead, you'll get an error message like the one in Figure A-2.

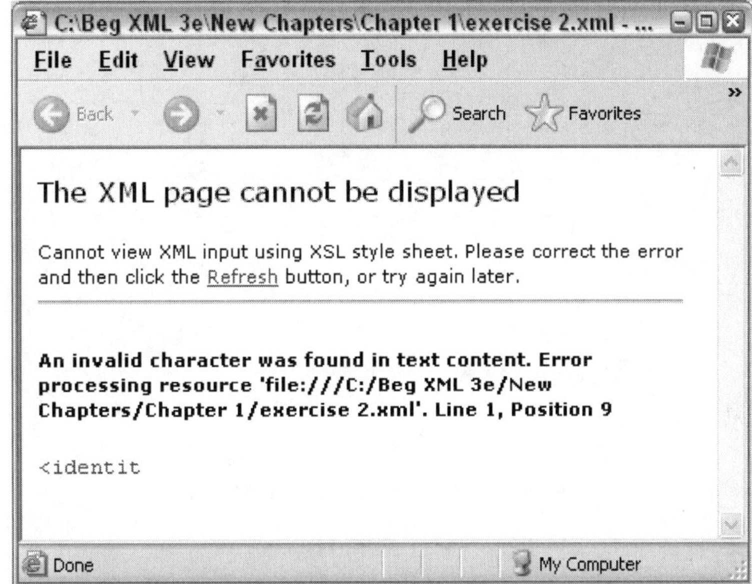

Figure A-2

In Chapter 2, we'll see why this encoding setting is so important.

Although XML is language-agnostic, allowing us to create markup in any language that we want, it's important to remember that XML is not able to translate markup from one language to another. So if we write an application that handles names, and we program that application to ask the XML parser for the information from the element called `last`, that's what the parser will do. If we try to feed our French XML document to that application, the parser will find an element called `nom`, but it won't be able to find an element called `last`. So the application won't be able to get the data that it needs. There is no way for an XML parser to know that a `nom` element is equivalent to a `last` element; as far as the parser is concerned, we've created two completely different document types, even if they are equivalent to a human mind.

This will be an important concept to remember, as we continue through the book.

Chapter 2

In this chapter, we learned about the basic syntax for writing well-formed XML documents.

Question 1

For the addresses in our Order XML, we used a common format of "Address Line 1, Address Line 2, City, State, and Zip Code." Other applications need to be stricter with their addresses, and have separate elements for street number, street name, and so on. Rewrite the last version of the Order XML using the following information, instead of the Address Line 1/Address Line 2 format:

- Street Number
- Street Name
- Apt. Number
- City
- State
- Zip Code
- Additional Information

Solution

As always, there are multiple ways this could be designed. One option might be to use attributes, to break up information about the street and the apartment, like this:

```
<Address>
  <Street number="123"
          name="Somewhere Ave." />
  <Apartment number=""
             type="" />
  <!--the apartment type would
      specify apartment, suite,
      room, etc. -->

  <City>Some Town</City>
  <State>TA</State>
  <Zip>000000000</Zip>
  <AdditionalInformation/>
</Address>
```

It's nice to have this flexibility, but for this example it would not be wise to design the address like that, because it isn't consistent with the rest of the document.

Instead, to fit in with the naming convention used throughout the rest of the document, it's probably better to use the following names:

```
<Address>
  <StreetNumber>123</StreetNumber>
  <StreetName>Somewhere Ave.</StreetName>
  <ApartmentNumber/>
  <City>Some Town</City>
  <State>TA</State>
  <Zip>000000000</Zip>
  <AdditionalInformation/>
</Address>
```

That turns the overall document into this:

```
<?xml version="1.0"?>
<Orders Count="2">
  <Order ID="0000000001">
    <?SernaProcessor ManualIntervention reason:Insufficient Funds?>
    <Type>N</Type>
    <Date>Jan 1, 2004, 14:29</Date>
    <Customer>
      <SernaDirect>
        <SubscriptionType>B</SubscriptionType>
        <SubscriptionLength>12</SubscriptionLength>
      </SernaDirect>
      <Address>
        <StreetNumber>123</StreetNumber>
        <StreetName>Somewhere Ave.</StreetName>
        <ApartmentNumber/>
        <City>Some Town</City>
        <State>TA</State>
        <Zip>000000000</Zip>
        <AdditionalInformation/>
      </Address>
      <CreditCard>
        <Number>4111111111111111</Number>
        <CardHolderName>John Q Public</CardHolderName>
        <Expiry>11/09</Expiry>
      </CreditCard>
      <Phone>5555555555</Phone>
      <Name>John Public</Name>
      <Email>jpublic@someprovider.com</Email>
    </Customer>
    <Number>x582n9</Number>
    <Products Count="1">
      <Product>
        <Model>X9</Model>
        <Price>129.95</Price>
        <ID>x9000059</ID>
      </Product>
    </Products>
  </Order>
  <Order ID="0000000002">
    <Type>N</Type>
    <Date>Jan 1, 2004, 16:00</Date>
    <Customer>
      <SernaDirect>
        <SubscriptionType>D</SubscriptionType>
        <SubscriptionLength>12</SubscriptionLength>
      </SernaDirect>
      <Address>
        <StreetNumber>89</StreetNumber>
        <StreetName>Subscriber's Street</StreetName>
        <ApartmentNumber/>
        <City>Smallville</City>
        <State>XQ</State>
        <Zip>000000000</Zip>
        <AdditionalInformation>Box 882</AdditionalInformation>
      </Address>
```

```
        <CreditCard>
          <Number>4512451245124512</Number>
          <CardHolderName>Helen P Someperson</CardHolderName>
          <Expiry>01/08</Expiry>
        </CreditCard>
        <Phone>5554443333</Phone>
        <Name>Helen Someperson</Name>
        <Email>helens@isp.net</Email>
      </Customer>
      <Number>a98f78d</Number>
      <Products Count="1">
        <Product>
          <Model>Y9</Model>
          <Price>229.95</Price>
          <ID>y9000065</ID>
        </Product>
      </Products>
    </Order>
  </Orders>
```

This doesn't put to work all of the different things we learned in this chapter, but it is a better overall design, when the document as a whole is taken into consideration.

Question 2

Sometimes the syntax used by XML can be a little troublesome to figure out. The following XML document contains a few syntactical errors, preventing it from being well formed. Correct them so that the document can be read by IE.

Hint: When I'm trying to correct a file like this, I often open it up in the browser and fix errors as the browser reports them to me. Be warned—some of the errors are a bit more difficult to figure out than others.

```
<?xml version="1"?>
<document>
  <--There are a couple of problems with this document.-->
  <Information>This document
  contains some < bold>information</bold>. Once
  it's corrected, it can be read by a parser.</Information>
</Document>
```

Solution

For this example, I purposely tried to pick some common errors that I find hard to spot when I'm working with XML.

When I have an XML document that isn't well formed, and I can't figure out why, my first step is always to load the document into a parser that gives good error information. IE is an excellent example, and I often use the browser to find my XML mistakes.

When I load this document into a browser, the first thing that it complains about is the version number, as shown in Figure A-3.

Figure A-3

XML parsers are very picky about the version number; it has to be exactly "1.0"—"1" isn't good enough. Correct the version number, as follows:

```
<?xml version="1.0"?>
<document>
  <--There are a couple of problems with this document.-->
  <Information>This document
  contains some < bold>information</bold>. Once
  it's corrected, it can be read by a parser.</Information>
</Document>
```

Resave this, and load it in the browser again. The file is still not correct, and the message in Figure A-4 comes up.

This doesn't seem to make sense. Why is the XML parser trying to read what's in the comments? The answer is that there is no `!` at the beginning of the comment, so the parser doesn't realize it's supposed to be a comment. As far as the parser is concerned, there is a < character, and there's no `!` after it, so this should be the beginning of an element. Because a dash isn't a valid way to start an element name, the parser incorrectly thinks we've given an element a bad name.

Correcting this problem is easy enough. Just add the `!`, as in the following:

```
<?xml version="1.0"?>
<document>
  <!--There are a couple of problems with this document.-->
  <Information>This document
  contains some < bold>information</bold>. Once
  it's corrected, it can be read by a parser.</Information>
</Document>
```

Figure A-4

The document is still not done, though. Loading this into the browser gives the error in Figure A-5.

In this case, the error message is exactly right. The mistake made here is an extra space added after the opening < of the `<bold>` element. Remove the space, as follows:

Figure A-5

```
<?xml version="1.0"?>
<document>
  <!--There are a couple of problems with this document.-->
  <Information>This document
  contains some <bold>information</bold>. Once
  it's corrected, it can be read by a parser.</Information>
</Document>
```

The document is almost complete, but there is one problem left. Viewing it in the browser now gives the error in Figure A-6.

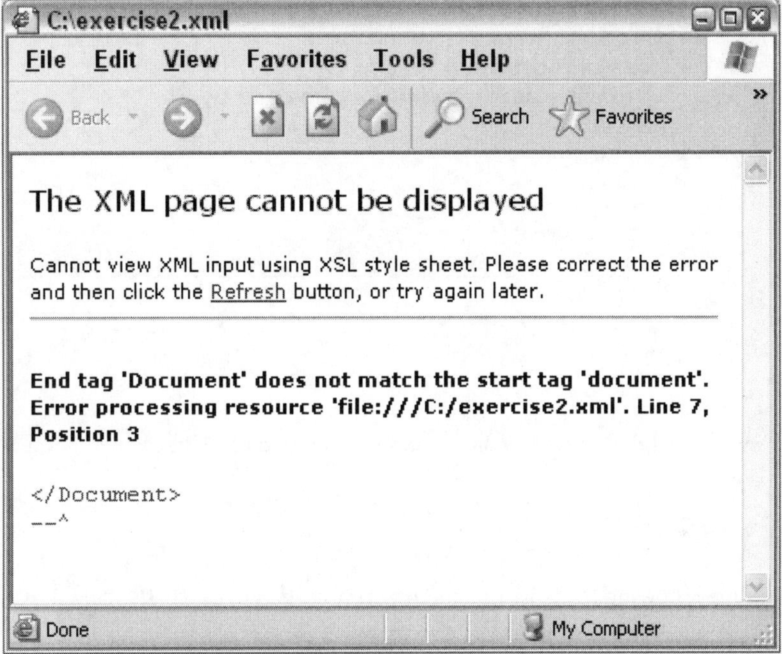

Figure A-6

Once again, the error message given by IE is very descriptive. Although the start tag was named `document`, with a lowercase "d," the end tag was named `Document`, with the "d" in uppercase. Changing the end tag to use a lowercase "d" fixes the document and gives the following XML:

```
<?xml version="1.0"?>
<document>
  <!--There are a couple of problems with this document.-->
  <Information>This document
  contains some <bold>information</bold>. Once
  it's corrected, it can be read by a parser.</Information>
</document>
```

The document finally loads properly in the browser, as shown in Figure A-7.

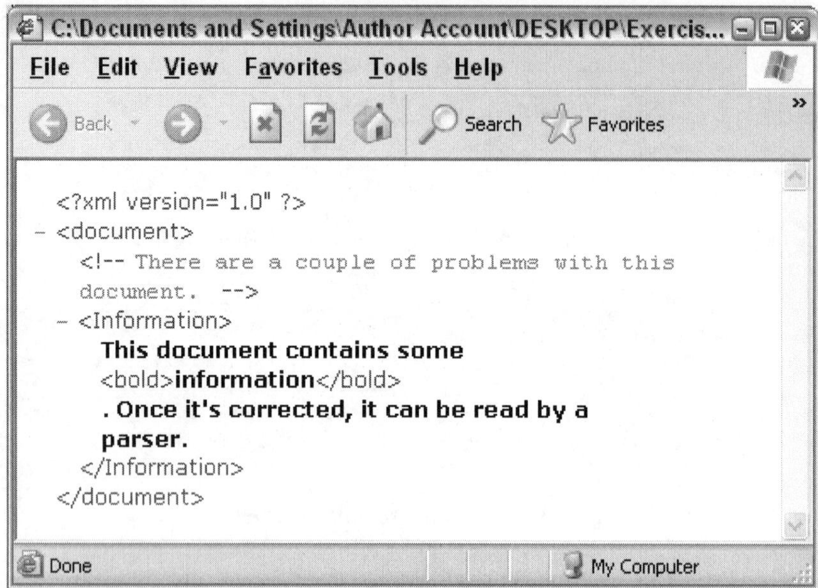

Figure A-7

Chapter 3

This chapter introduced the concept of namespaces, along with their implementation in XML.

Question 1

Earlier we had the following XML document, in which we had to cancel the default namespace:

```
<employee>
  <name>Jane Doe</name>
  <notes>
    <p xmlns="http://www.w3.org/1999/xhtml">I've worked
    with <name xmlns="">Jane Doe</name> for over a <em>year</em>
    now.</p>
  </notes>
</employee>
```

Assuming that this document is for the fictional Serna Ferna, Inc., company we've been using, create a namespace for employees, and use it in this document. Be sure to keep the XHTML elements in their namespace.

Solution

The URL we've been using for namespaces for Serna Ferna, Inc., has been `http://www.sernaferna.com`, followed by something to indicate the namespace being named. In this case, because we're creating a namespace for employees, so `http://www.sernaferna.com/employee` makes sense.

Because we have a <name> element embedded inside an XHTML <p> element, it makes sense to use prefixes, rather than default namespaces, so the resulting document could look like this:

```
<emp:employee xmlns:emp="http://www.sernaferna.com/employee">
  <emp:name>Jane Doe</emp:name>
  <emp:notes>
    <p xmlns="http://www.w3.org/1999/xhtml">I've worked
    with <emp:name>Jane Doe</emp:name> for over a <em>year</em>
    now.</p>
  </emp:notes>
</emp:employee>
```

I decided to leave the XHTML elements in a default namespace, because I'm much more used to reading XHTML without all of the embedded namespace prefixes. Notice that I also removed the `xmlns=""` attribute, which had been canceling the default namespace on the <name> element, but I then had to prefix the <name> element with the `emp` prefix.

Question 2

Going through the employee records, Serna Ferna, Inc., has realized that they don't have a good unique way to identify each employee. Create a global `id` attribute that can be attached to any XML element in the employee namespace you created earlier.

Put this attribute into effect by modifying the XML you created in Question 1, and marking the Jane Doe employee as employee number x125.

Solution

We already know the name of the attribute we want to create, the only question is what namespace we should put it in. We could put it in the `http://www.sernaferna.com/employee` namespace, if we think the attribute is about an employee, or we could use the `http://www.sernaferna.com/pers` namespace, if we think the attribute is about a person, or we could create a brand new namespace, if we think it's distinct from both of these namespaces.

As is often the case, there is no right answer. More information is probably required to figure out conceptually what namespace should be used. For the sake of discussion, let's assume that this attribute will be used to identify not just employees of Serna Ferna, Inc., but also customers, business contacts, and so on. In that case, it makes sense to include it in the `http://www.sernaferna.com/pers` namespace.

In this case, we could modify our earlier document to make the following:

```
<emp:employee xmlns:emp="http://www.sernaferna.com/employee"
              xmlns:pers="http://www.sernaferna.com/pers"
              pers:id="x125">
  <emp:name>Jane Doe</emp:name>
  <emp:notes>
    <p xmlns="http://www.w3.org/1999/xhtml">I've worked
    with <emp:name pers:id="x125">Jane Doe</emp:name>
    for over a <em>year</em> now.</p>
  </emp:notes>
</emp:employee>
```

Notice that I also added the attribute to the <name> element that's in the *Notes* section. Depending on how the data will be used, this may or may not be necessary, but I figured that it couldn't hurt.

Question 3

Create a new XML file for an employee named Alfred Neuman, with employee number x393. In the notes for Alfred mention that he has worked closely with Jane Doe, being sure to use the <name> element to refer to her.

Solution

Because there isn't really that much data in these files, Alfred's XML file will look very similar to Jane's. The only real data is the <name> element, as well as the <notes> field. The end result should look similar to this:

```
<emp:employee xmlns:emp="http://www.sernaferna.com/employee"
              xmlns:pers="http://www.sernaferna.com/pers"
              pers:id="x393">
  <emp:name>Alfred Neuman</emp:name>
  <emp:notes>
    <p xmlns="http://www.w3.org/1999/xhtml">Alfred has worked
    with <emp:name pers:id="x125">Jane Doe</emp:name> in the
    past, and she has had nothing but good to say about him.</p>
  </emp:notes>
</emp:employee>
```

Feel free to put whatever you want in the <notes> field.

Chapter 4

This chapter showed us how to utilize DTDs to easily validate our XML documents against a defined vocabulary of elements and attributes.

Question 1

Add another dinosaur, Triceratops Horridus, to the list of dinosaurs based on the declarations in the dinosaurs DTD. Once you have added the new dinosaur validate your document to ensure that it is correct.

Solution

In this exercise question we asked you to add a new dinosaur to the list: the Triceratops Horridus. The hardest part of the exercise was probably finding all of the information about the Triceratops. Once you found that, it was probably not much work to pattern the new information after one of the existing dinosaurs in the list. In the following we list the full XML document with the new <herbivore> element highlighted:

```
<?xml version="1.0"?>
<!DOCTYPE dinosaurs PUBLIC "-//Beginning XML//DTD Dinosaurs Example//EN"
  "dinosaurs6.dtd">
```

```
<dinosaurs version="1.0" source="Beginning XML 3E">
  <carnivore kind="Tyrannosaurus_Rex" habitat="forest swamp jungle">
    <species>Tyrannosaurus Rex</species>
    <length>42 feet</length>
    <height>18 feet</height>
    <weight>5-7 tons</weight>
    <speed>25 mph</speed>
    <weapon images="PictureOfTyrannosaurusTooth">
      <part-of-body>Teeth</part-of-body>
      <description>Though the Tyrannosaurus had many different sizes of teeth,
all were razor sharp and some grew to lengths of <b>9-13 inches</b>. Broken
teeth were replaced frequently by newer teeth. The powerful jaw exerted
in excess of 3000 pounds of pressure!</description>
    </weapon>
    <discoverer>
      <name>Osborn</name>
      <year>1905</year>
    </discoverer>
    <location>
      <country>Canada</country>
      <region>Alberta</region>
    </location>
    <description>&tyrannosaurus;</description>
  </carnivore>
  <herbivore kind="Stegosaurus_Armatus" habitat="forest swamp"
   period="Jurassic">
    <species>Stegosaurus Armatus</species>
    <length>25-40 feet</length>
    <height>14 feet</height>
    <weight>2-4 tons</weight>
    <speed>&speed-not-known;</speed>
    <weapon images="PictureOfStegosaurusSpike PictureOfStegosaurusPlate">
      <part-of-body>Spikes</part-of-body>
      <description>The Stegosaurus had two long rows of armor along its back.
At the end of its tail <b>four large spikes</b> were an excellent
defense.</description>
    </weapon>
    <discoverer>
      <name>Marsh</name>
      <year>1877</year>
    </discoverer>
    <location>
      <country>United States</country>
      <region>Colorado</region>
    </location>
    <description>&stegosaurus;</description>
  </herbivore>
  <omnivore kind="Gallimimus_Bullatus" habitat="lakeshore prairie">
    <species>Gallimimus Bullatus</species>
    <length>18 feet</length>
    <height>8 feet</height>
    <weight>1000 pounds</weight>
    <speed>35-60 mph</speed>
    <weapon/>
    <discoverer>
```

```
      <name>Osm&#x00F3;lska</name>
      <name>Roniewicz</name>
      <name>Barsbold</name>
      <year>1972</year>
    </discoverer>
    <location>
      <country>Mongolia</country>
      <region>Nemegtskaya Svita</region>
    </location>
    &gallimimus;
  </omnivore>
  <herbivore kind="Triceratops_Horridus" habitat="forest plains hills"
  period="Cretaceous">
     <species>Triceratops_Horridus</species>
     <length>30 feet</length>
     <height>14 feet</height>
     <weight>10 tons</weight>
     <speed>&speed-not-known;</speed>
     <weapon>
       <part-of-body>Horns</part-of-body>
       <description>The Triceratops had <b>two large horns and a third beak
horn</b>. These horns could be used for <i>defensive</i> purposes or to
<i>establish dominance</i> in a group.</description>
     </weapon>
     <discoverer>
       <name>Marsh</name>
       <year>1889</year>
     </discoverer>
     <location>
       <country>United States</country>
       <region>Colorado</region>
     </location>
     <description>The Triceratops had three large horns and a huge bony frill.
It's snout was shaped like a <i>beak</i> and it's two large horns were
<b>hollow</b>.</description>
   </herbivore>
</dinosaurs>
```

Question 2

Add a `feathers` attribute declaration for the `<carnivore>`, `<herbivore>`, and `<omnivore>` elements. The attribute should allow two possible values: *yes* and *no*. Make the attribute have a default value of *no*. If you would like to add a dinosaur that had feathers to your document, add definitions for the Avimimus Portentosus or for the Archaeopteryx Lithographica.

Solution

In this exercise question we wanted to add a `feathers` attribute to all three of our dinosaur elements. Because this attribute will appear for each `<carnivore>`, `<herbivore>`, and `<omnivore>`, we can add the new attribute to the `dinoAttributes` entity. We can do this by mimicking the `period` attribute already in the entity as follows:

```
<!ENTITY % dinoAttributes "kind ID #REQUIRED
                          habitat NMTOKENS #REQUIRED
                          period (Triassic } Jurassic } Cretaceous)
                          &#34;Cretaceous&#34;
                          feathers (yes } no)
                          &#34;no&#34;">
```

For extra credit, we will add a new dinosaur to our list that has feathers. We will want to refer to a picture of the feathers when we add our new dinosaur inside of our XML document. To prepare for this we will add an external entity to the end of the DTD that we can refer to inside of our XML document, as shown in the following:

```
<!ENTITY PictureOfArchaeopteryxFeathers SYSTEM
  "http://www.destinationeducation.com/images/dinosaurs/din_archaeopteryx.jpg"
  NDATA jpg>
```

Now that we have completed the changes to the DTD we can begin modifying our XML document. First things first, we need to refer to the new DTD inside of our DOCTYPE, as follows:

```
<!DOCTYPE dinosaurs PUBLIC "-//Beginning XML//DTD Dinosaurs Example//EN"
  "dinosaurs-question2.dtd">
```

Now we can safely add the information:

```
<omnivore kind="Archaeopteryx_Lithographica" habitat="forest plains  hills"
  period="Jurassic" feathers="yes">
  <species>Archaeopteryx Lithographica</species>
  <length>3 feet</length>
  <height>2 feet</height>
  <weight>Weight not known</weight>
  <speed>&speed-not-known;</speed>
  <weapon images="PictureOfArchaeopteryxFeathers">
    <part-of-body>Feathers</part-of-body>
    <description>The Archaeopteryx had feathers that could have been used to
help it <i>fly</i>. Additionally, its <b>sharp claws</b> and <b>teeth</b> could
help it devour prey.</description>
    </weapon>
    <discoverer>
      <name>Von Meyer</name>
      <name>Sir Richard Owen</name>
      <year>1863</year>
    </discoverer>
    <location>
      <country>Bavaria</country>
      <region>Solnhofen Limestone, Pappenheim</region>
    </location>
    <description>The Archaeopteryx is very controversial. It is said to be
the <i>missing link</i> between <b>Dinosaurs</b> and <b>modern
birds</b>.</description>
  </omnivore>
```

Here, we added another dinosaur, the Archaeopteryx Lithographica, which had feathers. When we added the declaration, we were sure to make use of our new `feathers` attribute. We also referred to the picture of the Archaeopteryx feathers when describing its weapons.

Question 3

Add a `prey` attribute declaration for the `<carnivore>` and `<omnivore>` elements. Make the attribute type `IDREFS` and make the attribute `#IMPLIED`. Once you have completed this, add a `prey` attribute to the Tyrannosaurus Rex and refer to one of the dinosaur `ID`s found in your dinosaur document.

Solution

In our last exercise question we added the `feathers` attribute to all three of our dinosaur elements. Adding the attribute to the `dinoAttributes` entity made this easy. This time, however, we only want to add the `prey` attribute to the `<carnivore>` and `<omnivore>` elements. It wouldn't make sense to add the `prey` attribute to the `<herbivore>` element as herbivores ate plants, not other dinosaurs.

Luckily, mixing attribute declarations and parameter entities is very easy to do. Simply change the `ATTLIST` declarations in the DTD. Take the following for example:

```
<!ATTLIST omnivore %dinoAttributes;
                    prey IDREFS #IMPLIED>
<!ATTLIST carnivore %dinoAttributes;
                     prey IDREFS #IMPLIED>
```

In our document, we can refer to our new DTD, and this allows us to add the `prey` attribute to any of the `<omnivore>` or `<carnivore>` elements inside of our document. For example, we could do the following:

```
<carnivore kind="Tyrannosaurus_Rex" habitat="forest swamp jungle"
  prey="Gallimimus_Bullatus Triceratops_Horridus">
```

Notice that in the `prey` attribute, we listed two dinosaurs. We were sure to use the values from some of the `kind` attributes in our document, which had the type `ID`. We were also careful to pick dinosaurs that the Tyrannosaurus Rex might have eaten, as they were all from the Cretaceous period.

Chapter 5

This chapter taught us how to create XML Schemas that can be used to schema validate our XML documents.

Question 1

Add a `units` attribute to the `<length>` and `<height>` element declarations. Once you have added the attribute declaration, add the `units` attribute in your instance document and specify the value `"feet"`.

Solution

There were several approaches that could be taken when answering the first exercise question. In order to add an attribute to the `<length>` and `<height>` elements, we needed to be able to combine a simple content element declaration with a complex content element declaration. Knowing that we would need to refer to the existing <union> declaration by name, we decided to make it a global <simpleType> as in the following:

```
<simpleType name="IntegerListAndUnknownString">
  <union memberTypes="dino:IntegerList dino:UnknownString"/>
</simpleType>
```

We named the new type IntegerListAndUnknownString which describes the union of the IntegerList and UnknownString types that it declares. We then modified the declarations for the <length> and <height> elements as shown in the following:

```
          <element name="length">
            <complexType>
              <simpleContent>
                <extension base="dino:IntegerListAndUnknownString">
                  <attribute name="units" type="string" default="feet" />
                </extension>
              </simpleContent>
            </complexType>
          </element>
          <element name="height">
            <complexType>
              <simpleContent>
                <extension base="dino:IntegerListAndUnknownString">
                  <attribute name="units" type="string" default="feet" />
                </extension>
              </simpleContent>
            </complexType>
          </element>
```

In each of the declarations we used a <complexType> with a <simpleContent> declaration. Inside of this we used an <extension> element, specifying that the base type was the new IntegerListAndUnknownString type in our dinosaur vocabulary. Once we completed our declarations, all that was left to do was modify our document as follows:

```
<?xml version="1.0"?>
<dinosaurs
  xmlns="http://www.example.com/dinosaurs"
  xmlns:name="http://www.example.com/name"
  xmlns:xsi="http://www.w3.org/2001/XMLSchema-instance"
  xsi:schemaLocation="http://www.example.com/dinosaurs dinosaurs-
   question1.xsd"
  source="Beginning XML 3E"
  version="1.0">
  <carnivore kind="Tyrannosaurus_Rex" habitat="forest swamp jungle"
  period="Cretaceous">
    <species>Tyrannosaurus Rex</species>
    <length units="feet">25 42</length>
    <height units="feet">18</height>
    <weight>5-7 tons</weight>
    <speed>25 mph</speed>
    <weapon>
```

```
        <part-of-body>Teeth</part-of-body>
        <description>Though the Tyrannosaurus had many different sizes
of teeth, all were razor sharp and some grew to lengths of <b>9-13
inches</b>. Broken teeth were replaced frequently by newer teeth.
The powerful jaw exerted in excess of 3000 pounds of pressure!
</description>
      </weapon>
      <discoverer>
        <name:name title="Mr.">
          <name:first>Henry</name:first>
          <name:middle>Fairfield</name:middle>
          <name:last>Osborn</name:last>
        </name:name>
        <year>1905</year>
      </discoverer>
      <location>
        <country>Canada</country>
        <region>Alberta</region>
      </location>
      <description>The Tyrannosaurus Rex was the <b>king</b> of the terrible
lizards. Though many now believe it was a hunter <i>and</i> a scavenger it
is no less fearsome.</description>
    </carnivore>
    <herbivore kind="Stegosaurus_Armatus" habitat="forest swamp" period
     ="Jurassic">
      <species>Stegosaurus Armatus</species>
      <length units="feet">25</length>
      <height>14</height>
      <weight>2-4 tons</weight>
      <speed/>
      <weapon>
        <part-of-body>Spikes</part-of-body>
        <description>The Stegosaurus had two long rows of armor along its
back. At the end of its tail <b>four large spikes</b> were an excellent
defense.</description>
      </weapon>
      <discoverer>
        <name:name title="Mr.">
          <name:first>Othniel</name:first>
          <name:middle>Charles</name:middle>
          <name:last>Marsh</name:last>
        </name:name>
        <year>1877</year>
      </discoverer>
      <location>
        <country>United States</country>
        <region>Colorado</region>
      </location>
      <description>The Stegosaurus Armatus was, perhaps, the most heavily
armored of all dinosaurs. It is very possible though that it was not very
smart, it's  brain is believed to have been the <b>size of a
walnut!</b></description>
    </herbivore>
    <omnivore kind="Gallimimus_Bullatus" habitat="lakeshore prairie">
```

```
    <species>Gallimimus Bullatus</species>
    <length units="meters">5</length>
    <height units="meters">2 3</height>
    <weight>1000 pounds</weight>
    <speed>35-60 mph</speed>
    <weapon/>
    <discoverer>
      <name:name title="Ms.">
        <name:first>Halszka</name:first>
        <name:middle/>
        <name:last>Osm&#x00F3;lska</name:last>
      </name:name>
      <name:name title="Ms.">
        <name:first>Ewa</name:first>
        <name:middle/>
        <name:last>Roniewicz</name:last>
      </name:name>
      <name:name title="Mr.">
        <name:first>Rinchen</name:first>
        <name:middle/>
        <name:last>Barsbold</name:last>
      </name:name>
      <year>1972</year>
    </discoverer>
    <location>
      <country>Mongolia</country>
      <region>Nemegtskaya Svita</region>
    </location>
    <description>The Gallimimus Bullatus, or <i>Chicken Mimic</i> was
very fast, perhaps even the fastest of all dinosaurs.</description>
  </omnivore>
</dinosaurs>
```

For each of our dinosaurs we modified the `<length>` and `<height>` elements by adding the new `units` attribute. For our Tyrannosaurus Rex, we specified "feet" for the `units` in both cases. For the Stegosaurus Armatus, we specified "feet" as the `units` of the `<length>`, but we did not specify the `units` attribute for the `<height>`. Because we created a default in our attribute declaration, a schema validator would still see the `units` as "feet." In the Gallimimus Bullatus we specified "meters" for both of the `units`. We then changed the length and height inside of the element content to be measured in meters.

Question 2

Add a `feathers` attribute declaration for the `<carnivore>`, `<herbivore>`, and `<omnivore>` elements. The attribute should allow two possible values: `yes` and `no`. Make the attribute have a default value of `no`.

Solution

In this exercise, we had to add a `feathers` attribute to each of our dinosaur elements. Because the attribute needed to be declared for the `<carnivore>`, `<herbivore>`, and `<omnivore>` we were able to save some time by adding the attribute declaration to our `DinoAttributes` `<attributeGroup>`, as shown in the following:

```
<attributeGroup name="DinoAttributes">
  <attribute name="kind" type="ID" use="required"/>
  <attribute name="habitat" type="NMTOKENS" use="required"/>
  <attribute name="period" default="Cretaceous">
    <simpleType>
      <restriction base="string">
        <enumeration value="Triassic"/>
        <enumeration value="Jurassic"/>
        <enumeration value="Cretaceous"/>
      </restriction>
    </simpleType>
  </attribute>
  <attribute name="feathers" default="no">
    <simpleType>
      <restriction base="string">
        <enumeration value="yes"/>
        <enumeration value="no"/>
      </restriction>
    </simpleType>
  </attribute>
</attributeGroup>
```

When we added the attribute, we had to specify that the only allowable values were `yes` or `no`. We did this using a string restriction with enumerated values. We also set the default value to `no`. Once we completed this, we decided to add another dinosaur to our list that actually had feathers; so we added the Archaeopteryx Lithographica:

```
  <omnivore kind="Archaeopteryx_Lithographica" habitat="forest plains hills"
    period="Jurassic" feathers="yes">
    <species>Archaeopteryx Lithographica</species>
    <length units="feet">3</length>
    <height units="feet">2</height>
    <weight>Weight not known</weight>
    <speed/>
    <weapon>
      <part-of-body>Feathers</part-of-body>
      <description>The Archaeopteryx had feathers that could have been used to
help it <i>fly</i>. Additionally, its <b>sharp claws</b> and <b>teeth</b> could
help it devour prey.</description>
    </weapon>
    <discoverer>
      <name:name title="Mr.">
        <name:first>Hermann</name:first>
        <name:middle />
        <name:last>von Meyer</name:last>
      </name:name>
      <name:name title="Sir.">
        <name:first>Richard</name:first>
        <name:middle/>
        <name:last>Owen</name:last>
```

```
      </name:name>
      <year>1863</year>
    </discoverer>
    <location>
      <country>Bavaria</country>
      <region>Solnhofen Limestone, Pappenheim</region>
    </location>
    <description>The Archaeopteryx is very controversial. It is said to be the
<i>missing link</i> between <b>Dinosaurs</b> and <b>modern
birds</b>.</description>
  </omnivore>
```

Question 3

Modify the <description> declaration to include an element wildcard. Within the wildcard, specify that the description element can accept any elements from the namespace http://www.w3.org/1999/xhtml. Set the processContents attribute to lax.

Solution

In this exercise, we wanted to modify the <description> element so that it could include any elements from the XHTML namespace. To do this, we needed to replace the existing element declarations with an element wildcard declaration:

```
<complexType name="DescriptionType" mixed="true">
  <sequence>
    <any namespace="http://www.w3.org/1999/xhtml" processContents="lax"
      minOccurs="0" maxOccurs="unbounded"/>
  </sequence>
</complexType>
```

After we completed the changes to the declaration, we needed to update our XML document. In our document we had the following:

```
<description>Though the Tyrannosaurus had many different sizes of teeth, all
 were razor sharp and some grew to lengths of <b>9-13 inches</b>. Broken teeth
 were replaced frequently by newer teeth. The powerful jaw exerted in excess
 of 3000 pounds of pressure!</description>
```

But we needed to modify this. In order for the content to be valid we needed to make sure that all of the elements used inside the description were from the XHTML namespace. To do this, we first added a namespace declaration to our root element. Then, we added the new prefix to all of our <b> and <i> elements:

```
<?xml version="1.0"?>
<dinosaurs
  xmlns="http://www.example.com/dinosaurs"
  xmlns:name="http://www.example.com/name"
  xmlns:xsi="http://www.w3.org/2001/XMLSchema-instance"
  xmlns:html="http://www.w3.org/1999/xhtml"
  xsi:schemaLocation="http://www.example.com/dinosaurs dinosaurs-
question3.xsd"
```

```
  source="Beginning XML 3E"
  version="1.0">
  <carnivore kind="Tyrannosaurus_Rex" habitat="forest swamp jungle"
  period="Cretaceous">
    <species>Tyrannosaurus Rex</species>
    <length units="feet">25 42</length>
    <height units="feet">18</height>
    <weight>5-7 tons</weight>
    <speed>25 mph</speed>
    <weapon>
      <part-of-body>Teeth</part-of-body>
      <description>Though the Tyrannosaurus had many different sizes of teeth,
all were razor sharp and some grew to lengths of <html:b>9-13 inches</html:b>.
Broken teeth were replaced frequently by newer teeth. The powerful jaw exerted
in excess of 3000 pounds of pressure!</description>
    </weapon>
    <discoverer>
      <name:name title="Mr.">
        <name:first>Henry</name:first>
        <name:middle>Fairfield</name:middle>
        <name:last>Osborn</name:last>
      </name:name>
      <year>1905</year>
    </discoverer>
    <location>
      <country>Canada</country>
      <region>Alberta</region>
    </location>
    <description>The Tyrannosaurus Rex was the <html:b>king</html:b> of the
terrible lizards. Though many now believe it was a hunter <html:i>and</html:i>
a scavenger it is no less fearsome.</description>
  </carnivore>
  <herbivore kind="Stegosaurus_Armatus" habitat="forest swamp"
   period="Jurassic">
    <species>Stegosaurus Armatus</species>
    <length units="feet">25</length>
    <height>14</height>
    <weight>2-4 tons</weight>
    <speed/>
    <weapon>
      <part-of-body>Spikes</part-of-body>
      <description>The Stegosaurus had two long rows of armor along its back.
At the end of its tail <html:b>four large spikes</html:b> were an excellent
defense.</description>
    </weapon>
    <discoverer>
      <name:name title="Mr.">
        <name:first>Othniel</name:first>
        <name:middle>Charles</name:middle>
        <name:last>Marsh</name:last>
      </name:name>
      <year>1877</year>
    </discoverer>
    <location>
      <country>United States</country>
```

```
      <region>Colorado</region>
    </location>
    <description>The Stegosaurus Armatus was, perhaps, the most heavily
armored of all dinosaurs. It is very possible though that it was not
very smart, it's brain is believed to have been the <html:b>size of a
walnut!</html:b></description>
  </herbivore>
  <omnivore kind="Gallimimus_Bullatus" habitat="lakeshore prairie">
    <species>Gallimimus Bullatus</species>
    <length units="meters">5</length>
    <height units="meters">2 3</height>
    <weight>1000 pounds</weight>
    <speed>35-60 mph</speed>
    <weapon/>
    <discoverer>
      <name:name title="Ms.">
        <name:first>Halszka</name:first>
        <name:middle/>
        <name:last>Osm&#x00F3;lska</name:last>
      </name:name>
      <name:name title="Ms.">
        <name:first>Ewa</name:first>
        <name:middle/>
        <name:last>Roniewicz</name:last>
      </name:name>
      <name:name title="Mr.">
        <name:first>Rinchen</name:first>
        <name:middle/>
        <name:last>Barsbold</name:last>
      </name:name>
      <year>1972</year>
    </discoverer>
    <location>
      <country>Mongolia</country>
      <region>Nemegtskaya Svita</region>
    </location>
    <description>The Gallimimus Bullatus, or <html:i>Chicken Mimic</html:i> was
very fast, perhaps even the fastest of all dinosaurs.</description>
  </omnivore>
  <omnivore kind="Archaeopteryx_Lithographica" habitat="forest plains hills"
   period="Jurassic" feathers="yes">
    <species>Archaeopteryx Lithographica</species>
    <length units="feet">3</length>
    <height units="feet">2</height>
    <weight>Weight not known</weight>
    <speed/>
    <weapon>
      <part-of-body>Feathers</part-of-body>
      <description>The Archaeopteryx had feathers that could have been used to
help it <html:i>fly</html:i>. Additionally, its <html:b>sharp claws</html:b>
and <html:b>teeth</html:b> could help it devour prey.</description>
    </weapon>
    <discoverer>
      <name:name title="Mr.">
        <name:first>Hermann</name:first>
```

```
        <name:middle />
        <name:last>von Meyer</name:last>
      </name:name>
      <name:name title="Sir.">
        <name:first>Richard</name:first>
        <name:middle/>
        <name:last>Owen</name:last>
      </name:name>
      <year>1863</year>
    </discoverer>
    <location>
      <country>Bavaria</country>
      <region>Solnhofen Limestone, Pappenheim</region>
    </location>
    <description>The Archaeopteryx is very controversial. It is said to be the
<html:i>missing link</html:i> between <html:b>Dinosaurs</html:b> and <html:b>
modern birds</html:b>.</description>
  </omnivore>
</dinosaurs>
```

Chapter 6

This chapter showed how to create RELAX NG compact schemas, which can be used to validate XML instance documents.

Question 1

Break the dinosaur2.rnc schema file into two schemas. In dinosaur3Main.rnc, place the main schema elements. In dinoInfo.rnc, place the dinoInfo pattern. At the top level, place an include directive in dinosaur3Main.rnc to include dinoInfo.rnc.

Solution 1

First, we'll place the dinoInfo pattern into its own schema file, dinoInfo.rnc:

```
dinoInfo = ( species, length, height, weight, speed, discoverer, location )

species    =  element  species { text }
length     =  element  length  { text }
height     =  element  height  { text }
weight     =  element  weight  { text }
speed      =  element  speed   { text }


discoverer =  element  discoverer { name, date }
name       =  element  name { text }
date       =  element  date { text }


location   =  element  location { country+ }
country    =  element  country { text }
```

Note that this schema does not include a `start` pattern, because it is not intended to be used as a stand-alone.

Next, we'll create the main schema, `dinosaur3Main.rnc`, placing the main schema elements:

```
include "dinoInfo.rnc"

start = dinosaurs
dinosaurs = element dinosaurs { (carnivore } herbivore)* }

carnivore = element carnivore { dinoInfo }
herbivore = element herbivore { dinoInfo }
```

This main schema contains the `start` pattern for our dinosaur XML files, and also includes the `dinoInfo.rnc` file on the top line. The two `dinoInfo` pattern references, found in the `carnivore` and `herbivore` patterns reference the `dinoInfo` pattern found in the `dinoInfo.rnc` file.

Question 2

Add a wildcard extension to the `dinoInfo` pattern, so that the users can extend the dinosaur schema by adding any elements they desire to `dinoInfo`.

Solution 2

First, here is a wildcard pattern that can accept any element, with any attributes or text, from any namespace. This wildcard element also allows any child elements, due to the recursive (any) reference.

```
any = element * { attribute * {text} } any } text }*
```

Next, we need to extend the `dinoInfo` pattern by adding the any pattern to the end of the existing `dinoInfo` pattern:

```
dinoInfo = ( species, length, height, weight, speed, discoverer, location,
any)
```

Note the `any` reference at the end of the preceding list. Here is the new and complete `dinoInfo.rnc` file:

```
dinoInfo =  ( species, length, height, weight, speed, discoverer, location,
any)

species     =  element  species { text }
length      =  element  length  { text }
height      =  element  height  { text }
weight      =  element  weight  { text }
speed       =  element  speed   { text }

discoverer =  element  discoverer { name, date }
name        =  element  name { text }
date        =  element  date { text }

location    =  element  location { country+ }
country     =  element  country { text }
```

```
#wildcard extension for dinoInfo, allowing any element
any = element * { attribute * {text} } any } text }*
```

The main schema, `dinosaur4Main.rnc`, remains the same as the previous version, including the `dinoInfo.rnc` file:

```
include "dinoInfo.rnc"

start = dinosaurs
dinosaurs = element dinosaurs { (carnivore } herbivore)* }

carnivore = element carnivore { dinoInfo }
herbivore = element herbivore { dinoInfo }
```

Chapter 7

This chapter covered XPath 1.0, and we learned about XPath axes and the functions in the XPath 1.0 function library.

Question 1

Name two XPath axes which, respectively, can be used to select element nodes and attribute nodes. If the context node is an element node, give the XPath location path, which selects the `number` attribute node of that element node. Show the answer in both abbreviated and unabbreviated syntax.

Solution

Element nodes are most commonly selected using the `child` axis. The `descendant` and `descendant-or-self` axes may also contain element nodes.

Attribute nodes are selected using the `attribute` axis.

Using abbreviated syntax, the location path `@number` selects the `number` attribute. Using unabbreviated syntax, the equivalent location path is written as `attribute::number`.

Question 2

XPath 1.0 allows wildcards to be used when selecting child nodes of the context node. What is the location path, which selects all child nodes of the context node? Give the answer in both abbreviated and unabbreviated syntax.

Solution

Using abbreviated syntax the asterisk, `*`, selects all child element nodes of the context node;in unabbreviated syntax that is written as `child::*`.

Chapter 8

This chapter discussed how XML documents can be restructured for data interchange or transformed for presentation using XSLT.

Question 1

If you need to process a node in the source tree more than once but in different ways each time, what technique does XSLT provide to achieve this?

Solution

XSLT provides the use of modes to allow a node in the source tree to be processed multiple times. An `xsl:apply-templates` element can have a `mode` attribute. The same value as the value of the `mode` attribute of the `xsl:apply-templates` element will match, and therefore only that template rule will be processed.

Question 2

What are the two XSLT elements that provide conditional processing? Describe how the functionality provided by these two elements differs.

Solution

XSLT has the `xsl:if` and `xsl:choose` elements to provide conditional processing. The content of an `xsl:if` element is processed if a test is true and allows a single choice to be made.

The `xsl:choose` element together with its child elements, `xsl:when` and `xsl:otherwise`, allows multiple tests to be applied. No test is applied on the `xsl:choose` element or the `xsl:otherwise` element. Each `xsl:when` element has an associated test. Each test on the `xsl:when` elements is evaluated in turn. If a test returning `true` is found on an `xsl:when` element, then the content of that `xsl:when` element is processed and all subsequent `xsl:when` elements are ignored as is the `xsl:otherwise` element. If no `xsl:when` element has a test which returns true, then the content of the `xsl:otherwise` element, if present, is processed.

Chapter 9

This chapter covered some foundational aspects of the upcoming XML Query Language, XQuery.

Question 1

What notation is used in an XQuery expression to indicate that its content is created dynamically?

Solution

Paired curly brackets, written as `{` and `}` are used to indicate that their content is evaluated at runtime. Other parts of an XQuery expression, for example, start and end tags of element constructors, are used literally in the output from a query.

Question 2

What are the component parts of a FLWOR expression and what do they each do?

Solution

There are potentially five parts of a FLWOR expression: the `for` clause, the `let` clause, the `where` clause, the `order by` clause, and the `return` clause.

In the `for` clause, a variable can be bound to multiple items in a sequence. In a `let` clause, a variable is bound to a single item. The `where` clause filters the results according to specified criteria. The `order by` clause specifies any ordering of the returned data. The `return` clause specifies the construct in the output for each variable, appropriately filtered and sorted.

Chapter 10

This chapter explored the increasing business need to store or expose data as XML through the use of a viable XML-enabled database.

Question 1

List some reasons why adding XML functionality to a relational database management system may be preferable to using a native XML database.

Solution

First, be aware that this issue can generate discussion of religious intensity. The following offers a possible answer to the question.

Most uses of XML will be in a setting where relational database management systems are already in use. Using an RDBMS may be essentially free (for example, there would be no additional license costs), whereas acquiring a native XML database might have additional license or training costs. In addition, most commercial relational database management systems have good and well-tested security, reliability, and scalability. These considerations, which are important to enterprise use in a production setting, may be less good in the early versions of native XML databases.

Question 2

What methods are available in SQL Server 2005 to manipulate data in a database column that is of type `xml`?

Solution

There are four methods in SQL Server 2005 which allow manipulation of type `xml`: `query()`, `insert()`, `update()`, and `delete()`.

Chapter 11

This chapter introduced the XML Document Object Model (DOM), noting the differences between interfaces and nodes as well as describing several of the most common DOM interfaces and objects.

Question 1

Describe an important difference between the `NamedNodeMap` object and the `NodeList` object.

Solution

The `NamedNodeMap` object is unordered and is used to refer to attributes, because the attributes of an element are not ordered. A `NodeList` object is ordered so it cannot be used to refer to attributes. A `NodeList` object often corresponds to the child nodes of a `Document` node or of an `Element` node, because those child nodes are ordered.

Question 2

List the methods of the `Document` object that are used to add `Element` nodes, which are, first, in no namespace and, second, in a namespace.

Solution

The `createElement()` method of the `Document` object is used to create new `Element` nodes where the element is not in a namespace. To add `Element` nodes where the element is in a namespace, use the `createElementNS()` method.

Chapter 12

This chapter covered the Simple API for XML (SAX).

Question 1

Calculate the weight, length, and total number of occupants on the entire train. Once the document has been parsed, print out the result of the calculations.

Solution

In general, this was a straightforward task; all we needed to do was record the values as we encountered them and add them to a total variable that could be printed out in the `endDocument` function.

Our first step was to rename our class to `TrainReader_Question1`. We also added declarations for our total variables and a `StringBuffer` to collect the element values:

```
import javax.xml.parsers.SAXParserFactory;
import javax.xml.parsers.SAXParser;
```

```
import org.xml.sax.*;
import org.xml.sax.helpers.*;

public class TrainReader_Question1 extends DefaultHandler
{

  private boolean isColor;
  private String trainCarType = "";
  private StringBuffer trainCarColor = new StringBuffer();
  private Locator trainLocator = null;
  private StringBuffer trainElementValue = new StringBuffer();
  private int totalWeight;
  private int totalLength;
  private int totalOccupants;

  public static void main (String[] args)
    throws Exception
  {
    System.out.println("Running train reader...");
    TrainReader_Question1 readerObj = new TrainReader_Question1();
    readerObj.read(args[0]);
  }
```

We then needed to modify our `startDocument` and `endDocument` functions. Inside of `startDocument` we reset our total values to 0. Within the `endDocument` function, we made sure to print out the results of the calculations.

```
public void startDocument()
  throws SAXException
{
  System.out.println("Start of the train");
  totalWeight = 0;
  totalLength = 0;
  totalOccupants = 0;
}

public void endDocument()
  throws SAXException
{
  System.out.println("End of the train");
  System.out.println("The train weighed " + totalWeight + " tons");
  System.out.println("The train was " + totalLength + " feet long");
  System.out.println("The train had " + totalOccupants + " occupants");
}
```

Next, inside of our `startElement` function, we reset our `trainElementValue` buffer if we were not working with a color:

```
public void startElement(String uri, String localName, String qName,
Attributes atts)
  throws SAXException
{
  if (localName.equals("car")) {
    if (atts != null) {
```

```
        trainCarType = atts.getValue("type");
      }
    }

    if (localName.equals("color"))
    {
      trainCarColor.setLength(0);
      isColor = true;
    } else {
      isColor = false;
      trainElementValue.setLength(0);
    }

  }
```

As we had done when collecting the value of the <color> elements, we made sure to append any data we received to a buffer. Although it is unlikely that we would receive multiple calls to the `characters` function for a single value, it is possible, and we must be ready for it.

```
  public void characters(char[] ch, int start, int len)
    throws SAXException
  {
    if (isColor)
    {
      trainCarColor.append(ch, start, len);
    } else {
      trainElementValue.append(ch, start, len);
    }
  }
```

Finally, in the `endElement` function we performed the calculations. We first copied the value of the buffer into the `elementValue` variable. This value could include "tons" or "feet", so we checked to see if there was a space and deleted everything from the space until the end of the string. In a real application, we would need to do more error checking here to make sure that we didn't receive a bad value. Once we obtained the right string, we parsed it into a numeric value and added it to the correct total based on the `localName`:

```
  public void endElement(String uri, String localName, String qName)
    throws SAXException
  {
    if (isColor)
    {
      System.out.println("The color of the " + trainCarType + " car is " +
        trainCarColor.toString());
      if ((trainCarType.equals("Caboose")) &&
        (!trainCarColor.toString().equals("Red")))
      {
        if (trainLocator != null)
         throw new SAXException("The caboose is not red at line " +
           trainLocator.getLineNumber() + ", column " +
           trainLocator.getColumnNumber() );
        else
          throw new SAXException("The caboose is not red!");
      }
```

```
  } else {

    String elementValue = trainElementValue.toString();
    if (elementValue.indexOf(" ") >= 0)
      elementValue = elementValue.substring(0, elementValue.indexOf(" "));
    int value = Integer.parseInt(elementValue);

    if ("weight".equals(localName)) {
      totalWeight += value;
    } else if ("length".equals(localName)) {
      totalLength += value;
    } else if ("occupants".equals(localName)) {
      totalOccupants += value;
    }
  }
   isColor = false;
}
```

In the end, we were able to quickly see how much the train weighed, how long it was, and how many occupants were on the train. If you ran the program against our sample documents from Chapter 12, you would see the following results:

```
Running train reader...
Start of the train
The color of the Engine car is Black
The color of the Baggage car is Green
The color of the Dining car is Green and Yellow
The color of the Passenger car is Green and Yellow
The color of the Pullman car is Green and Yellow
The color of the Caboose car is Red
End of the train
The train weighed 822 tons
The train was 300 feet long
The train had 71 occupants
```

Question 2

Print out a list of all elements declared in the DTD. To do this, descend the `TrainReader` class from `DefaultHandler2` instead of `DefaultHandler`. Register the `TrainReader` class with the parser so that you can receive `DeclHandler` events (hint: you will need to use a property).

Solution

Although this exercise question may have seemed more difficult than the first, the code was actually shorter. We first needed to import the helper class `DefaultHandler2`. Then, we modified our declaration to descend from `DefaultHandler2` (and change the name of this class for the example).

```
import javax.xml.parsers.SAXParserFactory;
import javax.xml.parsers.SAXParser;
import org.xml.sax.*;
import org.xml.sax.helpers.*;
import org.xml.sax.ext.DefaultHandler2;
```

```
public class TrainReader_Question2 extends DefaultHandler2
{

  private boolean isColor;
  private String trainCarType = "";
  private StringBuffer trainCarColor = new StringBuffer();
  private StringBuffer trainElementValue = new StringBuffer();
  private Locator trainLocator = null;
  private int totalWeight;
  private int totalLength;
  private int totalOccupants;

  public static void main (String[] args)
    throws Exception
  {
    System.out.println("Running train reader...");
    TrainReader_Question2 readerObj = new TrainReader_Question2();
    readerObj.read(args[0]);
  }
```

Then, before we parsed the document, we needed to register our class as a `DeclHandler` with the parser. Because the `DeclHandler` is an extension interface, the only way to register it was to set the property `http://xml.org/sax/properties/declaration-handler`:

```
public void read(String fileName)
  throws Exception
{
  XMLReader reader =
      XMLReaderFactory.createXMLReader("org.apache.xerces.parsers.SAXParser");
  reader.setContentHandler (this);
  reader.setErrorHandler (this);

  try
  {
     reader.setFeature("http://xml.org/sax/features/validation", true);
  }
  catch (SAXException e)
  {
    System.err.println("Cannot activate validation");
  }

  try
  {
     reader.setProperty("http://xml.org/sax/properties/declaration-handler",
       this);
  }
  catch (SAXException e)
  {
     System.err.println("Cannot set declaration handler");
  }

  try
  {
```

```
        reader.parse(fileName);
      }
      catch (SAXException e)
      {
        System.out.println("Parsing stopped : " + e.getMessage());
      }
    }
```

Finally, we needed to override the `elementDecl` function. Remember in the `DefaultHandler2` class, this function does absolutely nothing. Inside the function all we did was print out a message with the element name:

```
public void elementDecl(String name, String model)
  throws SAXException {
  System.out.println("Element declaration : " + name);
}
```

While the resulting output may not be very exciting, being able to access declaration events is. Many XML editors utilize this feature of SAX to generate lists of elements for tag completion. If you were to run the code on our sample documents from Chapter 12, you would see the following results:

```
Running train reader...
Start of the train
Element declaration : train
Element declaration : car
Element declaration : color
Element declaration : weight
Element declaration : length
Element declaration : occupants
The color of the Engine car is Black
The color of the Baggage car is Green
The color of the Dining car is Green and Yellow
The color of the Passenger car is Green and Yellow
The color of the Pullman car is Green and Yellow
The color of the Caboose car is Red
End of the train
The train weighed 822 tons
The train was 300 feet long
The train had 71 occupants
```

Chapter 13

This chapter covered RSS and content syndication, introducing the fundamental concepts, some of the techniques that can be applied, and how XML is central to content syndication.

Question 1

At the end of the description of the simple Python aggregator, it was demonstrated how it was relatively simple to extend the range of the elements covered, by adding support for `dc:source`. Your first challenge is to extend the application so that it also displays the author of a feed entry, if that information is available.

You should check the specs and some real-world feeds yourself, but the elements used for identifying the author of an item are usually one of the following: `author`, `dc:creator`, `atom:name`, or `foaf:name`. The `author` element appears in the "simple" RSS versions (0.9x, 2.0) and has no namespace. However, there is a slight complication, as there is also an element in RSS 2.0 called `name`, which is used for the name of the text object in a text input area (the text input area elements are rarely encountered in practice, but it does make for a more interesting exercise). So part of this exercise is to ensure that this element won't be mistaken for the name of the author.

Solution

The core of the solution is just a matter of following what was done in the chapter for `dc:source`, that is, adding an extra conditional to the `endElementNS` method in `feed_handler.py`. But there is also the little matter of distinguishing between `atom:name/foaf:name` (author) and `name` (text area). The potential for naming clashes has been taken into account by using the SAX `endElementNS` method rather than the marginally simpler `endElement`. Referring back to the `endElementNS` method in `feed_handler.py`, we will see it begins like this:

```
        def endElementNS(self, name, qname):
            "Collects element content, switches state as
                         appropriate (called by SAX parser)"
            (namespace, localname) = name
    ...
```

The `name` value passed to the method is actually a pair of individual values combined in a tuple. The `localname` part is what has been used in the conditionals so far, but the `namespace` string is also available. So as a necessary step we can check to see whether the unambiguous combination of `namespace` and `localname` is one that corresponds to the author. The extra conditional needed looks like this:

```
    ...
            if localname == "source": # dc:source
                self.current_item.source = '('+self.current_item.source+') '+ text
                return

            if (localname == "creator" or # dc:creator
                localname == "author" or # RSS 0.9x/2.0
                (localname == "name" and
                 namespace == "http://purl.org/atom/ns#") or
                (localname == "name" and
                 namespace == "http://xmlns.com/foaf/0.1/")):
                self.current_item.author = text
    ...
```

As you probably noticed by now, there was a little cheating in the text—a member variable `source` was included in the original code for the `Item` class (in `feed.py`), so when the `dc:source` extension was added, a destination for the value was already available.

There isn't really any good place available for the value of author to go, but it's straightforward to create one, in other words, an `author` member variable in the `Item` class. Here's what the code looks like (in `feed.py`):

```
    class Item:
        """ Simple model of a single item within a syndication feed """
```

```
    def __init__(self):
        """ Initialize properties to defaults """
        self.title = ''
        self.content = ''
        self.source = ''
        self.date = time.time() - BAD_TIME_HANDICAP # seconds from the Epoch

        self.author = ''

...
```

That's simply an additional member variable with its value initialized to an empty string.

This new code will extract and hold onto the author's name, but we will also want to see it in the display of items. This can be achieved by adding a single line to the `__str__()` method in the `Item` class, which provides a string representation of the class (like `toString()` in Java). Here is the code, again in `feed.py`:

```
def __str__(self):
    """ Custom 'toString()' method to pretty-print """
    return (self.source + ' : '
        + self.title +'\n'
        + self.content + '\n'
        + self.author + '\n'
        + self.get_formatted_date() + '\n')
```

The string that contains the name of the author is inserted along with a newline character, into the string representation of `Item` objects, which is used by `FeedReader` to display them.

In you now run the modified code, the results should contain items like this:

```
Binary Relations : WordPress
 While WordPress gives you choices for translating the names of the
 weekdays for use with the post calendar, ...
Morten Frederiksen
Thu, 20 May 2004 16:16:38 +0200
```

As you can see, a name has been added.

Morten's name was actually included in his RSS 1.0 feed as a FOAF extension as follows:

```
<item rdf:about="http://purl.org/net/morten/...">
 ...
 <foaf:maker>
        <foaf:Person>
               <foaf:name>Morten Frederiksen</foaf:name>
               <foaf:nick>mortenf</foaf:nick>

<foaf:mbox_sha1sum>65b983bb397fb71849da910996741752ace8369b</foaf:mbox_sha1sum>
               <foaf:weblog rdf:resource="http://purl.org/net/morten/blog"/>
        </foaf:Person>
 </foaf:maker>
...
</item>
```

It's worth mentioning again that the model used inside the demo application is specialized to particular kinds of feed data and as simple as can be, and hence seriously limited. In feeds such as Morten's, there is a lot more information potentially available structured in the RDF model (in RDF/XML syntax). The `foaf:maker` of the item is a `foaf:Person` with a `foaf:name` of `Morten Frederiksen`. This `foaf:Person` also has other properties, including a `foaf:nick` and a `foaf:weblog`. The `foaf:mbox_sha1` property is a disguised reference to Morten's mailbox (e-mail address). This has a unique value, which makes it possible for RDF tools to tell that any other `foaf:Person` with the same `foaf:mbox_sha1sum` is the same person, allowing them to combine (merge or "smush") any properties associated with this `foaf:Person` and reason with the information as required. RDF code libraries are available for most languages, so if you're considering building a more sophisticated aggregator, it's relatively straightforward to use the richness available through RSS 1.0.

Question 2

We saw toward the end of the chapter how the most common syndication formats show themselves, and earlier in the chapter we saw how it was possible to run an XSLT stylesheet over RSS feeds to produce an XHTML rendering. The exercise here is to apply the second technique to the first task. Try to write an XSLT transformation that will tell us the format of the feed, together with its title.

Solution

The following (`version.xsl`) is one possible solution. The stylesheet starts with a list of namespace declarations that cover the kinds of data that might be encountered:

```
<xsl:stylesheet version="1.0"
    xmlns:xsl="http://www.w3.org/1999/XSL/Transform"
    xmlns:rdf="http://www.w3.org/1999/02/22-rdf-syntax-ns#"
    xmlns:rss="http://purl.org/rss/1.0/"
    xmlns:foaf="http://xmlns.com/foaf/0.1/"
    xmlns:atom="http://purl.org/atom/ns#">

<xsl:output method="text" indent="yes"/>
```

The output method here is set to `text`. To keep the listing short, this stylesheet only delivers a plain text output.

To make the output more legible, it is preceded and followed by a new line, which is achieved by placing an escaped-text representation of the newline character (`
`) before and after the application of the detailed templates. The entry point into the stylesheet is through matching the root element, as can be seen here:

```
<xsl:template match="/">
    <xsl:text>&#xA;</xsl:text>
       <xsl:apply-templates />
    <xsl:text>&#xA;</xsl:text>
</xsl:template>
```

There now follows a series of templates that match according to simple rules intended to identify the feed format. First of all, here is a template to match RSS versions 0.9x and 2.0:

```
<xsl:template match="/rss">
    <xsl:text>RSS Version: </xsl:text>
```

```
    <xsl:value-of select="./@version" />
    <xsl:apply-templates select="channel/title" />
</xsl:template>
```

Text is output to state the name of the feed type (RSS) and then the value of the version attribute is extracted. An attempt is then made to match templates to anything with the path `/rss/channel/title`.

The following template will match the root element of an Atom feed:

```
<xsl:template match="/atom:feed">
    <xsl:text>Atom Version: </xsl:text>
    <xsl:value-of select="./@version" />
    <xsl:apply-templates select="atom:title"/>
</xsl:template>
```

Again the version is extracted, then anything matching `/atom:feed/atom:title` is passed to other templates to deal with.

The next template will match RDF files:

```
<xsl:template match="/rdf:RDF">
(RDF)
   <xsl:apply-templates />
</xsl:template>
```

Note the requirement for RDF/XML files to have a root called `rdf:RDF` was removed from the latest specification, though this requirement is still in place for RSS 1.0.

If the feed is RSS 1.0, it will have a `<channel>` element, which will be picked up by the following template:

```
<xsl:template match="rss:channel">
    <xsl:text>RSS Version: 1.0</xsl:text>
    <xsl:apply-templates />
</xsl:template>
```

Next is a template that will match the feed title of the three feed formats:

```
<xsl:template match="rss:title } atom:title } title">
        <xsl:text>&#xA;Title: </xsl:text>
 <xsl:value-of select="text()" />
</xsl:template>
```

The FOAF document described in the text was a red herring, but for the sake of consistency here's a template that will extract the first named person in a FOAF profile:

```
<xsl:template match="//*[position() = 1]/foaf:Person/foaf:name">
    <xsl:text>FOAF Name: </xsl:text>
    <xsl:value-of select="text()" />
</xsl:template>
```

The stylesheet ends with a template that will pick up loose ends that would otherwise go to the output:

```
<xsl:template match="rss:item } text()" />

</xsl:stylesheet>
```

Here are the results of running this transformation on the documents at the sample URIs, which were previously downloaded using `wget`:

`http://news.bbc.co.uk/rss/newsonline_world_edition/front_page/rss091.xml`:

```
D:\rss-samples>java -jar saxon7.jar rss091.xml version.xsl
RSS Version: 0.91
Title: BBC News } News Front Page } World Edition
```

`http://purl.org/net/morten/blog/feed/rdf/`:

```
D:\rss-samples>java -jar saxon7.jar index.html version.xsl

(RDF)
RSS Version: 1.0
Title: Binary Relations
```

`http://icite.net/blog/?flavor=atom&smm=y`:

```
D:\rss-samples>java -jar saxon7.jar index.html@flavor=atom version.xsl

Atom Version: 0.3
Title: the iCite net development blog
```

`http://blogs.it/0100198/rss.xml`:

```
D:\rss-samples>java -jar saxon7.jar rss.xml version.xsl

RSS Version: 2.0
Title: Marc's Voice
```

`http://swordfish.rdfweb.org/people/libby/rdfweb/webwho.xrdf`:

```
D:\rss-samples>java -jar saxon7.jar webwho.xrdf version.xsl

(RDF)
FOAF Name: Libby Miller
```

Chapter 14

This chapter looked at Web Services, a group of XML-based protocols for performing remote procedure calls.

Question 1

Imagine you are trying to contact an XML-RPC-based Web Service to submit a classified ad for a lost dog. The required information includes your name, phone number, and the body of the ad. What might the XML request look like?

Solution

There are two ways of doing this. The first example (shown next) is the simpler way, representing each of the parameters individually. I've started by including the name of the procedure to call (`classifieds.submit`) and then simply specified each of the parameters, in order. (I could also have added a `name` element that named each parameter, as I did in the second example.)

```
<methodCall>
  <methodName>classifieds.submit</methodName>
  <params>
    <param>
      <value><string>Nicholas Chase</string></value>
    </param>
    <param>
      <value><string>212-555-1234</string></value>
    </param>
    <param>
      <value><string>Lost: Large mixed-breed dog. Chunk out of one ear,
              missing an eye, limps on three legs. Answers to "Lucky".
              212-555-1234</string></value>
    </param>
  </params>
</methodCall>
```

In the second example, I've added the same information, but I've added it as part of a struct, with each member holding one parameter. Which one you'd choose in the real world will depend on the requirements of the procedure you're calling.

```
<methodCall>
  <methodName>classifieds.submit</methodName>
  <params>
    <param>
      <value>
        <struct>
          <member>
            <name>CustomerName</name>
            <value><string>Nicholas Chase</string></value>
          </member>
          <member>
            <name>CustomerPhone</name>
            <value><string>212-555-1234</string></value>
          </member>
          <member>
            <name>AdText</name>
            <value>
              <string> Lost: Large mixed-breed dog. Chunk out of one ear,
```

```
                missing an eye, limps on three legs. Answers to "Lucky".
                212-555-1234</string>
              </value>
            </member>
          </struct>
        </value>
      </param>
    </params>
  </methodCall>
```

Question 2

You are trying to call a REST-based Web Service to check on the status of a service order. The service needs the following information:

```
cust_id: 3263827
order_id: THX1138
```

What might the request look like?

Solution

In a REST system, you add all of the information to the URL and then submit that URL as a `GET` request. In our case, we're adding two parameters, `cust_id` and `order_id`, separated by an ampersand (`&`) as shown in the following:

```
http://www.example.com/checkServiceOrder?cust_id=3263827&order_id=THX1138
```

Chapter 15

This chapter covered SOAP, an XML-based protocol for performing remote procedure calls and passing information between computers. The chapter also looked at Web Services Definition Language, or WSDL, which provides another developer with all of the information he or she might need in order to access your service.

Question 1

Create a SOAP message that fulfills the following requirements:

1. It corresponds to an RPC called `getRadioOperators()`.
2. It passes the following information:
   - City and State or Postal Code
   - Radius
   - License Class
3. The server must receive and verify a call sign from the sender.

Solution

In this case, we're creating a simple SOAP message, which includes the request as the contents of the `Body` element as shown in the following code. We're calling the `getRadioOperators()` method, so that's the name of the root element for our payload, and each item is included in an element that corresponds to the name of the parameter we're passing. The sender's call sign is sent in the header, with the `mustUnderstand` attribute set to true. If the server doesn't understand that it needs to verify this information before processing the message, it must reject the message altogether.

```
<soap:Envelope xmlns:soap="http://www.w3.org/2003/05/soap-envelope">
  <soap:Header xmlns:s="http://www.example.com/radio/">
    <s:License mustUnderstand="true">
      WNEW
    </s:License>
  </soap:Header>
  <soap:Body xmlns:h="http://www.example.com/hams/">
     <h:getRadioOperators>
        <h:postalCode>02134</h:postalCode>
        <h:radius>5</h:radius>
        <h:licenseClass>General</h:licenseClass>
     </h:getRadioOperators>
  </soap:Body>
</soap:Envelope>
```

Question 2

Create a WSDL file that describes the document in Question 1.

Solution

Starting at the bottom, we've created a service that has an instance located at a particular URL, `http://localhost/hamsearch.asp`. That instance is "bound" to the `HamSearchBinding` `binding`, which specifies that the message is to be sent using the SOAP RPC style, and defines the encoding for the `input` and `output` messages, as well as their namespaces. The binding also specifies that it's using the `HamSearchPort` `portType`, or interface. This `portType` specifies the message types for the input and output messages, which refer back to element definitions in the schema at the top of the document as shown in the following:

```
<?xml version="1.0"?>
<definitions name="HamSearch"
    targetNamespace="http://www.example.com/hamSearch"
    xmlns:typens=" http://www.example.com/hamSearch "
    xmlns:xsd="http://www.w3.org/2000/10/XMLSchema"
    xmlns:soap="http://schemas.xmlsoap.org/wsdl/soap/"
    xmlns:soapenc="http://schemas.xmlsoap.org/soap/encoding/"
    xmlns:wsdl="http://schemas.xmlsoap.org/wsdl/"
    xmlns="http://schemas.xmlsoap.org/wsdl/">

  <types>
     <xsd:schema xmlns=""
        xmlns:xsd="http://www.w3.org/2000/10/XMLSchema"
        targetNamespace="http://www.example.com/hamSearch">
        <xsd:complexType name="HamSearchType">
```

```
            <xsd:sequence>
               <xsd:choice>
                  <xsd:group>
                      <xsd:element name="City" type="xsd:string" />
                      <xsd:element name="State" type="xsd:string" />
                  </xsd:group>
                  <xsd:element name="Radius" type="xsd:number" />
                  <xsd:element name="LicenseClass" type="xsd:string" />
               </xsd:choice>
            </xsd:sequence>
         </xsd:complexType>
         <xsd:complexType name="HamSearchResponseType">
            <xsd:sequence>
               <xsd:element name="NumHamsFound" type="xsd:number"/>
            </xsd:sequence>
         </xsd:complexType>
      </xsd:schema>
   </types>

   <message name="HamSearchRequestMsg">
      <part name="HamSearchRequest" type="typens:HamSearchType"/>
   </message>
   <message name="HamSearchResponseMsg">
      <part name="HamSearchResponse" type="typens:HamSearchResponseType"/>
   </message>

   <portType name="HamSearchPort">
      <operation name="HamSearch">
         <input message="typens:HamSearchRequestMsg"/>
         <output message="typens:HamSearchResponseMsg"/>
      </operation>
   </portType>
   <binding name="HamSearchBinding" type="typens:HamSearchPort">
      <soap:binding style="rpc"
            transport="http://schemas.xmlsoap.org/soap/http"/>
      <operation name="GetOperators">
         <soap:operation/>
         <input>
            <soap:body use="encoded" namespace="http://www.example.com/
hamsearch" encodingStyle="http://schemas.xmlsoap.org/soap/encoding/"/>
         </input>
         <output>
            <soap:body use="encoded" namespace="http://www.example.com/
hamsearch" encodingStyle="http://schemas.xmlsoap.org/soap/encoding/"/>
         </output>
       </operation>
    </binding>
    <service name="HamSearchService">
       <port name="HamSearchPort" binding="typens:HamSearchBinding">
          <soap:address location="http://localhost/hamsearch.asp"/>
       </port>
    </service>

</definitions>
```

Chapter 16

This chapter discussed how HTML has been reformulated as an application of XML in XHTML 1.0. The exercises for Chapter 16 required that you turn a sample HTML 3.2 document first into a strict XHTML 1.0 document, and then into a transitional XHTML 1.0 document for use on legacy browsers.

Question 1

Take the following HTML 3.2 example, and create a version in strict XHTML 1.0 without any stylistic markup.

```
<HTML>
<HEAD>
   <TITLE>Excerise One</TITLE>
</HEAD>
<BODY bgcolor=white>

<A NAME="top"></A>
<H1 align=center>XHTML</H1>

<FONT face=arial size=2>
  XHTML 1.0 is the reformulation of HTML in XHTML. There are three XHTML 1.0
  document types:

  <UL>
    <LI>Transitional
    <LI>Strict
    <LI>Frameset
  </UL>

  XHTML has also been split into <b>modules</b>, from which document types
  such as XHTML 1.1 and XHTML Basic have been formed.
</FONT>

<A href="#top">Back to top</a>
</BODY>
</HTML>
```

Solution

In order to turn this example of text into valid strict XHTML 1.0, we must make sure all element and attribute names are written in lowercase. XHTML (like all XML languages) is case-sensitive, and all element and attribute names should be lowercase.

Next, look at what goes before the root `<html>` element in a strict XHTML 1.0 document. We can start with the (optional) XML declaration (after all this is an XML document). Many validators will require that the character encoding of the document is specified, so we can use the `encoding` attribute on the XML declaration to indicate the character encoding used (we could also use the `<meta>` element to provide this information). After the XML declaration, add the `DOCTYPE` declaration, which indicates that our document is written according to the strict XHTML 1.0 document type.

```
<?xml version="1.0" encoding="UTF-8"?>
<!DOCTYPE html PUBLIC "-//W3C//DTD XHTML 1.0 Strict//EN"
    "http://www.w3.org/TR/xhtml1/DTD/xhtml1-strict.dtd">
```

The root `<html>` element should feature the `xmlns` attribute indicating the markup in this document belongs to the XHTML namespace as shown in the following:

```
<html xmlns="http://www.w3.org/1999/xhtml" lang="en">
```

We do not need to make any changes to the `<head>` element or its content (other than making sure the element names are lowercase):

```
<head>
   <title>Excerise One</title>
</head>
```

The `<body>` element is where we should start removing the styling markup. One of the aims of XHTML is to separate style from content, so remove the `bgcolor` attribute and its value; instead, we would be using CSS to indicate the background color for the document. The opening `<body>` tag should now look like this:

```
<body>
```

The next task is to move the anchor element inside the heading, because the anchor element is an inline element and therefore should be inside a block level element, such as a heading or paragraph (in the original version the anchor element was before the `h1` element). Remember also that in the strict XHTML 1.0 DTD, we should be using an `id` attribute for the fragment identifier instead of the `name` attribute. Finally, we need to remove the `align` attribute from the `h1` element as shown in the following:

```
<h1><a id="top">XHTML</a></h1>
```

Next, we have to remove the font element. As the first line of text represents a paragraph, it should appear inside the opening `<p>` and closing `</p>` tags as shown in the following:

```
<p>XHTML 1.0 is the reformulation of HTML in XHTML. There are three XHTML 1.0
document types:</p>
```

The HTML 3.2 specification actually says, "The end tag for LI elements can always be omitted." Of course, this is no longer the case with XHTML; we must include the closing `</li>` tags for each list item as follows:

```
<ul>
  <li>Transitional</li>
  <li>Strict</li>
  <li>Frameset</li>
</ul>
```

Following this list there is another paragraph, which we put inside opening `<p>` and closing `</p>` tags. You could replace the `<b>` element with a `<strong>` element, indicating strong emphasis if you wanted to, but it is not necessary.

```
<p>XHTML has also been split into <b>modules</b>, from which document types
such as XHTML 1.1 and XHTML Basic have been formed.</p>
```

As with the anchor element indicating the top of the document, the link that points to the top of the document should be contained within a block-level element, which in this case is a `<div>` element:

```
<div><a href="#top">Back to top</a></div>
```

We finish off the document with the closing `<body>` and `<html>` tags, as shown in the following:

```
</body>
</html>
```

Now we run the document through a validator to make sure that we have not made any errors.

Question 2

Take the same HTML 3.2 example, and create a second version that uses transitional XHTML and can work in most legacy browsers.

Once you have written your documents, validate them using the W3C validator at `http://validator.w3.org/`.

Solution

The strict XHTML 1.0 document version will not work on all browsers, so in this exercise we need to make a transitional version that will work on legacy browsers. The first thing to avoid is the optional XML declaration, because older browsers do not understand it, and some of them will actually display it.

You can start the exercise with a `DOCTYPE` declaration, as this will not cause a problem for older browsers:

```
<!DOCTYPE html PUBLIC "-//W3C//DTD XHTML 1.0 Transitional//EN"
    "http://www.w3.org/TR/xhtml1/DTD/xhtml1-transitional.dtd">
```

In the root element, it is best to avoid the `namespace` attribute. While older browsers should just ignore markup they do not understand, there is no real point in putting it in here.

```
<html>
```

We can leave the `<head>` element and its content as it was in the original. However, when we come to validate, some validators will complain if we do not indicate the character encoding; so we can use the `meta` element inside the `head` like so:

```
<head>
   <title>Excerise One</title>
   <meta http-equiv="Content-Type" content="text/html; charset=UTF-8" />
</head>
```

While the transitional DTD allows us to use deprecated stylistic markup, we should still avoid the use of the `bgcolor` attribute, as it is not essential to the meaning of the document. In fact, the default background of browsers is white, so the background will only be a different color for users that have specifically changed the default setting. Therefore, the opening <body> tag should now look like this:

```
<body>
```

With the transitional document, there is no need to move the anchor element inside the heading as we had to in the strict XHTML 1.0 exercise. Older browsers do not recognize the id attribute as a destination anchor, so you should not change the name attribute to an id attribute as we did in the last exercise. We could leave the align attribute on the <h1> element, but I chose to remove it as that would be in the style sheet if we had one. So, leave the next two lines of the example as it was:

```
<a name="top"></a>
<h1 align=center>XHTML</h1>
```

We can leave in the <font> element if we wish. I mentioned at the start of the exercises, however, to imagine that there would be a CSS to replace styling rules; therefore, we can remove them. It is good practice to put the sentence in a <p> element, so we could do that the following:

```
<p>XHTML 1.0 is the reformulation of HTML in XHTML. There are three XHTML 1.0
  document types:</p>
```

When it comes to the unordered list, you should close the line item elements, with a closing </li> tag, as shown in the following:

```
    <ul>
      <li>Transitional</li>
      <li>Strict</li>
      <li>Frameset</li>
    </ul>
```

Again for good practice, I would put the sentence into a <p> element.

```
<p>XHTML has also been split into <b>modules</b>, from which document types
such as XHTML 1.1 and XHTML Basic have been formed.</p>
```

Finally, we have the link back to the top, which can be left on its own. We do not need to put it into a block-level element in the transitional DTD. Don't forget to finish the exercise with the closing </body> and </html> tags, as shown in the following:

```
<a href="#top">Back to top</a>
</body>
</html>
```

Again remember to validate our document to make sure that we have not made any mistakes.

Chapter 17

This chapter introduced Cascading Style Sheets (CSS) and how it can be used with XHTML.

Question 1

The exercises for this chapter focus on one example: a purchase order. You will slowly build up a more complex style sheet for the following XML file (ch17_ex01.xml):

```
<?xml version="1.0" encoding="UTF-8" ?>
<?xml-stylesheet type="text/css" href="ch17_ex01.css" ?>

<purchaseOrder orderID="x1129001">

<buyer>
   <companyName>Woodland Toys</companyName>
   <purchaserName>Tom Walter</purchaserName>
   <address>
     <address1>The Business Centre</address1>
     <address2>127 Main Road</address2>
     <town>Albury</town>
     <city>Seaforth</city>
     <state>BC</state>
     <zipCode>22001</zipCode>
  </address>
</buyer>

<orders>
   <item>
      <sku>126552</sku>
      <product>People Carrier</product>
      <description>Childs pedal operated car</description>
   </item>
   <item>
      <sku>122452</sku>
      <product>BubbleBaby</product>
      <description>Bean filled soft toy</description>
   </item>
   <item>
      <sku>129112</sku>
      <product>My First Drum Kit</product>
      <description>Childs plastic drum kit</description>
   </item>
</orders>

</purchaseOrder>
```

First, create a rule to put the purchase order in a box, with a 1 pixel black border, 20 pixels of padding inside, and a 20-pixel margin to separate the box from the browser window.

Solution

Here you can see the <purchaseOrder> element is specified to be a block-level element. Use the margin and padding attributes to create some white space on either side of the 1-pixel black border.

```
purchaseOrder {
  display:block;
```

```
    margin:20px; padding:20px;
    border-style:solid; border-width:1px; border-color:#000000;}
```

Question 2

Create a rule that writes "Purchase Order Number" in a large, bold, Arial typeface as the heading (in case the user does not have Arial, you should add Verdana as a second option and the default Sans-serif font as the third option), and that collects the purchase order number from the `orderID` attribute.

Solution

To write out "Purchase Order Number" along with the value of the `orderID` attribute, first set the font you want, then use the `content` property to first write out "Purchase Order Number," and then use the special value of `attr(orderID)`:

```
purchaseOrder:before {
  font-family:arial, verdana, sans-serif;
  font-size:28px; font-weight:bold;
  content:"Purchase Order Number: " attr(orderID);}
```

This will, unfortunately, only work in Netscape 6+.

Question 3

Add the buyer's details to the purchase order, with the company name in bold and each part of the address on a new line in a smaller Arial font (and if the user does not have Arial it should look for Verdana or the default Sans-serif font).

Solution

To add the buyer's details, you need to create styles for several elements. Rather than repeat the styles for each element, you can use the type selector, which separates element names with a comma:

```
buyer, companyName, purchaserName, address1, address2, town, city, state,
zipcode {
  display:block;
  font-family:arial, verdana, sans-serif; font-size:14px;}
```

Then, you only need to write one rule for the element whose content should be displayed in bold:

```
companyName {font-weight:bold;}
```

Question 4

Write out the items ordered in a table.

Solution

The writing out of the table is fairly straightforward using the special values for the `display` property designed for presenting tabular data. Remember to add some padding if you want to make your table more readable.

```
orders {display:table; padding-top:30px;}
item {display:table-row;}
sku, product, description {display:table-cell; padding:10px;}
```

Chapter 18

This chapter showed us how SVG is not only an extremely versatile drawing format, but also highly programmable, thanks to XML and scripting support.

Question 1

By now, it's likely that you've thought of 1,001 different things you'd like to do with SVG, but to get you moving, here is a drawing task to help familiarize you with the basic shapes. Figure 18-11 shows a picture of a stylized windmill. Your mission is to write the SVG code needed to draw it. There's some description of how it was done below, but you if you like a challenge, you can try it before looking at those hints. Squared paper can help in working out the coordinates; don't forget the y-axis starts with zero at the top.

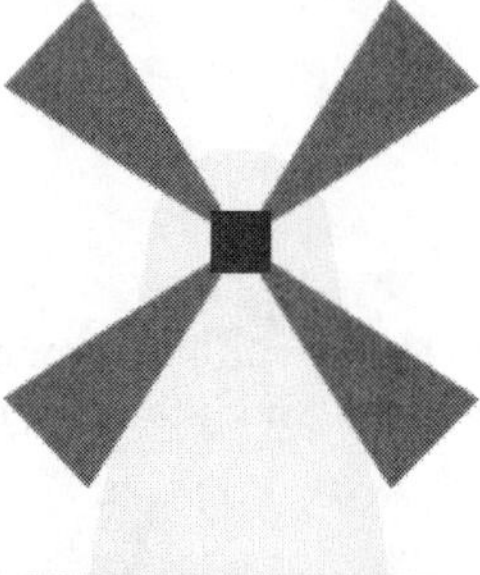

Figure 18-11

Hint

There are several different ways of doing this with SVG, but here the body of the windmill was constructed from a (yellow) `polygon` element with a (yellow) `circle` element half-overlapping on top. The four (blue) vanes are `polygon` elements with three points. The shape in the middle of the vanes is a (blue) `rect` element, with a transform to rotate it 45 degrees. At the bottom of the windmill is a (green) `line` element.

Solution

The windmill can be drawn using basic shapes like this:

```
<?xml version="1.0"?>
<!DOCTYPE svg PUBLIC "-//W3C//DTD SVG 1.1//EN"
    "http://www.w3.org/Graphics/SVG/1.1/DTD/svg11.dtd">

<svg xmlns="http://www.w3.org/2000/svg" version="1.1">

<!-- windmill body -->
  <circle cx="250" cy="230" r="30" fill="yellow" />
```

```
    <polygon points="200,340 220,230 280,230 300,340"
             fill="yellow" />

  <!-- vanes -->
    <polygon points="250,230 230,320 270,320"
             fill="red"
             transform="rotate(45, 250, 230)" />

    <polygon points="250,230 230,320 270,320"
             fill="red"
             transform="rotate(135, 250, 230)" />

    <polygon points="250,230 230,320 270,320"
             fill="red"
             transform="rotate(225, 250, 230)" />

    <polygon points="250,230 230,320 270,320"
             fill="red"
             transform="rotate(315, 250, 230)" />

  <!-- centerpiece -->
    <rect x="240" y="220" width="20" height="20" fill="blue" />

  <!-- bottom line -->
    <line x1="180" y1="340" x2="320" y2="340"
                    stroke="green" stroke-width="6" />

  </svg>
```

Here the different features of the windmill are drawn as eight different basic shapes. The `circle` and `polygon` that make up the body of the windmill overlap and are the same color, giving the effect of a single shape. Rather than figuring out the coordinates of the four vanes separately, the coordinates of one vane (as it would be positioned vertically) have been worked out and the point values copied into the others, with a `rotate` transform used to position them around a center point `(250,230)`.

There wasn't space in this chapter to properly describe all the alternative techniques available, but briefly here is an example of one other way the windmill could be drawn:

```
  <?xml version="1.0"?>
  <!DOCTYPE svg PUBLIC "-//W3C//DTD SVG 1.1//EN"
      "http://www.w3.org/Graphics/SVG/1.1/DTD/svg11.dtd">

  <svg xmlns="http://www.w3.org/2000/svg"
       xmlns:xlink="http://www.w3.org/1999/xlink"
       version="1.1">

    <defs>
      <polygon id="vane" points="250,230 230,320 270,320"
               fill="red"/>
    </defs>

  <! windmill body -->
    <path d="M 200,340 L 220,230 A 30,30 0 0 1 280,230 L 300,340 z"
    fill="yellow"/>
```

```
<!-- vanes -->
<use xlink:href="#vane" transform="rotate(45, 250, 230)" />

<use xlink:href="#vane" transform="rotate(135, 250, 230)" />

<use xlink:href="#vane" transform="rotate(225, 250, 230)" />

<use xlink:href="#vane" transform="rotate(315, 250, 230)" />

<!-- centerpiece -->
  <rect x="240" y="220" width="20" height="20" fill="blue" />

<!-- bottom line -->
  <line x1="180" y1="340" x2="320" y2="340"
                  stroke="green" stroke-width="6" />

</svg>
```

The triangular vanes are all of the same shape and color, so these attributes are given in a `defs` element (see section 5.3 in the SVG specification). The shape defined here won't be drawn immediately, but will provide the description that is referred to by `use` elements (section 5.6) further down the listing. Essentially, the `use` element will be substituted with the linked definition, and any additional attributes that are provided locally will be applied—here the `rotate` transform is defined for each vane. The reference is made through an element from the XLink namespace (`xlink:href`), so the namespace declaration at the start gives the namespace URI for the `xlink` prefix.

In this version, the body of the windmill is defined using a `path` element (see section 8 in the SVG specification). It trades brevity of code for simplicity, something that generally has to be decided case-by-case. The path uses an absolute `moveto` to get to the starting point (`M 200,340`); the line of the left-hand side of the windmill body is then drawn (`L 220,230`). The curve at the top of the windmill is drawn using an elliptical arc (`A 30,30 0 0 1 280,230`), the last pair of figures there being the right-hand side of the top (for details of how arcs work, see section 8.3.8 of the specification). A line is drawn to form the right-hand side of the windmill body (`L 300,340`). Finally, the path is closed by drawing a line back to the starting point (`z`).

Question 2

The Tangram puzzle described in this chapter had a square as the target shape to build from the seven pieces. If you search the web, you will find many more shapes that can be constructed from them. So the challenge here is to get the application to start with the pieces organized into the stylized cat as pictured in Figure 18-12. Everything else should stay the same—clicking Reset will still place all the pieces into the square box. Don't spend too much time on the details of this. Just try to figure out how you would go about doing it, bearing in mind that SVG is XML.

Solution

One solution to the question basically starts with the puzzle pieces ready-transformed to their positions in the cat shape. The coordinates listed in the `points` attributes are exactly as in the original. The `transform` attribute contains an initial translation and rotation to place them as required. Pressing the Reset button will still zero all these values, placing the pieces in the square box.

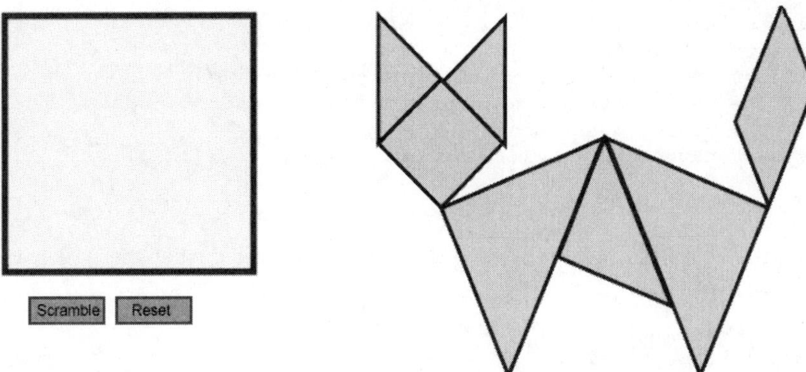

Figure 18-12

```
<polygon points="0,0 0,100 100,0"
    transform="translate(453.6,137.6) rotate(292.5,33.3,33.3)" />

<polygon points="100,0, 50,50 150,50 200,0"
    transform="translate(495,45) rotate(472.5,125,25)" />

<polygon points="50,50, 0,100 50,150 100,100"
    transform="translate(300,0) rotate(0,0,0)"/>

<polygon points="50,50, 100,100 150,50"
    transform="translate(285,-15) rotate(90,100,66.6)"/>

<polygon points="200,0, 100,100 200,200"
    transform="translate(245,76) rotate(22.5,166.6,100)"/>

<polygon points="0,100, 0,200 50,150"
    transform="translate(300,-100) rotate(0,0,0)"/>

<polygon points="0,200, 200,200 100,100"
    transform="translate(452,9.3) rotate(67.5,100,166.6)"/>
```

You might be wondering how those values were obtained. Using some cardboard, a ruler, and a protractor would be one approach. An easier way is to let the computer do the work. The hint is that it's XML you're looking at, so standard XML tools can be used. In the Tangram application, the pieces were moved by using code to dynamically manipulate the `transform` attributes of the `polygon` elements. These changes were made by modifying the DOM model in memory. It's not possible to view the contents of the DOM by saving the file from the viewer, but it is possible to expose it programmatically.

It is simple to get the browser to display a piece of text using the built-in `alert('text')` function. This causes a small window to pop up displaying the text and can be used to give an inside view of the part of the DOM that contains the `transform` attributes of the `polygon` elements.

In the original code, pressing any key caused a function to be called that would rotate the currently selected shape. A minor modification can be made to the script (`tangram.es`), to recognize when the "x" key has been pressed.

```
function init(evt) {
  // Get the Document
        svgDoc = evt.getTarget().getOwnerDocument();
 // Get the parent of the polygons
polyGroup = svgDoc.getElementById("PolyGroup");
polyGroup.addEventListener("keypress", keypress, false);
}
```

Here the event listener will cause the `keypress` function to be called when the "x" key is pressed. That function is as follows:

```
function keypress(evt) {
    var keyString = String.fromCharCode(evt.charCode);
    if(keyString == 'x') {
       alert(getPolygonDetails(polyGroup));
       return;
    }
rotatePolygon(evt);
}
```

The `charCode` property of the event object is obtained, and that code is converted into a string. The string is then checked to see whether it is an "x." If it is, the `polyGroup` object (the parent of the polygons, extracted previously) is passed to a function called `getPolygonDetails`. Whatever this returns will appear as the text in a popup window. If the character isn't an "x," the `rotatePolygon` function is called as in the original version.

What's needed are the attributes of the individual `polygon` elements. These are all child nodes of the polygon group and are easy to get from the passed `polyGroup` element. Each of these is examined in turn to make sure it is actually an element node. If it is, it will have a `nodeType` value of 1. In that case the attributes of that element can be obtained in turn, using the DOM `attributes.item(j)` method. The name of the node and its value are then added to a string. This will accumulate all the attribute names and values in the elements as the loops step through them. After each line, a newline character (`\n`) is added for the sake of appearances.

```
 var ELEMENT_NODE = 1;

function getPolygonDetails(group) {
    var string = "";
    var children = group.childNodes;
    var node;
    var attr;

    for (var i=0; i<children.length; i++){
        node = children.item(i);
        if (node.nodeType == ELEMENT_NODE){
            string += node.nodeName;
            for (var j = 0; j<node.attributes.length; j++){
                attr = node.attributes.item(j);
                string += " " + attr.nodeName + '="' + attr.nodeValue+ '"';
            }
```

```
                string += "\n";
            }
        }
        return string;
    }
```

Once the string has been built up, it is passed back to the preceding calling function (`keypress`), which uses it as the content of an `alert`.

If the puzzle pieces are moved around and then the "x" key pressed, a window will appear like the one shown in Figure A-8.

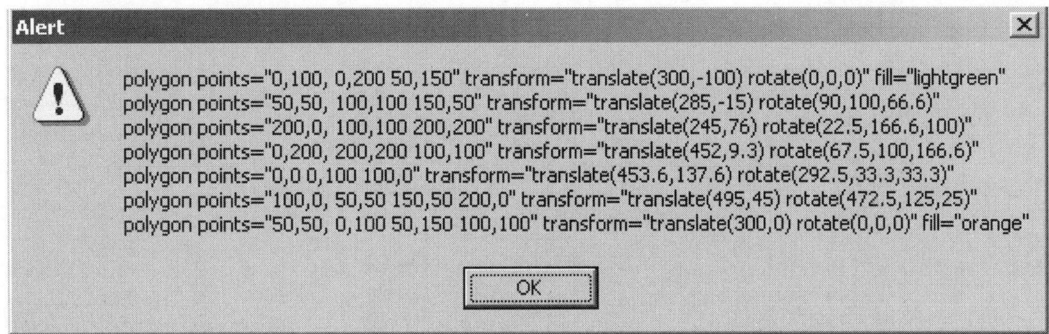

Figure A-8

Note that the order of the elements probably won't match that of the original, as selecting an element moves it to the last position in the list, so it shows up on top (following the Painter's Model).

Chapter 19

This chapter discussed the XForms model, including the creation of instance data, submission configuration of a form, XForms form controls, and XForms model item properties.

Question 1

Experiment in the code examples given in the chapter with the effect of changing the value of the `appearance` attribute on the `xforms:select` and `xforms:select1` elements. This, particularly, when viewed in more than one XForms viewer will give you an impression of the range of visual appearances available to an XForms developer.

Solution

There is no "solution" to this one, but you're encouraged to explore this area further on your own.

Question 2

Describe the differences in purpose of the `xforms:submit` and `xforms:submission` elements.

Solution

The `xforms:submit` element controls a form control visible to the users of the form to allow them to initiate submission of the form, typically by a mouse click.

The `xforms:submission` element is part of an XForms model and is not directly visible to the user. Attributes of the `xforms:submission` element control where the instance data is to be submitted and what method of submission should be used.

The XML Document Object Model

This appendix lists all of the interfaces in the Document Object Model (DOM) Level 2 Core, both the *Fundamental Interfaces* and the *Extended Interfaces*, including all of their properties and methods. Examples of how to use some of these interfaces appeared in Chapter 11.

> *You can find further information on these interfaces at* `http://www.w3.org/TR/DOM-Level-2`.

The interfaces defined in the DOM are illustrated in Figure B-1.

Notation

The notation used for the DOM interfaces is Interface Definition Language (IDL). So, for example, a property that is named "length" and returns an integer value might be defined in the DOM Level 2 Recommendation as follows:

```
readonly attribute unsigned long length;
```

This appendix uses the following, slightly more friendly approach:

Property	Type	Description
length	unsigned long (read-only)	A description of the property would go here

If you're not familiar with terms such as "unsigned long" or "unsigned short," don't worry; just think of either an "unsigned long" or "unsigned short" as an integer—that is, a number that doesn't have a decimal. Unless you're writing a DOM implementation yourself, it doesn't matter too much how big the numbers are, for the purpose of this appendix.

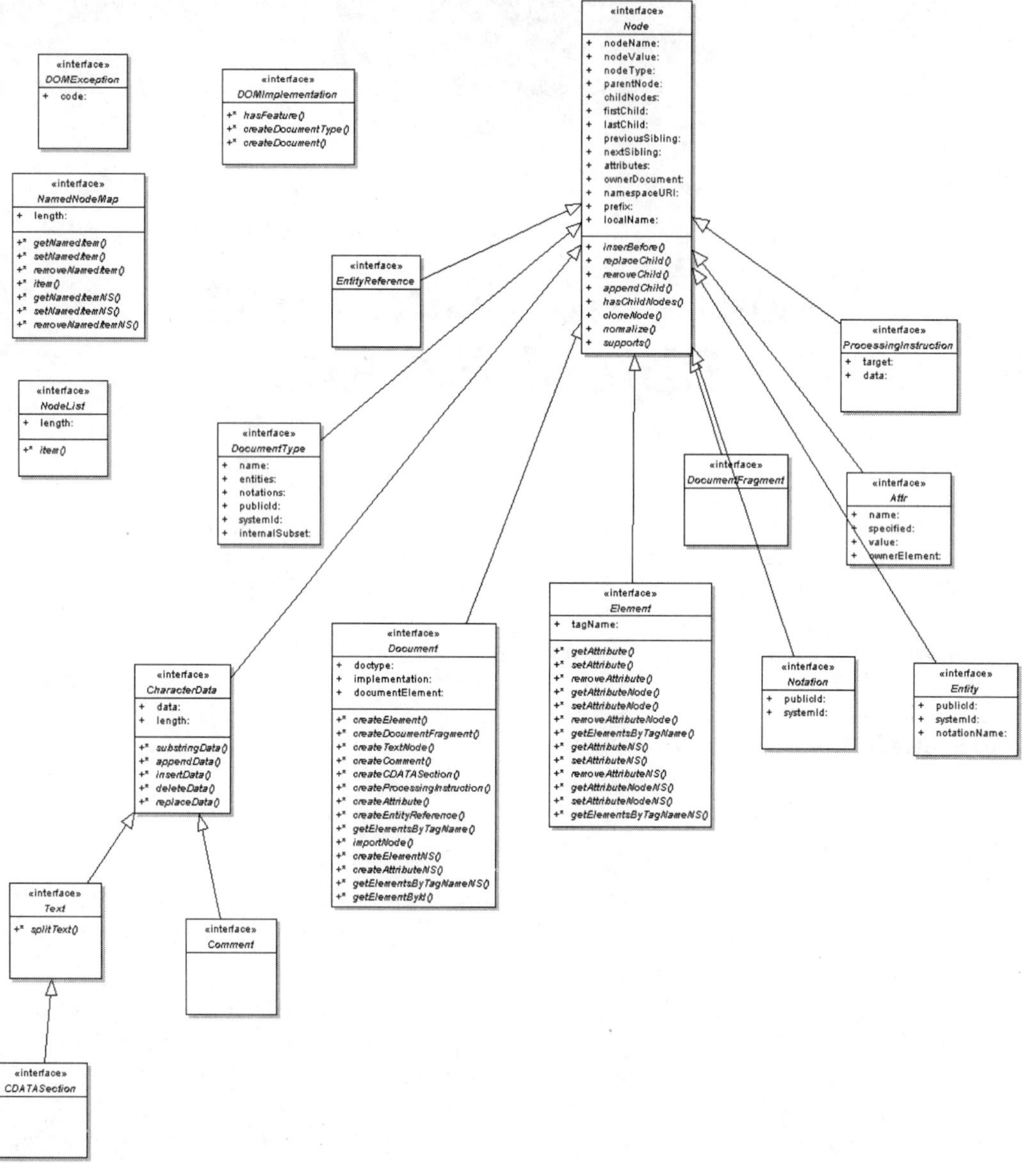

Figure B-1

Strings

To ensure interoperability, the DOM specifies a `DOMString` data type, which is a sequence of 16-bit characters. These characters must be in the UTF-16 encoding.

However, even though the DOM Recommendation always uses this `DOMString` data type, the actual data type used by a programming language may be an inherent string data type. For example, in Java, a

DOM implementation would use a normal `String`, as would a Visual Basic DOM implementation, because both Java and VB strings are UTF-16.

This appendix uses the `DOMString` type for consistency.

Fundamental Interfaces

The DOM Fundamental Interfaces are interfaces that *all* DOM implementations must provide, even if they aren't designed to work with XML documents.

DOMException

An object implementing the `DOMException` interface is thrown whenever an error occurs in the DOM.

Property	Type	Description
Code	unsigned short	Represents the *exception code* this `DOMException` is reporting

The `code` property can take the following values:

Exception Code	Value	Description
INDEX_SIZE_ERR	1	The index or size is negative, or greater than the allowed value
DOMSTRING_SIZE_ERR	2	The specified range of text does not fit into a `DOMString`
HIERARCHY_REQUEST_ERR	3	The node is inserted somewhere it doesn't belong
WRONG_DOCUMENT_ERR	4	The node is used in a different document than the one that created it, and that document doesn't support it
INVALID_CHARACTER_ERR	5	A character was passed that is not valid in XML
NO_DATA_ALLOWED_ERR	6	Data was specified for a node that does not support data
NO_MODIFICATION_ ALLOWED_ERR	7	An attempt was made to modify an object that doesn't allow modifications
NOT_FOUND_ERR	8	An attempt was made to reference a node that does not exist

Continues

Exception Code	Value	Description
NOT_SUPPORTED_ERR	9	The implementation does not support the type of object requested
INUSE_ATTRIBUTE_ERR	10	An attempt was made to add a duplicate attribute
INVALID_STATE_ERR	11	An attempt was made to use an object that is not, or is no longer, useable
SYNTAX_ERR	12	An invalid or illegal string was passed
INVALID_MODIFICATION_ERR	13	An attempt was made to modify the type of the underlying object
NAMESPACE_ERR	14	An attempt was made to create or change an object in a way that is incompatible with namespaces
INVALID_ACCESS_ERR	15	A parameter was passed or an operation attempted that the underlying object does not support

Node

The `Node` interface is the base interface upon which most of the DOM objects are built, and contains methods and attributes that can be used for all types of nodes. The interface also includes some helper methods and attributes that only apply to particular types of nodes.

Property	Type	Description
nodeName	DOMString (read-only)	The name of the node. Will return different values, depending on the `nodeType`, as listed in the next table.
nodeValue	DOMString	The value of the node. Will return different values, depending on the `nodeType`, as listed in the next table.
nodeType	unsigned short (read-only)	The type of node. Will be one of the values from the next table.
parentNode	Node (read-only)	The node that is this node's parent
childNodes	NodeList (read-only)	A `NodeList` containing all of this node's children. If there are no children, an empty `NodeList` is returned, not `NULL`.

Property	Type	Description
firstChild	Node (read-only)	The first child of this node. If there are no children, this returns NULL.
lastChild	Node (read-only)	The last child of this node. If there are no children, this returns NULL.
previousSibling	Node (read-only)	The node immediately preceding this node. If there is no preceding node, this returns NULL
nextSibling	Node (read-only)	The node immediately following this node. If there is no following node, this returns NULL.
attributes	NamedNodeMap (read-only)	A NamedNodeMap containing the attributes of this node. If the node is not an element, this returns NULL.
ownerDocument	Document (read-only)	The document to which this node belongs
namespaceURI	DOMString (read-only)	The namespace URI of this node. Returns NULL if a namespace is not specified.
prefix	DOMString	The namespace prefix of this node. Returns NULL if a namespace is not specified.
localName	DOMString (read-only)	Returns the local part of this node's QName

The values of the nodeName and nodeValue properties depend on the value of the nodeType property, which can return one of the following constants:

nodeType Property Constant	nodeName	NodeValue
ELEMENT_NODE	Tag name	NULL
ATTRIBUTE_NODE	Name of attribute	Value of attribute
TEXT_NODE	#text	Content of the text node
CDATA_SECTION_NODE	#cdata-section	Content of the CDATA section
ENTITY_REFERENCE_NODE	Name of entity referenced	NULL

Continues

nodeType Property Constant	nodeName	NodeValue
ENTITY_NODE	Entity name	NULL
PROCESSING_INSTRUCTION_NODE	Target	Entire content excluding the target
COMMENT_NODE	#comment	Content of the comment
DOCUMENT_NODE	#document	NULL
DOCUMENT_TYPE_NODE	Document type name	NULL
DOCUMENT_FRAGMENT_NODE	#document-fragment	NULL
NOTATION_NODE	Notation name	NULL

Method	Description
Node insertBefore(Node newChild, Node refChild)	Inserts the `newChild` node before the existing `refChild`. If `refChild` is `NULL`, it inserts the node at the end of the list. Returns the inserted node.
Node replaceChild(Node newChild, Node oldChild)	Replaces `oldChild` with `newChild`. Returns `oldChild`.
Node removeChild(Node oldChild)	Removes `oldChild` from the list, and returns it
Node appendChild(Node newChild)	Adds `newChild` to the end of the list, and returns it
boolean hasChildNodes()	Returns a boolean; `true` if the node has any children, `false` otherwise
Node cloneNode(boolean deep)	Returns a duplicate of this node. If the boolean `deep` parameter is `true`, this will recursively clone the subtree under the node, otherwise, it will only clone the node itself.
void normalize()	If there are multiple adjacent `Text` child nodes (from a previous call to `Text.splitText()`), this method will combine them again. It doesn't return a value.
boolean supports(DOMString feature, DOMString version)	Indicates whether this implementation of the DOM supports the `feature` passed. Returns a boolean, `true` if it supports the feature, `false` otherwise.

Document

An object implementing the `Document` interface represents the entire XML document. This object is also used to create other nodes at runtime.

The `Document` interface extends the `Node` interface.

Property	Type	Description
Doctype	DocumentType (read-only)	Returns a `DocumentType` object indicating the document type associated with this document. If the document has no document type specified, it returns `NULL`.
implementation	DOMImplementation (read-only)	The `DOMImplementation` object used for this document
documentElement	Element (read-only)	The root element for this document

Method	Description
Element createElement(DOMString tagName)	Creates an element with the name specified
DocumentFragment createDocumentFragment()	Creates an empty `DocumentFragment` object
Text createTextNode(DOMString data)	Creates a `Text` node, containing the text in `data`
Comment createComment(DOMString data)	Creates a `Comment` node, containing the text in `data`
CDATASection createCDATASection(DOMString data)	Creates a `CDATASection` node, containing the text in `data`
ProcessingInstruction createProcessingInstruction (DOMString target, DOMString data)	Creates a `ProcessingInstruction` node, with the specified `target` and `data`
Attr createAttribute(DOMString name)	Creates an attribute, with the specified `name`
EntityReference createEntityReference(DOMString name)	Creates an entity reference with the specified `name`
NodeList getElementsByTagName(DOMString tagname)	Returns a `NodeList` of all elements in the document with this `tagname`. The elements are returned in document order.
Node importNode(Node importedNode, boolean deep)	Imports `importedNode` from another document into this one. The original node is not removed from the old document; it is just cloned. (The boolean `deep` parameter specifies if it is a *deep* or *shallow* clone: deep means the subtree under the node is also cloned, and shallow means only the node itself is cloned.) Returns the new node.

Continues

Method	Description
Element createElementNS(DOMString namespaceURI, DOMString qualifiedName)	Creates an element, with the specified namespace and QName
Attr createAttributeNS(DOMString namespaceURI, DOMString qualifiedName)	Creates an attribute, with the specified namespace and QName
NodeList getElementsByTagNameNS (DOMString namespaceURI, DOMString localName)	Returns a `NodeList` of all the elements in the document that have the specified local name and are in the namespace specified by `namespaceURI`
Element getElementById(DOMString elementID)	Returns the element with the ID specified in `elementID`. If there is no such element, it returns `NULL`.

DOMImplementation

The `DOMImplementation` interface provides methods that are not specific to any particular document, but to any document from this DOM implementation. You can get a `DOMImplementation` object from the `implementation` property of the `Document` interface.

Method	Description
boolean hasFeature(DOMString feature, DOMString version)	Returns a boolean indicating whether this DOM implementation supports the `feature` requested. `version` is the version number of the feature to test.
DocumentType createDocumentType (DOMString qualifiedName, DOMString publicID, DOMString systemID, DOMString internalSubset)	Creates a `DocumentType` object with the specified attributes
Document createDocument(DOMstring namespaceURI, DOMString qualifiedName, DocumentType doctype)	Creates a `Document` object, with the document element specified by `qualifiedName`. The `doctype` property must refer to an object of type `DocumentType`.

DocumentFragment

A document fragment is a temporary holding place for a group of nodes, usually created with the intent of inserting the nodes back into the document at a later point.

The `DocumentFragment` interface extends the `Node` interface, without adding any additional properties or methods.

NodeList

A `NodeList` contains an ordered group of nodes, accessed via an index.

Property	Type	Description
Length	unsigned long (read-only)	The number of nodes contained in this list. The range of valid child node indices is 0 to `length` –1 inclusive.

Method	Description
Node item(unsigned long index)	Returns the `Node` in the list at the indicated index. If `index` is the same as or greater than `length`, it returns `NULL`.

Element

The `Element` interface provides properties and methods for working with an element.

It extends the `Node` interface.

Property	Type	Description
tagName	DOMString (read-only)	The name of the element

Method	Description
DOMString getAttribute(DOMString name)	Returns the value of the attribute with the specified `name`, or an empty string if that attribute does not have a specified or default value
void setAttribute(DOMString name, DOMString value)	Sets the value of the specified attribute to this new `value`. If no such attribute exists, a new one with this `name` is created.
void removeAttribute (DOMString name)	Removes the specified attribute. If the attribute has a default value, it is immediately replaced with an identical attribute containing this default value.
Attr getAttributeNode (DOMString name)	Returns an `Attr` node containing the named attribute. Returns `NULL` if there is no such attribute.
Attr setAttributeNode (Attr newAttr)	Adds a new attribute node. If an attribute with the same name already exists, it is replaced. If an `Attr` has been replaced, it is returned; otherwise, `NULL` is returned.

Continues

Method	Description
Attr removeAttributeNode (Attr oldAttr)	Removes the specified Attr node, and returns it. If the attribute has a default value, it is immediately replaced with an identical attribute containing this default value.
NodeList getElementsByTagName (DOMString name)	Returns a NodeList of all descendants with the given node name
DOMString getAttributeNS(DOMString namespaceURI, DOMString localName)	Returns the value of the specified attribute, or an empty string if that attribute does not have a specified or default value
void setAttributeNS(DOMString namespaceURI, DOMString qualifiedName, DOMString value)	Sets the value of the specified attribute to this new value. If no such attribute exists, a new one with this namespace URI and QName is created.
void removeAttributeNS(DOMString namespaceURI, DOMString localName)	Removes the specified attribute. If the attribute has a default value, it is immediately replaced with an identical attribute containing this default value.
Attr getAttributeNodeNS(DOMString namespaceURI, DOMString localName)	Returns an Attr node containing the specified attribute. Returns NULL if there is no such attribute.
Attr setAttributeNodeNS(Attr newAttr)	Adds a new Attr node to the list. If an attribute with the same namespace URI and local name exists, it is replaced. If an Attr object is replaced, it is returned; otherwise, NULL is returned.
NodeList getElementsByTagNameNS DOMString namespaceURI, DOMString localName)	Returns a NodeList of all the elements matching these criteria

NamedNodeMap

A named node map represents an unordered collection of nodes, retrieved by name.

Property	Type	Description
length	unsigned long (read-only)	The number of nodes in the map

Method	Description
Node getNamedItem(DOMString name)	Returns a Node, where the nodeName is the same as the name specified, or NULL if no such node exists
Node setNamedItem(Node arg)	The arg parameter is a Node object, which is added to the list. The nodeName property is used for the name of the node in this map. If a node with the same name already exists, it is replaced. If a Node is replaced, it is returned; otherwise, NULL is returned.
Node removeNamedItem(DOMString name)	Removes the Node specified by name and returns it
Node item(unsigned long index)	Returns the Node at the specified index. If index is the same as or greater than length, it returns NULL.
Node getNamedItemNS (DOMString namespaceURI, DOMString localName)	Returns a Node matching the namespace URI and local name, or NULL if no such node exists
Node setNamedItemNS(Node arg)	The arg parameter is a Node object, which is added to the list. If a node with the same namespace URI and local name already exists, it is replaced. If a Node is replaced, it is returned; otherwise, NULL is returned.
Node removeNamedItemNS (DOMString namespaceURI, DOMString localName)	Removes the specified node and returns it

Attr

The Attr interface provides properties for dealing with an attribute.

It extends the Node interface.

Property	Type	Description
name	DOMString (read-only)	The name of the attribute
specified	boolean (read-only)	A boolean, indicating whether this attribute was specified (true), or just defaulted (false)
value	DOMString	The value of the attribute
ownerElement	Element (read-only)	An Element object, representing the element to which this attribute belongs

CharacterData

The `CharacterData` interface provides properties and methods for working with character data.

It extends the `Node` interface.

Property	Type	Description
Data	DOMString	The text in this `CharacterData` node
length	unsigned long (read-only)	The number of characters in the node

Method	Description
DOMString substringData(unsigned long offset, unsigned long count)	Returns a portion of the string, starting at the `offset`. Will return the number of characters specified in `count`, or until the end of the string, whichever is less.
void appendData(DOMString arg)	Appends the string in `arg` to the end of the string
void insertData(unsigned long offset, DOMString arg)	Inserts the string in `arg` into the middle of the string, starting at the position indicated by `offset`
void deleteData(unsigned long offset, unsigned long count)	Deletes a portion of the string, starting at the `offset`. Will delete the number of characters specified in `count`, or until the end of the string, whichever is less.
void replaceData(unsigned long offset, unsigned long count, DOMString arg)	Replaces a portion of the string, starting at the `offset`. Will replace the number of characters specified in `count`, or until the end of the string, whichever is less. The `arg` parameter is the new string to be inserted.

Text

The `Text` interface provides an additional method for working with text nodes.

It extends the `CharacterData` interface.

Method	Description
Text splitText(unsigned long offset)	Separates this single `Text` node into two adjacent `Text` nodes. All of the text up to the `offset` point goes into the first `Text` node, and all of the text starting at the `offset` point to the end goes into the second `Text` node.

Comment

The `Comment` interface encapsulates an XML comment.

It extends the `CharacterData` interface, without adding any additional properties or methods.

Extended Interfaces

The DOM Extended Interfaces need only be provided by DOM implementations that will be working with XML documents.

CDATASection

The `CDATASection` interface encapsulates an XML CDATA section.

It extends the `Text` interface, without adding any additional properties or methods.

ProcessingInstruction

The `ProcessingInstruction` interface provides properties for working with an XML processing instruction (PI).

It extends the `Node` interface.

Property	Type	Description
target	DOMString (read-only)	The PI target; in other words, the name of the application to which the PI should be passed
data	DOMString	The content of the PI

DocumentType

The `DocumentType` interface provides properties for working with an XML document type. It can be retrieved from the `Document` interface's `doctype` property. (If a document doesn't have a document type, `doctype` will return `NULL`.)

`DocumentType` extends the `Node` interface.

Property	Type	Description
Name	DOMString (read-only)	The name of the DTD
Entities	NamedNodeMap (read-only)	A `NamedNodeMap` containing all entities declared in the DTD (both internal and external). Parameter entities are not contained, and duplicates are discarded according to the rules followed by validating XML parsers.

Continues

Property	Type	Description
Notations	NamedNodeMap (read-only)	A NamedNodeMap containing the notations contained in the DTD. Duplicates are discarded.
PublicId	DOMString (read-only)	The external subset's public identifier
SystemId	DOMString (read-only)	The external subset's system identifier
InternalSubset	DOMString (read-only)	The internal subset, as a string

Notation

The `Notation` interface provides properties for working with an XML notation. Notations are read-only in the DOM.

It extends the `Node` interface.

Property	Type	Description
publicId	DOMString (read-only)	The public identifier of this notation. If the public identifier was not specified, it returns `NULL`.
systemId	DOMString (read-only)	The system identifier of this notation. If the system identifier was not specified, it returns `NULL`.

Entity

The `Entity` interface provides properties for working with parsed and unparsed entities. `Entity` nodes are read-only.

This interface extends the `Node` interface.

Property	Type	Description
PublicId	DOMString (read-only)	The public identifier associated with the entity, or `NULL` if none is specified
systemId	DOMString (read-only)	The system identifier associated with the entity, or `NULL` if none is specified
notationName	DOMString (read-only)	For unparsed entities, the name of the notation for the entity. `NULL` for parsed entities.

EntityReference

The `EntityReference` interface encapsulates an XML entity reference.

It extends the `Node` interface, without adding any properties or methods.

XPath 1.0 Reference

XPath is a well-established W3C specification that describes a non-XML syntax for selecting a set of nodes from the in-memory model of an XML document. XPath version 1.0 reached W3C Recommendation status on November 16, 1999. The specification documents for XPath 2.0, which is a subset of XQuery 1.0, were in late Working Draft stage at the time of this writing. XPath, both 1.0 and 2.0, is an essential part of the corresponding XSLT specification. This appendix focuses on XPath 1.0.

An XPath location path contains one or more "location steps," separated by forward slashes (`/`). Each location step has the following form:

```
axis-name::node-test[predicate]*
```

In plain English, this is an axis name, then two colons, then a node test, and, finally, zero or more predicates each contained in square brackets. A predicate can contain literal values (for example, `4`, or '`hello`'), operators (`+`, `–`, `=`, and so on), and other XPath expressions. XPath also defines a set of functions that can be used in predicates.

An XPath axis defines how to select a part of the model of an XML document, from the perspective of a starting point called the "context node." The context node serves as the starting point for selecting the result of an XPath expression. The node test makes a selection from the nodes on the specified axis. In other words, a node test filters the nodes in the specified axis. By adding predicates, it is possible to filter any nodes already selected by selecting a subset of the nodes selected by the axis and node-test parts of the expression. If the expression in the predicate returns `true`, the node remains in the selected node set; otherwise, it is removed.

This reference lists the XPath axes, node tests, and functions. Each entry lists whether it is implemented in version 1.0 of the specification. At one time, there were significant variations among implementations with, for example, the Microsoft XML Core Services lacking full XPath 1.0 compliance. The situation has now improved to the point that any XPath implementation is likely to be essentially fully XPath 1.0 compliant. Microsoft Core XML Services versions 3.0 and later have full XPath implementations. Versions of MSXML before version 3.0 are not suitable for XPath 1.0 processing, in my opinion.

Other implementations, such as Xalan and Saxon, essentially fully implement version XPath 1.0.

Axes

Next, I list each axis with a brief description of the nodes it selects. The principal node type of an axis indicates what type of nodes are selected by a literal node test or the * node test (see under the *literal name* node test for an example). For some axes, XPath defines an abbreviated syntax. This syntax's form and its primary node type are listed for every axis.

ancestor

Description:	Contains the context node's parent node, the parent node's parent node, and so on, all the way up to the document root. If the context node is the root node, the ancestor axis is empty
Principal node type:	Element
Abbreviated Syntax:	No abbreviated syntax for this axis
Implemented:	W3C 1.0 specification (recommendation)

ancestor-or-self

Description:	Includes the context node itself and the nodes in the ancestor axis
Principal node type:	Element
Abbreviated Syntax:	No abbreviated syntax for this axis
Implemented:	W3C 1.0 specification (recommendation)

attribute

Description:	Contains all attributes of the context node. The attribute axis will be empty unless the context node is an element node
Principal node type:	Attribute
Abbreviated Syntax:	`@`
Implemented:	W3C 1.0 specification (recommendation)

child

Description:	Contains all direct children of the context node (that is, the children, but not the children's children)
Principal node type:	Element

Abbreviated Syntax:	The child axis is the default axis, so if no axis is expressed, it is assumed that a location path is using the child axis
Implemented:	W3C 1.0 specification (recommendation)

descendant

Description:	All children of the context node, including all children's children recursively
Principal node type:	Element
Abbreviated Syntax:	`//`
Implemented:	W3C 1.0 specification (recommendation)

descendant-or-self

Description:	Includes the context node itself plus the nodes in the descendant axis
Principal node type:	Element
Abbreviated Syntax:	No abbreviated syntax for this axis
Implemented:	W3C 1.0 specification (recommendation)

following

Description:	Contains all nodes that come after the context node in the document order. This means that, for nodes in the `following` axis, the start tag of the element to which the node corresponds must come after the context node's end tag. Descendant nodes of the context node are not part of the `following` axis
Principal node type:	Element
Abbreviated Syntax:	No abbreviated syntax for this axis
Implemented:	W3C 1.0 specification (recommendation)

following-sibling

Description:	Contains all siblings (children of the same parent node) of the context node that come after the context node in document order
Principal node type:	Element

Continues

Abbreviated Syntax:	No abbreviated syntax for this axis
Implemented:	W3C 1.0 specification (recommendation)

namespace

Description:	Contains all namespace nodes that are in scope on the context node. This includes the default namespace and the XML namespace (these are automatically declared in any document). The `namespace` axis is empty unless the context node is an element
Principal node type:	Namespace
Abbreviated Syntax:	No abbreviated syntax for this axis
Implemented:	W3C 1.0 specification (recommendation)

parent

Description:	Contains the direct parent node (and only the direct parent node) of the context node, if there is one. If the context node is the root node, the parent axis is empty
Principal node type:	Element
Abbreviated Syntax:	..
Implemented:	W3C 1.0 specification (recommendation)

preceding

Description:	Contains all nodes that come before the context node in the document order. This contains element nodes where the corresponding start tag--end tag pair are alreadyclosed (their end tag comes before the context node's start tag in the document). Ancestor nodes are not present in this axis because their end tag is later in the document
Principal node type:	Element
Abbreviated Syntax:	No abbreviated syntax for this axis
Implemented:	W3C 1.0 specification (recommendation)

preceding-sibling

Description:	Contains all sibling nodes (children of the same parent node) of the context node that come before the context node in document order
Principal node type:	Element
Abbreviated Syntax:	None
Implemented:	W3C 1.0 specification (recommendation)

self

Description:	Contains only the context node
Principal node type:	Element
Abbreviated Syntax:	.
Implemented:	W3C 1.0 specification (recommendation)

Node Tests

A node test describes a test performed on each node in an axis to decide whether it should be included in the node-set. If the Boolean value `true` is returned by the node test, the node is included in the node-set. If `false` is returned, the node is not included in the node-set. Appending a predicate can later further filter the node-set.

*

Description:	Returns `true` for all nodes of the principal node type for the axis
Implemented:	W3C 1.0 specification (recommendation)

comment()

Description:	Returns `true` for all comment nodes
Implemented:	W3C 1.0 specification (recommendation)

literal name

Description:	Returns `true` for all nodes of that name of the principal node type. If the node test is '`PERSON`', it returns `true` for all `PERSON` element nodes (if the principal node type is element)
Implemented:	W3C 1.0 specification (recommendation)

node()

Description:	Returns `true` for all nodes, except attributes and namespaces
Implemented:	W3C 1.0 specification (recommendation)

processing-instruction(name?)

Description:	Returns `true` for all processing instruction nodes. If a name parameter is passed (the question mark means that it is optional), it returns `true` only for processing instruction nodes of that name
Implemented:	W3C 1.0 specification (recommendation)

text()

Description:	Returns `true` for all text nodes
Implemented:	W3C 1.0 specification (recommendation)

Functions

Functions in XPath 1.0 are limited to fairly simple manipulation of node-sets, numbers, strings, and booleans. A common use of functions in XPath 1.0 is to filter a node-set that was selected using an axis and node test. To do that, an expression is written in square brackets, which can include literal values (numbers, strings, and so on), XPath location paths, and one or more functions defined by the XPath specification.

Each function in this section is described by a line of this form:

```
return-type  function-name (parameters)
```

For each parameter, you display the type (`object`, `string`, `number`, `node-set`) and, where necessary, a symbol indicating if the parameter is optional (`?`) or can occur multiple times (`+`). The type `object` means that any type can be passed.

If an expression is passed as a parameter, it is first evaluated and (if necessary) converted to the expected type before passing it to the function.

boolean **boolean** (object)
Converts any object passed to it to a Boolean.
`boolean(attribute::name)` will return `true` if the context node has a `name` attribute

Parameter:
object
Numbers result in `true` if they are not zero or NaN.
Strings result in `true` if their length is nonzero.
Node-sets return `true` if they are nonempty.

Implemented:
W3C 1.0 specification (recommendation)

number **ceiling** (number)
Rounds a passed number to the smallest integer that is not smaller than the passed number.
`ceiling(1.1)` returns `2`

Parameter:
number
The number that is to be rounded up to an integer

Implemented:
W3C 1.0 specification (recommendation)

string **concat** (string1, string2+)
Concatenates all passed strings to one string.
`concat('con', 'c', 'a', 't')` returns `concat`

Parameters:
string1
The first string

string2
All following strings

Implemented:
W3C 1.0 specification (recommendation)

boolean **contains** (string1, string2)
Returns `true` if string1 contains string2.
`contains('John Smith', 'John')` returns `true`

Parameters:
string1
The source string.

string2
The string whose presence in the source string is to be tested

Implemented:
W3C 1.0 specification (recommendation)

number **count** (node-set)
Returns the number of nodes in the passed node-set.

Continues

`count(child::*[@name])` returns the number of child elements of the context node that have a `name` attribute

Parameter:
node-set
The node-set that is to be counted

Implemented:
W3C 1.0 specification (recommendation)

boolean **false** ( )
Always returns `false`. This function is needed because an expression `False` tests whether the context node has child element nodes whose name is `False`

Implemented:
W3C 1.0 specification (recommendation)

number **floor** (number)
Rounds a passed number to the largest integer that is not larger than the passed number.
`floor(2.9)` returns `2`
`floor(-1.1)` returns `-2`

Parameter:
number
The number that must be rounded to an integer

Implemented:
W3C 1.0 specification (recommendation)

node-set **id** (string)
Returns the element identified by the passed identifier. In a compliant XPath implementation this will only work in validated documents, because for nonvalidated documents, the parser has no way of knowing which attributes represent `ID` values. The `ID` type is defined in a schema document

Parameter:
string
The ID value

Implemented:
W3C 1.0 specification (recommendation)

boolean **lang** (string)
Returns `true` if the language of the context node is the same as the passed language parameter. The language of the context node can be set using the `xml:lang` attribute on itself or any of its ancestors. `lang('en')` returns `true` for English language nodes

Parameter:
string
Language identifier

Implemented:
W3C 1.0 specification (recommendation)

number **last** ( )
Returns the last node in a node-set. The node returned is, for forward axes, .the last node in document order. For reverse axes the opposite is true.
`child::*[last()-1]` selects the penultimate child element node of the context node

Implemented:
W3C 1.0 specification (recommendation)

string **local-name** (node-set?)
Returns the local part of the name of the first node in the passed node-set (the part of a namespace-qualified name that occurs after the colon). For example, the local part of an `xsl:value-of` element is `value-of`

Parameter:
node-set
If no node-set is specified, the context node is used.

Implemented:
W3C 1.0 specification (recommendation)

string **name** (node-set?)
Returns the name of the first node in a passed node-set. This is the fully qualified name, including namespace prefix

Parameter:
node-set
If no node-set is specified, the context node is used.

Implemented:
W3C 1.0 specification (recommendation)

string **namespace-uri** (node-set?)
Returns the URI of the namespace of the passed node

Parameter:
node-set
If no node-set is specified, the context node is used.

Implemented:
W3C 1.0 specification (recommendation)

string **normalize-space** (string?)
Returns the whitespace-normalized version of the passed string. This means that leading and trailing whitespace is stripped and all sequences of whitespace characters are combined to one single space character.
`normalize-space(' some text ')` would return `'some text'`

Parameter:
string
If no string is passed, the value of the context node is converted to a string.

Continues

Implemented:
W3C 1.0 specification (recommendation)

boolean **not** (boolean)
Returns the logical inverse of the passed value.
`not(@name)` returns `true` if there is no `name` attribute on the context node

Parameter:
boolean
An expression that evaluates to a Boolean value

Implemented:
W3C 1.0 specification (recommendation)

number **number** (object?)
Converts the parameter to a number.
`number('3.6')` returns the number `3.6` from the supplied string parameter.

Parameter:
object
If no parameter is specified, the context node is used.

Implemented:
W3C 1.0 specification (recommendation)

number **position** ( )
Returns the position of a node in a node-set.
`position()` returns `1` for the first node in a node-set

Implemented:
W3C 1.0 specification (recommendation)

number **round** (number)
Rounds a passed number to the nearest integer. If the value is exactly half way between two integers it is rounded to the integer nearer to positive infinity.
`round(1.5)` returns `2`, `round(-1.7)` returns `-2`

Parameter:
number
The number that is to be rounded

Implemented:
W3C 1.0 specification (recommendation)

boolean **starts-with** (string1, string2)
Returns `true` if string1 starts with string2.
`starts-with(@name, 'D')` returns `true` if the value of the `name` attribute starts with an uppercase D

Parameters:
string1
The string to be checked

string2
The substring that must be searched for

Implemented:
W3C 1.0 specification (recommendation)

string **string** (object?)
Converts the passed object to a string value.

Parameter:
object
If no parameter is specified, the context node is evaluated.

Implemented:
W3C 1.0 specification (recommendation)

number **string-length** (string?)
Returns the number of characters in the passed string.
`string-length('Andrew Watt')` returns `11`

Parameter:
string
If no parameter is specified, the context node is converted to a string.

Implemented:
W3C 1.0 specification (recommendation)

string **substring** (string, number1, number2?)
Returns the substring from the passed string starting at the number1 character, with the length of number2. If no number2 parameter is passed, the substring runs to the end of the passed string. Characters are numbered from 1.
`substring('Andrew Watt', 8)` returns `'Watt'`

Parameters:
string
The string that will be used as source for the substring extraction

number1
Start location of the substring

number2
Length of the substring

Implemented:
W3C 1.0 specification (recommendation)

string **substring-after** (string1, string2)
Returns the substring following the first occurrence of `string2` inside `string1`. For example, the return value of `substring-after('2004/3/22', '/')` would be `3/22`

Parameters:
string1
The string to be searched for the specified substring

string2
The string that is searched in the source string

Continues

Implemented:
W3C 1.0 specification (recommendation)

string **substring-before** (string1, string2)
Returns the string part preceding the first occurrence of the `string2` inside the `string1`. For example, the return value of `substring-before('2004/3/22', '/')` would be `2004`.

Parameters:
string1
The string to be searched for the specified substring

string2
The string that is searched in the source string

Implemented:
W3C 1.0 specification (recommendation)

number **sum** (node-set)
Sums the values of all nodes in the set when converted to number.
`sum(student/@age)` returns the sum of the values of all `age` attributes on the student elements in the `child` axis starting at the context node.

Parameter:
node-set
The node-set containing all values to be summed

Implemented:
W3C 1.0 specification (recommendation)

string **translate** (string1, string2, string3)
Translates characters in `string1` to other characters. Translation pairs are specified by `string2` and `string3`. For example, `translate('A Space Odissei', 'i', 'y')` would result in `A Space Odyssey`, and `translate('abcdefg', 'aceg', 'ACE')` would result in `AbCdEf`. The characters `a`, `c`, and `e` are translated to the corresponding uppercase character, as specified in the string3. The final `g` gets translated to nothing, because string3 has no counterpart for that position in string2.

Parameters:
string1
String to be translated character by character

string2
String defining which characters must be translated

string3
String defining what the characters from string2 should be translated to

Implemented:
W3C 1.0 specification (recommendation)

boolean **true** ( )
Always returns `true`. This function is required in XPath because the expression `True` selects any child element nodes whose name is `True`.

Implemented:
W3C 1.0 specification (recommendation)

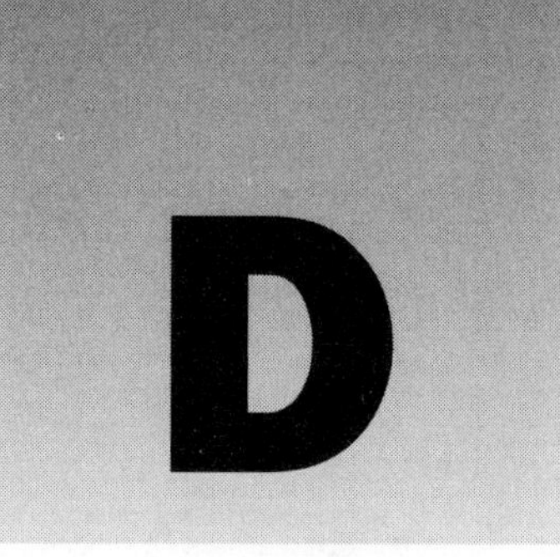

XSLT 1.0 Reference

This appendix provides a reference to the elements and functions that are part of XSLT 1.0. A reference to XPath 1.0 constructs, including functions that can also be used with XSLT, is in Appendix C.

The XSLT 1.0 specification became a W3C Recommendation on November 16, 1999. XSLT 2.0 is a W3C Working Draft at the time of writing.

XSLT 1.0 processors may or may not come with a description of the conformance to the XSLT 1.0 specification. However, most XSLT processors can be assumed to be close to 100 percent conformant to the W3C XSLT 1.0 specification. Some experimental XSLT processors, such as recent versions of Saxon, include a conformant XSLT 1.0 implementation, which was used in Chapter 8, and an experimental XSLT 2.0 processor.

Both the attributes on XSLT 1.0 elements and the parameters of XSLT 1.0 functions can be of several types. At the end of this appendix, you will find a list of the types used in the elements and functions of XSLT.

Elements

An XSLT stylesheet is itself an XML document, using elements in the XSLT namespace. The namespace URI is `http://www.w3.org/1999/XSL/Transform`. When XSLT is used, a namespace prefix is used in the element name as a proxy for the namespace URI. In this appendix we use the namespace prefix `xsl`.

For each XSLT 1.0 element we give a short description of its use, describe the attributes that can or must be used on the element, and indicate where in the stylesheet the element can occur (as a child of which other elements).

xsl:apply-imports

Used for calling a template from an imported stylesheet that would be of lower import precedence in the importing stylesheet. This element is typically used if you want to add

Continues

functionality to a standard template that you imported using `xsl:import`. The `xsl:apply-imports` element has no attributes.	
Implemented:	W3C XSLT 1.0 specification
Can contain:	No other elements
Can be contained by:	`xsl:attribute`, `xsl:comment`, `xsl:copy`, `xsl:element`, `xsl:fallback`, `xsl:for-each`, `xsl:if`, `xsl:message`, `xsl:otherwise`, `xsl:param`, `xsl:processing-instruction`, `xsl:template`, `xsl:variable`, `xsl:when`

xsl:apply-templates

Used to select a set of nodes, a node-set, to be processed. The processor attempts to find templates that match.		
Attributes:		
`select` (optional)	Expression describing which nodes should be processed. Defaults to `child::*`	
	Type:	Location path
	Attribute Value Template:	no
`mode` (optional)	By adding a `mode` attribute, the processor will process nodes using only templates with a matching value for its `mode` attribute. This allows us to process a node in the source tree more than once	
	Type:	Qname
	Attribute Value Template:	no
Implemented:	W3C XSLT 1.0 specification	
Can contain:	`xsl:sort`, `xsl:with-param`	
Can be contained by:	`xsl:attribute`, `xsl:comment`, `xsl:copy`, `xsl:element`, `xsl:fallback`, `xsl:for-each`, `xsl:if`, `xsl:message`, `xsl:otherwise`, `xsl:param`, `xsl:processing-instruction`, `xsl:template`, `xsl:variable`, `xsl:when`	

xsl:attribute

Generates an attribute in the result document. It should be used in the context of an element (either `xsl:element` or a literal result element). It must occur before any text or element content is added to an element node.

Attributes:		
name (required)	The name of the attribute	
	Type:	Qname
	Attribute Value Template:	yes
namespace (optional)	The namespace URI of the attribute node. By default uses the namespace of the element the attribute is placed on	
	Type:	uri-reference
	Attribute Value Template:	yes
Implemented:	W3C XSLT 1.0 specification	
Can contain:	xsl:apply-imports, xsl:apply-templates, xsl:call-template, xsl:choose, xsl:copy, xsl:copy-of, xsl:fallback, xsl:for-each, xsl:if, xsl:message, xsl:number, xsl:text, xsl:value-of, xsl:variable	
Can be contained by:	xsl:attribute-set, xsl:copy, xsl:element, xsl:fallback, xsl:for-each, xsl:if, xsl:message, xsl:otherwise, xsl:param, xsl:template, xsl:variable, xsl:when	

xsl:attribute-set

Used to define a set of attributes that can then be added to an element as a group by specifying the xsl:attribute-set element's name attribute value in the use-attribute-sets attribute on the xsl:element element.		
Attributes:		
name (required)	Name that can be used to refer to this set of attributes	
	Type:	Qname
	Attribute Value Template:	no
use-attribute-sets (optional)	For including one or more existing attribute sets in this attribute set	
	Type:	Qnames
	Attribute Value Template:	no
Implemented:	W3C XSLT 1.0 specification	
Can contain:	Xsl:attribute	
Can be contained by:	Xsl:stylesheet, xsl:transform.	

xsl:call-template

Used to call a template by name. Causes no change of context node as `xsl:apply-templates` and `xsl:for-each` do. This element can be used to reuse the same functionality in several templates.		
Attributes:		
`name` (required)	Name of the template you want to call	
	Type:	Qname
	Attribute Value Template:	no
Implemented:	W3C XSLT 1.0 specification	
Can contain:	`xsl:with-param`	
Can be contained by:	`xsl:attribute`, `xsl:comment`, `xsl:copy` `xsl:element`, `xsl:fallback`, `xsl:for-each`, `xsl:if`, `xsl:message`, `xsl:otherwise`, `xsl:param`, `xsl:processing-instruction`, `xsl:template`, `xsl:variable`, `xsl:when`.	

xsl:choose

Used for implementing the choose/when/otherwise construct. Compare to `Case/Select` in Visual Basic or `switch` in C and Java. The `xsl:choose` element has no attributes.	
Implemented:	W3C XSLT 1.0 specification
Can contain:	`xsl:otherwise`, `xsl:when`
Can be contained by:	`xsl:attribute`, `xsl:comment`, `xsl:copy`, `xsl:element`, `xsl:fallback`, `xsl:for-each`, `xsl:if`, `xsl:message`, `xsl:otherwise`, `xsl:param`, `xsl:processing-instruction`, `xsl:template`, `xsl:variable`, `xsl:when`.

xsl:comment

Needed for generating a comment node in the result document. The `xsl:comment` element has no attributes.	
Implemented:	W3C XSLT 1.0 specification
Can contain:	`xsl:apply-imports`, `xsl:apply-templates`, `xsl:call-template`, `xsl:choose`, `xsl:copy`, `xsl:copy-of`, `xsl:fallback`, `xsl:for-each`, `xsl:if`, `xsl:message`, `xsl:number`, `xsl:text`, `xsl:value-of`, `xsl:variable`.
Can be contained by:	`xsl:copy`, `xsl:element`, `xsl:fallback`, `xsl:for-each`, `xsl:if`, `xsl:message`, `xsl:otherwise`, `xsl:param`, `xsl:template`, `xsl:variable`, `xsl:when`

xsl:copy

Generates a copy of the context node in the destination document. Does not copy any child nodes or attribute nodes.		
Attributes:		
`use-attribute-sets` (optional)	For adding a set of attributes to the copied node, if it is an element node	
	Type:	Qnames
	Attribute Value Template:	No
Implemented:	W3C XSLT 1.0 specification	
Can contain:	`xsl:apply-imports`, `xsl:apply-templates`, `xsl:attribute`, `xsl:call-template`, `xsl:choose`, `xsl:comment`, `xsl:copy-of`, `xsl:element`, `xsl:fallback`, `xsl:for-each`, `xsl:if`, `xsl:message`, `xsl:number`, `xsl:processing-instruction`, `xsl:text`, `xsl:value-of`, `xsl:variable`	
Can be contained by:	`xsl:attribute`, `xsl:comment`, `xsl:copy`, `xsl:element`, `xsl:fallback`, `xsl:for-each`, `xsl:if`, `xsl:message`, `xsl:otherwise`, `xsl:param`, `xsl:processing-instruction`, `xsl:template`, `xsl:variable`, `xsl:when`	

xsl:copy-of

Copies a node, together with any attribute nodes and child nodes, to the result tree. If multiple nodes are matched by the `select` attribute, all are copied. If you have an XML fragment stored in a variable, `xsl:copy-of` is a useful element for sending the variable's content to the result tree.		
Attributes:		
`select` (required)	XPath expression that selects the nodes to be copied	
	Type:	Expression
	Attribute Value Template:	no
Implemented:	W3C XSLT 1.0 specification	
Can contain:	Cannot contain other elements	
Can be contained by:	`xsl:attribute`, `xsl:comment`, `xsl:copy`,, `xsl:element`, `xsl:fallback`, `xsl:for-each`, `xsl:if`, `xsl:message`, `xsl:otherwise`, `xsl:param`, `xsl:processing-instruction`, `xsl:template`, `xsl:variable`, `xsl:when`	

xsl:decimal-format

Declares a decimal format that controls the interpretation of a format pattern used by the `format-number()` function. Among the aspects of the format defined are the decimal separator and the thousands separator.

Attributes:

Attribute	Description	
`name` (optional)	The name of the defined format	
	Type:	Qname
	Attribute Value Template:	no
`decimal-separator` (optional)	The character that will separate the integer part from the fraction part. Default is a dot (`.`)	
	Type:	Character
	Attribute Value Template:	no
`grouping-separator` (optional)	The character that will separate the grouped numbers in the integer part. Default is a comma (`,`)	
	Type:	Character
	Attribute Value Template:	no
`infinity` (optional)	The string that should appear if a number equals infinity. Default is the string `Infinity`	
	Type:	String
	Attribute Value Template:	no
`minus-sign` (optional)	The character that will be used to indicate a negative number. Default is minus (–)	
	Type:	Character
	Attribute Value Template:	no
`NaN` (optional)	The string that should appear if a value is Not a Number. Default is the string `NaN`	
	Type:	String
	Attribute Value Template:	No
`percent` (optional)	Character that will be used as the percent sign. Default is `%`	
	Type:	Character
	Attribute Value Template:	No

per-mille (optional)	Character that will be used as the per-thousand sign. Default is the Unicode character #x2030, which looks like ‰	
	Type:	Character
	Attribute Value Template:	No
zero-digit (optional)	The character used as the digit zero. Default is 0	
	Type:	Character
	Attribute Value Template:	No
digit (optional)	The character used in a pattern to indicate the place where a leading zero is required. Default is 0	
	Type:	Character
	Attribute Value Template:	No
pattern-separator (optional)	The character that is used to separate the negative and positive patterns (if they are different). Default is semicolon (;)	
	Type:	Character
	Attribute Value Template:	No
Implemented:	W3C XSLT 1.0 specification	
Can contain:	Cannot contain other elements	
Can be contained by:	xsl:stylesheet, xsl:transform	

xsl:element

Generates an element with the specified name in the destination document.		
Attributes:		
name (required)	Name of the element (this may include a namespace prefix bound to a namespace in the stylesheet)	
	Type:	qname
	Attribute Value Template:	yes
namespace (optional)	To specify the namespace URI of the element to be created	
	Type:	Uri-reference
	Attribute Value Template:	yes

Continues

`use-attribute-sets` (optional)	To add a predefined set of attributes to the element	
	Type:	Qnames
	Attribute Value Template:	no
Implemented:	W3C XSLT 1.0 specification	
Can contain:	`xsl:apply-imports`, `xsl:apply-templates`, `xsl:attribute`, `xsl:call-template`, `xsl:choose`, `xsl:comment`, `xsl:copy`, `xsl:copy-of`, `xsl:element`, `xsl:fallback`, `xsl:for-each`, `xsl:if`, `xsl:message`, `xsl:number`, `xsl:processing-instruction`, `xsl:text`, `xsl:value-of`, `xsl:variable`	
Can be contained by:	`xsl:copy`, `xsl:element`, `xsl:fallback`, `xsl:for-each`, `xsl:if`, `xsl:otherwise`, `xsl:param`, `xsl:template`, `xsl:variable`, `xsl:when`	

xsl:fallback

Can be used to specify actions to be executed if its parent element is not supported by the processor.	
Implemented:	W3C XSLT 1.0 specification
Can contain:	`xsl:apply-imports`, `xsl:apply-templates`, `xsl:attribute`, `xsl:call-template`, `xsl:choose`, `xsl:comment`, `xsl:copy`, `xsl:copy-of`, `xsl:element`, `xsl:for-each`, `xsl:if`, `xsl:message`, `xsl:number`, `xsl:processing-instruction`, `xsl:text`, `xsl:value-of`, `xsl:variable`
Can be contained by:	`xsl:attribute`, `xsl:comment`, `xsl:copy`, `xsl:element`, `xsl:for-each`, `xsl:if`, `xsl:message`, `xsl:otherwise`, `xsl:param`, `xsl:processing-instruction`, `xsl:template`, `xsl:variable`, `xsl:when`

xsl:for-each

Used for looping through the node-set selected by the XPath expression in the `select` attribute. The context is shifted to the current node in the loop.		
Attributes:		
`select` (required)	Expression that selects the node-set to loop through	
	Type:	node-set-expression
	Attribute Value Template:	no

Implemented:	W3C XSLT 1.0 specification
Can contain:	`xsl:apply-imports`, `xsl:apply-templates`, `xsl:attribute`, `xsl:call-template`, `xsl:choose`, `xsl:comment`, `xsl:copy`, `xsl:copy-of`, `xsl:element`, `xsl:fallback`, `xsl:for-each`, `xsl:if`, `xsl:message`, `xsl:number`, `xsl:processing-instruction`, `xsl:sort`, `xsl:text`, `xsl:value-of`, `xsl:variable`
Can be contained by:	`xsl:attribute`, `xsl:comment`, `xsl:copy`, `xsl:element`, `xsl:fallback`, `xsl:for-each`, `xsl:if`, `xsl:message`, `xsl:otherwise`, `xsl:param`, `xsl:processing-instruction`, `xsl:template`, `xsl:variable`, `xsl:when`

xsl:if

The contained instructions are instantiated only if the test expression returns `true`.		
Attributes:		
`test` (required)	The expression that is tested. If it returns `true` the instructions contained in the `xsl:if` element are executed	
	Type:	boolean-expression
	Attribute Value Template:	no
Implemented:	W3C XSLT 1.0 specification	
Can contain:	`xsl:apply-imports`, `xsl:apply-templates`, `xsl:attribute`, `xsl:call-template`, `xsl:choose`, `xsl:comment`, `xsl:copy`, `xsl:copy-of`, `xsl:element`, `xsl:fallback`, `xsl:for-each`, `xsl:if`, `xsl:message`, `xsl:number`, `xsl:processing-instruction`, `xsl:text`, `xsl:value-of`, `xsl:variable`	
Can be contained by:	`xsl:attribute`, `xsl:comment`, `xsl:copy`, `xsl:element`, `xsl:fallback`, `xsl:for-each`, `xsl:if`, `xsl:message`, `xsl:otherwise`, `xsl:param`, `xsl:processing-instruction`, `xsl:template`, `xsl:variable`, `xsl:when`	

xsl:import

Imports the templates from an external stylesheet document into the current document. The priority of these imported templates is lower than the priority of templates in the importing stylesheet, so if a template in the importing document is implemented for the same pattern, it will always be instantiated rather than a similar template in the imported template being instantiated. An imported template can be called from the overriding template using `xsl:apply-imports`.

Continues

Attributes:		
`href` (required)	Reference to the stylesheet to be imported.	
	Type:	uri-reference
	Attribute Value Template:	no
Implemented:	W3C XSLT 1.0 specification	
Can contain:	Cannot contain other elements	
Can be contained by:	`xsl:stylesheet, xsl:transform`	

xsl:include

Includes templates from an external document as if they were part of the stylesheet document that contains the `xsl:include` element. This means that templates from the included stylesheet have the same priority as they would have had if they were part of the including stylesheet. An error occurs if a template with the same `match` and `priority` attributes exists in both the including and included stylesheets.

Attributes:		
`href` (required)	Reference to the stylesheet to be imported	
	Type:	Uri-reference
	Attribute Value Template:	No
Implemented:	W3C XSLT 1.0 specification	
Can contain:	Cannot contain other elements	
Can be contained by:	`xsl:stylesheet, xsl:transform`	

xsl:key

Can be used to create index-like structures that can be queried from the `key()` function. It is basically a way to describe name/value pairs inside the source document (like a `Dictionary` object in VB, a Hashtable in Java, or an associative array in Perl). However, in XSLT, more than one value can be found for one key and the same value can be accessed by multiple keys.

Attributes:		
`name` (required)	The name that can be used to refer to this key.	
	Type:	Qname
	Attribute Value Template:	no

match (required)	Contains a pattern that defines the nodes in the source document that can be accessed using this key. In the name/value pair analogy, this would be the definition of the value	
	Type:	Pattern
	Attribute Value Template:	no
use (required)	This expression defines what the key for accessing each value would be. For example, if an element PERSON is matched by the match attribute and the use attribute equals "@name", the key() function can be used to find this specific PERSON element by passing the value of its name attribute	
	Type:	Expression
	Attribute Value Template:	no
Implemented:	W3C XSLT 1.0 specification	
Can contain:	Cannot contain other elements	
Can be contained by:	xsl:stylesheet, xsl:transform	

xsl:message

Used to issue error messages or warnings. The content of the element is the message. What the XSLT processor does with the message is left to the implementation. It could be displayed in a message box or logged to an error log.

Attributes:

terminate (optional)	If terminate is set to yes, the execution of the transformation is stopped after issuing the message	
	Type:	yes/no
	Attribute Value Template:	no
Implemented:	W3C 1.0 XSLT specification	
Can contain:	xsl:apply-imports, xsl:apply-templates, xsl:attribute, xsl:call-template, xsl:choose, xsl:comment, xsl:copy, xsl:copy-of, xsl:element, xsl:fallback, xsl:for-each, xsl:if, xsl:message, xsl:number, xsl:processing-instruction, xsl:text, xsl:value-of, xsl:variable	
Can be contained by:	xsl:attribute, xsl:comment, xsl:copy, xsl:element, xsl:fallback, xsl:for-each, xsl:if, xsl:message, xsl:otherwise, xsl:param, xsl:processing-instruction, xsl:template, xsl:variable, xsl:when	

xsl:namespace-alias

Used to make a certain namespace appear in the result document without using the desired namespace prefix for that namespace in the stylesheet. The main use of this element is in generating new XSLT stylesheets.		
Attributes:		
`stylesheet-prefix` (required)	The prefix for the namespace that is used in the stylesheet	
	Type:	prefix/#default
	Attribute Value Template:	no
`result-prefix` (required)	The prefix for the namespace that must replace the aliased namespace in the destination document	
	Type:	prefix/#default
	Attribute Value Template:	no
Implemented:	W3C XSLT 1.0 specification	
Can contain:	No other elements	
Can be contained by:	`xsl:stylesheet`, `xsl:transform`	

xsl:number

Needed for outputting the number of a paragraph or chapter in a specified format. It has flexible features to allow for different numbering rules.		
Attributes:		
`level` (optional)	The value `single` counts the location of the nearest node matched by the `count` attribute (along the ancestor axis) relative to its preceding siblings of the same name. Typical output: chapter number. The value `multiple` counts the location of all nodes matched by the `count` attribute (along the ancestor axis) relative to their preceding siblings of the same name. Typical output: paragraph number of form 4.5.3. The value `any` counts the location of the nearest node matched by the `count` attribute (along the ancestor axis) relative to its preceding nodes (not only siblings) of the same name. Typical output: bookmark number	
	Type:	single/multiple/any
	Attribute Value Template:	no
`count` (optional)	Specifies the node-set that is to be counted	

	Type:	pattern
	Attribute Value Template:	no
`from` (optional)	Specifies the starting point for counting	
	Type:	pattern
	Attribute Value Template:	no
`value` (optional)	Used to specify the numeric value directly instead of using `'level'`, `'count'` and `'from'`	
	Type:	number-expression
	Attribute Value Template:	no
`format` (optional)	How to format the numeric value to a string (1 indicates 1, 2, 3, . . . ; a indicates a, b, c,)	
	Type:	string
	Attribute Value Template:	Yes
`lang` (optional)	Language used for alphabetic numbering	
	Type:	token
	Attribute Value Template:	Yes
`letter-value` (optional)	Some languages have traditional orders of letters specifically for numbering. These orders are often different from the alphabetic order	
	Type:	alphabetic/traditional
	Attribute Value Template:	Yes
`grouping-separator` (optional)	Character to be used for group separation	
	Type:	Character
	Attribute Value Template:	Yes
`grouping-size` (optional)	Number of digits to be separated. `grouping-separator=";"` and `grouping-size="3"` causes: 1;000;000	
	Type:	number
	Attribute Value Template:	Yes
Implemented:	W3C XSLT 1.0 specification	
Can contain:	Cannot contain other elements	

Continues

Can be contained by:	`xsl:attribute`, `xsl:comment`, `xsl:copy`, `xsl:element`, `xsl:fallback`, `xsl:for-each`, `xsl:if`, `xsl:message`, `xsl:otherwise`, `xsl:param`, `xsl:processing-instruction`, `xsl:template`, `xsl:variable`, `xsl:when`

xsl:otherwise

Content is executed if none of the `xsl:when` elements in an `xsl:choose` is matched.

Implemented:	W3C 1.0 specification (recommendation)
Can contain:	`xsl:apply-imports`, `xsl:apply-templates`, `xsl:attribute`, `xsl:call-template`, `xsl:choose`, `xsl:comment`, `xsl:copy`, `xsl:copy-of`, `xsl:element`, `xsl:fallback`, `xsl:for-each`, `xsl:if`, `xsl:message`, `xsl:number`, `xsl:processing-instruction`, `xsl:text`, `xsl:value-of`, `xsl:variable`
Can be contained by:	`xsl:choose`

xsl:output

Top-level element for setting properties regarding the output characteristics of the result document. The `xsl:output` element describes how the serialization from a created tree of nodes to a string happens.

Attributes:

`method` (optional)	`xml` is default `html` creates empty elements such as `BR` (with no end tag) and uses HTML entities such as ` `. `text` causes no output escaping to happen at all (no entity references in output)	
	Type:	xml/html/text/qname-but-not-ncname
	Attribute Value Template:	no
`version` (optional)	The version number that will appear in the XML declaration of the output document	
	Type:	token
	Attribute Value Template:	no
`encoding` (optional)	The encoding of the output document	

	Type:	String
	Attribute Value Template:	no
`omit-xml-declaration` (optional)	Specifies whether the resulting document should contain an XML declaration (`<?xml version="1.0"?>`)	
	Type:	yes/no
	Attribute Value Template:	no
`standalone` (optional)	Specifies whether the XSLT processor should output a stand-alone document declaration	
	Type:	yes/no
	Attribute Value Template:	no
`doctype-public` (optional)	Specifies the public identifier to be used in the `DOCTYPE` declaration	
	Type:	String
	Attribute Value Template:	no
`doctype-system` (optional)	Specifies the system identifier to be used in the `DOCTYPE` declaration	
	Type:	String
	Attribute Value Template:	no
`cdata-section-elements` (optional)	Specifies a list of elements that should have their content escaped by using a CDATA section instead of entities	
	Type:	Qnames
	Attribute Value Template:	no
`indent` (optional)	Specifies the addition of extra whitespace for readability	
	Type:	yes/no
	Attribute Value Template:	no
`media-type` (optional)	To specify a specific MIME type while writing out content	
	Type:	String
	Attribute Value Template:	no
Implemented:	W3C XSLT 1.0 specification	
Can contain:	Cannot contain other elements	
Can be contained by:	`xsl:stylesheet`, `xsl:transform`	

xsl:param

Defines a parameter in an xsl:template or xsl:stylesheet.		
Attributes:		
name (required)	Name of the parameter	
	Type:	Qname
	Attribute Value Template:	no
select (optional)	Specifies the default value for the parameter	
	Type:	expression
	Attribute Value Template:	no
Implemented:	W3C XSLT 1.0 specification	
Can contain:	xsl:apply-imports, xsl:apply-templates, xsl:attribute, xsl:call-template, xsl:choose, xsl:comment, xsl:copy, xsl:copy-of, xsl:element, xsl:fallback, xsl:for-each, xsl:if, xsl:message, xsl:number, xsl:processing-instruction, xsl:text, xsl:value-of, xsl:variable	
Can be contained by:	xsl:stylesheet, xsl:transform	

xsl:preserve-space

Enables you to define which elements in the source document should have their whitespace preserved. See also xsl:strip-space.		
Attributes:		
elements (required)	In this attribute you can list the elements (separated by whitespace) for which you want to preserve the whitespace content	
	Type:	tokens
	Attribute Value Template:	no
Implemented:	W3C XSLT 1.0 specification	
Can contain:	Cannot contain other elements	
Can be contained by:	xsl:stylesheet, xsl:transform	

xsl:processing-instruction

Generates a processing instruction in the destination document.		
Attributes:		
`name` (required)	The name of the processing instruction (the part between the first question mark and the first whitespace of the processing instruction)	
	Type:	Ncname
	Attribute Value Template:	yes
Implemented:	W3C 1.0 specification	
Can contain:	`xsl:apply-imports`, `xsl:apply-templates`, `xsl:call-template`, `xsl:choose`, `xsl:copy`, `xsl:copy-of`, `xsl:fallback`, `xsl:for-each`, `xsl:if`, `xsl:message`, `xsl:number`, `xsl:text`, `xsl:value-of`, `xsl:variable`	
Can be contained by:	`xsl:copy`, `xsl:element`, `xsl:fallback`, `xsl:for-each`, `xsl:if`, `xsl:message`, `xsl:otherwise`, `xsl:param`, `xsl:template`, `xsl:variable`, `xsl:when`	

xsl:sort

Enables you to specify a sort order for `xsl:apply-templates` and `xsl:for-each` elements. Multiple `xsl:sort` elements can be specified to provide primary, secondary, and other sorting keys.		
Attributes:		
`select` (optional)	Expression that indicates the criterion that should be used for the ordering	
	Type:	string-expression
	Attribute Value Template:	no
`lang` (optional)	To set the language used while ordering. (In different languages the rules for alphabetic ordering can be different)	
	Type:	Token
	Attribute Value Template:	yes
`data-type` (optional)	To specify alphabetic or numeric ordering	
	Type:	Text/number/qname-but-not-ncname
	Attribute Value Template:	yes

Continues

`order` (optional)	Specifies ascending or descending ordering	
	Type:	Ascending/descending
	Attribute Value Template:	yes
`case-order` (optional)	Specifies whether uppercase characters should come before or after lowercase characters. Note that case insensitive sorting is not supported	
	Type:	upper-first/lower-first
	Attribute Value Template:	yes
Implemented:	W3C XSLT 1.0 specification	
Can contain:	Cannot contain other elements	
Can be contained by:	`xsl:apply-templates`, `xsl:for-each`	

xsl:strip-space

Enables you to define which elements in the source document should have their whitespace content stripped. See also `xsl:preserve-space`.

Attributes:

`elements` (required)	Specifies the elements whose whitespace should be stripped	
	Type:	Tokens
	Attribute Value Template:	no
Implemented:	W3C 1.0 specification	
Can contain:	Cannot contain other elements	
Can be contained by:	`xsl:stylesheet`, `xsl:transform`	

xsl:stylesheet

It is the root element for a stylesheet. Synonym to `xsl:transform`.

Attributes:

`id` (optional)	A reference for the stylesheet	
	Type:	ID
	Attribute Value Template:	no
`extension-element-prefixes` (optional)	Enables you to specify which namespace prefixes are XSLT extension namespaces	

	Type:	Tokens
	Attribute Value Template:	no
`exclude-result-prefixes` (optional)	Namespaces that are only relevant in the stylesheet or in the source document, but not in the result document, can be removed from the output by specifying them here	
	Type:	Tokens
	Attribute Value Template:	no
`version` (required)	Version number	
	Type:	Number
	Attribute Value Template:	no
Implemented:	W3C XSLT 1.0 specification	
Can contain:	`xsl:attribute-set`, `xsl:decimal-format`, `xsl:import`, `xsl:include`, `xsl:key`, `xsl:namespace-alias`, `xsl:output`, `xsl:param`, `xsl:preserve-space`, `xsl:strip-space`, `xsl:template`, `xsl:variable`	
Can be contained by:	No other elements	

xsl:template

Defines a transformation rule. Some templates are built-in and don't have to be defined. Refer to Chapter 8 for more information about writing templates.		
Attributes:		
`match` (optional)	Defines the set of nodes on which the template can be applied	
	Type:	Pattern
	Attribute Value Template:	no
`name` (optional)	Name to identify the template when calling it using `xsl:call-template`	
	Type:	Qname
	Attribute Value Template:	no
`priority` (optional)	If several templates can be applied (through matches on their `match` attributes) on a node, the `priority` attribute can be used to determine which template is instantiated	
	Type:	Number
	Attribute Value Template:	no

Continues

mode (optional)	If a mode attribute is present on a template, the template will be instantiated only if there is a matching mode attribute on an xsl:apply-templates element whose select attribute's value matches the value of the template's match attribute	
	Type:	Qname
	Attribute Value Template:	no
Implemented:	W3C XSLT 1.0 specification	
Can contain:	xsl:apply-imports, xsl:apply-templates, xsl:attribute, xsl:call-template, xsl:choose, xsl:comment, xsl:copy, xsl:copy-of, xsl:element, xsl:fallback, xsl:for-each, xsl:if, xsl:message, xsl:number, xsl:processing-instruction, xsl:text, xsl:value-of, xsl:variable	
Can be contained by:	xsl:stylesheet, xsl:transform	

xsl:text

Generates a text string from its content. Whitespace is never stripped from the content of an xsl:text element.		
Attributes:		
disable-output-escaping (optional)	If set to yes, the output will not be escaped: this means that a string "<" will be written to the output as "<" instead of "<". This means that the result document will not be a well-formed XML document	
	Type:	yes/no
	Attribute Value Template:	no
Implemented:	W3C XSLT 1.0 specification	
Can contain:	Cannot contain other elements	
Can be contained by:	xsl:attribute, xsl:comment, xsl:copy, xsl:element, xsl:fallback, xsl:for-each, xsl:if, xsl:message, xsl:otherwise, xsl:param, xsl:processing-instruction, xsl:template, xsl:variable, xsl:when	

xsl:transform

Identical to xsl:stylesheet.	
Attributes:	
id (optional)	A unique reference for the stylesheet

	Type:	ID
	Attribute Value Template:	no
`extension-element-prefixes` (optional)	Enables you to specify which namespace prefixes are XSLT extension namespaces	
	Type:	tokens
	Attribute Value Template:	no
`exclude-result-prefixes` (optional)	Namespaces that are only relevant in the stylesheet or in the source document, but not in the result document, can be removed from the result document by specifying them here	
	Type:	tokens
	Attribute Value Template:	No
`version` (required)	The version of XSLT being used	
	Type:	number
	Attribute Value Template:	No
Implemented:	W3C XSLT 1.0 specification	
Can contain:	`xsl:attribute-set`, `xsl:decimal-format`, `xsl:import`, `xsl:include`, `xsl:key`, `xsl:namespace-alias`, `xsl:output`, `xsl:param`, `xsl:preserve-space`, `xsl:strip-space`, `xsl:template`, `xsl:variable`	
Can be contained by:	No other elements. It is the document element	

xsl:value-of

Generates a text string from the value of the expression in its `select` attribute.		
Attributes:		
`select` (required)	Expression that selects the node-set that will be converted to a string	
	Type:	Expression
	Attribute Value Template:	no
`disable-output-escaping` (optional)	You can use this to output < instead of `<` to the destination document. Note that this will cause the result document not to be well-formed XML. Normally used when generating HTML or text files	
	Type:	yes/no
	Attribute Value Template:	no

Continues

Implemented:	W3C XSLT 1.0 specification
Can contain:	Cannot contain other elements
Can be contained by:	`xsl:attribute`, `xsl:comment`, `xsl:copy`, `xsl:element`, `xsl:fallback`, `xsl:for-each`, `xsl:if`, `xsl:message`, `xsl:otherwise`, `xsl:param`, `xsl:processing-instruction`, `xsl:template`, `xsl:variable`, `xsl:when`

xsl:variable

Defines a variable with a value. Note that in XSLT, the value of a variable cannot change—you can bind a variable using `xsl:variable`, but it cannot be changed afterwards. The XSLT variable resembles a constant in some other programming languages.

Attributes:		
`name` (required)	Name of the variable	
	Type:	qname
	Attribute Value Template:	no
`select` (optional)	Value of the variable (if the `select` attribute is omitted, the content of the `xsl:variable` element is the value)	
	Type:	Expression
	Attribute Value Template:	no
Implemented:	W3C XSLT 1.0 specification	
Can contain:	`xsl:apply-imports`, `xsl:apply-templates`, `xsl:attribute`, `xsl:call-template`, `xsl:choose`, `xsl:comment`, `xsl:copy`, `xsl:copy-of`, `xsl:element`, `xsl:fallback`, `xsl:for-each`, `xsl:if`, `xsl:message`, `xsl:number`, `xsl:processing-instruction`, `xsl:text`, `xsl:value-of`, `xsl:variable`	
Can be contained by:	`xsl:attribute`, `xsl:comment`, `xsl:copy`, `xsl:element`, `xsl:fallback`, `xsl:for-each`, `xsl:if`, `xsl:message`, `xsl:otherwise`, `xsl:param`, `xsl:processing-instruction`, `xsl:stylesheet`, `xsl:template`, `xsl:transform`, `xsl:variable`, `xsl:when`	

xsl:when

Represents an option for execution in a `xsl:choose` block.

Attributes:	
`test` (required)	Expression to be tested

	Type:	boolean-expression
	Attribute Value Template:	no
Implemented:	W3C XSLT 1.0 specification	
Can contain:	`xsl:apply-imports`, `xsl:apply-templates`, `xsl:attribute`, `xsl:call-template`, `xsl:choose`, `xsl:comment`, `xsl:copy`, `xsl:copy-of`, `xsl:element`, `xsl:fallback`, `xsl:for-each`, `xsl:if`, `xsl:message`, `xsl:number`, `xsl:processing-instruction`, `xsl:text`, `xsl:value-of`, `xsl:variable`	
Can be contained by:	`xsl:choose`	

xsl:with-param

Used to pass a parameter to a template using `xsl:apply-templates` or `xsl:call-template`. The template called must have a parameter of the same name defined using `xsl:param`.		
Attributes:		
`name` (required)	Name of the parameter	
	Type:	qname
	Attribute Value Template:	no
`select` (optional)	XPath expression selecting the passed value	
	Type:	Expression
	Attribute Value Template:	no
Implemented:	W3C XSLT 1.0 specification	
Can contain:	Cannot contain other elements	
Can be contained by:	`xsl:apply-templates`, `xsl:call-template`	

Functions

Within expressions in an XSLT stylesheet, you can use the XPath functions we saw in Appendix C and also a number of XSLT functions. These XSLT functions are described in this section.

Each function is described by a line of this form:

```
return-type   function-name (parameters)
```

For each parameter, we display the type (`object`, `string`, `number`, `node-set`) and where necessary a symbol indicating whether the parameter is optional (`?`) or can occur multiple times (+). The type `object` means that any type can be passed.

If an expression is passed as a parameter, it is first evaluated and (if necessary) converted to the expected type before passing it to the function.

node-set **current** ( )

Returns the current context node-set, outside the current expression

Implemented:

W3C 1.0 XSLT specification

node-set **document** (object, node-set?)

To get a reference to an external source document

Parameters:

object

If of type String, this is the URL of the document to be retrieved. If a node-set, all nodes are converted to strings and all these URLs are retrieved in a node-set

node-set

Represents the base URL from where relative URLs are resolved

Implemented:

W3C 1.0 XSLT specification

boolean **element-available** (string)

Determines availability of a specified extension element

Parameters:

string

Name of the extension element

Implemented:

W3C XSLT 1.0 specification

string **format-number** (number, string1, string2?)

Formats a numeric value into a formatted and localized string

Parameters:

number

The numeric value to be represented

string1

The format string that should be used for the formatting

string2

Reference to an `xsl:decimal-format` element to indicate localization parameters

Implemented:

W3C XSLT 1.0 specification

boolean **function-available** (string)
Determines availability of a specified extension function
Parameter: string Name of the extension function Implemented: W3C XSLT 1.0 specification
node-set **generate-id** (node-set?)
Generates a unique identifier for the specified node. Each node will be given a different ID, but the same node will always generate the same ID. You cannot be sure that the IDs generated for a document during multiple transformations will remain identical
Parameter: node-set The first node of the passed node-set is used. If no node-set is passed, the context node is used Implemented: W3C XSLT 1.0 specification
node-set **key** (string, object)
To get a reference to a node using the specified `xsl:key`
Parameters: string The name of the referenced `xsl:key` object If of type String, this is the index string for the key. If of type node-set, all nodes are converted to strings and all are used to get nodes back from the key Implemented: W3C XSLT 1.0 specification
object **system-property** (string)
To get certain system properties from the processor
Parameter: string
The name of a system property. Properties that are always available in a conformant XSLT processor are `xsl:version`, `xsl:vendor`, and `xsl:vendor-url` Implemented: W3C XSLT 1.0 specification

node-set **unparsed-entity-url** (string)
Returns the URI of the unparsed entity with the passed name
Parameter: string Name of the unparsed entity Implemented: W3C XSLT 1.0 specification

Available XPath Functions

Check Appendix C for information on the XPath functions. They can all be used in XSLT:

`boolean()`	`ceiling()`	`concat()`	`contains()`
`count()`	`False()`	`floor()`	`id()`
`lang()`	`Last`	`local-name()`	`name()`
`namespace-uri()`	`normalize-space()`	`not`	`number()`
`position()`	`Round()`	`starts-with()`	`string()`
`string-length()`	`substring()`	`substring-after()`	`substring-before()`
`sum()`	`translate()`	`true()`	

Types

These types are used to specify the types of the attributes for the XSLT elements given in the previous tables.

`boolean`	Can have values `true` and `false`
`character`	A single character
`expression`	A string value containing an XPath expression
`id`	A string value. Must be an XML name. The string value can be used only once as an `id` in any document.
`language-name`	A string containing one of the defined language identifiers. American English = en-us
`name`	A string value that conforms to the naming conventions of XML. That means no whitespace. It should start with either a letter or an underscore (_).
`names`	Multiple name values separated by whitespace

`namespace-prefix`	Any string that is defined as a prefix for a namespace
`ncname`	A name value that does not contain a colon
`node`	A node in an XPath tree. Can be of several types, including: element, attribute, comment, processing instruction, text node, etc.
`node-set`	A set of nodes. Can be of any length.
`node-set-expression`	A string value, containing an XPath expression that returns nodes
`number`	A numeric value. Can be either floating point or integer.
`object`	Anything. Can be a string, a node, a node-set or a boolean.
`qname`	Qualified name; the full name of a node. Made up of two parts: the local name and the namespace identifier.
`qnames`	A set of qname values separated by whitespace
`string`	A string value
`token`	A string value that contains no whitespace
`tokens`	Multiple token values separated by whitespace
`uri-reference`	Any string that conforms to the URI specification

XML Schema Element and Attribute Reference

In this appendix, we provide a full listing of all elements within the XML Schema Structures Recommendation (found at `http://www.w3.org/TR/xmlschema-1/`). The elements are given in alphabetical order. Each element is described with examples and a table detailing all the attributes the element can carry. When attributes are required, it is noted in the attribute listings.

At the end of this appendix, we present a table of the attributes in the XML Schema Instance namespace that can be used in instance documents.

all

The `<all>` element is used within content model declarations. It indicates that all elements declared within it may appear in the instance document in any order and may appear at the most once. The `<all>` element is used within a `<complexType>` or `<group>` element. It can contain `<element>` or `<annotation>` elements. Note that when using `minOccurs` and `maxOccurs` on `<element>` declarations within an `<all>` element, you are not restricted to using a `maxOccurs` of `1` or `0`. You can make an element optional by setting the `minOccurs` to `0`.

Example

```
<xs:element name="Rucksack">
   <xs:complexType>
      <xs:all>
         <xs:element name="Sunglasses" type="xs:string" maxOccurs="1" />
         <xs:element name="Sweater" type="xs:string" maxOccurs="1" />
         <xs:element name="Book" type="xs:string" />
         <xs:element name="Lunchbox" type="xs:string" />
         <xs:element name="Flask" type="xs:string" />
      </xs:all>
   </xs:complexType>
</xs:element>
```

Attributes

Attribute	Value Space	Description
Id	ID	Gives a unique identifier to the element
MaxOccurs	1	The maximum number of times the <all> model group can occur
MinOccurs	0 or 1	The minimum number of times the <all> model group can occur

For more information: see §3.8.2 of the Recommendation.

annotation

The <annotation> element is used to provide additional data for XML Schema declarations. It may contain the <appinfo> and <documentation> elements, which are used to contain instructions for the XML Schema processing application or for additional documentation. It is contained by most elements (excluding itself); specific cases are detailed in the following examples.

Example

An example of using <annotation> with <documentation>:

```
<xs:element name="Person">
   <xs:annotation>
      <xs:documentation>
         Used to contain personal information. Note that the last name
         is mandatory, while the first name is optional.
      </xs:documentation>
   </xs:annotation>
   <!-- definition of Person element goes here -->
</xs:element>
```

An example of using <annotation> with <appinfo>:

```
<xs:element name="Person" type="PersonType">
   <xs:annotation>
      <xs:appinfo>
         <sch:pattern name="Top Level Person elements">
            <sch:rule context="/*">
               <sch:assert test="self::Person">
                  The root element must be a "Person"
               </sch:assert>
            </sch:rule>
         </sch:pattern>
      </xs:appinfo>
   </xs:annotation>
</xs:element>
```

In this second example, the <annotation> element is used to contain a Schematron schema inside the <appinfo> element.

For more information: see §3.13.2 of the Recommendation.

any

The <any> element is used within content model declarations. It is a wildcard element that acts as a placeholder for any element in a model group. Using the <any> declaration it is possible to specify from which namespaces allowable elements may come. This is useful, for instance, if unspecified XHTML, or MathML content might be included within the instance document. It may contain an <annotation> element, and can be contained by <choice> or <sequence> element.

Example

```
<xs:element name="XHTMLSection">
   <xs:complexType>
      <xs:sequence>
         <xs:any namespace="http://www.w3.org/1999/xhtml"
            minOccurs="0" maxOccurs="unbounded"
            processContents="lax" />
      </xs:sequence>
   </xs:complexType>
</xs:element>
```

Here, an XHTMLSection element in an instance document can contain any well-formed markup that is valid in the XHTML namespace.

Attributes

Attribute	Value Space	Description
Id	ID	Gives a unique identifier to the element
MaxOccurs	nonNegativeInteger or unbounded	The maximum number of times the model group can occur
MinOccurs	NonNegativeInteger	The minimum number of times the model group can occur
Namespace	##any | ##other List of (anyURI | ##targetNamespace |	##any means that the content can be of any namespace. ##other refers to any namespace other than the target namespace of the schema. Otherwise, a whitespace separated list of the namespaces of allowed elements,

Continues

Attribute	Value Space	Description
	##local)	which can include ##targetNamespace to allow elements in the target namespace of the schema and ##local to allow elements in no namespace. The default is ##any
ProcessContents	skip | lax | strict	If lax, validation is performed if possible. If skip, then no validation occurs. If strict, validation is enforced, and the validator needs to have access to the declarations for the elements used or a validity error will be raised. The default is skip

For more information: see §3.10.2 of the Recommendation.

anyAttribute

The <anyAttribute> element is used within content model declarations. It acts as a placeholder for any attribute within an element declaration. It allows any unspecified attributes to be present. These can be validated against a specific namespace. For example, XML Schema allows elements to have any attributes as long as they're not in the XML Schema namespace and are qualified with a prefix for another namespace. You might find this useful to allow the use of any XLink attribute within the specific element. The <anyAttribute> can be contained by <attributeGroup>, <complexType>, <extension>, or <restriction> elements; and like most elements it can contain an annotation.

Example

```
<xs:element name="Description">
   <xs:complexType>
      <!-- content definition goes here-->
      <xs:anyAttribute namespace="http://www.w3.org/1999/xlink" />
   </xs:complexType>
</xs:element>
```

Here, a Description element in an instance document can contain any attribute that is valid in the XLink namespace.

Attributes

Attribute	Value Space	Description
Id	ID	Gives a unique identifier to the element
Namespace	##any | ##other |	##any means that the content can be of any namespace. ##other refers to any namespace other than the target

Attribute	Value Space	Description
	List of (anyURI | ##targetNamespace | ##local)"	namespace of the schema. (The attributes must be namespace qualified.) Otherwise, a whitespace separated list of the namespaces of allowed elements, which can include ##targetNamespace to allow elements in the target namespace of the schema and ##local to allow elements in no namespace. The default is ##any
ProcessContents	skip | lax | strict	If lax, validation is performed if possible. If skip, no validation occurs. If strict, validation is enforced, and the validator needs to have access to the declarations for the elements used or a validity error will be raised. The default is skip

For more information: see §3.4.2 of the Recommendation.

appinfo

The <appinfo> element is used within <annotation> declarations. It allows information to be supplied to an application reading the schema. It may contain unique identifiers or additional tags to help an application perform further processing on the schema. Although the XML Schema Recommendation does not specify allowable uses for the <appinfo> element, many XML Schema designers use it to combine Schematron validation with XML Schema validation. For more information on combining XML Schema and Schematron validation, see http://www.topologi.com/public/Schtrn_XSD/Paper.html. Multiple <appinfo> elements may appear within a single <annotation> declaration.

Example

```
<xs:element name="Person" type="PersonType">
  <xs:annotation>
     <xs:appinfo>
        <sch:pattern name="Top Level Person elements">
           <sch:rule context="/*">
              <sch:assert test="self::Person">
                 The root element must be a "Person"
              </sch:assert>
           </sch:rule>
        </sch:pattern>
     </xs:appinfo>
  </xs:annotation>
</xs:element>
```

Attributes

Attribute	Value Space	Description
`Source`	`anyURI`	Specifies a URI where the parser can acquire the required `<appinfo>` content

For more information: see §3.13.2 of the Recommendation.

attribute

The `<attribute>` element is used to declare allowable attributes within elements. It is usually found within an `<attributeGroup>` or a `<complexType>` element and so defines the attributes for that particular content model. It can also be used in an `<extension>` or `<restriction>` element when deriving a new type. Attribute declarations may also appear in the root `<schema>` element to create global attribute definitions that can be referenced from other declarations. The `<attribute>` element may contain an `<annotation>` element. It may also contain an anonymous `<simpleType>` declaration, if no `type` attribute is specified.

Example

```
<xs:attribute name="Amount">
   <xs:simpleType name="positiveDecimalN.2" >
      <xs:restriction base="xs:decimal" >
         <xs:minInclusive value="0" />
         <xs:fractionDigits value="2" />
      </xs:restriction>
   </xs:simpleType>
</xs:attribute>

<xs:element name="Payment">
   <xs:complexType >
      <xs:attribute ref="Amount" />
      <xs:attribute name="currency" type="xs:string" default="US$"
         use="optional" />
   </xs:complexType>
</xs:element>
```

Attributes

Attribute	Value Space	Description
`Default`	`string`	A string containing the default value of the attribute that is used if the attribute is not specified in the instance document

Attribute	Value Space	Description
Fixed	string	If present, the value of the attribute in an instance document must always match the value specified by fixed
Form	qualified | unqualified	If qualified, the attribute must be namespace qualified in the instance document. Note that if the form attribute is present on the attribute element it overrides attributeFormDefault on the schema element. All global attribute declarations must be qualified regardless of the value of the form attribute or attributeFormDefault attribute. For an attribute to be qualified in an instance document, it must have a prefix associated with the namespace
Id	ID	Gives a unique identifier to the element
Name	NCName	The name of the attribute conforming to the XML NCName data type
Ref	QName	Refers a previously defined global attribute by name
Type	QName	The data type of the attribute
Use	optional | prohibited | required	If optional, the attribute may be omitted in the instance document. If required, it must be included. If prohibited, it cannot be included. The default is optional

For more information: see §3.3.2 of the Recommendation.

attributeGroup

The <attributeGroup> element is used to declare a group of attributes or to refer to an existing global <attributeGroup> declaration. This is useful when more than one element contains the same group of attributes. It may contain <annotation>, <attribute>, <attributeGroup>, and <anyAttribute> declarations. When the <attributeGroup> element is a direct child of the <schema> element it must be used as a global declaration for a group of attributes. Attribute group definitions can be nested, so an <attributeGroup> can contain or be contained by another <attributeGroup>. It can also be used as a reference from within a <complexType>, <redefine>, <extension>, or <restriction> declaration.

Example

```
<xs:attributeGroup name="myAttrGroup">
   <xs:attribute name="weight" type="xs:decimal" use="optional" />
   <xs:attribute name="height" type="xs:decimal" use="optional" />
```

```
</xs:attributeGroup>

<xs:element name="Person">
   <xs:complexType>
       <xs:sequence>
          <!-- element content here -->
       </xs:sequence>
      <xs:attributeGroup ref="myAttrGroup" />
   </xs:complexType>
</xs:element>
```

Attributes

Attribute	Value Space	Description
Id	ID	Gives a unique identifier to the element
Name	NCName	The name of this attribute group
Ref	QName	Refers to previously defined global attribute group; used within a <complexType> definition to include a group of attributes

For more information: see §3.6.2 of the Recommendation.

choice

The <choice> element is used within content model declarations. It is used to indicate that only one of its contained declarations can be used within the content model in the instance document. It may contain <annotation> and <element> declarations. Also, because we can nest content models it may contain <choice>, <sequence>, <group>, and <any> elements. Similarly, it can be contained by <choice>, <group>, <sequence>, or <complexType> elements.

Example

```
<xs:element name="IceCream">
   <xs:complexType>
      <xs:sequence>
         <xs:choice>
            <xs:element name="Strawberry" type="xs:string" />
            <xs:element name="Chocolate" type="xs:string" />
         </xs:choice>
         <xs:choice>
            <xs:element name="Cone" type="xs:string" />
            <xs:element name="Tub" type="xs:string" />
         </xs:choice>
```

```
        </xs:sequence>
    </xs:complexType>
</xs:element>
```

Attributes

Attribute	Value Space	Description
Id	ID	Gives a unique identifier to the element
maxOccurs	nonNegativeInteger or unbounded	The maximum number of times the model group can occur
minOccurs	nonNegativeInteger	The minimum number of times the model group can occur

For more information: see §3.8.2 of the Recommendation.

complexContent

The <complexContent> element is used when descending new complex types through to extension or restriction. It indicates that the resulting content model can carry attributes and can contain element content or mixed content or even be empty. This element is used inside a <complexType> declaration and can contain an <annotation>, <restriction>, or <extension> element.

Example

```
<xs:complexType name="CAN_Address">
  <xs:complexContent>
     <xs:extension base="Address">
        <xs:sequence>
           <xs:element name="Province" type="xs:string" />
           <xs:element name="PostalCode" type="CAN_PostalCode"/>
        </xs:sequence>
     </xs:extension>
  </xs:complexContent>
</xs:complexType>
```

Attributes

Attribute	Value Space	Description
Id	ID	Gives a unique identifier to the element
Mixed	boolean	If true, the content is specified as being mixed. The default is false

For more information: see §3.4.2 of the Recommendation.

complexType

The <complexType> element is used to specify the allowable type of content for elements. Complex type definitions are the key to the creation of complex structures and content models in XML Schema. They should be used when an element will contain anything that is more complex than simple character data, such as attributes and child elements. A <complexType> can be declared globally (for example, as a direct child of the <schema> element) or locally (for example, as a direct child of an <element> declaration). They can also be used from within a <redefine> element. A <complexType> may contain an optional <annotation> element. It may be derived from another type, in which case it must contain a <simpleContent> or <complexContent> element. Alternatively, you can specify the allowable content model directly using <group>, <all>, <choice>, or <sequence> element, followed by attribute declarations using <attribute>, <attributeGroup>, or <anyAttribute> elements.

Example

```
<xs:element name="ResearchPaper">
  <xs:complexType mixed="true">
     <xs:sequence>
        <xs:element name="Hypothesis" type="xs:string" />
        <xs:element name="Conclusion" type="ConclusionType" />
     </xs:sequence>
     <xs:attribute name="paperID" type="xs:integer" />
  </xs:complexType>
</xs:element>
<xs:complexType name="ConclusionType" block="#all">
  <xs:simpleContent>
    <xs:extension base="xs:string">
        <xs:attribute name="accepted" type="xs:boolean" />
    </xs:extension>
  </xs:simpleContent>
</xs:complexType>
```

Attributes

Attribute	Value Space	Description
abstract	boolean	This specifies whether the complex type can be used to validate an element. If abstract is true, then it can't; you have to derive other types from it for use in an instance document. Note that this behavior is distinct from using the abstract attribute on an element declaration (for more information refer to the *element* section later in this appendix). The default is false

Attribute	Value Space	Description
`block`	`#all` | List of (`extension` | `restriction`)	Enables the schema author to prevent derived types from being used in the instance document in place of this type. The values `extension` and `restriction`, prevent the use of types derived by extension and restriction, respectively, and `#all` prevents the use of any derived type
`Final`	`#all` | List of (`extension` | `restriction`)	This attribute restricts the derivation of a new data type by `extension` or `restriction` within the schema. The values `extension` and `restriction` prevent the creation of types derived by extension and restriction, respectively, and `#all` prevents the creation of any derived type
`Id`	`ID`	Gives a unique identifier to the type
`Mixed`	`boolean`	Specifies whether the content of this data type is mixed
`Name`	`NCName`	The name of the data type specified

For more information: see §3.4.2 of the Recommendation.

documentation

The <documentation> element is used within <annotation> declarations. It provides a consistent location for comments about the use or resources associated with declarations in your XML Schema. The <documentation> element allows any content (such as well-formed XHTML), and external references can be made using the `source` attribute. Though the XML Schema Recommendation does not outline specific uses for the <documentation> element, many XML Schema designers use it to produce automatically generated Help files for their XML Schemas. Multiple <documentation> elements may appear within a single <annotation> declaration.

Example

```
<xs:element name="Person">
   <xs:annotation>
      <xs:documentation>
         Used to contain personal information. Note that the last name
         is mandatory, while the first name is optional.
      </xs:documentation>
   </xs:annotation>
   <!-- definition of Person element goes here -->
</xs:element>
```

Attributes

Attribute	Value Space	Description
Source	AnyURI	Specifies the URI where the content of this element may be found. You don't need this attribute, if the content is specified within the documentation tag as in the previous example
xml:lang	Language	Specifies the language using a code defined by RFC 3066. Most languages can be identified by a simple two-letter code

For more information: see §3.13.2 of the Recommendation.

element

The <element> declaration is possibly the most important schema namespace element because it is used to declare the elements that can occur in the instance document. It may contain a <simpleType> or a <complexType>, creating a local type for the allowable content, or the type of content may be specified using the type attribute. The <element> declaration may also contain <unique>, <key>, or <keyref> elements to define identity constraints. As with most elements, it may also contain an <annotation>. Elements are declared within model groups using <all>, <choice>, or <sequence>, or can be declared globally as children of the <schema> element.

Example

```
<xs:element name="Customer">
   <xs:complexType>
      <xs:sequence>
         <xs:element name="FirstName" type="xs:string" />
         <xs:element name="MiddleInitial" type="xs:string" />
         <xs:element name="LastName" type="xs:string" />
      </xs:sequence>
      <xs:attribute name="customerID" type="xs:string" />
   </xs:complexType>
</xs:element>
```

Attributes

Attribute	Value Space	Description
abstract	boolean	Specifies that the element is abstract, and so it cannot appear in the instance document, but must be substituted with another element. The default is false

Attribute	Value Space	Description
block	#all | List of (substitution | extension | restriction)	Prevents derived types from being used in place of this element in the instance document (which can be done with the xsi:type attribute), and/or substituting another element in its place. The values extension and restriction prevent the use of types derived by extension and restriction, respectively, and #all prevents the use of any derived type
default	String	Enables us to specify a default value for the element, which will be used if the element appears in the instance document but is empty
final	#all | List of (extension | restriction)	This prevents the element from being nominated as the head element in a substitution group, which has members derived by extension and/or restriction as appropriate
fixed	String	If present, the value of the element in the instance document must always match the specified fixed value
form	qualified | unqualified	If qualified, the element must be namespace qualified in the instance document. The value of this attribute overrides whatever is specified by the elementFormDefault on the schema element. All global element declarations must be qualified regardless of the value of the form attribute or elementFormDefault attribute
Id	ID	Gives a unique identifier to the type
maxOccurs	nonNegativeInteger | unbounded	The maximum number of times the element can occur. Global element declarations cannot use the maxOccurs attribute
minOccurs	nonNegativeInteger	The minimum number of times the element can occur. Global element declarations cannot use the minOccurs attribute
name	NCName	The name of the element
nillable	boolean	If true, the element may have a nil value specified with xsi:nil in the instance document. The default is false

Continues

Attribute	Value Space	Description
`ref`	`Qname`	This attribute enables us to reference a globally defined element using the value of that element's `name` attribute
`substitutionGroup`	`Qname`	The element becomes a member of the substitution group specified by this attribute. Wherever the head element of the substitution group is used in a model group, we can substitute this element in its place
`type`	`Qname`	The type of the content of this element, which could be simple or complex. If the element contains a `<simpleType>` or `<complexType>` element, the `type` attribute must not be used

For more information: see §3.3.2 of the Recommendation.

extension

The `<extension>` element is used when descending new complex types. Using this declaration you can extend a base type by adding additional element or attribute declarations. When adding element content to a type, the extension element may contain a `<group>`, `<choice>`, or `<sequence>` element. When adding attributes, it will contain one or more `<attribute>`, `<attributeGroup>`, or `<anyAttribute>` declarations. Note that when an `<extension>` element is contained inside a `<complexContent>` declaration, it can introduce new element and/or attribute content, whereas when it is inside a `<simpleContent>` declaration it can be used only to add attributes to a type.

Example

Extending a complex type:

```
<xs:complexType name="CAN_Address">
  <xs:complexContent>
     <xs:extension base="Address">
        <xs:sequence>
           <xs:element name="Province" type="xs:string" />
           <xs:element name="PostalCode" type="CAN_PostalCode"/>
        </xs:sequence>
     </xs:extension>
  </xs:complexContent>
</xs:complexType>
```

Extending a simple type to produce a complex type with simple content:

```
<xs:complexType name="ConclusionType" block="#all">
  <xs:simpleContent>
    <xs:extension base="xs:string">
```

```
        <xs:attribute name="accepted" type="xs:boolean" />
    </xs:extension>
  </xs:simpleContent>
</xs:complexType>
```

Attributes

Attribute	Value Space	Description
base (required)	Qname	Specifies the base internal or derived data type that will be extended
Id	ID	Gives a unique identifier to the element

For more information: see §3.4.2 of the Recommendation.

field

The <field> element is used when creating identity constraints, such as <key>, <keyref>, and <unique> declarations. When creating identity constraints, you must specify a context, or scope, for the constraint using a <selector> declaration and the specific node that is constrained using a <field> declaration. It may contain an <annotation> element.

Example

```
<xs:element name="Employees">
  <xs:complexType>
      <xs:sequence>
         <xs:element ref="Employee" minOccurs="1" maxOccurs="unbounded" />
      </xs:sequence>
   </xs:complexType>
   <xs:unique name="employeeIdentificationNumber">
      <xs:selector xpath="Employee" />
      <xs:field xpath="@employeeID" />
   </xs:unique>
</xs:element>
```

Attributes

Attribute	Value Space	Description
Id	ID	Gives a unique identifier to the element
xpath (required)	Xpath	Used to select the element context affected by the identity constraint. The path is relative to the current element declaration

For more information: see §3.11.2 of the Recommendation.

group

The <group> element is used to declare a group of elements or content model declarations or to refer to an existing global <group> declaration. This is useful when more than one element contains the same content model. When the <group> element is a direct child of the <schema> element, it must be used as a global declaration for a content model group and it may contain a <sequence>, <choice>, or <all> declaration. It can also be used as a reference from within a <complexType>, <redefine>, <extension>, or <restriction> declaration. Because content models can be nested, the <group> element can also be referenced within a <sequence> or <choice> declaration.

Example

```
<xs:element name="Customer">
  <xs:complexType>
     <xs:group ref="FirstOrLastNameGroup" />
  </xs:complexType>
</xs:element>

<xs:group name="FirstOrLastNameGroup">
  <xs:choice>
     <xs:element name="FirstName" type="xs:string" />
     <xs:element name="LastName" type="xs:string" />
  </xs:choice>
</xs:group>
```

Attributes

Attribute	Value Space	Description
`Id`	`ID`	Gives a unique identifier to the element
`maxOccurs`	`NonNegativeInteger` | `unbounded`	The maximum number of times the element can occur
`minOccurs`	`NonNegativeInteger`	The minimum number of times the element can occur
`name`	`NCName`	Defines the name of the model group. If you are creating a named model group, the `ref`, `minOccurs`, and `maxOccurs` attributes are not permitted
`ref`	`Qname`	Refers to a previously defined global group. When using this attribute, we cannot specify a name, but we can set occurrence constraints with `minOccurs` and/or `maxOccurs`

For more information: see §3.7.2 of the Recommendation.

import

The <import> declaration is used to combine multiple XML Schemas. It enables you to import the declarations from an XML Schema for another namespace. If you are trying to combine XML Schemas that utilize the same namespace or have no namespace you should instead use the <include> declaration. The <import> element should be declared as a child of the root <schema> element, and has an optional <annotation>. An XML Schema may contain multiple <import> declarations.

Example

```
<xs:schema xmlns:xs="http://www.w3.org/2001/XMLSchema"
           targetNamespace="http://www.example.com/Order"
           xmlns="http://www.example.com/Order"
           xmlns:products="http://www.example.com/Products"
           xmlns:types="http://www.example.com/Types"
           elementFormDefault="qualified">

   <xs:import schemaLocation="http://file_Location/Products.xsd"
              namespace="http://www.wrox.com/Products" />
   <xs:import schemaLocation="http://file_Location/TypeLib.xsd"
              namespace="http://www.wrox.com/Types" />

  <!-- rest of schema definition here -->
</xs:schema>
```

Attributes

Attribute	Value Space	Description
Id	ID	Gives a unique identifier to the element
namespace	AnyURI	The namespace of the imported data
schemaLocation	AnyURI	The location of the schema to import

For more information: see §4.2.3 of the Recommendation.

include

The <include> declaration is used to combine multiple XML Schemas. It enables you to include the declarations from an XML Schema that has the same target namespace, or no target namespace. If you include an XML Schema with no target namespace the declarations will be treated as if they were declared using the target namespace of the including XML Schema. If you are trying to combine XML Schemas that utilize different namespaces, you should instead use the <import> declaration. The

<include> element should be declared as a child of the root <schema> element, and has an optional <annotation>. An XML Schema may contain multiple <include> declarations.

Example

```
<xs:schema xmlns:xs="http://www.w3.org/2001/XMLSchema"
           targetNamespace="http://www.example.com/ECommerce"
           xmlns="http://www.example.com/ECommerce"
           elementFormDefault="qualified">

    <xs:include schemaLocation="http://location of schema/Products.xsd" />
    <xs:include schemaLocation="http://location of schema/TypeLib.xsd" />

    <!-- rest of schema definition here -->
  </xs:schema>
```

Attributes

Attribute	Value Space	Description
Id	ID	Gives a unique identifier to the element
schemaLocation (required)	AnyURI	The location of the schema to include

For more information: see §4.2.1 of the Recommendation.

key

The <key> element, along with the <keyref> element, enables us to define a relationship between two elements. The key/keyref mechanism functions similarly to database keys, or to the ID/IDREF mechanism built into XML DTDs. For example, an element might contain a <key> that is unique within a specified context or scope. Another element can refer to the key using a <keyref> element. A <key> is always defined inside an <element> declaration. It contains a <selector> element that defines the context or scope of the key and a <field> element that defines the specific key node. Like other elements, it can also contain an <annotation>.

Example

```
<xs:key name="KeyDepartmentByID">
  <xs:selector xpath="Departments/Department" />
  <xs:field xpath="@departmentID" />
</xs:key>
```

Attributes

Attribute	Value Space	Description
Id	ID	Gives a unique identifier to the element
name (required)	NCName	The name of the key used

For more information: see §3.11.2 of the Recommendation.

keyref

The <keyref> element is used to specify a reference to a <key> (see the previous discussion of <key>). Like the <key> element it may be used within an <element> declaration. It may contain an <annotation> element, and can define the context of the key reference by including a <selector> declaration and <field> declaration.

Example

```
<xs:keyref name="RefEmployeeToDepartment" refer="KeyDepartmentByID">
  <xs:selector xpath="Employees/Employee" />
  <xs:field xpath="Department/@refDepartmentID" />
</xs:keyref>
```

Attributes

Attribute	Value Space	Description
Id	ID	Gives a unique identifier to the element
name (required)	NCName	The name of the key reference
refer (required)	Qname	The name of the key to which this key reference refers

For more information: see §3.11.2 of the Recommendation.

list

The <list> element is used to declare a specialized simple type, which is a sequence of whitespace-separated simpleType values. The itemType attribute defines the allowable type for each item contained in the list. Because you cannot create a list of lists, the itemType cannot refer to an existing list type. Moreover, because lists use whitespace to separate the values, item types that refer to any type that can contain whitespace can be problematic. For example, the XML Schema string type may contain spaces, such as "The XML Schema Recommendation". If treated as a list type, an XML Schema processor would see four separate values, not one value with four spaces. A `<list>` declaration must appear within a `<simpleType>` definition and can contain optional `<annotation>` and `<simpleType>` elements.

Example

```
<xs:simpleType name="AgesList">
   <xs:list itemType="xs:integer" />
</xs:simpleType>
```

Attributes

Attribute	Value Space	Description
Id	ID	Gives a unique identifier to the element
itemType	Qname	The base data type for each item in the list

For more information: see §3.14.2 of the Recommendation.

notation

A `<notation>` declaration is used to associate a particular type of file with the location of an application that can process it. Within XML Schemas, notations must be declared globally (the `<notation>` element must be a direct child of the `<schema>` element). A `<notation>` declaration has a global name that is specified using the `name` attribute. In addition to the `name`, the `<notation>` provides `public` and `system` attributes that can be used to specify the public identifier and system identifier, respectively. The public identifier is optional.

Example

```
<xs:notation name="jpeg" public="image/jpeg" system="JPEGViewer.exe" />
<xs:notation name="png" public="image/png" system="PNGViewer.exe" />

<xs:simpleType name="ImageTypeNotation" >
  <xs:restriction base="xs:NOTATION">
    <xs:enumeration value="jpeg"/>
    <xs:enumeration value="png"/>
  </xs:restriction>
</xs:simpleType>
```

Attributes

Attribute	Value Space	Description
Id	ID	Gives a unique identifier to the element
name (required)	NCName	The name of the specified NOTATION data type
public	AnyURI	Any URI; usually some relevant identifier, like a MIME type. MIME types (Multipurpose Internet Mail Extension) are used to identify file types on the World Wide Web. Some common MIME types for XML include text/xml and application/xml
system	AnyURI	Any URI; usually some local processing application

For more information: see §3.12.2 of the Recommendation.

redefine

The <redefine> declaration is used to combine multiple XML Schemas. It enables you to modify complex types, simple types, model groups, or attribute groups as they are included from another external schema. The external schema must have no namespace or it must have the same target namespace as the schema where <redefine> is used. Within the <redefine> element, you must refer to an existing type and amend it as necessary using extension or restriction. A <redefine> declaration must appear within the root <schema> element, and may contain <annotation>, <simpleType>, <complexType>, <group>, or <attributeGroup> elements.

Example

From one schema we have the following:

```
<xs:complexType name="NameType">
  <xs:sequence>
    <xs:element name="FirstName" type="xs:string" />
    <xs:element name="MiddleInitial" type="xs:string" />
    <xs:element name="LastName" type="xs:string" />
  </xs:sequence>
</xs:complexType>
```

We can redefine this in another schema like so:

```
<xs:redefine schemaLocation="http://file location/firstSchema.xsd">
  <xs:complexType name="NameType">
     <xs:complexContent>
```

```
            <xs:restriction base="NameType">
                <xs:sequence>
                    <xs:element name="FirstName" type="xs:string" />
                    <xs:element name="LastName" type="xs:string" />
                </xs:sequence>
            </xs:restriction>
        </xs:complexContent>
    </xs:complexType>
</xs:redefine>
```

Attributes

Attribute	Value Space	Description
Id	ID	Gives a unique identifier to the element
schemaLocation (required)	AnyURI	Specifies the location of the schema

For more information: see §4.2.2 of the Recommendation.

restriction

The <restriction> element is used when descending new complex types. Using this declaration, you can restrict a base type and limit the allowable content within <complexType> or <simpleType> declarations. There are three different situations in which we might use restriction: to restrict a simple type, to restrict a complex type using simple content, or to restrict a complex type using complex content.

When restricting <complexType> declarations you must start with a base type and create the derivation by removing elements or attributes. In addition, you need to go a step further; when creating your restricted <complexType> declarations you must *redeclare* all elements you want to keep. Because of this, restricting <complexType> declarations is far more difficult than extending them. By default, attributes are automatically included in the newly restricted type.

The rules for restricting a <complexType> are very involved. Instead of listing all the conditions and exceptions, we will focus on two basic rules: First, you cannot introduce anything new when restricting a <complexType>. Essentially, this means that you cannot add elements or attributes that didn't exist in the base type. When modifying existing declarations you must also be careful that the modifications are permitted. Second, you cannot remove anything that must appear in the base type. For example, if your base type declares that an element has a minOccurs value of 1 (the default), it cannot be removed in your restriction. This rule was created so that applications that are designed to handle the base type can also handle the restricted type without raising an error.

The <restriction> element may appear inside <simpleType>, <simpleContent>, or <complexContent>. In the first two situations, the element may contain a <simpleType> element, and one of the constraining facets: <minExclusive>, <maxExclusive>, <minInclusive>, <maxInclusive>, <totalDigits>, <fractionDigits>, <length>, <minLength>, <maxLength>, <enumeration>, <whiteSpace>, or <pattern>. When restricting a <complexType>, a <restriction> declaration may also contain <attribute>, <attributeGroup>, and

<anyAttribute>. If the <restriction> declaration appears inside a <complexContent> element, it may also include <group>, <all>, <choice>, and <sequence> declarations. The <restriction> element also has an optional <annotation> element.

Example

Here's how we can derive a simple type:

```
<xs:simpleType name="Char">
  <xs:restriction base="xs:string">
    <xs:length value="1" />
  </xs:restriction>
</xs:simpleType>
```

Here's the code for deriving a complex type with simple content:

```
<xs:complexType name="Person">
  <xs:simpleContent>
    <xs:extension base="xs:string">
      <xs:attribute name="age" type="xs:integer" />
    </xs:extension>
  </xs:simpleContent>
</xs:complexType>
```

```
<xs:complexType name="RestrictedPerson">
  <xs:simpleContent>
    <xs:restriction base="Person">
      <xs:attribute name="age">
        <xs:simpleType>
          <xs:restriction base="xs:integer">
            <xs:minInclusive value="1" />
            <xs:maxInclusive value="120" />
          </xs:restriction>
        </xs:simpleType>
      </xs:attribute>
    </xs:restriction>
  </xs:simpleContent>
</xs:complexType>
```

Here's how to derive a complex type with complex content:

```
<xs:complexType name="ShortAddress">
  <xs:complexContent>
    <xs:restriction base="Address" >
      <xs:sequence>
        <xs:element name="Name" type="xs:string" />
        <xs:element name="Street" type="xs:string" maxOccurs="2" />
        <xs:element name="City" type="xs:string" />
      </xs:sequence>
    </xs:restriction>
  </xs:complexContent>
</xs:complexType>
```

Attributes

Attribute	Value Space	Description
Id	ID	Gives a unique identifier to the element
base (required)	QName	The base type from which the new type is derived

For more information: see §3.4.2 and §3.14.2 of the Recommendation.

schema

This <schema> element is the root element within an XML Schema. Details, such as target namespace and global defaults, are specified within the <schema> element. It may contain <include>, <import>, <redefine>, <annotation>, <simpleType>, <complexType>, <group>, <attributeGroup>, <element>, <attribute>, or <notation>.

Example

```
<?xml version="1.0" encoding="UTF-8"?>
<xs:schema xmlns:xs="http://www.w3.org/2001/XMLSchema"
  targetNamespace="http://www.example.com/"
  xmlns="http://www.example.com/"
  elementFormDefault="qualified">
   <!--rest of content goes here-->
</xs:schema>
```

Attributes

Attribute	Value Space	Description
attributeFormDefault	qualified | unqualified	Enables you to specify a default for attribute qualification in the instance document. If qualified, the attribute must be namespace qualified in the instance document. Note that if the form attribute is present on the attribute element, it overrides attributeFormDefault on the schema element. All global attribute declarations must be qualified regardless of the value of the form attribute or attributeFormDefault attribute. For an attribute to be qualified in an instance document, it must have a prefix associated with the namespace

Attribute	Value Space	Description
blockDefault	#all | List of (extension | restriction | substitution)	Enables us to block some or all of the derivations of data types from being used in substitution groups. The values extension, restriction block type substitutions and the value substitution blocks element substitutions. This can be overridden by the block attribute of an <element> or <complexType> element in the schema
elementFormDefault	qualified | unqualified	Enables you to specify a default value for element qualification in the instance document. If qualified, then the element must be namespace qualified in the instance document. Note that if the form attribute is present on the <element> declaration, it overrides elementFormDefault on the <schema> element. All global element declarations must be qualified regardless of the value of the form attribute or elementFormDefault attribute
finalDefault	#all | List of (extension | restriction | list | union)	Enables you to disallow some or all of the derivations of data types from being created in the XML Schema. This can be overridden by the final attribute of an <element> or <complexType> element in the schema
Id	ID	Gives a unique identifier to the element
targetNamespace	anyURI	This is used to specify the namespace that this schema is defining
Version	Token	Used to specify the version of the XML Schema being defined. This can take a token data type, and is intended for use by XML Schema authors
xml:lang	language	Specifies the language, using a code defined by RFC 3066. Most languages can be identified by a simple two-letter code

For more information: see §3.15.2 of the Recommendation.

selector

The <selector> element is used when creating identity constraints, such as <key>, <keyref>, and <unique> declarations. When creating identity constraints, you must specify a context, or scope, for the constraint using a <selector> declaration and the specific node that is constrained using a <field> declaration. It may contain an <annotation> element.

Example

```
<xs:key name="KeyDepartmentByID">
  <xs:selector xpath="Departments/Department" />
  <xs:field xpath="@departmentID" />
</xs:key>
```

Attributes

Attribute	Value Space	Description
Id	ID	Gives a unique identifier to the element
xpath (required)	Xpath	A *relative* XPath expression (relative to the element on which the identity constraint is defined) that specifies which elements the identity constraint applies to

For more information: see §3.11.2 of the Recommendation.

sequence

The <sequence> element is used within content model declarations. It is used to declare a specific order of elements and content model declarations to be used within the content model in the instance document. It may contain <annotation> and <element> declarations. Also, because we can nest content models, it may contain <choice>, <sequence>, <group>, and <any> elements. Similarly, it can be contained by <choice>, <group>, <sequence>, or <complexType> elements.

Example

```
<xs:sequence>
  <xs:element name="FirstName" type="xs:string" />
  <xs:element name="MiddleInitial" type="xs:string" />
  <xs:element name="LastName" type="xs:string" />
</xs:sequence>
```

Attributes

Attribute	Value Space	Description
Id	ID	Gives a unique identifier to the element
maxOccurs	NonNegativeInteger or unbounded	The maximum number of times the model group can occur

Attribute	Value Space	Description
minOccurs	NonNegativeInteger	The minimum number of times the model group can occur

For more information: see §3.8.2 of the Recommendation.

simpleContent

The <simpleContent> element is used when extending or restricting complex types. It indicates that the resulting content model may contain attributes and text data, but cannot contain element content or mixed content. This element is used inside a <complexType> declaration and can contain an <annotation>, <restriction>, or <extension> element.

Example

```
<xs:complexType name="LengthType">
  <xs:simpleContent>
    <xs:extension base="xs:nonNegativeInteger">
      <xs:attribute name="unit" type="xs:NMTOKEN"/>
    </xs:extension>
  </xs:simpleContent>
</xs:complexType>
```

Attributes

Attribute	Value Space	Description
Id	ID	Gives a unique identifier to the element

For more information: see §3.4.2 of the Recommendation.

simpleType

The <simpleType> element is used to specify the allowable type of content for attributes and text-only elements. Simple Type definitions are the key to the validation of text content within XML Schemas. A <simpleType> declaration can be contained within an <attribute>, <element>, <list>, <redefine>, <restriction>, <schema>, or <union> declaration. It may contain <annotation>, <list>, <restriction>, or <union> declarations.

Example

```
<xs:simpleType name="FixedLengthString">
  <xs:restriction base="xs:string">
```

```
    <xs:length value="120" />
  </xs:restriction>
</xs:simpleType>

<xs:simpleType name="Size" >
  <xs:restriction base="xs:string" >
    <xs:enumeration value="S" />
    <xs:enumeration value="M" />
    <xs:enumeration value="L" />
    <xs:enumeration value="XL" />
  </xs:restriction>
</xs:simpleType>
```

Attributes

Attribute	Value Space	Description
Final	#all | List of (union | restriction)	Restricts how new data types may be derived from this simple type
Id	ID	Gives a unique identifier to the element
Name	NCName	The name of the data type that this element is defining

For more information: see §3.14.2 of the Recommendation.

union

The <union> declaration enables you to join numerous simple data types together. You can include existing types in the union by referring to them within a whitespace-separated list in the memberTypes attribute. They will be joined together along with any contained <simpleType> declarations to form the new data type. The <union> declaration must be contained within a <simpleType> declaration and may contain <annotation>, or <simpleType> declarations.

Example

```
<xs:simpleType name="CatsAndDogs">
  <xs:union memberTypes="CatBreeds DogBreeds" />
</xs:simpleType>
```

Attributes

Attribute	Value Space	Description
Id	ID	Gives a unique identifier to the element
memberTypes	List of Qname	A whitespace-separated list of simple data types that we wish to join together to form a new <simpleType>

For more information: see §3.14.2 of the Recommendation.

unique

The <unique> declaration enables you to specify that an element or attribute must have a unique value within a document or part of a document. The unique value might be the element content, a specific attribute's content, an ancestor's element or attribute content, or a combination of any of these options. You may specify the item that contains the unique value using the <selector> and <field> declarations. The <unique> element must be contained by an <element> declaration and may contain <annotation>, <selector>, or <field> declarations.

Example

```
<xs:unique name="employeeIdentificationNumber">
  <xs:selector xpath="Employees/Employee" />
  <xs:field xpath="@employeeID" />
</xs:unique>
```

Attributes

Attribute	Value Space	Description
Id	ID	Gives a unique identifier to the element
name	NCName	The name of the identity constraint for the unique value being defined

For more information: see §3.11.2 of the Recommendation.

XML Schema Instance Attributes

The XML Schema instance namespace is declared in an instance document to refer to instance-specific XML Schema attributes. (The namespace does not include any elements.) For example, the document can indicate to the parser the location of the schema to which it conforms using the `schemaLocation` attribute. The XML Schema instance namespace is available at `http://www.w3.org/2001/XMLSchema-instance`, and is declared in the document element like this:

```
<someElement xmlns:xsi="http://www.w3.org/2001/XMLSchema-instance">
```

All the attributes detailed in the following table would be prefixed by `xsi:` as in the previous case.

Attribute	Value Space	Description
`nil`	`boolean`	Used to indicate that an element is valid despite having an empty value. Necessary for simple types, such as dates and numbers, for which empty values aren't valid. For example, `<OrderDate xsi:nil="true"></OrderDate>`
`noNamespaceSchemaLocation`	`anyURI`	Used to specify the location of a schema without a target namespace, for example, `xsi:noNamespaceSchemaLocation= "name.xsd"`
`schemaLocation`	List of `anyURI`	Used to specify the location of a schema with a target namespace. The namespace of the schema is specified first; then after a space there is the location of the schema. Multiple schema/namespace pairs can be given as a whitespace-separated list, For example, `xsi:schemaLocation=" http://www.example.org example.xsd"`
`type`	`QName`	Enables us to override the current element type by specifying the qualified name of a type in an existing XML Schema. Note that the data type has to be derived from the one that the element is declared with. Also, the substitution of the derived type cannot be blocked by the element or type declaration, for example, `<returnAddress xsi:type="ipo:USAddress">`

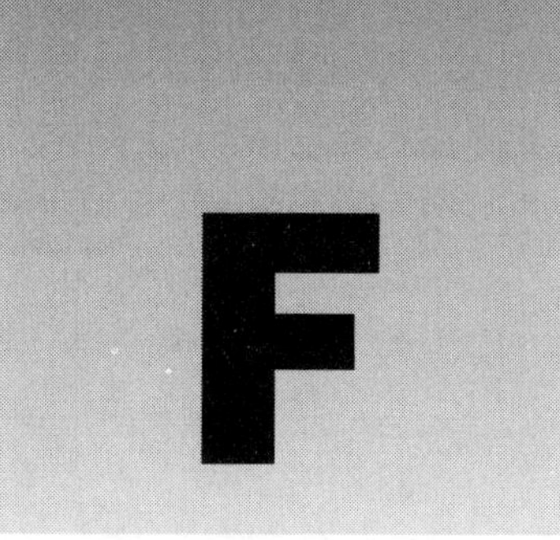

Schema Data Types Reference

In this appendix, we provide a quick reference to the W3C Recommendation for XML Schemas, Part 2: Data types. Data types were separated into a specification in their own right so that XML Schemas as well as other XML-related technologies (for example, Relax NG) can use them.

XML Schema defines a number of data types that can be used to validate the content of attributes and text-only elements. These data types allow you to specify that the content must be formatted as a date, a boolean, a floating-point number, and so on. The second part of the XML Schema Recommendation defines two sorts of data types:

- Built-in types, which are available to all XML Schema authors, and should be implemented by a conforming processor.
- User-derived types, which are defined in individual schema instances, and are particular to that schema (although it is possible to import and reuse these definitions into other XML Schemas). These types are based on the existing built-in types.

There are two subgroups of built-in type:

- Built-in primitive types, which are types in their own right. They are not defined in terms of other data types. Primitive types are also known as base types, because they are the basis from which all other types are built.
- Built-in derived types, which are built from definitions of other primitive and derived data types.

In the first part of this appendix, we will provide a quick overview of all the XML built-in data types, both primitive and derived. In the second part, we will give details of all of the constraining *facets*, or characteristics, of these data types that can be used to restrict the data types thereby deriving new types. Finally, we provide tables that illustrate which of these constraining facets can be applied to which data type.

XML Schema Built-in Data Types

The following table shows the primitive types that XML Schema offers, from which we can derive other data types.

Primitive type	Description	Example

`string`	Represents any legal character string in XML that matches the `Char` production in XML 1.0 Second Edition (`http://www.w3.org/TR/REC-xml`)	`Bob Watkins`
		
		If you need to include a character that is not easily typed, such as the copyright symbol, or that may not appear directly in content, you can use a built-in or character entity reference. The following are the five built-in entities:
		
		`<` or `<` for `<`
		(an opening angled bracket)
		
		`>` or `>` for `>`
		(a closing angled bracket)
		
		`&` or `` for `&`
		(an ampersand)
		
		`'` or `'` for `'`
		(an apostrophe)
		
		`"` or `"` for `"`
		(a quotation mark)

`Boolean`	Represents binary logic, true or false	`true, false, 1, 0` These are the only permitted values for this data type
`decimal`	Represents a subset of real numbers that can be represented using decimal integers	`3.141` The plus sign (+) and minus sign (-) may be used to represent positive or negative numbers, for example, -1.23, +00042.00
`float`	Standard concept of real numbers patterned after an IEEE single-precision 32-bit floating point type. Additionally, the values `INF`, `-INF`, and `NaN` are permitted	`-INF, -1E4, 4.5E-2, 37, INF, NaN` `NaN` denotes not a number and is neither less than nor greater than any other number. It cannot be compared with other numbers. INF denotes infinity
`double`	Standard concept of real numbers patterned after an IEEE double-precision 64-bit floating point type. Additionally the values `INF`, `-INF`, and `NaN` are permitted	`-INF, 765.4321234E11, 7E7, 1.0, INF, NaN` `NaN` denotes not a number and is neither less than nor greater than any other number. It cannot be compared with other numbers. `INF` denotes infinity

Primitive type	Description	Example
`duration`	Represents a duration of time in the format `PnYnMnDTnHnMnS`, where: `P` is a designator that must always be present. An optional + or -sign is allowed before `P`. `nY` represents number of years `nM` represents number of months `nD` represents number of days `T` is the date/time separator. If any time elements are included in the duration, `T` must be present. `nH` is number of hours `nM` is number of minutes `nS` is number of seconds. Seconds allows a fractional part (arbitrary precision) to appear after a decimal point. Based on ISO 8601	`P1Y0M1DT20H25M30.120S` 1 year and 1 day, 20 hours, 25 minutes and 30.120 seconds. Limited forms of this lexical production are also allowed. For example, `P120D` denotes 120 days

`dateTime`	A specific instance in time in the format:
	
	`CCYY-MM-DDThh:mm:ss` where:
	
	A leading minus (-) sign is permitted at the beginning of the value to indicate that the year is negative.
	
	`CC` represents the century
	
	`YY` represents the year
	
	`MM` represents the month
	
	`DD` represents the day
	
	`T` is the date/time separator
	
	`hh` represents hours
	
	`mm` represents minutes
	
	`ss` represents seconds. Seconds allows a fractional part (arbitrary precision) to appear after a decimal point.
		`2004-09-13T14:51:26`
		
		Represents the 13th of September 2004, at 2:51 and 26 seconds in the afternoon.
		
		`2004-09-13T14:51:26T-05:00`
		
		`2004-09-13T14:51:26Z`
		
		(Note that the year `0000` is prohibited in XML Schema version 1.0, and each of the fields `CC`, `YY`, `MM`, `DD`, `hh`, and `mm` must be exactly 2 digits)

Continues

Primitive type	Description	Example
	There is also an optional time zone indicator. The time zone must follow the format: `-hh:mm` A leading + sign or - minus sign followed by the number of hours and minutes indicates the difference between the local time and UTC. In addition, a `Z` may be used to indicate that the time zone is UTC. Based on ISO 8601	
`time`	Represents an instance of time that occurs every day in the format `hh:mm:ss.sss`. Fractional seconds can be added to arbitrary precision and there is also an optional time zone indicator (see `dateTime`). Based on ISO 8601	`14:12:30` Represents 12 minutes and 30 seconds past 2 in the afternoon
`date`	Represents a calendar date from the Gregorian calendar (the whole day) in the format `CCYY-MM-DD`. A leading minus (-) sign is permitted at the beginning of the value to indicate that the year is negative. There is also an optional time zone indicator (see `dateTime`). Based on ISO 8601	`2004-09-13` Represents the 13th of September 2004. (Note that the year `0000` is prohibited in XML Schema version 1.0)
`gYearMonth`	Represents a month in a year in the Gregorian calendar in the format `CCYY-MM`. A leading minus (-) sign is permitted at the beginning of the value to indicate that the year is negative. There is also an optional time zone indicator (see `dateTime`). Based on ISO 8601	`2004-09` Represents September 2004. (Note that the year `0000` is prohibited in XML Schema version 1.0)
`gYear`	Represents a year in the Gregorian calendar in the format `CCYY`. A leading + sign or - sign is permitted at the beginning of the value to indicate whether the year is positive or negative.	`-0001` Represents 1 BCE (or 1 BC). (Note that the year `0000` is prohibited in XML Schema version 1.0)

Primitive type	Description	Example
	There is also an optional time zone indicator (see `dateTime`). Based on ISO 8601	
`gMonthDay`	Represents a recurring day of a recurring month in the Gregorian calendar in the format `-MM-DD`. No preceding sign (positive or negative) is permitted. There is also an optional time zone indicator (see `dateTime`). Based on ISO 8601	`--07-12` Represents the 12th of July. Ideal for birthdays, anniversaries, holidays, and recurring events
`gDay`	Represents a recurring day of a month in the Gregorian calendar in the format `---DD`. No preceding sign (positive or negative) is permitted. There is also an optional time zone indicator (see `dateTime`). Based on ISO 8601	`---16` Represents the 16th day of a month. Ideal for monthly occurrences, such as pay day.
`gMonth`	Represents a recurring month in the Gregorian calendar in the format `--MM`. No preceding sign (positive or negative) is permitted. There is also an optional time zone indicator (see `dateTime`). Based on ISO 8601	`--01` Represents January
`hexBinary`	Represents hex-encoded arbitrary binary data	`0FB7`
`base64Binary`	Represents Base64-encoded arbitrary binary data. The encoding adheres to RFC 2045	`GpM7`

`anyURI`	Represents a Uniform Resource Identifier (URI). The value can be absolute or relative, and may have an optional fragment identifier	`http://www.example.com`
		
		`mailto://info@example.com`
		
		`mySchemafile.xsd`

`QName`	Represents any XML element qualified by a namespace. This includes a local name together with an optional prefix bound to a namespace and separated by a colon.	`xs:element`

Continues

Primitive type	Description	Example
	The XML Namespace Recommendation can be found at: `http://www.w3.org/TR/REC-xml-names/`. Namespaces are discussed in Chapter 3	

`NOTATION`	Represents the NOTATION type from XML 1.0 Second Edition. There must be a corresponding notation declaration within the XML Schema. Only data types derived from a NOTATION base type (by specifying a value for enumeration) are allowed to be used as references to notation declarations.
	Should only be used for attribute values and in XML Schemas without a target namespace
		`<xs:notation name="jpeg" system="JPEGViewer.exe" />`
		`<xs:notation name="png" system="PNGViewer.exe" />`
		`<xs:simpleType name="imageNotation">`
		`<xs:restriction base="xs:NOTATION" >`
		`<xs:enumeration value="jpeg"/>`
		`<xs:enumeration value="png"/>`
		`</xs:restriction>`
		`</xs:simpleType>`

To create new simple data types—known as *derived types*—you place further restrictions on an existing built-in type (or another simple type that has been defined). The type that you place the restrictions upon is known as the new type's *base-type*. Here is a list of the built-in derived types:

Derivative type	Description	Example
`normalizedString`	Represents whitespace normalized strings. Whitespace normalized strings do not contain carriage return (`#xD`), line feed (`#xA`) or tab (`#x9`) characters. Base type: `string`	`Hello World`
`Token`	Represents tokenized strings, which do not contain line feed (`#xA`), carriage return (`#xD`), or tab characters (`#x9`) and contain no leading or trailing spaces, and no internal sequences of more than two spaces. Base type: `normalizedString`	`One Two Three`
`Language`	Natural language identifiers, as defined in RFC 3066. Base type: `token`	`en-GB`, `en-US`, `fr`

Derivative type	Description	Example
`NMTOKEN`	Represents the `NMTOKEN` attribute type from XML 1.0 Second Edition. Should only be used on attributes. An `NMTOKEN` is a "name token" as defined in XML 1.0 Second Edition Base type: `token`	`small`
`NMTOKENS`	Represents the `NMTOKENS` attribute type from XML 1.0 Second Edition. Should be used only on attributes. `NMTOKENS` is a set of `NMTOKEN` values separated by an XML whitespace character. Base type: A `list` of items of type `NMTOKEN`	`small medium large`
`Name`	Represents XML Names as defined in XML 1.0 Second Edition. Base type: `token`	`html, sch:assert, Address`
`NCName`	Represents XML "noncolonized" Names (without the prefix and colon), as defined in the Namespaces in XML Recommendation. Base type: `Name`	`Address`
`ID`	Represents the `ID` attribute type from XML 1.0 Second Edition. Should be used only on attributes. Base type: `NCName`	`<address id="Address1" />`
`IDREF`	Represents the `IDREF` attribute type from XML 1.0 Second Edition. Should be used only on attributes. Base type: `NCName`	`<bill sendTo= "Address1" />`
`IDREFS`	Represents the `IDREFS` attribute type from XML 1.0 Second Edition. Should be used only on attributes. `IDREFS` is a set of `IDREF` values separated by an XML whitespace character. Base type: A `list` of items of type `IDREF`	`<employee Addresses="Address1 Address2" />`
`ENTITY`	Represents the `ENTITY` attribute type from XML 1.0 Second Edition. Should be used only on attributes. Base type: `NCName`	Note that the `ENTITY` has to be declared as an unparsed entity in a DTD

Continues

Derivative type	Description	Example
`ENTITIES`	Represents the `ENTITIES` attribute type from XML 1.0 Second Edition. Should be used only on attributes. `ENTITIES` is a set of `ENTITY` values separated by an XML whitespace character. Base type: A `list` of items of type `ENTITY`	Note that each `ENTITY` in the list has to be declared as an unparsed entity in a DTD
`Integer`	Standard mathematical concept of `integer` numbers, where no fractional value is allowed. Base type: `decimal`	`-4,0,2,7`
`NonPositiveInteger`	Standard mathematical concept of a nonpositive `integer` (includes 0). Base type: `integer`	`-4,-1,0`
`NegativeInteger`	Standard mathematical concept of a negative `integer` (does not include 0) . Base type: `nonPositiveInteger`	`-4,-1`
`Long`	An `integer` between -9223372036854775808 and 9223372036854775807. Base type: `integer`	`-23568323,` `52883773203895`
`Int`	An `integer` between -2147483648 and 2147483647. Base type: `long`	`-24781982,24781924`
`short`	An `integer` between -32768 and 32767. Base type: `int`	`-31353,-43,345,31347`
`byte`	An `integer` between -128 and 127. Base type: `short`	`-127,-42,0,54,125`
`nonNegativeInteger`	Standard mathematical concept of a nonnegative `integer` (includes 0). Base type: `integer`	`0,1,42`
`unsignedLong`	A `nonNegativeInteger` between 0 and 18446744073709551615. Base type: `nonNegativeInteger`	`0,356,38753829383`
`unsignedInt`	An `unsignedLong` between 0 and 4294967295. Base type: `unsignedLong`	`46,4255774,` `2342823723`

unsignedShort	An unsignedInt between 0 and 65535. Base type: unsignedInt	78, 64328
unsignedByte	An unsignedShort between 0 and 255. Base type: unsignedShort	0, 46, 247
positiveInteger	Standard mathematical concept of a positive integer (does not include 0). Base type: nonNegativeInteger	1, 24, 345343

Constraining Facets

The constraining facets defined in the XML Schema Data types specification are as follows:

- length
- minLength
- maxLength
- pattern
- enumeration
- whitespace
- maxInclusive
- minInclusive
- maxExclusive
- minExclusive
- totalDigits
- fractionDigits

length

This enables us to specify the exact length of a data type. If the data type is a string, it specifies the number of characters in it. If it's a list, it specifies the number of items in the list. If the base type is hexBinary or base64Binary, the length is measured in octets. It is always used inside a <restriction> element, and can contain an <annotation> element.

Example

```
<xs:simpleType name="USA_SSN">
   <xs:restriction base="xs:string">
      <xs:length value="11" />
   </xs:restriction>
</xs:simpleType>
```

Attributes

Attribute	Value Space	Description
`fixed`	`Boolean`	If `true`, then any datatypes derived from this type cannot alter the value of `length`. The default is `false`
`id`	`ID`	Gives a unique identifier to the type
`value`	`NonNegativeInteger`	The actual length of the data type. You may not use the `length` facet and `minLength` or `maxLength` facet in the same datatype declaration

For more information: see §4.3.1 of the Datatypes Recommendation.

minLength

This sets the minimum length of a data type. If the base type is `string`, it sets the minimum number of characters. If it is a list, it sets the minimum number of members. If the base type is `hexBinary` or `base64Binary`, the length is measured in octets. It is always used inside a `<restriction>` element, and it can contain an `<annotation>` element.

Example

```
<xs:simpleType name="Password">
   <xs:restriction base="xs:string">
      <xs:minLength value="5" />
      <xs:maxLength value="20" />
   </xs:restriction>
</xs:simpleType>
```

Attributes

Attribute	Value Space	Description
`fixed`	`Boolean`	If `true`, any data types derived from this type cannot alter the value of `minLength`. The default is `false`
`id`	`ID`	Gives a unique identifier to the type
`value`	`NonNegative Integer`	Sets the minimum length of the data type, which must be a nonnegative integer. You may not use the `length` facet and `minLength` facet in the same data type declaration

For more information: see §4.3.2 of the Datatypes Recommendation.

maxLength

This sets the maximum length of a data type. If the base type is `string`, it sets the maximum number of characters. If it is a list, it sets the maximum number of members. If the base type is `hexBinary` or base64Binary, the length is measured in octets. It is always used inside a <restriction> element, and it can contain an <annotation> element.

Example

```
<xs:simpleType name="DesiredItems">
   <xs:restriction base="ItemList">
      <xs:minLength value="0" />
      <xs:maxLength value="3" />
   </xs:restriction>
</xs:simpleType>
```

Attributes

Attribute	Value Space	Description
fixed	Boolean	If true, any data types derived from this type cannot alter the value of maxLength. The default is false
Id	ID	Gives a unique identifier to the type
value	NonNegativeInteger	Sets the maximum length of the data type, which must be a nonnegative integer. You may not use the length facet and maxLength facet in the same data type declaration

For more information: see §4.3.3 of the Datatypes Recommendation.

pattern

This enables us to restrict any simple data type by specifying a regular expression. It acts on the lexical representation of the type, rather than the value itself. It is always used inside a <restriction> element, and it can contain an <annotation> element. If the pattern facet is used in a declaration with the base type list, the pattern applies to the entire list, not each item.

Example

```
<xs:simpleType name="USA_SSN">
   <xs:restriction base="xs:string">
      <xs:pattern value="[0-9]{3}-[0-9]{2}-[0-9]{4}" />
   </xs:restriction>
</xs:simpleType>
```

Attributes

Attribute	Value Space	Description
Id	ID	Gives a unique identifier to the type
value	String	The value contained within this attribute is any valid regular expression. The regular expression is implicitly anchored to the start (head) and end (tail) of the string

For more information: see §4.3.4 of the Datatypes Recommendation.

enumeration

The `enumeration` facet is used to restrict the values allowed within a data type to a set of specified values. It is always used inside a `<restriction>` element, and it can contain an `<annotation>` element.

Example

```
<xs:simpleType name="Sizes">
   <xs:restriction base="xs:string">
      <xs:enumeration value="S" />
      <xs:enumeration value="M" />
      <xs:enumeration value="L" />
      <xs:enumeration value="XL" />
   </xs:restriction>
</xs:simpleType>
```

Attributes

Attribute	Value Space	Description
`Id`	`ID`	Gives a unique identifier to the element
`value`	`anySimpleType`	One of the values of an enumerated data type. Multiple `enumeration` elements are used for the different choices of value

For more information: see §4.3.5 of the Datatypes Recommendation.

whiteSpace

This dictates what (if any) whitespace transformation is performed upon the data type content before validation constraints are tested. It is always used inside a `<restriction>` element, and it can contain an `<annotation>` element.

Example

```
<xs:simpleType name="token">
   <xs:restriction base="xs:normalizedString">
      <xs:whiteSpace value="collapse" />
   </xs:restriction>
</xs:simpleType>
```

Attributes

Attribute	Value Space	Description
`fixed`	`boolean`	If `true`, any data types derived from this type cannot alter the value of `whiteSpace`. The default is `false`
`Id`	`ID`	Gives a unique identifier to the type

Attribute	Value Space	Description
value	preserve | replace | collapse	preserve means that all whitespace is preserved as it is declared in the element. If replace is used, then all whitespace characters such as line feed (#xA), carriage return (#xD), and tab (#x9) are replaced by single whitespace characters (#x20). collapse means that all whitespace characters, such as line feed (#xA), carriage return (#xD), and tab (#x9) are replaced by single whitespace characters (#x20), and then any series of two or more whitespace characters are collapsed into a single whitespace character. Note that a type with its whiteSpace facet set to replace or preserve cannot be derived from one with a value of collapse, and similarly, one with a value of preserve cannot be derived from one with a value of replace

For more information: see §4.3.6 of the Datatypes Recommendation.

maxInclusive

This sets the *inclusive* upper limit of an ordered data type (number, date type, or ordered list). So, the value stated here is therefore the highest value that can be used in this data type. maxInclusive must be equal to or greater than any value of minInclusive and greater than the value of minExclusive. It is always used inside a <restriction> element, and it can contain an <annotation> element.

Example

The following example enables you to pick a number between 1 and 10. The values 1 and 10 are permitted.

```
<xs:simpleType name="PickANumber">
   <xs:restriction base="xs:integer">
      <xs:minInclusive value="1" />
      <xs:maxInclusive value="10" />
   </xs:restriction>
</xs:simpleType>
```

Attributes

Attribute	Value Space	Description
fixed	boolean	If true, then any data types derived from this type cannot alter the value of maxInclusive. The default is false
Id	ID	Gives a unique identifier to the type
value	anySimpleType	If the base data type is numerical, this would be a number; if a date, then this would be a date. The value must be allowable in the base type

For more information: see §4.3.7 of the Datatypes Recommendation.

minInclusive

This sets the *inclusive* lower limit of an ordered data type (number, date type, or ordered list). The value stated here is therefore the lowest value that can be used in this data type. `minInclusive` must be equal to or less than any value of `maxInclusive` and must be less than the value of `maxExclusive`. It is always used inside a `<restriction>` element, and it can contain an `<annotation>` element.

Example

The following example enables you to pick a number between 1 and 10. The values `1` and `10` are permitted.

```
<xs:simpleType name="PickANumber">
   <xs:restriction base="xs:integer">
      <xs:minInclusive value="1" />
      <xs:maxInclusive value="10" />
   </xs:restriction>
<xs:simpleType>
```

Attributes

Attribute	Value Space	Description
fixed	boolean	If `true`, then any data types derived from this type cannot alter the value of `minInclusive`. The default is `false`
Id	ID	Gives a unique identifier to the type
value	anySimpleType	If the base data type is numerical, this would be a number; if a date, then a date. The value must be allowable in the base type

For more information: see §4.3.10 of the Datatypes Recommendation.

maxExclusive

This sets the *exclusive* upper limit of an ordered data type (number, date type, or ordered list). The `maxExclusive` value is therefore one higher than the maximum value that can be used. `maxExclusive` must be greater than or equal to the value of `minInclusive` and greater than the value of `minExclusive`. It is always used inside a `<restriction>` element, and it can contain an `<annotation>` element.

Example

The following example enables you to pick a number between 0 and 11; however the values `0` and `11` are not permitted.

```
<xs:simpleType name="PickANumber">
   <xs:restriction base="xs:integer">
      <xs:minExclusive value="0" />
      <xs:maxExclusive value="11" />
   </xs:restriction>
</xs:simpleType>
```

Attributes

Attribute	Value Space	Description
`fixed`	`boolean`	If `true`, then any data types derived from this type cannot alter the value of `maxExclusive`. The default is `false`
`Id`	`ID`	Gives a unique identifier to the type
`value`	`anySimpleType`	If the base data type is numerical, this is a number; if a date, then it is a date. The value must be allowable in the base type, or must be equal to the value of the `maxExclusive` facet in the base type

For more information: see §4.3.8 of the Datatypes Recommendation.

minExclusive

This sets the *exclusive* lower limit of an ordered data type (number, date type, or ordered list). The `minExclusive` value is therefore one lower than the lowest value the data will allow. `minExclusive` must be less than the value of `maxExclusive` and less than or equal to the value of `maxInclusive`. It is always used inside a `<restriction>` element, and it can contain an `<annotation>` element.

Example

The following example enables you to pick a number between 0 and 11; however the values `0` and `11` are not permitted.

```
<xs:simpleType name="PickANumber">
   <xs:restriction base="xs:integer">
      <xs:minExclusive value="0" />
      <xs:maxExclusive value="11" />
   </xs:restriction>
</xs:simpleType>
```

Attributes

Attribute	Value Space	Description
`fixed`	`boolean`	If `true`, then any data types derived from this type cannot alter the value of `minExclusive`. The default is `false`
`Id`	`ID`	Gives a unique identifier to the type
`value`	`anySimpleType`	If the base data type is numerical, this would be a number; if a date, then a date. The value must be allowable in the base type, or must be equal to the value of the `minExclusive` facet in the base type

For more information: see §4.3.9 of the Datatypes Recommendation.

totalDigits

This facet applies to all data types derived from the `decimal` type. The value stated is the *maximum* number of significant digits allowed for the number (the `totalDigits` value must always be a positive integer). Note that leading zeros and trailing zeros after the decimal point are not considered when counting the total number of digits. The facet applies to only the value and not text representation.

Example

```
<xs:simpleType name="InterestRatePercent">
   <xs:restriction base="xs:decimal">
      <xs:totalDigits value="2" />
      <xs:fractionDigits value="3" />
   </xs:restriction>
</xs:simpleType>
```

Attributes

Attribute	Value Space	Description
`fixed`	`Boolean`	If `true`, then any data types derived from this type cannot alter the value of `totalDigits`. The default is `false`
`Id`	`ID`	Gives a unique identifier to the type
`value`	`positiveInteger`	The maximum number of `totalDigits` allowed for the value

For more information: see §4.3.11 of the Datatypes Recommendation.

fractionDigits

This facet applies to all data types derived from the `decimal` type. The value stated is the *maximum* number of digits in the fractional portion of the number (the `fractionDigits` value always a *non-negative* integer that is less than or equal to the value of `totalDigits`). Note that trailing zeros after the decimal point are not considered when counting the total number of digits. The facet applies to only the value and not text representation.

Example

```
<xs:simpleType name="InterestRatePercent">
   <xs:restriction base="xs:decimal">
      <xs:totalDigits value="2" />
      <xs:fractionDigits value="3" />
   </xs:restriction>
</xs:simpleType>
```

Attributes

Attribute	Value Space	Description
fixed	Boolean	If true, then any data types derived from this type cannot alter the value of fractionDigits. The default is false
Id	ID	Gives a unique identifier to the type
value	nonNegative Integer	The actual value of the value fractionDigits attribute. This cannot be any larger than the totalDigits value for the current type or base type

For more information: see §4.3.12 of the Datatypes Recommendation.

The following table indicates which of these constraining facets may be applied to which built-in datatypes in order to derive new types.

Datatypes	length	minLength	maxLength	whiteSpace (allowed values)	pattern	enumeration	MinExclusive	maxExclusive	minInclusive	maxInclusive	totalDigits	fractionDigits
String Types												
string	X	X	X	preserve replace collapse	X	X						
anyURI	X	X	X	collapse	X	X						
NOTATION				collapse	X	X						
QName				collapse	X	X						
Binary Encoding Types												
boolean				collapse	X							
hexBinary	X	X	X	collapse	X	X						
base64Binary	X	X	X	collapse	X	X						
Numeric Types												
decimal				collapse	X	X	X	X	X	X	X	X
float				collapse	X	X	X	X	X	X		

Datatypes	length	minLength	maxLength	whiteSpace (allowed values)	pattern	enumeration	MinExclusive	maxExclusive	minInclusive	maxInclusive	totalDigits	fractionDigits
double				collapse	X	X	X	X	X	X		
Date/Time Types												
duration				collapse	X	X	X	X	X	X		
dateTime				collapse	X	X	X	X	X	X		
date				collapse	X	X	X	X	X	X		
time				collapse	X	X	X	X	X	X		
gYear				collapse	X	X	X	X	X	X		
gYearMonth				collapse	X	X	X	X	X	X		
gMonth				collapse	X	X	X	X	X	X		
gMonthDay				collapse	X	X	X	X	X	X		
gDay				collapse	X	X	X	X	X	X		

The following table indicates which of these constraining facets may be applied to which derived built-in data types in order to derive new types.

Datatypes	length	minLength	maxLength	whiteSpace (allowed values)	pattern	enumeration	MinExclusive	maxExclusive	minInclusive	maxInclusive	totalDigits	fractionDigits
Types derived from string												
normalizedString	X	X	X	preserve replace collapse	X	X						
token	X	X	X	collapse	X	X						
language	X	X	X	collapse	X	X						
Name	X	X	X	collapse	X	X						
NCName	X	X	X	collapse	X	X						
ID	X	X	X	collapse	X	X						

Datatypes	length	minLength	maxLength	whiteSpace (allowed values)	pattern	enumeration	MinExclusive	maxExclusive	minInclusive	maxInclusive	totalDigits	fractionDigits
IDREF	X	X	X	collapse	X	X						
IDREFS	X	X	X	collapse	X	X						
NMTOKEN	X	X	X	collapse	X	X						
NMTOKENS	X	X	X	collapse	X	X						
ENTITY	X	X	X	collapse	X	X						
ENTITIES	X	X	X	collapse	X	X						
Types derived from decimal												
integer				collapse	X	X	X	X	X	X	X	0
negativeInteger				collapse	X	X	X	X	X	X	X	0
positiveInteger				collapse	X	X	X	X	X	X	X	0
nonNegativeInteger				collapse	X	X	X	X	X	X	X	0
nonPositiveInteger				collapse	X	X	X	X	X	X	X	0
byte				collapse	X	X	X	X	X	X	X	0
short				collapse	X	X	X	X	X	X	X	0
Int				collapse	X	X	X	X	X	X	X	0
long				collapse	X	X	X	X	X	X	X	0
unsignedByte				collapse	X	X	X	X	X	X	X	0
unsignedShort				collapse	X	X	X	X	X	X	X	0
unsignedInt				collapse	X	X	X	X	X	X	X	0
unsignedLong				collapse	X	X	X	X	X	X	X	0

Index

Symbols and Numbers

A

B

C

D

E

N

O

Q

R

S

T

U

V

W

Z